Many Possible Worlds

Cameron Gordon

Many Possible Worlds

An Interdisciplinary History of the World Economy Since 1800

palgrave
macmillan

Cameron Gordon
Tax and Transfer Policy Institute
Crawford School of Public Policy
Australian National University
Canberra, ACT, Australia

ISBN 978-981-19-9283-4 ISBN 978-981-19-9281-0 (eBook)
https://doi.org/10.1007/978-981-19-9281-0

Cover illustration: Unfinished steel structure intact after quake, San Francisco. San Francisco California, ca. 1906. Photograph. https://www.loc.gov/item/2004680400/

This Palgrave Macmillan imprint is published by the registered company Springer Nature Singapore Pte Ltd.
The registered company address is: 152 Beach Road, #21-01/04 Gateway East, Singapore 189721, Singapore

To Josephine, my wife, the love of my life, found later in life.

Acknowledgements

I would like to thank the following people who kindly reviewed chapters of my book and gave me valuable feedback, almost all of which I incorporated in my revisions: Aditya Balasubramanian, Richard Flanagan, Timothy Hatton, John Hawkins, Helga Henckel, Timo Henckel, Maria Racionero Llorente, Ben Mercer, David Paynter, Will Steffen and Alan Zimmerman. The usual caveat about all the errors being mine applies.

I also want to thank the staff at Palgrave Macmillan who worked very hard to find reviewers for the proposal and have been most accommodating in the publishing and production processes. Thanks also to anyone else whose names I don't know. I know there are many who work in the background and I very much appreciate their anonymous labours. And thanks also to the anonymous reviewer(s) who gave very thoughtful, detailed and positive comments on both the initial proposal and the completed draft manuscript itself that resulted in some important improvements that I hope are reflected in the final book.

Finally, this book would never have been written if not for the third-year undergraduate class, *World Economy Since 1800,* that I taught at the Australian National University. That class inspired me to do a wide range of reading that I normally would not have undertaken, and showed me that there was a need for a truly interdisciplinary history of the modern economy. As always, teaching is a wonderful gift, and I am grateful for the opportunity to have taught the class and for the students who were part of it.

A Very Brief Reader's Guide

Roughly 250 years ago, a startling thing happened: material output, income and wealth began to take off in Europe, first leaving the rest of the world and, then, historical precedent, behind. As the twentieth century progressed, Europe and its white settler "offshoots" attained unprecedented levels of opulence, while the non-European world increasingly adopted "capitalist" methods to achieve its own parallel growth acceleration.

Economists have defined this transformation in a narrow economic frame, generally focusing on individual economic agents moving within and constrained by competitive markets, their institutional arrangements, and the behavioural incentives the overall system provides to economic actors. This book uses that model but goes beyond it to look at economic change as a constant interplay of individual and social evolution, a process here presented in one cross-cutting interdisciplinary narrative. Sociology, political science, economics, anthropology, biology, geography, organisational theory and environmental science, amongst others, all have legitimate claims to being part of a true interdisciplinary economic history. Immodestly, and certainly incompletely, I have attempted to tell the story of the world economy since 1800 using a set of multiple lenses.

The book approaches this task across 32 chapters. Chapter 1 discusses some general issues arising in the writing and practice of interdisciplinary history, while Chapter 32 presents overall conclusions. The remaining 30 chapters are organized in 10 subsets of 3 that take the following sequence, repeated ten times:

- One chapter presents a relevant core idea for a phase of economic history (e.g. Chapter 2 on "Understanding the Anthropocene").
- The next chapter presents a broad historical narrative pivoting around a critical or illustrative year (e.g. Chapter 3 on "1800").
- A final chapter then pulls out a relevant associated cross-cutting theme considered in the prior two chapters (e.g. Chapter 4 on "Political Economy": the making of a North/South planet).

This is not a tight structure, and there is much overlapping and cross-cutting. The intent is to break a long and varied history into relatively digestible chunks that highlight key motive forces and impacts. The book is meant to be read sequentially, of course. But one may focus on one of the 10 "sets" of 3. Individual chapters can also be read in isolation, but some cross-referencing may be required in some cases. To that end, there are relatively frequent parenthetical pointers to other relevant chapters.

Most chapters contain at least one text-box, of lengths ranging from a paragraph up to a page and half. These have varying aims. Technical models and diagrams are used very sparingly in this book. But in a few cases, boxes are used to present such material for those interested, to be safely skipped by those otherwise inclined. Much more often the box material expands on or illustrates something presented in the main narrative, such as how a particular country experienced a particular epoch under discussion, or going more deeply into a single topic referenced broadly in the text. In quite a few instances, the boxes focus on what is deemed to be an interesting sideline or story. In general, these boxes can be read or not read as preferred.

A final noted on the illustrations used here: they are an integral part of the narrative. Sometimes, they play the conventional role of providing a visual to supplement the historical description provided in words. But they are also meant to serve as visual narratives in their own right, a bit like poetry, provoking nonlinear thought and bringing in the right hemisphere of the brain to augment what the left hemisphere is reading. A concerted effort has been undertaken to use only images that have been determined to be free to use by being in the public domain or under licences that allow unlimited use. Whether the underlying licence requires it or not, full attribution of sources have been given, as well as the nature of the licence itself. If any errors have been made, please notify the publisher and these will be corrected in subsequent editions.

Contents

List of Figures

List of Tables

List of Boxes

CHAPTER 1

Practising Interdisciplinary Economic History

C. Gordon, *Many Possible Worlds*,
https://doi.org/10.1007/978-981-19-9281-0_1

Fig. 1.1 Can you make a story out of windblown fragments? (*Image source* U.S. National Archives [Project DOCUMERICA]. Original Caption: Magazines and Newspapers Litter the Intersection of Sixth & Broadway After Debris Was Spilled from a Passing Truck, September 1972. U.S. National Archives' Local Identifier: 412-DA-1397. *Photographer* Strode, William. Persistent URL: research.archives.gov/description/543890. No known copyright restrictions)

1.1 Stitching Histories Together

Humanity seeks to learn from its past in order to improve its potential future. Yet the "past" is not something standing there like a mountain, to be surveyed by the relevant professionals. It must be put together first. And it must be put together in such a way as to yield useful lessons. This is the central challenge to anyone seeking to do history, whether an historian or not. How this might be done depends on one's approach, of which there are at least three (Fig. 1.1).

1.1.1 *Surmising and Validating "General Laws"*

In this case, various generalisations about historical causes and effects are posited a priori and then tested against the available evidence. If the regularity of these generalisations across different situations and time periods is strong enough, the theorist may see fit to declare them to be general laws in a predictive sense (whether using that specific language or not), making statements like: if "x" is present, then "y" will be expected to follow. This process is generically referred to as "deductive" in that general propositions are purportedly laid out and then verified or falsified against available facts.

1.1.2 *Story-Telling to Bring Out the Comprehensible Patterns from Messy Reality*

All history provides a narrative to make sense of things. The deductive approach of general laws uses narrative mostly descriptively, rather like a recounting of the results of a laboratory experiment, with the investigator and the object of investigation completely separated. An alternative is to make the story an end in itself, rather than a means of understanding a reality that is somehow already there. Subject and object are intimately connected. In genuine scholarly inquiry, facts are extremely important, but induction (drawing out generalities from specifics) is just one element of an exercise that aims to arrive at a story whose telling yields comprehension of what is true versus what is false.

1.1.3 *Historical Imagination and the Singularity of the Past*

While the past's regularity is a typical focus of historical analysis, there is also the view that history is always about the uniqueness—the singularity—of all events, with the flow of human time being like a beach made up of peculiar and innumerable grains of sand. Drawing out patterns is certainly possible and desirable. But in each moment, as with each sand grain, there are particularities that will never repeat, even if patterns and conditions may be similar at particular points in time. Historical imagination, defined as the ability to bring back to life some past person, place or event, emphasises the power of human agency and contingency, i.e. that human beings and their choices cannot ever be completely boiled down to a set of regularities or even probabilities, and that therefore human decision and the whim of fortune are always present and powerful in determining historical outcomes, both large and small.

1.2 Historiographical Pitfalls

These general approaches are obviously not mutually exclusive. The ever-present difficulty with any of them is to put the contemporary observer, with all the benefits of hindsight and detachment, into the unique conditions of past epochs to come up with a true advance in understanding. In doing so, there are a number of methodological "pitfalls" that can catch even the ablest analyst.

1.2.1 Causal Determinism

Causal determinism, stated in its extreme form, is the philosophical idea that every event or state of affairs, including every human decision and action, is the inevitable and necessary consequence of antecedent states of affairs. If this holds, then all effects can be directly traced to some prior causes, and all causal relationships, even if complex, ultimately are fixed in some way. Determinism is quite different from determination, which asserts that events (including human actions) can be adequately determined by immediately prior events (such as an agent's motives). Determination is an essential part of most standard reasoning about cause and effect. Determinism makes definitive claims about how such determination unfolds (Hoefer, 2016).

One extreme is sometimes called "hard" determinism, holding that conceivably all outcomes can be known and predicted if we know all the antecedent causes. Further, if we had the power, we could conceivably control all future outcomes by controlling all antecedent causes. This is the idea held by some religious sects and some secular ideologies, including certain versions of Marxism. It is also, perhaps surprisingly, true of some older scientific traditions, such as Newton's conception of his own physics (Jones, 2011). In this extreme view, there is ultimately no room for human "will" or "agency" (i.e. human action or intervention, by conscious choice, producing a particular effect) because human action and decision are said to be entirely the result of prior causes, along with everything else. Most determinism is "soft" and allows for some "randomness", either probabilistic (where there is some random variation around causal outcomes) or because some degree of human agency is allowed for (where people do have scope to make a choice out of the range of possible options that are presented by broader underlying causes).

Whatever version is used, determinism posits direct, one-to-one causal changes that lend some element of inevitability between initial causes and final results once a causal chain is set in motion. Like almost all other philosophical concepts, it is impossible to definitively prove or disprove the general argument behind determinism. Its use in historical analysis should be made explicit and a case should be made that it holds in the time and place it is being applied to.

1.2.2 *Reductionism*

Reductionism asserts that one theory or phenomenon can be reduced to some other theory or phenomenon. As an example one might claim that all the activity of all biological entities can be reduced to, and explained as, collections of atoms and molecules. For example, it is often stated that all human mind processes are reducible to physics and thus that mental phenomena, such as consciousness, are simply physical phenomena (Ney, 2021).

Reductionism may be valid in particular domains, especially narrow and purely physical and material ones (e.g. looking at chemical changes purely in terms of molecules). It is harder to defend as an explanation for human history, and where employed its use should be made explicit and justified.

1.2.3 *Uniformitarianism*

Uniformitarianism is the assumption that the natural processes operating in today's world have always operated in the past and everywhere in the domain where they apply. The term was originally developed with respect to earth geological processes as a response to the doctrine of catastrophism that held that current geological environments were the results of unique catastrophic events, such as great floods or earthquakes. In earth sciences, uniformitarianism is widely accepted. But it is more debated in cosmology, where the constancy of cause and effect throughout space–time and spatiotemporal invariance of physical laws is not yet proven; and also in modern ecology, where old assumptions about the natural equilibrium of environmental processes have been challenged (Knight & Harrison, 2014).

If uniformitarianism applies in history, then close study of today's systemic relationships allows one to say much about how things operated in the past. But the assumption that the basic underlying dynamics of people and their societies have been largely or entirely invariant over tens of thousands of years is very hard to establish and quite debatable. Granted, some general continuity across human history and societies can be plausibly demonstrated and many cultural and institutional patterns and forms are exceptionally persistent. But there are many counter-examples as well.

As with reductionism and determinism, uniformitarianism can slip into an analysis implicitly and unconsciously. Much "deep roots" economic history, which often draws inferences about present conditions from data series across centuries or millennia (Spolaore & Wacziarg, 2013), may sometimes be implicitly converting present correlations into past causes and effects through an implicit and perhaps unconscious uniformitarianism.

1.3 "Truth" and History

Charles Tilly (1984) speaks of the "encompassing comparison" in historical inquiry. Rather than compare two separate things in isolation, as per classical social theory, he argues that one should look at parts in a larger whole and see how each shapes, and is shaped by, that whole. For Tilly, human history is made up of big structures and large processes that cannot be broken up and examined like an insect put under plate glass. Its totality has to be accounted for and assessed directly. Comparisons are still needed to get at causality, but they must be broad enough to be truthfully complete rather than misleadingly partial.

Picasso is often quoted as having said that art is the lie that tells the truth; or, more precisely, that art is the lie "that makes us realise truth…that is given us to understand" (Barr, 1946, 270). If by art one means artifice, the creation of a form that is by definition synthetic, then "history" is most definitely an artifice. But it need not, therefore, be false if it points to true things. The artifice just needs to be big enough to be reasonably accurate while being contained enough to be understandable.

Historical artifice is thus required to capture the shared journey of human beings across time. It can have an independent beauty that is admirable, as in, for example, Churchill's dulcet tones in his sweeping history of the Second World War. But the content is always contestable and with age, deep limitations may appear, as Churchill's often self-serving and Whiggish narrative is now recognised as having (Reynolds, 2005). Nonetheless, I declare up front that I do believe "truth" is still a relevant concept and still "discoverable"; although I also completely acknowledge that, inevitably, who one is seeps into the tale told and thus corrupts it to a degree, and that history, even of a particular time period, actually needs to be rewritten constantly, not just because new facts might be uncovered but because new lessons need to be learned and that need changes with a constantly evolving context. Even if human truth is only ever relative, shifting truth is still truth, and it is good to attempt to capture it as best we can.

References

Barr, A. H., Jr. (1946). *Picasso: Fifty years of his art*. The Museum of Modern Art.

Hoefer, C. (2016). Causal determinism. In E. N. Zalta (Ed.), *The Stanford encyclopedia of philosophy* (Spring 2016 ed.). https://plato.stanford.edu/archives/spr2016/entries/determinism-causal/.

Jones, S. E. (2011). A brief survey of Sir Isaac Newton's views on religion. In M. D. Rhodes & J. W. Moody (Eds.), *Converging paths to truth* (pp. 61–78). Religious Studies Center, Brigham Young University; Deseret Books.

Knight, J., & Harrison, S. (2014). Limitations of uniformitarianism in the Anthropocene. *Anthropocene, 5*, 71–75.

Ney, A. (2021). Reductionism. In *The internet encyclopedia of philosophy*. ISSN 2161-0002. https://www.iep.utm.edu/.

Reynolds, D. (2005). *In command of history: Churchill fighting and writing the Second World War*. Penguin.

Spolaore, E., & Wacziarg, R. (2013). How deep are the roots of economic development? *Journal of Economic Literature, 51*(2), 325–369.

Tilly, C. (1984). *Big structures, large processes, huge comparisons*. Russell Sage Foundation.

CHAPTER 2

Understanding the "Anthropocene"

C. Gordon, *Many Possible Worlds*,
https://doi.org/10.1007/978-981-19-9281-0_2

Fig. 2.1 Shooting for the moon (*Image source* Photo provided by Repository: San Diego Air and Space Museum. Original caption: "Here men from the planet Earth set foot on the Moon, July 1969. We came in peace for all mankind". *Note* No known copyright restrictions)

2.1 Travelling on "Spaceship" Earth

In the late 1960s, Buckminster Fuller published a book that captured the imagination of an era: *Operating manual for spaceship earth* (1968). Though not the first person to use such imagery, Fuller's vision was the most deeply elaborated, putting forth a story about the human race travelling throughout space on a vessel called "Earth". The age of space travel had begun in the 1950s, making the image especially resonant, with its subtext of human ingenuity liberating Homo sapiens from the bounds of the planet into the open skies of the universe (Fig. 2.1).

It was not just science, logic, knowledge and rationality that had achieved this. Political will and collective action had been the prime movers for actually making it all happen, with the superpower rivalry of the Cold War an additional impetus. The American "astronauts"—a technical updating of the mythical Argonaut—were rigorously trained and supported by a vast technical apparatus funded by the deep pockets of a nation with a single-minded purpose of exploring space and spreading earthlings throughout the cosmos.

Decades later this era would be humorously and somewhat sarcastically captured by Tom Wolfe in his 1979 book *The Right Stuff* which portrayed the astronauts more as cogs in a large organisational machine than as intrepid heroes. But that was a slightly later and more jaded age and for Fuller, and much of his reading public of the time, if humanity could travel in space, it also could manage the whole planet in a manner that was efficient, equitable and sustainable.

It was seen as a matter of urgency to do so, for the fate of the earth seemed to hang in the balance as environmental degradation, rampant consumerism and uncontrolled technological change—to say nothing of the possibility of nuclear annihilation—appeared to be spiralling out of control. These concerns were the impetus for Fuller's book, and parallel and interrelated discussions going on around the same time reflected similar concerns and fears. In 1968 Stanford professor Paul Ehrlich published a book called *The population bomb* that forcefully argued for immediate control of burgeoning population growth, lest the planet face famine and disaster. It was a modern-day echo of concerns expressed by the English political economist Thomas Malthus two hundred years earlier (see Chapter 4), now updated to say that technical progress alone was not going to solve the problem of fundamental resource limits. While past technical advance had staved off the famine that Malthus had so feared, it had also allowed an increase in numbers of people that were now pushing against the outer bounds of planetary stability. After initially being ignored, the book ended up selling 3 million copies and its author became an international celebrity (Mann, 2018).

Analysts from various disciplines, including economics, were also studying the broader ecological and economic aspects of modern-day growth, of which human population size was but one aspect. One result was the 1972 *Limits to growth* report of the so-called Club of Rome, which looked not just at population expansion but industrialisation, pollution, food production, and resource depletion, concluding that if growth was not reined in and managed, a serious economic and environmental crisis was inevitable within the next one hundred years (Meadows et al. 1972).

Though dire, neither Fuller, nor Ehrlich, nor the Club of Rome were actually pessimistic. In fact, they were all merely sounding the alarm that business as usual could not continue on as it had. Change was urgently needed but it was also possible and moreover possible along primarily technical lines. Far from rejecting the prevailing scientific, materialist, technological paradigm, these authors and others were calling for a re-orientation of these modalities away from a narrow focus on meeting human desires whatever they might be towards a greater "holism" (the concept that had been invented by Jan Smuts in 1926) and which included all of nature, human and non-human. In other words, while unchecked human invention leads to trouble, the same intellect behind it could also be employed to limit and regulate its less positive aspects and bring about a better future.

This was not an unchallenged view, despite its contemporary popularity. Putting aside the anti-scientific and anti-materialistic strains of the counterculture (see Chapter 24), there were some who believed that the existing system would correct itself. Economists were in the lead here, most arguing along traditional neoclassical theory lines that relatively modest policy changes involving markets and prices would be sufficient to correct any negative "externalities", e.g. putting a tax on polluting emissions to "internalise" these costs within the polluter's calculus, thus reducing emission levels to economically "efficient" levels. This particular idea was of early twentieth-century heritage, going back to the orthodox economist A.C. Pigou (1928) and hence given the infelicitous label of a "Pigovian tax". In this paradigm, course corrections were admitted as necessary but they were largely to be addressed by policy tweaks to the "market failures" of the existing economy which was thought to basically work well overall (Kumekawa, 2017).

Thus some economists dismissed the *Limits to Growth* Report entirely, on the basis that Malthusian predictions 200 years earlier of a population crisis were incorrect because they did not account for that fact that human ingenuity could change resource limitations entirely, something that had actually happened with food production throughout the nineteenth and twentieth centuries. This development contradicted Malthus' belief that agriculture could not grow faster than population and which was the basis of his predictions of certain and regular periodic famine. Almost all other natural resource limits also appeared to have been beaten by technical advance, especially with the creation of new synthetic materials to replace limited supplies of natural ones (e.g. rubber) (Neal & Cameron, 2016, 398–399).

There were even those who held that untrammelled markets had brought undreamed of prosperity thus far and would continue to do so if left relatively—or completely—free. The most extreme archetype for this point of view was expressed by the "Austrian" economists, who extolled the price mechanism as the ultimate guide of efficient allocation of societal resources, and markets the best guarantors of human freedom against the creeping authoritarian tendencies of states. To this way of thinking, incentives drove all economic behaviour, and even though most human behaviour was said to be self-seeking, it was also rational, and collective self-destruction in the form of planetary collapse was supposedly impossible because markets and competition could be depended upon to provide the incentives to overcome resource limitations in the creative and feasible ways they always had. Reports like *Limits to growth* were thus not only wrong but quite possibly dangerous because they opened the door to destructive State limits on invention and freedom of action. Ludwig von Mises and Friedrich von Hayek were the leading exponents of this market libertarianism. Hayek had won the Nobel Prize in economics in 1974 (sharing it with the much more politically progressive Swedish economist Gunnar Myrdal) giving his free-market views a boost in prominence and status (Offer & Söderberg, 2016).

2.2 Three Paradigms of the World Economy

Whatever one's point of view, the debate during the 1960s and 1970s was simply an inflection point around a very definite set of historical facts, namely a sharp and global break in patterns of human economic (and other) activity and impact that became manifest around 1600 and was fully evident by 1800, accompanied by an exponential increase in both human population and economic output. The fact of this break is indisputable and screams out for explanation. To vastly oversimplify, there can be said to be three explanatory paradigms, each one focusing on a different dimension of the phenomenon:

1. The break is fundamentally about human impacts pushing beyond ecological and environmental limits (the "Anthropocene")

2. The break is fundamentally about changes in human society ("Modernity and Modernisation")
3. The break is fundamentally about changes in the human economy (the "Growth Model").

These are not mutually exclusive categorisations, and causes and effects cross back and forth between economic, social, environmental and other categories. Nor is this a complete or comprehensive paradigm listing. But arguably these are the three most influential narratives employed to make sense of intensifying, deepening and expanding changes in human life and its natural setting over the past two and a half centuries, and particularly since the mid-twentieth century.

2.3 Paradigm 1: The Anthropocene (It's All About Earth System Limits)

The first paradigm focuses on the Earth itself, observing how its various "systems"—biological, geological, climatic, etc.—are being changed by different factors over time (Zalasiewicz et al., 2021). The time frame is very long run, to say the least, since the earth is thought to be around 4.5 billion years old. Geologists have a structure for ordering these vast time periods into two aeons, broken down into smaller eras, which themselves can be broken down into yet smaller epochs and ages. The latest period of geological time, the Quaternary, began 2.6 million years ago and includes the Pleistocene and the Holocene epochs, the Holocene beginning only 11,700 years ago or so. Human existence sits only in the Quaternary period and not even a very big part of that. The species "Sapiens", i.e. the human being, is currently thought to have emerged roughly 150,000 years ago, with other competing species of the line (e.g. Erectus, etc.) dying out around 70,000 years ago (Zalasiewicz et al., 2011).

In geological terms, therefore, we humans remain a blip; but not, arguably, in terms of impact on the planet. This is where the Anthropocene comes in, as a label for a proposed new epoch in which human activity is said to be driving planetary system outcomes, arguably to breaking point from the perspective of most of the higher species that live here. Eugene Stoermer used the term in the 1980s in reference to human influence on freshwater diatoms in the lakes of North America.

Nobel laureate Paul Crutzen, unaware of Stoermer's use of the term, independently used it at a 2000 conference to refer to broader human-influenced Earth System changes (Simpson, 2020, 54). Earth System scientist Will Steffen has done some of the major theoretical and empirical work arguing for its existence and is a major advocate for its recognition by the official geological bodies (Steffen et al., 2011, 2015). This has not yet happened so we officially remain in the Holocene epoch.

The notion that human beings were radically altering global natural systems (as opposed to local ones which they had been altering for centuries—see Box 2.1) began with observed changes in the global climate that became systematic beginning in the nineteenth century accompanied by the birth of the technical field of meteorology (versus the more informal study of weather that has been engaged in for millennia by farmers, navigators and others interested in it by necessity). Over the course of the twentieth century, as the record of weather observations grew and became more refined, climatologists began to notice significant and unprecedented patterns in the world climate, intensifying in the latter half of the 1900s and continuing and expanding ever since.

Average surface temperatures across the planet have risen unequivocally and with increasing intensity. As of this writing, the global average surface temperature is 1.2 degrees Celsius above pre-industrial levels, according to the most recent assessment of the World Meteorological Organisation. According to the IPCC (2019), the surface ocean has warmed by 0.87 degrees Celsius from the period 1850–1900 to 2006–2015. Associated with this warming have been global ice sheet melting, retreating glaciers and reduced snow cover across the Polar Regions (US NASA, 2020).

Box 2.1 When Did the Anthropocene Actually Begin?

The Anthropocene has two meanings. One is from a geological perspective in which the Holocene has arguably been terminated and a new epoch has begun. The other is from the perspective of the Earth System, which is now on a rapid, human-driven trajectory away from the 11,700-year period of stability that had prevailed during the Holocene.

But when did the Anthropocene actually begin? Human beings have had substantial impact on their local environments throughout much of the history of the species, often over wide areas. So one could say that "anthropogenic" environmental change is perhaps as old as humanity. But in a more general sense, the scale, scope and degree of such changes have built up over the past few centuries into a full Anthropocene, with both geologists and Earth System scientists providing more precise criteria for defining this shift (Zalasiewicz et al., 2015).

The trajectory of human economic and social development is broken down into the Paleolithic era (broken into Lower, Middle and Upper periods), followed by the Mesolithic, then Neolithic, and then the various metal ages. During each one the species exhibits increasing sophistication of materials and shaping of various tools, starting with stone and moving up into bronze etc. The Neolithic period represents a collective break between the human and other species in terms of collective socialisation, social organisation, technical prowess, culture and the use of language (Zalasiewicz et al., 2011). "Recorded" history begins in the Neolithic period, with growth in the scale of human organisation prodigious since then.

So too has been growth in the human impact on planetary resources and systems, especially biological, climatic and environmental ones. Such alteration and disruption are common to the large mammals, and even ancient humans, such as Australian aborigines, the oldest known continuous civilisation that is still ongoing, significantly altered their surrounding landscapes and biomes. The invention of agriculture in particular was a seismic change in the relationship between human activity and ecology, arguably unparalleled until the Industrial Revolution many centuries later (Harari, 2014).

But from geological/stratigraphic and Earth System perspectives, the Earth System only left the Holocene envelope of variability around the mid-twentieth century, a period referred to as the Great Acceleration (Syvitski et al., 2020). Interestingly, both geologists and Earth System scientists consider human impacts on and changes to the rest of the natural world prior to this time to be a feature of the Holocene. Thus, while the human species has always interacted with the environment in varied and often destabilising ways, it was when this trend became completely global and highly intensified that our modern ecological era could be said to have started (Steffen et al., 2016).

The climatic indications are incontrovertible, except by those ignoring, or being selective with, the available evidence (e.g. citing isolated anomalies such as one unusually cold winter in a particular country). The scientific establishment is in almost complete agreement that the proximate cause of global warming is an unprecedented rise in global CO_2, especially after 1950. The consensus is almost as great that human activity has been behind most of that rise (US NASA, 2020; Syvitski et al., 2020). Much of the current "debate" about climate change is thus heavily political in nature (see Box 2.2).

Box 2.2 The Climate Change Debate

Climate change has become a "hot" issue over the past couple of decades (no pun intended). In the realm of public and social media, it seems highly contested and contentious, leading many to refer to the climate change "debate".

This term suggests that the warming of the global climate and its anthropogenic origins are something for which no solid consensus exists. Is this really the case? Kitcher (2010) argues that there are actually three areas of pertinent discussion: (1) the issue of whether human activities are contributing to a significant average warming of Earth overall; (2) the probabilities with which various climate-driven phenomena (such as melting of polar ice sheets) will continue to occur and what their consequences for human beings will be; and (3) considerations about what might be done to deal with planetary warming.

With respect to (1), the scientific community is nearly unanimous, though, as always, there are a few scientists who differ with the prevailing view of the evidence available, and a very few who dispute that evidence overall (perhaps between 0.1% and 1% of qualified scientists in the area). This point is often lost or distorted in the hub-bub of media reporting, especially when amplified by the various political slants of most media outlets and put into the "balanced news" reporting model whose format is to have two "sides" covered, suggesting equivalence between the two, even if one side represents only a small minority of opinion. The problem can be even worse in the much more fragmented social media world of Facebook, Twitter and YouTube, to name the major platforms as of this writing. Public discussion indeed takes the form of a "debate" but the substantive points, about which experts in the field are in near-unanimous agreement, get lost in the noise, exacerbated by a widespread public cynicism about expertise in general.

For (2) there is more disagreement, but the accuracy and reliability of predictions in many areas of climate science are improving rapidly. As warming progresses, there is a convergence on particular scenarios as the facts on the ground, such as polar ice melting, are largely conforming to the courses suggested by the ongoing reports from the International Panel on Climate Change (IPCC 2007, 2021).

Issues surrounding (3) constitute the most genuinely contested and truly debatable area. But in the public domain, this conversation does not get very far because of reversions to questioning of whether climate change even exists or not, or even if admitted that it does, whether human beings are the cause.

In general one could say that the political issues have been conflated with the scientific ones, with both suffering as a result. Still the experts do agree nearly fully about the following facts: the global climate has been warming at an accelerating rate since the mid-twentieth century, and is continuing to do so; and human activity is a major contributor.

The arguments for anthropogenic (i.e. human-induced) changes to the climate and Earth System are based on a variety of metrics of both human activity and environmental change and their patterns of growth over the past 250 years. The International Geosphere-Biosphere Programme (IGBP, 2015) tracked 24 such metrics in total between 1750 and 2010, focusing particularly on a distinct period of especially rapid escalation after 1950, referred to as the Great Acceleration. The 24 metrics are divided into two sets of 12: "Earth system trends" (consisting of Carbon dioxide, Nitrous oxide, Methane, Stratospheric ozone, Surface temperature, Ocean acidification, Marine fish capture, Shrimp aquaculture, Nitrogen to coastal zone, Tropical forest loss and Domesticated land); and "Socioeconomic trends" (Population, Real GDP, Foreign direct investment, Urban population, Primary energy use, Fertiliser consumption, Large dams, Water use, Paper production, Transportation, Telecommunications and International tourism). A few selected observations for a subset of these metrics are presented in Table 2.1.

The patterns in these selected data are exhibited across all the series, namely strong growth between 1800 and 1950 (with clear beginnings in 1750) and an order of magnitude or more change between 1950 and 2000/2010—a hyperbolic pattern. The other striking thing about these data is how closely they track with each other over time. By itself this does not, obviously, prove any causality, being just statistical association. But much other research does point to human socioeconomic changes being primary drivers of recent Earth System changes (IPCC, 2021).

Although focused on planetary ecology and climate, the clear economic implication of this paradigm is that modern economic growth is having severe impacts on various Earth System components and processes,

Table 2.1 Changes in selected socioeconomic and earth system trends, 1800–2000

	Year				*Units of measurement*
Socioeconomic trends	*1800*	*1900*	*1950*	*2000*	
Population	0.96	1.66	2.53	6.12	Billions people
Real GDP	0.47	1.89	5.54	39.33	2005 US dollars (trillions) (1820 data for 1800)
Urban population	0.08	0.27	0.74	2.86	Billions people
Primary energy use	20.0	49.4	112.3	434.4	Exajoule (EJ)
Earth System trends					
Carbon dioxide	282.58	296.10	311.24	366.82	Carbon dioxide, ppm
Methane	735.50	875.58	1117.27	1724.18	Methane, ppb
Surface temperature	−0.3	−0.34	−0.05	0.4	Temperature anomaly, deg C (1850 data for 1800)*

* *Note* Global surface temperature anomaly (measured as combined land and ocean observations, relative to 1961–1990, 20 y Gaussian smoothed)
Source of data IGBP (2014)

with possibly catastrophic consequences. In many ways, the Anthropocene story is a negative mirror to the economics paradigm considered next. Affluence and technical change (and note that Real GDP is one of the socioeconomic metrics tracked above) are seen as drivers of human impact on planetary systems, and an existential problem is now arising due to the human disregard for natural limits of the Earth System.

The conclusion is not one of simple cause-effect logic but rather that accelerating system-level change in human systems has led to corresponding changes in Earth System parameters that amount to a complete system-level shift, rather than just incremental changes to single variables (technically referred to as "state and transition dynamics" based on complex system theory). This was essentially the point made by the *Limits to Growth* report. The proposed socioeconomic interrelationships between human activity and nature from a geological and climatological perspective are captured in the "IPAT" model, details of which are provided in Box 2.3.

Box 2.3 The IPAT model

A simplified mechanical model to explain the links between impacts on planetary systems and human activity is contained in the multiplicative formula:

$$I = P \times A \times T.$$

I = refers to Human impact on the global environment. This consists of:

(P) Population, i.e. how many people in total the earth is supporting at a given time;

(A) Affluence, which broadly refers to how rich people are on average and which is typically measured by GDP per capita in \$/person/year;

(T) Technology, which conceptually refers to the state of technical sophistication at a particular point in time, but which usually is boiled down to economic intensity of a particular resource or pollutant, e.g. energy joules per \$ of GDP (Ward et al., 2016).

According to this model, for most of human history, human impact on the earth was driven mainly by changes in population (P) and, to a lesser extent, technology (T), with the two closely related to one another. The development of human agriculture is a perfect example, where the development of techniques (such as crop rotation) and tools (such as ploughs) were technical advances that increased food output and productivity by allowing for planting and harvesting in fixed locations which in turn could support larger populations overall and in bigger and bigger agglomerations such as cities resulting in increased human impact on the environment.

Affluence (A), on a per capita average basis, is, however, believed not to have shifted too greatly until the onset of the Industrial Revolution (though as will be seen in Chapter 3, this is not an uncontroversial statement) with the average person's level of consumption not changing much from year to year. Thus until the past few centuries, human impact (I) on the environment was relatively limited when viewed from a planetary perspective (though not always from a localised one) because population growth was limited by agricultural productivity, which grew relatively slowly and sometimes temporarily reversed itself.

Modern economic growth has allowed for a vast increase in Affluence through rapid technical change, which in turn has allowed for a prodigious increase in population. Thus the modern economy has fostered rapid growth in P, A and T which has had a multiplicative impact on I; hence (according to the model), the trends in the various data in Table 2.1 and beyond became pronounced with the onset of the Industrial Revolution and especially the Great Acceleration after 1950 driven by increases in all three variables.

The IPAT model is less an explanatory device than an illustrative one, though it is consistent with the available data. It is an accounting identity, i.e. a relationship said to be true by definition, rather than a causal theory, but it is helpful in evaluating broad potential causality.

Regarding implied policy guidance, if human impact on planetary systems is to be reduced, policymakers have three variables to focus on. Environmentalists focus on all three to differing degrees, with some calling for large changes in human consumption and production patterns (reducing A); others emphasising population control and reduction through birth control and other methods (to lower P), Microsoft founder Bill Gates and former US Vice President Al Gore being notable proponents (Cox, 2014); and yet others calling for green technology and other technical changes to change the way that T impacts the environment, especially by reducing the intensity of resource use and waste outputs, Paul Hawken (2017) being one of many in this camp. Of course most analysts agree that all three elements are important.

An interesting area of relative agreement seems to be around T. If, in fact, technical change can support continual increases in A and P but do so in way that nonetheless keeps the cumulative I stable or reducing, then perhaps the human species can have its cake and eat it too, so to speak. Many economists are in this camp, as mentioned above. But so are some environmentalists, especially executives in the high-technology sector whose business model focuses on selling innovations as the solution to most problems.

One writer who combines dire pessimism about climate change with optimism about technology's potentially salvationist role is Paul Gilding, who argues that humanity is hurtling towards the environmental cliff but will pull out all the technical stops at the last minute and avert catastrophe when it becomes clear that there is no other choice but to take decisive action involving collective sacrifice and pooled effort. He uses the analogy of Winston Churchill in the Second World War who rallied Britain against the seemingly impossible odds of Hitler's onslaught as an example of how human beings are wired to flirt with disaster but always pull away from it at the last minute (Gilding, 2011). How applicable this analogy is remains to be seen, but at least it is a hopeful trope amidst an apparently darkening ecological picture. It may, however, be misleading as well, by suggesting that no fundamental change in human behaviour or comfort is needed.

Whether we are now in a new geological epoch called the "Anthropocene" or not, it is clear that unquestionably a significant break has occurred from past patterns from both a species and an environmental perspective and human activity of all sorts is playing a large role. The core economic issue here is whether it is possible to "decouple" economic growth and environmental impact. This remains an area of unresolved debate that will apparently only be settled by the current uncontrolled global experiment that has been ongoing for the past three centuries, and particularly since the mid-twentieth century.

2.4 Paradigm 2: Modernity and Modernisation (It's All About the Society)

The Anthropocene model could be said to be a working backwards from observed results. Earth System metrics are sharply changing along with metrics of human activity and the surmise based on that association is that human activity is a prime multivariate cause. Causality is difficult to prove across such simultaneously large and subtle scales, so strong associations, strongly demonstrated, are used instead. However, it is important to understand what has driven human beings towards such dramatic changes in their activities in the first place, something the Anthropocene model mainly describes rather than explains, although quite alot of scientific explanatory work has been conducted as well (McNeill, 2016; Steffen et al., 2016).

This is where a more sociological, historical and political perspective is useful. This comes in many flavours, but a broad label that applies is "modernity". Michel Foucault defines "modernity" as a social-political stance of being sceptical of tradition; individualistic; believing in and promoting social, scientific and technological progress; fostering professionalisation and formalisation of institutions and norms; employing a pro-market economy and an industrial mode of economic relations; fundamentally secular (though not necessarily intolerant of religion); politically "liberal" in the sense of upholding the nation-state (as opposed to a royal or feudal order, for example); using representative democracy as a governance model; and promoting and providing mass public education (Foucault, 1977, 170–177). There are many other definitions of modernity, but this one encapsulates some of its major social, political and economic features.

"Modernity" in its original sense is explicitly European and Western and as a concept has been justly criticised as excluding other non-Western traditions that in many cases are far older and cover a far greater proportion of the world's populations and cultures. Postcolonial theorists have argued for alternative sequences of modernity unfolding in the non-European realms (Chakrabarty, 1998, 2009; Chatterjee, 1995; Kaviraj, 1995). Foucault himself is one such prominent critic along these lines.

However, if the idea of the "modern" is detached from value judgements about supposed superiority or inferiority of one society versus another and looked at simply as a particular mode of social organisation and collective and individual human development, then it can be very useful when applied to the modern world economy which arguably has been moulded heavily by the West, spreading a form of global dominance, for good and ill, and very often by implicit and explicit force. This historical unfolding of Westernised modernisation, sometimes adapted and altered to fit local conditions, has been associated with the rapid change and expansion in human material growth and impacts already discussed above.

There is no concrete date for when modernity began but most historians see its roots in the "Early Modern" period in Europe between 1450 and 1750, a time which began with the Renaissance and its associated doctrine of Humanism which placed "Man" at the centre of the created world. God, of course, was still seen as above all as the Creator of all, but the perspective was shifting from the European medieval notion that downplayed human individuality towards one that celebrated the individual and broke "him" (and definitely not including females) out from a prevailing subordinated set of hierarchical social groups in a nominally interdependent order often referred to as "corporatism" (Monfasani, 2016).

Closely following upon the Renaissance was the Enlightenment which developed the doctrine (some might say ideology) of rationalism, upholding the power of human reason to unlock the workings of God's universe, a development that was closely linked to the Renaissance "rediscovery" of the "Pagan" classics of Greek and Roman times. This secularised the modality of reason, which in the Middle Ages had been devoted more exclusively towards theological ends, as with the Scholasticism of the medieval Church, exemplified by the great logical tome *Summa theologica* by Thomas Aquinas ([1237] 1997). Humanism also emerged from the Renaissance, adapting the Classical celebration of individuality that runs through much Greco-Roman art and myth. The creation of the printing press by Gutenberg in the mid-1400s was a major technical advance that helped widely disseminate knowledge of these developments (Fitzpatrick et al., 2004; Monfasani, 2016).

These intellectual currents coalesced into the "Scientific Revolution" with its nascent development of the scientific method, practical empiricism and secular inquiry into the natural world, all aimed at increasing human ability to manipulate nature (Dear, 2005). During the early part of this era, the Protestant Reformation broke apart the universal authority of the Catholic Church in Europe, loosening that institution's grip on both moral authority and temporal political power, and opening up varying and uneven episodes of political liberalisation in various European states of the time, especially newly Protestant ones. The Reformation also removed the Church's ability to universally suppress scientific theorising and investigation. Finally, the new Protestant theology put the individual in charge of his or her own faith and relationship with God, removing the requirement of any intermediary to do so. This set the stage for an enhancement of individualism (Rublack, 2017).

This "Early" modern period then flowed into the "Modern" period of European history itself, roughly beginning in 1750 (with much debate about the proper starting date) in which the general political and social arc is said to move decisively from personalistic, informal and concrete social ordering and direction, to more institutional, formal and abstract patterns, all of which have been posited as critical in driving a shift towards the market modes of production, consumption, distribution and social organisation that are so archetypal of the economy since 1800.

An important milestone in Western modernity was England's Glorious Revolution of 1688, with the triumph of the English Parliament as the central State authority over King James II, and its making Kingship conditional rather than purely dynastic by legislating that no Catholic could succeed to the throne as James had, and hence that no English kingship could be again be unconditional and based on familial prerogatives alone (Harris, 2006). The American Revolution and War for Independence of 1776–1787 are seen as extending these political developments. Arguably more of a rebellion against British colonial authority than a true revolution (more on that later in the book), the establishment of a Republic, without a monarchy and with political leaders chosen on the basis of limited franchise elections, along with a written Constitution and later ten amendments known as the Bill of Rights that enshrined supposedly universal "natural" rights, was another blow to modes of hereditary and traditional rule, at least amongst European elites. It was also a further prod to an individualist rather than monarchical or corporatist political ideology (Bailyn, 1967).

These two events can be said to be primarily political in nature, but an even more thoroughgoing socio-political-economic development came with the overthrow of the *ancien régime* in France during the French Revolution of 1789. *Ancien régime* is a French term that literally refers to the political and social system in France before the Revolution of 1789, but which has since come to mean any antiquated pre-modern socio-political system. 1789 was a political and ideological earthquake amongst the royalist European powers of the time, marking a decisive shift in power politics and ushering in a wave of political rebellions, revolutions, and a series of wars over the following decades that shook and eventually took down many of the European systems based on hereditary privilege and rigid traditional class power structures, a process that would be accelerated by the ravages of the First World War.

The French Revolution itself was explicitly and radically "rationalist", putting logic and intellect at the heart of the design and governing of the entire social order. It overthrew a king and royal family, Louis XVI and the Bourbon dynasty; but much more than that, it eliminated an entire system based on tradition that had evolved over centuries (Livesey, 2001; Roberts, 2000). In the beginning it was both egalitarian and individualist, at least on the surface. The slogan of the French Revolution (officially institutionalised later under the French Third Republic) was Liberté, Égalité, Fraternité (Liberty, Equality, and Fraternity). The Declaration of the Rights of Man, which became part of French law on 16 August 1789, offered principles that included equality of everyone under the law; freedom of expression and religion; and natural rights of all individuals. As Article 1 states: "Men are born and remain free and equal in rights. Social distinctions can be founded only on the common good". This declaration is still contained within modern French law (Livesey, 2001).

During the Revolution's most radical phase, a reordering of society along rational principles was attempted, including a new metric system to replace old weights and measures based on custom, a completely new calendar, and a new technical bureaucratic mode of administration, including reorganisation and renaming of provincial subdivisions of the nation (Cobban, 1964). The calendar did not last long, but the metric system was useful enough to be ultimately adopted worldwide, except in the United States, and the administrative advances remained influential as well, in France and elsewhere.

The French Revolution in many ways was the first example of secular internationalism, i.e. the notion that there were certain principles that united people across national and other group boundaries. Christianity, Islam and other religions had this potential flavour too, but by necessity their realms generally remained confined to members of the church in question. The Roman Empire had a universal quality given its breadth, scale, scope and grandeur, but this was filtered through a provincialism based on a distinction between "superior" Roman citizens and non-Romans (Livesey, 2001). To the extent that future globalisation required a universalistic intellectual framework, the French Revolution provided some of the seeds.

The French Revolution thus birthed many new models for social, political and economic institutions, but within a decade it had taken a new form in *Bonapartism*, driven by the rise of the militarily brilliant Napoleon Bonaparte as French Emperor and supreme leader. Although his reign was relatively brief, from 1799 to final defeat and deposition in 1815, Napoleon conquered much territory and administered it in a relatively formal way, imposing his new and fairly progressive legal code on the large areas of the European continent that he briefly conquered. In generally choosing relatives to be leaders of these areas, and in designating himself as Emperor, he was backwards looking. But otherwise his government was a force of European modernisation since many of the areas under French rule were exposed to new systems of law and public administration that disrupted and displaced existing social networks of power, both of which tended to vivify more abstract notions of "nationalism" and weaken existing systems of "personalism" with lasting consequences well after Napoleon's own demise (McLynn, 1998).

Additionally, intense resistance to his rule, especially in the principalities of Germany, and in Spain, were further stokes to a growing nationalist fire. Although short-lived, Napoleonic rule in Europe temporarily unified areas that were politically and administratively fragmented (especially in Germany), imposed codified rather than customary laws, and displaced tradition elites and powers. All this was largely swept away by Napoleon's defeat in 1815 and the subsequent Congress of Vienna that restored many, though not all, of the old orders, borders and rulers. However, the genie was out of the bottle and the old royal and noble orders were ultimately on their way out (Winks & Neuberger, 2005).

Social theorists and sociologists often collapse social and political developments such as these under the rubric of "modernisation", which has many definitions but which broadly refers to a transformation of society along a notionally progressive path of change. Modernisation is a paradigm with many competing schools of thought (see Chapters 3, 7, 9 and 11 for more about its theories and various facets). Its general thrust is that, as societies begin to build and bed down modern political states, which themselves are the outgrowths of changing social forces, there begins a steady co-evolution of social activity, intellectual, family, and political life, public and private institutions, economic relations and culture. Social and political modernisation will necessarily drive economic change that reverberates back into noneconomic spheres in a mutually reinforcing process (Inglehart, 2005).

Of course modernisation theory, framed monolithically, will always oversimplify very complicated and interrelated patterns, even within single societies. Some areas of social life seem to be relatively poorly explained by it, such as trends in religion, crime rates, or the status of women (Inglehart & Baker, 2000). And modernisation theory largely assumes that causality runs from society to economy, which is not always the case, with boundaries between the two often difficult to distinguish. There has also been strong Eurocentric and Western bias in much modernisation theory that ignores patterns of change that occurred outside of Europe, and independently of it (see Engerman and Unger [2009] for a discussion of correctives to this bias).

Clearly, societal changes took a distinct turn in the "modern" era and were a critical ingredient in the making of the modern world economy. Some of the relevant sociological models are considered in detail later, but one useful construct that will be employed in various ways throughout this book is that of the sociologist Norbert Elias, whose views are detailed more in Chapter 5. Elias explicitly bridges a dualism that plagues much social theory, that of the individual and the collective society of which the individual is part. In brief Elias argues that social change (which he refers to as sociogenesis) causes changes within individual psyches (which he refers to as psychogenesis) and back again in an ongoing homeostatic equilibrium that constantly evolves over time. The simplified mechanics of his approach are summarised in Box 2.4.

Box 2.4 Norbert Elias and Psychogenesis and Sociogenesis
Socialisation refers to the attainment and development of individual skills, abilities and awareness that allow one to be social with other fellow creatures. In human society, this involves internalisation of societal norms and behaviours (Cromdal, 2006). The sociologist Norbert Elias claims that modern society has resulted from, and continues to evolve out of, a long-term socialisation process that simultaneously changes individual character and psychology and the way that individuals relate to each other and form a collective.

Elias claims that human sociality has evolved over time to make us both more connected with each other socially while necessarily and simultaneously also more self-regulating and self-censoring as individuals. The ability to modify our behaviour as individuals in the presence of others allows us to adapt ourselves to the greater society and achieve greater levels of interpersonal connection and the social functionality and power that comes with that. But this comes at the cost of greater internal suppression and repression.

Elias splits this interplay between personal and societal into the component processes of "sociogenesis" (changes in the structural dimensions of social life) and "psychogenesis" (changes in the structural dimensions of the psychology of society's members and the constitution of their collective psychology). Elias sees this dual co-evolution as a distinct aspect of the formation of modern Western civilisation and refers to it as the "civilising process", a theme of his major sociological work, spread out over three volumes (Elias, 1969, 1982, 2000). He claims that Western civilisation was formed and continues to evolve out of this dual nature of human relatedness and personality formation, and that it has manifested in the West in a very particular way with outcomes that we now refer to as modernity. Importantly, Elias argues that this trade-off is neither good nor bad in and of itself. Nor does it have an "optimal" stable endpoint.

Elias came to his conclusions in part by extensively examining the contents of etiquette manuals in royal courts in European countries from 800 C.E. to 1900 C.E. to see how guidance on elite manners changed over time. What he found was that the earlier manuals allowed for all sorts of personal behaviour (e.g. spitting at table) that we would now consider disgusting for anyone to do in public, much less nobility. But over decades and centuries, a slow and gradual redefinition of shame boundaries took place, with personal shame now becoming the primary emotion for regulating social behaviour. As communities grew larger and more complex, socially unregulated "animal" behaviours (e.g. defecating and copulating in public) needed to be internally "pacified" to allow for the sorts of deeper group bonding required to conform to changing social norms underpinning increasingly interdependent societies.

Thus less complex societies required less social interdependence than more modern societies, with no pejorative or honorific meaning to be taken either way. With less social interdependence, people are freer to express individual animal instincts and personal drives, including direct violence or amorousness upon nearby others, (though this varies widely by culture). But this freedom limits the benefits that greater social interdependence brings, such as fine specialisation of labour and high levels of organisation that yield greater levels of material gain and cultural sophistication. Gaining these benefits requires increased individual self-censoring and self-regulating, enforced through changing social norms, often starting with elites and then ultimately filtering down to the masses.

Elias further refers to the "ambivalence of interests" of people both competing with and yet depending on one another simultaneously. This requires a lot of attunement with others, a "permanent monitoring" which consists of a constant evaluation of what others want so as to be able to coexist with them more profitably, safely and productively.

Thus in Europe individual violence increasingly became outsourced to the collective and ultimately the State. Whereas medieval knights felt no compunction in lashing out at the nearest available opponent, modernising societies reserved legal violence to the government and its agents. This created its own problems, of course, as any evolution in some sense always does. But the payoff was a wider social peace and greater ability to coordinate across ever larger and more diverse groups. Thus the beneficial interdependence gained through internal social pacification, such as the ability to walk down the street or sit at table with peers firm in the knowledge that all exchanges would be peaceable, required social norms that were increasingly repressive of instinctual drives. This also required new implicit and explicit standards of social civility and changes in the way that individuals themselves perceived and acted in the world. Over time, changes in norms and other social pressures were increasingly internalised by individuals as "second nature" (what Elias refers to as "habitus").

Since this is a homeostatic process, there is not a simple cause-and-effect relationship between psychogenesis or sociogenesis. It is the state of the overall equilibrium between the two that matters. This process is always dynamic, which is one reason that Elias resisted "systems" approaches, which he believed were too biased towards immutability, whereas he believed social orders and individual members of them to be always changing. While there is an evolution to be sure, Elias is careful to note that there is no inherently better or worse state of society and therefore no meaningful or valid hierarchies of different societies can be developed. And, to reiterate, Elias specifically focused on European society and its transition from pre-modern to modern modes. Non-European societies would surely follow their own distinct pathways of societal change, and Elias made no claims about these. (For descriptions of Elias's theory of the civilising process see Aya, 1978; Linklater & Mennell, 2010.)

Whether one agrees with Elias' exact formulation, it does seem reasonable to say that social change acts at both collective and individual levels and that the evolution of both individuals and their collectives affect each other. This assumes that individuals are changeable through social processes in some basic fundamental ways, and also that the nature of the social groupings they live in, up to and including their whole society, are also quite plastic. The modernisation paradigm from this social perspective implies that social changes drive economic history in some core way and that the modern economy is an outgrowth of this process.

2.5 Paradigm 3: The Growth Model (It's All About the Economy)

When most people speak about the world economy, they generally think first of the economics discipline, which is dedicated to its study. As with any field, economists share a set of simplifying assumptions about how the world works. Two particular ones relevant here are about (1) the boundaries between "society" and "economy"; and (2) the fundamental drivers of economic behaviour and change over time. Taken together these assumptions are key elements of what is often referred to as the "Growth Model".

With respect to (1), economists generally limit their scope of analysis to the "real economy" which refers to actually existing and produced, consumed and exchanged goods and services flowing through a given society. For the economy since 1800 especially, this typically refers to such activities conducted and priced through markets of some sort, formal and informal, though it also can encompass production, consumption and exchange that occurs outside markets (such as child-rearing within a family household). The boundaries between "economy" and "society" can actually be quite contested and clearly they have shifted with economic modernisation away from "informal" activities outside markets and towards "formal" ones conducted within them.

The standard baseline measure of economic growth is Gross Domestic Product (GDP) which measures the monetary value of all output produced in a region (usually a country) in a given period of time (often a year), assessed at prevailing market prices. To get a crude idea of how this total output value filters down to individuals, for a given economic unit, GDP is divided by the total population to get per capita GDP. Usually, a "real" GDP measure, which screens out the distorting effects of mere price inflation, is used.

This metric, limited as it is, grew dramatically after 1800. Table 2.2 shows the trends for selected years between 1820 and 2010 for various global regions, using the consensus number series developed by the economic historian Angus Maddison (though these are not completely uncontroversial, as Chapter 3 discusses).

Imperfect as they are, these data, nevertheless, clearly show that by 1820, the "West" in the form of Western Europeans and their four major white settler colonies of the United States, Canada, Australia and New Zealand (especially the US in 1820) were already substantially "richer" in terms of GDP per capita than the rest of the world. Although for much of history prior to that Asia especially was richer than Europe, a modern pattern of the two global regions switching relative economic places was already well established by the early nineteenth century.

This pattern only accelerated as the nineteenth century unfolded and the twentieth century began, something that economists refer to as the "Great Divergence", in which industrialising Western countries (and Japan) broke away from the rest of the world in terms of the market value of output produced per person. East Asian per capita GDP (which included China) barely moved between 1820 and 1900, while Western Europe more than doubled its per capita GDP and the offshoots more than tripled theirs (Pomeranz, 2000). By 1950 East Asia was still basically economically treading water, while strong growth continued in the

Table 2.2 Regional averages of GDP per capita, 1820–2010 (Selected years) (2011 US$)

Region *Year*	*Western Europe*	*Eastern Europe*	*Western Offshoots*	*Latin America*	*Asia (East)*	*Asia (South and South-East)*	*Middle East*	*Sub-Sahara Africa*	*World total*
1820	2307	818	2513	953	1089	929	974	800	1102
1850	2678	985	3474	1081	900	929	1000	800	1225
1870	3301	1575	4647	1319	989	850	1165	800	1498
1900	4724	2700	7741	1751	1086	994	1300	850	2212
1920	4884	1343	9741	2331	1160	1117	900	950	2241
1940	7185	3209	11,621	3024	1361	1235	2146	1100	3133
1950	7263	4082	14,773	3713	1122	1070	2393	1323	3351
1960	10,974	5779	17,472	4751	1735	1295	3110	1574	4386
1970	16,161	8241	23,210	6286	3042	1546	4801	1958	5952
1980	20,950	9933	28,787	8728	4212	1897	6742	2026	7233
1990	25,440	10,344	35,619	8132	6121	2574	6435	1801	8222
2000	32,536	8986	44,329	10,225	8164	3437	9640	1981	9915
2010	37,318	17,021	48,090	13,453	12,853	5367	16,716	3156	13,179
2016	38,511	19,446	51,668	14,090	15,698	6991	18,010	3491	14,700

Source Bolt and Van Zanden (2020), Maddison 2020 Update

"West", though at somewhat slower rates because they were increasing off a large and very wealthy base income level. What kicked off this process is referred to as the "Industrial Revolution", which is discussed in much greater detail in Chapter 3.

Then, around 1980, this process takes a different turn. The very wealthy "West" continues to grow but much more slowly, and it is the "East" that rapidly catches up in per capita GDP terms, a process referred to as the "Great Convergence". This process is said to still be ongoing, although as everyone attains high affluence, simple arithmetic dictates that growth rates must slow as the base they grow off of becomes larger (Allen, 2011).

Why caused all this to occur? According to the Growth Model, prior to 1750 or so there were only intermittent periods of sustained economic advancement that could go for stretches of years or decades, with associated increase in material standard of living for local or regional areas. Rising per capita GDP for some regions during some periods of time did occur, sometimes over quite large areas, such as the core of the Roman Empire or China. Additionally, Asian and Middle Eastern countries were generally significantly richer than European ones, and it was they that experienced the greatest amount of localised growth. But for all people everywhere the natural constraining forces that operated on all animals, especially famine and disease, and other more human limits, such as agricultural productivity and war, always brought the human material economy back to some form of subsistence level (Acemoglu, 2012).

The Industrial Revolution broke humanity out of this very long-term natural-biological homeostasis, and the Growth Model explanation for this revolves around a change in incentives. Economists generally posit a stable set of human traits across time, especially egotism, self-seeking and logical thinking. Given these traits a plausible story emerges in which the structure of constraints and encouragements (i.e. the incentives) in the "West" shifted in such a way that logical human self-seeking more and more became oriented towards decisions and activities that delivered ever greater material productivity, and which then became mutually reinforcing into a virtuous and self-propelling cycle. According to the theory, when incentives change, so does the behaviour, in relatively predictable ways given the core selfishness and logicality of most people. Know what the incentives are, and also the constraints, and one can basically know the economic direction of society, which is treated as being the sum of all the individuals in it, more or less (Acemoglu et al. 2002; Allen, 2009).

The Growth Model and its basic moving analytical pieces are described in Box 2.5. The thumbnail version is that the material economy can be likened to a great big machine (or perhaps a great big factory full of machines and workers) into which go inputs (such as human labour hours worked and physical units of land) which produces outputs (such as sewing machines and foodstuffs) which are then sold and traded in markets for consumption and investment, feeding the economy in an ongoing expansion. The inputs (e.g. soil and seed and farm labour) are transformed into higher-level outputs (e.g. wheat and bread) by "technology", here used in a very broad sense of some sort of process, whether it be "hard" (e.g. a winepress) or "soft" (devising more productive ways of organising people to do tasks) which rearranges inputs and changes them into newer "higher value" forms.

Box 2.5 The Growth Model (and the Production Function)

The Growth Model generically refers to a variety of models that posit an economy as resting on a production function. This function is typically written in generic form as something like:

$$Y = f(K, L)$$

where:

Y	refers to output over a given period;
"f"	refers to a "function" which is literally just a mathematical relation but one which is representative of some of process (often referred to as a "technology") that transforms inputs into Y;
K and L	refer, respectively, to two major inputs "capital" (such as factories) and "labour" (such as hours worked).

If we measure "Y" as "GDP", we can see that the equation implies that the major ways to increase growth in Y (and hopefully make it grow faster than population, which will then lead to growth in per capita GDP) come through the total amount of inputs available (in this case K and L) and through the efficiency and effectiveness of the available technology (f) that transforms those outputs.

A little more reflection reveals that the most effective way to boost growth is to improve the quality of technology. This is said to be the key aspect of the Industrial Revolution, and it remains a key goal of policymakers in our current "high tech" age.

Another way to achieve the same goal, which can be used in conjunction with technical progress, is to improve the quality of the inputs, especially L, through, for example, the creation of a better educated, better trained, and more skilled labour force through improved access to education and training; and K, through the provision of incentives to increase savings and investment. The lines between technology and capital can be conceptually blurry at times, but improvements in the quality of either are held to be generally good for increasing growth, according to this model. (For more see Acemoglu, 2008, 2012; Allen, 2009, 2011.)

An important term in the Growth Model is productivity. In crude terms, productivity refers to the amount of output produced per given unit of input. For example, one hour of human labour producing two finished cotton garments represents more productivity than that same hour producing just one finished cotton garment. In the Growth Model, productivity growth is especially important because, if achieved, workers and entrepreneurs, and hence society, can get more material gain for less material sacrifice (Crafts, 2004).

The Growth Model narrative holds up positive growth in material output as a desirable thing, driven by a supposedly natural human tendency to want a growing accumulation of material wealth and income. It also offers a model that purports to capture the way such increase can be achieved, namely through incentives to accumulate and produce more efficiently and productively. There are quite a few variants to this approach, but the theoretical core is remarkably consistent, boiled down to this statement: incentives, and their effect on deployment and development of capital, labour and technology, are the key drivers of modern economic change. Chapter 3 lays out how this played out in the form of the Industrial Revolution.

2.6 Consistent or Inconsistent Paradigms?

Each of the three broad approaches is based on the single core reality that the scope, scale and nature of human activity on the planet began to change significantly around 300 years ago and that the process has been continuing ever since. In one sense, the three paradigms can be seen as different lenses looking across a very multidimensional development. Society, Economy and Earth Systems are all changing rapidly, and it is necessary and desirable to examine all three dimensions simultaneously, which is what using these approaches together allow us to do.

But the values and causal assumptions of the three can be quite distinct in practice and in theory, at times even antagonistic to one another. Thus the economic lens is very materialistic in its viewpoint. Material output and input is the basic unit of all measurement, and increase in these indicators is seen necessarily as a sign and goal of human progress. Technical change is posited as providing technical solutions to a technical process of ever increasing (though generally diminishing) returns on investment that are, one way or the other, ultimately delivered to all human beings, even though external interventions into markets by government and other entities may be required at times. The economics lens also tends to be ruthlessly individualistic in a methodological sense. The individual is the key actor in the story and that individual's viewpoint, in a generic sense, is the privileged outlook of the model. Society and all social groupings are in general seen as merely sums of individual parts, and since the parts are selfish, greedy and rational, the wholes are too.

This methodological particularism is a big part of the hostility and scepticism that the mainline economics profession had towards the *Limits to growth* report, sentiments still regularly expressed towards contemporary no-growth or slow-growth movements. It is not that the seriousness of the ecological problem, nor its human genesis, is denied. But the nature of the problem is generally assumed to be one of incentives and either the incentives will cause the system to correct itself (rational people, even selfish ones, will not destroy themselves, or so it is presumed); or selective policy interventions that "mimic the market" can be used to guide the system back on track. The most important thing is to allow economic agents maximum freedom of action to pursue their interests at all times, intervening only and periodically when the entire system is put at risk because of "incomplete" or "imperfect" markets.

The Anthropocene paradigm is less specific in its assumptions about human behaviour, which allows it to be broad in its framing of causality, positing human activity as a prime mover of climate change, without getting into the details of what drives such activity. This approach encompasses multiple causes and effects. Indeed, a planetary perspective by definition has to look at many grand causes, of which humanity is but one. While more comprehensive in the way the impacts are defined, tracked and explained, there is much less analysis of why people are doing what they are doing. Individualism, materialism and the market mechanism can all be legitimately critiqued, but an Anthropocene perspective does not by itself provide a guiding light by which to formulate policy, other than, perhaps, the "precautionary principle" (Gollier & Treich, 2013) which, in its various versions, holds that where there is threat of serious damage, corrective action that might help without doing harm should not be refrained from simply because there is less than full scientific certainty about the nature of the problem at hand.

With respect to the social modernisation perspective, this chapter has collapsed into one single outlook a vast variety of sociological, psychological and political theories, not all of which are compatible with one another (and further elements of which are considered as the book progresses). Any societal perspective, however, grapples with what actually constitutes human society. As we've seen, economists essentially hold that it consists of an array of single beings added up. But it is obvious humans are highly social beings and that their collectives are often much different than the sums of their parts. Even the notion of an "individual" is in reference, and relation, to some sort of "society". Arguably, economists take a much too simplistic view of this problem, often defining it away. Sociologists and others do look at the issue but have not yet found a single key to reality either. It is clear, though, that changes in human society have been critical to changes in human economy.

The chapter ends, in a sense, where it began. Multiple paradigms and perspectives are required to track and understand the process of economic change over the past three centuries. It is not that one paradigm is "right" or "better" but that they should be applied more symbiotically than they have thus far.

References

Acemoglu, D. (2008). Growth and institutions. In L. E. Blume & S. N. Durlauf (Eds.), *The new Palgrave dictionary of economics* (2nd ed.). Palgrave Macmillan.

Acemoglu, D. (2012). Introduction to economic growth. *Journal of Economic Theory, 147*(2), 545–550.

Acemoglu, D., Johnson, S., & Robinson, J. A. (2002). Reversal of fortune: Geography and institutions in the making of the modern world income distribution. *The Quarterly Journal of Economics, 117*(4), 1231–1294.

Allen, R. C. (2009). *The British industrial revolution in global perspective*. Cambridge University Press.

Allen, R. C. (2011). *Global economic history: A very short introduction*. Oxford University Press.

Aquinas, T. ([1237] 1997). Summa theologica. In A. C. Pegis (Ed.), *Basic writings of St. Thomas Aquinas* (Vol. 2). Hackett Publishing.

Aya, R. (1978). Norbert Elias and "the civilizing process." *Theory and Society, 5*(2), 219–228.

Bailyn, B. (1967). *The ideological origins of the American Revolution*. Belknap Press.

Bolt, J., & van Zanden, J. L. (2020). Maddison style estimates of the evolution of the world economy. A new 2020 update. *Maddison Project Database* (version 2020). https://www.rug.nl/ggdc/historicaldevelopment/maddison/releases/maddison-project-database-2020

Chakrabarty, D. (1998). Minority histories, subaltern pasts. *Economic and Political Weekly, 33*(9), 473–479.

Chakrabarty, D. (2009). The climate of history: Four theses. *Critical Inquiry, 35*(2), 197–222.

Chatterjee, P. (1995). *The nation and its fragments: Colonial and postcolonial histories*. Oxford University Press.

Cobban, A. (1964). *The social interpretation of the French Revolution*. Cambridge University Press.

Cox, J. (2014, 24 January). *World's elites gather for Davos 2014: Contraception key in climate change fight: Gore and Gates*. CNBC. https://www.cnbc.com/2014/01/24/contraception-key-in-climate-change-fight-gore-and-gates.html

Crafts, N. (2004). Productivity growth in the industrial revolution: A new growth accounting perspective. *Journal of Economic History, 64*(2), 521–535.

Cromdal, J. (2006). Socialization. In K. Brown (Ed.), *Encyclopedia of language and linguistics* (pp. 462–466). Elsevier.

Dear, P. (2005). What is the history of science the history of? Early modern roots of the ideology of modern science. *ISIS, 96*(3), 390–406.

Elias, N. (1969). *The civilizing process: The history of manners* (Vol. 1). Blackwell.

Elias, N. (1982). *The civilizing process: State formation and civilization* (Vol. 2). Blackwell.

Elias, N. (2000). *The civilizing process: Sociogenetic and psychogenetic investigations* (Rev. ed.). Blackwell.

Engerman, D. C., & Unger, C. R. (2009). Introduction: Towards a global history of modernization. *Diplomatic History, 33*(3), 375–385.

Fitzpatrick, M., Jones, P., Knellwolf, C., & McCalman, I. (Eds.). (2004). *Enlightenment world*. Routledge Press.

Foucault, M. (1977). *Discipline and punish: The birth of the prison* (A. Sheridan, Trans.). Penguin Books.

Fuller, R. B. (1968). *Operating manual for spaceship earth*. Southern Illinois University Press.
Gilding, P. (2011). *The great disruption: Why the climate crisis will bring on the end of shopping and the birth of a new world*. Bloomsbury Publishing USA.
Gollier, C., & Treich, N. (2013). The precautionary principle. In J. F. Shogren (Ed.), *Encyclopedia of energy, natural resource, and environmental economics*. Elsevier.
Harari, Y. N. (2014). *Sapiens: A brief history of humankind*. Random House.
Harris, T. (2006). *Revolution: The great crisis of the British Monarchy, 1685–1720*. Allen Lane.
Hawken, P. (Ed.). (2017). *Drawdown: The most comprehensive plan ever proposed to reverse global warming*. Penguin.
IGBP (2014, October). *The great acceleration data*. International Geosphere-Biosphere Programme (spreadsheet), http://www.igbp.net/download/18.950c2fa1495db7081ebc7/1421334707878/IGBPGreatAccelerationdatacollection.xlsx
IGBP. (2015). *International geosphere-biosphere programme*. http://www.igbp.net
Inglehart, R. (2005). *Modernization, cultural change, and democracy: The human development sequence*. Cambridge University Press.
Inglehart, R., & Baker, W. (2000). Modernization, cultural change, and the persistence of traditional values. *American Sociological Review, 65*(1), 19–51.
IPPC. (2007). *Climate change 2007: Impacts, adaptation and vulnerability, contribution of Working Group II to the fourth assessment report of the Intergovernmental Panel on Climate Change*. Intergovernmental Panel on Climate Change.
IPPC. (2019). *Climate change and land: An IPCC special report on climate change, desertification, land degradation, sustainable land management, food security, and greenhouse gas fluxes in terrestrial ecosystems*. Intergovernmental Panel on Climate Change.
IPPC. (2021). *Human influence on the climate system: Contribution of Working Group I to the Sixth Assessment Report of the Intergovernmental Panel on Climate Change*. Intergovernmental Panel on Climate Change.
Kaviraj, S. (1995). *The unhappy consciousness: Bankimchandra Chattopadhyay and the formation of nationalist discourse in India*. Oxford University Press.
Kitcher, P. (2010). The climate change debates. *Science, 328*(5983), 1230–1234.
Kumekawa, I. (2017). *The first serious optimist*. Princeton University Press.
Linklater, A., & Mennell, S. (2010). Norbert Elias, the civilizing process: Sociogenetic and psychogenetic investigations—An overview and assessment. *History and Theory, 49*(3), 384–411.
Livesey, J. (2001). *Making democracy in the French Revolution*. Harvard University Press.

Mann, C. C. (2018, January/February). The book that incited a worldwide fear of overpopulation. *Smithsonian Magazine*.

McLynn, F. (1998). *Napoleon*. Pimlico.

McNeill, J. R. (2016). *The great acceleration: An environmental history of the Anthropocene since 1945*. Harvard University Press.

Meadows, D. L., Meadows, D. H., Behrens, W. W., & Randers, J. (1972). *The limits to growth: A report for the club of Rome's project on the predicament of mankind*. New American Library.

Monfasani, J. (2016). *Renaissance humanism, from the middle ages to modern times*. Taylor & Francis.

Neal, L., & Cameron, R. (2016). *A concise economic history of the world: From Paleolithic times to the present* (5th ed.). Oxford University Press.

Offer, A., & Söderberg, G. (2016). *The nobel factor: The prize in economics, social democracy, and the market turn*. Princeton University Press.

Pigou, A. C. (1928). *A study in public finance*. MacMillan.

Pomeranz, K. (2000). *The great divergence: China, Europe, and the making of the modern world economy*. Princeton University Press.

Roberts, J. (2000). Revolution from above and below. In T. C. Blanning (Ed.), *The Oxford history of modern Europe* (pp. 15–45). Oxford University Press.

Rublack, U. (2017). *Reformation Europe: New approaches to European history (Second edition)*. Cambridge University Press.

Simpson, M. (2020). The Anthropocene as colonial discourse. *Environment and Planning d: Society and Space, 38*(1), 53–71.

Smuts, J. C. (1926). *Holism and evolution*. Macmillan.

Steffen, W., Broadgate, W., Deutsch, L., Gaffney, O., & Ludwig, C. (2015). The trajectory of the anthropocene: The Great Acceleration. *The Anthropocene Review, 2*(1), 81–98.

Steffen, W., Grinevald, J., Crutzen, P., & McNeill, J. (2011). The Anthropocene: Conceptual and historical perspectives. *Philosophical Transactions of the Royal Society A: Mathematical, Physical and Engineering Sciences, 369*(1938), 842–867.

Steffen, W., Leinfelder, R., Zalasiewicz, J., Waters, C. N., Williams, M., Summerhayes, C., Barnosky, A. D., Cearreta, A., Crutzen, P., Edgeworth, M., & Ellis, E. C. (2016). Stratigraphic and earth system approaches to defining the anthropocene. *Earth's Future, 4*(8), 324–345.

Syvitski, J., Waters, C. N., Day, J., Milliman, J. D., Summerhayes, C., Steffen, W., Zalasiewicz, J., Cearreta, A., Gałuszka, A., Hajdas, I., & Head, M. J. (2020). Extraordinary human energy consumption and resultant geological impacts beginning around 1950 CE initiated the proposed Anthropocene Epoch. *Communications Earth & Environment, 1*(1), 1–13.

US NASA. (2020). *Climate change: How do we know?* United States National Aeronautic and Space Administration. https://climate.nasa.gov/evidence/

Ward, J. D., Sutton, P. C., Werner, A. D., Costanza, R., Mohr, S. H., & Simmons, C. T. (2016). Is decoupling GDP growth from environmental impact possible? *PLoS ONE, 11*(10), e0164733.

Winks, R. W., & Neuberger, J. (2005). *Europe and the making of modernity, 1815–1914*. Oxford University Press.

Zalasiewicz, J., Waters, C. N., Ellis, E. C., Head, M. J., Vidas, D., Steffen, W., Thomas, J. A., Horn, E., Summerhayes, C. P., Leinfelder, R. & McNeill, J. R. (2021). The Anthropocene: Comparing its meaning in geology (chronostratigraphy) with conceptual approaches arising in other disciplines. *Earth's Future, 9*(3), e2020EF001896.

Zalasiewicz, J., Waters, C. N., Williams, M., Barnosky, A. D., Cearreta, A., Crutzen, P., Ellis, E., Ellis, M. A., Fairchild, I. J., Grinevald, J. M., Haff, P. K., Hajdas, I., Leinfelder, R., McNeill, J., Odada, E. O., Poirier, C., Richter, D., Steffen, W., Summerhayes, C., … & Oreskes, N. (2015). When did the Anthropocene begin? A mid-twentieth century boundary level is stratigraphically optimal. *Quaternary International, 383*, 196–203.

Zalasiewicz, J., Williams, M., Haywood, A., & Ellis, M. (2011). The Anthropocene: A new epoch of geological time? *Philosophical Transactions: Mathematical, Physical and Engineering Sciences, 369*(1938), 835–841.

CHAPTER 3

"1800"

C. Gordon, *Many Possible Worlds*,
https://doi.org/10.1007/978-981-19-9281-0_3

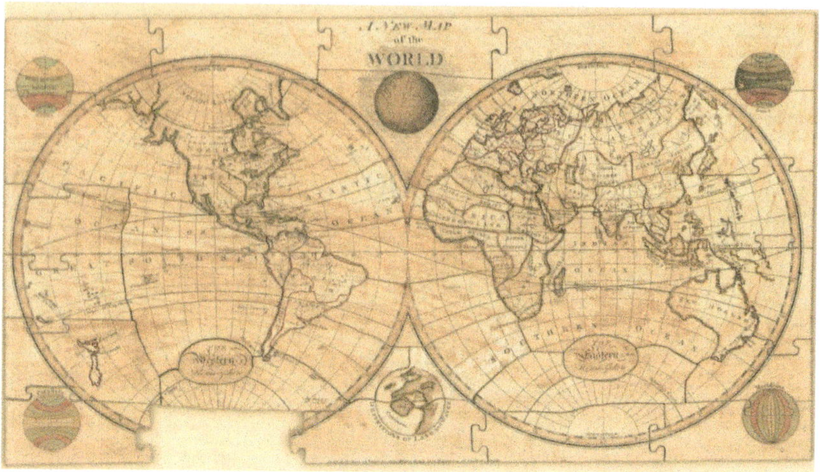

Fig. 3.1 A puzzle of the world—and the puzzle of the Industrial Revolution circa 1800 (*Image source* Wallis, J. [1800] *A New Map of the World*. London: John Wallis. [Map] Retrieved from the Library of Congress, https://www.loc.gov/item/85694393/. Map produced as a puzzle. No known copyright restrictions)

3.1 The Beginning of a "Modern" Economy

As the 1700s ended and the 1800s began, a clear shift in global economics was underway. A world that had been primarily agricultural in its basis was becoming more mechanical, technical and manufacturing oriented. The centre of wealth and political power was moving from Asia towards Europe. Most of all the scale, scope and size of production were growing. As the year 1800 commenced, world output and population had already been growing strongly, with both soon to explode over the course of the nineteenth century, the Europeans and their offshoots to quickly outpace almost everyone else in production of output (except for Japan and, to a lesser degree, a couple of the newly independent Latin American countries). World population now began to grow prodigiously across all regions, but Europeans increased their share of the total. And unlike prior times, output would expand consistently faster than population, in many European countries much faster, thus raising per capita output as well (Fig. 3.1).

The historically unprecedented nature of economic growth is shown in Table 3.1, using the Gross Domestic Product (GDP) per capita measure compared across all world regions.

These data, developed by the economic historian Angus Maddison and his successors (Maddison, 2007), are accepted as authoritative, though for the earliest periods, very notional and speculative and not nearly as accurate as the reporting to two decimal places suggests. Nonetheless, what they generally indicate is that consistent positive annual growth in per capita GDP was essentially non-existent during the first millennium of the Common Era (C.E.) in every region of the world, with very slow growth following in the five hundred years after that. China, India and Western Europe were the best performers between 1000 and 1500. A distinct shift then commences in 1500 with Europe and its offshoots still

Table 3.1 Rates of growth of real Gross Domestic Product (GDP) per capita (average annual compound growth rates [%])

	0–1000 C.E	*1000–1500 C.E*	*1500–1820 C.E*	*1820–1870 C.E*
Western Europe	−0.01	0.13	0.15	0.95
Eastern Europe	0.00	0.03	0.10	0.63
Former USSR	0.00	0.04	0.10	0.63
Western Offshoots	0.00	0.00	0.34	1.42
Latin America	0.00	0.01	0.15	0.10
Japan	0.01	0.03	0.09	0.19
China		0.06	0.00	−0.25
India		0.04	−0.01	0.00
Africa	0.00	−0.01	0.01	0.12
WORLD	0.00	0.05	0.53	1.30

Notes Western Offshoots consists of the US, Canada, Australia and New Zealand
Western Europe consists of Austria, Belgium, Denmark, Finland, France, Germany, Italy, Netherlands, Norway, Portugal, Spain, Sweden, Switzerland, the UK and other
Eastern Europe consists of all European countries outside Western Europe but not in the former USSR
Source Table B-22, p. 265, OECD (2006)

growing modestly but perceptibly more than other regions, the differential picking up in 1750–1820. In 1820–1870, there is decisive growth acceleration in Europe and its offshoots, with them pulling ahead of most of the rest of the world. (Though there may be a statistical bias in these figures towards the European countries in this latter period since many of them had started collecting economic data, from which these historical estimates are drawn, while many other parts of the world had not, the extent of this distortion is, however, likely to be relatively small [De Jong & Palma, 2018].)

This table should not be misinterpreted as saying that there was no economic improvement for anyone on earth until 1500 and later. The world population in the year 0 is estimated in the Maddison reports to be around 230.8 million people while by 1870 it had increased more than fivefold to around 1.27 billion (OECD, 2006, Table B-10, p. 241). Total production, wealth and income had to have increased substantially to support this fivefold increase in the number of people, and this was driven by definite technical and social advancements that helped to improve the average material quality of life generally.

However, between 0 and 1500, it is thought that there was not so much a rising standard of living but a rising level of subsistence. Human beings can subsist on very little, but economic change allowed this minimum level of material support to increase. Most people remained very poor, with little prospect of rising above poverty in their individual lifetimes; but their poverty slowly became less dire. The invention of agriculture tens of thousands of years earlier, and its various refinements along the way, allowed for this. The subsistence level for a hunter-gatherer society is assumed to have been much lower than that prevailing under later agricultural societies. Nonetheless, while humans on average were increasing their material baseline over the passage of centuries, collectively and locally they could still only temporarily rise above it before being brought back down to it (Galor, 2005). At least this is the generally prevailing theory as of this writing.

3.2 The Vantage Point from 1800

This is all a retrospective view. An observer placed in 1800 would have had some difficulty in predicting how quickly economies everywhere would change, the ways in which they would change, and how overwhelmingly economically dominant the European world would become. Contemporary observers had little actual "data" to consult. If they had, a distinct but subtle shift in global economic centre of gravity would have been clear. In 1700 the Maddison data indicate that India had the largest total GDP in the world, closely followed by China. France's GDP was less than one-fourth that of China and only one-sixth of India (though of course the precision of these numbers is fairly loose). By 1820, China and India had reversed positions, but were still the two largest economies (all using modern political boundaries). However, the UK was now in third place with a GDP one-sixth that of China, slightly ahead of France (Cox, 2015). Thus there were significant economic shifts going on between Europe and the rest of the world and within Europe itself.

Table 3.2 meanwhile uses the modern designations of "First" and "Third" worlds on global population distribution. Four-fifths of the world population were outside of what would become the "developed world" in both 1750 and 1800. Over these five decades, world population had already increased by almost a quarter, but growth was proportionately slightly stronger in the future "First World", leading to a slight increase in the percentage of people living there.

These are just numbers, but events on the ground at the time would buttress the trends exhibited in them, especially with regard to Europe's growing direct conquests of other parts of the world from an already fairly extensive base. Still the contemporary observer could not be totally certain as to how this would all ultimately play out. The future economic (to say nothing of political or social) trajectory arguably could have gone

Table 3.2 World population

Year	*(Millions of people)*			
	Third World	*First World*	*Whole World*	*Third World Share of Whole World (%)*
1750	626	165	791	79.1
1800	768	210	978	78.5

Notes Third World consists of Asia (including Japan—unlike in Table 3.1), Africa and Latin America/Caribbean) and Oceania (unlike Table 3.1)
First World consists to Europe, Russia, North America (but not Japan—unlike in Table 3.1)
Third World Share numbers are rounded to the nearest decimal point
Source extracted from UN (1999, Table 2, p. 6)

in a number of directions. There were still very significant independent power blocs outside Europe, including the Chinese empire, the independent Indian principalities, the Japanese under the Tokugawa regime, the Qajar dynasty of the Iranians, the Ottoman Empire, and the various countries of large and diverse Africa. In the Americas, European colonisation had already been entrenched for several centuries but things were changing there, British North America already broken into Canada and the newly independent US; Spanish South and Central America beginning a twenty-year process of breaking apart into multiple independent entities; and remaining French and Spanish possessions in North America and the Caribbean to pass out of their masters' control within a few decades (Stearns, 2001, 1264–1267, 1017–1026; White, 2013, Part 1).

The European order itself was to be roiled by the Napoleonic wars of 1800–1815, an outgrowth of the cataclysmic French Revolution of 1789. This development was a key driver that finished off the long-standing and once mighty Spanish empire in the Americas, since Spain came under French dominion thus loosening that country's hand over its colonies. These wars also and incidentally enlarged the territory of the newly established US, first with Napoleon's sale of the Louisiana territory to the American government in 1803 (to help finance his Continental war effort), followed by Spain's sale of Florida in 1821 (Spain once more independent by then but ailing and cash-strapped) (White, 2013, Chapter 1).

Given all this upheaval, many contemporary observers in the first decade of the nineteenth century might have thought that perhaps the Western and European project was at a turning point. Spain and Portugal were obviously powers of the past, but what were to be the powers of the future, and would they be European? Whether the French or the British would prevail in their mutual war was uncertain, with many ebbs and flows to follow. The Russian Empire was a rapidly emerging new world major power, but it had only really unified itself just two centuries earlier. It now possessed a huge internal landmass running from the eastern fringe of Europe all the way to the Pacific Ocean (Mason, 2011, 23–29). But it remained isolated and something of a mystery still to both Europeans and Asians, a unique and truly Eurasian entity.

The Asian world was in a similarly tumultuous state. China had been a true world power in earlier centuries, but in 1800 was in the middle of the White Lotus Rebellion (1794–1804), an event that separated Sichuan province from the rest of the country for a time. However, China had suffered through such crises before only to expand once more afterwards. Indeed, the country's borders had reached their greatest extent just before this turmoil. True, Burma, Vietnam and Korea, formerly vassal states to the Qing dynasty, had all broken free from Chinese domination. But the position of these countries was quite different compared to one another. Vietnam unified around this time and grew regionally assertive, while Korea was suffering the after-effects of a long war with Japan, emerging victorious but devastated internally. The Koreans drew inwards into what became known as the Hermit Kingdom. It was conceivable that China could reassert its control at least over Korea in the future, once it had recovered its own equilibrium. Japan had already drawn inward well before the time, though it was prosperous and stable under its Tokugawa rulers, with the capital of Edo having perhaps 1 million people, one of the largest cities in the world (White, 2013, Chapter 2).

Still, European penetration of Asia was growing in intensity and breadth at the beginning of the century, though the European powers sometimes also fought amongst themselves over the spoils. British traders were pressuring the Qing government for more access to its cities for trade, while the Dutch were pushing out the Portuguese enclaves on Java, and overtaking the English enclave on the southern coast of Sumatra. The Spanish colony of the Philippines was in conflict with Muslim traders and colonisers who were expanding in the Malaccas (White, 2013, Chapter 2). How this would ultimately play out was not completely obvious. China was clearly under great pressure, and its dominance in Asia was threatened, but the Europeans were divided as well.

African power movements of the time were much more complex. That vast continent had never been politically consolidated territorially and possessed a wide range of local environments, cultures, religions and societies. The major competition for external domination of the continent was between Muslim powers, concentrated mainly along the Northern and parts of the eastern coasts, and Europeans, who had established their own small coastal enclaves oriented towards trade, most notably the growing and highly profitable movements of slaves across the Atlantic. Such settlement began in the 1400s and 1500s by the Portuguese, joined by other European powers, especially the Dutch and the English, who began to establish white minority settler colonies. In Southern Africa, the two powers were coming into increasing conflict (White, 2013, Chapter 3).

The Muslim world was, according to most authorities, more economically developed than Europe in the early Middle Ages. But during the high and late Middle Ages, this tide turned with Islamic territorial reversals in Europe (e.g. the final elimination of the Islamic powers from the Iberian Peninsula in 1492), and many European countries catching up with and possibly surpassing Muslim wealth and income levels (Bosker et al., 2013). Muslim authority had never been as monolithic as European Christians had portrayed it. By the 1500s Islamic political and military power was divided and in relative decline in many places. Sunni Islam was the sect of the Ottoman Turks, and the Ottoman domain was now in slow but steady contraction. An Anglo-Ottoman alliance had ejected the French from Egypt but then Egypt became nominally independent of the Ottomans in 1805, though actually an English dependency. Muslim powers had once consolidated control of India under the Mogul emperors but the British firmly established their own imperial control over much of the subcontinent after a decisive victory over the French in 1757. The decline in global Islamic power was, however, not universal; inroads were being made in the populations of the Pacific, and there were continuing strong power bases in Africa (Egger, 2018, Chapters 5–8).

Taken together the "neutral" observer in 1800 looking at the world, even without access to statistics, would surely conclude that Europe was rising, but also that the world was likely to remain multi-polar politically and economically. China and the Islamic world were still influential on the world stage and relatively advanced in material terms, and the African continent remained mostly independent, though fragmented.

3.3 The Industrial Revolution and the Great Divergence: The Unified Growth Model (UGM)

Yet the changes that would unfold after 1800, already in motion, would play out much more dramatically and differently than those on the ground at the time might have predicted. "Europe" (broadly defined to include offshoots) materially leaped ever further relatively and absolutely ahead of the non-European regions. This development has been retrospectively called the Great Divergence. This was driven by what has been retrospectively referred to as the Industrial Revolution.

What really was the Industrial Revolution? A standard current-day explanation is offered by the Unified Growth Model (UGM) which holds that transition to a modern economy has had three distinct phases: the Malthusian Epoch, the Post-Malthusian Regime and the Sustained Growth Regime (Galor, 2005, 178).

The "Malthusian Trap" refers to the per capita GDP growth that prevailed globally before 1500. Pre-industrial economies, it is argued, were essentially limited by the amount of food that could be grown to feed a given population, and the availability of other natural resources necessary to house and otherwise support it. As noted earlier, there were long-term advances in subsistence levels, driven especially by innovations in agricultural technique and social organisation. And during times of natural resource and agricultural plenty, economic output per capita would slowly rise above subsistence as mortality and morbidity from disease and poor nutrition would wane and per capita production could thus increase.

However, this relative increase in growth would then cause birth rates to increase, death rates to decrease and total population to increase, setting in motion a counter-dynamic that began to bring per capita growth back down to subsistence levels, often temporarily shooting below them during the transition. As population growth created more mouths to feed overall, output per capita would begin to fall as available resources got used up. At this point, the human economy became overextended, leading to famine, greater disease, rising death rates and falling birth rates, a falling population and growing vulnerability to "exogenous shocks", e.g. catastrophic impacts of a crop failure that in more lush times could have been weathered by using stored food surpluses. Population ultimately had to fall back to a sustainable level given available baseline stocks of resources, at which point the economy would stabilise for a while, with the whole process to commencing once more later. In this way, humans were like any other animal population, subject mostly to the constraints and rhythms of the greater biological forces of which they were part (Galor, 2005).

However, some time during the eighteenth century, something changed to allow humans to break out of this biological cycle. The exact details of what happened are discussed in the next section, but according to the UGM, humans managed to reorganise their affairs in such a way as to open up the second phase of the human economy, the Post-Malthusian Regime, in which they used technological advances to break free of their biological constraints on material growth. This change is what has long been referred to as the Industrial Revolution. During this initial phase, running roughly between the middle of the 1700s to the latter half of the 1800s, the economy was still tethered to the overall size of the population, but technical advances dramatically increased agricultural productivity and manufacturing efficiency, allowing for much more to be produced from a given level of resources, thus loosening the demographic constraints to growth that had prevailed for centuries. These constraints have since been more fully overcome in the last phase, the Sustained Growth Regime, still ongoing (Galor & Weil, 1999; Pfister & Fertig, 2020).

To summarise, the UGM posits that the Industrial Revolution was primarily technological in nature driven by changes in incentives. Technical innovation increased productivity, increased the production of surplus beyond subsistence (while raising subsistence as well), and allowed for the accumulation of ever-greater material surpluses, in the process breaking the long tyranny of biological and demographic constraints.

3.4 The Industrial Revolution on the Ground

Is this what actually happened though? There is no question that economic growth shot up after 1750 or so; but was growth before that actually so slow and was the break with past patterns actually so sharp? Maddison's GDP data are considered to be amongst the best available comprehensive collection of national output over the very long term. But the information behind them is obviously fragmentary at best, nonexistent at worst for the earlier years. Thus there are many imputations and assumptions required, even for the more data-rich early nineteenth century. So one valid concern is whether the simplifications required to construct over 2000 years of GDP data may have oversimplified too much. Perhaps economic growth was more robust over the long run than the Maddison data suggest. (Of course the bias may also be the other way, and economic growth was actually less robust, in which case the story of a sharp "break" is strengthened.)

To get a better handle on this, economists have examined more detailed national accounts for selected countries and have found that European growth was both faster and more nuanced before 1750, and slower after that, than the Maddison estimates suggest. Fouquet and Broadberry (2015) find that between 1350 and 1420, the level of per capita income in the leading Western European economies (including Britain) rose by 40%, a modest but non-negligible growth rate of 0.8% per year over 70 years. Some countries had truly impressive growth before 1700, such as Holland, with per capita GDP rising by 70% from 1505 to

1595, and Sweden's almost equally strong growth in the beginning of the eighteenth century. England followed with its own strong growth in the second half of that century but was not the leader in this regard as has been so often supposed. These data do not overthrow the UGM story, but do moderate it, suggesting that if a Malthusian trap existed it actually began to end, in Europe at least, around four hundred years or so before the Industrial Revolution (Broadberry, 2013).

Other research zeroes in on British economic growth between 1770 and 1830 because the "Industrial Revolution" is often held to have been centred in that country (more on this in later sections). This research further modifies the UGM story by finding that English growth was much slower than those using the term "Revolution" had once proposed. Crafts and Harley (1992; also Harley & Crafts, 2000) are leaders in this revisionism, estimating that British per capita GDP growth during the late 1700s and early 1800s was around 0.48% per annum: good but not particularly unprecedented or even notably high. There has been much dispute over exact numbers (see, e.g., Berg & Hudson, 1994; Temin, 2000). But overall the current consensus is that European economic growth before between 1750 and 1830 was slower than was previously thought, and thus the Industrial Revolution was not so much a massive and sudden take-off there but a more diffused process of economic change, a sequence of strongly interrelated phenomena rather than a single event (Mokyr, 1999b, 30–31). But what were these "events" exactly? And why did they appear to occur first in Europe?

John Komlos (2000) argues that economic growth processes had existed for a long time in most places around the world, but that capital formation, population health, technical knowledge and agricultural surplus accumulation simultaneously reached a critical mass that allowed human productivity to achieve a scale and scope that it had never quite reached before. The term "revolution" is still apt in a way, but not in the sense of being a total rupture with past patterns. Britain in particular witnessed a significant restructuring of its workforce, transferring workers from agriculture to entirely new industrial occupations and into very new types of work and work conditions, over a number of decades, with the net effect of increasing both labour and capital productivity and per capita material growth (Griffin, 2013).

Indeed, the Industrial Revolution can be seen as a relatively gradual but profound shift in "economic structure" (to use the Kuznets [1966] concept), first in Europe, and then spreading to the rest of the world as the nineteenth century unfolded. The age-old pattern of rural labour accounting for the vast majority of national workforces, while also being primarily agricultural, was broken as more and more people were employed, directly or indirectly, in the production and servicing of manufactured goods which were located in or near cities (O'Brien, 2006, 2). It is estimated that in 1800 approximately 75–80% of the working population in what was to become the "developed" world was engaged in farming (Bairoch, 1988, 287). But this average conceals considerable variation across European countries, some of which had already gone a considerable distance towards industrialisation. In 1800, it is estimated that only 36% of the population was agricultural in England, 44% in Holland but still nearly 60% France (Johnson, 1997). Even relatively early in the Industrial Revolution, work in industrialising areas was moving rather quickly off the land, a trend that gained speed with the years.

Figures for relative shares of global economic activity during the 1800s illustrate this move away from farming and into manufacturing, and Europe's predominance in this trend. In 1750 around 33% of the world's total manufacturing took place in China with the Indian subcontinent close behind at around 25%. By 1913 Chinese and Indian shares of world manufacturing had dropped to roughly 4% and 1%, respectively, while the UK, the US and Europe accounted for three-quarters of the total (Allen, 2011, 6–8). This shift was already becoming pronounced by 1830 and by 1880 it was well and truly advanced (see Table 3.3).

All these people leaving the countryside had to go somewhere and another aspect of the Industrial Revolution was what some call the "urban transition". This was most marked in the UK, which was the leader in European, and thus global, industrialisation. From 1700 to 1830, the English population living in cities of more than 5000 inhabitants rose from 15% to 34% (Bairoch & Goertz, 1986, 285). During that same

Table 3.3 Shares of world manufacturing output (%)

	1750	*1830*	*1880*	*1913*
Europe	23.2	34.2	61.3	56.6
UK	1.9	9.5	22.9	13.6
China	32.8	29.8	12.5	3.6
India	24.5	17.6	2.8	1.4

Source Bairoch (1982)

time the urban share of the population (using the same definition of urban) was 10.7% in the "developed world" (all European countries and the Western offshoots), rising to 13.9% in 1850 (with a wide variation between individual countries). Urbanisation starts becoming hyperbolic in the latter half of the century, industrialising country urban population share reaching 41.6% in 1910 (Bairoch & Goertz, 1986, 289).

This level of urbanisation was achieved generally without the massive imports of foodstuffs from other countries that would have been required in the past. Instead productivity in agriculture grew and this allowed for sufficient internal creation of surpluses to support rapid city growth. Thus a growth cycle fed on itself: a steady increase in the amount of food output from a given hectare of land from a given amount of inputs, such as work hours and seed, combined with rapid innovation and productivity in manufacturing to produce increasing amounts of surplus that supported extensive urbanisation which created further increases in scale and efficiency of industry and further reductions in the total number of agriculture workers who were nonetheless producing greater amounts of food per labour hour (Johnson, 1997).

3.5 The Industrial Revolution: Why and How Did It Happen?

Indeed, steady productivity growth in all sectors is a hallmark of a modern economy in general and of the First Industrial Revolution in particular (Crafts, 2004). As later chapters will discuss (and as the UGM implies) there have been several shifts on industrialisation. The technological innovations of the First Industrial Revolution, which began around 1750, were myriad and profound, and so some scholars have described it as being primarily technological in nature (Landes, 1969). The inventions in early industrialisation, such as the steam engine, the power loom, and the use of coal as a power source (as opposed to wood and water), were important early innovations, with tremendous productivity impacts and flow-on effects (Griffin, 2013).

Many argue, however, that the First Industrial Revolution was about much more than just technical advance, impressive as that was. The sphere of domestic industry was especially affected, with sharp changes to female domestic roles, child labour and household structure, amongst other things. Cause and effect are difficult to establish, and it is not always that clear how technologically induced change in industry changed the household and vice-versa. There was also substantial variation across countries, the UK changing much faster and earlier than some of its counterparts, such as France, where social and economic changes were more gradual. Still there are those who claim that the social changes were much more profound, and truly revolutionary from the perspective of human being and society, than the technical ones (Griffin, 2013).

An additional issue is that much of the discourse about the Industrial Revolution remains tethered to the very limited measure of GDP growth, a measure arguably in need of revision or even superseding (Boarini & d'Ercole, 2013). But putting data limitations aside, it remains clear that a series of important and radical shifts in society and economy across the planet were rolling along and building through the nineteenth century, centred in Europe, driven by technical progress and rapid productivity growth. But why and how did it come about?

Let's return to the UGM as a starting point. The Model suggests that the transition from stagnation to growth is an inevitable outcome of the long process of human development and that the movement from subsistence to steady surplus economies resulted from forces within the human economy itself: in jargon, economic modernisation was endogenously created (or self-driven) and changing incentives were the motor (Galor, 2005).

The moving pieces of the Unified Growth economy are biology, demography and technology. Pre-industrial human economies are said to be biologically bound, with economic growth constrained to subsistence long-term because economic advance is driven either by good fortune (like a good growing season) or by simple technological improvement (implicitly admitted to be a constant human imperative). Both of these forces led to a temporary increase in surplus that was ultimately eaten up (literally) by population growth from a society that was typically very young, highly fertile, but also subject to high death rates. In good times population grew and was ultimately and always checked by growing beyond the ability to maintain a surplus. Human adaptation over the centuries did allow for slow overall population growth and increasing levels of subsistence, but a breakout to overcome the stronger forces of nature was not possible across a very long period (Galor, 2005).

This equilibrium was broken internally by a reinforcing interaction between the rate of technological progress and the size and composition of the population. Essentially, human adaptation began to slowly overcome the tyranny of demographic repetition, lowering fertility rates and family size so that their upkeep required fewer resources while also allowing for greater increments of surplus to be devoted to technical improvements. Gradually this increased pace of technological progress encouraged more total investment in human education. Both of these factors enabled societies to create more economic surplus per capita and caused them to be devoted to activities that steadily increased that surplus, rather than just be consumed through population growth in the form of larger families. This process culminated in the Industrial Revolution and the Great Divergence, though as noted, current scholarship indicates that these processes took several centuries to unfold and reach critical mass.

The model claims that natural selection in the form of these specific adaptations was a significant factor in moving the world economy from stagnation to growth. It also claims to be a "deep roots theory" finding persistent effects from small variations in historical and prehistorical conditions that accumulated into the Industrial Revolution and all the subsequent changes that have resulted in the present-day economic development across countries. In this schema, England's early industrialisation as compared to later movers, China especially, simply reflects initial differences in geographical factors and historical accidents. When conditions were right in any place, incentives to growth would shift, diffusing slowly over time through variations in institutional, demographic, cultural and other factors (Galor, 2005, 237–238).

Not even all economists, even neoclassically minded ones, believe in this tale. For example, Mokyr (1999b) refers to "the cartoon story of a preindustrial static society before 1750" (3). In fact, there is a myriad of possible drivers of modern economic change. A causal menu of potential factors driving growth is presented in Fig. 3.2.

There are so many factors here that one might say that this is an "overdetermined" model, offering too many explanations and thus explaining nothing. But in fact different theories focus on different factors, making differing claims about cause and effect, and this is all that the figure is meant to indicate. It is too strong to say that nothing has been learned about the Industrial Revolution and its Great Divergence (and its successor Great Convergence, discussed later), or that no definitive statements can be made. But given the complexity of the phenomenon, it is also fair to say that true consensus about causes has not yet been reached, if it ever will be.

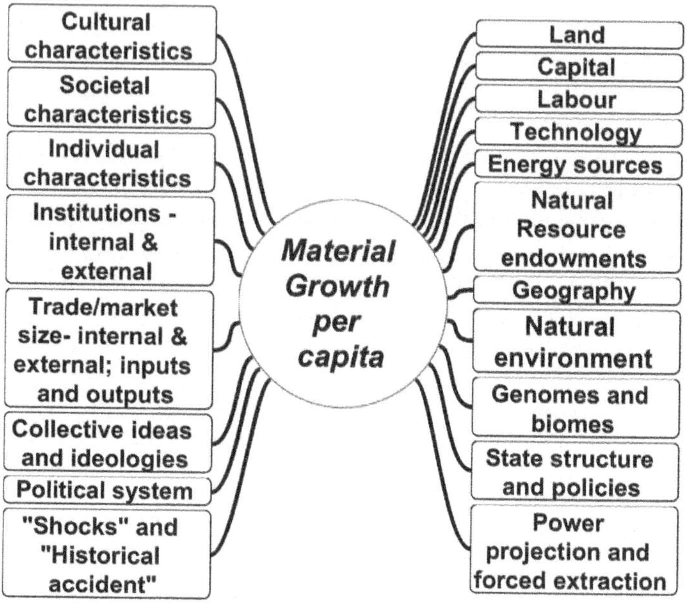

Fig. 3.2 "Menu" of factors affecting material growth per capita (*Source* Created by author)

Amongst economists the use of some kind of growth framework to approach economic history is a common feature, even though not all subscribe to the UGM. This rests on the notion, laid out in Chapter 2, that the economy can be viewed as akin to a great big machine, or, if one prefers, large factory, (technically referred to as a production function), in which inputs are fed into a technical process and transformed into higher-value outputs. Output for long-run economic growth is usually measured as per capita GDP and the major inputs are typically capital, labour and land, with the addition of other raw materials (such as minerals) in selected cases. Inputs are said to be scarce overall and varying in scarcity relative to one another in any given period.

These inputs generally are said to have the characteristic of "diminishing marginal returns", i.e. that past a certain point adding an additional unit of a given input yields less and less incremental output, all other things, such as current technology and use of other inputs, held constant. Also assumed is a high responsiveness of human beings to "incentives", which can be boiled down to the changes in the "opportunity cost" of doing one thing relative to other possibilities. Human beings are assumed to be generally highly selfish, greedy and "rational", and have generally been so across history, admitting significant cultural differences collectively, and variation across individuals.

The "why" of the Industrial Revolution in the UGM is technical progress that allowed for a reallocation of labour away from simply supporting family-based subsistence towards more technical advance which set up a virtuous circle of more and more surplus accumulation that got channelled into more technical progress, greater productivity and economic growth. Natural and social incentives that used to be oriented towards survival, subsistence and relatively immediate consumption, slowly shifted towards encouragement of production, investment and accumulation. In the UGM and most economics paradigms, capital is the critical ingredient of growth—it's quality, quantity and form. This logic goes back to Adam Smith and the Classical economists who saw the accumulation of capital as a prime mover in economic development (see Chapter 4). The very word "capitalism" enshrines this logic within its name.

"Capital", however, is not a new thing in and of itself. Some economic historians thus argue that the operative shift came when producers moved from creating and accumulating traditional forms of primitive capital which degraded quickly or were consumed entirely with their initial use (circulating capital to use the Classical term, and represented by things such as seeds for agriculture, raw materials for household production and simple tools in general) to more advanced "fixed" forms such as machines and structures, that were more productive, durable and able to be accumulated into large amounts that could produce economies of scale and other synergies (Mokyr, 1999b, 7–8). Many economists support this logic by noting the strong positive statistical correlation between an economy's overall supplies of capital and its GDP per capita growth rates. Others find that leading economic sectors in the past, such as mining, are often the most capital-intensive (Deane and Cole, 1969; Gerschenkron, 1962; Rostow, 1960).

Changes in technology are obviously prominent features of industrialisation, which some consider to be primary to all other changes, including capital accumulation and improvement. This includes not just inventions and new knowledge but techniques for organising labour and distribution and stimulation of consumer demand, amongst other things. The successful creation, implementation and diffusion of new technologies often required prodigious amounts of capital and for many economists capital supply and technical advance are thus closely linked (Landes, 1969; Mokyr, 1999a, 8).

Some see demographic adjustments as key to the capital accumulation process, which is also part of the UGM argument. E. L. Jones (2000) considers various arguments that Europe broke away from Asia in the sixteenth through eighteenth centuries, despite having a similar "preindustrial" economy, because Europe was able to use various customary checks on fertility (e.g. late marriage) to escape the prevailing universal condition of population growth absorbing almost all increases in production output. This population check allowed Europe to devote its surplus to accumulate the capital that allowed for greater technical progress and a better nourished (and hence more productive) workforce, dynamics that in certain ways reverse the UGM causality of technical change changing family size to the other way around.

Another story focuses on relative scarcity of labour to capital. The story is somewhat complex, but goes something as follows. Taking for granted that Europe pulled ahead of Asia, the argument is that this happened because Western Europe at the time had little labour to spare in comparison with Asia. This incentivised Europeans to find ways to save on labour (and the correspondingly high wages driven by its short supply) in their production processes, moving by necessity towards the development and use of machinery and other capital-based means of manufacturing. Other societies had plenty of labour but little capital and so focused on using their labour more effectively, but at the cost of losing the longer-term productivity increase that capital-intensive methods yielded. Many claims have been made in this regard, but except for some critical industries, especially in British cotton, it is hard to demonstrate a consistent case for it across countries (Pomeranz, 2000, 49–53). Another problem is that wage data for the period are often unavailable, and the data that do exist does not always indicate that Europe was "high-wage" or had the strong wage growth that would supposedly be consistent with a shortage of labour at the times this dynamic was supposedly playing out (Baumard, 2019, 37). Finally, in theory labour scarcity and high wages could equally have had a depressing effect on growth and productivity as much as a positive one, since more surplus in the short run would have to go pay for workers in high-wage areas, leaving less of it available for other purposes. All of these questions do not yet have particularly clear or universal answers (Mokyr, 1999b, 82).

Land scarcity is another element of debate. In an agrarian economy, land is always the ultimate constraint, and finding ways of coaxing more food from it has been a challenge since the invention of agriculture itself. Famine persisted in industrialising Western Europe until the middle of the nineteenth century, showing just how precarious the food supply was even in the recent past of the most economically advanced countries (Johnson, 1997, 4). But with low populations, the harder problem for much of global history was getting enough to people to work the land and having them working it as effectively as possible. Traditionally, this had been accomplished primarily through more intensive use of land, rather than from increased yields per unit of sown area, largely using the age-old system of leaving parts of fields fallow for regeneration and then harvest in later seasons (Boserup, 1965).

This situation is the background of the UGM's Malthusian trap in which human subsistence is kept bound closely to population size and land availability and productivity. However, as population grew over the centuries, and as human economic activity became more consuming and destructive of land and other resources (e.g. through deforestation resulting from timber use for housing in growing cities and other settlements) this calculation shifted, with usable land becoming short in supply, sometimes acutely so, and with old fallow field farming methods becoming outmoded. This would have incentivised economies in both the use of land and people, providing the necessary prod to industrialisation. Some, though, dispute this, Johnson (1997) claiming that land did not limit growth of agricultural output in Europe until well into the twentieth century, if then, because agricultural productivity was constantly raised by new technological means of increasing sophistication, even before industrialisation (6).

It is clear more broadly, though, that an ecological sustainability crisis was growing around the world, but in Europe especially, starting around the 1600s, and for which industrialisation offered a potential way out, though creating new problems as well. Pomeranz (2000) is the leading proponent of ecological crisis as a driver of European development, though still within a Growth Model causality. He argues that Europe and China (which are his main focuses) were roughly similar in overall wealth, income, technology and productivity at the turn of the eighteenth century, even with their very different cultural, geographical and historical circumstances. In fact, he says that is plausible to ask why China was not the first mover in industrialisation rather than England, given their similar advancement in "proto-industrialisation".

The difference he argues is that, broadly speaking, the core areas of the world prior to the Industrial Revolution, i.e. Europe and Eurasia, were experiencing modest per capita economic growth through the increased use division of labour and formal and informal market mechanisms of exchange (which we could refer to as "capitalistic"); but basic technological and ecological constraints of the time could not be overcome by this alone (Pomeranz, 2000, 107). Europe, however, had hit on a key innovation as the 1800s began through new techniques for developing and using coal as a new inanimate source of power for a whole array of activities beyond traditional heating. Coal was much more efficient and less land using than alternative energy sources of the time such as wood. Additionally, and more importantly, Europe also broke out of its own ecological and resource constraints by expanding its already substantial use of natural resources into non-European regions, solving its own ecological crisis through external expropriation.

The importance of coal to the English Industrial Revolution has long been known. English coal reserves were some of the most abundant in Europe, relatively cheap to extract, with deposits near population centres and of the right type for generating efficient power. China had coal but not in such convenient locations, and it was a much bigger country to boot so moving coal across such a large space added significant transportation costs (Clark & Jacks, 2007, 39). The innovation of coal-fired steam power that came to fruition in England was especially advantageous to industrialisation in that country. This coal power advantage, however, was according to Pomeranz, a foundation upon which New World trade and conquest built upon, a combination that made a critical difference. One author has made the analogy that with the Industrial Revolution Britain essentially became a giant urban area within Western Europe, fed with raw materials from European and international hinterlands and selling its production back out to those same hinterlands (Harley, 2003, 818).

In England particularly, coal provided a new energy source that gave power to industrial enterprise without sacrificing land needed to feed and house the growing population (Griffin, 2013). At the same time, the amount of land available for industrial use, directly and indirectly, was expropriated through state power both internationally (mainly through colonialism) and domestically (through, for example, enclosure of previously common lands, though this particular process was largely completed by 1750). Colonialism also allowed the capture of overseas raw materials and helped create a new kind of periphery feeding a new English and European core an ever-growing volume of land-intensive imports (which averted Europe's own land crisis) in exchange for an ever-growing volume of manufactured exports, often at exploitative terms (Pomeranz, 2000, 20).

The significance of the Atlantic trade in terms of financial profits and capital accumulation has been studied with these dynamics in mind, with mixed results. The traditional argument is that external resources gained by Europe through trade were much larger and more important to European industrialisation than those gained by force. Pomeranz acknowledges this possibility but claims that extracted resources played a much more important role in relieving the strain on Europe's scarce land and energy and gave the Europeans a critical advantage over the Chinese, their most salient economic competitor, which did not have similar access. He also claims that the payoff to this forced movement of resources to Europeans was far greater than purely consensual trade with less densely populated parts of the Old World.

3.6 From Competition Between Nations to a "World System"?

There is another way that "Divergence" and industrialisation can be looked at. Rather than be an indication of the failure (or success) of some countries to industrialise first, the unit of analysis can be shifted to a regional or global system, of which countries and areas are primarily component parts. Then the question can be reframed as to why the system sent growth to some areas and not others. The major implication of this idea is that it may be possible that some nations might not be able to succeed, while others cannot help but do so almost regardless of what they do or fail to do. This is because imperatives and agency are located at a supranational level, serving supranational ends.

Pomeranz (2000) does make use of schematic "core" and "periphery". His case, however, rests on standard economic logic about incentives and constraints, which explains global integration largely on the basis of national and regional incentives, in this case a European project to solve its own ecological crisis by extracting resources from other areas, using opportunities that were not as available to its Eastern counterparts at the time. He arrives at a point similar to "World Systems Theory", though by quite different logic. The sociologist Immanuel Wallerstein (1976) was the primary developer of the system idea, which starts with the argument that the proper unit of analysis is not the nation-state but the world system. This is already a departure from Pomeranz who begins with, as most economists do, nations in competition. Wallerstein's model of capitalist productivity instead rests on efficiency from a global division of labour introduced by capitalism itself. Pomeranz does note this, but sees it as one of a number of important elements rather than a central motive force.

Global economic relationships are not new, of course. International trading routes and relationships, some quite developed, go back thousands of years. But these were not interdependent within one global system in the Wallerstein sense. Autarky (self-sufficiency in production and consumption of necessities) was not only possible within those trading links but often necessary since international trade most times mainly encompassed "luxuries" rather than subsistence needs. Most pre-industrial economies were not productive enough to produce for, or rely on, other countries for the regular supply of essential inputs or outputs. Also the speed and reliability of international trade were not fast or consistent enough to allow for an international "supply chain", to use a modern term. Industrial production removed such autarkic elements almost completely over time, yielding much greater productivity than ever before, and also much larger interdependency which, worst case, yielded peripheral dependency.

Wallerstein's system consists of core, semi-peripheral and peripheral regions of the world economy. The core is where the high-value, high-income generating production and distribution occurs, with the periphery supplying low-value and low-income providing inputs. Semi-peripheral regions obviously are bridges of intermediate value-add and processing between the two. The system is partly organic, arising out of natural economic incentives and processes, and partly consciously designed, with the core using its muscle, i.e. its soft and hard power, to keep each region in its higher, middle and lower places.

Wallerstein is not deterministic in his theorising, as some others using the construct can be (more on this later). Some peripheral countries can grow into semi-peripheral or even core countries while others can slip down the other way. Still, over time the system dynamics predominate and these tend to harden as its scale and scope grow. The reason is that capitalism requires both globalised and localised division of labour, something reinforced by industrialisation. In a growth model context, by contrast, local conditions and initial starting points are what matter, working against fundamental constraints of scarcity that all human societies face and must contend with given their unique local incentives, resources and "accidents", all of which cause small differences in paths that can accumulate into large "divergences" at one time, "convergences" in others. With the world systems perspective, the dynamics of the whole are much more important for ultimate outcomes which may end up being very different from what initial starting points might suggest.

A plausible case may be made either way and arguably both perspectives are useful. Pomeranz and others make the case that China was as economically advanced as Europe in the 1600s and that therefore saying that Europe was better placed for a "take-off" is implausible. In fact, China was in some ways more advanced in its institutions, being widely known as the "inventor" of things such as paper money and credit. Similarly, China became a major naval power in the 1400s, before the Europeans had consolidated their advantage, and could have set off on a global imperialism of their own (Graff et al., 2013, 11). But in 1433 the Chinese emperor forbade further voyages overseas and destroyed ocean-going craft, a real turning point that closed off any possibility that it, not Europe, might have become the world imperialist (Neal & Cameron, 2016, 85). The Growth Model suggests that a large degree of "accident" was involved in Europe-China contest, the World Systems view by contrast suggesting that the divergence was more systemically orchestrated. The history is too complex to be forced into one paradigm or the other, but both are useful, certainly having applicability at different times and places.

3.7 Core-Periphery Examples: Monetary Standards and Slavery

An example of where a system dynamic might have been occurring is the pre- and early industrial world monetary system. Pre-industrial China and much of Asia were in practical terms using currency on a silver standard. In China, particularly, locally minted coins were made of copper, but silver increasingly became the standard of value as the country started importing monetary silver through Mexican and Spanish dollars in the early modern era. The monetary base of perhaps 40% of the world's economy in the period before the Industrial Revolution was in silver, and China's silver demand can be seen as a very important force in creating a pre-industrial global economy (Horesh, 2020).

Then a shift came, as Europe and its demand for Chinese tea and other goods gave it the leverage that it ultimately used to its advantage, in combination with colonialist force, to impose a gold standard on the world while disadvantaging the silver economies of China, Chinese tributaries and also India, which also used silver (Pomeranz, 2000, 161). Interestingly, the earlier vast gold and silver troves that the Spanish brought from their colonies into Europe during the 1600s and early 1700s were likely not that helpful to Europe's economic development, because of its inflationary effects. But this metals flow may have helped facilitate European trade overall by virtue of the large increase in liquidity it provided, helping to cement a systemic global financial edge (Palma, 2020). Also, by financing expensive European military adventures, this precious metals influx may also have helped European countries develop more effective militaries, a critical advantage in European expansionism overseas, especially once Europe stopped fighting itself for most of the century after the Napoleonic Wars (Morris, 2014; Pomeranz, 2000, 269–270). These are contestable propositions but they do suggest at least one economic arena that supranational forces may have been more important than national ones.

Another contrast between system and nation perspectives is around slavery and the slave trade. Slavery is an ancient practice, but many argue that a crucial turn in the institution came with its global expansion in the 1600s and 1700s driven by European colonialism and capitalistic development that helped "commodify" and "marketise" what was, up to then, more "informal" (though brutal either way). Slaves increasingly became financial "assets", accumulated through slave trading (and piracy), and arguably crucial to the funding of the Industrial Revolution, over and above the smaller advantages provided to Europe by the output of New World mines and plantations, for which slaves were the primary labour force. Many scholars dispute that the returns to these overseas activities were much larger than what was actually earned within Europe itself and through voluntary trade outside it (Pomeranz, 2000, 184–186). Regardless, Pomeranz (2000, 269) emphasises that the real value of slavery was to make European manufactures possible without much use of British land in exchange for ever-increasing amounts of land-intensive food and fibre (and later timber) at favourable prices. And most admit that slavery was key to some leading sectors, especially the British cotton cloth industry, which would have run into a severe bottleneck if not for raw cotton from US slave plantations (Mokyr, 1999b, 75). Putting the very important issue of morality aside for the moment, the slave system likely played a key role in creating a Eurocentric world system. And it looms much larger in a world system point of view than from a national perspective where many of its effects get excluded. (See more on the slavery issue in Chapters 6, 8, 11 and 13.)

3.8 What About "Society"?

The China–Europe debate points to an obvious question. If, say, China is somehow "different" from Europe but the main material economic features seem similar at the outset of industrialisation (the Pomeranz position, which is debated), what then is the basis of that difference? Could it be due somehow to the nature of their very different societies? Some make exactly this claim about England versus the rest of Europe, saying that the Industrial Revolution started in England (also debated) because its society was such that it was predisposed to the create formal, competitive and impersonal markets in goods and labour and capital, as well as democratic political institutions, both of which are supposedly essential to industrialisation in the first place (Bezanson, 1922). Could something similar have been happening with China relative to England also?

As with trends in growth itself, scholars have moved from broad sweeping claims to more targeted analysis of particular social factors. Some of these have already been alluded to, namely differences in family size. Many economic historians have examined the nature of individual consumption and the distribution of income over time, what economists refer to as the "demand" side, as opposed to the "supply" or production side. Some claim that a "consumer revolution" took place in Europe but not elsewhere, and it was this that was a crucial precondition for industrialisation. This "revolution" consisted of a combination of slowly but steadily rising household incomes, changes in consumer tastes towards non-essential goods rather than necessities only, and, an incremental increase in the availability of "luxury" goods made outside the home and sold in markets (De Vries, 1994). This is purported to have happened in 1500s and 1600s Europe. The rich had long had such tastes and the financial means to satisfy them, of course. But pre-industrial prosperity in the most advanced European countries helped raise the purchasing power of many others, creating a critical consumer mass where none had existed before. This new mass of consumers, it is argued, helped spur new investment in productive capacity and invention. This was not occurring in China or India, and this was the reason that they did not industrialise first, even though they had the capacity to do so (Clark, 2007).

The actual evidence for this has been disputed as possibly a statistical illusion due to biases in existing data towards more well-off households and misclassifications of purchase types as luxuries when they were actually necessities (Clark, 2010). Even if the proposed trends exist, others claim that the changes over time in income distribution and in consumer tastes were actually not markedly different between China, Japan and Western Europe (though it arguably was quite different in India) (Pomeranz, 2000, 136–146). Additionally, the timing of European change in tastes appears to have peaked too early to plausibly be seen as a cause of later industrialisation, existing, but independent of the industrial supply side change a century later (Mokyr, 1999b, 60).

Nonetheless, this "Industrious Revolution", to use the De Vries (1994) term to refer to a broader change in household behaviour from production of necessities by, in and for the household to a more market-oriented exchange model on which the household becomes more market-dependent for both consumption and production, is a significant social change (Mokyr, 1999b, 65). De Vries frames it as a change in preference from wanting leisure over goods in earlier times, to wanting goods over leisure in later times, and thus increasingly choosing to work more to get money to buy more things rather than go without and thus have more time off. As evidence he notes an ongoing diminution of "domestic production" altogether, and increased buying of ready-made goods sold at market, a change helped along by a growing number of shops, especially in England, which is where the phenomenon is heavily centred (see Chapter 5 for more on this).

These sorts of changes are still not fully "social" in the sense of transcending the notion of individuals as the core unit of social analysis. To put it more technically, individuals are assumed to be essentially "atomistic" in that their social connections are at best limited, mostly not reaching outside the household and generally more "transactional" in which exchange is conducted on a basis of mutual individual advantage. Sociological and other models that break out of this frame are considered in Chapters 4 and 5.

3.9 "Institutions"

Human activity is mediated by organisations of various sorts, and these have been another influence on economic growth. For this economists use a rather catchall and poorly defined term called "institutions". North (1990) uses the term to refer to the implicit and explicit "rules of the game" made by human beings to "shape human interaction". This is obviously extremely broad and encompasses things like human-made formal organisations, systems of law, and political rules and structures, but also any explicit or implicit structure that provides incentives to guide decision-making. Under this rubric, even things like culture and religion can be included.

Arguably, this is a concept that is too loose to be of much use. But in the study of economic growth, certain things come to the fore as important, especially property rights, corporate form and the nature and power of governmental entities (Acemoglu, 2008). With respect to the role that institutions played in industrialisation, property rights and business forms are leading candidates for many scholars. The structure and scale of the modern firm are deemed essential in some stories, with its ability to depersonalise and share risk and reward in the form of limited liability of ownership, as opposed to the unlimited liability of traditional sole proprietorship and partnership forms. And some very important means for organising production, especially the factory, emerged out of organisations of this type (Mokyr, 1999b).

Chandler (1992) sees the corporation as of vital economic importance, though more during the Second Industrial Revolution when large-scale enterprises, such as railways, boosted productivity and growth through economies of scale and scope delivered through vertically integrated production processes supported by large administrative apparatuses. Roy (1997, 78–114) disputes this, arguing that the corporate form was not in fact intrinsically more efficient that other forms, but at least in the case of building the American rail network, it became an institutional norm due to financiers demanding it before lending the substantial amounts of credit needed to build rail projects. (More will be said about railways in Chapter 8.) Everyone agrees, however, that the corporation certainly changed the shape of economic growth radically, even if it may not always have increased its rate.

The security of private property rights is often seen as even more fundamental. The very first narratives about England as a leader in the

Industrial Revolution often heralded that country's superior protections for such rights as the reason modern economic growth took hold there, especially after the Glorious Revolution of 1688 which enshrined parliamentarianism and the rule of law (see Chapter 2). However, subsequent scholarship has noted that other countries outside Europe, most notably China, had strong property right protection as well yet did not join the early industrialisation club (Pomeranz, 2000). The point has also been made that in some places, notably France, property rights were actually too strong, allowing incumbents to discourage competition and innovation by competitors, thus calling into question the previous holy grail that secure property right specifications were the be-all and end-all in the development of free enterprise (O'Brien, 1996).

Figure 3.1 also distinguishes between "external" (international) and "internal" (domestic) institutions. Thus European hegemony created through biased mechanisms of trade and extractive colonialism can be framed in terms of institutions. Pomeranz (2000) implicitly does this himself, in saying that during the sixteenth through eighteenth centuries, Western Europe and China both were broadly similar with respect to the economic effectiveness of their institutions (the individual manifestations obviously being quite different); but that the former became a "fortunate freak", to use Pomeranz's words, only when it hit upon its own coal revolution and transformed its institutional ability to take advantage of flows of various New World resources (207). Similarly, India can arguably be seen to be quite different from the two other regions in that it had considerably more ecological slack and therefore less need to develop the same economically efficient levels of organisation than Europe (Pomeranz, 2000, 213).

By the same token, China lived on a very thin ecological margin, making it very vulnerable to any decline in the ability of the State's then considerable capacity to manage such problems, with the country's economic decline in the mid-1800s coinciding exactly with a decline in the Chinese State's institutions. The fact that rich Yangzi Delta was much less affected by economic hardship in the midst of ecological challenge, despite being the site of the nineteenth-century civil wars and opium imports, can be attributed to its traditionally active local management of environmental affairs as compared to the more peripheral regions of China (Pomeranz, 2000, 239). By no means does Pomeranz reduce China-Europe differences to ones of institutions, for there are many factors involved in the former's decline and the latter's rise. But institutions played a pivotal role.

With respect to England, much of the earliest historiography emphasised the island's supposedly "unique" institutions. This tack has largely gone by the wayside. But economic historian Patrick O'Brien has an interesting argument about England's primacy and its development of a singular global naval supremacy, which is described in Box 3.1.

Box 3.1 Ships, Trade and British Hegemony

Britain had achieved global naval supremacy by the eighteenth century. Combined with its island position, O'Brien (2017) argues that its hegemony in this area allowed it an external security not particularly available to Continental countries like France. He also adds that, "Whig rhetoric" aside, the UK did maintain, per capita, a large standing army which, not needed too regularly abroad, served to maintain internal security against rebellious regions such as Ireland and Scotland.

Moreover, England at this point had a large empire, which grew larger over the course of the nineteenth century, which provided it with big external markets to sell output into and import input out of, on terms highly preferential to England. The large market for output is especially important because of the ability it afforded to make good returns on investment through larger potential sales, in turn encouraging English capital formation and innovation. All European imperialists did this, but England had a particularly favourable situation in this regard given its naval power.

One might point out that maintaining a large navy and relatively large army does cost money and that this would detract from its ability to deploy resources into industrialisation. Indeed, Britain did have a very high external debt level at times, especially after the Napoleonic wars, where the country recorded debt-to-GDP ratios of close to 300%, higher than even the later World Wars. And significant sums had to be appropriated to the British armed forces regularly.

But O'Brien argues that the UK also had high pools of savings and that the full faith and credit of the British government issuing these bonds was in fact enhanced by the power of the British Navy around the world. Foreign investors were willing to buy British bonds at low interest rates given the perceived safety of the issuer (not dissimilar to the position the US finds itself in today). Thus the higher cost of financing large armed forces was made up for by cheaper financing costs.

Moreover, this vast military power allowed cost-efficient maintenance of the Empire with its large captive markets, and the size of the navy itself was subject to economies-of-scale, making its upkeep cost-efficient as well. Overall Britain's military position created external and internal peace and stability that enhanced its ability to take advantage of some favourable domestic economic factors, such as abundant supplies of coal. This does not account for any additional potential direct economic effects (e.g. military innovations that diffuse into non-military applications), something examined more in Chapter 22. These were, though, probably fairly minimal at the time.

The discussion thus far has only just begun to look at the factors behind economic growth enumerated in Fig. 3.1. For example, no discussion has yet been offered of collective ideas and ideologies, or culture, and societal characteristics and political systems have been barely touched. These topics are deferred to the rest of this book, with this chapter devoted primarily to segments of the economics literature on modern growth and development (i.e. sticking mostly to Paradigm 3 of the Growth Model, as presented in Chapter 2).

This approach can take in almost everything, but in a particularly narrow way, assuming an essentially immutable human being who is self-interested, competitive and greedy, constrained by a natural environment, limited to species survival and extinction, that human ingenuity, led by the right incentives, manages to overcome. This focus is explicitly "materialist" in a philosophical sense, with economic forces, including within the human being, seen as purely material in the nature of cause and effect. There are, however, "idealist" approaches as well. Box 3.2 provides another example of how economists (in this case O'Brien once more) can turn even these in a materialist direction. Alternatives to this approach will be discussed in further chapters.

Box 3.2 An "Idealist" Conception of Industrialisation

Economic historian Patrick O'Brien, already discussed in Box 3.1, makes what is, in effect, a cultural argument for the rise of the Industrial Revolution in Europe in a 2013 paper. Economists sometimes refer to this an "idealist" explanation as opposed to the more materialistic notions embedded in growth theory.

O'Brien argues that with the rise of Christianity, the Catholic Church first suppressed polytheistic and animist systems of belief and thought and then, to consolidate its position against various threats (e.g. heresy and Islam) began to buttress its intellectual foundations by allowing in more logical reasoning modalities drawn from ancient Greek and other sources, and enhancing religious educational institutions and modes with secular bases (such as philosophy and law). "Natural Philosophy" thus became established and its status rose as various royal courts in the latter Middle Ages and Renaissance adopted it. The seeds of a separation between metaphysical (sacred) and physical (secular) knowledge and investigation, while not yet Church-sanctioned, became more explicit.

This distinction would flower once the Protestant Schism with the Catholic Church began. These new Protestant sects were often as intolerant of secular and heretical thinking as the Catholic Church but they broke open the monopoly of Church authority over secular and non-secular reasoning. One could add to this Protestant ideas about being able to discern divine truth directly as opposed to needing mediation from Church authorities, such as priests. These buttressed firmly established (or re-established) notions that the Greeks and Romans had developed about unencumbered individualism in the pursuit of knowledge and the ability of individuals to discover the workings of nature, and with this an ability to manipulate them.

O'Brien argues that the Scientific Revolution of the 1500s and 1600s was born out of these undercurrents and that this, in turn, helped give birth to the Industrial Revolution. O'Brien goes so far as to say that even "occult" disciplines such as magic, alchemy and astrology, helped advance the rational inquiry model so important to later science and industry.

Many economic historians disagree with various parts of the O'Brien argument. It does, however, sit well within a Growth Model framework since these cultural and intellectual changes are said to manifest in the form of changed behaviour, both individually and collectively, leading to the rational maximising actions economists assume underlie markets and growth. It also offers a "deep roots" trajectory as well, with changes in the distant past building up to sharp breaks in history, like the Industrial Revolution. The motive power of human ideas and the cultural transmission of concepts and practices in modern economic change are treated in more depth in Chapters 5 and 17. O'Brien provides a good example of the economist's approach to these things.

References

Acemoglu D. (2008). Growth and institutions. In L. E. Blume, & S. N. Durlauf (Eds.) *The new Palgrave dictionary of economics* (2nd ed.). Palgrave Macmillan.

Allen, R. C. (2011). *Global economic history: A very short introduction.* Oxford University Press.

Bairoch, P. (1982). International industrialization levels from 1750 to 1980. *Journal of European Economic History, 11*(2), 269–333.

Bairoch, P. (1988). *Cities and economic development: From the dawn of history to the present.* University of Chicago Press.

Bairoch, P., & Goertz, G. (1986). Factors of urbanisation in the nineteenth century developed countries: A descriptive and econometric analysis. *Urban Studies, 23*(4), 285–305.

Baumard, N. (2019). Psychological origins of the industrial revolution. *Behavioral and Brain Sciences, 42*, e189.

Berg, M., & Hudson, P. (1994). Growth and change: A comment on the Crafts-Harley view of the Industrial Revolution. *The Economic History Review, 47*(1), 147–149.

Bezanson, A. (1922). The early use of the term Industrial Revolution. *Quarterly Journal of Economics, 36*(2), 343–349.

Boarini, R., & d'Ercole, M. M. (2013). Going beyond GDP: An OECD perspective. *Fiscal Studies, 34*(3), 289–314.

Boserup, E. (1965). *The conditions of agricultural growth: The economics of agrarian change under population pressure.* Allen & Unwin.

Bosker, M., Buringh, E., & Van Zanden, J. L. (2013). From Baghdad to London: Unraveling urban development in Europe, the Middle East, and North Africa, 800–1800. *Review of Economics and Statistics, 95*(4), 1418–1437.

Broadberry, S. (2013). Accounting for the great divergence. *Voxeu.* https://voxeu.org/article/accounting-great-divergence

Chandler, A. D. (1992). Organizational capabilities and the economic history of the industrial enterprise. *Journal of Economic Perspectives, 6*(3), 79–100.

Clark, G. (2007). *A farewell to alms: A brief economic history of the world.* Princeton University Press.

Clark, G. (2010). *The consumer revolution: Turning point in human history, or statistical artifact?* (Working Paper). University California-Davis.

Clark, G., & Jacks, D. (2007). Coal and the industrial revolution, 1700–1869. *European Review of Economic History, 11*(1), 39–72.

Cox, W. (2015). 500 years of GDP: A tale of two countries. *New Geography.* https://www.newgeography.com/content/005050-500-years-gdp-a-tale-two-countries

Crafts, N. (2004). Productivity growth in the industrial revolution: A new growth accounting perspective. *Journal of Economic History, 64*(2), 521–535.

Crafts, N. F., & Harley, C. K. (1992). Output growth and the British industrial revolution: A restatement of the Crafts-Harley view. *Economic History Review, 45*(4), 703–730.

De Jong, H. J. & Palma, N. (2018). *Historical national accounting* (Maddison-Project Working Paper WP-12).

De Vries, J. (1994). The industrious revolution and the industrial revolution. *Journal of Economic History, 54*(2), 249–270.

Deane, P., & Cole, W. A. (1969). *British economic growth, 1688–1959* (2nd ed.). Cambridge University Press.

Egger, V. O. (2018). *A history of the Muslim World since 1260: The making of a global community*. Routledge.

Fouquet, R., & Broadberry, S. (2015). Seven centuries of European economic growth and decline. *Journal of Economic Perspectives, 29*(4), 227–244.

Galor, O. (2005). From stagnation to growth: Unified growth theory. In P. Aghion & S. N. Durlauf (Eds.), *Handbook of economic growth* (Vol. 1, Part A, pp. 171–293). Elsevier.

Galor, O. & Weil, D. N. (1999). From Malthusian stagnation to modern growth. *American Economic Review*, 89(2), Papers and Proceedings of the One Hundred Eleventh Annual Meeting of the American Economic Association (pp. 150–154).

Gerschenkron, A. (1962). *Economic backwardness in historical perspective: A book of essays*. Belknap Press of Harvard University Press.

Graff, M., Kenwood, A. G., & Lougheed, A. L. (2013). *Growth of the international economy, 1820–2015*. Routledge.

Griffin, E. (2013). *The 'industrial revolution': Interpretations from 1830 to the present* (Working Paper). School of History, UEA, Norwich.

Harley, C. K., & Crafts, N. F. (2000). Simulating the two views of the British Industrial Revolution. *Journal of Economic History, 60*(3), 819–841.

Harley, K. (2003). Growth theory and Industrial Revolutions in Britain and America. *The Canadian Journal of Economics/Revue Canadienne D'economique, 36*(4), 809–831.

Horesh, N. (2020). *Chinese money in global context*. Stanford University.

Johnson, D. G. (1997). Agriculture and the wealth of nations. *American Economic Review, 87*(2), 1–12.

Jones, E. L. (2000). *Growth recurring: Economic change in world history*. University of Michigan Press.

Komlos, J. (2000). The Industrial Revolution as the escape from the Malthusian trap. *Journal of European Economic History, 29*(2), 307–331.

Kuznets, S. (1966). *Modern economic growth: Rate, structure and spread*. Yale University Press.

Landes, D. S. (1969). *The unbound Prometheus: Technological change and development in Western Europe from 1750 to the present*. Cambridge University Press.
Maddison, A. (2007). *The world economy volume 1: A millennial perspective volume 2. Historical statistics*. OECD, Development Studies Centre OECD Publishing.
Mason, D. S. (2011). *A concise history of modern Europe: Liberty, equality, solidarity* (2nd ed.). Rowman & Littlefield Publishers.
Mokyr, J. (1999a). The Second Industrial Revolution, 1870–1914. In V. Castronovo (Ed.), *Storia dell'economia Mondiale* (pp. 219–245). Laterza Publishing.
Mokyr, J. (1999b). Editor's introduction: The new economic history and the Industrial Revolution. In J. Mokyr (Ed.), *The British industrial revolution: An economic perspective* (2nd ed., pp. 1–127). Westview Press.
Morris, I. (2014). *War! What is it good for? Conflict and the progress of civilization from primates to robots*. Farrer, Straus and Giroux.
Neal, L., & Cameron, R. (2016). *A Concise economic history of the world: From paleolithic times to the present* (5th ed.). Oxford University Press.
North, D. (1990). *Institutions, institutional change, and economic performance*. Cambridge University Press.
O'Brien, P. K. (1996). Path dependency, or why Britain became an industrialized and urbanized economy long before France. *Economic History Review, New Series, 49*(2), 213–249.
O'Brien, P. (2006). *Provincializing the First Industrial Revolution*. London School of Economics and Political Science, Department of Economic History.
O'Brien, P. (2017). *Was the First Industrial Revolution a conjuncture in the history of the world economy?* (Working Paper). London School of Economics.
OECD. (2006). Appendix B: World population, GDP and GDP Per Capita Before 1820. In *The world economy: Volume 1: A millennial perspective and volume 2: Historical statistics*. OECD Publishing.
Palma, N. (2020). American precious metals and their consequences for early modern Europe. In S. Battilossi, Y. Cassis, & K. Yago (Eds.), *Handbook of the history of money and currency* (pp. 363–382). Springer.
Pfister, U., & Fertig, G. (2020). From Malthusian disequilibrium to the Post-Malthusian era: The evolution of the preventive and positive checks in Germany, 1730–1870. *Demography, 57*(3), 1145–1170.
Pomeranz, K. (2000). *The great divergence: China, Europe, and the making of the modern world economy*. Princeton University Press.
Rostow, W. W. (1960). *The stages of economic growth: A non-Communist manifesto*. Cambridge University Press.
Roy, W. G. (1997). *Socializing capital: The rise of the large industrial corporation in America*. Princeton University Press.

Stearns, P. N. (2001). *The encyclopedia of world history* (6th ed.). Houghton Mifflin Company.
Temin, P. (2000). A response to Harley and Crafts. *The Journal of Economic History, 60*(3), 842–846.
UN. (1999). *The world at six billion*. Population Division, Department of Economic and Social Affairs, United Nations Secretariat.
Wallerstein, I. (1976). *The modern world-system: Capitalist agriculture and the origins of the European world-economy in the sixteenth century*. Academic Press.
White, C. M. (2013). *A global history of the developing world*. Routledge.

CHAPTER 4

"Political Economy": The Making of a North-South Planet

C. Gordon, *Many Possible Worlds*,
https://doi.org/10.1007/978-981-19-9281-0_4

Fig. 4.1 Europe as the centre of the world (*Image source* Goodrich, S.G. [1857]. *Peter Parley's common school history. Illustrated by engravings.* E. H. Butler & Co. Page 84. Contributing Library: Information and Library Science Library, University of North Carolina at Chapel Hill. No known copyright restrictions)

4.1 Classical Economics and "Political Economy"

The Industrial Revolution gave birth not just to a radical change in material circumstances. It also gave birth to a new intellectual current, based in England, which became known as "Political Economy". The dramatic changes taking place in the eighteenth and nineteenth century English and European economy and society demanded explanations, and men like Adam Smith, Thomas Malthus, David Ricardo and John Stuart Mill sought to provide them. Their efforts led to the creation of the field of "Classical Economics" which provides the origins of the discipline of economics, as we know it today (Fig. 4.1).

Interest in a systematic inquiry into the relationship between economics, society and the State did not start with them, however. Such inquiry originally grew out of the need for national leaders to effectively navigate the competition between European empires of the 1500s and 1600s. The acquisition of large overseas domains brought up numerous novel issues about international trade, investment, and financial flows that needed proper study and understanding in the service of strategic national interest. The doctrine of "Mercantilism" became a leading idea or, more properly, set of interrelated ideas, the most simplistic of which was "Bullionism", which held that states grew stronger relative to other states the more precious "specie" they held in reserve, basically following the old joke about the Golden Rule: he who has the most gold, wins. To maximise bullion reserves required aggressive accumulation of trade surpluses, through the use of protectionist trade measures and imperial ventures. More sophisticated versions were more subtle about means but the general end remained the same in either case. Meanwhile, in seventeenth century France, the Physiocrats were busy applying rational analysis and philosophical systematising in attempting to model the circulation of agricultural surplus through the rest of the French economy and its impacts on various sectors, a template which foreshadows the input-output models of the twentieth century (Barber, 1970, 17–22).

The Mercantilist efforts, however, were somewhat ad hoc, driven more by periodic exigencies than by detached analysis, while the Physiocrats had the opposite problem of being more intellectual but not practically influential. However, the growing complexity of international and domestic economics, and the shifts in economic structure that altered domestic and global interest group configurations called out for a more systematic study of the economy, using the apparatus of an emerging analytical science. It was this impulse that gave rise to Political Economy and the Classical Economists. Not by accident was the movement born in the UK, the country that was undergoing profound change domestically and internationally and which operated under a constitutional monarchy where group politics were especially arcane, corrupt and increasingly influenced by the growing power of commercial interests against older established powers.

4.2 Adam Smith and the Wealth of Nations

Of course the well-known father of the economics discipline is the Scotsman Adam Smith. Smith was a product of the so-called Scottish Enlightenment and Scotland itself was arguably more prosperous and culturally advanced than England during the 1700s, boasting four universities as opposed to England's two, and birthing a number of prominent intellectuals, of which Smith was one. In his magnum opus *The Wealth of Nations* (the short version of a much longer title), Smith ([1776] 2000) attempted to develop a system of thought and empiricism to apply to the economy of his day. Smith's specific theories and policy prescriptions were not new in and of themselves, but he imaginatively synthesised existing ideas, punctuated by catchy phrases for key concepts (such as the "invisible hand" and "division of labour", discussed more below) that changed thinking about the relationship between economic and political power rather profoundly (Fig. 4.2).

Although a systematiser, like most writers of his time, Smith is rather discursive and meandering in his presentation, it being systematic in a loose sense. Therefore, to some degree "Smithian" economics always necessarily contained a significant element of interpretation, both at the time and later on. Nonetheless, Smith's system of thought can be simplified into a few basic core assumptions that would greatly influence his successor classical economists.

(1) "*Moral sentiments*". Human beings are said to have three core bundles of motivations: self-love/sympathy; desire for freedom and sense of propriety; habit of labour and propensity to exchange.
(2) *"Natural value" v market value.* Things traded on markets have a fundamental value in terms of the labour effort embodied in them and the key question is how this aligns with the market-assigned price attached to it.
(3) *Productive and non-productive sectors.* Agriculture is productive in that it produces surpluses—a belief that the Physiocrats held; but so is the creation of tangible things—manufacturing—a sector that the Physiocrats thought was "sterile" and which was generally seen as derivative from agricultural activity. (Note: government and services are unproductive sectors according to Smith.)
(4) *Capital accumulation and growth.* Given that manufacturing is productive, it deserves to have resources devoted to it. But where do these come from? Agriculture uses land and labour in obvious ways. But manufacturing does not spring so directly from the ground in the same way, requiring more impetus, organisation and resources from outside. Smith thus referred to "advances" of capital

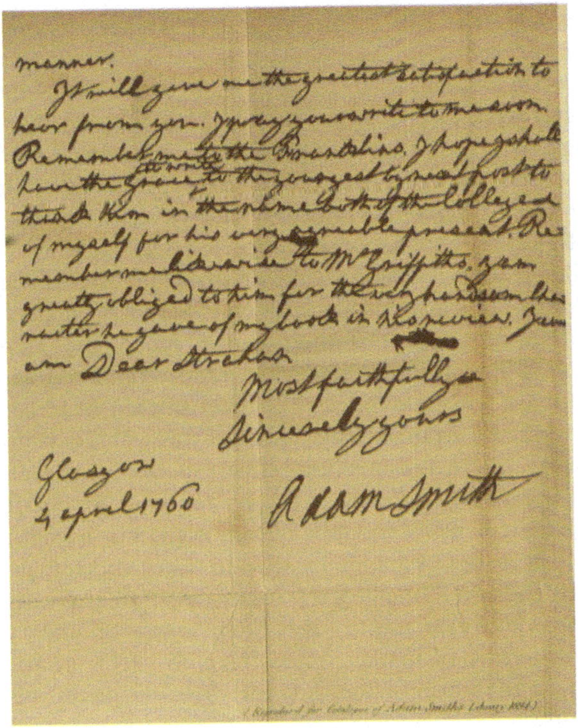
manner.
It will give me the greatest satisfaction to
hear from you. I pray you write to me soon.
Remember me to the [illegible]. I hope you shall
have the [illegible] to [illegible] to
thank him in the name both of the College and
of myself for his very agreeable present. Re-
member me likewise to Mr Griffiths. I am
greatly obliged to him for the very handsome cha-
racter he gave of my book in his review. I
am Dear Strahan
Most faithfully and
sincerely yours
Glasgow
4 April 1760
Adam Smith

Fig. 4.2 Page from a letter by Adam Smith (*Image source A catalogue of the library of Adam Smith: author of the 'Moral sentiments' and 'The wealth of nations'* [1894], Macmillan and Co. Contributing Library: University of Connecticut Libraries. No known copyright restrictions)

from entrepreneurs who desired to make a profit off their investments. These advances, if profitable, create their own "surplus" of new capital that can be reinvested back into productive activity that in turn leads to economic growth. Therefore, accumulation of capital, through entrepreneurial advances and self-generated profits, yield economic growth.

Taken together these key premises suggest the following conclusions:

(A) *Human beings can pursue their self-interest, through exchange, which at the same time will lead to social outcomes in which the common good is attained.* This result follows directly from Smith's assumptions about "natural" moral tendencies of human beings, who are seen as self-seeking, but also having concerns for others, and an innate desire to be productive. The Smithian actor's self-interest is thus not purely egoistic, but inherently involves at least some consideration for one's fellows as well. These posited tendencies, along with Smith's idea that private investors are better informed than bureaucrats about profitable opportunities, together suggest (though do not guarantee) that individual pursuit of private gain through markets, combined with competitive forces, will more effectively meet human material needs than State-directed arrangements, and that this will also be more socially efficient, in terms of meeting human social and ethical desires.

(B) *Market exchange allocates resources the most productively.* This is a restatement using modern terminology, but it captures Smith's idea that private exchange by self-interested individuals (as defined above) ends up funnelling resources across an economy away from unproductive uses and towards their most productive ones. How? By the setting of market prices through exchange to be roughly equal to their true value, i.e. the "natural price" of inputs and outputs.

(C) *The market is self-regulating.* Even if the market is truly best at productively allocating resources, will it be stable? Smith did not address whether this would be so (and neither did his Classical or even his Neoclassical successors) but he did implicitly suggest it would be. This suggestion requires some additional assumptions, which are considered in Sect. 4.4.

These conclusions taken together form the basis for the phrase "invisible hand", which encapsulates Smith's notion that self-interest in exchange through markets would guide people towards not just what was best for them individually, but what was best for society overall. This extraordinary claim does not fully follow from Smith's arguments, but seems to be more based on his interpretation of things he was seeing in the contemporary UK, and Scotland in particular, which was going through a social and economic renaissance at the time, concomitant with more formal market mechanisms displacing less formal social ones against a tableau of rapid economic change and growth. Economic growth and industrialisation were occurring, and Smith did identify some of the processes behind this. Whether all the conclusions that he drew from these observations were correct is another matter.

4.3 Rationalism and Its Emotional Tones

Like any writer, Smith did not write in a vacuum. He was very influenced by the intellectual currents of his time, especially, as noted, the Enlightenment. The simplistic notion of the Enlightenment as a single epoch in which (European) "Man" discovered the power of reason and knowledge to break free of old traditions, habits and superstitions has been discarded by historians studying the era. In fact during its actual flowering in the 1700s, contemporaries thought about the concept differently according to their national origins, French *philosophes,* for example, conceptualising human progress divergently from, say, their Italian counterparts (Outram, 2019, 1–2; Porter, 1990, 1–11).

However a common theme across these divergences is Rationalism, which broadly speaking refers to the view that human reason serves as the chief source and test of knowledge. There are varying degrees of this idea, the more extreme versions holding that everything can only be known through reason (essentially the position of Descartes), while less extreme versions hold it to be central to understanding, but not the only means of doing so (Markie & Folescu, 2021).

Rationalism also had different underlying implicit emotional tones and attitudes, depending upon the particular adherent. Leibniz, Pope and Rousseau were all optimists, believing that the reasoning faculties of humanity would always be associated with human advancement. Immanuel Kant, however, questioned this, writing in a 1784 essay that the full development of rational capacity was desirable but cautioning that it could be carried too far, a constant and never-ending logical analysis and questioning of all phenomena being potentially destructive and corrosive of the social order and human harmony (Outram, 2019, 2–4). Despite this caution, Kant was overall very supportive of the Enlightenment Project (to use twentieth-century theologian Alasdair Maclntyre's phrase) and strongly believed in the overall power of human reason in human advancement (Capaldi, 1998).

It is often forgotten that the contemporary Catholic Church was aligned with much of this positive attitude as well. Humanism, with its celebration of the human being as just below God, had been a prominent feature of pre-Reformation Catholicism, and the philosophical hostility towards Reason that the Counter-Reformation had engendered had largely spent itself by the 1700s. Protestantism by then was an accepted fact on the ground that could no longer be extirpated. Catholic leaders still saw the need to challenge it though and an optimistic (Catholic) Rationalism was one tool for doing so. Meanwhile, Protestant Christendom celebrated (in diverse and diverging ways) the power of individual investigation into spiritual and corresponding material realities (Rublack, 2017). In combination this created a theological environment in which God remained above all in heaven but human reason was a critical tool in doing His work, whether you were a Catholic or a Protestant.

Thus both religious and secular Enlightenment rationalists posited a "Universal Good", with Reason as the key tool for getting there. Leibniz coined the phrase "best of all possible worlds" to denote a new hope about where Reason would take humanity. The famous French philosopher Voltaire was a subscriber to this form of Rationalism during the early part of his life (De Boer & Sanders, 2005, 102).

The Lisbon earthquake of 1755 shook apart this optimistic consensus, literally. The rest of Portugal, Southwestern Spain and Northern Africa were deeply affected by this devastating quake, with Fez and Casablanca destroyed. But Lisbon, then a leading city of European civilisation, got the most attention from European philosophers. The event took place on All Saints Day, and in a bitter irony the full churches in the throes of holiday celebration vastly increased fatalities. Tsunamis wreaked havoc in Lisbon, Cadiz and especially Algiers and Tangier where the death tolls may have been highest (De Boer & Sanders, 2005, 88–94).

After this event, a rift soon opened up between the secularist Rationalists and the religious ones, and the optimists and the pessimists. Voltaire made the most decisive break, never formally renouncing his Catholic faith but now becoming being a fierce critic of religiosity in all its forms. He became an ardent exponent of Rationalism but with much more cynicism, bitterness, scepticism and pessimism about the world than his peers. For him the catastrophe of Lisbon seemed proof that a loving God working on Man's behalf did not exist (though not going the further step, apparently, of rejecting the existence of God altogether). He also rejected the optimism of Rousseau and others, believing that the "best of all possible worlds" was not going to arrive without struggle, and that the current human order was very far from good much less the best. The "positive attitude" school was ruthlessly ridiculed in his work *Candide* ([1759] 1959), in the form of the ridiculously and relentlessly positive character Pangloss who would airily refer to any disaster that came by labelling it with Leibniz's phrase. Although the term "Pessimism" was not actually coined until 1795 by Coleridge (Davis, 2002, 285), its time had arrived.

Not, however, for Smith, apparently. Smith did not proclaim himself as an optimist. And he did make many cutting statements about some of the circumstances of his times, including the tendency of businessmen to conspire amongst themselves to limit competition and engage in profiteering. Yet Smith's conclusions were ultimately very upbeat. For him economic growth was a good thing on all fronts, and the changes underway in his time and country were definite moves on the road of progress. His optimism certainly coloured his views of the world, and in time would be challenged by Thomas Malthus, considered more in a later section.

4.4 Science, Mechanism, Deism and the Self-Regulating System

Smith wrote during the era of the Scientific Revolution, which is another label that actually encompasses a number of diverse developments stretched out over many decades. The relevant dimension here is a systematisation of thinking and investigation that created the first true technical and mathematical "models" in the sense we know them today. The findings of Galileo, Copernicus and Newton culminated in a theory of physics that produced powerful hypotheses that actually worked in the real world. In this framework, there was still a God, but He worked by creating "natural laws" which were observable but not changeable by humanity. These governed all affairs, including social ones, and were "discoverable" through human experimentation and logical analysis (Cohen, 1976). The material efficacy of human-made theories in the created physical world seemed to affirm these conclusions.

Newton himself believed strongly in God and considered his works on theology (unpublished during his lifetime) to be as important as his works on physics and mathematics (Jones, 2011). So natural law did not start as a secular movement but was a unique departure in religious doctrine that soon became known as Deism. The basic idea is that an all-powerful Creator sits apart from the world and is unknowable and untouchable by human beings. This God does not act directly in the world but is constantly acting indirectly through the God-created natural laws of the created universe.

Although Christian in its original incarnation, the doctrine does not accord with the supernaturalism present in much of the Old and New Testaments in which God is constantly directly intervening in human affairs, often contravening the normal workings of nature. That version of God is also beyond human understanding but can nonetheless be known directly through divine revelation to an individual or group, and through the interpretation of the occasions of God's direct interventions in the world (e.g. the parting of the Red Sea for Moses or Jesus's walking on water). Deism ignores both things and thus makes God very distant from humanity, contact with Him being indirect only. But in return the doctrine does offer a decipherable natural law that binds human affairs and, if understood properly, can be a doorway to a powerful human manipulation of the natural order nonetheless aligned with God's purpose (Byrne, 2013). Theologically, Deism is potentially blasphemous for Catholic and non-Catholic Christians, but this seemed to cause relatively little institutional response or backlash (Byrne, 2013). Partly this was because the doctrine was not promoted independently and explicitly but came out implicitly in treatises on secular matters. For example, Newton mentioned a perfect supreme being in his scientific texts, including the *Principia* and *Optics* (Jones, 2011, 64–65), strongly implying a Deistic God but not arguing directly for one.

Deism also was bound up with a related contemporary doctrine of Mechanism, i.e. the idea that the material world is composed of small particles that act upon each other according to physical laws whose interactions could be analysed to provide an explanation of all happenings in the physical universe (MacIntosh, 2016). The analogy to the workings of the parts of a machine is obvious and this sort of thinking was the basis for the Deist analogy that God was a clock-maker and that the universe was a giant clock, set in motion by the First Mover and running smoothly ever after.

From here it is a short step to the idea that all physical systems are self-regulating according to the precepts of natural law. Clocks and other machines are designed to run smoothly for a specific purpose, operating along very specific lines. Ideally, they should never malfunction and run forever. A quest for the "perpetual motion machine" which, once set in motion, could run eternally without any further human intervention, had been an obsession of many theorists and tinkerers since the Middle Ages, with the Renaissance and Enlightenment bringing a new surge in such efforts (Ord-Hume, 1977).

A human-made perpetual machine was clearly a chimera, something that the later formulation of the laws of Thermodynamics would put to rest for scientists and other serious thinkers. But the possibility of a God-made mechanistic nature (or, later on, a randomly constituted one following laws of probability) appeared very real to eighteenth century observers. Nature and human society were seen as perfect divine machines whose operating principles could be uncovered and possibly even mastered after enough research and investigation. In this way, one could say that the modern notion of "system" was born in this time, with its "self-regulating" nature taken as axiomatic.

Although Smith did not explicitly promulgate his religious views, many have read his works as reflecting Deistic beliefs, some claiming that his reference to the "Invisible Hand" of the marketplace was actually a reference to God working through natural law. Certainly, his ideas contained many elements of natural law and the self-regulating system that permeated Western thought at the time (Becker, 1961; Dunn, 1941).

4.5 A Revised Role for the State

"That government is best which governs least". This phrase of Henry David Thoreau ([1849] 2016) captures Smith's policy prescriptions, namely that government should get out of economic, and most other, affairs. Smith was an opponent of Mercantilism and restrictions on international trade generally, opposing the Corn Laws (English protectionism for agriculture) of his time, as well as the Poor Laws (which provided very basic relief to the impoverished and famished).

To Smith these recommendations appeared as obvious implications of his assumptions and inferences. But these stances were a considerable break from contemporary ideas holding that active government intervention at home and abroad were required to advance the national interest. Smith by contrast was arguing instead that the State should pull back from regulating domestic and international economic affairs. This was a rather striking stance, extended remarkably even to the ongoing wars and colonialism conducted by his country's government and those of others.

What also appeared different about the economic philosophy of Smith as compared to his predecessors was his methodological stance of scientific neutrality. Prior economic theorising was typically given from a power perspective of a government or State actor (such as a trading company) and was thus highly contextual and explicitly political. General principles were sometimes offered, but always with respect to a particular situation. Smith, however, was claiming to be coming up with generalisable propositions much like Newton's physics. It is no accident that part of his (very long) book title contains the phrase "the wealth of nations", made plural to show this theory would work for all nations and not just the realm of the UK. This would seem to suggest that Smith was putting aside purely national interest considerations to present a theory that would benefit all that would apply it, even if they were competitors to the UK.

Of course there is much artifice in this stance. Smith was very much a partisan for his own corner of the world. He was in the main still aiming to advise a particular national government and was a good apologist for certain ascendant commercial interests who, as ascendant interests always prefer, were seeking a general banner under which they could claim their actions were serving general, not narrow aims. This is not to deny that Smith did aim to build a general theory that would offer general benefit. But he did have definite biases.

For example, Smith was relatively optimistic about the process of economic change, the emphasis being on "wealth" and "growth". As noted earlier there was a strong strain of philosophical optimism coming out of the Enlightenment, and Smith was certainly affected by this living through the Scottish Enlightenment himself. Additionally, Smith lived through times that were relatively prosperous, a benefit of the beginning of English industrialisation with its significant changes in the human and social and economic order. From his relatively comfortable position in the professional class, things did seem rather bright and the future very exciting.

The English political order was also one of relative constraint on monarchical power along with a flexing of parliamentary authority in domestic social and economic affairs, a diverse but sometimes unflattering portrait of the exercise of State might, with its factions and manipulations and unintended consequences. Although State policy was a key ingredient of British industrialisation (a fact considered more in Chapter 5), it wasn't always so clear at the time, and the dynamism of much private action was unmistakable. This may have suggested to Smith that the economic problem was misleadingly simple: get arbitrary government out of the way of self-regulating efficiency of private enterprise (Dunn, 1941).

4.6 Power, Politics and Economics

The modern (and simplified) version of Adam Smith, which does not do complete justice to his actual and somewhat more nuanced views, is that of "laissez-faire capitalism" in which the State is relatively non-interventionist. Smith himself emphasised the important role that social norms played in channelling competitive self-interested individuals towards collectively positive economic and social outcomes (see Carugati & Levi, 2021). The presence of such norms, combined with his underlying scepticism about government, led to his clear view that private economic action should be given maximum scope. It also is demonstrative of the "Political" part of "Political Economy".

However, Smith and his successors did not really explicitly define the term "politics" and rarely mentioned its cousin concept, power. The Western theory of politics derives from ancient Greek practice and theory, particularly that of Aristotle ([ca. 350 B.C.E.] 2000) in his work *Nicomachean Ethics*. "Politics" literally refers to the life of the "polis" or city-state of Greek times, which was not just a mere governance entity but a social community, seeking community agreement and collective resolution of its conflicts around values, norms and general direction. The word "Ethics" in Aristotle's title is indicative of his view that "right action was completely bound up with social activity. Politics in the Aristotelian sense broadly refers to the seeking and gaining of the necessary consensus on collective choice and action that truly reflects "corporate" interest in the sense of the "corpus" or "body" of the community (Clayton, 2005).

However, the Greek city-state of which Aristotle wrote was not a place of equal power. Women were completely disenfranchised in ancient Athens, as were many of its male residents, even long-standing ones, with only "citizens" given the right to participate in the political community, generally white men of property and recognised residence and proper class. In ancient Athens, the Aristotelian ideal was to have a cohesive community, reaching consensus on collective right actions. But the community itself was defined very narrowly to exclude non-citizens and even within this group not every individual had equal influence.

Power, therefore, is a term with multiple meanings depending upon the context. Social power can be loosely defined as the ability to influence or control over others to attain desired goals (Nash, 2009). Social power is not necessarily coincident with economic or political power. It was not so even in Athens, where commercial interest groups often had substantial economic and social influence even though they were politically disenfranchised. And it was certainly not so in the England of the Political Economists, where the balance between government, governance, politics and power was being altered significantly by the rise of a capitalistic and industrial economy. The Political Economists recognised the importance of these issues, but effectively ended up writing it out of the equation. Because government was diagnosed as being a hindrance to economic growth, and maximum freedom of individual action was seen as the key to economic growth, politics and power in the traditional sense ended up being slowly excised from their analysis. This superficially might have appeared to capture the reality on the ground given the increasing prominence of economic affairs under capitalism and industrialisation. What was really happening, though, was that power relationships were shifting, with emerging forms of economic power subsuming and altering what used to be separate realms of political, social, religious and other types of power (Varoufakis, 2015). Smith had set Political Economy on an "apolitical" path, a tendency that his successors tended to amplify and, later, the neoclassical economics codified. These issues nonetheless did not go away but morphed and intensified as industrialisation expanded, as will be considered more fully later.

4.7 Thomas Robert Malthus and Malthusian Economics

The next "great" in the Political Economy line, Thomas Malthus, took a more pessimistic view of economics than Smith, though also a narrower one, trying to understand not the entire sweep of economic growth but just the link between population and economic growth. It is from Malthus's name that we get the Malthusian Trap moniker in the UGM (see Chapter 3). Although Malthus is not nearly as wide-ranging as Smith in his ambit, his ideas about economic growth and population growth were, and continue to be, influential in the fields of study of human demography and the economy.

Temperamentally, Malthus was less sunny than Smith, at least judging by his writing. In fact, he was originally motivated to write a critique of the optimistic view of his contemporary William Godwin who held that while any additional person brought to earth had an additional mouth to feed, she/he also had an additional pair of hands to work with. Hence, overpopulation would never cause a problem in terms of overall sustenance. Malthus largely believed the opposite was true and felt the necessity of saying so. The content and tone of the writings of Malthus are one reason that economics has garnered the epithet of "The Dismal Science", although personally he was apparently warm and generous (Barber, 1970, 55–58).

While Thomas Malthus's life span overlapped with Smith's (1766–1834 v 1723–90), he was writing mostly during a more difficult time of his country's history. In 1792, France declared war on Austria and Prussia; and on 1 February 1793, the French National Convention declared war on Great Britain. Warfare between the two countries continued almost uninterrupted until 1815 (there was a brief interlude of peace which lasted from the Peace of Amiens in March 1802 until the renewal of war in May 1803, and another respite during 1814–1815). This "23 year war" had severe consequences economically, especially in trade, something very important to export-dependent England. Existing data on prices for key commodities in Britain and measures of exports and imports show overall a temporary but significant break in longer-run trends towards increasing trade (i.e. some sharp falls in imports and exports) and periodic spikes in various domestic prices. During the war period, Britain moved from being a net exporter to a net importer of food (Bordo & White, 1991). Smith, who lived during generally improving economic times, had more reason to believe in the benevolence and self-regulation of markets than Malthus, whose times were marked by significant periods of economic duress, if not crisis.

This context no doubt affected Malthus' model of the economy, which is actually pretty simple and almost predetermined. It is asserted that the size of the population increases geometrically, while agricultural output increases only arithmetically. Thus inevitably over time population will outstrip agricultural growth, with the end result that sufficient food to feed the population will fall short. It then follows that at this point population growth will be limited by either "positive checks" (a bit of a misnomer given that this refers to things like famine and disease) which bring population back down to sustainable levels by having significant numbers die off; or "preventive checks" (more aptly named as they refer to things such as voluntary choices by families to have fewer children).

Malthus did not provide evidence for his underlying assumptions but if granted they logically follow (Malthus [1798] 1872).

Malthus' first edition of his treatise argued that humanity would never be able to stop natural procreative tendencies through the exercise of preventive checks, thereby dooming populations to grow too large during good economic times before crashing against the inevitable positive checks. His subsequent editions softened this stance arguing that people were capable of learning and restraining their natural desires to have large families, especially when educated properly. Either way, though, the human economy was ultimately constrained by biology and environment. This is why Malthus favoured the Corn Laws in England, unlike Smith, because he felt domestic food supplies needed to be secured. It was also why he agreed with Smith (with nuances) on opposing the Poor Laws, since he felt this encouraged population growth (Barber, 1970, chapter 2).

Malthus did not consider the possibility that agricultural productivity itself could improve, breaking out of its arithmetic growth pattern, which is why he focused on restraining population growth alone. Of course productivity growth in other sectors such as manufacturing was outside Malthus's purview entirely. His model turned out to be wrong in its particulars, but its general dichotomy between population pressures versus resource constraints is still very influential. The longer run debate has, however, shifted from short-run dynamics to about how operative these competing forces will be over the long run, as the Anthropocene paradigm considers most forcefully (see Chapter 2).

4.8 David Ricardo and the Ricardian Synthesis

The next in line of great Political Economists is the towering David Ricardo. A friend of Malthus, Ricardo, made enormous sums of money in finance (in the family firm at first and then breaking out on his own) and sat in Parliament for the last few years of his life, having purchased a seat there. Ricardo had very firm opinions about the economic policies of the day and, although a reluctant writer, managed to pen some very influential economic treatises that firmly bedded down Classical Economics theoretically and methodologically. Ricardo was a true systematiser and theoriser in the modern sense and for that alone he is influential in the development of the field of economics (Weatherall, 1976).

Ricardo is a wide-ranging thinker, with many of his central ideas laid out in his seminal 1821 work, *On the principles of political economy*. His central ideas include:

(1) *Comparative advantage*. This term, invented by Ricardo, holds that countries should specialise in producing goods where they hold a relative cost advantage with respect to other potential trading partners. At the logical extreme, this implies domestically producing such goods exclusively and trading with other countries for the rest. This builds on a more limited idea introduced by Adam Smith of absolute advantage, in which countries should specialise in the production of goods only when they are absolutely, rather than relatively, more efficient. Comparative advantage also extended the Smithian notion of division of labour and specialisation into the international trade sphere.

Smith had remarked on how dividing up tasks in to component parts and then assigning workers specialist roles in those component parts could make for more efficient production, hence the term "division of labour". His example was of a "pin factory" in which workers vastly increased the factory's total output by moving from a system in which a single craftsman made a pin from beginning to end to one in which one person specialised in one phase of the production process (such as straightening the pin) and handed it off to another person "specialised" in another phase (such as adding a cap to the top). Ricardo applied this idea to entire national economies providing a systematic argument for "free" (or more precisely "unfettered") trade as a natural policy prescription. This was one basis for Ricardo's firm opposition to the Corn Laws, a position he shared with Smith. But Smith's opposition was based more on a presumption of inefficiency of state intervention in markets while Ricardo's was based on a theory of the efficiency of a globalised interdependent trade economy.

(2) *Economic "rents"*. Although the concept was not original to Ricardo, he developed most fully the idea that although "capital" was not in fixed supply like land was, entrepreneurs could supply it in a similarly monopolistic fashion and thus be able to extract excess returns on it. It was this excess that Ricardo called "rent" because it came not from any special ability but simply from the power

that comes with ownership. While Smith optimistically believed that greater profits automatically were ploughed back into production, thus creating more profit and more capital in a virtuous circle (provided there was sufficient market competition and a large enough market to sell into, the latter condition referred to by Smith as "the extent of the market"), Ricardo, perhaps because of his experience as a financier, saw the possibility that individuals might control key assets of a production process and thus be able to squeeze out margins for themselves, thus reducing the amount of surplus available for productive activity and further capital creation.

The fact that rent and "rentiers" (collectors of rents) existed provided Ricardo with a further argument against the Corn Laws and their restrictions on competition and the use of land. Regulations and restrictions like these would only provide more power to rentiers, and less to the true entrepreneur and the workers. Ricardo, however, did not fully consider the possibility that rent could allow private parties, as well as governments, to create economic inefficiencies through (to use a modern term) their "rent-seeking" activities. Like Smith, Ricardo remained a firm believer in the powers of market competition to cure most economic ills, including the minimisation of rents, a faith that history would not always bear out.

(3) *Diminishing returns.* Ricardo also posited a law of diminishing returns on the supply of land. His argument was that as economic growth expanded, lower and lower quality land would be pulled into the production process, reducing overall returns to the economy as a whole and falling profit for producers over the long run. By itself this would lead to stagnation, but in his schema, there were two equivocal counter-forces (equivocal because they had potentially both aggravating and ameliorating effects): foreign trade and technical progress. Of the two, unfettered trade, conducted along the lines of comparative advantage and specialisation, was the more genial force since it would (supposedly) increase market competition and also increase the extent of the market. Technical progress was more ambivalent in its effects. Obviously, productivity would be raised by it but so, possibly, could rents and rent-seeking since new inventions could initially provide new sources of rent to their inventors. Ricardo also saw the real

possibility of technological unemployment due to labour-saving innovations.

There is much more to say about Ricardo but overall he more fully articulated an impersonal, self-regulating system where market prices played a key role in keeping the system growing on a stable path. For sure Ricardo was a critical figure who decisively separated the "Political" from the "Economy" (Winch, 2001).

4.9 "Man" and "Nature" and Classical "Liberalism"

Implicit in Political Economy (and in fact most Classical and neoclassical economic theory) is a particular characterisation of human behaviour and the natural environment in which human beings operate. Malthus and Smith were influenced by an English philosophy called Utilitarianism that saw human beings as fundamentally aggressive, mutually antagonistic and greedy, though Smith had tempered all this with the suggestion that there is also a natural degree of sympathy towards others as well (Graff et al., 2013, 11). Meanwhile, "nature" was largely seen as hostile and intemperate, with resource scarcity being the fundamental reality for all species. Thomas Hobbes ([1651] 2010) wrote of humans in their primal state as having lives that are "solitary, poor, nasty, brutish, and short", and always at war with each other unless a strong authoritarian central government is established to control them. The Classical Economists did not take up Hobbes's authoritarian political leanings, but his attitudes towards nature, human and otherwise, were largely retained. Even many modern treatments of the Industrial Revolution, like the Growth Model, treat it as an exit from the "tyranny and niggardliness of nature" which leads to an "inescapable need to exploit each other" unless material mastery is attained (Mokyr 1999, 6).

Political Economy slowly merged with Utilitarianism. The Utilitarian individual was at once egoistic and primitive, chasing pleasure and avoiding pain almost compulsively, and thus ready to exploit others if given the slightest chance to do so. They operated under a niggardly Providence to boot, making the competition between people especially fierce. However, these same impulses could be channelled into creating a human-made bounty to make up for Nature's deficits by fostering the organic forces of competition as posited by the Political Economists. In many ways, the Utilitarian Man was a very useful construct for Classical Economics, simplifying away some very thorny societal issues of both theory and reality.

These intellectual undercurrents came together to birth a political doctrine to accompany the economic doctrine of Political Economy. It was called Liberalism and contained the following general propositions that: the individual should be given priority over the collective and is inherently the fundamental unit in society; individual freedom in all realms (social, political, economic, etc.) should be protected and promoted; governments should be bound by the rules and processes that also governed individuals; individual freedom of speech and toleration for differences in opinion are fundamental rights; and that government power and size should be as small as possible, limited to exercising the basic necessary functions, such as preserving public order and providing for the rule of law. The exact size of the state was not specified, allowing for some variation across values and circumstances.

What about the distribution of income? Perhaps output would be maximised by the market system. But would everyone get his or her fair share? For the Classical Economists, the difficult problem of distribution of resources would also be solved through the self-regulating forces of self-interest and competition, the "Invisible Hand" naturally rewarding factors of production appropriate to the real value contribution. In effect fairness and efficiency would collapse into one and be handled by the same market apparatus.

One idea of Smith's was especially influential here. This was the idea of a "wage fund", into which the returns from capital accumulation were deposited, and out of which workers got paid. The wage fund did not exist in actual form, but was a construct that Smith invented to buttress a notion of a natural alignment between the interests of wage earners and capitalists. Higher profits would boost the wage fund and in turn result in higher wages. In this construct, class conflict was largely wiped away.

4.10 Emerging Cracks in the Political Economy Edifice

In actual fact, things would not be so easy. The increasing organisation of economies along market, and then industrial, lines may have brought growth in wealth and income, at least for some people in some countries.

But it also brought a lot of social instability. The Classical economists argued that this was all part of a natural and forward-moving progression, compensated for by greater material benefit for everyone. But as the middle of the nineteenth century dawned, the naturalness and beneficence of this progression began to appear debatable.

Although the primacy of the individual was celebrated in both Liberalism and Political Economy, there was a recognition that social relations between individuals were important and necessary, captured in the concept of "civil society" which referred to the general collection of free associations and groupings that individuals chose to organise themselves into (Butler, 2015, xviii-xx). Adam Smith in particular spoke of some elements of civil society, though without using the term. One of his successor Political Economists, John Stuart Mill, addressed these social issues at some length with regard to the role of freedom of expression and tolerance (see Chapter 17). Mill went so far as to caution against an unbounded faith in markets and the giving of free reign to what he called "the commercial spirit" (Bevir, 2001).

But Classical Economics lost most of this social concept, and theoretically, the individual soon became an atomistic unit, exercising political power through electoral representative democracy (the archetypal Liberal state) and economic and personal choice through unregulated markets and a large domain of minimally regulated personal life. The disappearance of a social component would have important practical, political and philosophical consequences (see Chapters 17 and 28).

Additionally the actual material results promised by Liberalism were not being unequivocally borne out by experience. Mill in particular renounced the wage fund doctrine in mid-century in part because the statistical evidence that was now being collected and accumulated in a relatively systematic way (inspired by Classical Economics itself which provided a framework for defining and measuring such data) contradicted some theoretical predictions made by the Political Economists. The prodigious rise of trade unions during the 1850s and 1860s and the associated labour unrest behind it suggested that a century of industrialisation was still far from equilibrating civil society as a whole or transcending class conflict. These sorts of developments did not completely contradict Classical Economics but they certainly suggested that it was in need of modification to fit fast-changing facts. Thus even in its heyday, laissez-faire liberalism, which Thomas Carlyle had lampooned as "anarchy plus a constable" (Neal & Cameron, 2016, 211), was facing growing internal theoretical and evidentiary strains.

It was Marx, another Classical economist, who would challenge the whole edifice of capitalist-worker comity and bring forth the idea that wage earners and capitalists were necessarily opposed in terms of economic interests, something that could only be worked out through class struggle. That intellectual development will be considered in more detail later (see Chapters 6, 7 and 23). It marked a growing divide between a theory that said all was going well and according to plan, and an economic reality that contained many crosscutting pressures and inconsistencies.

4.11 The Making of a North-South World

The picture becomes even more nuanced when looking at the world entire, beyond Europe. Pomeranz (2000) notes that Europe and Eurasia were both under ecological stress at the dawn of the Industrial Revolution. But China in particular had developed different philosophies and institutions for dealing with it. That country had a dominant Confucian school of thought that wanted to curb physical nature (e.g. with hydraulic works) the same way that human nature was supposed to be curbed by strict ethical ideas and training. This, in some ways, mirrored the European ideas about greedy man and a stingy nature, but more broadly fit it into a fundamentally benign hierarchy between heaven and earth, ruler and ruled, that required active alignment of human policy and practice to keep things in overall balance. This contrasted with concurrent Taoist ideas of letting nature take its course, something that on the surface might suggest laissez-faire but which really argued for a complete submission to nature itself (Davis, 2002, 387). Both ideas were largely foreign to Europeans.

India was in a bit of different situation in the eighteenth century, ecologically and institutionally. The country still had very large amounts of forest, and even dense areas, such as Bengal, still contained significant uncultivated reserves. The country was also less unified and less organised than China in this period, with significant brigandage in much of the countryside. As a result, there were numerous instances of the authorities burning forests to deny sanctuary to outlaws, showing that Indian authorities were both less consistent as ecological stewards than the Chinese but also that the country had more ecological slack to play with (Pomeranz, 2000, 213).

Although the Divergence debate claims social and economic institutions in China (and much of the rest of Asia) were lacking with respect to Europe (see Chapter 2), current scholarship instead notes the sophistication of China's systems of ecological management. For example, during the China drought of 1743–1744, the country avoided famine due to state intervention based on long-standing mutual obligations to prevent such things from occurring, a structure not present in Europe at the time. Although China was "absolutist", its "Confucian statecraft" allowed government to take food security seriously and deliver it, showing that absolutism has differing degrees of emphasis and is not necessarily always socially negative. Mughal India during the 1700s was less impressive in this regard, but it too had many more standing mechanisms for collective food provision during tough ecological times than most European states (Davis, 2002, 297–300, 379). Pomeranz (2000) claims that ecological degradation was better handled in China than Europe up until the mid-eighteenth century.

After 1750 China and India both began to experience a combination of increasing ecological, political and economic stress. This is not necessarily due to inferior local institutions and practices, though such factors do play a role (e.g. serious soil erosion in Chinese agricultural areas due to mismanagement). A particularly severe El Niño-Southern Oscillation (ENSO), a recurring climate pattern involving changes in the temperature of waters in the central and eastern tropical Pacific Ocean, also hit China and India hard while largely sparing Europe (Davis, 2002). But Pomeranz (2000), as mentioned in Chapter 2, argues that on the eve of the Industrial Revolution, China, Japan and Europe were all essentially in the same boat, expanding their proto-industrial sectors through growing international trade and more intensive and extensive exploitation of domestic resources to relieve local ecosystem pressure. Europe, however, had already tapped into "New World" resources significantly and thus could avoid the diminishing rates of return and growing ecological costs that Asia was encountering. The result in early 1800s Asia was either stagnation (as in Japan, which was prosperous but whose population stopped growing by 1750) or a degree of going backwards (the situation in some regions of China and also India) (287).

Europe's avoidance of these eco-boundaries through overseas extractions, in the process imposing further environmental degradation in Asia, is particularly clear in India, which Britain colonised in stages. The East India Company, the public-private arm of British imperialism on the subcontinent (see Box 4.1), increasingly bound Indian weavers to a single local buyer, something that helped Company returns but depressed local artisan earnings and caused many of them to leave their occupations, a process furthered later by competition with the many Lancashire mills that had arisen due to a change in British legislation that mandated making cloth in England in lieu of the former practice of buying it from India. Indeed, Britain's trade with India was in constant surplus, imperial legislation artificially enlarging British markets there, India in turn financing its deficit through the forced export of opium to China that Britain had imposed, as well as exports of Indian tea, indigo and other farm goods to continental Europe. All this helped Britain to sustain its large Atlantic deficits while still exporting large amounts of capital to its favoured locations, especially the US, a country which could afford to protect its own markets without sacrificing its own large capital inflows from the "developed world" (Pomeranz, 2000, 285).

Box 4.1 The British East India Company

A unique structure of European colonialism was the government trading company. Governments generally conducted territorial exploration and conquests directly, but sometimes these, as well as later administration, trade and many other activities, were outsourced to newly created quasi-governmental "companies", which were really state-chartered commercial cartels. This was especially the case in the region of the Indian Ocean, with East India Companies established in London (1600), Amsterdam (1602) and Paris (1674). These companies were chartered by governments, but were given trade monopolies out of which everything needed to maintain the monopoly, ranging from administrators down to armies and weapons, were to come out of the profits from trade (Morris, 2014, 197). In this way, the State could lessen its own costs of imperialism (see Chapter 13).

The operations of these companies taught European states much about resource extraction, commercial development and financial and trade integration. For one thing they were run on a basis in which company shareholders were incentivised to minimise operational costs to maximise their own profits. This basis led to numerous "natural experiments" which provided the kernels of Political Economy theory.

This was especially true of the British East India Company whose operations were the most sophisticated, most successful and most long-lived of the various enterprises established by the colonialist governments. The Company had been granted a trading charter by Queen Elizabeth in 1600. By 1757 parts of the Indian subcontinent had come under Company control after the Battle of Plassey (Ramesh, 2017, 23). Even after the British Empire Act of 1846 granted Crown colonies autonomy in pursuing their own trade policies, the Act exempted the East India Company until 1858, when the Crown took over direct control after the disastrous Indian Mutiny (Foreman-Peck, 1983, 47).

It was due to careful analysis of British East India Company books by some of its more enterprising apparatchiks that Mercantilism became discredited, since such analysis found that more open trade actually generated greater profit rather than the protectionism advocated by Mercantilist doctrine. Further intellectual advances came in the nineteenth century, especially with the recruitment in 1819 of a number of high-powered analytical men, most notably the philosopher James Mill. While at the company, Mill published *Elements of Political Economy* in 1821. In 1823 Mill's son John Stuart Mill became his assistant, working there for next thirty-five years, until the Company was dissolved. Both father and son were, by all accounts, dedicated company men, putting in full days of diligent work. But as the official day ran only from ten till four, this allowed a great deal of time for extracurricular activity, which in J. S. Mill's case included the writing of his *System of Logic* and *Principles of Political Economy*. Indeed, the Company work, from its vantage point at the pinnacle of colonial administration of a large economy, was most useful to the formulation of the J.S. Mill's economic theories; and by providing a steady income, the Company provided structure and ease of mind to complete such works (Sampson, 1995, 19).

The fact that the activities of a commercial, but imperial, enterprise played such an important part in the formulation of Political Economy reveals how peculiar some aspects of that theoretical system actually were. Its notions about economic efficiency being derived from maximum freedom of enterprise at all levels were ironic, given that it was based, at least in part, on the experience of a partial command economy managed on behalf of a colonial master. British policy in India relied heavily on the export of raw materials from India for British manufactures, many of which were then exported back to the Indians. This could not to be said to be genuinely resource saving in an overall sense, though it did maximise the returns of Company shareholders and, by extension, English taxpayers. The system also distinctly contributed to the demise of existing

Indian manufacturing industry and that sector's continuing impoverishment. The Company forced Indian artisans, who were advanced money and material by the Company, on generally exploitative terms, to sell their finished goods only to the Company—hardly a model of market competition. Many scholars blame the destruction of the Indian handloom and spinning wheel, and the rise of tenant farming there, on this practice (Ramesh, 2017, 28).

Certainly, this was not a path to the "wealth of nations" for the colonised country. It also was a set of double standards in which competition and efficiency were good for some, but not for others. The very notion of the Company was one of monopoly, although one run on a rather modern notion of internal incentives. This was a novel idea and provides support for the core finding of economic theory of the time and later, which is that incentives matter. But as this finding is based in part on imperialism, it may not be as generalisable as economists like to make out.

The policies designed to favour British industry over local manufacturing took the Indian economy backwards. The percentage of the Indian population living in cities declined from its estimated 13–15% in the late seventeenth century to 9.3% in 1881 (Pomeranz, 2000, 294). England also imposed a new sort of enclosure in India that privatised "free goods" and removed commons, undermining household ecology (Davis, 2002, 345).

Pomeranz (2000) claims that India, Southeast Asia and some parts of China still could ecologically accommodate more people without major technological change or declining living standards, in part because of their more ecologically sound institutions (though these had many imperfections as well). Europe was in a very different situation, lacking environmentally adaptive institutions, facing much less ecosystem slack and thus forced to both innovate domestically and extract resources from outside. The use of coal for energy was the first major internal innovation that helped lessen the pressure, while Europe extracted external bounty on a scale that only New World colonisation could provide. This was especially so since Europeans had already rather extensively and intensively exploited their own natural resources, e.g. destroying many of the German and English forests and confiscating many English common lands. The coercive aspects of colonisation allowed for much greater scope and scale in extraction than mere consensual trade, and in some ways, the differences between Chinese and Indian economies during the 1800s indicate this, India faring worse in relative terms because of Britain's direct control there (Pomeranz, 2000, 11).

Davis (2002) goes further than this, arguing that the "divergence" and the ultimate breaking up of the world into a "North" and "South" of developed and undeveloped countries, was actually a deliberate product of European power interventions. This general argument is not new, reflected in, amongst other theories, the World Systems theory of Wallerstein (see Chapter 2). What is novel is Davis's contention that the impacts of adverse climate events such as flooding, droughts and famines (and to an extent the occurrence of the events themselves) were actually largely driven by Great Power decisions and systems that drew resources from China, Brazil and India (the major focuses of Davis's book) in such a way as to degrade existing local governance and traditional ecological management systems that were generally effective because they contained some measure of mutual obligation between elites and peasant classes. He further argues that the Europe-centred global financial and economic system entrenched "North" privilege. Perversely, much of this hard intervention was done under the auspices of a doctrinally laissez-faire Liberalism.

Davis argues that the West destroyed much of the third world's capacity to respond to ecological devastation, Japan's growth being an exception that proves the rule, because that country's modernisation was a choice forced by Western impingement. "Free trade" was built by force, by London especially, subsidised via large Asian trade surpluses built up through captive markets. Britain offloaded its obsolescent goods and manufactures on India in particular and stunted its industrial development in doing so. Meanwhile, Indian debentures bled capital reliably to English rentiers.

4.12 The Dual Nature of Technical System Making

Davis additionally notes that the nineteenth century saw the rise of a supposedly neutral technical system of global finance, colonial administration, technological development and management, infrastructure investment (especially the Indian railways) and climate terminology and schema that simultaneously created and masked a rapacious system of western exploitation that resulted in widespread poverty and death in the exploited countries. Broadly speaking the system worked through the usual application of raw military force by European nations in the takeover of non-Europeans (see Chapter 13), leveraged and enhanced with a global financial system, run out of London, that created modern debt peonage and extractive taxation, even in nominally "free" countries such as China (see Chapter 19).

While traditional narratives emphasise the "poor" choices of developing countries (short-term and long-term), and even Pomeranz notes the importance of national government agency in responding to implicit and explicit incentives inherent in ecological constraints, Davis emphasises the use of monopsony power of European nations to drive down prices of "South" country exports; the increasing monetarisation and marketisation of international trade which degraded traditional domestic trade mechanisms and forced both the uptake of Western debt and the forced exporting of critical foodstuffs overseas, even during times of drought and famine; and the imposition of the Gold Standard on the world which demonetised silver in China and India, reducing local money supply there and further forcing these countries into a disadvantageous international trade system (see Chapter 3). India, being a direct colony of the British, had systems of exploitation that were more direct and brutal (e.g. colonial viceroys commanding onerous tax levies and forced exporting of food during droughts). But the results in China were more or the less the same, even though the Chinese government was nominally independent. And similar things were happening in Brazil in the late 1800s after its independence from Portugal.

At the same time, the supposedly benevolent European colonial investment in technology and facilities, especially the railways in India, were often more nefarious than beneficial to local populations. Besides being built in the first instance for military control and imperial resource extraction, Davis argues that the Indian railroads helped spread infectious disease more efficiently, send forced exports overseas more quickly and were required to be built using British imported technology and run (mostly) by British expertise. The telegraph meanwhile facilitated quick movements in local and international commodity price changes often adverse to local people. Thus technology and infrastructure can as easily increase mortality as reduce it, depending upon the design of the systems of which it is part.

Even when there was just plain back climate luck, such as the Great Drought of 1876–1879, driven by a serious ENSO that afflicted Brazil,

India and China simultaneously, its negative impacts were synchronised and heightened through global movements of capital and prices, in ways that were more destructive and destabilising than ever before, and not just by pure accident, but as the direct and indirect result of imperial policy. Famines occurred in all three places, and Davis argues that while the drought may have been inevitable, starvation wasn't, and that had indigenous eco-management systems been left in place, or allowed to operate, it wouldn't have occurred. Sometimes this outcome was even said to be deliberate, famine having its political uses. Stalin and Mao have been accused in the twentieth century of deliberately allowing the starvation of regions and groups that were hostile to their regimes. Davis claims that this also occurred within Europe with the Irish Potato Famine, and outside of it at various times in China, India and Brazil. These are contested claims, and evidence can be brought to bear on both sides. But the notion that technical system making was by itself always a movement towards greater efficiency and equity can no longer be taken for granted.

Davis claims that Utilitarianism, with its emphasis on social control backing up a distorted version of political Liberalism in colonial territories (i.e. letting people starve while cutting budgets for local colonial services), was an official ideology that justified injustices in the name of an ideological efficiency. This hypocrisy was not completely unnoticed by contemporary English observers, even by a few within the imperial administrative system, and was part of the reason for the growing latter nineteenth-century disenchantment with Liberalism as a whole.

These techniques, in their totality, effected significant transfers of funds from the poor South to the rich North. At a minimum, Davis argues that the British drained India to finance not only its colonial administration there, but also its imperial adventures elsewhere, such as in Afghanistan. On the high end of economic estimates, economist Utsa Patnaik has calculated that Britain drained a total of nearly $45 trillion from India alone during the period from 1765 to 1938 (Hickel, 2018). Other estimates are considerably lower than this, and there are some historians and economists who claim that Empire was actually a net cost for colonial masters. But it seems clear that European colonialism did not have indigenous interests in mind in general and that it often delivered privation and burden instead, even when on the surface some physical improvements were being made and some economic development being encouraged (see Chapter 13).

4.13 The Self-Regulating System Point of View

Growth model theorists are obvious sceptical of stories like these, even the hybrid economistic approach of a Pomeranz. But then again, their paradigm is quite different, much more similar to the Political Economy of old with its neutral self-regulating systems, driven by incentives, with politics mostly incidental or embedded elsewhere. Mokyr (1999) is typical in this regard, claiming that British imperial protections and policies in a general sense conveyed only slight advantage to the mother country and had relatively little broad impact on the Industrial Revolution beyond some favourable treatment in some markets. He claims that British commercial relations with the US remained strong even after its independence in 1783, and that while India was an important market, it never reached the size that would make it singularly so, with 1784–1786 Asia (primarily India) absorbing 13.3% of British exports, a proportion essentially constant until 1854–1856. Even in the all-important British cotton industry, Asia was a disproportionately large buyer of British output but not much more than other important markets elsewhere. The non-imperial nations of Switzerland and Belgium (before the latter acquired its African colonies in the latter half of the nineteenth century) are pointed to as successful industrialisers without external hinterlands, while Holland and Portugal are pointed to as unsuccessful modernisers of the time, despite their large overseas territories. In fact, it is claimed that empire may have been more central economically before the Industrial Revolution than after it, as manufacturing became more important than trade in raw materials. Even the slave trade, which was highly profitable, is claimed not to have been significant enough in size to make a big difference in funding Western industry.

Unified Growth theorists speak more generally of so-called non-unified theories that focus on the roles of differences that geographical and institutional factors, ethnic, linguistic and religious fractures, and culture played in industrialisation, with colonialism simply being one of many causes, positive and negative, that alter the direction of the "production function" of the economy (Galor, 2005, 277) (see Chapter 2).

Growth theorists generally claim, though, that the "Great Divergence" between North and South after 1800 mainly boils down to differences in incentives. Allen (2011) argues that Europe excelled because of its superior industrial technology, which was readily adopted in high-wage Europe because it was labour saving, but was not cost-effective in other parts of the world where wages were lower. Thus Indians stopped competing against English textiles because the adoption of spinning machines there (which might have allowed them to compete) merely increased the capital costs of spinning more than they concomitantly lowered labour costs. Japan, facing more labour scarcity managed to break out of this trap by redesigning the machines for their own circumstances, but this did not occur in China or India, which had more labour available. Later on, steamships and railways intensified international competition, lowering transport costs and making Western technology cost advantages over Asian labour-intensive production even greater, quickening the Great Divergence. Once Chinese and other Eastern labour forces were redeployed into agriculture, they specialised more and more in primary products and became underdeveloped countries in the modern sense of the word.

Allen (2011) also claims that developments such as these were not due to a European conspiracy, or even much due to colonialism (although it played a role), but simply was the result of shifts in comparative advantage (55–56). Williamson (2013) comes to the same conclusion proposing a somewhat different neoclassical mechanism. He claims that during the nineteenth century a long-run terms-of-trade boom (i.e. a rise in the relative price of a country's exports to its imports) made peripheral countries deindustrialise. The export of raw materials became so profitable that it pushed such capital and labour away from import-competing proto-industrial sectors in countries like China and India, instead diverting them to primary-commodity production for export.

Other neoclassical economists point to different critical factors, but in the end systematic factors are at play and these, it is argued, are based on a sort of natural unfolding of system forces with people responding to changes as best they can. That everyone does not end up in a good place is simply a result of a process that, like God, favours neither saint nor sinner, though perhaps does have a bit of a soft spot for those who help themselves.

The role of geography in the Great Divergence is a focal point for many neutral system points of view, of both economic and noneconomic stripes. Jared Diamond (1997), an anthropologist, is oft-cited, with his argument that advantageous geographical conditions made Europe less vulnerable to the risk associated with climate and diseases, allowing for an early European take-off in contrast to the adverse geographical conditions in other regions (e.g. harsh climate, disease prevalence, etc.), often summed up as "lucky" versus "unlucky" latitudes.

In one version of this story, during the Malthusian trap, Europe's geography was actually disadvantageous, as it was a marginal peninsula, far from the rich centres of South and East Asia that ran long-standing trade surpluses with European merchants and nations. This was why Europeans were always seeking shorter routes to Asia, with explorers braving the sailing trip around the bottom of Africa, Portugal being the maritime innovator here in part because of its maritime culture fostered by being positioned on Europe's Atlantic fringe. This impulse helped open the way for Europe's colonial enterprises that overcame the inherent geographical barriers while also playing up Asian, African and especially Amerindian disease-pool disadvantages (whose populations had no resistance to European microbes and thus died off in droves when exposed to them) (Morris, 2014, 178). Geography is here claimed to be the great leveller over the long run and Europe, poorly placed for much of history, was well placed for the accumulation of subtle changes that constituted economic modernity.

Diamond (1997) adds the wrinkle that China's relatively uniform internal geography and its largely even coastline were more easily unified under a central imperial authority and that it was this authority, in the 1400s, that suppressed the fostering of its "lucky latitude" position as well as a formidable technological base, choosing to turn inwards. Britain, though geographically "unlucky", could not as easily be politically mastered and, being an island, was naturally turned outward in its economic and political focus.

It follows from this sort of reasoning that the various technologies and models Europeans developed for natural system analysis and management, which grew as their territorial ambits expanded, were certainly not motivated by self-sacrificing generosity, but neither were they exploitative conspiracies. The underlying ground of geography was literally a common very long run shaping factor across otherwise very diverse societies.

4.14 A Bottom Line?

In many ways, the two (broadly defined) viewpoints speak past each other, with very different assumptions about political economy of the world prior to and during the Industrial Revolution. On the one hand, there are true forces of nature that are well beyond the human species and even the human-made forces and which have lives of their own. Treating the economy as an essentially impersonal and mechanistic system growing out of and constrained by these limits has its merits, and is consistent with some of the evidence, some of the time.

On the other hand, humanity and nature are not actually so easily separated and conscious human intention is a big part of the human economy, maybe even more under an integrated global economic system that a set of un-integrated localities. To treat, for example, trade between metropolitan and colony essentially similar to it being a matter of choice between relative equals seems a stretch when applying it to, say, colonial India and Imperial Britain. One should appeal to the facts but resource extraction, either direct, through on-site expropriation, or indirect, through biased trade and tax arrangements, is often not captured in official trade and finance statistics, often deliberately. The English kept the trade and investment account books with its colonies and they were far from an honest broker.

Additionally determinism can creep in very easily on both sides. Blaut (1999) has criticised Diamond as a geographic determinist, ignoring flaws in his own data and drawing overly broad conclusions by ignoring contrary salient facts. The Growth Model arguably can fall into this trap as well, as does World System models like Wallerstein's. One has to use some sort of simplification of reality, so by itself a lack of "realism" is not a fair basis of critique. The question is how plausible and flexible the framing is in relation to facts on the ground. It does seem clear that European exploitation of non-European areas was a critical part of that region's success, but that other factors, including luck, played a role too.

The problem is not the choice of a particular paradigm per se but how one uses it. The ever-versatile economist Patrick O'Brien is an example of one who uses a Growth framework, but in subtle ways, indicating how any approach can be used with versatility. His work has already been highlighted in Chapter 3, but it is worth discussing a bit more here. For him the Industrial Revolution was gradual and not limited to Britain; but Britain still was a break out of sorts because of its unique naval and commercial hegemony, and the relative efficiency of its agriculture, which was already well advanced by the second half of the eighteenth century. A clear domestic comparative advantage already present in several sectors, combined with novel techniques of production that were emerging at the same time, and were helped along by improved financial intermediation, abundant coal and other minerals, and the trade and colonial advantages that naval supremacy helped secure. All this gave Britain a critical economic edge. A unique system of solid agrarian property rights, already in place for a couple of centuries allowed for even greater efficiencies in the use of agricultural lands (O'Brien, 2006, 6–8). These were the core elements of England's early industrialisation and its later supremacy.

But O'Brien does not minimise the institutional violence used to make these changes at home and abroad, referring to internal colonisation, expropriation of ecclesiastical and common land, and the accumulation of power by aristocratic elites. This constituted a "push" from above towards efficiency, with many losers. And it caused economic changes that created a growing "pull" from below in the form of potentially high wages for displaced country migrants to London and other maritime cities (O'Brien, 2006, 8–10).

The Elizabethan Poor Law was part of this, nominally a safety net, but in actual fact more of a repressive system of control over the labour of the disadvantaged. Parliament, at the commercial elite's behest, criminalised the formation of unions, riots against high prices, resistance to enclosures, attacks by Luddites and others on the new machinery and factories, disorderly conduct of every kind, and indeed most every type of infraction, even minor theft. O'Brien notes that in 1808 the numbers of soldiers mobilised against the Luddites in the Midlands and North of England exceeded troops under Wellington's command in the Peninsular (O'Brien, 2006, 21–23).

As O'Brien's work indicates, a Growth approach need not (and should not) be ahistorical with respect to the true ugly realities of the past. But even so it is not always the most applicable or accurate model of that past, and multiple frames are required to better understand the complex dynamics and changing circumstances of economic modernisation. Possibly the advice of the great physicist J. B. S. Haldane might be appropriate here where he speaks of the universe as not only queerer than one supposes, but queerer than one can even imagine, going on to quote from Shakespeare's Hamlet that there are more things in heaven and earth than are dreamed of in philosophy (Haldane, 1927, 286). As for the universe so it is for the world economy and its politics, which has aspects of self-regulation at times, and many more contradictory things besides.

References

Allen, R. C. (2011). *Global economic history: A very short introduction*. Oxford University Press.

Aristotle. ([ca. 350 BCE] 2000). *Nicomachean ethics* (Crisp, R., Translator and Ed.). Cambridge University Press.

Barber, W. J. (1970). *A history of economic thought*. Penguin Books.

Becker, J. F. (1961). Adam Smith's theory of social science. *Southern Economic Journal, 28*(1), 13–21.

Bevir, M. (2001). The long nineteenth century in intellectual history. *Journal of Victorian Culture, 6*(2), 313–335.

Blaut, J. M. (1999). Environmentalism and Eurocentrism. *Geographical Review, 89*(3), 391–408.

Bordo, M. D., & White, E. N. (1991). A tale of two currencies: British and French finance during the Napoleonic Wars. *The Journal of Economic History, 51*(2), 303–316.

Butler, E. (2015). *Classical Liberalism: A primer*. Institute of Economic Affairs/London Publishing Partnership.

Byrne, P. (2013). *Natural religion and the nature of religion: The legacy of deism*. Routledge.

Capaldi, N. (1998). *The enlightenment project in the analytic conversation*. Springer.

Carugati, F., & Levi, M. (2021). *A moral political economy: Present, past, and future*. Cambridge University Press.

Clayton, E. (2005). Aristotle: Politics. In J. Fieser & B. Dowden (Eds.), *Internet encyclopedia of philosophy*.

Cohen, I. B. (1976). The eighteenth-century origins of the concept of scientific revolution. *Journal of the History of Ideas, 37*(2), 257–288.

Davis, M. (2002). *Late Victorian holocausts: El Niño famines and the making of the third world*. Verso Books.

De Boer, J. Z., & Sanders, D. T. (2005). *Earthquakes in human history: The far-reaching effects of seismic disruptions*. Princeton University Press.

Diamond, J. (1997). *Guns, germs and steel: The fates of human societies*. Norton.

Dunn, W. C. (1941). Adam Smith and Edmund Burke: Complementary contemporaries. *Southern Economic Journal, 7*(3), 330–346.

Foreman-Peck, J. (1983). *A history of the world economy: International economical relations since 1850*. Harvester Press.

Galor, O. (2005). From stagnation to growth: Unified growth theory. In P. Aghion & S. N. Durlauf (Eds.), *Handbook of economic growth* (Volume 1, Part A, pp. 171–293). Elsevier.

Graff, M., Kenwood, A. G., & Lougheed, A. L. (2013). *Growth of the international economy, 1820–2015*. Routledge.

Haldane, J. B. S. (1927). *Possible worlds and other essays*. Chatto & Windus.

Hickel, J. (2018). How Britain stole $45 trillion from India. And lied about it. *Aljazeera*. https://www.aljazeera.com/opinions/2018/12/19/how-britain-stole-45-trillion-from-india/

Hobbes, T. ([1651] 2010). *Leviathan: Or the matter, forme, and power of a commonwealth ecclesiasticall and civill*. I. Shapiro (Ed.), Yale University Press.

Jones, S.E. (2011). A brief survey of Sir Isaac Newton's views on religion. In M. D. Rhodes & J. W. Moody (Eds.), *Converging paths to truth*, 61–78. Religious Studies Center. Brigham Young University; Deseret Books.

MacIntosh, J. (2016). Mechanism, in modern philosophy. In *The Routledge encyclopedia of philosophy*. Taylor & Francis. https://www.rep.routledge.com/articles/thematic/mechanism-in-modern-philosophy/v-1

Malthus, T. R. ([1798] 1872). *An essay on the principle of population: Or, a view of its past and present effects on human happiness; with an inquiry into our prospects respecting the future removal or mitigation of the evils which it occasions*. Reeves & Turner.

Markie, P., & Folescu, M. (2021). Rationalism vs. empiricism. In E. N. Zalta (Ed.), *The Stanford encyclopedia of philosophy* (Fall 2021 Edition). https://plato.stanford.edu/archives/fall2021/entries/rationalism-empiricism/

Mokyr, J. (1999). Editor's introduction: The new economic history and the industrial revolution. In J. Mokyr (Ed.), *The British industrial revolution: An economic perspective* (2nd ed., pp. 1–127). Westview Press.

Morris, I. (2014). *War! What is it good for? Conflict and the progress of civilization from primates to robots*. Farrer, Straus and Giroux.

Nash, K. (2009). *Contemporary political sociology: Globalization, politics and power*. Wiley.

Neal, L., & Cameron, R. (2016). *A concise economic history of the world: From Paleolithic times to the present* (5th ed.). Oxford University Press.

O'Brien, P. (2006). *Provincializing the first industrial revolution*. London School of Economics and Political Science, Department of Economic History.

Ord-Hume, A. (1977). *Perpetual motion: The history of an obsession*. Martin's Press.

Outram, D. (2019). *The enlightenment*. Cambridge University Press.

Pomeranz, K. (2000). *The great divergence: China, Europe, and the making of the modern world economy*. Princeton University Press.

Porter, R. (1990). *The enlightenment*. Macmillan.

Ramesh, S. (2017). An economic history of India. In S. Ramesh (Ed.), *China's lessons for India: Volume I: The political economy of development* (pp. 23–54). Palgrave Macmillan.

Rublack, U. (2017). *Reformation Europe*. Cambridge University Press.

Sampson, A. (1995). *Company man: The rise and fall of corporate life*. Times-Business/Random House.

Smith, A. ([1776] 2000). *The wealth of nations* (Cannan, E. (Ed.)). Modern Library.

Thoreau, H. D. ([1849] 2016). *Civil disobedience*. Broadview Press.

Varoufakis, Y. (2015). *The global minotaur: America*. Zed Books.

Voltaire. ([1759] 1959). *Candide* (Bair, L., Ed. and Translator). Bantam Dell.

Weatherall, D. (1976). *David Ricardo: A biography*. Martinus Nijhoff.

Williamson, J.G (2013). *Trade and poverty: When the Third World fell behind*. MIT Press.

Winch, D. (2001). *That disputatious pair: Economic history and the history of economics*. Centre for Economics and History at the University of Cambridge Working Paper.

CHAPTER 5

Self, Socialisation, Organisation, Culture

C. Gordon, *Many Possible Worlds*,
https://doi.org/10.1007/978-981-19-9281-0_5

Fig. 5.1 The dance of human sociality (*Image source* Image taken from Russell, W.H. [1865]. *The Atlantic Telegraph.* [1865]. Original caption: Interior of One of the Tanks on Board the Great Eastern: Cable Passing Out. https://historyarchive.org/images/books/books-t/the-atlantic-telegraph-1865/plates/25-interior-of-one-of-the-tanks-on-board-the-great-eastern-cable-passing-out.jpg. No known copyright restrictions)

5.1 Prelude: The Origins of the Term Industrial Revolution

Although the term "Industrial Revolution" is now a commonplace, it actually has a rather long and interesting history. Its first use is as early as 1799, when a French envoy to Berlin wrote that his country had entered upon one (Landes, 1999, 128–129). Its meaning in this context was a rapid advance in just one industry in one place in one time. For a long while after that, contemporaries used the phrase in this relatively limited sense (Griffin, 2013) (Fig. 5.1).

Fast-forward to 1884, when the English historian Arnold Toynbee gave a series of lectures to Oxford undergraduates between October 1881 and May 1882 under the title, *On the economic history of England,*

1760–1840. These were re-titled ***Lectures on the Industrial Revolution in England*** (Toynbee, 1884) and when published they proved so popular that they went through five editions, remaining in print until 1927 (Griffin, 2013, 16).

Toynbee argued that during the period 1760–1840 advances in English agrarian methods combined with various other economic changes to yield a "revolution" in production. These changes included: the replacement of medieval feudal and guild relationships with cash transactions and market exchange; the development of steam power; and the creation of a genuine manufacturing sector. All of which created a transformative rise of industry and capitalist competition, which constituted a true economic revolution. Alongside these, however, came social ills such as pauperism and social dislocation in Britain (Toynbee, 1884).

Cannadine (1984) has noted how striking are the parallels between the historian's own times and their accounts of British industrialisation (171–172). In Toynbee's era, there was a justified marvelling at the rapid material improvements of the past century. But there was also shock and dismay at the associated societal upheavals, which included a thoroughgoing remaking of the social order and the rapid urbanising of what remained of the bucolic English countryside. Toynbee's use of "revolution" played up the social factors as much as the economic ones in part because that was a current concern of his audiences who were grieving over what seemed the final loss of any possibility of reclaiming the "Merrie England" of days gone by. This grief perhaps seemed more acute then because there were still enough living manifestations of days past to make the losses of modernity clear and present. Even as late as 1850, the cotton industry was still a mix of old methods and rapidly spreading new ones, while fully half of the population was still employed in areas untouched by industrialisation (Griffin, 2013). Toynbee's idea that the modern system of industry, which had increased national wealth in England, had been achieved at the expense of the material and moral well-being of many resonated with the general public (Winch, 2010).

Toynbee also had unkind words for David Ricardo, claiming that his thinking had completely dominated Political Economy between 1817 and 1848, and, as a result, parliamentary economic and social legislation as well. Far from being salutary, Toynbee claimed that Ricardo's use of abstract deductive thinking with its appearance of inferring general laws of economic behaviour and outcomes was actually misleadingly unhistorical and devoid of the actual social implications of economic policy changes. Toynbee argued that Ricardo's theorising soothed middle-class opinion but provided theoretical underpinnings, through his theories of labour value, wages, and rent, for Marx's *Das Kapital* and Henry George's *Progress and Poverty*, both doctrines with incendiary implications. Meanwhile Ricardo's theories abetted legislative and voluntary civic association agitation that was changing the relationship of employers to their employees in ways that undermined the implicit and explicit obligations of social union (Bezanson, 1922, 5–6). Indeed, Ricardo's reputation suffered quite a bit more generally during this time.

Toynbee was no radical. But unlike more modern observers he saw the economy as just one part of a social organism, something that a rapidly emerging capitalism had disrupted, for better and for worse. This social aspect of the economy has largely been lost from much modern theory. This chapter draws some of this element back in.

5.2 Sociality

For the first three chapters of this book, human biology has been alluded to in terms of material needs and constraints, with the basic process of population growth identified as a critical turnkey of economic growth. It was supposedly the breaking out of natural biology and "natural selection" that caused the species to emerge out of thousands of years of stagnant "Malthusian Trap" into the Industrial Revolution and beyond.

Yet for all this talk of biology, a very important feature of humanity has thus far been mostly unspoken of, namely sociality. Much economic theory focuses on rationality as the supposedly distinguishing feature of the human species. However, it is arguably the sociality of humanity that better earns its title of uniqueness.

Sociality refers to a tendency of a species to live in groups, allowing for a high level of social interaction and high adaptability to different demands of the group on the individual (Pam, 2013). Human beings are able live in extremely large and complex societies even when genetically unrelated to most other members, and sometimes not even closely related socially. This ability appears to be mainly due to proficiency in the social (cultural) transmission of information, knowledge and behaviours, although genetics also plays a role (their relative contributions being a matter of ongoing debate). The scope, scale and complexity of human social organisation appear to go beyond anything else in the natural world (Tomasello et al., 2020).

Only a few dozen species out of thousands are highly social in the sense of having a need and ability to form permanent communities with ranges from dozens to billions of members. Some highly social species are highly intelligent, such as humans, dolphins, killer whales and nonhuman apes. But ants are arguably the most social, yet also have the least cognitive power, at least judging by their extremely limited brains, which are physically primitive enough so as to make biologists refer to them as "ganglions". Ant communities are not only large—one measure of sociality—but also highly interdependent—another measure—with the result that their colonies are called "superorganisms" because there are millions of insects acting together as if they made up one giant animal. This combination of limited individual brainpower and high social organisation is referred to as "civilisation by instinct" by biologists (Morris, 2014, 299).

Obviously, individual human beings have much more brainpower than other social species, but also as much or arguably sometimes more social organisation. Some authors even claim we break the scale, referring to human "ultrasociality" (Richerson & Boyd, 1998). But how much of this is driven by "instinct" versus other factors such as abstract thinking and intelligence?

Harari (2014) focuses, like many others, on the importance of human brainpower and cognitive ability. He says that 150 members is the "natural" limit of human social organisation, a benchmark about which there is little actual consensus, though it is typically assumed that human beings in their more "primitive" form have fairly low size constraints for the groups they organise themselves into. He then argues that a "cognitive revolution" allowed the species to create flexible language, which in turn provided for verbal communication about third parties, which in turn allowed for the creation of collective stories that allowed humanity to socially organise far above such "natural" levels. Thus two Christians or Serbs who have never met can cooperate based on a shared God or flag and this can be scaled up to millions, and even billions potentially. This focus on the power of thinking is very consistent with much standard economic theorising about economic modernisation that emphasises rationality and its presumed products such as technological innovation and invention.

An alternative view is to focus on instinct, which is what many anthropologists and some sociologists do. An influential example of this is the work of anthropologist Robert Carneiro's "circumscription" theory, refined by sociologist Michael Mann as "caging". The dynamic behind levels of social organisation come from how hemmed in a group finds itself to be. If the group is unable to run away from enemies, they either create a more effective organisation for themselves so they can fight back, or are absorbed into the enemy's more effective organisation (Morris, 2014, 80). Here one could say that the basic instinct of aggression is a core motivator for enhancing natural sociality. Powerful cognitive ability certainly enables much higher levels of organisation than other species can achieve, but an instinctual motivation for sociality is shared by all social species. This sort of reasoning is especially influential in some theories of human war making and the formation of the State. Box 5.1 discusses the topic of human aggression and war in more detail (see Chapter 22 for more on war generally).

Box 5.1 Human Aggression, Violence and War

In conflict situations, most species can be observed to revert to a primitive, midbrain processing of instinctual aggression. However an equally powerful resistance to lashing out is a deep inhibition towards killing one's own kind. For example animals with horns will fight others of their species in a rather ritual way while fighting without restraint against other species. This dual aspect of aggression is believed to be a survival mechanism that prevents a species from destroying itself while still being able to defend against incursions by outside rivals.

In human war making, this natural tendency is not necessarily a good thing. General S. L. A. Marshall, based on post-combat interviews conducted in his role as an official military historian, found that only 15–20% of the individual riflemen in World War 2 fired their own weapons at an exposed enemy soldier. More impersonal wide fire weapons, such as flamethrowers, did not incur such inhibition and crew driven weapons like machine guns were generally fired with little hesitation. His conclusion was that left to their own devices, most individual combatants were unable or unwilling to kill other human beings, even their enemies, unless there was a clear and present close threat, as in hand to hand combat.

Marshall's methods and data have since been criticised but his general conclusions have since been supported by other military researchers across different times and wars, and have been echoed by studies of law enforcement officers. Human beings are not, by nature, killers of other human beings without having some very good, personal, direct reason for doing so. This essential feature of humanity has, however, been treated as a barrier to overcome by military authorities, for obvious, if unpleasant, reasons. Thus the American Army after World War 2 radically altered its combat training, replacing firing at target markers with realistic, man-shaped pop-up targets that fall when hit. The idea is to condition a response to fire immediately on an enemy soldier when sighted, over-riding the natural instinct to refrain from such action. These and other methods helped increase the rate of fire to approximately 55% in Korea and around 95% in Vietnam.

However the overcoming of basic instinct comes with a cost, not least an inner tension that creates ongoing psychic torment. The Vietnam War led to unprecedented rates of Post-Traumatic Stress Disorder (PTSD) in returning veterans, and earlier wars of the twentieth century came with similar types of complexes. (See Box 14.1 in Chapter 14 for more on this). What war training experience shows is that human beings are malleable and quite subject to socially induced changes in behaviour that is supposedly innate. But also that there are some innate limits to this process as well, and costs to overriding these.

(This discussion has been drawn from Grossman [2014].)

5.3 Socialisation, Culture and Society

Human sociality across individuals within species covers a wide spectrum, from asocial—a state of avoidance and hostility to relating to others—to highly social—where connection is all important to a person in determining their well-being, actions and sense of self. The wide range of sociality exhibited across human beings may be unique across species (Ochs & Solomon, 2010). And because of the complex nature of human sociality, social identity and individual identity are not fully separable. Who we are as individuals depends upon who we are in connection with others—and vice-versa. Thus socialisation—the process of internalising the norms and ideologies of society—is a critical part of who we become as individuals (Cromdal, 2006). Individuation is a related concept, i.e. the level of awareness and coherence of a person as a unique individual, distinct and boundaried from others.

Developmentally, a key task for most humans as they grow and mature is to become fully individuated and autonomous, yet be able to maintain requisite and functional relationships with others. These needs go well beyond mere physical and instinctual drives, such as for food, shelter, and procreation. Primate studies have shown that deprivation of social contact can cause severe mental illness short-and long-term, a finding confirmed by experiences with neglected orphans left in orphanages during the Second World War and in Communist Romania, who ended up being severely emotionally disabled for the rest of their lives (Greene, 2020).

Of course one can be highly individuated and highly social at the same time—or highly individuated and asocial—or poorly individuated and asocial. And some individuals can move dramatically across both spectrums in very short time-frames. For example, otherwise well-adjusted people can temporarily lose their individuation and individual identity in crowds, with the "mob" acting as a unit with its own social forces, causing people to behave in ways contrary to the ways they would when left on their own or in very small groups. Thus social psychologists study group behaviours and processes as distinct from individual ones (Aronson et al., 2009). Sociologists similarly study social, as opposed to individual dynamics.

Culture, in a very loose sense, could be said to involve socialisation writ large. This is a term with many definitions but one of the simplest is as a synonym for "social learning". If an individual member of a group learns something (a behaviour, a belief, etc.) on its own, then this is individual learning. If, on the other hand, members of the group learn something from each other, that is social learning (keeping in mind that the educational means can vary widely, e.g. imitation, teaching and so on). Social learning is also sometimes called cultural learning or cultural transmission (Whitehead & Rendell, 2014).

While by no means the only definition of culture, this one is widely used and also conceptually relatively simple. There is some debate about whether some nonhuman animals also have cultural transmission or culture (see Box 5.2); but humans certainly have both at a deep and profound level. Their proficiency at cultural transmission especially is a key part of the human ability to build large and complex societies and to spread ideas, technologies, doctrines and practices across many different groups and wide areas.

Box 5.2 Do Non-humans Have Culture?
Although it is quite clear that human beings have very elaborate cultures, is it possible that other species have culture as well? This is a very live

debate within the community of ethologists, i.e. scholars that study animal behaviour, and especially amongst those who focus on the higher marine mammals of dolphins and whales.

These creatures are known to be highly social, highly intelligent and highly adaptable. They also often form close relationships with human beings, both on individual and group bases. To take but one example, between 1828 and 1843, shore-based whalers catching Baleen whales in Twofold Bay off the coast of Eden, Australia, formed an ongoing collaboration with Killer whales who would herd and exhaust the Baleen until they were easy prey for the whalers. In return the whalers would leave the stripped Baleen carcasses for the Killer whales to pick off of for a couple of days and then tow the carcasses back to the whaling station for disposal. The human-whale cooperation even extended towards the Killer whales towing boats by holding on to the ship lines with their teeth. Some of the helper whales were given names by the whalers (Whitehead & Rendell, 2014, 141–142).

There are numerous examples of both interspecies cooperation and equally complex and social coordination within marine mammal species. But are these examples of culture? Partly it depends upon the definition of the term. One definition points to cultural transmission based on collective ideas and concepts that are not linked to the genome (Whitehead & Rendell, 2014, 124). To the extent this is happening within whale and dolphin communities is impossible to say because internal mind workings of such creatures are essentially unobservable. Some claim the question is settled because cultural transmission relies on abstract language. But the highly complex and variable whalesong, or, for that matter, birdsong, are believed by some to constitute such language, though others doubt it. There are strong positions on these matters with nothing definitively settled empirically. And there are those who doubt even the criticality of language to the formation of culture, a position that boosts the hypothesis that certain nonhuman mammals could indeed have culture (Whitehead & Rendell, 2014, 205, 232–233).

Culture is clearly a concept applicable to humans. But it may be applicable to other species as well. To deny this possibility may be a case of "sapiens exceptionalism" because theoretically and empirically, no final answer has yet been arrived at (Whitehead & Rendell, 2014, 299) (Fig. 5.2).

Fig. 5.2 Bottlenose dolphins off the coast of North Carolina, USA (1979) (*Image source* page 127 of "Coast watch" [1979], \UNC Sea Grant College Program, Publisher: [Raleigh, N. C.: UNC Sea Grant College Program], Contributing Library: State Library of North Carolina, Digitizing Sponsor: North Carolina Digital Heritage Center [No known copyright restrictions])

5.4 Economic Change and Society

Human society encompasses all of this. Lichtheim (1972) defines "society" as the "entire structure of institutions and modes of life inherited from the past and constantly refashioned through the process of historical change" (10). How economic change affects society in this sense much exercised those writing during the time of the Industrial Revolution itself. Toynbee's views have already been mentioned. Emile Durkheim ([1897]

1951), one of the founders of modern sociology, wrote of organic solidarity, i.e. the ability of a social system to integrate all its diverse elements into a stable whole. He argued that society's underlying ground is a "conscience collective", a "system of beliefs and sentiments" held by everyone creating a common bond. When this breaks down, "anomie" results and he argued that this was increased by industrialisation with suicide often being the result at an individual level. Durkheim criticised Adam Smith's arguments for the division of labour as being exclusively from a wealth creation perspective, neglecting its impact on social cohesion. Industrial division of labour, with its attendant task specialisation, made society more materially interdependent, and correspondingly more efficient. But it came at the cost of undermining social bonds and shared meaning (Swedberg, 2008).

A contemporary of Durkheim's, and an even more towering figure in the formation of sociology as a field, was Max Weber. Weber has made a number of contributions to the discussion about society and its effect on economy, most famously (and controversially) his contention that the Protestant Reformation laid the foundation for modern capitalism in Northern Europe because of the Protestant work ethic which, according to him, incited large numbers of people to engage in work in the secular world, engaging in trade and accumulating wealth, and greatly aiding in the expansion of commercial enterprise, all of which laid the groundwork for industrialisation (Weber, 1930). This "macro" social argument focuses on a socially formed worldview and change in collective belief system.

This particular argument by Weber has not stood the test of time and evidence unchallenged (Etzrodt, 2008) (though some, notably Barro and McCleary (2019), claim that it does stack up empirically). His larger (and unfinished) work *Economy and Society* (1914) has been more generally accepted. Weber argued that "political" capitalism and "traditional" capitalism have existed for thousands of years but its more recent variant, Rational Capitalism, arose only with Western modernity. Traditional capitalism is centred on small, largely self-sufficient enterprises, trading with each other and using money to conduct exchange, mixed with barter and other means as needed. Political capitalism refers to profit making by State directed enterprises such as activities in pursuit of mercantilism or imperialism. Rational capitalism, however, is the intentional, conscious, methodical and privately directed profit-driven business activity, large-scale enterprises with specialised bureaucracies and trained staff, sometimes working with the State, for definite predictable and planned outcomes. It is this social-political structure, according to Weber, that allowed for industrialisation and competitive dynamism (Swedberg, 2008).

Unlike neoclassical economic constructs, economic action in the sociological sense is by not just individual at root (even additively) but inherently driven by social structure and values. Both Weber's hypotheses on Protestantism and Rational Capitalism are based on his premise that a collective scientific attitude had to replace superstition for technological progress to occur. In pre-modernity, supernatural forces were thought to affect the natural world and so manipulation of the latter involved supernatural beings. This attitude retarded scientific and technological and social progress. Modern society and its science and material progress arose with "the disenchantment of the world" in which events in the material realm were seen as unaffected by the spiritual, allowing people to focus on discovery of material regularities and patterns. Weber thought that this process began in the West first, and thus explained that region's economic rise, though why this occurred in the first place is not explained (Allen, 2009, 7–9).

Meanwhile Fiske (1992) looks at economic modernisation from a social psychological perspective, defining sociality as a state where relationships between people are intrinsic, i.e. valuable because of the social connection itself and not because of any extrinsic rewards (such as money gain) that may come from such connection. Relatedness is sought because it offers relatedness, end of story. But there are definite gradations, with important economic implications. Transactional relationships, motivated primarily by extrinsic reward, do exist, though even these, Fiske claims, derive in part from innate sapiens sociality. The transactional mode of relating is the sort of sociality that is obviously "economic" in the modern sense of the word and this mode has played a critical part in making modern capitalism possible and, in turn, making it dominant in many societies. This Market Pricing (MP) (to use his term) is only one of four fundamental social modes. Even where the MP mode is dominant, other more cooperative modes will co-exist with it and, indeed, will be necessary for the full range of human social need to be met. And, like all modes, MP itself evolves over time and across societies.

Baumard (2019), in contrast to these sociological and social psychology perspectives, argues that the most important change that occurred during the Industrial Revolution may not have been in the incentives to action (a position at variance with standard Growth model reasoning), or any changes in social structure, but a cognitive switch from a "scarcity mindset" to an "affluence mindset", which caused people to become more optimistic, patient and inquisitive than before, characteristics that supposedly foster innovation, accumulation and investment in long-term enterprises.

Baumard claims that an initial increase in pre-industrial living standards triggered a slow but steady modification in neurocognitive processes, especially in greater orientation towards future rewards, which changed the way human beings planned and allocated their activities and devotion of energies across their lifespan. This insight is based on Life History Theory (LHT), a branch of evolutionary biology that holds that organisms have a finite budget of resources across time. In high scarcity environments, people tend to be more violent, less trustful and more intolerant than in high abundance environments because there are greater evolutionary payoffs to seeking short-term gain, since "tomorrow" may never come. As background wealth and income slowly grew, people became more favourable towards speculative activities with more uncertain results, especially technological development, since they could afford to take more risks and defer rewards over a longer time-span.

Although focusing on the human collective, Baumard is not focusing on society in the sociological sense but on the biological evolutionary tendency of the human species. His view arises out of sociobiology and other similar types of thinking, e.g. Richard Dawkins' *The Selfish gene* (1976), which posits genetics as the prime mover of human social (and individual) evolution. In this case, the gene's hardwired imperative to reproduce and improve itself employs the human as a vehicle for doing so and so human action is driven accordingly, if unconsciously. Humans experience themselves as making "choices" but this is not only an inaccurate perception but also an irrelevant one. Baumard's unique wrinkle is to claim that systemic changes in preferences based on subjective worldview driven by changes in underlying resource constraints are the key mechanism that marks the critical turn towards the modern economy. This differs not only from purely biological approaches but also from much economic theory where the external changes in opportunity costs and incentives are the engine of behavioural change.

As mentioned in Chapter 2, Norbert Elias posits a theory that blends sociology and psychology by proposing a dynamic homeostasis in which the psychology of members of a society is co-created with the structure of society in an ongoing way, social forces interacting with and changing individual psyches (psychogenesis) and individuals interacting with and changing the broader society (sociogenesis). This is not a mere cognitive process, though that plays an important role, but is driven by the fundamental human drive for interconnection, which, in turn, is constantly shaped by the shape of society. For Elias the modern economy is part of a broader "civilising process" in which individuals increasingly attune to the needs and desires of others, thus increasing interdependence and the power of the collective to fulfil various social, psychic and physical needs of both individual and society. This social division of labour creates some new free space for individuals for personal expression, but also limits such action that threatens the level of social interdependence at the time (Elias, 2000).

An interesting question arises at this point regarding the relative importance of individual subjective experience as opposed to objective changes in material and other conditions. Baumard's worldview hypothesis proposes what are effectively subjective changes in group cognition, though these are driven by material changes, while Elias is more focused on a broader set of psychological and social dynamics. The importance of the subjective versus objective continues to be a matter of some debate. Sigmund Freud was the first to develop a model of the human psyche, something that had never been done before. (Elias builds on Freud but goes in quite distinct directions from him; see Box 5.3.)

Freud puts forward a tripartite model of the psyche consisting of an "Id" which is the seat of instinctual drive; the "Ego", which is the seat of higher intelligence, aware of reality as it truly exists; and the "Superego" which is the repository of social forces, especially those presented by parents. Human subjective life consists of a constant struggle between the "pleasure principle" of pure instinct, which is grossly egoistic in its seeking of total satisfaction of physical needs and desires; and the "reality principle" which is the seeking of functional accommodation with the world as it is. Freud also posits an underlying instinctual drive of the human species towards violence and aggression, a so-called Thanatos (death) drive. The development of a healthy Ego to mediate the struggle between these forces is a basic developmental task for all human beings (Lapsley & Steyld, 2011).

On the one hand, subjective experience is extremely important in the Freudian view since it drives human action. The goal of psychoanalysis is to bring to the surface the unconscious conflicts between the psyche's three parts, and bring them into proper balance, allowing "adjustment" of the individual to challenges presented in the real world. On the other hand, Freud has a mechanistic view of the human being that is almost Newtonian in its model of energy flows through a system. He is also rather fundamentally conservative in seeking the conformity of an individual with prevailing social norms and constraints. Thus one can go quite a few divergent directions with Freudian constructs towards and away from subjectivity, as will be discussed later. However, Freud's theory and some of his psychological successors potentially open the door to subjectivity as a causal factor in economic development, though few have gone through it.

Box 5.3 Freud, Elias, Civilisation and the Holocaust
Norbert Elias and Sigmund Freud both offer theories of development of human civilisation. And both speak of psychological factors in this development. But beyond this the two authors part in important ways.

Freud wrote a famous book, *Civilisation and its Discontents* ([1929] 1962), in which he argued that human civilisation was a thin veneer that developed to keep human instinctual drives under check, lest they come out into the open and destroy the whole social order. This comes out of Freud's model of the human psyche as fundamentally egoistic and hedonistic. People are basically narcissistic seekers of pleasure and struggle constantly to become well adjusted to the reality of society and the world.

This is not what Elias argued for he saw humans as individualistic and socially related simultaneously. Civilisation for him was not purely repressive of basic instincts but a product of those instincts, one of which was sociality. Thus for Elias, heightened internal psychic repression was a product of modernisation, but it was not repression for repression's sake, nor repression of inherently and immutably desired egoistic options. Instead, Elias saw preferences changing along with society and while instinctual drives do have some level of inalterability (being "first nature" after all), human instinct evolves well beyond this through the shared processes of social connection and interaction. Freud did not believe this, seeing human instinctual drives as effectively fixed.

Elias therefore sees modern civilisation as consisting of an extremely high level of social interdependence, with potential benefits such as high levels of personal security, division of labour, specialisation of effort, expanding commerce and output, and space for greater individual and creative expression. To have these benefits people do need to repress their egoistic drives to co-exist and co-operate with others better, and this does result in a constant inner tension. But it was not the sort of epic contest between "higher" and "lower" that Freud suggested, nor with his hard and fast lines between subjective and objective. Rather human social and individual experience is dynamic over time and able to go in unexpected directions.

One way to see the differences between Freud and Elias is to look at their attitudes towards the German Holocaust of European Jewry under Hitler. Both men were Jewish and both obviously were targets of this genocidal campaign, though both managed to escape to safety in England, Freud being welcomed there but Elias detained for eight months in a detention camp because of his German ancestry. Neither one defended or in any way justified the Holocaust. Freud and his family escaped to England from the Austrian Anschluss in 1938, but since he died the following year, he did not live to see the full unfolding of the Holocaust. But his theory clearly suggested that its occurrence was an example of a slide back into barbarism and of how thin the veneer of civilisation is against the dark instincts inherent in the human animal. Elias, living into the twenty-first century witnessed the Holocaust and actually did write about it. He saw it as an outgrowth of the German civilising process up to that time which in this case had became a "decivilising process." He obviously thought the Holocaust reprehensible but also an example of what can happen when psychogenetic and sociogenetic processes get out of whack.

(The discussion above is drawn from Dunning & Mennell, 1998; and Pratt, 2013).

One intermediate social scale that may often be more important economically than either end of the spectrum is the organisation. Indeed, even if there clearly are dominant mass social forces, or some generalised individual characteristics, these can manifest quite differently when refracted through membership of, or dominance by, an organised entity such as a church, corporation, civic association and, obviously, governments and State structures. Some of this debate has already been encountered in Chapter 3 in asking why Europe industrialised before China. A very common organisational hypothesis is that some European countries, such as Holland and England, had limited and relatively democratic government early on, which was an aid to first-mover industrialisation because such governmental forms are supposedly conducive to free enterprise, secure property rights and technical progress and investment.

Countries like France are said to have lagged because of a propensity, and history, of autocratic government, which, presumably because of its arbitrariness, is toxic to capitalist development (though the specific logic behind this is not always clear). China is said to have fallen behind for similar reasons but with a different historicity, its tradition of unified empire being more stable and hence good in preindustrial times, but then retarding when more dynamism and initiative were required for industrialisation (Dincecco & Wang, 2018; Ma & Rubin, 2019). Rosenberg and Birdzell (1986) go so far as to argue that the retreat and decentralisation of State power from various private realms in the West opened the floodgates to modern industrial capitalism by allowing innovative changes to the way private enterprise organised itself and created and invested capital. This echoes the positions taken by the Political Economists (see Chapter 4), though obviously is debatable.

5.5 Case Studies of Economy/Society Modernisation

To put some of these concepts into a bit more context for the great change that was the Industrial Revolution, let's consider four major topics regarding the collective and individual transformations involved in the Industrial Revolution.

5.5.1 *"The Great Transformation"*

The rise of market forms of organisation and distribution is known to be critical to industrialisation and the early stages of economic modernity. But how did these forms come about? Was it, as many economists maintain, a natural progression based on an evolutionary process surrounding incentives that drove changes in individual and then collective action?

Karl Polanyi (1944) posits the emergence of the market economy as the fundamental event for capitalism. Polanyi claimed that all economic functions—production, consumption and distribution—had previously been "embedded" in politics and religion before the advent of capitalism, and that these were subsequently "disembedded" by a epochal and traumatic "Great Transformation". This was driven in England by a State-led change in laws and interventions that destroyed old institutions and ways of being, replacing them with new forms that fundamentally altered humankind's economic relations. Markets thus went from playing

Table 5.1 Selected English legislative actions critical to industrialisation

1694—Bank of England established
1705—English Bankruptcy Act of 1705 recognizes concept of "honest bankrupts"
1720—South Sea Bubble bursts, ending speculative frenzy in London stock market. The Bubble Act in England restricts formation of joint-stock companies
1733—Sir John Barnard's Act outlaws "wagers, puts, and refusals" on the London stock market
1750—English enclosure movement of common lands enters most intensive phase
1769—English Parliament makes destruction of any building housing machinery a felony punishable by death
1799–1800—English Combination Acts of 1799 and 1800 ban trade unions

Source Drawn from Allen & Belt (1998)

a very minor role in human affairs to playing a central one, founded on what Polanyi calls the myth of human nature's propensity toward rational free trade.

A prime example of such action is a series of Enclosure Acts which enclosed common fields and privatised them, helping to force peasants into the emerging putting-out (later factory) system of production that organised people along division of labour lines. But there are many others. These changes were driven mainly by an emerging and powerful set of commercial interests, made more powerful by the changes once enacted. Table 5.1 notes of a few of the major English legislative acts in this regard.

While recognising the material progress wrought by this transformation, Polanyi was critical of the social-economic nature of many of these changes, arguing that the political task of the twentieth century was to "re-embed" into the economy the political and human values that were lost, especially rebalancing the concepts of reciprocity (e.g. distribution within a kinship group by way of gifts and mutual obligations); redistribution (typically by a political centre such as the State); and exchange (the market mechanism in particular) (Swedberg, 2008).

For Polanyi the self-regulating system of market totality does not arise out of some natural evolutionary human tendency. The "Market Society" was made not born and it needs to be remade accordingly. He disputes the idea that markets have always been a "natural" paradigm, even for organising human economies, much less entire societies, an assessment that some anthropologists and even economists support (Henrich et al., 2005; Suzman, 2017). Governments and private interests helped create the modern economy we know now and the particular interests who stood most to gain were key in influencing governments to do this, so there is no reason not to modify it accordingly to fit a more general social purpose.

5.5.2 *"The Industrious Revolution"*

The Industrious Revolution refers to a change in human socialisation that occurred in individual households. Although developed by an economic historian (De Vries, 1994), the model has content that can be considered sociological in nature.

The general idea is that the autonomy and boundaries of the household had to change to make a fully marketised and industrialised economy work. De Vries refers to this as the "permeability" of the household, which he argues increased with industrialisation. Thus in-home nonmarket goods production had to be discouraged, with household members encouraged to buy goods produced for sale in the market, converting householders into consumers to provide the requisite product demand to sustain large-scale production from the supply side. On that supply side, householders had to supply labour required by industrial production, i.e. becoming workers to keep the new industrial enterprises going, leaving their household routines behind.

This change in household composition, structure and direction was a combination of push (the industrial market system forcing households to change by, for example, expropriating or enclosing formerly common resources essential to household production and consumption) and pull (the same system offering attractive incentives for the household to discard its old ways, especially by offering higher wages and an array of previously rare or unavailable consumer goods, especially ones not possible to make at home).

On the push side, De Vries and others note the increasing inability to satisfy household needs through household production as the market model entered more and more consumption realms requiring the earning of more cash (gained only through participation in wage-earning employment) to buy things formerly home-produced. Polanyi emphasised the State interventions (such as enclosure) that did this, while De Vries focuses more on forces generated by the industrial process itself, such as concentrating employment at key locations, leading to the depopulation of rural areas with its home-based subsistence to the rise of more interdependent and less household-autarkic economies. The two are obviously closely interrelated.

On the pull side, De Vries notes that rising industrial wages and the increase in variety and quantity of affordable consumer goods changed both household tastes, increasing their desires for factory-made and market-provided goods rather than home-made crafts; and also the opportunity cost of leisure (i.e. it now cost more, in terms of foregone wages, to rest and so rest became less attractive).

Industrial-led household changes then led to further feedback factors, e.g. the rise of the "capitalist patriarchy" where the father works, and women and children stay at home. Very slowly but surely more and more households began to follow this model, further discouraging fully independent household production and reinforcing industrial modes of production. State policies such as mandatory primary schooling and, later, rules against child labour, at first motivated by economic goals (e.g. better educated labour was more productive) contributed to this change as well.

De Vries focuses very much on incentives driving essentially optimising and rational households into new behaviours that are framed as discretionary choices. Granted these choices are often highly constrained, such as by State enclosures and, later, public education mandates, and by economically driven demographic change. Still, according to De Vries, they are the products of rational calculation, agents doing the best that they could under the circumstances, given their preferences.

But it is equally plausible to look at more sociological mechanisms, such as social forces and socialisation. This is particularly applicable to the capitalist patriarchy and the nuclear family, which became strong norms for households to follow. Consumption preferences, especially the accumulation of market-provided goods, also are known to be highly social and collective in nature. The changes that occurred for households in the first part of the Industrial Revolution are pretty well documented and known. But their exact causes, certainly manifold, remain open to multiple views.

5.5.3 *"Factory Discipline"*

During this time, householders had to adapt to a most unnatural institution—the factory. Having people show up to work at regular times, sit down and work at repetitive tasks, and do it day in and day out, required new authority structures, changed attitudes, and radically new habituation.

All this is generically referred to as "factory discipline". Economic historian Gregory Clark (1994) notes that factory discipline varied considerably across the nineteenth century in Europe, and, in some industries such as coal mining, even into the early twentieth century. Some factories, in increasing numbers as time wore on, did indeed employ actual discipline in the form of strict and enforced rules about not talking while working, sitting in place, not taking breaks and, of course, strict working hours and days. Some factories, however, were far more relaxed, allowing flexible working hours, and no or few restrictions on how workers completed their tasks (e.g. talking and moving around and breaks were permissible). These structures were combined at times with piece-rate incentives or penalties (e.g. rewards for producing above a certain amount or deductions for failing to meet a set quota) and/or capital rental rates (a charge to the worker for using the machinery provided to them).

Clark notes some variety across industries, and says that the higher the value of capital provided to the worker by the employer, the more strict discipline tended to be, to limit the damage workers could do to valuable machines and tools and also to ensure that the capital did not lay idle too long. According to him, this was an opportunity cost issue: very expensive machines needed to be worked more regularly and consistently to generate returns to cover their costs while less expensive machines could be more loosely managed. In general the less systematic the production process, the less strict the discipline. Clark notes that some English miners could still mostly report to work when they felt like it even in the 1930s mainly because mining still had a "craft" rather than production line flavour to it. Nonetheless, strict discipline became more and more the norm in mining and most other industries.

Clark himself puts forward two hypotheses as to why factory discipline arose in the first place. One was "social coercion", namely that to make the factory system work, people had to be forced to conform to it, through the exercise of social, economic, political and institutional power. This is the intuitive response and the opinion of many non-economists (and of some economic historians), namely that factory discipline was about social control driven by the imperatives of technology requiring people to be broken in to submit to it. This is a paradigm that continues to resonate today with more modern technological change and associated changes in work practices.

Clark suggests supports an alternative hypothesis: that it was in worker's self-interest to become more disciplined because of the increased personal payoffs to them from factory production; but that discipline had to be imposed from the outside because of deficiencies in the workers' own self-discipline. In other words, "Factory Discipline" is optimal from both a system and an individual perspective, despite appearances to the contrary. Of course, this answer accords well with the traditional assumptions of economic models that hold the individual as the primary unit of analysis. It is also a debatable proposition.

5.5.4 Entrepreneurship

The story of the First Industrial Revolution contains many tales of bold inventors and investors staking all on a novel idea, with success far from guaranteed. These idealised stories suggest that it is the individual entrepreneur that is critical to economic breakthrough, at least in many instances.

Joseph Schumpeter, an economist with a sociological bent, provides a famous analysis of entrepreneurship in his book, *The theory of economic development* (1934), noting the social resistance from the environment that the entrepreneur usually confronts. Schumpeter valued invention and innovation, but believed that it was of little economic import without the activities of the entrepreneur who developed and made it commercially viable, funnelling resources into it with great risk and uncertainty.

This type of individual was not simply a maximising agent with particular preferences, but in a class of their own, with unique motivations to break out of norms and excel in unique ways. At the same time, this type of individual is critical to the social processes of capitalistic development, with an important social function, even though and at the same time internally motivated. From Schumpeter comes the call from many innovation theorists to provide resources and incentives to encourage the development of an entrepreneurial cadre.

The importance of entrepreneurship is seen as important to particular turns in production innovations, such as the invention and application of the steam engine. But even neoclassical economists recognise that the scale of such individual activity as was witnessed during the Industrial Revolution had to be driven by some underlying common factor or set of factors. As discussed, there are many candidate causes here, ranging from changes in incentives, differences in natural environments, institutions in their broad and narrow senses, and even, sometimes, dumb luck. Even today, with a large and growing literature in entrepreneurship, there is something of a mystery as to how to encourage and inculcate it. The entrepreneur is an exemplar of the dual social-individual character of the human being.

References

Allen, R. C. (2009). *The British industrial revolution in global perspective*. Cambridge University Press.

Allen, L., & Belt, F. H. (1998). *The ABC-CLIO world history companion to capitalism*. ABC-CLIO.

Aronson, E., Wilson, T. D., & Akert, R. M. (2009). *Social psychology* (7th ed.). Prentice Hall.

Barro, R. J., & McCleary, R. (2019). *The wealth of religions*. Princeton University Press.

Baumard, N. (2019). Psychological origins of the industrial revolution. *Behavioral and Brain Sciences, 42, e189.*

Bezanson, A. (1922). The early use of the term Industrial Revolution. *Quarterly Journal of Economics, 36*(2), 343–349.

Cannadine, D. (1984). The present and the past in the English industrial revolution 1880–1980. *Past & Present, 103*(1), 131–172.

Clark, G. (1994). Factory discipline. *Journal of Economic History, 54*(1), 128–163.

Cromdal, J. (2006). Socialization. In K. Brown (Ed.), *Encyclopedia of language and linguistics* (pp. 462–466). Elsevier.

Dawkins, R. (1976). *The selfish gene*. Oxford University Press.

De Vries, J. (1994). The industrious revolution and the industrial revolution. *Journal of Economic History, 54*(2), 249–270.

Dincecco, M., & Wang, Y. (2018). Violent conflict and political development over the long run: China versus Europe. *Annual Review of Political Science, 21*, 341–358.

Dunning, E., & Mennell, S. (1998). Elias on Germany, Nazism and the Holocaust: On the balance between "civilizing" and "decivilizing" trends in the social development of Western Europe. *British Journal of Sociology, 49*(3), 339–357.

Durkheim, E. ([1897] 1951). *Suicide: A study in sociology* (J. A. Spaulding & G. Simpson, Trans.). The Free Press.

Elias, N. (2000). *The civilizing process: Sociogenetic and psychogenetic investigations* (Revised Ed.). Blackwell.

Etzrodt, C. (2008). Weber's protestant ethic thesis, the critics, and Adam Smith. *Max Weber Studies, 8*(1), 49–78.

Fiske, A. P. (1992). The four elementary forms of sociality: Framework for a unified theory of social relations. *Psychological Review, 99*(4), 689–723.

Freud, S. ([1929] 1962). *Civilization and its discontents* (J. Strachey, Trans.). W. W. Norton
Greene, M. F. (2020, July–August). 30 years ago, Romania deprived thousands of babies of human contact. Here's what's become of them. *The Atlantic.*
Griffin, E. (2013). *The 'industrial revolution': interpretations from 1830 to the present* (Working Paper, School of History), UEA, Norwich.
Grossman, D. (2014). *On killing: The psychological cost of learning to kill in war and society.* Open Road Media.
Harari, Y. N. (2014). *Sapiens: A brief history of humankind.* Random House.
Henrich, J., Boyd, R., Bowles, S., Camerer, C., Fehr, E., Gintis, McElreath, R., Alvard, M., Barr, A., Ensminger, J, Henrich, N. S., Hill, K., Gil-White, Gurven, M., Marlowe, F. W., Patton, J. Q., & Tracer, D. (2005). "Economic man" in cross-cultural perspective: Behavioral experiments in 15 small-scale societies. *Behavioral and Brain Sciences, 28*(6), 795–815.
Landes, D. S. (1999). The fable of the dead horse; or, the industrial revolution revisited. In J. Mokyr (Ed.), *The British industrial revolution: An economic perspective* (2nd ed., pp. 128–159). Westview Press.
Lapsley, D. K., & Steyld, P. C. (2011). Id, ego, and superego. In V. S. Ramachandran (Ed.), *Encyclopedia of human behavior* (2nd ed.). Elsevier.
Lichtheim, G. (1972). *Europe in the twentieth century.* Praeger Publishers.
Ma, D., & Rubin, J. (2019). The paradox of power: Principal-agent problems and administrative capacity in Imperial China (and other absolutist regimes). *Journal of Comparative Economics, 47*(2), 277–294.
Morris, I. (2014). *War! What is it good for? Conflict and the progress of civilization from primates to robots.* Farrer, Straus and Giroux.
Ochs, E., & Solomon, O. (2010). Autistic sociality. *Ethos, 38*(1), 69–92.
Pam, N. (2013). Sociality. *Psychologydictionary.org.* https://psychologydictionary.org/sociality/. Accessed September 10, 2020.
Polanyi, K. (1944). *The great transformation.* Beacon Press.
Pratt, J. (2013). Elias, punishment, and decivilization. In J. Pratt, D. Brown, & M. Brown (Eds.), *The new punitiveness: Trends, theories and perspectives* (pp. 256–271). Routledge.
Richerson, P. J., & Boyd, R. (1998). The evolution of human ultra-sociality. In F. Eibl-Eibesfeldt (Ed.), *Indoctrinability, ideology, and warfare: Evolutionary perspectives* (pp. 71–95). Berghahn Books.
Rosenberg, N., & Birdzell, L. E. (1986). *How the West grew rich: The economic transformation of the industrial world.* Basic Books.
Schumpeter, J. (1934). *The theory of economic development.* Harvard University Press.
Suzman, J. (2017). *Affluence without abundance: The disappearing world of the Bushmen.* Bloomsbury Publishing USA.

Swedberg, R. (2008). Economic sociology. In S. N. Durlauf & L. E. Blume (Eds.), *The new Palgrave dictionary of economics* (2nd ed.). Palgrave Macmillan.

Tomasello, M. (2020). The adaptive origins of uniquely human sociality. *Philosophical Transactions of the Royal Society B, 375*(20190493).

Toynbee, A. J. (1884). *Lectures on the industrial revolution in England; Popular addresses, notes and other fragments*. Rivingtons.

Weber, M. (1930). *The Protestant ethic and the" spirit" of capitalism and other writings* (Parsons, T., Translator). Unwin University Books.

Whitehead, H., & Rendell, L. (2014). *The cultural lives of whales and dolphins*. University of Chicago Press.

Winch, D. (2010). Arnold Toynbee's industrial revolution. Keynote address to *Before and After Toynbee,* Cambridge Victorian Studies Symposium (September 23), Cambridge University.

CHAPTER 6

"1848"

C. Gordon, *Many Possible Worlds*,
https://doi.org/10.1007/978-981-19-9281-0_6

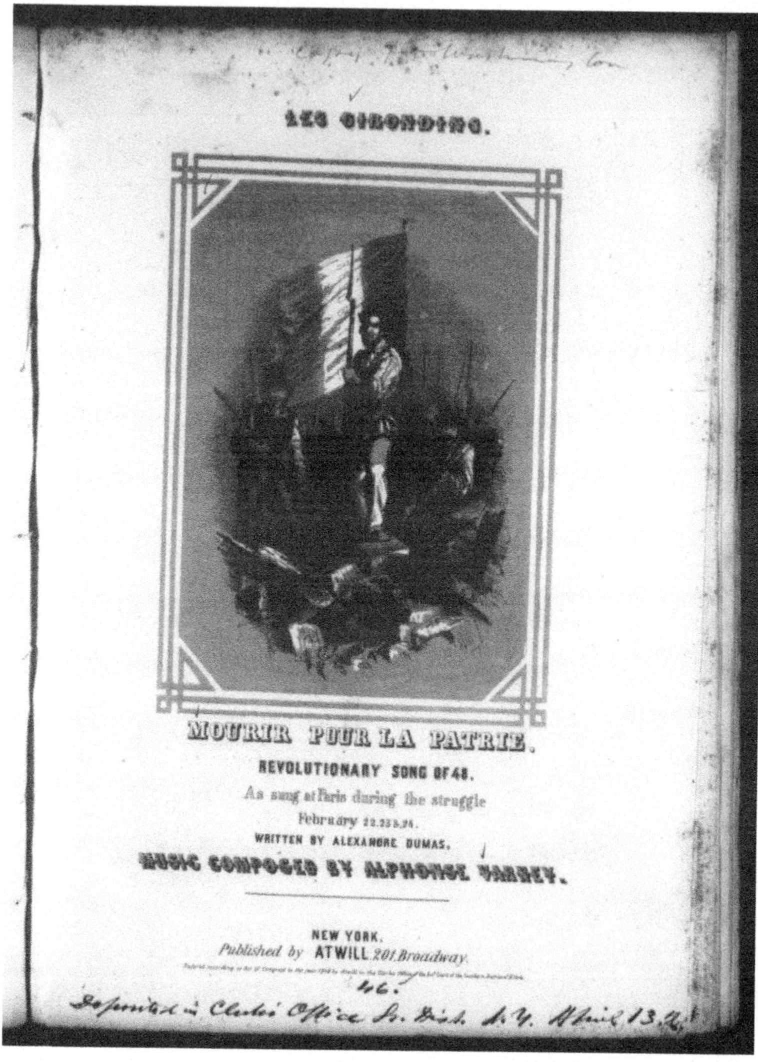

Fig. 6.1 Les Cirondins, Mourir pour la patrie, revolutionary song '48 (sheet music cover) (*Image source* Varney, A. & Dumas, A. [1848] Les Cirondins, Mourir pour la patrie, revolutionary song '48. Atwill, New York, monographic. [Notated Music] Retrieved from the Library of Congress, https://www.loc.gov/item/sm1848.440490/.Library of Congress, Music Division. No known copyright restrictions)

6.1 The Napoleonic Transition in Europe

Between the heady chaos of the French Revolution and the harsher variegated realities of the mid nineteenth century stands the figure of Napoleon Bonaparte. As much a political genius as a military one, Napoleon managed to take over the transitional and consolidating power sharing arrangement of the Directorate that arose to govern France at the very end of the 1700s and convert himself in short order to French Emperor in 1803 and, then, briefly, overlord of much of the European continent (McLynn, 1998) (Fig. 6.1).

Many at the time saw Napoleon's Empire as a betrayal of the ideals of the Revolution. Beethoven, who had dedicated his Third Symphony ("Eroica") to Napoleon, bitterly regretted it as soon as the man declared himself Emperor. Lord Byron, the great Romantic poet, was also greatly

Fig. 6.2 "The Double-Faced Napoleon" (*Image source* [page 29] in Maurice, A .B. & Cooper, F. T. [1904]. *The history of the nineteenth century in caricature*. Dodd, Mead. Contributing Library: The Library of Congress. Title of this figure is taken from the original caption in the source. No known copyright restrictions)

disappointed and expressed this in his poetry (McLynn, 1998). If one considers the Revolutionary slogan of "Liberte, Fraternite, Egalite", this disappointment is understandable, for Napoleon was neither egalitarian, nor a proponent of freedom and fellowship either. And by choosing an ancient title of Emperor, he hearkened back to the heritage of Rome, a heritage deeply antithetical to the principles of the revolution (Fig. 6.2).

On the other hand, Napoleon not only kept much of the Rationalism celebrated by the Revolution, but his power, both military and political, built upon and refined the new and radical mass politics and mobilisation that revolutionary politics had so fatefully set in motion. The Revolution had begun this process by striking a mortal blow against the prevailing French corporatism in which individuals were assigned membership in one of three "estates": the First Estate (clergy); the Second Estate (nobility); and the Third Estate (commoners). These functioned within a notionally organic order of hierarchical but reciprocal obligations. Pressures to conform to group norms were strong, sometimes officially legislated. But there was also some potential shelter within each group for individuals from the society as a whole and, potentially, from other competing groups. Louis XVI was appealing to just such a corporatism in convening the Estates General in 1789. Hoping to simultaneously ease the growing turmoil within French society while manipulating through divide-and-rule, he unwittingly signed his own death warrant, as the old social fabric could no longer be held within a mediaeval frame. The convening of outmoded social groupings in a quasi-legislative body unleashed the latent powers of the commoners against the monarchy and the old order (Cobban, 1964).

For a brief time, the overthrow of the monarchy, nobility and clergy promised a flowering of the individual, but the Terror resulted in a new sort of conformity demanded by a secular and notionally rationalist ideology, and by political, economic and social crisis that threatened to tear the country apart and smother the revolution in its cradle. These developments demonstrated that the removal of group authority allowed the possibility of untrammelled forging of individuals into a mass consciousness and collective instrument of State power, justified by an appeal to "The People" against existential threats. Napoleon was the man who rose to the challenge, moulding the masses into a unified force, developing some innovative techniques in legitimising his authoritarianism with republican forms; most notably the use of national plebiscites to legitimise major constitutional changes, including the 1804 inauguration of the French Empire itself, which centralised power while at the same time claiming popular consent. His nephew Louis Napoleon III would refine these methods further when his turn on a self-created throne came fifty years later (Roberts, 2000, 24).

Napoleon also built upon the new politics of competition in mass ideas that was replacing, or at least supplementing, the pure elite power machinations of the past. The central idea that governmental legitimacy must be sought first through the support of a "public", struck at traditional social orderings and politics, replacing them with new ideological groupings, e.g. of "Left" and "Right" (terms that originally emerged from the revolutionary French Assembly in which radical Jacobins sat on the left of the chamber while conservative Girondists sat on the right). Old terms were redefined, e.g. "Party" which used to refer to a "faction" within elite ruling interests. Political parties now became means of organising large groups of people according to an ideological allegiance. The Jacobins hated the rise of parties because they thought that it detracted from the pure power of the masses and allowed for manipulation by elites. Which they did, but in different ways than before because to rule now, even elites needed to be able to plausibly claim public approval and be able to periodically marshal the masses to their cause (Barraclough, 1967, 126–129).

Most significantly "patriotism", which used to be associated with "Patria" or "Fatherland" (sometimes called a "Motherland" instead) and which linked people on the basis of their connection to a particular land, became fused with "nationalism", a more abstract and new idea of mass identity and loyalty to a "nation" which transcended old ethnic, familial and group loyalties. All political divisions could potentially be subsumed under nationalism, and the 1848 revolutions showed that conservatives could use it as effectively for their own ends as liberals for theirs (Roberts, 2000, 26–32).

The greatest lesson of Napoleonism was to show what State power could do when it was unbounded by the traditional privileges of "intermediate bodies", and now animated by nationalism and backed by an effectively organised mass. Conservatives did not at first pick up on this paradox, i.e. that their ability to shape society could go well beyond what traditional authority relations had offered if they managed to gain control of a State apparatus and run it along "rational" lines to make its efforts more efficient and effective. This is why the 1815 post-Napoleonic settlement was formally a dynastic restoration, so feared was the Revolution and so hated was the Napoleonic power grab that followed it and which nearly succeeded but for the Emperor's overreach. However, those looking very closely could see that Napoleon's combination of mass appeal combined with a technocratic approach to State management could amplify State power for whoever managed to get their hands on it. Ironically the 1815 restoration of monarchy likely accelerated the demise of monarchical authority because it quickly became clear that it was no longer necessary to have a monarch and nobility to run an effective government and build a powerful nation. Additionally, fewer and fewer people believed in the notion that the nobles were a group inherently interwoven into the organism of society (Roberts, 2000, 25).

Partly for this reason, Napoleon's institutional refashioning of European old regimes and boundaries was not completely discarded, just repurposed. His conquests destroyed 300 or so small sovereign entities that did not re-emerge after the restoration (Roberts, 2000, 24). In some particular cases, this creative destruction (to borrow a term from an unrelated context) set the stage for the emergence of new industrial powers within mere decades afterwards. Before Napoleon's takeover of Prussia in 1806–1813, that country was a mix of absolutism and feudalism, though with some internal change under Frederick the Great who abolished serfdom in stages of royal lands between 1763 and 1784 and introduced compulsory schooling in some areas. Napoleon vastly expanded, accelerated and broadened reforms such as these, making sweeping institutional changes, sometimes called a "revolution from above", which removed guild restrictions on trade, abolished serfdom for peasants completely and introduced freedom of land tenure, all of which strengthened commercial interests and firmed up individual property rights. Additionally, freedom of occupational choice and business establishment was introduced, along with legal reform, emancipation of the Jews and substantial municipal self-government. Post-Napoleonic Prussian governments built upon these reforms (Becker et al., 2011, 97–98).

All of this was quite obviously favourable to commercial and industrial activity, and the Napoleonic reforms in Prussia jump-started its strong industrial performance in the latter half of the century. Meanwhile, Napoleon's development and imposition on the Continent of a uniform commercial law code, the Napoleonic Code, was another major

Fig. 6.3 The Napoleonic reorganisation of Europe (1810) (*Image source* Meyers, P. V. N. [1889]. *A general history for colleges and high schools*. Ginn & Company, p. 748. Contributing Library: The Library of Congress. Digitizing Sponsor: Sloan Foundation. No known copyright restrictions)

institutional reform with substantial positive economic impacts later on throughout the Continent (Lobingier, 1918–1919) (Fig. 6.3).

6.2 New Ideas About Old Institutions

A seismic shift in attitude, born out of the Enlightenment and pushed forward by the Revolution and Napoleon, came about in the attitudes towards slavery, serfdom and the rights of the individual, although it still came slowly and moved ahead in fragmentary fashion. A movement away from the corporatism of "divine right" monarchical forms (where static social orders sanctified rule of "superiors" over "inferiors") and towards individual rights as enshrined in the Declaration of the Rights of Man in France made traditional power relations, embedded in traditional social relations, intellectually untenable, threatening prior modes and relationships based on them.

Slavery was the most ancient of institutions, practised in the Classical world and still widespread in various parts of the globe during the eighteenth century. It was not always seen as socially just. Christianity on the one hand contained much that spoke against the practice, proclaiming that all are equal before God and thus undermining any moral authority that might be invoked for it. The Old Testament in particular bemoaned the bondage of the Jewish people under the Egyptian Pharaohs, and celebrated their deliverance from it by the hand of God. And the historical Jesus was most popular amongst the outcasts and disadvantaged and the early Christian churches found most of their adherents there. Much later, clerics in the Catholic Church did sometimes speak against slavery, most notably the Spaniard Bartolomé de las Casas, a 1600s landowner who became a Dominican Friar and went on to be a vocal critic of Spain's treatment of the Amerindians in the colonies and of the institution of slavery more generally (Rodríguez, 2020).

However, there was also an attitude within the New Testament that the things of this earth did not matter as much as the things of the Spirit, and that inner, not outer, liberation were primary. This attitude was consonant with the Hellenic tradition of Stoicism, which broadly held that the practice of virtue was its own reward and that the practitioner would be insulated from the effects of any earthly misfortune. One of its prime exponents, Epictetus, was, in fact, born a slave (Baltzly, 2019). Thus, a Christian political program against slavery never really coalesced until after well after the Reformation, and even then not until the greater political and social environment had already moved significantly in that direction. Even then there was not unity within the Protestant denominations, with slaveholding interests, especially in the Southern US, often citing Biblical authority for the holding of black slaves in particular (Snay, 1993).

The French Revolution markedly changed the intellectual atmosphere, building on Enlightenment rationalism and humanism while removing the old shackles of tradition on which slavery depended. Granted, this was only a minority view at first. The British banned the Atlantic Slave Trade in 1807, the Americans following in 1808. The British, with their naval superiority, took it upon themselves to police this injunction globally, even setting up an international tribunal system for the purpose, regularly interdicting slave ships, mostly of other, competitor, imperial nations and freebooters. Muslim slave trade off the west of Africa continued on for some time after this, as did illegal Atlantic slave trading, while formal slavery itself was not abolished in the US until 1863–1865, as a result of its bloody 1861–1865 Civil War, and not ended in Brazil until 1888 (Lovejoy & Anderson, 2020).

Revolution in Europe also inspired restiveness amongst slaves in overseas colonies, through communication of ideas and events carried by individual sailors, the Abolitionist notions being especially resonant where African slavery existed. Revolts occurred in 1808 South Africa partly for this reason (Sivasundaram, 2020, 92–94). There also stood the example of the only successful modern slave revolt (perhaps the only one in history), of Toussaint L'Ouverture against the French in Haiti in 1795. Having gained independence, L'Ouverture abolished slavery in Haiti in 1801. Napoleon sent an expedition to the Island after he took power and captured L'Ouverture, bringing him back to France, where he died in 1803. But his colleague Jacques Dessalines drove the French out for good, declared Haiti independent and abolished slavery permanently in 1804 (James, 1963).

Although no other slave rebellions achieved similar success, localised slave revolts, though ultimately put down, spawned communities of fugitive slaves, both becoming increasingly common elements of an enterprise under pressure due to the difficult social control problem for whites ruthlessly and brutally exploiting masses of human beings, mostly Africans, who far outnumbered them. The slave owners responded to rebellions and discord with growing repression, brutality and fear (Price, 1996). The Revolutionary ideas from France did not ignite slave revolts, but they certainly helped to undermine the supposed "natural" authority of the European masters, and provided further inspiration to those slaves who managed to gain knowledge of such ideas.

Abolitionism is thus a complex phenomenon on a number of levels. Prior to it, "free" and "unfree" were clear established social categories, and in some places like Mauritius, slaves had definite historically defined paths to buying their freedom, with high manumission rates as a result. Abolition, initially honoured more in the breach, sounded like an advance, but practically it often replaced bright-line categories that had clear pathways out of bondage, with a new continuum that could be murky and which typically included contract labour indentures that were theoretically consensual but born out of uneven power relationship and hard for the indentured party to break out of, especially if any significant "debt" (e.g. payments to former masters for accumulated food and board) had to be worked off (Sivasundaram, 2020, 284–286) (see Box 6.1).

The paradoxical rise of Britain as self-appointed liberator created some strange crosscurrents. In the British colonies, abolition combined with local self-rule movements, with the granting of British citizenship of some sort sometimes appearing to be the best way to achieve both, even though this course obviously contained discordant exclusionary and nationalistic elements from the point of view of the colonial subject. The Dutch and French were countries associated with steadfast slavocracy, while Englishness was becoming increasingly associated with the middle-class values of personal freedom as expressed through Classical Liberalism (Sivasundaram, 2020, 330) (see Chapter 4). Liberal abolitionism thus purported to be neutral and principled, but cloaked many particularly English styles of domination, domestically and abroad.

Table 6.1 Abolition of slavery in the Americas: by year

Country	*Year*
Haiti	1803
Chile	1823
Central American Federation	1824
Mexico	1824
Guyana (British)	1834
Uruguay	1846
Colombia/Panama	1850
Ecuador	1852
Peru	1852
Argentina	1853
Venezuela	1854
Bolivia	1861
Surinam (Dutch)	1863
United States	1863–65
Paraguay	1870
Puerto Rico	1878
Cuba	1886
Brazil	1888

Source Scanlan (2019) and Diaz-Diaz (1999)

Box 6.1 Abolitionism

In 1794 the French National Convention abolished slavery within the French Empire. Earlier, in 1787, the Abolitionist Society in England was established with the help of William Wilberforce, a man who conscientiously fought within Parliament and outside of it to outlaw first the Atlantic slave trade and later slavery within the British Empire itself.

The traditional story has been that the triumph of Enlightenment values in Europe (and, by extension, America) caused the rise of the worldwide Abolitionist movement in the West and the ultimate rejection of the institution on moral grounds. Wilberforce is one of the heroes of this story, with his tireless devotion to a noble cause, while the French Revolution's enshrining of the sanctity of individual "Man" and Republicanism removed the final struts of tradition that slavery apologists once stood on.

While there are elements of truth to this story, it is one-sided. The Abolitionist movement did not come in a crashing wave but went in stops, starts and periodic reversals and was highly conditional in its granting of freedom to slaves. Slavery and the slave trade actively existed in many parts of the world well into the late nineteenth century. And most former slaves not only gained freedom slowly, their post-slavery conditions were often little more than legalised servitude under a different name.

Moreover, much of the move towards abolition was driven by widespread rebellion by the slaves themselves rather than changes of attitudes on the part of their masters. While the Revolution in France led to the formal outlawing of slavery, this was in a context of an already widespread slave revolt across the French colonies in the Caribbean, especially Haiti. The British chose not to follow the French in their proclamation, their own sugar islands, especially Jamaica, being too valuable to experiment with such radical change which was, in any case, fiercely resisted by colonial slaveholders who exerted a powerful influence in Westminster. The Spanish, who would soon lose their Latin American holdings, attempted to ameliorate the terrible conditions of slaves through the so-called "Black Codes" which imposed some regulation on the treatment of those in bondage. But here too the slavocracy was in opposition and even these stopgap measures were ignored.

When Napoleon took power, he actually restored slavery in French colonies, though he could not do so in Haiti, which continued to fight for its independence, achieving it definitively in 1804. European colonialists, whether French, British or Spanish, could not permanently repress slaves in their colonies, which experienced regular slave upheavals, including major slave rebellions in Havana (1809), Matanzas (1825) and Güira (1826).

Jamaica, which already had many communities of escaped slaves, broke into a massive slave revolt in 1831. These and other disturbances caused the European metropolitans to question the economic viability of slavery, and this led to the passage of laws to remove the institution.

But while a formal advance, these were very tepid laws indeed, calling for gradual emancipation, full compensation for slave owners (without any corresponding remuneration to the slaves themselves), labour codes and controls after emancipation, and elaborate and costly manumission procedures, all of which precipitated what has been referred to as a "second horizon of slavery". Continued resistance to enduring slavery-like conditions throughout the 1820s and 1830s convinced colonial masters that gradualism and owner compensation had to be dropped, though restrictions on former slaves remained a common practice.

Thus, even the formal abolition of slavery was very piecemeal, slow and often more apparent than practically real throughout the world, both under colonialism (e.g. Spanish Cuba keeping the practice until 1886) and within former colonies, such as the US (which formally abolished slavery throughout the country after the North's victory in 1865 in its Civil War) (see Table 6.1).

Even when mass enslavement of Africans was made illegal in one place, European trade and investment often supported it and encouraged it elsewhere. A perfect example of this is the Atlantic slave trade. The offloading of slaves in British colonies was prohibited in 1807 and a similar formal prohibition came into force in the US the following year. But the trade continued almost unabated for several decades on ships flying the flags of foreign nations. Meanwhile, former slaves laboured on their former plantations as "apprentices" and British capital was invested in slave labour enterprises where they still existed, such as in the US until 1865 and Brazil, the last bastion of formal slavery, until 1888.

There is a separate debate about how important slave labour was to capitalist development, which is considered elsewhere. But it certainly persisted throughout the First Industrial Revolution and well into the Second, and was given up by the Europeans and Americans very grudgingly and, arguably, incompletely even after formal abolition.

(The above discussion and the information in Table 6.1 is drawn from Scanlan, 2019, 2020, and Diaz-Diaz, 1999.)

The French Revolution and Napoleonism were both theoretically antithetical to feudal relations as well, and here ideas had a bit more force. The last vestiges of feudalism were eradicated in France after 1789, and of course England had long since moved away from its formal practice. Even Prussia had begun to move away from feudalism, and Napoleon's occupation of the country finished the job. Revolutionary ideals continued to undermine the institution intellectually as the nineteenth century progressed, combining with the forces of economic modernisation, to lead to its formal abolition in Russia and parts of Central and Eastern Europe in the latter half of the century. But as with slavery economic forces already in train were more important in serfdom's demise. Industrialisation, with its reliance on formal market mechanisms of exchange and the commodification of labour obviously could not easily co-exist with feudalism, with its complex basis in mutually binding (though very uneven) obligations between serf and lord. This was not as great a conceptual problem with slavery which was, in a sense, the ultimate commodification of labour and which did in fact live alongside rising industrialisation in some places until close to the Second Industrial Revolution's start. In the end, though, economic and social modernisation rendered both institutions formally anachronistic and political anathema.

6.3 Colonial Ferment, Change and Upheaval

Worldwide throughout the late eighteenth and mid-nineteenth centuries, there was a dynamic rebalancing of European and non-European Empires that paradoxically went in two different simultaneous directions: decolonisation and colonial expansionism. Decolonisation in this period primarily arose from the decline of earlier external European Empires (Spain, Portugal, the Netherlands and France, though the French would compensate for their earlier losses by later gains elsewhere), and from the weakening of internal Empires in China, Russia, Persia and the Ottoman realm. These declines created vacuums into which popular resistance and independence movements emerged, and facilitated the incursion of other imperialists, especially the British and the French. It was a time of much overturning of tradition and experimentation with the new.

In Asia, Vietnam was finally liberated from the Chinese and unified by Gia-Long in 1802, creating a new imperial capital at Hue. The later phase of this reconquest was ironically achieved with French help, in the classic "the enemy of my enemy is my friend" stratagem and one typical of European Great Power politics, a process that would roll on throughout the century, to the longer-term detriment of the non-Europeans left in its wake, not least the Vietnamese themselves. Not dissimilar was the struggle in Southern Africa between the Dutch white Boer settlers and the British tactically allying with local peoples. Shaka built a strong Zulu state between 1816 and 1828, attacking and trying to drive out the Boers who retaliated, inflicting some damage and in the end weakening both to later English advantage. The British defeated the Zulus in 1879 and incorporated them into Natal, a self-governing British colony, in 1897 (Lehning, 2013, Chapters 4, 5).

Rivalry between the French and British in the Pacific Islands caused autonomous island communities to join together to exploit these divisions, reduce their own internecine conflicts and protect themselves, many adopting monarchies, an adaptation of a Western form introduced by missionaries and other western interlopers. Local modes of warfare were also transformed, as they were in many other places where colonisation was resisted, generally universally and sometimes fiercely (Sivasundaram, 2020, 50–65).

Imperial intrusion created many new local connections and alliances; for example, revolutionary and republican Mauritius was aided by the Sultan of Mysore to help ward off European incursions (Sivasundaram, 2020, 104–111). In many cases, it was sea travel, not land contact, which carried political messages, knowledge of distant events and the planting of revolutionary seeds far and wide. This was the case with Napoleon's overturning of Spanish dynastic rule which, in turn, helped drive Latin American revolts, news of which was then carried into Asia by sailors from the region, and transmitted even further as other indigenous crew members were picked up and dropped off along the way (Sivasundaram, 2020, 37–39).

Within Europe, Russia, outwardly imposing with its grand territorial scale of the early 1800s, was at the same time a society grappling internally with constant peasant revolt fostered by the country's particularly retrograde form of feudalism, overseen by a thin layer of quasi-westernised local elites attempting to impose modern ideals on a highly agrarian and traditional society. The result was a slow contraction in its Eurasian boundaries (ameliorated by occasional countering gains), accompanied by some progress, highly uneven, in social and economic modernisation. The Ottoman Empire's European ambit fared considerably worse, its nineteenth century history being a constant retreat from its remaining territories in the Balkans (Hobsbawm, 1987).

These declines did inspire some attempts at internal reform. The reformers generally meant to preserve their respective systems, but often merely destabilised them in the end. An example of this is the reign of Mohammed Ali who became Ottoman Viceroy in Egypt in 1805, despite the opposition of the Egyptian Sultan. Ali killed the Sultan and his family in 1811 and took complete control of the country, reforming the army and extending Egyptian power up the Nile into the Sudan. These moves would be thwarted and later reversed by the British who took direct control of the Sudan later in the century and obtained indirect control of Egypt by making it a financial vassal state, burdened by predatory debt (Cleveland & Bunton, 2018). Reformers also attempted to change conditions in China and Russia as well, though furtively and generally unsuccessfully.

The most notable decolonisation of the period came with the disintegration of the Spanish Empire in Latin America. Between 1804 and 1825, a wave of former colonies became independent of Spain, with the larger colonial administrative entities breaking up into smaller ones. This collapse was precipitated by the occupation of Spain by Napoleonic France, exacerbating a pre-existing Iberian malaise. These were rebellions, not revolutions, overthrowing a "foreign" overlord, but replacing it with overlordship by settler elites, often in the form of "caudillos", i.e. strong-men whose inclinations were not necessarily populist but fed off the discontent of colonial settler elites chafing under distant Spanish rule (De la Escosura, 2005, 2007, 2009). Nonetheless, the rhetoric of "freedom" was widely used, echoing the new republican ideals of the American and French revolutions, and nominal republican forms of government were adopted after independence. An exception to this pattern was the Portuguese colony of Brazil, to which the Portuguese royal family had escaped during Napoleonic times, and which Emperor Dom Pedro, son of Portugal's John VI, declared independent in 1822 (Adelman, 2009).

The American Revolution, running from 1776 to 1789, was a major loss for the British Empire during this time, though only a temporary setback to an English expansionism that had a century more to run. It was particularly notable because of its republican form in an era when this was still quite rare. But, as in Latin America, the form masked elitist and politically conservative elements. American Republicanism obviously had an especially profound influence on the Latin American independence movements (Lewis, 2000). It also served as a rallying example in other parts of the world, the soaring rhetoric of the Declaration of Independence a celebration of Enlightenment principles.

Where decolonisation was occurring it was not, it should be said, about respecting or freeing indigenous peoples. The rebellious Americans were white English settlers breaking from their former master, and some historians claim that the major impetus for the American Revolution was British restriction of settler expansionism into Indian territory outside established colonial boundaries (a policy done out of British self-interest, trying to keep the peace with certain large Amerindian federations while simultaneously battling the French for continental supremacy). The independent Americans would then fight a century-long nearly genocidal war against the original residents, herding them into scattered and fragmentary "reservations" whose boundaries continued to be reduced through constant cessions to land-hungry white frontiersmen, and continued displacement of their populations to ever more isolated and desolate environs (Zinn, 2005). As Chief Red Cloud said in a speech made shortly after the massacre of unarmed people, mostly women and children, by the US Army, one of many committed over the years as indigenous people were driven from one area to another, "They [the white men] made us many promises, more than I can remember, but they never kept but one; they promised to take our land, and they took it" (Brown, 1970, 249).

The Spanish Empire from its very beginning had been a ruthless and ongoing conquest of indigenous peoples (which is why the early Spanish "explorers" were more aptly known as "conquistadores" or "conquerors"). The end of that Empire was the scene of major upheavals led by local peoples. There was a widespread revolt of Maquihe Indians in Chile in the 1780s, and anti-Spanish movements in Columbia and Venezuela, with Indians massacring Spaniards in some areas. Although led by a wealthy Spanish settler, Jose Gabriel Condorconqui, the Tupac Amaru movement in Peru was made up of indigenous Peruvians who worked in the appalling conditions of the mines there. Condorconqui had adopted the name of a 16th-century Inca Emperor (hence the name of the movement) and over the course of the revolt he captured much of the Peruvian highlands, made connections with Bolivian resistance movements, attacked Cuzco and the capital, La Paz, and came close to routing the Spanish before finally being decisively crushed in 1782 (Tarver & Slape, 2016).

6.4 A Cementing of a World Economic System

The combination of declining Dutch and French, and rising British, Empires dynamically altered European-local power relations, with British ideas and institutions gaining increasing hegemony. The various imperial lacunae made the British imposition of an overseas version of Liberalism consisting of free trade, monarchy and bureaucratic monitoring of radicals that much easier to spread and implement. Not that it was easy, or taken without response by those being colonised. The rise of the British maritime Empire caused a rebalancing within the Middle East and Africa where there were already long-standing regional connections, e.g. between Oman and east Africa. Oman and Muscat played the British and French off one another to their advantage, while also fending off the waning but still active Persian Empire (Sivasundaram, 2020, 138–148). British land power was not to be underestimated either, though colonial conquests by land were generally more difficult, especially in India, which was a hard-fought affair unfolding over decades. Conquest there was not complete until the wars against the Sikhs of Punjab were fought in 1845–1846 and in 1848–1854 (Sindh was taken in 1843). Even then India remained a patchwork of formal and informal rule and was never totally quiescent. Wars against Afghanistan proved even more difficult and with outcomes even less complete (Sivasundaram, 2020, 230–242).

The creation of a vast British Empire "upon which the sun never set" was thus only partially finished by 1848. But already the first modern world economic "system", with a particularly British stamp and influence, couched neutrally but designed to benefit London most of all, took a firm shape.

Consider the world shipbuilding industry. The decline of the Persian and Ottoman Empires created vacuums not just in Europe but also in the Persian Gulf, complicated by the British/French rivalry and further coloured by the fact that actual maritime personnel, e.g. shipbuilders, pilots and sailors, came from widely scattered locations. Economies of scale and scope were hindered by this fact but not too much could be done about it until there was sufficient centralised authority over enough maritime locations, a situation that the British had attained by the 1830s, consolidating their position and imposing their institutional and legal mores over locals in the Indian Ocean and Arabian Seas. All Europeans were imperial of course, but British success was large enough to reshape the economic geography of the region. Thus, Bombay became the nexus for the Gulf maritime industries (amongst other things, as a shipbuilding centre). While this could be cast as "natural" comparative advantage, it was also imposed administratively according to the will of the Imperium (Sivasundaram, 2020, 163–165).

This was also an age of "science" in naval and maritime practice. Of necessity, this was already highly technical and systematic because of the need for stringent adaptation of a land mammal to the rigours of the sea. But now it became "scientised", leading to a wealth of fact collection and scientific observation. The move into the tropics brought the British face to face with handling and managing what to them were novel weather patterns like the monsoon, and thus coming up with new technical methods, especially the development of the new discipline of meteorology. This data was input into new constructs of causal modelling. These were exercises in applied scientific method but were joined with an instrumentalism designed for imperial control (Davis, 2002; Sivasundaram, 2020, 260–266). In particular, the setting up of observation centres at key points from Madras to Singapore created a non-indigenous system for undertaking British navigation of the seas, cutting out local knowledge and authority, and replacing it with infrastructure, such as lighthouses, controlled by the British with their own maritime and commercial interests put foremost (Sivasundaram, 2020, 280–283). Scientific "observation" thus dually became one of a number of forms of surveillance and racial ideology with technical clothing (Sivasundaram, 2020, 4).

Similarly, British imposition of Liberalism in the form of a "freedom of the seas" doctrine, while framed as based on equal application of universal principles under an emerging international law, was itself most favourable to a dominant sea power, which Britain then was, applying it in a way that was preferential to them. The Persian Gulf is a good example of how this operated. Prerogatives of Wahhabi regimes in that region were deemed as piracy and thus resisted and suppressed (as were other waterborne local rival projections of power elsewhere), while British maritime power was privileged because it was deemed "legal". A treaty was imposed in 1820 that enforced the abolition of slavery and "free trade", supposedly mutual in terms of freedom of both parties to call in at ports, but inherently unequal in terms of actual consent to its provisions and enforcement. It also imposed arbitrary boundary lines on the Arab signatories whose domains followed much different lines on the ground, and mapped out sea channels that were to British advantage, using British navigational expertise and notions, locking out local interests now deemed as "pirates" and "fanatics". The resulting bureaucracy and cartography so critical to the treaty's implementation was created and administered by the English (Sivasundaram, 2020, 122–138). A parallel process was used against the Barbary Coast "pirates" along the North African Mediterranean coast (Colas, 2016).

Militarism and humanitarianism was a characteristic English blend of the time, especially effective in subjugating the Australian aboriginals in Tasmania (and elsewhere). This was achieved by using a notionally technical formulation of "civilising" in which methods of control were presented as non-political technical improvements (Sivasundaram, 2020, 186–189), justified on Benthamite Utilitarian grounds, the quasi-official ideology of the Empire at the time (Davis, 2002). All of this was generally corrosive to indigenous local traditions and institutions, which had many imperfections of their own (such as a tolerance for slavery in some areas) but which were, nonetheless, products of the societies native to the areas. Especially hard hit were the authorities of traditional elders and leaders, as in aboriginal Australia. These were replaced with European practices that were typically exploitative and divisive and which did not improve existing social conditions, local patriarchies being replaced by European versions, for example (Sivasundaram, 2020, 172–175). In Australia, the indigenous population was practically wiped out over time.

None of this should be taken to suggest that the British were worse imperialists than the Spanish and Portuguese before them, the French, the Dutch or Belgians as contemporaries, or the Americans and others after them. Rather their style was more subtle and influenced especially by the emerging technical paradigm of the time. Nor is it suggested that there was no actual technical content or benefit to this technical model of imperialism. This was indeed part of the institution building of a modern economy in the making, a true integration along "rational" lines that would have significant consequences for the colonised areas, good and bad, as time wore on.

But neither was the process an outgrowth of beneficial natural selection or efficient incentives. Real force and power politics were involved and these are never "neutral" in a human social sense, if, indeed, "technicalities" can ever be divorced from their social context in the first place. Indigenous resistance to the growing European-led "globalisation" was not merely the cry of the less efficient being driven out by ever more productive modern forces. There was real power and agency being fought over, and issues of justice at stake, even though these were officially obscured.

6.5 "Structural Change" in Europe

Meanwhile, in Europe itself, industrialisation was bringing both growth but also a reshaping of the economy, a process that economists refer to as "structural change" (Kuznets, 1966). Available data, scanty as it is, shows a shift from primarily agrarian economies to more manufacturing based ones. Table 6.2 provides selected data on "structural" change in the two most important European economies during the first forty years of the nineteenth century, i.e. Britain and France. Economic structure is discussed in greater detail in Chapter 29, but it basically refers to how output and income is generated and distributed. What these rather cursory figures show is that both Britain—already acknowledged to be economically advanced—and France—generally considered as a somewhat lagging but nonetheless economically sophisticated European country—were both striding towards industrialisation. The French were doing this more gradually than the English, partly because the former had been wracked by constant continental war and political and social upheaval between 1789 and 1835. But it was happening in both places.

The figures are not precisely comparable, and are more detailed for Great Britain, but the traditional basic story is that the share of national income in both countries had shifted from agriculture to industry by the 1840s (more strongly for England) and there are data to show that the same was true for share of employment of the English labour force. "Services" is a category that even today remains a bit hard to define but during this period it includes primarily income generated by small retail enterprises like tailors and cobblers, and activities supporting trade and manufacturing, such as finance. In France, the proportionate decline in services in this period exactly matches the increase in industry, probably indicating a move away from small-scale household production into the factory system.

More recent scholarship on both French and English structural change during the first half of the nineteenth century confirm this basic story but provide some new nuances. Ridolfi and Nuvolari (2021) find that French economic performance and structure was quite close to that of England until the second half of the seventeenth century when the English economy broke out on an increasingly industrial path. Broadberry et al. (2015), in an extensive and detailed re-estimating of English national accounts, report that Great Britain was not as advanced in

Table 6.2 British and French economic structure, circa 1800 to 1845: selected statistics

Country	*Agriculture*	*Industry*	*Services*
GREAT BRITAIN % National Income share from sector in 1801	32	23	45
GREAT BRITAIN % National Income from sector in 1841	22	34	44
GREAT BRITAIN % share of labour force in sector in 1801	35	29	36
GREAT BRITAIN % share of labour force in sector in 1841	23	39	38
FRANCE % National Income from Sector 1789/1815	50	20	30
FRANCE % National Income from Sector 1825/1835	50	25	25
Addendum—2015 revisions of British sectoral data			
GREAT BRITAIN % share of national output from sector in 1801	31.3	32.7	36.0
GREAT BRITAIN % share of labour force in sector in 1801	31.7	36.4	31.9
GREAT BRITAIN % share of national output from sector in 1851	18.7	32.1	49.2
GREAT BRITAIN % share of labour force in sector in 1851	23.5	45.6	30.9

Source Data extracted from Kuznets (1966), Tables 3.1 & 3.2
Addendum data extracted from Broadberry et al. (2015), Table 9.1, page 344

services in 1801 as the Kuznets (1966) data above suggest. Their estimates, as reported in the addendum to Table 6.2, show that British output and labour force shares in 1801 were substantively more industrial but less services oriented than earlier thought with an economy overall a bit closer to French economic structure at that time, though the latter was still more agrarian. Their data also show a more profound sectoral shift in Britain during the first 50 years of the 1800s than earlier thought. Shaw-Taylor and Wrigley (2014) confirm these patterns.

Nonetheless, structural change and growth were clearly occurring and expanding in nineteenth century Europe, and it was quite clear at the time, as it is to those living through structural change today, that such changes created "winners and losers", especially for agricultural workers and those forced to migrate into cities and factories. Living standards are likely to have declined on average, even with steadily rising GDP per capita, up until around 1830 or so, because wages often grew much more slowly and working conditions were harsh (Voth, 2003). Gallardo-Albarrán and de Jong (2021) come to a somewhat more nuanced conclusion on English living standards during the early phase of industrialisation (1760–1850), however. Using an indicator combining four key dimensions of well-being, including material living standards, health, working time and inequality, they find decreasing welfare during the late eighteenth century where rising working time and income inequality outweigh improving health. But after 1800, steady real wage raises kick off a rising standard of living, although the cumulative effect was still not substantial by 1850.

6.6 The European Restoration and Its Rapid Breakdown

Thus it is quite likely that the breaking of numerous social and individual eggs to make an industrial omelette was a factor leading to the European unrest of 1830 and 1848, and the considerable ferment outside of Europe occurring at the same time. Historians sometimes refer to this period as "the springtime of the peoples", a time of widespread popular ferment, uprisings, rebellions and, occasionally, successful revolution. It was also a time of reaction, repression and retrenchment by the forces of established power, which often prevailed but generally not without some major changes to their way of exercising their authority (Kostantaras, 2020).

The Congress of Vienna of 1815 had sought to restore the pre-Napoleonic, pre-French Revolution European monarchical order, using the dual principles of Legitism (restoration of the legitimacy of prior dynastic orders) and the Balance of Power (in particular the Quadruple Alliance of Russia, Prussia, Austria and England united against any further outbreak of revolutionary fervour) (Ferrero, 1941). This reactionary plan had many internal contradictions, especially the notion of the enforcement of a Continental order carried about by competing and incompatible countries, with Prussia and Austria being long-time rivals within the German-speaking principalities and England being the Constitutional monarchy odd-man-out in the Quadruple Alliance. France was a dangerous pariah to be contained, and yet it remained one of the most important of the Great powers and a key element of any hoped-for stability in Europe. The plan was too clever by half, and ultimately doomed to fail, though it was surprisingly durable for a while. Not for the first and certainly not the last time would the great European states find themselves in such a situation.

In any case, there was no going back, however hard the established order might try. The old hereditary ruler models had long been creaking at the seams even before the French Revolution. Repressed groups, such as ethnic minorities, lower social classes and colonial subjects, shaken up by the Napoleonic era, were even more agitated by the dislocations of the Industrial Revolution. Industrialisation would also add entirely new social groupings, especially the "working classes" and the "capitalists" whose interests, despite Adam Smith's optimism, did not align easily, if at all.

It was a heady cocktail, primed to explode, and trouble broke out almost immediately after 1815. In 1820, there was a wave of uprisings in Naples, Piedmont and Spain, amongst other places. With the long decline of the Ottoman Empire, the Balkans broke out into open rebellion, the Serbians gaining their independence in 1817, and Greek independence coming after a long struggle between 1821 and 1832. Meanwhile, a rebellion occurred in Moscow in 1825. Even Parliamentary England faced unrest in the form of the Luddite movement in which agrarian workers destroyed machines employed in growing factory production, their name coming from Ned Ludd's initial riot in Nottingham in 1812. England's colonial overlordship of Ireland was on a constant boil, inflamed rather than quieted by the 1800 formal union between the two forced through by William Pitt in response to a plot by Wolf Tone to gain support from Revolutionary France for an Irish uprising. And these were not just lower-class movements. The elites sometimes joined in as well. In Spain, officers led the charge against established orders (Kostantaras, 2020).

1830 then saw the first major wave of true revolutions, after the 1789 pattern. Agitation was rising in various places in Germany, while Warsaw broke out in a revolt that was quickly crushed. The July Revolution in France overthrew the restored (and repressive) Bourbon monarch Charles X, replacing him with the constitutional monarchy under the so-called bourgeois monarch Louis-Phillippe. Belgium gained its independence that same year, while in 1831–1832, rebellions broke out in several Italian states. The Congress of Vienna arrangements were visibly tattering, especially now that France had become an ally of "liberal" powers, and the small states that had been created on her borders to contain her power were splintering and weakening (Ferrero, 1941; Kostantaras, 2020).

6.7 1848 from a Global Perspective

By mid-century, two potent political/intellectual forces had taken hold in Europe and, increasingly, across the world: popular democracy and nationalism. Dynastic rule and ethnic overlordship had been discredited, their decline aided and abetted by weakness in the powers that still supported them. Economic change further challenged the old and called out for something new.

1848–1849 was a true epicentre where these seismic forces collided to cause a political earthquake. Hapsburg Austria managed to survive afterwards only by becoming Austria-Hungary, granting co-equal rule over the new Empire to the formerly subservient Hungarians (who continued afterwards to nonetheless repress other "minorities" within their realm, such as the Czechs). Declining Austrian power also accounted in part for increasing restiveness in some Italian states, some of which granted constitutions to their subjects. In 1848, an uprising in Vienna drove the architect of the Congress of Vienna, Prince Klemens von Metternich, out of the capital. This was the same year that the Hungarians managed to gain their independence (Sperber, 2005).

The "springtime" of 1848 also witnessed uprisings in Paris, Berlin, Posnan, Madrid, Prague and Ireland, amongst other places. In most instances, except for Austria, which also abolished serfdom as a result of its own unrest, such risings were put down. France, once more, was an exception, its bourgeois king deposed and a republic briefly restored, only to have a new Emperor rise up later, a descendant of Napoleon no less, who got there through shrewd manipulation of the country's infant democracy (Sperber, 2005).

Britain had seemed to escape the turmoils of the continent in 1848, with major reforms in both Britain and Ireland effectively resisted until the late 1860s, at which point Britain enacted the sorts of constitutional change that had occurred immediately after 1848 in some places on the Continent. At the same time the 1840s had seen a major expansion of the Empire with the annexation of Hong Kong (1843), Labuan in Indonesia (1846), Natal (1843) and the Orange River (1848) in South Africa, Gambia (1843), Afghanistan (1842) and, in India, Sind (1843), the Punjab (1846–1849) and a series of smaller princely states such as Satara (1848) and Sambalpur (1849) (Taylor, 2000, 146–148).

Arguably, Britain had ridden relatively smoothly over the turbulent waters of 1848 because of the use of the Empire as a safety valve.

Transportation of prisoners to the colonies was renewed in 1848 as one strategy of containing Chartism (a mass, though unsuccessful, movement to petition parliament for democratic legislation) and also the post-potato famine disorder in Ireland, though most dissidents in both cases were just exiled rather than transported (Taylor, 2000, 153). Once those crises were past, voluntary movements to colonial possessions expanded, and by 1852, over half of outward emigration from Britain and Ireland went to British dependencies, relieving Britain of some of the population pressures that were testing continental Europe (Taylor, 2000, 159).

At the same time, the growth in domestic tax burden to finance a growing State both at home and abroad was halted to ease domestic political pressure. This was financed by heavy cuts to administration, policing, armed forces and services of British territories abroad. The commitment to import duty reduction (a cut in indirect taxation) was also continued, carrying on a process initiated under the Peel budgets of 1842 and 1846, and now reframed as a populist attack on colonial planters, conveniently ignoring the effects of such cuts on domestic agricultural interests (Taylor, 2000, 158).

While Metropolitan Britain had largely ridden out 1848, Imperial Britain did not pass through it unscathed. Riots and rebellions occurred in Ceylon, the Ionian Islands and the Orange River in South Africa. Most famously, there was the Mutiny in the Punjab. Martial law was introduced in all of these places. Even in white settler Canada, the Canadian parliament building was burned down in Montreal in protest of the burdens imposed by the new trade policies that helped British consumers but hurt colonial producers and residents, while in New South Wales, Australia, settlers protested the new influx of transportees and émigrés. The cuts in colonial budgets, combined with trade policies, hit some places very hard. Jamaica and British Guiana in particular ultimately had to suspend all public expenditure as their local economies collapsed due to the equalisation of the sugar duties, which now exposed them to direct competition to other sugar producers outside the Empire, including the slave-plantation economies of Brazil and Cuba. An unfortunately timed commercial crisis of 1847 did not help matters (Taylor, 2000, 152–160).

Outside of Canada and New South Wales, British dependencies were mostly Crown colonies, presided over by a governor with a military background and offering few civil liberties to its subjects (Taylor, 2000, 149). After the turmoil of 1848–1849, New Zealand, the Australian and Cape colonies all received representative assemblies and even the Crown colonies received extended elective franchises more generous than on the British mainland. But the power of the Crown was also considerably strengthened to deal with unrest and a taxation franchise was removed from most colonial constitutions after 1848 (Taylor, 2000, 176).

Even those countries not formally under European rule struggled with rebellion. In China, the declining Manchu dynasty was rattled by a number of fractious movements and nearly toppled by the Taiping Rebellion of 1853, a revolt in which rebels seized Nanking and whose activities spread throughout fifteen provinces. About 20–30 million people are estimated to have been killed during the entire episode before it was finally put down in 1864 with European help. In return, the Chinese government had to grant special European trading privileges and concessions, all of which were part of a larger pattern of quasi-colonisation of the country (White, 2013, Chapter 2).

Spanish America, although now independent and generally republican, was not spared revolutionary trouble, though with a delay in most places, turmoil occurring in 1851 in Chile, 1849–1854 in Colombia and 1855–1857 in Mexico. Brazil suffered through unrest in Pernambuco in 1848–1849, right on time. At issue in most of these places was not the republican form of government, which had widespread use (except in Brazil) and was generally supported, but social, political and economic pressures similar to those besetting Europe and a feeling that government was not being responsive to them (Lida, 2002).

6.8 Economic Causes of "1848": Long- and Short Term

What role was economic change specifically playing in all this? Again, data are relatively scant but Voth (2003) argues that while industrialisation and growth was occurring in Europe, an upward turning point in aggregate living standards was probably not reached before the 1830s (223). And whatever the aggregates were saying, the distribution of wealth and income was unevenly spatially and socially distributed. Of course, economic conditions in much of the non-European world were much worse (see Allen, 2009; Milanovic, 2016; Pfister, 2019, 2020).

Berger and Spoerer (2001) note that there were serious shortages of Continental European basic food supplies between 1845 and 1847 and famine and hunger riots broke out in Ireland, Flanders and Silesia. Looking at data for grain prices for 27 countries between 1820 and 1850, they find that most European countries experienced a severe price shock in 1846 or 1847. This was a major issue for lower-class households, which around 1850 still spent between two-thirds and three-quarters of their incomes on food.

The growing integration of European grain markets, due to cheaper land and sea transport and lowered barriers to trade, had mixed effects on food price shocks. On the one hand, the increasing globalisation of commodity and money markets could have increased the volatility and intensity of food price movements by allowing rapid synchronisation of price changes, adjusting them up or down rapidly over a wide area. Grain price volatility appears to have been especially pronounced in France and Prussia during 1845–1847, while prices in England and Sweden in these years were more stable. Although prices fell after mid-1847, they still remained above the average for 1838–1845, and for almost three years after that, accentuated by bad harvests, they had been increasing incessantly (Berger & Spoerer, 2001, 303). On the other hand, Chilosi et al. (2013) note that the increasing integration of grain markets during this time actually reduced price volatility by helping to smooth out supply and demand.

Overall the short-run economic times were obviously quite bad in Europe immediately prior to the 1848 turmoil, likely providing a proximate trigger to unrest. But how much was longer-run structural economic change an ultimate a trigger both on the Continent and outside it? The data are too fragmentary to be definitive but agricultural price spikes across the world, whatever their cause, seem to be a strong possible driver of political unrest in diverse locations arising at roughly the same time.

Outside of price movements, industrialisation was increasing output, wealth and income, but also increasing economic instability and social and economic dislocation. Synchronised global output and financial booms and busts were already beginning to become an established feature of the world economy by mid-century. Globalisation was said to offer economic buffers in the form of rapid movement of resources to fill temporary gaps. But in this early developmental period, such buffers did not operate evenly or very well and imperial policy and structures generally hurt poor and vulnerable populations in the colonies without necessarily aiding the toiling masses at home much either (see Chapter 4).

Moreover, industrialisation was creating new strains, especially in terms of mass differences in wealth and income accumulation. Of course, great inequality was nothing new, but generally it had been a case of most of the populace being equally poor, with a small elite (or a few small elites) holding most of the surplus. These elites were now generally richer than ever, and also more visible, no longer able to plausibly hide behind any "natural rights" arguments for their primacy, such as religious or royal privilege. New social categories—merchants, bankers, capitalists and entrepreneurs—were being created, and new disenfranchised groups, especially urban poor and factory workers, were growing alongside them. In this period, they were not necessarily worse off materially than their agrarian peasant predecessors, though some could be. They were all generally more insecure in their poverty, not having even the meagre traditional safeguards of the peasantry, such as an ability (generally) to raise subsistence for one's own household off of common lands, or the occasional *noblesse oblige* of their social superiors. Meanwhile, agricultural sectors were under pressure from both international trade and industrialisation and the peasantry was often squeezed by impersonal forces that did not have even an informal obligation to them. Underclass rebellions are as old as human civilisation, but synchronised political movements across wide and diverse areas are something of a modern phenomenon, and the rapid and uncertain disruptions caused by industrialisation do seem to be one of the causes.

6.9 Aftermath: The Developmental State

Although most of the 1848 revolutions "failed", the ruling classes in Europe could not ignore them. To prevent future unrest, European governments now became oriented towards pragmatic, "centrist" coalitions with a non-ideological rhetoric of economic growth as a desirable tonic to the social division of the past. European governments launched public works projects on an unprecedented scale, justified by the idea that government needed to create the preconditions for an economic expansion that ultimately neutralised what was then called the "social question". This was aided by business-friendly policy reforms in many countries, such as the abolition of regulations preventing the formation of joint stock companies, designed to open up and incentivise capital concentration and investment (Clark, 2012, 174–179).

This was also an era of "professionalisation" of government. Emblematic of this was the creation of new ministries of public works to supervise and strategically plan spending programs, as in Portugal, Spain and the Second Empire in France, the latter the archetypal developmental regime.

Prussia and Piedmont in Italy followed along similar lines, the Prussians reorienting their policy frame away from an earlier century of anti-statist talk towards strongly state-centred direction and protectionism (Clark, 2012, 178–183).

In general, positing an organic connectedness of economic systems was a commonplace of the era, to be supported by an increasingly "scientific" apparatus of data collection and analysis. The 1850s saw a big increase in the establishment or consolidation of government statistical offices focused on measuring the "national economy." The State allied with many prominent exponents of social and political change in this effort, partly to co-opt them but also to ensure the tabulation of the good, independent, high-quality data now seen as essential to the making of effective policy and planning. Reformists themselves thought more and more in statistical terms. Granted, this framework was often used cynically or tactically to cover a mere muddling through. But it also was a real conceptualisation of the State as distinct from society, a manager of public affairs rather than an outgrowth of politics, shifting to a primary focus on material rather than immaterial concerns (Clark, 2012, 183–85).

1848 created a new set of exponents, public and private, of "moral statistics", i.e. the collection of numerical information to track social and economic developments as a basis for policy reform and action. There was a growing interchange between State and civil society that was both intra-country and international, represented by the International Congresses of Statistics that began in 1851 and continued into the mid-1870s. This trend brought many social reformers into the government fold in a way that was not entirely cynical. There was a temporary, if somewhat narrow, consensus that the "Social Question" was in fact a technical problem subject to technical solutions, solutions to be informed by neutral information. This obviously paralleled economic planning which seemed to more definitely be subject to a statistically based policy approach (Clark, 2012, 196–197).

This could be said to be birth of the notion of "progress" (the word often used at the time) referring to the idea of material increase doing away with the ideological and confrontational politics of the prior fifty years. The revolutionary decades up to and including 1848–1849 left a lot of disillusionment in its wake, on both the revolutionary side, whose attempts to grab power were mostly thwarted or co-opted, and for the defenders of the status quo of all stripes, including reformists, who saw that a simple restoration of old ways not going to be sustainable in containing the social ferment of the era. The agitators licked their wounds and organised for another day, trying to come up with new ideas and methods, while those exercising power sought innovative ways of implementing economic liberalisation and promotion of growth as the way to overcome social problems and political conflict (Clark, 2012, 187–188).

6.10 Aftermath: Reform of the City

Whereas pre-industrial social rebellion was mostly centred in the rural areas of primarily agrarian societies, the new make-or-break battlefields were the rising cities in increasingly commercialised national economies. Table 6.3 provides data on urbanisation rates for the major European countries for 1800, 1830 and 1850.

These data show that Europe overall was urbanising rapidly, though unevenly. The UK was well in the lead here, as it was industrially, with almost two-fifths of its population living in cities by 1850. As noted earlier, Britain avoided revolutionary fervour during this time showing that urbanisation by itself did not necessarily cause rebellion. But it did cause change and dislocation in social relations in which a growing and displaced urban working class found themselves in expanding cities that were far from pleasant places to live in for those with few resources. Politically, this could be a volatile situation, and with an increasing proportion of the total population living in cities, if cities could be taken, the country was much more likely to follow than in times past.

Paris, Berlin and Vienna had all been sites of street fighting and barricades in 1848 and, in some cases, 1830 as well. Madrid avoided problems in 1848 but was beset by wide-scale disturbances in 1854. All four cities

Table 6.3 Urbanisation rates for selected European countries, 1800–1850 (% of population living in cities of populations over 5,000)

Country	*1800*	*1830*	*1850*
UK	19.2	27.5	39.6
France	12.2	15.7	19.5
Italy	18.0	19.0[a]	23.0[a]
Germany	8.9	9.1[a]	15.0[a]
Austria-Hungary	6.5	7.1	9.7
Europe	10.9	12.6	16.4

[a]These data have a higher degree of error

Source Extracted and reordered from Bairoch and Goertz (1986, p. 188, Table 3) were thus substantially redesigned and rebuilt in the 1850s, primarily with an eye towards social control. The Haussmann plan for Paris is the most famous example in which many old winding mediaeval streets, easily blocked by barriers built from cobblestones extracted from the road surfaces, were eliminated and replaced by long broad boulevards easily traversed by police and military authorities if need be. Haussmann also extended and modernised the city's sewerage system and began to provide clean municipal water supply, a positive addressing of a root cause of urban social unrest. Madrid had a similar rebuilding, though its water system would not be modernised for a few more decades (Jordan & Young, 1997).

The upheavals of 1848–1849 were not the only driver of urban modernisation. It was also informed by a new concept of improved "circulation" for goods and people, a notion central to the mechanistic conception of the economy posited by Liberal economists (who had borrowed it from the Physiocrats) and transferred into urban planning, planning itself being a novel idea. Revolution accelerated such trends because the association between overcrowding, poor sanitation, disease and political upheaval now seemed acute and in need of more immediate action and state intervention to reduce political instability, as well as being genuine problems in their own right (Clark, 2012, 188–190).

6.11 Aftermath: Managing Popular Consent

1848 also was framed primarily in terms of democratic republicanism versus authoritarian monarchy. Class egalitarianism was certainly an element, particularly in France, and would become ever more dominant as the century progressed, the publication of the Communist Manifesto in 1848 being a seminal moment (Boyer, 1998). However, the struggle was primarily political rather than economic at this point, because the economy was still in a great deal of developmental flux. The authoritarians got the message (generally, though not always universally) that some adaptation to the emerging masses would be required. The hard headed and heavy-handed methods of repression could not be given up, but they could be modulated and exercised with greater care and growing sophistication to ensure that the general public was kept onside without giving too much away.

This was especially clear with censorship, i.e. authorities vetting printed material prior to publication. This was widespread before 1848, calls for its abolition a central demand of all revolutionaries. After 1848, censorship regimes across Europe were removed and freedom of the press generally legalised. But this was only a relative freedom. For one thing, governments decided it was cheaper and easier to move from the "prior consent" of censorship to surveillance of political groups and newspapers that were most problematic, with penalties and controls imposed after publication and not beforehand (Clark, 2012, 190).

Additionally, governments set up press offices and agencies to coordinate the mass media of the day and influence its message. Prussia, for example, established a "Central Agency for Press Affairs" (Zentralstelle für Pressangelegenheiten) that distributed funds to friendly newspapers, and cultivated relationships with domestic and overseas papers transitioning from censorship to news and information management. Most other continental states, especially France, followed similar lines (Clark, 2012, 194). Whereas revolutionists saw power in the masses for overthrowing the State, governments saw a means of influencing them to buttress it.

6.12 A Summing Up: The World Economy at Mid-Century

By the middle of the nineteenth century, Europeans, at the forefront of industrial change (and imposing it on the wider world), were living through dramatic changes in ideas and circumstances regarding the rights of individuals and the proper relationship of governmental power to people (now citizens rather than subjects), a rise of purely private enterprise power that had not been experienced before, and new alliances between government and private economic interests.

One way to look at the period between 1780 and 1850 is as one of major flux in sociogenesis and psychogenesis, to use the terms of Elias (see Chapters 2 and 5). Social structures were modernising in rapid and yet uncertain and varying ways, and individuals were having trouble keeping up with the changes. Individualism was a growing mantra, yet it was set against an increasingly impersonal mass system of economic output, distribution and political management. The older orders had many flaws, but at least notionally there was a place for everyone, individuation being less important than the "good" of the order. Now the individual was being held up as an ideal but this individual was often only as good as their last pay check, to use a modern turn of phrase, their labour commodified, their status and importance reduced to an economic value computed in the marketplace, with no intrinsic importance outside of that, at least as far as modern economic thinking and practice was concerned.

The global economic order also was solidifying and changing, and new cores and peripheries were being shaped. Europe was in the economic and political ascendancy, though not yet fully consolidated in its position. Asia and Africa were in relative decline, helped along by outside force in many instances. These adjustments were occurring not just globally but regionally as well. Western Europe and England were gaining, with Central Europe divided between a rapidly expanding Prussia and a declining Austria-Hungary. Eastern Europe generally remained backwards. Russia was in some tumult, furtively modernising, with industrialisation coming in the late 1800s, and engaging in Great Power politics and sometimes getting the worst of it. Ottoman decline was leaving newly independent but small and backward states in its wake, creating sources of future instability. In the Americas, there was a whole raft of newly independent states and a rapidly rising, though still developing US, riven with many social, economic and political contradictions.

Modern state administration theory and practice was also beginning to come into fashion, its mores and modes still in development. This too was a worldwide phenomenon. Lagging non-western powers, such as the Ottomans, tried to adopt some of these modalities, as did the Chinese, to try to keep from further slipping into the peripheries in which they increasingly found themselves. In India, the English would soon impose their self-interested versions of "reform", usually at great cost to the locals and great benefit to themselves. But win or lose, a new ideal was emerging, and everyone had to compete to get ahead, or fall permanently behind.

Thus, "1848" can be seen as period of incomplete adjustment to the modern economic order that was still in the process of consolidation and emergence. But how did people, masses and elites, feel about it? The rise of economic output and the growing technical and statistical apparatus suggested the possibility of optimism about the future, that human beings were finally mastering their physical environment and that this would be sufficient for mastery over their social, moral and spiritual environment as well. Even the struggling disenfranchised saw reasons for hope.

Yet, there was also a case for doubt and pessimism. This was not yet fully manifested in 1848, but arguably it was possible to see in the events of the first half of the decade a decline in, if not the world, then the

West. Schopenhauer, with his message of the exhaustion of Western ideals and the consideration of Eastern (especially Indian) thought as a superior alternative, was mostly ignored in his day. But he would have a posthumous revival with admirers such as Zola, Tolstoy, Wagner, Thomas Mann and most spectacularly, Friedrich Nietzsche just a few decades later, all jumping off his ideas in diverse way. In particular, his notion of a declining West would be amplified at century's end, even though Schopenhauer himself did not see this as a totally bad thing (Gottfried, 1973). "Progress", at least within the thin lines of economic advance, seemed undeniable. But its direction towards a greater good was not a foregone conclusion. This conflict between optimism and pessimism would end up being the major philosophical divide of the nineteenth century. It is still going on today, in an atmosphere of considerably more cynicism and despair, and no more settled than back then.

References

Adelman, J. (2009). *Sovereignty and revolution in the Iberian Atlantic*. Princeton University Press.

Allen, R. C. (2009). Engels' pause: Technical change, capital accumulation, and inequality in the British Industrial Revolution. *Explorations in Economic History, 46*(4), 418–435.

Bairoch, P., & Goertz, G. (1986). Factors of urbanisation in the nineteenth century developed countries: A descriptive and econometric analysis. *Urban Studies, 23*(4), 285–305.

Baltzly, D. (2019). Stoicism. In E. N. Zalta (Ed.), *The Stanford encyclopedia of philosophy* (Spring 2019 Edition), https://plato.stanford.edu/archives/spr2019/entries/stoicism/.

Barraclough, G. (1967). *An introduction to contemporary history*. Pelican.

Becker, S. O., Hornung, E., & Woessmann, L. (2011). Education and catch-up in the Industrial Revolution. *American Economic Journal: Macroeconomics, 3*(3), 92–126.

Berger, H., & Spoerer, M. (2001). Economic crises and the European revolutions of 1848. *The Journal of Economic History, 61*(2), 293–326.

Boyer, G. R. (1998). The historical background of the Communist Manifesto. *Journal of Economic Perspectives, 12*(4), 151–174.

Broadberry, S., Campbell, B. M., Klein, A., Overton, M., & van Leeuwen, B. (2015). *British economic growth, 1270–1870*. Cambridge University Press.

Brown, D. (1970). *Bury my heart at Wounded Knee*. Henry Holt and Company.

Chilosi, D., Murphy, T. E., Studer, R., & Tunçer, A. C. (2013). Europe's many integrations: Geography and grain markets, 1620–1913. *Explorations in Economic History, 50*(1), 46–68.
Clark, C. (2012). After 1848: The European revolution in government. *Transactions of the Royal Historical Society, 22*, 171–197.
Cleveland, W. L., & Bunton, M. (2018). *A history of the modern Middle East*. Routledge.
Cobban, A. (1964). *The social interpretation of the French Revolution*. Cambridge University Press.
Colas, A. (2016). Barbary Coast in the expansion of international society: Piracy, privateering, and corsairing as primary institutions. *Review of International Studies, 42*(5), 840–857.
Davis, M. (2002). *Late Victorian holocausts: El Niño famines and the making of the third world*. Verso Books.
De la Escosura, L. P. (2005). *Colonial independence and economic backwardness in Latin America* (London School of Economics Working Paper 10/05).
De La Escosura, L. P. (2007). When did Latin America fall behind? In S. Edwards, G. Esquivel & G. Márquez (Eds.), *The decline of Latin American economies: Growth, institutions, and crises* (pp. 15–58). University of Chicago Press.
De la Escosura, L. P. (2009). Lost decades? Economic performance in post-independence Latin America. *Journal of Latin American Studies, 41*(2), 279–307.
Diaz-Diaz, R. (1999). Abolition and emancipation. In Latin America and the Caribbean. In K. A. Appiah & H. L. Gates (Eds.), *Africana: The encyclopedia of the African and African-American experience* (pp. 5–9).
Ferrero, G. (1941). *The reconstruction of Europe: Talleyrand and the Congress of Vienna 1814–1815* (T. R. Jaeckel, Trans.). G.P. Putnam's Sons.
Gallardo-Albarrán, D., & de Jong, H. (2021). Optimism or pessimism? A composite view on English living standards during the Industrial Revolution. *European Review of Economic History*, 25(1), 1–19.
Gottfried, P. (1973). Pessimism and the revolutions of 1848. *The Review of Politics, 35*(2), 193–203.
Hobsbawm, E. J. (1987). *The age of empire, 1875–1914*. Pantheon Books.
James, C. L. R. (1963). *Black Jacobins: Toussaint L'ouverture and the San Domingo revolution* (2nd ed., revised). Vintage Books.
Jordan, D. P., & Young, R. J. (1997). Transforming Paris: The life & labors of Baron Haussmann. *Urban History Review, 25*(2), 71.
Kostantaras, D. (2020). *Nationalism and revolution in Europe, 1763–1848*. Amsterdam University Press.
Kuznets, S. (1966). *Modern economic growth: Rate, structure and spread*. Yale University Press.

Lehning, J. R. (2013). *European colonialism since 1700*. Cambridge University Press.

Lewis, J. E. (2000). *The American union and the problem of neighborhood: The United States and the collapse of the Spanish Empire, 1783–1829*. University of North Carolina Press.

Lida, C. E. (2002). The democratic and social republic of 1848 and its repercussions in the Hispanic world. In G. Thomson (Ed.), *The European revolutions of 1848 and the Americas*. Institute of Latin American Studies.

Lobingier, C. (1918–1919). Napoleon and his code. *Harvard Law Review, 32*(2), 114–134.

Lovejoy, H. B., & Anderson, R. (2020). Introduction: "Liberated Africans" and early international courts of humanitarian efforts. In H. B. Lovejoy & R. Anderson (Eds.), *Liberated Africans and the abolition of the slave trade, 1807–1896* (pp. 1–24). Rochester University Press.

McLynn, F. (1998). *Napoleon*. Pimlico.

Milanovic, B. (2016). *Global inequality*. Harvard University Press.

Pfister, U. (2019). The inequality of pay in pre-modern Germany, late 15th century to 1889. *Jahrbuch für Wirtschaftsgeschichte/Economic History Yearbook, 60*(1), 209–243.

Pfister, U. (2020). The Crafts-Harley view of German industrialization: An independent estimate of the income side of net national product, 1851–1913. *European Review of Economic History, 24*(3), 502–521.

Price, R. (Ed.). (1996). *Maroon societies: Rebel slave communities in the Americas* (3rd ed.). Johns Hopkins University Press.

Ridolfi, L., & Nuvolari, A. (2021). L'histoire immobile? A reappraisal of French economic growth using the demand-side approach, 1280–1850. *European Review of Economic History, 25*(3), 405–428.

Roberts, J. (2000). Revolution from above and below. In T. C. Blanning (Ed.), *The Oxford history of modern Europe* (pp. 15–45). Oxford University Press.

Rodríguez, L. A. M. (2020). Bartolomé de Las Casas y el pensamiento decolonial: debates y precisiones. *Estudios, 41*, 210–226.

Scanlan, P. X. (2019). Emancipation and captivity in the British Empire. *History and Anthropology, 30*(5), 503–508.

Scanlan, P. X. (2020). *Slave empire: How slavery built modern Britain*. Robinson.

Shaw-Taylor, L., & Wrigley, E. A. (2014). Occupational structure and population change. *The Cambridge Economic History of Modern Britain, 1*, 53–88. Cambridge University Press.

Sivasundaram, S. (2020). *Waves across the south: A new history of revolution and empire*. William Collins.

Snay, M. (1993). *Gospel of disunion: Religion and separatism in the antebellum South*. Cambridge University Press.

Sperber, J. (2005). *The European revolutions, 1848–1851* (2nd ed.). Cambridge University Press.
Tarver, H. M., & Slape, E. (2016). *The Spanish empire: A historical encyclopedia.* ABC-CLIO.
Taylor, M. (2000). The 1848 revolutions and the British empire. *Past & Present, 166*, 146–180.
Voth, H. J. (2003). Living standards during the Industrial Revolution: An economist's guide. *American Economic Review, 93*(2), 221–226.
White, C. M. (2013). *A global history of the developing world.* Routledge.
Zinn, H. (2005). *A people's history of the United States: 1492–present.* Harper Perennial Modern Classics.

CHAPTER 7

"Revolution"

C. Gordon, *Many Possible Worlds*,
https://doi.org/10.1007/978-981-19-9281-0_7

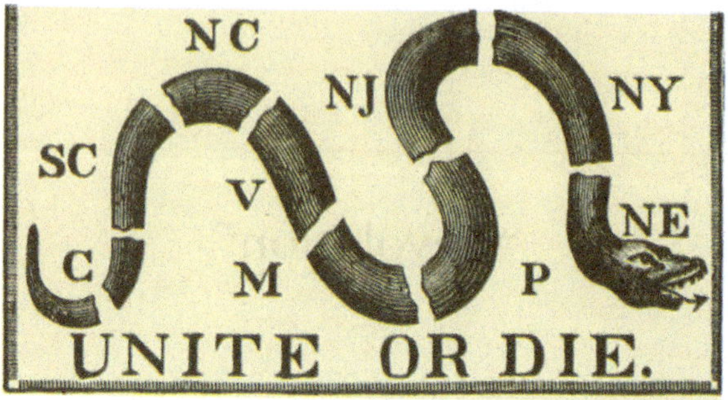

Fig. 7.1 "Unite or Die" flag from the American revolution (*Image source* Wikipedia Commons. No known copyright restrictions)

7.1 A Revolution Is Not a Dinner Party

What is a revolution, anyway? Mao famously said that it was "not a dinner party", or any other refined and peaceable activity, but "an insurrection, an act of violence by which one class overthrows another" (Mao, 1967, 11). The musician Gil Scott Heron sang "the revolution will not be televised" in a song of the same name on his 1971 *Pieces of a man* album (Flying Dutchman/RCA). Instead, he noted the revolution would be live and violent (Fig. 7.1).

These are the vibrant and unsettling words of activists. Scholars are more bloodless in their discussions, seeking to distinguish revolutions from other social, political and civil disturbances such as riots, coups, rebellions and general unrest. One can get caught in terminological weeds, but a good working baseline, to be used here, is that rebellion aims to overthrow a political regime in power, while a revolution aims for substantial social and political change as well. Either one is deemed successful if these respective things occur (Weede & Muller, 1998).

Power struggle is always present, and may be manifested in various ways with violence (such as riots) or not (such as bloodless coups). An actual change-over in the form of, and/or, personnel in, government generally occurs, but does not necessarily have to meet the definitional terms for a revolution as in the case of so-called revolutions from above in which incumbent rulers and ruling classes make radical and lasting policy and institutional alterations. What Mao and Heron are speaking of are true mass movements that bubble up from the lower reaches of society and coalesce into a genuine overthrow of existing social, political and/or economic structures, replacing them with a genuinely new alternative. Such revolutions generally are led by an elite group of some sort, often coming from an intermediate class. But their motive force and success come from the masses.

Theda Skocpol's (1979) definition is one of the more influential and will be the broad basis for the discussion here. She asserts that revolution is a rapid change in a society's social structure and institutions accompanied by some kind of mass mobilisation. Table 7.1 lists some major historical examples of such "revolutions from below", i.e. radical changes in social, political and/or economic structure based on some sort of mass movement.

The French Revolution of 1789, Russian Revolution of 1917 and the Iranian Revolution of 1979 would clearly fit this definition on all counts. But some important events might not: many of the individual Latin American independence movements in the first part of the nineteenth century saw political institutions change but were led by elites, not masses. In fact, these elites were often hostile to the indigenous populations and did not change the social structure of the settler population much either (Adelman, 2009). The American Revolution of 1776–1789 is also a bit of a hybrid. There was obviously dramatic political change, but the mass

Table 7.1 Selected major revolutions since circa "1800"

1789–1795 French Revolution
1830 revolution in France
1848 revolution in France
1910–1920 Mexican Revolution
1911–1927 Chinese national revolution
1917 Russian (October) Revolution
1927–1949 Chinese Communist Revolution
1941–1945 Yugoslavian revolution
1945–1973 Vietnamese revolution
1952 Bolivian revolution
1954–1962 Algerian revolution
1959 Cuban Revolution
1978 Iranian Shiite Revolution
1989–1991 Collapse of Soviet Bloc and Soviet Union
2010–2013 "Arab Spring"

Source Chosen by author based on events recorded in Stearns (2003) and Ishay (2019)

movement was regionally concentrated heavily in New England, the mid-Atlantic and Virginia, and hierarchical social structures, especially in the South and New York, were largely left in place after independence. Indeed just after American independence was achieved, President George Washington was faced with a rural popular revolt in New England, the Whisky Rebellion, which he successfully suppressed (Bailyn, 1967).

A common delineation is to term and date a revolution based on the timing of a successful overthrow of incumbent elites by a new elite, who may or may not accomplish this with violence and/or mass mobilisation, and who then go on to fundamentally change the structure of society and authority (Zimmermann, 1990). This categorisation would encompass most of the revolutions in Table 7.1. Some of the initial Latin American independence movements might fit as well, although there would be some judgement calls to be made for overthrows that changed little more than the names of the rulers. The military overthrows of civilian governments in twentieth century South and Central America would likely be excluded on this basis. Thus, Brinton ([1938]1965) makes a distinction between a coup d'état as opposed to "major" revolutions associated with social, political and economic change.

What about "reform"? This term is generally used to denote changes within an existing political power structure, with changes necessarily designed and implemented by those in power. But some reforms can be revolutionary in their impact, in ways not always intended by the reformers themselves. On the ground, even distinct revolutions have multiple phases, often including earlier reforms that were critical to the eventuation of revolution later on.

While the archetypal occurrences all are given dates that often become legendary ("1789", "1917" etc.), it can be hard to truly know when a revolution properly begins and ends. As an example, periodisation for the French and American Revolutions may seem quite straightforward as they contain very clearly delineated incidents of rupture, such as the American Declaration of Independence in 1776, or the storming of the Bastille in 1789. But when did either of these events really go past the point of no return, and when did they really end? Can, for example, the 1905 rebellion against Tsarist Rule be included as an integral part of the Russian Revolution of 1917, or a failed practice run? Arguments can be made both ways in this case, though the success of the latter certainly was linked to the failure of the former. Political and social ruptures may take years to fully unfold into their final form, and therefore are difficult to disentangle and date. It can be a bit like saying that the timing of a particularly violent lightning strike is equivalent to that of the storm that created it. To some degree, these are narrow historiographical issues and dating always requires some arbitrary, but necessary, decisions to make a telling of history possible in the first place.

As a side note, applying the term "revolution" to non-political shifts is quite common, as with the Industrial Revolution, Scientific Revolution, Commercial Revolution, etc. In some ways, these do seem like revolutions, arguably highly significant in the broad and deep disruptions and alterations they bring, perhaps more so than specific political revolutions themselves. But these are also very long-term processes, for which the term evolution might be appropriate. They also transcend political boundaries. For these reasons, Arnason (2016) argues that these much longer but highly change-inducing societal waves should be called "transformations".

7.2 Theorising About Revolutions

Lawson (2016) argues that there have been, thus far, four main generations of theories of why revolutions occur. Brinton ([1938] 1965) was one of the pioneers in systematically studying the "great revolutions" as following a sort of universal sequence, rather like the course of a disease, or epidemic, beginning with outbreaks of symptoms, cresting with mass contagion, widespread illness, population collapse and then rebirth and renewal, possibly transitioning with convalescence. Brinton and other scholars of his era introduced some structure into what had previously been a much more anecdotal affair. In particular, they created an interest in the determining the vulnerability of different kinds of state structures and social organisations to revolutions and other large-scale disruptions.

The second generation of revolutionary theorists, writing mainly in the 1960s, built on this foundation to focus on modernisation as a cause of revolt. Their historical focus moved from the "classic" European movements such as the French Revolution, to uprisings in the Third World. One important hypothesis was that periods of modernisation raised public expectations for greater social and economic opportunities. When there was a mismatch between the two, a revolution could occur. The evidence did not support this as a universal explanation since modernisation has often unfolded without revolution, such as in India (post-independence) and Canada. But it did serve as an effective counterpoint to the then-prevailing notion that economic modernisation was always a universal social and political good whose social consequences were incidental, an idea posited most forcefully by W. W. Rostow (1960).

The "structuralists" such as Theda Skocpol (1979) and Jack Goldstone (1982) constituted a third-generation digging more deeply into the links between modernisation and social stability or lack thereof. They searched for "macroconditions" that would result in revolution, and tried to determine how these might result in successful uprisings and how much these would then alter society afterwards. They offered a diverse menu of possibilities, including responses by social classes to economic change and the capacity of the state to respond to international conflict (Skocpol, 1979). While useful in understanding particular events, and less grandiose than the early universalist models, a general theory did not successfully emerge.

Because of this, a fourth generation of theorists saw revolutions as unique and complex amalgams of responses to international, domestic, social, economic and political systemic crises, which in turn created their own feedback loops. Zimmerman (1990) proposes a framework in which the final dependent variable, "outcomes of revolution", can be broken down into alterations in the independent variables of politics, the economy, the social-cultural realm and state power. Lawson (2016) considers these models as an improvement in terms of explanatory power and characterisation but still sees them as too simplistic, arguing that revolutions themselves go beyond characterisation as concrete stable events with clearly demarcated causal chains emanating into and out of them. The thrust of current theories of revolution could be said to boil down to a version of chaos theory, with seemingly random event structures that have determinants that are very sensitive to initial starting conditions.

7.3 Social Fabric, Social Capital and Social Movements

Another way to come at revolutions is to consider them as an outcome of a human social system driven to an extreme. The metaphor of "social fabric" is often used to characterise the state of a society. A strong fabric is associated with social stability, solidity and collective human growth, while a weak fabric is connected with unrest, a shaky social ground and collective retrogression (Hayden, 1982). This can be quite relevant when considering the relationship between economic change and societal functioning.

As noted in Chapter 5, Polanyi sees social meaning and economic exchange as inseparable from one another, "embedded" within a society. Polanyi argued that the market society created a new social orientation, with the concern for individual maximisation, now made a central motive of human civilisation. This displaced a much more socially natural way of being, as old as the human social collective itself, which was the sufficiency principle, namely a primary concern with whether there was enough material resources to go around. Under either regime, of market/maximisation or nonmarket/sufficiency, social rituals and ceremonies were essential to creating the social values and associated norms that fostered an implicit social contract between individuals and the greater whole which in turn made viable operation of a given economic system possible (Hayden, 1982, 641–642; Polanyi, 1944).

Polanyi is not a social determinist. Social processes cannot function without the emotional and psychological commitment of individual people. Thus psychological factors are crucial to the social interdependence needed for any production, consumption and exchange process. Unmanaged changes in these factors can undermine the unity and stability on which any economic process depends and, in so doing, alter individual and social psychology, either of which can lead to a breaking point (Hayden, 1982). Although Polanyi does not address this issue, extreme social imbalances fostered by capitalist economic modes can be seen as leading to revolution in some cases.

More contemporary models of social behaviour are found in the constructs of social capital and the social network. Social capital refers to the idea that there is creation of a valuable social asset with independent existence that develops out of social relationships. The closer the relationship between people and/or groups, the greater the potential value of social capital and the greater the likelihood is that the relationship in question will be maintained to mutual advantage. Thus, social capital represents investment in social relations that, if successful, yields social returns to both parties, in both monetary and non-monetary forms (Lin, 1999). An example of social capital in action would be a mutual trust level that arises between related parties working together over a long time to act with little need for monitoring of one another, hence lowering what economists would call "transactions costs."

Social capital is generally seen as arising from social networks. The term has a lineage going back to at least the middle of the twentieth century (Mitchell, 1974). Its basic thrust (there are many variations) is that apparently autonomous individuals (or organisations) are by definition part of a web of social relations and interactions. But unlike Polanyi's embeddedness, or Elias's interdependence, individuals act as autonomous and independent units, weighing relationships in a relatively rational manner, and not driven by independent social forces emanating from social groups or social categories. Thus, a social network consists of independent actors relating to each other for mutual gain and thus fundamentally transactional in the simplest sense. But with time and experience between parties, positions within the network can change, affecting individual member scope of action and ability to achieve desired goals, good and bad. This is similar to what can happen with social capital (Degenne & Forsé, 1999). Significant degradations in either one can lead to breakdowns of various sorts, including revolution, though the dynamics in these models are quite different than those in more sociological analysis.

All of these elements can come together to drive social movements of various sorts. How these movements come about, what drives them and how they relate to revolutions are all questions considered in the literature. One very influential economic theorist in the area of social movement dynamics is Mancur Olson (1971) who claims that social movements are always the sum of strategic actions by individual agents maximising their self-interest and choosing to join with or part from others depending upon the net economic benefit of doing so. "Successful" movements in this schema can always be measured by the achievement of specific extrinsic outcomes sought by the interest groups involved.

Acemoglu and Robinson (2006) offer an even broader framework in which they argue that democracy is preferred by the majority of citizens, but opposed by elites, and whether a democratic system or dictatorship prevails depends upon the shifting balance between the costs of repression, the credibility of promises of elite concessions and the relative strength of various social groups. Democracy consolidates when elites do not have a strong incentive to overthrow it, and can be the most stable of political set-ups because power is shared across a wide group of people. But it can fail when incentives shift in particular ways, and the same can occur to undermine oligarchical arrangements.

Public Choice and Rational Choice schools of this sort thus see revolution and other social movements as like any other "collective action problem" in which self-interested and rational maximising individuals require adequate incentives to sacrifice short-term gain for long-term gain, the latter necessarily having to be higher than the former. If a post-revolutionary outcome is a "collective good" and revolutions to achieve this require collective action, revolutionaries face a "free-rider" problem. Because the models assume that everyone is self-interested and revolutions involve significant sacrifice for uncertain gains that generally accrue to many others not involved in bringing the revolution to pass, self-interested potential participants in a revolution must be induced to take risks for something that could benefit everyone in the end but which they would rather get for free by letting others do the work. When the problem is framed this way, the literature suggests that true revolutions should almost never occur, even though they do. More narrow challenges to authority, such as coup d'etats where participants are few and identifiable, and where benefits and costs to those participants are fairly clear and chances of success reasonably high are explained better by this model (Weede & Muller, 1998).

One way of dealing with this inconsistency with history is to question the assumption that revolutionaries are only motivated by the public good, positing that revolutions occur instead because of the rewards and punishments involved for those leading it (Olsson-Yaouzis, 2012). This is somewhat more plausible and fits the historical record better for some instances, but it is still not necessarily that convincing. It is true that elites are critical in leading true mass revolutions. But is it plausible that they are primarily motivated by purely private gain, especially when the leading of such efforts often appear to have a very low probability of success at the time? Also elites are often dragged along by the masses more than being ahead of them, and the theory does not explain these occurrences at all. Even in the case of coups, these are led by elites who by definition are already privileged, which calls into question their desire to rebel in the first place (Weede and Muller 1998). A rational/public choice model may fit some political situations, but revolutions, and even many rebellions, do not seem to be one of them, even with significant theoretical modification.

Non-economistic models of social movements are obviously motivated quite differently, with social movements and groupings developing through social dynamics that are sometimes quite distinct from, and even overriding of, the motivations of their members. These constructs also emphasise that the individual agent is co-produced and co-defined by the greater collective and the movements they are part of. Construction of social identity is as important as individual identity, and the organisation of a social movement may in the end actually change the actions, motivations and preferences of the participating agents (Edelman, 2001). Norbert Elias's theory offers another relevant concept here: figuration. Human beings are not purely autonomous individuals but a product of both their individual psyches and the interdependent social (con)"figurations" of which they are a part at any given time. Bourdieu's concept of "fields" is roughly analogous (Friedland, 2009).

A revolution therefore acts at both individual and group levels, and its success or failure depends on changes feeding back and forth between societies and groups and individuals. Rationality is involved, but far from exclusively and is not a purely fixed faculty or set point. Even belief is potentially dynamic. This notion challenges some theories of revolution, and certainly most standard economics models, which reduce societies to self-contained systems, whether the unit of action analysis is at the individual, societal or some intermediate level (Featherstone, 1987).

7.4 Economic Impetuses of Revolution

Many revolutions contain a significant economic motivation, with an archetype of poor, starving masses pushed to the breaking point. Indeed, the iconic (possibly apocryphal) revolutionary spark, Marie L'Antoinette's dismissal of the peasant bread riots with her flippant remark of "let them eat cake", is indicative of the idea that economic lack against a background of plenty serves to ignite much social spasm and collapse.

Marx saw popular revolution as a product of increasing immiseration of the working classes, the proletariat itself being a creation of industrialisation. Goldstone (1982) notes that Marxist historians attributed the great revolutions in the West of England in 1640 and France in 1789 to a more general breakdown of the old regime caused by the growth of capitalism. These dynamics were not just domestic but international. Even if the rise of internal capitalist institutions and classes were not sufficient to cause enough discord to cause the poor to revolt, the expansion of international markets and shifts in economic "cores" and "peripheries" might cause enough social dislocation and loss to tip the social balance into violence and political upheaval.

De Tocqueville ([1856] 1955) flipped this materialist explanation on its head, claiming that revolution was a product of increasing prosperity raising expectations beyond what the economy actually delivered. Even if living standards were rising, if they were not going up as quickly as expected, trouble could arise.

Davies (1962) argues that Marx focused on long-term structural changes while De Tocqueville focused on short-term crises and that the two views are not necessarily incompatible. His own view is that economic modernisation causes political problems, even with persistent and ongoing poverty, only if people's expectations shift from accepting such conditions as being one's natural lot in life to expecting a better life. Since this is precisely the implicit and explicit promise of economic growth, this dynamic could be said to expand along with industrialisation and modernisation. Davies (1974) synthesised these views in his J-curve theory, i.e. that revolutions are most likely to occur when a long period of objective economic/social development is followed by a short reversal in material conditions. Graphically, this appears as an inverse "J" depicting economic performance, rising along with a line depicting expectations. All is well until the performance curve suddenly dips downward while the expectations line keeps rising, opening up a gap between performance and expectations that leads to revolution if the gap become too large and lasts for too long.

Some twentieth century modernisation theorists have taken up these threads in various ways. The transition from a traditional to a modern economy can be a particularly fraught time, where an initial growth phase may cause a decline in the standard of living of the majority of people, causing social dislocation as the older mode of production declines faster than the new mode can rise and consolidate. Even after growth becomes widespread, there may be a gap between expectations of the masses, the realities of everyday life and a much more visible, and extreme, increase in the well-being of the newly rich.

However, individual or even group discontent is likely only a sufficient, but not a necessary condition for revolution. Discontented masses certainly will cause social unrest, manifested in riots and local rebellions. But revolution requires much more organisation than that. So if revolution arises from below, the nature of mass discontent, social forces and social movements are critical.

Historians have observed two major and different types of modern organised revolutions: peasant revolts and urban workers' uprisings. The educational levels, abilities to organise, and economic strengths and vulnerabilities vary between these two groups and will affect their capacity, desire and ability to rebel and successfully revolt.

On the rural side, dispossession and dislocation are often key triggers to unrest, while the strength or weakness of peasant versus landlord self-organisation can make the key difference to a rebellion's ultimate success or failure. Russian landlords during the First World War, the French landlords during the Crown's bankruptcy in 1788–1789 and the Chinese landlords during the Japanese invasion of the 1930s were left exposed and weakened and thus eventually destroyed by rural uprisings because they did not have the capacity to resist or respond to them effectively. They thus were rendered unable to channel or put down rural uprisings (Skocpol 1979).

Meanwhile, for urban masses, the cost of food and availability of employment have been traditional triggers of social ferment, while solidarity and the ability to organise workers has been a key historical factor in whether this coalesces into a revolution. Of course, Marx predicted that countries where a critical mass of an urban proletariat existed was where revolution would naturally occur, leaving Lenin to fly by the seat of his pants when the first major "Marxist" revolution occurred in primarily rural and backwards Russia.

To complicate matters, while the overthrow of an existing state is one primary political objective of any revolution, paradoxically that state itself can be a source of revolution. Skocpol and Trimberger (1977) argued that a "revolution from above" consists of civil or military officials seizing control of existing administrative apparatus, using it to significantly reshape distributions of social, economic and political power. Although these are reforms in a technical sense, such changes can be quite radical. Examples include major land reform, abolition of traditional status distinctions and rapid industrialisation. The Mejii restoration of Japan in 1868 and Ataturk's takeover of Turkey in 1923 are two major examples of this, both with important economic consequences, domestically and internationally.

7.5 The Role of Ideas

Many of the "great" revolutions invented ideas and ideologies that often fed later tumults, e.g. 1789 in France, 1917 in Russia and 1949 in China. Modernity is the "Age of Ideology" to use Hobsbawm's (1994) phrase, which in many ways seems to be something almost inviting revolution with its elements of idealism, utopianism and Manichaeism. (Ideas and ideology more generally are considered in Chapter 17).

Max Weber's distinction between interests (material and ideal) and ideas is helpful here. Weber claims that interests are direct determinants of human action. Thus, if the masses are starving and they see the existing order as the reason for their starvation, their material interests will lead them to rise up, all other countervailing things (such as the power of the elites to supress rebellion) being equal. But ideas (and ideologies) are what Weber claims will shape the perception of what options and paths are available to effect change (Lizardo & Stolz, 2018).

As an example, one could say that the overthrow of the Tsarist government during First World War was inevitable from a material interests point of view. But its Marxist-Leninist shape was at least partly driven by how relevant actors, mainly in the revolutionary elites, thought about how it should proceed, ideas that also fed into those opposing it, including the Western powers that intervened in the Russian Civil War of 1919–1921. If another set of ideas had predominated, the revolution would have taken a very different shape. Tooze (2014), for example, argues that the Russian Revolution was on a social democratic trajectory, but that the cunning and bold power plays of Lenin's Bolsheviks, driven by a particular ideal, put it on a very different path.

Definitively proving the power of ideas in moving social change is almost certainly impossible. But Weber's construct does offer an intermediate ground that seems intuitive and defensible and which does clearly arise in some actual social and political upheavals, as it does in the example just mentioned. It offers a dichotomous model in which primarily material things (i.e. whether a revolution occurs or not) are explained in material term (material interests) while things that arguably involve more human conceptualising (i.e. the model for social and political organisation) have an idealist cause (ideal interests). Like any typology, this one has its limits and will never likely attract a consensus. But it offers a useful historical filter.

There can be power in both old ideas and new ones. After the French Revolution, the concept of revolution itself was universalised, taking on mythological proportions, with the notion that a revolution was an inevitable reckoning of the forces of historical progress. Selbin (2013) highlights four revolutionary sub-narratives including "civilising and democratising revolutions" (e.g. America in 1776); "social revolutions" (France, Russia and Cuba); "freedom and liberation revolutions" (Haiti and Mexico); and "lost and forgotten revolutions" (various crushed indigenous people's rebellions). These concepts may be more salient when looking back after the fact, however, with a series of events being reinvented to create an historical memory that informs (and misinforms) later ones.

7.6 Political Economy Revisited

Revolutions may or not be primarily political, but they inevitably change politics and political systems in one way or another. The American, French and Industrial Revolutions cemented the ideal of "representative democracy" as the best structure for the modern "polis" or political community (see Chapter 4). Economic and social modernisation both literally expanded the size of the polis and intensified the need to clarify and operationalise the relationship between political community, economic and social spheres, and the state. As Lichtheim (1972) points out, democracy effectively merges the State and political community together, with the paradoxical result, unforeseen by most early democrats, that the demands of the State on its people intensify, since it is "their" state in the first place and their responsibilities to it and for its decisions cannot be easily let go of, with resistance of non-compliance being somehow "against" the people rather than some detached authority.

In the aftermath of the French Revolution, democracy became a measuring stick for judging future revolutions and other regime changes. Representative democracy was the default ideal politically after 1789, but the ideal economic structure was not so well established, not least because of the constant upheavals and dynamism of capitalistic growth. The European revolutions of 1830 and 1848 were most definitely "democratic" in orientation, though most of them did not succeed. Because of this, nods to representative assemblies were made even in authoritarian countries such as Russia and the newly unified Germany. Although there was more than a fair share of cynical manoeuvre in much of this, it was also motivated by a genuine change in political norms (Lichtheim, 1972).

As the Industrial Revolution gained scale and scope, both the political elites and their opponents found that their programs needed to do so as well. For the elites, a "mass" politics was required to contain the discontent of the growing hordes, while those seeking change needed to develop counter-movements of similar breadth and depth. Democracy, or at least democratic procedures like elections and representative legislatures, found favour with both sides, allowing potentially greater legitimation for the rulers, and potentially greater power for the disenfranchised, achieved at relatively low cost. But reformers adopted such measures under a belief that the existing system could and should be preserved, even if modified. Revolutionaries did not accept this sort of compromise.

7.7 "East" v "West"

The political and economic theories considered so far are mostly "Western" and "European" in focus, although the theories themselves are generally assumed to be universal. The quite different social-political-economic structures of the "East" (i.e. non-European world) do not, however, necessarily conform to their logics. These regions were impinged upon by Western modernising forces, resisted and adapted to by their recipients in unique ways, and creating some unique political configurations as a result.

The ancient societies of Asia, which had true civilisations well before the Europeans, responded to penetration by Western power and ideas with quite turbulent and novel political developments that could take decades to unfold. Thus Fairbank (1986) posits a "long Chinese revolution" from 1850 to 1949, beginning with the Taiping rebellion, a cataclysm that weakened the dynastic Empire beyond repair, with later internal crises and geopolitical setbacks leading to its collapse in the early twentieth century; an interregnum of several decades of internal and external power struggle; and a unified successor state emerging only in the middle of the twentieth century with Mao's triumph. Even then the "Communism" in China was quite distinct from its western counterparts, so much so that it ultimately split from Russian Communism (see Chapter 25). Meanwhile, Eisenstadt and Aizenshṭadṭ (1996), in examining the Meiji restoration in Japan, prefers to use the Japanese term *ishin*, arguing that 1868 was more of an assertion of refashioned traditionalist claims rather than a Western revolution, blurring the distinction between revolution and restoration, and taking a very distinctly Japanese course from then on.

On the other side of the globe, the former Spanish colonies saw independence movements that, as noted, were not particularly "revolutionary". But this changed in the twentieth century when revolutions in Mexico (1910–1920 and beyond), Bolivia (1952), Cuba (1959 and beyond) and Nicaragua (1978–1979) led to rather unique applications of European models in postcolonial settings, irrespective of their broader ideological labels. Even with the European heritage of their elites, Latin American revolutions do not conform to European patterns. Indigenous populations in conflict with transplanted and multi-generational settler elites have led to, in some cases, a distinctively Latin American tradition of authoritarian rule and populism known as *caudillismo* in which, in the best case, personalism blends with a crusade for genuine social change, as initially was the case with Peronism in Argentina (Arnason, 2016). The worst case can yield a rent-seeking kleptocracy of an especially odious sort. This is where caudillismo usually ends up either way.

Africa also saw tremendous incursion by European influence in the nineteenth century, but "revolution" was largely inapplicable there because of the ruthless and effective dominance of colonial masters, and a very different history of state-community forms and relations. The continent was also incredibly diverse politically. Localised rebellions, sometimes quite strong, occurred, but colonial control always reasserted itself in the end because of the overwhelming firepower of the Europeans. Genuine African revolutions would come in the twentieth century, bound up with post-war decolonisation and Cold War competition between Capitalist and Communist blocs. The Indian subcontinent gained its independence during this time as well, and although its postcolonial order was not brought about by revolution in the classical sense, its formation and unfolding did involve considerable unrest and upheaval (see Chapters 23 and 25).

Arnason (2016) thus refers to the "civilisational context of revolutions" as a way of highlighting the importance of grand cultural factors in social and economic change, upheaval and modernisation, and revolution itself. Cause and effect remain highly contextual depending on the form of civilisation in the background.

7.8 Great Power Politics

The nineteenth and twentieth century national domestic developments in a globalising world took place in an international context that became ever more important as the world integrated more intensively and extensively, especially after 1800. Geopolitics has been critical to revolution and other political upheaval before this time but became even more important afterwards (Lawson, 2011).

Great Power clashes had varying degrees of decisive impact in the success of revolutions in Russia, China, America and France. The American Revolution in particular marked the beginning of a historically unparalleled shift in geopolitical and economic power inside and outside that country, with some historians arguing for the US Civil War of 1861–5 as the closing chapter in the American revolutionary process. For seven decades or so, the Russian revolution created a comparable shift, though it succeeded in the face of unified Great Power intervention against it, and thus was truly home grown, except for the return of Lenin to Russia that was arranged by the German government as a form of covert action against the Tsarist government.

The same can be said of the French Revolution. While often dated from 1789 to 1799, a period in which the European powers combined unsuccessfully to crush it, the Revolution could be extended to the end of the Napoleonic wars in 1815 to highlight its "imperialist" phase, while others, notably Furet (1981), argue for its ending with the consolidation of the Third Republic around 1880, with the contest between monarchy and republic definitively settled, and internal socio-cultural structure and geopolitical position established until the First World War.

The strong geopolitical view sees modern revolutions as being rooted in the international relations of states, with the comparative weakening of some states versus their rivals and the changing orders and alliances between regional or global hegemons and their dependencies, being the main underlying drivers. Lawson (2011) claims that successful domestic revolutions actually require Great Power counter-actions of some sort to develop a sense of historical importance and even motive force. Without such opposition, a revolutionary might be crushed or hollowed out by being absorbed back into the global status quo. Revolution has thus generally been closely associated with war.

This geopolitical perspective can be complementary to an economic "world systems" view in which globalisation increasingly regionalises the planet into a series of interdependent and specialised "cores" and "peripheries". In that case, the economic forces that help drive revolutions can be transmitted through the economic system of trade, finance, production and distribution, while international political forces can be transmitted through shifting geopolitical arrangements. The two can interact and, leaving "strong form" geopolitical theorists aside, local disruptions can be driven by varying combinations of domestic and international factors.

At the same time, greater international integration has been perennially argued to be a prophylactic against revolution, with interdependent nations supposedly less subject to it than isolated ones because they are more open to stabilising foreign resources, influences and ideas. This was the basis of much American thinking after Second World War devastation in which a unified and prosperous Capitalist world was seen as both a bastion against the forces of Communism and an attractive template for developing countries to conform to (see Chapter 25).

7.9 1848 as a Case Study

How might all these theories explain the revolutionary movements of 1848, which were so seemingly synchronised? An answer that will please nobody is that all of them have relevance. Economic change was clearly a major driver, but so too were the long processes of industrialisation and associated urbanisation and changes in economic structure, and short-term economic pinches in the form of grain price spikes and food shortages.

European imperialism meanwhile roiled many other parts of the world, especially (though not exclusively) areas where traditional powers, like China, were retreating and leaving power vacuums behind. Raw geopolitical projection of European force was vital to many of the alterations of political and social form in non-European realms. Within Europe, 1830 and 1848 were definite outgrowths of the decline of the Great Power restoration of 1815.

The intellectual ferment of the age is remarkable as well. The idea of Republicanism was a shining revolutionary beacon of the American and French revolutions. Liberalism was also on the scene, supporting an industrialising status quo on the one hand, while promoting democratic political arrangements on the other, in a heady contradictory mix that held up democracy as a tantalising and inspiring destination for those living under authoritarian rule or with significant disempowerment. Marxism had just emerged, and would provide both diagnosis and antidote for the sins of Capitalism that were all too evident amidst the rising but uneven tide of growth.

Perhaps the era was a result of a confluence of causes and effects, a perfect storm so to speak? One can make a case like this in a broad sense, and common causation of some sort seems likely given the breadth and depth of the revolutionary events of mid-century. Yet each revolution is truly unique as well and revolutions themselves are not discrete events or shocks, but processes of varying durations and intensities. Beyond doubt, they have impacted the course of the world economy in manifold ways.

Box 7.1 Economic impacts of revolutions

There has been a great deal of study of the potential economic causes of revolution. But how about its potential effects on the economy, both domestically and internationally?

Answering this question turns out to be perplexing for a number of reasons. For one thing, revolutions tend to have multiple causes and multiple effects, making it difficult at times to even tease out what something referred to as a "revolution" actually consisted of and when it actually occurred (see the main text of the chapter for more on these issues). Making the construction of a "before" and "after" comparison is thus fraught.

The intent of the revolution is also important. Some revolutions, such as in Iran in 1979 or Russia in 1917, arguably have objectives which are much more social than economic, the achievement of which might require the temporary disruption of economies and economic processes, such as the breaking up of large landholdings to redistribute to landless peasantry. This will have negative economic consequences in the short run that will hopefully lead to a positive net gain later, though, to use economist parlance, the improvements may come more on the equity than the efficiency side. In such a case, how should the economic impact of an individual revolution be judged? One might be able to identify discrete outcomes, such as a fall in per capita GDP. But if the major goals were noneconomic, this may be an intermediate rather than final effect, although certainly too much economic dislocation can make the revolution itself unsustainable. It is thus important to take noneconomic impacts into account, but these are hard to measure

Related to this is the time frame of analysis. Revolutionary impacts are long-term affairs, as already mentioned. Yet how long should the analytical frame be, and how can the revolutionary effects be separated out from post-revolutionary developments?

Having said all this, some study has been devoted to the economic impacts of the French Revolution. Many have pointed to the Revolution's economic modernisation dimensions, such as the abolition of the feudal system, legal and administrative system reform and creation of the metric system, amongst others. On the other hand writers like Cobban (1962) claim that the Revolution was actually anti-capitalist, as evidenced by its emphasis on egalitarianism. The exact nature of the Revolution is hard to pin down, but a truly encompassing analysis would have to tease out the diverse causes and effects to adequately determine whether it met its objectives. Economists therefore tend to narrow the focus to economic impacts, and break it down into its sub-components to allow for more definite and quantitative analysis.

The post-revolutionary performance of the French economy in the nineteenth and early twentieth centuries was somewhat lagging (see Chapter 4), especially given its relatively slow switch from an agrarian-rural economy to an urban-industrial one, the result being a per capita GDP growth rate that was generally behind Britain and, later, Germany. By these metrics, one could say that the Revolution retarded French economic progress. But this is no doubt too broad a statement and next to impossible to assess. Thus, Finley et. al. (2017) examined the economic impacts of the law passed by the French Constituent Assembly on 2 November 1789 that confiscated all Church property, redistributing it through auction. Between 1790 and 1795, over 700,000 ecclesiastical properties were put into private hands, amounting to 6.5% of French territory. They found that this process increased inequality. But they also found that districts with higher redistribution had higher wheat production productivity, more manufacturers of drainage and irrigation pipes, and less land left fallow. At the same time, the Revolution caused a great out-migration of people, many of them highly skilled. The authors found that high out-migration French departments had significantly lower GDP per capita during the nineteenth century, but higher growth during the twentieth century

These are only two aspects of a wide-ranging program of reform. These particular findings are mixed, indicating that for these two discrete elements there were some short-term costs economically, but longer-term gains. It is hard to generalise, even for these examples, except to say that, as with many other economic phenomena, there are economic trade-offs that come with revolution and that they morph over time

References

Acemoglu, D., & Robinson, J. A. (2006). *Economic origins of dictatorship and democracy*. Cambridge University Press.

Adelman, J. (2009). *Sovereignty and revolution in the Iberian Atlantic*. Princeton University Press.

Arnason, J. P. (2016). Revolutions, transformations, civilisations: Prolegomena to a paradigm reorientation. In J. P. Arnason & M. Hrubec (Eds.), *Social transformations and revolutions* (pp. 27–55). Edinburgh University Press.

Bailyn, B. (1967). *The ideological origins of the American Revolution*. Belknap Press.

Brinton, C. ([1938] 1965). *The Anatomy of revolution* (Revised ed.). Vintage Books.

Davies, J. C. (1962). Toward a theory of revolution. *American Sociological Review, 27*(1), 5–19.

Davies, J. C. (1974). The J-curve and power struggle theories of collective violence. *American Sociological Review, 39*(4), 607–610.

Degenne, A., & Forsé, M. (1999). *Introducing social networks*. Sage.

De Tocqueville, A. ([1856] 1955). *The Old Regime and the French Revolution*. Anchor Books.

Edelman, M. (2001). Social movements: Changing paradigms and forms of politics. *Annual Review of Anthropology, 30*(1), 285–317.

Featherstone, M. (1987). Norbert Elias and figurational sociology: Some prefatory remarks. *Theory, Culture & Society, 4*(2–3), 197–211.

Finley, T., Franck, R., Johnson, N., & Michalopoulos, S. (2017). Economic consequences of revolutions: Evidence from the 1789 French Revolution. *VoxEU/CEPR*. https://voxeu.org/article/economic-consequences-revolutions

Friedland, R. (2009). The endless fields of Pierre Bourdieu. *Organization, 16*(6), 887–917.

Furet, F. (1981). *Interpreting the French revolution*. Cambridge University Press.

Goldstone, J. A. (1982). The comparative and historical study of revolutions. *Annual Review of Sociology, 8*(1), 187–207.

Haldane, J. B. S. (1927). *Possible worlds and other essays*. Chatto and Windus.

Hayden, F. G. (1982). Social fabric matrix: From perspective to analytical tool. *Journal of Economic Issues, 16*(3), 637–662.

Hobsbawm, E. J. (1994). *Age of extremes: The short twentieth century*. Michael Joseph.

Horsefield, J. K. (1944). The origins of the Bank Charter Act, 1844. *Economica, New Series, 11*(44), 180–189.

Ishay, M. (2019). *The Levant express: The Arab uprisings, human rights, and the future of the Middle East*. Yale University Press.

Lawson, G. (2011). Halliday's revenge: Revolutions and international relations. *International Affairs, 87*(5), 1067–1085.

Lawson, G. (2016). Within and beyond the "fourth generation" of revolutionary theory. *Sociological Theory, 34*(2), 106–127.

Lichtheim, G. (1972). *Europe in the twentieth century*. Praeger Publishers.

Lin, N. (1999). Building a network theory of social capital. *Connections, 22*, 28–51.
Lizardo, O., & Stoltz, D. S. (2018). Max Weber's ideal versus material interest distinction revisited. *European Journal of Social Theory, 21*(1), 3–21.
Mao, Z. (1967). *Quotations from chairman Mao Tse-tung* (2nd ed.). Foreign Languages Press.
Mitchell, J. C. (1974). Social networks. *Annual review of anthropology, 3*(1), 279–299.
Olson, M. (1971). *The Logic of collective action: Public goods and the theory of groups* (Second Printing with a New Preface and Appendix). Harvard University Press.
Olsson-, N. (2012). An evolutionary dynamic of revolutions. *Public Choice, 151*(3/4), 497–515.
Polanyi, K. (1944). *The great transformation*. Beacon Press.
Rostow, W. W. (1960). *The stages of economic growth: A non-Communist manifesto*. Cambridge University Press.
Selbin, E. (2013). *Revolution, rebellion, resistance: The power of story*. Zed Books Ltd.
Stearns, P. N. (2003). *Western civilization in world history*. Taylor & Francis Group.
Skocpol, T., & Trimberger, E. (1977). Revolutions and the world-historical development of capitalism. *Berkeley Journal of Sociology, 22*, 101–113.
Skocpol, T. (1979). *States and social revolutions: A comparative analysis of France*. Cambridge University Press.
Tooze, A. (2014). *The deluge: the Great War, America, and the remaking of the global order, 1916–1931*. Penguin Books.
Weede, E., & Muller, E. (1998). Rebellion, violence and revolution: A rational choice perspective. *Journal of Peace Research, 35*(1), 43–59.
Zimmermann, E. (1990). On the outcomes of revolutions: Some preliminary considerations. *Sociological Theory, 8*(1), 33–47.

CHAPTER 8

Technology, Innovation and Invention

C. Gordon, *Many Possible Worlds*,
https://doi.org/10.1007/978-981-19-9281-0_8

Fig. 8.1 The dance of humans and machines (*Image source* The Fabricator: New Bedford Textile School yearbook [1922]. New Bedford Textile School). Contributing Library: Claire T. Carney Library, University of Massachusetts Dartmouth. Digitizing Sponsor: Boston Library Consortium Member Libraries. Original caption: "A Freshman mechanical student's dream of the deep after one of Mr. Crompton's lectures." No known copyright restrictions

8.1 A Technological Revolution?

When people think of the Industrial Revolution, the part that seems revolutionary is the technical change that accompanied it, especially in England. One historian has quipped that it constituted a wave of gadgets (Allen, 2009, p. 901), and the description seems apt, as the listing of some of the major inventions of the eighteenth to early nineteenth centuries in Table 8.1 confirms (Fig. 8.1).

Taken together, these and other inventions allowed humanity to more effectively extract raw mineral energy from the ground (at first in the form of coal), more and more efficiently convert if from latent to usable form (at first using steam), and apply it increasingly efficiently towards desired ends, including extraction and conversion of more energy, and the transformation of raw materials into a panoply of manufactures. Mechanisation generally made all production processes ever more efficient, at first concentrated in textiles, and moving out from there.

8.2 "Technology" and Productivity

This technological story is certainly compelling, not least because it is true. But it cannot be the whole story, because machines do not invent or use themselves, and even just restricting one's view to the economy, humans are not equivalent to their machines. Technical progress is easy

Table 8.1 Major inventions of the First Industrial Revolution's dawn

Invention	*Inventor(s), Country of inventor, Year invented*	*Economic and technological significance*
Steam Engine	Thomas Newcomen, England, 1712	Pumped water using a vacuum created by condensed steam, enabling draining of water out of deep mines and greatly expanding the ability to extract minerals, especially coal
Flying Shuttle	James Kay, France, 1733	Greatly reduced number of weavers by mounting the shuttle on wheels in a track using paddles to push the shuttle side to side
Spinning Jenny	James Hargreaves, England, 1764	Allowed workers to produce multiple spools of thread simultaneously. Further refinements led to spinning just one spindle at a time to between 80 and 120 spindles
Watt Steam Engine	James Watt, England, 1769	Added a separate condenser to move the piston much faster and efficiently, thus requiring much less coal to produce the same amount of power
Water Frame	Richard Arkwright, England, 1769	Improvement on an ancient instrument to produce cotton thread more rapidly and requiring no prior technical skill to operate
Spinning Mule	Samuel Crompton, England, 1779	A hybrid machine combining two earlier inventions, the spinning jenny and the water frame, particularly useful for muslin production

(continued)

Table 8.1 (continued)

Invention	*Inventor(s), Country of inventor, Year invented*	*Economic and technological significance*
Power Loom	Edward Cartwright, England, 1785	A mechanised loom using water power to speed up the weaving process. Scottish inventor William Harrocks and American inventor Francis Cabot Lowell introduced improvements that made its use commercially feasible and hence widely adopted
Cotton Gin	Eli Whitney, USA, 1793	Mechanised the separation of cotton fibres from seeds, greatly increasing efficiency
"Puffing Devil"	Richard Trevithick, England, 1802	First steam-powered train of its kind
Steam Engine Locomotive	George Stephenson, England, 1814	Steam engine locomotive running on rails initially used to haul coal out of mines

Sources Allen (2009) Landes (1969), and Mohajan (2019).

to quantify and date, but it is not so easy to periodise and measure the political, social and economic trends that support, enhance and shape it, and which can thus get lost in the telling of history (Lichtheim, 1972). Even from the point of view of productivity increase, which was prodigious, how much of this was purely technological in nature as opposed to coming from organisational and behavioural change?

The usage of the term "technology" in English was not common before the twentieth century and its meaning has shifted over time. It can encompass specific tools, knowledge, ideas and techniques, and/or refer to their application to practical purposes (Salomon, 1984). Lichtheim (1972) defines the word very broadly as encompassing humanity's "methods and tools for manipulating physical forces and material things" (397). Economists use the term in the context of their Growth Model, which, as noted in Chapter 2, puts forth the economy as if it were a giant machine or factory, taking inputs and converting them into higher level outputs. In this context, "technology" is any process used to actually transform inputs into outputs and technical change refers to alterations in these processes and an analysis of the attendant productivity results (i.e. how much output is gained from a single unit of input). In analytical terms and using a standard generic form of the production function "machine", output = f(inputs) --, "f", the functional form, is what "technology" refers to.

All of these definitions are very broad, but if one accepts the definition sitting within the Growth Model, in theory one can separate out the productivity effects of technical change from mere changes in the quantity and quality of inputs (i.e. producing more simply by having people work more and/or by providing more capital) by getting the right data and estimating the relevant causal relationships. To be highly simplistic about this, if we see that 100 "inputs" created 100 "outputs" with a given "f" (technology) and then, if "f" is changed somehow (e.g. an improvement in the efficiency of a machine) and now 200 "outputs" are created with those same 100 "inputs", we would say that the new "f" is twice as productive as the old one and that the change is due solely to the technical improvement. To oversimplify a bit, this is why many economists claim the Industrial Revolution to be purely, or mostly, technological in nature.

However, technology in this Growth Model is also highly nonspecific, with all manner of processes, inputs and outputs put under its banner, ranging from new types of machines and new organisational forms all the way down to small changes like using shorthand to lessen the amount of time spent inputting data into paper accounts. This disembodied nonspecificity, while potentially capturing some broad productivity effects, does not explain how technology actually "works" on the ground, including what causes technical change, what shapes it, and what might retard it. For this reason, the technology of the Growth Model is often called a "black box" because only the "before" and "after" stages are visible, and these relatively speculatively, everything else in between being hidden from view. Already mentioned, too, is the complete lack of social context, which some argue is absolutely critical.

Given all these caveats, however, a growth framework logically leads to the conclusions that technological change (and supporting capital investment) is a major route to modern economic growth since one can work and invest as much as before and yet get much more output from doing so. In simple mechanical terms, this is what the breakout from the Malthusian Trap represented, i.e. a productivity boom driven by technological improvement, broadly defined (see Chapter 3).

8.3 Entrepreneurs Versus Technology "Systems"

As to how new technology actually comes about, the traditional view of invention, innovation and technology is the model of the "heroic" individual, inspired and determined, who comes up with a breakthrough, sometimes against long odds and opposition from others. The economics counterpart to this idea is the entrepreneur, risking scarce capital on risky and unconventional propositions, an idea most famously developed by the economist Joseph Schumpeter ([1942] 1994) (see also Chapter 5). According to Schumpeter, entrepreneurship is risky because it necessarily involves some form of innovation to be successful, and its outcomes are thus highly uncertain because of the novelty of the entrepreneurial enterprise. The innovator's activities may not even result in a tangible outcome, which is often the case with much new technology. Even if such an outcome is achieved, there is no guarantee that it will make money for those putting capital at risk. Therefore, failure is much more likely than success. But the potential for return is very high, which is what motivates the entrepreneur. This is why Schumpeter refers to the "creative destruction" of the entrepreneur, the few successful ventures generally adding a total amount of value far higher in the form of sectoral transformation, than the total lost in the much larger number of failures.

Schumpeter's ideas are the original basis of the current term thrown "disruptive technology". This can include changes to inventions, processes and business models, amongst other things. What makes them "disruptive" is their potential to completely upend a market in a short period of time. There are many examples of such disruption strewn throughout the First and Second Industrial Revolutions, e.g. the railroads, electricity, steam engine, etc., some of which are considered in more detail below.

The Schumpeterian view emphasises the importance of the entrepreneur in providing the catalyst for this, and many economic historians have thus sought to make lists of such entrepreneurs, what their country origins are and what factors might have made one country more amenable to entrepreneurship than another. While still considered valid in some domains, such as less developed economies (including pre- and early industrial Europe), Schumpeterian views about innovation and invention have since been supplemented by broader and more holistic views thought to be more applicable to later stages of economic development. One paradigm is the that of the Large Technical System

(LTS) which stresses the networked aspects of advanced technology and a grander type of entrepreneur-planner-visionary who doesn't just invent new machines but builds entire new systems, such as Thomas Edison, who conceived of, raised capital for, and helped roll out the electricity network in the US. Such networks make diffusion of inventions widespread and vastly increase their market value and market power. Broader conceptions de-emphasise the role of individuals and speak more of general socio-technical systems encompassing society, regulation and cultural meaning, amongst other things, as the inherent context from which purely technical innovation cannot be separated (Goldsmith, 2014, 2).

Indeed, the human historiography of technological "ages" indicates the salience of such a view, in which epochs are labelled according to a set of commonly used materials and sources of energy, labour types, and tools and techniques that are dominant across a society. Examples include the Stone Age, the Bronze Age, the Machine Age and the Atomic Age. The history of technology certainly includes the story of individual inventions and inventors. But these are also part of a much wider whole of interrelated parts, including culture, politics and ways of thinking (Austen & Headrick, 1983, 168–169).

8.4 The Finance Connection and Beyond

As far as the public sector role, the role of the State is often central to technology development generally and network assets in particular. Thus, the ancient Romans built large infrastructure networks and urban centres almost entirely through state effort and direction, with long-lived economic effects. The Industrial Revolution saw a more hybrid model emerge of private enterprise supported by government policy. But this did not mean that government became less relevant. Regardless of who owns the asset, government must establish rules that both enable investors to confidently tie up large amounts of capital in the form of sunk costs while they await system operability and financial viability. Indeed, many technical innovations of the Second, Third and Fourth Revolutions—trains, electricity, petroleum, automobiles, airplanes, radio, television and the Internet—have been LTS projects in which government played a critical set-up and start-up role, providing crucial seed capital, protecting initial markets for entrepreneurs and regulating markets to help dampen and manage the inevitable market power of a few players in industries exhibiting large scale economies of scale (Goldsmith, 2014, 27–28).

While the First Industrial Revolution was mostly about small-scale investment, individual invention and diffusion based on relatively modestly sized enterprise, innovation and technological progress soon became more of a matter of increasingly large scale, requiring large mobilisations of capital and socio-political nous. As discussed in Chapter 6, the Developmental State in mid-century Europe was building extensive public work projects that private investors had neither the resources for, nor the commercial interest in, to initiate, though they were often all too happy to participate in follow-on investments and management once the foundations were built. Besides direct public investment, governments on the Continent especially took it upon themselves to subsidise private investment, directly and indirectly, and by making formation of corporate enterprise easier to accomplish and manage. Capital markets were already sophisticated by the middle of the nineteenth century, but they grew even more complex and powerful, driven by the need to build larger and more technically advanced background environments to support the growing economic machine of production and consumption, devoted to a quest for expanding material productivity.

Railroads are one example of where this happened, a case to be considered in more detail below in Sect. 8.6. But this was a widespread phenomenon and included sanitation, water, sewerage and waste management networks. Not all these industries used financial innovations. Rail, electricity and petroleum were the leaders, with their lessons learned and applied elsewhere. Finance became a significant sector in its own right and it sometimes seemed that the finance tail was wagging many private enterprise dogs. This is a trend that flowers late in the nineteenth century (see Chapters 9 and 12). The point to be made here is that industry in the general sense was becoming an affair of large operators moving around large technical systems, with money playing a big role in determining winners and losers, arguably not always optimally.

These trends once more raise questions about just how important the individual entrepreneur or innovator actually is, especially in later stages of economic growth. Obviously, there were visionaries back then, are still with us today and presumably will be with us in the future. But how much are they riding systemic waves versus making them is an open question, thus leading to "neo-Schumpeterian" schools of technical change. An example is the Great Successive surges of Development (GSD) school which argues that the Industrial Revolution was the first of a series of increasingly integrated economic-social positive long-run feedback loops between technological systems of production, infrastructure, finance and institutions (Goldsmith, 2014, 42–43). This is a true "systems" perspective that not only cuts away from the individual, but even whole sectors as prime actors.

8.5 Technology and Society

This line of thinking is reminiscent of other "long-wave" theories of economic undulation such as those of Kondratieff, which Schumpeter himself referred to, in which industrial economies establish and in turn become driven by large long-term cycles of critical variables such as input prices. When an economy gets to this long-term, large-scale level, individuals and institutions find themselves floating on economic oceans, their influence still important in terms of detecting patterns and setting courses, but not determinative in a broader causal sense (Sterman, 1986).

Even in narrow economic terms, and especially as capitalist enterprise becomes more sophisticated, technology is a collective, social affair, with individuals playing roles of varying degrees of importance. The relative importance of individual versus society in technological evolution is, however, highly contextual, manifested in many different ways across time and space. This story runs in two directions: how society affects technology and how technology affects society, with the tension between individual and collective present in both.

As to how society affects technology, economists focus on the causal role of institutions, using their very broad definition of them, in bringing invention, innovation and, most importantly economically, commercialisation, to the fore in some places rather than others. For an economist, this includes implicit incentives contained in resource constraints, e.g. an abundance or lack of inputs, such as labour, capital or a raw material like coal (see Chapter 3). England's Industrial Revolution is the scene of many debates on this field. On the one hand, It is claimed that England variously had a more hospitable geography, resource base, property rights regime, wage structure (mainly that labour was more expensive than capital and so capital intensive technology was encouraged) and, even, just plain dumb luck, all background variables that aided individuals rather than the other way around (Becker et al., 2011; Galor, 2005; Mokyr, 1999a). On the other hand, some focus on the characteristics of individual inventors and engineers, claiming that England had an advantage in having an abundance of skilled mechanics and technicians with a particularly practical bent, unlike equally intelligent France whose inventors were more ethereally rationalist in their ideas (e.g. Landes, 1969). Why this might be so (if it is so) is said to be something of a mystery, though economic historians in particular often try to explain it by way of differences in particular local incentives (Mokyr, 1999a).

Culture is seen by some as the critical difference in why some countries industrialised before others, and some did and some didn't at all. Mokyr (2016) defines culture as beliefs, values and preferences and suggests that radical changes occurred to these in Europe in the period from 1500 to 1700, something that he refers to collectively as a "cultural breakthrough". This preceded and enabled the Industrial Revolution by allowing for the rise of "useful knowledge" which served as the basis for economically productive technical change and creativity specifically applied to production. The scientific-cultural changes within Europe were the foundation for this shift and combined with specific institutional changes (e.g. enforceable contracts, sound property rights etc.) to produce the Industrial Revolution. While this was occurring across much of Europe, English "practical" culture is often invoked as the reason why that country pulled ahead of more "philosophical" France, other things being relatively equal (Mokyr, 2009). Goldstone (1996) meanwhile argues that the Industrial Revolution emerged in England and not China because the factory system would never have been allowed under China's social conservatism, even though the country was otherwise potentially well suited to its adoption. An important scholarly discussion revolves around Africa, which not only was largely left out of the Industrial Revolution but overall appears to have been left behind in a lot of technological advance that took place elsewhere (see Box 8.1).

Box 8.1 Africa's history of technological progress

Austen and Headrick (1983) argue that there are three stages of technological development in Africa: classical African agricultural and metal-using technologies; introduction of European and Asian proto-industrial technology that was mostly not taken up locally (especially the wheel and the plough); and the colonial and postcolonial period in which European industrial technology entered Africa but was never locally integrated. (165)

Why does Africa appear to have such a long history of relatively limited technological progress? Even where there was long and close contact with Eurasia before the Age of Imperialism, Africans generally rejected rotary mechanisms and most forms of non-human energy. Instead African technological systems were based mainly on human energy and linear-reciprocal motion for centuries

Africa is a highly heterogeneous place so generalisations must be tentative, but possible reasons for broad technological patterns in the earliest years include an abundance of iron, which made experimentation with copper economically unattractive; a paucity of tin, which impeded the development and implementation of various tools; and the difficulties of transportation which limited both technological development and the need for it, labour- and animal-intensive short haul methods being sufficient for most local needs (168). Other less economistic explanations exist, including ecology and geography (the basis of Diamond's thesis in *Guns, germs and steel* [1997]); demography; and cultural inertia. For some regions, certain factors loom larger than in others, e.g. the isolation of the sub-Saharan region from the rest of the world being a barrier to technological diffusion from outside. But even regionally definitive statements are hard to make (169). Of course, slavery and the slave trade looms large. In Africa, these appeared to be technology retarding. But this, if true, obviously applies more to later, rather than earlier periods of African history (172).

One particularly interesting hypothesis surrounds the sexual division of labour in Africa. Tending fields and spinning cotton have traditionally been women's work in most African societies, so the introduction of ploughs and spinning wheels may have been resisted partially because of their disruption of sex roles. Another socially based explanation rests on the generalisation that mothers in many African societies limit infant interactions with the world of objects, providing them with few toys, thus encouraging development of a higher degree of inter-personal relations but less experience in manipulating the physical world as compared to Europeans (174). These are all interesting possibilities, but the evidence is sketchy and the inferences mostly speculative.

With colonialism, Western technology was introduced but through means that discouraged or actively prevented local adaptations and innovations. While this was true in many other non-African colonies as well, Africa may have been uniquely affected because many societies on the continent generally did not consider technology all that important, for some of the reasons described above (176).

The nature and path of technological development, implementation and innovation in Africa is definitely distinct. But it is hard to generalise accurately even about what actually happened technically on this vast continent, with its many local exceptions to any possible continental rule, much less explain its historical cause and effect adequately. There is so much more to know, and this part of the world deserves much more attention than it has traditionally gotten.

Then there is the issue of how technology affects society. This can be looked at in "pure" economic terms (i.e. how social arrangements change to produce novel advances in output and distribution) or more generally in terms of how technology affects social development or advancement.

In the first instance, technical advance has driven and required much social rearrangement. Even the conditions for industrialisation appear to have relied heavily on prior social changes, often directed by State policy, as for example with the English enclosures of common lands which sped up the establishment of private property rights and displaced critical masses of people who then became part of proto-industrial labour forces (Polanyi, 1944). Changes in household form and activity in the form of the "industrious revolution" (De Vries, 1994), and the imposition of "factory discipline" on the workers represent major alterations to social structures and conditions that could be both cause and effect in the Industrial Revolution (Clark, 1994) (see Chapter 5).

Once the Industrial Revolution got going, the development and imposition of mass compulsory public education had the immediate goal of providing the basic skills, such as literacy and numeracy, that was becoming a prerequisite for much work, even in factories. As importantly, the uniform socialisation of sedentary schooling adapted people into regimented, directed work, while also creating a new counterpart category of "nonworking" leisure hours, with both "free" and "paid" time on a schedule and on command (Minge-Kalman, 1978, 459).

Equally significant was the rise of corporations, offices, and their attendant subcultures. Herman Melville depicted an eponymous clerk going through a nervous breakdown in his story *Bartleby the Scrivener* (1853) showing how widespread office work had become by the middle of the nineteenth century, the growing legal profession being a target of much satire and scorn throughout the era. Corporations were denounced by the essayist William Hazlitt as early as 1824, noting that although corporate bodies were legal "persons", they had no human attributes such as remorse or goodwill, and were especially pernicious for that reason. Hazlitt very early on writes of a person that would later became known as the "corporate man", more and more identified with the firm he works for and less connected to society and the greater good (Sampson, 1995, 17). Corporate culture was not pervasive in the mid-1800s or even, for most people, the late 1800s. But it would be pervasive soon enough and it was helping to shape society, an example of an organisational innovation with significant social consequences.

This raises a separate question of whether the social changes wrought in service of technology and productivity are necessarily good for society itself. The textbook answer is that technology itself is socially "neutral" and its social effects depend on how it is consciously or unconsciously deployed. But this is a caricature of a relationship that is subtle, complex, and multi-causal and multi-directional. Elias (1995) observed how new inventions and their diffusion could at least partially de-humanise the civilising process through the adaptation of human beings and societies to technological systems, rather than the other way around. He referred to this process under a broader rubric of "technisation", a term that narrowly refers to the human capacity to manipulate the physical world but suggests that the form this takes also can deeply affect the ongoing dance of development of the social structure and individual human psychology. Thus, for example, mechanical aids of all sorts are needed for humans to safely interact with increasingly sophisticated techno-systems, e.g. through the imposition of schedules, signals, training regimes and so on. The benefit of all this is (hopefully) greater productivity and material wealth and income. But the cost can be a sort of inner alienation from both oneself and from the larger society.

8.6 A Case Study: Railroads and Economic Growth

Many scholars studying the link between technology and economic productivity choose to focus on particular inventions and sectors and time periods. A major example of this has been the debate by economic historians over the role that the railways played in economic growth and development during the later stages of the First Industrial Revolution and the early parts of the Second. By the 1950s and 1960s, economic historians were strongly of the view that modern growth was determined by sufficient investment and capital formation on the one hand, and technological progress on the other. The dominant narrative was thus that the Industrial Revolution started in capitalist-friendly England, where the right incentives encouraged entrepreneurial activity and technological invention and application (Unger, 2018).

This crystallised into a consensus that the Industrial Revolution represented a rapid break from past growth, with technology and capital-intensity being the key. This was most famously encapsulated by W. W. Rostow's "take-off" thesis (1960), in which it was held that economies follow set stages of growth, with industrialisation being the transition from a slow-growth traditional economy to high-growth modernity. The railroad was seen as the key to this process, a quintessential modern gadget that caused a genuine rocketing into a new and unbounded age of rapid expansion and sophistication. Advances in weaving and milling were all very well and good, and important initial economic advances away from pre-capitalist modes. But these were simply updates of centuries-old activities. Railways represented a completely new way of moving around and this innovation in transport flowed through to modernise the entire economy. From the vantage point of the mid-twentieth century, railways were the first of a series of transport shifts in a line all the way up to the jet engine and rocket ship. The "Rail Age" was thus the first of a series of transformational epochs including the "Automobile Age", the "Jet Age" and the "Space Age" (Fig. 8.2)

A sacred symbol like this inevitably invites an iconoclast, and it came in the form of Robert Fogel, an economist who would later win the Nobel Prize for his 1964 book, *Railroads and American Economic Growth*. Fogel challenged the role of the railroads in an industrial "take-off". His method was to examine the "indispensability" of railroads to American economic growth during the late 1800s, by creating a measure called the "social saving" that the technology generated. Roughly speaking, this was a measure of how much extra GDP was created with the railways present in America, as compared to the hypothetical GDP that would have held if they had never been invented at all (or, perhaps more precisely, never deployed in America).

Fogel's choice of America for a case study was not accidental. Railways had been traditionally seen to be a particularly transformational development in the country, which by the late nineteenth century was one of the world's leading industrialisers and one of its fastest growing economies. For this to be true, it would have to be the case that the social savings from their presence would have to be very high. There was no precise threshold for this, but, if US annual GDP would have been, say, 50%

Fig. 8.2 Three trunk lines crossing each other—USA circa 1919 (*Image source* Manufacturer: Southern Bargain House, Richmond, Va. Date Postmarked: 1919 From Virginia Commonwealth University Libraries. URL: dig.library.vcu.edu/u?/postcard, 182. Notes provided from source: "This unique photograph presents to view the only point in the world where three trunk line trains cross each other at the same time, and over their separate tracks. At the top is shown a passenger train of the C. & O. Railway leaving Richmond for the upper James River Valley just beneath it a train of the S.A.L. Railway leaving the Main Street (Union) Deport for the South, and on the ground a train of the Southern Railway coming into Richmond from West Point on the York River. Rights: This item is in the public domain)"

lower without the railroads than with them, one could make a good case that economically they were indeed "indispensable."

What Fogel actually found was, that, by his estimates, US GNP (i.e. Gross National Product, a measure close to but not identical with GDP) in 1890 (which was the year he chose to do his with and without comparison, according to Fogel a year in which social savings should have been greatest) would have only been 2.7% lower without the railways existing as opposed to with them. This was not only a figure far from suggesting the railroads to be indispensable: it defied the consensus of the time about the economic importance of railroads in America, and, by implication, everywhere else. No one had actually tried to quantify their impact before and now that someone had, the results were underwhelming.

There was a great uproar about both Fogel's numbers and his method of "counterfactual" comparison, which consisted of comparing actual GNP at a point in time (the "factual") with an imagined state with one thing, in this case, railways, removed (the "counter" to the "factual"). "Social savings" inherently rested on this imagined comparison and it can be attacked as being too speculative to be of much use. To the extent that one nonetheless saw it as allowable (and it is now a standard practice amongst economic historians), many people attacked Fogel's way of doing it, and the simplifying assumptions that he used for it. A more detailed explanation of the counterfactual and social savings is provided in Box 8.2.

Box 8.2 Fogel, social savings and counterfactual history

The social saving method is a fairly simple application of supply and demand theory. In this case, one looks at the "supply" of transport by all means (or modes to use the technical term) used in the selected economy at a given time. Fogel looked at the supply of transport available in the US in 1890, which in actual fact included railroads. Then he estimated the supply of transportation in that time and place as if railroads were unavailable. The latter case is imaginary and represents a "thought experiment" in which one compares how an economy might complete its transport task by using only the contemporary rail alternatives, such as canals, and what size of GNP (Gross National Product, a measure similar, but not identical, to GDP) would result from this. The "savings" represents the amount spent on transport with railroads available, versus the same amount spent when they are not. The "social saving" more broadly considers how much better or worse society is with the railroads removed. The entire imagined "with" versus "without" comparison represents the "counterfactual" method.

Fogel collected all the data he could on the US economy in 1890 and modelled how railroads contributed to GNP levels in that year. He then eliminated railways from this model to see how the economy would be hypothetically affected and what bottom-line GNP would be in that case. Real historical data were collected but then a simulation had to be run using various assumptions and imputations about the transport choices a railway-less America would make, and how much this would in turn increase total expenditure on transport throughout the economy. He then modelled the effect of this increased transport cost on US GNP in 1890 to derive his social savings estimate.

Since railroads were, on average, the cheapest, fastest and most efficient travel mode in actual fact at the time, it was certain that removing them would increase overall transport costs. But the question was how impactful this would be on GNP. Fogel claimed he was stacking the deck in the railroad's favour by choosing a peak year of American agricultural production, when railways would be most utilised, and also by assuming "perfectly inelastic" demand for transport overall (i.e. complete inflexibility in the choice to transport goods, which meant that people would maintain their total use of transport rather than economise by transporting things less, even with the removal of one of their best available transport modes). These assumptions would supposedly ensure that any estimate come up with would arguably be on the high side and hence an overestimate of social saving due to railways. If all this is accepted, then the 2.7% of GNP social saving is even more disruptive to traditional wisdom.

Although this sounds somewhat fantastical, Fogel was actually just doing a retrospective benefit–cost analysis (BCA) which in practice does the same thing prospectively, imagining how much worse or better off a society would be in the future with the imagined presence of a chosen project as compared to its absence. His assumptions were especially simplistic (to make a point), he was "backcasting" rather than "forecasting" and the "project" he was assessing (the removal of the railways in America in 1890) was extremely large. But his method was very standard analytically within the economics profession. Its plausibility in this case is another matter.

Sources David (1969), Fogel (1979), and Gordon (2006).

Whatever its faults, Fogel's analysis was a bold attempt to delve more deeply into the true nature of the railroad as an invention, a technology, and a force for economic change. A fierce debate ensued, with four major lines of attack:

1. "Embodied" V "Disembodied" Effects
2. Role of Topography and Geography
3. Market access and network effects
4. Static V Dynamic Analysis

8.6.1 *Embodied and Disembodied Effects*

Fogel referred to his social saving measure as a disembodied effect because it was expressed in "pure" terms of how much it lowered unit (average) transport costs and how this flowed through to a resulting GNP number. Everything was boiled down to a monetised amount. This had the advantage of being relatively simple to interpret, based on a widely accepted metric, and amenable to easy comparison with other monetised costs and benefits if desired.

However, railroads, like any other technical advance, delivered its benefits, namely travel time savings, in a particular form, very different from similar time savings that might be delivered through the alternatives such as canals. These differences in form are referred to as embodied effects. Fogel's analysis implicitly held that the form of travel time savings did not matter; only the bottom-line transport cost savings did.

But in actual fact the form can and does matter a lot. Even the relatively insignificant net social saving that Fogel calculated might result in otherwise dramatic changes in a society and the shape of its economy. These, in turn, might have flow-on effects of their own. In other words, even if Fogel was correct that the total value of economic output in 1890 America might have remained fairly similar in the absence of railroads, the economic structure and processes of the US would very likely have looked dramatically different without the specific form of effects that railroads delivered.

Alfred Chandler (1977, 1980) and Oliver Williamson (1985) both argued that railroads produced not only transportation efficiencies, but organisational and institutional innovations that, when combined with the speedier and more regular delivery of goods and passengers, made a system of mass consumer and producer goods distribution possible; promoted the growth of mass manufacturing; led to the development of the large, vertically integrated corporation; helped develop deeper and more sophisticated financial and capital markets; and even established standardised time zones, which were created by the railroads to run clear and efficient schedules. None of this had happened with canals, the railroad's main competitor in many parts of the US. Canals simply did not move things and people as reliably or as quickly as rails to either require such extensive organisational planning and management, or require as much capital, which is why railways led to the changes mentioned above and canals largely didn't. This is most graphically illustrated with the time zone standardisations. Prior to railways, local times in most places were based mostly on the position of the sun in the sky, and local times in a relatively small area could have wide variances. This was fine for relatively slow canal and other watercourse travel. But it did not suit the railways that covered space so quickly, so frequently, and in such volume.

Effects such as these are impossible to capture in models that rest only on the final net disembodied impacts on consumption, production and relative prices alone. Yet these may be as important as average net gains or net losses. Furthermore, including these embodied effects may well change the bottom-line estimate of actual net economic impact. For example, the change in corporate form alone driven by railroad expansion had significant economic impact all on its own, quite apart from travel time savings. When the organisational lessons of the railroads were transferred to other sectors, these may well have delivered boosts to GDP that the disembodied social savings estimate ignored. Standardised time zones also led to important economic efficiencies that accrued to economic sectors outside the rails.

In general, the fact of embodied effects shows that even technological advance has many "non-technological" aspects to it, including institutional, organisational and social changes. The economic boundaries of technical change are actually not as clearly defined as might be supposed and measuring them in a disembodied way can be misleading.

8.6.2 Role of Topography and Physical Space

Fogel focused on the US, a country that had large natural endowments in the form of abundant internal natural waterways. Canals, rivers and, in some places, the Great Lakes offered good transport substitutes for railways. The UK was in a similar situation, with fairly good waterways, and additionally a compact, densely populated, urbanised geography. In these countries, and others with similar economic geographies, it made sense that the relative travel time and cost efficiencies offered by railways would be relatively modest.

Other countries were not so lucky, however. There were a whole series of studies that applied Fogel's exact methods to other countries and found social savings estimates that were often much higher elsewhere than in the US. Social saving was greatest in countries that relied most on roads, since at this time many surface routes were unpaved and horse-drawn wagon travel slow and uncertain. Here railways very vastly superior modes of travel, and thus offered much greater travel time savings, and operational reliability. Their hypothetical removal was much more costly than in countries where there were many navigable rivers, a terrain well suited to building canals and good facilities for coastal trade. In general, railways alleviated poor natural endowments. Where these endowments were rich, rails had relatively little effect. Where these endowments were poor, railroads saved society much more in terms of transport costs (Carlos & Frank, 1992; Coatsworth, 1981; Hawke 1970).

Australia is a particularly interesting counterpoint here, a country roughly 80% the size of the continental US, with many large, sparsely populated areas separating the major cities and economic production points; yet, unlike America, with very few large internal waterways of any sort, much less navigable ones. The Australian gold rushes in the latter half of the nineteenth century were well served by railway building, since these enabled much more efficient and less costly movement of high-value minerals to processing and export points than was possible over the available roads or rivers. Wool and much of the country's agricultural production did much better with existing water routes since production and consumption tended to be clustered around major watercourses anyway, such as the Murray-Darling system, and along the coast. Here rails mattered less. But when the minerals sector took off, railways helped strengthen linkages and efficiencies between the two sectors (Jackson, 1977, 84–90).

Along similar lines, economic historians dug out a variety of data on transport costs in non-rail sectors in the US. They found that rigidities in these sectors, both physical and economic, often made them more costly to use as rail alternatives than Fogel's simplistic baseline suggested. Canals, for example, could not be as easily adjusted to reach all the shifting origins and destinations of a rapidly changing economy, and canal operators, without railroads as competition, would likely have charged much higher prices to their users than Fogel had predicted (Lebergott, 1966; McClelland, 1968; O'Brien, 1983). Even in the US in 1890 these factors, when taken into account, yielded higher social savings estimates than 2.7%, by some measures almost twice as much.

8.6.3 Market Access and Size Effects

Adam Smith wrote of the importance of the "extent of the market" in providing sufficient and growing demand for a product and providing a critical mass of potential change to spur production and trade. Transport innovations therefore don't just reduce travel times. They reshape and re-form market size, extent and access. This particular effect can have critical impacts missed by a narrow social savings methodology.

One way to get a sense of this effect is by looking at travel time isochrone (also called isoline) maps. This refers to a map projection in which one delineates boundaries on a projection of a physical area, showing, from a given reference point, how far a traveller can get from that point in a given time period (e.g. a day). Two isochrone maps, created at the height of the Second Industrial Revolution and the heyday of rails, are shown in Figs. 8.3 and 8.4

These two maps are not directly comparable as they are created by two different authors using different data and different methods at different times but they illustrate a couple of basic points about the effect of transport innovations on market extent and access. (As an aside, Galton's 1881

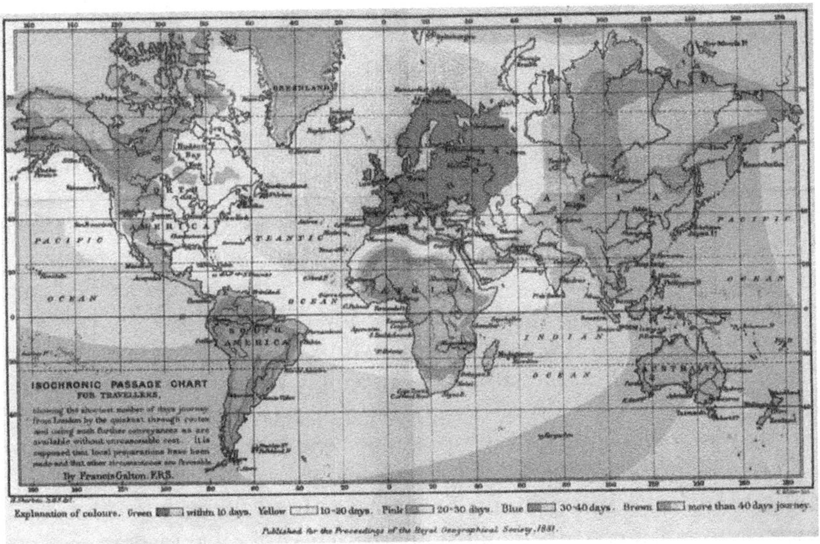

Fig. 8.3 Travel time contours from London (1881) (*Image source* Francis Galton's original "Isochronic Passage Chart." Francis Galton/Public Domain. Converted to Black and White by the author. Public domain)

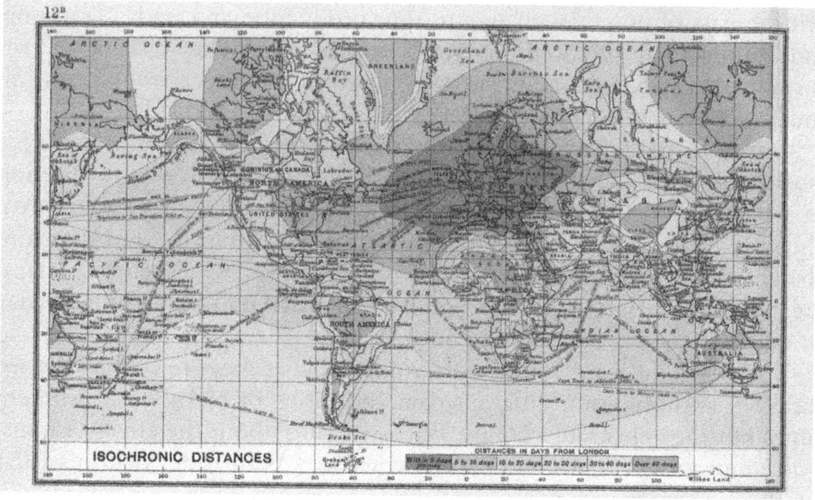

Fig. 8.4 Travel times from London 1914 (*Image source* Bartholomew, J. G. [1914]. Public domain)

map is the first known instance of an isochrone map, and Galton himself, known for his theories of genetics, claimed to have invented the device).

The first point is that travel time savings, driven by transport technology, increase potential market sizes. The clearest comparison between the two maps is continental Europe as a whole, the general limits of which could be reached in 10 days in 1881 but only 5 days in 1914 (the actual contours being roughly similar but not identical between the periods). A London producer of, say, glassware thus had many more potential customers to sell to in the latter period, simply due to more efficient and speedier travel to carry his or her goods to market, driven mainly by train and ship improvements for both passenger and freight movements. From a consumer point of view, this larger market area also brought in more competition from more distant locations, potentially driving down final prices (though not to their full potential where local transport monopolies or oligopolies existed). The increased extent of the market enabled by transport improvement also provided wider potential choice of labour, capital and raw materials to producers, increasing economies of scale and scope.

The second point flowing on from this that the shape of market areas changes as well. This is a more subtle effect, not necessarily a net gain for the economy as a whole in the way that a simple expansion of market size would be. But it certainly contributed to the growing dynamism and rapid pace of change in nineteenth and early twentieth century marketplaces and the quickly changing incentives, opportunities and challenges embedded in them. This dynamic is demonstrated graphically in Figs. 8.5 and 8.6, using a modern day example of a proposed adoption of High Speed Rail (HSR), the latest iteration of railway technology, in the European Alps region. The spatial effects are similar to what was happening with widespread adoption of rail systems throughout the world during the nineteenth century: systematic reductions in travel time "compressing" the time space of economies, from a human interaction perspective bringing geographic points closer together.

8.6.4 Static v Dynamic Effects

Finally, Fogel's analysis was explicitly "static" in its comparison. That is, Fogel compared one fixed year with the same hypothetical counterfactual year and subtracted the GNP of the second from the first to come up with a social savings estimate. In other words, the calculation was something like: GDP (1890—actual) *minus* GDP (1890—hypothetical, without rails) = social saving.

This is a simple approach and relatively easy to understand. But it is rather like comparing one Lego block model with another with some Legos removed, and works bests when comparing things whose behaviour is fairly well approximated by Lego blocks. Living economies, especially rapidly changing ones, are much more like organisms, more "dynamic" in that sense. In this case, a static comparison can be potentially very misleading. Williamson (1974, 1975) tried to model the dynamic effect of the railroads on the American economy over time by using a Computable General Equilibrium (CGE) model that was meant to capture the flow-through effects of railroads as they went back and forth through different American economic sectors across time periods. (Of necessity, this is still a relatively mechanistic approach, but arguably more accurate, something like comparing one working engine with another with some parts removed and the rest reconfigured). He then compared an estimate of this dynamic economy with and without railroads and came up with a social savings estimate that was more than twice as large as Fogel's, showing

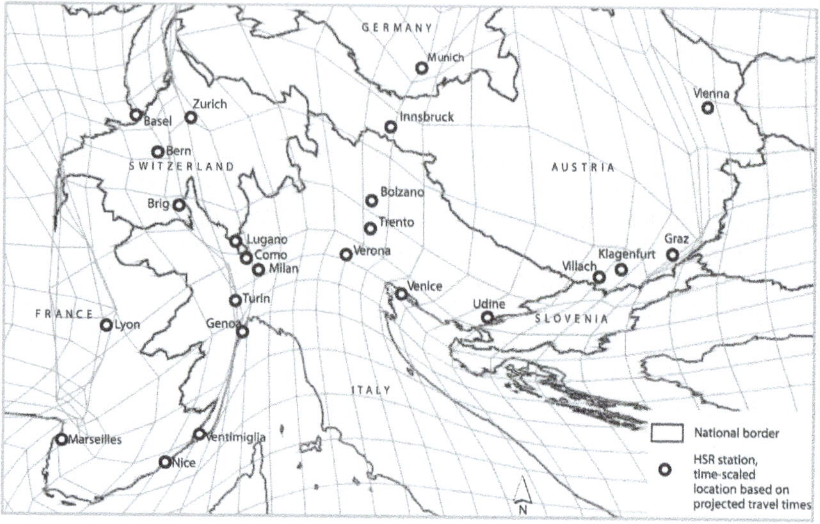

Fig. 8.5 "Compression" of the travel-time space of the European Alps using a modern example: the building of a High Speed Rail (HSR) connection. (Compare with Fig. 8.6) (*Image source* Ravazzoli et al. [2017] [Map by Elisa Ravazzoli] MDS-based rescaling of major points along HSR lines. © 2017 Ravazzoli et al. This open access image is used as licensed by the authors through a Creative Commons Attribution 4.0 International License [http://creativecommons.org/licenses/by/4.0/])

Fig. 8.6 European Alps "actual size" (*Image source* https://www.loc.gov/resource/g5700.ct001356/ Map of Europe [2004]. U.S. Central Intelligence Agency). No known copyright restrictions

that the dynamics had material effect. Fogel's assessment of the lack of "indispensability" of railroads to the US economy in one sense was not fully overturned by this exercise, but it did indicate the economic impacts of the American railways were considerably more important than Fogel had suggested.

Dynamic analysis is recognised by economists as being needed to more fully capture past and current effects of technological innovations as well as all manner of other economic influences and events (James 1984). Thus, many other scholars have estimated social savings and productivity impacts of railways using CGE modelling and have generally found higher results than those yielded by static comparisons. Donaldson (2018), for example, found the British railroads in the Indian Raj increased real agricultural income by 16%. But dynamic analysis is hard to do because of data limitations and the greater range of simplifying assumptions required to do it. That does not mean thus such issues can be safely put to the side in historical analysis. Fogel's work started a useful debate but was not an endpoint to it.

8.7 An Intermediate Reckoning

Was the Industrial Revolution a technological revolution primarily? Broadly speaking, yes, in that there were many inventions that were disseminated and applied with haste and force and scale and scope, and the resulting material environment was rather quickly unrecognisable from prior times after mere decades. The pace of invention gathered breakneck speed along with economic growth, at least as picked up by per capita GDP, in the "advanced" economies. Was the Industrial Revolution unique in terms of technological innovation? The results also suggest yes. But historians debate whether there were in fact earlier technological revolutions of similar breadth and depth, one leading candidate being the Middle Ages which witnessed a whole slew of new advances, under considerably different institutional, cultural and economic arrangements. Sapiens has certainly always been an innovating and materially manipulating animal across most of its existence. So the question may not be whether the Industrial Revolution was technological or not, but why it was so economically productive.

On that question it is clear that technology cannot be viewed in isolation from its larger social, economic, political and institutional milieu. Important changes occurred in this regard that quickened the quality and quantity of technological change into a critical mass that became the First Industrial Revolution and these changes in turn engendered socio-political alterations, all of which created the structure and productivity of the modern economy.

Was it worth it? As noted already, there was a rather constant social backlash to industrialisation with all its relentless pace and scale. The factory, and the laying of railway tracks through pristine countryside, the rapid growth of towns and cities, and the generally increasing impingement of human beings on the environment were noted by many contemporaries early on. Henry David Thoreau ([1845] 1917), in 1840s New England, living in isolation on Walden pond, wrote an entire book describing and criticising the changes that were already well advanced even in those relatively early times in a still relatively underdeveloped country. It is a tension explored in more detail in the next chapter.

References

Allen, R. C. (2009). The industrial revolution in miniature: The spinning jenny in Britain, France, and India. *The Journal of Economic History, 69*(4), 901–927.

Austen, R. A., & Headrick, D. (1983). The role of technology in the African past. *African Studies Review, 26*(3–4), 163–184.

Becker, S. O., Hornung, E., & Woessmann, L. (2011). Education and catch-up in the Industrial Revolution. *American Economic Journal: Macroeconomics, 3*(3), 92–126.

Carlos, A. M., & Frank, L. (1992). The profitability of early Canadian railroads: Evidence from the Grand Trunk and Great Western Railway Companies. In C. Goldin & H. Rockoff (Eds.), *Strategic factors in nineteenth century American economic history* (pp. 401–426). University of Chicago Press.

Chandler, A. D. (1977). *The visible hand.* University of Chicago Press.

Chandler, A. D. (1980). Industrial revolutions and institutional arrangements. *Bulletin of the American Academy of Arts and Sciences, 33*(8), 33–50.

Clark, G. (1994). Factory discipline. *Journal of Economic History, 54*(1), 128–163.

Coatsworth, J. H. (1981). *Growth against development: The economic impact of railroads in Porfirian Mexico.* Northern Illinois University Press.

David, P. A. (1969). Transportation innovations and economic growth: Professor Fogel on and off the rails. *Economic History Review, 22*(3), 506–525.

De Vries, J. (1994). The industrious revolution and the industrial revolution. *Journal of Economic History, 54*(2), 249–270.

Donaldson, D. (2018). Railroads of the Raj: Estimating the impact of transportation infrastructure. *American Economic Review, 108*(4–5), 899–934.

Elias, N. (1995). Technization and civilization. *Theory Culture and Society, 12*(3), 7–42.

Fogel, R. W. (1979). Notes on the social saving controversy. *Journal of Economic History, 39*(1), 1–54.

Galor, O. (2005). From stagnation to growth: Unified growth theory. In P. Aghion & S. N. Durlauf (Eds.), *Handbook of economic growth* (Vol. 1, Part A, pp. 171–293). Elsevier.

Goldsmith, H. (2014). *The long-run evolution of infrastructure services* (CESifo Working Paper, No. 5073). Center for Economic Studies and Ifo Institute (CESifo), Munich. http://hdl.handle.net/10419/105088

Goldstone, J. A. (1996). Gender, work, and culture: Why the industrial revolution came early to England but late to China. *Sociological Perspectives, 39*(1), 1–21.

Gordon, C. (2006). Assessing adequacy of America's transportation policies: Lessons from the debate about the role of railroads in the development of the American west. *Transportation Research Record, 1966*, 96–102.

Haldane, J. B. S. (1927). *Possible worlds and other essays.* Chatto and Windus.

Hawke, G. R. (1970). *Railways and economic growth in England and Wales 1840–1870.* Oxford University Press.

Jackson, R. V. (1977). *Australian economic development in the nineteenth century.* Australian National University Press.

Landes, D. S. (1969). *The unbound Prometheus: Technological change and development in Western Europe from 1750 to the present.* Cambridge University Press@.

Lebergott, S. (1966). United States transportation advance and externalities. *Journal of Economic History, 26*(4), 437–461.

Lichtheim, G. (1972). *Europe in the twentieth century.* Praeger Publishers.

McClelland, P. (1968). Railroads, American growth and the new economic history. *Journal of Economic History, 28*(1), 102–123.

Minge-, W. (1978). The Industrial Revolution and the European family: The institutionalization of childhood as a market for family labor. *Comparative Studies in Society and History, 20*(3), 454–468.

Mohajan, H. K. (2019). The first Industrial Revolution: Creation of a new global human era. *Journal of Social Sciences and Humanities, 5*(4), 377–387.

Mokyr, J. (1999). The Second Industrial Revolution, 1870–1914. In V. Castronovo (Ed.), *Storia dell'economia Mondiale* (pp. 219–245). Laterza Publishing.

Mokyr, J. (2009). *The enlightened economy: An economic history of Britain, 1700–1850* (pp. 83–84). Yale University Press.

Mokyr, J. (2016). *A Culture of growth: The origins of the modern economy.* Princeton University Press.

O'Brien, P. (1983). Transport and economic development in Europe, 1789–1914. In P. O'Brien (Ed.), *Railways and the economic development of Europe* (pp. 1830–1914). St. Martin's Press.

Polanyi, K. (1944). *The great transformation*. Beacon Press.

Ravazzoli, E., Streifeneder, T., & Cavallaro, F. (2017). The effects of the planned high-speed rail system on travel times and spatial development in the European Alps. *Mountain Research and Development, 37*(1), 131–140.

Rostow, W. W. (1960). *The stages of economic growth: A non-Communist manifesto*. Cambridge University Press.

Salomon, J. J. (1984). What is technology? The issue of its origins and definitions. *History and Technology, an International Journal, 1*(2), 113–156.

Sampson, A. (1995). *Company man: The rise and fall of corporate life*. Times-Business/Random House.

Schumpeter, J. ([1942] 1994). *Capitalism, socialism and democracy*. Routledge.

Sterman, J. D. (1986). The economic long wave: Theory and evidence. *System Dynamics Review, 2*(2), 87–125.

Thoreau, H. D. ([1845] 1917). Walden, or, life in the woods (Bowman, J. C., Ed.). Scott, Foresman and Company.

Unger, C. R. (2018). *International development: A postwar history*. Bloomsbury Publishing.

Williamson, J. G. (1974). *Late nineteenth-century American development: A general equilibrium history*. Cambridge University Press.

Williamson, J. G. (1975). The railroads and Midwestern development, 1870–1890. In D. C. Klingaman & R. K. Vedder (Eds.), *Essays in nineteenth century economic history*. University of Ohio Press.

CHAPTER 9

"1870"

C. Gordon, *Many Possible Worlds*,
https://doi.org/10.1007/978-981-19-9281-0_9

Fig. 9.1 Philadelphia: Centennial Photographic Co., 1876. Interior view of Machinery Hall (*Image source* and original notes "Machinery Hall was designed by Pettit and Wilson and constructed as one of the temporary buildings of the Centennial Exhibition. It showcased the technological advancements of the America's Second Industrial Revolution *from steam* and hydraulic power to electricity and the internal combustion engine. At the center of attention, the 56-ton flywheel of the Corliss Centennial Steam Engine drove a mile of shafting to provide steam power to exhibitors." P.2011.47.288 [Public Domain]. Raymond Holstein Stereograph Collection, library company of Philadelphia)

9.1 The Psychic Costs of Modernisation

In 1851, the Crystal Palace Exhibition opened in London. Fourteen years into Queen Victoria's long reign, this was a celebration of industry, showcasing the latest technology with all its flash and potential. Although the official title was the"Great Exhibition of the Works of Industry of all Nations", the show was really intended to celebrate Britain as excelling beyond competitor nations in both its economy and its growing Empire (King, 2007).

There had been prior commercial and industrial exhibitions but this was the largest to date. Moreover, the event was definitely not like traditional, practical and fast disappearing regional trade fairs. Those were mainly about conducting on-the-spot exchanges between normally distant buyers and sellers. Instead, the exhibition was designed as a mass spectacle celebrating the process of manufacturing in and of itself. Nothing on display was actually for sale. Rather the products shown were detached from their ultimate use value, presented as objects worthy of being spectated in their own right. It was an early homage to consumerism, the earliest of many such spectacles to come, (Fig. 9.1) providing a proving ground for the nascent mass advertising industry. The Crystal Palace was also a distant precursor of the shopping mall, employing a system of circulation that snaked entrants around exhibits in indirect ways to maximise the number of views while simultaneously speeding people along for maximum visitor throughput (Gardner, 2018) (Fig. 9.2).

The hall was novel in both its physical design and its construction process, the latter hurried between the date the idea of the exhibition was conceived of in 1849 and its opening set for a mere two years later. This ambitious deadline required mechanisation of as many of the building processes as possible. At its height 2,000 men were employed in the

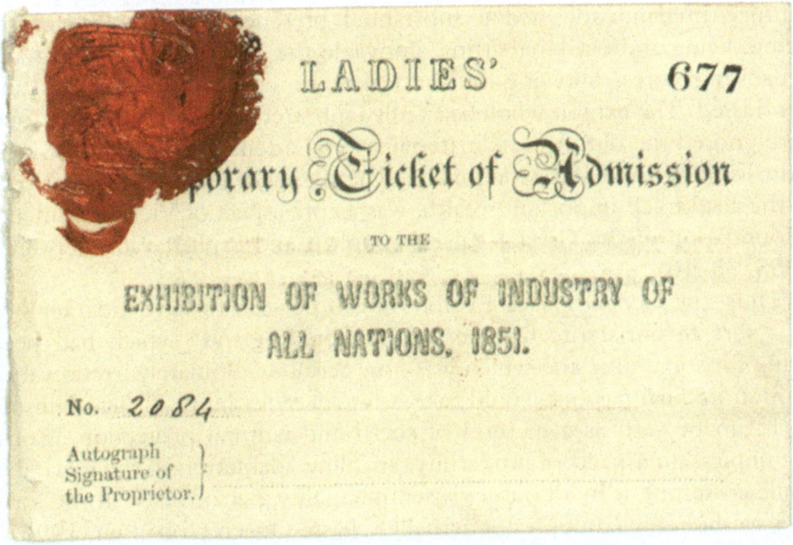

Fig. 9.2 "Ladies" admission ticket to the Crystal Palace Exhibition of 1851 (*Image source* The National Archives UK, Catalogue # BT 342/2 f.6. No known copyright restrictions)

construction work, which itself became a spectacle. During its run from May to October of 1851, over 6 million people had visited, and the event actually made money, against all expectations, in the process generating huge amounts of newspaper coverage and international publicity, another novelty of the whole process (King, 2007).

This triumphalism seemed justified, for Britain had an expanding Empire, a solidifying international political hegemony, strong economic growth and a new urban middle class, this last being the exhibition's main intended audience. Yet all this masked profound and disturbing social change. Britain was the first country in the world (outside of very small city-states and principalities of the past) to have a majority urban population, crossing this threshold at 50.1% in 1851, as compared to a 16.9% rate in 1800. Agricultural interests, both landlord and peasant, had not fared particularly well during this period, and their political influence was waning. As a result, agricultural protectionism would very soon be largely and finally eliminated after decades of battles over the issue (Briggs, 1955, 19–23).

This might have been a good time to reflect, especially since mid-century England still had a substantial presence of the old ways of being, living and working sitting alongside the newly industrialising and urbanising cores, allowing old and new to be visibly compared and contrasted. The exhibit wholeheartedly embraced and trumpeted the new and ignored the old. And its materialism and attendant consumerist individualism was loud and pronounced. The gospel of work, which was seen as the road to all-important wealth, was a core aspect of Victorianism and a foundation of the Crystal Palace's implicit and explicit values (Briggs, 1955, 35–40).

Thus, the Crystal Palace Exhibition can be seen to have a darker side as a sort of burial rite for the old "Green England" which had been dying for some time and which was now certainly ultimately irretrievable, though its final passing would take a few decades more. "Victorianism" itself can be seen as a method of social and cultural protection against the unpleasant aspects of modernity, enabling adaptation to the inevitable while cossetting it in a bourgeois sentimentality, personalised in the form of a symbolically (though not actually) chaste Queen (Johansen, 1996).

For amongst all the growth in English power and material well-being, the social, economic and intellectual changes of the period put immense pressure on individual psyches during this time. On the one hand, a lot was promised to, and expected of, the individual in this time of democracy and competition. Hard work promised status, comfort and power. But one had to work very hard indeed to keep from falling behind a constantly changing set of standards.

In 1859, Samuel Smiles published his book, *Self Help* that trumpeted self-reliance and hard work as the sure way to success. It was an idea bolstered by Political Economy (see Chapter 4), with its theories of market competition, complemented by its stepchild doctrine of Liberalism of limited government and maximal allowance of the pursuit of self-interest in all its forms. The book itself was remarkably successful, selling 20,000 copies in its first year, a number very large for its time and far beyond sales of other contemporary books, spawning an entire movement of "success" literature across the Western world. Yet, for all its apparent modernity, Smiles explicitly invoked self-help as a return to "old-fashioned…lessons" which, apparently, were being corroded by new policies, especially relief for the poor, that were judged as being a barrier to the forces of natural, competitive selection (Briggs, 1955, 116–119).

Darwin's *Origin of the Species* was also published in 1859, and implicitly offered similarly mixed social messages. The Enlightenment and the French Revolution had already secularised the default worldview of most Europeans, putting "man" at the centre of the world rather than "God". But this had the unintended emotional effect of putting more responsibility of the human being than many of them could handle, holding inevitable individual imperfection to an impossibly high standard with supernatural escape hatches now closed. Evolutionists (Darwin was not the first to use the idea, just the most systematic and empirical) had already been challenging even the earthly centrality of humanity. Now Darwin and those he inspired began the project of "Darwinism", the collation of ideas about the natural world inspired by Darwin, though not always in exact accord with his writings. "Social Darwinism" was the most influential offshoot, broadly holding that "natural selection" applied not only between species, as Darwin maintained, but within them as well, especially for the species known as Sapiens (Rogers, 1972). Humans were now estranged from, and in competition with, the natural biological world as well as the man-made social and economic one. In the face of this rapidly changing set of ideas, practices and conditions, "Self Help" was really the only possibility, even though it was far from a complete refuge from what Lichtheim (1972) has referred to as the psychic costs of industrialisation.

9.2 Material Modernisation in Europe

On the purely material front, things looked a lot more upbeat, at least from an overall average point of view. Materially England was in the forefront of European industrialisation, with Western Europe overall in global economic ascendancy by the time 1870 rolled around. The Maddison data indicate that European GDP was 46% of world GDP in 1870. Annual per capita GDP growth was 0.12% between 1720 and 1820; 0.86% between 1820 and 1870; and 1.22% between 1870 and 1920 (Carreras & Josephson, 2010, 32–34). Europe was rich and growing richer at an accelerating pace.

Table 9.1 provides comparative GDP per capita data for broad world regions (again derived from Maddison) for the period 1820–1870. These data show that white Europeans in Western Europe and their offshoot white settler colonies were becoming much wealthier relative to the rest of the world on a per person basis, arising from prodigious growth as compared to a now stagnant and declining East Asia.

The economic tide was rising, but it was not lifting all boats, even within Europe broadly defined. For one thing, the European "children" of the offshoots, were, as a group, outpacing their "parents" even by 1820, and the gap would only grow from there. The United States, which would surpass the UK in total GDP shortly after 1870, would be twice its size by 1913 (Carreras & Josephson, 2010, 32–33).

Meanwhile European continental "cores" and "peripheries" were developing, mirroring the same pattern across the rest of the world. In 1870, Eastern Europe's per capita GDP was less than half that of Western Europe's and there were further differences within these large groups and within countries themselves. Eastern and southern European countries were poorer, less industrialised and more agrarian than the western and central core. Spain and Portugal in particular, both once great powers, lagged considerably, while Russia was a chaotic mix of late economic modernisation in the cities and uneven growth in the countryside (Carreras & Josephson, 2010, 33–35).

But even the fortunate rich countries could not rest on their laurels. In 1815, the Netherlands still had the highest per capita GDP on the continent, but by the mid-1840s the UK had overtaken it. England would remain on the top for a couple of decades, after which German per capita GDP would overtake Britain's in 1908 (Carreras & Josephson, 2010, 35). Belgium, Switzerland and Denmark would all achieve their own stellar

Table 9.1 Regional averages of GDP per capita, 1820–1870 (US dollars at 1990 PPP [Purchasing Power Parity])

Decade	*Western Europe (WE)*	*Eastern Europe (EE)*	*Western Offshoots (WO)*	*Latin America and Caribbean (LA)*	*East Asia (EA)*	*South and South-East Asia (SSEA)*	*Middle East and North Africa (MENA)*	*Sub-Saharan Africa (SSA)*	*World*
1820	1,226	–	1,294	595	579	–	580	–	605
1830	1,344	–	1,489	–	–	–	–	–	–
1840	1,522	–	1,641	–	–	–	–	–	–
1850	1,589	–	1,809	–	599	–	–	–	706
1860	1,823	–	2,200	–	–	–	–	–	–
1870	1,976	719	2,421	754	543	516	720	–	837

Source Van Zanden et. al. (2014, Table 3.2)

growth at some time during the period 1870–1913. France, though prosperous and rich, was a growth laggard throughout the century (Carreras & Josephson, 2010, 44). To be rich was not synonymous with being secure in position on the economic ladder. "International competitiveness" had been born, in fact if not yet with that name.

Within "successful" nations there were winning and losing groups, reordering generally coming very fast given the dynamic turbulence of the growth process. Germany, only unified in 1871, was a case in point, being prosperous with a fast growing industrial region in the north, outpacing more rural areas in the south. The Austrian part of the Austro-Hungarian Empire grew more slowly than Germany and even France. But the Hungarian portion of the Empire was the most well-managed economy in Eastern Europe, though it suffered from the general agrarian crisis that afflicted most agricultural nations in the 1870s. Italy garnered a modest growth boost from political unification in 1861 but then grew very slowly before 1900 and with wide variation of wealth and income between its northern and southern halves (Carreras & Josephson, 2010, 44, 46–47).

9.3 The "Second" Industrial Revolution and the Role of the State

The latter half of the nineteenth century marks the beginning of the Second Industrial Revolution, typically said to have two phases, 1850–1870 and 1890–1914. Whereas the First Industrial Revolution, roughly running from 1780–1850, was driven heavily by the tinkering of inventors and process innovations by small businesses (such as the implementation of division of labour within new factories), by 1850 there was now an established socioeconomic complex called "Industry" of increasing complexity, scope and scale, becoming more systematic in its application of technical expertise and more and more applying scientific method, knowledge and research directly to production and distribution. Increasing proportions of national output were being produced and sold by large firms in markets that were becoming dominated by a few large players.

The first phase of this period was officially one of laissez-faire economics and a supposedly limited state. But strategic alliances between government and private sector were growing in number, and many businesses supported some sort of public regulation as a way to protect their market position, while also seeking direct and indirect public aid through tariffs, labour controls, and what would now be referred to as industrial policy (Stearns, 2001, Section V > B > 7).

Outside of the UK, many industrialising European states were recognising four planks of national industrial planning as a way of catching up with and overtaking the English: (1) creation of large domestic markets knitted together by transport investments (e.g. railroads) and the abolition of internal tariffs; (2) protection of domestic "infant industries" behind external tariff walls until these could viably be exposed to international (in this period read: British) competition; (3) establishment of domestic banking systems capable of stabilising the domestic currency and providing business with sufficient capital; and (4) establishment of mass education to skill up workers, enabling them to be more effective inputs into industrial production (Allen, 2011, 41–42).

Alexander Hamilton in America and Friedrich List of Germany made nationalist arguments for these policies based on overcoming initial inequalities in national bargaining power, maintaining, with a lot of truth, that Britain supported free trade because of its own massive bargaining advantages and market power (Graff et al., 2013). Landes (1969) characterises the period up to 1850 as one of "continental emulation", where European countries outside the UK were mainly copying English techniques in their protected "infant" manufacturing sectors. But by 1870, Continental industry could finally compete on an equal footing with England and then propel beyond her (Allen, 2009, 2). These "national" strategy packages were so effective in allowing countries to catch up to Britain by the end of the century that orthodox free trade policies began piecemeal to be rolled back everywhere, even in Britain, though still within a relatively liberal international economic framework (Allen, 2011, 41–42).

By 1870, it also became clear that manufacturing, while still essential, was only one part of the growth formula, especially as economies matured. Britain's role as the leading industrial nation became superseded by its role as shipper and financier in the latter part of the nineteenth century. It had a long way to go to the service economy of the late twentieth century, for the making and selling of goods still was the economic mainstay of development. But industrial production itself required new administration and other non-manufacturing activities such as consumer sales, marketing and distribution to support it, and services of various sorts were clearly going to be a growing part of the economic game (Stearns, 2001, Section V > B > 7).

Table 9.2 shows the shifts in the allocation of GNP for the major purposes of private consumption, government consumption and private capital in the larger and fastest growing economies of the second half of the nineteenth century. The data show that maturing economies required proportionately growing amounts of national output to be taken up by government expenditure for domestic purposes (e.g. defence, public works and education), and also investments by the private sector (mostly) for domestic capital formation. Total private consumption fell slightly as a share of national GNP. But since these economies were all growing, in absolute terms government spending, private investment and private consumption, all went up.

Table 9.2 Distribution of Gross National Product (GNP) by final use for selected countries (% share of GNP) last half of the nineteenth century (roughly)*

Country	*Time period*	*Private consumption*	*Government consumption*	*Gross domestic capital formation**
United Kingdom	1860–79	82.7	4.8	9.4
	1880–99	81.9	5.8	8.4
Germany^	1851–70	81.6	4.0	13.7
	1871–90	73.1	5.9	18.9
Italy	1861–80	87.3	4.2	10.0
	1881–1900	84.4	4.8	10.8
United States	1869–88	76.7	3.6	20.6
	1889–1908	73.6	4.4	21.4
Canada	1870 & 1890	86.5	5.6	15.2
	1890,1900,1910	82.1	7.4	18.5
Australia^^	1861–80	88.8		16.1
	1881–1900	90.0		17.1
Japan^^	1887–1906	92.0		10.1

Source Extracted from Kuznets (1966, Table 5.3, pp. 236–238)

Notes * Gross Domestic Capital Formation does not include capital imports or exports which will make Total Gross Capital Formation larger or smaller, depending on trade balance. For this reason, the percentages in this table will not add to 100% (though they do in the original table where the trade balance figures are included—excluded here for simplicity)

^German boundaries are as they existed during the periods in question

^^Australian and Japanese figures include only total consumption, not broken out between government and private

9.4 A Changing World of Work and Lifestyle

Adam Smith had written of the productivity advances that the division of labour would make possible. But even he admitted that this required people to perform a few simple operations over and over again, making them ultimately "as stupid and ignorant as it is possible to be for a human creature to become" (quoted in Mokyr et al., 2015, 38). The price of ever more material output was thus a radical change in class structure and human working life and arrangements. By 1870, these processes were well in train, with more to follow. There are several dimensions especially important during this period: organisation of work and production; hours of work; payment for work (i.e. wages); and changes in the general "standard of living".

9.4.1 *Work Organisation*

The mechanisation of the First Industrial Revolution was, at first, relatively limited in its impact on work. This was not only because it took time for new ways of doing things to diffuse through the economy, but also because of the nature of technical change at the time, which initially could only replace or impact a limited number of human activities. Indeed, division of labour at first was mainly about alterations to process than to technology. Adam Smith's pin factory example, it should be noted, did not employ new inventions, but just broke production into discrete tasks divvied out to specialised workers.

During the First Industrial Revolution, there were fears that displaced workers would be permanently unemployed and, now deprived of the former relative self-sufficiency of household production, subject to starvation as well. This was the basis for the outbreaks of machine smashing in England by the Luddites and others, conducted as a pre-emptive strike by labourers to keep the machines from gaining a foothold. It was a futile endeavour and, as it turned out, unnecessary as there ended up being (in general) more jobs available rather than fewer because of industrialisation, simply because growth accelerated thus boosting total employment. However, the categories and nature of work were transforming. The number of jobs available for craftsmen declined, but new positions as mechanics to fix the new machines, workers in the new factories and supervisors to oversee them more than took their place in number. As industrialisation picked up steam (no pun intended) and as the Second Industrial Revolution began, organisational changes created new categories of work, such as accountants and clerks employed by large-scale enterprises operating on an unprecedented scale. At the same time, dynamic product innovation and technological change created entirely new sectors for the economy, such as chemicals. This growing abundance of employment eventually ended most discussion of the so-called "machinery question", which was shorthand for the concern that technical improvement would permanently displace workers by the late nineteenth century (Mokyr et al., 2015, 36).

But just because people could generally find jobs (when there was not a recessionary period, and assuming that they were able-bodied, that is), this did not mean that they would like doing them. The shift to machines imposed a new discipline on production labour, the devices setting the pace, with human beings having to conform to unnatural, and sometimes inhuman, rhythms, subject to directive oversight by floor overseers who themselves were managed by increasingly technical performance-oriented hierarchies. This was an extension of the human–machine synchronisation of work that had begun with the invention and diffusion of the clock, carried to greater and greater extremes (Minge-Kalman, 1978).

The First Industrial Revolution witnessed the rise of factory discipline and the Industrious Revolution (see Chapter 5) helped along by the interrelated developments of geographical centralisation of production, the use of factories to organise work and the imposition of labour control within factories, all of which gained intensity and breadth as the 1800s unfolded. Economists generally explain these developments as most probably driven by the nature of technical change which introduced increasing returns to scale that could only be realised by spatial concentration of activity, and enhanced further by tight work routines. This, in turn, made the remaining home-based, and very small-scale craft production, uneconomical. For many workers, this meant unemployment and the rendering of an existing set of household assets, such as tools, land and animals, suddenly obsolete and nearly worthless. But from a system perspective, this released further labour resources into the factory-industrial system. There is debate about the relative contribution to productivity of factory labour force concentration and activity versus factory discipline, with some (particularly Marxists) emphasising the importance of the latter, neoclassical economists tending to emphasise the former (Mokyr, 1999, 104–105). Whichever may be the case, the nature of work dramatically changed with the expansion of industrialisation.

Division of labour was a set of interrelated processes closely related to scale and labour control. Varying degrees of skill were involved depending upon the task division employed, and for some jobs there might be a high level of training for technical specialist roles. For many others, training and skill were minimal, though a certain habituation was required to stay in place for fixed times doing repetitive work which gave those experienced at it some premium and protection since a "green" replacement would likely be much less productive for a good period of time. Routine and repetition itself might have independently contributed to productivity by lowering training and management costs and increasing speed of throughput. But it also separated groups of workers from one another by sorting different skill sets into different "comparative advantage" groups. Such specialisation meant that workers could completely master their given tasks more easily than a larger set of related actions and thus become even more efficient at them as well as ensuring a better matching of innate skill sets to tasks best suited to them (Mokyr, 1999, 107–108).

The net effect was a labour ecosystem that offered plenty of opportunities for employment overall, but with the mass of jobs at the lowest levels essentially making workers cogs in a greater machine. The productivity advantages were enormous, and there was sufficient dynamism that many new and interesting work categories arose along with the drudgery. But working life in general was now more standardised, regimented and fragmented than it ever had been before.

9.4.2 Hours and Wages and "Standard of Living"

Certainly, the imposed discipline required to work in factories, and, with the Second Industrial Revolution, offices, was not a natural default for human beings and arguably it required as much management innovation as it did new physical technology. Workers resisted this trend in many places in many ways, which is one reason that supposedly more docile and pliable women and children were brought in to factory work. More positive inducements were offered in the form of both incentive payments (which were used to varying degrees by factory owners in conjunction with discipline) and, of course, higher wages (Mokyr, 1999, 112).

Wages were rising generally along with per capita GDP. But were wages keeping up in real terms? Data are fragmentary and tend to be available only for particular categories of workers in particular countries at particular times, usually for more skilled and specialised ones, such as in the building trades and other professions that are likely to be on the higher end of the wage scale (OECD 2014). It is thus hard to be definitive but the rough consensus amongst economic historians is that wage growth was relatively slow in Europe until 1830/40 and that workers were not fully compensated in the form of wage payments for increases in their productivity (Crafts 2020). However, wage growth did pick up after that, on average, though the firm owners still generally pocketed more of the productivity gains in profit growth than the workers obtained through wage growth.

One also has to take into account how many hours per day were spent in work, and what level of subjective well-being was experienced. If industrial workers had more leisure time and/or better living conditions than before, this may be at least a partial compensation for stagnating pay packets. Again, available information on hours and standard of living is patchy and has the additional problem of being resistant to good measurement in the first place. Overall, though, the picture until mid-century is not particularly good for European workers, with the growth rates in their consumption of market goods seemingly very slow, and the disamenity costs of industrialisation (crowding, pollution, discipline etc.) growing. Some make the counterpoint that productivity increases were more than compensating for these "bads" with the "goods" of more availability of quantity, quality and variety of food, and improvements in housing. But this is a minority view, especially since working hours appear to have been rising too until around 1850, probably negating the impact of consumer benefits (Mokyr et al., 2015, 36). During the First Industrial Revolution, European adults are thought to have toiled on average more than 3,200 hours per year, high by the standards of human history. While working hours were not short in 1750, they increased by approximately 20% to 35% over the following hundred years (Baumard, 2019, 223–224). Gilmore (2021) has assembled a rather comprehensive database indicating that workers in manufacturing worked 60 to 90 hours per week in the nineteenth century, with declines to the current modern average of around 40 hours today taking place between 1920 and 1970 or so.

In sum, workers living during the First Industrial Revolution saw rapid change around them but relatively modest improvement, and sometimes deterioration, of their economic lot in life and their subjective experience of it. However, the start of the Second Industrial Revolution seems to bring about a positive change in fortune, at least for many European workers. For one thing, there was a growing amount of work available in relatively cushy office environments rather than factories, though the drudgery and toil of labour in the office should not be underestimated, as recounted in Charles Dickens' autobiographical *Sketches by Boz* (1836–1837), describing the unending routine, working with little break and getting paid very little for the effort (Sampson, 1995, 52).

Also, after 1850 technological improvements increasingly filtered down to consumers and urban residents in the form of a growing array of cheap consumer goods and delivery of new urban services. By the end of the century, modern life was closer to what we know today, with at least some people in some cities enjoying clean running water, central sewerage systems and proper home heating. All this created a growing urban middle class that was more comfortable than ever before in material (though not necessarily social) terms.

9.5 A Changing World of Home and Family

These trends in work were accompanied by significant changes to the family and the household. The pre-industrial household used to be a largely autarkic food and home goods producer, as well as the primary place of socialisation across most of the population. With industrialisation, it now shifted mostly to being a provider of labour input and consumption to an industrial economy, socialisation itself now being sourced out to mass processes of government (through public education) and the floors of factories and offices. This changed family size and structure and child-rearing practice dramatically, extending middle-class childhood from age five or six to age fifteen or sixteen, or even further for those families sending their children to university, since children no longer went to work when they were physically able to do so. The whole concept of adolescence, with parents supporting offspring after childhood but with a delayed onset of adulthood, could be said to be a product of the industrial revolution. Indeed, "childhood" itself now became a more formal standardised social institution with more rigid distinctions from adulthood (Minge-Kalman, 1978, 462–463).

This era also witnessed the birth of the "capitalist patriarchy". Patriarchy, in the form of male-dominated social, political and economic structures, was nothing new, characterising Western and many non-Western societies for centuries. But the imperatives of mass production, with its separation of work from home, and family from economic output, changed it in particular and peculiar ways. The term has a very specific meaning, referring to the housebound nuclear family, with the male head of household out most days earning money, and the women left to tend house and children, and with very strict gender roles extending out into the rest of society (Hart, 2016). This development was not entirely economically driven, and was often filtered through a unique cultural lens (e.g. in England in took the form of Victorianism, a rather complex set of mores, values and practices). And it applied less to the toiling classes in which often all members of the family had to work, including the female, though there was still gender-typing of household work, with women having to care for children and home, even if they also had to work for wages. Still it was heavily shaped by industrialisation as it unfolded.

The imposition of mass compulsory public schooling was another development that was unprecedented in human history and which played a part in the formation of nuclear family households. Social and political elites had always provided formal schooling for their own children and mission-based institutions, especially churches, provided religious and other education for its members. But mass education had never been a State role and most people were not exposed to formal education before the Industrial Revolution. However, the need for "human capital" improvement (as we would put it now) was soon seen as an essential ingredient for industrial success, and business interests were soon on board with making it a new government function. Mass education now had an economic justification, and social arrangements were permanently transformed as a result of its widespread implementation (Becker et al., 2011).

One other thing that was affecting home and family life was the state's role in enforcing public health. Public health as a discipline was born with the Industrial Revolution, because industrialisation led to unprecedented levels of workplace and residential densities that, together with pollution of air and water, caused new and regular outbreaks of epidemic disease. An industrial economy, unlike an agrarian one, could not simply ride out mass death and morbidity without being overturned entirely. Thus, an understanding of disease aetiology and rapid corrective and preventive action were both needed and only the State could fill the gap.

The United Kingdom, being a leader in industry, was also a leader in public health. In 1853, vaccination of infants was made compulsory, building on a voluntary vaccination act in 1840 and bolstered by further vaccination acts in 1858, 1867 and 1871 that stipulated various fines and terms of imprisonment for parents who failed to immunise their children. Meanwhile in 1855, the Nuisances Removal and Disease Prevention Act allowed local authorities to force property owners to remove public health dangers at the expense of the property owners involved, if they refused to cooperate. There was a concomitant rise of a temperance movement in the 1850s as well which successfully pushed for Acts in 1854 and 1864 that progressively restricted the hours that pubs could operate on Sunday (Stearns, 2001, Section V > B. > 7. > b.) Though not a public health measure per se (and not especially successful at combatting alcoholism), these acts began to deemphasise the pub as a complete centre of social life and together with various mandates on public health marked the rise of a middle class view of social probity, along with a more medicalised view of the care of self and others. The rise of a professional medical class and a health industry that was to become an authority for families and households, displacing folk methods and home care, had well and truly begun.

9.6 A Globalising Economy

By 1870 movements of people, goods and capital had all grown prodigiously and these volumes would accelerate between 1870 and 1914, driven by vast increases in output and aided and abetted by falling international and domestic freight rates by way of the various technical advances and infrastructure investments. International trade policy by 1870 was officially Liberal, one of minimal tariff barriers and various free-trade areas within the European empires especially. There was also increasing international capital mobility, i.e. the ability to move money easily between political jurisdictions. Here public–private institution building was important, as with local currency unions such as the Latin Monetary Union and the Scandinavian Monetary Union. The most significant development was the international Gold Standard and the increasing dominance of the English Pound Sterling as a unit of account and settlement for international trade. These developments allowed for cheaper, easier and more secure completion of international transactions between traders, and also greatly facilitated investment of rich country capital surpluses into peripheral deficit countries (Daudin et al., 2010).

The Gold Standard, coordinated by the Bank of England, essentially forced many countries to peg their currencies to a gold price determined in London. Although supposedly a neutral allocation mechanism, the system also had a highly political component, playing a big role in transfers of goods and capital often biased towards the British Empire and the European core. It also required active coordination across national central banks, despite the pretence of being automatically self-regulating, resulting in interventions that were sometimes in the interest of the overall system but not always (Eichengreen & Flandreau, 1997). The peripheral countries often did benefit from inflows of capital for needed social investment projects. But these were often at unfavourable terms and always contained the threat that such money could as quickly flow out as it flowed in.

These systemic innovations increased international price convergence of raw commodity and industrial goods prices across the world. That is, gaps between prices of commodities in geographically separated markets narrowed and synchronised more and more quickly because movement of goods across markets became less encumbered due to cheaper transport, easier finance and, for a time, lowered tariff and other trade barriers. A series of local markets was slowly being cleaved into one global market, and the process was well in place by 1870 (Daudin et al., 2010).

One can look at this process of world economy integration in purely "Smithian" and "Ricardian" terms, i.e. as an international division of labour across countries and regions based on increasing specialisation in production, with "free" trade filling gaps that could not be domestically met, and capital flowing to the most productive activities and areas. While countries had always traded with others for what they could not produce themselves, industrialisation and economic integration made trade a core component of all domestic economies. Most peripheral countries now became reliant on one or a few export goods for much of their national income, while even the advanced economies of the time became specialised in highly profitable exports of their own.

Cotton is one prime example of how this worked. The growing of raw cotton and its manufacture into textiles went from a globally dispersed enterprise done mostly as a cottage industry in the eighteenth century, to a scale industry with a few majors centres of raw production (primarily India and the "cotton south" of the United States) and a few major processors (mainly Britain). In 1770, cotton manufacturing in Britain made up just 2.6% of the value added in the economy as a whole; by 1801, the figure was 17%; and by 1831, 22.4%. Productivity of the cotton industry exploded, as did trade in its various wares, such as finished cloth (Beckert, 2015).

These wages of internationalisation were, however, not entirely sanguine or certainly not particularly neutrally efficient allocative mechanisms. For one thing, imperialism was growing apace with globalisation, with generally deleterious effects on the colonised (see Chapter 13). Nowhere was this clearer than with cotton where British colonisation of India forced that country into a junior, and much exploited, role within the international cotton supply chain, to say nothing of the major role that slavery played in the building and maintaining of the global industry until well past mid-century, the slave-based "Cotton South" of America being especially important (Beckert, 2015). All this belies that notion that the global economy, in cotton and much else, was simply an outgrowth of "natural" economic forces and incentives that allocated resources to their most efficient uses. One can rightly debate the relative roles of institutional and systemic equilibrating forces, but both are clearly in play.

Similarly, price convergences, particularly in India, but also in China, were driven in part by forced exports of local goods at locally unfavourable rates and in return for highly priced manufactures sold to captive imperial markets. At times, food exports out of colonised areas occurred during times of local famine and drought, leading to disastrous consequences for the locals. As but one example, grain surpluses in the US were burned in 1877–1878 because of low international prices, while starvation reigned elsewhere on the planet. This phenomenon was repeated many times over throughout the world and was especially acute in China, India and Brazil (Davis, 2002). One might add that price synchronisation could transmit price volatility as easily as smoothing it, the former increasing as the century progressed and often ruinous to local producers and distributors if the changes came too sharply and quickly.

Colonialism was also as much a reducer of unfettered trade as it was an increaser of it; or at least it diverted much trade to channels that were not always the most efficient ones, but those most favourable to colonial powers. On the one hand, within Empires, country boundaries were almost literally eliminated for trade and investment purposes as far as the metropolitan was concerned. But economic boundary permeability could be adjusted at will by colonial masters to suit themselves rather than the local populace in the provinces. And trade between Empires became less free between 1870 and 1914 when protectionism made something of a comeback within Europe (O'Rourke, 1997, 2000). Indeed, there is some indication that globalisation made more progress before 1870 than after it (see Uebele, 2011; Tena-Junguito et al., 2012; Chilosi & Federico, 2015), Federico & Tena-Junguito, 2017). Imperial rivalries contributed to this strategic hardening. The colonies were generally the losers in the strategic bargain (Hodgart, 1977; Davis 2002).

The increasing integration of world markets also brought the modern business cycle to the worldwide fore. Economics-driven feasts and famines were nothing new in human history, but they were generally closely tied to natural cycles, such as changes in the weather, crop yields, incidence of disease or to geological tumults like earthquakes (De Boer & Sanders 2005). Of course, wars were a constant factor in economic ups and downs. The notion that the human economy itself would create cycles all its own was not entirely modern, but the prominence of such dynamics was.

Thus, the Industrial Revolution brought prosperity but also major economic downturns and upturns occurring regularly, driven by the "normal" operations of the economy more than particular natural disruptions like crop failures. Even where there were "exogenous" disruptions, such as adverse weather events, their local impacts often were heightened and internationalised via interconnected capital and goods markets that were further magnified by the inherent and recurrent instability of a modernising financial system. Financial crises existed before industrialisation, with major financial market and institution failures happening in the 1500s and 1600s, the South Sea Bubble and "Tulipmania" in Holland being oft-cited examples. But now finance was much more sophisticated and efficient at moving sums around between markets, a generally good thing as far as production and trade was concerned, but also causing severe disruptions at times when speculative capital flowed into too freely, created artificial booms or, worse, flowed out suddenly, creating artificial busts (Kindleberger & Aliber, 2005).

All this corresponded with an increase in the movements of people. In the 1820s, free immigration to the Americas, to take a major destination for Europeans, averaged 15,380 people per annum, one quarter of them slave inflows. By the 1840s, the average annual numbers were 178,530, four times that caused by the slave trade (some flow continuing there despite the outlawing of the trade by various countries, most notably the UK and the US in the early nineteenth century) (Daudin 2010, 13). Growth in international migration from Europe to the rest of the world would increase throughout the century but with significant periodic domestic political backlashes in some places, especially the United States. Like trade protection, migration was opened up until around the nineteenth century's end when it was tightened up along nationalist and chauvinistic lines in the industrial core. These movements did in part reflect people grabbing better opportunities thrown up by economic growth, and were beneficial in that way. But they also were caused by the dislocations of that same growth and helped create turmoil and dislocation of its own (see Chapter 16).

9.7 The "Concert of Europe" in 1870

The first half of the eighteenth century had been difficult for Europe. The region had begun the century in the throes of a power struggle between England and France that was ended with the former's decisive victory and the imposition of a restoration "Concert of Europe" and an attendant "Balance of Power" between "Great Nations" in 1815. This order had never been particularly stable, shaken by revolutionary waves in 1830 and 1848, and it continued to teeter and rock after that on the twin waves of economic transformation and political change, domestically and internationally (see Chapter 6).

One major problem for the system was the decaying Ottoman Empire, which had been declining for a couple of hundred years. This had been handled in the eighteenth century by direct extension of Hapsburg and Romanov dynasties into the former Ottoman lands. But in the nineteenth century, this dynastic solution was a less acceptable default in an age of democracy, liberalism, nationalism and capitalism. The solution of the creation of minor national states such as Serbia seemed a reasonable response, but soon proved worse than the disease it was brought in to cure given the instability they contributed to (Roberts, 2000, 38).

Another challenge was Russia's decline, which outwardly still appeared formidable, but whose weakness became more obvious with each military defeat it suffered after its turning back the existential threat of the Napoleonic invasion. Most notable was Russia's loss in the Crimean War, ironically fought to preserve the Ottoman Empire and hence the Balance of Power. Russia took away from that experience that it had to modernise to preserve its Great Power status. Thus, in 1863, the Tsar decreed the emancipation of the serfs. This was not a full-blooded effort but it did indicate that staying in the past was no longer an option for the government (Roberts, 2000, 33–34). Russia, the Ottomans and Austria-Hungary were all isolated from the European mainstream, all being states with antiquated social and political structures, and restive but largely subservient masses. However, by 1870, they all had become set on the path of (late) industrialisation, with social, economic and political change being dictated, with mixed success, from above.

Meanwhile, Italian and German unification were both complete by 1870. The traditional narrative has been these developments were also driven by elites, not masses. Italian unification was heavily influenced by the industrial and new bourgeoisie of the country's north seeing advantage in bringing together a weak disparate collection of principalities (Riall, 2002), while in Germany the process was driven by Prussian expansionism, led by conservative and militaristic landowners known as the Junkers (Showalter, 2015). However, more recent scholarship suggests mass participation and changes in mass politics were as, or more important than, considerations of elites or economy (Banti, 2020; Riall, 2002). Either way the German effort was most successful economically and geopolitically, the newly unified country quickly becoming a military and economic powerhouse. Prussia, defeating France quickly and decisively in the Franco-Prussian War of 1870–1871, proclaimed the German Empire immediately afterwards.

All this ferment resulted in a rebalancing of the French, Prussian and Austrian spheres of interest in their Italian neighbour and between themselves, Austria being on the losing end in both cases. Italy was slow growing but now a single political unit with some potential. Russia was weak, and its weakness would be further exposed as the century turned over into a new one, but it remained an integral part of the Balance of Power. The Ottoman decline was awakening old passions and rivalries in the Balkans, but these were being managed in what seemed to be a relatively orderly fashion by the Great Powers.

In 1870, although the Concert of Europe had been considerably shaken up and re-formed in ways that could not have been anticipated in 1815, it seemed as if general peace, joined by economic growth and prosperity, had been achieved on the Continent. There were some costs to this process, especially in the wars that were fought to adjust it, obviously losses to the national economies that lost territory corresponding to gains by those than won them (France's loss of Alsace-Lorraine was rather major, and it is surprising in some ways that the French economy nonetheless performed rather solidly afterwards). None of this, though, seemed to stop the ongoing process of growth, and it was hoped that both economy and polity could be managed to keep on an upward trajectory (Fig. 9.3).

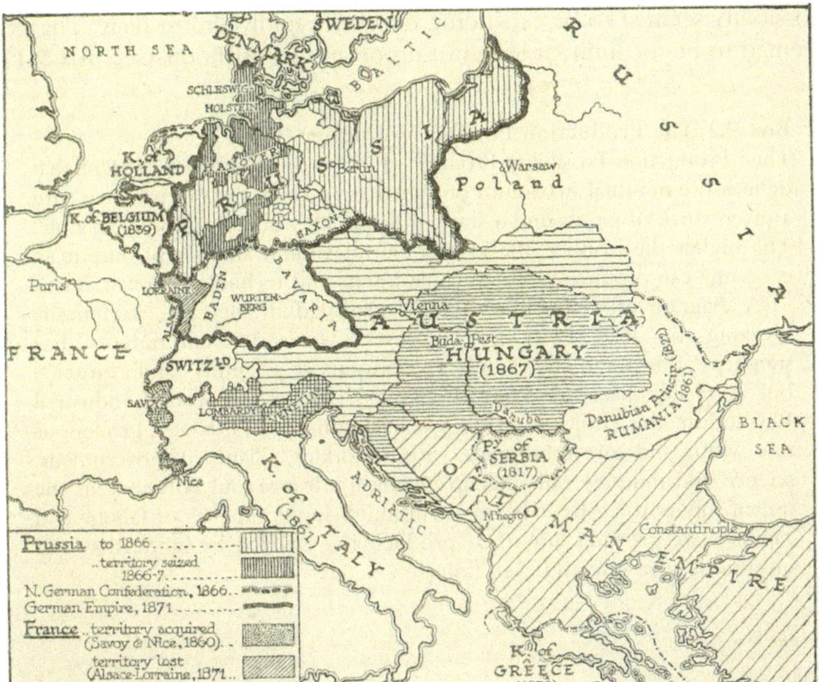

Fig. 9.3 The Concert of Europe circa 1870 (*Image source* Wells, H. G. & Horrabin, J. F. [1920]. The outline of history: Being a plain history of life and mankind. Cassell. Page 310. Contributing Library: University of California Libraries Digitizing Sponsor: MSN)

9.8 The "Production Possibility Frontier"

In 1870, one could truly say that an age of constant productivity improvement had arrived. Productivity, roughly defined as the rate of change in output yielded per unit of a given input (or set of inputs, in which case one refers to Total Factor Productivity—TFP), was certainly exploding in the Second Industrial Revolution. Pre-industrial times were closely constrained by supplies of available capital, land, labour and raw materials, with technical improvements causing some sharp temporary shifts in productivity now and again. But in this era, the frontier of economic possibility seemed to be expanding outward rapidly almost daily. The sky seemed to be the limit, at least in Europe and its offshoots (see Box 9.1).

Box 9.1 The Production Possibility Frontier (PPF)

The "Production Possibility Frontier—PPF" is an economics concept that defines the notional maximum output that an economy can produce with a given stock of inputs and a state of technology at a given point in time. The higher the frontier, the greater the maximum amount of output an economy can produce given available inputs and technology constraints

A diagram of a simplified PPF is provided in Fig. 9.4. Technically speaking, the PPF shows a "choice set" across different outputs. For simplicity, this graph shows only two outputs (e.g. "guns" and "butter") but in reality there are many thousands. During the Second Industrial Revolution, this choice set (PPF) kept shifting outwards at a prodigious rate within the core economies, with a working alliance of government, science and industry ramping up technical advance and efficiency in the use of inputs to make it happen. Although input supplies of labour and capital were growing fast, their productivity, enabled by innovation and invention, were growing even faster.

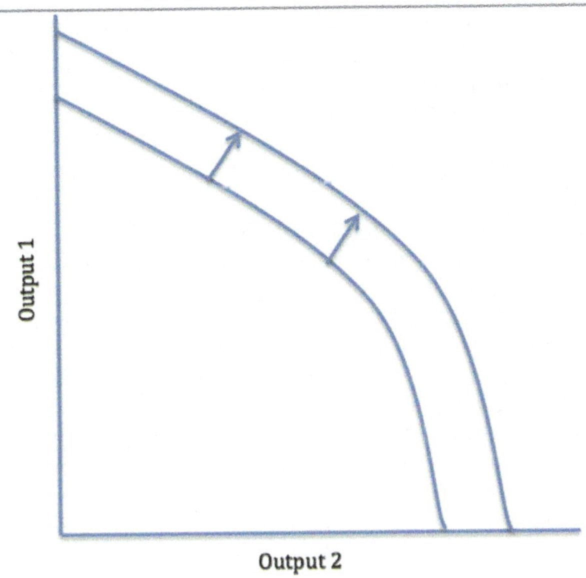

Fig. 9.4 The "Production Possibility Frontier" (PPF) (Created by author)

Because of this material progress, there were those who felt that the past problems of distribution were now superseded by the promises of endless production growth without any increase in hours worked per person (and possibly even a reduction in such hours), pushed ever forward by the genie of technological advance. The rapid social, cultural and political changes accompanying material growth could not be so easily wished away or dealt with. And some truly awful things were happening in parts of the periphery. Nonetheless, for those living with the core, things looked hopeful indeed.

References

Allen, R. C. (2009). *The British industrial revolution in global perspective*. Cambridge University Press.

Allen, R. C. (2011). *Global economic history: A very short introduction*. Oxford University Press.

Banti, A. M. (2020). *The nation of the Risorgimento: Kinship, sanctity, and honour in the origins of unified Italy*. Routledge.
Baumard, N. (2019). Psychological origins of the industrial revolution. *Behavioral and Brain Sciences, 42*, e189.
Becker, S. O., Hornung, E., & Woessmann, L. (2011). Education and catch-up in the Industrial Revolution. *American Economic Journal: Macroeconomics, 3*(3), 92–126.
Beckert, S. (2015). *Empire of cotton: A global history*. Vintage.
Briggs, A. (1955). *Victorian people: A reassessment of persons and themes, 1851–1867*. University of Chicago Press.
Carreras, A. & Josephson, C (2010). Chapter 2: Aggregate growth, 1870–1914: Growing at the production frontier. In S. Broadberry, & K. H. O'Rourke (Eds.), *The Cambridge economic history of modern Europe: Volume 2, 1870 to the present*. Cambridge University Press.
Chilosi, D., & Federico, G. (2015). Early globalizations: The integration of Asia in the world economy, 1800–1938. *Explorations in Economic History, 57*, 1–18.
Crafts, N. (2020). *Slow real wage growth during the industrial revolution: productivity paradox or pro-rich growth?* Warwick Economics Research Papers #1268 (May).
Daudin, G., Morys, M., & O'Rourke, K. H. (2010). Globalization, 1870–1914. In S. Broadberry & K. H. O'Rourke (Eds.), *The Cambridge economic history of modern Europe: Volume 2, 1870 to the present* (pp. 5–29). Cambridge University Press.
Davis, M. (2002). *Late Victorian holocausts: El Niño famines and the making of the third world*. Verso Books.
De Boer, J. Z. & Sanders, D. T. (2005). *Earthquakes in human history: The far-reaching effects of seismic disruptions*. Princeton University Press.
Eichengreen, B., & Flandreau, M. (1997). *Gold standard In theory & history* (2nd ed.). Routledge.
Federico, G., & Tena-Junguito, A. (2017). A tale of two globalizations: Gains from trade and openness 1800–2010. *Review of World Economics, 153*(3), 601–626.
Gardner, J. (2018). Beneath the rubble, the Crystal Palace! The surprising persistence of a temporary mega event. *World Archaeology, 50*(1), 185–199.
Gilmore, O. (2021). *The working week in manufacturing since 1820*. OECD.
Graff, M., Kenwood, A. G., & Lougheed, A. L. (2013). *Growth of the international economy, 1820–2015*. Routledge.
Hart, M. (2016). Capitalist patriarchy. In A. Wong, R. Wickramasinghe, R. Hoogland, & N. A. Naples (Eds.), *The Wiley Blackwell encyclopedia of gender and sexuality studies.*
Hodgart, A. (1977). *The economics of European imperialism*. Edward Arnold.

Johansen, S. (1996). The Great Exhibition of 1851: A precipice in time? *Victorian Review, 22*(1), 59–64.

Kindleberger, C. & Aliber, R.Z. (2005). *Manias, panics, and crashes: A history of financial crises* (5th ed.). Wiley.

King, E. (2007). The Crystal Palace and Great Exhibition of 1851. *British Library Newspapers*. Gale.

Kuznets, S. (1966). *Modern economic growth: Rate, structure and spread*. Yale University Press.

Landes, D. S. (1969). *The unbound Prometheus: Technological change and development in Western Europe from 1750 to the present*. Cambridge University Press.

Lichtheim, G. (1972). *Europe in the twentieth century*. Praeger Publishers.

Minge-Kalman, W. (1978). The Industrial Revolution and the European family: The institutionalization of childhood as a market for family labor. *Comparative Studies in Society and History, 20*(3), 454–468.

Mokyr, J. (1999). Editor's introduction: The new economic history and the Industrial Revolution. In J. Mokyr (Ed.), *The British industrial revolution: An economic perspective* (2nd ed., pp. 1–127). Westview Press.

Mokyr, J., Vickers, C., & Ziebarth, N. L. (2015). The history of technological anxiety and the future of economic growth: Is this time different? *Journal of Economic Perspectives, 29*(3), 31–50.

O'Rourke, K. H. (1997). The European grain invasion, 1870–1913. *The Journal of Economic History, 57*(4), 775–801.

O'Rourke, K. H. (2000). Tariffs and growth in the late 19th century. *The Economic Journal, 110*(463), 456–483.

Riall, L. (2002). *The Italian Risorgimento: State, society and national unification*. Routledge.

Roberts, J. (2000). Revolution from above and below. In T. C. Blanning (Ed.), *The Oxford history of modern Europe* (pp. 15–45). Oxford University Press.

Rogers, J. A. (1972). Darwinism and social Darwinism. *Journal of the History of Ideas, 33*(2), 265–280.

Sampson, A. (1995). *Company man: The rise and fall of corporate life*. Times-Business/Random House.

Showalter, D. (2015). *The wars of German unification*. Bloomsbury Publishing.

Stearns, P. N. (2001). *The encyclopedia of world history* (6th ed.). Houghton Mifflin Company.

Tena-Junguito, A., Lampe, M., & Fernandes, F. T. (2012). How much trade liberalization was there in the world before and after Cobden-Chevalier? *The Journal of Economic History, 72*(3), 708–740.

Uebele, M. (2011). National and international market integration in the 19th century: Evidence from comovement. *Explorations in Economic History, 48*(2), 226–242.

Van Zanden, J. L., Baten, J., Mira d'Ercole, M., Rijpma, A., Smith, C., & Timmer, M. (2014). *How was life? Global well-being since 1820*. OECD Publishing.

CHAPTER 10

La Belle Époque

C. Gordon, *Many Possible Worlds*,
https://doi.org/10.1007/978-981-19-9281-0_10

Fig. 10.1 "En Famille" (*Image source* From *Le Monde moderne* [1895]. The Centre for 19th Century French Studies—University of Toronto. Digitising Sponsor: University of Ottawa//External-identifier: urn:oclc:record:848128196. Public domain)

10.1 "The Beautiful Epoch"—For Some

Reminiscence is usually sweeter than the actual time lived through at the time. So it is with the "Belle Epoque", referring to a specific time in French history, but more generally denoting a sort of Indian Summer of European ascendancy in culture, society and economy. Starting in 1870 (1880, 1890 and even 1900 are alternative initial demarcations), it ended definitively in 1914 with the start of the First World War. It was a far from easy time to live through. But in comparison to the horrors of World War, it appeared as a veritable heaven (Fig. 10.1).

Or so it was if you were a European, and one of the fortunate middle or upper classes living in one of the fortunate countries there. This was a time of global conflict, rampant imperialism, business cycle fluctuation, mass migration, and social unrest, especially intense in what would later become known as the developing world. But for the relatively rich in economically favoured locations, riding their upward crest of the wave of "Great Divergence", existence entailed steadily growing personal wealth, income, technological and cultural amenity, and the building of impressive public works.

Granted, even for these lucky few it could be disorienting to contend with the rise of mass culture and mass society. Although the level of urban physical comfort was attaining levels that would be superficially familiar to us today, the sheer pace of change provided a background tension and uncertainty that was not easy to bear. Class positions were tenuous. What was gained could quickly be lost.

Partly for these reasons, and also because material pursuits were becoming the main social activity, modern escapism through tourism, spectacle, and print media grew up to meet the natural human needs for belonging, security and diversion. In visual art, Impressionism, with its emphasis on new forms of colour and light, combined provocative experimentation with a dreamy romanticism, emblematic of an age that was always moving forward but seeking to recreate the comforts of an imagined more organic past.

In the European core, economic growth rolled on. European GDP grew 2.15% per year between 1870 and 1913 and even with strong population growth of 1.06%, itself a by-product of prosperity, net per capita GDP growth was a decent 1.08% over the same period. More importantly, such growth was now widespread on the Continent, as opposed to the First Industrial Revolution's much more localised and patchy pattern. Not all countries were rich, but most people were enjoying a profusion of consumer products, lower priced food, and improvements in technology. It was, as one set of analysts put it, a "silver age" economically, strong, though no longer explosive in economic improvement (Carreras & Josephson, 2010, 57).

The globalisation of trade and finance accompanying economic growth was striking. Annual rates of growth in world trade between 1800 and 1817 are estimated to have been around 0.5%, adding up to a cumulative growth in trade over that period of around 9%. But between 1817 and 1865, the average annual growth in trade was almost 4%, cumulating into an almost 600% increase over the period. Things did slow down between 1866 and 1913 for various reasons, not least because growth rates off a high base are harder to accomplish than off a lower base, and partly due to resurgence in protectionism during the late 1800s and early 1900s.

Still, annual growth in trade volumes averaged over 3%, cumulatively rising by roughly 310% across these years, with foreign trade becoming a crucial part of every industrialised economy (Federico & Tena-Junguito, 2017, Table 1). By 1913, France had a trade to gross domestic product ratio of 35.4%, Germany 35.1%, and the UK 44.7%. Capital was flowing outward from these major developed economies, in the form of both foreign direct investment (FDI) and portfolio investment (i.e. investments in financial securities), in the process helping to build the burgeoning "neo-Europes" of North America, Argentina, Australia and South Africa, these becoming what one author has called the "'tiger' economies of the Victorian era". Chicago and Melbourne were exploding new growth cities, while Budapest, Barcelona and Kiev were old ones infused with a new sparkle (Hirst, 1997, 411).

Urbanisation also picked up speed and intensity. By 1910, the proportion of urban citizens in the European population was up to 41%, and over the course of the prior hundred years the city population of Europe had rocketed from 19 to 127 million. Cities were also growing larger and more numerous throughout the world, driven by the same forces of rising industry, growing commerce, and fewer work opportunities in the countryside (Bairoch, 1988, 217).

Not all European countries urbanised equally quickly during this time. England, having started early, went from a 20.3% urban population out of the total populace in 1800, to a 61.9% share in 1890. Comparable figures for Belgium were 18.9% and 34.5%; Germany 5.5% and 28.2%; France 8.8% and 25.9%; Spain 11.1% and 26.8%; Italy 14.6% and 21.2%; the Netherlands 28.8% and 33.4%; and Scandinavia 4.6% and 13.2% (De Vries, 1984, 45–46). But all countries, even "laggard" ones, were converging towards an increasingly urbanised baseline.

But even with fast absolute growth, one could easily fall behind relatively. Economic modernisation became more and more of a race, where simply staying put meant losing out, especially when considering the increasingly globalised economy. Larger economies had more influence in the world system and more ability to set the rules in their favour, so rapid growth became a political, as well as an economic, imperative. It was bad enough for countries like Britain to fall behind in relative terms (the US surpassing it in terms of income per capita in 1880). But China and India actually fell behind industrially, their populations growing much faster than their output, leading to falling per capita GDP in both countries. Populations were growing everywhere, though, especially in the non-European core. Demographic advance, however, did not necessarily translate into economic progress.

10.2 Social and Economic Life Inside the Core: The Case of France

While Britain was the economic heart of Europe, France was arguably its cultural heart. Yet in many ways, the beginning of a supposedly beautiful age (using the 1870 starting date) was inauspicious for the country. The Third Republic had just been established, finally fulfilling the promise of the French Revolution after two prior failed attempts. Yet the Republic was born out of ignominious defeat at the hands of a surging Prussia during the Franco-Prussian War of 1871, engendering a decisive overthrow of a second Napoleon, and resulting in the loss of Alsace-Lorraine to the newly unified Germany. For a time France's role as a Great Power in Europe was called into question. Taken together with the savage repression of the Paris Commune in 1871, it seemed that France was a society with no political centre, just division between extremes, the rightists being the stronger, though not necessarily better, force. Pessimism reigned culturally and intellectually immediately after the war, some of the leading artists and thinkers themselves having fought in it, and many others suffering through the Prussian siege of Paris (Chapman, 1962) (Fig. 10.2).

However, the new Republic ended up providing a viable and sometimes even satisfying political compromise and internal peace that would last fifty years. The Commune repression ended up discrediting both left and right extremes, actually strengthening the centre and leading to an internal stability not known since before 1789. The country, allying with Russia and later England, once again quickly regained its Great Power status, and accumulated an outwardly formidable imperial Empire in Africa and Southeast Asia as well. There was a flowering of literature, music, philosophy and science that was unparalleled while it lasted. Economically, real wages increased, economic growth was solid and respectable and French finance and the French Central Bank were second only to Britain in global importance (Watson, 1983, 761–762).

Such cultural, social and political equilibrium could not be taken for granted. The possibility of strong man populist rule under General Georges Ernest Boulanger was a constant threat, his charismatic appeal and growing electoral success ended only by a decisive election defeat in

Fig. 10.2 Map of France: describing the new limits according to the treaty of peace, 1874 (*Source* [1874], London, J. Wyld. Public domain image courtesy Yale University Library)

1889. Boulanger rode the wave of resentment that pervaded conservative society, especially amongst the Catholics and Royalists, smarting at the Prussian defeat and chafing against the social and economic modernisation that France was undergoing. Boulanger the man was a near miss, but Boulangism would continue to appeal to significant segments of the population. The examples of the Second Empire and the military crushing of the Commune remained ever present precedents for the political model of military coup as a regular interval, a template that some fellow “Latin” countries, such as Spain and her former colonies, seemed increasingly attracted to (Watson, 1983, 764).

Still, the Belle Epoque was a period where “Republicanism” was translated from a set of ideals to a working political system that gained the allegiance of the majority of the population. The conservative elements joined battle regularly with the Republic, not least over the secular "anti-clericalism" campaign that became an ongoing effort to put the Catholic Church in a non-political place, a holdover from the anti-religious French Revolution, and a continuation of older struggles between the Catholic majority and the country's Protestant minorities. But these traditionalist allegiances were at least to some degree replaced by a broader popular devotion to Republican institutions, manifested in allegiance to the Socialist or Radical Parties that were reformist but committed to the established institutions of government. Other planks included a loose official secularism that consisted of tolerance of all religions, but with unofficial quotas for hiring of Protestants in some government ministries, Catholics in others and no official prejudice against Jews, but with anti-Semitism an ongoing holdover from the distant past, as the Dreyfus Affair exposed all too clearly (Larkin, 1995).

These political and social elements were uniquely French (Weber, 1976). But France's economic developments mirrored changes going on elsewhere. France was industrialising and growing more gradually than Britain had, but it was doing so, and pretty well at that. Table 10.1 provides some basic data on French per capita GDP growth and structural change, before and during the Belle Époque.

Depending on the GDP measure used, French real GDP per capita rose by a total of over 40% or close to 75% between 1872 and 1910, a big range but impressive either way. The amount of national income produced by, and the share or people employed in, the agricultural sector, dropped significantly throughout the latter half of the nineteenth century and into the beginning of the twentieth century. French industrialisation, though not especially speedy, was ongoing, with national income derived from industry rising from one-quarter of the total in 1825/35 to over a third by 1908/10.

However, the service sector did not grow much at all in relative terms and if one looks at just the gross figures both industry and services were not especially productive since there was a greater share of labour force employed in these sectors than the proportions of national income they produced respectively. There are a number of possible reasons for this, but one factor is the relatively small scale of production and retail sales in the country during this time. (Something similar could be said for agriculture, though productivity advance was more impressive there). The French were known for their small artisanal shops and producers (bakers, food sellers etc.) which may have had a productivity penalty, though with

Table 10.1 Selected statistics on the French Economy, between 1825/35 and 1910/11

Time period	*Agriculture*	*Industry**	*Services*
A. National Income Distribution by major economic sector (% of total)			
1825/35	50	25	25
1872/82	42	30	28
1908/10	35	35	28
B. Labour force employment by major economic sector (% of total)			
1866	43	38	19
1911	30	39	31
*C. Real GDP per capita***			
1872		$2641 ($3419)–$3312 (2020 update)	
1882		$3067 ($3765)–$3647 (2020 update)	
1892		$3514 ($4101)–$3974 (2020 update)	
1902		$4105 ($4566)–$4423 (2020 update)	
1910		$4551 ($4878)–$4726 (2020 update)	

Sources
Panel A data: Kuznets (1966), Table 3.1, p. 88
Panel B data: Kuznets (1966), Table 3.2, p. 106
Panel C data: Bolt et al. (2018) (Maddison data)
*Transport and communications included
**First number is Real GDP per capita in 2011US$, multiple benchmarks; second number (in parentheses) is Real GDP per capita in 2011US$, 2011 benchmark; third number is Real GDP per capita in 2011US$, updated in 2020 (Bolt & Van Zanden, 2020)

the possible benefit of greater social cohesion and connections between community and production (Aminzade, 1984; Nye, 1987).

The French were also global leaders in cultural production, being taste and fashion makers, with an especially privileged place in the growing industry of ready-to-wear clothing. Whereas fashion had been reserved for the aristocracy in the past, homemade peasant clothing being the norm for everyone else, mass apparel production now could create and distribute high fashion for all. This was aided by the rise of retail department stores, the French being innovators here too, along with their attendant mass marketing campaigns. Fashion was now a new “dream world” in which consumers could vicariously satisfy their animal desires (Steele, 2004, 319).

There were interesting developments in gender relations and views emerging in France as well, with the economic system shaping cultural categories more directly than ever before, and vice versa. Mass production led to mass consumption in turn leading to mass culture and mass mores, this last category being expressed in material forms such as clothing. Older notions of female "vanity" and "immodesty" began to be replaced by contradictory appeals to middle-class women to be simultaneously "virtuous" and "seductive". It was presented as possible to do this by buying the right piece of clothing, purportedly amorously transgressive (for females) and yet not really challenging the masculine power strictures of the time. It has been argued that the creation of "fashion" as the "art of being feminine" made the limited emancipation of women going on feel safer to men while also preserving for women the old notion of obtaining power through sexual charm. An interesting example of this is the change in intimate apparel from being merely functional to becoming increasingly light and decorative, providing an emerging emphasis on sexual romance within companionate marriage (Steele, 2004, 322–323).

Women were making real advances professionally. There were growing numbers of female doctors, lawyers, artists and businesswomen. But these advances were accompanied by ongoing restrictions. Political culture in France continued to deem women as belonging to the private sphere of the home, not the public sphere of politics, which remained a man's game as always. The commentary on the Dreyfus Affair was primarily run by high-profile men, including literary figures such as Zola and Anatole France with only a few notable women thrown in, including Séverine, Gyp and the female journalists of *La Fronde*. However, these women were often dismissed as frumpy feminists and sometimes satirised in the press, unlike their male counterparts (Dubbelboer, 2015, 37).

More generally, in France and elsewhere, the new middle classes appeared to have arrived at a higher social plane, at least in material terms. Female fashion has already been mentioned (there were also standards for men). There was also a new plethora of etiquette books to train people in manners to go with their fashionable homes, stylish clothes and latest gadgets. As in fashion, these rules were based on the norms of the wealthy, adapted for the bourgeoisie. This extended to domestic architecture and urban design, cities being transformed to accommodate expanding populations. In older European cities, defensive walls were torn down and the newly vacant areas converted into parks and boulevards. Suburbanisation was also beginning, expanding along streetcar and commuter train lines allowing people to work in the city in the rapidly increasing number of office jobs, while returning at night to homes in more bucolic suburban neighbourhoods. Once more "upper class" standards of living were diffusing down into the middle classes, along with expectations of what was an acceptable material way of life (Julian 1982).

Working life was becoming more standardised and regimented, for both the working and middle classes, although conditions, hours and pay were obviously higher for the latter. The clock dictated when one should work but also when one was off work, and so new leisure hours were created by the industrial system, i.e. free evening hours after work, at least one day on weekends (usually Sunday, following older religious conventions), and, eventually, a week or two in the summer for vacation. Common mass leisure hours stimulated demand for common mass activities and new industries (sometimes supported by public funding) to provide them in the form of music and dance halls, trips to art museums, fairs, and "tourism", the new idea of travelling for travelling's sake. Organised sports and culture became mass affairs. Sport saw a plethora of new teams, written rules, officials, and stadiums. And new museums opened in major metropolitan centres so that art was no longer just for the upper class. Art was also now being displayed in cafes and becoming a social commodity in the process (Julian, 1982).

Technical change was no longer mostly just about industrial production. Many of the newest inventions were personal in nature and use, such as sewing machines, clocks, bicycles, electric lights, and typewriters. Some of these freed up home labour time for leisure, like the sewing machine. Electric lighting increased the ability to utilise dark hours for work or leisure, individual and *en masse*. Mass consumption, and a routine of life organised along its pursuits, crystallised concomitantly (Magraw, 1983; Somerwine, 2018; Weber, 1986; Wilde, 2020).

Meanwhile, immigrants were settling in growing numbers within Europe, and France in particular. During the French Revolution, Jews living in France were granted citizenship, and this official acceptance continued afterwards, the country thus becoming a magnet for those persecuted elsewhere in Europe. Paris was where they concentrated, almost half of French Jews living there in 1872. Between 1881 and 1925, around 3.5 million Jews emigrated from their home countries, mostly to various parts of North America, the US especially. But France admitted 100,000 of them, drawn there by a decent economy, official acceptance of Judaism, the official pronouncement of egalitarian and non-sectarian principles of the French Revolution, and the relative proximity to Russia and Eastern Europe where many had strong family ties. Perhaps unsurprisingly, given the primacy of the fashion industry, 30% of those arriving had apparel-making skills, and overall this was a group already well trained in this trade. As in many other places and for most immigrant groups, the Parisian Jews were exploited in sweatshops, were initially slow to learn French (Yiddish being their major language) and were ghettoised, in this case mostly settling in the Marais neighbourhood (Green, 1986).

Here in microcosm was a scene repeated around the world: foreigners settling in diverse places in the core, trying to assimilate, serving as critical labour inputs into growing economic sectors, and yet also kept in their separate social categories and neighbourhoods, sometimes forcibly, more usually informally, presenting as an "other" to the mainstream, exotic and "dangerous" all at once. Jewish immigrants in particular tended to be Socialist or Communist in their ideologies and in Paris they were behind some of the labour organisation and strikes of the period, especially late in the nineteenth and early twentieth centuries. This push–pull cycle stoked nationalist and pan-ethnic identification at the same time, a trend that would expand and which for Jews would develop into Zionism, a movement founded in the later nineteenth century and growing in appeal (Green, 1986).

10.3 Mass Media, "News" and Nationalism

During this era, the French, together with the Americans, were the world's biggest consumers of newspapers, their existence encouraged by liberal Republican press laws and their diffusion enhanced through low sales prices made possible by technological advances in printing and paper and cheaper transportation. Mass education and increased literacy provided the requisite numbers of readers for the 2400 titles of both periodicals and newspapers published every day in Paris in 1900, costing between 5 and 10 centimes per issue, the cheapest in the world. The period between 1890 and 1914 was indeed the golden age of the press in France. What was uniquely French about this was that the big journalistic names were almost all literary figures (Dubbelboer, 2015, 33).

Technical advances in printing made possible mass print journalism, giant presses capable of printing 10,000 papers per hour. This alone helped contribute to a massive growth in the number of newspapers, both in total numbers of different mastheads, and circulation numbers for particular mastheads. By 1890, some papers boasted circulations in excess of one million copies. New technologies allowed cheap reproduction of not just text but detailed illustrations, which featured prominently in the growing numbers of pictorial weeklies. Consisting at first mainly of prints made from woodcut engravings based on reporters' sketches, the new photographic technology led photographs to take their place more and more (Gabrial, 2008; PsPrint.com, 2021).

By the early twentieth century, newspapers were looking very much like modern ones, with banner headlines, photos and illustrations, and added sections for comics and sports. Even colour was making its way in, the first colour comic in an American newspaper appearing in 1894, and a commemorative edition of the *Milwaukee Journal* using blue and red to commemorate an election in 1891. However, colour printing remained too expensive to become a regular feature until the 1990s, though mass magazines were using it extensively by the middle of the twentieth century (PsPrint.com, 2021).

Mass media had arrived, and it was changing public consciousness. Benedict Anderson (1991) uses the phrase "print-capitalism" and argues that it is at the root of the modern nation-state and, by extension, nationalism in its modern form (see Section 11.5 for more on nationalism as an ideology). Before the printing press was invented, he argues that most people were illiterate and communicated and interacted across small geographical areas that tended to have their own specific dialects. The invention of printing press began to change this, and with the rise of mass produced and widely distributed books, local language became standardised across larger geographical units, e.g. French gradually replacing the regional languages of Breton, Burgundian and so forth. Over time, people began to identify more and more with their national "language" as the basis for an imagined political community (Anderson's definition of a "nation") and eventually the modern nation-state, and group allegiance to it (i.e. "nationalism") was born, even though in actual fact individual members of the supposed nation might generally have little to do with one another. Although print-capitalism predates industrialisation, the rising scale and integration of the world around economic processes, and the birth of a true mass media reaching populations with larger literacy rates than ever before arguably created mass nations, profoundly changing both individual and collective consciousness' of large groups of people over time. It was another mass phenomenon, in many ways conducted through mass production and mass consumption.

Newspapers played critical roles in this growing economy in a number of ways. Of course, they served as platforms for communication of information about consumer products and helped launch the new advertising industry. As already alluded to, they became taste and image-makers, helping to create new status categories and the attendant new demands for particular goods and services. The industry also became a large employer and contributor to national income in its own right.

Politically, newspapers became mediums of messages to form, convey and manipulate public attitudes about issues of the day and help mobilise the masses to turn out for particular causes. The whole notion of "news" itself is something that really only was born out of a literate society, and merchandised through an industrialised one. As far as its being "objective" or "factual", this conceit was not practised much at all (except for a brief few decades after the Second World War when major media outlets developed a purportedly "balanced" presentation of views) (Taibbi, 2019). By the end of nineteenth century, the newspaper industry within most countries had consolidated into a few national or regional companies controlling multiple newspapers, under the control of a few "press barons". In terms of industrial organisation, they were following the trends of scale and size that most other industries were falling into at the time.

These newspaper magnates were generally quite colourful and flamboyant—and partisan. They tried to shape stories, and even create whole new narratives to suit their political agenda. But like mass producers of other products, they did have to stay close to the tastes of their customers. Truth, whatever that might be, was dispensable. But selling papers was not and this involved a balancing of catering to the masses and manipulating them in profitable ways. In this sense, selling the news was just like selling anything else (see Fig. 10.3).

10.4 Girdling the Globe

France, despite its unique elements, was, like every other country, establishing its place in the broader world system, which by the end of the nineteenth century was already fairly well developed. Both the European continent and much of the world had been built out with the new infrastructure that enabled the deepening and widening of the globalisation that industrialisation had kicked off. The "mature" transport technologies, such as railways and canals, were already well entrenched,

Fig. 10.3 "Fake News" and other variants of old (*Image source* US Library of Congress, https://www.loc.gov/item/2012648704/. Illus. from Puck, v. 35, no. 887, [1894 March 7], centrefold. With detail below. No known copyright restrictions)

while surface roads were being extended and improved, along with urban streets, soon to be used by the twentieth century automobile. Britain was the leader here, as in many other areas, aided by its relatively compact geography and wide array of navigable rivers. Britain also had a long naval tradition, which aided its ability to innovate and implement new technologies on both short-haul boats and long-haul ships (Bogart, 2013).

Long-haul freight and passenger carriage was still the province of the ship and it is interesting to note that the Belle Époque began with the construction of the Suez Canal in Egypt in 1869 and ended with the construction of the Panama Canal in 1914. The Kiel Canal was completed in between, in 1897. The ships that went through these canals were growing bigger and faster throughout the century, steamships growing in power and fuel efficiency, enabling them to go farther for longer per energy unit. Thus, shipping freight rates fell dramatically, boosting international trade, lowering commodity and input prices which then provided further boosts to production (Younis, 2017, 486).

A parallel revolution took place in telecommunications, something that did not exist at all before the early 1800s. The first transatlantic submarine cable was laid in 1858, though it quickly failed and had to be replaced by a new one, while the first successful transatlantic telegraph cable was completed in 1866. Within 29 years of its first installation at Euston Station, the telegraph network crossed the oceans to every continent but Antarctica (see Fig. 10.4). The telephone made its first successful transmission by Alexander Graham Bell in 1876. These technologies would rapidly improve and diffuse, creating a truly "networked world" as the twentieth century began (O'Hara, 2010).

Chapter 8 has already reviewed some of the economic implications of these improvements, especially in railways. But the cultural and psychological implications were perhaps as important. Combined with mass printing, the ability to exchange ideas and information in real time made global discourse more intense and immediate than ever before, generating a new frame about the annihilation of space and time that continues today (Younis, 2017, 486). In the early twentieth century, Einstein's theory of relativity would bring scientific weight to this idea as well.

The standard view of these developments at the time was generally presented from the perspective of the technologist, celebrating the power of human ingenuity and the physical awesomeness of the changes wrought by human invention. The perspective was also almost entirely that of the

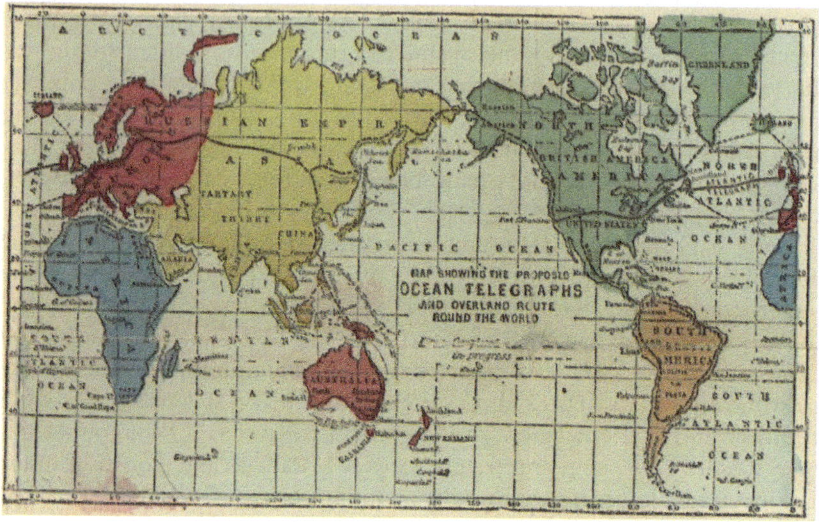

Fig. 10.4 The Atlantic Telegraph Line and plans for future overland lines (1865) (*Image source* The Atlantic Telegraph. Map Shewing the Atlantic telegraph, and other submarine cables in Europe and America. Map Showing the Proposed Ocean Telegraphs and Overland Route Around the World. Date: 1865. London: Bacon & Co. No known copyright restrictions)

Western investor and strategic Great Power elites. Interestingly, there was then much talk quite similar to the post-Cold War discussion of the "end of history" in which a (Western) civilisation based on "progress" had triumphed and in only a matter of time would take over completely, much to the world's good fortune (see Chapter 26).

Yet this triumphalism was one-sided and incomplete. Europe was becoming more important globally in demographic terms, the European population growing from 23% of the world total in 1800 to 36% in 1900, and so a Eurocentric viewpoint is not entirely indefensible. But Europeans were still only a minority of the world's people, and the polarisation of wealth, income and geopolitical power was also widening, another "Great Divergence" very unfavourable to the bottom half (Amin, 2000). The infrastructural knitting together of the planet enabled not just an extraordinary growth in productivity but also an ability to extract resources from peripheries to cores with remarkable speed and efficiency. This aspect was unremarked on by Western economic and political elites at the time, and often in the East as well, where many local leaders and groups were hoping to succeed at the Western game by imitating it. This was generally a vain hope during the period, except in Japan, discussed more in Section 10.6.

10.5 Internationalisation and Its Nationalist Backlashes

The Belle Époque was a sort of high point of Western society, but also one of the most extensive periods of migration in human history, with more than 50 million Chinese, 50 million Europeans and about 30 million Indians emigrating throughout the period. Migration theorists speak of push and pull and supply and demand factors (see Chapter 16). During this period, falling transport costs and rising economic opportunities drew many out of stagnant or economically declining areas, while political strife and dire need, sometimes starvation, pushed people out of their native lands.

Economistic narratives pose this as a matter of rational choice, driven by changing incentives, which it no doubt was for some. But much of the catalyst also came from the expansion of European imperialism, especially the subjugation of China and India, and, internal to Europe, the subjugation of the Irish by the British, European Jewry by the Russians, and so on (Younis, 2017, 487). The result was a growing nationalism that accompanied global integration and movements of people, capital and ideas.

The relationship between expansionism, immigration and globalisation in stimulating nationalism is an interesting one. Nationalism as an intellectual doctrine was a product of the revolutionary ages of earlier decades and advances in mass communication and exchange of ideas already mentioned. It provided a reference point for people in a world rapidly economically integrating in which old mores and ways of life were falling by the wayside. Nationalism was regularly and cynically manipulated by elites who sought to divide and rule fractious ethnic minorities and distract from growing social problems. And yet it also filled a genuine social and psychological vacuum that material modernisation alone was not able to address.

Oddly, the celebration of the "Nation" coexisted with the actual and conceptual nullification of political boundaries brought about by globalisation and integration. Nations were still the prime geopolitical actors on the world stage and typically had substantial power within their domestic domains. But capital moved freely between jurisdictions and increasingly powerful non-State actors, following supposedly neutral rules that were nonetheless regularly manipulated behind the scenes.

Nationalism also competed with internationalism of both right (global capitalism) and left (international communism). A fusion between these two strains came with various forms of "transnationalism", often centred on racial and/or ethnic affinities, e.g. "pan-Slavism".

Despite Great Power rivalries and age-old communal conflicts, pan-Europeanism was very strong during the Belle Époque, the French National Assembly calling for a US of Europe in 1871 for example. The actual ideas were often created by elites, and didn't always filter down to the masses. But some, particularly localised concepts such as pan-Slavism, often became widely adopted, especially by small national groups that were fighting much larger entities, as was the case in the Balkans. Somewhat paradoxically, therefore, mass culture thus was both an integrating and a dis-integrating force (Younis, 2017, 485–488). This tension would have serious consequences that would explode into the First World War.

10.6 An Exceptional Case: Japan

If nineteenth century Asia was mostly the picture of economic decline relative to Europe and spreading European imperialism, Japan at first looks to be a semi-exception to the pattern. After the Meiji restoration of the Emperor to full power in 1868 (more on this below), Japan began a process of rapid social, political and economic modernisation that was accompanied by rapid real per capita GDP growth.

Table 10.2 shows the Maddison GDP per capita data for 1820, 1870 and 1913, for China, Japan and India. These data are sketchy overall but they show that Japan was likely better off per capita than China at the beginning of the period, before it took off in the later in the century, leaving a declining China and India well behind (India declining in absolute as well as relative terms between 1820 and 1870), what Broadberry (2013) has referred to as an Asian Little Divergence.

It is important to mention that Japan was no less a victim of Western colonialism than the other countries. It was just the way Japan was

Table 10.2 Per capita GDP and per capita GDP growth rates for Japan, China and India, 1820–1913 (2011 $)

Country	*1820*	*1870*	*1913*
Japan	$1317	$1580	$2431
China	$882	$945	$985
India	$937	$850	$1073
Per capita GDP growth rates (average annual)			
	1820–1870	1870–1913	
Japan	0.37%	1.01%	
China	0.12%	0.10%	
India*	−0.20%	0.54%	

*India definition for 1820–1870 average includes Bangladesh and Pakistan
Sources Bolt and Van Zanden (2020) (2020 update to Maddison data). GDP per capita average annual growth rates calculated by author using CAGR formula. Results rounded to second decimal point

approached by the Western powers that was different. China was a much bigger target of Western interests given its size and its traditional trading power and wealth. Japan was more of a sideline and, at that time, much more isolated by its own choice than even relatively insular China. Japan lay on American trade routes into China and that country required a place to refuel their Pacific whaling ships. It was this fact that caused the American Commodore Matthew Perry to demand permission to trade and open diplomatic relations with Japan. These commenced in 1854 and very quickly other Western powers, including Britain and Russia, asked for "equal" treatment.

These pressures had profound repercussions on Japanese society, its leading members seeing their relative weakness and isolation as a disadvantage of the Shôgunate in which the Emperor had little power, the country effectively fragmented and governed by independent warrior-leaders. The Japanese were well aware of the humiliations of India and China at the hands of the Europeans, and knew that outright resistance was futile. Adaptation to Western ways, on Japanese terms, was deemed as essential (Eisenstadt & Aizenshtadt, 1996).

Japan did have to concede significant sovereignty to the West in important policy areas, signing treaties that limited its control over its own foreign trade and requiring that crimes against foreigners in Japan be tried in Western courts. But, unlike China, it did not suffer from piecemeal partition of its territorial periphery, nor humiliating military defeat followed by the imposition of savage peace agreements, as had happened after China's defeat in the Opium Wars. Japan's agency as a country in its own foreign affairs was thus constrained but not completely impaired and its domestic power groups swung into action decisively, executing what was in effect a bloodless coup that removed the Tokugawa shôgun ("great general") from power in 1868, bringing the Emperor back into control, though now much more as a delegator and coordinator of power than a strong central authority. This new order promptly set about building a strong army on the one hand, and a Westernised economy on the other. The emperor took the name Meiji ("enlightened rule") and so the takeover was referred to as the Meiji Restoration (Macpherson, 1995).

Japan in 1868, as noted, was far from a backwards or poor country. The available evidence suggests that both Chinese and Japanese birth rates were lower than European ones, that their death rates were lower as well and that they possessed a fairly high standard of living by Western standards (Pomeranz, 2000, 41). Japan's population was apparently stagnant from between 1720 to 1860, and some believe that its per capita income also stagnated; but if so, it was at a very high level (Pomeranz, 2000, 229). Moreover, Japan's per capita GDP annual growth rate between 1730 and 1800 has been estimated at 0.29%, higher than any previous rate over ten prior centuries and higher even than the average rate for the first half of the nineteenth century (Bassino et al., 2019). This was not as high for Britain at the time, but quite good when compared to most other countries.

The Tokugawa period of 1607–1868 was one of substantial internal reform as well, despite its corresponding external weakness. In the late sixteenth century, the peasantry was disarmed and only the samurai could carry swords, with land surveys conducted to identify owners and taxpayers to ensure a stable revenue base. The country urbanised and by the middle of the seventeenth century, Japan was the site of the most populated city in the world, Edo, and two other sizeable cities, Osaka and Kyoto. Urbanisation brought a growing commercial economy, sophisticated financial and credit systems, spreading literacy, and expansion of patronisation of arts and theatre. To substitute for Chinese silk imports, steps were taken to develop the silk industry in Nishijin in Kyoto (Eisenstadt & Aizenshtadt, 1996).

Thus, the Japanese were already used to social and economic modernisation when Western intrusions came and very hospitable to adopting novel ideas to advance their national power and interest. The Tokugawa administration was already decentralised, and so the Meiji Restoration was too. The emperor returned to central position, but ruled indirectly through the ambitious and change-oriented cadre that had overthrown the shôgun. The previous feudal lords had been requested to give up their domains, and in 1871, these domains were changed into the prefectures of a unified central state. Official class privileges were eliminated, and the government declared all classes to be equal. A national army based on universal conscription was created in 1872, with all men subject to call-up. A national land tax system with cash, rather than rice payments, was established, and feudalism was abolished (Macpherson, 1995).

The government also embarked on a public works spree of building railways, shipping lines, telegraph and telephone systems, and munitions works, while establishing domestic consumer industries such as glass making and textiles. In 1880, the government decided to sell most of these industries to private investors. The establishment of a national educational system, constitution and elected parliament accompanied these changes. Both political and economic reforms were based on Japanese adaptations of Western models, with heavy consultation of Western experts, but with the Japanese picking those elements off the menu they liked, altering them to fit Japanese needs and discarding anything that seemed not to suit or, if tried, found not to work (Macpherson, 1995).

Finally, and from the perspective of Japanese geopolitical power, the country had built up a powerful army and navy. By the beginning of the twentieth century, Japan had regained complete control of its foreign trade and legal system, and won two major wars, one against China (gaining control over Korea and Taiwan as a result), and the other against Russia. The Western nations agreed to revise the unequal treaties in 1894, acknowledging Japan as an equal in theory (Macpherson, 1995).

But white Europeans were not prepared to treat non-white Asians as equals in practice, even when they showed themselves adept at Western modalities. Japan signed a treaty with China giving Japan special rights on China's Liaotung peninsula, following the extraterritorial concessions demanded of China by the Western powers. In this, Japan showed itself as greedy and imperialist as any European power. But France, Russia and Germany combined to pressure Japan to give up her rights in Liaotung, taking them for themselves. Japan's defeat of Russia in the Russo-Japanese War of 1904–1905 was a sort of payback, with Japan firmly establishing itself as a colonial power in East Asia and major player in the Pacific. But after the First World War, the country would once again find itself treated as a second-class world citizen, even though it had been on the victorious side (Haggard et al., 1997; Macpherson, 1995) (Fig. 10.5).

◂**Fig. 10.5** The floor of a large Silk Factory in Japan (ca. 1868) (*Image source* University of Victoria, Hebert Geddes collection [public domain] https://vault.library.uvic.ca/concern/generic_works/50299f2c-93e7-4549-8061-fa97ac015aff. *Nots from Collection*: "Herbert Geddes was a manager for G.R. Gregg and Company, importers and exporters, in Vancouver and Winnipeg. He was sent to Japan and was based in Yokohama between 1908 and 1918. ...The collection consists of photographic glass-plate transparencies depicting life in Japan, including scenery, street scenes, workers, farming, fishing, silk production, stone carvers, wood carvers, metal workers, potters, and artists. These "Yokohama photographs" were sold to foreign tourists between about 1868 and 1912, before cameras and postcards were generally available." No known copyright restrictions)

The Japanese experience did show that Asian economies did not have to accept junior positions in the world economy. Western inventions and institutions could be redesigned and adapted to local circumstances without sacrificing totally its identity or culture (Allen, 2011), a lesson that the "Asian Tigers" followed in the 1970s, 1980s and 1990s. But the Japanese experience also provided a cautionary tale of the unintended social consequences that could emerge from this strategy, and the Western response to Japanese success revealed that even the following of Western rules by non-whites would never be a complete road to "success".

10.7 A Growing Bittersweet Decadence in Europe

Meanwhile, back in continental Europe the century ended with a sense of decadence, drawn from both the seeming tiredness of European civilisation, the exhaustion caused by constant change and superficial novelty, and possibly the ennui of mass culture more generally. This was reflected in "Decadentism", a literary movement that ended the era, having strong links with Modernism in art. It was emblematic of the age, the "decadents" setting themselves partly, but not fully, against prevailing assumptions of modern society, hedging their bets as it were, not sure that the present order was viable, but not sure that the possible alternatives were either. They remained individualistic, communicating with one another, but not forming a movement (Conversi, 2018).

Alienation was a dominant theme in many European works, such as the poetry of Constantine P. Cavafy and Stefan George, who evoked, unfavourably, late Roman and Hellenistic-Alexandrian times, with their omens of decline. In England, Oscar Wilde satirised the way things were, seeking to deflate it with sarcastic panache, while offering an individual path to, if not redemption, then a sort of conscious decadence by choice, and the relative freedom that came with it. There was something subversive about Wilde's eccentricity that was meant to carve out a bit of personal liberty within a decaying and otherwise conformist and homogenising order. This was best illustrated in a fable-like way in his only novel, *The Picture of Dorian Gray*, whose protagonist sells his soul to pursue libertine ways and have only his portrait age instead of himself (Conversi, 2018).

This was a time of explicit "individualism", and yet many individuals felt smaller and more unimportant than ever before, given the rise of large-scale economic enterprise, mass politics and mass communication. There were many who advocated for and participated in social rebellion and attempts at revolution. But Wilde retreated to a more individual path, something spelled out in his essay *The soul of man under socialism* ([1895] 2003), laying out a template which was formally anarchistic, calling for socialism, but without calling for the overthrow of established society, and mainly celebrating the right to artistic expression as part of an elevation of a human soul which Wilde felt was rapidly being corroded.

The sad thing about Wilde's personal experience here was that his individualism was ahead of its time, as his unsuccessful libel suit and subsequent conviction and imprisonment for homosexuality attests. *The Ballad of Reading Gaol* ([1897] 2003) is a testament of a man both defiant and broken, the logical result, perhaps, of a purely individualistic open rebellion against the social order in which, to quote from the poem, men "always kill the things they love". That being so, the bravest course is to do so openly, with a "sword" and not a "kiss."

Wilde ended up in Paris after his release from prison, dying at the age of 46. This choice of location is also emblematic, for Paris at the end of the century was at the very centre of "high" cultural affairs, and a tide of Francophilia swept throughout Europe before the First World War. In contrast with a later Americanisation, Francophilia was not primarily catering to "mass" tastes, but was more of a reshaping of elite tastes to fit into and refine a mass consumption culture. This manifested in a Paris art scene that was inventive, uniquely French and culturally pastiche (nowadays one would say culturally appropriating) all at the same time. Exoticism was prominent in both French and Western culture more generally., e.g. the craze for Japanese visual themes (Japonism) that was spawned by the mass production and diffusion of Japanese prints throughout Western Europe (Conversi, 2018).

Melancholia was an integral part of this high culture fused with mass culture. The Salomé myth was a regular theme of European writers and artists of the era, approached by August Strindberg, Oscar Wilde and Henrik Ibsen, amongst other major literary artists. Wilde's 1891 play *Salomé* was written in French, showing how central all things French were then. This Bible tale, about John the Baptist's death and Herodias's daughter Salome asking for his head, inspired several contemporary visual artworks as well. "Salomania" combined exoticism and material hedonism in a sophisticated mix, as well as continuing the sexist and racist tropes of the "femme fatale" (Conversi, 2018). Although the story was taken from the Gospels, the messages of hope and redemption were stripped away, brutality, futility and frisson emphasised instead.

Thus, the Belle Époque is in many ways a preview of the current post-modern era we live in today. Modernism was a vital force in all arenas, but was beginning to wear thin. Cultural commodification was not yet complete but it was having an impact on mores and meaning as the culture more and more took disparate elements and fused them into collages that were not necessarily coherent and might even be self-contradictory. Mass production, consumption and culture still had some decades to develop further and to spread and deepen, as did mass politics and mass communication, but their basic forms and structures had been created. Prosperity was everywhere, but so too was growing corruption and malfeasance (see Box 10.1). The present was materially rich, but empty. The future seemed bright, but an inchoate foreboding lay beneath it all.

Box 10.1 America and the "Gilded Age"

While the last decades of the nineteenth century were a "Belle Epoque" in France, they were labeled a "Gilded Age" in the United States. The two countries were, of course quite different: France, a European Great Power with centuries of history; America, a country that celebrated its centenary in 1876 and still rough and tumble in most aspects of its societal and economic development. Whereas material progress in France fused with what was seen as an attendant fruition of Western civilisation and a settling into the routines of the Third Republic, in America it was concomitant with great social and political ferment, rapid economic growth and, most discordantly, rampant corruption

The phrase "Gilded Age" came from an 1873 book by the American humourist Mark Twain and co-author Charles Warner, *The Gilded Age: A tale of today,* which satirised the post-Civil War period in the US, portraying it as an era of serious problems gilded over by heady economic expansion. Its application to an entire American era was a gloss by later historians but it well fit the times that were beset by major public and private scandals at local, regional and national levels. Ulysses S. Grant, the hero general of the triumphant north in the Civil War became the first US president to succeed the Lincoln administration (which included the accession of Vice-President Andrew Johnson to the presidency after Lincoln's assassination), entering office with a tremendous amount of goodwill and hope. His two terms in office between 1869 and 1877 quickly dissipated this, being marked by regular scandal (though Grant himself was personally honest) fed by the breakneck growth of completely unregulated railroad and banking sectors that sought successfully to buy federal government subsidy, contracts and favours like candy from a sweets shop. The difficult issues of racial equality and so-called "Reconstruction" in the American South that the end of slavery had brought to the fore ended not with resolution but with a contested presidential election in 1876 that was settled by an overt and unsavoury political deal that put any progress in entrenched national racial discrimination practices on a back-burner for almost a century

Meanwhile, overseas immigration into America's burgeoning cities became a flood, resulting in the rise of entrenched municipal political "machines" that were patronage based and thoroughly corrupt, New York City's "Tammany Hall" being the most notorious example, though far from alone, or, even, possibly, the worst. Speculative finance led to two major economic contractions in the form of the Panics of 1873 and 1893, which were not to be outdone until the catastrophic Great Depression of the 1930s. None of this stopped America's real GDP per capita growth from increasing by over two-thirds between 1870 and 1900 (according to the Maddison data)

The Gilded Age was also a period of tremendous increases in economic inequality in America, something occurring in most other industrialising countries but which was particularly pronounced in the US. While average wages and living standards were (roughly speaking) increasing for everybody, those at the top were accumulating proportionately much more of the gains than the large bulk of people below them.

All this bred a lot of cynicism amongst Americans, as hypocrisy, outsized rewards for little effort, crass ostentation, and the neglect of obvious social problems ballooned. Europe was grappling with similar issues, but America was on the move, a new power in the "New World", with new ideas and a willingness to take risks, at least according to its own "exceptionalist" mythology (see Chapter 20). All things were possible, it seemed, and economic growth and change would deliver any and all solutions, if not for the collective, then for the enterprising individual. In France the Belle Époque was experienced as a civilisational Autumn that felt like a bright burst before a foreboding Winter would come. America's Gilded Age, for all its faults, was experienced as a sort of eternal Spring in a country that had little sense of history.

(Discussion above draws on Cherny, 1997 and Edwards, 2005)

References

Allen, R. C. (2011). *Global economic history: A very short introduction*. Oxford University Press.

Amin, S. (2000). The political economy of the twentieth century. *Monthly Review (June), 52*(2), 1–17.

Aminzade, R. (1984). Reinterpreting capitalist industrialization: A study of nineteenth-century France: Proletarianization, small-scale industry and capitalist industrialization. *Social History, 9*(3), 329–350.

Anderson, B. (1991). *Imagined communities: Reflections on the origin and spread of nationalism* (Revised edition). Verso Books.

Bairoch, P. (1988). *Cities and economic development: From the dawn of history to the present*. University of Chicago Press.

Bassino, J. P., Broadberry, S., Fukao, K., Gupta, B., & Takashima, M. (2019). Japan and the great divergence, 730–1874. *Explorations in Economic History, 72*, 1–22.

Bogart, D. (2013). *The transportation revolution in industrializing Britain: A survey* (p. 121306). University of California-Irvine.

Bolt, J., Inklaar, R., de Jong, H., & van Zanden, J. L. (2018). *Rebasing Maddison: New income comparisons and the shape of long-run economic development*. Maddison Project Working Paper 10 (Maddison Project Database, version 2018).

Bolt, J., & van Zanden, J. L. (2020). Maddison style estimates of the evolution of the world economy. A new 2020 update". *Maddison Project Database*, version 2020. https://www.rug.nl/ggdc/historicaldevelopment/maddison/releases/maddison-project-database-2020

Broadberry, S. (2013). Accounting for the great divergence. *Voxeu*. https://voxeu.org/article/accounting-great-divergence

Carreras, A., & Josephson, C. (2010). Chapter 2: Aggregate growth, 1870–1914: Growing at the production frontier. In S. Broadberry & K. H. O'Rourke (Eds.), *The Cambridge economic history of modern Europe: Volume 2, 1870 to the present*. Cambridge University Press.

Chapman, G. (1962). *Third Republic of France: The first phase, 1871–1894*. Palgrave Macmillan.

Cherny, R. W. (1997). *American politics in the Gilded Age, 1868–1900*. Harlan Davidson.

Conversi, D. (2018). In the shadow of the Belle Époque: Progress, decadence, and the rush to war. *The European Legacy, 23*(5), 564–570.

De Vries, J. (1984). *European urbanisation 1500–1800*. Methuen.

Dubbelboer, M. (2015). Nothing ruins writers like journalism: Colette, the press and Belle Époque literary life. *French Cultural Studies, 26*(1), 32–44.

Edwards, R. (2005). *New spirits: Americans in the Gilded Age, 1865–1905*. Oxford University Press.

Eisenstadt, S. N., & Aizenshṭadṭ, S. N. (1996). *Japanese civilization: A comparative view*. University of Chicago Press.

Federico, G., & Tena-Junguito, A. (2017). A tale of two globalizations: Gains from trade and openness 1800–2010. *Review of World Economics, 153*(3), 601–626.

Gabrial, B. (2008). History of writing technologies. In C. Bazerman (Ed.), *Handbook of research on writing: History, society, school, individual, text* (pp. 27–40). Lawrence Erlbaum Associates (Taylor & Francis Group).

Green, N. L. (1986). *The Pletzl of Paris: Jewish immigrant workers in the "Belle Epoque."* Holmes & Meier.

Haggard, S., Kang, D., & Moon, C. (1997). Japanese colonialism and Korean development: A critique. *World Development, 25*, 867–881.

Hirst, P. (1997). The global economy-myths and realities. *International Affairs, 73*(3), 409–425.

Jullian, P. (1982). *La Belle Epoque: An essay*. Metropolitan Museum of Art.

Kuznets, S. (1966). *Modern economic growth: Rate, structure and spread*. Yale University Press.

Larkin, M. (1995). *Religion, politics and preferment in France since 1890: La Belle Époque and its legacy*. Cambridge University Press.

Macpherson, W. J. (1995). *Economic development of Japan 1868–1941*. Cambridge University Press.

Magraw, R. (1983). *France 1815–1914: The bourgeois century*. Fontana.
Nye, J. V. (1987). Firm size and economic backwardness: A new look at the French industrialization debate. *Journal of Economic History, 47*(3), 649–669.
O'Hara, G. (2010). New histories of British imperial communication and the "networked world" of the 19th and early 20th centuries. *History Compass, 8*(7), 609–625.
Pomeranz, K. (2000). *The great divergence: China, Europe, and the making of the modern world economy*. Princeton University Press.
PsPrint.com. (2021). *History of the printed newspaper*. https://www.psprint.com/resources/history-of-the-printed-newspaper/
Somerwine, C. (2018). *France since 1870: Culture, politics and society* (3rd ed.). Palgrave.
Steele, V. (2004). Femme fatale: Fashion and visual culture in fin-de-siècle Paris. *Fashion Theory, 8*(3), 315–328.
Taibbi, M. (2019). *Hate Inc.: Why today's media makes us despise one another*. OR Books.
Watson, D. R. (1983). Review: La Belle Époque: Domestic, military and foreign politics under the third French republic. *The Historical Journal, 26*(3), 761–768.
Weber, E. (1976). *Peasants into Frenchmen: The modernization of rural France, 1870–1914*. Stanford University Press.
Weber, E. (1986). *France: Fin de siècle*. Belknap Press of Harvard University Press.
Wilde, O. ([1895] 2003). The soul of man under socialism. In *Complete works of Oscar Wilde* (5th ed., pp. 1174–1197). Collins.
Wilde, R. (2020). Belle Époque or the "Beautiful Age" in France. *ThoughtCo* (Aug. 28) thoughtco.com/the-belle-epoque-beautiful-age-1221300.
Younis, M. (2017). United by blood: Race and transnationalism during the Belle Époque. *Nations and Nationalism, 23*(3), 484–504.

CHAPTER 11

"Civilisation", Gender, Race and Class

C. Gordon, *Many Possible Worlds*,
https://doi.org/10.1007/978-981-19-9281-0_11

Fig. 11.1 An example of civilisation's iconography: "The lion-killing hero of Khorsabad" (*Image source* Carus, P. [1900]. The history of the devil and the idea of evil, from the earliest times to the present day. Open Court Publishing Company. Page 209. Original caption used above. Public domain)

11.1 Civilisation: The Birth of a Concept

Civilisation is a term widely used but is also very difficult to define. It can be thought of as a sort of super-culture, the widest and broadest form of culture and social identification, encompassing beliefs, religion, values, language and institutions. Historically, civilisation is considered to be a distinct shift in humanity from more organic forms of human organisation (pejoratively referred to as "primitive") to more complex forms marked by urbanisation, technological adaptation, social complexity, long-distance trade and symbolic communication. The concept lends itself to both horizontal comparisons, i.e. between civilisations of different types, such as "Western" versus "Oriental", "English", "American", etc.; and vertical comparisons along an implicit (often explicit) hierarchy between uncivilised and civilised and less and more civilised (Fig. 11.1).

The term has been used for so long, and is so often associated with "Classical" (Western) societies such as Ancient Rome and Ancient Greece, that it is easy to forget that it actually was developed first during the eighteenth century, simultaneously amongst the French philosophes and the literary set of England. The *Oxford English Dictionary* (2020) puts a date on first use of the word as 1601 and its etymology specifically notes a 1772 recording of the term by Boswell asking his mentor Samuel Johnson whether he would include the word in the fourth edition of his folio Dictionary that he was then preparing. The great master replied that he would include only the word "civility", to which Boswell replied that "civilisation", derived from "civilise", was better because of its clearer counterpoint to the idea of "barbarity".

The idea of civilisation was born out of a combination of Enlightenment ideas about a progressive historical process, an ancient notion going back to the Old Testament and the Greeks; and the belief that there was a universal benchmark for evaluating development in different societies, a more novel idea. Given that Enlightenment thinkers conceived of the historical past as an outmoded and harmfully irrational period, to become civilised meant to be emancipated from the weight of historical prejudices (Ahlskog, 2010, p. 154).

The Political Economists were highly influenced by this concept, especially because the main formulators were products of the Scottish Enlightenment, notably David Hume and Adam Smith (see Chapter 4). An influential model of time was that human development had four stages, moving from less advanced to more advanced economic modes, with capitalism being the pinnacle. Smith's economic magnum opus is, in many ways, a supposed road map across these four stages, with Marx later adding what he thought was the true, post-capitalist, apotheosis of Communism (Ahlskog, 2010; Meek, 1976).

The Enlightenment was unfolding during a time of expanding European contact with, and domination of, the non-European world, and this raised an imagined need to explain why Europeans were so different from the rest of the world. eighteenth-century rationalism emphasised human mutability through the acquisition of knowledge and this suggested that Europeans were not innately superior but simply more learned. Anyone could learn the lessons the Europeans had uncovered and Europeans therefore thought that they had a mission to spread these lessons, just as the Spanish had earlier thought they were bringing Catholicism to the heathens they were encountering as they built their Empire. Adam Smith, and others of his ilk, was simply an evangelist of progress rather than Christ (Ahlskog, 2010, 155).

Yet, Enlightenment thought also brought to the fore old essentialist ideas about human nature, especially regarding those who weren't European. Ancient practices that were taken for granted because of their basis in tradition were now called into question, especially slavery and feudalism, since tradition was no longer a viable justification for social practice. The slave trade and slave colonies now became intellectually questionable at best, causing the vested interests involved to push a new doctrine of white European racial superiority on a supposedly scientific basis. The eighteenth century saw great ferment in the world of biology, with much cataloguing of data and attendant categorisation of biological differences, most notably "race". Supposedly neutral, these new categories were used politically to justify European supremacy, or at least the European role of helping shepherd their non-white, non-Western "lessers" into the modern world, if not ultimately as equals, at least as properly raised inferiors (Ahlskog, 2010, 148–150).

11.2 Civilisational Analysis

This is not to say that civilisation is not a useful concept, especially when shorn of value judgements as much as possible. If nothing else, the breadth and depth of the notion invites exploration of connections between diverse facets of human existence that narrower conceptions tend to leave out. "World history" is a contemporary discipline that has emerged in large part because of such an approach, tracking how distinct societies have grown and changed over time, seeing how they solved key problems in similar, but also different ways, and discovering how they have produced separate identities yet across common themes (Stearns, 2016).

This emphasis on breadth has also brought out more clearly the interdependence between differing social units, replacing older reified hierarchies of more and less advanced progressions. For example, nomadic groups have played vital roles in world history, especially because of their strategic placements between larger and more centralised socio-political units, and the flexibility of this particular form of social organisation may have arisen precisely as an adaptation to the larger forms around them. Thus differing social forms and units are not more or less advanced relative to each other, but represent the myriad adaptations that social Sapiens use at various times and various places (Stearns., 2016).

Similarly, there has been a re-definition of terms like "Western" in historiography, which leaves narratives like the history of Western Europe and the expansion of Western civilisation across the Atlantic valid but now more narrow, seen as only part of a larger world history context of changing and dynamic civilisational patterning (Stearns, 2003). In particular, civilisation can be used to break out of older "functionalist" traditions, which have their place but which generally are too limited or teleological in many instances to be used on their own. This is why "civilisational analysis" has become fashionable over the past few decades, allowing for investigation of large-scale, long-term social formations that can encompass multiple societies (sometimes referred to as macro-cultural, macrosocial and macro-historical units), even for societies quite different from one another (Arnason, 2009).

Granted, the meaning of civilisation is multiple and contested, even more so when getting down to comparisons across different societies, which is what civilisational analysis is all about at its core. The major civilisation groups are still generally treated as being Eurasian (including the subset of European), Byzantine, Islamic, Indian and East Asian, all of which can be seen (not totally favourably) as an expansion of the older more limited "Western" canon of Greece, Rome and possibly Semitic worlds versus "Eastern" cultures. Even within Western Europe, the Continent is distinct from the British Isles, France is distinct from Spain and so forth. And when does "Central" Europe begin and end and how does it relate to both its "Eastern" and "Western" boundaries? There is also the question of how Western European civilisation relates to that of Western Christian civilisation and that of Eastern rite Orthodoxy. Similar sorts of boundary and definitional issues arise with respect to whether one can speak of one Indian civilisation or a set of multiple Subcontinent socio-cultural groupings, and how East Asia should be characterised, especially with regard to the relationship between China and Japan (Arnason,

2003) (see Box 11.1 for a discussion of a more contemporary boundary debate).

Box 11.1 Are Turkey and Russia "European"?
Two countries have long been part of, and yet apart from, Europe: Turkey and Russia. Are these countries "European" civilisations or not?

Turkey, whose modern incarnation still has a small foothold on the European continent, is, nonetheless, seen by most "Europeans" as from a different civilisation: Muslim, Asian, Eastern. Cebeci (2019) deconstructs modern Turkey's application process to join the European Union (EU), begun in 1999 and stalled and essentially dead by 2006. He argues that although EU conditionality standards are framed in technical terms (e.g. having good democratic institutions, independent judiciary, modernised economy, etc.), they actually are based on a standard of civilisation pursued by Europeans for accepting certain countries to the international society in the seventeenth through nineteenth centuries, with the EU continuing to serve as a guardian and gatekeeper of European civilisation against outsiders.

This can be seen, Cebeci argues, in a number of ways. During a state's accession negotiations, the EU authoritatively decides the standards that the candidate country must adopt, putting an asymmetrical relationship between the EU and the candidates. These standards are not applied evenly or consistently. For example, Croatia has many of the same issues as a candidate country that Turkey has, and yet its application, though still pending, has not been as definitively frozen.

There are also parallels between EU treatment of modern Turkey and older European views of the Ottomans, which were equally asymmetrical and arguably biased. The Ottoman Empire had a centuries-old extensive presence in Europe but in its decline was crystallised in an image of "The Sick Man of Europe", a cultural pejorative that was not applied to an arguably equally weakening Russia. The Ottoman Empire was only accepted into the European state system with the Paris Peace Treaty of 1856 on the condition that Sultan Abdülmecid I adopt a set of political and economic reforms acceptable to Europeans, especially the granting of equal rights to non-Muslim minorities and improvement of the ecclesiastical rights of the Christian communities in the Empire. Such conditions were never imposed on Russia, its status being accepted as a fait accompli.

But here is where Russia is an equally interesting counterpoint and parallel all at the same time. Russia is arguably more geographically European than Turkey, and in some ways its treatment as a European power was never in doubt. Russia did not have to "prove" its European status, as the Ottomans had to. It is also "white" and "Christian", which obviously are very salient points in its favour viewed through a "European" lens.

Nonetheless Russia has always been very distinct in its civilisation: Orthodox Christian (which had a very separate trajectory from the Western Church, including the lack of a Reformation), Mongol origins, and a quite distinct social history and development. Indeed, Peter the Great and Catherine the Great explicitly adopted Western mores in large part to bring their country into line with what were seen as Western civilised standards.

The differences in treatment by European elites of Russians versus Turks in both their rises and falls are instructive. A rising Russia during the eighteenth century was let into the European power tent, regardless of inter-societal distinctions, the jointly agreed partitions of Poland by Russia, Hapsburg Austria and Prussia showing this. A similar accord was never reached with the Ottomans during their territorial gains of the same period. The Turks were seen as invaders penetrating into Europe from Asia, yet so too was Russia. The latter, however, was seen as sharing a common European foundation, which was not the case for the Muslim, Arab Turks.

As both Turkey and Russia have now reached a sort of mutual post-greatness state, oddly enough their treatment by the European Union has become more similar. Both are now seen as too "non-European" for admission into the "civilised" club of the EU. There are, of course, many reasons for this, the war in Ukraine intensifying matters. But the judgement of these two countries, with long involvements in European affairs and geographic footholds, as "alien" somehow is indicative of an underlying, and contestable, civilisational element that goes beyond mere national, economic and political criteria.

11.3 "Western" "European" Civilisation

The Industrial Revolution and the Great Divergence were centred in Europe, the heart of "Western Civilisation". European historian Norman Davies (1996) dates the development of a distinctly European civilisation as emerging between 330 and 800 C.E. Other scholars see it coalescing a little later with the solidification of unity in Western Christendom, and the melding of church and most royal authorities around 1000 C.E. (Bråkenhielm, 2002). Regardless of exact timing, and noting various "strains" (such as the split between the Eastern Rite churches and Catholic Church in Rome), it is clear that the diverse peoples and groupings of Europe did eventually come to see themselves as sharing a continental cultural identity enough to think of themselves as "Europeans".

The name "Europe" was derived from a Greco-Roman myth. Europa was a beautiful Phoenician princess, whom the God Zeus saw gathering flowers one day, immediately falling in love with her. Zeus transformed himself into a white bull and carried Europa away to the island of Crete, where he revealed his true identity and made her the first queen of the island. Davies (1996) claims this myth is significant because it shows the movement of Asian culture from Asia Minor to the European continent (an "abduction" by it); a template of culture metaphorically following the sun (moving east to west); and a change in cultural paradigm from long-run stasis (the ideal of the ancient Egyptians and, to a lesser degree, Imperial Rome) to the dynamism of constant movement of peoples and ideas heading in a forward direction.

"Europe" as an overarching transnational cultural identification has been around for a long time now. But there are numerous wellsprings from which the European identity has drawn. At least three major sources can be noted, two of them from "classical" civilisations (Daszkiewicz, 2007):

11.3.1 Ancient Greece

From this heritage comes human-centred as opposed to nature- or God-centred models of the world; empiricism and human reason as modes of inquiry and discovery; the distinction between divine and human law; the idea that humans can improve and shape themselves and that reason and the use of logic and words are methods for doing this; the ideal of human freedom as a goal desirable in and of itself (for only free humans can improve themselves); and the notion of citizenship and equal membership in a civic community (the "polis"). The Greeks were not completely unique in these particulars, but they were the first to develop a systematic philosophy with a unity and harmony that tied all these things together and made them compelling.

11.3.2 Ancient Rome

The Roman Empire provided some of the key institutions that laid the substrate for modern economic growth in Europe, especially systematic legal thinking and common law; successful methods of public administration; a tradition of urban development, allied with engineering prowess; the development of a professional army with a national identity (and not just open to "warrior" classes but an institution with the ability to make and train soldiers); tremendous influence on the development of a modern theory (and practice) of the State and statecraft (powerfully allied with Greek notions of democracy and representative government); and the idea of Great Leaders with special abilities: it was the Romans who called their Rulers "First Citizens"—"Principas"—from which the word "Principal" is derived (Fig. 11.2).

11.3.3 Christianity

Of course, the rise of the Catholic Church—first as official state religion of the Roman Empire under Constantine—and then as official religion of many of the post-Empire states of Europe—affected European identity both institutionally and ideologically. Arguably, the conferral of "divine right" on early European monarchs helped to integrate the state under an "impersonal" authority while the "Scholastic" movement in the Catholic monasteries (especially Thomas Aquinas) and "discovery" of the ancient Greek texts in the Middle Ages reinvigorated and disseminated rationalist and empiricist techniques.

11.4 Civilisational Sources and Aspects of Economic Growth

All civilisations have long lineages and multiple sources that shape them, and they encompass all aspects of human social organisation in some way. The prior section has mentioned several major sources of Western European civilisation, and this is still far from a complete or even consensus reckoning. The onset of industrialisation and capitalism was also drawn from this well. How are these strains related to one another and how was Western civilisation affected as a result?

Fig. 11.2 Augustus, Roman Emperor (*Image source* West, W. M. [1913]. *The ancient world, from the earliest times to 800 A. D.* [Revised edition]. Norwood Press, Page 461. *Contributing Library* The Library of Congress. Digitizing Sponsor: Sloan Foundation. No known copyright restrictions)

For example, did the West industrialise first because of its turn towards rationalism and individuality that emphasised individual inquiry, empiricism, experimentation and investigation as inculcated in Ancient Greek values and taken up in earnest with the Renaissance and Enlightenment? Was perhaps Christianity the crucial factor, the earlier church being a retarding influence but then a stimulative one after the institutional diversity created by the Reformation and particular aspects of Protestantism such as the Weber "work ethic"? Or can economic advance be traced to the Roman heritage of codified law, large-scale military and political organisation, and systematic public administration, things that ultimately laid the ground for later European Empires, "exploration" and colonisation of non-European areas, underneath state structures that could coordinate it all?

Analysts of various disciplinary stripes have considered these and many others as discrete elements (see Chapters 3, 4 and 5). A civilisational approach would consider these things more collectively, seeing capitalism and its sources as likely much more than a merely economic system, but a macro-cultural complex. To consider economic change as an alteration to civilisation is to test the possibility that there is something about the integrated social whole that is greater than the mere sum of its parts.

Consider the hypothesis that what was truly unique about Europe as an economic first mover was not industrialisation but its global expansionism, often referred to as European Imperialism (see Chapter 13). Did something about European civilisation change to cause this expansionism? That China had the means of conducting similar moves in the 1400s but did not, and the fact that colonialism was engaged in by so many diverse European countries suggests that this is a possibility. If so, why? Was it perhaps an inherent rapacity unique to European culture that caused it to break out in aggressive aggrandisement against weaker parts of the world, as the German playwright (and Marxist) Bertolt Brecht always claimed, and which found its full expression in unbridled international capitalism (Katz, 2015, 284–288)? Alternatively, it may be that European macro-culture was especially war-like and violent, factors that caused the region to stoop to conquer outward, with an edge in military technology, honed by the region's constant internecine internal warfare which helped to create powerful states capable of leading war campaigns and powerful weapons capable of achieving successful outcomes (Morris, 2014). This is often captured in the phrase, "war makes the state, and the state makes war" to summarise (and oversimplify) the work of Charles Tilly (1992) (see Chapter 22).

These are grand questions requiring grand approaches. The French Annales historian Fernand Braudel (1992) argued that economic change was not just about meeting material needs, including production and consumption, but also material life more broadly, which is embedded in all areas of living, whether within the market, outside of it or apart from it entirely. For this reason, Braudel referred to this as "material life" or "material civilisation". Braudel argued that between the fifteenth and eighteenth centuries, change in these material aspects of European social life was slow, but that it rapidly sped up in the nineteenth century to produce the material civilisation associated with modernity, speed being one of its distinguishing features. Braudel claims that the European intellectual and cultural planes were already fairly modern by Voltaire's age, but that the material elements of life were still pre-modern. The material plane changed drastically with industrialisation, not only catching up with advances in the other dimensions, but surpassing them and, in turn, transforming them all, with the material ending up on top of everything in a sense. Thus, Braudel argues that the raising of the material over the immaterial is a mark of a change in civilisation rather than just a change in economic modes, as most growth theorists would maintain (Dant, 2006, 291– 293).

This is one reason that modern sociologists and anthropologists spend so much time studying "material culture", because modern life has become so full of objects of every kind, creating a cultural and social force all their own. This is not simply a matter of changing consumption or production activity, as economists generally see it. Material objects do arise out of these processes, but they also have social meanings, and radical change in the array and availability of objects changes rituals around them and practical uses in everyday life, altering the social networks that people operate in, and changing the nature of collective and individual experience in some essential way. Unlike the economics model that holds that value derives from transactional exchange through the market conducted by rational atomistic actors, a sociological perspective sees the value of material objects as socially variable and a product of many factors. Capitalism and industrialisation and modernisation are thus necessarily far more than purely "economic" which itself is a socially constructed category in many respects (Dant, 2006, 298–299).

For Braudel, these dynamics add up to changes in civilisation, or at least the civilising process that underlies it. In the modern context, Elias (1995) studied the effects of the introduction and dissemination of the automobile throughout the developed world and argued that it had civilising effects in the form of greater mobility, convenience and material gratification. But it also produced unintended "de-civilising" effects not just in the form of auto-induced death and injury but also through an expanding "technisation" (see Chapter 8), which is defined as the process by which human beings learn to exploit inanimate objects for ever greater power over their environment. This required human beings to make significant, and rather unnatural, adaptations to the technology to get its fullest mechanical benefits, e.g. habituating to mechanical controls, the dictates of traffic signals and so on. This is an extension of Elias's theme of human development as a process of internalising greater self-regulation to realise greater social interdependence that yields a (sometimes mixed) blessing of more collective power to achieve ends, including the wonders of modern technology and economy.

The sociologist Max Weber also saw culture at a macro-level as the human way of lending meaning and significance to the world, a need not shared with other species (so far as we know). He went on to explore the social and cultural sources of modern capitalism in the West as contrasted to non-Western civilisations that were economically proceeding along parallel pre- and early capitalistic lines, but which did not continue in the same ways that the Europeans did. Weber's most famous hypothesis was that the Protestant Reformation spawned an individual "work ethic" which was the critical factor in setting Europe off on its higher labour effort and productivity which in turn set off the Industrial Revolution. The evidence does not completely support this particular surmise (see Chapter 5). But this is only part of Weber's broader agenda of seeing modern Western capitalism as linked to a whole set of transformative processes, economic and otherwise. Weber also posited the idea of "rationalisation", a somewhat ambiguous concept that refers to things such as formal organisation and methodical procedures, especially bureaucracy. Weber claims this to be a core innovation of Western modernity and a critical part of modern economic growth, though with decidedly mixed social effects. Indeed, while rationalisation helped radically to boost material life, it also set in train processes that could help strangle it in various ways (Kim, 2020).

Macro-cultural, "civilisational" frames like these may be revealing. But they also can be intractable or too broad to be useful for analysing economic change. Like any framing, this is not an either/or choice, the civilisation paradigm offering another dimension to consider, sometimes relevant, sometimes not, but to be kept in mind because the modernisation of society is so multifaceted, and operates at large and small levels at the same time. Still the pitfalls can be significant. For a more contemporary, and controversial, use of the civilisation concept to consider affairs of the world, see Box 11.2.

Box 11.2 Samuel Huntington's "Clash of Civilisations"
A modern "civilisational" paradigm is offered by political scientist Samuel Huntington (1993) who argued that the contemporary world had now entered into a period where civilisations were the new basic fault lines, rather than economic differences or ideologies (where ideology can be defined as a system of ideas, values and beliefs that cohere into a dominant worldview, sometimes contrary to observed reality; see Chapter 17).

Huntington thought of civilisation as the overarching cultural category of our time, an identification that he called "real" and "basic" and the least mutable of social forms. He particularly emphasised religion as a key part of culture (a view not shared by everyone). He admitted that economics, ideas and other factors play a role in economic and geopolitical conflict (this latter item the main focus of his analysis) but argued that civilisation had become the fundamental divide between group identities and motivations, often transcending nations, especially where religion is involved. He notes that it is relatively easy to be French and Arab (for example), but not so easy to be Christian and Muslim.

For Huntington, Europe and the West were thus now divided along civilisational lines, and future conflict would be fought along these. Although on the same continent, "European" countries such as Bulgaria, Serbia and even Greece are part of a different cultural/religious orbit, as is Russia and Turkey, he claimed. And, of course, strains between Christian and Muslim countries were another global conflict zone.

Writing in 1993, right after the end of the Cold War, Huntington's pronouncements resonated, since old ethnic, religious and cultural conflicts soon opened up across Europe after the long freeze of Soviet Bloc stasis and Superpower counter-balance (see Chapter 25). Huntington's claim that he had identified the core lines of future international conflict was then, and still is, not an uncontested view. His concept may have been too broad, obscuring many other fields of dispute that were much less lofty, such as fights over strategic resources, and he also ignored the biases of world "rules of the game" which implicitly sanctified the values of a "core" over a "periphery". Others have criticised Huntington for an ad hoc and poorly defined use of the word civilisation, which in his hands tends to be reduced mainly to religious differences. And he leaves out almost entirely economic and social development within civilisation groups, except as products of, and responses to, inter-civilisation conflict. Overall, this is probably less a true civilisational analysis, than a geopolitical strategic template put into relatively simplistic macro-cultural terms.

11.5 Modernisation and the Individual

Civilisation does not only have "macro" effects but "micro" ones as well. It is the structure that at least partly defines how individuals think of themselves as individuals, and how they interact with one another, all of which in turn has significant impacts on the operations of an economy.

Returning to Elias, civilisation is not just a collective identity at a fixed point in time, the essence of Huntington's "clash" as per Box 11.2, but a process through which individual conduct is changed through interaction with the collective. Elias proposed that individuals and groups acquire multiple identities (for example, their individual persona, their gender, kin-group, occupation, religion, ethnicity, nation and so on) through the experience of participating in complex social networks, shaped by long-term social processes, a process Elias refers to as "figurations". Therefore identity formation is a shared social experience, shaped by social and historical location, as well as a critical part of the formation of a collective civilisation itself (Smith, 1999, 82).

Interestingly, Michael Foucault, an author sometimes seen as opposed to this notion of organic and non-coercive civilising, actually shares a lot of similar assumptions with Elias, both agreeing that the centralisation and the complexity of networks of interdependence has increased greatly over time and that the modern response has been to elaborate and enhance the external indications of social status, and thus become deeply preoccupied with the nature of the self. Where Foucault differs with Elias is in seeing modernity as coercive in its effects on the individual, forcing each person to change in ways that they otherwise might not, rather than being the natural equilibration proposed by Elias. For him, modern sociality intrusively imposes disciplines of thought and behaviour in the name of rationality and science. He rejects the so-called "repressive hypothesis" put forward by Freud, with its claims of a natural human stifling a wide range of spontaneous impulses, especially sexual ones, which may be analysed or even liberated by new knowledge. Instead, modern social power relations are "productive" rather than "repressive" in their operations, i.e. they actually create and re-create our conception of experience of things and the technical paradigm actually increased rather than decreased discourse about many matters, sexuality most notably. There is thus not so much a dance between individual and society in modernisation, as Elias claims, but rather a much more integrated co-creation of the two, driven by power considerations (Foucault, 1977; [1978] 1998). He believes that the human being needs to resist the modernisation process and search for ways of breaking out this social structure (Smith, 1999, 86–93). In this sense, Foucault traces a lineage back to Weber's warnings about rationalisation. And Elias himself does admit that technology forces human adaptation to machines and technical structures, the basis of his technisation concept.

The political and social implications of these contrasting views are rather stark, but their basic view of individual identity is very close to one another, namely that it arises out of social processes that are characterised in modernity by increasing sophistication, subtlety and social attenuation. Foucault and Elias both see the human being as co-created out of social forces and individual characteristics, some of which arise purely out of nature. Both speak to the simultaneity of cultural, individual, social and civilisational development. And both depart from the economistic view of rational, self-interested maximisation as being the immutable character of at least the economic actor.

11.6 Economic Change and Changing Categories of Gender, Race and Class

Modern civilisation, whatever its dynamics, certainly brought sharp alterations to basic social categories, especially gender, race and class. All three are socially constructed to one degree or another. The debates have always been about how much so, versus being innately determined, in sociology referred to as essentialism.

11.6.1 Gender

Many leading figures in the Enlightenment argued that gender hierarchies were no more rational or tolerable than aristocratic ones, and during the earliest part of the French Revolution, significant legislative advances were made on the rights of women and children, such the granting of the right of divorce for females. But while these measures gave women more civil rights than anywhere else in Europe, male revolutionaries had a bifurcated view of equality, seeing authority relations amongst men as socially constructed (and thus changeable), but those between men and women as established by nature (and thus unchangeable). This schizoid line of thinking continued under Napoleon, whose 1804 Civil Code made adult unmarried women relatively free in business and legal affairs, but made them totally subservient to their husbands after marriage (as per Article 213) (Wiesner-Hanks, 2001b, 21–22).

Despite strong economic, social and political change, old patriarchal patterns proved (and still prove to be) hard to break. The Roman Republic developed extensive legal notions and institutions of patriarchy, with Roman fathers theoretically holding life and death power over their children, including married daughters ("patria potestas"), although it is thought not to have been exercised often (Carcopino, 2003). Roman institutions and thinking permeated ancient Europe, carrying on well after the fall of the Empire, and this patriarchy continued right along with it, picked up both other Roman-influenced entities such as the Catholic Church.

Patriarchy is however far from exclusive to the Romans. If using the term broadly to refer to unequal social power between men and woman, almost every culture has been patriarchal. More narrowly referring to institutionalised power of older men over women, children and men in dependent positions (sometimes also thus referred to as "patriarchalism" or "paternalism"), Western cultures were patriarchal until the beginning of the nineteenth century, and still not entirely free of it today (Wiesner-Hanks, 2001b, 15).

An interesting debate about the distant economic past is whether matriarchy preceded patriarchy. Friedrich Engels said "yes", theorising that matriarchal cultures held goods in common but with the advent of agriculture, men began to claim ownership, through the creation of private property, of agricultural surplus and means of production in an attempt to continue such control through their heirs, exercising increasing dominion over women. With the abolition of private property under Communism, such dominion, he argued, would be unnecessary. The modern historian Gerda Lerner has argued instead that men made women the first property in order to control their procreative power and so patriarchy preceded other forms of hierarchy (Wiesner-Hanks, 2001b, 16).

Either way patriarchy continued with the Industrial Revolution, though altered by it. Although one might think that a system based on market exchange and economic value would reduce female inequality since everything was reduced to the value of the product of labour, which shouldn't differ by gender, in some ways industrialisation worsened the position of the woman in economic society, while in other cases merely changing its form without bettering it. The decisive marketisation of much household production during industrialisation removed women from many tasks they used to be informally employed in, except for child rearing and housekeeping, making them more, not less, excluded from the economy. After a turbulent period of dislocation for both men and women, where women and children were sometimes favoured over men for the new factory jobs, by the mid-nineteenth century, domestic service outpaced factory work as a source of urban area jobs for women and laws were passed in various jurisdictions restricting women's (but not men's) hours of work in many formal occupations (Smith, 2001, 28).

This situation evolved as manufacturing scale rose, giving rise to new office jobs, and as the service sector expanded, generating non-factory employment that provided work for (unmarried) women. Gender segregation was practised, with stereotyping of jobs that supposedly appealed to women's desire for clean work and their perceived greater submissiveness. Some of these jobs, such as secretarial, bank teller and librarian work, which had initially been done by men, were now reserved exclusively for women, and as females moved up into these positions, the positions themselves moved down in status, pay and room for advancement. Meanwhile, the professionalisation of fields like medicine and the law removed women from these sectors since they were excluded from the training and licensing that was now required (Smith, 2001, 28).

In parallel, the rising technical organisation of production and employment also changed the form of gender inequality, though not its thrust. The skill levels required for many jobs, in the factory or outside of it, were rising, while at the same time, many other jobs were becoming more routinised than ever. At the same time, job tasks, functions and categories were becoming increasingly systematised and codified so they could be managed and staffed more effectively. Thus, some jobs that had traditionally been done by men were reclassified and given to women, at lower status and pay, as machinery made the work (weaving and secretarial work being examples), more monotonous. Men were also seen as more "mechanical" and thus brewing and stocking knitting were converted into male-dominated occupations in some parts of Europe as they became more machine-based. At the same time, the very use of "skilled" and "unskilled" work classifications was often code for enforcement of gender divisions. So, women were judged as too "unskilled" for glass cutting, yet "skilled" enough for lacemaking, which was actually a more complex task. Mechanisation and standardisation thus expanded, reinforced and formalised discrimination against women (Wiesner-Hanks, 2001a, 60).

Changing class groupings and roles, discussed separately below, also came into the mix. Urban prosperity created new urban middle classes prosperous enough to be supported by only one income-earner, perhaps supplemented with part-time informal work by wives and children. But these sole supporter roles were reserved for men, and the male-led nuclear family, which began to emerge out of the initial turmoil of early capitalism, now became institutionalised, formally and informally, in a new middle-class ideology of "separate spheres" of work for men, home for women. This general template of female subordination and gender-stereotyped division of household labour went back centuries, but now became a more rigid ideal that ironically was no longer a luxury reserved for the rich (Smith, 2001, 32). The working classes, as always, generally could only look in on such practices from afar, even though they increasingly aspired to them. Most women in poor households had to work at whatever they could find, often continuing to do informal household production or service-provision on a piecework basis as well as paid employment outside the home.

Both men and women were socially typecast in this period, "feminisation" and "masculinisation" being terms referring to the process. Men dominated sport, politics and business, women being shunted into household-related public spheres of charity work and genteel (middle class) social action on behalf of children and other forsaken souls (Stearns, 2001). Female political activism however started in these reserved realms. Care of orphans and prostitutes soon expanded to temperance and anti-smoking movements, and the woman's suffrage movement became a growing crusade as well, beginning in Norway in the 1830s, then France in the 1840s and Britain and Sweden in the 1850s. Suffragism became a foundation for a growing feminist movement fighting for women's rights, organising globally with the formation of the International Council of Women in 1888 and the International Woman Suffrage Alliance in 1904. These currents coalesced into the "New Woman" controversy over marriage, famously dramatised by Henrik Ibsen in his 1879 play, *A Doll's House*, which portrayed the entire institution of marriage as nothing more than an economic arrangement repressive of women. English suffragist Cicely Hamilton, in her 1909, *Marriage as a Trade* pamphlet, argued that marriage differed from prostitution only in the social approval attached to its status (Mayhall, 2001, 49–51). All this activity did result in an increasing legal emancipation of women in various spheres in various countries. But the pace was gradual and piecemeal, and informal discrimination continued.

Mary Beard (2018) finds patriarchy still deeply embedded in contemporary Western European civilisation, in part because of its foundation in the Ancient World, where women were not allowed a voice, except to advocate for the supposedly parochial interests of women such as the welfare of children or their own sex. Even if women did speak (their silence was preferred), they did not need to be listened to according to ancient mores. Although there are differences between contemporary Western and ancient Greco-Roman cultures, this notion has carried through to current times and it certainly was well practised during the Industrial Revolution, First, Second and beyond. Beard argues that we need to question the whole conception of power itself, which currently uses male categories.

11.6.2 Race

Human beings have long identified themselves as belonging to groups of one sort or another. Some of the oldest designations include religion and ethnicity, both encompassing culturally contingent features, such as a common language, or sense of a common history or belief.

Modern biology has shown that "race" actually does not exist genetically, and so despite its salience for recent and contemporary history, it is an empirical fiction. Yet, the heyday of industrialisation was also the heyday of racialism and racism. Prejudice is nothing new for humanity, of course. Religious, cultural and ethnic discrimination and stereotyping is as old as civilisation, as is the oppression of human by human, as the practice of slavery shows. But using skin colour and other outward physical characteristics as the basis for this oppression is only hundreds rather than thousands of years old. "Racism", i.e. categorising and discriminating against people according to the "race" they have been assigned, seems to have been born as a biological concept out of the European Religious Wars, first between Muslims and Christians and then between Protestants and Catholics; though arguably the ancient practice of anti-Semitism during the early Catholic ascendancy after the fall of the Roman Empire is a form of racism very long-standing, or at least ethnic persecution (Horne, 2018).

Even then the Spanish, in the horrific practices of their Empire, tended to be sectarian first, racist second, killing heathens without necessarily considering their race in the first instance. There were a number of Africans amongst the Conquistadores, while Cuba had a large free black population. The English, on the other hand, developed their Empire more explicitly along racial lines, for example allowing Church of England dissenting sects (such as Quakers, who established the colony of Pennsylvania) and Catholics (who set up Maryland), to settle in the Americas, but allowing blacks in only as slaves. The French and the Dutch were similarly racially oriented, engaged in slave holding and slave trading and treating both transported and transplanted Africans and conquered indigenous peoples appallingly and as racial, not just social or ethnic inferiors, generally not even as humans. However, race-based slavery appears to be more of a European than a non-European practice, with Islamic slaveholders, for example, keeping 25,000 whites in bondage at one point (Horne, 2018).

The turn towards official doctrines of racial superiority and inferiority that had begun to emerge in the 1500s and beyond, reached an apotheosis in the nineteenth century right along with industrialisation and European imperialism. Its purpose was low but its rhetoric was high-pitched. Alfred Thayer Mahan's essay, *A Twentieth-Century Outlook* (1897), predicted a race war, while Charles Pearson's, *National Life and Character* (1893), warned other whites of the dangers of newly ascendant and dangerous non-white races. The First World War and its aftermath brought more tomes of this sort, amongst them Oswald Spengler's, *The Decline of the West* (1914–18), H. M. Hyndman's, *The Awakening of Asia* (1919), Madison Grant's, *The Passing of the Great Race* (1922), Lothrop Stoddard's, *The Rising Tide of Color Against White World-Supremacy* (1920), and Maurice Muret's, The *Twilight of the White Races* (1925)

(Younis, 2017, 497). Racism became tightly bound up with defences of "Western Civilisation".

While non-whites were thus to be feared by Europeans as imminent threats, they were, paradoxically, also seen as natural inferiors who needed to be paternalistically managed, or ruthlessly exploited. Rudyard Kipling's *White Man's Burden* was published in 1900 and expressed the condescending paternalistic view so typical of the British Imperial tradition. Many other treatises were not even this genteel. The results for the colonised subjects on the ground were the same either way, imperial hagiography of the time notwithstanding. Even within the white race, there was said to be operating fierce forces of "natural" competition that winnowed out the weak and left only the strong remaining. The doctrine of Social Darwinism thrived in this era, to be replaced by the more "scientific" field of eugenics in the twentieth century (Byrd, 1971; Koch, 1984; Paul, 2003; Rogers, 1972). Even with a posited range of ability within the white race, in general the least amongst whites were said to be naturally superior to the best amongst non-whites.

Not incidentally, the nineteenth century was also an era of rampant nationalism as well. Nationhood and so-called "national characteristics" were emotive-intellectual responses to the building pressures of the age. Nationalism often became fused with nationality and ethnicity, as when people would refer to the "English", "German" or "American" races. This was also true of transnational affinity. Across Europe and its settler territories, notions of supposed pan-racial affinity spread alongside imperial nationalism. A parallel pan-racial solidarity emerged in the places being colonised or threatened with colonisation, as with pan-Africanism and pan-Islamism. Such affinities were not mutually exclusive, and could coexist, sometimes rather contradictorily (Younis, 2017, 484–485).

Racial identifications within present and former colonies created some interesting juxtapositions, such as the "Greater England" notion of unity between white England, Imperial white Dominions and the US. Imperial nationalism in England was a particularly peculiar form of racial transnationalism, calling for political union between Britain and its settler territories. Cecil Rhodes went so far as to call for the US to be absorbed back into a united Anglo-Saxon Empire, the Anglo-Boer War being a spur to ideas of this type. It wasn't just hardened imperialists that engaged in this racist utopianism. W. T. Stead, H. G. Wells and Andrew Carnegie all expressed variants of such views (Younis, 2017, 486–488). There was also pan-Hispanism in Latin America, "Latin Europe" in the Latin language European nations, pan-Germanism across German speakers and pan-Slavism in Slavic territories. There are clear ethnic as well as racial crosscurrents here, but Osterhammel (2014) notes that whiteness was an underlying commonality, set against a notional non-white "threat".

European imperialism was triumphing across the globe, and, as noted, the subjects at this point could most successfully resist by formulating counter-doctrines of racial identification. But Ethiopia's victory over Italy at Adwa in 1896 and Japan's victory over Russia in 1905 were felt across the colonised world as signs that non-whites could take on whites and win. In Indian villages, newborns were named after Japanese generals and African American and South African church denominations took the name "Adwa" (Younis, 2017, 490). In the European core, the defensive response was an increase in doctrines of (white) racial superiority. These racialisms would butt up against the paradoxical and concurrent internationalisms and universalisms of the era: Liberalism on the right, and Socialism and Communism on the Left.

Racism was both a cause and effect of industrialisation. Communications and travel technologies greatly increased the capacity to interact in real time with one another, creating a discourse about the annihilation of space and time that both increased the sense of global interconnection but also fragmentation based on fear of the "other" (Younis, 2017, 486). Mass culture and the rise of newspapers created new ways of creating (and manipulating) mass identities (see Chapter 10). Economic changes were upending established social categories and institutions and undermining old traditions and ways of thinking. And practices like colonialism, the exploitation of immigrants, squalid urban poverty and regimented factories with seething labour conflict created a cognitive and moral dissonance that had to be reconciled to the supposed "progress" of modern industrial civilisation. Race and racism, scientifically justified, provided one such tonic, often consciously exploited by the power structure.

11.6.3 Class

Finally, there is social and economic class. Class is surprisingly hard to define with certitude, but sociologists note that it necessarily involves comparisons between groups in a society. While gender might have an element of biological absolute definition (though this is now widely disputed), and "race" is most definitely a pure social construct, even when justified "scientifically", class is always relative and always social.

Capitalism increasingly removed many older differences between social and economic categories of class, such as "clergy" and "nobility", fusing them into economic designations such as "workers" and "capitalists". The Political Economists were not unaware of class but for them, economic growth was an opportunity that would alleviate or even eliminate old class conflict. This was the thrust of Adam Smith's idea of a "wage fund" fed by capitalist profits to pay growing worker wages, both expanding along with productivity, and effectively putting the two classes on the same side (see Chapter 4).

Reality was not so simple, and the new economic order called for new theories of class. Weber posited that power was based on, and applied to accomplish to three things: social honour, material resources and authority. Industrial society transformed these long-standing drives into highly rationalised and formalised forms, converting the overall power quest into one primarily of accessing and using material resources, from which social honour and authority followed. In capitalism, the market exchange was where this happened, and under an industrial system, it was pursued and exercised through "rationalised" mechanisms such as bureaucracy. All this caused people what he called "instrumental rationality", a much more nuanced and full-bodied notion of procedural rationality that economists use, and thus often misunderstood by them. Whereas economists assume people use logical processing and calculation to achieve definite ends, Weber thought that, in an industrial age, rational analysis, discourse and decision-making had in fact fragmented into a number of different types. Weber's use of the concept is not entirely clear or consistent but its main thrust is that, just as modern society has become formalised and procedularised in ways that are almost ritual, and sometimes even detached from ends (a sort of procedure for procedure's sake), the cognitive and logical processes of individual human beings had become so too (Wright, 1997).

Marx, on the other hand, saw economic class as a central part of the economic problem. Capitalism was just the latest stage of a historical process of intensifying class struggle, with class itself being a means of exploitation. The ultimate and last stage would be a classless (and stateless) society in which such exploitation ceased. The flaws and saliences of Marxist thought, in theory and application, are considered later on in Chapters 21 and 23. The key point here is that the Marxist concept of exploitation goes beyond simple conflicts over distribution of economic income. That could be characterised as a technical problem in which resources could be redistributed leaving existing classes in place. Instead, class relations are the fundamental problem in and of themselves. Marx argues that class is always completely a product of the economic system of the time and that the capitalist system created its own particular classes of capitalist and proletariat that would inevitably clash, resulting in the collapse of the entire system into a communal collective. With that, class of any sort would end forever (Wright, 1997).

Regardless of theoretical viewpoint, unquestionably capitalist development redefined class entirely and in many ways still is. As far as discrimination on the basis of class (or race or gender), the economic costs of all these must be high, though hard to estimate. There is the idiosyncratic theory of "rational" discrimination, which claims that its practice is based on particular preferences of rational maximising agents and whose effects are costly to both discriminator and discriminated, and thus ultimately withering away with market competition and optimisation (Becker, 1971). But outside the economics profession, and probably even within it, this is a minority view. In sociological terms, class is one category of social power, a complex of social relations, ideas, economics and history, and discrimination of any sort is an injustice to be rectified.

11.7 "Axial" Movements, Modernisation and "Multiple Modernities"

Although this chapter has focused on "Western" civilisation, civilisation itself is much more general, shared by virtually all people. Going back to much earlier history, the Axial Civilisation paradigm claims that a big break in global human social patterns took place from about the eighth to the third century B.C.E. Prior to this (and rather grossly overgeneralising), human societies tended to have no distinctions between divine and human orders. Then, across diverse societies, Eastern and Western, cultures began to independently and concurrently make distinctions, between the human being and nature, between the sacred and the mundane and between the individual and the collective. The human being began to be seen as a creature with autonomy and agency of thought and action, able to exert control over the world while also subject to its forces (Arnason, 2003).

This characterisation has been widely criticised on various grounds, but its generalisations have some utility in potentially identifying universal processes that brought all societies into a modern age, or at least elements such as industrialisation, bureaucratisation and secularisation. In this civilisational take, the modern vision of human autonomy is built on older cross-cultural traditions of beliefs about human capacities to accumulate power, wealth, self-determination and mastery of nature. This is not a straightforward development and contains contradictions and conflicts between individualistic and collectivist conceptions of autonomy and competing models of rationality.

Thus, some claim that there are now "multiple modernities" (Eisenstadt, 2003), that are bouncing off one another, partly joined by common Axial threads, and thus with old notions of linear hierarchy of progress inapplicable (Arnason, 2009). One can view many ongoing debates through this lens. An example is the Western argument that democracy and capitalism necessarily go together, which is often set against Asian counterexamples, like China and Singapore, which suggest that they don't have to. The default is to couch this in oppositional terms, one "right", another "wrong"; or, perhaps, a set of viable trade-offs on a policy menu. However, there is much to be said for a broader approach to modern economic change. Deep social structures and traditions have interacted with economic forces in mutually reinforcing and conflicting ways across history, so even if one can say that we are on some kind of unprecedented material frontier, there are multiple ways that this manifests, and none of these are wholly independent from one another in a systemic sense.

Civilisation was once a very standard frame for historical analysis. It has been dropped because it originally contained the conceit that one set of societies was "better" than another, and this conceit continues in many quarters. It also contained many exclusionary and discriminatory assumptions. But if this misdirection is consciously put aside and refrained from, civilisation can offer a wide-reaching paradigm in which to analyse complex changes across multiple macro-cultures, economic and otherwise.

In some ways, this sort of thinking was applied to the modern economy in its earlier stages. Thorstein Veblen (1919) argued that industry and science had brought about a machine age that had transformed not just the economy but created a new sort of scientific civilisation in which systems of thought, based on machine logic and necessarily taken as given because of the opacity of the workings of modern technical systems, had pushed aside more pragmatic thinking and acting based on workmanship and the relative clarity (though greater informality) of craft production. Veblen was not alone in such thinking (which is oversimplified here to focus on a couple of primary elements). He was not being critical of this development per se. Nor was he, as many of the pre-Raphealites of the time were, inclined to go backwards to a purportedly golden and simpler age. But he was arguing that Capitalism, at least in its industrial form, was not just a new economic system but also an entirely new civilisation, and needed to be thought of as such.

Not that civilisation, even an elevated one, doesn't have its downsides. One could recount a story called *Peace And War* by Kahlil Gibran (1932). To paraphrase the tale, three dogs are conversing, dreamily comparing themselves and their "dogdoms" and noting how peaceful and artistic they all are, and how far they have progressed since their forefathers. Their dreamy idyll is suddenly broken by the appearance of the dogcatcher. At which point they all scatter and run with the third calling out "For God's sake, run for your lives. Civilization is after us".

References

Ahlskog, J. (2010). The political economy of colonisation: Carl Bernhard Wadström's case for abolition and civilisation. *Nordic Journal for Eighteenth-Century Studies, 7*, 146–167.

Arnason, J. P. (2003) *Civilizations in dispute: Historical questions and theoretical traditions*. Brill.

Arnason, J. P. (2009). Civilizational analysis: A paradigm in the making. In R. Holton & W. R. Nasson (Eds.), *Encyclopedia of life support systems: World civilizations and history of human development*. EOLSS Publications (in cooperation with UNESCO).

Beard, M. (2018). *Women & power: A manifesto* (updated). Profile Books.

Becker, G. S. (1971). *The Economics of discrimination*. University of Chicago Press.

Bråkenhielm, C. R. (2002). The idea of Europe in the perspective of world views and values. An Introduction. *SPIEL, 21*(2), 187–202.

Braudel, F. ([1979] 1992). *The structures of everyday life: The limits of the possible*. University of California Press.

Byrd, R. H. (1971). *Social Darwinism and British imperialism, 1870–1900* (Doctoral dissertation) Texas Tech University.

Carcopino, J. (2003). *Daily life in ancient Rome: The people and the city at the height of the empire*. Yale University Press.

Cebeci, M. (2019). Deconstructing the EU's "standards of civilisation." *Uluslararası İlişkiler/International Relations, 16*(64), 77–91.

Dant, U. (2006). Material civilization: Things and society. *British Journal of Sociology, 57*(2), 289–308.

Daszkiewicz, W. (2007). Greek and Roman roots of European civilisation. *Studia Gilsoniana, 6*(3), 381–404.

Davies, N. (1996). *Europe: A history*. Random House.

Eisenstadt, S. N. (2003). *Comparative civilizations and multiple modernities* (Vol. 1). Brill

Elias, N. (1995). Technization and civilization. *Theory Culture and Society, 12*(3), 7–42.

Foucault, M. (1977). *Discipline and punish: The birth of the prison* (Sheridan, A., Trans.). Penguin Books.

Foucault, M. ([1978] 1998). *The history of sexuality: The will to knowledge*. Penguin.

Gibran, K. (1932). *The wanderer: His parables and his sayings*. Knopf.

Horne, G. (2018). *The apocalypse of settler colonialism: The roots of slavery, white supremacy, and capitalism in 17th century North America and the Caribbean*. New York University Press.

Huntington, S. P. (1993). The clash of civilizations? *Foreign Affairs, 72*(3), 22–49.

Katz, P. (2015). *The partnership: Brecht, Weill, three women, and Germany on the brink*. Nan A Talese/Doubleday.

Kim, S. H. (2020). Max Weber. In E. N. Zalta (Ed.), *The Stanford encyclopedia of philosophy* (Winter 2020 Edition). https://plato.stanford.edu/archives/win2020/entries/weber/

Koch, H. W. (1984). Social Darwinism as a factor in the 'New Imperialism.' In H. W. Koch (Ed.), *The origins of the First World War* (pp. 319–342). Palgrave.

Mayhall, L. E. N. (2001). Feminisms. In P. N. Stearns (Ed.), *Encyclopedia of European social history from 1350 to 2000* (Vol. 4, pp. 44–54). Charles Scribner's sons (Gale).

Meek, R. (1976). *Social Science and the ignoble savage*. Cambridge University Press.

Morris, I. (2014). *War! What is it good for? Conflict and the progress of civilization from primates to robots*. Farrer, Straus and Giroux.

Osterhammel, J. (2014). *The transformation of the world: A global history of the nineteenth century* (Camiller, P., Trans.). Princeton University Press.

Paul, D. B. (2003). Darwin, Social Darwinism and eugenics. In J. Hodge & G. Radick (Eds.), *The Cambridge companion to Darwin* (pp. 214–239). Cambridge University Press.

Rogers, J. A. (1972). Darwinism and social Darwinism. *Journal of the History of Ideas, 33*(2), 265–280.

Smith, B.G. (2001a). The development of gender history. In P. N. Stearns (Ed.), *Encyclopedia of European social history from 1350 to 2000* (Vol. 4, pp. 3–13). Charles Scribner's sons (Gale).

Smith, D. (1999). "The civilizing process" and "the history of sexuality": Comparing Norbert Elias and Michel Foucault. *Theory and Society, 28*(1), 79–100.

Stearns, P. N. (2001). Men and masculinity. In P. N. Stearns (Ed.), *Encyclopedia of European social history from 1350 to 2000* (Vol. 4, pp. 37–43). Charles Scribner's sons (Gale).

Stearns, P. N. (2003). *Western civilization in world history.* Taylor & Francis Group.

Stearns, P. N. (2016). World history, identity and political change. *Foundations of Science, 21*(1), 105–115.

Tilly, C. (1992). War in history. *Sociological Forum, 7*(1), 187–195.

Veblen, T. (1919). *The place of science in modern civilisation.* B. W. Huebsch.

Wiesner-Hanks, M .E. (2001a). Gender and work. In P. N. Stearns (Ed.), *Encyclopedia of European social history from 1350 to 2000* (Vol. 4, pp. 55–67). Charles Scribner's sons (Gale).

Wiesner-Hanks, M. E. (2001b). Patriarchy. In P. N. Stearns (Ed.), *Encyclopedia of European social history from 1350 to 2000* (Vol. 4, pp. 14–24). Charles Scribner's sons (Gale).

Wright, E. O. (1997). *Class counts: Comparative studies in class analysis.* Cambridge University Press.

Younis, M. (2017). United by blood: Race and transnationalism during the Belle Époque. *Nations and Nationalism, 23*(3), 484–504.

CHAPTER 12

"1900"

C. Gordon, *Many Possible Worlds*,
https://doi.org/10.1007/978-981-19-9281-0_12

RANCH AND RANGE

ISSUED EVERY WEEK

Vol. 16. No. 7. SEATTLE and SPOKANE, WASH., JANUARY 18, 1900. $1.00 Per Year.

NEW 20th CENTURY
De Laval "Alpha" Cream Separators

In wishing the Creamery and Dairy interests of the country and every one in any way associated with such interests a Happy and Prosperous New Year the De Laval Company avails of the opportunity to briefly announce the further expansion and improvement of its machines in conjunction with the opening of the new year.

The word De Laval has always been synonymous with progressive development. Every year has marked some new improvement or step of advancement bringing the "Alpha" De Laval machines still nearer to literal perfection. 1900 is to be no exception, bringing with it the general adoption to the "Alpha" disc system of the new Split-Wing Tubular Shaft invention thus effecting more even and thorough distribution of the milk in the separating bowl than heretofore accomplished. This improvement effects generally every feature of separator practicability, affording considerably greater capacity with still more exhaustive thoroughness of separation—particularly under the harder conditions of heavy cream and low temperature, while the accompanying change in bowl construction obviates all previous possibilities of clogging.

Hand in hand with this expansion and greater utilization of the "Alpha" disc system of separation various mechanical improvements and touches of betterment have been put into practice during the past few months, including a new method of bowl locking and unlocking, which precludes the springing of bowl spindles and the throwing of bowls out of balance from careless or impractical handling in such connection, and new oiling arrangements which effect a material saving of oil heretofore wasted and render literally impossible the heating or setting of machines and the splattering of oil around them.

Everything that twenty years of experience in both Europe and America has yet been able to devise or suggest has now been done toward making the TWENTIETH CENTURY "ALPHA" DE LAVAL SEPARATORS perfect for their purpose, and great as has been the universally conceded superiority of the De Laval machines heretofore the new standard is now raised still higher.

The new improvements apply to all styles and sizes of machines, both Dairy and Creamery, Hand and Power. The following week the new capacities will be announced, prices remaining the same as heretofore.

The De Laval Separator Co.

Western Offices:
Randolph & Canal Sts., CHICAGO

General Offices
74 Cortlandt St., NEW YORK

Fig. 12.1 Commerce and a new century (*Image source Ranch and range.* [North Yakima, Wash.], 18 January 1900. Chronicling America: Historic American Newspapers. Lib. of Congress. https://chroniclingamerica.loc.gov/lccn/2007252185/1900-01-18/ed-1/seq-1/. No known copyright restrictions)

12.1 Prelude: When Does a New Century Begin?

The arrival of the twentieth century seemed to many to be very auspicious. So much had been transformed over the past century that the human world, at least in the rapidly growing rich corner of it, would have been almost unrecognisable if someone from 1800 had been suddenly transported to 1900 (Fig. 12.1).

Ambiguity and uncertainty were, however, just beneath this beneficent surface, as reflected in something so arcane as the date of when the century actually began. In America, on the bleeding edge of material modernity, a controversy ensued over whether the dawn of a new century was on 1 January 1900 or 1 January 1901. Some people and some newspapers celebrated it on the first date, others on the second (US LOC, 2021).

Minor though this might seem, the calendar dispute was emblematic of the fact that technical innovation created as many uncertainties as it supposedly resolved; in this case, increasing adherence to clock and calendar time superseding older organic cycles and clashing with them simultaneously. It was but one of many such ambiguities of a rapidly maturing industrial economic system.

12.2 Material Expansion as of "1900"

A century of spreading industrialisation had, by 1900, led to faster material growth than ever before, especially in the West. Much of the rest of the world (outside Japan) was stagnating, making the differences between "East" and West" starker than ever. Tables 12.1, 12.2 and 12.3 provide data on per capita GDP, total GDP and shares of world GDP by major global regions.

Collectively, these data tell a story of a world growing dramatically richer in material terms between 1820 and 1900, both in absolute terms of total GDP and in the relative terms of per capita GDP. Per capita world GDP doubled over the course of 80 years, while total GDP almost tripled. But these gains were distributed unevenly. The rich "West", consisting of Europe and its Western Offshoots, became wealthier, while the rest of the world generally stagnated or declined. Thus in 1820 Europe, both Eastern and Western, accounted for 31.6% of global GDP, a share that increased to 36.6% when adding the Offshoots and Latin America. This was well below Asia's collective share of 55.6%. In 1900, by contrast,

Table 12.1 Per capita GDP by region—1820, 1850, 1870, 1900 (2011 $)

Region	*Western Europe*	*Eastern Europe*	*Western Offshoots*	*Latin America*	*Asia (East)*	*Asia (South and South-East)*	*The Middle East*	*Sub-Saharan Africa*	*World total*
Year									
1820	2307	818	2513	953	1089	929	974	800	1102
1850	2678	985	3474	1081	900	929	1000	800	1225
1870	3301	1575	4647	1319	989	850	1165	800	1498
1900	4724	2700	7741	1751	1086	994	1300	850	2212

Source Bolt and Van Zanden (2020)

Table 12.2 GDP by region—1820, 1850, 1870, 1900 (2011 $) (millions)

Region	*Western Europe*	*Eastern Europe*	*Western Offshoots*	*Latin America*	*Asia (East)*	*Asia (South and South-East)*	*The Middle East*	*Sub-Saharan Africa*	*World total*
Year									
1820	305.4	74.3	28.2	31.9	410.0	258.9	42.0	52.0	1,202.7
1850	442.8	115.9	93.0	31.9	410.0	258.9	42.0	52.0	1,446.5
1870	615.9	223.1	214.2	49.7	404.9	278.7	58.1	56.0	1,900.6
1900	1100.0	525.7	668.8	106.8	496.5	364.0	72.8	73.1	3,407.7

Source Bolt and Van Zanden (2020)

Table 12.3 GDP share of total (%) by region—1820, 1850, 1870, 1900 (2011 $)

Region	*Western Europe (%)*	*Eastern Europe (%)*	*Western Offshoots (%)*	*Latin America (%)*	*Asia (East) (%)*	*Asia (South and South-East) (%)*	*The Middle East (%)*	*Sub-Saharan Africa (%)*	*World total (%)*
Year									
1820	25.4	6.2	2.3	2.7	34.1	21.5	3.5	4.3	100.0
1850	30.6	8.0	6.4	2.2	28.3	17.9	2.9	3.6	100.0
1870	32.4	11.7	11.3	2.6	21.3	14.7	3.1	2.9	100.0
1900	32.3	15.4	19.6	3.1	14.6	10.7	2.1	2.1	100.0

Source Bolt and Van Zanden (2020)

Europeans produced 47.7% of world GDP, the Offshoots producing an additional 11.3% all on their own (with Latin America essentially unchanged in relative terms at 3.1%). Asia collectively was down to a mere 25.3%, less than half its share eight decades earlier.

The per capita GDP story is in some ways even starker. Asian GDP per capita was essentially unchanged between 1820 and 1900, while Western Europe doubled its per capita GDP and the Offshoots almost tripled theirs. These were continuations and accelerations of trends already well entrenched by earlier industrialisation. Asian per capita GDP was already below the world average in 1820 though close to it. By 1900, it was less than half the average. Western Europe was more than twice the average in 1820, slightly improving on this in 1900 (though in absolute terms obviously much richer in the later period). But the Offshoots, also around double the world average of per capita GDP in 1820 were around three and a half times above it in 1900. Broad averages such as these obviously obscure great differences between countries within each region and between classes of people within countries. But one's chance of being materially rich were much greater in the European realms than the non-European ones.

The economic "machine" (or production function in Growth Model terms) driving this change in growth and distribution of planetary output was radically shifting as well. The way to get rich in this world was to industrialise. But there were a variety of ways to do this, with different associated economic structures. Comparing two of the largest European economies, France's industrialisation was different from Britain's, coming later, rolling out more slowly, based on a greater proportion of small and medium-sized enterprises, with less intense and rapid urbanisation, and with less coal-dependence. Nonetheless, national economic outcomes by 1913 were similar, both France and England becoming rich advanced economies. The French pattern may have been more typical of what was taking place elsewhere, mainly because of lower reliance on coal (Britain being something of an outlier in its coal abundance). French per capita GDP growth in the 1800s was comparable to Germany's, and actually a bit better than the UK when measured over the entire century. French patterns of growth may also have yielded a better for average quality of life for its citizens (Neal & Cameron, 2016, 232).

Meanwhile, Western Europe was richer than Eastern Europe, and Russia, being truly Eurasian, was in a class by itself, much more agrarian, rural and with relatively little industrial spark coming from below, most of the initiative and investment being driven by the State. Unlike many European countries, Russia was self-sufficient in food and was a major exporter of it, as well as of other primary goods such as minerals. The overall economic growth rate picked up considerably after mid-century, and the country's average GDP per capita by 1913 was well below that of even Eastern Europe, but comparable to Latin America and Japan. After 1885, it also appears that peasant standards of living were rising, so food exports were not coming at the expense of local food supplies.

Some speculate that all this indicates that Russia may ultimately have been on a US-style development path of initial reliance on natural resources wealth exports and development and exploitation of internal markets, until the World War and Revolution derailed it all (Neal & Cameron, 275). Certainly, both America and Russia occupied large continuous landmasses and both formally and informally encouraged internal migration from established to undeveloped areas, while also displacing, and sometimes exterminating, long-standing indigenous populations. In Russia, the emancipation of peasants from serfdom in 1861, incomplete though it was, still provided a new pool of people available for internal colonisation. And from 1881, government policy encouraged westward migration, creating new urban centres east of the Urals, paralleling similar moves of people in the US to new and rising Midwestern industrial centres. Siberian migration similarly paralleled movements of people within America into the Rockies and California (Barraclough, 1967, 86).

Despite these considerable differences between patterns of industrialising economies, the broad economic results were similar, namely growing GDP, both total and per capita, and a relative shift away from agriculture and towards manufacturing and services. Table 12.4 illustrates this for France and the US. The two countries are obviously quite different socially and economically (America being considered in much fuller detail in Chapter 20, while France has been considered in some detail in Chapter 10). Yet, their broad structure, at least when considered by sectoral employment, exhibited a parallel proportionate convergence into manufacturing and services. The agrarian world of the pre-industrial past was thus rapidly disappearing across the core, even though local manifestations differed.

Table 12.4 Employment shares by sector, France and the US 1800 and 1900

% of total employment	*France*			*United States*		
	Agriculture (%)	*Manufacturing (%)*	*Services (%)*	*Agriculture (%)*	*Manufacturing (%)*	*Services (%)*
1800	64	22	14	68	18	13
1900	43	29	28	41	28	31

Source Piketty (2014), Table 2.4

12.3 A Global Trade System

Trade was also growing prodigiously. Figure 12.2 provides a graphic from a contemporary source indicating overall trends and composition of worldwide commercial trade in goods between 1800 and 1910 (with detailed composition data for 1885 and 1910).

Trade growth and output growth are intimately related. This is straight out of Adam Smith and David Ricardo. Smith spoke of efficiency gains from a "division of labour" and an expanding "extent of the market", while Ricardo foretold the efficiency that comes with the specialisation of national production in one's "comparative advantage" in goods and services, selling these into the world market, and then trading with other countries for things not produced as relatively efficiently at home (see Chapter 4). Industrialisation created rapidly growing output that was then leveraged into a higher turnover of goods and services in domestic and international economies. What we would now refer to as "supply chains" become more complex and international, with many goods now passing through production stages from raw material to final output across many countries, boosting international trade statistics and increasing the multiplier effects of each unit of output produced.

In the early 1830s, Europe accounted for 62% of world exports, slowly drifting downwards to 56% in 1913 (Federico & Tena-Junguito, 2017, 610). Europe and its offshoots in total held around 4/5ths of total trade in both 1885 and 1910. The British Empire accounted for more than a quarter of trade both years, though with a slight relative decline over the period, with Germany and the US increasing in importance. Between 1870 and 1914, these two up-and-comers of the Western world were doing their own version of what Britain had done earlier in the century, namely growth through exporting and industrialising, though without the

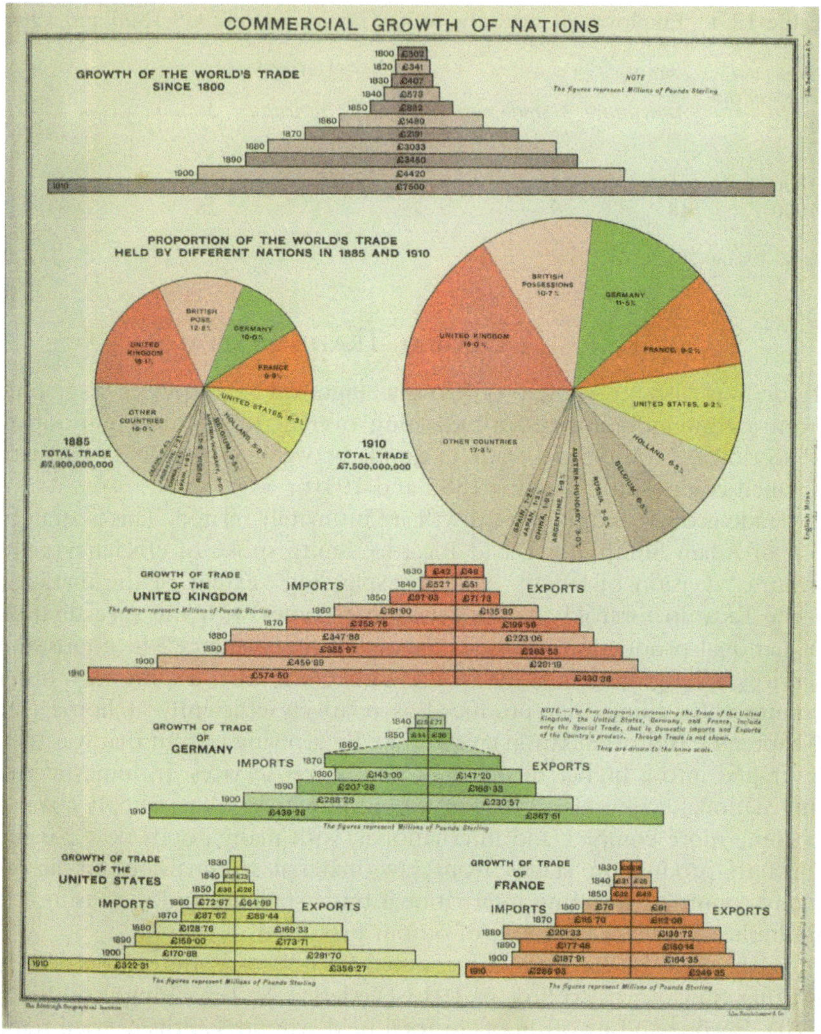

Fig. 12.2 World trade volumes 1800–1910 (and trade composition by nation in 1885 and 1910) (*Source* Bartholomew [1914]. No known copyright restrictions)

benefit of big empires (though America did have a large internal territory to exploit).

There were, though, very key differences between these countries and Britain and between each other. Germany's growth was much more purely an industrial affair, more similar to England in that way, with it becoming a strong exporter of iron and steel exports and later chemicals and dyestuffs, amongst other high-value add goods. Indeed, Germany became one of Britain's main competitors in markets that country used to dominate. The upward trajectory of America, on the other hand, was unique enough to be referred to as the "American path". This rested on a combination of trade protectionism to develop domestic "infant" industries which had a strong initial foundation based on local demand, combined with exports of primary agricultural and mineral goods, especially cotton in the earlier stages. Both Germany and the US used protectionism and both relied on exports, but US flows into the world economy early in the Industrial Revolution were quite low because internal demands soaked up much domestic output (Foreman-Peck & Millward, 1994).

12.4 International Finance and System Driven Turbulences

From 1820 to 1913, around ten billion pounds were invested in areas across the globe (Graff et al., 2013, 39). The integration of the developed world financial system under a Gold Standard, with London as the financial centre and the Pound Sterling as an international unit of account helped to facilitate this movement of capital and the much larger amounts of money required for international trade. It was not a "neutral" system, for England designed the system with its own advantage in mind (see Chapters 9 and 18). But the British underwrote it with enough liquidity and capital, much of it drawn from its own colonies, to keep investment funds and short-term capital globally mobile, something of benefit to Britain but also to the rest of the industrialised core and a fortunate few in the periphery.

Figure 12.3 shows a contemporary map of the contours of the world money system in 1910 (along with formal tariff zones). A big feature of "1900" was "free trade" in the form of low tariffs formally applied across much of the world. However, such trade was not as "free" as it seemed, partly because of the presence of large empires with their internal preferential trade blocs and also because large industrial corporations generally dominated movements of both money and goods (Graff et al., 2013). Still, the era did usher in a world market unified as no other one in history had ever been.

This increasing integration had its dark side however. Much capital investment funded by rich countries in poorer ones was generally in the form of debt. The terms were not necessarily easy or fair on the borrower and there were regular defaults throughout the period that could create dislocations for lender and borrower alike. And mobile money could move as quickly out of economies as it could move in. These factors combined together, and with periodic unexpected events such as crop failures, to result in regular global financial cycles of both boom and bust. Neal and Cameron (2016) record ten major international business cycles between 1800 and the start of the First World, roughly one every fifteen years: 1825–1826; 1837–1838; 1846–1847; 1857; 1866; 1873; 1882; 1893; 1900–1901; 1907 (295).

This instability had attended industrialisation from an early time. The 1840s had been marked by trade depression and political unrest. It had been followed by a long period of general growth and prosperity (though concentrated more in the European world than the non-European one). Then in May 1873 the Vienna Stock Market collapsed. This triggered a series of bank failures, contraction in money and credit, and collapse for many leveraged businesses, such as the September 1873 failure of Jay Cooke and Company, a leading American railway investor. The US, at this time heavily dependent on foreign capital, was especially hammered by the "Panic of 1873" in which 98 banks, 89 rail companies, and 18,000 businesses failed, putting one seventh of all Americans out of work by 1876 (Faulkner, 2018, 264–265).

Although not technically continuous, economic historians often refer to the "Long Depression of 1873–96" because of its steady price deflation and lowered growth rates and because it was sandwiched between two major economic "panics". Between 1850 and 73, the German economy grew 4.3% a year; between 1873 and 90, it grew only 2.9% a year. For the US, the comparable figures were 6.2% versus 4.7%, and for Britain 3.0% to 1.7%. The contractions were sharp, but as these figures indicate on average, the bust times only slowed long-run positive GDP growth, rather than reversing it. Moreover, technical progress continued apace with new industries, such as chemicals and electricity emerging, and with wages overall rising while prices fell (Faulkner, 2018, 266).

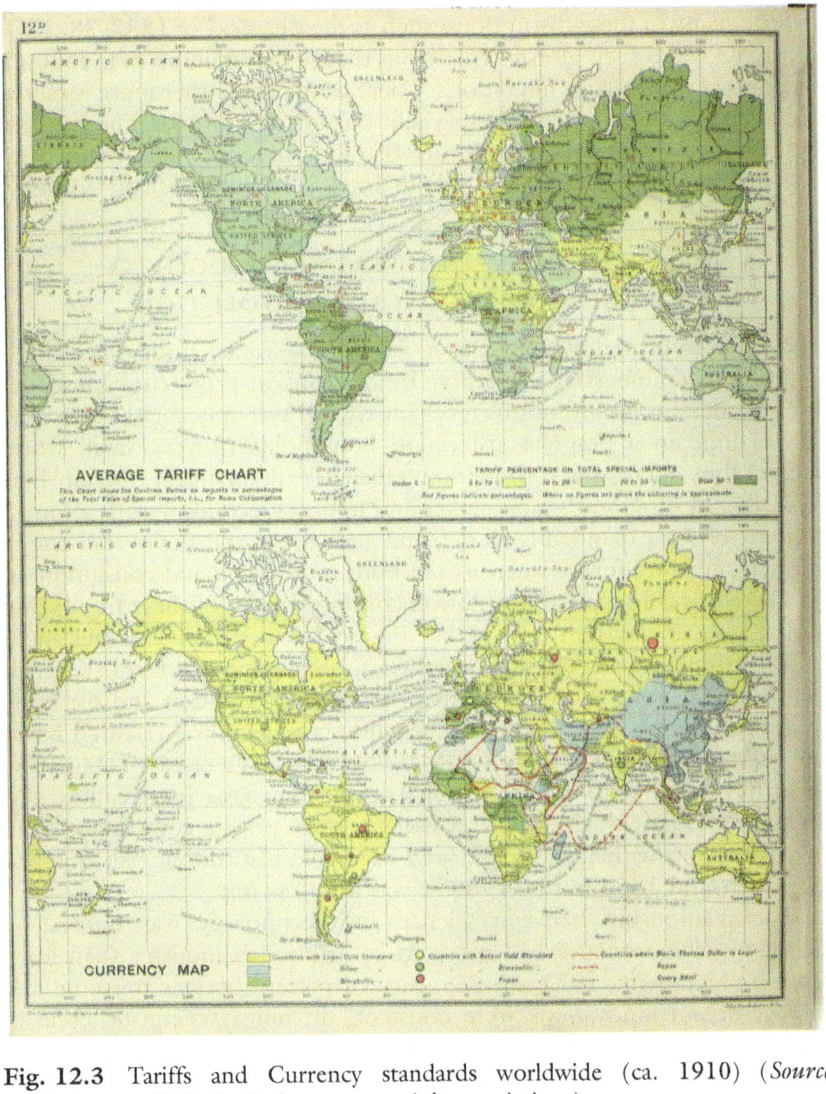

Fig. 12.3 Tariffs and Currency standards worldwide (ca. 1910) (*Source* Bartholomew [1914]. No known copyright restrictions)

Still, many of these disruptions, such as the "Panics" of 1837–38, 1873 and 1893, were deep global depressions that ruined millions of livelihoods and caused some major migrations. There were many other more localised occurrences, some extreme, especially outside of Europe. The modern business cycle was a regular feature of modern economic growth, with financial leverage playing a key role in amplifying both ups and downs.

12.5 Science–Industry–Productivity: The Second Industrial Revolution

The First Industrial Revolution could be said to be primarily technological and commercial in nature. Innovations in production processes and manufacturing inventions mechanised and systemised tasks that used to be done in a bespoke fashion in households or very small workshops, thus increasing production efficiency dramatically. Meanwhile, replacement of a mostly nonmarket and informal economy with a formal market version expanded both demand and supply and the overall size of markets, creating further increases in both production and consumption.

The Second Industrial Revolution continued both of these trends, but added scale and system to it. A key ingredient was the increasing application of science and scientific method to economic processes. Whereas before much innovation came out of practical application and tinkering by individual inventors and entrepreneurs, now technical research based on a systematised knowledge base developed by large research teams and institutes devoted to pure research became the basis for creating new technologies that were commercialised by huge private companies, often in partnership with government and academic institutions. All this had begun around 1850 but by 1900, it was in full swing.

The relationship between science and technology was tightest in Germany where science had more to contribute to industry than learn from it (Lichtheim, 1972, 32–35). But the pattern became universal and science-driven innovations were constant, driving a synergistic cycle of knowledge advance, practical application, commercialisation and material growth. Amongst the many examples that one can point to the extraction of nickel, discovered by Ludwig Mond in 1890, which then allowed for its addition to steel, strengthening that material dramatically and thus allowing for its much wider use. The introduction of the electrolytic process in 1887 made production of aluminium commercially viable, the metal then becoming a critical input into the nascent aviation industry.

The invention of electricity introduced a whole new source of light, heat and power, all of which transformed the chemical industry, electrolysis particularly, as already mentioned, a critical part of the extraction of aluminium and also a critical input into the bulk production of caustic soda. Edison's invention of the incandescent bulb in 1879, Siemen's invention of the dynamo in 1867 and the opening of the world's first electrical power plant in New York in 1882, brought electric power to the residential masses and made industrial use of it much wider than before. To this could be added the rise of the petroleum industry and its increasing use as a fuel for the infant automobile industry (Barraclough, 1967, 46–47).

The creation of modern pharmacueticals is perhaps the most socially prominent science-led innovation, built on the major advances achieved in late nineteenth century chemistry. The great age of bacteriology began around 1870 from the development of aniline dyes that allowed for identification of different bacteria through differential staining methods. Microbiology and biochemistry then emerged, and the first antibiotic, Salvarsan, was invented in 1909. Vitamins and hormones were discovered in 1902, the mosquito was identified as the carrier of malaria in 1897, aspirin was first marketed in 1899 and antiseptic and aseptic techniques became part of standard medical practice (Barraclough, 1967, 48–49).

These technical breakthroughs added to the considerably lower-tech "public health revolution" of mid-century focusing on better sanitation and disease quarantining and together they effectively completely removed the "urban penalty" that cities had been burdened with throughout history, their density formerly being a petri dish for infectious disease (see Chapter 16). All this eliminated any effective public health ceiling on city growth (Easterlin, 1995), and that growth was further fed by the advances of the safety elevator (mid-century) and the skyscraper built of reinforced steel (late century) that eased the technical constraints on housing the masses on very small footprints.

Low-tech, medium-tech and high-tech changes, sometimes rapid, sometimes more gradual, came together to transform economies and societies in other ways. Bulk production of basic slag for artificial fertiliser, a by-product of the steel making process, and new methods of food preservation derived from the innovations of sterilisation and pasteurisation developed for medical practice, helped to create a food-canning industry availing itself of new processes of tin-plating. Perfection of refrigeration techniques and infrastructure investment, such as the penetration of the

Alps by the Mont Cenis and St Gotthard rail tunnels in 1871 and 1882, allowed for the growing urban areas to be fed both properly and more richly than ever before. The Alps tunnels, along with canning and refrigeration, permitted bulk export of southern European fruits and vegetables to the industrialised north, further integrating regions into a production and consumption web more tightly than ever (Barraclough, 1967, 48–49).

Indeed, whereas the First Industrial Revolution could be said to have made the earth the limit of human productivity, the Second effectively made the sky the limit, so to speak. To take only a single example, the natural nitrogen-waste-food cycle has been estimated to be able to support an outside global population limit of 2.4 billion people sustainably, at modern rates of consumption. The Haber–Bosch nitrogen extraction process, which led to the creation of artificial fertilisers, effectively removed this particular constraint (Immerwahr, 2019, 57). (At least this was true in the short term. The broader, deeper, longer-term destabilisation of the Earth System was not so well understood then; see Chapter 2).

12.6 Big Capital and Labour Movements

Scientific advance, joined with production economies of scale combined with financial instability to concentrate and centralise capital in an unprecedented manner (Faulkner, 2018, 266). With the depressions of 1873 and the 1890s, many smaller enterprises were knocked out of the marketplace, and the remaining industry participants sought new ways to survive economic cycles of boom and bust. One solution to get through tough times was to dominate markets and production through vertical and horizontal integration, under either one company or, more commonly, industrialist-formed cartels of interlocking companies. In either case, the goal was to harness production economies and control pricing and production. All this was accompanied by the use of new "scientific" methods of management, production and labour processes and finance (Stearns, 2001, Section V. > B. > 7).

To even gain a foothold in the new industries generally required large amounts of accumulated capital to begin with. Barriers to entry were high enough that small enterprise could not even hope to compete. This was true of the new steel and chemical manufacturing enterprises that were innovating and growing most rapidly in Germany and the US and which required large investments of funds to even begin production. Electricity, chemical dyes and railroads, to name but a few, were mainly scale enterprises. In some cases, such as utilities, there was a tendency towards "natural monopoly" in which average production costs were lowest where there was only one producer in a given market. For "network assets", like electricity, and urban tram lines, there was a "lock-in effect": once a given company built a network of a certain size, it was close to impossible for any new network to compete with it since it could not hope to match the connections of the incumbent.

The increasing domination of markets by large firms with strong market power was certainly good for business and was a critical component of maximum production efficiency (though, as economic theory indicates, this is generally accompanied by squeezing consumers and smaller business operators, creating associated "welfare losses", to use economics lingo). It also led to an increasing political power for the corporate sector. It was not, however, automatically accompanied by rises in worker wages or their standards of living. These did come in some places and times, especially where labour shortages occurred. But the process was uneven, and in the economic busts, very hard to come by. Available evidence suggests that overall wage growth was stagnant until around 1850, though it did pick up after that.

In fact, distribution of market surplus had to be fought over, and was. The creation of an industrial labourer class and the clear fact that the gains of industrialisation were far from equally shared even in the heart of rich Europe and its settler colonies stimulated a growing labour movement. This movement took two forms: labour unions and labour-based political parties. Some of the wellspring for unionisation began with more generalised mass democracy movements, such as the Chartist movement in the UK during 1838–1850. But the greater impetus came from worker grievances that could only be addressed by worker organisation and action.

The latter part of the nineteenth century was thus increasingly an era of class conflict. The rapid pace of standardised work routines, a faceless corporate management structure, rigorous pursuit of efficiency, all led to push back. The resistance began first with strikes, often spontaneous and loosely commanded. The terrible depression of the 1870s pushed many workers against a wall, leaving them idle, desperate and angry, with little to lose. "Industrial Action", to use a standard euphemism, gathered strength with each passing decade. In 1892, French workers struck 261 times against 500 companies involving 50,000 workers. By 1906, the peak French strike year before 1914, 1,309 strikes brought 438,000 workers off the job. British and German strike rates were higher still; in Britain, more than 2,000,000 workers struck between 1909 and 1913 (Sørensen et al., 2020, "The rise of organized labour and mass protests").

This sort of unrest, and the need to organise it, birthed the labour union. At first unionism tended to be confined to the more educated and relatively free artisan worker, leading to the so-called craft union, which was divided along skill lines. But as work became more standardised and the ranks of the unskilled grew, mass unionism surfaced throughout Western Europe. Unions, fought hard by employers and governments, especially in the US, had political and legal as well as economic impact. As the franchise gradually increased throughout Europe, the percentage of the electorate that was in industrial work rose as well, furthering worker political influence. Legal changes, spreading widely in Western Europe after 1870, reduced political barriers to unionisation and strikes, and gradually legitimised both institutions (Allen & Belt, 1998).

More and more, individual unions began to confederate with one another, creating both mass unions in individual industries, and general federations formed at the national level, such as the British Trades Union Congress and the French and Italian general confederations of labour. New labour market institutions arose, such as collective bargaining procedures with employers, though in an incremental and patchwork pattern. Some unions provided education, housing or temporary relief to their members.

More and more, unions became a powerful pressure group for changing government policy. One direction this took was the formation of labour political parties. Obviously, such parties were most obviously appropriate to parliamentary democracies and in 1900 and the years leading up to it, these were mostly in the English-speaking world. In 1891, trade union members in the British colonies of Australia formed localised labour parties. They later amalgamated to form the Australian Labor Party (ALP). In 1899, the labour party in the Colony of Queensland briefly formed the world's first labour government, lasting one week. More successfully, Andrew Fisher was a minister in the first labour government nationally in Australia in 1904, and led the first labour majority government there in 1910. This was well ahead of the UK. There, the British Labour Party was created as the Labour Representation Committee, as a result of an 1899 resolution by the Trade Union

Congress. That party would not form a national government until 1924 (Bongiorno, 2011; Van der Linden, 2017).

12.7 The First Age of Modern Inequality and the Rise of Radicalism

Social and economic inequality is nothing new. But older patterns of resource distribution tended to be within a context of low growth, relatively low average wealth, and relatively long periods of social stability. With industrialisation came rapid changes in socioeconomic conditions and rapid and obvious concentration of wealth at the top end of the hierarchy.

Table 12.5 shows how wealth concentration increased over the course of the nineteenth and early twentieth centuries within Europe. The patterns are quite clear: the rich kept getting richer, accumulating greater shares of the bounty of the First and Second Industrial Revolutions than the mass of the population.

Wealth and income inequality affected the social and political fabric of the growing industrialising core in a number of ways. Although living standards did steadily increase on average for the mass of the population within Europe and its offshoots, private opulence was growing even faster, creating a fair amount of social resentment. This was added to by the fact that economic instability created a lot of insecurity amongst the growing working and middle classes who saw the richest tiers seemingly insulated from such problems. And changes in work environment, especially higher intensity of work pace and regimentation and control of work process, even if compensated through higher pay and/or shorter hours, created grievances in their own right.

One response, already discussed in the previous section, was labour organisation and political activism, an essentially reformist program. But there were those who called for an overthrow of the existing social, political and economic order. The Communists are considered in more detail in later chapters and in 1900 were still not a major factor in politics, either underground or above. Some trade unions linked instead to the rising socialist parties, in places like Germany and Austria, though here they generally aimed to change the system by working through it. In other countries, especially France and Italy, syndicalism became a prominent

Table 12.5 Share of the top 10%, 1% and 0,1% in total wealth for selected European nations and Europe as a whole, 1810–1910

Year	*France*			*United Kingdom*			*United States*			*Sweden*			*Europe*	
	Top 10%	*Top 1%*	*Top 0,1%*	*Top 10%*	*Top 1%*	*Top 0,1%*	*Top 10%*	*Top 1%*	*Top 0,1%*	*Top 10%*	*Top 1%*	*Top 0,1%*	*Top 10%*	*Top 1%*
1810	79.90	45.60	17.10	82.90	54.90		58.00	25.00		83.90	55.90		82.20	52.10
1820	81.80	46.70	19.00											
1830	83.20	47.50	17.10											
1840	80.40	46.00	15.50											
1850	82.40	50.30	19.40											
1860	83.70	52.00	18.30											
1870	81.80	50.40	18.30	87.10	61.10		71.00	32.00		87.20	57.30	29.60	85.40	56.20
1880	84.60	49.50	21.10											
1890	84.70	51.10	20.20											
1900	87.30	58.70	28.10											
1910	88.50	60.50	29.00	92.00	69.00		81.10	45.10	24.80%	88.20	61.10	29.40	89.50	63.50

Source Piketty (2014), Tables 10.1–10.6 and background table S.10.1

doctrine, urging that direct action through strikes should topple governments and usher in a new age in which organisations of workers would control production (Van der Linden, 2017).

The Anarchists were, however, the force causing greatest disruption in Europe and the New World as the nineteenth century ended and the twentieth began, occasionally allied with labour unions (Syndicalism being greatly influenced by it). Anarchism, simplified, calls for the elimination of any formal social organisation from above. Some anarchists were idealistic and pacifist, such as Prince Kropotkin, who published a major treatise on the subject in 1900. But others were violent, practising what would later be labelled as terrorism. Assassination was a regularly employed instrument, and amazingly successful. In 1900 alone, anarchists killed Italy's King Umberto, while attempts were made on the Prince of Wales, the Shah of Iran and the German Emperor (West, 1982, 17). Elisabeth, Empress of Austria was stabbed, but not killed, by an anarchist in 1898. In 1901, an anarchist bullet dispatched William McKinley, making way for his Vice President Theodore Roosevelt to ascend to the American Presidency. Bombs were also another way of spreading terror. In 1894, Emile Henry detonated a bomb at a Paris Cafe, killing one and injuring twenty, one of a number of such attacks throughout the late nineteenth and early twentieth centuries (US LOC, 2021b; Fig. 12.4).

Anarchism is in many ways a particularly modern movement in its means and ends, almost Romantic in its notions. The primary method was the action of the individual against other individuals, whether this was a ruler or a group of innocents. Its modus operandi was theatrical, and the mere occurrence of the act and public knowledge of it was somehow supposed to begin the unravelling of the State and its subsidiary apparatuses, private and public. How this was supposed to happen was not clear, but the emotive impact was definite. In fact, one could argue that anarchism was a creature of a media culture, a unique institution of industrial modernity. In more traditional ages of personalistic rule and traditional institutions, the killing of a king or queen could usher in real change (though as history shows not always of the intended or desired sort). This was less so in an age where even the monarchies had to consider, and sought to shape, the opinions of the masses and where "systems" made even high-placed individuals more replaceable than ever before (see Box 12.1).

Fig. 12.4 Anarchist "terror" (*Image source* July 9, 1914. The Day Book [Chicago, IL], Noon Edition, Image 9. Chronicling America: Historic American Newspapers. Original caption: "A New York building wrecked by the explosion of a bomb which was made by Joseph Caron, said to be an anarchist"). No known copyright restrictions

Box 12.1 The new image-makers

Chapter 9 has chronicled how advances in the printing press and paper production allowed for rapid reproduction of cheap periodicals, while vast improvements in transport and the rise of cities created ideal conditions for easy distribution of the printed word to concentrations of readers created by increases in literacy rates engendered by mandatory public education.

The possibility of quick dissemination of ideas and information was greater than ever before, and it was well utilised. Photography was a key component of this process. As the American press magnate William Randolph Hearst supposedly famously said when trying to gin up anti-Spanish sentiment to foment American involvement in the Cuban revolt against Spain: "You provide the pictures, I'll provide the war." Photography was becoming a recognised high art form by the beginning of the twentieth century, with the Linked Ring Brotherhood promoting it as such, and the emergence of high-profile art photographers such as Robert Demarchy in France and Alfred Stieglitz in America (West, 1982, 102). But its real importance came with its alliance with the newspaper.

The photograph communicated impactful messages in ways words could not and newspapers could deliver them to millions of people within the day. Thus newspaper barons became a new class of private power-broker, often millionaires (such as Hearst) from prior fortunes made off burgeoning industrial enterprise, others made rich by the new business itself. Newspapers were a highly profitable business, driven by a powerful combination of rising circulation sales, subsidised by mass print advertising, a vital component of mass marketing.

These developments had clear implications for mass politics and mass communication. Interestingly enough, the exercise of mass manipulation of public opinion was sometimes more actively and subtly practised in authoritarian countries, like Germany, than in democratic ones, like Britain and France, perhaps because in the former there was less of that safety valve that genuine electoral institutions offered and thus more of a need to make sure public discontent was minimised and public approval maximised. While outright repression was more available in the autocracy, it was also more costly and risky than having the people, if not on board, at least quiescent. Making people think the way you wanted was a cheaper and safer course, it if could be achieved. Either way, mass campaigns, whether selling products, stimulating demand, or forming opinion, were becoming more pervasive, more sophisticated, and more effective. The twentieth century would see the full flowering of this rather bittersweet fruit.

(Discussion above drawn from Curran & Seaton, 2009, 47–63)

12.8 Pollution and Waste

One oft-neglected aspect of modern industry is the concomitant rise of the waste cycle that accompanied the ever-increasing rise in production and consumption. The Classical Economists had already posited that the extensive and intensive resource exploitation of capitalist growth would be necessarily accompanied by diminishing marginal returns. In other words, returns squeezed out of human and physical capital and the raw materials upon which they operated would incrementally decline and eventually be exhausted or even turn negative. This is why they all wrote of a long-term "stationary state" in which economic growth would cap out at a zero rate, though with attendant high wealth and income.

What they failed to consider was that this resource exploitation would have to be accompanied by a growing waste trail into the air, water and earth. To use more modern terminology, economic growth increases emissions, discharges and solid waste creation. This waste-stream side of growth was an equally diverse manifold to the output side.

Air pollution was the earliest problem confronted by the English State during its first wave of industrialisation. Smoke from coal burning and burgeoning factory production became intense and at first was left to the workings of plaintiffs and defendants in the courts of common law, especially under existing common law nuisance and tort provisions, i.e. smoke being the nuisance and its damage being the harm (tort) to be adjudicated and dealt with through successive judiciary suits.

Ronald Coase's (1960) somewhat magical view of property rights notwithstanding (in which private party legal actions and court adjudication are argued to be sufficient to wipe away the inefficiencies of such negative "externalities", assuming that there were no transactions costs and well-specified property rights) English common law was actually not that effective in eliminating the pollution problem. And so, a variety of pollution laws were passed, dealing specifically with airborne and waterborne effluents. In 1863, the Alkali Act was passed in England, the first known effective air pollution regulation in the world (Allen & Belt, 1998). The initial act created the position of Alkali Inspector, assisted by four sub-inspectors, to curb air discharge of muriatic acid gas (gaseous hydrochloric acid) created by alkali works and later expanding to a more general remit with subsequent amendments in later years (MacLeod, 1965).

Although it would take many decades for environmental protection to become an accepted governmental function, the environmental consequences of economic growth were recognised early on, especially since its consequences were plain to see and were interfering rather mightily with daily life and economic productivity. Urban and industrial smog became widespread and intense by the 1900s, with attendant public health deterioration that at least partially undid the advances of the sanitation and pharmaceutical movements. Data on emissions was not tracked during this time so information on them during the First and Second Industrial Revolutions is speculative. The information we do have (Tables 12.6 and

12.7) shows an industrialised world explosion in carbon dioxide (CO_2) emissions (a close to 30-fold rise in Western Europe between 1820 and 1910) and sulphur dioxide (SO_2) emissions (roughly eightfold between 1850 and 1910). Global increases were strong, but not as high, mainly because of how non-polluting most of the non-European world was due to its slow economic growth.

Meanwhile, "waste" was beginning to become its own economically separate category from "output". It was a new industry, in fact. Traditional economic activity tended to recycle and reuse waste products from one process in another, e.g. the use of animal tallow for candles, etc. Early industrialisation began to more fully separate producers from their waste products into separate economic streams. But these still remained closely related to one another and followed traditional channels, such as the two-way barter conducted by the travelling "pedlar" who took rags, bones, ashes and so forth from households in trade for household goods such as tinware, then transferring the waste products to smaller scale, or even factory producers, who relied on them for raw materials. "Waste" before 1850 might be thought more properly of as scraps, with a secondary use as scrap material, rather than "garbage", i.e. an undifferentiated mass of undesirable cast-off materials with no use value at all that generated disposal costs (Liboiron, 2012).

"Trash" came into its own economically through a variety of means. The fall of household production and the rise of commercially made and readily available consumer products undermined the household skill sets of mending and repair that had kept goods in service for well past their original intended life. The pedlar's trade was slowly eliminated as purchase and discarding of ready-made goods came to be more widely practised (Strasser, 1999). And the rising efficiency and falling cost of consumer products led to a sheer volume of both goods purchases and disposal into waste streams that required methods of greater scale than traditional means could deliver. Meanwhile, industry was creating greater volumes of more diverse and toxic effluents, and it generally was cheaper, especially in the absence of any regulation, to discharge these into the environment rather than reuse or recycle them, except when there was a clear use for a by-product, such as the aforementioned use of steel slag for fertiliser. In any case, some of these materials were too hazardous to be safely handled by the amateur or small-scale waste handler.

There were some interesting economic relationships forged between urban household waste and industrial use, however, so the picture

Table 12.6 Regional totals of CO_2 emissions, 1820–1910

(Values in Petagrams Carbon (Pg. C, peta = 1015)

Year	*Western Europe (WE)*	*Eastern Europe (EE)*	*Western Offshoots (WO)*	*Latin America and Caribbean (LA)*	*The Middle East and North Africa (MENA)*	*Sub-Saharan Africa (SSA)*	*East Asia (EA)*	*South and South-East Asia (SSEA)*	*World*
1820	13.4	0.2	0.2	0.0	0.0	0.0	0.0	0.0	13.8
1830	23.4	0.3	0.6	0.0	0.0	0.0	0.0	0.0	24.3
1840	30.3	0.6	1.6	0.0	0.0	0.0	0.0	0.0	32.5
1850	47.4	0.9	5.4	0.0	0.0	0.0	0.0	0.0	53.7
1860	74.5	2.6	13.1	0.0	0.0	0.0	0.0	0.2	90.4
1870	110.1	8.1	27.4	0.0	0.1	0.0	0.0	0.0	145.7
1880	158.1	18.1	56.4	0.0	0.1	0.0	0.6	0.6	233.9
1890	207.0	30.9	114.4	0.4	0.3	0.1	1.8	1.3	356.1
1900	279.4	55.7	189.9	1.1	0.7	0.6	5.3	4.0	536.9
1910	352.0	74.8	366.7	5.9	1.1	4.8	16.2	8.8	830.2

Source van Zanden et al. (2014), Table 10.3

Table 12.7 Regional totals of SO_2 emissions, 1850–1910

(Value in Petagrams SO2 (Pg SO2), where Peta = 1015)

Year	*Western Europe (WE)*	*Eastern Europe (EE)*	*Western Offshoots (WO)*	*Latin America and Caribbean (LA)*	*The Middle East and North Africa (MENA)*	*Sub-Saharan Africa (SSA)*	*East Asia (EA)*	*South and South-East Asia (SSEA)*	*World*
1850	1.3	0.1	0.3	0.0	0.0	0.0	0.2	0.1	2.0
1860	1.9	0.1	0.7	0.1	0.0	0.0	0.2	0.1	3.1
1870	2.8	0.3	1.4	0.1	0.0	0.0	0.2	0.1	4.8
1880	4.0	0.6	2.8	0.1	0.0	0.0	0.2	0.1	7.7
1890	5.3	1.1	5.5	0.1	0.0	0.0	0.3	0.1	12.4
1900	7.2	1.7	9.5	0.1	0.1	0.0	0.4	0.1	19.2
1910	9.3	2.3	16.7	0.5	0.1	0.2	0.9	0.2	30.2

Source van Zanden et al. (2014), Table 10.1

should not be oversimplified. With mass printing of books, newspapers and government documents, the growing paper industry became a major consumer of urban rags. Slaughterhouse bones from city abattoirs yielded many useful chemical-side compounds (Barles, 2014, 205). Thus, a human-made industrial ecology arose in place of the more organic (though not always cleaner) one that had prevailed for centuries before.

Still, enough excess garbage was being produced in urban areas to require the rise of an entirely new field: waste management. A new industry of garbage collection arose, at first ad hoc, and sometimes with periodic municipal "purges" of a particular problem neighbourhood (Liboiron, 2012). This function became more systematic with time, but was at first mostly privately provided by third parties, with distinct differences in level of service according to social and economic class of the neighbourhood. Interestingly, the earliest efforts focused on waste recovery and reuse, but by the early twentieth century, these began to be dropped in favour of simple removal, mostly into sanitary landfills. The main reason for this was economic: waste recovery was almost always financially unremunerative. The die was thus cast for the modern waste removal industry with us today (Barles, 2014, 210–217).

12.9 Northern Industrialisation and Southern Deindustrialisation

The discussion thus far has focused on the rich Western world, where industry was a permanent and growing condition of production, consumption and, more and more, everyday life. It was highly disruptive to small local economic operators even there. Older and smaller-scale ways of production, even those that were of a vintage of only two or three decades old, were being pushed out rapidly. By 1907, for example, the cotton weavers in German textiles, two-thirds of whom were domestic outworkers in 1875, now were no longer in the trade or were swallowed up in ever larger-scale urban factories. The import of cheap foodstuffs from overseas production processes created a European agricultural crisis and rural depopulation that lagged on even after the difficult 1873–1896 period (Barraclough, 1967, 52). Large industrial enterprise was the "winning team" and as an individual you either joined it, whatever it might be offering, or you fell by the wayside.

Worldwide, economic integration concentrated specialisation in particular geographic areas, creating some big "winners" but also some big "losers", especially for non-Europeans. There were a few peripheral countries that did benefit from newly discovered and newly valuable natural resources. For example, Chile accounted for three-quarters of global nitrate production in 1900, then a critical input into fertiliser production, whereas thirty years previously it had produced none. Even here many of the gains went to European offshoots. Australia's Mount Morgan copper and gold mine opened in 1882 and the largest lead and zinc deposit in the world was uncovered in Broken Hill and began to be mined the year after (Barraclough, 1967, 54). Gold and silver in the US and South Africa are other examples of a few notable mining winners. Thus, the first globalisation of the nineteenth and early twentieth centuries was very complex and nuanced, quite different from the general tenor of the Classical Economists who suggested a sort of uniform positive thrust to modern economic change through economic specialisation.

Industrialisation itself, wherever it occurred, had many different forms, ranging from large factories to workshops with partial mechanisation, shaped greatly by the prevailing social and cultural contexts in which industrialisation took place (Clarence-Smith, 2012, 31). Thus, for example, Tirthankar Roy (1999) argues that "traditional" industry in India actually was the foundation for later modern change there, as with the brass industry workshops of Moradabad that later adapted to become modern metal industries in forms and lines fairly independent of much of Europe or the rest of the world. Sub-Saharan Africa and Latin America however displayed much less continuity between artisanal and subsequent industrial production. Even in India, outside the trades mentioned, there was wide variation in the forms of industry, geographic location, specialisation and well-being of local enterprise.

A key causal question thus is how global integration and institutional change affected modernisation paths and probabilities in "peripheral" locations. Did "free trade" before 1913 aid the development of local industry, by increasing the extent of the market and allowing for national and regional efficiencies of specialisation at scale, for example? Or did it hurt, by driving out local entrepreneurs through a flood of cheap imports? Was international capital mobility a blessing because it provided the needed seed funds for local industrial development to begin? Or was it a curse which hampered and debilitated local financial markets and institutions, replacing them with heavy overseas debt burdens, often paired with restrictions on the use of capital, formally or informally, such as forcing foreign expertise and technology on the developing country, as happened with India and its railroads?

These are not questions with a single answer, and the context matters a great deal. The complexity and growing interdependence of supply chains contained both perils and promises. Import substitution (i.e. the local production of a product that otherwise would have to be imported from overseas) was generally difficult to engage in and uncertain of success at this time. Export processing, in which a country placed itself in a position to add value at an intermediate or final processing stage, was more feasible. Japan is often held up as a prime example, focusing first on processing tea and silk for export as part of the economic strategy undertaken by the newly restored Meiji emperor in 1868, capturing a substantial part of China's international market share and providing a base for further modernisation. Japanese governments on the other hand abandoned unprofitable state-directed efforts to create heavy industry in the 1880s (Clarence-Smith, 2012, 49). (see also Chapter 9).

But what Japan could do was not necessarily a path open to everyone. Some goods, like sugar and palm oil, were more amenable to transformation at source than others, like coffee and rubber. Countries whose natural resource base lay in one versus the other had less or more chance to employ an export-processing schema. The degree of sophistication in such processing also had a big impact on technical flow-throughs later. Bulk rubber exporting involved fairly simple smoking and drying of raw material into sheets for export, with little lateral application to other economic activities, and thus little benefit to the local economy beyond the extraction of the material itself. But more sophisticated industrial treatment was required to turn the same raw rubber into liquid latex, a process that required higher skill in labour and which potentially represented more local technology transfer, assuming processing stayed in-country (Clarence-Smith, 2021, 50–51).

So, was there peripheral deindustrialisation before 1913? Clarence-Smith (2012) goes so far as to say that this conclusion is "impossible" (57), arguing that developing economies instead turned to export-processing manufacturing, which benefited from free trade, along with the industrialisation of key services, factory production of intermediate and light capital goods, and selective and temporary import substitution as needed. However, his own evidence does not support this unequivocally, for only sometimes and in some places did a considerable amount of handicraft and informal production survive in the periphery, and even then only in some places did it evolve in an industrial direction. This can be taken, as it is by Clarence-Smith, as a sign of a robust economy, but it can also be seen as indicating a retarded one. A definitive bottom-line may not be possible, but the broader economic data, including that cited earlier in this chapter, suggest that even if the developing world avoided deindustrialisation completely, it did not share much in industry's rising tide.

Indeed, it is very difficult to decisively disentangle the rich and powerful one-third from the poor and powerless two-thirds in the cause and effect of the Great Divergence. One extreme of thought is that Europe got it "right," through a combination of luck and smarts, while the rest of the world mostly got it "wrong" (Japan excepted) through bad luck and dumbness of various sorts, the proportions of luck to inherent qualities varying by the one giving the account. The existence of Imperialism and Western exploitation cannot be denied, but the tendency has been to narrowly define "returns" to imperial investment and generally find that the net number ranges from relatively small to negative. On the other extreme is the story that the Great Divergence was a massive transfer of wealth from poorer parts of the world to Europeans, with tremendous crippling of the current and future potential of those poorer peoples along the way. Chapter 13 considers Imperialism in more detail separately, but the co-incidence of Divergence and Imperialism certainly suggests a significant link between the two.

Either way, if globalisation is held responsible for delivering an extraordinary array of economic "goods", it certainly has to be true that it is equally responsible for delivering the many "bads" that happened to fall more heavily on non-white non-Europeans. The new financial and economic arrangements of the global order were not neutral with respect between rich investor and poorer recipient, though inherent biases could be quite subtle and not entirely uniform. Poorer regions could and did benefit from rich country investment. But they also suffered from it.

12.10 The Conundrum of "Rational Planning"

While Smith's term "Invisible Hand" is used to characterise (and oversimplify) the First Industrial Revolution, the Second Industrial Revolution has been referred to as the age of the "Visible Hand" (Chandler, 1977). This was part of a shift from the mechanisation of more organic practices into a full "system" which increasingly encompassed all relevant parts of the human-nature nexus. Such a system required considerable human oversight, despite conceits of self-regulation to the contrary.

The Concert of Europe and the Balance of Power were themselves systems of a sort, the latter in particular being a mechanism that functioned rather paradoxically by counter-poising equal and opposite forces against one another to maintain a supposedly stable equilibrium. After a turbulent early and mid-century, the Balance settled into a regular series of Congresses to settle disputes and a proliferation of treaties and permanent international organisations to coordinate for mutual benefit, such as the Universal Postal Union and the Geneva Convention.

The market economy was not dissimilar, except having (in theory) many small powers engaged in hard but mutually beneficial competition with one another that delivered efficiency greater than the sum of its parts. In practice, the significant players in various markets were mainly large oligopolies and monopolies, operating complex organisations internally and interacting within rapidly evolving financial and operational networks. This is most apparent in the infrastructure arena, where transport, communication and energy systems, amongst others, were being assembled and expanded by various private entities, with large injections of public support, and sometimes direct government provision. Once built, these networks had to be maintained and operated, all of which required expert systems. It was not quite modern technocracy, but well on the way to it (Goldsmith, 2014).

Indeed, "rationality" and "rational planning" seemed possible and necessary for everything, economic and otherwise. Poverty, for example, had always been with us, as the Gospels reminded everyone. But now, rather than being a sanctified spiritual state (as many Christians had maintained) or an inevitable part of a larger organic order, the nineteenth century reformers reduced it to a purely material realm and believed that technical improvements could be used to eliminate it (Clark 1969, 52). The State was now seen as having a role to play in meeting the basic needs of an uprooted industrial class, dependent on the shifting vagaries of the marketplace and no longer able to fend for itself in bad times. The recently unified Germany proved to be a leader here, granting some of the earliest social benefits, such as age pensions and health insurance, and setting a pattern that would be followed elsewhere, including in Liberal Britain. Public health was another arena of legitimised state authority (see Chapters 10 and 15).

The background for this was that there was no longer self-sufficiency for most households as there had been, at least notionally, in more "primitive" times. Traditional economic safety valves such as the commons that had helped to take the edge off hard times in the past, even in feudal societies, were now gone. Mutual obligations between "lower" and "higher" social classes that were at least notionally there to bind one class to another, if often in the breach rather than the norm, were gone too. Industrialisation and market capitalism had swept much of this away and was continuing to do so. In a sense, a new need for formal support of the individual and household had been created because of the removal of more organic sources of self-regulation and self-provision. This had obvious benefit, massive increases in productivity most notably. But the market was never going to provide everything, and the State became a default alternative for filling gaps, which it did partially, mainly where doing so would preserve its own power and status. (Large companies sometimes attempted to practise a corporate paternalism towards their own employees but this was too limited, and often too self-serving, to be a viable alternative to the government.)

Although not particularly apparent at the time, the dawn of the 20th-century economy sat on a conundrum. Rational planning was seen as both possible and necessary in all areas of human affairs. The marketplace took care of the private, individual sphere, while the State would manage the collective areas that markets could not penetrate, or deal with efficiently. And yet, as the economy grew in sophistication and complexity and penetrated more and more of the greater society, the attempt to manage human affairs simultaneously solved some problems while creating new ones. The rapid growth in material output and technical prowess seemed to validate the possibility of human control over its own affairs. And yet, the human mechanisms to do this were becoming more independent of their masters, and the problems themselves were rapidly growing in complexity. Of course, there were also areas of human being and endeavour that were outside rationality and logicality entirely, and thus at odds with the entire paradigm to begin with. Older societies had explicitly at least tried to deal with these (e.g. spirituality) but modern ones denied their existence, although such denials did not actually make them go away.

References

Allen, L., & Belt, F. H. (1998). *The ABC-CLIO world history companion to capitalism*. ABC-CLIO.

Barles, S. (2014). History of waste management and the social and cultural representations of waste. In M. Agnoletti & N. Serneri (Eds.), *The basic environmental history* (pp. 199–226). Springer.

Barraclough, G. (1967). *An introduction to contemporary history*. Pelican.

Bartholomew, J. G. (1914). *An atlas of economic geography*. Oxford University Press.

Bolt, J. & van Zanden, J. L. (2020). Maddison style estimates of the evolution of the world economy. A new 2020 update. *Maddison Project Database*, version 2020. https://www.rug.nl/ggdc/historicaldevelopment/maddison/releases/maddison-project-database-2020

Bongiorno, F. (2011). Australian labour history: Contexts, trends and influences. *Labour History, 100*, 1–18.

Chandler, A. D. (1977). *The visible hand*. University of Chicago Press.

Clarence-Smith, W. G. (2012). The industrialization of the developing world and its impact on labour relations, 1840s to 1940s. In K. Hofmeester & P. de Zwart (Eds.), *Colonialism, institutional change and shifts in global labour relations* (pp. 29–66). Amsterdam University Press.

Clark, K. (1969). *Civilization: A personal view*. Harper and Row.

Coase, R. H. (1960). The problem of social cost. *Journal of Law and Economics, 3*, 1–44.

Curran, J., & Seaton, J. (2009). *Power without responsibility*. Routledge.

Easterlin, R. (1995). Industrial revolution and mortality revolution: Two of a kind? *Journal of Evolutionary Economics, 5*(4), 393–408.

Faulkner, N. (2018). *A radical history of the world*. Pluto Press.

Federico, G., & Tena-Junguito, A. (2017). A tale of two globalizations: Gains from trade and openness 1800–2010. *Review of World Economics, 153*(3), 601–626.

Foreman-Peck, J., & Millward, R. (1994). *Public and private ownership of British industry, 1820–1990*. Clarendon Press.

Immerwahr, D. (2019). *How to hide an empire: A short history of the greater United States*. Random House.

Goldsmith, H. (2014). *The long-run evolution of infrastructure services*, CESifo Working Paper, No. 5073, Center for Economic Studies and Ifo Institute (CESifo), Munich. http://hdl.handle.net/10419/105088

Graff, M., Kenwood, A. G., & Lougheed, A. L. (2013). *Growth of the international economy, 1820–2015*. Routledge.

Lichtheim, G. (1972). *Europe in the twentieth century*. Praeger Publishers.

MacLeod, R. M. (1965). The Alkali Acts administration, 1863–84: The emergence of the civil scientist. *Victorian Studies, 9*(2), 85–112.

Neal, L., & Cameron, R. (2016). *A Concise economic history of the world: From paleolithic times to the present* (5th ed.). Oxford University Press.

Piketty, T. (2014). *Capital in the 21st century.* Harvard University Press (*companion data at:* http://piketty.pse.ens.fr/en/capital21c2

Roy, T. (1999). *Traditional industry in the economy of colonial India.* Cambridge University Press.

Stearns, P. N. (2001). *The encyclopedia of world history* (6th ed.). Houghton Mifflin Company.

Strasser, S. (1999). *Waste and want: A social history of trash.* Metropolitan Books.

US LOC. (2021a). *New century celebrations: Topics in Chronicling America.* United States Library of Congress, https://guides.loc.gov/chronicling-america-new-century-celebrations

US LOC. (2021b). *Anarchist incidents (1886–1920): Topics in Chronicling America.* https://guides.loc.gov/chronicling-america-anarchist-incidents

Van der Linden, M. (2017). *Transnational labour history: Explorations.* Routledge.

Van Zanden, J. L., Baten, J., Mira d'Ercole, M., Rijpma, A., Smith, C., & Timmer, M. (2014). *How was life?: Global well-being since 1820.* OECD Publishing.

West, R. (1982). *1900.* Viking Studio Book.

CHAPTER 13

Imperialism

C. Gordon, *Many Possible Worlds*,
https://doi.org/10.1007/978-981-19-9281-0_13

Fig. 13.1 Western empires—the fairy-tale version (*Image source* Golding, H. [1925]. *The wonder book of empire*. Ward, Lock & Co, Limited, book cover). Image is in the public domain

13.1 The "Age of Imperialism"

The Industrial Revolution ushered in many disruptive changes to the world economy, mostly still unfolding. One such development was "imperialism" (Fig. 13.1).

Domination and exploitation of one group's territory by another is nothing new. Indeed, the ancient Romans and Greeks practised a raw form of such domination, "colonialism", well before the advent of the modern nation-state. The root of the term Imperialism comes from the Latin term "imperium", meaning "to command", while the word "colony" is derived from the Latin "colonus" referring to "farmer" (Kohn & Reddy, 2017).

There is some debate about whether ancient imperialism, especially that of the Roman Empire, was qualitatively different than its nineteenth century version. Winn (2008) argues that imperial violence of all sorts is excessive by definition, going beyond the force needed to achieve national goals to achieve total submission of the vanquished, fighting beyond military need for the sake of glory (70–71). Yet, this seemingly irrational primitivism was also part of the equally systematic and rational strategic administration and control that was such a distinctive part of the Roman state. Virgil captures this dual aspect, trumpeting the peace, order and civilisation it achieved (at least from the Roman point of view) while noting the terrible price that must be paid for it in terms of personal freedom and heroism, hearkening back to Greek attitudes trumpeted by Homer (Winn, 2008, 73–76).

Thus, modern imperialism was in some ways an extension of the Roman variety, combining impersonal State building prerogatives with darker human drives. What the Industrial Revolution added to it was more deliberateness in service of an economic order, and much greater degrees of mechanisation and systematisation of conquest and control.

In this way, imperialism was modernised along with everything else. It was practised by all the major (and some minor) European powers in the 1800s, but a cleavage now opened up between an older dynastic version and a modern bourgeois version arising out of the new nation-state. Russian and Austria-Hungarian expansionism was thus in service to traditional political and economic orders that were based on fealty to personal rulers and the expansion of their personal domains. French and British expansion was driven by a nation-state that transcended dynasty and replaced it a State power imperative notionally based on a domestic commitment to liberal democracy. The dynastic states relied on imperialism as a way of underwriting their pre-modern orders using overseas resources and, especially in Austria-Hungary, as an outlet for sublimating internal tensions between domestic ethnic majorities and minorities at home. The nation-states were more focused on industrialisation and their expansionism was more purely economic in motivation, at least in the beginning. Germany was a hybrid that straddled these modes (Lichtheim, 1972, 15–23).

Both models became caught up in an increasingly self-propelling dynamic of Great Power politics, with overseas territories being a mark of status, a defensive bulwark against competitors, and a source of economic and manpower resources for defending the imperium while underwriting its expansions. For these reasons, Lichtheim (1972) defines the "Age of Imperialism" as one where "the imperial urge has become articulate and self-conscious" (23). To this, one may add a quantum leap in scale, scope and sophistication of imperial domination informed and shaped by industrialisation. Historians have dated the "Imperial Age" in various ways but all distinctly refer to a modern period that is generally agreed to have ended in 1914, and which starts anywhere from the late 1600s (generally assumed to be the last vestiges of a Commercial Revolution that peaked in high Middle Ages (see Lopez & Lopez 1976) to the late 1700s (the beginning of the Industrial Revolution) (Bayly, 2004). The economic globalisation of the 1800s and early 1900s further drove and cemented a network of hierarchical interdependency between European colonisers and colonies that was unprecedented in its complexity and all-round economic impacts.

13.2 Forms and Styles of Imperialism

The forms that European colonisation took were myriad. Conceptually, there are four dimensions to the degree of formality in rule of colony by the coloniser, and the degree of directness of such rule (Table 13.1).

Option 1, direct and formal rule, is the form of imperialism most popularly associated with nineteenth- and early twentieth-century European expansionism. This way of control is often referred to as "colonialism", in which colonies are established by a foreign nation in overseas lands, the coloniser directly exercising formal foreign dominion over the local

Table 13.1 A matrix of forms of imperialism

	Direct rule	*Indirect rule*
Formal	1 (Colonialism)	2 (Vassal state)
Informal	3 (Theoretical only)	4 (Network dependency)

populations. The rise of industry and manufacturing saw a global explosion of this type of domination by European powers, succeeded by similar forms of dominion by some European settler colonies over other lands, especially by the Americans (Duiker, 2010, Chapter 2).

While this first form was quite obvious and predominant, other forms of imperialism that were not "colonial" in the formal direct sense were unfolding as well, and colonialism in this time often began with informal indirect rule morphing into more direct and formal rule in stages over a number of years. In India, for example, British expansionism manifested first through option 2 (indirect/informal) in many parts of the subcontinent, where local rulers became vassals to varying degrees to the British both formally and informally. This type of indirect formal rule continued throughout the Raj period and India became a patchwork realm of direct and indirect colonisation (Ramesh, 2017). Figure 13.2 provides an 1894 map showing British across South Asia up to that point.

The Indian case is quite interesting in many ways, as British institutions of control morphed over time. Following the mercantilist model of earlier Commercial Revolution imperialism, parts of modern-day India came under British rule beginning in 1757, under the control of the East India Company, an entity that had been granted a trading charter and monopoly by Queen Elizabeth I at the end of December 1600. The Charter Act of 1813 broke this monopoly, allowing private British citizens to trade directly with India, weakening the Company's monopoly power somewhat but not its function as an instrumentality of British rule. The disastrous Great Sepoy Mutiny of 1857 led to the Company's dissolution, with governance of India (where such direct authority was exercised) taken over by the British crown in 1858 (Ramesh, 2017, 23–24).

On the other hand, option 4 (indirect/informal) could be said to have been used with China almost exclusively, where overall sovereignty was nominally respected, but with major limitations on it imposed either generally or in specific locations, in the latter case in the form of "extraterritorial" trading concessions in major cities that combined colonial forms with supposedly purely commercial agreements (Hong Kong being an exception of outright colonial rule by Britain over a detached piece of Chinese territory). The Opium Wars, where Chinese economic dependence on Britain for this devastating narcotic was brutally imposed through military force, could be seen as a particularly nefarious example of "indirect" control (Brandt et al., 2014).

Fig. 13.2 The expansion of British in South Asia in the nineteenth century (***Image source and notes*** British Library digitised image from page 155 of "History for ready reference, from the best historians … Their own words in a complete system of history … With … maps … by A. C. Reiley" Date of publication: 1895 Publisher: C. A. Nichols. British Library's catalogue: 002,078,454 [physical copy] and 014,860,646 [digitised copy]. No known copyright restrictions)

Logically, option 3—direct and informal—is implied and included for completeness. But it is the least coherent form practically. It might in theory be possible to directly rule an area informally but no one seems to have done it and it is hard to see how it would work.

The choice of control mode depended partly upon the nature of the territory being colonised. For example, Indian society is more complex than Chinese society and in India there has never been any pre-industrial continuous development of either national institutions or a central bureaucracy (Ramesh, 2017, 23). Thus, it was easier and more natural for the British to follow a patchwork formal and informal takeover there as opposed to its approach in China, where the country and its government was left nominally intact. In India, changing conditions sometimes led to changing methods of control, as happened after the 1857 Mutiny which showed that delegated colonisation was no longer effective.

Much also depended on the culture, politics and social ordering of the coloniser, which can be referred to as a "style" of rule. This would include the cultural and institutional norms and practices that imperial powers transmitted to their imperial subjects through their ruling policies and institutions (Oto-Peralías & Romero-Ávila, 2017). For example, the British colonisation of North America in the 1600s and 1700s was direct and formal (option 1) but the style was one that reflected the institutional diversity of the constitutional monarchy of the home state. Thus, each American colony was administered by different agents on behalf of the Crown, each under differing terms and conditions, and with considerable leeway given in the way that colonies themselves were run on the ground. Economically, the colonies were explicitly designed to serve the central British authority but as they were not directly controlled from the centre but run by a devolved set of local (white) settler elites, an autonomy was established that served as a foundation for the settler rebellion against English overlordship in the late 1700s. As England began to tighten both its political control and level of extraction of local resources, local colonists resented the change in their levels of autonomy and saw it as their right to rebel against what they saw as a violation of an implicit contract between rulers and the ruled. The loose leash on the colonists had also allowed the building of locally controlled institutions and resources that could be easily mobilised for revolt when the time came (Fitzmaurice, 2003).

The French colonies in the Caribbean Sea (the "Sugar Islands") were, by contrast, more tightly controlled from a centre that focused purely on economic extraction of local raw materials for the benefit of the French Empire. Part of this was due to the fact that these particular colonies were small islands with agricultural monocultures, and completely based on slave labour (unlike the mix of free and unfree labour modes in British North America). Profits were repatriated mostly back to France, with little left behind. These economic facts by themselves helped to drive the choice of a directly exploitative imperial form. But this was also due to specific assumptions that the French had about their own cultural superiority, and a stronger tradition of a central State, leading to a style of colonial administration that was much tighter and controlling than of the geographically adjacent British colonies (Aldrich, 1996).

These are very broad and incomplete observations with many exceptions and nuances. In general, though, there were wide variations in style and form of rule during the Age of Imperialism, sometimes even by the same colonial overlord. Whatever the form or style, the essential inequality and exploitative nature of imperialism remained the same wherever it was applied.

13.3 Motivations for Imperialism

Even during the imperialist age itself, a sharp debate emerged over the motivations for the explosion of European expansionism that was then taking place. Three major threads have emerged in the literature since then.

13.3.1 Geopolitical

The nineteenth century was an era of European "Great Power Politics". The imperialist era was dominated by multiple and relatively evenly matched large and rapidly industrialising powers in Europe: France, England, Germany in particular; rising new powers outside Europe—the US and Japan; and declining formerly great non-European powers—China, and the Ottoman Empire, as well as a few European formerly greats—Spain, Portugal and the Netherlands. There was also Russia, which was in a category of its own, being Eurasian, declining in some ways (and losing quite a bit of territory between 1800 and 1914) but growing and developing domestically in economic and social terms, though quite unevenly.

No one power could claim true global hegemony (i.e. complete leadership and influence) during this time, with the exception of the British Empire, which covered close to a quarter of the globe by the end of the century, possessing a navy that ruled the waves, and a currency, the Pound Sterling, which served as a global means of exchange and a unit of global account under the prevailing Gold Standard (with the French Franc running a close, though declining, second) (McKeown, 1983). However even Britain had uneven global control, its military power on the European continent limited by Germany and France, its naval superiority nonetheless hemmed in by a traditional competition with Russia in Asia, the Pacific and the Caucasus, and the rising nations of Japan and America in the Pacific and the Atlantic. This very unstable power mix of rising and declining powers unsettled the old post-Napoleonic "Concert of Europe" established by Metternich, and unleashed an impetus for a new balance that could only find immediate expression in competition for dominance of "untouched" and relatively open "peripheries".

The so-called "Scramble for Africa" is where this dynamic is most evident. Africans ruled approximately 90% of Africa in 1800 (though trade and enclave colonisation by Europeans had been going on for centuries). By 1900 virtually the entire continent except for Ethiopia (genuinely independent for centuries) and Liberia (established by the US in 1822 as a colony for emancipated slaves and technically independent since 1847 but largely an indirect American colony) was directly controlled by European nations. Figure 13.3 shows how the political map of Africa was transformed by colonialism in a mere five decades. This rapid and rather sudden acceleration of European conquest, while especially acute in Africa, was reflected globally as well. In 1500, Europeans controlled 7% of the land surface of the planet; by 1800, this share had risen to 35% (Duiker, 2010; Chapter 2; Mason, 2011).

There is considerable evidence for the geopolitical dynamic of imperialism as this was a rationale explicitly invoked by the Powers themselves, especially during the periodic Great Power conferences that met to bring competing nations into explicit agreement on spheres of influence and colonial boundaries and arrangements. General war threatened to break out a number of times because of conflicts between European imperialists on the continent of Africa especially, and the outbreak of the First World War is seen by many as a culmination of this process in which the Great Powers finally confronted each other directly after decades of doing so on their colonial out-lands (Mason, 2011).

13.3.2 Cultural/Ideological

A contemporary justification for European imperialism was that the superior white races of Western civilisation were bringing good things to people generally characterised by Europeans as not being fully civilised. This was an era of Social Darwinism, which was an official justification for a racist and elitist attitude used by Imperial powers to justify their

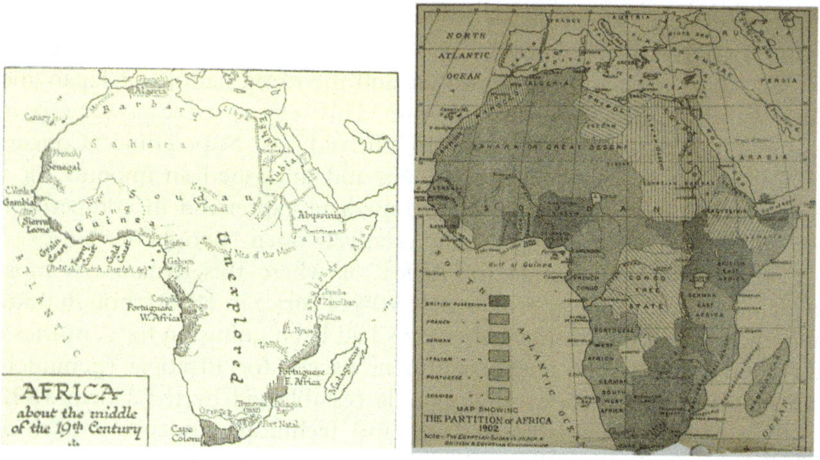

Fig. 13.3 The European takeover of Africa (*Authors note* The left panel map, circa 1920, shows a prevailing colonialist attitude that continued well into the twentieth century, designating much of the continent "unexplored", reflecting earlier European tropes about the "dark continent", made so because of European ignorance of its peoples and also its racist bias. *Source* Wells, H. G., & Horrabin, J. F. [1920]. *The outline of history: Being a plain history of life and mankind.* Cassell. P. 321; Contributing Library: University of California Libraries; Digitizing Sponsor: MSN. Right panel: Rose, J. H. [1916]. *The development of the European nations, 1870–1914.* G.P. Putnam's sons. P. 809. Contributing Library: University of California Libraries. Digitizing Sponsor: Internet Archive. No known copyright restrictions)

colonialism, as well as their exploitations of workers and other groups within Europe (Koch, 1984). This more "scientific" ideology replaced, or at least sat over, the more traditional religious bigotry of older Empire building, especially by the Spanish who had sought to convert the natives of their conquered realms into the Catholic faith, usually killing many more than they converted.

These attitudes got filtered through unique and particular European ethnocentrisms. The French, for example, simultaneously aimed for domination and assimilation of many of their subject peoples into "superior" French culture, with French citizenship being notionally granted to some colonial subjects, though very qualified, for only a select number, and far from automatically granted, limited to those geographic areas considered to be integral parts of the metropole. This was the case for Algeria, which ended up having representation in the French National Assembly, with the country's territory divided into départements considered to be part of Metropolitan France, dues to its location directly across the Mediterranean from France itself and because of its inordinately large French settler community. This "democracy" was, however, granted mainly to white French settlers, not the locals, who were generally ruthlessly governed from afar. This model was a result of both French nationalism and cultural chauvinism combined with the Republican ideology of the French Revolution whose principle of representation for French citizens regardless of location or status could not be so easily dismissed by colonial policymakers (Winnacker, 1938).

By contrast, the British were culturally and politically more isolationist, generally aiming for association instead of assimilation, i.e. collaborating with local elites to dominate the subjected culture, while keeping that culture separate from "superior" British norms. Even where local elites almost slavishly adopted British mores, such as in many parts of India, their foreign overlords never accepted them in any way as English. Colonial subjects, even white English settlers, never were offered direct representation in the British Parliament, the exception being Ireland, whose residents wrested some political concessions during their struggle for independence. True equality was never acknowledged in either case: locals were not given any other choices except what the dominant power offered them (Bleich, 2005).

In general, cultural/ideological motivations are generally seen as secondary to geopolitical and other motivations, used as justifications more than impetus for imperialism. But they did have an important indirect effect by helping to shape style and form of domination.

13.3.3 Economic

How much imperialism was motivated by economic rather than noneconomic concerns was a topic of heated discussion during the time, and still a topic debated today. British political economist John A. Hobson, for example, wrote a widely read book entitled *Imperialism: A Study* ([1902] 2018) that argued that Western industrialism led to production of more goods than there was domestic demand for, with colonies providing the necessary overseas markets for these surpluses, markets that could be captured purely for the benefit of the coloniser. This line of thinking gave rise to an "underconsumptionist" theory of capitalism, later used by some to explain the Great Depression of the 1930s. This doctrine held that the natural tendency of capitalist enterprise was always to produce too much, something that if not addressed externally, would lead to economic collapse in the end. For Hobson, diversion of excess output into captive foreign markets was the means of escaping such a collapse. Karl Marx had earlier made an argument in *Das Kapital*, paralleling Hobson's, saying that the capitalist class by definition needed to constantly find new markets for its output (Marx et al., 1965). Hobson simply placed these "new markets" overseas in colonies.

The change in the nature of European imperialism in Africa lends some support to these ideas. Before 1800, European penetration of Africa was largely trade-based, exploitative but also containing some mutual gains from trade for both African and European, especially as the territorial control was mostly limited trading outposts. After 1800, Europeans dropped any mutual gains, moving to direct imperial extraction of raw materials from colonies, with high value-add done by the coloniser, accompanied by forced selling of manufactures and other processed goods back to its underdeveloped colonies. This had been a feature of British North American colonisation too, but those colonies were still allowed a considerable amount of political autonomy and the ability to reap local gains from trade.

Marx made a further inference, based on a surmise his fellow Political Economists made that competitive markets would ultimately drive investment returns down to zero at the margin, resulting in a long-term "stationary state" in which there would be no further growth. Marx reasoned that this impending no-growth state was a "contradiction" that would bring the capitalist system down, rather than settle into the stable long-run homeostasis implicitly assumed by the Classical Economists. Lenin jumped off Marx's inference to argue that imperialism was thus a natural and inevitable stage of late capitalism, an argument that was one of his few genuine original contributions to economic theory (as opposed to the genuinely original, if often ruthless, political theory, he developed to explain and guide the Bolshevik Revolution and its aftermath and which was merged with Marxism to form Marxism-Leninism). In true "dialectical" fashion, Lenin went on to argue that this stage would inevitably lead to conflict between the industrial capitalist economies resulting in their ultimate mutual destruction (Lenin, [1917] 1939; McDonough, 1995). The Leninist conception in particular is probably over-determined, i.e.

it explains too much and leaves too little room for alternative causes. More contemporary research indeed questions the applicability of the more mechanistic economic doctrines of imperialism that arose during its "Golden Age" (Etherington, 1982).

But many economic historians have perhaps implicitly replaced those with a quasi deterministic view of the coloniser as a rational maximiser, conducting ex-post cost-benefit analyses to determine whether colonial masters in their golden age actually had a positive payoff. This framework has spawned a broad literature on the "returns" to imperialism, with rather mixed findings. The British Empire has been the most widely studied and various analysts have estimated that the British had either a net gain, a net loss or a net wash to show for their imperial toils (Edelstein, 1976; O'Brien, 1988; Offer, 1993). At a minimum, this shows the limitations of data and the sensitivity of parameters for conducting the complicated task of calculating rates of return over wide-spreading and complex colonial empire.

But there are more fundamental problems with the "returns" literature. First, the assumption of "rationality" does not seem to fully apply to an enterprise that has a significant "non-rational" component, even with some clear economic functions that it served in a global economy, at least for the colonisers. Second, only material returns that can be collapsed into monetary units are considered. European colonisers gained control over people, geographies and economic resources that they used in many different ways, partly as "reserves" with "option values" to be drawn on in case of emergency, such as war, and partly as levers in a broader geopolitical strategy in which they were jockeying for position amongst their peers. These things have a lot of value that cannot easily or reliably be incorporated into a commercially based single monetised metric, and as a result are generally ignored under the returns rubric.

Certainly, the coloniser obtained stocks of available labour and raw materials and potential markets for European imports that were most useful during a time of rising mass production and other economic dislocations. Foreign territory also offered at least perceived strategic and geopolitical advantage and, when the chips were down, extra soldiers to fight rivals, something well-utilised by Britain and France in the First World War and, in the British case, as a cross-subsidisation of its ventures to expand the Empire, especially the bleeding of India to fund its Afghan wars (Davis, 2002, 337).

Whether or not imperialism was a losing proposition economically in the short term, for the colonial masters engaged in it, its moral and social costs ended up being incalculable for both sides, falling most heavily, obviously, on the colonised.

13.4 The Burdens Imposed by Colonial Rule

It must still be admitted that Empires cost a lot of money to conquer, run, protect and administer. And they encompassed very large amounts of people and territory at their height (see Figs. 13.4 and 13.5). The "returns" literature necessarily takes this into account to arrive at a "net" bottom-line. And some scholars rightly note that there was some transfer of wealth and knowledge from the imperial nation to their conquered charges. Did this transfer at least reap some dividends for locals in terms of economic growth after these colonies gained their freedom? If so, what was the cost paid, long- and short-term, by colonial subjects?

Even when restricting the focus to purely economic aspects, this is probably an impossible question to answer definitively, much less quantitatively. But the general history suggests much more movement of resources away from colonised to coloniser than in the other direction. For one thing, Europe had run persistent negative balances of trade with Asia for centuries, a situation that only reversed with imperialism (Neal & Cameron, 2016, 125). Although some argue that this was simply a result of efficient flow of resources due to "incentives" arising out of a newly integrated world economy (e.g. Allen, 2011, 61–62), it is hard to resist the conclusion that Europeans did indeed extract a great deal from their nominal charges to be able to overturn a centuries-old negative balance of trade, and that this had long-run consequences even after independence.

This can be seen in both direct and indirect ways. In India, for example, allocation of domestic economic, financial and ecological resources were in part devoted to railways that seemed to be benign from the outside, but which were built mainly for exports of mainly raw materials to the home country, and military control by British colonial forces. Thus not only were these railways not British "gifts", as they were financed by what even some contemporary British observers considered to rapacious local taxation, but their primary immediate functions were for command and extraction (Davis, 2002, 373). They were also built using imports

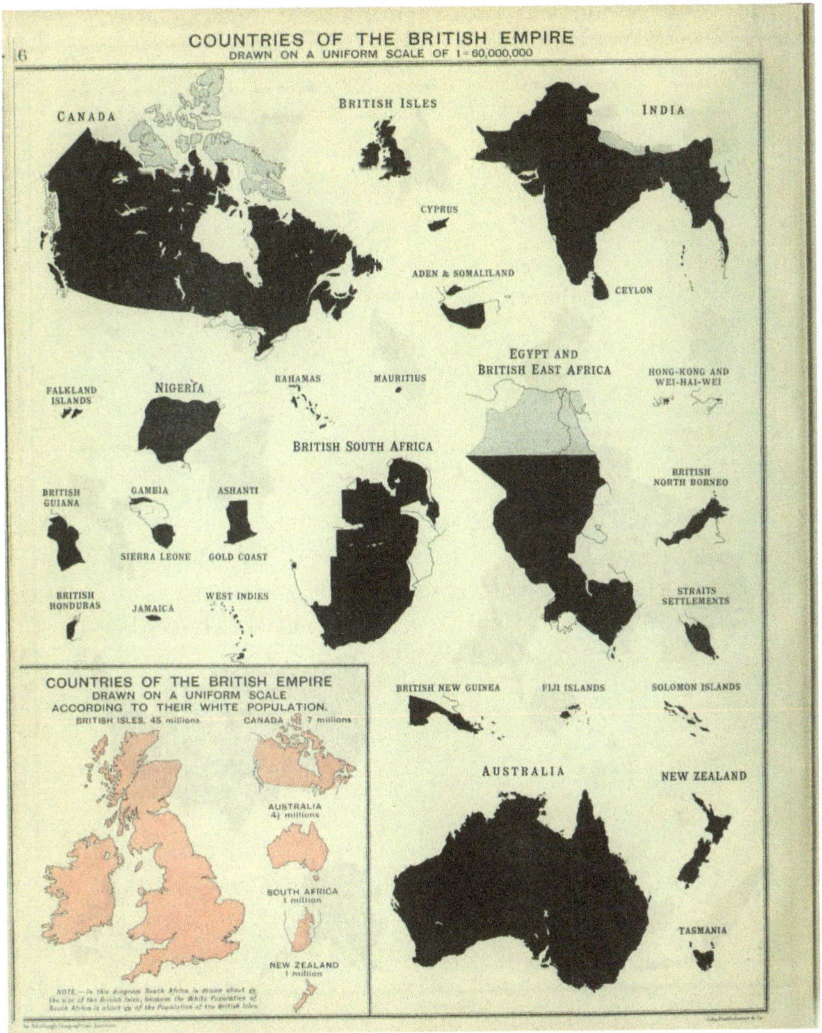

Fig. 13.4 The British Empire circa 1914 (*Image source* Bartholomew [1914]. No known copyright restrictions)

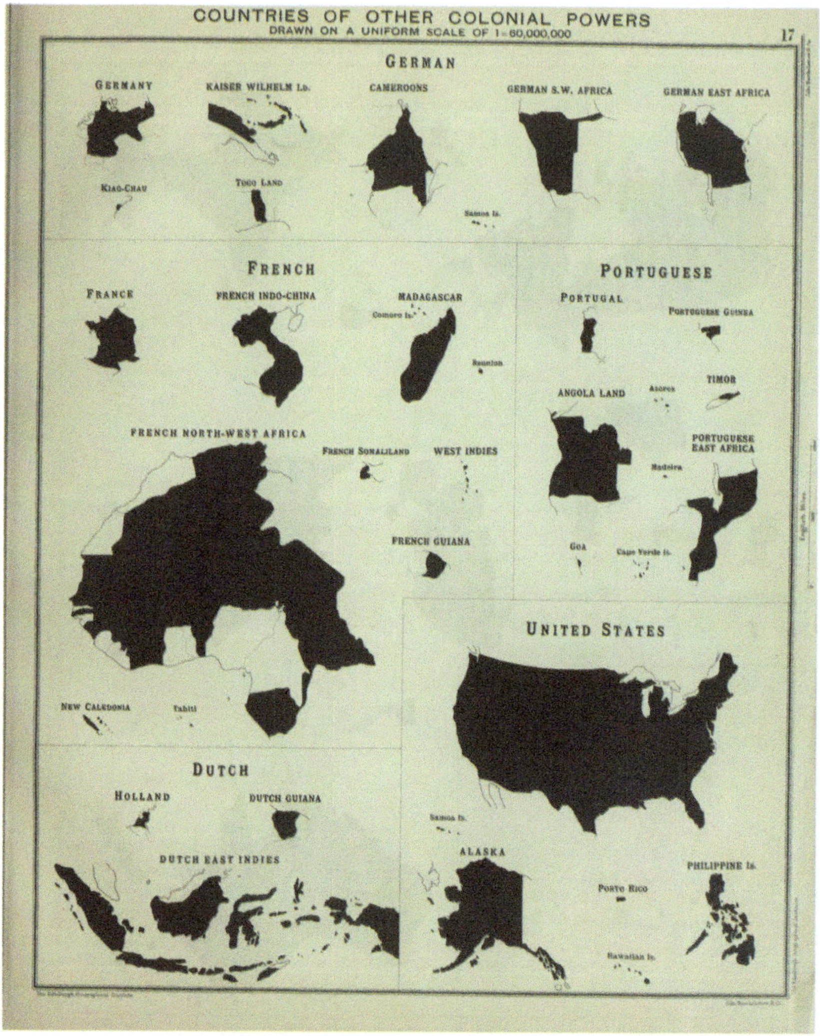

Fig. 13.5 Other European and offshoot empires circa 1914 (*Image source* Bartholomew [1914]. No known copyright restrictions)

of British expertise and technologies, with no chance for any development of local industry in the area and their building caused some serious environmental damage (Davis, 2002, 332).

India was also economically integrated into a European-dominated economic order, while not being given local autonomy to adjust policy and institutional response, a situation that often resulted in some real disaster. India became a major food exporter to the UK, especially after the building of the Suez Canal lowered transport costs between the two nations, even during periods when Indian famine raged. At the same time, India produced opium to finance its mostly forced negative balance of trade with the UK, feeding into the highly profitable British exploitation of China. The shift to a Gold Standard depreciated India and China silver-based currencies as demonetised silver flooded world markets, hurting both countries, to English advantage. Payments to the UK were fixed in Gold especially squeezing India (Davis, 2002, 332).

There has also been a lot of consideration of environmental exploitation by colonists, Pomeranz (2000) and Davis (2002) studying India and China and, in Davis's case, Brazil as well. Pomeranz claims that the major benefit to Europe of overseas colonisation was the relief of its own ecological pressures through the exploitation of other's lands. Meanwhile, Davis argues that the systematic collection of meteorological evidence, an outgrowth of the new field of meteorology, was as much an exercise in depoliticising a system of imperial control as one of science, and part of a much broader program of British data collection and systematic analysis and planning across its colonies that presented a supposedly neutral tableau but which British experts often manipulated to their own advantage when drawing up agreements, financial instruments and so forth, both within their Empire and outside of it. Colonial poverty was also cast as just a fate of nature, sitting comfortably with Social Darwinism, along with the new sunspot theories of business cycles that carried a sort of natural selection to economics that removed human agency, politics and power relations (Davis, 2002, 234). Furthermore, national weather and climate statistics are not the proper unit of meteorological analysis, and while some of this can be chalked up to ignorance and the vagaries of administrative convenience, the use of national categories helped to cover a broader exploitation justified in the British Colonial Office by a rigid Benthamite Utilitarianism along with strong Eurocentric bigotry (Davis, 2002, 262).

Imperialism, along with marketisation and global integration, generally is very bad for climate vulnerability overall, but was especially problematic in the colonies. In India fiscal autonomy for local governments was directly or indirectly removed by their British masters and international terms of trade declined as cores and peripheries emerged. While marketisation of formerly nonmarket (and non-monetised) relationships turned instead into debt peonage locally since food entitlements now had to be settled in international markets where an imperial money supply (the Gold Standard) worked against Indian silver (Davis, 2002, 309). The result in many parts of India was a form of deindustrialisation and an undermining of the local economy (Ramesh, 2017, 27–28). (See also Chapter 11).

Obviously, one should not go to the other extreme and say that the colonies received absolutely nothing from their masters. Railways, for example, did offer some productivity benefits for the Indian economy, along with a legacy of a built-out system after independence, even though it is clear that there could have been much more development benefit to Indians if the system had been built and managed differently and catered more to local needs (Bogart & Chaudhary, 2013). There was also some positive transfer of institutions and knowledge from Europe, such as more secure regimes of private property rights (Allen, 2011). More generally, the global system of trade and finance did allow for some efficient reallocation of resources from rich countries to poor ones. And even where economic failure can be pointed to, it is not always the result of deliberate administrative decisions, whether in the foreground or background. Economic incentives may not always be as relevant as some claim, but neither are they as irrelevant as others maintain.

Still, imperialism was in the end a game of the subjection of unwilling peoples to outside control. From an economic and social justice point of view, it can never be justified. From an economic efficiency point of view (itself a somewhat repugnant lens given the context), it was at best a very mixed blessing for those subjected to it, likely with much more curse than blessing in the equation.

13.5 Imperialism and Postcolonial Economic Growth

After the various colonies gained their independence, the long-run impacts of a colonial heritage on per capita GDP growth appears decidedly mixed. This question is usually answered via a Growth Theory model, with its underlying production function in which present and future growth is determined by inputs and technology and anything that might affect these in the background, such as "institutions". Indeed, the New Institutional Economics literature (Acemoglu et al., 2001, 2002; Dell, 2010; Engerman & Sokoloff, 2000; Nunn, 2008) posits that the profound current differences between previously colonised areas of the world such as Latin America and Africa can be traced back to differences in colonial era institutions and their persistent ongoing and cumulative effects over centuries. This framework has led economic historians in particular to consider different colonies as "natural experiments" in which one can compare the growth paths of different countries. This could be done by looking at the differences between colonies with different imperial regimes and/or masters (e.g. French versus British); "comparable" never-colonised countries and colonised ones (e.g. agrarian economies); or performance measured relative to some "optimal" theoretical standard of economic growth in a particular time period. Results can then be parsed further to analyse the possible causes of postcolonial differentials by isolating differences in technology, capital and labour.

In practice, there are many devilish details in such an enterprise. Not least, it is quite difficult to find a genuinely "controlled comparison". For example, an ideal would be two countries with roughly similar populations, endowments, geographic conditions and historical starting points but with each one colonised by different countries pursuing different regimes during similar time periods, or one colonised and the other left independent. Obviously, such pairings are rarely available.

Despite the difficulties, economic historians have given it their best shot. What have they found? Let's briefly consider two broad cases, focusing on the issues of comparability and the appropriate benchmarks for comparing results from different colonial regimes, something economic historians refer to as "mirrors".

13.5.1 Latin America

In the 1500s and 1600s, the Spanish Empire colonised most of South, Central and a large southern swathe of North America. By the early nineteenth century, Spain had been kicked out of the entirety of South and Central America by a wave of local national independence movements, mostly led by white settler elites, while still occupying some Caribbean islands such as Cuba and Puerto Rico, which would later be lost to the US around the turn of the twentieth century.

From an economic history point of view, Latin America offers the most promising case study for natural experiments and controlled comparisons and so most such work has been done for this region. The area has many commonalities imposed by colonisation, e.g. the shared Spanish language, Catholicism and broadly similar colonial institutions, policies and practices during the time of imperial domination. At the same time, there also are wide geographical, natural resource and even ethnic divides underneath the common colonial heritage which in theory allow for controls for these variables when comparing one colony to another.

Additionally, there is the comparator of the British colonies in North America, especially the US, which became independent within a roughly similar time frame to the Spanish colonies. The postcolonial period also fits very neatly within the Industrial Revolution period, potentially offering a "clean" case for how pre-industrial colonisation affected industrial development for newly independent nations.

In theory, then, one can "control" for different conditions within the Spanish Empire, pre- and post-independence, and between that Empire and its regional counterparts outside. In other words, one can ask how, first, the "common cause" of Spanish colonialism affected future growth postcolonially under different local independence conditions; and second, compare such growth with "similar" developed independent countries, especially the US which is in the same hemisphere and thus at least notionally of the same region. As already mentioned, the US itself has a colonial heritage that could be said to be "successful" as far as the settler, though not the indigenous, population is concerned.

De la Escosura (2005, 2007) has done some of the most comprehensive work here.

Data for comparative growth rates are uneven, but De la Escosura's best estimates of Latin American growth suggest that the region overall has had some very strong economic performance over the past 200 years. However, it has been uneven both across particular countries and time periods. He notes that after a slow start with independence, Latin America per capita GDP grew significantly between 1860 and 1890, with accelerating growth up to First World War. In fact, the region experienced greater output growth per capita in the 1880s and 1900–1913 than did the countries grouped in the modern Organisation for Cooperation and

Economic Development (OECD). The Interwar years were poor, but they were poor for most other areas too.

Growth then picked up again between 1938–1980, with a "Golden Age" between 1950–1973, though during that latter period, while Latin America managed to reach US growth rates, it did not match OECD growth rates overall. Obviously, the US was a very "mature" economy by that time, so its lower growth rates were more a sign of that fact rather than of any structural weakness. This interpretation would not hold, obviously, for most Latin American countries. Overall, the 1880s, 1900–1930s and the 1950s–1970s were times where Latin America consistently performed above the US and OECD averages. Other than that, its economic performance could be said to be substandard (though of course with local variations both above and below average).

But what is, really, the relevant benchmark? In assessing how "good" or "bad" postcolonial growth is in Latin America, what standard of comparison should be used? The US or OECD countries are often the metric, but perhaps these are not always the proper choice analytically, especially since these are more developed regions, some of which had no experience as colonised countries themselves, and thus may falsely reflect a relatively poor performance that would not look so bad if a more proper benchmark was used.

To use the standard terminology, what "mirror" should a country look into that best reflects the true long-term economic effect of its colonial past? Rather than use a US mirror, perhaps an Asian or African mirror should be used since this is an apples-to-apples approach (i.e. developing-to-developing country, and colonised-to-colonised) rather than an apples-to-oranges approach (developing-to-developed country and colonised-to-coloniser).

To that end, De la Escosura (2009) conducted some additional work that was more disaggregated, looking at individual Latin American countries, but also bringing in other aggregate economic areas outside the region to offer additional "mirrors" with which to reflect back the nature of postcolonial Latin American economic performance. As has been noted, Latin America's postcolonial economic performance measured against the US has been uneven. Using multiple comparisons or mirrors shows a more varied picture, however. From this vantage point, Latin America's postcolonial economic performance was, for the past two centuries, overall below that of former offshoot colonies that have fully entered the developed world (the US especially), and below the colonisers themselves (with the odd exception of Spain itself because of its own very poor performance after losing most of its Empire at the beginning of the 1800s). But they are above many other former colonies in other regions.

It should be added that Latin America is highly heterogeneous and some particular countries have performed above regional averages, with others being below. So while regional comparisons have value, they also obscure local patterns that may be crucial in both measuring and understanding economic performance more deeply. De la Escosura himself argues that Latin American countries should be compared against their own potential of what might have been if they had never been colonised, rather than against other countries such as the US. While very sensible, an issue with this benchmark, of course, is that the "counterfactual" is purely hypothetical, presenting similar issues to those encountered when considering the economic impacts of the railways (see Chapter 8).

Overall, when measured by postcolonial GDP growth, the Spanish colonial heritage has been mixed. The region has done very well in some periods, very poorly in others, with individual countries having their moments, high and low. The measure of performance also differs according to "mirror" used.

This might suggest that colonialism, at least the Spanish version of it, has not proven to be consistently economically harmful to those once under its heel (social, political and other dimensions obviously a very important separate issue). It may even have been helpful in certain ways by transferring technology and advanced institutions that set the former colonies up for better performance than they might otherwise have had in the newly industrialising world post-independence. Or maybe not, depending on period, region/country and mirror choice.

Causality around "institutions" is where many of the fiercest debates take place. These are also the hardest to measure and evaluate. An influential school of thought with respect to Latin America has been the "Structuralists" who maintain that colonialism by definition structured economic systems according to centre-periphery hierarchies. Colonisers put themselves at the centre of their Empires, at the top of the value-add chain, giving themselves a comparative advantage in manufactures, commerce and trade while leaving their colonies mainly to export raw materials back to their masters. In Latin America, there was little investment in education of the population (except for local elites, mainly foreign in origin) or other social institutions, with no provision for local autonomy in governance. After the end of Spanish rule in Latin America, colonial economic patterning persisted (it is argued) shaping the future growth paths and potential of the former colonies (Cárdenas & Helfand, 2011).

Some Structuralists take an especially negative, and more deterministic view of this patterning. The Dependency School, and its associated Underdevelopment variant, holds that Spanish colonialism left newly independent countries with largely extractive economies, based on export of raw goods such as minerals and agricultural products. As a result, these economies became export-oriented, stuck at the lower rungs of the value chain, with poorly educated masses, concentrated land-holdings (a definite relic of the Spanish colonial *hacienda* system of large plantation agriculture), and highly unequal distributions of income with associated rural poverty (Bértola & Rodríguez Weber, 2015). Resulting and relatively low urbanisation rates retarded industrial development further. Thus, Latin American countries started out as highly dependent on the international economy, yet without gaining many of the benefits of such integration, i.e. they remained "peripheral" and "dependent" on world economic systems beyond their control.

These arguments make some logical and conceptual sense. But the evidence for them is mixed. Some point to the US as a counter-example, where colonial structures were not nearly as centralised nor as extractive as their Spanish counterparts, claiming this as proof that colonial institutions do matter, but that post-independence choices matter as well, and that economic dependency is not a foregone conclusion. Yes, the US gained independence with a more developed local manufacturing and commerce sector, more tradition of local self-government and broader interdependent (rather than dependent) integration into the world economy. Latin American colonies lacked these things and as a result, they performed more poorly. But individual countries made very different choices after their freedom from colonial rule and there was much material prosperity amidst the poverty depending on the country, and post-independence policy set, in question. Latin American growth has overall been better than many other former colonies of other nations, and weaker than some non-colonised counterparts, which indicate imperialism's burden. But the fact that some Spanish colonies have done better than other colonies in the region and elsewhere also shows there is some national agency available to counteract this.

De la Escosura makes an essentially neoclassical case about the effect of colonial institutions before and afterwards in former Spanish colonies.

He argues that the Spanish colonial system had benefits as well as costs. The costs were the burden of colonial rule itself, where Spain taxed local populations high amounts to maintain local institutions while repatriating a large surplus for itself. Additionally, institutions were not modernised over time for there was little incentive to improve administration under a mainly extractive regime.

The benefits the Spanish brought, however, were unified government (which had economies of scale in provision of administration), a common defence and economic integration (though subservient) to an internal imperial market. One could argue that these particular scale benefits were more pronounced for the Spanish Empire than for the more administratively diverse and geographically far-flung British Empire, which in some areas, like India, was especially fragmented on the ground.

After independence, Latin America fractured into many smaller nations that, for a period, fought amongst themselves. The burden of imperial administration was now gone—a cost savings—but the new cost of independent administration of many smaller local states versus their much larger and fewer prior imperial subdivisions, combined with increasing war between the newly independent entities, more than wiped out these savings. Thus, it was not until the latter part of the nineteenth century that Latin American nations began to catch up, as internal wars settled down, self-administration costs fell and subsequent institutional modernisation, helped by regional peace and international economic growth, paid dividends. Additionally, the global market was becoming more integrated overall and Latin American nations themselves gained benefits from better market opportunities for exports and significant inflows of foreign capital for infrastructure and other investments (De la Escosura, 2005, 2007).

In a sense, neoclassical logic can line up with Structuralist logic in that there are good general arguments for colonial institutions affecting postcolonial growth trajectories, and much evidence that these colonial practices imposed lingering costs after independence that could be quite significant. But there the similarity ends because in one approach incentives largely trump institutions, while in the other institutions, especially in a world system, limit choices so much in some peripheries that the concept of incentives is hardly applicable.

13.5.2 Africa

Africa is in many ways a more interesting case because it was ground zero for the Age of Imperialism, being almost completely colonised during the latter half of the First Industrial Revolution and the first half of the Second. But Africa's postcolonial economic performance, and its causes and effects, is harder to assess in a number of ways. For one thing, during much of the continent's pre-colonial economy, the trading of slaves was a significant part of some local economies, especially those interfacing with Europe and the Muslim world. Between 1450 and 1900, some twelve million people were transported as slaves from Africa to the Americas, in exchange for various European goods, including weapons such as guns. This was a key part of the so-called "Triangular Trade" which was the foundation of mercantilist style trade Empires run by England, France, Spain and Portugal (Klein, 1999). African slaves also were a key input into the output production of foreign colonies, such as the Sugar Islands, which sent their raw materials back to Europe to be converted into manufactured goods, which were then traded for more slaves in Africa—and also forcibly sold to the colonies as well through mandated policies. England, for example, tried to limit local manufacturing in the American colonies and forced all trans-shipments to go through England to other parts of the world rather than directly from America to nearby ports (Klein, 1999).

Still until the 1800s, slaves were traded commodities within a European imperial nexus that involved relatively little occupation of African territory by foreign overlords. From this mostly trade-based imperialism based largely on mutually advantageous trade (though morally reprehensible when slaves were involved) with local people under local authority (almost all people enslaved were captured and brought initially to the Europeans by Africans, the Europeans then taking this immoral cargo to sea for the brutal "Middle Passage" to the "New World"), the Europeans moved abruptly to direct formal colonisation of Africa over the course of mere decades.

The exact causes of this sudden shift are not completely clear but generally involve a combination of an increasing competition between the two long-standing powers of France and Britain, the rise of two new imperial competitors in the forms of a newly unified Germany and Italy, and vacuums of power created by the declining Ottoman Empire, which had waning control over Egypt and the southern Mediterranean Sea.

Africa also was politically fragmented and generally poorly armed when compared to the modern armies and nation-states of Europe. Once one power grabbed a piece of territory, others rushed in, and before long almost every place was "taken".

In one sense, Africa offers a clear-cut case study for analysing the economic impacts of imperialism because its colonisation was rapid and intense and, like Latin America, confined to a single continent. There were also numerous colonial masters on the continent, at least theoretically providing for controlled comparisons, sharpened by the fact that these masters had relatively distinct governance styles. So the specific role of colonial institutions on later economic growth seems to be more prone to study in Africa than some other areas, Latin America possibly excepted.

But Africa is also devilishly unique in many respects, not least because of the slave trade legacy that continued for some time even during its colonisation. The role of slavery in capitalist development in the global "North" is a matter of ongoing controversy (e.g. Beckert, 2015). Here, the issue is how this particular trade might have negatively affected Africa, it being a major supplier of its own population to the world supply of slaves (with some relatively small exceptions of Muslim slave traders bringing slaves to Africa, including some white ones). The literature on this is surprisingly sparse but focuses on two likely effects, namely depopulation, which would have been concentrated in selected areas; and the phenomenon referred to as "social death", which points to the violence to African societies that enslavement brought with it (Whatley & Gillezeau, 2011). There certainly must have been at least some severe localised economic effects, if not also more general ones, but not much attention has yet been paid to them by scholars.

Additionally, Africa is a bit of puzzle for modern economic historians for it developed quite differently than many other places pre-colonially, its integration into the world economy quite idiosyncratic (not least its role as a major source of slave labour), its technological progress taking very different forms, and its relative lack of adoption and diffusion of technological innovations, even ones that it had been exposed to for long periods, difficult to explain in conventional terms (Austen & Headrick, 1983; Jerven, 2011) (see Chapter 8).

Some analysts, such as anthropologist Jared Diamond (1997) explain all this as a result of geographical and physical disadvantages inherent to Africa, e.g. climates that foster disease with asymmetric negative effects on economic development, as opposed to Europe, which had diseases but ones that were not as economically disabling. Over the very long run, these relative differences, it is argued by Diamond, caused Africa to fall behind a (slowly) ascendant West. If taken to an extreme, this might suggest that foreign colonialism in Africa was largely irrelevant.

Sweeping templates like this are always dangerous and heavily contested, especially since the African continent itself is perhaps one of the most highly varied in the world in terms of natural features, climate, and resources, human and otherwise (Blaut, 1999). Africa's overall performance in terms of per capita GDP growth since independence has been generally been at the bottom of most regional growth league tables, which seem to be proof that colonialism matters economically, and that really bad colonialism usually leads to really bad postcolonial outcomes, for European colonisation of the continent was especially ruthless and particularly abhorrent in many places, such as the Belgian Congo.

13.6 Assessing the Modern Legacy of Imperialism

Morally imperialism was a traumatic atrocity, for which there is still much atoning to be done. It was also a large dimension of the first periods of European and then worldwide industrialisation, and an integral part of the pre-1914 international economic and financial system.

As far as economic causes, European imperialism is a complex beast and the arguments about its economic origins are not yet settled. But its primary motivation surely was exploitation of all sorts and on that front, it was remarkably effective for the exploiters, though the exact scale and scope of conquest and exploitation (which includes environmental transfers) is still being analysed.

As far as economic effects, this too is still debated. Surely transfers went both ways, people and materials and finances sucked out of the periphery but European cultural heritage, capital and goods being sent back in return. Using a purely economic lens, the possibility of adapting Western tools to modernise along the Western lines of capital investment, education and military organisation to beat the West at its own game could be a promising one, as in Japan (Lichtheim, 1972, 25). But up until the post-World War II period, not many were able to make use of this strategy, especially when they remained under direct rule by outsiders. And the social and cultural and political costs even of this path, and even if done successfully, are notable.

Longer term, there are nations that seem to be good examples of imperialism being very negative in terms of retarded GDP per capita growth, others where a reasonably good performance was found in the end, and everything in between. Because of the relative uniformity (this being, as always, a relative term) of colonialism in Spanish Latin America, the clearest results are found there and it seems that overall postcolonial economic growth has been negatively affected on the margins, though still yielding a respectably positive per capita GDP growth since the exit of the direct colonisers (the indirect American colonisation of the area not included, and a separate issue). Africa seems to be an opposite case, though in many ways, taken as a region, that continent is a puzzle to economic analysts on many fronts, its pre-colonial development being even more poorly understood than its postcolonial path. In Asia, there remains an immense diversity of experience. The two giants of India and China have finally overcome much of their colonial past in pure economic terms. But what might have been, there and everywhere else, if there had not been such severe exploitation by the West is a tantalising question, worthy of more attention.

Economic changes in national income aggregates and associated social metrics are however not the most important legacies of European "high tide" imperialism in any case. The noneconomic (social, political, etc.) impacts loom much larger. These noneconomic impacts are that much harder to actually quantify, which may account for the general focus, even by critics, on boiling things down to economic metrics alone. Of course, this propensity also may be a broader sign of the current times, and whether such a narrow perspective is an indication of the progress of humanity, time will tell.

References

Acemoglu, D., Johnson, S., & Robinson, J. A. (2001). The colonial origins of comparative development: An empirical investigation. *American Economic Review, 91*(5), 1369–1401.

Acemoglu, D., Johnson, S., & Robinson, J. A. (2002). Reversal of fortune: Geography and institutions in the making of the modern world income distribution. *The Quarterly Journal of Economics, 117*(4), 1231–1294.

Aldrich, R. (1996). *Greater France: A history of French overseas expansion*. Macmillan International Higher Education.

Allen, R. C. (2011). *Global economic history: A very short introduction*. Oxford University Press.

Austen, R. A., & Headrick, D. (1983). The role of technology in the African past. *African Studies Review, 26*(3–4), 163–184.

Bayly, C. A. (2004). *The birth of the modern world, 1780–1914: Global connections and comparisons*. Blackwell Publishing.

Beckert, S. (2015). *Empire of cotton: A global history*. Vintage.

Bértola, L., & Rodríguez Weber, J. (2015). Latin American economic history: Looking backwards for the future. In F. Boldizzini & P. Hudson (Eds.), *Routledge handbook of global economic history*. Routledge.

Blaut, J. M. (1999). Environmentalism and Eurocentrism. *Geographical Review, 89*(3), 391–408.

Bleich, E. (2005). The legacies of history? Colonization and immigrant integration in Britain and France. *Theory and Society, 34*(2), 171–195.

Bogart, D., & Chaudhary, L. (2013). Engines of growth: The productivity advance of Indian railways, 1874–1912. *The Journal of Economic History, 73*(2), 339–370.

Brandt, L., Ma, D., & Rawski, T. (2014). From divergence to convergence: Reevaluating the history behind China's economic boom. *Journal of Economic Literature, 52*(1), 45–123.

Cárdenas, M., & Helfand, S. (2011). Latin American economic development. In S. N. Durlauf & L. E. Blume (Eds.), *The new Palgrave dictionary of economics, online edition*. Palgrave MacMillan.

Davis, M. (2002). *Late Victorian holocausts: El Niño famines and the making of the third world*. Verso Books.

De la Escosura, L. P. (2005). *Colonial independence and economic backwardness in Latin America* (London School of Economics Working Paper 10/05).

De La Escosura, L. P. (2007). When did Latin America fall behind? In S. Edwards, G. Esquivel, & G. Márquez (Eds.), *The decline of Latin American economies: Growth, institutions, and crises* (pp. 15–58). University of Chicago Press.

De la Escosura, L. P. (2009). Lost decades? Economic performance in post-independence Latin America. *Journal of Latin American Studies, 41*(2), 279–307.

Dell, M. (2010). The persistent effects of Peru's mining mita. *Econometrica, 78*(6), 1863–1903.

Diamond, J. (1997). *Guns, germs and steel: The fates of human societies*. Norton.

Duiker, W. J. (2010). *Contemporary world history* (5th ed.). Cengage Learning.

Edelstein, M. (1976). Realized rates of return on UK home and overseas portfolio investment in the age of high imperialism. *Explorations in Economic History, 13*(3), 283–329.

Engerman, S. L., & Sokoloff, K. L. (2000). Institutions, factor endowments, and paths of development in the new world. *Journal of Economic Perspectives, 14*(3), 217–232.

Etherington, N. (1982). Reconsidering theories of imperialism. *History and Theory, 21*(1), 1–36.

Fitzmaurice, A. (2003). *Humanism and America: An intellectual history of English colonisation, 1500–1625*. Cambridge University Press.

Hobson, J. A. ([1902] 2018). *Imperialism: A study*. Routledge.

Jerven, M. (2011). A clash of disciplines? Economists and historians approaching the African past. *Economic History of Developing Regions, 26*(2), 111–124.

Klein, H. (1999). *The Atlantic slave trade*. Cambridge University Press.

Koch, H. W. (1984). Social Darwinism as a factor in the 'new imperialism.' In H. W. Koch (Ed.), *The origins of the first world war* (pp. 319–342). Palgrave.

Kohn, M., & Reddy, K. (2017). Colonialism. In E. N. Zalta (Ed.), *The Stanford encyclopedia of philosophy* (Fall 2017 Edition). https://plato.stanford.edu/archives/fall2017/entries/colonialism/

Lenin, V. I. [1917] (1939). *Imperialism, the highest stage of capitalism: A popular outline*. International Publishers.

Lichtheim, G. (1972). *Europe in the twentieth century*. Praeger Publishers.

Lopez, R. S., & Lopez, R. S. (1976). *The Commercial Revolution of the Middle 773 Ages, 950–1350*. Cambridge University Press.

Marx, K. ([1867, 1885, 1894], 1965). *Das Kapital: A critique of political economy* (F. Engels & S. L. Levitsky, Trans.). H. Regnery.

Mason, D. S. (2011). *A concise history of modern Europe: Liberty, equality, solidarity* (2nd ed.). Rowman & Littlefield.

McDonough, T. (1995). Lenin, imperialism, and the stages of capitalist development. *Science & Society, 59*(3), 339–367.

McKeown, T. J. (1983). Hegemonic stability theory and 19th century tariff levels in Europe. *International Organization, 37*(1), 73–91.

Neal, L., & Cameron, R. (2016). *A concise economic history of the world: From paleolithic times to the present* (5th ed.). Oxford University Press.

Nunn, N. (2008). The long-term effects of Africa's slave trades. *The Quarterly Journal of Economics, 123*(1), 139–176.

O'Brien, P. (1988). The costs and benefits of British imperialism 1846–1914. *Past & Present, 120*, 163–200.

Offer, A. (1993). The British empire, 1870–1914: A waste of money? *Economic History Review, 46*(2), 215–238.

Oto-Peralías, D., & Romero-Ávila, D. (2017). *Colonial theories of institutional development: Toward a model of styles of imperalism*. Springer.

Pomeranz, K. (2000). *The great divergence: China, Europe, and the making of the modern world economy*. Princeton University Press.

Ramesh, S. (2017). An economic history of India. In S. Ramesh (Ed.), *China's lessons for India: Volume I: The political economy of development* (pp. 23–54). Palgrave Macmillan.
Whatley, W., & Gillezeau, R. (2011). The impact of the transatlantic slave trade on ethnic stratification in Africa. *American Economic Review, 101*(3), 571–576.
Winn, J. A. (2008). *The poetry of war*. Cambridge University Press.
Winnacker, R. (1938). Elections in Algeria and the French Colonies under the Third Republic. *The American Political Science Review, 32*(2), 261–277.

CHAPTER 14

Modernity

C. Gordon, *Many Possible Worlds*,
https://doi.org/10.1007/978-981-19-9281-0_14

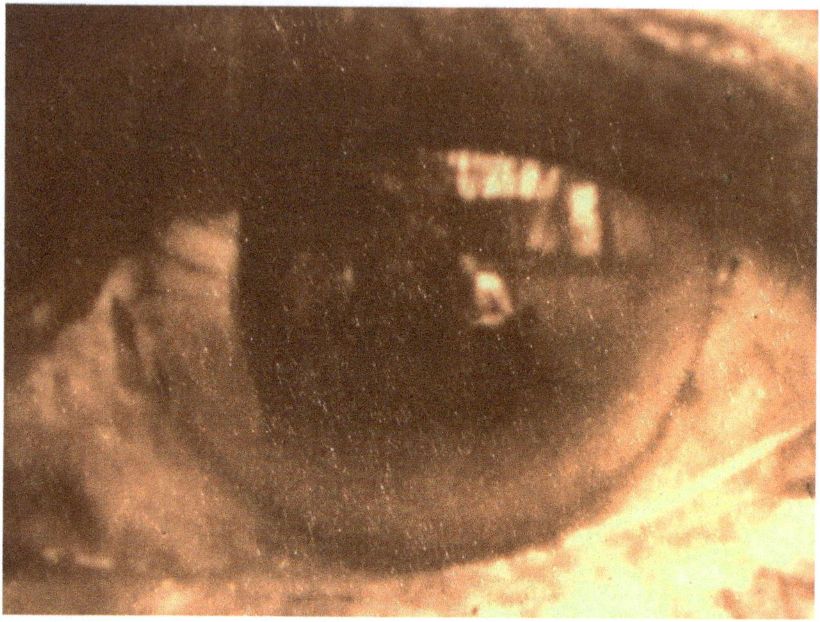

Fig. 14.1 Geronimo—detail showing photographer reflected in his eye (ca. 1904) (*Author notes* This picture of the eye of the American Indian Geronimo, the pupil of which is reflecting back the image of the photographer, typifies the combination of objectified self- and other-reflexivity which is perhaps the most iconic characteristic of modernity [see Sect. 13.9]. *Image source* Library of Congress, Prints and Photographs Division, Washington, DC 20540 USA, hdl.loc.gov/loc.pnp/pp.print. Persistent URL: hdl.loc.gov/loc.pnp/cph.3a19902. hdl.loc.gov/loc.pnp/ppmsca.31491. Call Number: LOT 4863, no. 14 [item]. No known copyright restrictions)

14.1 Modernity's Etymology

The Roman statesman Cassiodorus is credited with the first use of the term "modern" ("modernus") in the fifth century C.E. to contrast the Roman Empire's Christian era with its preceding pagan history. The term then fell into disuse until the seventeenth century when members of the French Academy were debating about whether contemporary culture, defined by French Enlightenment thinkers as marked by the use of reason, logic, and science to perfect the human individual through knowledge and its systematic application to the natural and human social world, was superior to classical culture, which contained some of the same values without the scientific apparatus. Both usages definitively created a hierarchy of value against which societies could be compared to an ideal of permanent progress based on new rational principles superseding older traditions (Lange, 2017, 37–38) (Fig. 14.1).

The nineteenth century French poet Baudelaire and his contemporaries began to reify the concept into "modernity", in this context a romantic state in which individual deviance from social norms was trumpeted as a true expression of individual freedom and fulfilment. Baudelaire's romantic conception was sidelined by the era's widespread Enlightenment-inspired trust in science and the use of scientific inquiry to understand human problems and come up with scientific solutions (Lange, 2017, 38). Thus, the founders of sociology used "modernity" to signify an ongoing transformation of social relations within which the individual sat and adopted the template of a progression from lower to higher orders in temporal linearity. While the sociological perspectives of Marx, Weber, Durkheim and Tönnies offered differing ideas about the exact nature of the process of change in social relations and its general direction and consequences, they all saw the binding of society into a working unit as the critical societal task to be accomplished across all societies, and they studied how modernity had fundamentally altered this task.

However, they had differing emphases and beliefs about the forces for change. Marx believed in the primacy of economic relations, especially ownership of the "modes of production", and thus believed that modernity could be reduced to capitalist production and market organisation. Durkheim believed that economics was not primary, but that the way in which society was organising production in his time, namely industrialism, was driving social modernisation in a particular way, creating new social strains and inner contradictions that he referred to as *anomie*, a state of social disintegration in which general social rules break down and individuals are unable to anchor themselves, resulting, he claimed, in increased suicide and crime rates. Weber meanwhile emphasised human need for meaning and indicated that the "rationalisation" of society was a key feature of modernity that led to a "disenchantment with the world" that also brought many social advances (Lange, 2017, 39; Yeo-chi King, 2018, 117). Tönnies in some sense straddled the middle, saying that traditional groups would always co-exist and interact with more modern, functional and transactional groupings (Adair-Toteff, 1995).

The Political Economists had a quite different emphasis. Although Adam Smith did have a rather substantial theory of human "moral sentiments", these were not taken up much into what would later become neoclassical economic theory. Smith's successors, especially Ricardo, dropped most elements of social theory, confining their attention to the atomised decisions of what we would now call "economic agents" and the way that these affected, and were affected by, changing structures and incentives of economic processes, especially markets. The division of labour and specialisation of economic function across workers and productive units was the motive force behind increasing economic productivity. The expanding "extent of the market" furthered this process by ensuring sufficient demand for the increasing supply of output. Taken together these shifted the constraints and incentives that economic agents had faced and led to new collective configurations between agents. These were much more transactional in nature than relational in the sociological sense, coming together and breaking apart depending upon economic conditions. Many sociologists essentially agreed with this analysis, but saw the social effects of economic change as much more subtle and complex, pointing out its mixed social consequences. Marx straddled this debate, sharing with the Political Economists their belief in the primacy of economic over social factors, while also subsuming individuality entirely under social conditioning. Thus, Marx's social analysis of capitalism was catastrophic, positing a deep "alienation" of the human being, yet also believing that this would necessarily force resolution into a higher socioeconomic stage that would automatically solve the individual struggle since that individual was just a pure product of social forces in the end.

These debates have not been settled, and probably never can be definitively. Which is why the contemporary usage of the term "modernity" strips much of this colouring away to use it as a demarcation of an historical era. Giddens (1990) offers the loosest but in some ways the most practical contemporary definition in this sense, as referring to "modes of social life or organisation which emerged in Europe from about the seventeenth century onwards and which subsequently became more or less worldwide in their influence" (1) This is the basic way in which the term will be used in this chapter.

14.2 Commodification, Marketisation, Industrialism, Bureaucracy

Pre-modern societies are generally presented as having largely informal social connections, broken into groups in which members are personally familiar in some way with other members, trust flowing out of that familiarity, and pressures for in-group conformity being very high. Such societies are also thought to have fairly low social interdependence beyond the small group, because such groups generally are relatively self-sufficient, units mostly unto themselves, their internal trust and coordination relying on personal familiarity which imposes limits on its scope and scale, and limiting close cooperation across groups not closely related to one another.

Assuming this is true (it is not a settled point), modern social relations, by contrast, are more formalised, and more institutionalised, thus allowing social groupings to be much larger and to consist of members that are generally unknown, or at least unfamiliar personally to one another yet which nonetheless can foster effective cooperation within and outside the group, even across thousands of individuals or more. Broader social interdependence is much higher as a result, allowing for greater social and economic division of labour, yielding the material productivity that Adam Smith spoke of in the economic sphere, and the ability to mobilise large masses of people for specific purposes, something Weber and Polanyi, among others, remarked upon.

Elias notes that this is a subtle social and economic bargain (see Chapter 5). On the one hand, social and economic division of labour and specialisation can lead to standardisation. Efficiency in production and consumption is served by a certain amount of social regimentation and routinisation. Yet simultaneously, individual pressure to conform to norms is lowered since people are now mostly unknown to each other, many social tasks are delegated to a larger group or mass, and thus more individual freedom of expression and action can be accommodated within certain parameters. This tension between individualism and social interdependence is not straightforward, evolves over time, and, according to Elias, does not have a true "end" point but is in constant homeostasis. This view is in contrast with more static, functionalist or teleological models, of which Enlightenment thinking is an example. There remains a significant difference of opinion on these matters.

By the early twentieth century, economic modernity had intensively and extensively manifested in specific ways within the European core. Capitalism had always rested on the foundation of commodification and marketisation, terms that refer to the conversion of as many things as possible into quantifiable bundles on which a price could be set and then traded within market exchange mechanisms using money. While certainly economically efficient, this process led to an increasing "dis-embedding" of formerly embedded social relationships as the market mechanism governed more of economic and social life, increasingly separating economic tasks from social ones. Commerce, trade and the economy have existed long before capitalism, but prior to capitalism these activities were always bound up with social categories, networks and relationships in some way. This took many forms, such as feudalism, but the basic fundamental unity of economic and social was a constant. The various processes, taken over a long time period, that created a truly and purely market-based economy covering all aspects of production, consumption and distribution, broke this unity. In so doing, social and economic interactions ultimately became fully separated from one another and the economy took on a logic all its own (Polanyi, 1944).

In a sense one could say that it was capitalist organisation that created the "transaction" itself, or at least made it a central paradigm for human society. Of course, physical existence remained as it had before, in a pure sense. That is, trees, houses, animals, etc., were all in the forms they always had been. But the way that humans related to these things, and to each other, were now separated into quantities with qualities measured according to a monetary benchmark, everything fundamentally reduced to that dimension. This freeing of economic activity from social bounds definitely yielded a vast increase in quantity and variety of material output now available to the masses, overall weakening organic human bonds and social fabric, though strengthening the individual in some respects as well. One could argue that society itself was slowly but surely being subsumed into the economy almost entirely. Material gratification became both a substitute for various social losses, and also a new basis for pleasure and identity (Fig. 14.2).

Commodification and marketisation were fundamentals of Capitalism and remain so. But the full productivity fruits came with industrialisation, whose initial characteristics Neal and Cameron (2016) summarise as the incorporation of an extensive use of mechanical power in production; the widespread use of new inanimate energy sources in economic activity;

Fig. 14.2 A representation of "marketisation" and "commodification" (*Image source* From page 483 of *Breeder and sportsman* [1882]. Contributing Library: San Francisco Public Library; Digitizing Sponsor: California State Library. No known copyright restrictions)

widespread use of materials not normally occurring in nature; and, then, as a result, increasing scale of production (161). To these core ingredients of the First Industrial Revolution, the Second added systematic application scientific theory and method to this process to intensify and expand the industrialisation process (164) (See also Chapters 9 and 12).

Industrialism, which broadly refers to any economic and social system based on large-scale industrialisation, does not necessarily have to be capitalistic, as the twentieth century experiment with State Socialism under the Soviet Union proves (see Chapters 23 and 25). Whether capitalism itself had to proceed along these lines is a question with an unknowable answer. But it is clear that the industrial methods of organising production (and, also, more fully later on, distribution and consumption) had formidable societal consequences related to, but separate from, the commodification and marketisation that helped bring capitalism about.

Fig. 14.3 "Industrialism" on the ground in Canada (late nineteenth century) (*Image source* Deseronto Archives. RATHCO-06–30 "Panoramic view of the town of Deseronto, Ontario, entitled "Fig. 3. Machine and Blacksmith shops-sash, door and blind factory-general woodworking department-locomotive shops and stables-Deseronto", as published in *The Lumberman* [Chicago, September 5 1891. A locomotive is visible on the turntable to the right of the image, while the machine and blacksmiths shops are in the foreground at the left side." No known copyright restrictions])

Industrialism additionally came with an order-of-magnitude increase in urbanisation, regimentation of work and leisure, and unprecedented levels of spatial concentration of specialised economic activity and markets, among other things. Many of the early critiques of capitalism actually were arguably mostly focused on industrialism (e.g. William Blake's reference to factories as "dark Satanic mills") and many of the political and social reforms addressed industrial, not capitalistic, ills (Fig. 14.3).

The rise of modern industry and advancing capitalism of necessity required an increasing use of rational and intentional human planning and organisation, both public and private, across an increasing array of economic and social endeavours. Despite the pretensions of laissez-faire of classical Liberalism, even the government in the UK of the time found it necessary to intervene in new problem areas of capitalist, industrial development, such as regulation of public health and pollution, while other countries, Germany especially, offered various social guarantees for old-age pensions and care that used to be provided for through informal social and family arrangements (though doing so at this time on a very tentative and incomplete basis). Private enterprise itself was growing to stupendous size supported by an ever-more sophisticated finance sector. All of this required bureaucracy and all the standardisation that came with it. This was an aspect that Weber was especially concerned with, his use of the term bureaucracy referring to an increasing rationalisation that requires a coordinating apparatus that subsumes human originality and expression (Fig. 14.4).

Again, one can ask whether these aspects were a necessary outgrowth of capitalism. Once industrialism took over, it does seem that bureaucratisation and formal planning were required to run, maintain, manage and expand it, and the productivity and production scale increases enabled by it necessitated further bureaucratisation. Nonetheless, it is possible

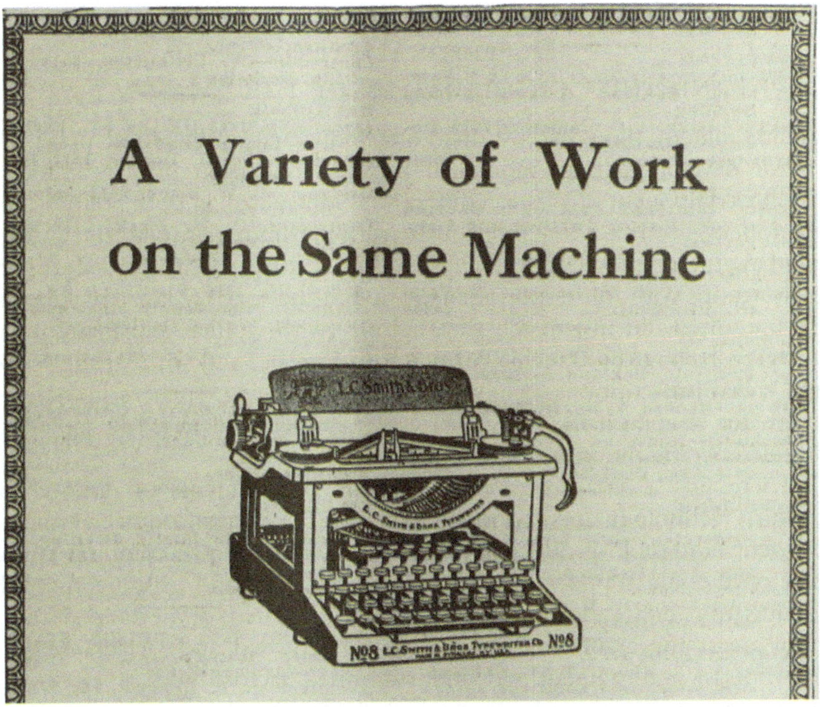

Fig. 14.4 The typewriter: the essential tool of bureaucracy and planning (*Image source* Contractors' and Dealers' Association of California [1914]. *Building & engineering news*. L. A. Larson. P. 632. Contributing Library: San Francisco Public Library. Digitizing Sponsor: San Francisco Public Library. No known copyright restrictions)

to imagine an historical path that might be capitalist and even industrial, but smaller scale, sacrificing some output growth to maintain a more balanced social order, and with lower social and ecological cost. Indeed, some countries such as France did follow a somewhat gentler path of economic growth during the nineteenth century, with smaller scale enterprise and a strong, though dwindling, residual of traditional social organisation. And in our current times, there is much talk about trying to turn back economic scale, or at least more adequately address the many noneconomic (and some economic) failings that have arisen over the past decades.

14.3 Modernity, Intensification, Depersonalisation and the Consolidation of the "Masses"

Enlightenment thought enshrined the individual as the focal point of human development and individualism is generally thought of as an inextricable component of Western modernity. Liberalism, in both politics and economics, promotes free individuals, with maximum latitude to try their hand at attaining their desired aims, and to bear the success (or failure) of their actions with full responsibility. Though the social realities of Liberal Europe often did not match the rhetoric (with women and many men not even having the franchise in much of Europe, and with strong legal and social proscriptions against many ways of being, such as homosexuality, for example), the individual was nonetheless idealised in capitalist and democratic thought.

There was a paradox though. For the achievements of nineteenth century technology and economy rested on the breaking down of independent household production units; the privatisation of common lands that once could support marginal fringe dwellings and existences; rapid urbanisation and industrialisation that depopulated or developed over rural areas; the cramming of people into crowded and faceless neighbourhoods; and standardised and routinised factory and office work. Economic and social modernism relied upon increased social interdependence and a scale of anonymous interoperability that demanded people fit into uniform and standardised roles and responsibilities. The individual was trumpeted but freedom now constituted (to invert a famous quote of the time by Anatole France) the right to sleep under any bridge over the

Seine River if you were outside the terms and conditions of the market system. Or at least the expression and experience of being an individual was more and more reduced to the ability to earn maximum income to purchase maximum consumption.

This was a slow process, with many variants, but what it meant to be an individual within society was being redefined. On a visit to New York in 1904, Max Weber observed the teeming crowds working, living and walking in the city and concluded that all individualism, whether in housing or eating, had become expensive (Sampson, 1995, 111). This was true in a literal sense, as so much was being mass-produced, mass-distributed and mass-consumed, and thus a choice that deviated from the standardised offerings would entail extra cost, if available at all. Henry Ford captured this essence in his famous quote about customers being able to have any colour of his Model T car (itself the only one offered to allow for mass production economies) so long as it was black (Ford with Crowther, 1922, 72).

But it was also true in a more fundamental way as most aspects of daily life became channelled through mass processes of some kind. This had begun with the factories but it had spread ever outwards to the mass public education, mass communication, mass entertainment and mass culture being delivered to the growing masses in growing urban centres.

Urbanisation was the most visible and literal massing of population, which followed a hyperbolic growth pattern paralleling industrialisation. The share of world population living in urban areas almost doubled from just under 7% in 1800 to 12% in 1900 and rose again to 29.4% a mere fifty years later in 1950. Europe was on the cutting edge with its share of urban population tripling between 1800 and 1900 (10%–29%), Britain experiencing a similar rate of growth but from a much higher base during the period (20.3%–61.9%). Not only were cities growing in relative terms, they were exploding in absolute terms as well, becoming ever bigger in size, and with some entirely new cities coming out of nowhere in the European Offshoots. New York added over 6 million people to its population during the nineteenth century, coming to rival London in size by 1900. Chicago, which wasn't even established in 1800, had almost 2.5 million people living in it one hundred years later. In a pattern that would reverse itself in the latter half of the twentieth century, it was the "West" where much of the urban growth was happening, outpacing the traditionally more densely populated countries of Asia. In 1800, 9 of the world's 30 largest cities were in Europe. By 1914, 12 were, and the US, not even ranking a century earlier, could claim 4 of the top spots (Zinkina et al., 2017, 165–169).

This dramatic "urban transition" led to a number of things. Cities aggregated to themselves greater shares of population, economic activity and cultural creation and thus become centres of political, economic and cultural power in their respective nations. The sheer density and aggregation of people in them altered methods of production, distribution and consumption, accelerating and enhancing the ability to do them all on a mass basis. The pace of daily life picked up and intensified. The process was a relatively tight circle. Scale and technical innovation drove productivity, which in turn drove urbanisation and intensifying use of resources, human and otherwise. Meanwhile, basic needs for a literate and relatively docile workforce led to mass mandatory education, which was easier to deliver in urban settings. At the same time, urbanisation required and facilitated revolutions in public health, urban built environment and public amenity.

The material upside to all this was quite obvious. Life expectancy, literacy and public health were all improving, especially for those on the leading edge of growth and development. Clean running water in to the home was becoming more of a typical feature in major European cities, street and indoor lighting was improving, especially with the advent of electrification, and the proliferation of consumer goods and amenities were becoming panoply. A new urban middle class rose up that was relatively upwardly mobile, well educated, well fed and reasonably well paid. The new proletariat was not as well off as the bourgeoisie, but was nevertheless gaining access to much of the same bounty (Mokyr, 1999b).

But every lightening has a dark side. This could be taken most literally as electric light created the 24-hour workday, combining with factory regimentation to yield shift work, including the dreaded night shift (which as the author can attest from youthful experience is quite disruptive, even for the young man he was then). This was good for productivity, but not entirely beneficial for the human animal and its circadian rhythms (Bowers, 1982, 1998).

Improvements in transport technology meanwhile were spreading residential and work districts outwards from the city core, while refinements in steel production, the invention of the elevator in 1857, and electricity's ability to move those elevators up and down quickly, were driving the city itself upwards. Suburbanisation, at this time in parallel with urbanisation (later displacing it—see Chapter 24), and densification were now both features of the modern world, to be driven later to logical, or illogical, extremes. Different classes of people were affected differently, the professional classes coming off fairly well materially, with urban poor and working people being crammed into tightly packed quarters, though fortunately having urban diseases moderated by the public health revolution of mid to late century. What all classes, except the high elites, shared, was more time spent in built environments, and correspondingly less exposure to green space and open sky, with clock tempos replacing organic ones (Young, 2015).

Everyone, high elites included, were also exposed to greater degrees of impersonality in life, a sort of generalised depersonalisation. Demarcations between work, leisure and home space and life became more sharply drawn and detached from one another as household production and consumption (to use economics terms) declined, which was a liberation of sorts. But bespoke individual rhythms and pursuits were increasingly replaced by the mass consumption, mass leisure, and mass work conducted in offices and factories and entertainment venues, the time periods for employment, fun and family strictly demarcated by clock and schedule (Mokyr et al., 2015, 39–40).

This is not to say that the pre-industrial past was idyllic. It certainly wasn't. Nor is it to say that the industrial era life was not an improvement over the past. Materially, on an average basis, it certainly was, and many old restrictions on individuality that had been based on social conformity were loosening up. There was also more to fill one's time with, much of it diverting and enjoyable. It was, however, a marked departure from much of previous human history, bringing its own unique problems as well as advantages, taking quite a lot of getting used to, yet changing so rapidly that one never could quite do so.

14.4 Mass Media and the Changing Self-Image of "Modern Man"

Technical advance did more than change just the outer conditions and experiences of human beings. It also changed their inner life as well. In the nineteenth and early twentieth centuries, new means of visual remembering and recording in the form of the photograph, combined with mass printing and distribution, made images of one's self and one's world a mass phenomenon as well. Mass production of cameras was kicked off in 1900 when Kodak introduced the Brownie camera, sold for the price of $1, bringing cheap photography to the masses, at least the middle-class ones (West, 1982, 30). Now anyone could capture the moments of their lives, or, if they chose, become an artist, and without any particular training or large commitments of time and resources. “Art” was on its way to becoming not just mass-produced but individually produced for the masses and mass-consumed as well.

The medium of film expanded the industrial proliferation of recorded memory and experience and made it more compelling as well. Photography had already helped feed a mass newspaper industry, while film led to a new industry all its own, together becoming key components of mass consciousness and politics (see Chapter 12). The first “cinema war” was also one that was heavily photographed, i.e. the Spanish-American War of 1898. Thus, a new adjunct was available to supplement newspaper coverage, which was already of a several decades old vintage. Early “newsreels” of the war purported to capture history as it happened, but actually contained large components of invention, such as model ships being exploded in tanks to simulate the battle of Santiago Bay, and the staging for the camera of the charge up San Juan Hill. These would be regular features of newsreels and, later, television coverage of future wars (Hastings, 2000).

It should be noted that these early filmmakers were doing what newspaper editors did (and still do), i.e. merging eyewitness reports with information received from other sources. But film was even more powerful in the way it could remake as well as record the boundaries of fact and fiction in history. Soviet filmmakers in the 1920s, for example, retrospectively created most of the imagery of the October Revolution, propagandising and moving opinion in ways little different from those used in the West, though through a very obviously different propagandistic lens. The power of film is derived from the illusion that something still “is”, experienced right now in the psychic present rather than the objectively referential past (Nowell-Smith, 1990, 161–162, 164–165). Photography does this too, but less powerfully due to its static presentation (Fig. 14.5).

By the twentieth century’s dawn, mass media already provided a powerful and effective distribution tool for shaping and forming mass perception and film and photography made subjective perception seem more real and present than ever before. Moreover, collective and individual reality could be merged, with everyone seeing the exact same images over and over again, along with the same text and explanation.

Fig. 14.5 Filmic encouragement (*Image source* Library of Congress Prints and Photographs Division Washington, DC 20540 USA. http://hdl.loc.gov/loc.pnp/pp.print. Digital Id: cph 3a11230 hdl.loc.gov/loc.pnp/cph.3a11230. No known restrictions on publication. https://lccn.loc.gov/2012645951 Created / Published c1912. Item notes: Please applaud with hands only. "Positive paper print from lantern slide used in motion picture theaters as announcement. Each text superimposed on humorous photograph, and the whole shown in a fancy carved frame)

Such developments were arguably a key ingredient in the formation of ideologies of all sorts, and especially in their dissemination.

More subtle changes in the relationship of a person to their own self were unfolding as well. Photography and film theoretically now offered the possibility of observing and relating to one's self the same way one did with others, as a social object serving as a means to individual ends. One could "objectively" look at one's image and see what it reflected back. These images could be commodified and sold on the open markets for definite though shifting monetary values, determined by mass demand.

And, at least seemingly, one could potentially commodify and market one's self, or at least one's image, in both a literal and figurative sense.

14.5 Modernity and the Problem of Violence

The changing nature and level of violence in modern versus pre-modern society is one arena where "progress" is a very contested fact. Elias himself claimed that civilisation involved an outsourcing of violence from the individual (and small group) level to the collective (usually the State) where, hopefully, it could be used for more targeted and socially necessary purposes, though this could not be guaranteed. A current argument rages about whether violence is declining overall as modernity progresses. The optimists (Pinker, 2011; Morris, 2014 being two prominent examples) avail themselves of a wide (though very fragmentary) set of data on all classes of violence, from murder to war, to claim that modernisation has lowered overall violence levels, and presumably will continue to do so. In their schema, modernisation is an antidote to violence, quite similar to classical notions about civilised nations versus barbarians. Episodes such as two World Wars and the Holocaust are seen as unfortunate variations in a nonetheless civilising trend.

But others, such as Hannah Arendt, who survived the Nazi era as German Jew, have been much more pessimistic. Arendt took Durkheim's notion of *anomie* in a direction that he did not consider. Durkheim, looking at the modernising society of his time, saw the loss of common social bonds as disorienting, and this *anomie* could precipitate individual suicide, although ultimately Durkheim believed the society would make changes to resolve this problem. Arendt living through a particularly virulent era of "mass society" degradation argued that the dissolution of shared meaning could go beyond such localised and personal effects to result in a nihilistic individualism in which people would feel free to do whatever they felt like within new collective channels of crowd movements. She noted how an ideology of nationalism could be especially effective in aiding this dynamic, and how this was a core feature of much Totalitarianism, Nazism being a particularly odious example. As both nationalism and mass movements are modern developments, modernisation can be seen as a prime and novel cause of such sanctioned collective violence, rather than the purely moderating force that the optimists believe it to be (Lange, 2017, 48).

There are middle grounds to these poles, especially since the data are ambiguous. The supposed strength of Pinker (2011) and others like him is his use of broad data sets that cover all categories of violence. But this is a weakness as well since the data quality and coverage is uneven at best, modern periods being much better covered than earlier ones, though with substantial gaps even there, and so much of violence itself is contextual and very difficult to capture quantitatively, and subject to classification and measurement bias. Overall it seems that the types of violence and the modes through which they are delivered have changed over time due to changing social environments, with some types more common now than in the past and vice versa. Some categories, such as "ethnic" violence, which requires application of a modern concept of "ethnicity" that is an abstraction and extension of long-standing "in-group" and "out-group" categories, did not exist at all in pre-modern times. Human violence is age-old, but it has been modernised along with everything else (Lange, 2017, 53–54).

Box 14.1 The psychological syndromes of modern war

Amongst the many things that modernisation has changed is war (see Chapter 22). Here the focus is on one aspect, namely the psychological impact of industrialised war on the individual combatant's psyche.

War has always been traumatic for the soldiers fighting it. But the psychological, as opposed to physical, effects on combatants was not even an area of study until the rise of depth psychology, a field that offered models of the human psyche and methods for analysing it in "scientific" fashion. This was concomitant with the systematic rigours of modern mechanised war that created unique conditions of sustained psychological stress.

The apotheosis of this came with World War I, with its gas weaponry, sustained and massive artillery bombardments and trench warfare, all creating novel mental stresses on fighting men leading to apparently unprecedented mass and individual mental breakdowns. During the Battle of the Somme, for example, 39,000 men suddenly lost their ability to fight, a phenomenon that occurred in other battles as well, though not quite on that scale. The commands of the various armies saw that this level of strain and dysfunction could not be sustained and they employed psychologists to determine what was going on and what could be done about it, launching the sub-discipline of military psychology in the process.

The initial hypothesis that this disorder was a result of physical damage caused by the concussive effect of exploding artillery shells on the brain was quickly rejected, with emotional causes identified instead. A new diagnosis was arrived at: shell shock. The term was first used in a *Lancet* article in 1915 and various methods of treating the disorder were tested, none wholly or consistently effective. While recognised as *bona fide* by psychologists, shell shock was not socially acceptable. It was not even officially accepted. The diagnosis could not be used as a defense in court-martials of enlisted men in the British Army, or even be mentioned in court proceedings. A number of men were executed for desertion even though the record showed that they had clearly been psychologically disabled at the time. British officers were treated less harshly. But even then "Neurasthenia" was the term used in their records, a term deemed to be less demeaning.

The World War I experience suggested to military professionals of the time that the issue was limited to those who had innate pre-existing weaknesses that battle conditions brought out. This thinking changed during World War 2 when it became clear that any man, subjected to systematized, mechanised war, would, in some way, and to varying degrees, fall apart. It took the Vietnam War to give rise to of a new diagnosis of "Post-Traumatic Stress Disorder (PTSD)" to replace the old "shell shock", a syndrome that later was seen to apply to non-war traumas as well. Treatments now shifted to psychotherapeutic and psychodynamic modalities, as opposed to the more behavioural and physical treatments of the First and Second World Wars. While there was still some shame attached to the diagnosis, it was recognised by authorities as being like any other battle injury, and worthy of the same compensations and ameliorations.

Thus modernisation in war is like any other modernisation process. It changes human psychology at individual and collective levels, and creates new social categories and agreements about their manifestations.

(The discussion above is based on Grossman, 2014; Kardiner, 1941; Young, 1997).

14.6 The First Age of Anxiety and the Weight of Western Civilisation

When W.H. Auden published his poem, "The Age of Anxiety" in 1947, it quickly became an emblem of the prosperous, mature phase of Western industrialisation that followed Second World War. Auden won the Pulitzer

Prize for it in 1948 and Leonard Bernstein used the phrase as the title of his Second Symphony, which came out in 1949. The Cold War was well underway then (see Chapter 25), cementing the status of late modernity's prime symptom (Maxwell, 2010).

Anxiety is sometimes loosely defined as fear of the imagined, and there were plenty of fears, imagined and real, in the atomic age. But free-floating fears of an imagined future were also a regular aspect of this earlier, and outwardly more progressive age. It was a more idealistic and hopeful time, but not really any simpler given all the major transformations of technology and working life. While the main threat of the First Industrial Revolution had appeared to be mass unemployment because not all agrarian refugees found industrial jobs and many craft jobs were being mechanised, this had not eventuated. Indeed, as industrialisation grew, it created many more new jobs than it destroyed. Partly this was because technology mainly changed labour processes (e.g. shifting to division of labour from craft production) rather than replacing human labour altogether (Mokyr et al., 2015, 36).

But the fear about net job losses soon morphed from one of permanent unemployment to displacement into unpleasant and unfamiliar work and home environments. Of course, the threat of unemployment and privation was still ever present during one of the periodic economic busts that occurred. But as the nineteenth century turned over into the twentieth there were generally plenty of opportunities for re-employment, especially during boom times. And strong economic growth, at least in the West, brought increases in living standards (on average) as well. Job types, though, were changing frequently, involving a loss of familiar work that one was good at, to be replaced with new and uncertain alternatives. Security of tenure, or at least the security of having a life's work in one location, was forever gone. So too was stability in one's home surroundings, since both countryside and cityscape were constantly developing. As with the changes of today, this could be exciting, empowering and freeing, and some thrived in such an atmosphere. But nothing felt secure or familiar for long, and the threat of sudden change was always there.

In particular, standardised work and large enterprise implied that everyone was ultimately replaceable. The metaphor of the machine was prominent in this machine age, and with standardised parts, machines could be kept functioning just fine without depending on any particular component. The same went for people. The Scientific Revolution had displaced "Man" from the centre of the universe, and now the Industrial

Revolution seemed to be displacing him from the centre of human life as well; hence the background anxiety. Things were constantly changing, often for the better, but one could never be sure of how this would manifest. A general optimism in the doctrine of "progress" (for Westerners) was a partial remedy for this affliction, but not a very secure one.

The musings of British author and critic Dame Rebecca West, in her book *1900* (1982), gives an idiosyncratic view of how the first year of the newest century appeared almost kaleidoscopic to many, especially those in the settled middle classes. During 1900, some events suggested the persistence of a dying old world, such as Paris suffering a "water famine" (a shortage of potable water) in July, an outbreak of Bubonic Plague in Glasgow in August and later the excommunication of Leonid Tolstoy by the Russian Orthodox Church for publishing *Resurrection*. These all hearkened backwards to a time just passing, of the importance of religious tradition, social propriety and order, and a still present intrusion of natural world disease and scarcity into modern and increasingly urban living. And yet many more other occurrences of the same year pointed towards exciting new frontiers. The *Zeppelin* made its maiden voyage hinting at a future of air travel. Max Planck formulated his quantum theory, and blood groups were discovered. Sigmund Freud published his landmark work *The Interpretation of Dreams*, and Henri Bergson published *Laughter*. H.G. Wells was writing visions of the progressive future, while George Bernard Shaw put out three more of his socially critical plays. In music, Ravel, Faure, Holst, Mahler and Sibelius created new works with innovative forms, while Cezanne, Monet, Picasso, Renoir and Toulouse-Lautrec painted new paintings defying old ways of displaying reality (West, 1982, 17–20, 30–32, 42). Discovery, experimentation and ferment seemed to be accelerating in all areas of human endeavour.

Exciting prospects nonetheless were unsettling. A hearkening back accompanied this array of newness, evocations of a supposedly unsullied and simple past, often referred to as "primitive" if that past was non-Western. The early nineteenth century Romanticism of the free but exposed individual was now being overtaken by an idealised nostalgia for a romanticised bygone era. Some of this has been considered in Chapter 10. Its relevance here is that many elites, artistic and otherwise, were rejecting modern mores, even while using them in their work. Paul Gaugin's book *Noa Noa* about his Polynesian travels and the inventively modern depictions of this "simpler" society that he used in his paintings; Diaghilev's *Ballet Russe* which pushed against Classicism in dance by supposedly returning to naturalistic movement of the body in its performances; William Morris trying to bring traditional forms back into English design; and the pre-Raphealites creating their own versions of pre-modern artistic expression were all enunciations of discomfort with modern change. Some, like Gaugin, were trying to escape from Western civilisation into an idealised "primitive" East. Others, like Morris, hoped to turn modern society back into its supposed state before industrialisation. Still others were trying to create private enclaves to shelter themselves against relentless external forces. World-weariness and primitivism were two sides of the same coin. Both represented a sort of "internal emigration" which the artist, at least, could seem to control (Lichtheim, 1972, 108, 118).

This search for a restoration of the individual to an organic collective, because it was mythical was, of course, futile. Seeking solace looking backwards, and romanticising a past that never really was, is nothing new, of course. But it took unique modern forms that tried to contain new and old at the same time. Some have even argued that Victorianism in England, and its celebration of chivalry and honour and probity, was an attempt to deny the existence of the modern world, falsifying the past in order to evade the present (Winn, 2008, 143). Yet the Victorian also celebrated English progress, a future of boundless promise that was just as imaginary as the legendary times of old. All of the most advancing European powers grappled with a similar desire to make sense of a present rapidly changing, in sometimes disturbing and unsettling ways.

14.7 Modernity Outside Europe

What of the non-European world, where, during the nineteenth and early twentieth centuries, most of the people, though not most of the wealth and income, resided? How did "modernity" manifest there?

In the Philippines, Rafael (2017) looks at various, and conflicting, interpretations of how "modern" colonial institutions sat within a pre-modern, hierarchical feudal society, both before and after independence. He finds a contested story but one that points to a sort of postcolonial incoherence that is found in other places where Europeans entered societies with a very different sort of historical evolution from them, interrupting that history in profound and contradictory ways. By contrast, China encountered Europe with an ancient unity and a highly developed society, philosophy, state administration and outlook, similar in some ways to Europe, though obviously very different in others. It had its own "progress", but one that was uniquely "Chinese". Europe disrupted this progression in a necessarily distinct way from places like the much more decentralised Philippines.

China's internal solidity had advantages and disadvantages, on the one hand keeping the country unified but on the other limiting its ability to respond to the outward challenges. China was a "civilisational state" rather than "nation-state" at the turn of the nineteenth century, based on universal "kingship" and adhering to long-standing Confucian values. China was already beginning its own re-examination of its mores, and the coming of the Europeans accelerated and reshaped those trends in diverse directions, moving away from Confucianism (e.g. with the dropping of civil service exams in 1905) and with some elements of society moving towards Western-style reform, and others engaging in an "anti-modern" return to a version of indigenous Chinese culture (Yeo-chi King, 2018, 113–114). The result was a uniquely Chinese adaptation of modernity to fit its own long-standing models, to its current day "project of modernity" in which a form of capitalism is divorced from both democracy and liberalism (Ikenberry, 2020, 288).

Meanwhile, the diverse Islamic world during the Industrial Revolution saw the European model as a sort of frontier for what was possible for their own societies, in which reformers recognised the need for change, and in a society that always had reform elements. Indeed because "Islam" had always contained within it a direct yet subtle and changeable homeostasis between "Religion" and "State", it had developed much political theory about these realms that Western observers incorrectly conflated into a simplistic characterisation of church and state being one. Further, because the Islamic world had used a multiplicity of governance structures encompassing diverse cultures under a broad religious banner, Muslim thinkers were quite comfortable with the possibility that "modernity" was a process not entrenched in a singular culture, a concept that is actually quite recent in the West, and not at all present for the imperial Europeans of the time. Thus, the old notion of "Napoleon's theorem" that modernity was first brought to the core of the Muslim world by Napoleon's occupation of Egypt has now been discredited. In fact, eighteenth century Ottoman society, the realm most touched by Europeans during the period, contained thriving intellectual cultures, a quasi-bourgeois class, and considerable dynamism, despite a fading central power structure (Salvatore, 2015, 138–142).

In Japan, Western force caused an insular, hierarchical but innovative system to bend and reorder but not, fundamentally, break, which was a saving grace that allowed that order to choose it's own effective adaptation path. In the end, the Meiji followed a "best of everything" Westernisation, e.g. a British-style navy, Prussian style army, the national banking system of the US, with poor results, and then shifting to the Belgian Central Bank model, a privately owned central bank under strong central government control (Neal & Cameron, 2016, 267). This model proved to be very influential for later Asian modernisations, as in Singapore and the "Asian Tigers" of the 1980s and 1990s, with considerable emphasis on country specialisation within a very mature world system.

In any case, "Eurocentrism" itself is not purely European, since European culture, including its Enlightenment, was an amalgam of many influences, European and otherwise. Putting aside the more temporally distant influence of Hellenism on Eurasian cultural origins, the long-standing Islamic presence on the Iberian Peninsula in particular deeply influenced both Catholicism and European culture, as well as provided an avenue for much importation of practical and theoretical knowledge that the Muslim principalities so carefully fostered and preserved. During the Age of Imperialism, colonialism was a two-way street of exchange of knowledge, ideas and techniques, even though very unequal in power direction. The rise and refinement of various scientific branches (meteorology, botany, etc.) based on collection of data from imperial outposts at least partly as a means of colonial control has already been mentioned (Davis, 2002). In addition Europeans tested and developed many techniques of social control and management in their colonies, bringing these back to the home countries in due course (penology and criminology being two prime areas) (Rattansi, 2017, 94–96). And as time progressed, colonial subjects came in their numbers as émigrés to the metropole, creating cross-cultural currents in both colony and coloniser.

Thus the idea that there emerged "multiple modernities" as discussed in Chapter 11, seems resonant even with the period of "high" European modernity, maybe especially so. As to whether "modernisation" is "a-cultural", as Taylor (1992) claims, this seems too sweeping a claim to make. The wide dissemination of a certain mode of economics obviously increases the shared experiences of diverse peoples in that realm, and the rapid manufacture and dissemination of symbolic content (in the current era, things like streaming video programs, etc.) does lead to some cultural homogenisation. But a single global culture remains a chimera, likely to never arrive, and not applicable to the time of history being discussed here.

References

Adair-Toteff, C. (1995). Ferdinand Tonnies: Utopian visionary. *Sociological Theory, 13*(1), 58–65.

Bowers, B. (1982). *A history of electric light & power.* P. Peregrinus in Association with the [London] Science Museum.

Bowers, B. (1998). *Lengthening the day*. Oxford University Press.

Davis, M. (2002). *Late Victorian holocausts: El Niño famines and the making of the third world*. Verso Books.

Ford, H., with Crowther, S. (1922). *My life and work*. Doubleday, Page & Company.

Giddens, A. (1990). *The consequences of modernity*. Polity Press.

Grossman, D. (2014). *On killing: The psychological cost of learning to kill in war and society*. Open Road Media.

Hastings, M. (2000). *Going to the wars*. Pan.

Ikenberry, G. J. (2020). *A world safe for democracy: Liberal internationalism and the crises of global order*. Yale University Press.

Kardiner, A. (1941). *The traumatic neuroses of war*. Hoeber Inc.

Lange, M. (2017). *Killing others: A natural history of ethnic violence*. Cornell University Press.

Lichtheim, G. (1972). *Europe in the twentieth century*. Praeger Publishers.

Maxwell, G. (2010, April 10). WH Auden's "The age of anxiety". *The Guardian*. https://www.theguardian.com/books/2010/apr/10/auden-age-anxiety-leonard-bernstein

Mokyr, J. (1999a). The second industrial revolution, 1870–1914. In V. Castronovo (Ed.), *Storia dell'economia Mondiale* (pp. 219–245). Laterza Publishing.

Mokyr, J. (1999b). Editor's introduction: The new economic history and the industrial revolution. In J. Mokyr (Ed.), *The British industrial revolution: An economic perspective* (2nd ed., pp. 1–127). Westview Press.

Mokyr, J., Vickers, C., & Ziebarth, N. L. (2015). The history of technological anxiety and the future of economic growth: Is this time different? *Journal of Economic Perspectives, 29*(3), 31–50.

Morris, I. (2014). *War! What is it good for? Conflict and the progress of civilization from primates to robots*. Farrer, Straus and Giroux.

Neal, L., & Cameron, R. (2016). *A concise economic history of the world: From paleolithic times to the present* (5th ed.). Oxford University Press.

Nowell-Smith, G. (1990). On history and the cinema. *Screen, 31*(2), 160–171.

Pinker, S. (2011). *The better angels of our nature: The decline of violence in history and its causes*. Penguin.

Polanyi, K. (1944). *The great transformation*. Beacon Press.

Rafael, E. F. (2017). Philippine problems are problems of modernity, not of transition: A Luhmannian critique of Randolf S. David's theory of modernity. *Philippine Sociological Review, 65* (Special Issue: Imagined democracies), 151–170.

Rattansi, A. (2017). *Bauman and contemporary sociology: A critical analysis*. Manchester University Press.

Salvatore, A. (2015). Modernity. In G. Bowering (Ed.), *Islamic political thought: An introduction* (pp. 135–151). Princeton University Press.

Sampson, A. (1995). *Company man: The rise and fall of corporate life*. Times-Business/Random House.

Taylor, C. (1992). Modernity and the rise of the public sphere. *The Tanner Lectures on Human Values, 14*, 203–260.

West, R. (1982). *1900*. Viking Studio Book.

Winn, J. A. (2008). *The poetry of war*. Cambridge University Press.

Yeo-chi King, A. (2018). "Modernization" and "modernity": The construction of a modern Chinese civilizational order. In A. Yeo-chi King (Ed.), *China's great transformation: Selected essays on confucianism, modernization, and democracy* (pp. 111–128). The Chinese University of Hong Kong Press.

Young, A. (1997). *The harmony of illusions: Inventing post-traumatic stress disorder*. Princeton University Press.

Young, J. (2015). Infrastructure: Mass transit in 19th- and 20th-century urban America. *Oxford research encyclopedia of American history*. Oxford Research Encylopedias.

Zinkina, J., Ilyin, I., & Korotayev, A. (2017). The nineteenth-century urbanisation transition in the First World. *Globalistics and globalization studies* (pp. 164–172). Uchitel Publishing House.

CHAPTER 15

"1914"

C. Gordon, *Many Possible Worlds*,
https://doi.org/10.1007/978-981-19-9281-0_15

Fig. 15.1 Kaiser Wilhelm and his six sons (*Image source* Hau, G. W. [1915]. *War echoes; or Germany and Austria in the crisis*. Chicago, M. M. Malone. P. 196. Contributing Library: The Library of Congress. Digitizing Sponsor: Sloan Foundation. No known copyright restrictions)

15.1 A Long Nineteenth Century

Historians of Europe speak of a long nineteenth century (1789–1914) beginning with the French Revolution, representing an overturning of a traditional order in the most powerful nation-state on the Continent at the time, ushering in 120 years or so of rationalism, scientific progress, materialism, and explicit "Balance of Power" politics in Europe. The dominant elite paradigm was based on mechanistic notions of the "natural order", i.e. equilibrium determined by a balanced interplay of opposing but interrelated forces. This was supposed to be true of all areas of human affairs, especially Great Power relations. Even though Europe remained largely monarchical in government, and old class elites remained dominant, the old idea of unquestioned traditional authority was replaced with an idea that authority should be based (at least implicitly) on the ability to achieve material and social progress, the two being conflated. This was something that industrialisation seemed to be achieving.

1914, the year marking the beginning of the First World War, put an end to all that. The faith in untrammelled progress, and the supposedly rightful power position of elites in attaining it, was totally shattered. While scientific and technical advance continued, its march now seemed more ominous than hopeful, as it was science and industry that made the "Great War" more destructive than any in prior history. The balancing act that was supposed to prevent such a catastrophe had not only failed to do so, it seemed to have encouraged it. The scope of political, economic and social destruction was clear after the war was over, with many old states eliminated completely, and the European dominance of world affairs, already slipping before the war, was now deeply fractured (Fig. 15.1).

15.2 A High Tide of Systems Thinking and Mechanism Ideals

It wasn't supposed to turn out this way. The pre-war narrative was one of scientific triumphalism and a genuine expectation that human rationality and ingenuity would solve all problems. This appeared most clear in the field of mathematics, the supposed queen of human thought. The idea that the workings of the universe could be completely captured in conceptual mathematical models went back to the ancient Greeks, starting at least with the Pythagoreans, who believed that nature was designed according to mathematical principles and that the patterns in numbers could be used to reveal the order in nature itself (Kline, 1980, 15). These premises were developed and systematised in Plato's philosophy of the "Ideal" which seemed to be manifested in Euclid's *Elements*, a concise collection of geometrical proofs that became an exemplar of how the physical world could be encapsulated into logical, analytical models that could then be manipulated to yield mathematical results to be effectively applied back in the physical world (Kline, 1980, 29).

The medieval "rediscovery" of the Greek classics by Western Europeans laid the foundation for the Scientific Revolution, with its practices of systematic observation, analytical model building and empirical testing whose power was first demonstrated in astronomy, with Kepler's and Galileo's calculations about the movement of planets and the true centre of the planets—the Sun, not the earth—followed by Newton's physics which laid a powerful foundation for a whole slew of other theoretical and practical innovations. These were most effectively applied during the Industrial Revolution, a time that led to the establishment of "Science" as an institution. These developments were joined with Cartesian rationalism (see Chapter 17) to create an integrated system of logical thought that coalesced into what amounted to an ideology of progress ending in an imagined pinnacle of human understanding and benign control over the planet and perhaps the cosmos.

At the dawn of the twentieth century, mathematicians seemed to be at the gates of paradise, having developed a unified theoretical apparatus that was complete in and of itself, with the power to uncover the secrets of creation, and thus allowing for human manipulation of them. In an address to the Second International Congress in Paris in 1900 at which the major mathematicians of the day had gathered, Henri Poincaré boasted that "absolute rigour has been attained". This high level of confidence was not completely universal, since some mathematical issues, such as doubts about the axiomatic process used by Euclid, had emerged and were not yet worked out. But most agreed that it was only a matter of time before these inconsistencies would be resolved and total logical and theoretical certainty achieved (Kline, 1980, 195).

Meanwhile, the stream of inventions created by industrialised science seemed to be concrete testimony to the fact that human logic and reason actually got results. The person living in the developed heart of 1914 Europe was literally living in a different world than the one encountered in 1814, or even 1854. Electricity, pharmaceuticals, mass production, clean running water in the home, mechanised transport—none of these things had existed and now they were commonplace in many parts of the world. It was true that there was still much diffusion of these technologies to be accomplished and that some areas of the world, even within Europe, were barely touched by modernisation at all. But although a universal human existence of prosperity, stability, safety and comfort might yet take some decades to achieve, its arrival could not be doubted.

Even in purely human affairs, mastery and management seemed possible. The Gold Standard as an international financial coordinating mechanism seemed to allocate capital in an efficient and, most importantly, a self-regulating manner (see Chapters 12 and 19). Government administration had been transformed from an ad hoc exercise of power to an evidence-based technical exercise that identified specific problems and then went about solving them. Public policy was now thought to be amenable to the same scientific management principles already well entrenched on the shop floor and in the executive suite (see Chapters 26 and 29).

15.3 Nineteenth Century Europe in Political Transition and the Rise of "Geopolitics"

Even that most unpredictable arena of relations between nations, of war and peace, was delicately but soundly pivoting on its own Balance of Power. Although Europe consisted of a strange hodgepodge of national states, with mass nationalism and economic liberalism coexisting with older autocratic forms of government and Empire that were dynastic and personal, these diverse entities nonetheless seemed to work out their disagreements in a rational, balanced and, most importantly, systematic manner. Yet all of them also had managed to compete with one another, without a general continental war occurring, since 1815 (The Crimean War of mid-century being a partial exception), and it was all thought to be due to the "Balance" set up by the Concert of Europe after Napoleon's final defeat.

Because Europe dominated much of the world during this time, the "Balance of Power" became a true world system, the first one in history. Indeed the term "geopolitics" was invented in this era, a sort of emblem of the age (Spencer, 1988). This was just one of the many "mechanistic" and "rational" systems of human activity that was supposed to preserve a stable field within which maximum freedom of action was possible for the competing and often inconsistent human needs and desires operating within that field, Adam Smith's "Invisible Hand" writ large. Indeed politics, the market, international finance—all collective human endeavour, in fact—were supposed to follow the same principles. As in all these areas, human capriciousness and the irreconcilable conflicts that could result were admitted to exist. But even these were thought amenable to natural processes that worked behind and beyond such frailties.

Part of what made the Balance of Power system viable in the first place was that it was explicitly a club, whose members came up with its joint rules, enforcing them on each other. One of these rules was that club members had to take all other member's interests into account when pushing their own self-interest. This would supposedly ensure a healthy competition that would nonetheless avoid descent into a scenario of sharks eating each other in a tank. Another rule was that non-member interests, especially small countries, could be ignored if desired. These less-than-great powers often provided the spoils divvied up between the great ones, a helpful and sometimes essential dispute-settlement aid. Inclusion in the Great Power club thus brought rights of participation that were counterbalanced with a responsibility to keep the system functioning well. In particular, Great Powers were not to seek the elimination of their rivals in victory, but only make adjustments that would maintain the balance. For example, Bismarck defeated Austria in 1866 and France in 1871. But while losing territory, both countries were kept strong enough to remain active members of the club. Thus Bismarck sought to press and safeguard German unity within the existing power framework rather than overturning it completely, something that Hitler would try to do later, and that Napoleon had tried to do before (Best et al., 2004, 13).

The protocols for coordination between members were fairly elaborate, with different levels of status and power. Thus Heads of State and Foreign Ministers met at Congresses, which were periodically convened to work out especially knotty issues that might lead to imminent war (for example, the 1878 Congress of Berlin that determined the territories of the states in the Balkan Peninsula after the Russo-Turkish War of 1877–1878). This was distinguished from the lesser conferences convened for less urgent matters, and which generally only exchanged ambassadors (diplomatic officials of the highest rank), not ministers (Best et al., 2004, 10).

There were also "courtesy" Great Powers like Italy, treated as such to lure Rome into one alliance or another. The Austrian Empire morphed into something similar as the nineteenth century unfolded. In 1866, the Empire had one of the largest armies on the Continent, and was a genuine power critical to maintaining the conservative order (and remember that Talleyrand, the architect of the Concert of Europe in 1815, was Viennese). In 1914, it had one of the smallest armies, and was now Austria-Hungary, with its clunky dual monarchy and separate governments, parliaments and budgets. Still, it was important for the Great Powers to maintain Austria-Hungary's integrity because of the vacuum that would open up if it fell apart (Best et al., 2004, 10–11). By contrast, the non-European Ottoman Empire was not even a courtesy member. Its rapid decline was desirable from a Great Power perspective, though its shrinkage still had to be managed to make sure that the spoils of its lost territories were parcelled out in ways that did not lead to more general conflict.

In this sense, the Balance system was something like a business cartel, where firms balance their common interest against their individual gains or losses, remaining united as long as their longer-term advantage is maintained by sticking together. The cartel model became widespread throughout many business markets during the growing concentration of oligopolistic industry during the Second Industrial Revolution. The Gold Standard can also be seen as a global financial cartel across national governments. Cartels in general could deliver growth and stability in their respective domains. But they also were prone to individual members seeking to use the rules to restrain their competitors while still pressing their own advantage at the same time. For this reason all cartels tend to be unstable, and the Great Power club proved to be no exception.

A great source of underlying strain was the political, economic and social diversity across the Great Powers. By and large, the "modern" countries were democratic while the backwards ones were not. But even the popular basis of the democracies varied considerably, with French and British franchises and representative structures quite distinct from one another with different governance systems, principles of government and social organisation. The Central and Eastern countries were largely nondemocratic but with varying degrees of representative forms, Germany again combining both some advanced democratic institutional typologies with very autocratic ones. Even this broad division covered a wide diversity of social and political arrangements (Lichtheim, 1972, 14–15) (Fig. 15.2).

These domestic arrangements could leak into Great Power issues. For example, the Western European powers had managed to combine nationalism and popular democracy, bringing the populace on board with, and allowing them varying degrees of influence over, state policies of domestic and international power maintenance. This allowed for a largely genuine self-determination for domestic majorities and varying degrees of protection for minorities that was more lacking the eastern periphery. The Austrian Hapsburg and the Russian Romanov dynasties had great difficulty in managing their ethnic minorities, not least because of the lack of a true nationalism (as opposed to ethnic loyalty) to unite them. Internationally, when these countries tried to expand on the world stage, this tended to enhance their domestic problems by upsetting delicately balanced and volatile internal ethnic accords. Their expansions also were more on

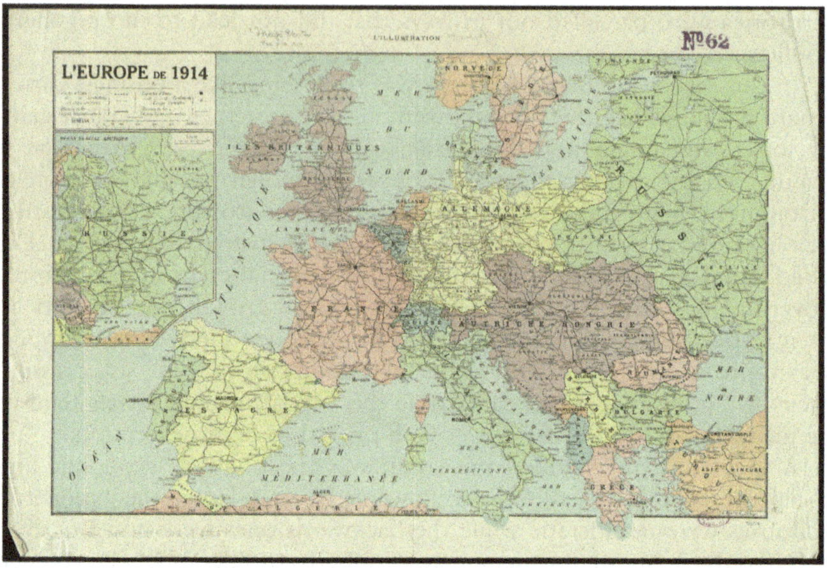

Fig. 15.2 Europe on the eve of First World War (*Image source* "L'Europe de 1914", Peltier, Georges, [1914?] Boston Public Library, Norman B. Leventhal Map Center Collection, No known copyright restrictions, No known restrictions on use)

the order of reshaping spheres of influence around the metropolitan, as opposed to the global projects of the French and the British, which were much more economic in nature, especially in facilitating and directing large capital and trade flows, and projecting geopolitical power within a globalising system (Lichtheim, 1972, 15–19).

To complicate matters, economic change was creating new social classes, especially the proletariat with its rumblings of socialism, another universalism that added to the heady mix of the modern era. This too was filtered through the unique circumstances of each country, with labour union-led syndicalists being more active in the "Latin" countries, especially Italy and France, with anarchists having a stronghold in backwards Spain (though Spain itself was not a Great Power, even in a courtesy sense). In Russia, populist socialism embedded in the elites slowly gave way to Marxism, while Social Democrats in Germany tried to put socialism into electoral practice in a place where such practice was highly constrained (Lichtheim, 1972, 16).

Indeed, the critical cultural and political shifts of the 1800s, such as Napoleonism, and even those of the 1700s, 1600s and 1500s, were diffusing at different rates throughout the Continent. The principles and forces of the French Revolution had not seeped deeply into Germany, Russia and Austria-Hungary and as a result they had largely staved off the 1830–1848 revolutionary waves, having to pay the piper after the First World War. The Protestant Reformation had entirely skipped Russia due to its Orthodox faith, while only lightly penetrating many of the staunchly Catholic countries of the east and southern regions of the German speaking realms, especially Bavaria and Austria (Lichtheim, 1972, 22). The conflicted societal incoherence of the major countries of Europe was masked by the Balance of Power arrangements that in the end could not hold them all together.

15.4 A Complexifying Order

The Great Power system was designed to manage relations from above, elite to elite. But the pressures from below were becoming unmanageable, with the legacy of the French Revolution making the job of management of nations by elites that much harder, even under democracy. The legacies of rationalisation, secularisation, urbanisation, industrialisation and, in particular, a mass society, all had to be negotiated by national leaders with their own peoples, a difficult balancing act, though in differing ways for autocrats versus democrats. Bismarck straddled both old and new, a Prussian Junker with confidence in his entitled power who nonetheless had a keen sense of domestic popular sentiment. This combination took his country a long way, but the contradictions could not be managed by his less artful successors, with fateful consequences.

The external pressures on the Balance of Power system were even more acute. On its eastern and southern fringes, five new nations emerged into full independence and sovereign status in South-eastern Europe between 1871 and 1914. All were former Ottoman territories and poor and backwards, but also Christian, nationalistic and purportedly constitutional regimes. Serbia, Montenegro, and Bulgaria were Slav. Romania and Albania were not (Roberts, 2000, 39). As many tinderbox issues occurred as a result of the Ottoman disintegration, this divergent multiplicity of new small principalities did not bode well for future stability.

Then there were the rising non-European powers of the US and Japan. By the end of the 1800s neither country could be treated as a minor entity. But neither were they allowed into the Great Power club. In 1893, the British finally upgraded its legation in Washington to a full embassy, with ministers now having the status of ambassadors (Tooze, 2014, 34). The British even recognised the Monroe Doctrine (which was the US declaration that only it could interfere in the Americas) during the Venezuela dispute in 1895, and the Americans participated in the conference on equatorial Africa in 1884–1885. Nonetheless Italy as a courtesy power outranked America, which had no formal status, because only it was European. The Americans saw this when they could not prevent European gunboat diplomacy during a second Venezuela crisis in 1902–1903 (Best et al., 2004, 10).

Meanwhile, Japan's defeat of Russia in 1905 caused an elevation of its standing and yet no permanent decline in Russia's status because everyone in Europe expected Russia would regain its strength and power, while not being so sure about Japan, which, in any case, was non-white and Asian. Even Italy's miserable 1896 defeat at Adwa in Ethiopia did not eject it from the Great Power club, although the country's second-rate status was fully cemented after that. Thus despite an underlying conceit of self-regulation, the "balance" was far less stable and self-regulating than it was made out to be. It survived the turmoil of 1830 and 1848 but even in its supposed heyday it required constant renegotiation and active participation by its members (Best et al., 2004, 10–11, 13).

Even its own members did fully trust the workings of their club, periodically concluding various bilateral and other arrangements between nations, designed to shore up their own position within the Balance of Power while gaining a perceived advantage by working outside of it. An example is Germany's alliance with Austria-Hungary, which was meant to give the former a check and control on the latter, even though they were already nominally aligned. These additional agreements, however, exacerbated conflict and drove blocs against one another, as they would fatefully when the assassination of the Archduke Franz Ferdinand in Sarajevo set in train interlocking alliances and counter-alliances that led to the unanticipated Great War, something the Great Power system was supposed to prevent (Hewitson, 2014, 230–232).

Indeed, there is a good argument to be made that the Great Power system was in fact failing between 1905–1914. Although Congresses continued to operate, armed power plays by individual states, using brinkmanship and unilateralism in the Balkans and North Africa became more and more the order of the day. The new small Balkan powers, especially Serbia, were distinctly uncooperative with Great Power plans, Serbia fighting successfully with the Ottomans to secure territory for itself, upsetting arrangements to stabilise the Balkan frontier there (Best et al., 2004, 21, 23–24). The Balance of Power thus addressed the European "core" and ignored its "periphery", the latter becoming increasingly powerful and restive (There is a parallel to the dynamics of the Cold War and the Superpower duopoly, a dog that became wagged by proxy wars and flashpoints in otherwise "unimportant" places; see Chapter 25).

The fraying of the system is clearest in in Asia, especially the Pacific, which, during the latter half of the nineteenth century, saw the decline of a China-dominated international East Asia. This opened up the area for the full force of Great Power politics, mainly between Russia and Britain. The forced opening of Japan had been part of this; but ironically this had led Japan to become an expansionist non-European rival, a development that had not been anticipated. Though never admitted into the club, Japan became the primary local challenger to China, conquering Taiwan in 1894, South Manchuria in 1905 and Korea in 1910 (Best et al., 2004, 59). The United Kingdom saw Japan as a useful counterweight to Russia, and to the Americans, who were projecting their newly found power into the region as well. But the fact that these developments were not seen as fundamentally destabilising to the whole Eurocentric order was an artefact of ideology. European countries thought of themselves as meant to rule and any failing by Europeans, or challenges from non-Europeans, were fundamentally temporary. First World War chaos and its aftermath would make clear the hollowness of this assumption (Fig. 15.3).

15.5 A New Industry of Arms

Despite the tension in global politics, the theology of "Progress" brought with it a complementary doctrine of faith that modernisation—economic, political and social—would bring a lasting time of peace and wealth and happiness. Ivan Bloch's *War in the Future* (1898) and Norman Angell's *The Great Illusion* (1910) made what at the time were novel arguments that the integration of the modern economy would sweep away the need or desire for armed conflict. The various international congresses and conferences that averted war and promoted cooperation seemed to confirm this (Best et al., 2004, 15).

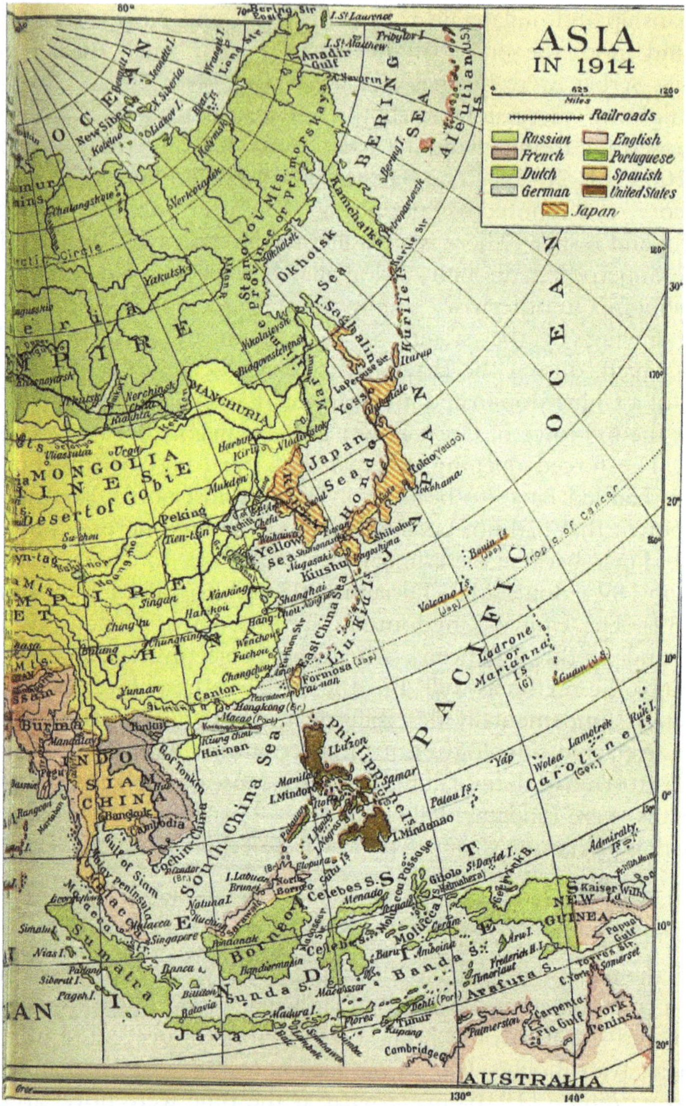

Fig. 15.3 Asia-Pacific in 1914 (*Image source* Hazen, C. D. [1919]. *Fifty years of Europe, 1870–1919*. H. Holt and company. p. 315; Contributing Library: Cornell University Library; Digitizing Sponsor: MSN. No known copyright restrictions)

Yet, things were not so rosy as they were said to be. Economic integration itself brought its own conflicts and challenges, creating tensions as well as smoothing them. For one thing, global interdependence made countries more vulnerable to external competitors, a fact which could as easily lead to a country to attempt to geopolitically neutralise its rivals before things got of hand, rather than foster good relations with them in the meantime. Economic interdependence thus exacerbated the propensity to make a military "quick strike" to take rivals out and solidify position (Eloranta & Harrison, 2010, 137).

Industrialisation, combined with the fiscal and administrative modernisations that occurred in most states by the mid-nineteenth century (see Chapter 6), also allowed countries to increase their military capacity without an excessive fiscal burden on their populations. This made the permanent maintenance of large standing armies more feasible, as a strategic reserve "just in case". And industrialised warfare seemed to offer the possibility of very rapid conflicts with rapid conclusions, though a study of the grinding American Civil War of 1861–1865, one of the earliest examples of industrialised conflict, would have disabused that notion. The "Great War" proved after the fact that industrialisation made wars longer and more destructive, especially if fought by relative equals. It also showed that war and preparations for it were more bearable economically but more total and destructive when and if it came (Eloranta & Harrison, 2010, 138).

Meanwhile, the French Revolution had birthed the mass popular army, which now became widespread. After Waterloo, there was an initial reversion to the small professional army because the notion of a people at arms seemed to have a double indemnity. First, it smacked of democracy and even revolution. Second, it betokened a form of war that could become unlimited in both its methods and its length, as the Napoleonic conflicts had demonstrated (Strachan, 2000, 94). This aversion to mass armies was, however, short-lived, as mass societies and economies required large forces to protect and extend their overseas power.

Mass armies demanded mass arming. Although competition in the production and development of armaments is as old as war itself, the idea of an "arms race" appears to be an idea that first came about in the 1850s (Gray, 1971). Pre-industrial wars involved much technical innovation, often with decisive results on the battlefield. But their main impetus was to harden, strengthen and leverage the basic fighting unit, which was the armed man, both singularly and collectively. Industrial production changed all that. Technical progress now made that chimera of a "miracle weapon" seem truly attainable, while industrial progress seemed to require a large stock of ever-more destructive armaments to equip a large standing army, able to mobilise quickly while being relatively cheap to maintain during peace. In fact, a country with a large technically sophisticated force could use it as a signal of strength that might carry the day without firing a shot, while being decisive if war did come after all.

Hence, the "race" to beat one's competitors in producing and developing arms. Once begun the modern arms race created its own momentum, as an independent source of conflict as well as an outgrowth of it. Whether the pre-1914 build-up "caused" the Great War is still debated. Conflict theorists tend to argue that arms competition can play a significant role in leading to war, but that other causes must be present to decisively tip the balance in its favour (Diehl & Crescenzi, 1998). It certainly does not help to create a peaceable atmosphere, aphorisms about preparing for war being the best way to prepare for peace notwithstanding.

It did definitely destabilise the pre-war European order in bellicose ways. The problem of arming oneself for the needs of modern war became like everything else, a matter of scale and production. The nineteenth century saw the rise of a global arms industry and "military-industrial complex" (see Chapter 22) where arms production and strategic planning themselves became signals for perceived and actual aggressive intent, as well as a symbol used to whip up popular agitation. German plans to build a fleet to challenge the British are a case in point, the British taking this almost as an act of war in and of itself. Similarly, "innocent" technical improvements, such as railway expansions, could also have menacing overtones. Even international financing moves, such as France's 2.5 billion Franc loan to Russia to build 5,000 kilometres of strategic railways by 1918, were seen as aggressive (Best et al., 2014, 17–18). The various arms limitations negotiations that were commenced to contain this dynamic ended up being as conflict-inducing as they were peace-inducing since they codified, in the eyes of the weaker participants, the perceived unfair advantages of the stronger nations.

There was a symbiosis—or parasitism, depending upon perspective—between government spending and the growing arms industry. As governments increased their military budgets, there was, of course, more business for private arms suppliers who, with the increasing technical sophistication of arms production, became more and more indispensable to war planners, as well as forming a pressure group for arms sales all in their own right. In the background was the march of scientific progress and economic growth that enabled a growing army and armaments cache to be maintained and replenished at a relatively fixed burden relative to GDP and public tax revenues. For example, the French defence budget stayed roughly around 30% of total state spending between 1815 and 1914, although its relatively sluggish GDP growth meant that the relative burden on the population did increase a bit over this time. In Britain, the defence-spending share was an average of around 37% across 1870–1913, with stronger British economic growth allowing this steady relative burden to fund more absolute military power as time went on (Eloranta, 2007, 260).

Thus, while relative spending and burdens in the Great Powers were in general static over time, the absolute size of armies and armament stocks increased prodigiously. Table 15.1 shows the growth in the major Entente and Central power army and navy personnel sizes and their warship tonnage between 1880 and 1914. A doubling or more was typical. And yet the military budgets never blew out of proportion as far as relative tax burden was concerned. It was a very efficient arms race in that way, but no less disastrous because of that.

Not foreseen by any strategist was the fact that mechanisation would shift the balance of power to the defender, not the attacker, since more efficiently lethal arms made defence more sustainable than an attack; unless, of course, success was rapid. The "short war illusion" was fed by a flawed premise when looking at raw metrics of military capability. High military capacity relative to one's opponent suggested quick tipping points. But it did not take into account a fact that would become clear all too soon, namely that victory in modern warfare turned on economic capacity as much as it did military prowess (As an aside, Hitler took the lessons of First World War and turned the logic of mechanisation on its head, using it to more efficiently concentrate force rapidly in the so-called blitzkrieg. But he would find the fundamental calculations would be the same in the end after his gamble on complete and rapid victory was proven illusory).

15.6 Reasons War Came

When general war finally came, the Great Power system itself could be said to have contributed to it, as much as it could be said to have helped

Table 15.1 Army and navy combined personnel sizes and warship tonnage for major First World War combatants

Russia	*Military and naval personnel (combined)*	*Warship tonnage*
– 1880	791,000	200,000
– 1914	1,352,000	679,000
France		
– 1880	543,000	271,000
– 1914	910,000	900,000
Britain		
– 1880	367,000	650,000
– 1914	532,000	2,714,000
Japan		
– 1880	71,000	15,000
– 1914	306,000	700,000
Germany		
– 1880	426,000	88,000
– 1914	891,000	1,305,000
Austria-Hungary		
– 1880	246,000	60,000
– 1914	444,000	372,000

Source selected from Kennedy (1989, Tables 19 and 20, p. 203)

delay it. Thus Germany saw itself as encircled within the Great Power system, and simply adopted what it considered a corrective policy to re-balance things, in its favour to be sure, but simply its due to account for growth in its economic and military power. Meanwhile, the other powers saw the German stance as too aggressive. But they ignored the fact that if Germany had wanted greater advantage than it already possessed, it could have moved against France in 1905, when Russia was defeated and France was weaker militarily. In that particular instance, Germany felt compelled to play by the rules and general war was averted (Best et al., 2004, 20). But that delay made war that much worse when it came.

Thus, playing by the rules and breaking them remained a matter of perspective. If you were already a dominant power, as the British Empire was, or an old contender and current co-inheritor of the existing order, as France was, German games were seen as nefarious; and, it must be said, German diplomacy was often extremely self-defeating in this period. The Germans begged to differ. Germany occupied a central position on the Continent, was rapidly industrialising, and could claim a pedigree and set of historical roots that were just as old as those of England or France. Other aggressive up-and-comers like Japan and the US were not European and so were never part of the club. But they were making rapid gains in their own domains. Why, German leaders thought, shouldn't Germany be given the same latitude within Europe? This is the problem with an elite club, especially a chauvinistic European one. There is no outer force to correct or reveal how distorted the perceptions its members had of themselves might become.

The contradiction within the Great Power system was that Germany could not be allowed to expand too much precisely because of its importance and centrality. The weaker Great Powers got greater sufferance because of their incidental positions. Austria-Hungary, though allied to Germany, was not a threat in and of itself, while Russia, also declining, was on the periphery of Europe. The balance required constant relative equality only between the key players. Any imbalance caused by power increasing in a central player was a grave threat.

In fact, the Balance of Power was an illusion. It was supposedly a self-regulating mechanism that could not long tolerate much dynamism, and these were very dynamic times. Hobsbawm (1994) notes that it was the very nature of the modern integration of globalised power politics and economics and finance to make everything more "total" in nature, especially in war. While Napoleonic warfare still assumed, in line with eighteenth century war-craft, that the principal focus of a nation's identity in times of war was with its army, the growth of the nation-state and its latent ability to devote total national resources to a military effort meant that the defeat of an army in the field might not itself prove decisive to the war. The capture of the nation's capital and other resources was now needed to ensure true and decisive national defeat (Strachan, 2000, 91).

This is the paradox: the First World War was the first genuinely total war even though it did not begin as an ideological crusade, as its successor conflict would end up being. Although the Central Powers were autocratic, democracies like France and England allied with autocratic Russia on the Allied side. It was only later, after Russia was knocked out of the war and all the major Allies had liberal democratic forms, and joined by the Americans, under President Woodrow Wilson, that the war became cast as a Wilsonian crusade for democracy, and also an answer to the new threat of Bolshevism.

But these were the late after-effects of the topsy-turvy Great War. Ultimate aims unconsciously became unlimited, for politics and economics had fused under global capitalism, and to seek superior position within that system meant total elimination of your opponents to maintain dominance. The powers thought they were fighting over old spheres of influence, which implied limited ends that could be met by limited means. But such spheres had now merely become tactical theatres in the competition of a globalised world (Broadberry & Harrison, 2005, Chapter 1).

This at least partly explains why some opportunities for a negotiated peace that arose after the War had begun were left unconsidered. The German invasion of Belgium, for example, was a primary proximate driver of England declaring war against Germany, but not the only one. Britain had decided to make Belgian neutrality a policy decision, subject to expedience, even though the country was a signatory to the 1839 London Treaty guaranteeing its independence. England could have finessed that transgression in some way if it had wanted to. But if England remained neutral it faced the prospect of a purely Russo-French bloc emerging victorious and hostile to the British Empire, a prospect more concerning than a German victory over an English-French-Russian alliance (Best et al., 2004, 25–26). This was a parallel to the German logic, that if a first-mover advantage was not seized, all was lost, and there would be no opportunity to limit losses in a general negotiation afterwards, as had been the case for European wars in prior centuries.

Finally one must add to this mix the dynamism of the modern idea of nationhood and nationalism, born out of the French Revolution, and now deeply motivating the "masses". Striking was the response of the Left when war came, nominally internationalist and pacifist, committed to refusing to fight for the capitalist class in its wars for profit. Yet almost all the left parties in Europe rolled over in a show of patriotism, its members joining their respective national armies in enthusiastic droves, though there were also some significant splits as well (Oppelland, 2017). Nationalism was an idea that mixed well with a mass age, allowing the individual, even in democracies, to melt into a noble cause and, after the war dragged on, allowed the State to conscript people into a necessary defence.

15.7 During the War

The actual progress of the War itself is well-trodden narrative ground: defensive war in the west, with massive casualties ground out in trench warfare with very static front lines; German defeat of Russia in the east, a front which always exhibited more mobility but no less lethality; the late entry of the Americans which brought its productive power to bear; a last minute desperate offensive by German Field Marshall Erich Ludendorff that aimed for "total war" but failed; and the Armistice between the victorious Allies and the defeated Central Powers that brought no true lasting peace (Hardach, 1977).

What is more important from an economic point of view is how the processes of the war transformed the economy and the State, both during times of war and in the peace that would follow it. The Great War also weakened an old European world order, and with it the pre-war global economic order (Fig. 15.4).

The new ways of industrial war could be seen in Germany's opening gambit, the Schlieffen Plan, which chose a theatre of operation, north-west Europe, which had the greatest concentration of railway track in the world. The plan involved moving over 3 million men and 600,000 horses in 11,000 trains during a period of 312 hours. This technical efficiency came with a sting in its tail, however, one that should have been obvious after a little reflection that no one of importance seemed to make. The railway was good for delivering masses from the rear to the railheads near the front. But beyond that their armies slowed to the pace of the slowest man and horse. Railways on balance thus probably contributed more to defence than to attack because rapid reinforcement of potential weak spots prevented the exploitation of offensive opportunities (Strachan, 2000, 87). The knockout blow hoped for by the Germans was always a vain hope.

Similarly, in 1866, Prussia had been the only army with a central general staff entrusted with development of war doctrine and overall plans during peacetime (all other armies had their staff officers in the field). The mass armies of First World War could never have been run without these and so in 1914 all the combatants employed a general staff. Gigantism in field operations had some precedent, for in 1812, Napoleon led 614,000 men into Russia. So this problem of coordinating such unprecedented numbers was a big reason for the development of doctrine and general staffs in the first place. But now the scale was even larger, and the notion that a commander-in-chief could actually personally lead their armies into battle, as both Napoleon and Wellington had, despite the size of their forces, was a literal impossibility (Strachan, 2000, 99). There was also a misleading impression, reinforced by the regularity and timetables of

Fig. 15.4 Corner of a battlefield, Haelen, Belgium (*Image source* Forms part of: George Grantham Bain Collection [Library of Congress]. No known restrictions on publication. Repository: Library of Congress, Prints and Photographs Division, Washington, DC 20540 USA, hdl.loc.gov/loc.pnp/pp.print [Persistent URL]: hdl.loc.gov/loc.pnp/ggbain.17368. Call Number: LC-B2- 3248–14 Title from data provided by the Bain News Service on the negative. Photograph shows dead soldiers and horses in a field after the Battle of Haelen which was fought by the German and Belgian armies on August 12, 1914 near Haelen, Belgium during World War I. No known copyright restrictions)

railways, that war was now a matter of management, like any other large-scale activity (Strachan, 2000, 88–89). The actual course of the war would disabuse everyone of the notion that war could be run like a machine or a large company, but too late to do any good.

From a purely military perspective, mechanised war created not only a massive logistics task, but also a huge increase in supply and manpower requirements. Until 1916, the huge British Army in France could still rely on volunteers to fill its ranks. But State power expanded greatly after that because it was necessary to go well beyond markets to raise sufficient fighting forces, feed them, and also to feed the people at home (Roberts, 2000, 41).

Technical change was a large part of this. A single Vickers machine gun, one of many technical innovations deployed with devastating effect, could fire 600 rounds a minute, an amount of ammunition that had previously been sufficient to supply half a battalion of troops. Machines like these required replenishment far beyond anything previously, and stockpiles of munitions were depleted within months, necessitating vast and rapid ramp-ups in production of war materiel, increases in imports for both war and civilian needs, and cutbacks in private consumption. Despite the success of the recent film and show *War Horse*, which shows the terrible toll on draught animals of the period, while millions of horses did die, mainly due to exhaustion, they were now militarily irrelevant (Morris, 2014, 249). 700,000 horses were kept idle behind the lines in First World War action because cavalry now proved strategically useless across the Western front (Lichtheim, 1972).

Technical advance did not stand still even during the war and technology bred the need for more technology, further increasing its "totalness". Advances in artillery and troop defence techniques increased offensive powers dramatically. But for every improvement made by attackers, defenders responded, digging multiple lines of trenches, manning forward positions lightly, and most of all, coming up with new weapons or improvements on existing ones. The new "tank" came too late and was too untested to make a strategic difference, but fire control and aviation did not. While aircraft had not even existed at the beginning of the century, and none was used in war until 1911, by 1918 two thousand planes were buzzing above the Western front (Morris, 2014, 248–249).

Meeting these needs required extraordinary government authority over private activities of all sorts and mandated the centralised organisation of production processes to suit war needs and mass drafting and mobilisation of men for fighting. Separations between State, economy and society evaporated and State capacity, power and ability reached scales, scopes and depth that had never been seen before. This process went furthest in authoritarian Germany and Austria-Hungary, but it was highly advanced in Britain as well, though, interestingly, less so in France. The Americans, once they formally joined the hostilities in 1917, would also go far down this path of command organisation and reap efficiencies in war production that outdid the rest of the Allies (Blum et al., 2014). And the intensity of resource use was unprecedented. According to one calculation, Britain, France, Russia, and (eventually) the US spent $36,485.48 for every enemy soldier killed. The Central Powers were much more efficient, spending $11,344.77 per corpse. But it was the German side that lost. It simply did not have enough time or resources to outlast the other side (Morris, 2014, 250).

Although the wartime measures were wound back after the war ended, a new pattern of large State and large private enterprise cooperation had been cemented that would not be entirely discarded in peacetime, and would be revived on an even greater scale during the following round of global conflagration. Despite the pretences of Liberalism, industrial capitalism had never truly been very laissez-faire, even in its formative stages. But governments had not been particularly efficient or effective in projecting power into private economic spheres, and such efforts were not ideologically supported nor especially popular. Now, it was seen that government could ally with business to transform economy and society in a crisis, and that the people could be convinced of its rightness and necessity (see Box 15.1).

Box 15.1 Total war, public relations and the making of mass opinion
Mass production had led to the rise of the large corporation and the need for mass distribution and stimulation and marshalling of mass consumption. These developments, when combined with mass media, created new methods of mass marketing. These were soon applied to political discourse and consensus building, and an entirely new enterprise called "Public Relations" was born.

A term probably first used in the US in the late nineteenth century, a Boston publicity agency, The Publicity Bureau, established in 1900, has been seen by some as the first American public relations agency, its first major corporate client being the telecommunications monopoly American Telephone & Telegraph. The German industrial giant Krupp set up a news bureau in 1893, while in Britain the Marconi company sent out its first news release in 1910 (Watson, 2012, 43). Large corporations had seen the necessity of communicating directly with the public, in both democracies and autocracies, to advance their own private political agendas and also to maintain their public image, the latter goal being seen as good for business.

One of the field's founders, Ivy Lee, saw Public Relations as a way of providing factual news to reporters for the benefit of his clients. Edward

Bernays, a nephew of Sigmund Freud's who had moved to America as an infant, took a different tack, reviving the old term "propaganda", but now using it to refer to material to be provided to the public that was designed not so much to inform them with selected factual disclosures, but more to persuade them, using techniques based on his uncle's theories of the human unconscious. Unlike Lee, Bernays believed that elites had to shape public opinion to avoid the "chaos" that he thought that untrained and undirected masses would bring. Bernays' ideas were a key part of the new emerging idea of a "public opinion" that was not just there to be passively discovered but something to be actively moulded by leaders in the interest of a common good and order (Olasky, 1984, 3–4).

While Bernays and other public relations experts were often hired by large companies and rich individuals to help shape private images and achieve private goals, such as increasing consumption of particular products or improving the public's view of a particular individual, the First World War provided an opportunity to use these methods to mobilise the public behind the war effort. This came into full flower in the US, where the European war was unpopular and where Woodrow Wilson had won a second term in 1916 based on a promise to keep the country out of it. Public opinion on this matter thus had to be turned around quickly, and the Committee on Public Information (1917–1919), also known as the Creel Committee after the last name of its director, was an independent agency of the government of the US created to do just this. The Committee used every modern medium then available to enthuse the populace about for the war effort, demonise opponents to the war, and create demand for "Liberty Loans", which were war bonds sold directly to individuals. A young Bernays worked for the Committee's Bureau of Latin-American Affairs, its office located in New York, where he focused on building support for war from American businesses operating in Latin America. Here, he would learn many lessons, refining and expanding on them in his own post-war career in the business and turning out to be wildly successful (Watson, 2012, 44).

The First World War made it very clear that policy and politics required consent of the masses and that this consent could be effectively shaped by leaders using the most advanced and "scientific" techniques. There were still economic classes and formations based on race, ethnicity and religion to varying degrees. But total war fused required the population to be fused into a mass movement. To accomplish war aims, the State had to mobilise masses of people behind the cause, both ideologically and physically. Authoritarian and democrat came to this conclusion, and they became better than ever at bringing the population onside. Interestingly, democracies had the most need to do this, despite their philosophical focus on individual rights, because popular governance implicitly required greater buy-in from individuals and hence made greater demands on them than autocracies needed to (Lichtheim, 1972). But no government wanted the "people" against them, whatever its persuasion, whether at war or at peace. They now had mass tools to keep this from happening.

The drag of a peasantry on modern economies was also made quite plain during the Great War. Germany was in a particularly tight corner in this regard. Highly advanced and industrialised at the outbreak of the war, Germany was nonetheless also one of the more agrarian economies amongst the industrialised economies, and this proved to be a big obstacle to its ability to supply itself food, even with a highly productive agricultural sector. General mobilisation drew away an estimated 40% of the male agricultural labour force and the need for military draught animals hampered food output still further (Blum et al., 2014). More backwards countries, especially Russia, had even worse problems in this regard. The War made clear that the size of an agrarian sector had to be minimised for economic modernisation, full stop, though a productive agrarian sector was still a good thing to have. In Russia, that country's surrender to the Germans was at least partly due to peasants ultimately refusing to provide portions of their crops to urban populations as the war became desperate. The decimation of the rural workforce through conscription and battlefield casualties didn't help matters. This is partly why Stalin later resorted to forced collectivisation of agriculture, which removed the freedom of the peasant to withdraw from supplying the economy in war or peace. Brutal and awful as it was, and despite some massive initial failures, it did succeed in its political objective, making Stalin's victories in Second World War more assured (Eloranta & Harrison, 2010, 147).

The fusion of economy, polity and society that modern capitalism had forged made it clear that major conflicts would likely forever more be wars of attrition based on total economic capacity, and not just military engagements (Fig. 15.5). France had gone from devoting 10% of its GDP to military spending in 1913 to 50% in 1917, while Germany had gone from the same level to 59%. Even Britain, not having war touch its own soil, went from 8% to 37% (Eloranta & Harrison, 2010, 145, Table 6.6).

This understated the mobilisation of resources since command and regulation over private activities had also vastly expanded and these were not always included in defence statistics. "Total war" had arrived, never to retreat completely, sometimes even during peace.

15.8 After the War Was Over

First World War hostilities finally did end, at least officially, although the "Interwar" period following it was not very pacific. With it died an older, more personalistic and romantic conception of war. The initial poetry of First World War soldiers hearkened back to an imagined Middle Ages that made horses "steeds", friends "comrades", and the dead "the fallen". Phrases such as the "man-at-arms" and the "chalice of courage" were the favoured sorts of imagery, and the ordinary soldier and his death was exalted with words like "dignity" and "glory". By the end of the war, poets such as Siegfried Sasson and Wilfred Owen had a far darker vision. The wholesale, mechanised and senseless carnage of the War discredited such noble images and these were replaced by despair and senselessness (Winn, 2008, 13, 18). One of their poetic number, Robert Graves, who was nearly killed himself, accordingly entitled his 1929 post-war memoir, *Goodbye to all that.*

The post-war world had been changed irrevocably, though it would take another twenty years of turmoil and an even worse Second World War to complete the change. For one thing, great amounts of human and physical capital (to use the bloodless economics terms) had been destroyed, leaving victor and defeated greatly weakened. Nine million combatants and twelve million civilians were estimated to have died during the War, and substantial property damage was sustained especially in France, Belgium and Poland. Estimated total direct financial losses range from 180–230 billion US dollars (in 1914 values) (in 2021 values, roughly $4.7 trillion to $5.9 trillion) with indirect losses of property and capital thought to be around 150 billion dollars ($3.9 trillion), though more recent estimates of total economic losses arising from the war are as high as 525 billion 1914 US dollars ($13.7 trillion in 2021 values). Serbia-Montenegro and Romania lost 5.7% and 3.3% of their overall population in the conflict, while Turkey, France and Germany lost more than 3% each. Total Allied losses of life were actually higher than those of the Central Powers, 5.4 million compared to 4 million (Blum et al., 2014).

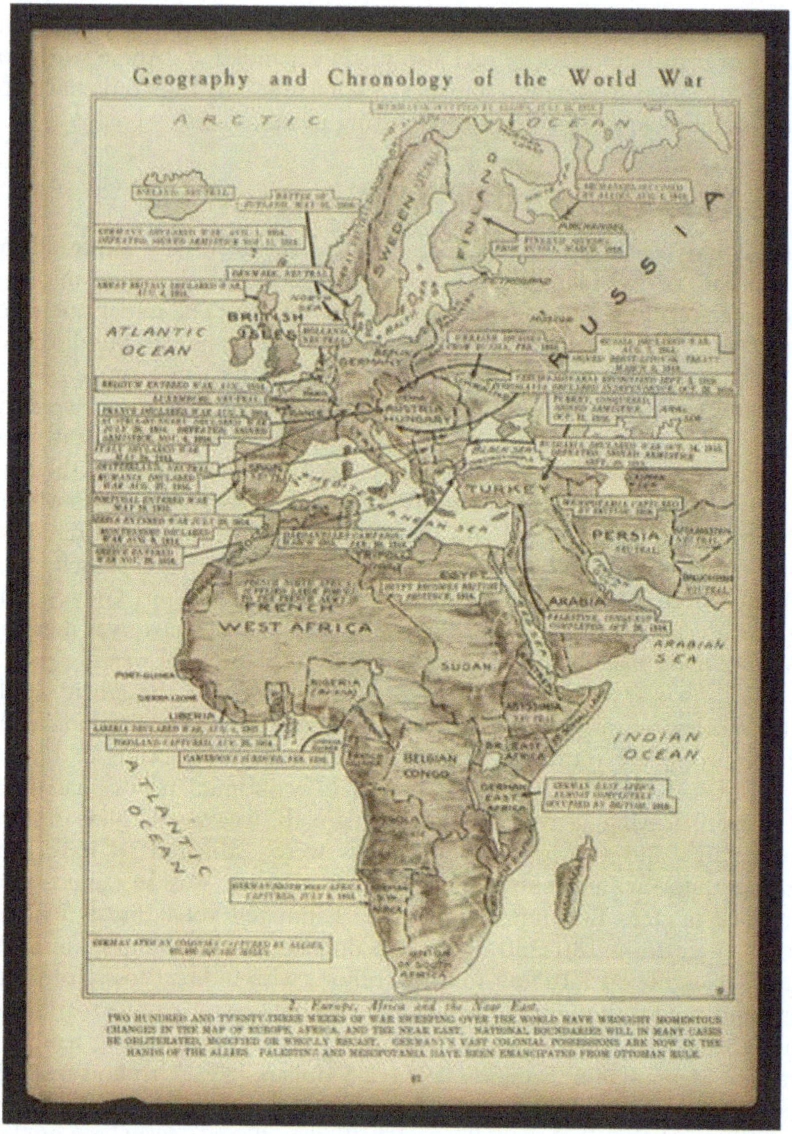

Fig. 15.5 A wider war (*Image source* The war of the nations: portfolio in rotogravure etchings: compiled from the Mid-week pictorial. New York: New York Times, Co, 1919. Book. Retrieved from the Library of Congress, www.loc.gov/item/19013740/. No known copyright restrictions)

When considering these intangibles as "assets", France was very hard hit, losing 7.2% of its pre-war human capital and 24.6% of its domestic physical assets, 49% of its overseas assets and 31% of its national wealth. Germany was even worse off, losing 54.7% of its national wealth and 6.3% of its human capital. England got off comparatively lightly with a 3.6% loss of human capital and 14.9% of national wealth (Eloranta & Harrison, 2010, 149). For this reason, economic recovery from the war was long and hard. European countries that won the war took around 3 and 1/2 years from the end of the war to recover their pre-war GDP per capita, while the losers took almost 10 years (Eloranta & Harrison, 2010, 154, Table 6.9).

The exception to this pattern was the US, which had entered the war late, fought on other people's soil, and had, even before entering, become the global financier and materiel supplier for the Allied war effort. The country had started out as a net debtor internationally but became, after the war, the world's largest creditor. England had already been declining relatively even before the war. Now its status as world hegemon with Sterling as the world reserve currency was severely hampered, though the US was not yet quite willing or able to take on this mantel.

The World War was also good for Japan, during which its own exports replaced those of its cut-off European competitors while forcing domestic import substitution within Japan to replace lost supplies of European iron, steel and chemicals, both of which built up a new industrial base. Japan used its position as an Allied Power to attack Germany's Jiaozhou lease on Shandong Peninsula in 1914, following this up in 1915 with its "Twenty-One Demands" on China, claiming Jiaozhou for itself and calling for other concessions, many not granted because of Allied counter-pressures. Nonetheless Japan extended many loans to China in 1916–1918, further binding that country to itself. The Allies did not like Japan's expansionism but didn't do much to constrain it since there was a need for Japan naval assistance, especially in the Mediterranean (Best et al., 2004 61). Japan was, however, bitterly disappointed with the 1919 peace, gaining control over Jiaozhou only with a promise to return it to China (which took place in 1922), taking over German Pacific colonies only as League Mandates, and having its call for a clause opposing racial discrimination in the Covenant of the League of Nations vetoed by Australia and the US (Dickinson, 2013, 62–67).

Japan did soften its militarism in the early 1920s and liberalised its political system, introducing universal male suffrage in 1925, allowing

Socialist parties to stand in the 1928 election. The decision to transfer Jiaozhou to Japan, even temporarily, was, however, explosive in China. A nationwide boycott of Japanese goods ensued, dubbed the May Fourth Movement, showing that mass protest and popular mobilisation were strong in China, a precursor of resistance to come (Best et al., 2004, 62–64).

The European Empires remained in place, except for Germany's, but they were in a process of deterioration, though this was not apparent to most at the time. Ironically their imperial subjects had arguably saved the European Allies, at least at the margin. During the First World War British Dominions contributed over 1 million troops to the British war effort, India 800,000 and West Africa 80,000. Huge numbers of Indians and Africans also served in British labour corps. For France 600,000 troops and 200,000 labourers came from French possessions. Of course imperial extraction of raw materials was intensified during the war, as were forced foreign currency earnings. All this was a continuation of peacetime practices by imperial powers, e.g. the Indian Army being used as an imperial police force that could be deployed to defend interests in Southeast Asia and The Middle East, just as it had earlier been used to help shore up Afghanistan (Best et al., 2004, 83–84).

Expectations within the colonies that such loyal subject service might lead to better conditions, or even freedom, were quickly dashed with the Peace. Before the war it was the white colonies in the British Empire that got the most freedom by being granted relatively independent Dominion status. This was not the case in the non-white colonies. They remained governed by their colonial masters with only minor power-sharing concessions to locals, even those that had offered significant sacrifices on behalf of their Empires. India was a most notable example in this regard. Meanwhile, Ho Chi Minh came to Paris in 1919 trying to carry his message asking for American support for independence for Vietnam to Woodrow Wilson, but the letter was never even seen, much less answered. Even if it had been, nothing would have been accomplished. Nonetheless, the Wilsonian language of equality, self-determination and internationalism could not be so easily ignored, nor could the abilities and aspirations of non-white and non-Western peoples around the world (Shimazu, 1998).

The immediate post-war order now also contained two new pariah states: Weimar Germany and the new Soviet Union. Germany was cast out of the Great Power club for good and, for that matter, the arena of civilised nations as far as the victors were concerned, at least temporarily.

The Soviets were more permanently banished from both realms. But there was a strange wrinkle here. The collapse of Tsarism and the removal of Russia from the war had actually made the "democratic" alliance against Germany more pure and unhindered. Wilson could thus make the claim that the War was a "fight for democracy" more plausible and in that sense more ideological, although his British and French Allies remained more immune to this thinking. Lenin's regime was of course explicitly ideological. For both, total defeat of their enemies was the only option. And so a greatly weakened Russia remained completely outside the global political and economic system until the Second World War (Ostrower, 1996).

First World War destruction had seen Europe change from possessing a common culture and thought pre-1914 (at least at the elite level) with which it had dominated the world, literally, to fragmentation and a weakened position that would ultimately remove the area from its former glory and power, ultimately to be replaced by the formerly peripheral countries of America and Russia after a second conflagration worse than the first.

References

Best, A., Hanhimäki, J. M., Maiolo, J. A., & Schulze, K. E. (2004). *International history of the twentieth century and beyond* (2nd ed.). Routledge.

Blum, M., Eloranta, J., & Osinsky, P. (2014). Organization of war economies. In U. Daniel, P. Gatrell, H. J. Janz, J. Keene, A. Kramer, & B. Nasson (Eds.), *1914–1918-online: International encyclopedia of the First World War*. Freie Universität Berlin. https://encyclopedia.1914-1918-online.net/article/organization_of_war_economies

Broadberry, S., & Harrison, M. (Eds.). (2005). *The economics of World War I*. Cambridge University Press.

Dickinson, F. R. (2013). *World War I and the triumph of a new Japan, 1919–1930* (Vol. 39). Cambridge University Press.

Diehl, P. F., & Crescenzi, M. J. (1998). Reconfiguring the arms race-war debate. *Journal of Peace Research, 35*(1), 111–118.

Eloranta, J. (2007). From the great illusion to the great war: Military spending behaviour of the great powers, 1870–1913. *European Review of Economic History, 11*(2), 255–283.

Eloranta, J., & Harrison, M. (2010). Chapter 6: War and disintegration, 1914–1950. In S. Broadberry & K. H. O'Rourke (Eds.), *The Cambridge economic history of modern Europe: Volume 2, 1870 to the present*. Cambridge University Press.

Gray, C. S. (1971). The arms race phenomenon. *World Politics, 24*(1), 39–79.

Hardach, G. (1977). *The First World War, 1914–1918*. Allen Lane.
Hewitson, M. (2014). *Germany and the causes of the First World War*. Bloomsbury Publishing.
Hobsbawm, E. J. (1994). *Age of extremes: The short twentieth century*. Michael Joseph.
Kennedy, P. M. (1989). *The rise and fall of the great powers*. Random House.
Kline, M. (1980). *Mathematics: The loss of certainty*. Oxford University Press.
Lichtheim, G. (1972). *Europe in the twentieth century*. Praeger Publishers.
Morris, I. (2014). *War! What is it good for? Conflict and the progress of civilization from primates to robots*. Farrer, Straus and Giroux.
Olasky, M. N. (1984). Retrospective: Bernays' doctrine of public opinion. *Public Relations Review, 10*(3), 3–12.
Oppelland, T. (2017). Governments, parliaments and parties. In U. Daniel, P. Gatrell, O. Janz, H. Jones, J. Keene, A. Kramer, & B. Nasson (Eds.), *1914–1918-online international encyclopedia of the First World War*. Freie Universität Berlin, Berlin. https://encyclopedia.1914-1918-online.net/article/governments_parliaments_and_parties
Ostrower, G. B. (1996). *The league of nations: From 1919 to 1929*. Avery Publishing Group.
Roberts, J. (2000). Revolution from above and below. In T. C. Blanning (Ed.), *The Oxford history of modern Europe* (pp. 15–45). Oxford University Press.
Shimazu, N. (1998). *Japan, race and equality: The racial equality proposal of 1919*. Routledge.
Spencer, D. S. (1988). A short history of geopolitics. *Journal of Geography, 87*(2), 42–47.
Strachan, H. (2000). Military modernization. In T. C. Blanning (Ed.), *The Oxford history of modern Europe* (pp. 77–100). Oxford University Press.
Tooze, A. (2014). *The deluge: The great war, America, and the remaking of the global order, 1916–1931*. Penguin books.
Watson, T. (2012). A (very brief) history of public relations. *Communication Director* (January), 42–45. European Association of Communication Directors (EACD).
Winn, J. A. (2008). *The poetry of war*. Cambridge University Press.

CHAPTER 16

Global Demographic Change

C. Gordon, *Many Possible Worlds*,
https://doi.org/10.1007/978-981-19-9281-0_16

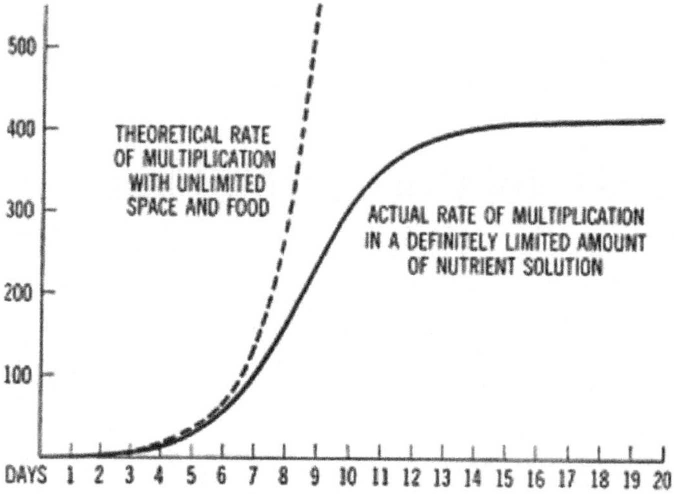

Fig. 28-1. Multiplication of yeast cells: abscissas, time in days; ordinates, number of cells (in millions).

Fig. 16.1 An example of population growth curves—limited and unlimited (*Image source* Marsland, D. [1964]. *Principles of modern biology*. Holt, Rinehart and Winston. Contributing Library: Cornell University Library, Digitizing Sponsor: MSN. No known copyright restrictions)

16.1 Industrialisation and the Modern Demographic Transition

For millennia, the general pattern of world population was one of high-mortality and high fertility, i.e. families with large numbers of offspring (on average) paired with high death rates across the population. This is a gross generalisation, with many exceptions over time and space. But its net effect was to keep global population growth relatively slow, as a relatively high percentage of people born would end up dying prematurely, often in infancy (Fig. 16.1).

Numbers are sketchy, but between 1000 and 1750 C.E., the world population likely tripled, more or less growing at a rate of 1.3% per decade. The Industrial Revolution brought with it a revolution in human demography as well. Over the course of a century or so, the world, led by "Europe" broadly defined to include its offshoots, exhibited a low-mortality, low-fertility population pattern. Average family sizes decreased because of falling birth rates, but death rates fell even more. The result was a population explosion. Between 1750 and 1960, it more than quadrupled, a decadal growth rate of 7.0% (Kuznets, 1966, 35).

Table 16.1 shows population by world regions, in years between 1700 and 1950. The numbers are sorted from smallest to largest total percentage increases between 1700 and 1870, a period encompassing the entirety of the First Industrial Revolution, and the first phase of the Second.

What these data show, taking into account all the usual caveats about limits on data quality, error bounds and so forth, is that the periods of the First and early Second Industrial Revolutions brought high population growth to the industrialising areas, surpassing the traditionally high rates of Asia. Europe and its offshoots grew much faster than the world average between 1700 and 1870, while Asia and Africa generally grew below it. Although non-European parts of the globe always retained a majority share of the total world population, the fast relative growth of the European regions meant that the centre of population gravity shifted towards it in addition to the even more prodigious economic shift taking

Table 16.1 World population estimates by regional totals ('000s), 1700–1950

Year	*1700*	*1820*	*1870*	*1913*	*1950*	*Total % increase 1700–1870*
Africa	61,000	74,208	90,466	124,697	228,342	48.3%
Total Asia	401,800	710,366	765,056	925,932	1,381,859	90.4%
World	603,410	1,041,092	1,270,014	1,791,020	2,524,531	110.5%
Total Western Europe	81,460	132,888	187,532	261,007	305,060	130.2%
Eastern Europe	18,800	36,415	52,182	79,604	87,289	177.6%
Total Latin America	12,050	21,220	39,973	132,187	165,837	231.7%
Former USSR	26,550	54,765	88,672	156,192	180,050	234.0%
Total Western Offshoots	1,750	11,230	46,133	111,401	176,094	2536.2%

Source OECD (2006, Table B-10, p. 241)

place there. The Western Offshoots of the US, Canada, Australia and New Zealand grew explosively, off a low base admittedly, but still impressively, their collective population rocketing up by over 25 times over 170 years.

This striking "demographic transition" accompanying the Industrial Revolution (to use the jargon) has two components: a fall in birth rates and a fall in death rates. Demographers refer to the former as the fertility transition, which more precisely refers to declining fertility (birth) rates per family (Mason, 1997). The latter, which is referred to as the mortality transition, refers to the fact that people started dying less and less from all causes (Jedwab & Vollrath, 2019).

This change did not take place smoothly or immediately. The fertility rate in France began to decline around 1760, and it took until around 1875 until this general pattern took hold in most rich countries. Meanwhile, mortality rates at first fell in many places with industrialisation but then began to rise again before resuming a strong downward trend in the late 1800s (Fernandez-Villaverde, 2001, 6).

An example of this pattern can be seen for Britain, which has been one of the most studied countries given its leading role in the Industrial Revolution and a place with some of the best early data. Figure 16.2 graphs changes in the crude birth rate (number of births per thousand of population) and the crude death rate (number of deaths per thousand of population) for England and Wales between 1751 and 1914.

British reproduction rates increased between the middle of the seventeenth through to the beginning of the nineteenth century before starting to decline afterwards, a pattern exhibited more or less in other European countries, with differences in exact timing. Meanwhile British death rates were more smoothly downward in trend, though with some local spikes, until mid-century when there was a brief step up in mortality, with a renewed spiky decline back to initial levels and then a surpassing of these.

This trend of an overall widening average gap between fertility and mortality rates occurred in most industrialising countries. Falling fertility rates obviously will lower population growth, all other things being equal, while falling mortality rates will raise it. If the gap is large enough, total population will increase, which is what happened to the rich country population during the 1800s and early 1900s.

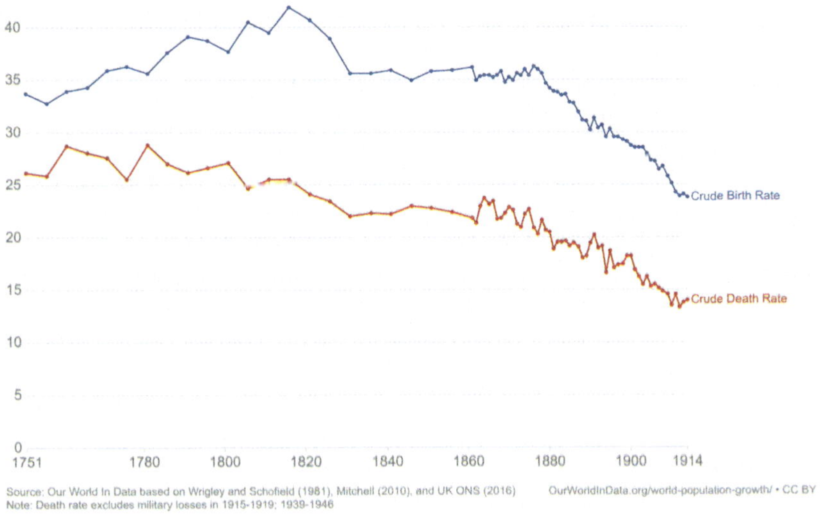

Fig. 16.2 Demographic Transition in England and Wales, 1751–1914 (*Image source* Our World in Data, used under a CC BY license)

16.2 Demographic Forces and Economic Modernisation

A theme of this book thus far is that industrialisation and economic modernisation is determined by a complex set of interrelated causes and effects. These processes were driven by, and in turn drove, the entire range of dimensions in the human and natural environment. Human demography, i.e. the statistical characteristics of human populations (age, gender, etc.) was no exception.

It is easy to see why from a Growth Model perspective. The model simplifies the economy into one big production function which generically can be represented as Y = f (K, L) (see Chapter 2). This economic "machine" converts "inputs" into output (Y). Demography sets the baseline parameters of the quality and quantity of "L" (labour), which in turn affects the productivity and growth of the economy and its ability to produce a given level of output from a given set of inputs. According to the specifications of the Unified Growth Model, all of pre-industrial history was sharply constrained by the size of the population, and this was growing fast, having the effect of keeping the labour force growing (more L by definition increasing GDP) but also increasing the number of mouths to feed as well. Until a way was found to increase labour productivity, most people were kept in a slow-growth economics dynamic and in relative poverty for centuries.

A big reason for these pre-industrial limits had to do with long-standing limits on the levels of technology (the "f" in the equation) and "K", the stock of capital. To vastly oversimplify a model that already is highly simplified, earlier economies could be said to be almost purely demographic in nature, in which the primary motive force behind production and productivity was the human being, augmented by tools, machines and ideas, but not significantly expanded beyond it. Industrialisation broke that tight causality, allowing human labour to produce orders of magnitude more in output than labour input could do on its own. This led to a dramatic increase in the creation and accumulation of surplus output well above what was needed for subsistence, much of which was diverted into increasing the supply of capital (K). In economic terms, K and L are "complementary", which simply means that capital is generally more productive when more labour is available, and vice versa. Capital formation expanded and intensified during the nineteenth and twentieth centuries, and this process helped intensify advances in technology which further increased the supply of capital, increasing labour productivity, and thus surplus output, setting in motion a virtuous circle of rising productivity and per capita GDP where industrialisation took place.

The demographic component of this whole process is remarkable. A whole range of population characteristics that had been relatively invariant for millennia (with some significant cultural and temporal variation) shifted significantly in a matter of mere decades. In the new industrial era, lifespans rose, death rates fell, and population grew, at least in the modernising countries (Galor & Weil, 1999). This larger and longer living population was better nourished and housed which fed back into demography, improving the health of the population, which in turn led to a healthier labour force further increasing labour productivity, independently and on top of technological change and other factors. Overall, Europeans were, on average, living longer, getting healthier (with some temporary setbacks caused by the urban disease pool until the public health revolution set in), and were also getting more training and public education, all of which led to further demographic change, such as later marriage ages and a reduction in family sizes (on average).

At the same time, the world economy was becoming more integrated and flows of people across international boundaries ramped up considerably. This too had further demographic impacts, especially in local areas that were either losing significant numbers of people, with particular skill sets, and those that were gaining them. This heavy migration had further flow-on effects in the economy and society at large.

16.3 Possible Causes of Falling Fertility

As noted in Chapter 4, the more formal study of demographics began with the Classical economist Thomas Malthus. The Malthusian model of population growth is posited as a balance between "positive checks" which reduce population through increased mortality rates, e.g. famine, disease and war; and "preventive checks" which reduce the birth rate, e.g. celibacy and the postponement of marriage.

Malthus was initially pessimistic about reducing fertility rates, which he thought were resistant to downward change because he believed that the underlying "passion between the sexes" would always lead to larger families. In other words, he took the fertility rate as a biological given, an observation that loosely seemed to accord with the early modern society he lived in. He also saw mortality rates as being determined by the biological and natural environment as well, basically unchangeable by human action. This too was plausible for the time he was writing in. Malthus did later revise his views of preventive checks in particular, admitting that mores on family size were changing, though he did not shift on the nature and predominance of positive checks.

Nonetheless, Malthus's reasoning was too simplistic. He did not know that the average fertility rates of his time, of five to seven births per woman, were well below the maximum number of 15 to 16 births possible biologically. This suggests that even less "developed" societies practice some discretion regarding the age at marriage, length of periods of breast-feeding (which suppresses ovulation), sexual abstinence and folk methods of birth control to control the fertility rate (Campbell & Wood, 1988). Malthus's declining pessimism about preventive checks over time does suggest he began to see that human behaviour in this arena was more changeable than he had thought.

On positive checks, though, Malthus ended up being dead wrong, particular about famine and disease (war being another story). In fact, agricultural productivity would take off during the Industrial Revolution, greatly reducing the occurrence of famine in modern and modernising societies (at least on average: poorer population cohorts often did experience starvation, though this tended to be due to lack of access to food, not a paucity of it overall). Meanwhile, he did not anticipate at all the possibility that morbidity and mortality from disease was also going to fall sharply in the century ahead.

Of course, Malthus was not alone in this lack of foresight. Nobody could really forecast the demographic impacts of the dramatic economic and social changes that were being unleashed by industrialisation. Our current theories of the fertility transition obviously have the benefit of hindsight, having the somewhat easier job of explaining why things happened, rather than predicting a very uncertain and dynamic future. Such theories have typically offered as a three-stage model: the first stage consisting of pre-transition societies characterised by high fertility and mortality; a second transitional stage, consisting of societies with declining mortality and, after a lag, declining fertility; and a third and final stage, consisting of post-transitional societies, which lave low-mortality and fertility (Bongaarts & Potter, 2013, 173–176).

However, this triptych is probably too simple because there are many possible causes of the fertility transition, with multiple directions in causality. Declining mortality itself has effects on fertility decisions and these do not always track neatly with economic stages of growth. And many things drive fertility rates, e.g. the reduced role of the family in economic organisation, the growing independence of women from traditional roles, and the shift from customary behaviour to calculative rationality, which can have causes partially independent of economic growth as well as being dependent on it. It has, therefore, long been known that a simple Malthusian model is obviously no longer completely adequate to explain modern conditions. It turns out more subtlety is required in post-Malthusian models as well.

Economists studying demography use the standard neoclassical assumptions of agent rationality and self-interested maximisation to examine how industrialisation shifted the incentives to cause couples to have fewer children. In other words, they apply microeconomics to the problem. Guinnane (2011) makes the general point that, as per economic theory, as income rises, opportunity costs of time rises as well, and time is a major cost of child rearing. Thus, the income growth that came with industrialisation may be the major driver of fertility decline during the period (596). This remains the preferred generic explanation by many economists of the observed link between economic development and fertility rates.

The Unified Growth model offers a parallel incentives-based explanation. Economic growth and technological progress improved the returns to all inputs into production and consumption, "human capital" included. Households now had a greater incentive to "trade off" quantity of children for quality because higher-quality children would have greater economic returns for the family than lower-quality ones. This would result on average in smaller families. "Quality" in this context is strictly economic, referring to the health and education of each child, and returns to each child's earnings over a lifetime. In smaller families, higher-quality children with higher relative rates of return per child were possible, while in larger ones, total returns could be higher (since there were more children in total) but with lower return per child. Parents would trade-off one dimension against the other to come up with the "optimal" number of children at which the family's life-cycle material welfare, net of cost, would be maximised. Industrialisation had increased both health and earnings potential of children so that optimal family size was now lowered. In pre-industrial times, labour in general had low productivity whatever its quality so it made more sense to have many children, especially in a high-mortality environment. This made less sense in industrial times since labour quality did matter much more and mortality rates were lower (Galor & Weil, 1999).

(Fernandez-Villaverde, 2001) suggests a number of more specific drivers of the fertility transition, which could either lower or raise lower fertility rates, but which economic growth generally pushed towards a lowering:

1. *Changes in marriage patterns*. Later dates of and/or lower rates of marriage will lower fertility rates (This, of course, does not consider childbirth out of wedlock);
2. *Labour participation of women*. The more that women work in the formal sector and/or the higher their wages are, the lower fertility rates will be since the opportunity cost of birthing and bringing up a new child is higher.
3. *Urbanisation and the movement from farming to industry*. As families move away from agriculture into factories and cities, informal child labour on farms is no longer possible and this will reduce

fertility rates because the productivity benefit of having a new child is lessened.

4. *Fall in infant mortality.* Assuming parents have a desired family size, if more children are surviving infancy, then fertility rates will fall.

Additional causal possibilities include: innovations in, and more widespread availability of, contraception; changes in the direct cost of childbearing (such as for food and housing) and/or changes in its opportunity costs (mainly increased time-value); increased "net returns" to child quality, which in this context basically refers to the ability to have, and be happy with, fewer but healthier children, independently of and in addition to the trade-offs between quality and returns mentioned above; and reductions in the value of having more children as a way of ensuring against the risk of not being provided for during the parents' old age, because of the rise of state social insurance, private insurance and savings vehicles (Guinnane, 2011, 598).

The evidence for these propositions is variable. Regarding increase in direct costs, these do not appear to have changed enough over the relevant period to produce the observed fertility decline. Food, clothing and housing expenditures, which made up the bulk of household budgets, did not exhibit significant price rises, though obviously they were quite volatile at times. The textile innovations of the Industrial Revolution meanwhile led to more mass production of lower-priced clothing, making that component of household expense lower on average. The biggest increases in direct costs came from urbanisation, which required market purchases of many goods that were formerly home-produced (Guinnane, 2011, 602–603). Murphy (2015) finds that in nineteenth century France, education in general, and female education in particular, seems to be crucial, with other noneconomic factors such as secularisation playing significant supporting roles.

The opportunity costs, child quality and insurance functions that economists ascribe to family size decisions are even murkier as causal effects. Factories made increasing use of child and female labour in its earlier period. From a returns point of view, the new opportunities for putting children to work should theoretically have led to more children being born, not less. By contrast, the employment of women should have led to fewer children being born, since the opportunity cost of women's time was now increased. But child labour began to be discouraged as the century wore on, and mandatory public schooling was becoming a norm. This would have raised the "quality" of children, as well as lowering monetary returns to having them, and may thus have encouraged smaller families. Female labour, meanwhile, was growing in some industries, such as textiles and low-level clerical work, but declining in others, and there was a decisive shift in middle-class values towards the stay-at-home mother that occurred later in the century as well. Additionally, and finally, European governments were bringing in state social insurance, though this was a quite patchy affair. This would have led, *ceteris paribus* ("all other things being equal", as economists say), to smaller families since children were now less needed to care for parents in their old age. There are cross-cutting effects here, but taken together one could probably say that theoretically these trends encouraged lower quantities of children per household, with an emphasis on greater quality (Guinnane, 2011, 603–606). Taken singly, though, none of these individual causes seem to definitively explain the fertility transition, though they are generally consistent with it.

All these factors could be said to represent "endogenous" fertility effects in that they are potentially at least partly driven by changes within the economic system. There is a possibility that some of the historical dynamics in the rich countries of the 1800s included "exogenous" declines in infant and child mortality, which were unexplained and random events. Although there were some negative economic and political events that shook countries during different periods of time and induced lowered fertility, these were temporary and localised. The rich world overall did not experience an "exogenous shock" deep, broad or long enough to explain the observed fertility transition. Demographic shocks do occur, but this period does not seem to fit that mould (see Box 16.1).

Box 16.1 "Exogenous" demographic shocks

Things like war, disease and business cycles often act as exogenous (external) shocks to both the economy and demography of a given country or region. When sufficiently big in scale and scope, the effects can be far-reaching on a population, both at the time they occur but also in how they alter future demographic trajectories. This ties back to the historical concept of "deep roots" in which "historical accidents" can have cumulative impacts over time that are quite significant. This is particularly true for demographic shocks in which future population characteristics are intimately tied up with earlier population characteristics and an event that knocks normal demographic processes significantly off their expected path can alter the course of a population for decades and even centuries to come.

For example, First World War devastation removed millions of working age men from the populations of France, Britain, Russia, Italy, Germany and Austria-Hungary, with profound social and economic effects. For one thing, with fewer men at home during the war, and then a large removal of them due to combat deaths afterwards, meant sharply lower birth rates in these countries for a generation or more. The Great Depression tamped down birth rates further, so that the demographic effect of the war years was further magnified, with significant effects on growth and productivity in the affected countries, and the world.

Second World War destruction was even greater and countries, such as Russia, that suffered very large civilian and military casualties, had similar demographic dampening during the subsequent peace. But in this case, strong post-war prosperity helped drive a worldwide "baby boom" in the post-Second World War years that boosted the size of the labour force for a generation or more, and which is now boosting the retirement cohort in developed countries significantly as this boom group ages out (see Chapter 24).

Of course, causality between economics and demographics runs in both directions and sometimes in unforeseen or poorly understood ways. Growth and productivity between 1945/6 and 1973 was historically unprecedented. How much was the demographic boom a cause of this, and how much was it an effect? There are many such questions in economic history, the fertility transition and the Industrial Revolution being just one of them.

16.4 The Mortality Transition

Then there is the other side of the coin, which is the Mortality Transition, i.e. the movement of societies from high-mortality rates to low-mortality rates. This is also subtle but the causes of death rates are a bit easier to parse out being more single-dimensional than family size choices.

Richard Easterlin (1995) claims that the Industrial Revolution led directly to what he refers to as a "Mortality Revolution", i.e. the profound and sustained falls in the death rate of the population that came with economic growth. Easterlin's logic begins with the observation that rising income and wealth from industrialisation, along with modernisation's improved technology and material progress, combined to bring better nourished and healthier populations that lived longer and died off less rapidly. This would be reflected in a fall in the death rate.

However, this is only part of the story. Easterlin notes that while income and wealth growth was conducive to improving public health and lowering mortality, urbanisation, another facet of industrialisation, worked in the opposite direction: rural areas with less density had lower mortality than the dense urban disease cesspools wrought by the rise of cities which caused greater disease exposure to the people living in them. Again this suggests that public health improvement was at least partially independent of economic improvement.

He proposes the following causal model:

> Economic Growth → higher per capita income → higher disease resistance → higher life expectancy (lowered mortality).

And

> Urbanisation → greater exposure to disease → lower life expectancy (higher mortality).

The problem faced in the Industrial Revolution was how to reverse the offsetting negative public health dynamic of urbanisation to keep it from overcoming the first positive dynamic of greater income. Easterlin focuses on the nature of technology used in the initial round of public health improvements that came about mid-century. The Industrial Revolution was driven by the three inventions of steam power, wrought iron and textile machinery and subsequent diffusion of these throughout the economy. The Mortality Revolution was driven by the germ theory of disease, the understanding that pure food, water and air were essential to limiting disease transmission, and the resulting innovations and investments in public sanitation (e.g. urban sewerage systems and mosquito control). The net outcome was a steady narrowing of rural/urban life expectancy differentials, an overall increase in average life expectancy and a falling mortality rate.

Easterlin argues that the technological changes that were behind public health were simple enough that they can be traced to the sort of thinking and investigation that arose during the Scientific Revolution, namely a set of procedures and attitudes that included reliance on effective proven empirical methods, respect for facts, careful making and recording of observations of differences resulting from trial-and-error comparison, and an ability to draw associations based on all that. This is much more basic than the science of the Second Industrial Revolution which collected and systemised a set of knowledge within a consistent theoretical framework while employing controlled experiments. Public health, Easterlin argues, did not require something so sophisticated to have lasting and significant measurable effect.

Thus Easterlin claims that both the Mortality Revolution and the Industrial Revolution came from a common source: the Scientific Revolution, which birthed a scientific approach to the quest for human knowledge. He argues that this is what really was driving falling mortality, especially since the Mortality Revolution has since spread across less developed and more developed areas alike, suggesting a common cause that works independently of economic development.

Europe did see significant improvement in public health over the course of the nineteenth century. The last major outbreak of bubonic plague in Europe was 1812–1816. In 1871, the Austrian government terminated its plague frontier. New diseases and epidemics driven by urban density replaced some of these older plagues as threats, especially cholera, which arrived in Europe from China in 1831–1832 and delivered devastating outbreaks to the teeming industrial slums of England. But the public health revolution got on top of these outbreaks within a couple of generations. Then technical advances in immunology started an anti-microbial revolution that continues to this day, providing effective vaccines for many of the "sanitary" diseases of modernity and other more ancient ones (Rosen, 2015, Chapter 6). Smallpox vaccination became available in 1796, helping to lower infant mortality, with many German states (though not Prussia) making such vaccination compulsory in the early nineteenth century.

Government provision of social insurance also played a role, research indicating that such schemes were also associated with reduced infant mortality and had some effect on adult mortality as well. The main channel for bringing these effects about were probably through what modern experts would call health promotion, i.e. educating people about good hygiene and health practice brought about through contact with health professionals (Bauernschuster et al., 2018, 4–6). However, insurance and medication advances overall for the most part really only became widespread in the late 1800s.

Overall, industrialisation and the economic growth it brought were good for death rates, but urbanisation was not. Public health improvements did most of the amelioration of the "urban penalty" initially, and this was then augmented by the provision of social insurance and support and pharmaceutical innovations, which played increasingly prominent roles as time went on.

In general, economic historians and demographers have confirmed the powerful role that the mortality transition played in the overall demographic shift that has been so important to economic modernisation. McKeown and Record (1962) have forcefully argued that improvement in economic and social conditions were major contributors to nineteenth century mortality declines in industrialising regions, nominating improved diet as the most important in relative terms. Their conclusions have been confirmed by later scholars such as Floud et al. (2011). Other recent work confirms that role that public health measures played in bringing down the urban penalty (Alsan & Goldin, 2019; Gallardo-Albarrán, 2020) and cast new light on the specific mechanisms at work.

16.5 Migration

Migration refers to the movement of peoples from one place to another. Economist Jeffrey Williamson notes that world migration has been going on for aeons but free mass migration is only of more recent origins, essentially for the past two and a half centuries. Its modern causes have been mainly economic, to improve the migrant's conditions one way or another (Williamson, 2006). This does not include movements of refugees who by definition are escaping from persecution of some sort (Fig. 16.3).

The scale of mass migration during the First and Second Industrial Revolutions is impressive by any measures. Tables 16.2 and 16.3 provide a few such metrics.

At its peak between 1881 and 1910 Europe had a gross migration flow (i.e. total number of people leaving, not accounting for people migrating in) of 8.4 million people per decade, representing a turnover equal to 2.2% of total population each decade. One of the largest recipients of this outflow was the United States. 5.91 million were flowing in on a

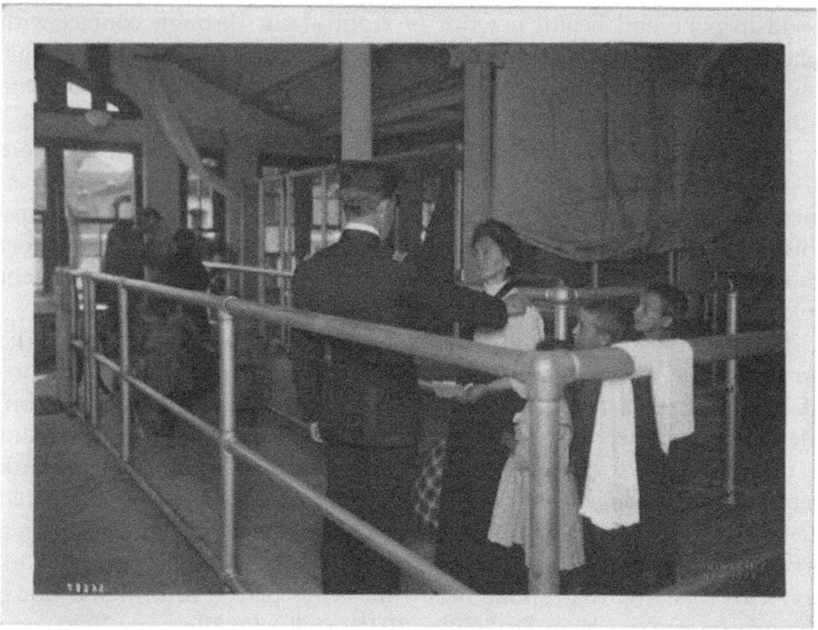

Fig. 16.3 Immigrants undergoing medical examination in Ellis Island New York, circa 1902–1913 (*Image source* Levick, Edwin—Photographer. 1902–1913 Photographs of Ellis Island, 1902–1913. Repository: The New York Public Library. Photography Collection, Miriam and Ira D. Wallach Division of Art, Prints and Photographs. Persistent URL: digitalgallery.nypl.org/nypldigital/id? 416754. No known copyright restrictions)

gross basis during the same period, representing a staggering 8.5% of that country's population each decade.

Although much of the migration flow of the period before 1914 went from Europe to its offshoots, Table 9.3 shows that the phenomenon was global as well, changing the demographic mix of some countries dramatically. By 1910–1911, the United States had a foreign-born population equal to 14.7% of its total population. But Argentina had an even more staggering 29.9% share. Meanwhile, even though many were migrating out of Europe, enough were migrating in to create significant blocs of immigrants within the "Old World". France, for example, had 3% of its

Table 16.2 European migration, 1801–1910

Emigration from Europe—total flow per decade (millions)	*1801–1820*	*1821–1850*	*1851–1880*	*1881–1910*
a. Gross flow	0.12	0.98	2.89	8.49
b. Net flow	0.12	0.90	2.37	5.89
As % of average population				
a. Gross flow	0.1	0.4	1.0	2.2
b. Net flow	0.1	0.4	0.8	1.5
Immigration into the US—total flow per decade (millions)				
a. Gross flow	0.12	0.82	2.57	5.91
b. Net flow	0.12	0.75	2.11	4.10
As % of average population				
a. Gross flow	1.7	5.5	7.2	8.5
b. Net flow	1.7	5.0	5.9	5.9

Source Kuznets (1966, Table 2.4, p. 32)

Table 16.3 Share of foreign-born population (in per cent)

	1870–1871	*1890–1891*	*1910–1911*
Europe			
Germany	0.5	0.9	1.9
France	2.0	3.0	3.0
UK	0.5	0.7	0.9
Denmark	3.0	3.3	3.1
Norway	1.6	2.4	2.3
Sweden	0.3	0.5	0.9
New world			
Australia	46.5	31.8	17.1
New Zealand	63.5	41.5	30.3
Canada	16.5	13.3	22.0
United States	14.4	14.7	14.7
Argentina	12.1	25.5	29.9
Brazil	3.9	2.5	7.3

Source Hatton and Williamson (2005)

total population foreign-born by 1910–1911 and Germany had a 1.9% share, far higher than the UK's 0.9% portion.

With regards to such voluntary migration, scholars have identified push factors—namely people escaping from negative conditions such as poverty and economic instability—and pull factors—namely people moving towards positive things such as better opportunities. Obviously, these two dimensions interact, since a pull towards another place may be magnified if local conditions at home deteriorate.

This mass migration had been preceded by the more forced movement of 11.3 million journeying to the New World before 1820. Of these, 8.7 million were slaves while many others were indentured servants. Europeans leaving for the New World after this averaged around 300,000 per year, more than doubling during the next two decades, and rising to over a million a year after the turn of the century. Important migrations also took place within Europe, such as the Irish migration into Britain, which yielded an Irish-born share of almost 9% in British cities by 1851 (Williamson, 2006). Leonard and Ljungberg (2010) estimate that European urban growth between 1870 and 1914 was driven almost entirely by migrants (118).

16.6 Economic Impacts of Migration

Migration had many important effects on economic growth, not least by contributing to the growth of the labour force. This was particularly important in earlier phases of the Industrial Revolution where factory and agricultural labourer need not be skilled, or even well versed in the local language. There was much demand for labour in many countries, especially cities, which immigration met.

Additionally, much unskilled immigrant labour may have had the additional advantage of being inexpensive relative to local sources. In such cases, there was a redistribution of income from native to foreign-born workers, which would be a net cost to the economy. But lower wages also could contribute to productivity by lowering the price of a key factor of production.

Not all migrants were unskilled moreover. Germans, for example, often had deep reservoirs of knowledge and ability in particular industries and could help certain types of businesses take root in new countries, e.g. brewing in the US. This further aided the countries that received them (Warner, 2010). And local immigrant communities gave particular flavours to their new urban neighbourhoods and sometimes rescued them from urban decline, something very important in Europe, where, as noted, migration helped keep some of the Continental cities growing rather than stagnating. Later on, particularly after 1950, many cities, especially in the US, were revitalised by in-migration from overseas (Ford et al., 2008).

Economists generally see migration as a positive economic force overall, especially as there tends to be a self-selection bias in migrants towards those exhibiting resourcefulness and initiative. The data on the role of migration on the economies of industrialising countries during the Industrial Revolution is, however, mixed. Hatton and Williamson (1998) find no net impact on the US economy of the late nineteenth century, arguing that immigration mainly lowered wages. Others find positive returns.

Much does seem to depend on local context, as usual. Migration can depress an economy if its timing coincides with a recession or negative business conditions (assuming immigrants compete with locals for jobs which is not always the case as they often they take jobs that locals do not want). The conditions of local labour markets receiving substantial numbers of new migrants are thus very important. If there are significant labour shortages, particularly in specialised skill areas, migration can be a boon to the receiving country. If not, it can be a negative.

16.7 Migration as a Safety Valve for Capitalism

Massey (1988) argues that migration was an important regulator of many national economies, especially during bad times in the business cycle when surplus labour could be released into other countries where there were jobs. He claims that this was a critical factor in the economic modernisation process.

Massey notes that most accounts of the Industrial revolution underplay the role of migration, ignoring its substantial role in the internal equilibration of the European economy, society and polity. Between 1846 and 1924, roughly speaking, 48 million people left Europe, equal in total to a 12% of the European population in 1900. Not all of this was driven by flows out of underdeveloped economies. Britain was one of the largest contributors, despite being an early industrialiser and one of the richest countries of the time (385–386).

This safety valve operated inside and outside of Europe, between countries and also regions within countries. International migration interacted with internal migration, the latter often falling when internal movement from rural to urban areas was occurring within a nation (389). Economic development destabilised European societies because it disturbed or overrode the social norms underlying existing stability. Migration provided a buffer for this social problem by letting the disaffected go somewhere else (390–391). Driven at first by economic factors, migration ultimately became increasingly self-propelling, especially as migrant networks bedded down and expanded worldwide. These large permanent overseas ethnic enclaves reduced the economic, social and psychic costs of emigrating (396–397).

Of course, migration created pressures and tensions as well as lessening them, so the story is not quite as simple as Massey suggests. Migration waves displaced local populations in many places and, as noted, could drive down wages of local workers. Large influxes of foreigners could also be seen as threatening by incumbent residents, leading to political and social backlashes. Many countries greatly restricted inflows of immigrants during the nineteenth and early twentieth century as a result. Most notable was the US which had been one of the largest recipients of immigrants in the rich core, but which had long had an active anti-immigrant "Nativist" movement. Anti-immigration forces ultimately succeeded in imposing sharp quotas on immigrants in a series of acts during the early 1900s (Vialet, 1980).

16.8 The Shifting Well-Being of the World

Industrialisation ushered in a period of strong global population growth concentrated in Europe and its white settler colonies. The global demographic result was that between 1800 and 1930 the white proportion of the world's population expanded from 22% to 35%. Vital statistics were also improving for whites, though with an uneven dispersion. By 1870 within Europe, only Scandinavia had a life expectancy close to or above 50. At this time, life expectancy was still not closely correlated with GDP per capita, being driven more by other related factors such as urbanisation rates, changes in labour market structures, uptake and diffusion of sanitary measures and even cultural differences. But rising economic prosperity exerted more and more general influence on mortality rates and by the turn of the century many European countries had reached the Swedish life expectancy average, though the Scandinavians continued to maintain their life expectancy gap over the prevailing European average (Leonard & Ljungberg, 2010, 110, 114–115).

Although a life expectancy of 50 sounds very short by modern standards, it marks a large advance over previous eras. Once more, data are imperfect, but in England life expectancy has been estimated to be 28.5 years in 1681, 36.6 in 1751, 40.8 in 1831 and 41.3 in 1871. One sweeping estimate of average life expectancy throughout recorded history is 25 years until the middle of the 1700s. As late as 1840 life expectancy in high-income countries was still only 41 years (Komlos & Snowdon, 2005, 98). Figures such as these are highly speculative, and certainly there are societies and even communities within societies where longevity was a norm even in ancient times. But life spans were certainly taking a strong secular upward swing starting in the 1800s.

However, as was the case in other social and economic dimensions, the non-white, non-European generally did not share in this bounty. Table 16.4 provides estimates for comparative life expectancy in India and England for selected years between 1363 and 1913. These imperfect data show that there was little difference between the two countries in medieval times, but a gap had opened up by the early modern period that only increased with industrialisation.

Economists have sought to track and measure biological metrics as complements to measures of well-being, mainly physical stature and weight. The idea here is that these physiological characteristics relatively reliably capture poor health, nutrition, living conditions and economic opportunities. Height is especially closely related to nutritional status until adulthood, which in turn is a function of the supply of food, disposable family income and food's relative price (Komlos & Snowdon, 2005, 102–104).

The economic study of biological markers has led to a new field called anthropometric history that examines patterns in human body size and

Table 16.4 Historical life-expectancy estimates for India and the UK, 1363–1913

Year	*India*	*UK*	*Ratio India/UK (%)*
1363	24.0	24.3	99
1543	24.0	33.7	71
1738	24.0	34.6	69
1813	24.0	40.8	59
1913	24.8	53.4	46

Source Extracted from Komlos and Snowdon (2005, p. 99)

its various correlates over time. Fogel (1999) systematised this research agenda by positing a synergism he refers to "technophysical evolution". The idea, put simply, is that human control over the environment is now so great that the species can influence not just its external environment, but also its actual body size, efficiency and longevity. This is a provocative statement, not a consensus, but is one of many hypotheses that anthropometrics has set about investigating.

The findings of anthropometric history are fairly diverse and contested, and data series are limited. Much of the best height data, which is the most studied metric, comes from military records, where the most detailed and reliable records are kept. These are obviously potentially limited in their applicability to more general populations but they have been supplemented by other sources and modified and adapted through the use of econometric modelling. One clear trend is that heights in European offshoots in the New World were much taller than for Europeans themselves, until there was a convergence between the two in the twentieth century. The reasons for this were lower population density, lower levels of income inequality and greater food resources. Another robust finding is that city dwellers generally were shorter than rural residents, and for similar reasons (Cuff, 2004). Finally, heights were generally shorter for populations in the global "South" that were touched by European imperialism and suffered from lagging economic development.

One has to be careful about generalising from limited and rather speculative figures such as these. But they are illustrative of the fact that the North–South gap that opened up with industrialisation was—and is—more than just economic. Indeed rich countries increasingly arrogated health and biological well-being for themselves.

References

Alsan, M., & Goldin, C. (2019). Watersheds in child mortality: The role of effective water and sewerage infrastructure, 1880–1920. *Journal of Political Economy, 127*(2), 586–638.

Bauernschuster, S., Driva, A., & Hornung, E. (2018). *Bismarck's health insurance and the mortality decline* (IZA Institute of Labor Economics Discussion Papers, No. 11628).

Bongaarts, J., & Potter, R. E. (2013). *Fertility, biology, and behavior: An analysis of the proximate determinants*. Academic Press.

Campbell, K. L., & Wood, J. W. (1988). Fertility in traditional societies. In P. Diggory, M. Potts, & S. Teper (Eds.), *Natural human fertility: Studies in biology, economy and society*. Palgrave Macmillan.

Cuff, T. (2004). Historical anthropometrics. In R. Whaples (Ed.), *EH.Net Encyclopedia*. http://eh.net/encyclopedia/historical-anthropometrics/

Easterlin, R. (1995). Industrial revolution and mortality revolution: Two of a kind? *Journal of Evolutionary Economics, 5*(4), 393–408.

Fernandez-Villaverde, J. (2001). *Was Malthus right? Economic growth and population dynamics*. SSRN Working Paper. https://papers.ssrn.com/sol3/papers.cfm?abstract_id=293800

Floud, R., Fogel, R. W., Harris, B., & Hong, S. C. (2011). *The changing body: Health, nutrition, and human development in the western world since 1700*. Cambridge University Press.

Fogel, R. W. (1999). Catching up with the economy. *American Economic Review, 89*(1), 1–21.

Ford, L., Klevisser, F., & Carli, F. (2008). Ethnic neighborhoods and urban revitalization: Can Europe use the American model? *Geographical Review, 98*(1), 82–102.

Gallardo-Albarrán, D. (2020). Sanitary infrastructures and the decline of mortality in Germany, 1877–1913. *The Economic History Review, 73*(3), 730–757.

Galor, O., & Weil, D. N. (1999). From Malthusian stagnation to modern growth. *American Economic Review, 89*(2), 150–154. Papers and Proceedings of the One Hundred Eleventh Annual Meeting of the American Economic Association.

Guinnane, T. W. (2011). The historical fertility transition: A guide for economists. *Journal of Economic Literature, 49*(3), 589–614.

Hatton, T. J., & Williamson, J. G. (1998). *The age of mass migration: Causes and economic impact*. Oxford University Press.

Hatton, T. J., & Williamson, J. G. (2005). *Global migration and the world economy: Two centuries of policy and performance*. MIT Press.

Jedwab, R., & Vollrath, D. (2019). The urban mortality transition and poor-country urbanization. *American Economic Journal: Macroeconomics, 11*(1), 223–275.

Komlos, J., & Snowdon, B. (2005). Measures of progress and other tall stories: From income to anthropometrics. *World Economics, 6*(2), 87–135.

Kuznets, S. (1966). *Modern economic growth: Rate, structure and spread*. Yale University Press.

Leonard, C., & Ljungberg, J. (2010). Population and living standards, 1870–1914. In S. Broadberry & K. H. O'Rourke (Eds.), *The Cambridge economic history of modern Europe: Volume 2, 1870 to the present* (pp. 108–130). Cambridge University Press.

Mason, K. O. (1997). Explaining fertility transitions. *Demography, 34*(4), 443–454.

Massey, D. (1988). Economic development and international migration in comparative perspective. *Population and Development Review, 14*(3), 383–413.

McKeown, T., & Record, R. G. (1962). Reasons for the decline of mortality in England and Wales during the nineteenth century. *Population Studies, 16*, 94–122.

Murphy, T. E. (2015). Old habits die hard (sometimes). *Journal of Economic Growth, 20*(2), 177–222.

OECD. (2006). Appendix B: World population, GDP and GDP per capita before 1820. In *The world economy: Volume 1: A millennial perspective and Volume 2: Historical statistics*. OECD Publishing. Organisation for Economic Cooperation and Development.

Rosen, G. (2015). *A history of public health* (Rev. Exp. ed.). John Hopkins University Press.

Vialet, J. C. (1980). *A brief history of US immigration policy*. Congressional Research Service, Library of Congress, Report # 80-223 PW.

Warner, A. G. (2010). The evolution of the American brewing industry. *Journal of Business Case Studies, 6*(6), 31–46.

Williamson, J. G. (2006). Global migration. *Finance & Development, 43*(3).

CHAPTER 17

Ideas and Ideologies

C. Gordon, *Many Possible Worlds*,
https://doi.org/10.1007/978-981-19-9281-0_17

Fig. 17.1 HIPO inspecting identity cards when people cross Langebro (bridge) in Copenhagen. Date: Winter 1944–1945 (*Image source* National Museum of Denmark/The Museum of Danish Resistance: erez.natmus.dk/FHMbilleder/Site/index.jsp. No known copyright restrictions)

17.1 A Political Economist Grapples with the Individual in a Mass Age

From the beginning industrialisation was a time of great social change in which society itself was becoming unrecognisable from even the relatively recent past, and the experience of the individual within it radically altered as well. On the one hand, society and economy were becoming integrated as never before, with scientific knowledge and technological progress delivering collective material that was truly astounding. The physical well-being of any given individual was better than ever before, at least on average, and largely in the global "North". Yet the scale of social organisation and human institutions, along with the sheer pace of change, had the potential to bury the individual entirely (Fig. 17.1).

The Political Economists had answered this quandary by offering the solution of competition within free markets, majority voting in electoral democracy, a minimalist state and the granting of maximum formal individual rights. This generic package (specific details varied according to context) was labelled Liberalism, and it purported to protect the individual from public and private oppression through processes, procedures and institutions that would naturally limit excess by both the State (through democracy and personal legal rights) and private actors (through competition) (see Chapter 4).

It was a plausible and appealing idea. But like all ideas, it didn't always work in practice and the devil of making it work was in the ever-changing details. It was easier to assume these difficulties away, which were what analytically minded thinkers like Ricardo essentially did and his successors continued to do; or to have a relatively blind faith in their workings, which is what some politicians did. The great political economist, John Stuart Mill, however, was satisfied with neither of these extremes. He sought to resolve them within the framework of Liberalism, working with the mid-nineteenth century world as he found it rather than as he may have hoped it would be. In particular Mill wrote extensively about the individual right to free expression, tolerance of dissent and the balance between political democracy and free market capitalism, making him one of the few Political Economists to focus as much on the former as the latter.

Mill was grappling with a problem that Political Economy ended up largely dropping, namely the role of the individual in making collective decisions for the collective good, and the balancing of individual rights within a broader society. Liberalism largely assumed that this problem would take care of itself within an electoral process accompanied by a marketplace economy. But Mills did not take this for granted.

In many ways he couldn't, for he wrote in a time of growing mass politics, communications and media. In his various treatises, he observed the role that newspapers especially were playing in political discourse and he did not entirely like what he saw. His main target was the taxes that the English government imposed on newspapers, something he argued inhibited competition within the press and retarded the start-up and distribution of periodicals amongst the masses. It was a view shared by many others and was perfectly consistent with prevailing doctrines of laissez-faire. Most of these levies were thus repealed by the middle of the century.

But Mill's concerns about the role of the press as a proper mediator between governed and government went further than this. Referring to England in 1840 he noted that "hardly anything now depends upon individuals", class instead being the main power bloc in a democratic society. In determining the pulse of public opinion, Mill claimed that the middle class was the rising pivot of the political system and that the press was catering too much to its views. So there was something of a paradox in that public opinion was more important than ever but its expression was being distorted by a press increasingly beholden to the political influence offered by the property and "intelligence" of a particular economic grouping. This group's influence was made even greater in that it tended to ally with the traditional aristocratic class to form what Mill called "bourgeois opinion" (Baum, 2001, 519–520).

Mill made additional institutional arguments that the commercial operations of the press of his day would tend to under-represent the true sentiments of public opinion because their owners were more interested in return on their investment than in exercising their social function. At the same time, newspapers, he said, would pander to popular sentiments to sell papers. Indeed Mill warned that mass politics was already here, and he was not entirely sanguine about it (Baum, 2001, 520).

Mill thus recognised the importance of both socioeconomic class and institutions in the functioning of both the marketplace and the State, and tried to fit this into the constraints of the Liberalism that was emerging during his times. Indeed, this was the critical role that Liberalism assigned to "civil society" (the social space where individuals voluntarily entered into various groupings and associations), yet which most theorists, except for Mill, ignored. In fact, the individual was most strengthened by well-functioning and freely chosen connections with others, and the proper workings of democracy relied on this. It could not be taken for granted, and there were many examples Mill could see of how the Industrial Revolution was interfering with it.

This is why Mill was so adamant about the necessity of free expression of ideas and its importance to a functioning electoral democracy. The popularised thumbnail description of the views that he expressed in his essay *On liberty* (1859) is that there should be a free and unfettered "marketplace of ideas" (not a phrase he used but a later gloss) in which people bring their personal notions to a free forum of exchange, engendering an intellectual competition in which the best idea wins. This political competition, joined with the supposed economic competition of the time, constituted the two main pillars of Liberal Democracy.

This, however, misrepresents Mill's actual thinking. For he recognised the importance of social power and argued that groups with more of it could dominate any such competition. While he strongly believed in representative democracy and supported maximum freedom for individuals to express their opinions, even false ones, he saw the danger of a majority repressing a minority and argued that allowances must be made for such minorities. In this sense, he was not at all comparing political expression to the workings of the economic marketplace (Gordon, 1997, 238–239). His view was much more organic than this. Full freedom of expression was a critical component of ensuring that civil society worked as it was supposed to, hopefully minimising the ability of special interests to manipulate and dominate it.

Thus, Mill was a true economic philosopher, trying to develop and apply systems of ideas to be used in service to the greater good. He was "progressive" in the sense of being committed to the genuine forward movement of society, at least as he saw it. He was also a pragmatist and an idealist at the same time, believing in the worthwhile nature of the material bounty being delivered by the economic and political systems of his time, while also critiquing some of these arrangements, especially with his defence of individual rights, and women's rights in particular (about which he wrote at length in, *The subjection of women* in 1869, using ideas that he developed jointly with his wife Harriet Taylor Mill; see Box 17.1). Mill's thought is thus a good example of the way basic ideas such as freedom and individualism, were being reshaped by the economic change of the Industrial Revolution and how, in turn, these ideas were shaping the policies and political programs.

Box 17.1 Mr Mill and Mrs Taylor

John Stuart Mill went against a number of contemporary sacred cows in his writings, especially his stance on equality for women. But he was also a social rebel of sorts too. All the while he was no radical in either arena, his dissents and protests generally staying within the conventional bounds of his time, if occasionally uncomfortably. This is best exemplified by his relationship and marriage to Harriet Taylor, and the nature of their intellectual collaborations.

Harriet Taylor was initially married to John Taylor, a prosperous junior member of a firm of druggists. The marriage was friendly enough, and Taylor was a reasonably well-behaved and respectful man when it came to his wife. But Mrs Taylor did not find him sexually or romantically attractive and found the imposition of conjugal rights forced on her by the institution of marriage as constituted in England at the time (though not pressed in practice by Mr Taylor) offensive and morally wrong.

In many ways, this situation was quite typical of many English Victorian marriages. What was different was Mrs Taylor's outspokenness about her views, as well as her frank defiance and independence in carrying out a liaison with John Stuart Mill, something that started out as intensely Platonic but which became much closer in due course (though historians still debate as to whether the relationship between Mill and Taylor, before or after their marriage, was ever consummated). John Taylor forbade Harriet from seeing Mill at one point. This merely caused her to take a hiatus to Paris for six months to decide whether to break off the marriage and get together with Mill, stay with Taylor, or go her own way. In the end, she stayed married to Taylor, though they remained separated in an amicable way. At all times, Taylor allowed her to continue her relationship with Mill and continued to support his wife financially, including her turning point journey to Paris.

When Taylor died, bequeathing everything to Harriet, she and Mill were now free to do as they pleased. Somewhat surprisingly, they decided to get married, though only after Harriet went through the traditional two-year mourning period for her dead husband. Both felt that the institution of marriage did not support the partnership of equals that they both wanted, but they were also conventional enough not to stray too far out of bounds. And, in any case, marriage in the Victorian era, though outwardly strict, nonetheless encompassed a very wide array of practices, which in some cases even approximated what might now be called open relationships. In this spirit, Mill wrote a formal document disclaiming all his rights, material, conjugal and otherwise, that getting married would legally confer upon him. He and Harriet would join in matrimony, but on their terms.

Once married, John worked closely with Harriet on all his major works, save, *The system of logic*, published in 1843. He thought her an equal to his own intelligence and gave her equal credit in writing all his other works. She made many suggestions and he took them all, even when they contradicted positions he had taken previously. Most notably, in the second edition of *Principles of Political Economy*, he dropped his opposition to a guaranteed minimum income (which he had felt would discourage incentives to work) because of Harriet's objections to his stance. This was one of many changes he made, always deferring to her advice. Mill outlived his wife by fifteen years, but he always maintained that his work was a collaborative effort with her (This discussion is based on Rose, 1983, 101–141).

The Mill-Taylor union is an example of how Mill took positions in his daily life that flowed out of his philosophy, especially the ideas that nothing is innate, and that there was no inherent superiority to class, race or sex, or anything else in the human world, save, perhaps natural intelligence, which also was distributed to individuals independent of social categories (Fig. 17.2).

Harriet Taylor, c1830

Bust of John Stuart Mill

Fig. 17.2 Harriet Taylor and John Stuart Mill (*Image source* Miniature oil portrait of Harriet Taylor [nee Hardy], 1807–1858. London School of Economics (LSE) Library Persistent URL: http://archives.lse.ac.uk/Record.aspx?src=CalmView.Catalog&id=IMAGELIBRARY/1350. John Stuart Mill [1806–1873]; husband of Harriet Taylor. London School of Economics Library, http://archives.lse.ac.uk/Record.aspx?src=CalmView.Catalog&id=IMAGELIBRARY/1353). No known copyright restrictions

17.2 Industrialisation and Changing Ideas About Economy and Society

Liberalism and Political Economy increasingly fused with Utilitarianism (Chapter 4). Primarily a product of the UK, the philosophy was most fully articulated by Jeremy Bentham. Bentham was a social reformer who thought he had found a rational way to design a society that fully accounted for individual wants, independent of arbitrary tradition, and yet accomplished socially desirable ends. This rather remarkable goal, which the French Revolution had tried to effect on the ground but couldn't, could only achieve intellectual coherence by two daring assumptions, the first the assertion of a highly simplified human psychology, the second the adoption of what philosophers call an instrumental ethical standard. Bentham, influenced by the earlier English philosophers David Hume and Thomas Hobbes, held that humans were ruled by a desire for pleasure and an aversion to pain. Human happiness boiled down to the attainment of both goals. This led to a criteria by which to judge right action: one should do things that promote happiness, or pleasure, and not do things that cause unhappiness, or pain. He then asserted that overall social happiness, which he referred to as "utility", should be the fundamental social goal, to be used in judging public policy and private action. This was summed up by the famous epigram that actions should be taken that promote a maximum amount of overall happiness for as many people as possible—"the greatest good for the greatest number" (Driver, 2014, Section 2.1).

Bentham's ethics were purely instrumental. There was no intrinsic right or wrong in the world, only the positive and negative consequences of actions. Some principles, like liberty, are good, but for Bentham this was not because they should be adhered to regardless, but because they yield the best outcomes, which for him boiled down to the greatest utility. It should be noted that if a time comes when these principles become instrumentally bad, i.e. they reduce total utility, they should be discarded (Driver, 2014, Section 2.1).

Utilitarianism was quite emblematic of the European intellectual atmosphere of the time which was primarily materialistic in its philosophy (which, simply put, is a view that the world is entirely composed of matter), and mechanistic in its outlook. Utilitarianism encompassed a free-floating individual, and indeed based a measure of the social good on it. But this was within an overall framework of a coordinating system that supposedly guaranteed "optimal" social outcomes.

Mill, whose ideas opened this chapter, diverged from this purely atomistic view of individuals, seeing their voluntary civil interconnections as a critical component of obtaining the greater good. Mill was also a philosophical Utilitarian, though with more nuance than Bentham. He supported democracy and competitive markets precisely because he thought they offered the best avenues for people to develop their individual talents and pursue their greatest opportunities to maximise their personal well-being. Yes, "the greatest good for the greatest number" was an objective he supported, like most Utilitarians. But he parted ways with Bentham who rather inconsistently thought that a democratic society required a certain "civilisational" level and degree of education for the citizenry and that an enlightened "instructed minority" was needed to ensure that public debate would proceed along the best possible lines, which included the protection of minority opinions but also the driving out of false views (Baum, 2001, 505–506). Mill agreed that democracy required a certain level of culture to function well, but he did not qualify his full commitment to individualism, and saw any elite manipulations of the masses as problematic.

Bentham also held that there were only quantitative differences between pleasures, not qualitative ones. Mill's hedonism (and indeed Utilitarianism is hedonistic in the sense of elevating human pleasure-seeking, however that may be defined, to primacy) introduced a qualitative hierarchy, intellectual pleasures being higher, better, animal or sensual pleasures, lower. This difference is captured in the famous aphorism that it is better to be Socrates unsatisfied than a pig satisfied. This hierarchy makes Utilitarianism more palatable to many, but it is not philosophically justified by Mill and so more a matter of opinion than logic (Driver, 2014, Section 2.2).

As already noted, Mill did passionately defend various human "rights". On its face, this sounds like a contrast with Bentham and his purely instrumental reckoning of human accounts. But like Bentham, Mill defends rights on an instrumental, not intrinsic, basis. True, his own biases, by privileging "purer" pleasures over "coarse" ones, allows for some defences of things, like gender equality, that were ahead of his time and sound principled and idealistic to modern readers. And Mill himself appeared to be a fair-minded thinker of some personal rectitude. One could even say that he was an idealist temperamentally. But philosophically his moral statements, because they ultimately rest on human psychological states, rest on the same shaky instrumentalist ground that all Utilitarianism does (Driver, 2014, 2.2).

Mill not only thought that people had tastes which were properly subject to refinement according to an external standard or ideal, but he strongly believed in their inherent sociality, that they inherently cared about and had feelings for others, and that social connections yield utility in and of themselves. Thus, if others are harmed by our actions, or even just harmed, this causes pain to us, thus reducing out utility. Bentham did not explicitly reject this possibility but he spoke as if it didn't exist. Mill also believed in natural human mental predilections like conscience and a sense of justice that could motivate people in addition to the pleasure-pain dichotomy. In this respect he echoes Adam Smith's theory of "moral sentiments" (see Chapter 4). This also underlies much of Mill's arguments about women's rights and free speech, and, if granted, reinforces his conclusions about them. Still, the basis for any "right" remains changeable "utility" or "happiness" (Driver, 2014, Section 2.2). Overall, Mill's theory of human psychology was more social as well as more "meritocratic" than Bentham's, while Bentham's pleasure-seeker was more atomistic and egoistic than Mill's.

One could say that Mill's thought is an example of both the possibilities and limits of Liberalism and Political Economy as a coherent and consistent philosophical system. Mill's modifications and amendments to Political Economy in many ways strengthened its inner consistency and its applicability to real world institutional and social issues. Yet the subtleties of his thought were mostly lost as Liberalism became more of a mainstream ideology rather than just an idea-set and some of his notions, such as about freedom of expression, became distorted in translation. Meanwhile the Benthamite version of crude Utilitarianism took hold amongst the British political leaders well before then, especially when dealing with colonial subjects, who had little power on the domestic political scene (Davis, 2002).

17.3 Ideas and Economic Change

This ushers in a core question in economic history regarding the role that human thinking and ideas play in economic change, and vice versa. Most would admit that Industrialisation was both a product of changing ideas and an impetus for intellectual change as well. The tradition of empiricism that came out of the Scientific Revolution laid part of the foundation underlying the rise of innovation, industry and science. The individualism that the Protestant Reformation and the French Revolution, respectively, encouraged and then idealised was enshrined in Liberalism and Democracy, along with the concept of human "rights" and "natural law" Rationalism, which was a product of French philosophy during the Enlightenment, was almost literally deified during the French Revolutionary interregnum, bringing about a radical secularism to French society that was partially rolled back after the Revolution but which became deeply embedded within French culture and influential beyond it.

There is no general consensus on how systems of thought might have enough power to effect or alter economic change. Norbert Elias (see especially Chapter 5) maintains that all aspects of the individual human psyche, including ideas, are constantly co-evolving along with the social structure, and thus all social change, including in the economy, is determined by both material and immaterial factors. Thus, individual human "psychogenesis" (the process of systematic and ongoing evolution of the human psyche) and "sociogenesis" (a similar and parallel process of change in the social structure) are intimately and constantly co-evolving in a homeostatic process.

Others, economists in particular, have focused on the power of specific intellectual movements as critical drivers of economic modernisation, though mediated through relatively simple self-interested, rational individuals who are influenced by external incentives. O'Brien (2013), for example, claims that the Scientific Revolution itself was driven in part by shifts in Western worldviews that the Protestant Reformation caused, helping lead to the sorts of abstraction and attempts to manipulate the physical world that turbocharged technical change. This tinkering then transformed the material world in ways that radically reshaped the incentives and constraints that agents faced, leading to the Industrial Revolution. Mokyr (2016) makes parallel points about the rise of "useful knowledge" in the West and its role in the European Industrial Revolution (see also page 135). For Elias, Mokyr, O'Brien, and many others examining ideas and economic change, changes in thinking have to work through channels of some sort to have a real effect in the actual, rather than just imagined, world. O'Brien's and Mokyr's channel is technical change, Elias's social interdependence. In this sense, ideas have economic effect only indirectly, through changes in human actions and choices and the channels through which ideas act on these.

The causality of ideas and real-world changes is often debated. To take one seminal example, Max Weber's theory that the Protestant Reformation and its "work ethic" were the critical ideational change that set off the process of Industrial Revolution was intended to explicitly contrast against Marx's theory that all ideas and beliefs are products of economic structures rather than by-products. Marx would maintain that it was the economic system of the time, in this case commercial capitalism, which generated Protestantism, and not the other way around. Some of Weber's fellow non-Marxist sociologists made somewhat similar claims. Mannheim, for example, claimed that "life conditions" produced ideologies and behind these were group interests of various sorts (Sargent, 2017).

One may ask how are ideas, once formed, diffused across a society? This is important because if ideas are not transmitted far and wide enough, or are spread in ways that fail to motivate people in critical masses, then they will count for little in material terms (putting aside the Marxist determinism discussed above). And the channels themselves can have significant effects on both the shape of ideas and those receiving them. Religious ideas are diffused through churches and religious education in the first instance, and their motivating element has traditionally been some posited supernatural effect, such as a reward or punishment in the afterlife. When the Church was dominant in Western society such supernatural models reigned supreme, though, as O'Brien noted, they nonetheless contained seeds useful for later scientific thought.

Scientific ideas, meanwhile, are diffused in various ways, and the method of diffusion has changed over time, going from less formal communications and sharing across individual inventors in limited social networks, to more formal coordination through government, universities and scientific institutes. As one gets into more contemporary eras, mass social and institutional mechanisms designed to shape public opinion, tastes and thinking take centre stage, especially for popular ideas, e.g. the film industry, newspapers and so forth. Historically, the channels of diffusion and impact are not neutral with respect to the ideas themselves. Distortion, intentional and unintentional, conscious and unconscious, creeps in, the effects accumulating over time. As an example, this was the core of Mill's concerns about newspaper ownership during his own times.

17.4 Changing Conceptions of the Self in Society

A critical debate during the Industrial Revolution was the nature and role of the individual in the economy and the society. At one extreme was Karl Marx and his system of thought as spelled out in various works, most notably his master work, *Das Kapital*, unfinished at his death (Marx, 1965).

Marx was a thoroughgoing philosophical materialist, like all Classical Economists, seeing economic dynamics as purely physical. He also conflated economics and society into one, also not unlike his economist peers. But whereas they posited an autonomous, if methodologically somewhat robotic, individual at the heart of society, Marx claimed that the individual, and all the broader social context in which they moved (beliefs, ideas, institutions, government, culture, etc.) were part of a "superstructure" determined by the underlying economic "substructure", i.e. the ownership of the means of production.

Marxian economics is considered in more detail in Chapters 23 and 25. The salient point here is that Marx did not believe in individualism in even a theoretical sense. Individual consciousness was a product of social forces and the individual simply changed along with the society. Marx borrowed Hegel's theory of history as a series of progressions between opposing forces that yield new "syntheses" as time moves forward (though there are some who claim that it was Marx's collaborator, Friedrich Engels who was mainly responsible for the introduction of Hegelianism in the first place). Marx claimed that the ultimate end of history was a Stateless, classless society emerging necessarily through Hegelian historical process, out of the class struggle engendered by capitalist development. Revolutionary change, where working classes would overthrow capitalist classes, was inevitable and necessary to ensure the final stage of Socialism (common ownership of the means of production) (Barber, 1970, Chapter 5).

This was obviously in sharp contrast to the Utilitarian and Liberal notion of an independent individual whose existence sat apart from society, although in relation to it. However, Marx, Bentham and the Political Economists actually all agreed on the Enlightenment era notion that the human being was "perfectible" along rational, logical lines. The difference in starting premises yielded drastically different means of how this should be achieved. For Liberals and Utilitarians, the default solution was a competition between individuals in markets and in democracy, although as already shown, the optimality of these processes could not be taken for granted, with Mill and Bentham diagnosing the various ways that problems might arise and how they might be addressed. The Marxists did not have this issue since for them the individual was completely a product of social forces. For them the society would be perfected and perfect individuals would naturally result as a by-product. This "solution" didn't really work either, since the obvious question was who would perfect the society. Marx had avoided the issue by assuming that an "inevitable" historical process would do the job. History falsified this notion completely, leaving the problem to Marx's successors, most notably Lenin and Stalin.

Either way there was thought to be a progressive order from lower to higher that human destiny followed. Nineteenth century natural sciences, especially biology, mirrored this notion of hierarchy and progress, but they too threw the autonomy and true nature of the individual into question, Darwin being the seminal figure here. Darwin was heavily influenced by Malthus's writings leading him to examine the survival or extinction of a species as part of an evolutionary change dynamic. Darwin's basic work was highly empirical, based on extensive fieldwork done on arduous fact-finding journeys (see Fig. 17.3) and made theoretically systematic, though with a number of ambiguities that still arise when considering his work today. Marx respected Darwin and his approach so much so that he dedicated the first volume of *Das Kapital* to him (Paul, 2003).

Darwin's main conclusion was that all species were mutable—they can and do change over time—and that this change takes place over long periods of time through natural selection, i.e. the retaining of characteristics that are useful for survival in a given environment, and the losing of characteristics that are not useful. Across generations those with the non-useful characteristics will die out, supplanted by those with the useful ones. The idea of evolution was not new, but Darwin's extensive observational research to demonstrate its existence in nature was novel, although because the changes take place so slowly they actually cannot be directly observed but only inferred from interpretation of a long chain of historical evidence.

Darwin's framework seemed to fundamentally, and scientifically, establish evolution as a powerful metaphor with which to view the rest of modern society and its rapid disruptive change. "Darwinism" refers to the many ways in which this metaphor has been applied, some of which can be in contradiction to Darwin's own thoughts (Paul, 2003). Darwin's *On the Origin of the Species* (1859) did not look at human

Fig. 17.3 Charles Darwin's voyage on the Beagle temporarily waylaid in 1834 (*Note* During one of Darwin's South American journeys, the captain of the Beagle, the ship Darwin was traveling on, decided to inspect Beagle's keel, and so landed at Santa Cruz on16th April 1834 to do so. Some damage was found and expertly repaired and they were off again within a matter of hours. *Image source* Darwin, C., & Darwin, F. [1896]. *The life and letters of Charles Darwin: including an autobiographical chapter*. D. Appleton. Plate inserted between pages 160 and 161. Contributing Library: Harold B. Lee Library. Digitising Sponsor: Brigham Young University). No known copyright restrictions

beings specifically, focusing only on physical characteristics of nonhuman species. Nonetheless, the book caused an absolute uproar since it flew against both traditional religion and Enlightenment humanism that put the human being at the centre of the natural order. Sapiens was just one of innumerable species, mutable like all the rest of them.

Darwin's later book, *The Descent of Man* (1871), did however focus on humans and applied and expanded his theory of natural selection to them much more broadly, expanding his purview to spiritual and moral traits as well as physical ones. This second work is impossible to boil down into a few salient points and has many subtleties and makes many claims, some of which, such as the position that women's subordinate position in society is the product of natural selection, are rejected today. The basic rejection of human "exceptionalism" with respect to the rest of the biological order is in both works, and the elaborations of the second work help lay the foundation for a doctrine that became Social Darwinism. The term refers to the application of Darwinian natural selection, sometimes very crudely, to the development of human society. English philosopher Herbert Spencer actually worked out his own theory of human social evolution before Darwin and, in fact, Darwin borrowed Spencer's phrase "survival of the fittest" for his own work (Rogers, 1972).

The basic idea behind Social Darwinism is that "better" humans (more capable and intelligent) will slowly become dominant over "lesser" humans (less capable and intelligent) through a process of competitive natural selection. Spencer, like Darwin, was influenced by Malthus' ideas and felt that government should keep out of the way of the evolutionary process to ensure the best outcomes were achieved. Many carried this idea further arguing that "natural selection" should be encouraged through formal and informal human breeding programs, and eugenics, the supposed science of determining racial categories and ordering them according to their "natural" abilities, was born in this time, to fully blossom (if that is the right word) in the first half of the twentieth century. In its more apocalyptic forms a deterioration of the "quality" of the human race might well lead to the extinction of the entire species as it lost its ability to be the "fittest" (Paul, 2003; Rogers, 1972).

What is interesting about all this is the fundamental misinterpretation of Darwin's work, arguably even by Darwin himself when he broadened his purview to human affairs. Putting aside the fact that Darwin rejected the idea of human "race" as a category, the evolutionary process is not, in fact, teleological in any sense. Adaptation does allow for survival of one species given certain conditions, as opposed to those who do not make the requisite changes. But there is no direction to this process, no fulfilment of a destiny, or even an increasing "optimisation", but simply a movement across one set of conditions to another. Moreover, there is the real possibility of multiple suitable adaptations at one time, rather than complete extinction of all but the "best". So the notion of a "natural" linear progression in human society in which the "best" rise to the top, is a definite gloss, indicative of the tenor of the times in which "progress" was a widely held belief.

Marxism and Darwinism both put the individual in a subsidiary position with respect to a greater whole, economic superstructure for the former, species for the latter. Liberalism's rejection of Marxist sociology is understandable and intellectually defensible since it is matter of disagreement over fundamental premises, which are always debatable. The failure to fully incorporate the possible implications of Darwinism is a bit more inexplicable. After all only the survival of the species matters there and individual actions have little effect on that, except collectively.

Obviously, there was a strong element of people seeing things the way they wanted them to be, and justifying that, as opposed to an analysis of the way things really are. Social Darwinism can be seen as a way of grafting together the system logic of natural selection with the political-economic doctrine of Liberalism. Thus, competition in free markets and individual preferences exercised through representative democracy could be said to be winnowing out the inefficient and the regressive in favour of the efficient and the progressive. If this is admitted, it is a short leap to say that some sort of Darwinian process is therefore operating on human society to weed out the "inferior" human being from the "superior" one. This causal chain is not entirely felicitous and is somewhat self-contradictory since evolution is about groups not individuals. But it fit well the prejudices and discoveries of the time.

For all these doctrines, individual psychology is not modelled or considered in any substantial way, either being irrelevant, as in Marxism; an outgrowth of larger adaptive processes whose individual manifestations need not be bothered with, as in Darwinism; or vastly oversimplified and homogenised, as in Liberalism and Political Economy. The subjective life of the individual is just not that important to any of these theories, regardless of how important it might be to the individual self.

That forces within the human personality could shape human behaviour and choice is not itself a new notion. Indeed, ancient Greek tragedy contained many characters with fatal flaws coming to meet unfortunate ends because of them and many of Shakespeare's finest plays can be considered as human character studies. But the idea of studying these forces rationally and scientifically was a modern idea that flowered with the rise of rationalism and science. Mesmerism in France, just prior to the French Revolution, is one of the more notable attempts to understand, codify and manipulate the human unconscious to shape and improve human conduct and well-being. Medical doctors then became more directly involved with this effort, and with much more purely physiological models, as the 1800s progressed. The culmination of this lineage came with Sigmund Freud, a neurologist by training (hence the term "neurosis"), who invented the field of depth psychology (though not psychology in the broader sense of the systematic study of human mental processes) essentially single-handedly, though it would be reinvented by his various successors (Tallis, 2001).

Freud is very much a product of his time and place, especially with his essentially patriarchal ideas, his late Victorian prudishness and his Central European pessimism about human nature. The mechanism underlying his ideas paralleled the highly elaborated Newtonian mechanics of his era with its energetic balances, most notably the Laws of Thermodynamics positing the conservation of energy within any physical system, i.e. that no energy that was inside a system could be lost or gained (though it could be transformed) unless it was added or subtracted from the outside. Freud extended this model to the Psyche, stating that is was a system whose energy had to go somewhere, and if it was not allowed its proper channels, it would find improper ones, all of which would be below mental awareness. The purpose of Freudian analysis was to re-channel this energy by raising unconscious dynamics to consciousness and finding proper and socially acceptable and functional sublimations for instinctual drives (Zaretsky, 2015, 15–37).

Depth psychology, as it became known, could go in a number of directions philosophically. To many at the time, it suggested the possibility of a total analysis of an overall system in which both the whole and its individual members could be thoroughly dissected, and resulting actions predicted. In practical terms, there was the possibility that technical experts could find ways of "adjusting" people to the social and economic systems they found themselves part of and coming up with a set of "average" profiles that in turn would serve as a basis for adjusting the system further (Zaretsky, 2015). This was the way that the Freudian model would be used during much of the twentieth century, in domains ranging from consumer marketing to the management of public opinion.

In a way Freudianism offered a bridge between the social determinism of Marxism, the species determinism of Darwinism, and the individualism of Liberalism. However, it also held that human behaviour was at least partially unconscious and irrational in nature. This did not sit in accordance with Liberalism or the Political Economy of the time, or even its Marxist Offshoots. Further, the Freudian template fractured the psyche into component parts, suggesting that personality was a fragmented affair. All of this could potentially lead to problems philosophically and practically. How could a system necessarily be stable and yet forward moving if irrational forces drove individuals? The answer to this question depended at least partly upon how amenable the psyche was to rational analysis and how predictably responsive it was to external prods and stimuli. This would lead to techniques to shape and mould the individual psyche for both personal and individual ends, not all of them benign.

17.5 Ideas Versus Ideologies

In the quest for social and individual perfectibility, it was perhaps inevitable that many of the ideas discussed thus far crossed over a line into versions of "ideologies". The word "ideology" first was coined by French philosopher A.-L.-C. Destutt de Tracy during the French Revolution to mean a "science of ideas" keeping in the spirit of the official Revolutionary rationalism. This was not just an intellectual pursuit but a mission to rid people of their prejudice and make them genuinely rationalist; which is to say governed completely by a faculty that supposedly gave them the capacity to be truly free individuals. Destutt de Tracy and his adherents designed a system of national education and state planning that was official doctrine of the French Republic during the Directory (1795–1799). The roots of the term indicate that ideology's main features were established early on in modernity, namely a system of thought offering a comprehensive theory of the human and external world that is combined with a generalised and abstract social and political program for change. Often this is joined with a political and social struggle led by a cadre of committed and well-indoctrinated ideologues. Ideologies are thus much more than mere ideas or even a system of explanatory and descriptive thought, because they are intimately tied to a program of social action seen as superior to the status quo and thus demanding implementation. In the extreme they offer arguments that cannot be refuted, and which adherents are not allowed to disagree with (Cranston, 2020).

Some idea systems amenable to becoming ideologies aren't necessarily ideological in and of themselves, as for example with Darwinism, which, apart from Social Darwinism, remains a reputable and testable model of biological adaptation. Marx's thought obviously lent itself to ideological interpretation, and with its hyphenate Leninism, Marxism become an official ideology for the Soviet Union. But Marxian economics itself is no more (and no less) ideological than Ricardian economics, for example. Both offer models of the economy based on simplifying assumptions that are debatable, but nonetheless yielding hypotheses with testable predictions of cause and effect.

Ideologies are sometimes compared to religions in that both contain "total" thought systems concerned with questions of truth and of conduct, while also (potentially) demanding loyalty while condemning apostasy. However, ideology always claims a basis in reason and material reality alone as opposed to religion which evokes faith and revelation and, of course, a belief in the spiritual. Arguably, however, both the Reformation and the Counter-Reformation invested Christianity with a new militancy, a new intolerance and a new emphasis on creeds and conversion that had distinct ideological aspects (Cranston, 2020).

Some note that ideologies can be likened to culture, or at least a truncated version of it in the form of a cult. Swidler (1986), however, refutes this by saying that although ideology offers highly organised meaning systems, as cultures do, culture is not unified and, in fact, genuine culture contains diverse and divergent symbols, rituals, and principles informing action, while a cult does not (277–278).

These boundary issues cannot be totally settled. The French Revolution certainly established a model of both practice and theory for ideology. Rationalism itself, which encompasses a diverse set of ideas about the power of unaided human reason, was lifted up to a matter of faith during the period, elevated, in fact, about the other human senses, including what was seen with the eyes and heard with the ears or felt with the heart. As an ideology, or quasi-ideology, Rationalism became almost a caricature, with the true believer recanting a reality that was straight in front of them and everyone else, in favour of an argued-for but chimerical, and sometimes fantastical, alternative conceived in the mind. The willingness to commit atrocities on behalf of the greater good called for by the ideology, in the form of the Terror during the French Revolution, was another distinguishing feature to be developed further and repeated many times later on.

Although the categories of political right and left were born with the French Revolution, in fact these positions were tellingly divorced from more traditional social and political divides, such as monarchy versus republic, or church versus State, with such issues moved into a strategic and tactical arena of determining how best to reach a promised utopia. Utopianism is thus another feature of ideology, though these two can also be distinct projects. Karl Mannheim spoke of utopia as a desired but plausible vision for a society's future that could provide meaning and inspiration in the present. For him, utopianism was a vital animating part of human consciousness, something that made the human being more than a creature acting on a set of impulses.

But this good characteristic can be made maladaptive if one loses sight of the present and lives, unconsciously, in an imaginary future. To oversimplify, utopia is a vision from which one is properly and rationally detached, whereas ideology is a vision from which one is not (Sargent, 2017, 32–34). In this sense most things could practised ideologically and the growth of abstract theory in the seventeenth century, with its tendency to construct systems and principles, caused the emergence of an ideological style which exploded in 1789 and then expanded from there.

Not all utopias are grandiose or mythological. Liberalism offered a very bourgeois and rather practical nirvana of prosperity, proper manners and neutral and efficient outcomes that may even support a sort of survival of the fittest. Its implicit utopianism derived from the fact that it did not really accord with many facts on the ground even during its own time, a gap that increased as the technical nature and scale of industrialisation grew. Technological prowess arguably enhanced the trend towards a concrete ideology based on a Scientism that did deliver definite material results, though not the promise of a unified understanding of, and power over, all aspects of human existence. The mechanistic models of science suggested definite (if complex) causes and effects, which, when finally discerned, would be subject to manipulation and command by human expertise. The possibility that human social phenomena might not operate in the same way as purely physical things, did not really occur to most thinkers of the time, though there were influential philosophers, like Henri Bergson with his "vitalism", who suggested that life in general went far beyond its apparent mechanics. But these views remained sidelines to the materialist mainstream of "Progress" (Greco, 2005).

A consequence of the industrial era scientific paradigm writ large and applied to everything is that there are "right" and "wrong" answers, and "objective" data, and facts, totally separated from opinions and perceptions. Interpretations of facts might vary, as could explanations, but ultimately the "correct" answer would emerge from falsification and/or verification based on empirical investigation over time. This form of "scientific" attitude could enhance an intolerance on political and social issues that was not unlike differences between those of contrasting faiths. Scientific method and systematic observation was also often abused and misdirected to serve political agendas, as was the case with eugenics.

Thus, philosophers like Michael Oakeshott saw ideology as a form of Rationalism. But this was not a consensus view. Edward Shils claimed that ideology was a form of Romanticism, being a chase after a deeply felt ideal combined with a scorn for the actual. In fact both characteristics can hold, especially since humans contend with both their heads and their hearts. A worst-case potential outcome is one of Rationalist systematisation, applied with industrialised scale and merged with an unhinged emotionalism that leads to an efficient and brutal primitivism (Cranston, 2020). Some would argue that this is the essence of Nazism in Hitler's Germany or Stalinism in Russia.

17.6 Violence and Ideology

And thus once more the topic of modernity and violence arises (see Chapter 14). Taking for granted that ideology is a product of modernisation, did it also necessarily engender violence? The French Revolution witnessed perhaps the first occurrence of ideologised violence in the form of the Terror and Terrorism itself is sometimes more than just a tactic but a social worldview.

The rise of the "masses" is a key causal component here. Even during the terrible age of the Religious Wars and the savage religious intolerance they bred, nonetheless there were distinctions made then between believers and nonbelievers. And, at least notionally, one could be spared by converting to the dominant side—though Jewish and Muslim converts tended to be perennially distrusted, e.g. the Spanish Muslims who had taken on the Catholic faith under the "Reconquered" Iberian Peninsula in the 1500s and 1600s. With the rise of mass politics and mass war, this notional refuge was no longer possible.

With the advent of Second World War maelstroms, entire peoples could be regarded as an "enemy" and thus a target for violence, even elimination. Kershaw (2005) claims that the fusion of popular sovereignty with nationalist ideology, colonial imperialism and the revolutionary version of socialism in nineteenth century Europe caused a generalised and accepted use of violence in the service of ideology. Imperialism used violence as a regular instrument of policy, justifying this with a doctrine of racial superiority, buttressed by Social Darwinism and eugenic pseudoscience. The French Revolution notions of "Liberte, Fraternite, Egalite" both turbocharged mass nationalism and required an artificial division of global peoples into those who had the "truth" and those who needed to be converted—or conquered—into it. Pre-Enlightenment discrimination could be justified on the basis of tradition or some sort of received wisdom, but this was no longer possible under a new rationalism carried under a national banner. Meanwhile, the Marxist versions of Socialism were inherently revolutionary in outlook, and thus violent in method, which those in power used as an excuse to use violence as a matter of course in response to challenges, whether there was actual cause to do so or not (Kershaw, 2005, 111–112). These dynamics intensified after the First World War.

The grim apotheosis of this process is the Nazi state, with many less extreme, though still very noxious, versions arising in other places and at other times. The Nazi case rested on multiple decades of refinement in the technical planning, method and control so vital to industrial society. Planners in state and party offices, academics in universities, data-collectors and processors, doctors and medical specialists, industrial armaments and chemical product manufacturers—all these and more were needed to devise and run the technocratic enterprise of a world turned upside down, a true anti-utopia (Kershaw, 2005, 118–119). Nazism is an extreme, to be sure. But it is a product of trends that had deeply penetrated society up to that point.

And ideology was a critical starting point for it. Bauman (2000) interprets the Holocaust as a ghastly attempt at social engineering intended to bring the actual social order around to conformity with a design of the "perfect" society. Which implies that such a thing is actually feasible, a sort of insanity of its own (Rattansi, 2017). The modern belief in the saving and secular grace of technology is the root of such thinking and it becomes especially dangerous when elevated (or perhaps one should say brought down) to the level of ideology.

17.7 An Evolutionary Strategy?

Although secular, there are those that claim that ideology, or at least a common framework of thinking, is critical to any highly elaborated large-scale society. This sort of thinking is reflected in Harari's (2014) proposition that the human race went through a "cognitive revolution" in its semi-distant past which allowed people to develop social links beyond kin and village relations, based on identification with an abstract idea or symbol, such as a national flag or religious icon.

To put it another way, human bonds rely on trust in one another, and trust is difficult to develop and maintain with strangers. This is what some people argue is the main function for religion after a certain point in human history, generally considered to be the Axial Age in which the major monotheistic religions were born (see Chapter 11). These were the first truly "universalistic" dogmas that introduced a divide between the deity and the human being, possibly setting the stage for the ultimate rise of both science and ideology. They also, according to some, set the stage for a new adaptation that allowed human beings to trust members of much larger groupings than ever before (Bahçekapili et al., 2019).

Thus, it is possible that the modern age is, at least from an adaptation point of view, one that relies more on secular rather than "sacred" religion. Gorski (2019) refers to the use of the term "civil religion". By itself, this is not modern. Rousseau is said to have originated the term and the Romans exercised a form of it in the mandatory civic rituals of the Empire that otherwise permitted a great deal of personal freedom in religious practice, even in occupied territories such as Jerusalem where the Jewish religious and civil hierarchy and worship modes were allowed to continue so long as the Roman deities, especially the Emperor, were made sacrifice to as well. But these demands were still purely ritual, exercises performed as efficacious in themselves and not explicitly requiring any inward creed or outward confession. Hence, the "civil" aspect of the Roman religion consisted of a ceremonial obligation that helped socially bind together a diverse Empire while allowing for a multiplicity of local practices; or at least was intended to, since the "fully" religious subject peoples, such as the Christians and the Jews, found such rituals problematic and refused to abide by them, leading to their various and periodic persecutions by Roman authorities. Until, that is, the Christians themselves became dominant, in which case the target of persecution shifted from the Christians to the "pagans" and, perennially, the Jews (Carcopino, 2003).

Roman practices were, in fact, seen as a model by Machiavelli who believed that Christianity and Republicanism were incompatible but also that a Republic could not survive without some sort of religion. Hence, something like the civic cult of the Roman Empire was needed for the modern republic. Rousseau agreed with this idea and sketched out a dogma that was rather similar to Deism and which spelled out broad virtues that would uphold the social contract upon which civil society depended. He also spelled out some useful proscriptions, such as a ban on "intolerance."

Older faith-based religions and secular ideologies are distinct from civil religion. In a secular, industrial age, the former is no longer plausible to enough people, and the latter is too clearly artificial to be acceptable in a political democracy or even many mass-based autocracies. But people have to believe in something, and a society is bound together in part by shared beliefs. This is what a civil religion can offer, as it did for the Romans. The experience of the past two centuries is in some ways a story of struggle involving all three, still being worked out.

17.8 The Void of Meaning

All of this discussion is primarily functionalist in nature. In that sense, it is very much in keeping with the materialism of the modern age which sees everything in terms of cause and effect in a physical world, where purpose is boiled down to outcomes, anything without one attached to it deemed irrelevant and superfluous.

In this schema, the immaterial is an illusion, maybe useful or maybe not, but which has no real independent existence of its own. Meaning is generally put in that category. The Classical economists did not really address meaning, Adam Smith's "moral sentiments" notwithstanding. Marx was explicitly deterministic about the material basis of everything, meaning included, while his rival Political Economists were generally agnostic about it, seeing it as a potential source of subjective pain or pleasure, but still with extrinsic value only.

The sociological tradition did not give it much quarter either. Weber wrote extensively on the topic but for him there were no transcendent prior values within the universe itself. Human beings needed meaning in the world, but they made it for themselves. Weber saw this as a fundamentally irrational and thus impenetrable process, but no less necessary to address for all that (Kim, 2020). The depth psychologists, who plumbed its function within the psyche, mostly joined him in, while looking at meaning from a psychological perspective instead. Viktor Frankl, a survivor of the Nazi death camps, built a whole school of therapy around the human quest for meaning, naming it "Logotherapy" after "Logos", the "Word", in the Old and New Testaments. A sense of meaning was so vital that for many in the camps, including him, it could mean the difference between surviving and perishing (Frankl, [1959] 2006). But even here meaning mainly had a functional not a transcendent basis. Amongst the major psychologists only Carl Jung gave the immaterial an independent existence in a transpersonal spiritual realm (Jung, [1959] 1969).

For a time, the mere march of technological and economic change seemed meaning enough all by itself, especially with a background assumption that it represented a climb to some sort of pinnacle. Darwinian natural selection seemed to confirm that indeed it was just this, though as already mentioned the conclusion actually comes from outside the theory itself. With religion in decline, ideology sometimes filled the vacuum of the nagging feeling that something was missing. Whether it was Socialist paradise or a techno-utopia, there were still compelling things to believe in.

The problem was—and is—that materialism will only get you so far. Eventually, things never quite work out as planned, leading to a crisis that might end in despair. This was what happened in the European world in the aftermath of the First World War. Worse, things might work out as predicted. All your material needs might be met and exceeded, all the technical problems solved. But then what? A materialist worldview has nothing else to offer and knowing that you yourself are making up a story to fill the void doesn't work if you know it's just a story. Thus the existentialists of the mid-twentieth century tried to answer this conundrum by celebrating life's futility as a sort of titanic quest in which survival itself created a reason for carrying on.

But this merely kicked the can down the road, so to speak. Eventually, everyone cries out: what is it all about? Economic development alone does not quiet or ultimately comfort this cry. Ideas, ideologies, beliefs and faiths all arise in part to get this comfort, this closure. And the mystery of existence remains.

References

Bahçekapili, H. G., Yilmaz, O., & Sevi, B. (2019). *Evolutionary perspectives on religion*. Unpublished Working Paper.

Barber, W. J. (1970). *A history of economic thought*. Penguin Books.

Bauman, Z. (2000). *Modernity and the holocaust*. Cornell University Press.

Baum, B. (2001). Freedom, power and public opinion: J. S. Mill on the public sphere. *History of Political Thought, 22*(3) (Autumn), 501–524.

Carcopino, J. (2003). *Daily life in ancient Rome: The people and the city at the height of the empire*. Yale University Press.

Cranston, M. (2020). Ideology. In *Encyclopaedia Britannica*. https://www.britannica.com/topic/ideology-society. Accessed November 4, 2020.
Davis, M. (2002). *Late Victorian holocausts: El Niño famines and the making of the third world*. Verso Books.
Driver, J. (2014). The history of utilitarianism. In E. N. Zalta (Ed.), *The Stanford encyclopedia of philosophy* (Winter 2014 Edition). https://plato.stanford.edu/archives/win2014/entries/utilitarianism-history/
Frankl, V. ([1959] 2006). *Man's search for meaning*. Beacon Press.
Gordon, J. (1997). John Stuart Mill and the "marketplace of ideas." *Social Theory and Practice, 23*(2), 235–249.
Gorski, P. (2019). *American covenant: A history of civil religion from the puritans to the present*. Princeton University Press.
Greco, M. (2005). On the vitality of vitalism. *Theory, Culture & Society, 22*(1), 15–27.
Harari, Y. N. (2014). *Sapiens: A brief history of humankind*. Random House.
Jung, C. G. ([1959] 1969). *The archetypes and the collective unconscious* (Collected Works, Vol. 9, Part 1). Princeton University Press.
Kershaw, I. (2005). War and political violence in twentieth-century Europe. *Contemporary European History, 14*(1), 107–123.
Kim, S. H. (2020). Max Weber. In E. N. Zalta (Ed.), *The Stanford encyclopedia of philosophy* (Winter 2020 Edition). https://plato.stanford.edu/archives/win2020/entries/weber/
Marx, K. ([1867, 1885, 1894] 1965). *Das Kapital: A critique of political economy* (F. Engels & S. L. Levitsky, Trans.). H. Regnery.
Mokyr, J. (2016). *A culture of growth: The origins of the modern economy*. Princeton University Press.
O'Brien, P. (2013). Historical foundations for a global perspective on the emergence of a western European regime for the discovery, development, and diffusion of useful and reliable knowledge. *Journal of Global History, 8*(1), 1–24.
Paul, D. B. (2003). Darwin, social Darwinism and eugenics. In J. Hodge & G. Radick (Eds.), *The Cambridge companion to Darwin* (pp. 214–239). Cambridge University Press.
Rattansi, A. (2017). *Bauman and contemporary sociology: A critical analysis*. Manchester University Press.
Rogers, J. A. (1972). Darwinism and social Darwinism. *Journal of the History of Ideas, 33*(2), 265–280.
Rose, P. (1983). *Parallel lives: Five Victorian marriages*. Penguin Books.
Sargent, L. T. (2017). Ideology and utopia: Karl Mannheim and Paul Ricoeur. In Z. Czigányik (Ed.), *Utopian horizons: Ideology, politics, literature* (pp. 19–39). Central European University Press.

Swidler, A. (1986). Culture in action: Symbols and strategies. *American Sociological Review, 51*(2), 273–286.
Tallis, F. (2001). *Hidden minds: A history of the unconscious.* Arcade.
Zaretsky, E. (2015). *Political Freud: A history*. Columbia University Press.

CHAPTER 18

"1929"

C. Gordon, *Many Possible Worlds*,
https://doi.org/10.1007/978-981-19-9281-0_18

Fig. 18.1 Christmas poor relief appeal tent. Sydney, Australia, December 1938 (*Image source* acms.sl.nsw.gov.au/item/itemDetailPaged.aspx?itemID=24071. From the collection of the State Library of New South Wales www.sl.nsw.gov.au. Sam Hood, photographer. No known copyright restrictions)

18.1 "The Economic Consequences of the Peace"

A young economist working at the UK Treasury on war finance ended up attending the 1919 Peace Conference in Versailles. His name was John Maynard Keynes and he was appalled at the terms of the treaty he saw being drawn up. He felt that the reparations the Germans were being made to pay were a bad idea, or at least were set at too high a level; that all Allied war debts should be forgiven; and that provision should be made to plan and coordinate for Europe's post-war economy. His outrage was high enough that he resigned from his position before the treaty was signed, although his poor health was a contributing factor as well (Strachan, 2003, 333).

Keynes elaborated on his ideas in a book titled, *The economic consequences of the peace* (1919). It ended up being a bestseller, though it had little practical impact on either the final Treaty or its implementation. His argument that the peace was too harsh to be economically viable resonated with many, especially in Germany, where both leaders and the masses felt the Versailles settlement unfair. The book infuriated others, especially the French, who had wanted to impose even harsher terms on the Germans.

The merits of Keynes's arguments were debated then and still are even today. What is certain is that his book's popularity reflected the genuine fact that no one, victor or vanquished, was satisfied with the post-war order, and for often diametrically opposed reasons. The Great Depression a mere decade later seemed to validate Keynes's critique (Fig. 18.1).

18.2 Remaking a Problematic Europe

It also was indicative of the fact that the prior world economic order had been gravely wounded by the War and that a return to the status quo *ex ante* was not an option. The vast devastation of the war itself created acute immediate problems (see Chapter 15). But the intermediate political and economic outlook was not much better, being gravely uncertain at best.

No peace treaty can ever be without flaws, and only hindsight is 20–20. But Versailles arguably did not really attempt to deal with post-1919 economics. And the political settlement verged on incoherent. The cessation of hostilities in a worldwide conflict did not, unlike in 1815, result in any sort of stable order afterwards. French wartime commander, Marshal Ferdinand Foch, is apocryphally quoted as saying of the settlement that it was not peace, but an armistice for 20 years. Apparently he didn't actually say this, but the quote pithily captures the state of affairs after the war.

The problem was deeper than a lack of consensus on terms. While Keynes had argued that economically the Treaty was too harsh, others focused more on the military and political aspects and found it to be too lenient. The lessons of 1815 were that if the vanquished had been central to European affairs before the conflict, that centrality had to be preserved for the good of the order, though with suitable chastening and modification. But the Napoleonic Wars, as destructive as they were, could not hold a candle to the human, material, social and economic toll of the First World War. Passions on both sides ran high and no one was in a particular mood for forgiveness, or even enlightened self-interest. The winning alliance itself was riven with disagreements, with imperfectly aligned interests to say the least, while the losing side, Germany especially, seethed with resentment. These factors alone made any kind of sensible peace settlement difficult to achieve.

There were other issues as well. Napoleon had been the personal enemy whose damage the 1815 settlement sought to repair. His elimination, even though it took two tries, enabled a defeated France shorn of him to be seen as country of strategic importance, to be dealt with relatively impartially. In 1919, Germany was seen as an impersonal threat, regardless of its current leader or system. The country had been rocketing to power so rapidly during the last decades before the War (it had only been fully unified in 1871) that the removal of the Kaiser and the monarchical system were not seen as sufficient to tamp down its power to disrupt and destroy. In effect it was the Germans that were demonised, rather than the leaders who had started the war. Though the Allies did not agree exactly on how much Germany should be punished, all agreed that it should be. Yet the vision of what came after that was lacking. Whatever one's opinion was, a post-war Germany remained too critical to the European economy and polity to be totally sidelined. Even a weakened Germany would have significant latent power, a situation that could neither be denied nor, as it turned out, adequately dealt with.

Then there was the problem of what a new European system should look like. The Balance of Power concept and the Concert of Europe had been discredited. The European ascendancy it had delivered in the nineteenth century had not lasted, and forces within the system blew it apart. Yet Versailles essentially carried on the Balance of Power concept (though dropping the "Concert of Europe" part), attempting to impose it on a radically altered landscape. Germany and Russia had been eliminated from the balance, leaving only a greatly diminished France and Britain, two powers that were competitors as much as allies. In short, an old order had been literally blown to pieces, as it had been after Napoleon. But nobody agreed on what should take its place, and no one was willing to enforce the imperfect replacement that was established.

Even from a prosaic territorial point of view, Europe's boundaries remained unsettled into the mid-1920s, with the victorious powers punting on a few critical issues, and rapidly changing facts on the ground doing the rest. Figure 18.2 shows a contemporary 1922 map of what had been the war's eastern front. This was the front where the greatest post-war adjustments were made, with Austria-Hungary broken into two new small nations and the remaining territories of its Empire parcelled out to a number of new, equally small buffer states. These were supposedly drawn along principles of local "self-determination", but their populations had been so mixed in many places that this was impossible in practice. Meanwhile, the Ottoman Empire had disappeared, its old Balkan territories merged into the new unsteady amalgam of Jugo-slavia (later known as Yugoslavia).

Fig. 18.2 Adjustments to Europe's east in 1922 (*Authors note* "Jugo-slavia" was ultimately renamed as "Yugoslavia". *Image source* Unstead, J. F. [1922]. *Europe of to-day 1922*. Moffat, Yard and Company, p. 129. Contributing Library: The Library of Congress; Digitising Sponsor: The Library of Congress. No known copyright restrictions)

Even three years after war's end, many eastern boundaries were still uncertain, as the map indicates. Turkey and Greece had just concluded their own war after the Great Powers, with Greek connivance, had tried to reduce Turkey to a rump state, a fate reversed by Kemal Ataturk's decisive rallying of his people, almost single-handedly, into a new secular Turkish state (Travlos, 2020, 2–5). Russia and Poland were still at war, the latter to emerge from the brink of defeat to emerge considerably larger than this contemporary map indicates. The Russians themselves had undergone a civil war in the interim and their own state and territory was in the process of consolidation. The Baltic states of Lithuania, Latvia and Estonia had gained their independence along with Poland. Ukraine was very briefly free after Russia had signed the Brest-Litovsk peace treaty with Imperial Germany in 1918. But the fall of the German Kaiser nullified this agreement and Ukraine was rather quickly incorporated into a new Soviet Union and a resurgent Poland (Gatrell, 2006).

Western Europe was not as radically altered territorially, the main change being Germany's return to France of the Alsace-Lorraine region it had taken in 1870 Franco-Prussian war. The Allies put off the issue of how much to weaken and constrain the German economy by having the Rhineland occupied by Allied troops for fifteen years and the Saar Valley temporarily detached, its final status to be decided by a plebiscite in a decade's time. These were stopgap arrangements used to paper over significant disagreements between Britain and France over the future of Germany and a vain hope that adequate resolution could be found in a hopefully better future. Figure 18.3 shows a 1922 map of the overall German settlement.

The longer-term economic repercussions of this European reordering, above and beyond the pure destruction of the War, were manifold. For one thing, all the new national boundaries broke up larger and previously integrated economic areas. The collapse of Austria-Hungary, for example, turned a large free trade bloc into the fragments of the now small nations of Austria and Hungary, while moving the Empire's remainder to the entirely new nations of Czechoslovakia and Yugoslavia. The creation of these new nations lengthened Europe's tariff barriers by close to 20,000 km (Graff et al., 2013, 169).

Meanwhile, the new states themselves were not always economically or politically viable. The new Austria was left to support the expensive city of Vienna, which had previously been the capital of a much larger nation. Austria-Hungary had been an ethnic melting pot with an Empire. But

Fig. 18.3 Provisional German boundaries in 1922 (*Image Source* Schapiro, J. S., & Shotwell, J. T. [1922]. *Modern and contemporary European history [1815–1921]*. Houghton Mifflin company, p. 852. Contributing Library: The Library of Congress. Digitising Sponsor: Sloan Foundation. No known copyright restrictions)

there had been no genuine fusion of nationalities. Its break-up resulted in only semi-coherent mini-states that could not as effectively contain ethnic divisions (Lichtheim, 1972, 154).

Uncertainty like this was bound to be economically dampening and while things did settle down by the mid-1920s, it seemed unlikely to stay settled for long because there was no long-term coalition in place to keep it settled. The most problematic issue was post-war Germany. Unlike France in 1815, which had its original national borders only mildly adjusted and was re-integrated decisively into the new Balance of Power, Germany was treated as a pariah state, without taking the necessary arrangements to weaken it enough to keep it that way. This proved to be a denial of strategic reality that would prove fatally costly. But perhaps it could not be otherwise given the power vacuum that had opened up and also the war-weariness of Britain and France in particular (Lichtheim, 1972, 148–150). As mentioned already, the Napoleonic Wars had been ghastly but the Great War defied all description. Its moniker as the "War to end all wars" proved false but at the time it expressed a hope that its dreadfulness would be impossible to repeat simply because of revulsion.

Interestingly, although all the European dynasties had collapsed, only Russia's changeover was truly revolutionary, arising from an alliance between the peasant soldiers turned militant through desperation with the more sophisticated urban groups, both forged into the new movement Bolshevism by the great opportunistic cunning and force of will of Vladimir Lenin. This situation contrasted with that in the other fallen Empires, now non-monarchical (though not necessarily democratic) and which in most places peasants remained a conservative domestic political bulwark to be reckoned with. Russia was made a pariah along with Germany, but even more so. Thus, two of the struts of pre-war European political order had been turned into loose cannons at best, with the Soviet Union having no hope of ever being invited back in at all.

18.3 An "Interwar" Order

Prior to 1914, the world order was decisively European, and British centred. European Empires controlled much of the world and much of the global financial system was dominated by London, with a Gold Standard using the Pound Sterling as its reserve currency. After 1919 things appeared to have picked up where they left off, inside and outside of Europe. For one thing, the French and British Empires remained formally intact, and the Gold Standard resumed. Britain even restored the value of the Pound to its value in gold set before the war, a policy technically referred to as "pre-war parity".

But the colonies of the extinct German Empire were parcelled out to the victors in the form of League of Nations "mandates". Japan was grudgingly given its share of these but generally the Western powers did not consider this non-white nation to be an equal in any shape or form. China had briefly become a Republic in 1911 and was now in turmoil as it sought to find its future, a vacuum into which Japan strode. Japan had been a fast rising Asian power before 1914 and was rising even faster now, this time against the background of a considerably weakened Europe and China.

The great world powers now also definitively included the US, a country that had also been rising before 1914 and whose upward trajectory was vastly accelerated by the war. The Great Power system had been upended, but there were still Great Power politics, and America was now its leader. Versailles had put post-war Europe under the management of the US, Britain and France, a complex enough proposition as it was, given the untested nature of American global stewardship and the denuded power of the fractious Anglo-French duopoly. But the US soon rejected the pact after having designed it, because of its domestic population's reticence about taking responsibility for world affairs. The UK and France, meanwhile, perpetually quarrelled over terms and conditions. Italy, although weak, was nonetheless a critical junior partner in keeping Germany's potential ambitions in the Mediterranean and Balkans in check. That country's fall to Fascism in 1923 removed a further supporting plank in the coalition that was supposed to enforce the agreement (Lichtheim, 1972, 148–149).

In hindsight 1919–1939 is thus called the "Interwar period" and it is an apt title beyond its literalness of denoting an interval between two major wars, because it suggests a transition period between one order and another that happened to require two massive military conflagrations to sort out. It should also be noted that the two dates given here are applicable to Western Europe, not to eastern European countries like Czechoslovakia, which had been partitioned by the Germans in 1938, or to China, which had hostilities with Japan beginning in 1932, or even to Spain, which had gone through a Civil War in 1936–1939. For them, the Second World War came early and the Interwar period was ended earlier. On the other side are countries like Turkey and Russia where the First World War did not end with Versailles, and the period started later. In any case, the failure to bed down a stable working post-war order, weakened old pathways without providing strong new alternatives, resulting in collapse.

18.4 Interwar Global Finance

The Interwar global financial system was no less transitional or dysfunctional. The reinstated Gold Standard was only a shadow of its former self. World finance, once centred in London, now had to share the stage with New York, since America had gone almost overnight from being an international debtor to an international creditor. The US also was now an industrial and economic powerhouse, not yet totally dominant, but still a force to be reckoned with and whose trends and developments now reverberated throughout the world, for better and for worse. However, the US did not have the inclination to take full responsibility for its latent role, while England no longer had the capacity to take up its pre-war hegemonic function. Turbulence and instability were the results.

Two issues that dominated the international credit markets were war debts and German reparations. Both involve long convoluted stories whose details are well recounted elsewhere (see Marks, 1978). The constant thread through both was that nobody could truly afford to meet their obligations and yet nobody did anything to fundamentally deal with this basic fact. Both reparations and debt were in the end constantly rolled over through ongoing re-negotiations and refinancing, driven by periodic crisis (Webb, 1988, 746).

Much of the American war debt taken on by the British and France had been offered through US banks, and both the American government and the banks saw its repayment as a commercial, rather than a political proposition. The US was thus not flexible on adjusting terms or even forgiving some portion of the obligation, something the other Allies did not particularly understand since it was felt on their side that they had all sacrificed for a common cause (Blum et al., 1970, 883).

The need to pay back the large debt overhang, on top of the substantial expense of wartime reconstruction, made the collection of German reparations inordinately important to Britain and France. The German capacity to pay reparations at the time is a debatable historical point. Germany did not make things easier on itself with an extensive non-reparation domestic debt run up in the late 1920s and early 1930s. By 1929, Germany had borrowed 12 to 15 billion marks abroad in gold value, rising to around 25 billion in 1931 (Webb, 1988, 757). Regardless of German capacity, the German political will to make sacrifices for reparations was lacking all along. So the Americans expected their Allies to pay back their debt, and the Allies expected the Germans to help them do it, and the Germans were never on board in the first place. This was a financial charade that was bound to fail and did completely with the onset of the Depression.

The interwar Gold Standard was another problem for the smooth functioning of the international economy. Even in its "classical" heyday before the war, and despite pretensions behind it being "self-regulating," the Gold Standard had always required a tremendous amount of back-room coordination and trust between participating governments and domestic central banks to avert the payments crises that loomed regularly and to keep capital, and gold especially, flowing to the places where it was most needed. Both trust and coordination was now in short supply, and so too was the generalised economic growth and prosperity that had characterised the two Industrial Revolutions (Cooper, 1992).

This was compounded by poor policy choices, especially by the British who took it as a matter of pride that the value of the Pound should be set at the same amount of gold that it had been before 1914, the so-called pre-war parity. The British economy paid dearly for this decision. England still relied heavily on exports to earn its national income and would have benefited from a weak pound in foreign exchange terms (which would make its exports cheaper to overseas buyers). It now caged itself in with a strong Pound and adherence to a Gold Standard that limited the country's ability to increase its domestic money supply to help reflate economic activity. The result was that the unemployment rate in Britain never fell below 10% throughout the 1920s. France did the opposite, resetting the gold value of the Franc too low, helping its domestic economy but distorting global trade flows. Since the Gold Standard fixed exchange rates, these distortions were set in place for the duration, unable to freely adjust for greater efficiency or to respond to the unexpected, of which there was much during this time (Eichengreen & Flandreau, 1997).

Overall, the Interwar Gold Standard was a set of "golden fetters", to use Eichengreen's (1996) phrase, that hampered a nation's economy to adjust its money supply and interest rates to meet changing local and international conditions. When these conditions took a dramatic secular turn for the worse in the 1930s, these restraints made a very bad situation that much worse. Even before then, the system's rigidities, combined with the shadow dance of reparations and war debt, made for a dysfunctional world financial order.

18.5 American Prosperity and the Roots of the Great Depression

Economists have used the rather clumsy term "path-dependence" (Puffert, 2008) to refer to the idea that in history once a process gets rolling it can move along a historically determined path to accumulate into big outcomes. The crisis of the 1930s is filled with such dependencies, as the prior sections have discussed. A spark that definitively marked the beginning of the tortured path came in the US with the Stock Market Crash of 1929. And while it is too much to blame America or the Crash for the Great Depression, there are unique aspects of the US economy in the 1920s that helped propagate the crisis of the 1930s, the Crash setting off a train of events that cratered that country's financial system and, soon after that, the world's.

On the surface, the 1920s was an era of prosperity in the US. There was strongly rising economic output per person on average, a growing labour force with a generally falling unemployment rate, and rising industrial output and productivity. However, the boom was distributed unevenly across the country, favouring cities over rural areas, and manufacturing over agriculture. Agriculture effectively suffered from a recession much of the decade due to low farm prices and soil erosion in some areas.

Also although the US was rich and powerful, it was in some ways still a developing country institutionally, socially and economically. This was especially true of its financial sector, which was dynamic, freewheeling and inherently unstable. At first, this appeared benign. The US had brought in a wave of innovations in domestic financial products and consumer marketing during the 1920s. Charles E. Mitchell ("Sunshine Charley"), president of National City Bank in the 1920s, introduced the practice of mass marketing of securities through branch offices, salespeople, and advertising. He also brought these offices out into the field, far from the money centres of New York (Klein, 2001, 54–58).

Meanwhile, although the practice of buying on instalment over time had been around since the late nineteenth century it had not been widespread. By 1927 in the US, it has been estimated that more than 75% of automobiles were purchased this way, more than 70% of furniture, 75% of radios, 90% of pianos, 80% of phonographs and about 80% of household appliances. American consumer credit, which prior to the First World War was limited to a few banks and lending societies, pawnbrokers and some merchants selling items on instalment, became in the 1920s a whole new industry with a new financial institution, the sales finance company, which came to dominate American consumer credit. From less than a hundred such firms in 1920, there were more than a thousand by 1928. One of the largest was the General Motors Assistance Corporation (GMAC), a special type of lender that was being created by large manufacturers to finance purchases of their products by their customers, technically referred to as vendor finance (Klein, 2001, 111–112).

Another financial innovation came in the market for corporate shares (stocks in American parlance). The whole idea of share ownership by individual retail investors, and the sale of shares directly to those investors by corporations, was novel prior to the 1920s. Around 1900 only about half a million people owned shares. (If individuals owned any securities they generally owned bonds.) By 1928, 15 million out of a population of 122 million owned shares (Klein, 2001, 125–126).

This rising demand was mirrored by the rising number of share offerings by companies on financial exchanges. As late as 1924 only 9% of new security issues took the form of common shares, most other listings being bonds. But in 1928, this proportion rose to 22% as a growing public appetite for shares was being fed with new issues. Investment companies, existing since the 1890s to aid monopoly and oligopoly company finance, exploded in number, this time not to fund real investment but mainly to create new entities to issue shares and reap financial profits from trading them between related entities. 40 investment trusts had come into existence by 1921, with another 139 created between 1921 and 1926, and another 140 established in 1927 alone (Klein, 2001, 129).

To paraphrase Galbraith (1972), the investment trusts did not create new enterprises. They just created new intermediaries that allowed people to buy into old ones, using ever more available easy credit to do so in the form of margin buying of shares. Whereas earlier innovations in corporate form were driven by the seeking out of operational efficiencies or increases in market share, these new financial trusts were driven by pure financial gain on the part of their issuers, creating more securities to sell to investors who would then sell them on to others at hopefully ever higher prices. Investment trusts were one way to do this. Reorganisation of corporations into holding companies, which then issued their own shares based on the shares of the held companies, was another way to accomplish the goal. Mergers between companies also allowed for quick and easy insider profits, as did "pyramiding", which referred to the creation of new spin-off securities that had little new value behind them other than new legal existence of issuing entities that could issue new shares. While very profitable in the short run, the link between underlying real assets and their financial claim certificates grew ever thinner and more tenuous (Rutterford, 2009). This process of "financialisation" (see Chapter 29) blossomed in 1920s America and would become a growing feature of modern capital enterprise after the Depression ended.

To all this must be added the rise of what would now be called a "shadow banking" system, i.e. the creation of credit outside of the banking system which the US Federal Reserve (America's central bank, colloquially referred to as the "Fed") oversaw. Just as consumers were buying products on credit, so too were investors. Brokerages were now becoming major lenders to share buyers through "call loans" that allowed investors to buy shares on "margin", i.e. pay only a portion of the share price, as low as 10%, with the broker buying and holding the rest as collateral. This form of credit was entirely outside of the Fed's control and it exploded as the decade closed. It also worked well only when share prices were continually going up (Bierman, 1999).

18.6 The Great Crash

One major result of this was an American share market boom. The Dow Jones Industrial Average (DJIA) was the most prominent American index of the time because it covered the performance of the shares of the largest 30 industrial companies in the US. The DJIA hit its peak of 381 on 3 September 1929 and had risen almost three-fold over the decade.

The Great Crash of 1929 doused this fire. On October 24 (Black Thursday), share prices dropped almost 20% before being supported by buying from a pool of bankers. Although the market closed with only a small loss that day (down 6 points to 299), trading was nearly 12.9 million shares, about triple the normal volume. Panic took over and on the following Monday the DJIA fell 38 points to 260, then the biggest one-day drop ever. The next day (Black Tuesday), it slid another 30 points. By November 13, the Dow was at 198. At its bottom, it would drop to about 10% of its pre-crash value (Galbraith, 1972). Note that the DJIA did not recover its September 1929 high of 381 until November of 1954.

Share trading volumes changed even more dramatically, going up proportionally more than share prices fell because of all the panic buying that ensued, with a corresponding inability to actually complete trades in many cases because the numerous sellers could often find no buyers for their shares. On Black Tuesday, October 29, 16 million shares were traded—a record—and thirty billion dollars of equity value vanished into thin air (Galbraith, 1972).

Groucho Marx said that all he lost was two hundred and forty thousand dollars, quipping that he would have lost more but ran out of money. Although a highly paid film star, with a salary of $2,000 a week (roughly $31,000 in 2021 dollars), he nonetheless figured he had lost the income of 120 weeks of work. His fellow Marx Brother, Harpo, told of how he liquidated every asset he owned except his harp and croquet set, joking that his market holdings after the Crash "were probably worth a medium-sized bag of jelly beans" (Klein, 2001, 231). If privileged people like film stars could be so badly affected, things were much worse for the ordinary American.

18.7 Full-Blown Financial and Economic Crisis in America

But this was only the beginning of the crisis. The sharp fall in the US stock market quickly rippled out to cause sharp declines in real asset values, such as houses and factories. The Crash ushered in a full-blown financial crisis in the US banking sector creating negative loops between the real and financial economy. As businesses failed, borrowers could no longer pay back their loans, and assets held by banks as collateral fell in value, with banks failing as a result, wiping out shareholder deposits, leading to sharp cutbacks in new lending and the calling in of existing loans, putting further pressure on businesses that needed new credit or had existing loans outstanding. Many of these businesses would fail, further squeezing banks and causing more bank failures, in a vicious downward cycle.

An image indelibly connected with the Great Depression is the sight of people standing in line outside of their bank, waiting hopelessly to take their money out. These "bank runs" were not unique to Depression and had occurred before during prior "Panics" (see Fig. 18.4). But in the Depression, these became so widespread that in the US large segments of the banking system simply collapsed.

First consider the extensiveness of the crisis. The erasure of $2.5 billion in corporate equity value in US share markets by 1933 was equal to 2.4% of 1929 nominal GDP. This loss of capital had been bought with highly leveraged money and sudden erasure of that amount of collateral decimated American banks, 9,000 of them suspending operations between 1930 and 1933 (Romer, 1993). To put this in perspective, in 1930, 5.6% of all operating banks in the US had failed. In 1931, another 10.5% had failed; in 1932, another 7.8% failed; and in 1933, the first year of the new Roosevelt Administration, 12.9% failed (Bernanke, 1983, 259).

This had come about because of the borrowing frenzy by all sectors of American society in the 1920s. Outstanding corporate notes (i.e. very short-term bonds) rose from $26.1 billion in 1920 to $47.1 billion in 1928. Non-federal government public debt rose from $11.8 billion in 1920 to $33.6 billion in 1928. 1929 US National Income by comparison

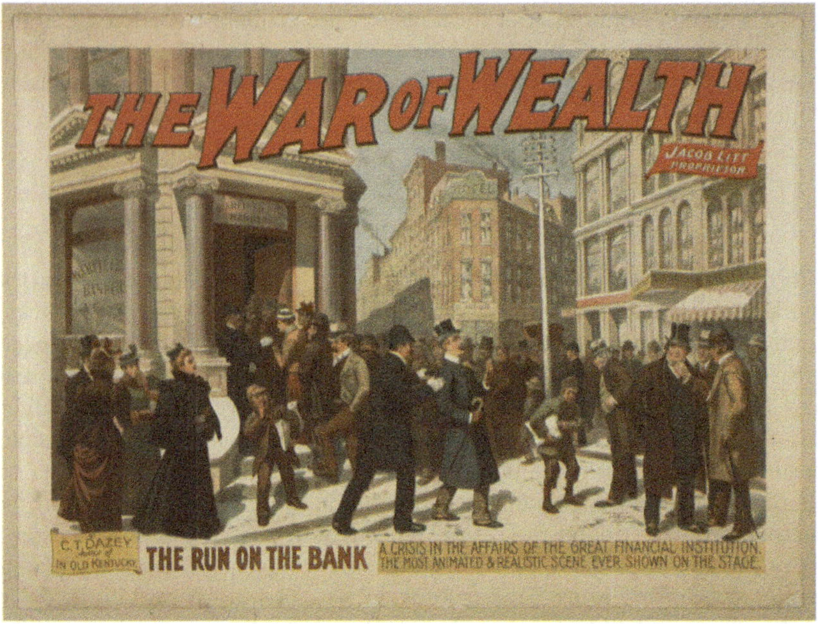

Fig. 18.4 A fictional bank run of 1895—a precursor of the Depression's massive wave of them (*Image source* US Library of Congress: The war of wealth. Call number: POS - TH - 1895.W37, no. 1 [C size] [P&P]. Reproduction number: LC-USZC4-591 [color film copy transparency]. LC-USZ6-380 [b&w film copy neg.]. Original created by C.T. Dazey, Published by: Cin'ti; NY: Strobridge Lith. Co., c1895. No known restrictions on publication)

was $86.8 billion. Even strong banks often could not withstand a general "contagion" of fear and a liquidity crisis in which the relative cost of debt service of borrowers skyrocketed, going from 9% of national income in 1929 to 19.8% in 1932–1933, mainly because nominal debt burdens had not gone away while national income had shrunk by close to a quarter during the period (Bernanke, 1983, 260).

Financial intermediation refers to the mediation of the "real" economy (where things actually get made and consumed) by financial institutions that borrow, lend and help create liquidity that is then used to finance new real productive activity in a hopefully virtuous circle. In theory, this should make the real economy more efficient by providing seed capital and liquidity to (hopefully) worthwhile production that otherwise would not be able to take place, and by transferring idle funds from those with no current use for them (savers) to those in need of them to pursue commercial enterprises (investors).

In practice, this process often goes wrong and it did so catastrophically in the US after the Crash. For one thing, America was "overbanked", i.e. it had too many small banks, competitively pumping up their lending business by extending too much credit to too many uncreditworthy people and not making adequate provisions for the inevitable defaults. A shakeout was unavoidable even if the good times had lasted, which they never do. This shakeout, when it came, was horrendous, taking out the good with the bad and everything in-between. Many banks had managed their risks so poorly in the 1920s that many were technically insolvent when the various implosions of the early 1930s commenced the rolling cycle of bank runs and mass shutdowns, exacerbated in some cases by financial legerdemain and corruption. Credit extended by institutions outside the formal banking sector, i.e. shadow banking, and outsized corporate borrowing and brokerage credit all added to this mix. There was simply too much money pumping out of the financial system, driving poor financial and business decisions that reverberated back and led to a credit collapse corresponding to, and greater in magnitude than, the prior boom (Calomoris & Mason, 1997; Grossman, 1994; Wicker, 1980).

Lax financial regulation and poor monetary policy also played a part. A raging debate that began between Friedman and Schwartz (1963) and Temin (1976) has spawned a large, contentious but now somewhat converging literature which concludes that the US central bank did make significant policy errors and that banking oversight was deficient and counterproductive. What remains contested is how large a part this played in the American banking crisis and the ensuing Depression. Friedman and Schwartz maintain that American central banking policy was the fatal factor, Temin being much less convinced of this. All scholars concede that financial policymakers hurt rather than helped matters, both in the lead-up to the crisis and during its initial unfolding.

With the financial bust-up, deflation, referring to a generalised fall in the price level, became another scourge. If gradual and orderly, deflation can be managed. But falls in both the prices of goods and the wages of workers fell precipitously. This deepened the fall in production as firms struggled to make profits because of ever-lower nominal prices commanded by the goods they did manage to sell, while the dwindling number of workers who managed to keep their jobs found their nominal wages slashed. If prices and wages had fallen proportionately and in lockstep, the real effect of deflation would have been close to nil, as lower prices adjusted for inflation would have cancelled out lower after-inflation wages and vice versa. But such things happen only in textbooks and downward prices and wage adjustments were sharp and chaotic, causing unstable profit and cost trajectories for firms and unsteady real incomes for workers. Even worse, deflation created incentives to hoard money rather than to consume and invest because the purchasing power of cash was rising while returns on other financial instruments were uncertain or falling. This reticence to spend reduced aggregate demand, increasing unemployment, with wages and worker income falling more as a result, and then further reducing prices. Total consumption in the economy fell as a result of falling incomes driven by deflation and mass unemployment, reducing sales and profits, leading to more job losses and wage cuts, and on downward in a vicious downward circle (Bernanke, 1983, 1995).

Deflation also worsened the financial crisis because debtors now found their repayments more burdensome when adjusted for deflation, because they had to pay back in dollars actually appreciating in purchasing power, and this raised the number of defaults. These defaults caused banks to involuntarily shift large parts of their portfolios from financial to real assets, through mortgage foreclosures on homes and loan foreclosures on factories, machinery and the like. But these things were falling in nominal price terms and often could not be sold or liquidated at all, leaving financial intermediaries with losses and worthless holdings on their balance sheets. Banks, for which deposits were financial liabilities (because they had to be paid back to depositors on demand), saw the real burdens of these rising because nominal deposits had to be paid out in nominal dollars which were dearer rather than depreciating because of deflation (Bernanke, 1983, 1995). These effects were significant enough that some contemporary observers, including the great economist Irving Fisher, felt that they were the prime cause of the Depression (see Box 18.1). Few subscribe to this idea now, though everyone does now recognise how damaging this particular debt deflation impact was and that it did play an important role in the overall crisis.

Box 18.1 Irving Fisher

One of the greatest economists of his era, and widely acknowledged to be the father of the field of financial economics more generally was Irving

Fisher. Fisher had been born in 1867 to a Congregationalist minister, but later became an atheist. He studied both mathematics and political economy at Yale and received the first economics doctorate ever granted by that institution. What followed was a brilliant academic career, in which he wrote one of the first American works on mathematical economics, followed by a series of books published between 1896 and 1910 on financial accounting and monetary theory which earned him an international reputation.

In 1898 Fisher developed tuberculosis, leaving Yale for three years, and, in his customary manner, seeking out an innovative cure. He found one in the "fresh-air regime" of Dr. E. L. Trudeau in Saranac, New York. This experience led him to become a disciple of healthy living, writing a book on the topic, *How to Live*, which became a bestseller. He joined the cause of Prohibition in the US (i.e. the movement to make the sale of alcohol illegal), and also advocated against the use of tobacco, for the chewing of food thoroughly, and for the filling of houses with fresh air, all of which he believed would restore the primitive and natural animal vitality that was the human birthright.

None of this activism slowed down Fisher's prodigious academic output, which included his seminal 1911 publication *The Purchasing Power of Money*, and his establishment of the Number Institute in the 1920s, which employed a staff of economists, and issued a weekly report sent out to newspapers worldwide. Fisher published *The Making of Index Numbers* in 1922, another seminal work in the area, that served as the basis of the creation of another enterprise of his called the Index Visible Company, which in 1926 merged with its chief competitor into a company that later became Remington Rand.

Through all this Fisher became a wealthy man. Ever the reformer, Fisher used his wealth to support many causes, most of which stand up well with the passage of time. The exception was his organization of the American Eugenics Society. However this was a very popular and respected movement during his era, a reflection of the contemporary belief in Social Darwinism (see Chapter 17) and in the ongoing social project to perfect the human being using science and technology, a program that appealed to a technical wizard like Fisher.

For all his technical expertise, knowledge and renown, Fisher lost much of his wealth along with everyone else during and after the Great Crash of 1929. Indeed, Fisher's reputation suffered greatly because of his pronouncements at the time that the market had plateaued after the Crash and that recovery was near at hand, a prediction he repeated for many months after the initial collapse. He eventually was forced to recognise that the Depression would not end up being resolved through a natural recovery and developed a theory referred to as the Debt Deflation theory which essentially held that deflation, by increasing the real burden of outstanding debt repayments, created an overhang on the economy that stressed the financial system and led to the hoarding of cash, both of which prolonged the Depression. Because of his incorrect prognostications about the Crash, his theory gained little traction, but has since been seen as explaining a lot about the financial crisis that unfolded in the US and other countries.

(The discussion above is largely drawn from Klein, 2001, 86–87; Okrent, 2010, 98–99.)

Effectively financial disintermediation was occurring in the US, i.e. an absolute rollback of the financial sector from its excessive prior levels. As but one quantitative example of how this looked, mortgage loans by life insurance companies fell from $525 million in 1929 to $10 million in 1933) (Bernanke, 1983, 273). Other financial metrics showed similar magnitudes of collapse.

This financial implosion was a combination of emotion and rational action in a crisis. On the one hand, people panicked as they saw bank after bank close, a "contagion of fear" causing them to head to their local bank, which might actually be sound in some cases, simply because they were afraid of what might come next. When everyone took the same action, the institution would fail, as would many others. This panic reaction was reinforced by good logical reasons to convert financial assets into cash. Of course, the newly unemployed and insolvent had immediate need of cash and thus had to draw down their savings quickly. But with deflation, a cash hoard was good to have, since cash was appreciating in purchasing power value, making the proverbial money under the mattress more valuable with time rather than less (Mishkin, 1978). It was safer too since so many banks were insolvent, and prudence would demand taking money out to the safe haven of home rather than leaving it in the hands of what were now seen as institutions run by crooks, con-men and the merely incompetent and unlucky (Calomiris, 1993; White, 1984; Wicker, 1980).

Corruption was a large factor in the making of the Depression, of which there had been ample amounts before the Crash. Wicker (1980) focuses on one example, the failure of Caldwell and Company, and a large Southern bank whose failure precipitated a regional South-eastern bank crisis in the US in 1930. His analysis of its balance sheet reveals a number of questionable transactions, particularly its investments in controlled companies, effectively empty shells created by Caldwell to move financial statement entries around as it suited them. These constituted two-fifths of the bank's total assets. Caldwell was in no way unique in such practices, engaged in by institutions ranging from local depository institutions, all the way up to large corporations.

Even without financial crisis, the American economic boom during the 1920s was much less strong than it appeared. While the cities and factories were humming along, the agricultural depression of the 1920s in the US weakened rural and regional farm banks and local communities, softening them up in advance of the Depression and making the crisis worse when it came. The rise of mass consumption arguably caused overconsumption that caused overinvestment in expensive plant and equipment, setting up the real economy for a fall regardless of the financial sector's health. Bank and securities regulation was on the one hand too lax as there was no legal requirement separating investment and commercial banking, but also too strong, prohibiting branch banking off a larger unit, which arguably incentivised the proliferation of smaller, weaker, "unit" banks that became especially prone to failure in times of stress. There was also a concomitant lack of uniform oversight of securities issuance and trading, allowing for rampant speculation and the creation of asset bubbles. Finally, the already mentioned deficient workings of the Gold Standard and the lingering effects of the World War's dislocations put the icing on a rotten cake (Garraty, 1986; Romer, 1990, 1992, 1993). One is spoiled for choice in identifying culprits in the tragic mess that resulted (Fig. 18.5).

18.8 A Worldwide Conflagration

The American financial crisis quickly spread to the banking and financial systems in other countries. In May 1931 there was a run against Creditanstalt, a large Austrian bank. The panic then shifted to Germany. In 1931 a major German financial institution, the Darmstadter- und Nationalbank, failed, leading to a general run on all the country's banks and the forced closure of all German financial institutions on July 13. These did not completely reopen until August 5. Even then the German central

Fig. 18.5 Son of depression refugee from Oklahoma now in California (1936) (*Image source* US Library of Congress, Call number LC-USF34- 009872-E [P&P]. Reproduction Number: LC-USF34-009872-E [b&w film nitrate neg.] LC-USZ62-130927 [b&w film copy neg. from print], 1936 Nov., Lange, Dorothea, photographer. No known copyright restrictions)

bank had to provide substantial infusions of money to banks and forced the Darmstadter to merge with another weak bank, the Dresdner Bank. This crisis caused a credit crunch as banks called in loans and refused to give new ones. This caused German interest rates to shoot up. Many businesses failed as a result. Being a major industrial economy, Germany was already seeing mass unemployment due to the collapse in industrial production and product demand. This financial crisis just made things much worse. In late summer the crisis spread to Britain and on to other countries. The basic dynamics were always the same: depositors deserted banks in droves, depriving them of their main source of liquidity. Meanwhile bank assets, such as loans and investments in securities, all fell sharply in value or were wiped out completely. Even when banks got their collateral back from defaults on secured loans, through foreclosures on mortgages on farms, houses and factories, the value of the real assets they got back were now much less than the value of the loan itself, leading to big losses for the lenders (Adalet, 2003; James, 1984b).

Germany was in a particularly acute situation. It had relied heavily on an inflow of foreign capital during the 1920s, especially bank loans. When times were good, these flowed in like water. With bad times they flowed out just as quickly, if not more so. Thus the German banking system was subject to external pressures not operative in the US and the financial contagion it received from that country hit its sector that much harder (James, 1984a).

Everywhere financial crisis was joined with a real economy crisis, and it was almost impossible to say where one ended and the other began. In America investments by business dropped from $16.2 billion to $0.4 billion since between 1929 and 1933, farm prices fell 53%, and international trade fell by two-thirds. Industrial production was savaged everywhere. Table 18.1 provides indices of total industrial production in nine major industrial economies between 1927 and 1935. Only Sweden and Britain managed to exceed their 1929 levels, in the latter case mainly because the economy had been so bad throughout the 1920s. The picture is especially acute between 1930 and 1932. German industry contracted by two-fifths compared to 1929, the US almost half, Canada by close to a third.

Economies like Germany that depended heavily on industry were thus very badly done by. Other economies that were less industrialised, like Italy, had delayed reactions. But almost no economy of significance was

Table 18.1 Indices of total industrial production, 1927 to 1935 (1929 = 100)

	1927	*1928*	*1929*	*1930*	*1931*	*1932*	*1933*	*1934*	*1935*
Britain	95	94	100	94	86	89	95	105	114
Canada	85	94	100	91	78	68	69	82	90
France	84	94	100	99	85	74	83	79	77
Germany	95	100	100	86	72	59	68	83	96
Italy	87	99	100	93	84	77	83	85	99
Netherlands	87	94	100	109	101	90	90	93	95
Sweden	85	88	100	102	97	89	93	111	125
U.S	85	90	100	83	69	55	63	69	79

Source Parker (2008)

Table 18.2 GDP Growth between 1929 and 1932 (%) for selected countries

Country	*GDP Growth*
Austria	−19.8
Germany	−15.8
Belgium	−7.1
Spain	−3.8
France	−14.7
Finland	−4.0
Sweden	−4.3
UK	−5.1
USA	−27.0
Japan	1.3
WORLD	−9.8
Unweighted average for countries above	−10.0

Source Aiginger (2009, slide 10)

spared from a contraction in GDP in the very earliest years, as Table 18.2 indicates.

18.9 Outmoded Policy Responses and Policy Experimentation

Governments around the world, especially the free market democracies, were caught flat-footed in trying to respond to this crisis. The initial responses of most governments were to cut spending and raise taxes in a bid to balance government budgets. Germany (before Hitler), the US and Britain, amongst others all took this tack in the first years of the Depression. A "sound finance" doctrine of the time called for "conservative" fiscal management believing that this would restore individual and business confidence. Instead, higher taxes on businesses and workers and reduced government spending exacerbated the economic contraction (Vernon, 1994). Western governments of the time also subscribed to a sort of economic Darwinism in which periodic recessions were thought to "weed out" inefficient producers. Andrew Mellon, Secretary of the Treasury under US President Herbert Hoover (President at the outset of the Depression) famously said, "Liquidate the workers, liquidate the farms, liquidate the factories" (DeLong, 1990). "Neoclassical" economic thinking of the time reinforced this view because it predicted that ultimately markets would "re-equilibrate" and the whole economy would return to full employment, despite the unfortunate "adjustment" costs, so long as government kept its fiscal house in strict order.

To take the UK as an example, a new Conservative government took over in 1931. In an effort to balance the budget and restore confidence in Sterling, Philip Snowden, Chancellor of the Exchequer, issued an emergency budget, which immediately instituted a round of cuts in public spending and wages. Public sector wages and unemployment pay were cut by 10%, and the income tax rate was raised from 22.5% to 25%. The pay cuts caused some unrest, including a "mutiny" in the Royal Navy (though it was not violent and quickly subsided). The economy did not improve as hoped, however (Middleton, 2010).

Conventional thinking thus came into increasing question as the Depression wore on.

Thus governments in the Western democracies began to improvise, driven by the social unrest and economic privation that was spreading everywhere. The idea of government spending as a temporary replacement for private spending was not a new idea but it had always been thought of as an emergency stopgap of limited scale and duration. However it was increasingly resorted to by governments around the world and began to take on an air of permanence, growing in size and scope. Price and wage controls to halt deflation, though anathema to free market ideology, was another policy, though tried more fitfully, and less successfully.

One noted policy response was that of the US government, under President Franklin Delano Roosevelt (FDR), who was elected in 1932, during the worst of the Depression. Herbert Hoover had been President when the crisis began and he took a relatively timid approach (though historians have noted that it was not as laissez-faire as supposed at the time). The results of this light government touch spoke for themselves since a third of the banks had gone out of business and the general unemployment rate was around 25% when Roosevelt actually took office in 1933 (Schlesinger, 1960).

Roosevelt had not campaigned on a very specific platform and his party, the Democrats, were not known as policy innovators. But Roosevelt took dramatic action immediately. One his first acts was the Emergency Banking Act (enacted on 6 March 1933 immediately after his inauguration as President) which closed the banks under a national "banking holiday" to help stabilise the system and suggest a strong hand in charge. He then created the Federal Deposit Insurance Corporation (FDIC) (1933) allowing government to insure individual deposits and hence stop banking runs. And in short succession his government abandoned the Gold Standard, created a number of national emergency "individual relief" programs to feed, clothe and house people, and created new agencies designed to put people immediately back to work. The acronyms of these agencies, collectively often referred to at the time as an "alphabet soup", are indicative: the Civilian Conservation Corps (CCC), Public Works Administration (PWA), Works Progress Administration (WPA), Federal Emergency Relief Administration (FERA), Civil Works Administration (CWA), to name a few. Special attention was also paid to the agricultural sector, which was in the US, as in most countries, in crisis well before the Depression due to overproduction and consistently low international commodity prices. Various laws designed to attend to this included programs to set crop prices through the Agricultural Adjustment Act (AAA) and increase liquidity for farmers with the Commodity Credit Corporation (Daniels, 2015). There were even programs for unemployed artists and writers that led to the creation of a number of iconic works (see Fig. 18.6).

These are only some of the major examples of an effort collectively known as the "New Deal". FDR's programs were eclectic and ad hoc, unevenly effective, and during his first term especially, enormously popular. FDR won his second term in a 1936 landslide that was so big that his defeated Republican challenger Alf Landon compared his defeat afterwards to a Kansas tornado (Kansas was his home state) that left nothing standing afterwards (Schlesinger, 1960, 643). The New Deal's

Fig. 18.6 The Federal Theater Project, one of many New Deal programs (*Image source* US Library of Congress, Prints and Photographs Division Washington, DC 20540 USA http://hdl.loc.gov/loc.pnp/pp.print. Call Number: POS - WPA - NY.S58, no. 1 [B size] [P&P]. Original Creator: Spellens, Irving, artist. Federal Theatre Project [New York, N.Y.], sponsor. Date Created/Published: NYC: WPA Federal Art Project [between 1936 and 1939]. Medium: 1 print on board [poster]: silkscreen, color. Poster for the show of the same title at the Adelphi Theatre in New York. Reproduction Number: LC-DIG-ppmsca-31218 [digital file from original item] LC-USZC2-5393 [color film copy slide] LC-USZC4-2090 [color film copy transparency]. No known restrictions on publication)

eclecticism, panache and vote-getting garnered a lot of attention abroad, particularly since it suggested that it was possible for capitalist democracies to survive and even thrive by intervening to correct systemic balances that did not seem capable of correcting themselves and gain a popular mandate for doing so.

18.9.1 Alternative Visions

Some countries went in a very different direction. Following fiscal orthodoxy, the conservative but democratically elected government of Weimar Germany cut government spending and raised taxes as the Depression took hold, further depressing atrocious economic conditions. This was an unpopular approach and the governments undertaking them had very small margins in the legislature, working with fractious coalitions. A series of conservative prime ministers quickly rose and fell and soon began to rule by presidential decree rather than parliamentary process (as allowed by the Weimar Constitution) justifying it by the emergency conditions they were facing but eroding the already tenuous democratic tradition in the country in the process. Politics were also highly polarised between Communist and Social Democratic left and Fascist right and street violence was a regular occurrence. Adolf Hitler constitutionally took power as Chancellor in 1933 but almost immediately imposed a one-party state, with firm state control of the German macroeconomy (and of most everything else). Unlike the Soviet Union (discussed next), private property and private industry largely remained in place, but the government became a major buyer of goods and services, especially for rearmament, and intervened heavily in private labour and capital markets. The German economy did come out of Depression quickly after this, seemingly confirming the notion of the time that modern capitalism was broken and that there were alternatives that worked much better (although the war economy model was unsustainable and undesirable for obvious reasons) (Kershaw, 1991).

Hitler's Germany was nationalist and right wing, along the lines of Fascism, a concept difficult to define exactly but a nonetheless distinct ideology from either Capitalism or Communism. Mussolini in Italy also ran a Fascist government, and other governments in Europe had fascist leanings (see also Chapters 21 and 23) (Paxton, 2007). The other model of Communism was in full operation in Josef Stalin's Soviet Union. We now fully know the brutality of the Stalin regime. But back in the 1930s, when information was harder to pry out, Russia was seen by many as a brave new world, economically and politically. The USSR had minimal trade with the rest of the world and thus did not suffer too much from international trade contraction or capitalistic business cycles. The economy was centrally planned by the State, there was no private enterprise or property of any significance, and Stalin had used a strong central state to mobilise national resources on a push for rapid industrialisation, building, for example, one of the largest steel works in the world in an extraordinarily short period of time (Gatrell, 2006; Suny, 1997).

Unemployment in the West freed up a lot of Western expertise that went to Russia to work on various projects, such as the GAZ automotive factory in Nizhny Novgorod, built with the help of Henry Ford (the founder of the Ford Motor Company). Many Westerners were idealistically motivated, desiring to help build an alternative to what appeared to be an increasingly doomed capitalistic democratic system (Siegelbaum, 2008). Of course the use of slave labour in the large political prison system (referred to as the "Gulag"), the inefficiencies of many of the state enterprises, and a couple of major famines in the early 1930s were carefully hidden from public and Western view, as was Stalin's ruthless political purges and general paranoia. However the Soviet Union had indeed moved rapidly from the quasi-industrial agrarian economy of the Tsars into a large-scale industrial economy in a short period of time, even if the costs were considerable, its morality reprehensible. Most importantly it was not outwardly suffering through the dislocations that the Depression had delivered in the Capitalist world.

These were extreme examples but their seeming economic success, together with the ravages of the Depression, indicated to most that the model of the Liberal Democracy and Liberal Economy which had seen the world through the First and Second Industrial Revolutions was no longer fit for purpose. The real debate was how capitalism could be reformed, if, indeed, reform was possible at all.

18.9.2 "Macroeconomics" and "Social Democracy"

Prior to the Great Depression, the consensus view amongst Anglo-American economists was that "neoclassical" economics, the successor to Political Economy and Classical Economics, was a sufficient explanation for all economic phenomena and the best theoretical basis for formulating public policy. This theory hypothesised that even a crisis of this magnitude should correct itself. The logic was based on the simple model of supply and demand that was used to capture the workings of single markets. For example, if one had a bushel of apples to sell, and it was not selling, all one had to do was lower the price until all the apples were sold. Price would thus "equilibrate" supply and demand. What applied to single markets applied to all markets taken as a whole. The Great Depression, it was said, was simply an example of wages and prices being too high to bring supply and demand into line. All one had to do was wait until prices and wages naturally reached a low enough level that would "clear" excess supplies of goods and excess supplies of labour.

As the Depression deepened into a truly existential challenge, there seemed to be need of a new theory. Into this breach came the theories of macroeconomics posited by John Maynard Keynes. After Keynes there would be two branches of economics, one for the entire economy (macroeconomics) and one for specific markets (now called microeconomics, though before the Depression sometimes fittingly called "price theory").

Keynes' theory is rather subtle but at its heart posited that there can be extreme cases where an economy contracts so severely that total (or aggregate) demand will not respond to the usual economic factors that can help an economy right itself (e.g. falling prices). In these cases the government had to exercise a new function: intervening temporarily to prop up aggregate demand with external "stimulus", mainly deficit-financed spending of the sort being used under the New Deal. The title of the Keynes magnum opus began with the words "general theory", to distinguish it from the special case and more limited theory that Keynes posited neoclassical economics as. In this sense Keynes was no radical. He believed in existing economic theory but thought that it, like capitalism itself, needed to be reformed to account for new circumstances.

It also should be noted that Keynesian thinking was not explicitly leaned upon during the Great Depression. Governments were busy improvising responses, throwing existing playbooks out, and didn't have any core text to refer to. Their actions were consistent with Keynes's ideas but not informed by them. In any case, Keynes didn't publish his "General Theory" until 1936. The ideas of "Keynesianism" (which was not entirely aligned with Keynes, who also could be ambiguous in some of his thinking) would really come after Second World War reconstruction though its credence had been earned because of the Depression experience.

There was also a parallel evolution of political theory. Classical capitalism had birthed Liberalism. Reformed capitalism ended up birthing "Social Democracy", i.e. democratic political processes underpinned by social "safety nets", a mixed private and publicly managed economy template, and a political ethos that emphasised social egalitarianism, while still maintaining the commitment to wide liberties in areas of personal and public expression that had been a core feature of Liberalism (see Chapter 4). Western countries varied as to how far they took both Keynesianism and Social Democracy, but the combination provided a post Second World War consensus in the Capitalist world that lasted for several decades (see Chapter 28).

18.10 The Ongoing Mystery of the Great Depression

The Great Depression touched almost every facet of the global economic and political system. It was a full-blown, international epic. Almost nothing was unaffected by the crisis and almost everything was transformed by it: financial markets and institutions, organisational forms, international trade, public tax and spending, politics and political ideologies, and on and on. The event shook everything within industrial capitalism down to its fundamentals, nearly wrecking it. This was not merely a superficial, if severe, economic shock, quite a few of which had occurred in the past. Rather it was something akin to a seismic shift, which got deep into the inner workings of economies, institutions, and ways of thinking, turned them upside-down and inside-out, and left matters altered forever.

The fact that there is still lively controversy and continuing scholarship about the causes and effects of the crisis adds to the ongoing currency of the event. The clash of different models and views of the world, of different empirical methods and findings, and the limits of modern analysis, are all richly demonstrated by the continuing study of the Great Depression.

On the one hand, there is substantial agreement on the importance and effects of individual events causes. For example, one survey of economists and historians found that most of those surveyed agreed that the high protectionist US 1930 Smoot-Hawley Tariff was destructive (a view that was echoed by contemporary economists); that the US Federal Reserve Bank (that country's central bank) could have done more to support the US economy with a looser monetary policy immediately after the Crash of 1929; and that the Interwar Gold Standard exacerbated the crisis, amongst numerous other propositions (Whaples, 1995). Kindleberger (1987) persuasively argues that the crisis was the result of multiple causes, including protectionism in international trade, excessive financial speculation followed by inept policy responses, overproduction, and so on, coming unfortunately all at once and in an environment where there was no international financial and economic policy coordination despite its being desperately needed.

But all this remains more a description of what occurred rather than an explanation of "why" and "how". It amounts to saying that the Depression was just bad luck on a large scale, which is not a terribly satisfying or comforting answer since its does not preclude such a cataclysm occurring again (as the Global Financial Crisis of 2008 demonstrates).

Was the Depression a sign of an economic system (capitalism) that was fundamentally untenable, as many of diverse political persuasions argued at the time? The continuation of capitalism ninety years later obviously suggests otherwise, particularly as the crisis elicited substantial reform to its workings both domestically and internationally. But were these reforms therefore the reason that the Depression ended? It seems not to be entirely so since the world economy was still quite weak overall until the onset of the Second World War which, destructive as it was, "ended" the Depression and allowed for a complete rebuilding of the world economic system. What the reforms did do was keep radical movements against capitalism, from the right and the left, contained in some countries, especially the US, Britain and France. And they set a template for a post-war restructure that kept the system relatively stable in ways that the old configurations did not.

Some maintained, then and now, that the Great Depression showed that capitalism is ultimately self-destructive and that while this crisis ended up being dodged, in the end a transition to something more sustainable, stable and humane is ultimately necessary. This was the essence of Marxism with its model of the historical inevitability of capitalist collapse. The end of the Cold War and the Socialist Bloc's own problems during it have put this particular notion to rest. But the Depression stimulated some interesting debates at the time which it is worth paying attention to now, especially as capitalism has not been without serious crisis since then.

Either way, although the Depression itself ended, its impacts still reverberate. It remains a case to go back to inform current events, as well as being an epoch of historical interest in its own right.

References

Adalet, M. (2003). *Fundamentals, capital flows and capital flight: The German banking crisis of 1931* (Working Paper). University of California.

Aiginger, K. (2009, September 21). *Comparing the current crisis to the Great Depression*. OECD Nero Conference, Paris, presentation (OECD_crises_210909_short.ppt).

Bernanke, B. (1983). Nonmonetary effects of the financial crisis in the propagation of the Great Depression. *American Economic Review, 73*(3), 257–276.

Bernanke, B. (1995). The macroeconomics of the Great Depression: A comparative approach. *Journal of Money, Credit and Banking, 27*(1), 1–28.

Bierman, H. (1999). The reasons stocks crashed in 1929. *The Journal of Investing, 8*(1), 11–18.

Blum, J., Cameron, R. E., & Barnes, T. G. (1970). *The European world: A history*. Little, Brown.

Calomoris, C. W. (1993). Financial factors in the great depression. *Journal of Economic Perspectives, 7*(2), 61–85.

Calomiris, C. W., & Mason, J. R. (1997). Contagion and bank failures during the Great Depression: The June 1932 Chicago banking panic. *American Economic Review, 87*(5), 863–883.

Cooper, R. N. (1992). Fettered to gold? Economic policy in the interwar period. *Journal of Economic Literature, 30*(4), 2120–2128.

Daniels, R. (2015). *Franklin D. Roosevelt: Road to the new deal, 1882–1939*. University of Illinois Press.

DeLong, J. B. (1990). *"Liquidation" cycles: Old-fashioned real business cycle theory and the Great Depression*. National Bureau of Economic Research, Working Paper # 3546.

Eichengreen, B. (1996). *Golden fetters: The gold standard and the Great Depression, 1919–1939*. Oxford University Press.

Eichengreen, B., & Flandreau, M. (1997). *Gold standard in theory & history* (2nd ed.). Routledge.

Friedman, M., & Schwartz, A. (1963). *A monetary history of the United States, 1867–1960*. Princeton University Press.

Galbraith, J. K. (1972). *The Great Crash, 1929* (3rd ed.). Houghton Mifflin.

Garraty, J. A. (1986). *The great depression*. Harcourt Brace Jovanovich.

Gatrell, P. (2006). Chapter 14: Economic and demographic change: Russia's age of economic extremes. In R. G. Suny (Ed.), *The Cambridge history of Russia, volume 3: The twentieth century*. Cambridge University Press.

Graff, M., Kenwood, A. G., & Lougheed, A. L. (2013). *Growth of the international economy, 1820–2015*. Routledge.

Grossman, R. S. (1994). The shoe that didn't drop: Explaining banking stability during the Great Depression. *Journal of Economic History, 54*(3), 654–682.

James, H. (1984a). The causes of the German banking crisis. *Economic History Review, 37*(1), 68–87.

James, J. A. (1984b). The use of general equilibrium analysis in economic history. *Explorations in Economic History, 21*(3), 231–253.

Kershaw, I. (1991). *Hitler: Profiles in power*. Pearson Education.

Keynes, J. M. (1919). *The economic consequences of the peace*. Macmillan & Co.

Kindleberger, C. (1987). *The world in depression 1929–1939*. University of California Press.

Klein, M. (2001). *Rainbow's end: The Crash of 1929*. Oxford University Press.

Lichtheim, G. (1972). *Europe in the twentieth century*. Praeger Publishers.

Marks, S. (1978). The myths of reparations. *Central European History, 11*(3), 231–255.

Middleton, R. (2010). British monetary and fiscal policy in the 1930s. *Oxford Review of Economic Policy, 26*(3), 414–441.

Mishkin, F. S. (1978). The household balance sheet and the Great Depression. *The Journal of Economic History, 38*(4), 918–937.

Okrent, D. (2010). *Last call: The rise and fall of Prohibition*. Scribner.

Parker, R. (2008). An overview of the Great Depression. In R. Whaples (Ed.), *EH. Net. Encyclopedia*. https://eh.net/encyclopedia/an-overview-of-the-great-depression/

Paxton, R. O. (2007). *The anatomy of fascism*. Vintage.

Puffert, D. (2008). Path dependence. In R. Whaples (Ed.), *EH.net Encyclopedia*. http://eh.net/encyclopedia/path-dependence/

Romer, C. (1990). The Great Crash and the onset of the Great Depression. *Quarterly Journal of Economics, 105*(3), 597–624.

Romer, C. (1992). What ended the Great Depression? *Journal of Economic History, 52*(4), 757–784.

Romer, C. (1993). The nation in depression. *Journal of Economic Perspectives, 7*(2), 19–39.

Rutterford, J. (2009). Learning from one another's mistakes: Investment trusts in the UK and the US, 1868–1940. *Financial History Review, 16*(2), 157–181.

Schlesinger, A. M. Jr. (1960) *The age of Roosevelt: The politics of upheaval*. Houghton-Mifflin.

Siegelbaum, L. H. (2008). Roadlessness and the "path to communism": Building roads and highways in Stalinist Russia. *Journal of Transport History, 29*(2), 277–294.

Strachan, H. (2003). *The First World War*. Penguin.

Suny, R. G. (1997). Stalin and his Stalinism: Power and authority in the Soviet Union, 1930–53. In I. Kershaw & M. Lewin (Eds.), *Stalinism and Nazism: Dictatorships in comparison* (pp. 16–24). Cambridge University Press.

Temin, P. (1976). *Did monetary forces cause the Great Depression?* Norton.

Travlos, K. (2020). Chapter 1: Introduction. In K. Travlos (Ed.), *Salvation and catastrophe: The Greek-Turkish War, 1919–1922* (pp. 1–22). Lexington Books.

Vernon, J. R. (1994). World War II fiscal policies and the end of the Great Depression. *Journal of Economic History, 54*(4), 850–868.

Webb, S. B. (1988). Latin American debt and German reparations after World War 1: A comparison. *Weltwirtschaftliches Arhiv, 124*(4), 745–774.

Whaples, R. (1995). Where is there consensus among American economic historians? The results of a survey on forty propositions. *Journal of Economic History, 55*(1), 139–154.

White, E. (1984). A reinterpretation of the banking crisis of 1930. *Journal of Economic History, 44*(1), 119–138.

Wicker, E. (1980). A reconsideration of the causes of the banking panic of 1930. *Journal of Economic History, 40*(3), 571–583.

CHAPTER 19

Global Finance

C. Gordon, *Many Possible Worlds*,
https://doi.org/10.1007/978-981-19-9281-0_19

Fig. 19.1 Counting money stacks in the US Treasury circa 1907 (*Image source* US Library of Congress. Title: U.S. Treasury. CALL NUMBER: LOT 10,801 [P&P]. REPRODUCTION NUMBER: LC-USZ62-91643 [b&w film copy neg]. CREATED/PUBLISHED: c1907. DIGITAL ID: [b&w film copy neg.] cph 3b37981 hdl.loc.gov/loc.pnp/cph.3b37981. CONTROL #: 96510963. No known copyright restrictions)

19.1 Open Markets in Money and Things

The Industrial Revolution ushered in what is often referred to as a first age of globalisation. By this is generally meant a large expansion of international trade in goods, along with a concomitant movement of people. Simultaneously, however, financial globalisation burgeoned as well, by which is meant a large increase in the flow of money, both in short-term movements of cash and longer-term movements of capital (Fig. 19.1).

Neal and Cameron (2016) note that international capital movements are driven by sources, motives and mechanisms (301). The Industrial Revolution transformed and accelerated all three. The primary motive for the capital movements associated with industrialisation was straightforward: to finance the burgeoning buying and selling of goods across international borders, and capital for making investments. Pre-industrial economies had much less need for "external" finance simply because trade volumes were lower, with financing gaps largely funded by what would now be referred to as "vendor finance", i.e. the seller of goods extending short-term finance to the buyer, outstanding balances usually met upon completion of the transaction. Domestic investments were generally more labour- than capital-intensive, of lower scale and obviously much more primitive technically, their financing needs hence lower.

Modern economic growth ushered in volumes of trade and capital investment that not even rich large countries could fund on their own, including even the British Empire of the nineteenth century. The ratio of world trade to output was about 2% in 1800, rising to 10% in 1870, 17% in 1900 and 21% in 1913 (Galor, 2005, 216). Financing this rising tide of production and consumption required investment, with many countries importing foreign capital in amounts equal to between 3 and 5% of GDP annually. One estimate is that by 1913 the ratio of global net foreign liabilities to global GDP was around 25%. Another estimate for the same year divides gross world assets by global GDP and finds this ratio to be about 20% in 1913. This latter number has been dwarfed by early twenty-first century ratios of roughly 75% but was nonetheless unprecedented at the time (Bordo & Meissner, 2007, 2–4).

As a result fund sources and mechanisms multiplied and flourished, continuing and extending a process that had begun in earnest with the European Commercial Revolution of the 1500s and 1600s, though China was the scene of many antecedent monetary and fiscal innovations. The nineteenth century saw the invention of many new financial instruments and institutions for creating and extending credit. Investment banks, though not present in Britain, blossomed on the Continent, such as the Société Générale pour favoriser l'Industrie Nationale des Pays-Bas, created in 1822 to promote Low Country industrial development, along with a proliferation of German private banks devoted to a similar national purpose, and the establishment of the Crédit Mobilier in France in 1852 to finance railways and industry. These were all novel credit institutions driven by the need to finance large infrastructure and other economic development projects (Allen, 2011, 42).

19.2 Financial Integration: Good or Bad?

Late nineteenth century Liberalism held economic globalisation in all its forms as beneficial to all participants, at least on an average and ongoing basis. The argument for unfettered capital flow was the same as that offered for "free trade", i.e. that goods and capital, when allowed unhindered flow, will be allocated to their most efficient uses. Also, a global capital pool is deeper and more diversified than a single domestic one and hence offers better risk sharing. Finally, free flowing capital moving across globally integrated capital markets increases efficiency by serving as a check on bad government policymaking (Bordo & Meissner, 2007, 12).

These are identical to arguments that are typically offered for unfettered capital markets now. These views seemed compelling at the time, mainly because there seemed to be many examples of economies that did indeed benefit from receiving foreign investment and funds to finance trade. Russia's adoption of the Gold Standard in the late 1800s, by more tightly integrating the country into the world financial system has been said to lower its cost of capital, increased its imports of capital by around 1% of its national product and raised its annual GDP growth rate by around a half a percentage point. Canada and the other dominions of the British Empire (all white settler entities), and the US prior to the Civil War, clearly needed and benefited greatly from heavy and regular foreign capital inflows which underwrote both their trade deficits and much of their public investment (Bordo & Meissner, 2007, 12, 35).

Much capital flowed from the richer countries to the poorer ones, especially since the highest returns were generally to be found there as the Second Industrial Revolution intensified. The non-European countries that were still nominally independent responded to the European imperial incursions all around them by institutional and infrastructural modernisation, financing the process through the issuance of foreign debt that was often eagerly taken up by rich country buyers. The Ottoman Empire and Egypt, which broke away from Ottoman rule in the beginning of the nineteenth century, were early movers in this regard, seeking to reorganise their armies, centralise their administrations, reform their social structures and build public works, all of which required extensive borrowing (Stearns, 2001a, 2001b, Section: Relationship between development and debt).

However, this often came with a sort of debt peonage to Western creditors that could constitute an alternative form of imperialism. By the mid-1870s, the extensively debt-financed modernisation campaigns of the Ottoman Empire, Egypt and Tunisia had all resulted in defaults on large loans taken from European bankers. Financial and political controls were established by European powers that restricted expenditures and sovereignty of regional governments in each of these countries (Stearns, 2001a, 2001b, Section: Relationship between development and debt). Of course, the bondholders in the lending countries, particularly France and Germany, were also sometimes burnt badly financially. These countries, however, retained their full political sovereignty.

In the extreme foreign money could as quickly flow out of an economy as it had flowed in, referred to as "hot money", or suddenly stop coming in, known as a "capital stop". Indeed, capital mobility is highly associated with financial crisis. Global crises occurred regularly, about once a decade, in 1816, 1826, 1837, 1847,1857, 1866 and 1873, then slowing their pace a bit with others in 1907, and 1921 (Kindleberger & Aliber, 2005, 24). There were multiple smaller more localised crises during between 1800 and 1913, and some of the "panics" of the time were major enough in magnitude and duration that they were only outdone by the Great Depression and the Global Financial Crisis of 2007–8.

Of course, it can still be argued that the economic development benefits outweighed these costs. Subsequent research has called into question much of this optimism. When looking across a wide sample of countries during the period, there seems to be little association between improved economic performance and levels of foreign capital inflows. Some countries had very good experiences with high levels of capital inflows, others had very poor experiences, and there is everything in between (Bordo & Meissner, 2007).

There was also a parallel geopolitical argument for economic and financial integration as well, that it would result in world peace, or at least less likelihood of general war. Politicians and theoreticians of the time argued that global interdependence in trade and finance would make prolonged war impossible and the outbreak of war less probable. The collapse of trade and finance, it was argued, would bring any fighting to a quick halt if it did occur, and the prospect of such a collapse would shift the general benefit–cost calculation away from hostilities (Tooze, 2014, 199). But this was purely from the perspective of the rich nations. The majority of the world's population lived through constant European incursions and conquests which in some cases were enhanced and sometimes even driven by capital flows, since there could be substantial pressure on governments to protect national assets overseas. The peace that capital mobility advocates were speaking of was thus about the European continent only and maybe for the major white settler offshoots. Even this possibility proved chimerical after the First World War broke out (see Chapter 14).

19.3 North/South Finance and Financial Hegemony

As a private business, commerce and finance have always relied on trust between the parties involved and in any intermediaries employed. As the international order complexified, it became more and more difficult to have personal connections upon which to base this. Thus an established commercial social milieu arose, and by the 1800s, international traders and financiers constituted a "cosmopolitan bourgeoisie", their value-add cemented by their client networks, close relationships with governments, and ability to move sums of money around quickly and easily, for a cut. Many of this class were Europeans, but there were significant numbers of Chinese, many operating out of the British enclave of Hong Kong (Foreman-Peck, 1983, 57).

This global financial trade network of individuals and institutions was a natural outgrowth of the exigencies of international commerce, in which a buyer of goods in one country had to pay a supplier of goods in another country in advance, with significant and uncertain lags in when the product would be received. It was risky for the buyer to pay upfront or the seller to ship upfront, for in the case of non-payment or non-delivery, it would be very costly, and perhaps impossible, to seek redress of breaches of contract, especially in the days when information and goods could still flow relatively slowly over sometimes uncertain sea and land routes. Thus an array of financial middlemen arose to take on the risk for buyer or seller or both, creating financial instruments that they would hold in trust, releasing funds or goods, as the case might be, only after a transaction was completed. This created a system of international third party accreditation of credit from private broker/dealers, who kept their own books. This was essential for the ongoing integration of the world economy, although the intermediaries themselves had interests there were not always aligned with their clients, or the public (Graff et al., 2013, 90–96).

The rise of this private nexus was associated with the creation of an international payments settlement system, conducted as a sort of public–private partnership. The first apotheosis of this system came with the peak of European imperialism and the British Empire especially. Coordination between public and private actors was essential and its form was a nominally technically neutral system ("numbers don't lie") with embedded interests and a notional "centre" for coordinating and manipulating things. British industrial and imperial leadership led to England being the economic centre, London its hub. The result was the Gold Standard, (discussed in more detail in the following section) and technically gold served as the world unit of account and means of transactions settlement. But in practice, Sterling was the first call for financing trade and investment, the Pound being a world reserve currency, with movements of gold being secondary (Graff et al., 2013, 100–108).

Arguably, this financial-imperial dimension was a core plank of building a broader core-periphery world economic system. England thus served as a "hegemon", a supremely dominant power that this sort of integrated centralised economic-financial network required. Whether a modern global economy needs to be designed around a hegemonic power is not completely clear from a conceptual point of view. This is, however, how things rolled out, and continue to into the present day. Certainly, a one-hegemon arrangement does have the advantage of consolidating the essential system maintenance and preservation functions required to operate for the general public good, and which might not be done otherwise (McKeown, 1983; Oneal & Oneal, 1988).

But as always, power tends to corrupt, or least tends towards becoming self-serving, an opportunity England availed itself of frequently. Britain kept the global financial accounts in the 1800s, and generally to its own advantage, reinforced by the power it exercised as a colonial master of dominions that covered around a quarter of the globe's territory at its peak. Britain also managed financial relations within its own Empire ruthlessly to maintain its privilege. Territories inside the Empire operated under what was called "Imperial Preference" which was a sort of internal free trade area, but one that was biased towards the mother country and, secondarily, the white Offshoots. India in particular served as a safety valve to maintain the capital surpluses so necessary for English financial dominance as a banker to the rest of the world and major source of investment capital (Graff et al., 2013, 138–140, 193).

England financially squeezed its non-white colonies in particular, in a number of other ways. For one thing, the internal colonial exchange rates were regularly manipulated to British advantage. Liability accounts of the colonies were calculated in London, and not fairly, with the interest and principal owed to England generally overstated. Hard bargains for colonial goods were driven through the monopsony power of a centralised English buyer cartel, e.g. the Wool Association of the UK buying Indian wool, for deflated prices, with no such leverage on the colonial seller side. The fact that a British colony never defaulted on any its own debt during this time is often trumpeted as a sign of how well the London-based imperial financial network functioned. But it also could be seen as a sign of how little agency colonial borrowers actually had, especially those not in relatively self-governing dominions, such as India. External debt by colonies, even when domestically issued, was mostly in foreign currency, often Sterling, or set in terms of pre-defined amounts of gold through "gold clauses". Either way the borrower had to come up with hard foreign currency and/or gold and was often short of it when principal or interest payments rolled around (Bordo & Meissner, 2007, 5–8). For borrowers outside the imperial system, this often took the form of default, sometimes resulting in a form of a peonage, as discussed above. Inside it, default was not allowed and the master simply expropriated the necessary resources. Either way the debtor often paid dearly (Fig. 19.2).

Even if a country was not a colony of England, the Gold Standard itself disadvantaged the countries that had monetary silver standards when settling trade and financial balances. Silver was a cheaper metal and yet international accounts had to be settled in gold or gold-backed currencies, resulting in heavier burdens of real payments for imports, and depreciated prices for exports when converting from silver into gold. India had a silver standard and this served as an additional disadvantage it faced. But China, nominally sovereign, also suffered from biased global economic arrangements because of its own silver standard. Either way the result was disadvantage for the weaker countries (Davis, 2002, 332).

This is not to say the England was necessarily any worse than the other major Europeans powers of the time, such as the French. Britain was simply more powerful and the greater the power the greater the privilege. And some peripheral countries nonetheless did benefit from the greater flow of resources facilitated by London-based finance system. The US was a major beneficiary, as were some Latin American countries, such as Argentina, which were major exporters of critical inputs in broader

Fig. 19.2 Colonised currency (*Image source* Von Bergen, W. [1889]. The rare coins of America, England, Ireland, Scotland, France, Germany, and Spain ... a complete list of and prices paid for rare American ... coins, fractional currency, colonial, continental and Confederate paper money; a list of all counterfeit U. S. Treasury and national bank notes and Canadian banks notes, and how to detect them; the market value of all nations' coins and bank notes in U.S. money; a list of and prices paid for rare English, Irish, Scotch, French, German and Spanish coins. Illustrated with about 150 cuts. W. Von Bergen. Page 162. Digitizing sponsor: The Library of Congress. No known copyright restrictions)

production processes and thus had some market leverage in the terms of their export trade. And of course where there was true agency on the part of peripheral countries, they were not entirely blameless for whatever conditions they found themselves in. For example, some of the proceeds from foreign debt were wasted in corruption and vanity projects. Better management by the recipient governments could have avoided some of the resulting defaults while making more productive use of the funds.

In general, the benefits of financial integration during its first high water mark are more nuanced than many professed at the time, and certainly not particularly neutral in the technical sense as many believed. The integration was also not quite as complete as it seemed, and some have argued that the early global economy was actually a system of distinct regional blocs cemented through the UK, but sometimes operating independently of it. As time went on these regional blocs became more directly connected to one another, weakening British power and its "buffer function" role, especially the US and Japan grew in strength (Graff et al., 2013, 144).

19.4 The Rise of Central Banking and the Lender of Last Resort (LOLR)

As noted, a major problem with worldwide economic growth was its cyclical instability. This facet of the nineteenth and early twentieth century financial system was far from unnoticed by contemporary policymakers. Credit creation boomed, powered by an explosion in the number and size of financial intermediaries, financial instruments and the huge growth of corporate forms and entities (which led to a burgeoning issuance of corporate shares that acted as a sort of alternative money which could be used to create more financial leverage as well as financing real investment). This made sense given the powered up growth in real economic activity, which gobbled up liquidity. But this credit creation also expanded the effective money supply, a quantity that included official money backed by Gold, but leveraged to a much higher total, and was in fact growing faster than real output. It was clear that this monetary expansion was the source of many booms and busts.

Two different views of how to manage this problem arose, both of which are remarkably similar to present divides on the issue, though using different labels. The Currency School advocated a firm limit on the expansion of the money supply to avoid inflation and speculation, a notion very similar to the contemporary Monetarist theories of today. It was thought that if money supply growth were constrained, the booms and busts that over-exuberant leveraging resulted in would be too. The Banking School took a different tack, arguing that increases in money supply would not be inflationary so long as they were financing real business transactions. In this case money and credit growth was playing its proper role of greasing real economic growth, with the result that monetary overheating and crashing would be limited (Kindleberger & Aliber, 2005, 68) (This is somewhat similar to the positions current Modern Monetary Theory (MMT), which holds that so long as there is sufficient capacity in the real economy, debt and credit will not be inflationary or overly stimulative under certain conditions [Mitchell et al., 2016]).

This all sounded well and good but either path had its challenges. The Currency School position had the problem of establishing what the "right" rate of growth in the money supply actually was. Set a growth rate that was too low and the economy would underperform in real terms; set it too high and the economy would overheat. The Banking School had a somewhat parallel problem: how could you tell in advance what was "real" finance versus purely "speculative"? Business investment was inherently uncertain, and while it might be clear in retrospect what was financial wheat and what was chaff, it was far harder to determine that in prospect.

Either way there was a fundamental issue of control. Who would actually regulate these relationships between real and financial sectors, and how would they do it? The levers were clear enough, i.e. managing the growth of money and credit and regulating its price, i.e. the interest rate. But the details were hard to work out, especially in a time of rapid economic transformation and an exceptionally dynamic finance sector. As is the case today, this was a process of feeling one's way, and there were many hidden, and not so hidden, bumps to contend with.

The spectacular collapse of the South Sea Company after a huge run-up in the price of its financial instruments (the whole incident being referred to as the South Sea Bubble) led some of the first financial regulation on record. The English Parliament passed the Bubble Act of June 1720, strengthening it with further amendments in 1749. This act made the establishment of an incorporated business more difficult and was not repealed until the nineteenth century (Kindleberger & Aliber, 2005, 92). The Act did not end further crises. Though it did have the intended limiting effects on the formation of fraudulent enterprises, it also caused some unintended limiting of legitimate ones, the literature being ambivalent about its overall net effect on the British economy. Still it was an attempt to ensure that finance would not so easily be funnelled into mere money speculation and it did have some success on that score.

Meanwhile on the money and credit control side, the Bank of England, a private institution, had already assumed substantial money supply and credit control functions within the English economy. Financial crises in the first decades of the 1800s resulted in significant strengthening of the Bank's powers when it came up for rechartering, codified in the Bank Charter Act of 1844. This Act took much of the Currency School's views to heart, and provided a monopoly to the Bank on the issuing of the national currency, along with restrictions on other private banks from doing so (Horsefield, 1944).

The Act is sometimes promulgated as a watershed in establishing the first true national central bank. This is somewhat of an overstatement, given that it really just continued a process begun in 1694 of giving the Bank of England central banking functions, rather than a sudden shift (Whale, 1944, 109). But the idea that a domestic economy required a central bank to govern its monetary operations was certainly cemented with the Act, becoming a global model given Britain's economic and geopolitical predominance.

A national central bank, however, still only had responsibility for the domestic economy. In the case of the British Empire and the centrality of London to a new world financial system, this domestic institution nonetheless had some significant de facto powers for setting money supply growth and interest rates for the rest of the world. The tension between the interests of England and other countries has already been mentioned. But the necessity of the Bank of England's maintaining a reputation for impartiality in order to maximise its overall international power and freedom of action did cause the Bank to act in the global interest more than it otherwise might have. The Bank was also keen to make sure, to the extent that it could, that crises either did not occur, or get out of hand when they did. The modern term of "Lender of Last Resort" (LOLR) did not exist then but this was a key function of the Bank, both domestically and internationally, though not always understood as such at the time. Indeed the Bank did intervene at critical junctures with injections of liquidity and capital to avert absolute catastrophe, though it could not prevent all disturbances (Humphrey, 1975).

There was a more fundamental issue as well, namely the balance between system stability and growth. More of one implied less of the other. Growth is beneficial, but tends to create crises, which are costly. So at what point was the balance right? This issue remained mostly implicit until the Great Depression definitively showed that international markets could not always be relied upon to correct themselves adequately, especially without a strong hegemon. Before then central banks did not see management of what would become known as the "macro-economy", domestic or international, as one of its functions. Afterwards, they did (see Chapter 17). But the answer to the question has not necessarily become much clearer with time.

19.5 The Classical Gold Standard and the Global Politics of Money

With the rise of civilisation, money in its more familiar form became a widely used mechanism for exchange. Commodity money, i.e. the use of a precious metal such as gold or silver, became the first norm, with governments issuing coins made out of a chosen metal (usually gold) as a way of both standardising weights (e.g. a particular coin always being a certain number of grams) and ensuring quality (purity) (e.g. a particular coin always being 99.99% pure). Governments did sometimes seek to cheat on both dimensions to get "extra" money, e.g. debase the metal of a coin by mixing cheaper metals into the base for coinage, e.g. copper, with gold or shaving bits of weight off of a coin. Indeed the term "debasement of money" referred originally to the process of moving a metal to a lower base, though in the modern era debasement refers to any cheapening of money, whatever its form (Chown & Chown, 1994).

A monetary invention with even greater potential was paper money, invented in China during the Tang dynasty period (618–907 C.E.). It emerged as traders discovered that depositing their earnings with their home trading companies and receiving bearer notes (*bequan*) in exchange were much more convenient—and secure—than carrying metal coins around. The *bequan* were such a success that the central government invited merchants to deposit their metallic money in the Government Treasury in exchange for official "compensation notes", called *Fey-thsian* or "flying money" (Horesh, 2012).

By the time of the Industrial Revolution, European countries had moved largely to a sort of hybrid in which low value coins intended for domestic circulation were made out of non-precious metals, and paper money (as well as paper financial instruments such as bonds) were the basis of most global capital movements and other large funds transactions, but with gold increasingly being the officially accepted standard of underlying value. With Britain's global ascendancy, the Gold Standard in its "classical" incarnation was born.

Gold as a basis of currency value was, as noted, as old as commodity currency itself. The Gold Standard system was, however, new because all the major economies in Europe and many large and small ones outside of it, now made their currencies convertible into gold at a specific value per unit, pegged off a single reserve currency, in this case Sterling. Thus, a holder of one British pound Sterling could in theory go to the British treasury and redeem (i.e. convert) that pound into its set value of grams of gold. Because all countries on the Gold Standard did this, at any given time exchange rates between different currencies were fixed to one another as determined by their respective relative values to the official gold price.

This central linkage was new and it was made possible by British hegemony as a clearinghouse bank and (unspoken) LOLR. The Bank of England had huge amounts of liquidity to keep the system liquid, especially during hard times. It also served as the world's largest market for gold, allowing it to manipulate gold supplies as well as liquidity and interest rates, as needed (or desired). And the Pound Sterling's role as a world reserve currency—a basic unit of account and underlying medium of exchange globally—provided the Bank with a second line of defence in times of trouble. The Bank of England sacrificed a measure of its own profitability (as noted above it remained a private entity but with central banking functions) to maintain the system stability from which it benefited most, but not exclusively so (Eichengreen, 1996, 37).

This system was supposedly self-regulating and automatic, promoting efficient movement of capital to settle goods trade accounts and international investments. However, even in this Classical age, things did not always operate as theory said they should. The English philosopher and Classical Economist David Hume had argued that a "price-specie-flow" mechanism operated in which domestic prices and/or gold reserves would adjust in response to changes in business conditions to keep prices and gold supplies allocated where they needed to be and in the most efficient manner (McGee, 1989). This theory underlay the Gold Standard.

And yet Hume's theory was already going out of date by the time the Gold Standard emerged. Hume wrote in a time when most trade was in tangible goods, and much international money supply was still in gold coin, allowing for a close and rather automatic balancing between prices, money exchanges and specie settlement. As the nineteenth century progressed, "invisibles" (services, especially those involved in making financial transactions possible) were becoming increasingly important in world trade and domestic and international transactions were predominantly made with paper money and other instruments, often never having to settle in gold at all. Thus, the Gold Standard was based on a scheme that worked best when there was little disjoint between volumes of money and real trade, as was the case back in the day when the total amount of gold (and other monetised metals) and total amount of circulating money were essentially equal to one another, and most monetary transaction was done through exchange of gold.

This was no longer the case in the nineteenth century. The result was that the behaviour of trade balances, international relative prices of goods, and movements of gold did not seem to always behave in the ways that theory predicted. In other words, money flows did not purely follow the trends of the real economy, but had dynamics of their own, and gold flows were relatively detached from both of them except at a gross level when central banks were settling accounts between themselves. Besides which Hume's theory assumed perfectly competitive markets for international trade in goods as opposed to an environment in which a few large enterprises often had oligopoly or monopoly power. Meanwhile the rise of London as the primary global financial centre, the manipulation of central bank discount rates, and the increasing mobility and preponderance of short-term capital, rather than long-term investments (though both were growing in absolute terms) all queered the theoretical presumption of purely competitive markets for capital, with interrelated single markets of varying competitiveness being the reality (Eichengreen, 1996, 32–34).

Despite the Bank of England's supposed neutrality, it could not resist taking advantage of its privileged position when it came to international debt management. There were myriad defaults on peripheral world sovereign debt held by France, Germany and other countries. But English investors generally came out unscathed, and not by accident. The Bank frequently exercised its prerogative as a central clearinghouse to hold foreign deposits hostage to have debt workouts play in England's favour. The Bank also could hold lower cash reserves (which had little or no return) than its counterparts because of the centrality of its position in global financial markets. In fact, the Bank was consistently under-reserved relative to the risks it had to manage, and this threadbare cupboard was exposed at times; for example, during the close-run Barings Crisis of 1890, the Sterling Crisis of 1906 and the US financial crisis of 1907, all of which the Bank shepherded the world through, but, it should be noted, with the essential coordination and cooperation by other central banks, especially France's, which, though not as privileged, nonetheless made its own crucial investments in overall system stability, without which the Gold Standard may well have cratered before 1914 (Eichengreen, 1996, 43–49). England's financial power was real, but not quite always as strong as it looked.

By 1890 the financial system of capital flows was growing more turbulent, with short-term liabilities more and more outweighing long-term investment flows. Short-term money could move a lot faster than longer-term funds, and their movements were more difficult to police. Britain's fiscal hegemony was already fading as its own relative growth slowed down and new competitors for top position, especially Germany and America, were rapidly coming up. The US was particularly problematic in terms of generating international financial crisis, especially as it was growing proportionally more important in the world economy, and yet had little interest in playing a role in managing the greater good. The US by 1890 had acquired 15% of the world's gold reserves and was a large economy in its own right in monetary terms. But America's economic development was still somewhat uneven and it had no central bank of its own. These two factors led to an unstable domestic money supply that was heavily reliant on foreign funds and which, in times of crisis, sucked in a great amount of gold from overseas, putting the European currencies in a precarious position since the ability to cover demands for conversion of their currencies into gold was insufficient during times of such outflow. The country also had a somewhat unstable commitment to the Gold Standard, with periodic political crises, driven by agrarian discontent, moving national policy into bimetallism (a dual gold and silver standard), then complete conversion to silver, dalliance with a movement away from a bullion standard entirely, and finally back to bimetallism. The US banking system was also highly fragmented and competitive, good in some ways for domestic credit, but prone, then as now, to financial bubbles. This is in contrast with much more stable Australia and New Zealand, which also did not have central banks, though they were, of course, much smaller economies. However, their domestic banking systems were much better developed. And, of course, they operated within the British Empire (Eichengreen, 1996, 54–55, 61–62).

19.6 Infrastructure and Money

Financial dynamics of this time were also affected by the massive increase in worldwide infrastructure investment, both public and private, as well as the rise of capital-intensive industry and a whole raft of "network" goods such urban mass transit, railways and electricity. The building of these real assets requiring vast amounts of capital raising and provided a tremendous impetus to the creation of all manner of financial assets to do so.

The financing of huge integrated public works was not unprecedented, but one had to go a long way back to find it. The Roman Empire built a quasi-market economy, based on a long period of stable government, out of which it constructed an integrated transport and urban physical network that would not be matched again in Europe until after 1800. The Empire's paved road network at its peak was slightly in excess of 80,000 kilometres with a further 320,000 kilometres of unpaved minor roads reaching out to its peripheries. Road specifications and the legal status of public rights of way were standardised and codified, and roads were constructed to be as straight as possible, designed to minimise long-term maintenance requirements. The Roman governance and financing system for all this was sophisticated, the State financing construction through taxes, but devolving maintenance funding to local authorities, thus incentivising their good stewardship. The Empire also funded the arterial connections and major systems, such as water, while the municipality was responsible for roads within its boundaries and other ancillary facilities (Goldsmith, 2014, 12–14).

With the Industrial Revolution, there were new empires, but these were outside the European continent, and the wider world was a much more competitive and multi-polar place. There was a new, and even more massive need, for wide-scale infrastructure building, but without the central apparatus of a Roman Empire. This new program was built on a more decentralised basis, using the novel mechanism of corporate enterprise, which was busily building networks that required large amounts of capital upfront before being sure of the viability of the business or its uptake by a critical mass of consumers. For example, Alexander Graham Bell's invention of the first commercially viable telephone in 1876 kicked off a long process of arranging finance to build the telephone network that would make the telephone a useful device and a profitable business. Bell's first companies could not find adequate capital but ultimately attained the necessary seed money from a railroad financier looking for new investment opportunities. Bell then had to fiddle with the right charging model for his services, changing from charging per connection to charging for each call, and then using his patent monopoly and profits to expand and to buy rival technologies. Corporate restructuring followed when the company separated long distance from local services (Goldsmith, 2014, 25).

By contrast, unlike Bell, who built his own network, Thomas Edison decided to gain technical monopolies through patents, which he then licensed to local operating companies, equipping them with his own devices, and accepting payment in local operator shares. The US financial panic and crash of 1893 caused a crisis for Edison that his business model never really recovered from (though Edison's own personal wealth continued to grow), especially since the financiers, the merchant bank of J.P. Morgan primarily, stepped in to split off the manufacturing equipment arm to become General Electric. There were many variants, but the typical network finance path started with money coming in from what would now be called venture capitalists, leading, if successful, to the establishment of a profitable network with monopolistic features that then generated sufficient returns to be able to rely on internal financing generated through growth in demand and profits. This financing through corporate retained earnings was leveraged with corporate financial engineering to create new interrelated entities with their own shares that could be sold to raise new capital from shareholders or serve as collateral for bank finance (Goldsmith, 2014, 26).

Railways were another industrial-financial nexus, a new technology whose construction boom covered the world with railways within 70 years. What really facilitated the diffusion of railways globally was finance and corporate organisation. This came on the back of the turnpikes and canal boom in England, with private financing incentivised by the English government, helped along by the repeal of the Bubble Act in 1824 which allowed for the creation of limited liability joint stock companies. Transport (and, to a lesser degree, communications) were technologies that lent themselves to a positive feedback loop between industrial and financing activity, with early service providers and facility operators funding local infrastructure which benefited them directly and expanding from there. The ravenous appetite for capital that resulted created a market for an expanding set of financial intermediaries, while the limited liability company created a growing market for trading in shares. This process was not actually all that efficient, with initial competition for first-mover status and desperate shake-outs afterwards into monopoly and oligopoly consolidations leading to financial excess and overbuilding which caused huge amounts of capital to be wasted due to duplication of lines, and a total loss for some participants. But the networks got built in the end, and the winners made a lot of money. British incentivising of private actors was not the only way to accomplish this. The French government, for example, took a leading role in planning the core network, an approach that avoided many of the excesses elsewhere and which has carried through to its building of its modern high-speed rail network (Goldsmith, 2014, 31–32).

The infrastructure and network asset boom drove a whole raft of financial innovation and blew up the scale of financing to unprecedented levels, done on a private–public basis with varying balances between the two, quite different, by necessity, from the earlier Roman Empire model. The boundaries between financial and industrial firms were often blurred, sometimes deliberately so. The profit motive was a powerful coordinator of all this network building, whatever the arrangements were. This profit incentive system was far from "wornout", to use Dos Passos's later phrase; but it did show some signs that even at this relatively early point it might be "tending more and more to strangle on its own power and complexity" (Dos Passos, 1932, vii). That dynamic would become more apparent during the later twentieth century and the ramp up in "financialisation".

19.7 Falling Standards

The Classical Gold Standard pre-1914 had required a lot of coordination between central banks, something easier when the major European banks had more capital, were largely in creditor positions, experiencing strong economic growth, and with England acting as a hegemon at the centre of the global economy and itself a major creditor. This period was actually not that long, with Eichengreen and Flandreau (1997) dating it between 1870–1914, squarely within the high tide of the Second Industrial Revolution.

World war broke all this comity up, though it was gradually unwinding even before then. Between the end of the war and 1933/4, the year when most countries abandoned the Gold Standard, the major creditor of the time was the US. But America would not step into the system management role that the Bank of England had done earlier. Britain was now an international debtor and considerably weakened by the war. France was in even worse shape. The background geopolitics was of conflict and instability and tended away from cooperation between powers and towards enmity and suspicion. The result was a revised Gold Standard, which, unlike its earlier incarnation, was more of a burden than a benefit to world finances for a number of reasons. As noted the world central banks were not as cooperative as they once had been and the new major American power was the least cooperative of all. Countries had made unwise choices about the exchange rates in gold they would set their currencies in after the war, notably the British Pound Sterling having too high a value, the French franc having one too low, the result being distorted trade flows. And when global economic conditions deteriorated, the system of fixed exchange rates could not adjust to respond to them (Cooper, 1992). (See Chapter 17).

Once the Depression hit, a dysfunctional system became deadly. Many countries found themselves in a squeeze on their international obligations as the Depression unfolded and the Gold Standard worsened matters for capital account deficit countries, which needed capital more than ever, and yet had to export their increasingly scarce gold to meet their international obligations. Before 1914, and, to a much lesser extent, between 1919 and 1929, capital surplus countries sometimes chose to help out the system by exporting some of their own gold to those in need, sometimes physically, more often just by internal bookkeeping transfers. In this way, many gold crises were averted since transactions were settled as if there was adequate gold on each side, whether there was or not. With the Depression, these niceties were abandoned, the safety valve closed, and those with excess gold hoarded the metal, much as individuals were hoarding their cash if they had it (Temin, 1993). Gold surplus countries like France and the US did this, making everyone worse off in the end, including themselves. Most countries, including the US, had domestic central banks, which in theory might have increased coordination globally. But these generally had policies, such as large reserve requirements (i.e. requirements to hold high levels of gold in their vaults) that made the international supply of gold more immobile than ever. Deficit countries could afford to lose very little of their gold supply before they were forced into deflationary reductions in their domestic money supply to keep their international accounts balanced. Domestic central banks were also generally prohibited in most countries from buying and holding the debt of their own governments, further restricting the ability to "monetise" it (i.e. having the central bank buy up the debt) and lessen its burden. Domestic government debt thus had to be sold internationally, in a time of weak or sometimes non-existing demand for it. If the necessary funds could not be raised or could be gotten only at high interest rates, further cuts in domestic money supply and government spending became required, deepening the local contraction, and causing further credit squeezes and pressure for gold outflows internationally (Bernanke & James, 1991, 36–39).

Fiscal philosophy of the time made things worse, being dominated by "sound money" principles, a slight adaptation of the Currency School ideas of the nineteenth century, which called for low money supply growth, high interest rates and balanced government budgets to "correct" the crisis. It was the wrong policy at the worst possible time, but nobody knew this then. There was no ability to resist or combat deflation when it came, nor any firewalls against the effects of international shocks on domestic banking systems (Bernanke & James, 1991, 40–41).

Trends in the world supply of physical gold didn't help matters. The gold rushes of the 1800s did not occur in this period (see Box 19.1), so global supplies of gold stay relatively fixed. Since domestic money supply and world supply of gold were directly related, it was not auspicious that worldwide gold supplies were growing during the 1930s at a rate of around 2% annually, while most domestic money supply on average needed to be growing faster than that to sustain any hope of economic recovery. This limitation of the Gold Standard, i.e. that it was tethered to the rather arbitrary growth in worldwide gold supplies, became another fatal flaw during the Depression (Bernanke, 1995).

Box 19.1 Gold Rushes

Precious metals have always been a source of inspired greed in many people and the potential to discover new sources of them in theory provide an opportunity to gain vast wealth in an instant, rather like winning the lottery. This possibility is increased under systems of precious metal currency, as was the case under the Gold Standard. Here profit opportunity is greatly enhanced, since all one has to do is discover the metal (gold or silver) and then sell it into international markets or to the monetary authority at the prevailing price.

Of course, it is far from easy to make such grand sums, not least because discovery, extraction, purification, and shipping of the metal are difficult and high-cost. Still the prospect encouraged a wave of "Gold rushes" (and some "silver rushes" too) in the nineteenth and early twentieth centuries, in which masses of people would quickly migrate to sites of new discoveries to find their fortune. Although existing very intermittently before industrialisation, such rushes became a frequent occurrence afterwards, often reaching manic levels, in part because of the vastly greater ease of travel in which gold-seekers could quickly move to the locations of the latest finds.

Gold rushes are legendary for their intense local impacts, of which there are many vivid stories. One less chronicled, but no less colourful, episode is the gold rush that took over Australia in the mid-1870s. Like many episodes, an interesting and volatile ethnic politics played out. In

1874, Cooktown, in Queensland, once a small town, had 94 hotel licenses issued in that year alone to house all the many people pouring in, seeking to stake their claims. By 1875, 9,000 people were doing so, 7,000 of them Chinese. By 1877, there were 19,500 miners, of which 18,000 were Chinese. This was only the latest increment of Chinese gold seekers in Australia, part of more than 40,000 in total who had arrived since 1853 who called Australia the "new gold mountain". Like most would-be miners, they had to borrow heavily to get to the country. And, like most, a relative few had moderate success and paid off their debts, while many others failed and remained in debt peonage.

These Chinese migrants also had to contend with discrimination and violence from white "diggers". And they also fought amongst themselves. While Europeans saw Chinese people as an undifferentiated mass, the Chinese themselves were divided into various ethnic and regional groups. A particularly bad series of internecine battles at this time was known as the Tong Wars, triggered at first by Cantonese miners retaliating against Pekinese who had been suspected of raiding their camp. Pekinese deaths resulted, followed by retaliation against the Cantonese. Fighting continued until police arrested the ringleaders. After this the Cantonese and the Pekinese formed an alliance against a Macau group that had moved in during the earlier fighting. This was but one of many examples of the turmoil that the gold rushes brought, for most miners in much greater quantities than the gold they had hoped to find.

(Discussion above drawn from Forbes, 2014, 195–196).

The return to Gold after the War had been shambolic in many ways. Its full restoration was actually quite slow. Britain and France had returned to it quickly, but it took until 1928 before most countries had done the same. The system was tottering by 1931, only three years later, and it disappeared entirely by 1936 (Bernanke & James, 1991, 35–36). Thus, the transition between a fully restored post-war Gold Standard and no Gold Standard was actually very brief. The end, when it came, thus came rather quickly. First Argentina and Uruguay suspended gold payments in December of 1929, while Hungary, Paraguay and Brazil became unable to maintain their currencies at par. In these latter cases, the Gold Standard was not yet formally abandoned but practically it could no longer be supported. In 1930 Chile, Venezuela, Peru, Australia and New Zealand fell below the gold export point, which amounted to the same thing. Then a watershed came with Britain detaching from gold in September

1931. By the end of October 1931, all of the British Dominions, (save South Africa), the rest of the British Empire, and a number of Scandinavian, European, African and Latin American nations had followed suit. Six months after that Japan, Greece, Siam and Peru were off of gold as well. Germany had already imposed foreign exchange controls in July of that year (Eichengreen & Sachs, 1985, 928–929).

As the Gold Standard began to unravel, there was a seemingly perverse dynamic where the countries that were last to leave the gold standard had more gold outflows than countries that left earlier. Bernanke (1995) explains this by saying that people had greater confidence in the currency stability of countries which had "bitten the bullet" earlier, than countries, like the US, that held on longer and which were increasingly seen as maintaining something that was fundamentally untenable. Not decisive in itself, this dynamic simply made the system's collapse faster and steeper.

A final nail to the gold coffin came when the US left gold in 1933. That process has its own dramatic details, typical of the cagey Roosevelt who tended to blow one way, then another, prone to making sudden gestures. America had already suddenly pulled out of a worldwide economic conference held that year, putting paid to any attempt at a unified global response to the crisis (Stein, 1969). That turned out to be a mere sideshow to the end of global financial integration and a common monetary standard. By 1936, the Gold Standard was dead entirely (Bernanke & James, 1991, 36).

The link between the gold standard and domestic banking crises is fairly well established. Countries that stayed on the gold standard were more likely to have banking panics than countries that went off it (Choudhri & Kochin, 1980). Countries that went off of the Gold Standard also generally recovered from the Depression much more quickly than countries that did not. Once countries went off of gold, they generally had markedly improved economic performance. Without having to conform to the Gold Standard's constraints, countries could freely inflate their domestic money supplies to fend off deflation. Some banking systems did much worse than others, even so, including "unit" systems, as in America, with lots of small banks and thus lots of banking failures; and "universal" or "mixed" systems, as in Germany and Austria, where banks typically held equity positions in many of their borrowers and thus were badly hit by large falls in share market values. The failure of Austria's Creditanstalt was an extreme example of this (Bernanke & James, 1991, 54–55).

The big lessons that were later gleaned from the collapse and perverse incentives of late-stage gold-ism found their way into the system of international exchange erected at the Bretton-Woods conference in 1946. The elements of this agreement included a managed exchange rate for currencies, subject to agreed upon parameters; free capital movements, subject to government intervention if need be; the construction of an international LOLR to deal with unanticipated and nationally unmanageable crises; and an unfettered trade in the current account (Cooper, 1992, 2125). (See Chapter 27).

19.8 Reparations and "Hot Money"

The strange dislocations of the War reinforced the dysfunction of the Gold Standard. After First World War fighting had ended, the US was the economic and financial powerhouse of the world. But it was reluctant and largely unable to step into the role formerly played by the Bank of England. For one thing, it had only just established its first central bank, the US Federal Reserve System, in 1913, and this system was both inexperienced and organised regionally, more focused on domestic than international needs. Politically the country was also isolationist (at least with respect to Europe) and did not want to get entangled in global financial leadership, though private US banks, like J.P. Morgan, were more than happy to profit from global ventures.

The European Allies were deeply indebted to American bankers, but not in a good position to repay their debts, having suffered major human, social and material losses. The US government had chosen to take a rather hard line on repayment of the debt that country had extended to its nominal Allies (though the US never actually joined the Allies, choosing instead to be an "Associated Power") (see Chapter 14). The Allied governments thus tried to get what they could out of Germany, which was required by the post-war settlement to pay reparations, eventually set at $US33 billion in gold. Germany, however, was in a poor position to pay, as it had ceded territory to Belgium, Czechoslovakia, Denmark, France and Poland; given up its overseas colonies; and accepted an Allied military force on the west bank of the Rhine River for fifteen years. In any case, the German government was not really willing to pay reparations even if they could (Marks, 1978).

Thus began a long and distorted travail over global movements of capital to milk Germany to pay Allied war debts to the US which in turn rescheduled German reparations payments to allow that country to make the payments to the Allies that would ultimately flow back to the US anyway in the form of debt repayments, all with nations that in some way or another did not have the capacity to pay their full burdens. This perversity of financial flows (which was frankly unsustainable in any case) would have major negative consequences for the global economy.

Reparations were enshrined in Article 231 of the peace treaties between the Allies and Germany, Austria and Hungary. Germans thought of this as the "War Guilt clause", though nowhere was guilt mentioned and the Austrians and Hungarians did not think of their indemnities that way. Theoretically, reparations were assessed against damage done (this too was defined in specific ways) and were unlimited, but the actual amounts were considered in an annex and partly based on Allied views of Germany's capacity to pay. The final amount of 132 billion gold marks for German reparations was a compromise figure, suggested by the Belgians, a splitting of the difference between a lower British and higher French figure (Marks, 1978, 231–232, 236).

The first major crisis in reparations took place in 1923 when the Reparations Commission voted 3–1 to declare Germany in default of its obligations and, in another vote by the same margin, to have the Rhineland occupied to force payment. However while the French were keen, the British stood largely aloof, acquiescing in allowing French and Belgian troops to use British controlled railways in the Rhine to move troops in to occupy Düsseldorf and the western Ruhr cities of Duisburg and Ruhrort, but otherwise refusing to take sides. This decision prolonged the crisis and sent mixed signals to the Germans (Marks, 1978, 243–244). The Ruhr, just east of the Allied-occupied zone, was targeted due to its pre-eminence as Germany's coal mining, metallurgical, heavy engineering and armaments production centre.

This move prompted the German government to suspend the cash payment of reparations in August. A concerted passive resistance campaign took place in the Ruhr, met by complete collapse of production there and suppression by Franco-Belgian troops (with over 130 deaths). Interestingly, the occupation yielded profits for the three Allied powers to the tune of 900 million gold Marks. Britain also benefited temporarily from disruption of German exports, though British officials did not admit this, even to themselves (Marks, 1978, 245–246) (Fig. 19.3).

But overall the occupation had negative consequences. The subsequent US-sponsored Dawes repayment plan reduced reparations, and

Fig. 19.3 Notice of French invasion of Essen, Ruhr Valley, Germany, 1923 (*Image source* US Library of Congress, Prints and Photographs Division, hdl.loc.gov/loc.pnp/pp.print. Part Of: Bain News Service photograph collection (DLC) 2,005,682,517 hdl.loc.gov/loc.pnp/pp.ggbain. Call Number: LC-B2- 5919–13. No known copyright restrictions)

was pushed mainly by American financiers, especially J. P. Morgan and Company, largely to the benefit of American investors, and unhappily given in to by the other powers, particularly France. The Germans had yielded, but resentfully and incompletely. The last Belgian and French troops left the Ruhr Valley in mid-August of 1925 (Marks, 1978, 248–249).

Thus began a process of continued loosening of German obligations, while maintaining the increasingly thin facade that these would actually be paid someday. In the Spring of 1929 (before the Great Crash later that year), the Young plan cut reparations roughly in half, eliminated the Reparations Commission and placed reparations disbursements and settlements with a new Bank for International Settlements (BIS) in 1931 (which still remains today still exercising its other stated function of the time, which is to foster central bank cooperation). German acceptance of this plan was rewarded with Allied evacuation of the Rhineland on 30 June 1930. US President Herbert Hoover brokered a one-year moratorium on reparations payments on 1 July 1931 to stem capital flight from Germany, benefiing US investors but hurting French interests. Though never formally cancelled, reparations were moribund by 1932 and later ignored by Hitler, who also repudiated some of the loans taken to make reparation payments before he took power. All in all just 20 billion gold marks, the equivalent of $US5 billion, were paid out, though even this ignores Hitler's later loan repudiations (Marks, 1978, 250–254).

The US had not ratified the peace treaty with Germany and thus had no claim to any reparations, which is one reason that it ended up being a mediator between the Allies on the issue. Yet the Americans were playing a dangerous double game, basically trying to preserve their own private creditors and the myriad investors in German securities who wanted to keep the credit system there solvent, making money all the way by infusing it with short-term loans and other capital. This increasing reliance of German banks on foreign capital was to have devastating results during the 1930s. Foreign loans were not just supporting the German central government; they were supporting every sector of the German public sector, and much of the private sector and much of the banking sector as well. This excess of foreign money was good in the sense that it kept the German economy humming (and underwrote a series of public investments by various levels of government). But it was bad in the sense that it kept German banks from addressing the fundamental weaknesses in their core businesses. It also left the German economy very vulnerable to any sudden cut-off in foreign funds. The Depression was magnified greatly in that that country as a result (Adalet, 2003).

Foreign capital didn't flow into Germany because of the goodness of foreign lenders' hearts. It flowed in because German interest rates were much higher than elsewhere, never lower than 1% more in Berlin than in New York and often multiple points higher. And German capital holders themselves were no more committed to the German financial system than foreigners. There is convincing evidence that a good portion of sudden capital outflows from 1929 to 1931 was not true foreign money being withdrawn but German money disguised as foreign money retreating to safe havens (James, 1984).

Germany in this sense is a sort of case study of the international financial system after the First World War. It contained, in a real sense, the worst aspects of international management and regulation, and of freewheeling untrammelled capital flows. The Gold Standard and the Versailles settlement were both half-baked and only half-functioning throughout the period, tending to hamper necessary adjustments rather than enabling them. Meanwhile, global money was flowing more rapidly and freely than ever before, with very destabilising results. The relative prosperity of the 1920s papered over these deficiencies, which would become all too obvious during the 1930s (see Chapter 17).

19.9 Goodbye to All that

The global system of international trade and finance had only partially re-integrated after First World War. After the Great Depression it fragmented. It had already been hindered by the US being in a near-hegemonic position but refusing to take up its mantle; Britain's taking up the hegemonic mantle but no longer being equal to it; Germany being hobbled internally and externally by reparations that it was unable and unwilling to pay and which its major European creditors were counting on to pay US debts; and an international web of "hot money" that flowed into countries, especially Germany, too much coming in during the 1920s, too much flowing out with the Depression. This was compounded by the distortionary and deflationary effects of the Interwar Gold Standard that, before its complete collapse in the early 1930s, caused many countries to resort to piecemeal protectionism to protect against excessive external demands on their gold reserves and prop up local demand for domestic industries (Eichengreen, 1996).

By the late 1930s, the main characteristics of the post-Gold Standard world were balanced exchange agreements, which often subjected long lists of goods from other countries to quotas along with elaborate schedules of split exchange rates. In Europe, Hitler's Germany made itself the centre of such an arrangement, especially eastward. The French and the British fell back defensively into protectionism within their internal imperial frameworks, while the Japanese were creating a new Empire for themselves out of the ruins of China. The Americans retreated into isolationism, focusing on captive imports from, and exports into, a subservient Latin America. Imbalances in the global capital accounts did largely disappear by the mid-1930s, but by fiat, not market forces (Ritschl & Straumann, 2010, 171–172, 175–176). They certainly were not "efficient" and they hampered growth.

Meanwhile, with the end of reparations in 1932, France and the UK declared default on their inter-Allied war debt to the US in December of that year; although the British in particular drew a hard line with their Dominions on the debt they held with London, an hypocrisy that led to a political crisis in Australia in 1931–32, as local elements of the political structure there demanded that Australian war debts be treated like the British were treating their own debts to the Americans. Rather quickly, though, the Australians capitulated. The US meanwhile enacted a credit ban on the French, cutting that country off from American capital, and causing that country to hoard gold, further straining the operations of the Gold Standard and increasing its deflationary impacts abroad by draining the availability of gold for deficit countries. The Germans were defaulting on more and more of their commercial debt, and by 1935 had reached a default rate of 80% to 90%. The result was increasingly tight capital and exchange control agreements the world over (Ritschl & Straumann, 2010, 171, 177).

General military conflict would soon arrive. It would be left to the settlement after the Second World War to try to correct the mistakes of the past. The problems of hot money and persistent imbalances in capital and trade flows were amongst the issues dealt with at the 1946 Bretton-Woods conference. Improvements and adjustments were made that helped usher in several decades of prosperity. But nothing lasts forever, and the inherent challenges of the global capital markets would end up returning later with a vengeance, both familiar and new.

References

Adalet, M. (2003). *Fundamentals, capital flows and capital flight: The German banking crisis of 1931.* University of California, Berkeley, Working Paper.

Allen, R. C. (2011). *Global economic history: A very short introduction.* Oxford University Press.

Bernanke, B. (1995). The macroeconomics of the Great Depression: A comparative approach. *Journal of Money, Credit and Banking, 27*(1), 1–28.

Bernanke, B., & James, H. (1991). The gold standard, deflation, and financial crisis in the Great Depression: An international comparison. In R. G. Hubbard (Ed.), *Financial markets and financial crises* (pp. 33–68). University of Chicago Press.

Bordo, M. D., & Meissner, C. M. (2007). *Foreign capital and economic growth in the first era of globalization.* National Bureau of Economic Research, Working Paper 13577.

Choudhri, E. U., & Kochin, L. A. (1980). The exchange rate and the international transmission of business cycle disturbances: Some evidence from the Great Depression. *Journal of Money, Credit and Banking*, 12(4). *Part, 1*, 565–574.

Chown, J. F., & Chown, J. (1994). *A history of money: From AD 800*. Routledge.

Davis, M. (2002). *Late Victorian holocausts: El Niño famines and the making of the third world*. Verso Books.

Cooper, R. N. (1992). Fettered to gold? Economic policy in the interwar period. *Journal of Economic Literature, 30*(4), 2120–2128.

Dos Passos, J. (1932). *Three soldiers*. The Modern Library.

Eichengreen, B. (1996). *Golden fetters: The gold standard and the Great Depression, 1919–1939*. Oxford University Press.

Eichengreen, B., & Flandreau, M. (1997). *Gold standard In theory & history* (2nd ed.). Routledge.

Eichengreen, B., & Sachs, J. (1985). Exchange rates and economic recovery in the 1930s. *Journal of Economic History, 45*(4), 925–946.

Forbes, C. (2014). *Australia on horseback: The story of the horse and the making of a nation*. Pan Macmillan Australia.

Foreman-Peck, J. (1983). *A history of the world economy: International economical relations since 1850*. Harvester Press.

Galor, O. (2005). From stagnation to growth: Unified growth theory. In Aghion, P. & Durlauf, S. N. (Eds.), *Handbook of economic growth* (Volume 1, Part A), 171–293.

Elsevier.

Goldsmith, Hugh (2014). *The long-run evolution of infrastructure services*, CESifo Working Paper, No. 5073, Center for Economic Studies and Ifo Institute (CESifo), Munich. http://hdl.handle.net/10419/105088

Graff, M., Kenwood, A. G., & Lougheed, A. L. (2013). *Growth of the international economy, 1820–2015*. Routledge.

Horesh, N. (2012). From Chengdu to Stockholm: A comparative study of the emergence of paper money in East and West. *Provincial China, 4*(1), 68–99.

Horsefield, J. K. (1944). The origins of the Bank Charter Act, 1844. *Economica, New Series, 11*(44), 180–189.

Humphrey, T. M. (1975). The classical concept of the lender of last resort. *Federal Reserve Bank of Richmond Economic Review, 61*, 2–9.

James, J. A. (1984). The use of general equilibrium analysis in economic history. *Explorations in Economic History, 21*(3), 231–253.

Kindleberger, C. & Aliber, R.Z. (2005). *Manias, panics, and crashes: A history of financial crises* (Fifth Edition). John Wiley & Sons, Inc.

Marks, S. (1978). The myths of reparations. *Central European History, 11*(3), 231–255.

McGee, R. W. (1989). The economic thought of David Hume. *Hume Studies, 15*(1), 184–204.

McKeown, T. J. (1983). Hegemonic stability theory and 19th century tariff levels in Europe. *International Organization, 37*(1), 73–91.

Mitchell, W., Wray, L. R., & Watts, M. (2016). *Modern monetary theory and practice: an introductory text*. Newcastle, NSW: Centre of Full Employment and Equity.

Neal, L. & Cameron, R. (2016). *A Concise economic history of the world: From paleolithic times to the present* (Fifth edition). Oxford University Press.

Oneal, J. R., & Oneal, F. H. (1988). Hegemony, imperialism, and the profitability of foreign investments. *International Organization, 42*(2), 347–373.

Ritschl, A., & Straumann, T. (2010). Business cycles and economic policy, 1914–1945. In S. Broadberry & K. H. O'Rourke (Eds.), *The Cambridge economic history of modern Europe: Volume 2, 1870 to the present* (pp. 156–180). Cambridge University Press.

Stearns, P.N. (2001a). *The encyclopedia of world history* (6th ed.). Houghton Mifflin Company.

Stearns, P.N. (2001b). Men and masculinity. In Stearns, P.N. (Ed.), *Encyclopedia of European social history from 1350 to 2000 (volume 4)*, 37–43. Charles Scribner's sons (Gale).

Stein, H. (1969). *The fiscal revolution in America*. University of Chicago Press.

Temin, P. (1993). Transmission of the Great Depression. *Journal of Economic Perspectives, 7*(2), 87–102.

Tooze, A. (2014). *The deluge: the Great War, America, and the remaking of the global order, 1916–1931*. Penguin books.

Whale, P. B. (1944). A retrospective view of the Bank Charter Act of 1844. *Economica, New Series, 11*(43), 109–111.

CHAPTER 20

Exceptionalism

C. Gordon, *Many Possible Worlds*,
https://doi.org/10.1007/978-981-19-9281-0_20

Fig. 20.1 Bicycle riders in parade on the Fourth of July at Vale, Oregon July 1941 (*Image source* US Library of Congress; Lee, Russell, photographer. United States. Office of War Information. Overseas Picture Division. Washington Division; 1944. Repository: Library of Congress, Prints and Photographs Division, Washington, DC 20,540 USA, hdl.loc.gov/loc.pnp/pp.print, Part Of: Farm Security Administration - Office of War Information Photograph Collection (Library of Congress) Persistent URL: hdl.loc.gov/loc.pnp/ppmsca.01538. Call Number: LC-USF33- 013,082-M4 No known restrictions on publication)

20.1 American "Exceptionalism"

In 1831, the French traveller and writer Alexis de Tocqueville wrote about his visits to the US, a country then only 50 years old, but capturing a lot of international notice. He wrote that America was "exceptional", differing from other nations qualitatively because of its unique origins, national credo, historical origins, and distinctive political and religious institutions (Koh, 2003, fn. 4, 1481). De Tocqueville was, however, merely remarking on what Americans already thought of themselves, and had done so since the founding of the nation. There had always been an idea that their country is somehow totally different and frankly superior to others, now and across history, a notion that remains today (Fig. 20.1).

De Tocqueville did not actually coin or use the term "exceptionalism", that coming later. But his observations about America established the germ of an idea. All countries are unique in some way. But the premise of exceptionalism is that some countries are uniquely unique, possessing some inherent, non-replicable quality that makes them rise above all others in ways that no one else can imitate or adapt. The concept can also be applied to a people, a culture or anything else.

Such thinking did not begin with America, and certainly does not apply only there, as will be discussed more below. But certainly, Americans have possessed a strong sense of it since the very beginning. The creation of the US itself was held by its "Founding Fathers" as a truly unique outcome in history, and this has carried on through to the present day, not least because of the global predominance of the US throughout the twentieth century and into the twenty-first century (even though its relative power is now waning). The 1900s is sometimes referred to as "the American century", and the country's massive military power and its ongoing centrality to the world financial and economic system brings it continued dominance, even today in a more multipolar world. In comparison to the British imperial era of the long nineteenth century, which had precedents in the Roman and Alexandrian Empires, American dominance in global affairs across all dimensions, especially after the collapse of the Soviet Union, has been historically unequalled. Some have even referred to it as a "hyperpower" (Cohen, 2004).

Such thinking often took on a messianic tinge. The country's expansion across the North American continent during the nineteenth century was not simply treated as one of numerous examples of similar internal expansions, as with China and Russia. Instead, John O. Sullivan coined the term "Manifest Destiny" in 1845 which posited the idea that America was "destined" to be great, and deserving of such greatness, even though its territorial growth came about through a patchwork of events that was often purely fortuitous, such as Napoleon's sale of the Louisiana Territory to the US as a way of raising revenue for his Continental wars. This idea was invoked again during the first period of American overseas expansionism in the late 1800s and early 1900s (Fig. 20.2).

Many historians, especially American ones, have continued this treatment of the history of the US as an unfolding of a special destiny, or at least an outgrowth of its truly unique characteristics. David Potter's book, *People of Plenty* (1954), for example explained differences between Europe and America in terms of American abundance (Tyrrell, 1991,

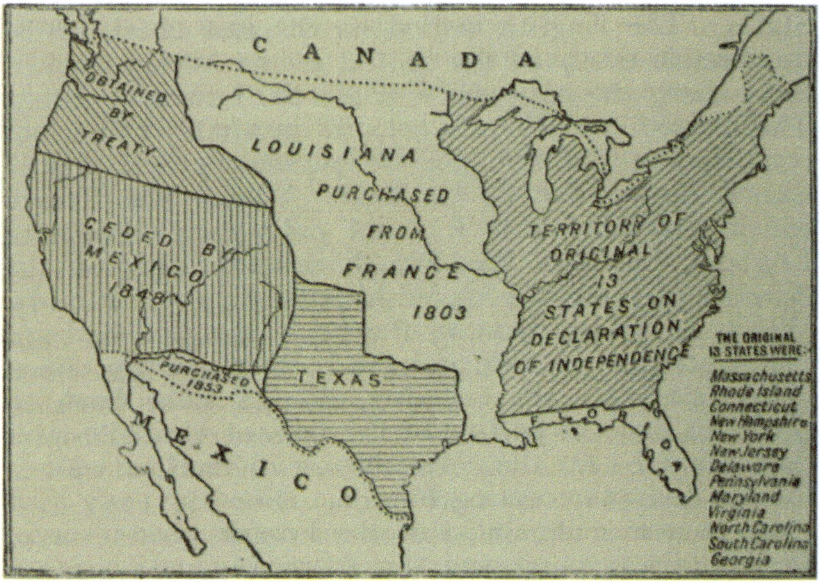

Fig. 20.2 American expansion on the North American Continent (*Image source* Brooks, L. (1922). *A regional geography of the world, with diagrams and entirely new maps*. University Press. Page 427. Contributing Library: Robarts—University of Toronto, Digitizing Sponsor: University of Toronto. No known copyright restrictions)

1034). Potter also claimed that Americans were special geniuses for "compromises" in his study of the origins of the American Civil War (Potter & Fehrenbacher, 1976). Potter recounted the shrewd apportionment of new territory into slave and "free" jurisdictions to maintain the delicate political balance within the American union, individual agreements that themselves were explicitly labelled as the "Compromise of 1820" and so on. This balancing act collapsed with the Civil War of 1861–1865 so it must be wondered how valuable this supposed talent actually was, especially its role in preserving an institution as odious as slavery. In any case, such balancing was not really unique, as the Concert of Europe in 1815 attests, to give one example. But the argument does indicate a tendency to elevate American patterns into especially unique, and sometimes preferred, ones.

Lipset (1996) thus treats American exceptionalism as both a doctrine and a method of analysis. His more methodological points are considered in a later section. But he makes the point that American historiography is very nation-state oriented by definition and that broader schemes of history, like the interdisciplinary "Annales" school of the French, do not appeal much to American scholars. He argues, in fact, that the US was organised around an ideology that was explicitly nationally bounded. "Americanism", in his view, is an "ism" in the way that Communism or Liberalism is. But it is unlike those schemas in putting a specific nation at the centre of historical process. However, this is not mere nationalism, with nationality related to a geographic community. A person cannot become un-English or un-Swedish, but one can be un-American if one rejects "American values". Conversely, people not American by birth or heritage can become "Americans" if they adopt the creed of the nation. Of course, one can be a "traitor" to any country, but except in America, the traitor still retains their fundamental nationality. Even Edmund Burke, when making a speech to the House of Commons proposing reconciliation with the colonies, observed that Americans were not simply transplanted Englishmen but culturally distinct and claiming to be so.

Burke, like many others, stressed the unique character of American religion with its messianic elements, which goes back to the Puritan colonies at Boston and Plymouth, both of which set out explicit self-defined missions in the New World. Both colonies were settled by members of the dissenting Congregationalist church, but John Winthrop and the colonists of the Massachusetts Bay Company were "non-Separating" Congregationalists while William Bradford and the settlers at Plymouth were "Separating" Congregationalists. Out of this division came two salient and contradictory notions that fused later into American self-identity. One was the vision of America as "a city upon a hill", the phrase used by Winthrop in 1630 to refer to the idea of a collective salvation through a special communal covenant with God in which that community (the Bay Colony in this case) served as the instrument of God's will. It was insisted that the colonists were on an errand into the wilderness as promised in scripture, a truly messianic vision. On the other side, the dissident Roger Williams, driven out of the Bay Colony to establish his own settlement in Rhode Island to the east, maintained the strong idea of separation of church and state and insistence that each individual must be redeemed individually. Williams also claimed that the Bible spoke only to spiritual, not material journeys (Madsen, 1998, Chapter 2).

This tension between religious visions, one messianic, the other individualistic, would carry on into the formation of national consciousness, going in some interesting directions along the way. Benjamin Franklin changed the concept of Puritan theology's "providence", which had described God's direct intervention in the human world, instead using the term to describe a rational principle that controls the operation of the world, very much in accord with the Deism that dominated his times and those of the other "Founding Fathers". This was an understanding of divinity that was peculiarly pragmatic and individualistic in which a world governed by rational principles can be improved by rational government, an enterprise supposedly best suited to the new American nation unhindered by the complexities and decadence of European history and institutions. Franklin and others believed that the US could thus be an exemplary nation to others, leading the world in improvement; this was "providence" for him. Franklin also embodies an impulse to create oneself anew, conflating the nation of America with the exemplary American who by definition is a beacon to the world and his fellows (Madsen, 1998, Chapter 2).

These philosophical struggles were not unique to America. Macpherson (1962) claims that seventeenth century English political thought contained two major strains, one being the social contract idea of John Locke in which free individuals form a pact with one another to ensure that freedom; and Thomas Hobbes's formulation that free individuals are antagonistic to one another and for a functioning society to work a strong central government must restrain them. The common element of both is what Macpherson calls "possessive individualism", i.e. that people inherently own their own person. This notion was the common element across a diverse range of political theory that followed, and was the basis for Liberal Democracy in which people negotiated their own trade-offs between their sanctity of self and sacrifices of it for the greater good, through competition through electoral political systems and free markets.

American political thought was obviously an outgrowth of English thought. But the Americans took it in unexpected directions, combining possessive individualism with the religious and nationalist elements already discussed. Luna (2002) refers to the "double-edged" nature of American exceptionalism stemming from a conflict between individualism, egalitarianism, populism and moralism. Individualism emphasises autonomy, privacy and freedom from state interference, while moralism demands sobriety, self-restraint and personal responsibility (753). These values helped spawn many of the great crusades that swept through America periodically, not least the Temperance movement that resulted in the constitutional amendment to ban alcohol, effective between 1920 and 1933 (Okrent, 2010). Yet far from unifying the country, this particular combination of moral crusade and maximalist individualism spawned bitter cultural battles that pitted different visions of society against one another. These battles continue in differing guises to the present day.

Yet oddly, whatever the divisions at home, Americans often try to carry their same messages overseas, acting as if unity has been achieved domestically even when it has (usually) not been and assuming that the country is an exemplar there to teach the rest of the world. The Anti-Saloon League, an umbrella lobbying group in the US, which lobbied successfully for the Nineteenth Amendment to the Constitution making alcohol illegal throughout the country, tried to export Prohibition worldwide through the establishment of the World League Against Alcoholism. American Prohibition was divisive from the start and was repealed less than fifteen years after it had started. But this did not stop the commencement of a confident international crusade on its behalf (Asbury, 1968, 144–145). To be fair, strong independent "temperance" movements existed outside the US at the time. But these tended to be domestically oriented. It was the US that took up the cause of world conversion (Okrent, 2010, 75). Wilsonianism can be seen as another example of such crusading, as can the official anti-Communism of the Cold War (see Chapters 15 and 25).

The discussion thus far is about exceptionalism as used in its ideological or idealist sense, evaluating values or practices against a supposedly unique belief system, with irreconcilable absolutes, all of which carry with them a strong call to force conformity to a rule. Yet the strong American sense of transcendent uniqueness and moralism leads sometimes to broad and glaring lapses in application of principle, creating exceptionalisms within exceptionalisms. For example, while the American Bill of Rights allows for safety against unreasonable search and seizure, in jurisprudential practice "drug exceptionalism" has allowed for abrogation of this and other constitutional rights in the case of drug offences. Judicial interpretations in the US have carved out strong exceptions in this arena to the First Amendment rights of religious freedom, the Sixth Amendment right to counsel, the Eighth Amendment limitations on detention and punishment and the Fourteenth Amendment's guarantee of equal protection under the law (Luna, 2002, 754, 758). (See also Box 20.1).

Even on its own terms, American exceptionalism is thus inconsistent. And being framed in terms of the nation, the concept ignores the rich diversity of America both regionally and across different social groups. "Regionalism" itself is often cited as a peculiarly American trait and there are many local exceptionalisms, Texas, New York and California being leading examples. Interestingly, though, de Tocqueville himself remarked on this localism, arguing that it was an integral part of America's "exceptional" nature. Thus, one can see this seeming inconsistency as exceptionalism in its own right.

Some argue also that exceptionalism is an elitist idea, excluding the ways in which African-Americans, Spanish-Americans, women and so forth experienced the country. This critique includes the working classes, including its white members. In the 1960s and 1970s, novelists such as Phillip Roth and John Updike explored the multi-edged and fractured vision of the white working class male during a time of relative economic decline, both nationally and in small-town deindustrialising communities, which heightened an implicit sense of betrayal that tended to be directed towards the "other" rather than leading to a questioning of what was going wrong (see Chapter 29). Exceptionalism can be uniting, but it can also be divisive and disorienting, depending upon the point of view.

But in some ways, all this is beside the point. Exceptionalism can and has had motive force whatever its truth may be. American policymakers and many citizens believe in it, whether it can be proven or not, and it continues to have demonstrable impact (see Box 20.1).

Box 20.1 The American style of imperialism

Alone amongst imperial powers, the US has always explicitly rejected the idea that it was an Empire or practising any sort of colonial expansionism. At least when the expansion was overseas; the takeover of the North American continent was seen as "Manifest Destiny", a perfectly natural and just process dictated by the exceptional fate that was the American prerogative (see text).

Despite this conceit, America has been a highly successful coloniser and expansionist. But it has done so in its own unique and inimitable way, though sharing some characteristics with its European counterparts. One shared basis was racism. Even Turner's famed "frontier hypothesis" (1894), i.e. that the frontier, as the American nation marched across the continent, served as a leveller and regenerator, applied to white men only.

The US did not take over empty land, but displaced whoever was already there, and then filled it with white settlers, only to push on to the next "empty" (read "populated with indigenous people") space. Indeed, it was only when the US census declared the frontier effectively "closed" that it began to count mainland Indians at all, in 1890 (Immerwahr, 2019, 78).

When the US did move into overseas territories, it often brought its segregationist policies along. A good example is the Panama Canal Zone in which Canal construction and operation was run under race and skilled-based segregation, in part to impede labour organising (McGreevey, 2017) (see Fig. 20.3). Before Alaska became a US state, the American territorial government practised segregation against the Eskimos (Immerwahr, 2019, 183).

What especially distinguished American colonialism abroad, however, was that the US generally preferred indirect takeover, seeking to reshape local societies into a version of its own image, using direct control where necessary but transitioning rather quickly to more distant and subtle forms of control. In 1940, colonised populations overseas made up 13% of the Greater US. But Americans did not call this vast collection of territories an Empire and did not stitch them together in the ways that the Europeans did. First, the US held some of this territory only temporarily. The Philippines, which had been gained from the Spanish during the Spanish-American War of 1898–1900, was granted independence in 1945, a goal that had always been explicitly stated from the outset. But the US had transformed that society in explicit ways that bound it economically and militarily tightly to the America afterwards. Other American territories were given US Statehood rather than independence, something many Americans saw as even better than freedom. Thus, Hawaii and Alaska were both admitted to the Union in 1959. Some even thought that Japan, occupied and administered by the US military between 1945 and 1952, should be made a State. And one congressman proposed that Iceland, occupied by US forces during the Second World War , should be similarly admitted to the Union (Immerwahr, 2019, 226–230).

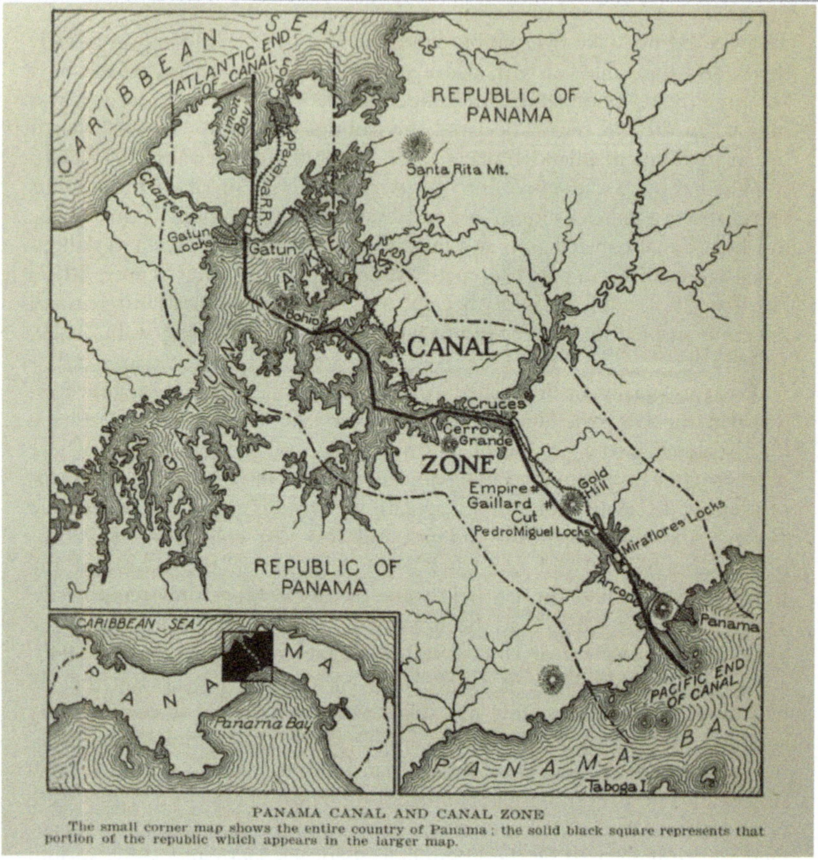

Fig. 20.3 The Panama canal zone (*Image source* O'Shea, M. V., Foster, E. D., & Locke, G. H. [1917]. *The world book; [electronic resource] organized knowledge in story and picture*. Hanson-Roach-Fowler Co. Digitizing sponsor Internet Archive. Contributor: Internet Archive. No known copyright restrictions)

Enclaves are an especially preferred strategy for control, with military occupation on strategic grounds quite widespread. The US held the Japanese island of Iowa Jima until 1968, and Okinawa until 1972, well after the Japanese occupation ended, under what one scholar has referred to as the "strategic island concept" (Immerwahr, 2019, 345). Even if a country is not formally occupied, US military installations around the globe are islands of American power within their boundaries and are often combined with significant sovereignty over their nominal hosts outside them. Locations deemed of vital importance are integrated into the American jurisdiction, but not directly ruled and under a highly varied set of legal arrangements, such as Guam, American Samoa, the Northern Marianas and Puerto Rico, all of which are American territories in which residents have American citizenship but whose governments do not have the full rights of Statehood, and each of them having their own unique arrangements (Immerwahr, 2019). These would be colonies under most other rubrics, but not for Americans.

Perhaps the most interesting example of American control is in neighbouring Latin America. Whereas the Spanish had run the area directly as colonial masters, the Americans managed to develop a quasi-colonial hegemony over the area, nominally respecting local sovereignty (except when it wasn't) and effectively directing the economies of the regions to varying degrees. This began with the Monroe doctrine, proclaimed by then US President James Monroe in 1823 in which he asserted that the American hemisphere was no longer to be considered an area for further interference by Europeans, a rather audacious note struck by a country only a few decades old. This doctrine became the basis for increasing interference by the US in Latin America, taken up a notch by President Theodore Roosevelt who engineered Panama's independence from Colombia so that the Canal Zone could be acquired and presided over the Platt Amendment which codified US military intervention in Cuba at will. This was the essence of the so-called Roosevelt corollary in which the US appointed itself as the guarantor of regional "stability" (Best et al., 2004, 134–138).

The official US policies towards Latin America varied over the twentieth century, but the results were consistent: regular US military intervention and occupation, interference with the domestic politics of South and Central American countries and a heavily imbalanced economic dependence of the region on America. The US intervened in the Mexican Civil War of the 1910s, entered and occupied Haiti from 1915–1939 and did the same in the Dominican Republic from 1916–1924. Such involvement continued after the Second World War, with the overthrow of a moderately Socialist government in Guatemala in 1954, an invasion and overthrow of the government of the Dominican Republic in 1965, and the CIA-aided overthrow of the democratically elected Socialist government of Salvador Allende in Chile in 1973. Further, the new UN charter of 1945 implicitly codified the Monroe Doctrine by preserving the right of regional bodies to collectively or individually deal with regional issues—outside the purview of the UN (Best et al., 2004, 139, 150–151).

Informal rule and attempts to influence other countries are not unique to the US. But the Americans are perhaps alone in being both extensive in its use of informal rule and simultaneously vociferous in its anti-colonial rhetoric and promotion of democratic forms of independent government that sit at odds with many of its policy actions. Whether this is truly exceptional or not is debatable. But it does appear distinctively American.

20.2 Varieties and Limits of Exceptionalism

Exceptionalism thus far has been spoken of mainly in terms of an idea about a country. Being naturally comparative, it can also be thought of as an assessment benchmark of degrees of uniqueness. And it need not be limited to country comparisons. The standard academic method for assessment is to collect relevant data, qualitative or otherwise, on a particular benchmark category (or set of categories) for a given and clearly defined entity which is then compared against other defined entities in that benchmark area to see what differences arise. If the differences are great enough, and distinctive in certain ways, one can make the case for how and why the entity in question is uniquely unique, i.e. exceptional (Luna, 2002).

This comparison is typically, but not exclusively, done between nations, and can be at a very high level, such as the national economy, or focused more narrowly, such as on an element of culture in one country versus others. What matters is that there is some standout attribute found in one place and nowhere else. Thus, for example, Zimring and Hawkins (1999) develop what they refer to America's violence exceptionalism as a rubric encompassing that country's supposedly disproportionate level of lethal or life-threatening violence when compared to nations of similar levels of development. Similarly, Pratt (2008) examines of what he calls Scandinavian exceptionalism with respect to the low-imprisonment societies there as compared to similar economic and cultural cohorts, and especially in contrast to America, which has amongst the highest imprisonment rates in the world, even against authoritarian outliers such as Russia or Iran. Pratt's analysis is simultaneously "micro", honing in on the penal system, and "macro", in seeking sources of national uniqueness in broader arenas.

This includes the US's individualist egalitarian tradition that allows for a higher tolerance of more degrading and inhumane punishments, as opposed to the more collectivist egalitarian tradition in Scandinavia where maintenance of relatively close group norms is important (119–120).

The standards of this juxtaposition can range from strong to weak. In theory, a truly "controlled" comparison is what is desired. This can take many forms. An example of one frame is to compare countries (such as Britain and America) that have achieved similar outcomes (such as superpower status) and contrast them across all relevant factors to see if there really is something exceptional about the ways they respectively got there. Whatever the form, this kind of rigour is almost impossible to implement because of data limitations, especially of immeasurable things such as culture, and because for many of the most interesting questions, there really is no possible comparison. For example, there is no precedent for the sort of global hegemony the US attained after the end of the Cold War, even against the earlier pinnacles of the British and the Romans.

For this reason, analysts generally ask a weaker question of how a particular country might be special in comparison to other countries. This is what the examples already cited are actually doing. This sort of exercise can be posed in response to an explicit statement or hypothesis that is then confirmed or denied. Or it can emerge more inductively from a data analysis. The problem with looking for "exceptionalism" in this way is the obvious bias inherent in the term itself, which arguably is a leading construction in the first instance. To ask about the exceptionalism of a particular country generally brings with it a hidden or unconscious agenda of whether a particular country is "right" ("wrong") in a higher (lower) moral or ideological sense, somehow exemplary with respect to its peers or the rest of the world (Nolte & Aust, 2013, 409–410). However, the ongoing use of the term, and belief in it, mostly by those who think they are indeed exceptional, argues for the need to study it, whatever the limits of the concept might be.

The construct of exceptionalism has been used in many contexts, in both its weak and strong senses. The British, for example, considered themselves as a "race" apart and superior to other peoples, and, as seen in Chapter 3, the debate about the "uniqueness" of Britain as the "home" of the Industrial Revolution can be boiled down to an argument about British exceptionalism, at least in the economic arena. This certainly was the flavour of some of the earliest narratives about industrialisation, such as Toynbee (1884).

Similar debates have surrounded French exceptionalism, especially in the political and social sphere, e.g. its tradition of governmental centralisation, the uniqueness of the French Revolution, the notion that France has a split personality regionally and so on. Arguments have made about Russian exceptionalism, German exceptionalism ("What is truly German?" was a common question asked once the country unified in 1871) and Spanish exceptionalism (Kammen, 1993, 24–25).

The focus can be transnational as well. "Latin" culture, shared across France, Italy and the Iberian Peninsula, and then exported to "Latin" America, is a theme of much work. Europe's uniqueness against the rest of the world is particularly well-trod ground, with many scholars from different disciplinary and ideological backgrounds asserting European exceptionalism, a new flurry of such analysis coming after the formation of the European Union (Nolte & Aust, 2013, 408). The European variant of Western Civilisation is often contrasted with settler offshoots, and "Western" culture is contrasted with "Eastern" culture with various nations and regions under both regions being contrasted with one another and so on.

Pronouncements of positive exceptionalism in particular tend to be boosted by actual economic, military and political success and some sort of global or regional dominance, which seems to "prove" the case for it, forgetting, of course, that history is cyclical, and that those on the top one time end up on the bottom some other time. Indeed, all the claims for past exceptionalisms generally fade as circumstances change, prior claims to special status seeming less compelling when one's time in the sun is over, only to be replaced by new claims made by the newly ascendant.

A major objection is that the whole idea is culturally biased. And although the bias can be towards any culture, the modern era ones are explicitly Western. Some sort of bias is inevitable since the perceptions of any given analyst will be coloured by the time they live in and the place they are from, at least to some degree. But when a bias becomes systematic in a particular mode of analysis, then the possibility of abandoning that mode must be seriously considered.

Edward Said's (1978) concept of "Orientalism" is relevant here. The term traditionally refers to an academic field of study, but Said expands it to refer to a worldview distinguishing between the "Orient" and "the Occident" as fixed and eternal categories, the former being "lower" than the other. This framing, by extension, leads to an ideology used in service of political domination, especially Western imperialism in all its forms (1–2). A related category, not addressed by Said but implicit in his work, is "Eurocentrism" which generally refers to a focus on European countries and/or European culture (perhaps extended to "Western" culture) as a paradigm for the rest of the world. One thus must ask whether "exceptionalism" is inevitably "Orientalist", "Eurocentric" or both.

20.3 Is America Economically Exceptional?

Narrowing the focus to the shape and trajectory of modern economic growth, many analysts have asked whether America was "exceptional" in ways that have shaped its own economic history, and that of the world. This is parallel to similar sorts of questions posed about European industrialisation (see Chapter 3), though the term is not generally used there.

There are two distinct periods to consider in answering this question: before world hegemony and after world hegemony. Prior to the First World War , the US can be seen as a rapidly developing nation that became a contender for world economic power by the turn of the twentieth century, but was not necessarily going to achieve it. Was this rapid trajectory a result of "unique" American characteristics, or just a confluence of the various growth-inducing factors pointed to by the Growth Model menu? If it is just the latter, then in theory others could replicate the American experience by doing the "right" things (though always within the constraints of historical uniqueness and "path dependence"). America may have been exceptionally lucky, doing the right things at the right times, but not exceptional in and of itself for all that. If the former holds, then one would want to know what truly exceptionally American factors were present that could not (by definition) be found elsewhere.

Scholars have identified many possible explanations for the prodigious American economic progress prior to the First World War. Chandler (1980) makes an institutional argument, claiming that in Europe, the large military and governmental establishments there provided much of the administrative training that became so essential to the operation of modern industrial economies while in the US this task fell upon the private sector much more. Also Europe had a much larger Statist tradition, and the government played a much larger role than it did in the US in financing, locating and operating the transportation and communication infrastructure.

Many economic historians have emphasised the agricultural and resource wealth of the US as key drivers of later success. Wright (1990) notes that American industrial success actually began quite late in the 1800s because the country was able to parley its natural resource advantages, which helped promote its first phase of growth through the more traditional means of export specialisation within a world market, into increasing technological and human capital advantage, something that became more science-based as the twentieth century wore on.

There are other resource-rich economies with large geographic scale, especially Russia. America, however, was able to exploit its advantages in particular ways that created the ingredients for extraordinary growth that capitalised on both the returns to resource abundance and the ways in which these returns were exploited, creating powerful technological and trade advantages accumulating over time. Focusing just on agriculture, Johnson (1997) argues that this sector is a foundation for industrial success in most other countries, but that American agriculture was especially productive, and it was this fact that created powerful flow-on effects for its own somewhat hyper-charged development.

Some note America's relative isolation from the European world as a key advantage that distinguished the US from other internal Empires like Russia or China. America, being situated on a continent far from other continents, and having few indigenous adversaries powerful enough to provide existential challenges, allowed for relatively easy expansion that was aided by some truly lucky breaks, as noted above. This advantage could have fed into others, such as the ability to fully and freely exploit a vast store of natural resources just that much more than others with similar endowments that nonetheless had to divert significant resources to external defence.

One influential argument that takes this geographic feature and turns it into a sort of exceptionalism is Frederick Jackson Turner's already mentioned "frontier thesis" (1894). Turner claimed that the steady existence of an American boundary line between settled and unsettled areas (of course referring to whites, as the indigenous peoples had been settled across the country for centuries) created a "frontier" that was a unique characteristic distinguishing the US from older and more class-bound European societies leading and creating its special brand of individualism, egalitarianism and pragmatism.

Granted, most societies had such boundaries at one time in their history, and the push of groups moving from one area to another has been going on since time immemorial. The existence of such escape hatches has always played a periodic role in keeping social equilibrium and exploiting "extra" resources once constraints have been reached. The general push into such margins intensified with proto-industrialisation and then industrialisation, a dynamic that is a key part of the Pomeranz (2000) argument about why Europe diverged from East Asia in the 1800s (see Chapter 3).

For Turner, however, such incursions elsewhere merely brought the existing society, with its all class and other struggles, along with it. America, on the other hand, was already a relatively classless society and therefore new settlement in frontier areas there took place on a blank canvas in which all things were possible to the new settler, at least potentially. This possibility led to the unique American culture, unlike any seen anywhere else. The challenge of maintaining this culture, after the US Census Bureau declared the frontier finally "closed" in 1890 (i.e. when the last lands without white settlement had run out—see Box 20.1), was the main impetus behind Turner's thesis in the first place (Cronon, 1987).

Others, like Turner, have also analysed the supposedly unique aspects of America's founding, but limiting the focus to their role in America's economic growth. Some have argued that it is America's lack of a feudal past that sets it apart, an aspect that certainly can used to explain its economic success relative to Russia, another very large, resource-rich country. Others emphasise a liberal consensus along the lines of Locke's "social contract", a paradigm that fostered respect for individual property rights, and a definite product of the Enlightenment philosophy of its founders. Some point to the power of America's unique political system, especially its federal structure and division of national executive and legislative functions. More small bore analyses focus on America's unique economic circumstances, of which natural resource endowments have already been mentioned, but to which can be added its unique history of organised labour (which was non-Socialist and relatively small, thus organising workers for industrial work but without the adversarial edge of its European counterparts), or the general and long-standing abundance of job and business opportunities during the country's formational decades (Litke, 2013, 5–6).

While all these factors are plausible in explaining America's strong economic success, and no doubt a combination of them came into play, most of them still do not prove American exceptionalism, since, for the most part, they have been evident in one society or another, in one way or another. The "frontier thesis" is especially problematic, not least because countries like Russia, Australia, Canada and possibly even Mexico all had large "untapped" hinterlands whose exploitation was a core feature of their development process. In these cases, the "openness" of such places (again, from a settler point of view) could be said to be equal to what was found in America. The wiping out of indigenous populations by settlers is also a common feature. The main difference is the justification used for expansion, America's story being especially "providential". But it is hard to see how this alone would have made a critical economic difference, though it may have made a cultural one.

In general, it does seem that the US economy is different but not exceptional. It is unusual enough to be seen as something of a real curiosity in the Political Economy of industrialisation. But there has been enough variance in national patterns and timing of capitalist development, including differences in the attitudes of social elites with regards to upwardly mobile industrialists, the structure of State power and the composition of various national working classes, that the exceptionalism hypothesis seems to be a stretch. Indeed, there is a parallel in the historiography of the First Industrial Revolution, where a British exceptionalism was first offered but then was increasingly (though not universally) displaced by a multi-causal, multi-locational explanatory model (see Chapter 3).

The situation perhaps looks somewhat different for America after the Second World War however. At that point, American power was towering and the country was indeed in a unique position not just for the time but also across the historical record, exceeding even British and Roman Empire power at their respective peaks. America's rapid rise from a new and largely agricultural country in 1789 (the date of the ratification of the US Constitution) to a global hegemon by 1945 could be used as proof as some kind of specialness given the profundity of the trajectory.

The American power advantage after the Second World War was so great and with so little real precedence, especially when taking economic output and productivity into account, that it seemed to call out for an explanation and justification. That Henry Luce wrote his famous editorial about the "American Century" in his publication *Life Magazine* linking the "meaning of America" to "the meaning of our time" in February 1941, with the Depression only just and uncertainly over and the country still formally isolationist during an otherwise flaming World War, is testimony to how distinct American power seemed even then, most notably to the Americans themselves. The fact of American hegemony afterwards, whatever its source, helped cement the ideology of exceptionalism both inside and outside the country.

The very design of the post-war global order was arguably shaped and informed by such ideology. While "universal" principles were put forward, carve-outs were made for America as a unique nation. This is clear in international human rights and humanitarian law conventions and treaties from which the US exempted itself from, then and now (something referred to as "exemptionalism"). The explicit maintenance of double standards for America, in which it judges itself and its allies by more permissive criteria than for others, is well established. This includes the denial of jurisdiction to human rights law within its own domestic law, insisting on the self-contained authority of its own domestic rights tradition, a rather brazen stance that many other countries practice but few proclaim so loudly and proudly (Ignatieff, 2005, 3).

Some of this is typical power politics, as all countries have exercised latitude to protect their specific legal and national traditions. But only the US, for example, demands an exemption on the exercise of the "right to life", a core human rights principle, but one said not to apply to American capital punishment. American judges regularly disregard the relevance of foreign jurisprudence, an attitude anchored in the idea that the supposed birthplace of modern democracy has nothing to learn about rights from any other country (Ignatieff, 2005, 6–8). This modern American exceptionalism (an exemptionalism) has been explained or justified on geopolitical realist grounds, based on America's exceptional power; cultural grounds, based on an American sense of Providential destiny; institutional grounds, based on America's supposedly unique institutional forms and paths; and political grounds, based on what is claimed to be a distinctive conservatism and individualism of American political culture.

Many twentieth century American presidents have articulated a strongly messianic vision of the American role in the world, a tradition, as already shown, going back to the "city upon a hill" vision and continuing with the rhetoric of Manifest Destiny and Woodrow Wilson's call to use American power to "make the world safe for democracy". The fact that Wilson called for the League of Nations to have a "Covenant" rather than a "Charter" shows his religious framing of world politics, a product of being a pastor's son (Ostrower, 1996, 10). The American public rejected Wilsonianism at the time, showing the limits of exceptionalist ideology. But it also reflected the country's lack of a completely hegemonic position at that moment. Later, when America had the power to project its mores and values on to the rest of the world with relative impunity, it chose to do so often, a religious sort of fervour propelling the country into engagements that a more realist calculation might have kept the country out of (Ignatieff, 2005, 11–13).

But again, while American attitudes and hegemonic success do appear historically unique in one sense, even this is not really exceptional in a general sense, though the American version of it is unusual. The Soviets, the French, the British and the Germans, amongst others, could all be said to have had their own versions of such a sense of mission, and the hubris that is the downfall of all great powers at one point or another.

20.4 The Limits of Exceptionalism as a Method of Analysis

Returning to question of methodology, is exceptionalism, then, a useful research paradigm? There are some reasons to doubt that it is.

First, there are the problems common to all comparative analysis. Lipset (1996) notes that generalisations may invert when the unit of comparison changes. He uses the example of Canada which, when evaluated by reference to the US, appears as more elitist, law-abiding and Statist, but more anti-Statist, violent and egalitarian when compared to Britain. The scale of examination matters too. All societies on a micro-scale are distinct, while when observed at a great enough distance, they often appear similar. The claim to American, or any other exceptionalism, may be entirely dependent on the scale of inquiry (Litke, 2013, 12).

Another obvious problem is methodological cherry-picking and prior assumptions. One generally finds what one is looking for when doing exceptionalist comparisons. If you want to prove a country is an outlier due to differences, it is all too easy to prove your conclusion, or reject it as desired, selecting and interpreting the data accordingly. Purer comparisons without such a bias are obviously better in this regard, but theoretical structure is needed to reach a plausible explanation. Arguably an exceptionalism framework provides too much structure in this regard.

This problem is made worse when one is defining exceptionalism to mean that there is some standard from which an exemplar deviates (as opposed to deviation from an empirical pattern set by similar countries). As an example, Marxists puzzled over why socialism never took hold in America, despite Marxist theory saying it should have according to the "laws" of historical progression. The problem with this formulation is obvious, but other systems of thought, including neoclassical growth theory, can fall into somewhat lesser but no less real pitfalls when defining ideals. Ideals and the models based on them (e.g. the stateless society of Marxism, or market optimality of neoclassical economics) are, by definition, imaginary, and while it is useful to have benchmarks, one can presume the conclusion if not careful. This general problem is prone to be magnified when looking at a society through a lens of exceptionalism (Litke, 2013, 6–8).

It does not have to be this way, though. As an example, the Growth Model (see Chapter 2), out of the hands of market fundamentalists, can be used in an inherently non-exceptionalist way. The approach has its limits but the model is in some ways open, offering a long menu of factors that are said to aid output and productivity, such as education, human capital, political institutions, culture, finance, levels of capital investment, quality of capital, innovation, entrepreneurial talent and so on. Successful economies have varying degrees of these factors, with the ones with the right mix at the right time growing more than those who don't.

Granted, every country is unique in its own way. And there are certainly a variety of ways to be rich, depending on timeframe and circumstances, with no one cookie cutter formula for obtaining growth. There really is no successful country that is somehow inherently exceptional, and the same can be said for unsuccessful ones. In modern times, both Singapore and Switzerland are exceptionally well off but have taken very different routes from different starting points in different contexts to get there. Singapore has done quite well being an autocratic state albeit with nominally democratic forms, while Switzerland is a genuine decentralised democracy of long-standing. Both have excellent education systems, though Singapore built theirs from the ground up in a short period while Switzerland's evolved over centuries. No country can repeat the "formula" of either country since every country is unique in their time and place, but general lessons can be learned and adapted.

In general, exceptionalism can be seen as an ideology, and has been practised as such at various times and places. Thus, the forms that such an ideology has taken, and the way it has shaped choice, action and consequences, seems to be a legitimate thing to study. But claims for actual exceptionalism are more difficult to make and examine and it appears to be a very problematic way of structuring an analysis. As an academic frame, it is probably best left to the side.

References

Asbury, H. (1968). *The great illusion*. Greenwood.

Best, A., Hanhimäki, J. M., Maiolo, J. A., & Schulze, K. E. (2004). *International history of the twentieth century and beyond* (2nd ed.). Routledge.

Chandler, A. D. (1980). Industrial revolutions and institutional arrangements. *Bulletin of the American Academy of Arts and Sciences, 33*(8), 33–50.

Cohen, E. A. (2004). History and the hyperpower. *Foreign Affairs, 83*(4), 49–63.

Cronon, W. (1987). Revisiting the vanishing frontier: The legacy of Frederick Jackson Turner. *The Western Historical Quarterly, 18*(2), 157–176.

Ignatieff, M. (2005). Chapter 1. Introduction: American exceptionalism and human rights. In M. Ignatieff (Ed.), *American exceptionalism and human rights* (pp. 1–26).

Immerwahr, D. (2019). *How to hide an empire: A short history of the greater United States*. Random House.

Johnson, D. G. (1997). Agriculture and the wealth of nations. *American Economic Review, 87*(2), 1–12.

Kammen, M. (1993). The problem of American exceptionalism: A reconsideration. *American Quarterly, 45*(1), 1–43.

Koh, H. H. (2003). On American exceptionalism. *Stanford Law Review, 55*, 1479–1527.

Lipset, S. M. (1996). *American exceptionalism: A double-edged sword*. WW Norton & Company.

Litke, J. (2013). *Twilight of the republic: Empire and exceptionalism in the American political tradition*. University Press of Kentucky.

Luna, E. (2002). Drug exceptionalism. *Villanova Law Review, 47*, 753–807.

Macpherson, C. B. (1962). *The political theory of possessive individualism: Hobbes to Locke*. Clarendon Press.

Madsen, D. L. (1998). *American exceptionalism*. University of Mississippi Press.

McGreevey, R. (2017). US Imperialism, 1898–1914. In *Oxford research encyclopedia of American history*. Oxford Research Encyclopedias.

Nolte, G., & Aust, H. P. (2013). European exceptionalism? *Global Constitutionalism, 2*(3), 407–436.

Okrent, D. (2010). *Last call: The rise and fall of Prohibition*. Scribner.

Ostrower, G. B. (1996). *The league of nations: From 1919 to 1929*. Avery Publishing Group.

Pomeranz, K. (2000). *The great divergence: China, Europe, and the making of the modern world economy*. Princeton University Press.

Potter, D. M. (1954). *People of plenty: Economic abundance and the American character*. University of Chicago Press.

Potter, D. M., & Fehrenbacher, D. E. (1976). *The impending crisis, 1848–1861*. Harper & Row.

Pratt, J. (2008). Scandinavian exceptionalism in an era of penal excess, part 1: The nature and roots of Scandinavian exceptionalism. *The British Journal of Criminology, 48*(2), 119–137.

Said, E. W. (1978). *Orientalism.* Pantheon Books.

Toynbee, A. J. (1884). *Lectures on the industrial revolution in England; Popular addresses, notes and other fragments.* Rivingtons.

Turner, F. J. (1894). The significance of the frontier in American history. In *Annual Report of the American Historical Association for the Year 1893.*

Tyrrell, I. (1991). American exceptionalism in an age of international history. *The American Historical Review, 96*(4), 1031–1055.

Wright, G. (1990). The origins of American industrial success. *American Economic Review, 80*(4), 651–668.

Zimring, F. E., & Hawkins, G. (1999). *Crime is not the problem: Lethal violence in America.* Oxford University Press.

CHAPTER 21

"1945"

C. Gordon, *Many Possible Worlds*,
https://doi.org/10.1007/978-981-19-9281-0_21

Fig. 21.1 The sequel: the Second World War (*Image source* The National Archives UK, Propaganda poster by an unknown artist. Catalogue Reference: INF 3/140. No known copyright restrictions)

21.1 Economic Prelude to Another World War

W. H. Auden wrote a poem at the very start of the Second World War, looking back over the years preceding it. Entitled "September 1, 1939", Auden plaintively recounts: "As the clever hopes expire/Of a low dishonest decade", despite it all "We must love one another or die" (Auden, 1939). This appeared a vain hope for Europeans at the time, just then embarking on another ruinous conflict, this time of unprecedented scale. It must have seemed even more so for the Chinese, who had been fighting the Japanese throughout the decade, the Spanish who had suffered through their bloody civil war of 1936–1939 and the Abyssinians, invaded by Mussolini's army in 1936. The thirties was a decade of economic collapse, instability, conflict and suffering. In retrospect, its conclusion in conflagration was only a matter of time (Fig. 21.1).

In looking for the possible causes of the Second World War, the analyst is spoiled for choice. The inadequacy of the Versailles settlement, the lack of a stable overarching geopolitics, poor foreign policy choices by the major powers of the day (e.g. isolationism by the US and "appeasement" by France and Britain) and the rigours of Depression—all these and more came together to result in catastrophe. But Auden's phrase captures a definite mood in which nobody wanted to truly deal with the clear and ongoing problems right in front of them. What he said of the thirties could also be said of the twenties, except to say that was high dishonesty rather than low. Relative prosperity was the only difference between the two, masking the budding and building irreconcilable differences in almost all parts of the world that would be impossible to ignore before too long (Fig. 21.2).

Although the Western democracies were experimenting, with varying degrees of success with temporary reforms (see Chapter 18), their time appeared to be passing. Maybe these tweaks lessened some suffering here and there. Maybe they would succeed if given sufficient time or, perhaps, sufficient resources. But time and resources were both in short supply. Fascism and Communism had emerged as utopian alternatives for some. However, nobody proposed doing away with machines, mass production or industrial organisation, for these were essential to GDP growth which the Depression had brought way too little of. Industrialism was taken by most as an accepted fact, a triumph of modern science and technology whose ability to bring material plenty was now obvious to all. The question was one of how it should be socially, economically and politically harnessed.

Table 21.1 provides some background on economic growth within Europe in the years 1913, 1925 and 1938. These data are not directly comparable to the Maddison data generally used in this book because they use Gross National Production (GNP) rather than a Gross Domestic Product (GDP) measure, are measured in 1960 US dollars and do not

Fig. 21.2 Some low dishonesty at decade's end (after Auden—see text) (*Image source* Collectie Spaarnestad: www.spaarnestadphoto.nl/ Nationaal Archief / Spaarnestad Photo, SFA002017138. Poster in a London travel agency advising people to book their holidays in spite of the tense situation in Europe (Hitler, Germany, the Second World War. About 1939)

Table 21.1 European GNP—selected countries (at market prices) 1913, 1925, 1938 in millions of 1960 US dollars

	1913	*1925*	*1938*	*% change 1925–1938*
Austria	–	4,314	4,320	0.1%
Hungary		3,025	4,137	26.9%
Austria-Hungary	26,050	–	–	NA
France	27,401	36,262	39,284	7.7%
Germany	49,760	45,002	77,178	41.7%
Italy	15,624	18,510	23,701	21.9%
Russia/USSR	52,420	32,600	75,964	57.1%
UK	44,074	43,700	56,103	22.1%
Europe total	256,845	257,434	376,947	31.7%
Western Europe*	163,780	179,830	231,560	22.3%
Eastern Europe*	93,060	77,600	145,390	46.6%

Source Bairoch 1976, pp. 281, table 4; 295, table 10
* The border between "Western Europe" and "Eastern Europe" to the iron curtain, with "Eastern Europe" being identical to the Eastern Bloc (Bulgaria, Czechoslovakia, the German Democratic Republic, Hungary, Romania, Poland and the USSR plus Albania). All the rest of Europe makes up "Western Europe" (Bairoch, 1976, pp. 317, 319) Note: If current Maddison 2020 data were used, making the historical border adjustments employed by Bairoch, the figures above would be somewhat different but likely of similar orders of magnitude.

use quite the same methodology. Also Bairoch adjusts the data for historical boundaries as they were at the time, an adjustment not always made in Maddison.

Having said that, the data do illustrate a few salient points. The dramatic fall in economic status of Austria-Hungary after its breakup is obvious. The two separate and much smaller nations had a combined GNP only roughly half that of the former Empire. While some of this is obviously due to loss of territory, Austria's economic growth between 1925 and 1938 was truly dismal, its GNP not moving at all over the period (though more fine-grained data would show this to be a net result of rising GDP up until the Depression and falling GDP after that, a pattern repeated for most other countries). France grew only tepidly, a total of 7.7% over 13 years. The UK had a better outcome of 22.1%, but this was off of its miserable growth before then. England's GNP was actually lower in 1925 than it had been in 1913, so its growth after that was making up for lost ground, and even then only partially. These three countries were all democracies (although Austria's government had taken on a Fascist cast in the mid-1930s). By contrast, Germany, which had been taken over by Hitler in 1933, had grown almost twice as much as England, the gain coming mostly under his reign. The Soviet Union performed even better, its GNP growing by close to three-fifths. Both Germany and Russia had grown well above the European average, and both had governments that did not follow the Liberal Democracy model, while the Soviets also completely rejected the capitalist economy.

There are some issues with data quality, especially for Russia, which some other sources show as having much lower growth than reported here. And this information was not available in this form to those at the time. But to contemporaries, it did seem that alternative systems had avoided the Depression. Even Italy, which had gone Fascist under Mussolini in 1922, and whose growth had been no better than Britain's, at least did not have the visible unemployment that had plagued England since the end of the war. Although the Second World War was not just about economics, in terms of economic performance, clear ideological battle lines had been drawn.

21.2 First Stages of the War

The war began with two sides, the Fascist powers, drawn together in an alliance known as the Axis, and an anti-fascist alliance constituting the Allies. As for the Axis powers, Fascism is devilishly difficult to define but Paxton (2007), one of the more authoritative sources on the topic, identifies its elements as consisting of a preoccupation with societal decline that is to be fought with a cultic focus on unity and purity, orchestrated and enforced through a mass-based party with hegemonic power, using an ideology of militant nationalism. This sort of movement generally works in collaboration with traditional elites, making it appear conservative, especially in its opposition to democracy. However, the focus on the complete elimination of the rule of law, and the use of presumptively redemptive violence against an "other" defined by the government, point to its radical orientation. Fascism emphasises the primacy of the social whole and the subordination of the individual to it. This whole is defined as a single organism, into which the individual melts, thus differentiating it from older corporatist models of semi-autonomous social groupings in organic balance (such as the Three Estates of pre-Revolutionary France: see Chapter 7). Fascism also posits direction of society by a supreme leader, whose instincts and intuitions are said to be superior to abstract and universal reason, thus justifying his supreme power and the invalidation of any individual or group challenge to it.

These are, however, generic points. The Fascist nations were quite different from one another in many respects. Hitler's Germany was the most extreme, "Hitlerism" essentially replacing "Nazism", a sort of leader cult with absolute and untrammelled power in the Fuhrer's hands (Kershaw, 1991, 6). The violence and dynamism of the Hitler state was truly extraordinary, with Hitler being in a position to make extraordinary changes to the entire social, political and economic order of Germany, a position he used to its full extent. By contrast, Mussolini's Italy was more constrained by pre-existing power groups, such as the Church and the Monarchy, that were never fully eliminated or suppressed as they were in Germany. Both leaders were supposedly antagonistic to capitalism, especially the Nazis whose party name included "Socialist" modified by "Nationalist". But the Socialistic elements of the Nazi movement were fully eliminated in 1934 by Hitler after he took power the previous year and Mussolini's regime was hardly egalitarian, despite some rhetoric to the contrary. And, in any case, both leaders required the skills and capacity of industrialists to accomplish their broader missions (Paxton, 2007).

Japan and Spain were also classified as Fascist states, though only Japan joined the Axis. Japan was nearly as expansionist as Germany, though seeking regional dominion in Asia rather than the world control that Hitler sought. Japan .also is more properly referred to as military dictatorship, led by a radicalised army that deposed the fragile Japanese democracy, and which encouraged a cult of the Emperor, the latter playing no small part in bringing the country to war, though he was not its mastermind. However, the focus on a melding of individual into a State-led mass and its alliance with other Fascist powers qualify it for the Fascist label.

German, Japanese and, to a lesser extent, Italian economic policies were not truly viable alternatives to capitalism. In fact, all three regimes kept private property rights essentially intact (although the State always had the right to override them), allied with corporate enterprise and left many markets functioning, although modifying them significantly. State planning was employed to varying degrees, with Germany having explicit multi-year plans like the Soviets. But economic function and direction, while heavily State-based, relied on many private elements whose elimination was not a strategic objective, as was the case in Russia. The common element of all three was an economy based on war and exploitation of foreign peoples and resources. Hitler's program was radically nationalist and racist, Japan's dressed up in a pseudo Asian transnationalism in the form of the "Co-Prosperity Sphere", and Italy's pretending to a modern restoration of the ancient Roman Empire. But it seems unlikely that these governments would have survived military success in the forms they were started with, and they achieved only total defeat, which destroyed them. Although Fascism as a political method and style lived on after the war because of the ability to gain and manipulate political power, there was no Fascist social, political or economic model that lived on after the utter defeat of its main adherents (see Chapter 23). Mussolini's program is somewhat excepted since he and his minions did formulate some quasi-philosophies on various topics, though these were thin and inconsistent, to say nothing of romantically chauvinistic (Baker, 2006).

Opposing the Axis were the Allies. At first, the primary Allies were Britain and France, both traditional political democracies with capitalist economies. Both countries had suffered during the Depression, experiencing the mass unemployment and deflation that most countries had. France, however, quickly fell to the Germans in June of 1940 (along with smaller Western powers such as the Netherlands and Belgium) and its democratic government quickly shut itself down, giving dictatorial power to a quasi-Fascist order under the First World War hero Marshal Petain. This was not the result of any demands made by the Germans but indicative of a domestic exhaustion with the democratic politics that had been so fractious in France during the Interwar period (Keegan, 1989).

After the fall of France, there was a roughly eighteen month interlude during which the only major active combatant against the Axis was the UK (though backed up by the considerable resources of its Empire, both material and human,). Germany occupied much of the Continent, Japan had a free hand in Asia, and the Soviet Union had expanded its own territory largely back to the limits of Russia's Tsarist Empire (Keegan, 1989). The Soviets had signed a "non-aggression" pact with Germany in August 1939, Stalin cooperating but not allying with Hitler to allow the two of them to partition Poland and then leave Germany free to fight in the west. Bizarrely, the Soviets, did come very close to joining the Tripartite Pact of Germany, Italy and Japan in November 1940 when Molotov visited Berlin in his official capacity as Soviet Foreign Minister, despite the avowed anti-Bolshevism of Fascism. But the parties could not agree on spheres of influence (Lichtheim, 1972).

This interregnum was inherently unstable. For one thing, the US, though formally neutral, was actively aiding the British war effort materially, while also in geopolitical and economic conflict with Japan in the Pacific. The American government was an active part of the anti-Fascist Alliance, providing great amounts of materiel and aid, just not yet directly engaged militarily. For another thing, German expansionism remained unbridled, Japanese militarism hyper-charged, and there was bound to be conflict between America and at least one of these countries sooner or later.

In any case, Hitler, ever the gambler, brought matters to a head. He had always planned to move against Russia and invaded that country on June 22, 1941. The US was brought into the war against Japan after that country's attack on the American Pacific Fleet in Pearl Harbor, Hawaii, on December 7, 1941. Hitler foolishly and rashly declared war against the US immediately. If not for that America might have remained out of active fighting in Europe for some time given the strong isolationism that still prevailed (Keegan, 1989).

21.3 Course of the War

The Axis powers had immediate military success in their respective spheres of influence, taking over vast swathes of territory between 1939–1942. Italy, which entered the war shortly after Germany successfully invaded France in 1940, was far less effective, its military incompetence causing Germany to have to bail out its ally various times. But this the Germans did successfully and as 1942 dawned, it did seem outwardly as if the world had been successfully taken over by the Fascist powers (see Fig. 21.3).

Even at its height, however, this Empire was built on sand. The Germans and Japanese proved to be their own worst enemies, treating their conquered peoples atrociously, to say the least, and creating enemies of them. It could have been different. Ethnic minorities in the Soviet Union greeted the Germans as liberators at first and many might well have joined the German cause had they not been subjected to German extermination and slave labour campaigns. The local reactions in Asia to the Japanese was not quite as uniformly positive, especially given Japan's recent imperialism in the region. But the displacement of European colonial masters was popular and could have been built upon, especially since it showed local peoples that European power was not invincible, and that Asians could defeat them. This potential was squandered completely with

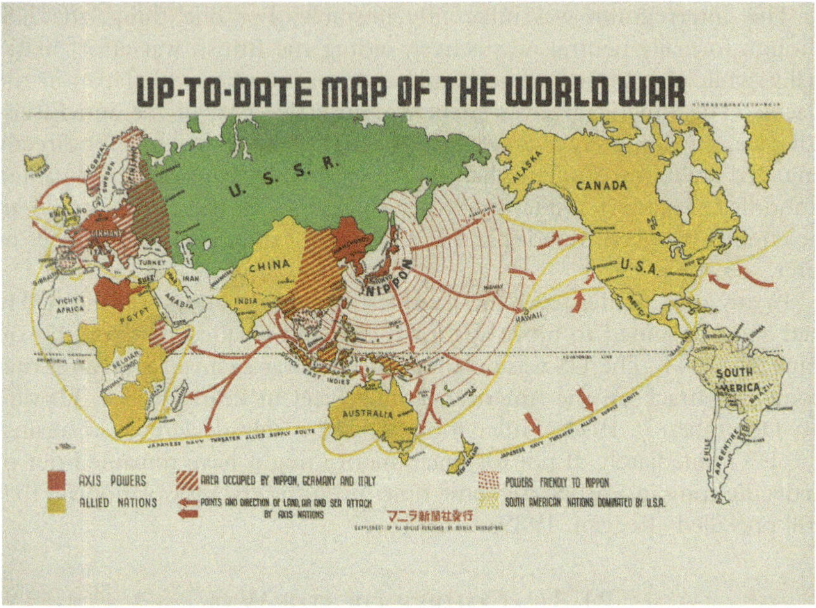

Fig. 21.3 The Axis-view of the war at its high point (for them) (*Image source* Up-to-date map of the world war (1942) by Manila Shinbun-sha. Original from The Beinecke Rare Book & Manuscript Library. Public domain)

Japan's brutal occupations of its newly subject peoples. For both Germany and Japan, the military, logistical and political task of holding control over massive amounts of spread-out territory was difficult enough, and probably untenable in any case. But it was made that much harder by turning subject peoples firmly against the occupying forces, requiring two wars to be fought at once, one against the external Allies and the other against the subject peoples and their various resistance movements (Davies, 2006).

And, as with First World War , this was "total war" in which the total resources of the combatants mattered more than anything else. The Axis was not well placed in this regard. Table 21.2 provides selected data on armed forces and GDP size and percentage of GDP devoted to war spending for the Allies and the Axis across the war period in which the Allied and Axis forces were in their final forms, from 1941–1945.

Table 21.2 Selected data on war spending and armed forces for Allies and Axis Powers

	1941	*1945*
Allied Powers		
– Total GDP (billions 1990 $)	$1798	$2342
– Total Armed Forces (thousands)	12,103	28,620
– [USSR GDP (bns 1990 $)]	[$359]	[$343]
– [USSR Armed Forces (thousands)]	[7100]	[12100]
% National Income spent on war effort by USA	11%	44%
% spent by UK	53%	53%
Axis Powers		
– Total GDP (billions 1990 $)	$911	$466
– Total Armed Forces (thousands)	12,956	15,560
% National Income spent on war effort by Germany	52%	70% (1943)
% spent by Japan	27%	76% (1944)

Source Data selected from Harrison (1998), Tables 1.3, 1.5., 1.8

In terms of pure military force, the Axis held the edge in terms of size of military forces in 1941, even when including the massive Soviet Army on the other side after Hitler's June invasion (prior to which the Axis combined armed forces were even larger relative to the Allies). By 1945, the combined Allied forces in sheer numbers were almost twice as large as those under Axis command. This, of course, does not account for force quality, which was sharply degraded on the Axis side by the end of the war, the best soldiers and commanders dead or disabled, last inadequate reserves pressed into service and, in Germany, even children and the elderly put into combat roles in 1945 in a last-ditch and futile defence effort.

This declining military edge was exacerbated by what was a consistently disadvantageous economic position. In terms of combined GDP, the Allies always had a far greater advantage economically than the Axis, even with France knocked out, with the exception of the USSR whose economic size was far below its raw military manpower. In 1941, the combined GDP of the Allies was two times that of the Axis. By 1945, it was 5 times. The UK and the US on peak war footings spent over half and over two-fifths of national income on the war in 1945. This was a hefty commitment, but Germany and Japan had to dig even deeper, 70% of German national income (in 1943) and 76% of Japanese national income (in 1944) spent on war activities. Military prowess did not make up for relative economic disadvantage and in this sense an Axis defeat was only a matter of time, even had it not over-reached. The lessons of the First World War would have shown this but were ignored; besides which the Axis economies were fundamentally devoted to war, with no sustainable moral or political objective other than varying degrees of maniacal domination (Fig. 21.4).

As an aside, Japan and Russia, although on opposite sides technically, did not engage in direct hostilities until the very end of the war. The two had fought in significant border skirmishes throughout the 1930s, but signed a non-aggression pact in April of 1941, only months before Hitler's Soviet invasion and the Japanese attack on Pearl Harbor. Even after joining the Allies, Stalin did not move against Japan until Japan's final defeat was near, invited in by the US as an insurance policy against

Fig. 21.4 (World) War is hell. Original caption: "Ten Minute Break" 1944 May 12. (*Image source* World War II sketchbooks from the Victor A. Lundy Archive, v.1. [p. 15]. Victor A. Lundy Archive (Library of Congress). Information about the archive is available at www.loc.gov/pictures/item/2010650114/). No known copyright restrictions

the Pacific war dragging on for another year or two, just before the use of atomic weapons made such insurance superfluous. It is interesting to speculate how the war might have gone differently had Russia attacked Japan much earlier (Davies, 2006).

21.4 A Series of Difficult Questions

Unlike the First World War, the alliance this time took a couple of years of fighting to take final shape, but ended up with a rather similar configuration or autocratic powers on one side and an odd amalgamation of capitalist democracies and an autocracy, this time a Communist one, on the other. Another parallel was the presence both times of an "Atlantic" alliance of the US and Britain, but the second time without France for most of the war. Whereas Italy and Japan had been against Germany in the First World War, they were now allied with it, and now Fascist rather than democratic. In both wars, an ideological template emerged, though much more explicitly and immediately during the latter conflict, with the Allies (more formerly the Grand Alliance) being an anti-Fascist league, united in a common purpose of defeating a Fascist threat.

Germany was seen as a prime aggressor in both wars, with Japan added as a co-conspirator the second time around. During the First World War, Germany had in fact invaded, and occupied, neutral Belgium. But though the Versailles Treaty put the onus for the war on Germany in the famous "war guilt clause" (which actually said nothing explicitly about that issue but implied it), many saw the Great War as emerging from more multi-causal roots. During the Second World War, German culpability was far more obvious and singular, especially given the presence of a vast killing complex of death camps whose names—Treblinka, Auschwitz, etc.—would become synonymous with mad atrocity.

The end of general war brought a short sense of relief in the Allied countries, a terrible deflation in the defeated ones, and in China, no real end at all since the Communists and the Nationalists resumed their fight for control of the country after the defeat of the Japanese. With the unifying bond of anti-Fascism gone, a number of difficult questions arose about the war just fought. Five major ones included:

(1) Who caused the war and how should they be held to account?
(2) Who was responsible for winning the war?

(3) Who was responsible for atrocities committed during the war and how should those responsible be handled?
(4) How could another world war be prevented and what sort of international order would help do that?
(5) How could another Great Depression be prevented and what sort of international order would help do that?

21.4.1 Causes of the War

In one sense, Hitler and Hideki Tojo, Prime Minister of Japan, during most of the war were clear aggressors and morally unsavoury characters to boot. Hitler killed himself in his Berlin bunker as the Russians advanced on the capital, but Tojo lived after the war's end and he and many other top leaders in the German and Japanese governments were tried at special tribunals and given sentences, often death (Tojo, for example, was hanged). The most famous post-war trials were held at the German city of Nuremberg, the site of massive annual Nazi party rallies during Hitler's reign. Here the top German war leaders were tried as war criminals by an Allied tribunal. Some were hanged, others jailed for many years. These trials were designed to show that the rule of law would prevail and were the first trials for "crimes against humanity". In that sense, they were unprecedented as the concept of "justice" after prior wars was purely up the victors, rather than accounted for under any general code or principle (Neumann, 1949).

Certainly, the people tried had much to account for. But the trials also simplified the complexity of the root causes of the war, personalising it, in very American fashion, as these were trials instigated, designed, and largely run by the Americans. There was also a great deal of moralising by the victors, which was appropriate given the horrendous acts that had been committed. But this stance also pushed aside more objective causal and systemic analyses of why the war took place, putting the onus almost entirely on the individual leaders of the Axis powers and, to a lesser but important degree, the willingness of their populations to follow them. Reality is never this simple and this limited perspective would have important consequences for immediate post-war events and interpretations.

21.4.2 *Who Won the War?*

Diagnosis of war wins and losses is never definitive. From a purely military point of view, especially in Europe, the Russians had sacrificed the most. As historian Norman Davies (2006) points out Soviet forces absorbed perhaps twenty times the combined British and American losses in all theatres, while inflicting 75% of all German casualties. Around 200,000 British military personnel died in the European war; the Russians lost nearly 9 million. Even as late as 1944, the Germans were still losing 3 out of 4 men on the Eastern—not the Western—front. (Box 21.1 provides a few further details of Soviet military losses relative to Allied ones). Moreover, Russia was the one country that sat between both European and Pacific theatres of war. Thus, though it only declared open war against Japan in 1945 (after the some hot border exchanges in 1939), it played an important containment role against Japan throughout the war.

It seems pretty clear that the Red Army was a key, perhaps decisive, element of the final military victory. But that presented a rhetorical problem since the Soviets were autocratic, anti-capitalist and their leader, Josef Stalin, was arguably almost as morally offensive as Hitler in the way he treated his own, and other, peoples.

Additionally, as noted earlier, it was the other Allies, particularly America, that provided the economic heft so important in a war of attrition. America had indeed become "the arsenal of democracy", and of the Soviet war machine as well. American material aid was critical in both supplying the Red Army and meeting some of the basic civilian needs of the Soviet people.

In fact, the Grand Alliance was a truly joint effort, with all the countries complementing one another well and jointly providing the inputs necessary to defeat the Axis. However, this fact was lost after the war ended and ideological interpretations hardened.

Box 21.1 More on Soviet losses

Davies (2006) points out that the seven bloodiest battles of the war were fought between German and Soviet forces. Those following Hitler's invasion of the USSR were the worst, killing 1,582,000 men. By contrast, 4,650 died at Alamein in North Africa. The Western allies were responsible for a mere 20% of the 3.5 million German military fatalities, whereas the Soviets accounted for 80%.

The Soviet casualty rate was actually comparable to that suffered by Tsarist forces during the First World War. Unlike that war, however, the Russian government did not collapse, or come anywhere close to collapsing, even though there were moments when the country was gravely threatened.

In some ways this was in spite of, rather than because of, Stalin's efforts. Stalin had greatly weakened the high command of the Red Army during the 1937/8 purge trials, and he had wilfully ignored clear intelligence that the Germans were massing at the border in 1941, clearly preparing for something. Yet the Soviers did not bother even to shelter key assets such as the planes of the air force which were decimated by the Wehrmacht's sudden and rapid assault. Stalin's repression also turned the USSR's ethnic minorities into fertile recruiting ground for the Nazis. As they swept through the Baltic countries and the Ukraine in particular, Germany more than wasted this opportunity, a very fortunate break for Stalin. The Soviet Union lost at least 9 million combatants, perhaps 10% of them shot by the NKVD to encourage the others. As Marshal Zhukov said: "In the Red Army it takes a very brave man to be a coward." The British military death toll was 144,000, slightly higher than the American.

Despite these unsavoury elements, Russian unity, its sacrifices and its fighting prowess are not to be disdained or discounted. They made the critical difference against the fierce power of the German war machine.

21.4.3 Atrocities

Of course the atrocities committed by Hitler and Tojo were utterly reprehensible. But so, arguably, were those committed by Stalin. Davies (2006) estimates that Stalin continued to destroy up to one million of his own people per year in continued political repression and the Gulag system throughout the war years, and had been destroying many before and after then as well. Around 16 million Soviet non-combatants perished overall during the Second World War. About 3.25 million Soviet soldiers died in Nazi custody but the Ukrainians, millions of whom were killed both by the Nazis and by the Soviets, suffered the largest number of civilian casualties in Europe. Other populations, such as the Poles, were similarly caught between the two powers at various times and suffered accordingly.

But if one is tempted to say that the autocratic ideological powers were the source of all evil, Western and democratic acts and attitudes could be problematic as well. As Davies indicates, the Waffen-SS recruited three times as many Dutchmen as the Ukrainians who are stereotyped as archetypal Nazi collaborators. Before the war, the Polish ambassador told Hitler that if he solved the Jewish problem "we will erect him a beautiful monument in Warsaw". After the war, Polish thugs killed hundreds of Jews in an apparent effort to complete the German genocide. Rape during wartime was not just committed by Communists, who called such crimes "negative phenomena in the army of liberation"; during the final attack on Germany, 500 American servicemen a week were charged with the offence.

Nor was torture restricted to totalitarian states. It was practised on German POWs at a secret interrogation centre in Kensington Palace Gardens known as the "London Cage", for example. The conduct of the Allied war against civilians in the field was at times just as brutal as the Axis war, with massive carpet bombings of German and Japanese cities leading to hundreds of thousands of civilian deaths with little military payoff. This was not just the judgement of hindsight. War planners at the time were uncertain of the utility of these raids.

Davies (1994) refers to A.J.P. Taylor's notion of a "Nuremberg Consensus" in which the history of the war had been written by the victors, and a subset of victors at that, primarily the Anglo-Americans. The totality of the victory left the moral and political assumptions of the victorious Allies largely unchallenged. The War had been framed as a fight of Good against Evil, and unlike the nuances of the First World War's aftermath, the narrative remained that the forces of evil, and those alone, had been beaten and then tried in the docks of the war crime tribunals.

Davies refers to this as the "Allied scheme of history" and claims that it dominates conventional wisdom. While it is understandable, coming out of the stark situation of the Second World War, it obscured and continues to obscure a fuller accounting of what actually happened to lead to the war, what happened during it and what happened after it. These are difficult questions with stark differences of opinion over many things. But they are, Davies argues, still covered over by pseudo-certainties born from the Second World War, which, in turn, built on some legends of the First World War as well.

This is not at all to suggest moral equivalence between the actors. But the victors treated the atrocities of the losers much differently than their own, as is typically the case. And this imbalance has continued through to the present day, on both sides, particularly egregious in some places such as Japan, which still omits many details of its own war crimes from its school textbooks and official documents.

21.4.4 Preventing Another World War and Another Depression

The leading immediate question after final victory was how the world should be shaped to ensure that there would not be a Third World War, perhaps even worse than the Second. An equally important concern was about how to avoid another Great Depression, which some now thought would resume as large armies demobilised and vast government war expenditures wound back.

After the war, the "Grand Alliance" nominally in charge of post-war restructuring found its members in radically differing positions. There was the US, which was now the largest economic power in the world and arguably the largest military power (though the Red Army had the most troops, it was technologically much less sophisticated); the UK, now in steady decline and devastated by the privations of war (rationing would not end there until 1954); and the Soviet Union, a Communist anti-capitalist and dictatorial state. France rounded out the major Allies, but, unlike in the First World War, did not really count. China under the Nationalists was also included but it was too divided and enfeebled, and under the Nationalist regime too corrupt, to have much independent influence, though obviously with tremendous strategic position and latent power. On the other side, the Axis had, of course, been utterly destroyed.

It was clear then that the centre of gravity had shifted away from the continent of Europe, even though a hard military border emerged in the middle of it. Russia, more Eurasian than European, was dominant in the East, America, of European heritage but non-European, in the West. Although there was nominal multi-laterism, it was unsurprising even at the time that the post-war order would really be determined by the Americans and the Russians between them. Whatever that order looked like, it was hoped that the twin evils of war and famine would be avoided (see Chapter 25).

21.5 Same War, Different Meanings

The Second World War was a global war. But that did not mean that everyone experienced the war in the same way. In Europe, Judt (1992) notes that France, relatively speaking, was well off in terms of physical and human damage, because while it suffered a terrible defeat earlier, it was largely spared any fighting after that and an occupation that was relatively light by comparison to German occupations elsewhere. The Balkan Croats gained a form of temporary independence, and were in any case heavily pro-Fascist, so for them the war on balance was something of an improvement, though not, obviously for Jews, political resisters and others out of favour with the authorities. To a lesser and more conflicted extent, this was also true for the Slovaks who got their own rump republic after the Germans had taken over Bohemia-Moravia in 1939. There are many other examples of countries that the war touched relatively lightly, including the so-called neutral countries of various political persuasions—Portugal, Spain, Switzerland and Sweden—all positioned quite differently from the warring parties.

After the war's end, countries now strove to be on the "right side" of history, and the moulding of post-war memory became critical. All agreed that the Germans were perpetrators. After that, though, it got more complicated. The Moscow Declaration of 1943 declared Austria as the "first victim", even though most Austrians had been enthusiastic about the 1938 Anschluss. Nuremberg narrowed the moral focus further to German Nazis, a pose that satisfied Churchill's anti-Prussian bias and left many non-Nazis, even ones who had benefited deeply from the regime, off the hook. Other non-German collaborators didn't want their roles too closely examined either, as in Vichy France, or in Holland, where there had been both active resistance and enthusiastic joining of the SS by some Netherlanders. The Soviets, too, had things they rather would not have looked at, especially their role in the division of Poland after the non-aggression pact was signed (Judt, 1992, 87).

In general, all countries had incentives to recast their war years in a heroic mode, mainly to restore the civil society that Fascism and war had torn apart. The Communists in particular now made the war purely an "anti-Fascist" crusade, transferring blame for all wartime evils to "Fascists". A similar simplification took place in the West, though along different lines. Some prominent local fascists were ostentatiously punished, but many were let off or ignored, because they had desperately needed skills essential to the rebuilding of destroyed countries, and also because a stable social fabric was deemed more necessary than justice, especially in the fight against Communism (Judt, 1992, 91–93).

A sort of collective and selective amnesia took hold and after 1948 nations (except Britain) devoted themselves to an official "European adventure." This effort rested on a series of "foundation myths": Nazism was strictly German; Germany had been de-Nazified; those responsible had (mostly) been fully punished. Austria returned to full independence in the 1955 State Treaty, relieved of any responsibility for its acceptance of Anschluss or participation in the Holocaust, while Sweden's and Switzerland's economic dealings with Germany, including the provision of critical war materials, were conveniently ignored; so too was Swiss insistence on distinguishing Jews from non-Jewish German refugees during the War, and the forced return of the former to the Nazis. Vichy was seen as an aberration, and Mussolini was seen as an accident, especially since the country took an active part in its own liberation after 1943, supposedly cleansed of Fascists afterwards. Franco's Spain was treated as a pariah for a while, given its Fascist colouring, although it did not join the Axis. Cold War politics ultimately allowed it back into the Western fold by the mid-1950s, despite its authoritarian system and Fascist past (which raises the interesting speculation of whether or not Mussolini might not have survived along with Franco, had he not taken Italy into the war) (Judt, 1992, 96–97, fn. 14, 114).

Additionally, the post-war movements of people were much more dramatic than after the First World War 1 when it was mostly Greeks, Turks and Armenians who moved in response to redrawn borders, and the Turkish genocide of the Armenians. After the Second World War, 15 million Germans were expelled from their home areas, and Poland and Hungary, as well as West Germany became ethnically homogeneous as never before. The Czechs transferred hundreds of thousands of Hungarians out of Czech regions, some into the depopulated Sudetenland, this being accepted at the time due to it being done by a "liberal" government before the Stalinist consolidation of power there in 1948 (Judt, 1992, 88–89).

Other than minor belligerents covered by a 1946 Paris treaty, the Allies never completed any treaty at all with their former enemies. Only in 1951 did the Western Allies declare their "state of war" with Germany over. This absence of formal peace further confused an already obscure memory of the war itself, although it did avoid the controversies that might have come with a formal peace, as had been the case with Versailles (Judt, 1992, 94–95). In all these, and other cases, the need to get on with things, and the ongoing power of a simple moral framing of the war, along with the Manichaeism of the Cold War, erased from consciousness the subtleties of the pre-war, wartime and post-war experiences. This simplification served the purpose of smoothing the transition to a new order; as it always does, but at a great cost.

References

Auden, W. H. (1939). September 1, 1939. http://poemdujour.com/Sept1.1939.html

Bairoch, P. (1976). Europe's Gross national product: 1800–1975. *Journal of European Economic History, 5*(2), 273–340.

Baker, D. (2006). The political economy of fascism: Myth or reality, or myth and reality? *New Political Economy, 11*(2), 227–250.

Davies, N. (1994). The misunderstood war. *The New York Review of Books,* (June 9 issue).

Davies, N. (2006). *No simple victory: World War II in Europe 1939–1945.* Penguin Books.

Harrison, M. (1998). The economics of World War II: An overview. In M. Harrison (Ed.), *The economics of World War II: Six Great Powers in international comparison* (pp. 1–42). Cambridge University Press.

Judt, T. (1992). The past is another country: Myth and memory in postwar Europe. *Daedalus, 121*(4), 83–118.

Keegan, J. (1989). *The Second World War.* Century Hutchinson.

Kershaw, I. (1991). Hitler: Profiles in power. *Pearson Education.*

Lichtheim, G. (1972). *Europe in the twentieth century.* Praeger Publishers.

Neumann, F. (1949). The war crimes trials. *World Politics, 2*(1), 135–147.

Paxton, R. O. (2007). *The anatomy of fascism.* Vintage.

CHAPTER 22

War

C. Gordon, *Many Possible Worlds*,
https://doi.org/10.1007/978-981-19-9281-0_22

Fig. 22.1 Allied bombing raid during the Korean War (*Image source* Catalog #: 10_0015926, Title: Korean War, Date: 1950–1954. Repository: San Diego Air and Space Museum Archive. No known copyright restrictions)

22.1 War…What Is It Good for?

Absolutely NOTHING.

That's the answer that Edwin Starr gave in his 1970 hit song. And many would say that it is good for worse than nothing, given all the misery, destruction and suffering that war brings (Fig. 22.1).

The impacts of the myriad changes in the nature, form and impacts of war since industrialisation are not quite so easily boiled down to this conclusion however. Mechanised mass warfare can arguably be more costly than ever in direct terms, though warfare is always tragic. Fighting and preparing for war has become intricately and intimately tied up with modern economic and political structures and processes, in ways both positive and negative. Modern war-craft has transformed both private and public institutions, especially the State, in myriad ways, for better and for worse.

Morally and ethically most would agree that war is reprehensible, and something very much to be avoided and condemned. Yet, the economics of war is too subtle and complex for such blanket judgements. Further analysis is required.

22.2 A Changing Face of War

By definition war is about destruction—of people, places and things. Industrialised and technologised war has been exceptionally destructive in this sense. Pre-modern war could be just as brutal and savage, and sometimes more so, given the lack of any international conventions regarding the rules of war, and different mores about collective punishment and the treatment of combatants and non-combatants alike that appear barbaric today. Thus, the ancient historian Polybius reports of widespread atrocities after the Romans took besieged cities, using deliberate carnage designed to inspire terror, and leaving behind not just corpses but frightening symbols such as dogs cut in half. The historian Plutarch believed that Caesar's conquest of Gaul involved killing at least one million of the enemy, and some modern scholars have characterised it as genocide. Rome's destruction of Carthage after its definitive defeat is legendary, including the mowing down of most of that country's agriculture, with salt poured into the fields, and much of the populace taken away as slaves (Winn, 2008, 71–73, 81).

War was also a frequent occurrence in the Classical world, the Greek city-states constantly fighting amongst themselves, except when united against the common threat of the Persian Empire. The Romans avoided the fate of disunity by forging a strong nation for which to fight for, and for which it was (supposedly) sweet to die for. But its warfare was just as constant and more deadly because of its scale, scope and one could add, motivation driven by national ideology (Winn, 2008, 71).

Both the Greeks and Romans perfected and improved war weapons, tactics, strategy and organisation. Their medieval and modern successors continued this trend. Europeans were in the forefront of these advances, mainly because they were doing plenty of fighting amongst themselves and with others. Some say Europeans fought more frequently than other regions and nations, including China, which was quite a military innovator in its own right, and with plenty of conflicts of its own. This is a contested proposition, but the technical and organisational innovations in making war more destructive proceeded apace either way. In fact, warfare throughout the centuries has been a constant process of improvement (if that is the right word in this context) in its means and ends, motivated on both sides by a constant desire to get the edge over one's enemy, something that Morris (2014) refers to as a "Red Queen" process, evoking the character in *Alice in Wonderland* who is always driving people to run faster and faster just to stay in the same (competitive) place.

By 1800, the outlines of modern military and methods of war had been laid down. This model consisted of standardisation in weaponry, in training (and breaking down) of men, and in comprehensive organisation of command from top to bottom all the way down to the field level. All of this was driven by the requirements of directing what were now true mass armies, recruited and conscripted from national populations and inflamed by a new and rising nationalism. Napoleon, an innovator in so many ways, broke his own army down into smaller units, each marching on a separate line, able to fight stand-alone battles if they had to, but also able to rapidly converge again into a single concentrated force. These interrelated units combined force and flexibility, and also were easier to supply, foraging for their own small unit needs as required, which, in the days before centralised logistics operations, was particularly essential (Morris, 2014, 213).

Armies would soon become more mechanised and industrialised, with the result they could be much more intensively destructive over a very compressed time period. Pre-modern wars could exhibit coordinated regimentation, the Romans being especially good at this. But modern ones now took on an assembly-line quality that industrial methods allowed, in this case churning out efficient destruction instead of production. Even smaller or peripheral countries could deliver bloody industrial war. The War of the Triple Alliance between 1864 and 1870, of Argentina, Brazil, and Uruguay allied against Paraguay, claimed about half a million lives, and the American Civil War (1861–1865) took around three-quarters of a million, the latter in particular employing the latest in military and logistics technology of the times, especially the military use of the railroad. Still the Europeans dominated warfare in this era, and through ocean-going ships and steam power extended their reach across the entire planet (Morris, 2014, 232).

22.3 "Total War"

The advent of First World War brought a new concept of warfare: Total War. The term was first developed fully by Field Marshal Erich Ludendorff, joint commander of Imperial German forces (and by the end of the war, virtual military dictator of the country) to indicate a complete direction of society to pursue military aims and objectives. His ideas were not totally original, and even the term itself has antecedents. It can be seen as an extension of the aphorism credited to the nineteenth century war strategist theorist Carl von Clausewitz, that war is politics by another means, suggesting a continuum of inter-nation conflict that runs the gamut from small bore diplomacy up through the internecine combat of entire nations. Ludendorff, however, went a step further, arguing that politics *is* war and war *is* politics and that there is no separation between the two at all, and thus no continuum, a misunderstanding that he argued was fatal to Germany in its limited preparations for and conduct of the Great War. That war, he argued, had always required totality of effort to win, using all the resources of society, and complete mobilisation of civilian as well as military resources (Segesser, 2014). Germany's failure to do this led to its failure to win the grander conflict, however good it was at fighting battles.

Ludendorff's ideas were more musings than a systematic theory and the term "Total War" remains ill-defined and controversial, often politically coloured. But it is a concept that continues to resonate because of the terrible experience of the two World Wars, the second of which was truly "total" for many of those living through it. Despite his advocacy, Ludendorff himself held back from conducting such a war for Germany, especially mass mobilisation across all sectors of society, because this move contained potential revolutionary tendencies in what was then a country led by conservative social elites and an imperial monarch. The idea was more amenable to Hitler, who was a true revolutionary, even if in a perverse sense, though he too was very sensitive to popular opinion (O'Shaughnessy, 2009). Hitler thus kept more productive capacity tied up in the production of civilian goods than his Armaments Minister, Albert Speer, preferred, until the situation got truly desperate, by which point it was too late. Hitler also held back using women in armaments factories and other war economy roles, because of his patriarchal sentiments that women belonged in the home sphere, not the broader social one (Hancock, 1991).

Certainly, the deaths directly and indirectly caused by war in the modern era have been staggering. One credible estimate is that approximately 231 million people died in wars and conflict during the twentieth century. Deaths during First World War hostilities ranged between 13 and 15 million. During Second World War fighting they reached 65–75 million (Leitenberg, 2006, 1, 9). If one adds the associated injuries, physical destruction and other flow-on effects, it is clear that, whether total or not, war has indeed become something of a hell on earth.

There are some (e.g. Morris, 2014) who argue that nonetheless modern war has become less fatal and violent, in relative terms, than ever before, their terrible force concentrated and more impactful in an immediate sense, but also more efficient in gaining objectives, needing to injure and kill fewer enemy to win. This is a highly controversial point, limited not just by data gaps, but also significant measurement and definitional issues. One of the standard databases, the *Correlates of War*, includes only battlefield deaths and not civilian casualties, while other repositories count freelance violence (such as by terrorist groups) but not State-led campaigns against their own populations (Leitenberg, 2006, 8). Thus, numerical claims such as that made by Morris are deeply questionable. Certainly, there can be little doubt that modern mechanised war has expanded the actual and potential scale, scope and speed of military destruction, and the ability to commandeer resources from all levels of society, to magnitudes never before possible.

22.4 War and the Economy According to the Growth Model

All this would seem to indicate that war has no "positive" economic effects whatsoever. Consideration of the possibility that it might has a questionable moral ring to it. But this is an issue that economists have devoted considerable time to studying. In their eyes, war can be seen just like any other "exogenous" shock to an economy, such as an earthquake, pandemic or fire. These types of events destroy much, but they also clear the path for other forces to assert themselves, sometimes positively, sometimes negatively. An analogy can be made with a forest fire: much old growth is eliminated but superior new growth can take its place.

In this way, Economists pose the question as one of how war potentially affects long-term economic growth; and, subsidiary to this, how it might affect shorter-term business cycle variations. There are two major economic strains of thought about the former, and one about the latter: the Phoenix effect; Institutional Clearance; and Military Keynesianism.

22.4.1 The Phoenix Effect

The Phoenix is a mythical bird that rose from the ashes. The Phoenix Effect refers to the hypothesis that war can increase post-war economic growth above any trend it might have had otherwise if three things happen:

(1) Destruction of old capital during the war is replaced by new and more productive capital after the war.
(2) The domestic savings rate increases.
(3) Technological innovation is spurred.

How does this work? The logic is drawn from the basic Growth Model assumption that the economy takes inputs and turns them into outputs via a generalised production function (generically represented by $Y = f(K, L)$ (see Chapter 2). This model posits that GDP is based on a transformation of given inputs via technology into economic output. Technology (f) and capital (K) are the main drivers of economic growth. Thus invention devoted to making war can potentially boost technological innovation more generally (considered in more detail in later sections). If so, this will boost productivity to the extent that military innovation flows into civilian application. War can also increase the supply of K through heightened domestic savings rates that create more financial surplus that can be devoted to investment (see Box 22.1). This too will raise economic growth. And although much K is destroyed during a war, hence reducing economic growth while it is taking place, if this K is replaced by better quality and more advanced K after the war, (and even better if replaced by more K than before), then this too increases economic growth.

Some arguments have been made that Germany and Japan's economic renaissance after the vast destruction of Second World War fighting was due in part to the fact that its older, decaying and obsolescent infrastructure and facilities were mostly flattened, allowing for the construction of modern, more technically advanced systems that, in fact, put them at a better competitive advantage with existing competitors like the US (or to a lesser extent the UK) that did not suffer such destruction and were stuck with older and less efficient capital and public works.

There is actually evidence that the Phoenix effect does hold, especially, and somewhat counter-intuitively, for very long and destructive wars. The reason is that vast destruction requires vast new investment and innovation that offers the possibility of a complete update of an old system to a more productive new one. There can also be economies of scale in such mass reinvestment (Organski & Kugler, 1977).

These findings refer only to net longer-run effects. Obviously, there will be great costs to be borne as a direct result of war and during the lags of reconstruction, with lowered and even negative growth during this transition. But as economists would put it, while the destruction of war certainly will knock trend economic growth down temporarily, it will put it back above trend in time afterwards if a Phoenix effect is operating.

Box 22.1 A Note on War Finance

One of the levers of the Phoenix Effect is an increase in the savings rate. War certainly requires a lot of funding above and beyond normal requirements. Whether it will increase a society's saving rate depends upon the method used to finance it.

The three major means that a government has for financing war are (1) national debt, (2) taxation, and (3) printing money. (3) is quite attractive to many war-torn governments, especially those with few resources, but this will generally only result in increased inflation and thus is only an effective means of finance in the very short-run. Printing money will not increase the savings rate because there is no direct call on real social resources when this method is used. In fact, this method will almost certainly reduce societal savings, since inflation incentivises people to spend now rather than save later to stay ahead of the decreasing purchasing power of their currency, and erodes the value of the various financial assets that savers generally put their money in. Though money may instead be diverted into real assets, such as land or housing, as a hedge against inflation, these sorts of investments tend not to be very productive, and certainly don't represent the most efficient returns available. And in a war the environment is generally not amenable to such investment anyway.

Method (2) is different. Taxation takes money directly out of private hands and puts it into government coffers. Private consumption is obviously reduced as a result, which is arithmetically identical to having the private savings rate go up. In this sense taxation can be seen as a form of "forced" savings where private resources, instead of going to private savings vehicles or spending, go into the State budget instead. Whether this is productive or not depends on the use of the government revenues raised. To the extent these are devoted to the creation of productive capital investment, such as the creation of arms factories that can later be converted to civilian use, the increase in savings increase capital formation that, according to the Growth Model, increases growth.

As for method (1), from a government perspective, the issuance of public debt would seem to be the exact opposite of savings. But from a private and societal point of view, and if the debt us held by domestic investors, this form of finance can also increase private domestic savings rates and potentially raise domestic capital creation and accumulation. This was the approach of the US government during World War 1 with its various "Liberty Loans", which were small denomination, interest-bearing bonds designed for individual investors (see Fig. 22.2). These bonds were amongst the first to be aggressively marketed through mass advertising, celebrity endorsements and hard direct sales campaigns, combined with a tremendous amount of workplace pressure in which people were implicitly or explicitly threatened with firing or other sanctions if they didn't subscribe to one of the various loan campaigns (Case, 1922). In effect the US government was "forcing" savings from individual investors into interest-bearing instruments that helped fund the war effort, and after the war the proceeds with interest were returned to the investor to spend, or invest, as they liked. By forcing savings to higher levels than would normally have been achieved, this had the net effect of increasing the amount of funds available for capital investment which in turn increased post-war growth in the United States beyond what it would have been.

Fig. 22.2 Honor Roll, Victory Liberty Loan (*Image source* Library Company of Philadelphia archive, Accession number: P.2284.265a. No known copyright restrictions. Image notes: Under a Victory Liberty Loan flag, there are empty spaces to write the names of people who had bought Victory Liberty Loans. The fifth in the Liberty Loan series, Victory Liberty Loans were used by the American Government to pay war debts. Created in 1919)

The case is different, however, for war debt that is held by overseas investors. For the British and French Allies the First World War debt they ran up led to a crushing burden of interest and principal payments that were diverted away from the domestic economy to foreign investors, especially the Americans. This debt reduced capital and savings for the debt issuers and transferred resources to those countries holding the war bonds.

(The discussion above is drawn largely from Bordo & White, 1991)

22.4.2 *Institutional Clearance*

Another argument for the possible long-term growth enhancing effects of war is based on Mancur Olson's theory that, over a long duration, vested special and narrow interests can take over government and other institutions and use them to direct resources away from productive enterprise and towards activities that benefit only these narrow interests, something that economists refer to "rent-seeking". Olson refers to this process as institutional sclerosis, after the medical condition of narrowing and hardening arteries that can occur with age and poor diet in the human being (Olson, 1971).

Many have applied Olson's theory to war, claiming that war can be productivity-increasing if it wipes out sclerotic institutions and replaces them with new "clean" institutions no longer dominated by narrow, rent-seeking groups. Again, arguments have been made along these lines for Germany and Japan after Second World War which saw a nearly complete wiping away of pre-war government and private institutions, replacing them with new governmental, legal and administrative arrangements, often quite radically. Such effects are very difficult to disentangle from broader ones, especially when the changes are dramatic enough that a fairly complete overhaul of the economic and political order has been accomplished. The analysis of the period after the Second World War is complicated by the fact of a long period of general prosperity across all Western countries (and even across the Socialist bloc Europeans as well) which drove up capital investment everywhere (Koubi, 2005).

The institutional clearance argument is generally an adjunct to the Phoenix effect. In both cases, there is a bit of a paradox since the more destructive the war, the greater the opportunity and need for capital and institutional replacement after it. These effects can't be taken for granted though, since old capital and organisations will not necessarily be replaced by better ones, if at all.

22.4.3 *Military Keynesianism*

The two effects discussed so far are microeconomic and longer-term in nature. There is also the question of how spending for war might affect the short-term macroeconomy. The idea here is that the spending associated with war stimulates the aggregate demand in an economy (see Chapter 18), making use of spare domestic productive capacity, keeping it from lying idle, and thus yielding a higher per capita GDP in the short run. This is just like any other "Keynesian" spending effect, in which government spending is used to fill a temporary recessionary gap, except that in this case the purpose of the spending is military, and the drive for such spending is more structurally embedded rather than a temporary explicit policy decision to provide domestic "stimulus" to "smooth" out a business cycle.

The initial genesis of the idea came out of the fact that the Great Depression appeared to end definitively not so much as a result of any countercyclical government program, and certainly not from any market self-correction, but through massive war spending, especially in America which was relatively lightly touched directly by the war's destructive power. Indeed "Doctor New Deal" had never produced anywhere near full employment before the war began, even though it did stave off disaster. Although historically unprecedented for a peacetime America, the levels of government spending to fight the Depression were not especially high. When "Doctor Win-the-War" commenced however, military spending ballooned, rising 600% between June 1940 and 1941, before the US had even entered the war formally, and reaching 42% of a much expanded GDP in 1943–1944. This spending was associated with massive rises in labour productivity, even with 15 million workers inducted into the military. Real GDP grew by a total of 52.4% between 1939 and 1944, and unemployment came down from 14.6% in 1940 to 1.2% in 1944 (Cypher, 2015, 451).

War spending thus seemed to boost economic growth dramatically. But it could not last forever. Or could it? In essence, this is what broader conceptions of Military Keynesianism refer to, namely macroeconomic policies with a structural military spending component that boosts both military and domestic spheres at the same time, whether there is a war going on or not. For some American policymakers who believed in the social Keynesianism of the Great Depression, but also were anti-Communist, Military Keynesianism represented an improvement, especially in the Cold War context in which military spending could be increased without (hopefully) having economically damaging "hot" wars to fight (Cypher, 2015, 452–453).

Econometric studies of military Keynesianism tend to find fairly weak multiplier effects over time. But these studies are limited in explanatory power because they tend to focus on relatively broad and very short-term estimates of official defence spending and its correlation to changes only in very short-run growth. Much military spending, in the US at least, occurs in entities outside the Department of Defense (DoD) and thus looking just at DoD expenditures understates the true size of total military expenditure. Also, to properly capture the timing of effects, one shouldn't look at when spending is authorised by the US Congress (which is what the official budgets record) but when it is actually expended. These confounding effects tend not to be adjusted for (Cypher, 2015, 466–472). Most of the existing econometric studies fail to take into account the broader set of policies such as subsidies for military contractors, either because these are hidden from budgets or, even if not, their much broader potential economic "multiplier" effects may fail to be fully accounted for (Custers, 2010). And there are some careful studies (e.g. Almunia et al., 2010) that do find strong multiplier effects for defence spending.

Whatever the short-run impact might have been, there certainly was a coincidence of high economic growth and high military expenditure growth through the first part of the Cold War period that shouldn't be dismissed, as some critics of the theory of Military Keynesianism are quick to do. Real US GNP advanced at an annual growth rate of 8.4% between 1941 and 1945, and 5.1% annually during the Korean War (Ohanian, 1997, 24). In the latter case, very little debt was issued, as opposed to the Second World War. Partly this was because it was a smaller war and could be financed by taxation alone. It was also due to the fact that President Harry Truman viewed Second World War financing methods as mistaken, and he wanted to maintain a balanced budget throughout the Korean conflict (Ohanian, 1997, 26). There were differences in scale of course, with the average number of individuals in military service being 9 million (14% of the total labour force) in the Second World War, versus 3.5 million in Korea (4%) (Ohanian, 1997, 30). Whether debt-financed, or tax-financed, war spending was at least concomitant with good macroeconomic performance in the US throughout the 1950s and most of the 1960s.

It also is now thought that Military Keynesianism represented a particular configuration of labour, business and government power which put Keynesian business cycle smoothing in a central position during a particular period in the history of the world economic system where the maintenance of full employment and a Cold War-induced constant state of military readiness was seen as essential to the survival of both capitalism and democracy (Cypher, 2015, 473; Nitzan & Bichler, 2006). The US war in Vietnam was a negative turning point for this order. That war was a military failure for America, temporarily bringing down the prestige of anti-Communist military activity generally. The war was also a clear proximate cause of a deterioration in US macroeconomic performance, bringing higher inflation but with increasingly less growth in the late 1960s, emblematic of the beginning of the end for Keynesian business cycle "fine-tuning" in general and its militarised version in particular (see Chapter 28). No doubt military spending continues to have some economically stimulative effects, but are not part of a concerted Keynesian macro-agenda as they once were.

22.5 Military Technology and Dual Uses

As already mentioned, military history is dominated by a series of ongoing innovations and inventions. Progress in weaponry and force delivery are especially impressive in the twentieth and twenty-first centuries, starting with the development of massive artillery ("big guns") and associated machines that helped to guide and target these guns during First World War combat; the invention of the airplane and the creation of an entirely new mode of air warfare, later extended into space, especially through the development of intercontinental ballistics systems during the Cold War and beyond; atomic weapons; increasingly sophisticated guidance systems, beginning with radar and sonar, and moving on into satellite communications, Global Positioning Systems (GPS) and digital warfare; and the list goes on and on (Hacker, 2005).

By itself such innovation mainly increases destructive rather than creative capacity. War strategists speak of applying and directing force and "fire", and innovations in military machinery have clearly vastly increased the scale and scope of its application and direction. To take but one (non-atomic) example, the Allied bombing of the German city of Hamburg in 1943 created the first known "firestorm" (a new term) in which the intensity of the on-ground fires created by the bombing created a vortex and whirling updraft of super-heated air resulting in a 460 metre high tornado of fire. The bombing of Dresden in 1945 would be even more devastating, flattening and sometimes melting buildings and occupants (De Bruhl, 2010). This phenomenon would be repeated many times in both theatres of the War, culminating in the even more devastating experiences of the dropping of atomic bombs on Nagasaki and Hiroshima in Japan by the US. It should be noted that mass conventional bombings could and did impose equally harsh loss of life and destruction, but minus the radiation and more economical delivery of nuclear weapons.

Clearly, the strictly military and destructive use of military technology is effective. But how about its potential for the "dual use" of such technology for non-military purposes, something which is most relevant for economic growth? Dual use applications of such technology exist and can be productive—as with jet aircraft—but are not always clearly so—as with nuclear technology. Some technologies—the Internet especially—are not yet clear contributors to overall productivity on a net basis, though many have clearly changed the face of society.

Ruttan (2006) argues that these large-scale "general purpose technologies", often birthed by military applications, take a long time to show up in productivity statistics, often decades. But they nonetheless can have profound positive consequences from an economic growth point of view. In particular, the military has very long-time horizons, often relatively unbounded budgets, and a willingness to underwrite technical advance that may begin with only a very general promise, things that private investors would not be willing to touch. Some of these investments may "win", some may "lose" in terms of military payoff, but in the meantime can generate broader public goods and productivity impacts.

Ruttan argues, in the US context, that American military programs played significant roles in the development of passenger jet aircraft, semi-conductors and mainframe computers. Military programs, according to him, were essentially solely responsible for development of nuclear weapons and associated technology, space travel and rocketry, GPS and, of course, the Internet. This is because military programs bring investment at a scale and ongoing regular commitment that purely private investment lacks and without which some technical progress, especially that requiring large initial expenditures and long and uncertain payoffs, would likely never take place.

Additionally, even where payoffs might ultimately be certain, the "public good" quality of the final outputs would probably prevent private investors from collaborating on them since the private returns they would receive would only be justified if the public returns, i.e. those available to all, could somehow be captured privately as well. GPS and the internet are both things that, arguably, had clear and obviously beneficial outcomes to the society at large once built, but which would not be profitable enough before such a network reached critical mass, to be of interest to purely private investors.

There is some debate about whether certain technologies would have developed anyway, without the aid of the military. For example, nuclear science was already well in train before the Manhattan project of the Second World War, and the actual fission of the atom was only a matter of time. Military involvement sped this up but was not the ultimate cause of it. Computers precede the military programs devoted to them and would certainly have continued to develop, perhaps producing the same innovations, though arguably much later in many cases without government support. And of course military involvement may as easily misshape technical progress as shape it. For example, would nuclear fission have taken a more humane and productive course if it had been freed from military involvement?

Finally, military expenditure has an opportunity cost because it diverts tax revenues from both private hands and other public uses, either one of which may have ended up yielding outcomes with higher returns. This is a potential objection to all State-financed technology development. But military programs in particular are generally not known for their cost-effectiveness, though Ruttan notes that broader definitive benefit-cost analyses on specific military programs have yet to be done.

22.6 War-Making and State-Making

There remains a broader question of how military innovation more broadly, what Hew Strachan (2000) refers to as "military modernisation", might feed into economic innovation and how this might contribute to broader economic growth.

Military modernisation refers primarily to organisational improvements, such as the professionalisation of the officer corps, the widespread adoption of the Prussian "General Staff" model and institution of military academies. Reorganisations and improvements in "logistics tails" (referring to supply systems for armies in the field), and the standardisation of tactical and strategic doctrines, are further improvements.

Mass mobilisation of the general population was another organisational innovation.

These are obviously closely related to but distinct from new technical innovations, whether militarily inspired or not. The railways, for example, allowed for the rapid raising and movement of armies on a vast scale, and this required concomitant innovation and reorganisation of military management systems. Clearly, these organisational changes had vast impact on military tactics, strategy and operations. But these also diffused through the wider society and economy.

A very influential sociological model of this process, which has been widely adopted by economists, comes from Charles Tilly (1975), pithily summarised as "war made the State, and the State made war". According to Tilly, in Europe after the sixteenth century, an expansion of military capacity (and constant internecine conflict) allowed wars there to become bigger and deadlier, but also shorter. During peacetime, European states restored their economic capacities and built up mass armies and navies that rested on a number of key foundations. These included: a modernised fiscal capacity to maintain and manage large standing forces; the disarmament of civilian populations to allow the specialisation in the use of force by a formal state-sponsored military establishment (a development that also reduced the prevalence of costly and destabilising small-scale private wars); and civilian bureaucracies with sufficient skill and capacity to oversee military leaders and constrain them to working for State objectives, while simultaneously expanding the ability of these leaders to prosecute war effectively. This last innovation established a model of civilian rulers with civilian interests managing war at a political level, which in turn required some degree of popular consent. Taylor and Botea (2008) summarise this overall process as: war → extraction → repression → state formation (28).

It is possible to argue that the peculiarly European genesis of military modernisation helped to lead to the industrial take-off of that part of the world; as well, of course, of the projection of European power over much of the rest of the world, although Tilly himself does not make that leap. The theory is consistent with the broader developments of the Industrial Revolution in which war, governmental and economic capacity all increased apace. While not exactly an argument for war, Tilly's thesis does allow one to say that modernised war was an integral part of economic modernisation through its role in changing the nature of the State and the relationship to its people.

This does not necessarily mean that all this is true. One critique of Tilly's model is that it is time and culture-bound, i.e. that it works well in the historical time and place he created the model for, but that it does not apply to other eras and areas so well. The modern developing world, with its generally differently articulated and less centralised states, does not seem to fit Tilly's progression very closely. Others note that war weakens and disintegrates states as easily as it strengthens and integrates them, and one can find counter-examples even in Europe during the period that Tilly is interested in. Thus Tilly's story may have to be modified to say that successful war makes a successful state and vice versa (Taylor & Botea, 2008, 29), something that Tilly himself alludes to. But then what makes for such success exactly? And can a successful state emerge without war, and if so, how? Tilly asserts a causal chain that is plausible but not necessarily proven or exclusive. The same can be said for broader claims about the links between the Tilly hypothesis and broader industrialisation in Europe.

22.7 Military-Industrial Complexes

The US Manhattan Project (named after the Manhattan Division of the US Army Corps of Engineers to which the project was assigned) which successfully created the first atomic bomb, set off the establishment, in America, of a whole raft of publicly funded national laboratories, working with academia and government, to develop new ideas, projects and applications with dual uses (Nelson, 2014, 24). This so-called "Big Science" became integrally tied up with "Big Business" and later helped to launch "Big Technology", i.e. large tech companies with deep pockets, often financially replenished with government contracts, that themselves could properly fund and conduct long-term Research and Development (R&D) and systemic innovation. This itself was a continuation of trends during the Second Industrial Revolution, in which government funded basic scientific research that in turn was commercialised by business. Germany was the epitome of this model in the late nineteenth century.

Although much policy and economic analysis still focuses on bright lines between "private" and "public", and especially "State" versus "non-State", the truly relevant unit of analysis when it comes to the military economy may be this larger complex of the public military, the private military contractors, academia, research institutes and the government as a whole, including the relevant internal and external pressure groups. This is what US President Dwight D Eisenhower warned about in his 1960 farewell Presidential address with his reference to the military-industrial complex (Fig. 22.3).

In his address, Eisenhower warned of "the acquisition of unwarranted influence, whether sought or unsought, by the military-industrial complex", and "the potential for the disastrous rise of misplaced power". He called on the American people to "never let the weight of this combination endanger our liberties or democratic processes". What Eisenhower was referring to was a situation where segments of the economy were

Fig. 22.3 Eisenhower and the Military-Industrial Complex head off into space (*Image Source* US NASA. Image Number: jsc2001e25132. Date: August 19, 1958. Original notes: President Dwight D. Eisenhower is pictured with Dr. Hugh Dryden [left] and Dr. T. Keith Glennan. NASA was created on 1 October 1958, to perform civilian research related to space flight and aeronautics. President Eisenhower commissioned Dr. Glennan as the first administrator for NASA and Dr Dryden as deputy administrator, swearing them in on 19 August 1958. Government created image put into public domain)

permanently devoted to military production, justified by the Cold War, but also creating a powerful set of interest groups capable of perverting the American political system (Engel, 2011, 177).

Coming from Eisenhower, this warning was a bit hollow. On the one hand, that a hero of Second World War and very popular President would say such a thing gave it great credence. But Eisenhower arguably had helped to build up and entrench the power of this complex, and not only because during his term, he spent close to 10% of GDP annually on official defence spending (Bernstein & Wilson, 2011, 3). (The actual level of military spending, including that conducted outside the DoD was probably even higher.) He also expanded war-fighting capacities through the "Massive Retaliation" and "New Look" doctrines that aimed to replace labour-intensive conventional defence and offence with sophisticated capital-intensive conventional and atomic means of delivering military force more economically. By 1958, Eisenhower explicitly promoted the aim of "full spectrum dominance" by creating the National Space Administration (NASA), justifying it in terms of peaceful space exploration but with major research aims focused on rocketry and weapons development, especially important in the "missile age" of the Cold War (Cypher, 2015, 461). This was the beginning of a process which has culminated with the creation in 2019 of an entirely new service branch of the US military called the Space Force, that "organizes, trains, and equips space forces in order to protect U.S. and allied interests in space and to provide space capabilities" (US Space Force, 2020, "What is the mission of the Space Force?").

Interestingly, a prior draft of Eisenhower's address had referred to the "military-industrial-scientific complex" (Kampmark, 2011, 11), a longer and a bit less felicitous phrase, but arguably more accurate in capturing the true nature of the relationships involved. The US government was conducting plenty of its own research directly, but much more was funnelled through contracts and grants to academic institutions via the Defense Advanced Research Projects Agency (DARPA), a major funder of basic research with a military edge, and also another Eisenhower creation. This echoed the earlier industrial alliances of the late nineteenth century, which were much more commercial in general, but which also received strategic public funding, especially in pre-1914 Germany, a state that felt it had much catching up to do militarily and economically.

The Second World War had merely accelerated this integration of the scientific research establishment into broader governmental commercial and military strategic aims. Indeed, the invention and use of atomic weapons was a product of scientific research and one that was viewed as critical in shortening the war, and essential in preventing a Fascist victory. A 1945 government report delivered to President Franklin Roosevelt, *Science: The Endless Frontier*, argued for a continuing and growing partnership between State and science to preserve American dominance not just in military terms, but in world trade terms as well. By 1949, the Pentagon's Research and Development Board (RBD), created to adapt science to war, had around 250 full-time staff members and 1,500 consultants, out of which DARPA was a natural outgrowth. By 1963, David E. Lillenthal, the first chairman of the Atomic Energy Commission, noted that the scientist was no longer a creative individual pursuing an idea but one of a number of "organization men" working in "platoons" (Kampmark, 2011, 11–12).

Brunton (1988) is more specific in his definition of the elements and characteristics of this complex, though he focuses mostly on the military and industrial parts, not its scientific component. As he sees it, the complex is an institution that combines a habituated way of thinking or behaving within an organisational frame that is a going concern, with military procurement in peacetime done largely through private contractors, and a "revolving door" between public and private entities along with a "preparedness" ethos (as captured in the epigram ascribed to George Washington that the only way to prepare for peace is to prepare for war). The complex also consists of formally incorporated defence lobbying organisations and defence-oriented trade associations, backed up by veterans' groups and patriotic societies that serve as ongoing pressure groups for the state support for "strategic" industry, i.e. a base of private defence firms (600–601).

Brunton finds that even in relatively laissez-faire America, this complex began to be built up early in the twentieth century, mirroring developments within industrialising Europe. Defence R&D was small but rising between 1900 and 1940, and by the late 1930s, a significant core of federally supported private research had been established. The US National Bureau of Standards, created in 1901, was explicitly modelled after the German (Reichsanstalt) national physical laboratory, soon to be joined by the Bureau of Mines (1903), the National Advisory Committee for Aeronautics (1915) and the National Research Council (1916). Also, the basic procurement law was changed in 1901 to provide special allowances for direct negotiation instead of competitive bidding. A foundation for a larger structure of continuing government support for industries deemed strategic and an underwriting of public-private research and development activity had thus been bedded down in America even before the First World War. The international political and economic background for this was an environment of international rivalry where military development and economic competition were blurred, whether there was a general state of war or peace (Brunton, 1988, 601–604).

22.8 "Iron Triangles"

American military production is now the largest such sector in the world. To get to this point, a strong, and somewhat shifting self-reinforcing "Iron Triangle" had been formed in the US that helped to define national policy at the juncture between defence and economic development. Its Cold War formation consisted of a three-sided alliance. The first leg was composed of military contractors, sub-contractors and their industrial unions. The second consisted of high-level military personnel spread through the US military forces and commands along with civilian policymakers within the defence arms of the executive branch (whether these had military policy designations or not: the Atomic Energy Commission and NASA, though nominally civilian agencies, were both heavily focused on military spending and affairs). And the third leg was comprised of legislative branch staff in the relevant policymaking committees of the US Congress (Cypher, 2015, 456).

This American triangle has shifted over time, now expanded into the national security, intelligence and information technology sectors, and with a much larger retinue than before of nominally neutral but heavily defence-funded institutes and research organisations, inside and outside of the academy. There are varying forms of this alliance in other countries as well, adjusted for local private sector economies and public governance forms. But the basic idea remains the same.

This rounds back to questions of war, economic growth and efficiency (leaving aside the equally important ethical and moral issues that are mostly outside the scope of this book). The military-industrial complex can be simplified into its three major components of military hierarchy, administrative bureaucracy (public and private) and corporate/national wealth (Moskos, 1974, 502). This complex may have had positive economic returns beyond each of the components taken in isolation.

This could be said to be the essence of Tilly's war-making/state-making hypothesis.

But the internal political economy of this complex must be considered as well. In its latest forms, it is quite possible that preponderance towards individual "rent-seeking" and resource wasting, which was certainly always there, may now be outweighing the important technological and economic improvements that were delivered in the past, the Iron Triangles now encouraging permanent war, and being fundamentally corrupting. This chapter must leave the answer to these questions open for the moment. Certainly, the shape of things past, present and future have been greatly altered by the modernisation of war and the military, whatever the net gains and losses might be.

References

Almunia, M., Benetrix, A., Eichengreen, B., O'Rourke, K. H., & Rua, G. (2010). From Great Depression to Great Credit Crisis: Similarities, differences and lessons. *Economic Policy, 25*(62), 219–265.

Bernstein, M. A., & Wilson, M. R. (2011). New perspectives on the history of the military-industrial complex. *Enterprise & Society, 12*(1), 1–9.

Bordo, M. D., & White, E. N. (1991). A tale of two currencies: British and French finance during the Napoleonic Wars. *The Journal of Economic History, 51*(2), 303–316.

Brunton, B. G. (1988). Institutional origins of the military-industrial complex. *Journal of Economic Issues, 22*(2), 599–606.

Case, J. H. (1922). Preparation for war and the Liberty Loans. *The Annals of the American Academy of Political and Social Science, 99*(1), 121–129.

Custers, P. (2010). Military Keynesianism today: An innovative discourse. *Race & Class, 51*(4), 79–94.

Cypher, J. M. (2015). The origins and evolution of military Keynesianism in the United States. *Journal of Post Keynesian Economics, 38*(3), 449–476.

De Bruhl, M. (2010). *Firestorm: Allied airpower and the destruction of Dresden*. Random House.

Engel, J. A. (2011). Not yet a garrison state: Reconsidering Eisenhower's military—Industrial complex. *Enterprise & Society, 12*(1), 175–199.

Hacker, B. C. (2005). The machines of war: Western military technology 1850–2000. *History and Technology, 21*(3), 255–300.

Hancock, E. I. M. (1991). *National socialist leadership and total war, 1941–1945*. Martin's Press.

Kampmark, B. (2011, July–August). Science and war: Remembering the military industrial complex. *New Zealand International Review, 36*(4), 11–14.

Koubi, V. (2005). War and economic performance. *Journal of Peace Research, 42*(1), 67–82.

Leitenberg, M. (2006). *Deaths in wars and conflicts in the 20th century* (Cornell University Peace Studies Program Occasional Paper #29 (3rd ed))

Morris, I. (2014). *War! What is it good for? Conflict and the progress of civilization from primates to robots.* Farrer, Straus and Giroux.

Moskos, C. C. (1974). The concept of the military-industrial complex: Radical critique or liberal bogey? *Social Problems, 21*(4), 498–512.

Nelson, C. (2014). *The age of radiance: The epic rise and dramatic fall of the atomic era.* Scribner.

Nitzan, J., & Bichler, S. (2006). *Cheap wars* (MPRA Paper 5549, University Library of Munich, Germany).

Ohanian, L. E. (1997). The macroeconomic effects of war finance in the United States: World War II and the Korean War. *The American Economic Review, 87*(1), 23–40.

Olson, M. (1971). *The logic of collective action: Public Goods and the theory of groups* (Second Printing with a New Preface and Appendix). Harvard University Press.

Organski, A. F., & Kugler, J. (1977). The costs of major wars: The phoenix factor. *American Political Science Review, 71*(4), 1347–1366.

O'Shaughnessy, N. (2009). Selling Hitler: Propaganda and the Nazi brand. *Journal of Public Affairs: An International Journal, 9*(1), 55–76.

Ruttan, V. W. (2006, October 9). *Is war necessary for economic growth? Military procurement and technology development.* Clemens Lecture Series, Saint Johns University (Collegeville, MN USA).

Segesser, D. M. (2014). Controversy: Total War. In U. Daniel, P. Gatrell, O. Janz, H. Jones, J. Keene, A. Kramer & B. Nasson (Eds.), *1914–1918-online international encyclopedia of the First World War.* Freie Universität Berlin.

Strachan, H. (2000). Military modernization. In T. C. Blanning (Ed.), *The Oxford history of modern Europe* (pp. 77–100). Oxford University Press.

Taylor, B. D., & Botea, R. (2008). Tilly tally: War-making and state-making in the contemporary third world. *International Studies Review, 10*(1), 27–56.

Tilly, C. (1975). Western state-making and theories of political transformation. In G. Ardant (Ed.), *The formation of national states in Western Europe* (Vol. 8, pp. 601–638). Princeton University Press.

US Space Force. (2020). *United States Space Force.* https://www.spaceforce.mil/About-Us/FAQs/Whats-the-Space-Force/.

Winn, J. A. (2008). *The poetry of war.* Cambridge University Press.

CHAPTER 23

Comparative Economic, Social and Political Systems

C. Gordon, *Many Possible Worlds*,
https://doi.org/10.1007/978-981-19-9281-0_23

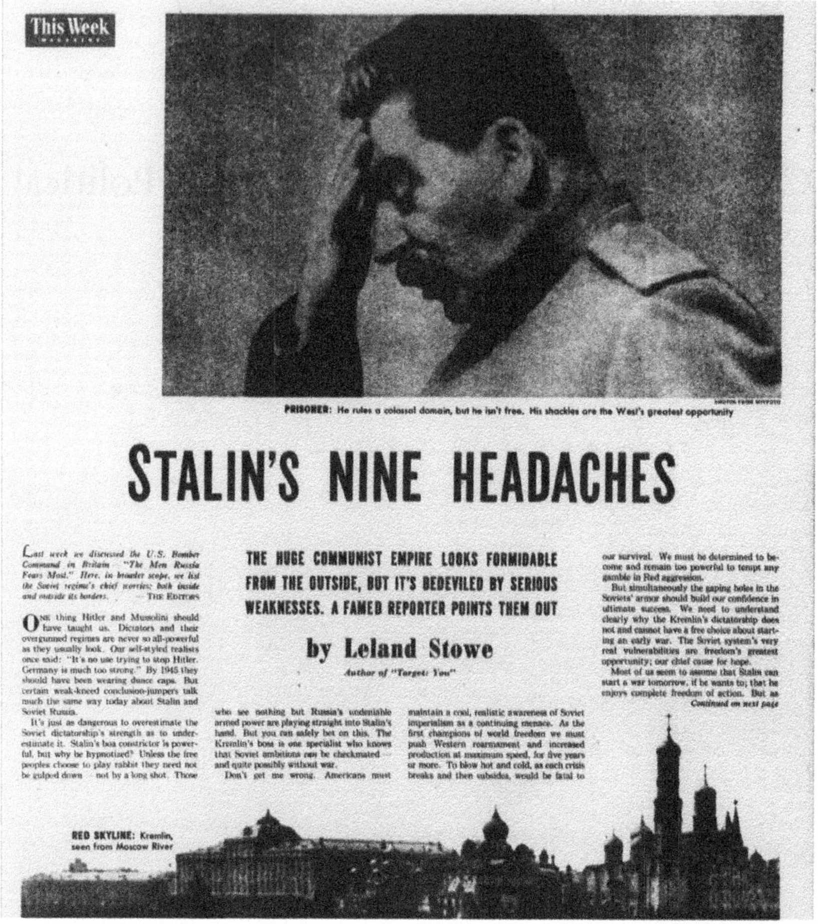

This Week

PRISONER: He rules a colossal domain, but he isn't free. His shackles are the West's greatest opportunity

STALIN'S NINE HEADACHES

Last week we discussed the U.S. Bomber Command in Britain "The Men Russia Fears Most." Here, in broader scope, we list the Soviet regime's chief worries: both inside and outside its borders. —THE EDITORS

THE HUGE COMMUNIST EMPIRE LOOKS FORMIDABLE FROM THE OUTSIDE, BUT IT'S BEDEVILED BY SERIOUS WEAKNESSES. A FAMED REPORTER POINTS THEM OUT

by Leland Stowe

Author of "Target: You"

ONE thing Hitler and Mussolini should have taught us. Dictators and their overgunned regimes are never so all-powerful as they usually look. Our self-styled realists once said: "It's no use trying to stop Hitler. Germany is much too strong." By 1945 they should have been wearing dunce caps. But certain weak-kneed conclusion-jumpers talk much the same way today about Stalin and Soviet Russia.

It's just as dangerous to overestimate the Soviet dictatorship's strength as to underestimate it. Stalin's boa constrictor is powerful, but why be hypnotized? Unless the free peoples choose to play rabbit they need not be gulped down — not by a long shot. Those who see nothing but Russia's undeniable armed power are playing straight into Stalin's hand. But you can safely bet on this. The Kremlin's boss is one specialist who knows that Soviet ambitions can be checkmated — and quite possibly without war.

Don't get me wrong. Americans must maintain a cool, realistic awareness of Soviet imperialism as a continuing menace. As the first champions of world freedom we must push Western rearmament and increased production at maximum speed, for five years or more. To blow hot and cold, as each crisis breaks and then subsides, would be fatal to our survival. We must be determined to become and remain too powerful to tempt any gamble in Red aggression.

But simultaneously the gaping holes in the Soviets' armor should build our confidence in ultimate success. We need to understand clearly why the Kremlin's dictatorship does not and cannot have a free choice about starting an early war. The Soviet system's very real vulnerabilities are freedom's greatest opportunity; our chief cause for hope.

Most of us seem to assume that Stalin can start a war tomorrow, if he wants to; that he enjoys complete freedom of action. But as

Continued on next page

RED SKYLINE: Kremlin, seen from Moscow River

Fig. 23.1 Every system has its headaches (*Image source Evening star*. March 18, 1951, Page 7, Image 112 [Washington, DC], 18 March 1951. Chronicling America: Historic American Newspapers. Lib. of Congress. https://chroniclingamerica.loc.gov/lccn/sn83045462/1951-03-18/ed-1/seq-112/ No known copyright restrictions)

23.1 Industrialism Versus Capitalism

What was the core feature of the Industrial Revolution? A default answer is to say capitalism, and the creation and diffusion of a capitalist system. But Adam Smith, the high theoretician of the changes wrought during this time did not actually use the word "capitalism"; instead, he referred to "commercial society" (Naggar & Naggar, 2005, 90). He did make many references to capital and its productive power, but was referring to them as a means towards the ends of division of labour, increased trade and expansion of the "extent of the market", not an end in and of itself. Interestingly, Marx did not use the word either in his earliest writings, though he was using it extensively, and generally pejoratively, by the time he wrote his major treatise *Das Kapital* (1867) (Fig. 23.1).

Capitalism now has come to refer to a process of change, expansion, consolidation and transformation that is subtle, complex and evolving over multiple generations. During the earliest parts of the First Industrial Revolution, industrialisation was the primary and most obvious element of change, in its literal sense being the widespread development of manufacturing within a region, a growing displacement and relative decline of the agricultural sector, and an increasing innovation in and use of methods and means devoted to boosting industrial productivity, such as scale and concentration of activity, division and specialisation of labour function and tasks, and technological and organisational process improvements, amongst other things. All of these changes were much more capital-intensive than the heavily labour-intensive pre-industrial economies that came before.

Simultaneously the socioeconomy was undergoing parallel processes of "commodification" (the transformation of things into objects of trade), "monetisation" (the conversion of things into monetary quantities) and "marketisation" (the use of market mechanisms and exchange to allocate resources), all of which involved a more general privatisation of resources formerly held in commons or outside a market nexus now being pulled into it. These are the sorts of changes that Polanyi (1944) discusses in the context of England, an earlier industrialiser.

During the second half of the twentieth century, a shift within the developed world towards a "post-industrial" economy began to become pronounced, spreading in the twenty-first century to many areas outside the developed core (see Chapter 29). Manufacturing and industrial production remained a large and growing component of the overall economic engine, even within advanced countries in which these activities exhibited a great deal of relative decline in proportion to overall GDP. But services, information and other less purely physical outputs and inputs became more and more prominent in the total value-add of more and more economies.

All of these diverse processes and broad changes over the past 250 years are still referred to using the rubric of "capitalism". This moniker makes some sense as a retrospective way of distinguishing an epoch in production, consumption and distribution that took a distinct and dramatic turn away from the quite different economic and social arrangements that prevailed before the First Industrial Revolution. That these changes were overwhelmingly reliant on and driven by capital accumulation justifies using "capital" as an integral part of the title.

However, when comparing systems across time and space, the label is far too simplistic. Capital and industry are common elements of economic and social change since the Industrial Revolution. But even with that foundation, socioeconomic complexes have differed greatly from one another at various points, while generally delivering at least sufficient levels of economic and social functionality for their times.

23.2 Social, Political, Economic and Cultural Comparisons

"Man does not live by bread alone", to paraphrase the Book of Matthew in the Gospels, and this remains true even as the emphasis on bread and other material things has become paramount, one could even say monomaniacal. Table 23.1 summarises some of the key elements of comparative economic system analysis. The table starts most obviously with the structures and processes most central to the economy, namely ownership and control of the inputs and outputs underlying material production and distribution. But it also breaks out the social, political and cultural elements that are integral linkages between the economy and the broader society.

As discussed in Chapter 4, Political Economy purported to examine the economy and polity as a unity. Liberalism proposed that free markets sitting within a political democracy best balanced the two spheres. In this mutually reinforcing dualism, political power was exercised by a majority of individuals via electoral representative democratic institutions, while economic power was determined and exercised via the sum total

Table 23.1 The elements of comparative systems analysis

Sphere	*Issues arising*
Economic	Existence and strength of property rights Ownership/control of capital and production processes Ownership/control of labour Distribution and control of surplus Means and control over allocation of resources
Political	Political rights and responsibilities of individuals Processes and institutions of collective decision-making Structure and power of the State Delineation of State and non-State sectors
Social	Social power structure shape—hierarchy versus flatness Social relations Civil society Position of the individual relative to society Cooperation versus competition
Cultural/meaning	Hegemony Collective communication mechanisms
Cross-cutting issues	Industrialisation and industrialism Scale of enterprise Capital-intensification Technological advancement High-level planning and bureaucracy

of commercial transactions in an unfettered marketplace. This is sometimes referred to as the methods of "voice" for hearing and acting on individual preferences mediated through the collective. The individual was the fundamental unit, with society essentially the sum of the parts. Thus, individual civil rights and private property rights were legally guaranteed by a minimally active State, whose major function was protecting and adjudicating such rights. Political power was also supposedly separate from economic power, though some of the Political Economists, like Mill, discussed ways in which economic changes could undermine political democracy (see Chapter 17).

Communism in its original Marxist form was theoretically even simpler. Here, economic processes (referred to as a substructure) underlay everything else, including political power. Ownership of the means of production was determinative of all economic forms and shapes and thus, in turn, all political, social and cultural ones as well. While Liberalism sought to offer a doctrine to explain the world as it was, however unrealistically in many ways, Marxism was utopian, claiming that politics would resolve itself as economic evolution followed its natural course towards a stateless society without class or politics. This utopianism posed some grave problems for the new Soviet Union that required the formulation of new political theory, as discussed below.

Both Political Economy and Marxism simplified away from discussions of society and social relations, putting economics at the fore in both cases in their different ways. Interestingly, the Political Economists started with some intriguing formulations of this dimension while rather quickly dropping it from the mainstream, while Marxism first ignored it and brought it in later. Adam Smith noted that humans had a natural social tendency that formed part of the "moral sentiments" for one another, and Mill knew the importance of "civil society" to both economy and politics. Civil society is a term that has multiple meanings, but generally refers to socially based institutions that do not fit within either the governmental or commercial realms. In some usages, this boils down to analysis of politics by other means (Edwards, 2009). Further discussions of civil society, however, got dropped from the mainstream as economics developed into its more formal "neoclassical" version, while Liberalism became narrowly focused on democratic procedures and institutions rather than broader social processes.

19th-century Marxism ignored the issue because of its deterministic bias. But as Communist movements expanded, and then took power in Russia, it became clear that society and politics needed to be more fully addressed. An influential concept is Antonio Gramsci's concept of "egemonia" (hegemony) that refers to a social order held in equilibrium by a moral and intellectual consensus informing all strata in daily life. This "consensus" takes generations to develop and cannot be done simply through political or social revolution or imposition from above (Lichtheim, 1972, 269).

Gramsci's concept encompasses both civil society and some cultural elements such as shared meaning in social and individual meaning in life. Hegemony, in the Gramscian sense, is a powerful foundation for social cohesion and the guiding of purposeful collective action. If hegemony is somehow at cross-purposes with the political and economic system, or failing to function in some way, the political, social and economic outcomes could be quite bad. Weber shared this concern, noting how important it was for human social animals to have meaning in their lives and thus the social necessity of providing it.

Liberalism as a doctrine took for granted some of the emerging values of the growing English middle classes of the time, e.g. self-reliance, social modesty, personal ambition, and conservatism, as the unspoken glue that held a democratic capitalistic society together. Without these values, it is hard to see how either chaos or autocracy of some sort could be avoided, which indeed was an outcome for many countries during the turbulent 1930s (see below) and which may be happening in some countries today (see Chapters 30 and 31). As noted, Soviet Marxism, following Marx's original writings, ignored civil society and hegemony, to its great detriment.

The last column of Table 23.1 notes the cross-cutting issues of: Industrialisation and industrialism; scale of enterprise; capital-intensification; technological advancement; and high-level planning and bureaucracy. In the early decades of the Industrial Revolution, it was, perhaps, possible not to go down some of these branches even if already on the industrial path. By the late nineteenth century, it was almost certainly impossible to avoid any one of them. Rapid material growth was the order of the day and all of these were the necessary means of organising industry to achieve it. European imperialism and global integration made it impossible for any country to seal off itself from these processes. Even where some agency was possible, as in Japan, and tweaks could be made, the large scale industrial path seemed unavoidable. Even if some kind of alternative pathway could have been conceived, there simply was no time to wait to see if it worked in terms of the narrow frame of GDP per capita expansion, especially with the forces of economic, political and military competition constantly working away.

The other items in the more singular categories of the table above remained more negotiable. For example, it was quite possible theoretically to have strong and well-defined private property rights and yet simultaneously have the means of production owned by some sort of collective, such as a government or a union. Thus, one can conceivably have a "socialist" industrial economy that protects the sanctity of private property while also nationalising or collectivising industry and agriculture.

These were the sorts of debates and developments that would dominate the twentieth century.

23.3 Political System Choice and the Role of the State

In the first part of the twentieth century, Rosa Luxemburg, the German Socialist, argued that socialism without political democracy is bound to be monstrous precisely because there would be no expression of social values. This became very clear with the excesses of both the Socialist fight against capitalism, and later with the actual situation in the Soviet Union. For a long time, Luxemburg and other democratic socialists were on the sidelines in both the East and the West. Perceived political necessity was the reason. In Russia, Lenin bypassed such objections by taking an elitist view that only a Communist "vanguard" could, and needed to, do what it liked to achieve victory, regardless of what the working classes at the time might want, especially in a hostile capitalist world (Lichtheim, 1972, 389). Communist movements outside Russia, even before having to hew to the Soviet line, also saw political danger, and even oblivion, by making too much accommodation with democracies or societies that were Capitalist, especially since Marxist theory posited these as necessarily arising purely out of underlying economic conditions. But these were false political, social and economic dualisms. What the course of twentieth century history has indicated is that the economic system does not necessarily lead to a particular political and social system or vice versa, that a choice needed to be made, and that the choice was very important.

In Russia, events of the ground forced the Soviet Communists to grapple with the issue rather immediately. Marx had predicted that the Revolution would take place in his native Germany, or in his co-author's (Engels) home of England, both highly advanced industrial economies with a growing proletariat and capitalist class. Conflict between these two classes was supposed to be the motive force in the toppling of capitalism and its replacement with Communism. Instead, its moment came in backwards Russia. To put it in Marxian terms, the proper historical conditions had not been present for Revolution, and yet it had occurred anyway. Which meant that the falling away of the State was not yet possible, and the proletariat was not large enough to take over. What now?

The solution to that conundrum fell to Lenin, who developed political theories to fill the vacuum in Marxian economic theory. The fusion of Marxism-Leninism became the official doctrine of the Soviet Union and represented theoretical and practical extensions to classical Marxism. One of Lenin's most significant theoretical innovations with respect to the State was the formulation of the Communist Party as the key authority overseeing and directing societal change. Political theory and practice prior to this had political parties as working through the State in some way (if they existed at all). Now the State would be ancillary and subsidiary to the Party. In some ways, this was a novel reformulation of a development already taking place elsewhere, with mass political parties becoming the primary mediator between people and leaders, whether there was a democratic system or not. Lenin however put the Party above the State and also gave it a political monopoly. The "One Party State" proved to be a popular idea on both left and right in the twentieth century amongst the radicals, and one that roiled both the traditional left (Social Democrats) and right (militarists and monarchists) which tended to establish parties designed to compete with other rival parties (Meyer, 2013).

Although Marx had thought that Communism would arise naturally out of inevitable historical process, Lenin saw that active organising was necessary to bring it about, and he was afraid that workers would be content with the gains in living and working conditions obtained through trade-union activity and bourgeois concessions. He did not trust them to develop the proper "class consciousness" on their own. This was the basis of using an elite party "vanguard" which was a key player in reformulating the society from top to bottom. Hegemony was in fact an active component of this change process, but more done through forced mass manipulation rather than the sort of consensual evolution that Gramsci favoured. In any case, Lenin was focused on the very survival, first of Russia itself, and then his Communist government, which was under existential pressure for years after the Revolution.

From the standpoint of political expediency, Lenin's ideas, ruthless and brutal as their execution could be, worked extraordinarily well in bringing him to power against considerable odds. As a longer-term viable and desirable political-economic-social order, they left much to be desired. Thus, many Communists inside and outside Russia saw this combination of political dictatorship and enforced cultural transformation as a bridge too far, even if in aid to a noble cause. Gramsci took an intermediate position, accepting Party dictatorship, but only through the State and only when it was exercising its powers in economics and politics. In civil society, Gramsci believed that an attractive new cultural superstructure to replace the old needed to be organically established, with maximum personal freedom necessary in its ongoing achievement (Lichtheim, 1972, 265–267).

There were some on the left who rejected the State and organised society in its entirety. Even Marx had seen the stateless society as the ultimate height of human social development, though he provided few details of it. One anti-State movement, Anarchism, was a powerful nineteenth century movement, engaged in a significant amount of terrorist activity (see Chapter 12), that was even more individualistic than Liberalism purported to be, in the extreme rejecting not just the institutions of marketplace and night watchman state, but any forced social order of any sort (Miller, 1984, 2–7). A limitation of this approach, though, was its lack of scalability. It seemed impossible to have anything more than self-governing small communities that might, perhaps, federate. Some saw this as a very attractive prospect, and a communal society movement arose where groups of like-minded people tried to break off from the larger society to establish self-sufficient communes where egalitarian self-government could be implemented. The success of these attempts were limited and temporary, outside of some older religiously motivated communities which had an ideological singleness of purpose and which survived through selective ongoing contact and exchange with the outside world (e.g. the Amish and the Mormons) (Miller, 1984, Chapter 3).

Syndicalism was an alternative notion that replaced the State and the economic system with self-government and production through labour unions (see Chapter 12). Unlike pure anarchism, this did have the possibility of operating at significant scale, since unions in some places were growing into mass organisations with political clout. In places like England, this drive became co-opted into the existing political order, where a Labour Party was established. In less politically and economically developed peripheries, especially Spain and Italy, the movement remained purer and more influential into the 1920s and 1930s. In Spain, Anarcho-Syndicalism was prominent, especially in industrial Catalonia, already a region with a significant history as a separate region and culture all its own (Van der Welt, 2016).

This was all leftist alternative thinking, but there were plenty of ideas on the right as well, though these were less well formulated, especially as they tended to fall back on traditional concepts and practices that required less elaboration, or might even have their appeal weakened by such elaborating. Nineteenth century conservative thought hearkened back to an "organic", or "corporate", State in which society was seen as a collection of "natural" groups, set in a hierarchy of roles and responsibilities under a central authority. These were conservatives in the literal sense of the word, pushing back against the economic and political changes of the time and trying to re-establish a version of the past.

But a radical right would emerge after the end of the First World War. Both old and new right attacked individualism as an ideology antithetical to true social unity. Both attacked the utilitarianism that underlay Liberalism. But the new right, especially under that diverse label called Fascism, sought to remake the social order just as radically as the left aimed to, though with different aims. Where the two factions of traditional conservatives and Fascists allied, they were generally successful in overthrowing governments. But it was the Fascist radicals that generally prevailed in the end over those seeking a restoration of an old order (Weiss, 1967, 11).

23.4 The Fascist Challenge of the Interwar Period

Prior to the First World War, the industrial mode of production, while rapidly evolving, was well diffused throughout the "developed" world and adopted by or imposed on its "developing" counterpart. There were distinguishing features of one country's industrialism versus another's, e.g. the relative involvement of the State in fostering capital formation or the nature of the banking system and corporate form, etc. But the greater distinctions seemed to be across national political organisation, seeming to suggest that there were political variants of one economic system. Thus, England, France and Italy had their "democratic" versions of capitalism, while Germany, Russia and Austria-Hungary had their "autocratic" versions, the main difference being the extent of State power in private and public spheres, economic and noneconomic.

The Great War shook all this up mainly because of the Soviet Revolution, which now explicitly suggested a dualism between Capitalism and Communism, in addition to the existing division between democracy and autocracy. Not everyone was happy with this choice. A "Third Way" school emerged, seeking some alternative between Communism and Capitalism, and democracy and autocracy. The Great Depression accelerated and solidified this trend. Many of the major "Third Way" formulations arose from the right in reaction to the Soviet model, which appeared to be avoiding Depression but which was nonetheless anathema to some (Gandesha, 2020).

Fascism was the major innovation. It rejected free-market capitalism. It rejected democracy. But it also rejected a return to the conservative past of God, King and Country. All of these had seemed to fail, and Stalin was seen as not having a desirable answer to contemporary ills. Fascism was especially appealing in places where there was a hard-core of anti-modernising forces, yet where modernisation had also advanced rather far. Germany and Italy fitted this definition well, and Fascism emerged in both places, though with different trajectories and under somewhat different conditions. Democracy had short histories in both countries and was resisted by significant anti-modern traditionalist groups that were, however, not strong enough to overturn either democracy or Capitalism. Even had these older rightist forces been more powerful, their promise of a return to a halcyon past had appeal only to selected groups and their pre-industrial frames offered no real compelling economic program that would work in an industrial age.

The fact that the Depression brought starvation, homelessness and mass joblessness in the midst of obvious economic surplus discredited both Liberalism and Capitalism; yet there was significant fear of Communism by many segments of society, even much of the working class. Fascism brought old right and elements of the non-Communist left together in a mass movement that appealed to a legitimate discontent, and appeared to offer solutions that were comforting and radical at the same time. Their salience was in offering an overthrow of purportedly corrupt elites and replacing them with an order that would give people back meaning, sustenance and justice. Their economic programs were hodgepodge and poorly developed but this proved to be an advantage since conflicting objectives could be fused into a single ideology to bring opposites together. That Nazi was short for "National Socialism" said it all with Hitler promising the egalitarianism of Communism combined with a unifying nationalism that would unite the people into a resurgent and revitalised mass, led by a charismatic leader (Kershaw, 1991).

While political and economic programs were vague, the theatrics, the atmospherics and especially the "egemonia" were, however, decisive. The existing frameworks of traditionalism could be combined with propaganda campaigns to make people feel that they were on their collective way up and out of a hole that Liberal democratic Capitalism had led them into. The combination of contradictory elements actually broadened the appeal. As Mussolini, a former newspaperman, put it in 1919, before he took power, "I am a revolutionary and a reactionary" (Weiss, 1967, 31).

In Hitler's case, this was based on an appeal to a mythical Aryan past and a hatred of an inferior "other", especially the Jews (a "racial" designation) and the Bolsheviks (an ideological one). Anti-Semitism was not essential to such an appeal, as the Italian example shows, although there was plenty of it in Europe and this did form a core part of most Fascist and proto-Fascist movements in Eastern Europe and in Vichy France, in that last case driven by a mix of long-standing native race hatred and the demands of the German occupiers. But racism and the making of absolute villains who are genetically and/or ideologically incapable of changing their ways, is an essential ingredient in the Fascist mix, however it is formulated. Even a specific group can have its definitional boundaries adjusted as needed; as Goering put it: "We decide who is Jewish" (Weiss, 1967, 26).

Once in power, Fascist governments employed the systematic use of terror, repression and violence to mould, guide and drive their populaces. The Fascist aesthetic is one of death and violence, and its appeal, much like mass advertising, is emotive (Weiss, 1967, 74). A Spanish Fascist slogan during the Spanish Civil War encapsulates this succinctly: "Down with Intelligence! Long Live Death!" (Weiss, 1967, 66).

Oddly enough, Fascism is not anti-modern per se. It is just against those elements of modernisation, such as individualism, that it views as problematic for keeping social order. In Europe, the movement that was the most revolutionary in the changes it made, namely Nazism, was able to do so precisely because Germany had modernised enough that a fall-back on established power centres and themes was not sufficient to enable viable rule or sufficient popular support. Italy was a hybrid case where Mussolini made major changes to society but always had to collaborate with the entrenched forces of Church, Military and Monarchy. Indeed, he nominally served at the pleasure of his Fascist Council, and it was this Council that deposed him in 1943 when the war was going irretrievably badly. Spain is an interesting case, apparently Fascist in form, but arguably more an example of military dictatorship ruling over a conservative coalition whose component members, especially the Army and the Catholic Church, were given significant authority and freedom in their delineated realms (an exception being the Monarchists, who supported Franco, but who did not get the return of royalty that they were hoping for) (Weiss, 1967, 92, 74).

Although there were Fascist movements in England, France and the US, these arguably did not prevail because social and political as well as economic modernisation there had gone too far, or, as in the US, the traditional power groups behind a potential Fascist coalition rule did not have any history of power beyond their own domains (e.g. the Church). Fascist elements did control the French Vichy rump state briefly after defeat at German hands, but this must be judged as an obvious anomaly.

Economically, Fascism was based on conquest and exploitation to varying degrees (see Chapter 21). It was unsustainable as an ongoing system, as its rapid and massive military defeat after a temporarily successful territory grab definitively proved. But in keeping with the Fascist "corporatist" line, a number of collective group initiatives were established that in theory had some potential for future political alignments (putting aside the Party itself, supposedly representative of the "people" as a whole, but really just a power and control mechanism for the Fascist elites). The Italians were at the forefront in this respect, creating many ideological and paramilitary leisure-time organisations, such as the *Dopolavaro* ("After Work"), which inspired the Nazi *Kraft durch Freude* ("Strength Through Joy") program. Leisure and free time was especially important to control and channel. These realms could certainly not be denied, but the Fascists tried to organise them in ways harmonious with their political and social objectives. Otherwise, such activities could result in independent, individualistic and thus dangerous, ideas, experiences and movements. Work, family and all other facets of the "domestic" sphere were subjected to such regimentation. In this arena, as in all others, the objective was to impose an undifferentiated mass experience and mythology created from above, but participated in from below (Weiss, 1967, 98) (Fig. 23.2).

Despite all the rhetoric about nationalism, socialism and corporatism, both Mussolini and Hitler (and, to a lesser extent, the military dictatorship in Japan) had to rely on the superior productive power of their local big businesses to achieve their rearmament and war-making ends. There was, of course, substantial government intervention in markets and business activity. But this generally was not nearly as extensive as that imposed on individual personal lives or labour organisation, all of which was strongly controlled and directed by the State, generally to the disadvantage of the worker and the individual, though the froth of rearmament did keep everyone employed. This was more about opportunism than any

Fig. 23.2 Italian dictator Mussolini with a working worker. Italy, Ostia, 1931 (*Image source* Nationaal Archief [The Netherlands]. Collectie SPAARNESTAD PHOTO/Het Leven. Dictator naast spittende arbeider/Dictator and digging worker. Spaarnestad Photo, SFA022003531. No known copyright restrictions)

consistent "mixed" or left-right character of a new Fascist model (Weiss, 1967, 104–105).

Overall, Fascism was really more of a temporary reaction to events of the time rather than the viable Third Way that many hoped for and which its leaders promised. Its real enduring appeal was in the realm of collective meaning. Lichtheim (1972) sums up true Fascism (as opposed to

Fascist-appearing conservative orders, like Franco's) as masquerading as a "neopagan worship of life" (112). Fascist forms were abominations. But they did speak to an ongoing human need for collective meaning, which is one reason why proto-Fascist fringes continue to resonate with some in times of trouble and change.

Meanwhile, within the capitalist democracies that survived, there was agreement that the capitalism and democracy subsumed within Liberalism had to be transformed in its current form. "Social Democracy" was one approach on the civil society and political side of things (see Chapter 18). "Fordism" was an especially appealing doctrine on the social-economic side, suiting those invested in the status quo but mindful of the need to contain the pressures impinging upon it. The basic idea here was that large industrial enterprise should expand its proven talent for organising private production and take on the broader planning of social material relations, with the State enlisted to put floors beneath wages and prices to provide the necessary stability that the untrammelled free market could not deliver by itself. No country really carried this through, but there were partial attempts, such as the National Recovery Administration (NRA) undertaken by Roosevelt, which sought to fix wages and prices through a government-led coalition of business and labour (Maier, 1977). This was an extension of earlier "corporatist" and "cooperative" models of capitalism, such as Herbert Hoover's vision of self-organised capitalism, the so-called "Sunkist" model named after the American agricultural cooperative that Hoover saw as a way of corporate enterprise managing itself for both profitability and the greater good of stable growth (Davis, 2006, 380). The War interrupted these attempts, which were furtive in any case, though some elements of them re-emerged in the "Keynesian" post-war order (see Chapter 28).

23.5 "Cold War" and "Comparative Economic Systems"

The end of the Second World War saw the creation of a Manichean competition between Communist and Capitalist systems, along with a new non-Fascist "Third Way" non-aligned camp that tried to thread the needle between the extremes by coming up with their own domestic versions of the best of both worlds. The accompanying decolonisation wave that came with the collapse of the European Empires also forced former European colonies in all parts of the world to create working

Table 23.2 The Cold War comparative economic systems template

	Command	*Market*
Capitalism	"State capitalism"	"Free-market capitalism"
Socialism	"Central planning"	"Market socialism"

Source Based on Naggar and Naggar (2005, p. 90)

modern economies largely from the ground up, driven towards one system or another by the state of play between the new Superpowers of the Soviet Union and the US (see Chapter 25).

It was in this era between 1945 and 1991 that an economic field known as "Comparative Economic Systems" (CES) arose. What this template implies is that the possibilities of selection of economic systems were now collapsed into four quadrants, with choices between Capitalism and Socialism on the one hand, and sub-modalities for allocating resources to their "optimal" uses, Command and Market, on the other. Thus four types of modern politico-economic systems existed: market capitalism, command capitalism, market socialism and command socialism. Table 23.2 provides the template.

The central question of the time was obviously about which broader system was "best" (or optimal), Capitalism or Socialism? The Austrian economists Ludwig von Mises and Friedrich Hayek contended that a socialist system was impossible to maintain over time because the necessary information needed for such allocation could arise spontaneously only from a market price system with economic decisions large and small responding to the constant rise and fall of prices coming out of economic competition. However, the economist Oskar Lange proved (in theory) that central planners could, in fact, gain such information from inventory rather than price movements and these could be monitored as the basis for adjustments to state-administered prices to keep supply and demand balanced, exactly as in the marketplace. This suggested that either system could be used to achieve the same material ends, the ultimate choice of system being inherently political (Persky, 1991).

Practice was quite different from theory however, for both capitalist and socialist economies. Lange had noted the danger of bureaucratisation in the Socialist model, and this was already the plague of Soviet central planning, a phenomenon that was noted (well after Stalin of course) by economists within the Soviet bloc itself, especially as the system began to break down in the late 1970s and early 1980s. *The Turning Point*, by two Soviet economists, Nikolai Smelev and Vladimir Popov, written in 1982 and published in English in 1989, gave many actual examples of planning failures caused by unintended consequences and perverse incentives created by a massive bureaucracy without private markets. This was an academic account of a phenomenon that had plagued the Soviet system in Russia and its satellites since the inception.

But bureaucracy was also a capitalist problem, if not quite as large, especially in the large-scale oligopolies and monopolies that increasingly dominated in the West. John Kenneth Galbraith noted how extensive large-scale private planning already was under oligopoly, and pointing out that planning takes place under capitalism but as a negotiation between a number of smaller private "sovereigns" (often with government connivance) than a single state sovereign (Hanson, 1971, 331). Whatever the faults of central planning, it was at least notionally done for the public good (though often failing miserably in this regard). This private planning had no regard for such issues, and lacking full competition, often could not deliver full efficiency either.

This then led to the second choice element, which was the allocation mechanism of command and control, or market mechanisms. The two superpowers were at the extreme ends, the US notionally a free-market capitalist economy, the Soviet Union clearly a central planning Communist one. There were modified alternatives on either side. France was often noted to be an economy using a great deal of State command in its Capitalism, while some of the Eastern bloc countries in the 1960s experimented with allowing more markets into their socialism, though often with severe repercussions (see Chapters 24 and 27).

Comparisons of the optimality of these two systems and their allocation variants were often reduced down to the standard benchmark: GDP growth per capita. Data limitations were problematic here. The official economic accounts of the Communist bloc were often distorted for political purposes, and much information was unavailable. Socialist countries also generally reported material outputs rather than market values (which obviously did not exist, at least domestically) and so their performance was hard to compare with Capitalist ones (Hanson, 1971).

The competition between the two superpowers, though still stated in ideological terms, more and more became based on claims about which one would deliver superior economic growth. Although attempts to overthrow Capitalism and impose world Socialism was still normally part of Eastern bloc policy, more and more it was argued that Communism would beat Capitalism at its own growth game and deliver a worker's paradise along with it. Khrushchev famously boasted that "we will bury you", referring to his claim that the Russian economy would grow faster than the American one in the end, making Capitalism redundant. This political theatre was echoed in the famous "kitchen debate" between Khrushchev and then Vice-President Richard Nixon about the superiority of American consumer goods offerings, leading the Soviet Premier on a drive to increase consumer good availability in his own country after he returned to Russia (Reeves, 2001).

Krushchev's threat obviously did not eventuate. Soviet living standards likely doubled from 1946 to 1960, arguably a Russian "golden age", though this compared to a tripling of American income over the same period (Morris, 2014, 279). The 1970s were not as kind to Russia or the Eastern bloc, and although the West also performed poorly at the time, the strains and stresses were much deeper in the East. More will be said on this in Chapters 24, 25 and 27.

Then there was the so-called Non-aligned bloc, mostly in the Third World (so named because it was neither First World [Capitalist] or Second World [Socialist]). How did this bloc perform? This has not really been adequately assessed systematically. India's experience has been the most studied, given its level of underdevelopment, population size, democratic political system and history as a British colony. Post-war, the country chose what might be loosely categorised as a democratic Command Socialism that was nonetheless outside of the Communist model. Alternatively, it could also be seen as a sort of blended Market Socialism, with large-scale planning at the macro-level and individual enterprise and property rights at many micro-levels. Regardless of categorisation, India sought to industrialise using a State-led series of Five-Year plans, emphasising both rapid GDP growth and a lifting of people out of poverty, while leaving many private political and economic rights in place. The results of this effort were decidedly mixed and there were distortions and unintended consequences along the way. Industrialisation proceeded but was uneven. Poverty was lessened but not greatly. Economic growth was very strong under some plans, weak in others. Interestingly, the earlier plans delivered growth that was superior to that achieved during the country's economic liberalisation starting in 1991 (Ramesh, 2017, 30–32).

During the time Yugoslavia was much studied, interesting because it was a Communist country, relatively well developed and relatively prosperous. The country under Tito hewed a line very independent of the Soviet Union. Indeed, Yugoslavia was a founding member of the Non-aligned bloc. Yugoslavia was explicitly Socialist, and non-democratic, but it did allow some freedom in the realms of production, consumption and distribution. Its productive units (basically firms) were supposedly run along cooperative lines, rather than as the command and control pods of a Communist central plan, or the entrepreneurial enterprises of Capitalism. Contemporary reviews of this experiment were fairly positive (Carson 1977); ex-post reviews not so much (Pleština, 2019) (see Box 23.1 for more details).

Box 23.1 Yugoslavia as an independent Socialist model

The immediate start of the Cold War offered what appeared to offer a particularly stark contrast between free market unplanned economies and a Stalinist central command and control model of industrialisation that had neither markets nor private property per se. This Socialist bloc solidity, always more fractured than it appeared, began to unravel in the 1950s as particular Communist countries began to chart their own courses for their own reasons. One of the earliest experimenters, and of the most interest to the West rather than the East, was Yugoslavia.

Yugoslavia was the only Eastern European country to obtain its freedom from Nazi rule without any direct outside intervention, and with little outside assistance from the Soviet Union or any other nation. This multi-ethnic state, riven with ethnic, political and religious conflict, had emerged from a brutal fight against the Nazis as still unified under the charismatic leadership of the Communist leader Josef Broz Tito, a man who pulled off a feat that few others could have. For that reason alone, Yugoslavia was probably always going to take an independent line from the Soviets, or, for that matter, the West. After an initial few years following a Stalinist foreign policy and domestic economic central planning regime, the country was cut off from Russian trade and aid, the Yugoslavian Communist Party was expelled from the Cominform (officially known as the Information Bureau of the Communist and Workers' Parties, and an institution designed to coordinate policy across the Eastern bloc), and the Yugoslavian model was demonised in propaganda as a deviationist apostate. The only real crime was Tito's determination to keep his maneuvering room with Stalin, whose government had not installed him in power and to which he owed nothing (Uvalić, 2018).

There were, however, other reasons behind the country's unique path. The country was a post-World War I experiment melding a diverse range of nationalities, religions, and regional levels of economic development into one country. Tito's combined achievement of throwing off the Nazi yoke while keeping this often internecine mélange intact cemented his reputation as a truly remarkable figure, a genuine "father" and preserver of his country. Indeed this charismatic leadership, what one author has called a key element of a Yugoslavian "civil religion", was perhaps even more necessary after the war than during it, with nationalist and religious rivalries having the potential to tear the country apart, and which promptly happened shortly after Tito died (Flere, 2007). All the Eastern bloc countries had ethnic divisions of some sort, but the internal nationalisms of Yugoslavia needed to be kept balanced in a dynamic fashion, and a simple towing of a Stalinist or Russian Communist line would likely have rather quickly come to ground.

Additionally, Interwar Yugoslavia had always been economically more closely integrated with Western Europe than Russia or Eastern Europe. Immediately after the War, the Soviet Union was briefly dominant, accounting for almost half of Yugoslavia's foreign trade. But the nature of the country's exports and imports were already Western-oriented, a trend that would be increased as its economy industrialised and critical inputs and technologies from the West needed to be imported, in exchange for exports that remained primarily agricultural and lower-value, leading to a chronic balance-of-trade deficit. This pattern remained even after relations with the Soviet Union were normalised following Stalin's death and flows of Eastern bloc and Soviet trade resumed (Obadic, 2014, 331–332).

For all these reasons Yugoslavia was bound to chart an independent course and it did exactly that. The two major elements of its Socialist model were worker control of production, referred to as "self-managed socialism"; and integration of market mechanisms into the economy, loosely referred to as market socialism, which included price liberalisation, a degree of openness to international trade, and the gradual development of a commercial legal code. These market-based reforms were accelerated in a grand manner in 1964–1965 (Estrin, 1991, 187–189).

This model seemed to perform well. Between 1952 and 1979, annual GDP growth per capita averaged around 6%, per capita consumption rising by almost 4.5% (Estrin, 1991, 190). However this efficiency was bought at a cost of high unemployment, something that was theoretically supposed to be impossible in a Socialist state. Combined with the effects of structural change in the economy, between 1952 and 1975 the average unemployment rate in Yugoslavia is thought to have fluctuated around a very high mean of 11.4% (Shonick, 2009, 725).

For these reasons a major shift in policy was made around 1975 with markets de-emphasised and worker control strengthened (Estrin, 1991, 189). However by that time, the deteriorating situation in the world economy, including the first of two oil price shocks, had become severe and perhaps insurmountable. Yugoslavia had attempted to deal with these pressures in various ways. It already had a guest worker program with West Germany, the only Communist country with such an arrangement, and this had alleviated the unemployment situation (Shonick, 2009, 732). But the country also had already taken on substantial Western debt that it could not adequately service due its chronic trade deficit. The policy shift did not improve the Yugoslavian economy. The death of Tito and the end of the Cold War delivered the final blows to the entire economic, social and political order (Obadic, 2014).

During the Cold War, though, Yugoslavian Socialism did provide a model of an alternative that tried to deliver worker power, State planning to achieve social ends, and the use of markets to improve economic efficiency, while maintaining strong ties with the West. Estrin (1991) judges the experiment as one that failed ultimately, but not necessarily because it was fatally flawed. On the plus side he argues that self-management, in the form it took during the 1950s and 1960s, may well have increased economic growth by replacing worker-manager conflict with cooperative relations, helping to achieve a rapid rise of labour productivity. Its design then was one in which business enterprise policy-making was subject to employee influence, while the execution of that policy remained the domain of management, a good combination. However this balance shifted with the 1974/1975 reforms in ways that muddied incentives, with declining labour productivity throughout the 1980s as a result, though there were multiple factors involved. Estrin also claims that the shift away from market mechanisms might have gone too far, bringing some social benefit but sacrificing too much efficiency in the process. These conclusions must remain speculative, but certainly Yugoslavia did not adjust adequately enough to changing world economic conditions, and proved unable to counter stagnation and a rising inflation (192–193). Its own inner contradictions as a nation also were formidable problems that became unmanageable in the end. Still, there may be some lessons to be drawn from particular innovations that were employed.

Table 23.3 The basic building blocks of the New Comparative Economics

Individual agents with bounded rationality and self-interest
Organisations and institutions within which agents operate (the principal-agent problem)
Factors that lead to changes in organisational structures: economic-political-legal systems; social norms, culture and level of economic development; input and output markets; organisational goals

Note Now that there is no choice of "system" per se. It is presumed that capitalism is efficient and that efficiency is by definition the main metric by which to judge an economic order. Given this, the choice is thus to optimise institutional frameworks given existing background factors such as level of economic development and local organisational arrays. This is basically equivalent to what the Growth Model is concerned with, and the policy menu is quite consistent with it (see Chapter 2). Comparative Economic Systems, even in its reduced Cold War form, assumed that there was a question to be answered about how best to organise an economic system. NCE assumes that this question has been fundamentally answered by history and that now the key issue is in the details of implementation

Source Based on Dallago (2004)

23.6 Post-Cold War "New Comparative Economics"

The end of the Cold War and the fall of the Soviet Union seemed to provide a final verdict: Capitalist economic organisation is the only viable system there is. From a theoretical perspective, the field of Comparative Economic Systems (CES) has collapsed even further into the "New Comparative Economics" (NCE). Now a capitalist system is assumed to be the optimal choice, but the analytical task is to compare different institutional forms within its application to different societies, seeing how well these bundles perform. Put simply, this current field represents a study of comparative institutional efficiency of a capitalist economy. Political system choices, which were a point of high rhetoric during the Cold War have re-emerged in importance, though now narrowed down to one of a number of institutional settings (Dallago, 2004, 65). Table 23.3 provides an indicative framework.

Thus, for example, many now compare the performance of the older liberal democratic capitalist systems, such as the US and Britain, with alternative capitalisms, such as the State capitalist templates of the Asian Developmental State exhibited and perfected by East Asian countries such as Japan and South Korea in the latter half of the twentieth century. Chalmers Johnson (1982) defined the Developmental State as one focused on economic development and the policy measures needed to accomplish that objective joined with far-sighted intervention by expert bureaucrats. The Chalmers case study was Japan, which fell into a long-run economic stagnation during the 1990s, still ongoing. South Korea has performed much better but it, and the East Asian region more generally, have faced problems that have caused a reassessment of the Developmental State in its original form (Wong, 2004). Either way, the focus of economic systems thinking now is to take capitalism as the base off of which various institutional and policy settings can be adjusted and adapted over time.

This shift in thinking occurred almost immediately after the collapse of the Soviet Union in which economists referred to the so-called "Transition" economies, i.e. formerly socialist states that were now primed to join the Capitalist ranks. Such "transition" was assumed as both inevitable and desirable, there being no other possible alternatives to it, except for regression. Many Western economists argued that "shock therapy" was needed to bust open the old ossified command structures to open up to the therapeutic forces of free markets. In a relatively short time, even shock therapy apologists admitted that this rapid course of transition was a mistake. But this merely reinforced the new "consensus" that one must create effective institutions within a capitalist economy and this cannot be rushed. Rather predictably, the optimum is said to be the combination of building both democracy and a market economy (Djankov et al., 2003, 597). Based on these inferences this is the recommended program for countries today offered by development agencies and theorists.

23.7 Going Forward

In the immediate aftermath of The Cold War's end, there was some discussion by former Comparative Economic Systems theorists about what the field should now study. The possible non-separability of the economic sphere from the society's social, cultural and political systems were noted and the question was asked: what are we comparing now (Malle, 1993, 97)?

Some discussion focused on whether or not to discard the behavioural assumptions of the Centrally Planned Economies, which revolved around the interesting implicit issue of how much a system might affect the individual and the reasonableness of assumptions about individual motivations and behaviour given the system in place. The hypothesis that the inertia, neglect, sloppiness, lack of professional ethics, rent-seeking behaviour and envy so characteristic of Central Planning would be transformed into their virtuous opposites (as defined by neoclassical economics) just because of a switch to markets, was questioned, presciently as it turned out. The study of Italy after its Corporatist experiment in the 1930s was suggested as one possible case study that might be useful for transition economies (Malle, 1993, 99).

It turns out that little of this proposed research has eventuated. Certainly, the failures of past systems are well-known, and some, such as Fascism, were still-born to begin with. But the successes of the current system are often assumed rather than objectively tested, the performative benchmarks narrow (e.g. per capita GDP), and the varied experiences of the non-capitalistic economies cast aside as if they never happened. That these were not wholly successful, and even quite unsuccessful in some respects, does not mean that they should be forgotten and that there is nothing to learn from them. And in any case, such an approach is ahistorical.

It may not be possible to build a true or complete alternative to industrial, or post-industrial, global capitalism given the nature of the world as it is. With eight billion people on the planet to support, a return to small-scale production and organisation is almost certainly not feasible, even with the drastic reductions in consumption that are recommended from an Earth Systems point of view (see Chapter 2). But substantial revisions to Capitalism are quite possible and desirable beyond what much of the standard development offers.

And in some ways, the noneconomic spheres of the economic system are more important than ever before. This is not just because of their economic implications. The emphasis on "bread" needs some correction for, important as it is, it has never been as important as it has often been presented. The forms and possibilities of alteration are highly contested, as are even the nature of the problems being faced. The twentieth century, as turbulent as it was, at least offered grand theories, overarching dreams and spirited, although sometimes disastrous, competitions. The twenty-first century appears very mono-cultural economically and even politically, with mass economies and societies, democratic or autocratic forms seemingly almost incidental. One can draw the conclusion that the important issues are decided and that the task now is to tweak the dials to get at least workable outcomes, if not inspiring ones. But now may be the time to experiment more rather than less to respond to the ever more pressing problems of the age.

References

Carson, R. L. (1977). *Comparative economic systems*. M.E. Sharpe.

Dallago, B. (2004). Comparative economic systems and the new comparative economics. *The European Journal of Comparative Economics, 1*(1), 59–86.

Davis, M. (2006). *City of Quartz: Excavating the future in Los Angeles* (New Edition). Verso Books.

Djankov, S., Glaeser, E., La Porta, R., Lopez-de-Silanes, F., & Shleifer, A. (2003). The new comparative economics. *Journal of Comparative Economics, 31*(4), 595–619.

Edwards, M. (2009). *Civil society* (2nd ed.). Polity Press.

Estrin, S. (1991). Yugoslavia: The case of self-managing market socialism. *Journal of Economic Perspectives* 5(4), 187–194.

Flere, S. (2007). The broken covenant of Tito's people: The problem of civil religion in communist Yugoslavia. *East European Politics and Societies, 21*(4), 681–703.

Gandesha, S. (2020). The Spectre of the 1930s. In J. Rayner, S. Falls, G. Souvlis, & T. C. Nelms (Eds.), *Back to the '30s?: Recurring crises in capitalism, liberalism, and democracy* (pp. 1–34). Palgrave Macmillan.

Hanson, P. (1971). East-west comparisons and comparative economic systems. *Soviet Studies, 22*(3), 327–343.

Johnson, C. (1982). *MITI and the Japanese miracle*. Stanford University Press.

Kershaw, I. (1991). *Hitler: Profiles in power*. Pearson Education.

Lichtheim, G. (1972). *Europe in the twentieth century*. Praeger Publishers.

Maier, C. S. (1977). The politics of productivity: Foundations of American international economic policy after World War II. *International Organization, 31*(4), 607–663.

Malle, S. (1993). What are comparative economic systems today? *Aula, 15*(3), 95–102.

Marx, K. ([1867, 1885, 1894], 1965). *Das Kapital: A critique of political economy* (F. Engels, S. L. Levitsky, Trans.). H. Regnery.

Meyer, A. G. (2013). *Leninism*. Harvard University Press.

Miller, D. (1984). *Anarchism*. JM Dent & Sons.

Morris, I. (2014). *War! What is it good for? Conflict and the progress of civilization from primates to robots*. Farrer, Straus and Giroux.

Naggar, T., & Naggar, A. K. (2005). Comparative economics: A reference guide. *The American Economist, 49*(2), 90–95.

Obadic, I. (2014). A troubled relationship: Yugoslavia and the European Economic Community in détente. *European Review of History—Revue européenne d'histoire, 21*(2), 329–348.

Persky, J. (1991). Retrospectives: Lange and von Mises, large-scale enterprises, and the economic case for socialism. *Journal of Economic Perspectives, 5*(4), 229–236.

Pleština, D. (2019). *Regional development in communist Yugoslavia: Success, failure, and consequences*. Routledge.

Polanyi, K. (1944). *The great transformation*. Beacon Press.

Ramesh, S. (2017). An economic history of India. In S. Ramesh (Ed.), *China's Lessons for India: Volume I: The political economy of development* (pp. 23–54). Palgrave Macmillan.

Reeves, R. (2001). *President Nixon: Alone in the White House*. Simon & Schuster.

Shonick, K. (2009). Politics, culture, and economics: Reassessing the West German guest worker agreement with Yugoslavia. *Journal of Contemporary History, 44*(4), 719–736.

Uvalić, M. (2018). The rise and fall of market socialism in Yugoslavia. In *Biannual IAFEP (International Association for the Economics of Participation) Conference*. University of Ljubljana, Slovenia, July.

Van der Walt, L. (2016). Global anarchism and syndicalism: Theory, history, resistance. *Anarchist Studies, 24*(1), 85–106.

Weiss, J. (1967). *The fascist tradition: Radical right-wing extremism in modern Europe*. Harper & Row.

Wong, J. (2004). The adaptive developmental state in East Asia. *Journal of East Asian Studies, 4*, 345–362.

CHAPTER 24

"1968"

C. Gordon, *Many Possible Worlds*,
https://doi.org/10.1007/978-981-19-9281-0_24

Fig. 24.1 The push against the "old" normal (*Image source* Vector image of the poster made for student and worker's strikes in Paris in 1968. Black-and-white drawing of a poster satirising the authorities' calls for a return to normal during the political upheaval then. Public Domain. *Source* https://freesvg.org/return-to-normal-poster-vector-illustration)

24.1 The Great Post-War Prosperity

The Second World War was the most destructive war ever fought. Yet, only five years after its end, the world economy was beginning a general period of extremely strong growth that would last roughly two decades. The growth trend was rather universal, although poverty remained endemic in much of the developing world. In the rich economies, Capitalist economies overall grew faster than Socialist ones. And even within

Table 24.1 Year-to-year percentage change in world per capita GDP, by region (1951–1975)

Year	*Western Europe*	*Western offshoots*	*Eastern Europe*	*USSR*	*Latin America*	*Asia*	*Africa*	*World*
1951	5.2	5.3	4.5	−1.3	2.6	5	2.6	4.1
1952	3.1	1.9	0.1	4.7	0.8	6.2	1.7	2.9
1953	4.5	2.7	4	2.6	0.8	4.8	1.5	3.1
1954	4.8	−2.2	3.2	3.1	3.6	2.1	2.6	1.5
1955	5.6	5.1	5.3	6.7	3.5	2.5	1.2	4.3
1956	3.9	0.5	1	7.7	1.5	4.6	1.8	2.8
1957	3.7	0	6.4	0.3	4.7	2.2	1.4	1.7
1958	1.6	−2.3	4.6	5.6	2.1	4.1	0	1.1
1959	3.9	5.3	4.1	-2.9	−0.4	2.7	3.1	2.7
1960	5.6	0.9	5.1	7.5	3.6	3.4	2.1	3.6
1961	4.4	0.6	4.8	3.9	1.9	-0.5	−0.1	2.1
1962	3.9	4.4	0.8	1	1.3	2.7	1.6	2.9
1963	3.8	2.9	3.9	−3.7	0.2	4.5	4.6	2.2
1964	5.2	4.3	5.1	11.4	3.9	6.5	2.8	5.1
1965	3.3	4.9	3.4	4.4	2.2	2.7	2.9	3.1
1966	2.9	5.1	5.6	3.7	2.2	4.7	0.3	3.3
1967	2.9	1.4	3.3	3.3	1.8	2.5	−0.6	1.6
1968	4.7	3.7	2.7	4.8	3.2	4.1	2.4	3.4
1969	5	2.3	2.3	0.4	3.7	7	5.1	3.4
1970	3.8	−0.7	2.7	6.7	4.1	6.4	5.6	2.9
1971	2.6	2	6.5	1.7	3.3	3.1	1.9	2.1
1972	3.8	4	4.2	−0.4	3.8	3.4	1.1	2.7
1973	5.1	4.7	4.1	7.4	5.5	5.4	0.9	4.5
1974	1.7	−0.8	5	1.9	3.4	0.1	2	0.4
1975	−0.8	−1	2.6	−0.7	0.6	2.6	−1.4	−0.3

Data source Maddison 2007, Table 7b, p. 237
Note There is an update of some of these historical series contained in Maddison 2020 which would result in slight changes to growth rates above. The earlier series is used here because of the accounting for the USSR.

high-growth countries, prosperity was not universally distributed. Table 24.1 shows annual per capita GDP growth rates for the major world regions (Fig. 24.1).

One can see that the 1950s and early 1960s were periods of especially strong per capita growth in both Capitalist and Socialist Eurasia (including the USSR) and that there were some years where the "East" performed better than the "West", at least in a gross sense, though Soviet growth in particular was quite erratic year-on-year in comparison to Western and even Eastern Europe. During the same period, Asia taken as a collective was doing even better overall, coming in above the world growth average. Latin America and Africa were underperformers. Of course, this obscures a wide variation across individual countries.

Western European performance was truly stellar after several years of reconstruction: so good that it is generally referred to as an economic "Golden Age". This period is typically dated as occurring between 1950 and 1973, with a marked slowdown beginning in 1969, depending on the country. The start was characterised by a period of "super-fast" growth in a few places that moderated into merely strong growth by the mid-1950s, West Germany the leading example. Ireland and Spain were amongst a set of countries that began rather backwards economically but had a speed-up in growth after the implementation of major policy reforms (Crafts, 1995, 434–436).

The UK was the main laggard in Europe, partly because it was already a high-income industrial economy. There is also evidence that its educational system was not as good as many Continental ones, and its economic policy during this time was more focused on short-run outcomes rather than long-run growth (Crafts, 1995, 442–445). The exact reasons for the difference are not totally clear, but these are only relative in any case. The 1950s in Britain were still times of prosperity, just not quite as good as in most of its Western European neighbours.

Why did the Golden Age in Western Europe occur? There clearly was a broad investment drive to rebuild war-torn economies, installing better and more sophisticated capital and technology that helped boost productivity in a sort of Phoenix Effect (see Chapter 22). This was also a second age of global integration, with international technology transfer, capital flows, trade and product market growth greatly facilitated by the newly reconstructed financial order in the form of Bretton Woods (see Chapter 25), which helped to lead to a convergence of input costs between Europe and America, and the rise of Multinational Corporations (MNCs) (Crafts, 1995, 437–439). Whatever the noneconomic merits or demerits of these developments, they generally were very good for growth since they increased the speed and ease of allocation of resources to high-return opportunities.

Western Europe also benefited greatly from its close association with the US. Relatively unscathed directly by the fighting, America emerged as an economic colossus. In 1950, American real per capita income was 40% above that of the UK and close to double that of the average of the Western European economies. The country had provided substantial (though not monumental) aid to Europe after the war, and had integrated the area into an America-dominated world economy that was caught in its post-war economic updraft (Harley, 2003, 819).

The Socialist economies were essentially walled off from this international system. For example, the Soviet Union and its Eastern European bloc were both offered aid through the so-called Marshall Plan (see Chapter 25), but Stalin rejected it, and forced those Eastern bloc countries leaning towards accepting, especially Czechoslovakia, to reject it as well (Westad, 2017, 94–95). There were a variety of reasons for this stance. It was motivated partly by ideology, partly by mistrust of the West, and partly because American Marshall Plan aid had some rather significant strings attached that were designed to encourage free-market economies and ties to the US, conditions that were obviously unpalatable to Russia.

But even when the West handed hard cash and influence over nominally without strings, the Russians demurred. The USSR was given a $1.2 billion quota in the new International Monetary Fund (IMF) that was established as part of the Bretton Woods order in 1946 (see Chapter 25), but ultimately declined membership in the new institution, leaving the quota and the voting rights behind as well (Graff et al., 2013, 232, fn. 16). The Soviets attended the initial sessions of the Bretton Woods Conference but did not continue participating (Pechatnov, 2017). Ultimately, the two systems were too different from one another for easy economic integration and coordination, even if there had not been such mutual hostility. There was also a sense that too much contact with Capitalism would only destabilise the Socialist bloc, and that growing trade and investment between the two should be avoided. This is exactly what did happen in the last decades of the Cold War (see Chapter 27).

Socialist Eurasia nonetheless had strong growth in the 1950s and 1960s. In part, this was because most of the countries involved, Czechoslovakia and Hungary being exceptions, were still very much developing countries and State-led industrialisation as a way of moving away from an agrarian economy, even if inefficiently done, still yielded advances in productivity and output, and there was plenty of both under the Stalinist economic model. Militarisation of the economy, though ultimately a deadweight loss, certainly provided its own short-term stimulus, as did the rebuilding of war-torn economies in the East, in a region where such damage was amongst the greatest (Westad, 2017, 187–88). Also the coming of relative peace, followed by the death of Stalin and the end of the heavy hand of Stalinism helped Russia and its satellites reorient economic planning away from a single-minded focus on industrial development towards diversification into the production and distribution of consumer goods.

24.2 A Demographic Boom

One thing that both the Communist and Capitalist developed world shared during this time was an explosion in birth rates after the war, what one demographer has referred to as a "birthquake". In most developed countries, the number of births increased profoundly between the late 1940s and the late 1960s, with an upward burst in marriage and fertility rates interrupting a trend in declining birth rates going back to the nineteenth century. Then, just as suddenly as it had started, the decline in birth rates began again in the 1970s. Collectively, this phenomenon is known as the "baby boom", with a very definite beginning, middle and end (Van Bavel & Reher, 2013, 257).

This was not predicted. Indeed, post-war planners assumed that population growth would be relatively sluggish, based on low fertility trends that had seemed entrenched. The reasons for this demographic break are still not entirely clear. Some leading explanations include the return of soldiers resuming work and family life; strong economic growth, which increased future earnings prospects and thus made couples more able to afford new children; the removal of female labour from the workforce after the demobilisation of the Second World War war industries which, combined with returning males and sexist cultural attitudes and discrimination, put many women back into the household inclined or pushed to have more children; and a greater post-war sense of optimism and more liberal sexual mores (Van Bavel & Reher, 2013, 258).

The available date show that the proportion of excess births (i.e. births above trends extrapolated from the past) was highest in the Western offshoots, i.e. New Zealand, Australia, Canada and the US. Norway and Iceland also had similar trends. Austria, France, Czechoslovakia, Switzerland and Finland had booms not quite as strong, followed by England and Wales, Sweden, Ireland and the Netherlands, all distinctly mild in their baby booms. Bulgaria, Hungary, Greece, Italy and Portugal and Spain had no genuine baby boom at all (Van Bavel & Reher, 2013, 263).

Although the birthquake appeared as a relatively short and sharp burst over a couple of decades, in retrospect it had demographic roots going back to the 1920s. This fact invalidates the simplistic notion that it was simply a bunching of deferred births from the Great Depression and the Second World War. That is certainly likely to explain the baby bulges of 1946–47, but not the sustained increase in birth rates that gathered steam in the 1950s and early 1960s, driven by men and women who were too young to have married during the war, some of whom were not even born during the Great Depression. The crowding out of women from the labour force once the men returned from overseas certainly played a role in this longer-term trend, especially in the US where there was a sharp drop in female labour force participation rates after the war. The rise in birth rates was also accompanied by rising nuptiality (which refers to the rate of marriage in the population) and fertility both within and outside marriage, across a diverse range of countries, which suggests a quite complex set of causal factors that may not ever be completely disentangled (Van Bavel & Reher, 2013, 270, 274–275).

24.3 Suburbanisation

The First and Second Industrial Revolutions were periods of intensive urbanisation, accompanied by rural depopulation in relative, and sometimes in absolute, terms as well. The number of cities grew, their sizes became unprecedentedly large, and they became extremely dense. This trend was driven by many factors, one of which was increasing economies of scale in production. Factories and offices became vast concentrations of people and activity in small areas, relying on workforces that would ideally live close-by given the relatively slow local urban transport modes of the time, which were largely pedestrian-based until the late nineteenth century.

As the Second Industrial Revolution crested, local transport technology became increasingly mechanised within urban areas, reducing the average time it took to travel a set distance, allowing for residential location further away from workplaces. This process began with the establishment of tramlines in various urban areas in the late 1800s and first decades of the 1900s (Post, 2007). But these were centralised modes of common carriage. The introduction of the automobile, a decentralised mode, allowed for individual on-demand movement from point to point, no longer bound to concentrated collection nodes of people at scheduled tram stops. This technological change came together with increases in income and changes in tastes, driven by the rise of a middle-class norm of capitalist patriarchy and nuclear families each living in their own houses, to establish a demand for houses on small plots that was not possible to satisfy within the city limits. Now that people no longer needed to live within a city to get to their work this demand could be satisfied in the burgeoning new suburbs (Gordon, 2017).

After the end of the Second World War, government policies further encouraged the creation of new decentralised residential areas and enabled the purchase of land and homes away from the urban core, in turn leading to new conurbations that had their own employment base. Two major levers here were the extensive building of public arterial roads that often bypassed city centres and made access to exurban locations faster and easier; and the provision of easy finance for house purchase and house construction (Fig. 24.2).

The US was a leader and innovator in both areas. President Eisenhower initiated the Interstate Highway System (formally known as the National System of Interstate and Defense Highways) that would ultimately provide 41,000 miles of new roads providing high-speed, limited access, nonstop arteries that went around or cut through ageing urban cores. As an example, the driving time between Chicago and Indianapolis was cut from six hours to three (Manchester, 1973, 928–929). Other developed countries, both East and West, made comparable road investments.

In fact, the new road system was about both speeding travel between large cities and making new suburban locations outside these cities more accessible and attractive to development. The expanding greater metropolitan areas of major cities were producing more and more of

Fig. 24.2 Dublin suburban sprawl—1954 (*Image source* The National Library of Ireland, http://catalogue.nli.ie/Collection/vtls000033928, The State Express Tobacco Factory and environs, Date: Tuesday, 27 April 1954, Morgan Aeriel Photographs collection, NLI Ref: NPA MOR16. No known copyright restrictions)

the national income and employment in America, while smaller secondary towns and mid-level cities, once essential overnight stays or rest stops on the long, slow journeys between desired destinations, found themselves stranded along now bypassed roads, leading to economic withering in many of these places. This enhanced the economic decline of rural and town areas that had begun with advanced industrialisation, and while it was most prominent in the US, it was a worldwide phenomenon.

The scale of new residential construction accompanying road building was even more prodigious. In Europe, some of this was to replace bombed out and destroyed housing from the War. But after this phase was completed by the mid-1950s, most housing was for new economic and population growth, most of it placed in new suburban areas outside city centres in the form of homes that were owner-occupied. For example, of all the homes standing in the US in 1960, one-quarter had been built in the 1950s. In 1960, 62% of Americans claimed home ownership, a jump from 44% in 1940, the biggest increase ever recorded there. In the US, most of the building was done by private enterprise, in contrast to Western Europe where governments did much of the construction. But the American build-up was assisted by a vast post-war increase in government subsidy, through federal mortgage guarantees with low interest rates, no down payment housing schemes offered under the so-called "GI Bill" of 1944 (which contained many benefits for returning veterans), as well as loan insurance to lenders and developers through the Federal Housing Administration, and a new mortgage interest deduction on individual income taxes (Cohen, 2003, 237) (Fig. 24.3).

Fig. 24.3 Driving across the wide open spaces (Canada) (*Image source* Postcard: Rogers Pass, BC, c.1962. THE SWISS PEAKS. *Hermit Mountain and Mount Tupper as seen from the Trans-Canada Highway Glacier National Park, British Columbia. Color Photo by Bruno Engler Original caption: View looking north from the Trans-Canada Highway [Hwy. 1] in Glacier National Park of Canada near Rogers Pass National Historic Site [9520 TCH, Rogers Pass, BC]. Public domain*)

The rise of the suburbs transformed the daily life, economies and political balances of countries everywhere. Cities began a relative and sometimes absolute decline in both economic and political importance that would become increasingly severe in the late 1960s and early 1970s when a full-blown economic crisis unfolded. The rise of the service sector and the "post-industrial" economy, fed, and was fed by, suburbanisation, as manufacturing in the industrial economies slowly became supplanted by various kinds of service businesses that did not require the scale or concentration that industry had required (see Chapter 29). In any case, employees did not need to live close to work anymore and companies did not need to locate in decaying, high-cost cities anymore either. Employers and employees would sometimes effectively meet in the middle in the growing number of "office parks" sprouting throughout suburbia (Whyte, 1988, Chapter 21).

One American region that was emblematic of the suburban, auto-driven age was Southern California. Already boosted by the massive World War 2 defence spending which flowed into the area's aviation and weapons industry, Southern California was further economically lifted and transformed by new Federally guaranteed mortgages, veterans benefits, government protected Savings and Loans institutions devoted exclusively to local home finance, new roads and high wage technical jobs. The battle between the old "traction trusts" which had built the pre-war urban tram networks and the new auto-focused development interests were also played out there. As in every place else, the latter prevailed. In this case, a "Rail Rapid Transit Now!" campaign supported by the old downtown city interests was narrowly defeated in the Los Angeles City Council with the margin of defeat provided by the votes of the surging San Fernando Valley and other suburban regions that relied on auto-based development (Davis, 2006, 121–122).

Socially, there was a racialist and conservative tinge that coloured the shift away from cities—pun intended. Once more America was on the unfortunate cutting edge in this regard, though not the only Western (or Eastern) country to practise de facto residential segregation. The 1920s through to 1960s was a period of creation of suburban "utopias" in the US outside of teeming multiracial cities, most notably, but not exclusively, in Southern California where municipal incorporation was relatively easy and where an extended land boom made newly incorporated communities self-financing—for a while. During the 1960s onward, the dynamic shifted to defending white suburbs against the cities rather than just moving outside them (Davis, 2006, 169–170).

The racism underlying suburbanisation in the US was not just implicit, but explicitly intended and designed in. Although the standard story is that American cities in the North became racially segregated informally (as opposed to the South where segregation was an official policy), through individual prejudices, socioeconomic differences and discriminatory policies by banks and other private firms, in fact mid-twentieth century Federal, state and local housing policies in the US all contained explicit provisions for discrimination on the basis of race. This began at the national level under "New Deal" programs designed to combat the Depression to build publicly funded, public housing. These programs explicitly and systematically excluded African Americans from residing in the newly built complexes. After the end of Second World War, the US housing finance programs also explicitly discriminated against giving publicly insured housing loans to African Americans, while US courts regularly upheld "covenants" that were part of the contracts of sale of homes in the many new suburban subdivisions which forbade the sale of homes to minority groups. Although these formal practices were finally outlawed with the passage of various national civil rights laws in the mid- to late 1960s, they helped to entrench an American pattern of deep racial residential segregation that continues to reverberate today (Rothstein, 2017).

24.4 A "Youth" Generation

Industrial era universities had traditionally been institutions for socialising the very top elites, with most everyone else left out. Figures for Great Britain are illustrative. In 1926, there were around 25,000 university students in Britain, most of these graduating from exclusive private primary and secondary schools. By 1939, there were still only 70,000 or so in total. A quantum leap began after 1945 with the opening of a raft of new institutions and expansion of old ones opening their doors to the general public. By 1964, there were 300,000 students in Great Britain. In 1950, university students had accounted for 1.5% of their age cohort. By 1970, this had risen to 15%. Class-based Britain was something of laggard in terms of university education penetration, but its growth was representative of a trend across all advanced industrial economies, East and West, in which the provision of higher education became critical in training the required scientists, engineers, doctors and other technical personnel (Faulkner, 2018, 412). Thus, just as the First and Second Industrial Revolutions had seen an expansion in the primary and secondary school sectors to service the skill needs of industry, the Third Industrial Revolution would see a similar expansion of the tertiary sector to service the needs of what would later become known as the "knowledge economy".

This development had a number of consequences. One effect was to push up the age at which children left home, went to work and got married. In effect, it helped to create a socially novel transitional phase of adulthood in which a person was not yet fully independent of their parents but not fully dependent either, a phase that is still with us (Sawyer et al., 2018). They lived together on campuses that were run by authorities external to the family home and with a duty not just to educate but also to care for people that were not children but not yet grown-up. In the US, until the 1960s, American universities were deemed by law courts to be acting *in loco parentis* with respect to their students; that is, as delegated parental authorities that could regulate the personal lives of pupils, without any respect for their incipient rights to due process. Interestingly, American courts began to afford constitutional protections to university students during the 1960s, corresponding with the time of peak campus unrest there (Lee, 2011).

While the legal doctrine was different in other countries, the basic tension was the generally the same, universities now overseeing large numbers of young adults for an extended period of time in an intermediary role that was poorly defined and as part of an evolving socialisation process. By the 1960s, large numbers of young people were congregated together, connected to and yet insulated from the mainstream of society, neither living at home under parental oversight, nor quite out on their own with full adult rights and responsibilities. From a sociological point of view, tertiary education institutions were becoming unique vehicles of socialisation for a particular age group and primarily for middle-class students, which was generally the largest group attending college that also lived on campus. Universities were still generally elitist but that elite was now considerably larger and an economically and politically more pivotal social group to educate and direct. The activism that occurred in the sixties was partly created by the cultivation of a norm of political participation (student government being the main channel) that became widened by the issues of the day. These developments led to an ideological orientation towards protest on the part of many young people (Sherkat & Blocker, 1994).

Growing household wealth and income also played a role. There was more disposable income for everyone, including university students, many of whom did not work, nor have to, while attending school, yet who still commanded significant discretionary spending power. Especially in the rich West, mass marketing and product development was increasingly directed towards the "youth demographic" who had more leisure time and money than ever. Young people were marketed to directly now, with their own products, fashions and services, and could make purchases themselves, without parental interjection or permission. This was not just the province of university populations. Teens and pre-teens living at home were marketed to just as much, though they obviously lived less independently (Frank, 1997).

This rise of youth autonomy was taking place in the context of what was still generally a rather conservative adult culture. The radical social-political experiments of the Interwar Period were unappealing to many who now just wanted to get on with their lives and enjoy the newfound prosperity of the time. The life of suburbia was ironically one in which the shared experiences of young and old were attenuated more than ever, the young spending the greater part of their days in educational institutions and in their own leisure activities in their own rooms in new and bigger homes, the father off to work most of the week, the mother at home in charge of the household but alone during much of her activity. Particularly in the socially conformist 1950s new parents had at least childhood memories of war and Depression that their children had no inkling of, and apparently never would have given the boom times and a Cold War that was tense but at least not "hot". Many of the parents of the 1950s and 1960s had some personal experience of war and privation, things that their children could only imagine. And the values and mores that resonated for parents, such as a return to safety and stability, seemed merely stifling and useless to many of their children (Baxandall & Ewen, 2000). The more traditional hierarchical pattern of elder authority was being eroded by this shift.

A parallel dynamic, though differently manifested, was unfolding in the Communist countries. These had suffered much greater privation and destruction from the War than America (though not as compared to some of their Western European counterparts) and their post-war transition under Stalinism was brutal in many respects. Yet, here too children of the mid- and late 1950s experienced a world of relative peace, stability, economic growth and material prosperity. To this was added guaranteed employment and social services, though not any political freedom or, ironically for so-called worker's paradises, power in the workplace since production quotas were imposed from above as were wages, the latter not generally growing as fast as the former. Still, to the young parents of the age this seemed, if not a paradise, a welcome change from decades past when even mere survival was far from assured. To many children though it seemed stultifying, an attitude they brought with them in the 1960s when they attended universities, which they too did in record numbers (Risch, 2015).

Overall on both "sides" of the (developed) world, there were now more youth than before because of the "baby boom" that had occurred after the end of the War, and thus a new bulge in the proportion of young people relative to older generations. This bulge would come of age in the 1960s, yet without formal political power in most countries. In the democracies, the voting age was generally 21 until the end of the decade or later, so most university students did not even have the franchise (Bergh & Eichhorn, 2019, 1). Voting was not relevant in the authoritarian East, although elections were held and the voting age in some Eastern bloc countries was actually lower than in the West; thus the lack of political power was especially acute there, particularly because much older people held the higher positions in the various hierarchies, with little prospect of turnover.

This was also true to varying degrees in the West especially in the 1950s. President Eisenhower was 62 years old when he took office as President of the US and almost 70 when he left. In France, the leading figure was Charles de Gaulle, in his mid-fifties when he led the country briefly after the end of the War and in his late sixties, when he came back as President with greatly enhanced powers in 1958 under the new Fifth Republic. Other major Western leaders were not much younger. Only in the US, with the election of John F. Kennedy, was there a leader in his mid-forties. But he was assassinated in 1963 (Kurlansky, 2004).

The Cold War (see Chapter 25) added to this environment of rigidity by extolling and demanding tight conformity to one set of values that was said to be "good" against the other said to be incontrovertibly "evil". Generational patterns do not break down neatly but the actual practices of any society could never match the claims of ideology. Cynicism and discontent were natural outcomes that crystallised in the 1960s, with youth, rather naturally, being attracted to rebellion against this imposed dichotomy.

24.5 Materialism and Consumerism

Meanwhile, the material quality of life was changing drastically. This was the first pure consumerist phase of capitalism, in which the share of consumption in overall GDP was becoming more and more important, while manufacturing was declining in relative terms across the developed and richer developing countries. While growing consumption was a hallmark of the entire industrialisation epoch, the period of capitalism after Second World War disruption was truly one of consumers. Mass consumption was already well-entrenched of course, major innovations in marketing and distribution beginning in the late nineteenth century. But the Great Depression had added a macroeconomic urgency to making sure that all the output being produced had a market, and advances in technology allowed for the production of many different types of goods designed to appeal to different consumer tastes and categories. While not quite the "mass customisation" of today, companies were producing at scale and yet able to tweak production lines to create slightly different versions of a mass-produced good. The automobile was the archetypal example, having moved from Ford's Model T (as Chapter 14 noted, available in any colour "so long as it's black") to annual model changes across multiple car lines produced by Ford and other auto manufacturers. But diversity in product lines was rapidly increasing in all industries.

At the same time, product branding and marketing had reached new heights and refinements. There seemed to a multiplicity of different offerings in the marketplace, made by different entities. But the reality was what economists call "monopolistic competition" in which producers try to gain pricing advantage through brand loyalty for what amount to small differences in product quality and characteristics. This approach was actually quite effective in making sales, and helped to advance a growing advertising industry devoted to creating demand for individual products within a line where all the offerings were very similar to one another. But it also helped open a door towards cynicism and malaise. A lot of fuss was made over things that in the end did not seem that important, even though an adman would be saying otherwise. This gap between reality and sales pitch would quickly become corrosive in areas outside product sales (Cohen, 2003).

Allied with rising incomes and the suburban household building boom, consumerism and consumer culture reached a new pinnacle. The Cold War politicised this development in an unprecedented way. Mass consumption was no longer just a personal indulgence, but a civic responsibility fundamental to the capitalist system, and an outward sign of that system's superiority. Once more this dynamic was greatest in America, which was in head-to-head competition with the Soviet Union, and where politicians were constantly crowing about America's political and economic superiority and its more democratic distribution of a much wider array of goods than was available in Russia (Cohen, 2003, 236–237). The Soviets bought into this idea as well, being just as materialistic in outlook, and attempted, with mixed success, to increase the offerings of consumer goods to its own citizens.

Thus private consumption and public benefit, it was widely argued, went hand in hand, implicitly promising a progressive goal of social equality without requiring any politically difficult redistribution of existing wealth. Rather, it was argued, an ever-growing economy built around the twin dynamics of increased productivity, product innovation and mass purchasing power would expand overall choice for everyone, without any sacrifice by anybody (Cohen, 2003, 237). This "gain without pain" was a panacea born relatively young in the Industrial Revolution (see Chapter 8). But it was now being delivered retail rather than wholesale, so to speak (Fig. 24.4).

24.6 The Organisation Man

The economist John Kenneth Galbraith wrote a book in 1966 called *The New Industrial State*. Its message was not entirely new but it did resonate with a time brimming with consumerism, large corporations and industrial scale in scientific and technical endeavour, all of which in an earlier era were causes for optimism and celebration but which in the Cold War did not seem quite so auspicious. Galbraith described how what he called a "technostructure" consisting of committees of managers, engineers and specialists operated a vast production organisation that controlled supposedly competitive markets and bent consumers to its corporate planning objectives. Mass marketing and advertising conditioned consumers to

Fig. 24.4 Allen's festive windows, Newcastle, UK 1963 (*Image source* Tyne & Wear Archives & Museums. "This photograph is from the Robert Sanderson collection which was kindly donated to Tyne & Wear Archives & Museums. This is a photograph of the illuminated windows of Allen's department store in South Shields. This is a 35 mm slide. It was taken in 1963. [Copyright] We're happy for you to share this digital image within the spirit of The Commons. Please cite 'Tyne & Wear Archives & Museums' when reusing")

buy products churned out in the interest of corporate profits and investment, while academics were turned into tame operatives through research funded by public–private grants oriented towards keeping the technocracy going rather than bold initiatives of knowledge for knowledge's sake.

It was not a pleasant picture, but this was only one of numerous tracts that came out bemoaning the numbing routine and regimentation of modern corporate life. The term "organisation man" was coined by the sociologist William Whyte in a 1956 book of the same title. Whyte's book was based on extensive interviews with the CEOs of major American corporations, and his central argument was that the average American had become collectivist and conformist to the norms of their organisation rather than being the rugged individuals that American myth liked to proclaim. Whyte proposed that most individuals in corporate hierarchies sacrificed their own creativity to fall in line with the prerogatives of the group. This metaphor became part of American popular culture. *The Man in the Gray Flannel Suit,* a 1955 novel by Sloan Wilson that was made into a 1956 film starring Gregory Peck, depicts the struggle of a young World War II veteran trying to align his neat and tidy suburban family and work life with some unpleasant after-effects of his war service. In Hollywood fashion, there is a rather unconvincing happy ending, but all was not well in many people's real lives. And, of course women, even though many of them worked in corporations and government agencies as well, were not included in this discourse.

Interior and exterior design reinforced this notion that humans were cogs in a larger machine (see Fig. 24.5). The machine might be benign, but it was a machine nonetheless. Architects set a pattern of corridor offices with rows of cells, each with their own window, later followed by the open-plan. The design began in America and Germany and spread to Britain in the sixties, supposedly offering the possibility of supervising hundreds of employees, specialised by function, each in their appropriate place, in panopticon fashion. In the late 1950s, some German companies used the *Burolandschaft,* or "office-landscape", with huge open floors split up by screens, foliage and desks scattered apparently at random. This purportedly discouraged hierarchies and yet was implemented in obviously very hierarchical organisations (Sampson, 1995, 266). The disconnect was obvious, and jarring. As one wag put it, organisational design in the industrial era had been using the Catholic Church and Caesar's legions as models (Sampson, 1995, 124). And yet this was supposedly the age of the individual. However this concept, along with everything else, was no longer what it had once been.

24.7 Ennui and a Crisis of Meaning

Not surprisingly, an individual and collective crisis of meaning began to take hold. It wasn't just the juxtaposition of a mass culture against an ideology of individualism in the West, or a profession of profound social ideals that were never lived up to, and often repressed in the East. Nor was it down only to the relentless materialism that ignored, denied or commodified immaterial needs, or even just the disorienting rapidity of change that seemed to promise utopia and the threat of nuclear or environmental annihilation the next. It was all of this in the context

Human Computers 1947
NASA Langley Research Center 1/28/1947 Image # EL-2001-00471

Fig. 24.5 Human "computers" in the office (*Image source* US NASA. Photograph published in Winds of Change, 75th Anniversary NASA publication [page 48], by James Schultz. Image Number: NIX-EL-2001–00,471. Original caption: The female staff at Langley performed mathematical computations for male staff. No known copyright restrictions)

of a profusion and confusion of a commercial world where everything was presented as equal in meaning to everything else and where grand promises were made on behalf of goods and services that in no way plausible way could deliver the joy, serenity and meaning they were sold as providing.

Mass media was the tableau on which much of this incoherence played out, often to absurd lengths. American culture, being something of a pastiche already, demonstrated this forcefully. For example, on January 30, 1966, *the Ed Sullivan Show*, an extremely popular "variety" television program, featured a young active duty Green Beret medic in full-dress uniform singing *The Ballad of the Green Berets*. The song was a patriotic paean to the Vietnam War, but one that never even mentioned Vietnam, and which was the number one pop song in the US for the year, selling

8 million copies, more than any other performer during the period, even the Beatles. Yet that same year the anti-war songs of Peter, Paul and Mary were almost as popular. In its quest for seeking mass appeal, the Sullivan show also regularly juxtaposed clashing acts that added up to collective incoherence, in one case having the iconic counterculture rock band the *Doors* performing their sexually provocative and drug referencing song, *Light my fire,* followed by the crooner couple Steve and Eydie Gorme singing, *Getting to Know You,* and Yul Brynner performing a medley from the musical, *Gypsy.* (Appy, 2015 123–125).

America was the most mass media and mass culture saturated nation on earth, but other countries were also grappling with the cultural contradictions of the age. André Malraux, a rebel in his youth, but in 1968 a member of de Gaulle's right-wing government, spoke of how the current civilisation was an affair of machines which could teach everything except how to be a human being (Kurlansky, 2004, 186). West Germany, surging back to a prominent place in the global political and economic order, was confronted by a Nazi past that had not been fully dealt with and which was continuing to be ignored, a shadow that intimated that the whole post-war order might be morally and socially bankrupt. In Japan too, an unpleasant past was buried and political and economic corruption seemed endemic amidst the general wealth.

Dissatisfaction with modernity was nothing new but the lack of connection and the sense of uselessness of life and personhood were becoming profound in many quarters. One could work and get a good job and buy anything desired. And yet the individual was totally replaceable. A deep gender divide prevailed, and many women were provided a different sort of emptiness, typically stuck in suburban homes, raising children and trying to find something to fill their time. Their existential crisis could not generally be met in the workplace since they were largely excluded from it once married. And the duties of the household seemed menial at best, everything bought from the outside, its self-sufficiency gone, disconnected from local communities except on a transactional basis. Meanwhile posterity itself, which used to be what children were offerings to, could be eliminated at any moment in a nuclear holocaust.

Not accidentally, the pharmaceutical industry grew prodigiously in this time, selling what we would now call "lifestyle drugs", with women the largest customers. Meprobamate, an exceptionally effective tranquilizer better known by its trade name, Miltown, was sold to both men and women, though it was most popular with the latter. A drugstore in Hollywood posted a huge red sign in its window saying "Yes, we have Miltown!" Meanwhile, the popular American comedian Milton Berle quipped that he was thinking of changing his name to "Miltown Berle" (Manchester, 1973, 929).

24.8 A Year of Global Unrest

The president of Columbia University in New York, Grayson Kirk, coined the phrase "generation gap" in a speech he gave at the University of Virginia in 1968, the same year that his own campus would be taken over for a time by rebellious students (Kurlansky, 2004, 186). Despite the apparent prescience of the term, Kirk was very much an establishment man who wished to manage events rather than respond to them. This would have been made clear simply by looking at Kirk's 1966 commencement address at Columbia University in which he referred to American history as "on balance, a success story without parallel" that merely required an updating of "old beliefs" (Cerny, 1971, 258). The conflict between the society as it actually was and the idea that technological and economic progress were sufficient by itself was soon to erupt in spectacular fashion.

It had been a long time coming in many ways. The 1950s socioeconomic order was never as peaceable as it was made out to be, the pressures for social conformity masking a great deal of ferment underneath, ferment which broke out into the open in various ways at various times, two major examples being the fight for equal rights by African Americans in the US; and the various and serious outbursts of nationalism and worker discontent in the Eastern bloc, which were generally ruthlessly suppressed by the authorities, sometimes with joint military action, as in Hungary in 1956.

Generalised unrest was less common, at least in any organised sense. Indeed, some of the resistance to social homogenisation remained individualistic. The so-called "Beatniks" of 1950s America were distinctly Bohemian, seeking personal experience of freedom rather than organised revolt. Jack Kerouac, the novelist and leading "Beat" light was quoted as saying that Beatniks loved everything, from Billy Graham (an American Christian evangelist) to Zen, apple pie, and Eisenhower: "we dig it all". This was said tongue in cheek but made the point that the "Beat" movement, such as it was, was more literary and experiential than political (Manchester, 1973, 892).

The movements of the 1960s were different. Individual seekers of Enlightenment remained but many of them now joined together in collective movements seeking change. The Free Speech movement, which was initiated with the 2 December 1964 occupation of Sproul Hall by more than a thousand students on the Berkeley campus of the University of California, protested an impending expulsion of campus activist Mario Savio. This particular ferment inspired later unrest on the campus of the Free University in West Berlin in June 1966, the London School of Economics in March 1967, major German universities in June 1967, and on to almost all the Italian universities between mid-1967 and January–February 1968. From there, it spread to universities in Warsaw, Paris, New York, West Germany, most of the higher education sector in France, various campuses in Britain, and finally to Madrid and Santiago in fascist Spain, before circling back to Berkeley again (Faulkner, 2018, 413–414). Mexico and Japan also experienced significant disruptions and in Mexico, a number of students were shot and killed in a major demonstration in Mexico City.

"May '68" in France saw brief takeovers of the University of Nanterre outside Paris and in the Latin Quarter around the Sorbonne. The French student unrest was joined by the labour unions and in the end, seven million went on a general strike that for a time seemed to threaten the entire political order within France. This labour uprising is generally seen as the event that broke the so-called "Fordist compromise" in France that required labour peace and the suppression of labour-capital class conflict to deliver higher labour productivity in return for higher wages, a bargain that was part of a larger global "Keynesian" order that came unstuck in the 1970s. It also ignited a series of debates within Europe about worker self-management and labour relations that challenged some fundamental notions of Capitalism itself, accompanied by strike activity in much of Southern and Western Europe. In the end, the established regimes in France and elsewhere survived (a revolution did not take place) but ideas and practices, especially in the labour realm, had been altered significantly (Mercer, 2020).

One unifying theme of these protests was opposition to the US prosecution of the Vietnam War. In America, a large motivator was that the male students were subject to being drafted to fight there. Outside America, a pushback against American global dominance more generally was also part of the revolt. But there were other themes too. Many students felt profound unease over the role that business corporations played in society and the economy, and the Vietnam War seemed to point to everything that was wrong with the relationship between Capitalism and the universities especially. This was acutely felt in American society where leading companies, higher education institutions and the government seemed tied together in immoral war profiteering and exploitation. Some activists took the fight to the corporations directly. On 28 April 1970, thousands of anti-war activists converged on the annual shareholder meeting of the Honeywell Corporation, a major defence contractor, disrupting the meeting. There were also protests against the Dow Chemical Company, the producer of napalm, especially when their corporate recruiters came to campuses (Waterhouse, 2017, 14–15).

In this time of Cold War, anti-capitalist elements of protest movements could be pronounced, especially outside the US. The Cultural Revolution in China and Maoism added an interesting and volatile mix to the proceedings (see Box 24.1). But local movements were shaped by other more localised concerns as well. In West Germany (and East Berlin), social protest was characterised by an anti-authoritarian thrust, directed against every kind of State repression. The condemnation of Fascism was especially acute because many Nazi Third Reich figures remained in the power structure and the parents of many protesters had hidden their roles and attitudes during the Nazi era. Italy and Japan were in similar straits, though in Italy anti-Fascism was joined with calls to change ongoing conservative and Catholic Church inspired social policies towards things like divorce, and abortion, as well as opposition to military service. Because of the strength of the Italian Communist Party, Marxist ideology was quite influential there. Japanese protest, meanwhile, tended to be more focused on the absurdities of modernisation. A very popular protest song, produced underground by students in 1968, was called *Drunkard Come Back from Heaven*, a comic ditty about death on the roads, which had increased dramatically in Japan due to rapid economic growth and increased automobile travel. Another song, *Let's Join the Self-Defence Forces*, was a parody of the Japanese military and of militarism more generally (Heilbronner, 2016, 691–693).

Box 24.1 China's Cultural Revolution, the New Left and the Counterculture

Although the Cold War froze many things in place, such as the dualistic Superpower competition and "Mutually Assured Destruction" (see Chapter 25), in other ways it created crosscurrents that interacted and interfered with each other in dynamic and volatile ways. Communism as an ideology splintered in the East with the Sino-Soviet Split, while in the West a "New Left" arose to add to the already fracturing Old Left. Chinese Communist theory and practice was shaken up by the Cultural Revolution and then melded into Maoism and these deeply influenced New Left and other thinkers. All of this got swept up into the 1960s "counterculture". It was heady mix that veered into incoherence and violence at times, but also unique and interesting experimentation.

The beginning of the Cold War was marked by the monolith of Stalinism, which was imposed to varying degrees on the Communist states. There were already numerous Communist doctrinal variants, such as Trotskyism, and differing visions offered by more humanist, democratic Socialists such as Rosa Luxemberg. But these were stranded in the world of theory. The official Soviet doctrine of Marxism-Leninism, and Stalin's heavy hand on policy and authority, was what held sway. Thus debate about various doctrinal points in the Socialist bloc was relatively limited and outside of it Communist movements were required to stay within the lines or face ostracism by Moscow.

This monolithic state of affairs in the East frayed rather quickly with Tito's break with Stalin in 1948, though that was political more than doctrinal. Then Mao seized power in China and aligned with the Soviet Union. China followed a Stalinist line on the surface but from the beginning Mao experimented with local initiatives to better suit both the nature of rural, peasant Chinese society, and his own personal philosophy of the power that put faith in the collective will to move material mountains. By 1960 or so Mao had broken completely from Russia and a totally separate school of Communism known as Maoism developed that would dominate within China and influence many outside of it.

Maoism does not have precise outlines, but its distinctions from Marxism-Leninism are several. Whereas Marxism-Leninism was tailored towards the industrial proletariat, Maoism was oriented towards the countryside peasant. The Russian economic model was one of large-scale heavy industry, while Mao's version was more small-scale and based on small industrial collectives. Following Marx, Soviet policy remained conceptually fixated on fomenting potential revolutions in the industrialised West, where capitalism was most advanced and where supposedly conditions were greatest for its collapse. Mao was always focused on countries more like his own, in the underdeveloped and agrarian "Third World". Finally, Marxism-Leninism was thoroughly materialist, hewing to the idea that economic "substructure" always drove politico-social "superstructure". Mao thought changes in culture could change the economy, and indeed often behaved as if such changes were the primary mechanism for doing so.

Mao's first major innovation along these lines was his "Great Leap Forward" between 1958 and 1962 in which small blast furnaces sprouted throughout the countryside against the Stalinist bias towards large-scale factories in or near cities. Economically this was disastrous and was replaced by a new and radical shift in policy and theory with Mao's "Cultural Revolution" between 1965 and 1968. Partly this came about as Mao sought to re-assert his personal prestige power after suffering a blow to his authority with the disastrous famine and scarcity that his "Leap" had engendered. But it also was an expression of Mao's romantic trust in the power and wisdom of the masses, his distrust of educated elites, and his belief in "permanent revolution".

The Cultural Revolution was an unprecedented move in which grass-roots were set against Party elites, young set against old, country against city, all under a cult of personality. Mao's tactics were bold, brilliant, ruthless and reprehensible all at the same time. He mobilised students and young adults across the country into "Red Guards" that were explicit agents of the Revolution totally apart from the Party, the Army and other normal existing channels of power. There was already a Chinese version of the Marxist technique of regular self-critique of "revisionism" and the rooting out of "revisionist tendencies", but this was taken to a different level when students were instructed to come up with instances of "counter-revolutionary" thoughts or actions they had come across in their elders. This was an upending of normal hierarchies of both Marxism-Leninism, in which trained Party cadres would normally be the ones leading others in the self-critique, and of Chinese cultural norms of the authority of elders over the young. This began mildly at first but soon students were denouncing teachers and, encouraged by Mao, forming into groups to actively ferret out counterrevolutionaries. Indeed in 1966 the Party officially sanctioned what were in effect local youth uprisings. A parallel process was taking place in work units, with workers denouncing bosses and work teams sent to distant locations to carry on actions against supposed reactionaries and deviationists. Urban educated people of all sorts were now automatically suspect, and were sent for "re-education" in rural labour camps, with denunciations a regular occurrence.

This extraordinary program literally tore the society apart. By mid-1968, the economy had stopped functioning due to chaos in offices, factories, and schools. Famine, collective violence and privation had led to many deaths, likely around 1 million, though estimates range as high as 20 million. Mao called in the People's Liberation Army to restore order in the cities and disbanded the Red Guard. Mao's actions had severely damaged the country and sharply limited its direct overseas influence as it became totally self-involved; indeed numerous Chinese ambassadorships were left vacant after many ambassadors were recalled to China to face very uncertain fates. However Mao had achieved one of his primary political aims of purging his enemies from top leadership positions, and settling scores with old enemies. To the extent that Mao believed this process would transform China into a modern Socialist utopia, he and everyone else were obviously gravely disappointed.

However the Cultural Revolution solidified the principles of Maoism and met with some especially receptive audiences overseas. The "New Left", a collection of heterogeneous left groups in the West that had become thoroughly dissatisfied with the existing pro-Moscow Communist parties, was affected greatly by Maoist doctrines. Many orthodox Marxists in the West became very disillusioned after the Soviet repression of the Hungarian Revolt of 1956 and yet did not want to reject Communism, while other Communist and non-Communist direct action and activist movements such as Anarchism and the Situationists rose up in response to societal turmoil of the 1960s. This New Left was broadly anti-establishment, socially activist, grass roots based and often anti-authoritarian, though individual group platforms were so diverse that there were often more arguments within the movement than against its purported foes. The 1960s counterculture, which covers a whole set of ideas and movements that rejected established mainstream culture and values, and often the entirety of Western culture, was also ripe ground for Maoist ideas. The boundaries across and within the counterculture are amorphous, members ranging from more life-style oriented "drop-outs", like the "Hippies", and political activists in the nuclear disarmament, civil-rights, student, and Anti-Vietnam War movements.

The New Left and counterculture found great resonance with Maoist notions of universal anti-elitism, permanent rebelliousness, romanticism, and its associated appeal to personal purity, anti-institutionalism, and the glorification and idealisation of the "masses", the commoner especially. In a sense both Maoism and its Western fellow travellers shared a common bond in being an anti-societal movement designed to tear down a rotten society in order to rebuild it from the ground up, remaking and reconditioning the corrupted human being as the way of doing so. Maoism appeared to provide a template, a set of techniques and a home country and inspirational leader all in one. The emphasis on action rather than intellect was very appealing to those who felt that the time for thinking and talking was well over, especially many on the Left used to long, vapid and endless terminological and doctrinal debates. Ironically, even Maoism's anti-urbanism resonated in a highly urbanised West, where many of the leaders came from large cities that appeared to be in the belly of the beast of an anti-human industrial technocracy that was essentially the same whether labelled Socialist or Capitalist.

Maoist techniques were especially popular, including self-criticism, re-education, people's communes and guerrilla theatre and propaganda, widely adopted by left activists of all stripes. These certainly were impactful in an immediate sense, just as the Cultural Revolution in China was. The impact of both program and techniques was, however, mostly disruptive and destructive. At the time though China was very much closed off to the West and the goings-on inside it were largely hidden from the outside world. What seemed to be the case for outsiders was that something exciting, new and liberating was happening in China. The fact that the causal links between the actions of the Cultural Revolution and stated social and economic outcomes was vague and murky was actually an advantage, attractive in an age in which feeling trumped logic, the subjective was above the objective, and, to use a phrase of the time, "the personal was political". If Marxism-Leninism appealed to the mind, with its literally "heady" ideals, Maoism appealed to the heart with its exciting emotions.

The fruits of Maoism, both inside of China and outside of it, obviously fell far short of the promise. Chinese Communism became understandably conservative after Mao's death in 1976, ultimately going down more of an autocratic State Capitalist path under Deng Xiaoping, egalitarianism and idealism dropped rather completely. The revolutionary Maoist movements that were most successful outside China, namely the *Khmer Rouge* in Cambodia, and the *Sendero Luminoso* in Peru, were brutal, violent, cult-like affairs that discredited the whole approach on the left and right alike. But some of its cultural elements, fused with New Left ideas, live on, especially an appeal to individual "purity" of some sort (colloquially known as "political correctness"), an emotive approach to politics, and an equating of disruption with progress.

(The discussion above is drawn from Davis, 2018; Lovell, 2019; MacFarquhar & Schoenhals, 2006; Meisner, 1999; Schoenhals, 2005).

When student rebellion occurred in the Spanish-speaking world in 1968, it was tied up with opposition to military dictatorship and oppressive political regimes operating in the present, not the past. Spanish student demonstrations were triggered by a government-sanctioned mass held in Madrid for Adolf Hitler. The University of Madrid closed because of student demonstrations and did not reopen for classes until thirty-eight days later. Brazilian protests were in opposition to the four-year-old military dictatorship there (Kurlansky, 2004, 82–83). In Mexico City, the single-party regime was determined that the October Olympics hosted by the city would go on without a hint of unrest and made the choice on October 2 to have troops surround a major downtown square where student protesters had gathered. 5,000 troops deployed to the square were ordered to open fire, killed at least 100, and arrested and wounded hundreds more (Faulkner, 2018, 436).

There were student protests in the Eastern Bloc as well. Youth trends got around globally, fuelled by mass media and normal social transmission. The biggest student movement occurred in Czechoslovakia where it fused with the "Prague Spring" reforms of the new Communist leader Alexander Dubcek that included an opening up of borders and liberalisation of local press laws. The Soviet Union sent out mixed messages during much of 1968 on the Czech reforms. Somewhat similar rumblings were happening in Poland, and again the Soviets prevaricated. The whole Eastern bloc, and Russia itself, was undergoing cultural, social and economic changes at this time not dissimilar to the West, and adaptation of some sort for the Communist system seemed called for, especially from a youth generation perspective (Svec, 1988).

In the end, it was not to be. The Warsaw Pact invasion of Czechoslovakia was met by student resistance and noncooperation, but to no avail. Dubcek was not, in this immediate instance, removed from power, though he and key members of his politburo were recalled to Moscow and pressured into towing the Soviet line. By the end of the year, the Czech borders were once again closed, the press muzzled, and dissidents back underground or in prison. Dubcek would be retired from authority in 1969 and retired completely in 1970. Poland's movement was not quite as dramatically put down but it too was not allowed to unfold. The possibility of reforming official Communism from within, which was a real hope before then, was definitively killed for a generation after 1968 (Kurlansky, 2004).

Youth unrest in both the East and West shared similar themes: opposition to authoritarianism, repression, militarism and a desire for greater individual expression and freedom. There was however a different kind of disappointment on the part of some of the Communist youth, who had hoped that their governments would realise the grand stated aspirations of Socialism, aspirations that Western governments left mostly to the private actor. The Polish demonstrations were also motivated by opposition to an anti-Semitism campaign launched by the Communist government as a means of funnelling popular dissatisfaction into an old sectional hatred, even though anti-Semitism was actually against official Communist doctrine and most Polish young people had little tradition of it (Kurlansky, 2004, 123).

24.9 The Aftermath

1968 is said by many to be the most "Sixties" year of the "long 1960s", with some claiming that it constituted a sort of worldwide "cultural revolution" paralleling that occurring in China but in its own distinct ways (Heilbronner, 2016, 690). Its cultural legacy is seen as enduring. As a political and economic movement, on the other hand, its main objectives, varied and sometimes contradictory to begin with, are seen largely not to have eventuated.

Is this a fair assessment? It is probably too strong to say that the 1968 protests added up to a true revolution in a cultural sense. But it certainly set off many changes in cultural discourse, and categories of social identity and thought. Certainly, the decade saw a continuation and reformulation of an earlier Romanticism that rejected the prosaic, utilitarian, mechanistic, rationalisation (in the Weberian sense) and commercial orientation of modern industrialism, whether Communist or Capitalist. One could say that there was a culmination of an attempt to "re-enchant the world" (to turn Weber's phrase on its head), with a new and reformed individual and collective meaning. Rather than turning backwards, as some of the nineteenth century Romantics had, there was now an attempt to liberate society from the ills of modernity, without wholly rejecting it, and even using some of its aspects for anti-modern ends (Löwy, 2020, 138).

Also, while full of motive force, the movements never really joined up with one another either intellectually or tactically and strategically. There were many different goals to be achieved, such as an end to racism and racial discrimination (a core focus of the American Civil Rights movements, the fight against Apartheid in South Africa and many others), an end to gender oppression (which the "second wave" feminist movement was focused on), workers' rights, economic justice, environmentalism, pacifism and so on. These were all noble ends, and a reaction against the simplified societal views offered under the rubrics of Communism and Capitalism. But they were difficult to bring together consistently, and often conflicted with one another. For example, the peace movement was notoriously sexist in practice, and racial divides split economic justice campaigns.

Whatever its past and present defects, the old unified revolutionary movement of Communism had a singular focus, a set of techniques that were field-tested, and an emphasis on the collective, a problematic aspect in many ways, yet a very useful orientation when organising a fight against an entrenched incumbent system. Individualism was the hallmark of much of the 1960s, sometimes allied with group liberation, but still largely aiming to free the person more than the society. For these reasons, and others, the legacy of the 1960s has been probably mostly in selected cultural and social spheres, rather than the economic and political arenas.

The role of mass media in, and on the movements, has generally been quite profound. Some of the 1960s "counterculture" activism became explicitly about media manipulation, and arguably little else at times. Exemplary of this (positively and negatively) were the antics of "Yippie" leader Abbie Hoffman ("Yippie" being short for "Youth International Party", not formally organised and arguably a media tag more than a party). Hoffman staged a "sweep-in" in the East Village neighbourhood in New York, mopping and sweeping up some of Manhattan's dirtiest streets, with one person even polishing a policeman's badge. Hoffman called this and other of his displays a "goof" and argued that a modern revolutionary group needed to head "for the television station, not for the factory" (Kurlansky, 2004, 98). This sort of spectacle may have been effective in its way but potentially has ended up replacing genuine politics, which is about the struggle for and negotiation of power relations within a society, rather than mere media performance and perception.

Media dynamics certainly shaped the Civil Rights and anti-War movements. On the one hand, television scenes of American sheriffs in Southern states beating peaceful protestors or military atrocities in Vietnam were effective in turning citizens against the coarsest abuses of power by their governments. But the various movements also needed such televised violence more and more in order to be politically effective. An unsuccessful protest was increasingly one that did not provoke a reaction from the authorities at all, or, worse, was not covered by the press. Moreover televised violence became normalised and lost its impact after a while. Martin Luther King, near the end of his life, concluded that violence, though he was against it, might have to be left to run its course if anything was to change, and even then change was not certain (Kurlansky, 2004, 115). Some argue that society itself, and its sense of genuine connection, has been replaced by enervating spectacle for spectacle's sake, a trend made evident in the 1960s (Löwy, 2020, 143–144). Events of the recent past seem to lend some weight to this assessment.

Still, for some groups there has indeed been substantial cultural advance that can be directly traced to the Sixties. Although racism and sexism continue unabated in many ways, the concept of "civil rights" is at least notionally beyond reproach and some groups are now accepted as equals in theory, if not always in practice. Significant struggles for woman's, LGBTIQA+, indigenous and other rights became established then and have since advanced. While there remain many gaps in true social equality, the basic idea of it is largely uncontested within the mainstream. The more contemporary battles tend to be over the legitimacy of various social categorisations, a battle subsumed under the broader label of "Culture Wars".

Economically on the other hand, one is hard pressed not to say that the movement was a failure, at least to the extent that the goal was reformulation or overthrow of capitalism, technocracy, industrialism and mass production, consumption and distribution. There was, as noted, labour unrest that achieved some temporary change and some reforms in government policies here and there. But a powerful organised pushback by the powers that be, in the form of Neoliberalism, came during the 1970s and the various movements that fought the establishment in the 1960s certainly could not prevent its reaction in the decades that followed (more on this in Chapter 28).

Perhaps, this is not the most important point, however. The universality and power of the social movements of the 1960s and early 1970s are impressive and they embodied many human currents that the prevailing order did not address at all, or at least not fully or adequately. Many interesting ideas and practices, worthy of further consideration and action, emerged. That many of these have been mostly sidelined or failed to be implemented should not to be taken necessarily as an indication of their lack of importance or utility.

References

Appy, C. G. (2015). *American reckoning: The Vietnam War and our national identity*. Penguin Books.

Baxandall, R. F. & Ewen, E. (2000). *Picture windows: How the suburbs happened*. Basic Books.

Bergh, J. & Eichhorn, J. (2019). Introduction. In Eichhorn, J., & Bergh, J. (Eds.). *Lowering the voting age to 16: Learning from real experiences worldwide*. Springer Nature.

Cerny, P. G. (1971). The mismatched President: LBJ and the USA. *Government and Opposition, 6*(2), 255–262.

Cohen, L. (2003). *A consumers' republic: The politics of mass consumption in postwar America*. Knopf.

Crafts, N. (1995). The golden age of economic growth in western Europe, 1950–1973. *Economic History Review, 48*(3), 429–447.

Davis, M. (2006). *City of Quartz: Excavating the Future in Los Angeles* (New Edition). Verso Books.

Davis, M. (2018). "Among the ordinary people": New Left involvement in working-class political mobilization 1956–68. *History Workshop Journal, 86*, 133–159.

Faulkner, N. (2018). *A radical history of the world*. Pluto Press.

Frank, T. (1997). *The conquest of cool: Business culture, counterculture, and the rise of hip consumerism*. University of Chicago Press.

Gordon, C. (2017). Carbarism: Civilising the automobile. *World Transport Policy and Practice* 23(1).

Graff, M., Kenwood, A. G., & Lougheed, A. L. (2013). *Growth of the international economy, 1820–2015*. Routledge.

Harley, K. (2003). Growth theory and Industrial Revolutions in Britain and America. *The Canadian Journal of Economics / Revue Canadienne D'economique, 36*(4), 809–831.

Heilbronner, O. (2016). Music and protest: The case of the 1960s and its long shadow. *Journal of Contemporary History, 51*(3), 688–700.

Kurlansky, S. (2004). *1968: The year that rocked the world*. Ballantine.

Lee, P. (2011). The curious life of in loco parentis at American universities. *Higher Education in Review, 8*, 65–90.

Lovell, J. (2019). *Maoism: A global history*. Random House.

Löwy, M. (2020). Revolutionary romanticism in the twentieth century: Surrealists and Situationists. In A. Hemmens & G. Zacarias (Eds.), *The Situationist International: A critical handbook* (pp. 138–146). Pluto Press.

MacFarquhar, R., & Schoenhals, M. (2006). *Mao's last revolution*. Belknap Press of Harvard University Press.

Manchester, W. (1973). *The glory and the dream: A narrative history of America, 1932–1972*. Little Brown and Company.

Meisner, M. J. (1999). *Mao's china and after: A history of the people's republic.* (3rd ed.). Free Press.
Mercer, B. (2020). *Student revolt in 1968: France.* Cambridge University Press.
Pechatnov V.O. (2017) The Soviet Union and the Bretton Woods Conference. In: Scott-Smith G., Rofe J. (Eds.), *Global perspectives on the Bretton Woods Conference and the post-War world order.* Palgrave Macmillan.
Post, R. C. (2007). *Urban mass transit: The life story of a technology.* Greenwood Publishing Group.
Risch, W. J. (Ed.) (2015). *Youth and rock in the Soviet Bloc: Youth cultures, music, and the state in Russia and Eastern Europe.* Lexington Books.
Rothstein, R. (2017). *The color of law: A forgotten history of how our government segregated America.* Liveright Publishing.
Sampson, A. (1995). *Company man: The rise and fall of corporate life.* Times-Business/Random House.
Sawyer, S. M., Azzopardi, P. S., Wickremarathne, D., & Patton, G. C. (2018). The age of adolescence. *The Lancet Child & Adolescent Health, 2*(3), 223–228.
Schoenhals, M. (2005). "Why Don't We Arm the Left?" Mao's Culpability for the Cultural Revolution's "Great Chaos" of 1967. *The China Quarterly, 182*, 277–300.
Sherkat, D. E., & Blocker, T. J. (1994). The political development of sixties' activists: Identifying the influence of class, gender, and socialization on protest participation. *Social Forces, 72*(3), 821–842.
Svec, M. (1988). The Prague spring: 20 years later. *Foreign Affairs, 66*(5), 981–1001.
Van Bavel, J., & Reher, D. S. (2013). The baby boom and its causes: What we know and what we need to know. *Population and Development Review, 39*(2), 257–288.
Waterhouse, B. C. (2017). The personal, the political and, the profitable: Business and protest culture, 1960s–1980s. *Financial History*, (Spring), 14–17.
Westad, O. A. (2017). *The Cold War: A world history.* Penguin Random House UK.
Whyte, W. H. (1988). *City: Rediscovering the center.* Doubleday.

CHAPTER 25

Cold War

C. Gordon, *Many Possible Worlds*,
https://doi.org/10.1007/978-981-19-9281-0_25

Fig. 25.1 "Checkpoint Charlie" between East and West Berlin (*Image source* https://worldhistorypics.weebly.com/ Donated to the public domain, taken on 4 August 2016 by Gary Lee Todd)

25.1 The Beginnings of a Manichean World

In one of the great, unintended consequences of history, the Germans, during First World War fighting in full swing, arranged to return V.I. Lenin to his home country by sealed train from Switzerland, across Germany, and through Finland. This was one of numerous schemes undertaken by both sides to destabilise the other through what would now be referred to as covert action. British agent T. E. Lawrence's activities riling up Arab nationalism in the Ottoman territories, and a clumsy German effort to bring Mexico into the war on the side of the Central Powers by offering it back territories that it had lost in the prior century are other examples. Most such actions either were of negligible importance strategically or tactically (as with Germany's efforts to lure Mexico). Or they were effective but not decisive, (which could be said of Lawrence's campaign, which weakened the Ottomans and made British operations there easier and faster, but did not make too much overall strategic difference) (Strachan, 2003) (Fig. 25.1).

Lenin's move into Russia is entirely another matter. That Russian Tsarism was headed for collapse is indisputable. But Bolshevism was not the path it would have taken without Lenin. Here is one of those relatively rare examples of an individual being both a product of history and a prime mover of it at the same time. Kerensky's Provisional Government had been installed after the fall of the Tsarist autocracy but was only weakly constituted. The government actually did legislate a large number of economic reforms (though couldn't implement them). But it made a fatal error in continuing to prosecute a war that the country was well past being able to fight any more. It was a decision made in response to Allied pressure to keep Russia from making a separate peace, and a hope that Germany would soon wear itself out, especially after the entry of the Americans into the war (Kochan, 1970, 193–195, 205–206). Yet, it was a blind alley.

The choice doomed the Provisional Government. But what would replace it was an open question. Tooze (2014) makes much of the election, held after the Provisional Government's power broke down but before it collapsed, as a sign of the nascent democracy that would have taken root if Lenin had not managed to subvert both the election and its aftermath. This is true as far as it goes, but Lenin was one of the few Russian politicians that both opposed continuation of the war and was willing to go to any lengths to end it. As Hobsbawn (1994) has put it: the choice was not between a liberal or illiberal or Communist or non-Communist Russia, but Russia or no Russia (64).

This was an opportunity to take power and Lenin seized it. It was only later, after surviving (barely) a civil war and an invasion by the country's former allies, that his political program was clear. The doctrine that would become formally known as Marxism-Leninism, more colloquially as Communism, as expounded by Lenin was explicitly universalist and triumphalist. It was an idea system that thought itself superior to Capitalism both morally and economically, and it offered no room for coexistence.

The liberal democracies had been fighting against leftism of all sorts throughout the nineteenth century and Lenin's Soviet project gave them a new enemy to focus on. The Allied intervention in the Russian Civil War after the Revolution was driven mostly by a counter-ideological obsession with the dangers of Communism, since at the time Russia presented little direct military, economic or geopolitical threat to any country, even to its closest neighbours. The Allies thus had a real hope that Communism could be crushed in its cradle, to use the phrase attributed to Churchill at the time. Tactically, the Allies sought to stabilise eastern and central Europe and shield them from the entry of Communist regimes into the new power vacuums of destroyed old orders, of which the new Soviet states briefly established in Hungary and Bavaria were most concerning (Barraclough, 1967). Strategically, the Allies sent in forces to help domestic opponents end Lenin's bogeyman regime once and for all.

It thus should not be forgotten that it takes two to make a duality. The strong Western desire to eliminate an ideological rival combined with the exceptionalism of American thinking (see Chapter 20) to help to co-create a strict division between permanently rival camps. "Wilsonianism" was an explicit response to Leninism, Wilson's Fourteen Points being a direct response to the challenge of Bolshevism, his proposed League of Nations aiming to establish an international liberal framework, from which both Russia and Germany were initially excluded, that would buttress the world order from the dangerous leftist ideas that were now official state policy in an actual government and society, however weak they might be at present (Lichtheim, 1972, 146–147). The religious fervour of Wilson's ideas are notable, Wilson explicitly choosing the term "Covenant" for the founding document of the League, over the more conventional term "Charter" that was later used for the United Nations founding document. Wilson was a pastor's son and religiously trained and thus his own experience and attitudes coloured the way his policies were framed. But the salvationist tone and terminology were also very much was a product of American culture (Berg, 2013, 171; Winn, 2008, 188). It was matched by the equally millenarian thinking of the religious secularism of Marxism. Thus was an epic battle created and joined.

25.2 Prelude to a Dichotomy

This mutual existential hostility was briefly interrupted by the challenge of militarised Fascism during the 1930s (see Chapter 23). Russia had already moved from the official stance of "World Revolution" that Lenin had favoured to the policy of "Socialism in one country", i.e. Russia. This had been motivated initially by pragmatism, as the Soviet Union simply did not have the resources to remain a pariah state trying to foment revolution in other countries. Stalin preferred to devote what the country had to rapid (and brutal) industrialisation. Millions were sent to the forced-labour camps that Stalin made an integral part of the Soviet economy before his death in 1953. In 1989, the Soviet historian Roy Medvedev estimated that about 20 million died as a result of the labour camps, forced collectivisation, famine and executions. Another 20 million were victims of imprisonment, exile and forced relocation (Gatrell, 2006; Suny, 1997).

After Hitler's takeover of power in Germany, Fascism now replaced Capitalism as the greatest immediate existential threat to the Soviet Union, and its survival demanded working with supposedly antithetical capitalist systems for an indefinite period of time to fight this threat. Stalin therefore directed Communist parties overseas to engage in broad, anti-Fascist "Popular Fronts", cooperating with non-Communist, democratic organisations that used to be seen as more dangerous than the conservatives or liberals (Buchanan, 2002).

In the West itself, Communism was still officially antithetical, but Russia remained weak internationally and Stalin's insularity obscured internal realities, allowing Westerners to idealise the system and Western governments to become somewhat less hostile; (although Soviet espionage remained active, it was directed mostly against its internal opponents, e.g. Leon Trotsky, who was exiled and finally murdered by Soviet agents in Mexico City in 1940). Hitler and Mussolini's expansionism and rearmament was a much greater concern. And the Depression revitalised left movements, forcing the liberal democracies to share some power with them. This was the opening that the "Popular Front" initiative worked through.

The Second World War forged an active formal alliance between the West and Stalin, because both sides found their survival at stake against a common enemy. The "Grand Alliance" between Russia, Britain and the US against Germany (with the Soviet Union only moving against Japan near the very end of the war) was born. The 1939–1941 Non-aggression pact between Hitler and Stalin was conveniently forgotten, Stalin obviously not wanting to call attention to his venality and short-sightedness in that matter, and the West desperately needing Russia to stay viable in its savage fighting against the Germans. On the British side, the pre-war Western policy of "appeasement", which had explicitly been about keeping the general peace on the French and British borders in exchange for leaving Hitler a "free hand in the East", ultimately at Russia's expense, was now cast as an epithet against giving in to evil. It was a fine mess that everyone had played a part in making, but that was then. Now was about the enemy of one's enemy making friends and prevailing in the end (Davies 2006). (See Chapter 21 for more on Second World War).

25.3 Making of a Cold War

As bad as the War was, it turned out to be the easy part. Even before its end, it was recognised that the spoils of war would need to be divided up and a new order arranged. Regular conferences between the "Big Three" (the US, UK and Russia) were conducted between 1943 and 1945, in Tehran, Moscow, Yalta and Potsdam, the first one focusing on war strategy, but later ones turning more to discussions of post-war affairs as Allied victory became imminent (Hobsbawm, 1994, 42–45).

In fact none of the Allies really ever trusted one another despite their mutual wartime interdependence. After Germany and Japan were defeated, the Alliance thus began falling apart quickly. There were three elements to this. The first, typical of all post-wars, was the settling of scores between victors and vanquished, and the working out of national and regional interests and spheres of influence between the winners themselves. The second revolved around the exercise of hegemonic power in a post-war world system. The third revolved around ideological competition.

As contentious as the settling of scores and dividing spoils was, these actually can be seen as a rather straightforward, and even predictable, a sort of completion of the incomplete 1919 settlement, adjusted for the radically new facts on the ground. Stalin wanted to restore the bounds of the old Tsarist Empire in both the Pacific and Eastern Europe, and proceeded to do so. The fate of Germany was an area of tension, both between Russia and the West, and between Britain, France and the US, exactly as it had been after First World War, though under different circumstances. The competing British and French colonial interests in their newly restored Empires also now came back into play, abutting against Russian areas of interest, such as Iran.

The big difference now was that the global hegemonic power structure was completely altered and now explicitly ideological. The Europeans, and the British especially, had finally and decisively dealt themselves out of being global power brokers, although the initial post-war restoration of the imperial realms, and the pretence of England and France having veto power in the Security Council of the recently established United Nations, initially obscured that fact. The old order had been effectively unipolar,

Britain as the hegemon, with challengers from a variety of rising nations. That had precedent in prior times, such as Roman Empire dominance of Europe centuries before. Multipolarity, with multiple powers competing for dominance was also a known norm. The new "bipolar" geopolitical arrangement between the two "superpowers" of America and Russia, with ideological justifications on both sides, was an unprecedented situation.

What ended up happening was the establishment of a state of "Cold War" which transpired over a number of phases. Between roughly 1946–1949 when the pressing order of business was post-war political and economic reconstruction and stabilisation, the US and the Soviet Union were establishing the terms of their relationship in arenas (such as the occupation of Germany) that were theoretically built on the equality and cooperation of the two countries. This was the most fluid of times, though lines quickly hardened. From 1949 to 1953, China fell to the Communists and turned to Russia for assistance while the Soviets developed their own atomic weapon, leaving Stalin in a strong geopolitical positions and a free hand to set policy and direction for what was now called the "Eastern Bloc". In this period, the ideological division of the world was solidified. Between 1954 and 1965, there was a post-Stalin period in which the rules of nuclear competition between the US and Russia were effectively worked out, putting "hot" war between the two off the table while establishing the working parameters of a permanent "cold" war. China also split from the Soviet Union during this time, decisively fracturing the Communist world into competing blocs. These three periods will be the focus of the discussion below, the latter and final Cold War decades between 1965 and 1989/1991 being considered in Chapter 27.

In the first period, there was some possibility of a less hostile accommodation between Russia and the US, but for various reasons this was not to be. Both superpowers played a part in this, though there is heated debate about relative responsibilities. On the US side, President Harry Truman proclaimed the "Truman Doctrine" in 1947 that committed America to defend "free peoples" wherever they might be fighting for "liberty". Anti-Communism was now born as an official foreign policy of the American government. That this was a peculiarly American view can be contrasted with the lowered intensity of ideological competition in other Western allies, even those such as France and Britain and Italy on the supposed "front lines". France and Italy had strong Communist parties, accepted by the political mainstream, and thus generally also had more pragmatic approaches to the Soviets. Some groups, such as refugees from Soviet occupation zones, or defenders of the old orders (e.g. Royalists in Greece, or the Catholic Church more generally) were rabidly anti-Communist, but their attitudes did not spread to the whole of their respective societies. Nobody trusted Russia, but then that was nothing new. As one historian has put it: containment was everyone's policy, but anti-Communism mostly America's (Hobsbawm, 1994, 234–237).

On the Russian side was Stalin's machinations and heavy-handedness. Stalin's foreign policy could be mercurial, cynical and ham-fisted, often all at the same time. He did not automatically align with Communist movements overseas, unsuccessful in his attempt to prevent the Communist takeover of Yugoslavia by Tito, while remaining committed to Nationalist China until the very end; the Russian Embassy in the Nationalist capital of Nanking was the last to evacuate from there before Mao's forces took over (Hobsbawm, 1994, 168–169, 227).

Stalin wanted security in the form of controlled client states in Eastern Europe and buffers in other strategic areas, such as Iran. In Europe, Stalin employed the "People's Republic" model, invented in 1924 by Soviets for taking Mongolia into its orbit, a place that was not easily integrated into the Soviet realm and which had been used to Chinese domination. Stalin felt the same way about Eastern Europe, wanting it Communist and aligned to Russia, but not comfortable with it as directly part of the Soviet Empire. Additionally, he did not believe that every country there was ready for Socialism and it is conceivable that he might have accepted Communist dominated coalitions in some places instead of fully Stalinist regimes if geopolitics of the time had been less heated (Westad, 2017, 81, 88) (Fig. 25.2).

All this suggested that Stalin was a tough player who was best met with toughness in return. But it also suggested that in at least some instances, he was more a practitioner of Realpolitik rather than of Communist orthodoxy. In any case, he went to great lengths to ensure that developments in Soviet areas of strategic interest went his way. The brutal and bloody Soviet methods employed to ensure pliant governments in the Eastern bloc, especially Czechoslovakia and Hungary, were an example of this, alarming the Western powers in the process.

The greatest flash point between America and Russia during this time was, predictably, Germany. Stalin preferred a unified but neutralist, agrarian, demilitarised country, for obvious reasons. The French had similar views, for similarly obvious reasons. But the US and Britain had other ideas, the Americans especially. Germany was divided into four

Fig. 25.2 Churchill lowers the Curtain in Missouri (1946) (*Image source* Missouri State Archives. Collection Name: MS192 Gerald Massie Photograph Collection. Photographer/Studio: Massie, Gerald R. Description: British Statesman and former Prime Minister Winston Churchill delivers his Iron Curtain "Sinews of Peace" speech at Westminster College Date: 5 March 1946 Rights: Permission Granted Credit: Courtesy of Missouri State Archives. Image Number: MS192_047_111.Tif. Institution: Missouri State Archives. No Known Copyright Restrictions)

occupation zones, between Russia, France, England and the US, and Berlin was similarly divided. Western German occupation zones were supposed to pay some reparations to the Soviets in the East. But in May 1946, the US unilaterally suspended payments from their zone and three months later, the British did so from theirs. Accusations went back and forth about treaty obligations being reneged on, for the Soviets had violated some of their own commitments to send food from its occupation zone to the West. Britain and America than called a conference in London in February 1948 to which the Soviets were not invited and which the French only reluctantly joined. A new currency was issued for the Western occupation zones, forcing the Soviets to introduce a new currency of their own in their zone to avoid being flooded with the old notes (Westad, 2017, 108–111).

At this point, division of Germany was inevitable given the sharp disagreements between the victors, the West German state being unilaterally declared in 1949 and the East German state shortly thereafter. While unavoidable, actualisation of division merely deepened mistrust and hostility on both sides. Stalin's unsuccessful attempt to drive the other Allies out of divided Berlin through a blockade of the city between 1948–1949 worsened matters. After this, both Germany and Europe were split into hostile, competitive blocs, one dominated by America, the other by the Soviet Union. This situation continued for another forty years.

And then, of course, there was the atomic bomb. Before 1949, the US was the only country with the weapon. But in that year the Soviet Union successfully tested its own nuclear device, developed through a mix of native research and successful espionage to steal Western atomic secrets (Nelson, 2014, 236). This duopoly of nuclear armament, combined with the unfolding of a fierce Russian-American competition had the effect of internationalising the conflict and giving it an apocalyptic tone. The creation of two major "superpowers", with opposing ideologies and economic/political systems commanding the most destructive weapons yet devised, had divided Europe and now the two were busying marshalling allies, and containing enemies, across the world. Yet, this competition could result in massive destruction on both sides if not managed properly.

Nikita Khrushchev's son, Sergei, tried to make sense of this turn many years later noting that whereas once conflicts could be settled by armed clashes, echoing Karl von Clausewitz's dictum that war is a continuation of politics by other means, the invention of nuclear weapons created not a possibility of victory for one side or another, but only the reality that both sides would lose. However, neither side knew how to behave differently, and so behaved as they always had, just without going to war, at least not directly with one another. According to him, this new phase was war without war and hence was called "cold war" (quoted in Nelson, 2014, 190) (Fig. 25.3).

Fig. 25.3 Cold War division in Europe (*Image source* United States Central Intelligence Agency [1963] European Communist States. 3-63 [Washington] [Map] Retrieved from the Library of Congress, https://www.loc.gov/item/75694114/. Credit Line: Library of Congress, Geography and Map Division. No known copyright restrictions)

25.4 Economic Performance of Competing Models

Although there was an explicit delineation between economic systems, one being Capitalist, the other Socialist (the term used by the Communist bloc itself), there was a common reliance on industrialisation to increase material output. The relative levels of economic development were quite different between countries, whichever camp one was aligned with, but there was little doubt that moving from an agrarian to an industrial economy and then into services was the road to riches. Tables 25.1 and 25.2 show some basic statistics for the two blocs during this time.

These numbers illustrate a number of things. Most striking is the level of development and economic size of the US relative to the USSR and the rest of the world. Even in 1910, the US was already far more sophisticated and industrialised than the USSR was in 1928 and roughly comparable

Table 25.1 Structural change in the US and USSR in the first half of the century

	USSR		*USA*	
% of total labour force employed in:	*1928*	*1958*	*1910*	*1950*
Agriculture	71	40	32	12
Industry	18	38	41	45
Services	11	22	27	43

Source Kuznets (1966, Table 3.2,. pp. 106–107)

Table 25.2 Economic measures for the two superpowers, China, and India—1958 (US $ of factor costs)

Country	*GDP (billions $)*	*Population (millions)*	*Product per capita*	*National GDP as % of world GDP*
USA	406.5	174.9	2,324	33.8
USSR	144.8	206.8	700	12.0
China	55.0	657.0	84	4.6
India	28.9	414.3	70	2.4

Source Kuznets (1966, Table 7.1, pp. 360–361)

to what the latter had become by 1958, at least considering the sectoral distribution of the labour force in the two countries. But in 1958, the US economy produced roughly a third of the world's output, the Soviet Union being a far distant second at only 12%. The US continued to progress industrially and maintained this gap over Russia, though both grew in absolute terms. Thus, to call the two countries "superpowers" is somewhat misleading, since economically there really was no comparison.

However, the tables also show that the Soviet model of Socialism could successfully impose industrialism on a backward country and bring it into the twentieth century. There were immense social costs of the Stalinist model used to achieve this goal, in Russia itself a massive gulag system of forced labour and large-scale political repression. It was not a particularly efficient or humane system. But it did modernise the Russian economy and did so relatively quickly, its means being state central planning of resource allocation conducted in the absence of private property rights and the formal prohibition of markets, though sometimes with limited exceptions for small-scale production and exchange activities. This was accompanied by State social investment in education, health and general welfare, with universal guaranteed access to these along with an entitlement to employment, though with generally limited individual job choice (Gatrell, 2006).

The actual economic performance of this model was arguably not bad from the crude point of view of per capita GDP. Data for the Socialist countries is poor, and subject to political manipulation, but Besnik Pula (2015) has taken Maddison GDP estimates and compared Russian and Eastern Bloc GDP per capita figures between 1946 and 1969 with the Latin American countries. These two areas, he argues, both had later starts economically and generally followed State-centred economic planning, though Latin America was generally capitalistic, with some populist variants. He finds that the USSR caught up with Latin America by 1950 and gained significant distance over it by 1969. During the later years of this time, the USSR also exhibited impressive technological advancement in areas such as space exploration and rocketry, even pulling ahead of the US in some domains.

Pula also compares Eastern bloc growth with East Asia, which in modern times has been held up as an area that grew from underdevelopment to advanced status through capitalist modalities though with an active state as well. During the 1950s and 1960s, the region was overall quite poor, and growth was concentrated only in Japan, South Korea,

Hong Kong and Taiwan. Between 1946 and 1969, even the Asian growth outliers grew more slowly than the USSR and Eastern Europe, Japan being an exception.

25.5 A Development Model for the Developing World

Table 25.2 also indicates, though, that outside the Communist and Capitalist "cores", poverty reigned. China, the most populous Communist country accounted for less than 5% of total world output in 1958. India, the largest democracy and prime member of the Non-Aligned bloc accounted for roughly half that. A common link between these two countries was a heavy use of central planning.

The Soviet model, which more precisely during the first years of the Cold War was the Stalinist version of it, was attractive to the poor countries that made up the majority of the global population, then as now. In the Eastern bloc, this model was, of course, imposed directly by the Soviets, and in the areas and countries that were quite agrarian, the economic structural results were similar to those achieved in Russia, namely rapid urbanisation and industrialisation. In Bulgaria, around 25% lived in cities just after the end of the War, while 50% did so by 1965. Entire new urban centres of production were built, such as Nowa Huta in Poland, Dimitrovgrad in Bulgaria and Stalin City (Sztálinváros) in Hungary, each with big plants and factories in their centres, and large apartment blocks for workers and their families placed nearby. Social services of all sorts were integrated into the factories and provided free or at nominal charge (Westad, 2017, 188–189). As noted above, per capita GDP growth was respectable.

Outside Russia, newly Communist China initially also attempted to follow a Stalinist model of State-driven industrialisation and the direct provision of social services. However, China was far poorer than even the least developed parts of Eastern Europe, had a much bigger population, and had already been war-torn for a generation after Mao took power. Communist victory in China had also been quickly followed by a draining involvement in the Korean War of 1950–1953. Nonetheless, Communist China received substantial aid and advice from the Soviets, and Mao believed in and applied the Russian model for some time before becoming disenchanted with its slow pace. Mao also insisted on cultural modernisation as much, or more, than he did economic growth. That was a dimension that orthodox Marxism-Leninism thought secondary (Gabriel, 1998). For these and other reasons, the Chinese Communists split with the Soviet camp around 1960, a story that will be covered more in Chapter 27. But during the initial years of Stalinist economics, there was advance in industry, although Mao did not follow that path for too long before going his own way.

It was possible to choose only some, not all, items off the Socialist menu. In the post-war developing world, it was not so much Communism that was attractive as it was the Soviet central planning model for development which seemed more suited than market models (Westad, 2017, 156–157). There was much about Russia's own history before and after its revolution that was appealing to the non-European countries of the global south. Under the Tsars, Russia had remained primarily agricultural but even then its development was mostly State-driven. Economic reforms in Russia began in the late nineteenth century, with the building of the Trans-Siberian Railway across the country stimulating the growth of supporting and related industries; a move to the Gold Standard in 1897 creating more financial stability and attracting more overseas investment capital; and a push to move away from traditional commons-based agriculture (mainly through liberalisation of ownership laws and provision of incentives) improving agricultural productivity a bit (though with mixed results) and encouraging some movement to the cities resulting in increasing urbanisation (Gerschenkron, 1962).

While some of these reforms were designed to more closely align Russia with the capitalist order, even before Lenin Russia was acclimated to a long-standing authoritarian state apparatus that was highly interventionist and regulatory, and the primary agent for forcing progress in a country that was poor and economically backwards. Tsarism had been pushing for capitalistic development, with all its attendant inequality and social division. The Communist model aimed for economic and social modernisation without, in theory, these capitalistic negatives. And although the comparison is not historically fair, the Communists had actually delivered much more industry than the Tsars. Thus the Russian experience appeared to be applicable to some leaders in the developing world, especially its State-driven industrialisation and planning methods which could be detached from ideology.

India was an interesting example in this regard. In 1950, India had only just emerged from colonial rule several years earlier, with the new majority Muslim nation of Pakistan breaking away violently at the same time. India's forced integration into a London-dominated global trade and financial order had had many undesirable effects from an Indian perspective, but capitalism nonetheless showed an economic power that the newly independent nation wanted to harness in its own way and for its own benefit. In contrast to China, India launched itself as an independent political democracy, the largest in the world, choosing central planning for its macroeconomy (a National Planning Commission was set up in 1950), while still maintaining private property rights and markets. After partition, India retained most of the cotton, jute processing and industrial production capacity, while Pakistan retained a good share of the sources of raw materials. India thus had an industrial base to work with, but it was relatively small and undiversified, the loss of Pakistani resources a blow to productive capacity. Indian poverty, meanwhile, was of long-standing with relatively little improvement. The overall planning objectives were therefore designed to bring balanced economic development across various sectors, and improve the country's socioeconomic framework (Ramesh, 2017, 30).

India's first five-year plan successively sought to invest in agriculture, irrigation, transport, communication, social services, electrical power and, finally industry, while controlling imports through government licensing and targeted planning in selected industries. Like many newly independent countries of the time, India chose what was called an import-substitution path, i.e. developing the ability to manufacture items for its own use, hopefully building up a domestic industrial base that retained profits and skills in the country. The second five-year plan, commenced in 1956, built on this foundation to try to reduce income and wealth inequality via educational investment and improved employment allied with the development of basic and heavy industries. Initial growth was good but below the plan objective and overall it appeared that pockets of industry were grafted on to an essentially underdeveloped rural and small-scale handicraft economy. To correct this, the third five-year plan increased investment in heavy industry even further. The growth result was still below plan. However, the average economic growth rate over the course of the first fifteen years of India's planned economy exceeded the economic growth rate in the eight years after economic liberalisation policies were implemented in 1991 (Ramesh, 2017, 30–31).

25.6 American Hegemony in the Capitalist Bloc

In the self-defined Capitalist "Free World", America was in a commanding position to shape the Capitalist order to its preferred form after the end of the war. Charles Maier (1977) labels this program as "Productivist", in that it aimed to suppress political and economic conflict by evading resource distribution conflicts via policies devoted to increasing productivity and growth. Lichtheim (1972) calls this the American version of Liberalism that contained an unquestioned promulgation of economic growth as a consensus objective across all groups since, so the argument went, a bigger economic pie was always good because that left no one worse-off and everyone better off even if they just kept the share of the growth pie they always had before.

Like the British before them, the Americans saw that its own hegemony was best achieved by creating a global economic and financial system that was designed around American interests but with enough benefit to go around to get relatively willing buy-in from other countries. There are roughly three dimensions to this new world order building: (1) fiscal (referring to direct government spending and aid); (2) monetary (referring to global capital flows and finances); and (3) geopolitical (referring to competition with other nations). This section provides an overview of the first two, the geopolitical dimensions discussed later.

On the fiscal side, the US stood alone amongst its Western allies in being economically, militarily and politically stronger after the war than before it. This was a repeat of the post-World War 1 order, except the gap between America and Europe was now even wider and American isolationism, while still a domestic political force, was diminishing quickly in the face of the fiercely interventionist policy of Anti-Communism. Western Europe was on its back after the end of hostilities, its industrial production in 1946 only 60% of its pre-war levels, and still only 70% a year later. Its 1946/1947 food supply was only 80% of 1938 levels, with a population 10% greater (20 million more people) even after all the war deaths are accounted for. Britain had liquidated almost its entire overseas investment portfolio in order to finance imports during the war and the economic devastation on most of the Continent meant that Western European capacity to import English food and other goods was equal to only approximately 30% of its 1938 imports, England's trade position further hurt by a concomitant decline in terms of trade (DeLong & Eichengreen, 1991, 19).

European recovery from the Second World War came faster than after the First, however; despite the larger initial losses incurred, it took six years for per capita national income in Britain, France and Germany to reach pre-war levels after the end of the First World War but only four after Second World War hostilities ceased. Continuing localised conflicts after the first war were one big reason for this earlier lag, in addition to the relatively incoherent and inconsistent post-war international order that generated as much volatility as it did certainty (see Chapter 18). Part of the reason for the more rapid recovery after the second war stemmed from a relatively fast cementing of post-war boundaries, ironically achieved in part through the rigid division of Europe under the two superpowers. But it was also helped along by the substantial American aid to its European allies after the war, much of which was delivered through the Marshall Plan, officially known as the European Recovery Program (ERP) but informally having the moniker of its chief advocate and architect, US Secretary of State and Second World War General, George Marshall (DeLong & Eichengreen, 1991, 22, 27) (Fig. 25.4).

The US was already the major funder of most international relief efforts in the West, in 1945–1947 contributing $4 billion per year through multilateral agencies run through the new United Nations (UN). The Marshall Plan was of a similar annual magnitude but was a multiyear direct commitment of $US13.2 billion between 1948–1951, with $3.2 billion given to the UK, $2.7 billion to France, $1.5 billion to Italy and $1.4 billion to the Allied occupation zones of Germany. 60% of this aid in the first year was spent on primary products and intermediate inputs mostly related to food (DeLong & Eichengreen, 1991, 14).

Much was made at the time of the scale of the Marshall Plan. But the money spent amounted to 2.5% of the recipients' combined GDP, a significant but not enormous amount. As this money flowed through the European economies, there were significant additional multiplier effects for local economies. But even this multiplied increment was not as epic as the marketing implied. The longer-term economic and political significance came from the purposes to which the aid was directed and the terms attached to it. Aid had to be matched 1:1 by recipients who placed local currency in a fund to be used only for purposes approved by the US government. Britain used the bulk of its funds to retire public debt. France was pushed to balance its budget and its counterpart funds were not released until 1948 when steps were finally taken to raise domestic taxes. Nations undergoing inflation were similarly fiscally constrained by

Fig. 25.4 Marshall Plan aid in West German action (*Image source* U.S. International Development Cooperation Agency. Agency for International Development [1 October 1979–ca. 1998] [Most Recent], Department of State. International Cooperation Administration [30 May 1955–November 1961] [Predecessor], Foreign Operations Administration [1 August 1953–30 June 1955] [Predecessor], Economic Cooperation Administration [1948–30 December 1951] [Predecessor], Mutual Security Agency [1951–1 August 1953] [Predecessor]. Persistent URL: arcweb.archives.gov/arc/action/ExternalIdSearch?id=541691. Original Title/Caption: West Berlin, Germany. Marshall Plan aid to Germany totalled $1,390,600 and enabled that country to rise from the ashes of defeat, as symbolised by this worker in West Berlin. Even a year before the end of the Marshall Plan in 1951, Germany had surpassed her pre-war industrial production level, ca. 1948–ca. 1955. No known copyright restrictions)

aid conditions until they had offered a plan to address it. The US also restricted aid dollars used for nationalisation, putting pressure on the UK Labour government to scale back its own plans in this area. Also each recipient had to sign a bilateral pact with the US, to agree to balance budgets, restore internal financial stability, stabilise exchange rates at acceptable levels and put more free-market mechanisms into their mixed economies (DeLong & Eichengreen, 1991, 45–48).

Economically the Marshall Plan may have quickened the pace of Western European private investment and supported investment in public works (beyond post-war replacement of damaged and destroyed assets which had been done fairly quickly and extensively before the institution of the plan) while also helping to eliminate supply bottlenecks (DeLong & Eichengreen, 1991, 6). Aid was offered to Communist states as well, though given the strings attached, it was never at all likely that it would be taken up in the East since the conditions were incompatible with the fundamentals of Soviet economic and political aims. The American government was likely quite happy when Soviet Foreign Minister Molotov quit the initial aid talks. Although the Marshall program is sometimes presented as selfless, it was like any other policy in promoting enlightened self-interest of the donor, in this case the US. The main objectives were to contain Communism in the West by keeping local economies growing, and to reshape those economies along Productivist lines (Maier 1977, 624).

On the monetary front, the Bretton Woods system, named after the resort in New Hampshire where the initial conference establishing it was held, was another American directed effort to restore the global financial system in a more functional way, organised along American ideals and concepts. The three new institutions created as part of this program were the International Monetary Fund (IMF), a new global Lender of Last Resort (LOLR) which maintained and distributed an international pool of capital to provide to countries facing economic or financial crisis; a "World Bank" (formally named the International Bank for Reconstruction and Development) to lend to underdeveloped nations seeking to climb up into industrialisation and economic modernisation; and a system of fixed exchange rates by major economies, with a new Gold Standard based on the US dollar as a world reserve currency and the American government being a guarantor of the system's stability (Bordo, 1993).

Much more will be said about this post-war global financial system in Chapter 28. Suffice it to say here that these reforms were designed to correct the glaring deficiencies of international economic coordination during the Interwar period. They also were part of American-led effort to ensure that the US was the unrivalled hegemon of the Capitalist world and that its version of a domestic free-market economy would be the dominant one. This version ended up consisting in general (there were many national variations) of a market system dominated by large corporations and large labour unions that negotiated their respective wage and price demands to attain both stability and growth. Both labour and capital interests, in theory, had to pare back their first-best demands to reach this general optimum. In practice, capital was favoured over labour because capital was deemed the most essential ingredient of growth. Internationally, the dollar-based fixed exchange rate system with its IMF backstop would manage capital flows to avoid having "hot money" undermine domestic equilibrium. Domestic governments would play their part by adopting a new "Keynesian" function of smoothing the ups and downs of the business cycle through countercyclical central government spending. Leftist movements were allowed, but they could not be Communist and must always work within the implicit rules of the system. Where Communists ended up being participants in the electoral process (as in France and Italy), they would not be allowed into any positions of real power (Maier 1977).

Although there were many ideological and political elements here, as there always are, these were now subsumed under a "technical" framework. A good example of this was the creation of the Organization for European Economic Cooperation (OEEC), which was succeeded later by the Organization for Economic Cooperation and Development (OECD). This was a coordinating and policy research body, designed to share information and knowledge, but whose unstated agenda was to ensure the primacy of economics over politics, and to turn issues of political economy into questions of "optimal" policy "settings" to achieve output and efficiency (Maier 1977, 628).

25.7 Varieties of Capitalism

This new order represented the early stages of the "Washington Consensus" (described more in Chapter 29), which could be summed up as a program promoting an American version of neoclassical growth. In its Cold War context, it represented a moderate form of Market Capitalism counterpoised against a Command Socialism alternative (see

Chapter 23). This consensus emphasised maximum currency stability, free trade, anti-Communist and pro-business labour unions, and domestic policies favourable to capital formation and business enterprise. However, many Western countries, including Marshall Aid recipients, were not entirely happy with this simplified choice. Despite America's great advantage, its power was not unlimited and, as in the Communist bloc, there ended up being a number of different Capitalist models which were not explicitly command economies or particularly egalitarian, but which shaped their political economies in ways that diverged from the American model (Maier 1977).

This occurred even in West Germany and Japan, the countries that the US occupied for a number of years after Second World War and where the Productivist program could be implemented most directly. In the three Western occupation zones of Germany, the US was somewhat constrained by its Allies, but not much. Through prodding and pushing and incentivising and threat of force, trade union organisations were formed that ended up being politically moderate and focused on wage restraint. In Japan, American control was unchallenged as it was the sole occupier of the country (with a few very small token exceptions of non-American forces posted in very small geographical areas invited in mainly for show). The US occupied and directed Japan for seven years, much of it under the virtual vice-royalty of General Douglas MacArthur. Here too, the Communist left was marginalised, the non-Communist left restrained (Dower, 1999).

In both places, economic growth was paramount, reinforcing a political structure that set aside class conflict and replaced it with an enforced consensus of capital-intensive industrialisation along with, in these two examples, export-led dynamism. This showcased the success of the Productivist agenda, while geopolitically sidelining both nations, making them rich and fitting into the global economic order as efficient accumulators of capital, but not as centres of geopolitical or military power (Maier 1977, 629). Even under direct occupation, however, the unique characteristics of German and Japanese society filtered and shaped American interventions and led to capitalist societies different from that in the US, more dominated by closely held conglomerates that were heavily intertwined with financial institutions, and with State sectors more directly involved in coordinating business and labour interests. Local culture and norms were reshaped by US occupation and hegemony, but these could not be totally refashioned in an American image.

Meanwhile, both France and Italy had large and influential legal Communist parties that ran in elections. They were, however, kept from participating in government, largely at US behest, with the American Central Intelligence Agency going so far as to conduct covert operations in French and Italian elections to keep the Communists from gaining any balance of power. Although Social Democracy in America was fast fading from its brief day in the New Deal sun (see Chapter 18), the US government focused on building a Social-Democratic centre in Europe to contain and subvert the more active radical left that had to be contended with there. In so doing, the US had to accept greater degrees of local nationalisation of industry and State social support than it would have preferred. This was true even for its close ally Britain, in which the British Labour Party simultaneously served as a moderating "third force" between political extremes, while building a national welfare state and government control of key industries (Maier 1977, 626–627).

Some countries in both Western and Eastern Europe still had to deal with a peasantry that had to be safeguarded at an acceptable economic level while industrialisation sped up. Authoritarianism and the Stalinist development model in the East forced the peasantry into the industrial sector. But France and Italy still had significant agrarian sectors and a certain amount of backwardness, and State planning in both countries had been the most effective means of modernisation before the War and a tool both countries retained. This was a deviation from the American model but had to be tolerated, especially since it delivered growth, and was more suited to local politics. State planning offered the potential of better aligning economic growth with social priorities (e.g. housing), and the French in particular sought to do just this, with mixed results, though remaining firmly capitalist, and also distinguished from the strong central command non-Communist socialist model that India pursued. Such State planning was not socialism—workers had no say—but it was not Productivism either. A political issue that such governments had to contend with was that the planner could not hide behind the supposed impartiality of the market place, something that would create some problems when growth faltered in the 1970s (Lichtheim, 1972).

Overall, Washington's politics of productivity did reorient the Western economies in the post-war era in ways that they might not have, while national preferences and approaches remained. These differences grew as American predominance waned (Maier 1977, 632).

25.8 Major Geopolitical Elements of the Cold War

The third element of the Cold War, geopolitics, is the dimension that understandably gets the most attention, then and now. This had three major elements that evolved over time.

25.8.1 The "Balance of Terror" and "Mutually Assured Destruction" (MAD)

Even when America had a nuclear monopoly, atomic weaponry presented a strategic problem that was historically unprecedented. The pure destructive power of the first generation of nuclear weapons was not that much different from conventional weaponry, as shown by the savage bombing campaigns that the Allies visited upon Germany and Japan (and the earlier bombings delivered by the Axis on their enemies) (Nelson, 2014, 208). Nuclear weapons however delivered that destructive force much more intensely, immediately and cheaply in military terms (Schlosser, 2013, 75). Allied air raids on cities like Hamburg required sorties by hundreds of planes. But only one plane each was required to drop the bombs on Hiroshima and Nagasaki, with equally devastating results achieved in an instant. In addition, there was the terrifying new effect of radiation sickness, which, combined with an equally terrible effect of thermal burns from the extreme heat of atomic explosions, accounted for perhaps one-sixth of the deaths from the Japanese explosions (Schlosser, 2013, 54).

However, while nuclear weapons offered massive and cheap concentration of destructive force, this effect could not be modulated. Even with their initial nuclear monopoly, the American government felt hamstrung in using the new weapon to "contain" the Soviets, although some of this reluctance came from the fact that the Americans had very few working bombs in their early inventory at the time. Once this atomic monopoly was broken, and weapons could be produced more economically in bulk, one had to be content with the corresponding inability to modulate the defensive or offensive response of any country attacked with them. And although moral and ethical considerations are rarely central in the pursuit of war, the obvious carnage of a nuclear strike did give pause to leaders contemplating their use.

After the Soviets announced that they had developed an atomic bomb, Truman responded by saying that the US was developing an even stronger thermonuclear bomb, even though at the time the country had only a very rudimentary understanding of how such a weapon might work. Some scientists saw this as provocative, resulting in the locking in of an arms race, which is exactly what happened (Nelson, 2014, 236). Such a race was probably inevitable, as they always seemed to be in the industrialised military age (see Chapter 22). But now, there were two powers (soon to be joined by others) with weapons so destructive that any use of them would lead to widespread destruction for all sides and perhaps the extermination of the human race entirely. Traditional calculations of "victory" in war-craft were now obsolete.

It took a little while for military strategists to catch up with this fact. As it turned out, most of these either came from the scientific community of the new military-funded "think tanks", rather than the armed forces general staffs, at least in the US. What emerged were two interrelated doctrines. The first was that of "Mutually Assured Destruction" (appropriately abbreviated as MAD) which was pretty much as it sounded: if the US and the USSR engaged in a nuclear conflict, they would inevitably destroy each other and much of the rest of the world. This led, in the fevered minds of the theorists, to the "Balance of Terror", a term developed by Wohlstetter in a 1959 *Foreign Affairs* article, who argued that because of MAD, nuclear weapons actually served as a deterrent (a phrase used first by the economist Jacob Viner) to war, rather than a spur to it, so long as the two superpowers aimed to balance their forces enough so as to avoid getting a "first-strike capability" that would eliminate the other before it could get off its own weapons in response. This, the theorists argued, was why the Cold War was "Cold" rather than "Hot". There was also the hopeful possibility that the MAD would incentivise mutually agreed disarmament of at least some degree, since after a certain point, additional weapons added no additional strategic advantage (Nelson, 2014, 278, 291; Wohlstetter, 1959).

25.8.2 Proxy Wars, decolonisation and Non-alignment

Whether these cerebral-sounding doctrines amounted to military strategy in the more traditional sense of the word, or were just *ex post* rationalisations of a path that the superpowers found themselves trapped into can be debated. The threat of nuclear destruction, intentional or otherwise, remained ever-present, involving numerous near misses of various sorts. There were dozens of nuclear weapon accidents that by the sheerest of luck avoided being catastrophic in their own right, or misinterpreted as a hostile nuclear act requiring response in kind (Schlosser, 2013). There were also a number of tense superpower standoffs, the closest call being the Cuban Missile Crisis of 1962, where the US and USSR appeared at one point very close to direct combat. Very fortunately, the two countries never went to actual war with one another, nor did any of the other nuclear powers that came into existence during the Cold War period.

The superpower military power struggle was, instead, channelled into so-called "proxy wars" in which the two superpowers clashed with one another through smaller countries allied to one side against another. The Korean War (1950–1953) was the first major proxy war of the era, and one that came dangerously close to another use of American atomic bombs as a "defensive" measure, after their first use over Hiroshima and Nagasaki. President Truman explicitly ruled in, during a press conference on 30 November 1950, the possible use of nuclear weapons in the Korean conflict and General MacArthur had a plan that he called a "cinch", namely to create a belt of radioactive cobalt through nuclear explosions across the border of Manchuria, running from the Sea of Japan to the Yellow Sea, creating a band with an active radioactive life of decades, which MacArthur felt would form a barrier to Chinese invasion of Korea. MacArthur's replacement, General Matthew Ridgway, also requested nuclear weapons, though to be used much less grandiosely (Nelson, 2014, 244–245).

That these options were so seriously considered may be due in part to the Soviet's still fledgling nuclear program of the time, and its inability to mount either a first or counter-strike. But they did continue to be on the strategic table even after Soviet strike capability was assured.

After the Korean War, proxy wars continued, always with occasions of serious consideration given to the use of nuclear weapons, but with increasingly more reticence given the soon entrenched prospect of MAD. The Vietnam War was the most extensive of the proxy wars, in which the US, indirectly facing off against Russia and China, backed different sides of what was essentially a local civil war that got completely taken over by Cold War politics and ideology. The "domino theory" of the time held that the "loss" of Vietnam to the Communists would set off a cascade of other states being taken over by the Communist bloc (Appy, 2015). But more fundamentally, this war followed a familiar template of

Fig. 25.5 A proxy war that didn't go to plan (*Image source* US National Archives. ARC Identifier: 531,441. Location: Still Picture Records LICON, Special Media Archives Services Division [NWCS-S], National Archives at College Park, 8601 Adelphi Road, College Park, MD 20,740-6001 PHONE: 301-837-3530, FAX: 301-837-3621, EMAIL: stillpix@nara.gov. Production Date: 7 February 1965. NAIL Control Number: NWDNS-111-SC-613587. Local Identifier: NWDNS-111-SC-613587 Original Title: Secretary of Defense Robert S. McNamara's press conference, at the Pentagon, 7 February 1965 Creator: Department of Defense. Department of the Army. Office of the Chief Signal Officer [18 September 1947–28 February 1964] [Most Recent]. Use Restrictions: Unrestricted)

the era in which one side hoped to embarrass the other and pull back its international spheres of influence by backing a "client" that would hopefully prevail. What actually ended up happening was the superpowers would find that their actual power was much more limited than they had thought, and the events in distant places rarely went according to plan (Fig. 25.5).

The fighting of proxy wars became intimately bound up with the collapse of the European Empires in the 1950s and early 1960s. As Fig. 25.6 shows, in 1945 European colonialists controlled much of the

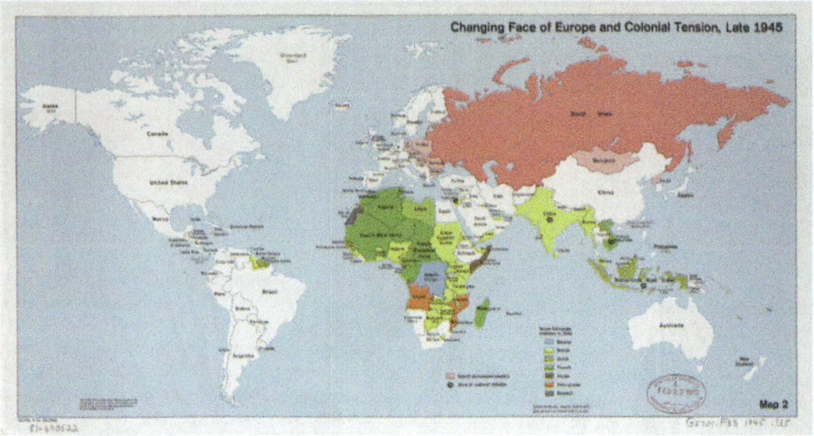

Fig. 25.6 European colonial empires circa 1945 (*Image source* United States Central Intelligence Agency [1945] Changing face of Europe and colonial tension, late. [Washington, DC: Central Intelligence Agency] [Map] Retrieved from the Library of Congress, https://www.loc.gov/item/81690522/. No known copyright restrictions)

developing world. By rights, this restoration should not have happened. The Asian colonies had had the experience of their European masters temporarily displaced by the Japanese in Asia, and while Japanese occupation was not the freedom hoped for, it did show that Asians could defeat Europeans. During the War, the French Empire in Asia and Africa passed on to the fragmented control of Vichy France, with Japanese seizure of some French Asian territories (though often leaving French administration in place), and the taking of some African colonies by the "Free French" under Charles de Gaulle as a base for operations to fight the Axis powers. This had weakened the entire French colonial enterprise considerably when the French Empire was restored after the war. Britain's African Empire had remained intact, but the Japanese temporarily displaced them in some of its Asian territories. After the war, both the British and the French emerged essentially bankrupt, unable to financially or militarily maintain their large overseas holdings, something that had become increasingly problematic before the war anyway due to rising tides of local nationalism and soon to become untenable. But Cold War tensions called for these Empires to be brought back to their previous breadths as a way of containing the Soviets, despite an officially avowed American anti-imperialism (see Chapter 20). In the struggle against the USSR, the US under Truman did not want to weaken its Western allies, and lay open new territories to Soviet influence. So the post-war strategic picture in 1945 was one of numerous colonial "flashpoints" in which local populaces resisted going back under the yoke of alien overlords (Fraser, 2013).

The tide, however, ended up being impossible to hold back and "decolonisation", the movement of former colonies to at least nominal independence in the 1950s and 1960s, was the result. As Fig. 24.7 shows, by 1968 most of the former colonies had broken free of European rule, with only the Spanish and the Portuguese holding major territories in Africa, and a smattering of other principalities held by Europeans across the world. By 1975, even many of these became free (Fraser, 2013).

What this process did was vastly increase the scope and scale of superpower interference and assistance in developing world affairs. Not all of this was negative. There was a large increase in foreign civilian and military aid from both superpowers, with some developing countries being fairly proficient in playing one side off the other for maximum local gain. But there was also plenty of overt and covert conflict, armed and otherwise, overthrowing of governments, and a general atmosphere of a strategic chessboard in which the tally board of Communist versus Capitalists satellites outside the respective dual cores was a constant competition whose shifting numbers alternately alarmed and reassured according to the side you were on (Fig. 25.7).

There was some pushback against this stark choice by the developing nations. Newly independent countries in Asia sponsored the Bandung Conference of 1955 with the aim of creating a space for Asian nationalism that could remain free of (white) superpower machinations. With all this in mind, China and Japan were invited, but the US, Soviet Union and European colonialists were excluded. A model of neutralism for decolonising nations outside Europe was set that soon expanded into the global vision of the Non-Aligned Movement (NAM) which included not just former colonies but countries such as Yugloslavia in which Josip Broz Tito was trying to forge a Socialist order not purely dictated by the Soviets or opposition to America (see Chapter 23). It was from this that the term "Third World" emerged denoting a collection of countries placing themselves outside of the bipolar alliances (Fraser, 2013, 473–474). However, the attempt to carve out independent space in a dualistic order could be a fraught exercise, the Indonesian experience being a cautionary tale (see Box 25.1).

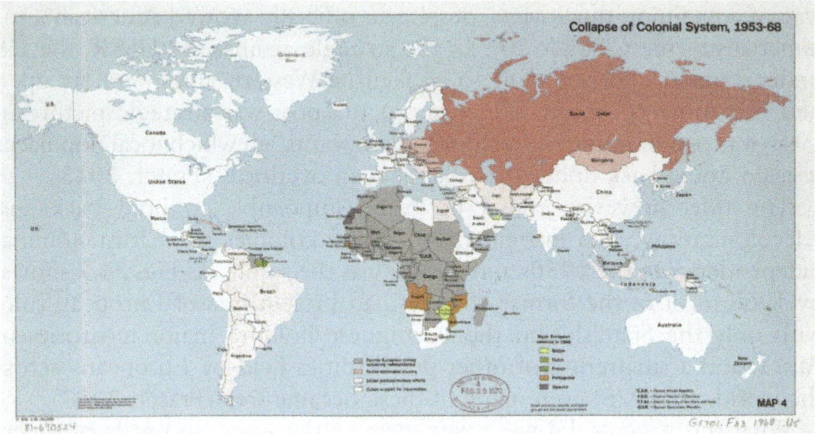

Fig. 25.7 Collapse of the colonial system between 1953–1968 (*Image source* United States Central Intelligence Agency [1978] Collapse of Colonial System, 68 [Washington, DC: Central Intelligence Agency] [Map] Retrieved from the Library of Congress, https://www.loc.gov/item/81690524/. No known copyright restrictions)

Box 25.1 Indonesia and the Cold War

During the Cold War, the decolonising emerging nations of the "Third World" were a crucial proxy battle ground in the competition between Capitalism and Socialism. Some of these countries ended up fairly firmly in one camp or the other. Some countries "switched" sides. Others stayed "neutral", sometimes explicitly within the Non-Aligned Movement, sometimes not. One country that moved across all three orbits was Indonesia

Indonesian nationalists fought for their independence from the Dutch after the end of World War II, with Sukarno being the leader delivering it. Sukarno had fought a civil war against the large and powerful Indonesian Communist Party (PKI) and had emerged victorious as the sole leader of the people, and a seeming friend of the United States, which pushed the Dutch towards granting Indonesia its freedom in 1949, thus allowing him to become the country's first president (Westad, 2017, 327)

If the Americans thought, however, that they had a firm ally, they were mistaken. As with many emerging country leaders, Sukarno was a nationalist above all else. Moreover, although he had defeated the PKI as a rival during the fight for independence, the party remained large and powerful and representative of a significant swathe of the Indonesian people, claiming 3 million members and 20 million non-member followers at its height in 1965, making it the third largest Communist Party in the world (Boden, 2008, 124–125). Sukarno could not ignore the Communists, but he did not have to bow to them either, since he had defeated them before. In any case towing a Communist line was not possible because of the counterbalancing power of the military forces and Islamic parties. Sukarno chose to use anti-colonialism as a way of uniting these diverse factions behind him (Boden, 2008, 113)

Immediately after independence, Indonesia had the moral support of the United States but relatively little material support, as Washington's attention was focused elsewhere in Asia, namely Korea, China and Indochina. Stalin was uninterested in the Third World generally and non-Socialist nations in particular, so gave no assistance to Indonesia. Sukarno thus turned his attention to the Non-Aligned Movement, playing against the two superpowers by hosting the Bandung conference in 1955 at which "Afro-Asian" countries gathered to develop a program to break free of post-colonialism. This independence irritated the Eisenhower administration, but it was appealing to the Soviet leadership after Stalin's death, especially Khrushchev who, after he consolidated control of the Premiership, saw the Third World as fertile ground for conversion to Socialism and who therefore appealed to the various non-Socialist but Non-Aligned States there (Westad, 2017, 327)

It was at this point that Indonesia became a major recipient of Soviet aid. Sukarno's doctrine was known as *Marhaenism*, combining Islamism, nationalism and Marxist socialism. This did not make it perfectly aligned with the Socialist camp but it did make it a promising candidate for Russian assistance and influence, especially after the US Central Intelligence Agency (CIA) chose to make Indonesia a target for destabilisation, though unsuccessfully at this time. Soviet aid between 1959 and 1965 (after Sukarno was deposed in a coup) amounted to 21% of the total amount provided by Moscow to all non-socialist developing countries, and one-third of all such aid devoted to Asia (Boden, 2008, 117)

Long-term loans at favourable interest rates were preferred over grants by the grantor, but, interestingly, there were few strings attached. This was mainly a strategic decision, longer-term potential rather than immediate shifts in Indonesian policy towards Socialism being the Soviet goal. Besides which, Sukarno had to take care in how he used this aid, since the Islamists and Army were wary of the Russians. Most of the aid did not go towards economic development projects but to a military build-up, a path disliked by the Soviets but tolerated nonetheless. Most of the specific projects funded were not completed in any case. But Sukarno did launch a "guided economy" (*ekonomi terpimpin*) program, which leaned towards socialist-style planning, a strengthened public sector and restrictions on foreign corporation investment, especially from the Netherlands. This "anti-Imperialism" was consistent with stated Soviet policy aims, but held Soviet engagement in Indonesia at arms-length. (Boden, 2008, 118–120, 124–125)

Then came a chaotic period, in which Sukarno was overthrown. This was a long process, initiated at first by left-wing Army officers but ultimately captured by the rightist Soeharto, who took power and then began a root-and-branch elimination of the PKI and many actual and imagined sympathisers. The army and associated militias slaughtered at least 500,000 alleged leftists and detained around a million more. After consolidating control, Soeharto turned the country decisively towards the United States, receiving substantial American aid and inviting in substantial foreign investment. A domestic economic restructuring commenced, guided by American educated technocrats known as the "Berkeley Mafia" after the alma mater that many of them obtained their degrees from. Poverty fell from 45% to 11% between 1970 and 1996, and life expectancy rose from 47 to 67 between 1966 and 1997. Infant mortality was cut by 60% and by 1983, primary school enrolment was 90%. But corruption was widespread as well, and the perpetrators of the anti-left massacres were never punished, many still exerting a great deal of power and influence (Lindsey, 2021)

Some have argued that Indonesia was a proving ground for a new stage of the American proxy Cold War, augmenting the usual covert action with a strong business-friendly post-coup program driven and guided by foreign corporate investors, a set of methods collectively referred to as the Jakarta method. One of the main advantages of such an approach was that it limited the official American involvement that the armed interventions used in Korea and Vietnam required, yet arguably achieved better results from a geopolitical point of view (Bevins 2020). This is probably a bit of an overstatement, since business-friendly proxy war by covert methods well preceded the Soeharto episode. But the use of technocratic elites to develop and help implement supposedly neutral but Western-friendly economic policies certainly was refined in Indonesia, and later used by General Pinochet in Chile after his US-backed coup against Allende in in 1973, with similarly impressive macroeconomic, and from the US point of view, geopolitical results

25.8.3 Propaganda and "Hearts and Minds"

Hobsbawm (1994) has called the "short" twentieth century the Age of Ideology, and the Cold War was certainly a pinnacle of opposing ideologies. Fluctuating direct and indirect large-power control over peripheral territory was nothing new. But now intellectual, emotional and psychological justification was seen as just as necessary as political, military and economy control.

During the Cold War, ideas of racial and cultural superiority, while still underneath the surface, were no longer acceptable justifications for domination and submission. Japan's temporary success in dislodging Western imperial rule had decisively shattered the illusion that such rule was impregnable, while the racialist genocide perpetrated by Nazi Germany made overt racism of any sort highly suspect at best, although it remained alive and well covertly. Thus, racial supremacy could no longer be a basis to be taken seriously as a justification for international divisions. Even domestic policies, as regarding *de facto* and *de jure* racial discrimination in the US, or apartheid in South Africa, were now seen as handicaps in the global ideological war, and these defects became talking points in the ideological competition between blocs (Fraser, 2013, 473).

Something had to replace these prior justifications, and innate economic and moral system performance became the favoured line of argument. In fact, both sides chose this metric as the proper one, though with somewhat different reasoning. Western modernisation theorists, such as W.W. Rostow, heartily embraced concepts such as "nation building" and it was not by accident that his very popular and highly influential 1960 book, *The stages of economic growth,* had the telling subtitle of, *A non-Communist Manifesto.* Rostow's theory was a sort of mirror image of standard Marxian historical progression, except here US capitalism represented the final stage of human economic evolution, with its supposedly widely distributed abundance and absence of class conflict, the very embodiment of Productivism (Appy, 2015, 99–100). Of course, such final stage triumphalism was already explicitly baked into "scientific" socialism. This ideological war waxed and waned, being very strong in the late 1940s through the late 1950s, then settling into a period of regularisation in the early 1960s to mid-1970s where it was felt that the two systems could coexist, though Capitalist and Communist advocates each would argue that their side would eventually modernise past the other.

25.9 The "National Security State" and "Big Science"

Large-scale institutionalised scientific endeavour, in partnership with government and large businesses, was a pattern that had emerged during the Second Industrial Revolution, especially in Germany. The First and Second World Wars had extended this paradigm in major militarised ways, setting the stage for a post-war economic model of "Big Science", "Military Industrial Complex" and "National Security State" (see Chapter 22). The "Atomic Age" took these facets and expanded and transformed them.

The Second World War task of making nuclear fission theory practicable, applying it to build an actual working nuclear weapon, and then developing, testing and manufacturing such a weapon was well beyond what business or academia could do working alone, or even in tandem, and certainly not within the very tight time frame required. The prospect of having the Axis powers develop an atomic bomb first was so terrifying, that the US engaged on a crash program to make it happen. The US Army Corps of Engineers was given the task of pulling scientists together under military direction, and the Manhattan Project was the result, named after the Manhattan Engineer District of the Corps where the project was headquartered, though most of the actual testing, building and developing would take place out in parts of the American West. The project would ultimately employ 130,000, pull in the some of the greatest physicists in the world and cost billions of dollars (Nelson, 2014, 149).

After the war's end, one might expect that this vast apparatus would be wound back. In fact, unlike what happened with conventional forces in the US, which were sharply demobilised within two years (though they did get partially built up again later), spending on atomic research, development of new weapons systems, and other related activities expanded exponentially. There were a number of reasons for this. Modern military technology of all sorts, and nuclear weapons in particular, had an expense and technical complexity that made them hard to reproduce quickly and made obsolescence, at least the perception of it, occur quickly. Thus, a 1980s jet fighter cost forty times the small aeroplanes of the 1940s, and there was a constant need for upgrading these newer craft (Overy, 2000, 232).

Additionally, a policy of "enough is never enough" took hold amongst policymakers. The new Atomic Energy Commission (AEC) in the US, nominally in charge of peaceful use of the atom, but actually an adjunct of the Department of Defence, created multiple laboratories and production facilities so that bombs and weapons could continue to be made and delivered even if some were destroyed in a nuclear first strike. Hanford Laboratory in Washington State had a twin in South Carolina, the Savannah River Plant, while Los Alamos was matched with Livermore, and Oak Ridge with a similar facility in Kentucky. This massive complex alone at one point consumed more than 11% of America's nickel and 34% of its stainless steel. By 1957, the AEC's total budget almost quadrupled between 1947 and 1957 (Nelson, 2014, 282). This apparatus, deeply intertwined with business and academia, constituted a hyper-charged military-industrial complex (see Chapter 22).

To this was added permanent State secrecy, binding on all parties and across any political, social, economic or other matter deemed "sensitive", with extraordinary penalties delivered for breaches. This alone was a significant departure from the assumed basis of liberal democracy, which was based on full political debate and fully informed consent by the public through their equally fully informed elected and delegated representatives, except in the case of (temporary) emergencies. What was even more extraordinary was that the national security apparatus itself was hived off from normal executive and legislative authority. In 1950, the US National Security Council (NSC), a post-war creation, drafted a top-secret document referred to as NSC-68. Declassified only in 1977, the document explicitly called on the government to use higher military spending to contain Communist expansion throughout the world. This became a justification for both permanently increased military spending and the running of covert operations by intelligence and other agencies, most of which was strictly classified (Nitzan & Bichler, 2006). This was not just an American practice. British Prime Minister Clement Atlee secretly funded the development of nuclear weapons for his country, all without informing Parliament (Lichtheim, 1972).

From the point of view of mere scale, "Big Science" had become bigger than ever. But it also had been changed in terms of the prior normal practice of open peer review and unrestricted publication and dissemination of knowledge through academic journals. This tradition had already been breached just before the war as some physicists self-censored publication of their nuclear fission results because of the fear that such disclosure would help the Nazis develop an atomic bomb. Hungarian-American physicist Leo Szilard, inventor of the idea of the nuclear chain reaction in 1933, in 1939 urged his fellow physicists working on fission not to publish their results. Many were shocked at the request, and some complied while others did not. The wartime nuclear war program institutionalised and regularised such secrecy (Nelson, 2014, 112).

25.10 A Paradigm of "Control" and the Cold War Paranoiac

The Cold War and the Atomic Age had broader social and cultural effects as well. From a sociogenesis and psychogenesis point of view, in many ways this era represented an apotheosis of the scientific paradigm into a near-religion. The secrets of the atom, one of the fundamental building blocks of creation (though quantum physicists would beg to differ), had now been opened by human intelligence and ingenuity.

Such prowess served as a visible reinforcement and at least partial restoration of the "Progress" doctrine that had prevailed throughout the nineteenth century and which had been so badly shattered by the First World War and Interwar periods. The carnage of two World Wars, the Holocaust and the intervening economic and political instability had further battered notions of inevitable forward-moving human evolution. But the reaching of unheard of levels of prosperity and the new and deeper marvels of science during the 1950s restored some hope in it, although only on a purely material basis.

Americans in particular emphasised the more optimistic ideas, leading the way in popularising and proclaiming faith in nuclear technology as ushering in a new and wonderful epoch. "Fat Man" and "Little Boy", the names of the bombs dropped on Japan, were now monikers for popular salt and pepper shakers shaped like bombs. X-ray machines became standard equipment in shoe stores, used to reveal the precise anatomy of a customer's foot and obtain the optimal shoe size to fit it. A popular 1947 toy was the *Lone Ranger Atomic Bomb Ring*, a plastic spinthariscope (that is, a radiation detector), made in the shape of an atom bomb, which held radioactive polonium used to spark the ring's screen to show the atomic reaction. The AEC chief, Lewis Strauss, predicted that nuclear power would deliver "electrical energy too cheap to meter" (Nelson, 2014, 230).

This positive attitude was shared on the other side of the Iron Curtain. The Soviets had Marxist-Leninist materialism as an official ideology and were profound believers in anything scientific. Their victory over the Nazis, the making of their own atomic weapon, their rapid rise to undreamed of world power, justified even more their faith in the social and economic progress that technology and rational organisation could deliver. Their own nuclear establishment, also mostly top-secret, boomed (Norris, 1992).

Yet this optimism was tempered by the reality that science had made it possible to destroy the world at any time with the touch of a button. War was now so apocalyptic and simultaneously so technical, that "control" of the system was imperative, a concept that had never been applied to a phenomenon that was inherently so fundamentally irrational. But it was strange sort of rationality. Nuclear systems analysts on both sides were busy trying to ensure that missiles could be delivered effectively and immediately as needed, chasing an elusive "first strike" capability and making war, if it occurred, more destructive than ever. At the same time, they were trying to eliminate the possibility of any technical mistake from occurring that would trigger an unintended Third World War. And these were both developed under the notion that a balance of "terror" was needed to keep the world from going MAD. The obvious contradictions of this enterprise, which seemed to immediately invalidate its rationality and control, indicating its insanity and incoherence instead, seemed obvious and yet unspoken by the planners and scientists themselves, at least publicly.

This quest for precision and control in a system that seemed liable to be out of control at any second, led to some truly bizarre juxtapositions. One example was the policy of US Defense Secretary Robert McNamara to develop a supposed ability to target and hit any individual facility or location in the Soviet Union. This capacity supposedly allowed modulation of nuclear war to attain the desired damage while also deterring a first strike by the other side because this refined capability would (it was said) still exist even if Soviet missiles had hit America in a first strike. The system backing this up was appropriately named the Nuclear Utilization Target Selection or "NUTS". McNamara was being intentionally ironic here, for as he later admitted, while each individual strategic decision during the Cold War seemed rational at the time, they were done in isolation and incrementally led to a huge arms race and arsenals that were far beyond making any strategic difference, military or otherwise (Nelson, 2014, 288–289). Yet, McNamara never admitted as much while in office. Nor did anyone else.

This state of affairs rather naturally led to societal and personal anxiety, along with its close companion, paranoia. Soviet Russia had long been wracked by this syndrome since its inception, Leninism positing a hostile capitalist world encircling the sole Socialist state, with Stalin adding new levels of insanity to Russia's internal power struggles (though paradoxically it was Stalin who developed the insular notion of "socialism in one country" to tamp down Trotsky's revolutionary internationalism). Solzhenitsyn (1974) quotes a trial record from one of Stalin's purge trials, in which all the defendants were charged with "wrecking" because they were engineers who had managed to sharply improve fuel efficiency in their operations, as stipulated in the preliminary official plan they were designed to carry out. But by tying up capital resources to achieve this, they were accused of depriving Soviet industry by such tying up and thus part of a wider capitalist conspiracy (379–380). Such examples are so numerous, that they are literally legion, a situation well captured by the former Communist, turned author, Arthur Koestler, in his 1940 novel, *Darkness at noon*.

Meanwhile in the US, domestic paranoia was already an accompaniment to the Bolshevik Revolution in 1917. Anarchists, Communitarians, Radicals, Anti-clericals, Republicans, even the odd Jacobin were part of general nineteenth century establishment fears (and countervailing underclass hope) of violent overthrow and turmoil. But with an actual revolutionary system in place in an actual country, this fear grew into existential terror. Under the supposedly progressive Woodrow Wilson administration, a ban was placed on the American Socialist party, a peaceful party that had run in many local elections, even winning a few of them. The pacifist Eugene V. Debs, the party's Presidential candidate for two election cycles and obtaining relatively good results, was thrown in prison, as were many other supposed left subversives, many under the newly minted Espionage Act of 1918. Wilson's Attorney General, A. Mitchell Palmer, conducted many raids and prosecutions whipping up what were called "Red Scares". That America had no threatening internal revolutionary movement to speak of (though it did have quite a few labour activists and unionists, including the International Workers of the World, a syndicalist union that was crushed for good during the War) did not matter (Skoll & Korstanje, 2013).

This was a situation that would repeat itself forty years later. In the US, an era of "McCarthyism" began, a new Red Scare named after one of its chief proponents, Senator Joseph McCarthy, a Republican from the state of Wisconsin. The hunt for Communists inside and outside government was a bipartisan effort however. President Truman, a Democrat, instituted loyalty oaths for Federal employees and banned the Communist Party of the US after the war, policies continued under Eisenhower. Although the Senate later censured McCarthy, ending his career (and prompting Eisenhower to quip that McCarthyism was now McCarthywasm (Manchester, 1973, 879)), the President had not stood against the Senator's legislative witch-hunts, and anti-Communism in the US continued, though not quite as virulently.

Ideology aside, the threat of nuclear annihilation naturally kept citizens on edge. This was encouraged, unintentionally or not, by many official agencies. The US Federal Civil Defense Administration set up model houses, inhabited by mannequin families, positioned in various rooms of the house, furnished with typical suburban furniture, including refrigerators stocked with food. These were placed at nuclear test sites, supposedly to see how an atomic blast would affect homes and the people who lived in them. But the main purpose of these tests, which were filmed, was to send the message that if you didn't prepare, you had only yourself to blame if taken out in a nuclear holocaust. The main way to avoid the fate of the mannequin families in their filmed mannequin homes was, it was said, to set up a proper underground shelter, stocked with supplies, and to be always vigilant as a sort of local cold warrior (Nelson, 2014, 283) (Fig. 25.8).

The longer-term impacts of all this were manifold. Militarisation of society, East and West, became normalised. Paranoia became entrenched in politics, especially in the US, which political scientist Douglas Hofstadter (1965) argued long had a "paranoid style" in its politics going back to its founding); and Russia, which even under the Tsars had operated some form of extensive political surveillance and secret police apparatus that gave lessons to its Communist successor. But the phenomenon solidified across many other societies.

Particularly concerning was the effect on liberal institutions upon which Liberal Democracy rested, such as political parties, universities, mainline churches, labour unions and civil society groups more generally. These are generally conservative, in that they seek to uphold the established order. But they also hold and contain dissent into manageable channels and are at least notionally committed to upholding "neutral" values such as the right to have and freely express one's opinion within "acceptable" and "safe" ranges. Anti-Communism in America perniciously weakened these institutions in the sense that most of them stood by while various conventions of the rule of law, due process and norms of civil exchange were damaged (Hedges, 2011).

Fig. 25.8 Comic book nightmares of the nuclear apocalypse (*Image source* Ace Comics 1952. Copyright expired and not renewed)

The irony of all this was that the fight against Communism in the West fundamentally helped to undermine the old doctrines of laissez-faire government, maximal personal liberty, freedom of expression and ideas and democratic consensus-making that underlie Liberalism. The scientific-technical apparatus behind the making, maintenance and expansion of a nuclear arsenal helped to accelerate the scale and scope of production and distribution throughout the economy, increasing the links between State and private industry. These developments had helped further weaken what was already something of a fantasy of a purely competitive market with sharp delineations between public and private enterprise. Meanwhile, the security apparatus had promoted a culture of secrecy and Anti-Communism had narrowed the right of dissent. The later collapse of the Socialist bloc made it appear that the Capitalist system had triumphed. But its underlying political economy had already been transformed radically from its Industrial Revolution origins, something that would become clearer after the end of ideological competition.

References

Appy, C. G. (2015). *American reckoning: The Vietnam War and our national identity*. Penguin Books.

Barraclough, G. (1967). *An introduction to contemporary history*. Pelican.

Berg, A. S. (2013). *Wilson*. G.P. Putnam's Sons.

Boarini, R., & d'Ercole, M. M. (2013). Going beyond GDP: An OECD perspective. *Fiscal Studies, 34*(3), 289–314.

Boden, R. (2008). Cold war economics: Soviet aid to Indonesia. *Journal of Cold War Studies, 10*(3), 110–128.

Buchanan, T. (2002). Anti-fascism and democracy in the 1930s. *European History Quarterly, 32*(1), 39–57.

Davies, N. (2006). *No simple victory: World War II in Europe 1939–1945*. Penguin Books.

DeLong, B., & Eichengreen, B. (1991). *The Marshall Plan: History's most successful structural adjustment program*. Centre for Economic and Policy Research (CEPR) Discussion Paper Series 634.

Dower, J. (1999). *Embracing defeat: Japan in the aftermath of World War II*. Penguin.

Fraser, C. (2013). Decolonization and the Cold War. In R. H. Immerman, & P. Goedde (Eds.),*The Oxford handbook of the Cold War*. Oxford University Press.

Gabriel, S. (1998). Economy of Great Leap Forward. *China Essay Series Mount Holyoke College*.

Gatrell, P. (2006). Chapter 14: economic and demographic change: Russia's age of economic extremes. In Suny, R.G. (Ed.), *The Cambridge history of Russia, volume 3: The twentieth century*. Cambridge University Press.

Gerschenkron, A. (1962). *Economic backwardness in historical perspective: A book of essays*. Belknap Press of Harvard University Press.
Hedges, C. (2011). *Death of the liberal class*. Vintage Books Canada.
Hobsbawm, E. J. (1994). *Age of extremes: The short twentieth century*. Michael Joseph.
Hofstadter, R. (1965). *The paranoid style in American politics: And other essays*. Knopf.
Kochan, L. (1970). *Russia in revolution*. Paladin.
Kuznets, S. (1966). *Modern economic growth: Rate, structure and spread*. Yale University Press.
Lichtheim, G. (1972). *Europe in the twentieth century*. Praeger Publishers.
Lindsey, T. (2021, August 21). Soeharto: The giant of modern Indonesia who left a legacy of violence and corruption. *The Conversation*. https://theconversation.com/soeharto-the-giant-of-modern-indonesia-who-left-a-legacy-of-violence-and-corruption-164411
Maier, C. S. (1977). The politics of productivity: Foundations of American international economic policy after World War II. *International Organization, 31*(4), 607–663.
Manchester, W. (1973). *The glory and the dream: A narrative history of America, 1932–1972*. Little Brown and Company.
Nelson, C. (2014). *The age of radiance: The epic rise and dramatic fall of the atomic era*. Scribner.
Nitzan, J., & Bichler, S. (2006). *Cheap wars* (MPRA Paper 5549). University Library of Munich, Germany.
Norris, R. S. (1992). The Soviet nuclear archipelago. *Arms Control Today, 22*(1), 24–31.
Overy, R. (2000). Chapter 8: Warfare in Europe since 1918. In T. C. Blanning (Ed.), *The Oxford history of modern Europe* (pp. 214–233). Oxford University Press.
Pula, B. (2015). Postwar economic growth under central planning. *Global Field* (blog). https://globalfield.wordpress.com/2015/03/30/postwar-economic-growth-under-central-planning/
Ramesh, S. (2017). An economic history of India. In S. Ramesh (Ed.), *China's Lessons for India: Volume I: The Political Economy of development* (pp. 23–54). Palgrave Macmillan.
Schlosser, E. (2013). *Command and control: Nuclear weapons, the Damascus accident, and the illusion of safety*. Penguin Press.
Skoll, G. R., & Korstanje, M. E. (2013). Constructing an American fear culture from red scares to terrorism. *International Journal of Human Rights and Constitutional Studies, 1*(4), 341–364.
Solzhenitsyn, A. I. (1974). *The gulag archipelago, 1918–1956: An experiment in literary investigation*. Harper and Row.

Strachan, H. (2003). *The First World War*. Penguin.
Suny, R. G. (1997). Stalin and his Stalinism: Power and authority in the Soviet Union, 1930–53. In I. Kershaw & M. Lewin (Eds.), *Stalinism and Nazism: Dictatorships in comparison* (pp. 16–24). Cambridge University Press.
Tooze, A. (2014). *The deluge: the Great War, America, and the remaking of the global order, 1916–1931*. Penguin books.
Westad, O. A. (2017). *The Cold War: A world history*. Penguin Random House UK.
Winn, J. A. (2008). *The poetry of war*. Cambridge University Press.
Wohlstetter, A. (1959). The delicate balance of terror. *Foreign Affairs, 37*(2), 211–234.

CHAPTER 26

Time and "Progress"

C. Gordon, *Many Possible Worlds*,
https://doi.org/10.1007/978-981-19-9281-0_26

Fig. 26.1 The twists and turns of time (*Image source* Bernard Spragg. Passing Time 2010 [Placed by photographer in Public Domain] Anton Parsons Passing Time sculpture, Christchurch, NZ, University of Canterbury campus. Taken on June 9, 2011 Photographer note: Passing Time is by Auckland-based sculptor Anton Parsons, a graduate of the University of Canterbury's School of Fine Arts. The work consists of a twisting ribbon of randomly linked boxes—with each box depicting one of the years between 1906 [founding of CPIT] and 2010 [the date of the sculpture's installation]. The work can be walked around, walked through, touched and sat on. "The winding form of the sculpture—placed on a street within the original 1851 grid plan commissioned by the Canterbury Association for their new settlement—is also a nod to the winding Avon River, an irregular feature of the landscape over which a street grid was placed," says Anton Parsons)

26.1 The "End" of History?

Just after the end of the Cold War, there was much discourse about what the whole episode meant. The obvious conclusion, given the rhetoric and ideology on both sides, was that a great ideological contest had been decided. Capitalism had won. Socialism had lost (Fig. 26.1).

Whether things were really this cut-and-dried, certainly there was a reason for Liberal Capitalist democracies to crow. But like the aftermath of most wars, the brief euphoria of victory doesn't last. There was the complex matter of what the post-war order would look like, considered in the following chapter. But there was also the need to determine the meaning of it all. Marx, it turned out, had been wrong about the ultimate inevitability of Communism. But could one thus conclude that the pinnacle was instead "Really Existing Capitalism" (to paraphrase how the Socialists had referred to their own actual systems) forevermore? Or would the tides of history, sooner or later, move humanity on to something else? And what might that be? Whatever happened, was this part of forward-moving historical trajectory, as both Capitalists and Socialists had maintained, or something else entirely?

In mid-1989, six months before the fall of the Berlin Wall, the political scientist Francis Fukuyama, wrote an article called *The end of history?* He followed this up with a 1992 book entitled *The end of history and the last man*. The article and book interpreted the end of the Cold War not just in terms of a literal end of one political-economic realm, i.e. the USSR and the Eastern Bloc, leaving the other one, i.e. the US and Western Europe, standing alone. They also framed the event much more broadly as an ideological triumph of Capitalism and liberal democracy over state socialism and dictatorship.

This was an obvious interpretation of events that had been made by many others. The 1989 article nonetheless got a lot of attention because of its seeming prescience. Although Gorbachev had been attempting to liberalise the Soviet economy and polity for several years and had publicly announced that his country would no longer intervene in Eastern Europe, Fukuyama nonetheless had published his bold prediction a few months before the fall of the Berlin Wall, a development that had been wholly unanticipated. It seemed that Fukuyama was on to something.

However, Fukuyama also got attention for another claim he went on to make, in both the article and more extensively in his book, that the end of the Cold War also meant the end of "progress" itself. There was, he claimed, no need to further refine or develop the underlying principles and institutions of Capitalism and Liberal democracy because these had prevailed and in so going had settled all of the really big questions of historical process.

This was a statement that went beyond mere triumphalism, of which there was plenty at the time. Instead, Fukuyama argued that Capitalism, because of its basis in modern science and markets, had established an ever-expanding horizon of economic possibilities that could not be improved upon. The Soviet system had tried and failed and so had all other comers. Meanwhile, just as Capitalism could meet all of humanity's material needs, liberal democracy had prevailed in meeting its immaterial needs. True, there is Capitalism without, or at least very limited, democracy, Singapore being a prime example. But Capitalist democracy has prevailed because only it allows people to compete for and gain social recognition in a genuine and meaningful way while also delivering maximum material prosperity. Hierarchical systems, even successful capitalist ones, cannot truly do both.

With Capitalism providing maximal material gain and Liberal democracy providing maximal individual social recognition, no alternative political-economic arrangement of human social institutions can be come up with that is superior and hence further progressive change in this particular sense is impossible. Fukuyama concludes thus that (1) liberal democracy and capitalism are the highest forms of human evolution and that (2) the end of the Cold War therefore represents an achievement of this end. It is this teleological fulfilment that the "end of history" refers to. Fukuyama was at pains to point out that historical events will continue to happen. But they will no longer be steps along a road running towards destiny since destiny has already been fulfilled.

There is, however, a strangely unsettled coda added to this. Drawing from the philosophy of Nietzsche, Fukuyama argues that a settled and comfortable age presents a challenge to the individual. If one simply sinks into the benign and final order of capitalist democracy, one is forced to become the "Last Man" who gives up pride in favour of a comfortable self-preservation within the broader collective. This, Fukuyama says, is what will provide a challenge to the final order. People will attempt to assert their individuality in novel and often destructive ways in order to become "First Men" rather than the comfortable faceless last ones of utopia. Fukuyama maintains his view that what should triumph has triumphed. But he then proposes that human individuality may not stay as settled as the social-political-economic order and could potentially sow the seeds of its unravelling.

Fukuyama's thesis has both adherents and detractors. His entire thesis, that Capitalism and liberal democracy were true apotheoses in human evolution, is inherently unprovable, however plausible it might seem to some. Others noted that there were many other unsettled collectives still to fight over, such as Samuel Huntington's idea (1993) that post-Cold War nations would move from struggles over ideology to fights over "civilisation", especially religion (see Chapter 11). Huntington's work is also simplistic and debatable, but represents one of a number of challenges to the historical reductionism that Fukuyama can be accused of resorting to.

26.2 Is There Progress in Time?

One challenge is to the entire idea of "progress" itself, which implies a direction to history and time that is contestable. Fukuyama is expressing belief in an Enlightenment idea that society is in the process of an upward march, an inherently good thing (Mokyr et al., 2015, 40–41). This sort of thinking about directional teleological temporal process is, in fact, deeply rooted in Western thinking. It was the Ancient Greeks, through the philosophy of Aristotle, that posited teleology in all processes, i.e. an evolution of everything towards its "natural" end, a construct that imposes an implicit forward and linear progress within history towards some ultimate (and desirable) destination (Clayton, 2005). Judaeo-Christianity is also built around history as movement across a line towards fulfilment, in this case of a divine aim. The mediaeval Catholic Church further integrated Greek teleology into its theology through its re-discovery of Classical authors.

Forward-moving time, while a widely held belief in the Western world, is not so widely held to in many non-Western societies. Philosophical and religious traditions in China and India have traditionally worked with cyclical time, the wheel of history turning over again and again. To be sure, these cycles might be impossibly long in human terms. In Hinduism, a "Kalpa" indicates a cycle that lasts billions of years in which the universe is born, destroyed and then reborn, in a series of cycles that span eternity (Needham, 1965). But a repetitive cycle, even a very long one, is by definition antithetical to "progress." Even within the Western canon, the ancient Greeks, teleological though they could be, did not really hold to linear time, also believing in cycles. This is why Plato's *Republic* ([ca. 375BCE] 2004) laid out institutions and practices to "freeze" political progress in place under "philosopher-kings" before the inevitable forces of decay set in to break it all down as a set up for the cycle in human political systems to start all over again.

Such temporal nonlinearity had been banished rather completely in the European mainstream by the nineteenth century, in which "Progress" could be said to have become an "official" quasi-ideology across much of the society and most of its elites. Technological and economic developments seemed to prove its existence, as output grew, diseases were cured, and innovations and inventions abounded. Social and political developments were not quite so rosy, but even here Liberalism and Capitalism were making steady inroads within Europe. Even the autocracies utilised some democratic forms and implemented reforms for economic modernisation. Utopianism, whether expressed by Socialists, Communists or Republicans, was a natural outgrowth of the Enlightenment which held that human spiritual, cultural and intellectual evolution was heading towards a rational and uplifted Man. Darwin, subtly misread by his interpreters (for his adaptation did not have a direction other than survival of a particular species over a particular time under particular conditions), was a framework that could hold all these conflicting views together as it was interpreted to suggest that natural processes would have the "best" solution win out, even though getting there might involve much pain and suffering for individuals, groups and even societies.

Yet projections into the far future, especially linear extrapolations no less, really can never be justified on evidence or logic alone because the far future is inherently unknowable and unpredictable in a fundamental sense. Most of the pronouncements about the future made by establishment figures at the height of the Second Industrial Revolution were projections that went far beyond available data or logic while also being selective even about conditions in the present. Socialist and Communist critics were arguably making similar overstatements in their dire claims about the current order, while being too optimistic in their expectations for their own preferred scenarios.

The First World War blew apart Western confidence in "Progress" for a generation at least, with many swinging towards a deep teleological pessimism or hedonistic nihilism. Oswald Spengler's, *Decline of the West*, published in 1918, was a massive and influential work that followed off of some of Nietzsche's observations but much more systematically and historically, making the claim that the West had passed its prime and was now in inevitable regression. It found very receptive audiences.

The Second World War, in a strange way, began to put Western confidence back together again. A fateful challenge had been met and bested. The Cold War competition was an anxious time but also prosperous and technologically sophisticated. When the Cold War ended it seemed that, indeed, the West truly had prevailed against all comers. Fukuyama's thesis said as much. Yet, interestingly, Fukuyama also brought in a slice of Nietzschean pessimism, positing an emotional component of the human being that resists order, even a good one. This particular aspect of Fukuyama's thought was, however, largely lost in the brief euphoria of the 1990s.

26.3 Is There Time in Progress?

Interestingly, the findings of twentieth and twenty-first century physics are ambiguous about time's motion. Einstein's theory of relativity found that time is inseparable from the space it occupies, rather than an independent and immutable separate dimension sitting apart from existence. This opened the door for direct investigation of time through the study of physical space as captured by Einstein's mathematical equations. Gödel's solution of them suggested that time might be in fact be cyclical, with a "strong" version suggesting that a particular event occurring somewhere in the universe has already occurred infinitely many times, and will be occurring in the future infinitely many times. The "weak" version suggests that the same event never gets repeated but that there is nonetheless an infinite sequence of oscillations of the universe in which a contraction phase leads to an expansion phase that in turn initiates another contraction phase, and so on to infinity. This debate is captured under the label of "eternal return" and is not yet definitively settled (Heller, 2002) (Fig. 26.2).

Relativity and its subsequent iterations eliminated the very notion of time as an objective fact. Einstein's relativity theory and the various empirical tests that proved its validity showed that, unlike Newton's schema of eternal time independent of the rest of the universe, time itself was actually born with the universe in an hypothesised "Big Bang". In fact, time is just the fourth dimension of "spacetime" (the other three being the conventional dimensions of space) and that a movement through space is also a movement through time. The "relativity" that Einstein introduced was just this inseparability, with any decomposition of spacetime into space and time depending on the motion of the observer making the distinction. Only spacetime itself is invariant (Hawking, 1988). In a cosmic sense, history as measured by time is also dependent on the state of motion of a given observer. Since everyone is actually in a different state, even if infinitesimally so, everyone literally has a different history to report and experience. Therefore, if there is the passage of time in "progress", the meaning and experience of it is a very human construct.

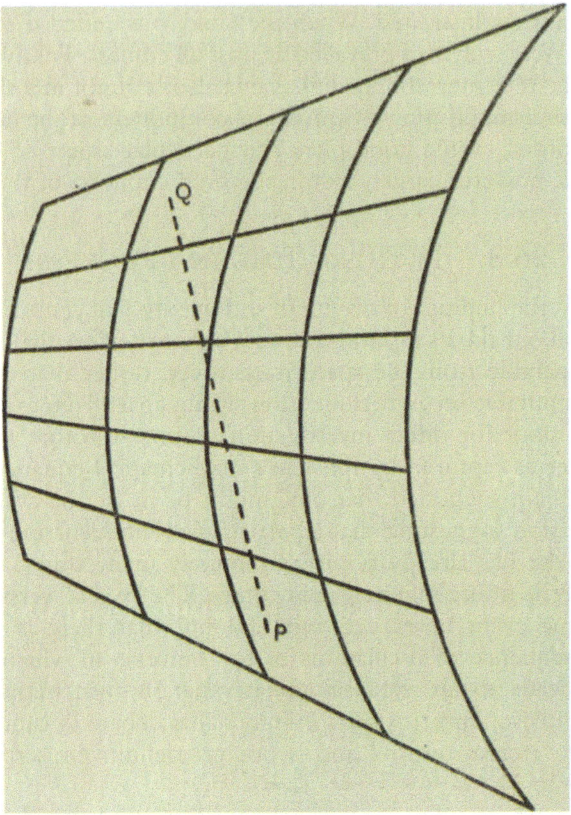

Fig. 26.2 "Spacetime" (*Image source* Eddington, A.S. (1920). *Space, time and gravitation: an outline of the general relativity theory*. Cambridge University Press. P. 100, Fig. 14. Contributing Library: PIMS - University of Toronto. Digitizing Sponsor: University of Ottawa. No known copyright restrictions. Original caption: A contrast between the old "linear" time of Newtonian mechanics and the curved "spacetime" of relativity)

26.4 The Industrialisation of Time

The measurement and division of time into units is one such construct that is very long-standing. The twenty-four-hour day is believed to go back to the Sumerians, with some speculating that the number of hours was drawn from the fact that, excluding thumbs, there are 24 segments on the eight remaining fingers on the human hand. The Babylonians refined this system and added the 60-minute hour. The Greeks came up with more precise divisions of hours, minutes and seconds, with the word "hour" having Greek origins, and the Greeks and others devised yearly calendars with months based on lunar cycles (Audoin, 2001).

Having more precise measures of time did not, however, mean that most people adhered to, or were even touched much by them. In Europe, Davies (1996) has claimed that the rise of the great mediaeval church institutions, especially the monasteries, began to transform daily time-keeping habits, slowly moving them from varying durations of sunrise and sunset to a more fixed daily routine of equalised hours, based on the regimens of the monks, and slowly becoming secularised. Urbanisation advanced this practice as more and more people moved into urban, rather than pastoral activities. The Scientific Revolution then provided an intellectual basis for this shift, with Newtonian physics positing its "objective" (and empty) time and space within which action took place and physical forces unfolded against one another. The whole universe was one great "celestial clock" in this model.

The social historian E. P. Thompson (1967) argues that industrialisation advanced this process even further as the increasing standardisation of factory discipline and expanding exposure to it on a growing factory labour force caused people to move away from task orientation (Thompson's term) towards clock time orientation. In pre-industrial eras, temporal duration of tasks could vary widely, was punctuated by significant idle time, with work intensity driven and affected by natural cycles (e.g. harvest time or daylight versus night time hours). As people moved away from agriculture to supervised work in factories, tasks were transformed into divisions of labour, their performance now kept to clock time and a regimentation soon internalised, making its way into general consciousness. Industrialisation, he argues, led people to live a "time-oriented" life driven by the clock and the newly monetised value of time.

Thompson's work has been criticised as being over-generalised. Not everyone during industrialisation was subject to the rigours of the factory or other regimented work, and natural and biophysical rhythms were not totally obliterated by them. But it seems clear that the measurement and experience of time did become increasingly standardised for most of the population, as was most everything else during industrialisation. The diffusion of affordable personal timekeepers and public clocks was the first of a series of technologies that altered behaviour and conceptions of time, extending into radio, television and computers and the Internet (Ogle, 2019, 317).

The distinction between time and temporality thus assumed a new importance, the former referring to the division into units as measured formally by clocks and calendars, or more organically by the passage of sun and moon, the latter as a form of experience by historical actors (Ogle, 2019, 315). In the study of history, the subjective is as important as the objective, with economic change affecting both in an interactive way. Time increasingly became synonymous with money, literally and figuratively.

As industrialisation deepened and intensified, so too did the regimentation of time. In the early twentieth century, the stopwatch driven time-and-motion studies of "Scientific Management" commodified time as an input into production. This was an approach that broke production worker tasks into micro-units, mechanically timing each one of them, then seeking to minimise task time and maximise output by reconfiguring labour processes using the data collected. Workers were driven sometimes to excess through the use of penalties and incentives. With the rise of mass production, and especially assembly lines and other "Fordist" mechanisms, "throughput" became a prime metric of the efficiency of industrial production, with speed being an essential ingredient (Braverman, 1974). This approach was taken to an even greater illogical extreme in Stalin's Russia through the so-called Stakhanovite movement in which workers were exhorted to match the achievements of a few ultra-productive "superworkers" (Shlapentokh, 1988). Outside the workplace, standard time zones were an industrial invention, imposed by the railways to make their operations easier and more coherent (see Chapter 8).

This progression (or possibly regression) was satirised by Charlie Chaplin's 1936 film, *Modern Times,* which depicts the absurd rigours to the factory floor that includes a comically unsuccessful trial of a feeding machine that would enable the worker to forego meal breaks during his working day. This is contrasted with the much more fluid and relaxed time of Chaplin in his "tramp" incarnation, though the price for such freedom is being broke (and in the movie the tramp is also accidentally and unjustly accused of radicalism as well) (Box 26.1).

Box 26.1 The changing ways of spending time

For the ordinary person in ordinary life, time is bounded by the day and the hours, minutes and seconds within it. As already noted, economic change has affected the way that time has been experienced, planned for, and measured. How has the use of time at the personal level changed?

Humans are certainly limited by natural constraints since there are 24 hours in a day, 8 of which are generally required for sleeping, on average. Considering that there are 168 hours in a week, and 56 are slept away, there are 112 hours to "play with" (or work with). The data that are available, which are based on "time budgets" derived from survey data or inferred from other information, indicate that 70 of those 112 waking hours were spent working in 1870, in the rich countries, which was the height of the Second Industrial Revolution in those places.

Fast-forward to 2000, and the average workweek is around 40 hours. This represents a drop of 30 hours of weekly working over 150 years, at least as far as paid employment is concerned. The decline was slow but relatively steady. It was also accompanied by an increase in days off, with workweeks contracting from a typical 6 down to 5. There has also been an increase in holidays and vacation days.

These are all average trends and even here one can see a considerable range across countries, the Americans working the most, the French amongst the least, both on a daily basis and across the year. There are also gender differences, women still averaging fewer paid hours than men, but having more hours of unpaid work doing family and household chores. There are other differences across the socioeconomic spectrum. But in general people in industrialised countries have had more time "free", during their days, their weeks, and their months, amounting to 4 hours daily, roughly equal to the time that used to be spent working in 1870. What they have done with this daily time in particular is, generally, to look at screens more. Shopping also is now a leisure activity rather than just a task undertaken to secure necessities.

Does this mean that people are now more "relaxed"? This is a more subjective question but most people would probably say no. The rise of work insecurity and social instability has increased anxiety. More fundamentally people could be said to be using their "spare" time for consumption activities, whether taking in a "virtual" product in the form of "binge-watching" streaming media (for example), or going online shopping to secure various "wants." This can be more intense even than paid work, and possibly less satisfying from the point of view of meaning or a feeling of achievement. It may be diverting but diversion and relaxing is not necessarily the same thing. And it certainly is not resting, i.e. true down time, which is so necessary for human wellbeing.

(Discussion above is drawn largely from data in Huberman & Minns 2007. Data on screen time is from Blodget, 2014.)

26.5 The Technisation of Time Past, Present and Future

The obsession with ever-faster motion over space and time came together in the aesthetics and philosophy of the Italian Futurist movement of the early nineteenth century. Inspired by the rapid mechanisation of all levels of society, particularly the chronophotographic (time-based) studies of the mechanics of animal and human movement as recorded in the works of late nineteenth century scientist and photographer Étienne-Jules Marey, the Futurists were obsessed with speed and violence, which for them went together. Filippo Tommaso Marinetti, the prime theorist of the movement, saw modernity as consisting in essence of ever-increasing speed, motion and industrial development, fused into one. Marinetti's founding 1909 manifesto lashed out against cultural tradition, rejected the past (though he also was hostile to feminism, and thus retrograde in that area) and celebrated the destructive power of war, which was seen as sweeping away the detritus of society to make way for the new. Futurism was an inspiration for Italian Fascism with its strange melding of appeals to ancient verities and modern technology (Mosse, 1990) (Fig. 26.3).

A scientific and technical approach was thus spreading to everything, though it remained decidedly Newtonian in cast, despite the nascent findings of relativity. Time's arrow according to the scientific paradigm, to use the physics phrase, remained most definitely linear and forward moving. And with human technological power, it now appeared that the future could be planned for, directed and mastered by the use of technical methods. Formerly mysterious and capricious, the future could be modelled and responded to just like anything else. Beginning around the seventeenth century, statistics and probability became an established field with a growing foundation in theory and expanding set of techniques of determination. A new concept called "risk" was created that denoted a hazard that could be defined and delimited through data collection of past

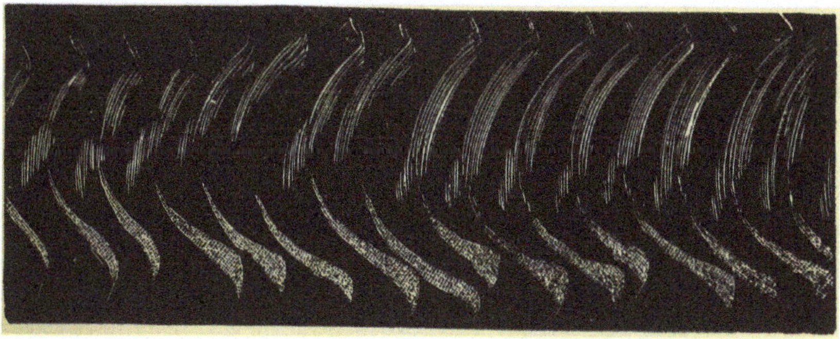

Fig. 26.3 Time and motion in the abstract (*Image source* Marey, E. (1874). *Animal mechanism: a treatise on terrestrial and aërial locomotion*. D. Appleton & Co. Page 193. Original caption: "Fig. 80 shows the tracing furnished by a wing of a humming-bird moth, arranged so as to touch the cylinder with its posterior edge." Contributing Library: Smithsonian Libraries Digitizing Sponsor: Biodiversity Heritage Library. No known copyright restrictions)

occurrences, projected into the future with calculable probabilistic tools. A whole series of financial instruments arose from this to help manage risk, insurance being the most important. To support this, a whole field of actuarial studies arose to assist in the underwriting of risk by insurance companies (Gigerenzer et al., 1989).

Thinking about Political Economy also became more technicised and put into a linear, progressive framework. After all science and knowledge could never go backwards, could they? Additionally, past experience was less and less useful as a guide for a future since the present was now changing all the time, its contours made unrecognisable and unstable by technical advances. The present was, by definition, obsolescent, and the future was where fulfilment would be found—or disaster if one didn't stay on top of things. Even knowing what the present consisted of took much more than common sense and observation. Formal models were required to fix where one was and projections were needed to figure out where one was going, at least probabilistically (Ogle, 2019, 319).

Intellectual schemes of historical teleology were increasingly popular in the era of high industry, and by extension utopias and dystopias. The motif of international competition enhanced this line of attack. The West was in decline, or Britain, or America or the white races, with the "other" constantly sneaking ever closer. The attempt of one nation or another to stay on top of the order of the day is an ancient one, as are justifications for "natural" superiority. But now these were implicitly depoliticised, replaced with technical paradigms in which levers needed to be adjusted to retain optimality and balance.

Subtly and stealthily thinking about reality was replacing reality itself, with abstract concepts fixed in a linear plane of progress replacing subjective human experience. Economic growth and development paradigms themselves were temporally directional. While one could go backwards, the desired end was always to go forward. This idea was picked up even more forcefully by the modernisation theorists of the latter half of the twentieth century and while some terminology has changed, the thinking largely has not.

26.6 Politics as a Technical Problem in Search of a Technical Solution

When the post-war "Golden Age" of the world economy rolled around in the 1950s and 1960s (see Chapter 24), economic, social and political problems seemed to be issues to be addressed by the technocrat, and time was reduced to a planning horizon. Ironically, for an age of Cold War ideology, sociologist Daniel Bell was able to write a book entitled, *The end of ideology* (1960), in which he claimed that the grand theories of the nineteenth and early twentieth centuries, which themselves were outgrowths of the Enlightenment, had run their course, to be replaced with more narrow theories that could be operationalised and optimised for specific results. The changes of the future would mainly be piecemeal technological adjustments of the existing system. The reason for this was the generalised and permanent affluence that was now the status quo. Different groups would continue to bargain with each other, but there were no more grand problems to solve.

Meanwhile, the economist John Kenneth Galbraith wrote, *The affluent society*, in 1958. He started by noting that the eighteenth century Classical Economists wrote during a time when there was widespread poverty and a need to increase the efficiency and scale of production of basic goods. Modern society (the US was the country he specifically wrote about) however had widespread affluence and production "wants" rather than "needs". Economics now was about allocation under plenty not scarcity, a condition that completely changed the orientation of the field. Galbraith followed this up with a 1967 book, *The new industrial society*, in which he claimed that the industrial sectors of modern capitalist societies now allocated resources mostly through the planning mechanisms of large corporations rather than the traditional mechanism of market supply and demand. He also argued that modern technological production required systematic long-term planning because of the substantial risk flowing from the massive capital investments required for economies of scale. In many ways, Galbraith was echoing similar arguments that business historian Alfred Chandler (1977) would make regarding the role of the large vertically integrated corporation in the Second Industrial Revolution.

Though not explicitly agreeing with Bell's conclusion that politics were no longer relevant, Galbraith's conclusions implied something similar. Galbraith noted that both Communism and Capitalism required extensive planning, though obviously markets and private property remained a central facet of the latter rather than the former. And in these prosperous times, both systems appeared to be churning out a surplus well above any natural human needs or even reasonable desires. Conflict obviously existed within and between nations, but materially it seemed as if there was little to fight about. Indeed, many commentators of the time found the parallel technocracies of the two systems striking, despite their different orientations and institutions. After the end of the Cold War, these technocracies would remain.

26.7 Round and Round It Goes

One can see how similar the lines of thinking offered during the Cold War are to the arguments that were made by Fukuyama after it. The end of "history" is apparent in both cases, in the sense that the major problems of society are now reduced to material ones, directly and indirectly, and these are judged as having been substantially solved. After the Cold War, even the choice of political values was moot, with capitalist economic organisation maximising output and democratic organisation maximising individual voice.

It thus makes sense that history can be said to be over when considering the fact that practical technical models do not deal well with time. All they can really do is determine direction and make tentative predictions about mechanical cause and effect, given starting and ending points and the forces of exogenous and endogenous variables. How long these processes might take, and how the passage of time might interact with its unfolding, is not accounted for, nor need it be.

This is subtle point but it can be understood by analogy. Imagine a pinball machine where one inserts a ball and then moves various levers to move the ball around a surface, with the ball finally exiting and with a final score recorded. One could experiment with this machine by trying a wide range of lever pulls, recording the differences in scores for each combination. With enough trials, one could compile a good record of the outcomes that various sets of pulls are likely to achieve, allowing the operator to pick a set of game moves that are predicted to have an "optimal" result (i.e. the highest score). Because of the randomness of various factors, such as friction, one cannot be definitely certain of outcomes, but their probabilities (effects) and their relationship with lever pulls (causes) can be mapped out and correlated to one another.

To play each game takes a certain amount of time. But note that nowhere is the passage of such "time" captured or incorporated. The pinball machine is invariant to time—its structure is given—and the time each game takes is irrelevant. This dimension could be tracked and tabulated, and if duration of the game is a variable of concern, one could devise strategies to optimise both score and speed, and determine trade-offs between the two. But time is still reduced to just another variable of interest. Its nature is not understood and, in this construct, irrelevant causally, except as it pertains to other factors, e.g. one lever or part of the board might be "stickier" than others and thus delay the ball in such a way as to affect how it moves and thus changes the score that might have resulted from faster movement.

If one thinks about it, this is really what the Production Function of the Growth Model is, a sort of giant pinball machine, sitting outside time, whose workings have inputs yielding outputs, but without any sense of history. Again, all that really matters is the interaction of variables and in the pure world of Growth Theory, there is one result or another, but time is ignored. Time, as with the sticky levers example above, may change "path dependence". But this is still all about timeless outcomes from timeless starting points. Hence growth modellers speak of "steady state" equilibrium outcomes that last forever until something perturbs the state. And one can map out the "transition dynamics" of how things unfold from one steady state to another. But again, whether this happens instantaneously or over a long period of time is mostly irrelevant, even if one puts in feedback loops and other effects, because the only state one is aiming for is the optimum.

In this framework, there really is the "end of history" in that there is no time and hence no history to speak of. There is simply a gap between the state where one is and the state that one wants to get to. There are intermediate events in the transition, but these are just events, in the sense Fukuyama denotes. Everything is just a giant planning problem, rather than human history. This is where Galbraith, Bell and then Fukuyama all agree. The paradigm continued into the 2000s with the so-called The Great Moderation idea that the economy was finally moving beyond business cycles and their instability in a natural progression that only required some monetary policy tweaking and a bit of fiscal policy to keep growth humming along. Capitalism was the only alternative, and when suitably adjusted by experts, it just kept getting better (Graff et al., 2014, 329, fn. 13) (see also Chapter 28). The Socialists thought the same thing about their system when their bloc existed, though the variables and levers were different. But they were gone now. Capitalism, and the removal of historical process, had finally been realised.

There is, however, another way to look at things. The Zen tradition has always maintained that time only exists because of identification with an "I" or an ego. If one stops trying to resist the flow of events by dropping the "I", timelessness, without cause and effect, is left. A "piece" of water may appear to move over a surface, but this is an illusion of waves which is actually only all water moving up and down. Similarly with the "self", moving through successive experiences seems to provide a link between youth and old age when there is simply all things moving like a wave. This symbolic self is where the notion of "progress" sits (Watts, 1957, 122–123).

This speaks to the idea that time only is there if there is someone to experience it. Buddhists reject the existence of the "I". The modern technical paradigm mechanises it, and makes it disappear that way. That is, if one assumes that there is some kind of invariant agent acting as one factor amongst many, time and history disappears and all one has left are the events. For the Zen master, once it is realised that the "self" is an illusion, "Enlightenment" is there. Can the same be said for the Growth theorist?

References

Audoin, C. (2001). *The measurement of time*. Cambridge University Press.

Blodget, H. (2014). The historical change in how we spend our time. *World Economic Forum Agenda*. https://weforum.org/agenda/2014/12/the-historical-change-in-how-we-spend-our-time

Braverman, H. (1974). *Labor and monopoly capital: The degradation of work in the twentieth century*. Monthly Review Press.

Chandler, A. D. (1977). *The visible hand*. University of Chicago Press.

Clayton, E. (2005). Aristotle: Politics. In Fieser, J. & Dowden, B. (Eds.), *Internet encyclopedia of philosophy*.

Davies, N. (1996). *Europe: A history*. Random House.

Gigerenzer, G, Swijtink Z., Porter, T., Daston, L., Beatty, J. & Krüger, L. (1989). *The empire of chance: How probability changed science and everyday life*. Cambridge University Press.

Graff, M., Kenwood, A. G., & Lougheed, A. L. (2013). *Growth of the international economy, 1820–2015*. Routledge.

Hawking, S. W. (1988). *Brief history of time: From the big bang to black holes*. Bantam Books.

Heller, M. (2002). Time of the universe. In G. F. R. Ellis (Ed.), *The far-future universe: Eschatology from a cosmic perspective* (pp. 53–64). Templeton Foundation Press.

Huntington, S. P. (1993). The clash of civilizations? *Foreign Affairs, 72*(3), 22–49.

Mokyr, J., Vickers, C., & Ziebarth, N. L. (2015). The history of technological anxiety and the future of economic growth: Is this time different? *Journal of Economic Perspectives, 29*(3), 31–50.

Mosse, G. L. (1990). The political culture of Italian futurism: A general perspective. *Journal of Contemporary History, 25*(2), 253–268.

Needham, J. (1965). *Time and Eastern man*. Royal Anthropological Institute of Great Britain & Ireland.

Ogle, V. (2019). Time, temporality and the history of capitalism. *Past & Present, 243*(1), 312–327.

Shlapentokh, V. (1988). The Stakhanovite movement: Changing perceptions over fifty years. *Journal of Contemporary History, 23*(2), 259–276.

Thompson, E. P. (1967). Time, work-discipline, and industrial capitalism. *Past and Present, 38*, 56–97.

Watts, A. (1957). *The way of Zen*. Vintage Books.

CHAPTER 27

"1989" "1991"

C. Gordon, *Many Possible Worlds*,
https://doi.org/10.1007/978-981-19-9281-0_27

◂**Fig. 27.1** After the Wall was over (*Image source* US National Archives [National Archives Identifier 6460121]. Original caption: At a newly created opening at Potsdamer Platz, an East German policeman looks at a small Christmas tree on the west side of the Berlin Wall. No known copyright restrictions)

27.1 Separate Worlds

In 1950, the sphere of "Really Existing Socialism" covered about one third of the world's population, though the single country of newly Communist China made up for a large proportion of this. (This label was used by the bloc to indicate that despite the shortfalls of Socialist governments when compared to the ideal, at least they were up and running.) Large as it was, it was a very self-contained universe, even in the two decades that followed which saw an explosion of economic growth worldwide across all economic systems. Only around 4% of capitalist economy exports were sent annually to "Centrally Planned Economies", a figure not varying much between 1950 and 1980. During the 1960s, two-thirds of Communist country exports stayed within their own bloc and emigration and tourism between the two worlds was minimal, expanding only slowly in careful increments as foreign tourism was cautiously encouraged by individual Socialist nations. The almost complete isolation between the two worlds was striking given the prodigious growth in transport and communications technology and the general trend of growing economic integration between the Capitalist countries (Hobsbawm, 1994, 373–374) (Fig. 27.1).

What was odd about this extreme demarcation was that it was almost entirely a product of historical accident. Immediately after taking power, Lenin had offered extremely generous terms to Western investors in his typically opportunistic willingness to work with anyone to achieve his longer-term agenda. But this was met with a capital strike by foreign investors and Western intervention in the Russian civil war. Already backwards and insular, the new Soviet Union was a pariah state from the get-go and thus forced to trod its own path with relatively little outside input or exchange (Hobsbawm, 1994, 375).

It is interesting to speculate on how things would have developed if Western money and expertise and influence had been allowed to flow in. Perhaps these capitalist "useful idiots" (in Lenin's terminology) would have unwittingly fed and built up his Communist nation into the overwhelming adversary he hoped it would be. More likely, the path of both Russian development and Communist ideology would have been altered into a more capitalistic and market-oriented form similar to modern day China. It is impossible to be for sure, but it seems likely that either way, a polarised Cold War world, fractured along rigid dichotomous lines, would not have resulted in quite the way it actually did. In this sense, the Capitalist countries unwittingly co-created that outcome from the birth of the first Socialist government in Russia.

27.2 A Golden Age of the Socialist Bloc

But a divided world is what ended up happening. And if one was looking at the global map as a geopolitical chessboard, which was what most everyone was doing at the time, arguments could be made that the Soviet bloc was "winning" the Cold War thirty years into it. By 1975, peaceful revolutions in Spain and Portugal gave independence to their respective former colonies in Southern Africa, which immediately turned to the Soviet Union for help. Decolonisation already had provided a fair number of new client states to the Communists, though there had been quite a number remaining in the Western ambit, and some, like Ethiopia, that flipped back and forth. American had finally withdrawn its forces from Vietnam in 1973, with the North Vietnamese finally reunifying the country under Communist rule two years later (Best et al., 2004, 481–482). Even President Nixon, who had skilfully played the Soviets and Chinese off against one another, had resigned in disgrace because of his involvement in various forms of corruption and cover-up that became known collectively as "Watergate".

From the outside, the Soviet economy also appeared to be performing well at this time. Russia was reporting steady increases in its manufacturing capacity and the beating of many old output records across its national plan. Large new oil and gas reserves had been discovered in the 1960s and the general commodities price boom of 1972–1973, followed by the first oil price shock of 1973–1974, greatly benefited the earnings generated by Russian oil and commodities exports. Though still subject to scarcity and poor quality, Soviet citizens were getting greater selections of consumer goods, and hard currency earnings from oil helped to finance a few imports of popular overseas products (Easterly & Fischer, 1995).

Per capita GDP growth had been improving steadily after the death of Stalin in 1953. Although the official statistics are recognised as being overstated, growth was certainly very strong during the 1950s and according to Western intelligence reports good during the 1960s as well, though other accounts differ on this last point (Harrison, 1993). The 1970s were not so rosy, but, as indicated above, external circumstances masked this fact, helping to fund decent increases in resources devoted to consumer good production and significant consumer price subsidies. As far as Russian citizens were concerned the first half of the 1970s was one of rising material prosperity and growing geopolitical power.

The Soviet system also was delivering on improving various social well-being indicators. A big push was on to build new housing stock after the war, adding to Soviet investments in cultural and educational institutions during the 1930s and 1940s, yielding concomitant increases in literacy rates and a growing stock of well-trained technical personnel. These economic and social advances were also being made in the Eastern bloc in Europe, funded by ongoing and significant foreign aid and import purchases from the Soviet Union (White, 1986). It was true that the USSR and its Eastern Allies still lagged behind the West in terms of GDP per capita. But European Communist country citizens could point to guaranteed employment and health entitlements as partial compensation for the gaps between Eastern and Western wealth and income and civil liberties. For a very brief time, it even appeared that these gaps might close soon as most of the developed Capitalist countries struggled with stagflation and domestic political unrest (see Chapter 28).

27.3 Pressures Beneath the Surface

All this is, however, a superficial picture, for the Soviet-Eastern bloc was struggling with significant underlying structural problems (China was too, though the nature of their struggle was quite different and is considered separately later). A fundamental issue, common to both Capitalist and Socialist economies of the time, was an ongoing shift in economic structure. Manufacturing as the primary road to economic success had begun to become outmoded for developed countries in the early 1960s. Developing countries, especially in Asia, were now creating their own manufacturing base with a lower-cost labour force that was nonetheless sometimes as skilled as those found in the West. To stay competitive, developed countries had to boost manufacturing productivity, lower their own wages, and/or shift into new services industries that offered high value-add but with little global competition. During the 1970s and early 1980s, most advanced Capitalist economies could do none of these things very well, and deindustrialisation and rising prices were the result (see Chapter 29).

Strictly speaking the Communist bloc did not face these problems since everything, including wages, were set by the State and trade and investment remained mostly within the bloc itself. But the motor of growth was the same, namely to deliver more output for a given amount of input, i.e. productivity increases, and the core of the economy remained heavy manufacturing-based in the face of a need for a structural shift to services. Technological and organisational innovation was required in the Communist system just as much as in its Capitalist counterpart, but the centrally planned economies had much less means of encouraging this than the West did. The commodity-income boom obscured this fact for a while, and also lulled the Communist planners into a false sense of security about the current efficiency of their economies and the need to make reforms.

Indeed the whole success of the Communist model up to this point was based on its reliance on State-driven command industrialisation, which was developed mostly during Stalin's rule, with tweaks and modifications made along the way. During the first post-war decades, this model delivered the fast growth that results from imposing manufacturing on an otherwise backwards economy. But command industrialisation is by definition inefficient and there is a separate issue of the concomitant need to raise agricultural productivity, a devilish issue that the Soviets never really adequately mastered and that, by extension, its client states largely did not either (Hobsbawm, 1994, 382–383). As the 1970s unfolded, the traditional Marxist-Leninist model could only deliver more of the same inefficient heavy industry that it had before and this was no longer adequate to deliver economic growth, or, increasingly, even meet requisite economic demands of a population more attuned to prosperity than mere survival.

Of course bureaucratisation, a perennial issue, grew worse. Employment in the planning sector and its many organs grew faster than in other truly productive sectors. Even Khrushchev, the last real "boss" of the USSR, could not tame this beast and during the Brezhnev reign, it truly went out of control. There was considerable and growing corruption and malfeasance. But the bigger problem was that the central planning apparatus was fixed on diverting more resources from less productive activities (such as backwards agriculture or home production) to more productive ones (mainly manufacturing) rather then delivering innovation that would increase productivity. With the low-hanging fruit mostly gone, the real struggles of adjustment were now much more complex and subtle, and thus well beyond the existing capacity and training within the technocracy (Westad, 2017, 367–369).

Also, Stalinism had required the forced expropriation of vast amounts of labour from the peasantry (in the form of collectivisation and expropriation), the workers (in the form of forced levies and substandard wages) and from the vast prison complex of the gulags (estimated to have a population ranging from 4 to 13 million). The general population (outside the gulags) was often willing to make inordinate sacrifices during the 1930s, the struggles of Second World War, and the post-war building of a global superpower immediately afterwards (Hobsbawm, 1994, 381). By the 1970s, the gulag complex had been vastly reduced (though not eliminated), existential crisis was past, the remaining positive myths of the Stalin era mostly extirpated. Soviet citizens now expected their government to deliver comfort and benefit, rather than calls for sacrifice. Even if the planning structure had known and wanted to do what was necessary to reform the economy (which they weren't), the people were not going to be very receptive to it.

27.4 A Disruptive Economic Opening to the West

An additional burden for the Soviet Union was the need to keep substantial resources tied up in a vast military apparatus in order to compete with the US and to control its often restive European satellites. Given the very closed nature of the Communist bloc, the Soviets also needed to serve as financiers and primary exporter to, and importer from, these satellite states. The Soviets were hardly generous in their terms of aid or trade, but they also did not always gain from them either in order to preserve their pre-eminence as a Socialist hegemon. This was a costly undertaking and not one Russia could afford for too long.

The turmoil of 1968 had demonstrated to the Party that a firm hand needed to remain over the Eastern bloc, with the resulting formulation of the so-called Brezhnev Doctrine, which held that a challenge to Communism in any single Eastern European ally was a challenge to all Communism and would be dealt with by military intervention. This doctrine was essentially an official codification of long-standing policy, going back to the Soviet intervention to crush the rebellion in Hungary in 1956 and a worker's revolt in East Germany in 1953. Being a public commitment it solidified a costly requirement of constant active deployment of the Soviet army in Europe. At the same time, Brezhnev also made the decision to try and gain military superiority over America in particular weapons systems areas, and managed to do so here and there. But it was an expensive and strategically useless choice, since MAD could function with much smaller forces, as the resolution of the Cuban Missile Crisis in 1962 showed (Hobsbawm, 1994, 246). Being able to destroy your opponent 50 times over rather than 40 did not really add much advantage but cost a great deal. The richer US economy could absorb these expenditures much more readily than the poorer Soviet one.

To finance this burden, and to continue to make needed investments in social and economic overhead, fast and ready cash, especially in scarce Western currency, was required, a need intensifying during the 1970s. The resources available within the Socialist world were no longer sufficient. There were two major ways this money was raised: through specialising in the export of raw materials, especially oil, that earned hard currency revenues; and borrowing from the West. The pitfall in commodity specialisation was a dependence on the booms and bust of commodity prices. When these were high, as they were during much of the 1970s, the public coffers were full. But this dependence caused the Eastern bloc to leave its decreasingly efficient manufacturing sector unimproved, thus losing whatever export prowess in making and exporting high value goods it had been building up. It was a classic example of "Dutch Disease", it being easier for Russia to sell oil out of the ground at great profit to finance its own and the bloc's development, than it was to work on technical advance and cultivate new markets (Epstein, 1986).

Meanwhile, high profits from oil sales caused the Soviet bloc to become hooked on cheap international credit, liquidity which it desperately needed, especially when buying goods and services from the West (American grain being one big Russian purchase item, bought to deal with a series of bad wheat harvests during the decade). Because most of the borrowed money went into consumption, rather than investment in infrastructure or industry, when oil prices fell again, and the debts came due, the liquidity squeeze became unmanageable. Some tightening of Russian central planning in the early 1980s did actually manage to reduce indebtedness, though without addressing the underlying structural problems, and thus being a mere stopgap (Hobsbawm, 1994, 474–475).

In the Communist bloc, foreign debt presented a special challenge because it let new forces into a system whose equilibrium required a large amount of insularity. As long as the bloc was autarkic, as it was during the Bolshevik period, or essentially bilateral between similar command economies, as it was during the first decades of the Cold War, resource flows and obligations could be managed by administrative shadow transfers and forced adjustments. But the reliance on Western purchases, capital, and currency introduced market dynamics that nonmarket economies could not handle for any length of time, without ultimately being taken over by them. The Brezhnev era appeared to be a high water mark in economic performance, internal social development and international power and prestige. But it was underwritten by unsustainable foreign credit and commodity sales income from the West. When these fell over, social, economic and, ultimately geopolitical conditions did too. This was highly problematic in Socialist countries where social stability and guarantees were the core promise of the system. Combined with an already corrosive rise in corruption, many lost faith in the Communism movement entirely, especially in Russia and Eastern Europe (Hobsbawm, 1994, 471).

27.5 "1989"

As economic, social and political pressures grew, they first burst out most forcefully in Eastern Europe. From the Soviet perspective, the European satellites were expensive burdens to be borne but economised on as much as possible. In the satellite countries themselves, the perspective was obviously quite different. Russia was an overlord and a constraint to domestic freedom. The Soviet sacrifices for maintaining world Socialism was not something the populace of these smaller countries saw very sympathetically, to say the least. The Soviets thus were hoping to reduce the resources sunk into the Eastern bloc but were frustrated in achieving this due to the uncooperativeness of its notional clients.

Eastern European pushback, grievance and rebellion had been constant throughout the Cold War. But in 1989 localised movements coalesced into a wave that overtopped the political dam. Poland and Hungary led the way, as they often had in the past. In Poland a "round table" between the Communist government and civil society groups, especially the "Solidarity" union movement, met early in 1989 and passed resolutions to permit independent trade unions, hold elections in June, and make further economic reforms. The resulting June 4 elections ended in utter defeat for the Communists. Meanwhile the Hungarian government had already allowed a multiparty system and other basic democratic freedoms, and then opened their borders, through which several million East Germans passed, hoping to enter West Germany. In this single swoop, the "Iron Curtain" had been torn down (Ther, 2016, 50).

But this was a mere start. In East Germany popular demonstrations broke out which the East German Army refused to put down. The Berlin Wall was opened on November 9, quickly bringing along the end of the German Democratic Republic, soon followed by the collapse of the Communist regime in Bulgaria and the so-called Velvet Revolution in Czechoslovakia that same month. Meanwhile, the government in Moscow confirmed the existence of the Molotov-Ribbentrop Pact in December 1989, opening the door to independence for the Baltic republics, while dictator Nicolae Ceauşescu lost control of events in Rumania and he and his wife were executed on December 25 (Ther, 2016, 50).

These developments followed on from the significant loosening of Russian oversight that had come with the reformist Premier Gorbachev coming to power in the USSR in 1985, aiming to restructure the Soviet Political Economy. Gorbachev allowed reform-minded governments in Hungary and Poland free rein to implement their own "perestroika", often pushed along by events on the ground, hoping that successful reforms there would lessen their need for Soviet resources. His loosening of control destabilised already tottering internal orders, opening the door to further turmoil in the Bloc as others deviated from Marxist-Leninist orthodoxy. Gorbachev's goal was to reform the system of both Russia and its satellites under the ongoing political monopoly of the Communist Party. But the hardest line Eastern bloc Communist party leaders saw the threats inherent in this course, Erich Honecker in East Germany and Gustav Husák in Czechoslovakia openly resisting reforms in their own countries (Ther, 2016, 67). Their predictions turned out to be right and Gorbachev's wrong. But by the time this was clear it was too late to turn back the tide, if indeed it even could have been.

Gorbachev's reform program was necessitated by the miserable economic performance of 1980s Soviet and Eastern bloc economies. From 1983 on, as the price of crude oil dropped as sharply as it had previously risen (from $US66 to $US20 per barrel), the Soviet Union, once flush with commodity sales money, now struggled to pay for its imports of grain and staple goods. The Soviet Union's budget deficit ran over

10% of GDP, higher than any other Eastern Bloc country. Inflation rose throughout the bloc as well, official price controls notwithstanding, with shortages a frequent occurrence. The Communist governments could now no longer maintain even slow economic growth and basic standards of living, caught between deficits and cratering productivity. By the end of the 1980s, Eastern Bloc industries took roughly five times as long as Western European ones to manufacture appliances and cars, not even adjusting for their consistently lower-quality. Consumer good availability had increased in theory, but they could not be obtained with any certainty, raising expectation and disappointment levels concurrently. Formal public entitlements remained untouched, but rising costs, cuts in food subsidies, and fixed wages increased squeezes on workers. These "pocketbook" issues caused immediate problems, arising first in Eastern Europe and Poland especially, where protests in 1970, 1976 and 1980 were all triggered by government increases in the prices of basic foodstuffs to cover mounting budgetary costs in the face of stagnating growth (Ther, 2016, 58–59).

Capitalism had undergone some existential crises of its own, surviving by altering its own shape significantly. There were some Communist bloc economists who had once believed in the possibility of similar economic reform on their side of the world, most notably the Hungarian Janos Kornai. But he and others came to the conclusion by the 1980s that the system was too deteriorated to salvage (Kornai, 1986). Even if this was not the case the governmental responses within the Socialist bloc had been too limited and remained so.

Given Russia's resource constraints and the magnitude of changes in the world economy it seems unlikely that a Communist Eastern Europe could have held together for very long. The Soviets simply could not afford simultaneous commitments to a large standing army to control Europe, associated investments in satellite armies, and international competition in the Superpower arms race. They might not even have been able to afford even one of these. A leader other than Gorbachev might not have pursued a similar loosening in the Russian grip over its buffer states, but this could not have gone on for too long. Perhaps an alternative scenario would have been something like "1999" rather than "1989" but the Socialist Bloc in Europe was likely coming to an end one way or the other, mainly because, in addition to its many other problems, Russian overlordship was never accepted or liked by most of the population. It was an historical epoch whose time had definitely passed.

27.6 "1991"

Might it still have been possible, however, for the Soviet Union to carry on, without its satellites? It could be argued that a more competent autocrat than Gorbachev might well have preserved the Soviet Union, with significant alterations in its institutional and perhaps even territorial form, while letting go of the burden of the Eastern bloc. Maybe the Soviet Union could then have lived on as a nominally Communist country, like China has, while remaining a nuclear superpower.

However, such a leader was not available and Russia's economic and political structures were so rigid and economically inefficient that this alternative seems implausible. By the 1970s the foundation of the Soviet economy was not just declining, but slowly starting to come apart. The rapid military build-up, falling commodity prices, foreign debt burdens and structural efficiencies all depleted available resources, not helped by crop failures. But other countries have survived such things, and by themselves these did not add up to an inevitable existential threat.

The Soviet problem was really one of deep institutional and societal sclerosis that combined with external pressures to end in collapse. What had once been a dynamic, if often unpalatable, system, had become more and more inert, contradictory and regressive. By the time Brezhnev had become Premier, the system had become what has been called a "crony communism" characterised by corruption and political control by in-bred elites (Westad, 2017, 365–367).

The Brezhnev era lasted until 1985, the ageing and increasingly senile Premier dying a few years before then, after which a few placeholder leaders revolved through the Premiership, at which point Mikhail Gorbachev took over. He inherited growth that was perhaps 2% annually, with increasing shortages of consumer goods and growing budget deficits due to military expenditures and the continuance of expensive price subsidies (which, of course, worsened the goods shortages). At 54 years old, Gorbachev was the youngest Premier in decades. Gorbachev came in trying to politically and economically reform both the Soviet Communist system and the Communist systems of the Eastern European satellite nations. He loosened State control of the economy, allowing for some private small-scale industry, while providing more commercial incentives and flexibility within state central planning (this was "perestroika" or "restructuring"). He also loosened control of the press and freedom of expression (referred to as "glasnost", or "opening"). He also followed a tacit reversal of the Brezhnev Doctrine in Eastern Europe. His intention was to preserve the Communist system by freeing it from internal and external pressures caused by State inefficiency, military repression and unresolved simmering social conflict, not dissimilar to what China was aiming to do with its own loosening under Deng Xiaoping, though there was far less political liberalisation in the latter country (Best et al., 2004, 386–388; Westad, 2017, 543–546).

Instead, this pulling of threads resulted first in "1989", as discussed above, and then a rapid series of events that deeply destabilised and finally destroyed the USSR. After the fall of the Berlin Wall, there was the reunification of Germany in 1990; the outbreak of armed conflict in, and beginning of the disintegration of Communist Yugoslavia in the Summer of 1991; the full independence of Lithuania, Latvia and Estonia following a coup d'état against Gorbachev in August; the end of Communism in Albania; and, finally, the official breakup of the Soviet Union in December 1991 (Ther, 2016, 50–51).

During this time, and outside Russia, Gorbachev was hailed as a shining figure, both before and after the Soviet collapse. He was awarded the Nobel Peace Prize in 1990 and signed significant arms control treaties with the US just before the end of his reign (Westad, 2017, 548). However, inside Russia he was and still is considered to be more of a tragic figure, and hated by those who still see the USSR, somewhat rightfully, as an apogee of Russian power in the world, with Gorbachev as the man who destroyed it all in short order. A joke that made the rounds during Gorbachev's rule is indicative. It begins with Stalin, Khrushchev, Brezhnev and Gorbachev on a train, which comes to a sudden stop. Stalin says, "Shoot the conductor". Khrushchev says, "No, we should rehabilitate the conductor and reform the train staff". Brezhnev says, "Let's cover the windows with curtains and pretend that the train is moving". And Gorbachev says, "No, comrades, we should all get out and push!" (Davies, 2010). The punch line captures both Gorbachev's noble intent but also his naiveté. For while the flaws of the other Premiers' "solutions" are obvious, they, unlike Gorbachev, at least know what the problem is, i.e. that the train is not moving and cannot be moved, and thus resorting to false substitutes and scapegoats. Gorbachev alone believes that mere human beings can actually push a stopped train, showing that he doesn't understand the true problem in the first place.

One could look at this from the perspective of the Elias "civilising process" (see Chapter 5). The USSR was relatively unique historically in that a large part of the whole enterprise was designed to force changes in social structure (sociogenesis) and to reshape individual human psychology (psychogenesis) entirely. The fundamental postulates and principles of Marxism-Leninism included the acceptance of State ownership and State responsibility for all social life and the surrender of all ethnic, nationalistic and regional autonomy to a centralised authority. Out of this Lenin had tried to create a "New Socialist Man", and in many ways had done so. But this New Man only could function in the context of total faith in, and control of society by, the Party, and by being totally subservient to it. Gorbachev tried to create a more independent and individualistic person, but this more individualistic type of person would never obey a monolithic party, nor be comfortable with the old Marxist-Leninist postulates. Being a Party product himself, Gorbachev could not see this contradiction (Sheehy, 1991, 287).

Moreover, the New Man that Soviet society had actually created did not even really match the ideal Marxist-Leninist theory. "Homo Sovieticus" was a "personality implant" devised to condition people to being dependent on the Communist Party that gave them everything in return for their submission to it. Private activities in private spheres were limited or eliminated. Buying and selling was "speculation", and conformism was rewarded over initiative and talent. Since things were allotted not bought or sold, "money" was an abstraction that meant little to Soviet citizens. All this was supposed to result in a selfless socially minded individual, willing to sacrifice for the common good. Instead, levelling down to a common minimum standard became the individual's goal, not rising up above the ranks to join in a higher purpose. This personality type was especially encouraged by the Brezhnev regime, under which Gorbachev rapidly advanced (Hobsbawm, 1994, 478–479; Sheehy, 1991, 204–205). Thus, Gorbachev was not only an adherent to Marxism-Leninism, but to the distorted version of the ideal person that it had turned out, though largely unconsciously.

Gorbachev had the typical Marxist faith in human improvability and rational action given the right conditions. Once in power he offered himself as an exemplar to emulate, now preaching free expression and initiative for individuals, things he had never been associated with much before. He remained committed to the Communist Party as the "vanguard" for that transformation; yet the Party was the problem. This was a tension never resolved, and, as one person described it, Gorbachev was always "in the last row of the avante-garde" (Sheehy, 1991, 319).

Gorbachev appealed to the intelligenstia and the elites as his natural Allies in this movement, key vanguard groups of which he was part. This was natural, but quickly ran into problems once perestroika and glasnost got underway. Gorbachev released new information about the truths about Stalinism and post-Stalin developments. But, as with Khrushchev’s denunciations of Stalin in 1956, these merely offended and confused those who had participated and benefited from the old system, while delivering no new benefits to those who had not, something Khrushchev had at least partly been able to deliver. Many families were torn apart as children confronted parents asking why they had been lied to. Something similar had happened in Germany in the 1960s, when children confronted their stolid parents about what they had done before the War (Hobsbawm, 1994, 477–479).

These disruptions appealed to the elites but not to the masses who only saw old verities dethroned, the conditions of life now made unstable (and, significantly, soon deteriorating after a few initial years of stasis), and any sense of social justice and classlessness, the stated pinnacle goals of the system and the biggest justification of socialism’s superiority to capitalism, thrown out the window. Meanwhile, more free press coverage exposed examples of long-standing corruption, exacerbating growing cynicism about Socialism’s faults, while offering little hope for positive change. Perestroika itself largely allowed new opportunities for leveraging continued apparatchik power because the Party and apparatchiks remained the vehicles through which resource decisions were really made. The public, either as individuals in their workplaces and civil society, or as voters in now actually competitive elections, couldn’t change anything real in those arenas, leading to even greater frustration (Sheehy, 1991, 343).

The intelligenstia, initially on board with the program, began to carry the process to the logical conclusions that Gorbachev was not prepared to go. The elimination of Party political monopoly was never put on the table. Yet pluralism and glasnost naturally led there. The economy continued to stagnate even with perestroika, proving to entrenched interests that the policy should be abandoned, while demonstrating to reformers that it was too half-hearted, incompletely designed, and poorly executed, which it was. The general public didn’t like it, not least because it didn’t deliver on its promises, while the progressive elites grew frustrated with what seemed to be a lack of real commitment (Hobsbawm, 1994, 484).

Gorbachev was a compromising reformer whose program became hopelessly compromised. He tried to create some quasi-market institutions such as freedom for some enterprises and shadow price incentives. But he left most of the central planning institutions in place, with the same people in power to allocate and distribute things, and the same basic entitlements (meagre as they were) given through workplaces and the like. This, combined with people's total lack of experience of "supply", "demand" and "price", actually drove people more towards nonmarket transactions like barter and social networking that they were most familiar with and that had always been a necessity anyway in the closed and intertwined power circles of Soviet society. They mostly did not take up the market ways they were being encouraged to pursue, even though any hope of success lay in their doing just that (Sheehy, 1991, 330–332).

Overall Gorbachev had awakened the masses but he had failed to channel their energies, and in some sense he had no coherent place to channel them to, being a committed Socialist playing with markets but not willing to use them fully, and a pluralist still committed to Party control rather than true democracy. As one Russian said, right as things were ending, "Before, we had two channels of belief - Communism and false romanticism - and they were secure. Now nobody believes and nobody is happy" (Sheehy, 1991, 333). As for Capitalism, this was not seen as a good alternative given its brazen hedonistic consumerism and lack of any stated egalitarian or higher values at all. Besides which, eight decades had been spent fighting it. Thus, the end of Communism had many causes but perhaps most of all it was a crisis of collective and individual meaning.

As matters got more desperate, Gorbachev kept trying new things, including a limited and ultimately fatal move to genuine national electoral politics in 1989–1990. Here he was weakened even further because he was too arid personally for mass appeal, after his initial novelty wore off. Boris Yeltsin, who became head of the Russian Soviet Socialist Federal Republic, had more popular appeal, being earthy, impulsive, action-oriented and prone to take the public pulse in the streets rather than in the elites and the Party institutions as Gorbachev had. Both had peasant backgrounds but Gorbachev had left behind his roots in many ways, while Yeltsin remained very much a product of them (Hobsbawm, 1994, 485).

A key moment in the collapse came when Gorbachev, with his now strengthened formal powers as President of the Union (a new constitution had been written earlier) came to loggerheads with Yelstin, head of the

Russian Republic. Yeltsin declared Russian independence in response to a power structure coup that had taken Gorbachev down in an attempt to put the old apparatchiks back in control. This was the definitive end of the Soviet Union. For the first time in its history, Moscow broke away from its own Empire. All Gorbachev had done in the end was re-awaken old nascent ethnic identifications and nationalisms, something that Lenin himself had seen as essential to repress if the Soviet Union was to hold together. It did not, and the rest, as they say, is history (see Figs. 27.2 and 27.3 to see how the USSR became a smaller and weaker Russia-centred "Confederation").

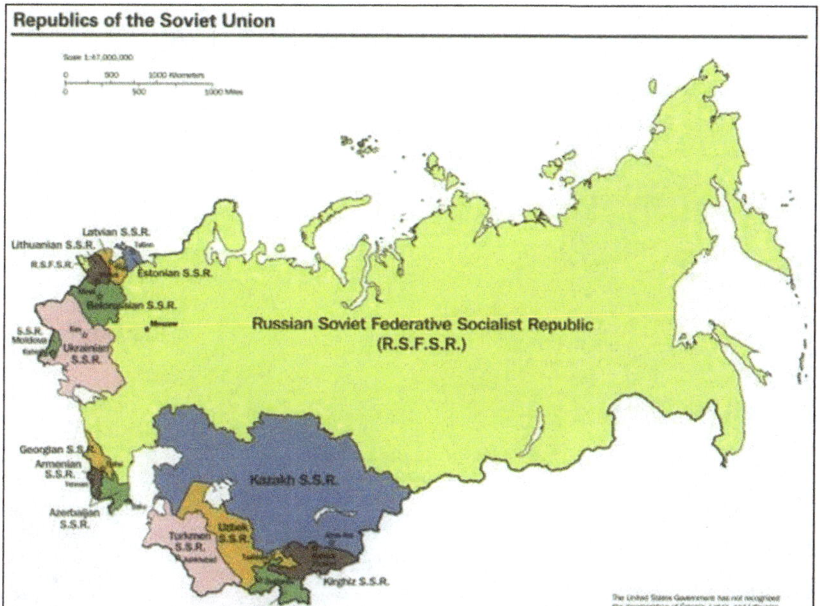

Fig. 27.2 The Soviet Union in 1991, just before its demise (*Image source* United States Central Intelligence Agency [1991] Republics of the Soviet Union [Washington, DC: Central Intelligence Agency] [Map]. Retrieved from the Library of Congress, https://www.loc.gov/item/2005626536/. No known copyright restrictions)

Fig. 27.3 The Soviet Union's replacement: the Russian Federaion in 2000 (*Image source* United States Central Intelligence Agency [2000] Asia [Washington, DC: Central Intelligence Agency] [Map]. Retrieved from the Library of Congress, https://www.loc.gov/item/2001621192/. No known copyright restrictions)

27.7 The Chinese Exception

The earliest and most dramatic rupture in the global Communist bloc was the Sino-Soviet split that took place over the course of the late 1950s and early 1960s. There were many proximate causes of this split, but its ultimate sources were cultural and social. China was very different from Russia and Europe and its offshoots generally. It was very poor, highly agrarian and yet had already been penetrated (mostly imperialistically) by Capitalism. In that sense it appeared similar to Tsarist Russia before Communism, and like many underdeveloped countries, the command industrialisation offered by Stalinist Marxism-Leninism was appealing (see Chapter 25). With the Soviet Union at the head of a new world vanguard, adoption of this model and entry into an alternative fold was very compelling (Fig. 27.4).

However, pre-Communist China had been very different from Tsarist Russia in numerous ways. Both were large countries with traditions of autocracy. But China had been unified for centuries before the nascent Muscovy had even been born. It had known wealth and sophistication at levels Europeans could only dream of until the Commercial Revolution set off the birth of Capitalism in the high Middle Ages. Most importantly it had a distinct, highly elaborated and highly developed civilisation that had been absorbed by the society from top to bottom, along with the motivating philosophy of Confucianism, coloured by Buddhist and Taoist traditions. Its state and civic institutions were sophisticated, subtly regulating all dimensions of society. Because both Russia and China exhibited high levels of social, economic and political hierarchy and had very large peasantries in perennial poverty, Western observers conflated the two countries. In the process they misunderstood both. China had long had a sense of cultural superiority to Europe and, perhaps more importantly, a sense of self-sufficiency from it, and the rest of the world (Skocpol, 1979).

It was only when the Imperial system finally fell that the Chinese adopted Western modalities, first republicanism, then nationalist autocracy and, finally, Communism; but in all of those cases, with a distinctly Chinese flavour. Prophetically a London *Times* correspondent wrote in the 1950s that there would be no Communism left in the twenty-first century, except in China, where it would survive as a national ideology, a restoration of order, peace, welfare, greatness and civilisation: in other words, all the principles of the Tang dynasty (Hobsbawm, 1994, 466). In China, as in many other developing countries, the bargain that Communism offered was interpreted somewhat differently than in Europe. Social

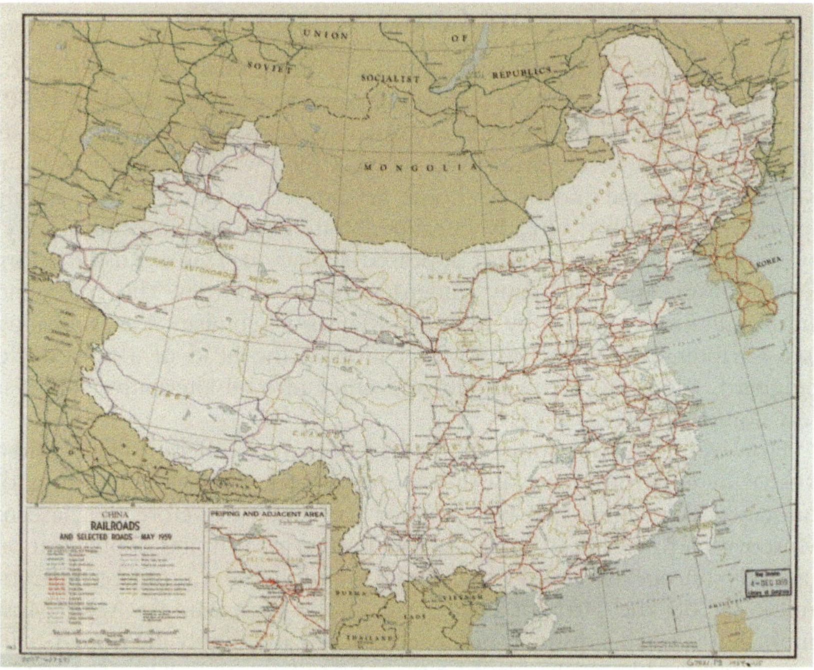

Fig. 27.4 Mao's China in 1959 (*Image source* United States Central Intelligence Agency [1959] China railroads and selected roads, May [Washington, DC: Central Intelligence Agency] [Map]. Retrieved from the Library of Congress, https://www.loc.gov/item/2007627271/. No known copyright restrictions)

progress was paramount, and a lack of visible economic progress would be tolerated for a long time so long as that was delivered.

All this was filtered through the "accidents" of history in the form of individual leadership. Just as Stalin had markedly changed the course of Russian Communism, Mao markedly changed its Chinese course. But even here, this was in turn shaped by the nature of the society being worked on. For example, Chinese agriculture was quickly collectivised after Mao took power, with little resistance from peasants, something quite distinct from the Russian experience in which virtual civil war and years of struggle were involved. Similarly, Chinese industrialisation was initially accompanied by very little urbanisation, again contrary to the Russian experience. Rural population in China did not fall below 80%

until the 1980s (Hobsbawm, 1994, 469). Finally, the various Maoist social experiments were also, initially, rather readily acceded to. One must be cautious, of course, about gross generalisations. But China was a very different environment on which to impose and implement a new system, and the results were quite different as a result.

And, indeed, Mao had personal beliefs and characteristics that made decisive historical differences. Other leaders, including those in his close retinue, such as Zhou Enlai, would likely not have so quickly dropped Soviet style central planning, as Mao had in part because he thought its results were being delivered too slowly. Similarly, the Great Leap Forward, with its vision of decentralised industrialisation, in the form of home-based iron smelters and industrial communes, would not have been conceived of, much less implemented by, anyone other than Mao. The disastrous Cultural Revolution of the 1960s (see Chapter 24), which was more the imposition of a new social order than an economic plan, was most definitely truly unique "Maoism" (Westad, 2017, 250–259). Mao had a belief that was distinctly Chinese and yet all his own, and quite different from the practical opportunism of Lenin's visioning, believing that revolutionary fervour all by itself could overcome absolutely any social obstacle. Some referred to this as a "collectivist mysticism" in which a truly believing and motivated whole could completely liberate the individual of past programming (Hobsbawm, 1994, 467). Indeed Mao thought that the primary problem with Chinese society was that all the old ideas and mores from the long Imperial past had become deeply ingrained in people and needed to be rooted out entirely and replaced with new modern versions. It was the Soviet New Man on steroids, and it became very influential in the New Left politics of the 1960s and 1970s West (see Chapter 24).

This romanticism was one thing when applied within Chinese society, which the philosophically materialist Soviets did not care much about. It was more worrying to Russia in an international geopolitical setting. Mao never cared too much about whether nuclear weapons might be used, believing that because of his country's population size, enough Chinese would survive it to carry on a sizeable post-apocalyptic cadre (Hobsbawm, 1994, 229). The Russians and Chinese would likely have split in some way, given how different they were as countries and societies. But Mao was a definitive figure in the process, delivering a rupture both earlier and more dramatically.

With Mao's death, this romanticism and all its wreckage was finally put to pasture, especially once Deng Xiaoping took power. Social issues were by no means ignored. But political and economic reconstruction took centre stage, and at a time when Marxism-Leninism and command industrialisation were everywhere in retreat, although the Socialist bloc still nominally remained existent. On 4 June 1989, the same day the Communists were soundly defeated in national elections in Poland, the Chinese armed forces crushed the growing democracy protests on Tiananmen Square. This violent suppression was a result of many things, not least a reaction to the Soviet authorities' apparent loss of control inside and outside the Soviet Union, a process the Chinese leadership had closely observed. To them glasnost seemed the primary threat to the political stability which they deemed a necessary condition for economic growth, something the disaster of Maoist experimentation had seemed to demonstrate definitively. Indeed, the party leaderships of the GDR (East Germany) and the ČSSR (Czechoslovakia) discussed the possibility of a "Chinese solution" for their own unrest, but were in no real position to enforce it, especially without Soviet help, which Gorbachev had ruled out (Ther, 2016, 69).

Deng Xiaoping also had already begun his own version of perestroika. Given the country's long-standing poverty, economic reform seemed much more critical than political liberalisation. But here he proceeded incrementally and strategically. Gorbachev had opened up the entire Soviet economy all at once. Deng chose an enclave, focusing on Hong Kong, which Britain handed back to China in 1997 under the unique "One country, two systems" policy, and which built upon some more limited loosening within China that had taken place in the turbulent aftermath of Mao's death. Hong Kong was left with its own internal economic and political arrangements under Chinese sovereignty, leaving it a free trade and international finance entrepôt within a Communist country. There was strong incentive for China to agree to this since at the time Hong Kong generated around 10% of China's overall GDP (Brandt et al., 2014).

An enclave strategy also allowed experimentation with managed risk. Deng simultaneously set up Special Economic Zones (SEZs), first just outside Hong Kong and then in other areas in Southern China, which drew in foreign investors with very favourable terms and inducements, and brought in surplus Chinese labour from the countryside and teeming cities, paying them wages that ran ten times or more the local standard but which were still exceptionally low by international standards (Brandt et al., 2014). In doing this, Deng was effectively following the imperialist practice of "concessions" in port cities and industrial areas that the Europeans had imposed. But this was a sort of reverse imperialism, controlled by China on designed to be on China's own behalf, while still offering considerably advantages to the foreigners.

When the end finally came for the Soviet Union, China survived as a Communist state, and the Deng experiment broadened, continued and ultimately was applied nationally. Whether it is still "Communism" or not is debatable. It certainly bears little resemblance to the Marxism-Leninism of its birth or the Maoism that succeeded it. But then again, Chinese Communism had long gone its own way, even at the height of the Cold War.

27.8 The "New World Order"

The Cold War, thankfully, ended "cold", with relatively little interstate or intrastate violence. It could have ended differently in many places, in Leipzig, Prague or Sofia in 1989 if the leaders had chosen to use military force, possibly provoking local civil war. The same could be said for the Soviet collapse. There are various reasons for this relative quiescence, especially the memories of the various, mostly older, Communist bloc leaders, who had experienced Stalinist terror first-hand and were reluctant to deploy armed forces and tanks against their own people. The fact that Russia was taking a hands-off approach (retrospectively referred to as the "Sinatra Doctrine" by the Russian foreign minister in 1989 because Gorbachev had allowed its European Allies to do it "their way") was obviously a critical factor as well. The writing seemed to be on the wall, and some of the old elites, especially in the economic sector, hoped to be able to retain their positions in a more capitalist system (Ther, 2016, 72).

In fact, the revolutions of 1989 were concerned primarily with changing the political system to achieve democracy, not striving to change society radically or impose a new social order. In this sense, they were actually fairly conservative. Even by the 1950s, the idea that Socialism would supplant Capitalism had become implausible, as disunity with the Bloc made it impossible to speak with one voice, and the prospect of nuclear annihilation caused the Superpowers to move towards "peaceful coexistence" (Hobsbawm, 1994, 488–489). In 1989 Eastern Europe, Communism and Socialism was quickly withering away and only Capitalism and Democracy, across the border, was on offer. After a political transition had been negotiated in its various countries, the hopeful phase of fraternisation, celebration, and euphoria ended quite quickly, with many of the mass participants soon losing hope and enthusiasm (Ther, 2016, 74).

In Eastern Europe, foreign capital and experts quickly moved in (Czechoslovakia being in particular vogue in the beginning), and neoliberal market structures were quickly adopted (see Chapter 28), disappointing many of the veterans of the protests of 1968 and the more youthful protagonists of the later movements. Jürgen Habermas in 1990 complained of a complete absence of forward-looking ideas as the natural ills of market organisation crept in, such as public spending cuts, growing social inequality, and greater disadvantages for women as older traditional discriminatory practices returned after Socialist egalitarianism dissolved. The 1989 protesters believed in the accomplishments and ideals of Socialism but were against the corrupt, deadening, oppressive institutions that worked in its name. They did not, mostly, expect that these ideals would be lost when a democratic order was established (Ther, 2016, 75). Having not lived under Capitalism, many were surprised and disappointed by that system's limits, whatever its other strengths were. Reality is always different from the ideal, and such disappointments are inevitable.

In the Soviet Union, the transition was far worse. Internal calls for radical and sudden economic deregulation, made by people who had no idea of how Capitalism actually functioned, were buttressed by the opinions of English and American "shock therapy" economists who believed in the benign transformative power of unfettered markets. Some of these programs were more ideological than empirical, inspired by free-market luminaries like Milton Friedman and Friedrich von Hayek who condemned any notion of a mixed economy and thus had nothing to offer on how to actually build one. But standard neoclassical economics pretty much argued in the same direction, though with a few caveats about "externalities" and other "market failures". Although the former Communist states were referred to as "transitional" economies, there was very little "transition" to speak of in Russia, and not too much outside of it either. The Russians suffered sharp and immediate disastrous falls in living standards, health and well-being, and the era witnessed the rise of the Oligarchs, native Russians who accumulated Russian assets on the cheap during the chaos to become massive private power centres (Hobsbawm, 1994, 491–493; Marangos, 2003).

Geopolitically, a vast power vacuum opened, and, for the third time in a single century, the US was there to fill it. After First World War hostilities ended America had pulled back from European and global entanglements, though not regional ones, especially in Latin America and the

Pacific. After Second World War denouement the country had stepped in to build an order around itself in a bifurcated world. Now the US seemingly faced no significant constraints to its exercise of power at all. America was a superpower without challenge, and now also had, at least notionally, significant internal resources freed up to it by a so-called peace dividend which could be potentially devoted to various purposes at home and abroad. Internationally, President George H.W. Bush, having served as Ronald Reagan's Vice President and prior to that head of the CIA in the 1970s, pronounced the "New World Order" (NWO), which, though dressed up in heady rhetoric amounted to American unilateralism of action and imposition of the "Washington Consensus" abroad (Williams, 2007).

Thus, the 1990s was the era of the NWO. Major changes to multilateral institutions were not required. Instead, existing institutions turned more America-focused or were expanded to incorporate formerly neutral or opposing powers. The Czech Republic, Poland and Hungary joined the North Atlantic Treaty Organisation (NATO) in 1999, followed in 2004 by Slovakia, Slovenia, Romania, Bulgaria and the Baltic states. Eastern Europe now clearly aligned itself with the West (Ther, 2016, 52). Other institutions, such as the Association of Southeast Asian Nations (ASEAN), also expanded and tilted westward, now shorn of the complexity of member countries being spread across competing Communist, Capitalist or Neutralist blocs.

One complication to this was nationalism, which the fall of Communism, in Europe especially, helped to reawaken. The "refrigerator theory" that nationalist conflicts had been frozen by Communism and then began to "thaw" after its collapse, is part of the explanation. But in fact, nationalist tendencies had been rumbling even under Communism, with Czechoslovakia federalising in 1969 to meet Slovakian concerns expressed during the Prague Spring, and Yugoslavia granting a new federal constitution in 1974. Armenians and Azerbaijanis fought each other as respective constituent Soviet republics within the USSR in the 1980s, conflicts broke out in Soviet Central Asia, and 320,000 Turks fled Bulgaria, as the government under Todor Shivkov repressed the Turkish minority. These tendencies broke out into hot war in some places during the 1990s, especially in the former Yugoslavia. Serbia Premier Slobodan Milošević was the prime agent in trying to build "Greater Serbia" out of the ruins of Yugoslavia with the persecution of Albanians in Kosovo and, later, the conflicts in Croatia and Bosnia and Herzegovina (Ther, 2016, 65). NATO became deeply involved in that conflict, shifting from a defensive Cold War alliance to a new and more ill-defined post-Cold War role.

Economically, the end of a divided world and its replacement with the NWO led to a rush of "free trade" deals and new economic blocs. The European Union expansion was greatly helped along by this, as was the North American Free Trade Act (NAFTA) successfully negotiated by the new Democratic President Bill Clinton, and signed in 1994. Global supply chains now were completely unhindered and allowed to find their cheapest labour and locations anywhere in the world, and offshoring of developed high-wage employment to low-wage locations sped up as a result (though it had been going on for decades) (Jean-Yves & Loïc, 2013, Chapter 4). *New York Times* journalist Thomas Friedman wrote the definitive apologia for free trade and "anywhere" supply sourcing in his 2005 book, *The World is Flat*, although some ironically noted that a round world was actually more geographically integrated and less bounded than a flat one.

This integration was helped along in Europe because a relatively skilled and industrially sophisticated Eastern European bloc now became fully accessible to the rich parts of Europe once these countries joined the EU. The policy choice of the Chinese to become the factory for the rest of the world, and its increasing ability to deliver the quantity and quality needed to do so, along with specific integration pacts, such as NAFTA, now brought in new low-wage, low-regulation hinterlands for Western, and especially American, producers. Without the drag of a Communist bloc, international business and business-friendly governments could proceed with more ambitious global projects such as the World Trade Organisation (WTO), established in 1995, which institutionalised and expanded the earlier free trade arrangements of the General Agreement on Trade and Tariffs (GATT) and created an authority with supranational sovereignty to oversee it (Jean-Yves & Loïc, 2013, Chapter 4). This internationalisation was not novel, but the speed, scale and scope of this new phase of globalisation was striking. It might have happened much earlier without a Cold War. It was certainly making up for lost time.

27.9 The Meaning of the Cold War's End

By 1989, the Cold War order had lasted for a long time in terms of human life, roughly 50 years, or two and half generations. It had gone through many undulations of tension, producing at least one global existential crisis, in Cuba in 1962, and many other near misses, not all of them known to the general public at the time or even now. There had also been some deadly "hot" proxy wars, and sharp rhetoric on both sides. One could not say that it was comfortable, but the Communist-Capitalist rivalry had grown familiar, with international and various domestic social, political and economic orders built around it.

Many theorists during the Cold War's heights thought that the there might end up being some sort of polyglot ecosystem of global Political Economy with institutional convergences, noting the rise of planning in Western governments and large Western companies, and the experimentation with market forms in Socialist countries. Certainly nobody thought that one side would prevail militarily over the other in a hot war, to impose its own system by force. The results of any such attempt would be "MAD". Hence the default was towards evolution of some kind over some years.

What almost no one predicted, in either Communist or Capitalist camps, was the sudden collapse of Socialism. Despite the presence of huge Western intelligence apparatuses and legions of analysts poring over data and situation reports, the presumption right up until the collapse was that the Superpowers, whatever their weaknesses, did indeed seem to be super in their powers, evenly balanced strategically, and thus impervious to rapid structural decay. But one must be gentle in making judgements in hindsight. After all, the Great Depression was also almost entirely unanticipated, as was the French Revolution, to take two other cataclysmic historical events.

It is important not to forget the historical concept of "contingency", i.e. that things could have turned out differently than they actually did, had circumstances, even minor ones, been different. In his imagined memoirs of the man Claudius, who would become emperor of Rome, Robert Graves ([1934] 1978) has his main character reflecting of the reign of his predecessor, the Emperor Caligula, and how events might have transpired if Caligula had been a better person. But he stops his speculations, noting them to be idle. If Caligula had been different than he actually was, then he would never have survived at all, or been chosen as Tiberius's successor. To speculate otherwise, the character says, is to engage in "impossible contingencies". "Claudius" cements his point through the use of an analogy of the Wooden Horse of Troy foaling, an obvious impossibility, and thus pointless to consider (325).

This is how people seem to treat the way that the Cold War actually ended, any alternative being an "impossible contingency". In prospect, its endpoint was uncertain close to the last minute. It is only in retrospect that things appear to be inevitable. Of course, one cannot change the past. But one shouldn't be too rigid in positing inevitability either.

References

Best, A., Hanhimäki, J. M., Maiolo, J. A., & Schulze, K. E. (2004). *International history of the twentieth century and beyond* (2nd ed.). Routledge.

Brandt, L., Ma, D., & Rawski, T. (2014). From divergence to convergence: Reevaluating the history behind China's economic boom. *Journal of Economic Literature, 52*(1), 45–123.

Davies, C. (2010). Jokes as the truth about Soviet socialism. *Folklore: Electronic Journal of Folklore, 46*, 9–32.

Easterly, W., & Fischer, S. (1995). The Soviet economic decline. *The World Bank Economic Review, 9*(3), 341–371.

Epstein, E. J. (1986). Petropower and Soviet expansion. *Commentary, 82*(1), 23.

Graves, R. ([1934] 1978). *I, Claudius*. Penguin Books.

Harrison, M. (1993). Soviet economic growth since 1928: The alternative statistics of GI Khanin. *Europe-Asia Studies, 45*(1), 141–167.

Hobsbawm, E. J. (1994). *Age of extremes: The short twentieth century*. Michael Joseph.

Jean-Yves, H., & Loïc, V. (2013). *OECD insights: Economic globalisation origins and consequences*. OECD Publishing.

Kornai, J. (1986). *Contradictions and dilemmas: Studies on the socialist economy and society*. MIT Press.

Marangos, J. (2003). Was shock therapy really a shock? *Journal of Economic Issues, 37*(4), 943–966.

Sheehy, G. (1991). *Gorbachev: A one-man revolution*. Mandarin.

Skocpol, T. (1979). *States and social revolutions: A comparative analysis of France*. Cambridge University Press.

Ther, P. (2016). *Europe since 1989: A history* (C. Hughes-Kreutzmüller, Trans.). Princeton University Press.

Westad, O. A. (2017). *The Cold War: A world history*. Penguin Random House UK.

White, S. (1986). Economic performance and communist legitimacy. *World Politics, 38*(3), 462–482.

Williams, A. (2007). *Failed imagination? The Anglo-American new world order from Wilson to Bush* (2nd ed.). Manchester University Press.

CHAPTER 28

Neoliberalism

C. Gordon, *Many Possible Worlds*,
https://doi.org/10.1007/978-981-19-9281-0_28

Fig. 28.1 Neoliberalism: not just a museum piece (*Image source* Loz Pycock-Follow, The Museum of Neoliberalism, Lee, Lewisham, England.Photo taken on January 12, 2020. Photographer has applied a CC BY-SA 2.0 license. https://www.flickr.com/photos/blahflowers/49390291577. No modifications have been made)

28.1 What's so "Neo" About "Neoliberalism"?

The Industrial Revolution gave rise to a new philosophy of Political Economy called Liberalism. Liberalism in its original form reduced politics and economics to a simple formula of laissez-faire in government policy; electoral democracy in which popular will was determined by majority at the ballot box and exercised through representative institutions; formal protections of individual freedoms through a defined set of civil rights; the legal guarantee of private property; the promotion, and even privileging, of activities that led to capital accumulation; the use of market mechanisms, wherever possible, to allocate and distribute resources across an economy; and a commitment to unfettered international trade and capital flows (Fig. 28.1).

The doctrine remained alive but underwent considerable modification during the twentieth century. In particular, political democracy in the

West became augmented by Social Democracy, which can be simplistically summarised as the proposition that economic rights are as important to democratic functionality as political ones. Thus, if some groups are too poor to participate in civil society, lobby their representatives, or even get to a polling place, while other groups can do all of this and more because of their economic advantages, then the society can be said to undemocratic and this will undermine the democratic nature of the political system. These inequalities need to be rectified to an extent that allows for genuinely equal inclusion and ability to exercise democratic rights. A "welfare state", providing basic material entitlements to the poorest while redistributing resources away from the richest to limit their unfair economic advantage, became one of the primary vehicles for accomplishing social democracy. There were many variations between countries on implementation, but this package became widespread during the 1950s, 1960s and 1970s while free-market Capitalism became modified by more interventionist government policies (Huber et al., 1993; Klitgaard, 2007).

The social discontent of the 1960s, and the economic stagnation of the 1970s led to a weakening of these modifications. Yet there was not just a simple return to the Liberalism of old. Too much had changed for that to happen. Instead, "Neoliberalism" became the norm. This was an obvious reference to the classical Liberalism of the nineteenth century. But what made it "Neo"?

There was much that was assumed away in the original conception of Liberalism, even during the time of its dominance, especially the existence and importance of group and social categories, e.g. economic and social class, race and gender, and the ability or inability of such to exercise collective power when organised. The rise of mass political parties during the 1800s was ignored in the theory, as was the mass media, large corporate entities, and all the other whys and wherefores of social power more generally. There were a few thinkers in the Liberal tradition that did grapple with these things, John Stuart Mill most notably (see Chapters 4 and 17). But these nuances were increasingly lost in translation.

These are rather gaping omissions. They can be forgiven initially by the fact that the doctrine was formulated during early industrialisation, a time of smaller scale enterprise, relatively small accumulations of capital and wealth (except for the wealth of traditional elites, such as the monarchy and nobility), some immediate continuity with traditional household social relationships and institutions, and the presence of relatively free-market competition that Adam Smith had trumpeted, despite his warnings of the monopolistic and collusive tendencies of businessmen (Rothschild, 1994). But even by mid-century, society was rapidly diverging from the "stylised facts" required to make the theory work. In this sense, Liberalism as an applicable theory needed updating even in its own heyday. It certainly needed major revision for applicability to the latter half of the twentieth century. In this narrow sense, Neoliberalism could be used as a term to indicate an updating of an old doctrine to make it more relevant and useful to changed conditions.

However, Liberalism, even its Classical form, always had a substantial ideological component in which the basic conclusions were assumed and selectively justified *ex post*. Neoliberalism as it has been practiced refers less to an updating and adaptation for modern times, and more to an update to an ideology. Earlier challenges to Liberalism, such as Fascism, Communism and the Depression, had forced reforms, like the welfare state, in order to preserve the Capitalism and Liberal democracy bundle preferred by Liberals. But a combination of political, economic and social shifts ended this particular form of adaptation. In fact, the "Neo" part of Neoliberalism emerged as an ideological rejection of the earlier moderations of classical liberalism, with that rejection now altered in the face of a radically changed economy and society that bore absolutely no resemblance to the context out of which the original version was born. This required many specific policy and institutional changes to the tenets of the original doctrine, radically changing it in the process, despite the evocation of Liberalism in name.

Thus, neoliberalism as a term refers to three different developments. First it can be spoken of as a revised theory or model of the Political Economy of Capitalism. Second, and more commonly, it refers to an ideology or system of thought, which in many cases could be said to be a utopian vision of a market system that will solve all problems, economic and otherwise, if only its imagined pure version is allowed to operate without restraint. Third, and finally, it refers to a concrete political and policy program that began in the late 1970s and continues today that is devoted to rolling back the interests of labour in favour of capital, eliminating governmental social programs and "safety nets", maximally deregulating private enterprise, including policy addressing market failures such as lack of competition, and removing as entirely as possible any progressive resource redistribution through government taxation or spending mechanisms, even to the extent of imposing regressive redistribution from bottom up to the top. Specific planks implementing this include removal of anti-trust policy, privatisation and contracting out of public services, regressive tax cuts, domestic and international capital market liberalisation, anti-union legislation and public sector worker employment cuts (Harvey, 2007). All this is to be accomplished by dismantling some government and social institutions, reshaping existing ones, and building entirely new ones, e.g. the World Trade Organisation (Slobodian, 2018).

28.2 The Bretton Woods International Order

Neoliberalism in all these senses is a reaction against the particular order that arose out of the Bretton Woods world economic and financial system order that was constructed after the end of the Second World War (see Chapters 24 and 25) (Fig. 28.2).

From the vantage point of 1945, the twentieth century world economic and political order up that point had been a disaster. Two world wars, the second far more devastating than the first, had taken place, sandwiching a ruinous global Great Depression in between. This was in contrast to the nineteenth century that had seen not just one but two Industrial Revolutions and a strong rise in economic growth in a widening number of "rich" countries.

Simplistic logic from the point of view of the economic status quo suggested that a restoration of the nineteenth century order, with its accompanying prodigious growth and income, was desirable. But, putting aside some of the more unsavoury aspects of this order, such as imperialism, such a restoration was no longer possible. Too much had changed. Europe had been the centre of the old order, but now it had torn itself apart not once but twice. The US had long been rising and now was completely dominant in economic and military power. Britain, though still retaining an Empire and having been a pivotal member of the Allies, was a shadow of its former self. The old Europe-based world order, with Britain as the hegemon, was obviously out of the question.

Could the old order be restored but with American hegemony instead? This too was not viable. The experience of the Interwar period seemed to demonstrate that while the international system of capital and trade flows did require a hegemonic power, the old system could not simply

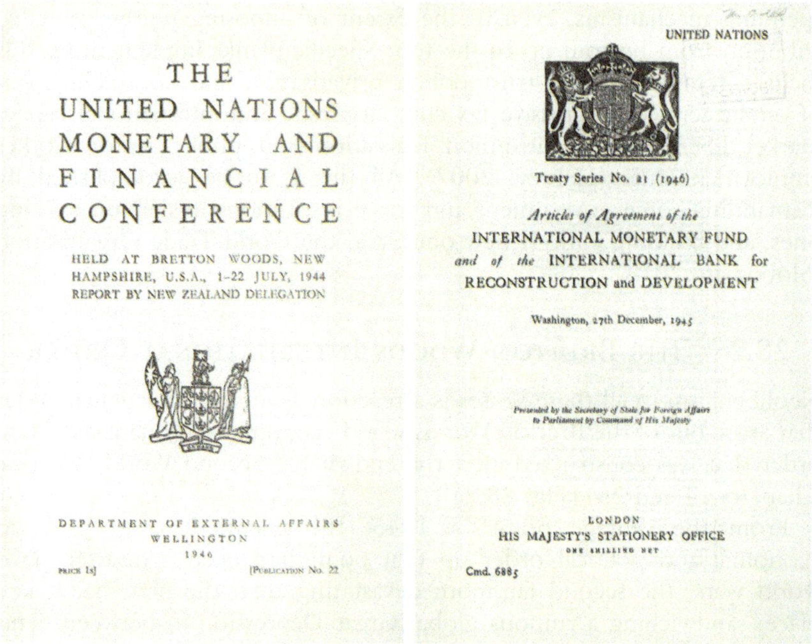
THE
UNITED NATIONS
MONETARY AND
FINANCIAL
CONFERENCE

HELD AT BRETTON WOODS, NEW
HAMPSHIRE, U.S.A., 1-22 JULY, 1944
REPORT BY NEW ZEALAND DELEGATION

DEPARTMENT OF EXTERNAL AFFAIRS
WELLINGTON
1946
PRICE 1s] [PUBLICATION No. 22

UNITED NATIONS

Treaty Series No. 21 (1946)

Articles of Agreement of the
INTERNATIONAL MONETARY FUND
and of the INTERNATIONAL BANK for
RECONSTRUCTION and DEVELOPMENT

Washington, 27th December, 1945

Presented by the Secretary of State for Foreign Affairs to Parliament by Command of His Majesty

LONDON
HIS MAJESTY'S STATIONERY OFFICE
ONE SHILLING NET

Cmd. 6885

Fig. 28.2 Coversheet of a document outlining the articles of Bretton-Woods (*Image source* Archives New Zealand, Reference: AECO 18,675 PM23 Box 2 3/2. http://archway.archives.govt.nz/ViewFullItem.do?code=20470599 Attribution 2.0 Generic [CC BY 2.0])

swap the US for the UK, and New York for London, without restructuring some fundamental rules and institutions. Indeed such a de facto swap, very roughly speaking, had been attempted after the First World War, and the result was that the entire system collapsed within a mere fifteen years, bringing economic debacle with it. What hadn't existed then but needed to be put in place now was a financial backstop for international liquidity, i.e. an international Lender of Last Resort or LOLR (see Chapter 19). The economic turbulence of the 1920s and 1930s also indicated that some measure of steady and geographically well-distributed international economic growth and development was needed to ensure that there was sufficient international demand to buy the exports that are a critical component of growth overall. The elimination of the possibility of ruinous trade wars was a final recommended strategy.

These basic ideas were embodied in the institutions created by Bretton Woods and its aftermath. These included a new International Monetary Fund (IMF) as a monitor of global liquidity, and provider of short-term capital and bridging loans to meet national financing needs that could not be met through the normal capital markets; the International Bank for Reconstruction and Development, colloquially known as the World Bank, to provide loans and grants to developing countries to help boost their growth and structural advancement; and the General Agreement on Trades and Tariffs (GATT), which was designed to lower tariff and other trade barriers between countries on an ongoing basis (Bordo, 1993).

It was this system that America designed, slotting itself into a hegemonic centre. Nominally, the Gold Standard with its fixed exchange rates was re-established. More precisely, the new system made most of the major currencies convertible to gold, guaranteed by the US dollar which now served as the global unit of account and the official reserve currency of the entire system. This formalised the more informal (and somewhat more fragmented) hegemonic order of the nineteenth century in which the British Pound Sterling and the British Treasury and Bank of England served a similar role, but unofficially and with less of the economic dominance that America had in its unprecedented post-war position. Adding to this the substantial American aid to European governments after the war (especially the Marshall Plan—see Chapter 25), one had a system designed to maximise currency stability, international trade and a growth-based liberalism that Maier (1977) has referred to as Productivism. In theory, this system was supposed to enhance the welfare of all, while cementing and continuing the predominance of the US within the Capitalist world. The conceit was that this was apolitical, providing a technical solution to the technical problem of growth, political stability and recovery on a global basis. The key to holding this together was constant growth of sufficient magnitude to remove zero-sum class and interest conflicts both domestically and on the global stage. This growth was also critical to American plans for its hegemony to be maintained with as little contribution from itself as possible. In this, they were even more parsimonious than the British had been in their time of dominance (Maier, 1977, 623, 631–632).

28.3 The Keynesian Consensus and Domestic "Fine-Tuning"

The domestic economic management mechanism to avoid zero-sum distributional conflict through strong, steady and stable growth was the exercise of Keynesian countercyclical policy by domestic governments throughout the developed world. Although Keynes had not published his "General Theory" until 1936, his ideas were very timely given the ravages of what seemed to be permanent Depression. Keynes' ideas are subtle and complex, and sometimes unclear and somewhat contradictory. After the war, a pared down interpretative synthesis of his thought emerged, not fully reflecting, and sometimes even inconsistent with Keynes' actual philosophy. It was this understanding that became the basis for the post-war "consensus" economic policy of the Western world. Replacing the disastrous laissez-faire approach to economic booms and busts that had prevailed into the 1930s, Keynesianism was shorthand for the use of government expenditure to smooth out the business cycle and the "output gaps" that occurred when total demand for goods and services was either too low or too high to buy up all the supply on offer. Never again, it was hoped, would the situation of the Depression, when total demand in the economy appeared to be permanently too far below total supply, transpire. Instead, national governments now would inject public money into their domestic economies temporarily in times of recession, either through tax cuts or through expenditure increases, to boost total spending to plug the gaps between "aggregate demand" and "aggregate supply". (This was supposed to work in boom times during which aggregate demand exceeded aggregate supply as well, except here the task would be to remove money from the economy to bring the two into equilibrium. This policy was undertaken much less in practice because it was politically much more attractive to put money into voters' hands than take it out of them). Such policy was thus referred to as "countercyclical", as it was designed to work against harmfully excessive turns in the business cycle.

The New Zealand economist A.W. Phillips added another influential piece to this economic policy consensus. In studying data for wage inflation (i.e. the growth in nominal wages, i.e. wages not adjusted for inflation, over time) and unemployment rates, he found a strong inverse relationship between the two. That is, higher wage inflation was associated with lower unemployment rates and vice versa. The Phillips pattern

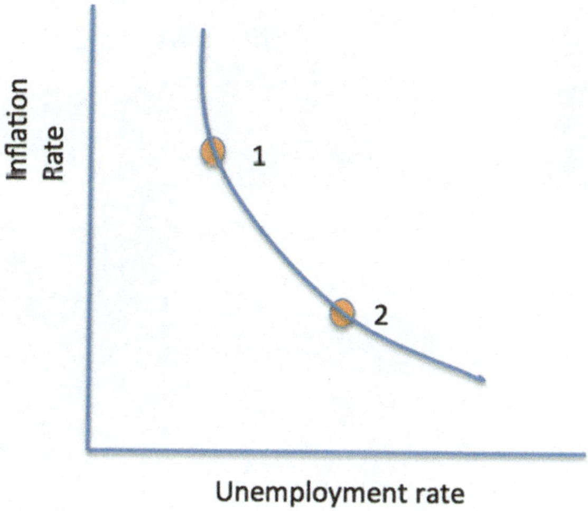

Fig. 28.3 The "Phillips Curve" (Created by author. See text for explanation)

held for England, but it was subsequently replicated for many other countries and it seemed to suggest a universal pattern whereby policymakers could "trade-off" between wage growth and unemployment through the use of Keynesian countercyclical spending and taxing.

To take a hypothetical example, if the data for a country suggested that an unemployment rate of 4% was associated with wage growth of 3%, and an unemployment rate of 5% was associated with wage growth of 2%, then it was inferred that it was possible to pick one of these two points (in actuality these would be just two pairs from a whole series of points) by moving money into or out of the economy until the desired point was reached. From this statistical correlation came the view that the macroeconomy was seen as a sort of machine whose dials could be adjusted by technical experts based on data and modelling. This adjustment became known as "fine-tuning" (Booth, 2001). This concept soon broadened out to trade-offs not just between wages and unemployment but inflation more generally and unemployment, as in Fig. 28.3. Here policymakers have a whole range of combinations between the two to choose from, with point 1 chosen if a lower unemployment, but higher inflation rate is preferred, and 2 chosen if a higher unemployment but lower inflation rate is the goal.

Fig. 28.4 Professor A.W.H (Bill) Phillips and his Machine circa 1958–1967 (*Image source* London School of Economics Archives. Extracts from http://archives.lse.ac.uk/dserve.exe?dsqServer=lib-4.lse.ac.uk&dsqIni=Dserve.ini&dsqApp=Archive&dsqCmd=Show.tcl&dsqDb=Catalog&dsqPos=0&dsqSearch=(RefNo=%27IMAGELIBRARY/6%27. No known copyright restrictions)

With this mechanistic paradigm of the economy in mind, Phillips himself had built a hydraulic machine (see Fig. 28.4) in which the "circular flow" of income through an economy was represented by water pumped around through a series of clear plastic tubes, with economic outflows representing savings, taxes and imports, and inflows representing investment, government spending and exports. Water flowed through three tanks connected to each other by various pipes, the flows being adjusted until a final hydraulic level, representing the total level of income, interest rates, foreign trade balance and currency balance, was reached. In this way, actual economies could be simulated and equilibrating flows via policy adjustments could be calculated, e.g. the right amount of tax cut to balance the economy and achieve the desired unemployment-inflation pair associated with it. Plotter pens, measuring these effects, traced the time path of all the flows in and out, along with the equilibrium levels. For its time, the machine proved to be extraordinarily accurate (Barr, 1988).

28.4 Business, Labour, Accords and the Social Wage

Sufficient growth would ensure that zero-sum conflict between classes and groups was avoided, fine-tuning would ensure enough employment and price stability to allow businesses and individuals to adequately plan for their futures in an environment of business cycle stability. However, the distribution of domestic wealth and income between capital and labour still needed to be modified through explicit policies. The rising inequality of the nineteenth century had brought rampant social and class conflict with it. This was bad enough, but the Depression had made it clear that the entire capitalist system could be torn apart by unresolved social discord. Also, one could no longer easily ignore the needs and desires of labour, and focus solely on the interests of capital, because labour interests were more organised and stronger than they had ever been. There was now also a Communist world supposedly devoted to the workers, providing a further threat to Capitalist democracies if the labouring classes became too discontented.

The Classical Economists had largely sidelined issues of distribution, growth being much more important to them. Adam Smith had invented the notion of the "wage fund" to indicate that capital accumulation would automatically provide for at least sufficient wages for workers and that capitalists and labourers had some common, rather than competing, interest in keeping a business enterprise growing and profitable, since growing profits would lead to growing wages (see Chapter 4). This ad hoc concept was not particularly convincing, and did not even grow logically out of Smithian premises, being asserted rather than proven. Some later Classical Economists, most notably John Stuart Mill, challenged it, while Marx, of course, rejected it completely with his model of an assumed inherent implacability between proletariat and capitalist.

The development of the capitalist economy did demonstrate a prodigious capacity to produce capital. But it also demonstrated that high profits did not at all guarantee higher wages, or even that workers would earn enough to have the necessities of life. The early welfare programs of the Second Industrial Revolution, with its furtive age and unemployment pensions and "poor relief" here and there, had been initial government interventions to support the very worst off of those unable to work and who could no longer count on sufficient organic care from the family and community which industrialisation was busy reshaping and, in many ways, undermining. The idea of ensuring that even gainfully employed people might require social support because they might not be sufficiently compensated privately was a later development driven especially by the Great Depression and the crisis in liberal democracy that it engendered. The post-war welfare state was a natural extension of this experience (Friedland & Sanders, 1986).

This general issue in capitalist development is referred to as the "social wage", which refers to the net amount of resources workers actually get as compensation for their labour, accounting for resource flows from the society as a whole, public and private, and netting out any payments made by labour into it, especially taxes (Friedland & Sanders 1986). Free-market capitalism held that the private wage was all that mattered, using the theorem of neoclassical economics that in purely competitive markets, the wage paid would be exactly equal to the marginal product of the labour provided. This was an economically efficient outcome, according to theory, and could also be said to represent a Utilitarian form of social justice, i.e. the market delivering to workers exactly what their labour was truly worth as a contribution to production.

The turmoils of the 1930s discredited this notion since the system was not able to provide employment to, at its height, on average, 1 out of 4 willing and able-bodied workers (see Chapter 18). Those who remained working often could not live on what they were making. Communism solved the problem by making the State the employer of first and last resort and provision of employment and a decent social wage was formally guaranteed, though the latter obligation was often not lived up to. On the right, the Fascists also explicitly guaranteed employment, though the

State did not necessarily provide it, much private enterprise remaining. The conceit was that labour was one of the "corporations" of society, to be balanced out against others, including capital interests, the State being the final arbiter. It was a counterfeit framework that suppressed labour activism and unionism through government-sponsored unions and political repression, and it was racist and exclusive as well. But Fascism and Communism at least acknowledged the wage was not just a private matter, but a social one as well, something that the capitalist democracies had largely evaded.

The post-war democratic capitalist settlement addressed the social wage in two ways. Expansion of the welfare state continued and expanded to serve those on the fringes of the market, such as the very poor, disabled or old along with new temporary short-term support for the cyclically unemployed displaced in business cycle downturns. To ensure that the employed had decent enough income not just to stay off the safety net but also to be able to afford a home and the purchases of necessities and a few luxuries as well, formal and informal "accords" between big business and big labour were arranged, with government serving as an intermediary. The fact that large labour unions had established their own political parties in some countries, or were active funders and supporters of centre-left parties in others, helped the formation of these agreements. The accords would nominally be about wage moderation offered by unions in exchange for profit and price moderation by business. But in practice profits were moderated less than wages, since wages were seen as costs to be minimised while profits were seen as capital inputs to be maximised. Where private wages were deemed insufficient in providing a politically and socially acceptable standard of living, the gap was made up through greater welfare spending and other labour benefits offered by government. Even when this was funded with higher taxation, there is evidence that such accords, formal and informal, may actually have been good for growth because of the macroeconomic stability and high investment levels they encouraged (Crafts, 1995, 441).

28.5 A Turn for the Better; then a Turn for the Worse

With all these planks in place, the 1950s, 1960s and very beginning of the 1970s exhibited some of the broadest and faster per capita growth rates ever seen throughout the Western developed world. (As already

Table 28.1 Annual growth rates in fifteen Western European countries (%), 1890–1994

Time period	*GDP*	*GDP per capita*
1890–1913	2.2	1.4
1913–1950	1.4	0.9
1950–1973	4.8	4.0
1973–1994	2.1	1.7

Source Temin (2002), Table 1, p. 4 (calculated by Temin using Maddison data available at the time; the rates above would change somewhat if the most current Maddison data were employed but the orders of magnitude would be roughly similar)

discussed in Chapter 25 the Socialist bloc also had strong growth in this period, though on average not as high and starting from a lower base).

Table 28.1 shows some broad time periods for growth in Western Europe. 1950–1973 stands out as a truly "Golden Age" in which both total GDP and GDP per capita grew on average very quickly after the ruins of war. There were country differences, to be sure. France, for example grew, much more strongly than Britain did during this time, as did West Germany. But the mean was a very high one, and whether below or above it, prosperity was steady for all.

However, there was a marked slowdown starting in 1973 for Europe (and as other figures would show, elsewhere in most of the developed world). Growth rates more than halved, both in total and per capita terms across 1973–1994 as compared to 1950–1973. Historically, this was still a good performance compared to the decades between 1890 and 1950, comparable even to the high water mark of the Second Industrial Revolution in 1890–1913. Thus, one can interpret the Golden Age as an ebullient aberration from a nonetheless solid upward trend.

However, the picture is not as rosy as it first appears. In particular, inflation accelerated throughout the developed world at the end of the 1960s and throughout the 1970s. In the US, the broadest measure of inflation, the GDP deflator, went from an average of 1.4% a year in the first half of the decade to 4.1% a year in the second, with a 4.8% rise in prices in 1969 and 5.5% in 1970. Between 1969 and 1970, the weighted average increase in prices across the developed world was 6%, and it would steadily climb beyond this during the 1970s (UN, 1975, 4).

Meanwhile, output and employment growth was slowing as inflation was increasing, a combination that was historically relatively novel. In the seven major industrial economies of the time, GDP grew only 2.2%

between 1969 and 1970, less than half the average for the 1960s, and growth would continue to deteriorate over the decade, accompanied by rising domestic unemployment rates. This was not a smooth process, and cyclical instability became a hallmark of economies, with two major recessions occurring in the industrialised world during the 1970s (UN, 1975, 4). The 1970s thus became known as an era of "stagflation" in the developed world, a term meshing together "stagnation" and "inflation". It was most definitively an end to the "Golden Age" of steady growth and its accompanying stable prices and unemployment rates.

28.6 What Happened?

To some degree, the extraordinarily broad and fast growth of the 1950s and 1960s could never last. Partly this was mere arithmetic; as economies grew larger, relative growth rates had to decline sooner or later. This mere fact alone would ultimately doom the Productivist dream of removing all social conflict by distributing an ever-larger material pie to capital, labour and other remaining interests. Once growth slowed sufficiently, or went into reverse, economic conflict could no longer be bought off and the political problem of distribution would have to be faced one way or another.

And it was inevitable that ever increasing growth would lead to ever increasing demand which in turn led to rising prices for basic commodities that served as inputs into industrial production, resulting in the commodities price boom in 1973–1974, a development that macroeconomists refer to as a "supply shock". Even before this point, domestic demand was rising too rapidly relative to domestic supply, leading to labour shortages and rising wage demands that began to break up the various "accords" between big business and labour and driving up domestic inflation. In turn, this upset the stable "Phillips Curve" trade-off between inflation and unemployment that Keynesian fine-tuning relied on to keep the economy stable and practice "fine-tuning". Stagflation had the further effect of eroding government budget revenues because of lowered rates of economic growth leading to less taxable income being generated. Inflation caused interest rates to rise as well. These tax and interest rate developments made Keynesian "pump-priming" more costly as government budget deficits limited the ability of governments to borrow and spend. And with both inflation and unemployment rising, the Keynesian solution of pulling money out of the economy to cool things down was made infeasible. In fact, such a move would likely only deepen a downturn without any guarantee of lowered inflation (Fig. 28.5).

America and the US-centred financial and economic system was meanwhile also on the ropes. Although Bretton Woods had been meant to allow for unfettered capital flows, the reliance on a global supply of US dollars tethered to gold had from the beginning required significant capital regulations and limitation of trade and payments liberalisation. Fort Knox in Tennessee held almost three-quarters of the world's gold reserves. But as mighty as this sounded, it was not enough to allow

Fig. 28.5 The 1970s "Energy Crisis" (*Image source* U.S. National Archives' Local Identifier: 412-DA-12965. Photographer: Falconer, David. Project DOCUMERICA; Persistent URL: https://arcweb.archives.gov/arc/action/ExternalIdSearch?id=555417; Repository: Still Picture Records Section, Special Media Archives Services Division [NWCS-S], National Archives at College Park, 8601 Adelphi Road, College Park, MD, 20,740–6001. Original Caption: "Turn Off the Damn Lights" Stickers Mirrored the Seriousness of the Energy Situation in Oregon During the Fall of 1973. This Sticker, in a Portland Business Office, Was Used in Newspaper Ads as Well as on Television, Billboards and Car Bumpers 10/1973. No known copyright restrictions)

anywhere near full convertibility of the US dollar into gold and other currencies for all who wanted such conversion. America was increasingly reliant on other central banks to not call in their gold, a "Gold Pool" created for that very purpose which became more and more strained until it was dissolved in 1968 (Hobsbawm, 1994, 240–42).

The fundamental problem was that the US had moved from being an international creditor and net goods exporter after the end of the Second World War, into a growing net debtor and importer. Like Britain before it, the US had to supply capital to the world to keep the international financial system going, but no longer had the requisite funds. And unlike after 1919, America lost even the will to try to do so. President Richard Nixon suspended gold convertibility of the dollar in 1971 to avoid having an American gold crisis, thus ending the Bretton Woods system and the Gold Standard entirely, although, crucially, the US dollar remained the world reserve currency (Bordo, 1993).

The other thing that upset the post-war order was the changing relationship between global North and South. In 1945, the European Empires still covered much of the globe and the colonisers could freely extract resources from the colonised. By 1971, few "Third World" countries were still directly under the control of Western nations, and the pressure of overheated Northern demand for raw Southern commodities briefly put those few developing economies that were major commodity exporters (along with a few developed countries in a similar position, such as Australia) in the economic driver's seat. The growth compact of Western Productivism had always relied on cheap inputs from, and relatively low consumption levels in, the global South to keep from crimping resource availability for the rich world (Araghi, 2010, 41). The commodities boom ended this pattern. The oil embargo by the mostly middle eastern-based Organisation of Petroleum Exporting Countries (OPEC) in 1973–1974, imposed in response to Western support for Israel in the 1973 Middle East war, indicated a new rebalancing, showing that the underdeveloped countries would no longer be easily compliant with Western needs and demands.

Geopolitically, a movement called the New International Economic Order (NIEO) arose from this state of affairs. Promulgated first in a United Nations declaration in 1974, the NIEO was a proposal for a transnational governance reform to change the institutions and relations of the global economy to redirect more of the benefits of transnational integration from North to South. A group of 77 developing nations, the

Group of 77 (G77), pushed and advocated for it. It was an extension of the decolonisation movement that had swept through the world during the 1950s and 1960s (see Chapter 25), and it sought to create a democratic global order of truly sovereign states and more equitable resource distribution. For a brief moment, its prospects looked good (Gilman, 2015).

28.7 A Changing Political Economy

All these developments demonstrated that Productivism, and its various institutional arrangements, was ultimately a chimera anyway. For one thing, it addressed only the material dimension of society. The mounting cultural strains of the 1960s and 1970s (see Chapter 24) were in some ways fed by a burgeoning yet empty material abundance. Other issues, such as civil rights or war and peace, are inherently political and conflictual, and never amenable to mere redistribution of the "extra" growth.

And it should be remembered that although there had been an implied, and in some countries, an explicit, social contract between Big Labour and Big Capital in the developed countries, this was not the same thing as a pro-labour policy nor did it represent a complete addressing of distributional concerns. Even at the height of prosperity, profitability was of more concern than wage growth. Also, many groups were left out, such as the non-unionised (though during prosperity they often benefited from spillovers of union terms and conditions into the general labour market), those suffering from discrimination (e.g. African-Americans in the US and women everywhere), and small and medium-sized enterprises. There was a relatively peaceful labour market, rising wages, and a decent portion of income and wealth accumulating within the working and middle classes. But latent class and social conflict remained under the surface.

The deteriorating economic conditions of the late 1960s and 1970s shattered this quiescence, along with the implicit and explicit business-labour compacts underlying them. Stagflation brought out the inherent capital bias of Productivism and its basic lack of interest in equitable distribution of resources. Policymakers of the time, and historians afterwards, have often emphasised that wages needed to be kept down to keep developed economies internationally competitive and keep inflation under control. But it should be remembered that, even with stagflation, the developed world remained extraordinarily wealthy. The social wage could have been maintained by raising taxes on the highest income people, on capital income, or both, and in many countries this would have just been a restoration back to taxation levels existing during the immediate post-war period. Governments could also have used their power to rein in business profits as well as wages. This could have been combined with targeted inducements to investment through the tax code to minimise reductions in capital accumulation. Adjustments to a changing world had to be made, involved risk, and pain was inevitable. But they did not have to take the path they took, which were generally focused on sacrifices by labour and the disadvantaged rather than by capital owners and the well-advantaged. The end of the Golden Age showed that the distribution of income and power had never actually gone away as a central issue of the modern economy. The evaporation of growth merely brought it back to front and centre.

In fact, there was a great deal of political organising within business to move things more definitively in their favour, as the post-war order broke apart. The most notorious example is to be found in the US, with a plan outlined in a 1971 memorandum authored by corporate counsel Lewis Powell and provided to the US Chamber of Commerce, one of the leading business advocacy groups there. It besmirched business passivity in the face of growing activism by left groups, academics and others hostile to business interests (Powell, 1971). Though it overstated the case in one way, since business interests were already well organised and active in protecting their parochial interests as corporations, the memo called for a novel and integrated program of corporate activism designed to remake government and society to be thoroughly amenable to company enterprise and freedom of action more generally. Powell was later nominated and confirmed to the US Supreme Court by President Nixon. His memo only became public years later after it was leaked to the investigative journalist Jack Anderson (Ferguson, 2017, 35–53).

The Cold War context is significant here, the Powell memo fitting into the more general narrative of the survival of free enterprise being at stake. In many ways, Powell was using tactics that the Communists were often correctly accused of, proposing the use of front organisations, interlinked alliances and propaganda fed through mass media, though this was also standard practice in any mass marketing or policy public relations campaign. Powell's strategy thus outlined the creation of alternative think-tanks, advocacy groups and business pressure channels that would produce research reports, change legislation and mould public opinion to move against unions, government regulation and progressive taxation, all with indirect but hidden links to the standard pro-business lobbies, heavily funded and staffed by them. All this was framed as a corrective to growing leftist influence in academia, mainstream research organisations (such as the Brookings Institute and the Ford Foundation) and the media (Powell, 1971).

There was also a parallel and independent movement within academic economics departments and the official economic planning apparatus, away from the Keynesian consensus towards more free market orientations. This too was not inevitable or purely neutral, and was also coloured by the atmosphere of the Cold War. Economics could have moved leftward as easily as rightwards to respond to the situation of the time. But that seemed to establishment authorities, and even portions of the population, in the US particularly, a give-in to the Communists, and in any case was not the way that standard, neoclassically trained economists were trained to think anyway. These academic turns had political content, often unacknowledged, and some of their chief individual proponents were often active in seeking policy changes according with their theories.

One major example was the economist Milton Friedman, who was awarded the Nobel Prize in Economics in 1979. The Economics prize had taken a distinct rightward tilt in its direction during the 1970s, awarded to the arch-free marketer economists Freidrich von Hayek in 1972 (the Swedish development economist Gunnar Myrdal sharing it as an apparent gesture of political balance, and one that would become increasingly rare). Friedman's award was a distinct signal that planning-oriented or Keynesian economics was no longer favoured by the establishment (Offer & Söderberg, 2016).

Friedman was very much in favour of the deregulation, low taxation and small government planks of the Neoliberal doctrine, and a fellow traveller of Hayek's views about the primacy of the marketplace in all things (although Hayek's thought had its own subtleties (Caldwell, 2008). But Friedman made significant contributions to neoclassical economics and occasionally followed neoclassical logic to unorthodox conclusions. For example, he was a proponent in the US of a measure for a negative income tax scheme that would have ended up providing a very basic income for everyone who needed it, with the ultimate end of eliminating much of the welfare state apparatus that provided more conditional support. Friedman felt this would be administratively much more efficient and in line with his small government philosophy. The proposal failed to pass a strongly

Democratic Congress during Richard Nixon's Presidency because the Democrats thought it didn't go far enough (Moffitt, 2003). He was, nonetheless, a vocal and effective advocate for rolling back the State in all areas of society and economy, and his academic status provided an imprimatur to such thinking. He wrote a very popular non-academic book entitled *Free to Choose* (1990) which was a paean to the Liberalism of old, updated for contemporary times, and was a policy adviser on economic liberalisation for a number of governments and electoral campaigns.

Friedman's signature policy was Monetarism, which held that the money supply should be grown at a fixed rate by the Central Bank in order to limit inflationary tendencies and provide certainty to economic agents in their forward planning. This was a position in monetary affairs consistent with the more general idea of "rational expectations", developed most vocally by the economist Robert Lucas (who would win the Nobel Prize in 1995). Put simply this idea held that private economic actors would ultimately be able to figure out what governments would do, adjust their expectations accordingly (this was the rational expectations part) and then take appropriate actions in response, in the end nullifying the desired effects that government was seeking. This was a repudiation of fine-tuning, since it predicted that only unexpected, and hence temporary, changes in government spending and taxation would affect inflation and unemployment in the short run, after which rational agents would adjust their plans. Lucas later went even farther than this by positing the doctrine of "Ricardian Equivalence" which held that any government policies funded by deficit spending and requiring borrowing would not be stimulative in the Keynesian sense since rational agents would know that the debt would have to be paid back, requiring taxes to go up in the future, which would cause such agents to duly save to make these extra tax payments, rather than spending any proceeds they might temporarily receive through government tax cuts or expenditure increases (Chrisodoulakis, 2015, 171–184).

These lines of reasoning were quite resonant in an era when inflation was running out of control, unemployment was increasing and government seemed helpless to do anything about either one. They suggested that government should be minimised and where allowed to act, as in the setting of the money supply, set on autopilot. They suggested a return to the "night watchman" state of classical Liberalism. Neoliberalism went further, though, taking a decidedly pro-business and anti-labour cast with respect to government policy. The first major political successes came with the election of Margaret Thatcher as Conservative Prime Minister in 1979 and the election of Ronald Reagan as Republican Party candidate for President in 1980 (an election which also saw the US Senate fall into Republican hands for the first time since Eisenhower). Reagan's success in particular was helped along by a raft of new conservative front organisations, very much in accord with the Powell memo strategy, with the new Heritage Foundation's policy plan followed very closely by the first Reagan administration (Jones, 2012).

Reagan's rhetoric sounded on the surface like classical Liberalism, with a call for tax cuts and smaller government. But his actual policies were Neoliberal in creating regressive, rather than neutral, tax cuts, cutting expenditures for working and middle class groups, while increasing spending dramatically for the military, and aggressively deregulating the financial sector, continuing a process that had already begun in the 1970s (see the following section). He shared this agenda with Thatcher, and both were particularlly anti-union, Thatcher aiding in breaking up union power in the coalmines, the press and other industries, while Reagan broke the national air controller's union in a major strike it held in 1981 (Jones, 2012).

Thatcher also engaged in a strict monetarist policy in her first term as Prime Minister, being advised by major English monetarists who in turn were advised by Milton Friedman. This policy mainly had the result of provoking a severe recession without yielding the promised fall in money supply growth that the theory suggested it would (money supply rather mysteriously grew instead). Thatcher later disowned monetarism, and Friedman, although she continued her other neoliberal policies unapologetically, especially deregulation, privatisation and union battling (Frazer, 1982). In the US, President Jimmy Carter, near the end of his first (and last) term, had appointed Paul Volcker as head of the Federal Reserve Bank to follow monetarist policies that resulted in short-term interest rates rocketing up to 20% and also causing a severe economic downturn. American money supply growth did fall and inflation was broken with it, though how much this was due to the recession and how much to the change in money supply growth was not clear (Goodfriend & King, 2005). Thus, Reagan did not need to experiment with Monetarism since his Democratic predecessor had already done so.

The market utopianism of these policies was hidden by a general backlash against government activism, driven by the discontent of the increasingly economically dislocated voters. Original Liberalism had not been explicitly anti-union, but Neoliberalism was, largely because of the implicit belief that unions held back the innate innovative power of the market. Welfare states had been created by the old liberal democracies to ensure that capitalism could survive. Neoliberalism held that the welfare state was not only unnecessary but destructive. Sound money principles had also underlay the old Liberalism, with government budget deficits greatly discouraged at all costs, and banking supposedly run on conservative principles. Now deficits arising from tax cuts were seen as self-financing, more than made up with synergistic growth resulting from the growth power of private enterprise such cuts would unleash. Fiscal conclusions like these would never have been accepted by nineteenth century Chancellors of the Exchequer. Moreover, tax cuts were intentionally designed to benefit the rich because they were deemed as inherently more productive than the non-rich, a taxation principle that was not even in accord with neoclassical taxation theory which generally calls for a broad tax base with minimum distortion and with minimum administrative cost of collection. Neoliberal tax cuts violated all of these principles in one way or another (Graff et al., 2013, 302). All this was justified by a claim of an almost magical impetus to growth.

Neoliberal ideology and policies became increasingly influential and a foundation of most establishment political parties, left, centre and right, thus denuding such traditional labels of any meaning. The British Labour Party's official abandonment of its commitment to the "common ownership of the means of production" in 1995, and the cautiously pragmatic policies of the UK Labour Party and the US Democratic Party during the 1990s are examples (Romano, 2009). Deregulation, tax reduction, cuts in the welfare state, privatisation, "mimicking the market" in most government interventions rather than direct provision of services or command and control measures were now bipartisan planks, the main differences being in degree, including towards unionisation, with the left parties not attacking unions but not helping them much either.

In fact, labour and social democratic parties had been moving towards deregulation and lowered taxation in the name of growth for some time. The Americans, always on the conservative end of the Golden Age consensus, had set the tone in their domestic policies as far back as the promise of "a rising tide to lift all boats", a phrase used by Chairman of Economic Advisers Walter Heller in justifying the broad set of regressive tax cuts proposed by US President John Kennedy in 1962, and passed in 1964 after his assassination (Mozumi, 2018). The Australian Labor party under Prime Minister Bob Hawke and his Treasurer Paul Keating pursued economic deregulation and tax reductions very much opposed by the unions who backed the party in the 1980s. Indeed, some of the greatest moves towards neoliberalism came under nominally social democratic rather than rightist parties in the 1990s and 2000s (Kelly, 1992).

28.8 Globalisation and Financialisation

A full embrace of "Free Trade", a core pillar of classical Liberalism, further cemented the Neoliberal program on both sides of politics by the 1990s (i.e. those established political parties that dominated the electoral and legislative processes, from which much of the rest of society was left out). Once more the Neoliberal version of this doctrine was quite different than the classical liberal version. In the nineteenth century, there was a Gold Standard and imperial trading areas of different Empires, generally smaller scale domestic enterprise, and a powerful and expanding industrial base centred in what was to become known as the developed world. Free trade in the 1990s was pursued in an environment of a deindustrialisation in the North, firms chasing lower costs, higher profits and unregulated labour and environmental standards in the global South. Global corporations were now much more powerful as well, often more powerful than governments, with multilateral agreements reached increasingly in secret negotiations with texts withheld even sometimes from legislators, and often providing for supra-national sovereign "technical" authorities, tribunals and bodies (Slobodian, 2018).

Indeed, globalisation and deregulation were offered as two sides of the same coin of purportedly unlimited growth. Deregulation would unleash the entrepreneurial spirit, raising wages and profits for the truly deserving investors who would create the new "knowledge economy", while totally unfettered trade would see manufacturing jobs in the North be replaced by even higher paid service jobs there. Both processes would lower consumer costs and raise incomes in the developed world, while spreading manufacturing to the impoverished developing world and raising its per capita GDP.

A critical foundation for all this lay in the restructuring of the Bretton Woods system. Bretton Woods had been inherently conservative in its attempt to balance global capital flows with domestic economic growth on the rock of global LOLR institutions backstopped by American hegemony. Unfettered money flow was not seen as an unalloyed good, as the experience of late 1920s and early 1930s showed especially, and the official designation of the US dollar as a world reserve currency and the use of a Gold Standard were mechanisms to manage and regulate the flow of capital in the interest of systemic stability. America benefited from this arrangement most of all, but its gains were in part based on the system delivering gains to others as well. A lack of political will in America to continue to sacrifice some of its own interest on behalf of the greater good led to a crunch point in which the dollar was taken off of gold in 1971.

With this change, capital flows grew prodigiously, but without much constraint, fuelled further by financial market deregulation across the developed economies, especially in the money centres of New York and London. The result was an explosion of "hot money", footloose and fancy-free across borders, with continuous financial innovation by financial intermediaries seeking to evade financial regulations of the day. Financial institutions pushed an agenda of financial liberalisation (more neutrally known as deregulation) both domestically and internationally in more and more countries. Financial crises driven by sudden inflows or outflows of capital (often both) became regular occurrences. "Hot money" crises at first focused mainly on exchange rate speculation, the first occurrence being the British Sterling crisis of 1973, in which a plunging Pound and plunging exchange reserves required an IMF bailout for that once mighty country (Girón & Correa, 1999).

Debt crises were becoming even more frequent than currency crises, the two deeply intertwined. The US dollar remained the world reserve currency and most international commodity prices were still set in dollar terms. Under Bretton Woods, "dollar gaps", i.e. shortages, had been a perennial problem. Without gold, now the problem turned from having too few to too many dollars. Huge amounts of them flowed into the Arab oil exporting countries in the 1970s because of the huge spikes in oil prices. As these countries could not absorb anywhere near the full amount of this money into their domestic economies, global banks kindly stepped in to recycle them in the form of foreign loans to other countries. The Latin American debt crisis of the 80s was the result, "petrodollars" funding loans to Latin American governments that got overextended as a result and ended up in default. Other crises would follow, growing in scale and scope to the present day. These crises tended to result in systemic threats that governments felt they "had" to fix with public money; or perhaps it was more a result of responding to the increasing political power of financiers, domestically and internationally, the industry growing proportionately faster than the rest of the economy and whose increasingly unregulated ability to move money around created a very powerful influence on policymakers and others. Certainly, it was some of both (Girón & Correa, 1999).

Even before the end of Bretton Woods, financiers were champing at the bit to grow their businesses and get around national and international regulatory constraints. The growth of offshore tax and corporate havens began in the 1960s in various forms, one prominent example being the use of Panama and Liberia for ship registration to get around various national requirements to build ships domestically. "Dwarf states" like Singapore or Middle East enclaves like Kuwait were especially useful to transnational corporations and financial institutions, which created shell entities and shell securities to leverage excess dollars into new securities that were promptly sold to third parties to generate even more revenues. As but one of many examples, "Eurodollars", i.e. US dollar deposits held overseas and not repatriated, became a major source of global tax avoidance and securitisation (Hobsbawm, 1994, 278, 282). The growing role of financial institutions in global and domestic capital movements also gave them increased political leverage and power (see Box 28.1).

Box 28.1 The default of New York City

A vivid illustration of the shifting balance of power between governments and financial institutions came with the default of New York City on some of its municipal bonds in 1975. New York had been free spending during the whole Golden Age, vastly growing its workforce, its public programs and the wages of its employees over this time. For a while this was not a problem, since both the United States and the City were economic powerhouses, New York hosting a strong finance industry, a plethora of Fortune 500 headquarters, and a rising and prosperous middle class.

But the City was steadily losing its manufacturing base, something masked for a while by strong compensating service industry growth, and the corporate head offices and much of the middle class were moving to the cheaper and lower-taxed suburbs. Municipal unions struck often for higher wages, which they received, and government program commitments continued to blossom. City spending was rising while tax revenues did not keep up. By 1975, New York was plugging operating budget holes from its capital budget and issuing Tax-Anticipation Notes (TANs) that were not based on actual future tax revenues (which were already fully borrowed against) but on hoped-for revenues that likely would never come.

That the fiscal crisis came was not a surprise. What was unexpected was the reaction of the banks. Departing from prior routines, they simply did not show up to one of the scheduled debt auctions. There was no negotiation, or warning or threats, just a capital strike, with banks no longer showing up to the regularly scheduled TAN auctions.

The follow-up was equally unprecedented. New York City asked the US Federal Government for funds to cover its funding gaps and the Federal government refused (leading to a famous New York *Daily News* headline, referring to US President Gerald Ford: "Ford to City: Drop Dead"). The responsibility then fell to New York State, which established the Emergency Financial Control Board (EFCB), led by investment banker Felix Rohatyn, with some, but minority, municipal union representation on the Board itself. The unions had contributed some of their own pension funds to the rescue package, as had the banks and the State, but in return strict austerity conditions were imposed, with major cuts in police, fire, sanitation, transit and other services, public wage freezes, and deferral of maintenance to the city's infrastructure. The design of the package was clearly oriented mostly towards making the banks and debtholders whole, with city residents put last. The responsibility for the crisis clearly lay with city leaders, and the necessary fiscal restructuring required sacrifice. The International Monetary Fund (IMF) or private banks dealing with defaulted nations had often imposed austerity packages of this sort for other country leaders in trouble. This was the first time, however this kind of package was being imposed within the US, and by the private financial interests of the country on its largest city. It was a striking occurrence and it laid a template for the future that was a plank of the larger Neoliberal program.

(Discussion above draws on Tabb 1982)

See Fig. 28.6.

Fig. 28.6 Municipal services under a financial crisis regime (**City services under default conditions**: U.S. National Archives' Local Identifier: 412-DA-5774 Photographer: Calonius, Erik Project DOCUMERICA), Persistent URL: https://research.archives.gov/description/548261. No known copyright restrictions. Original Caption: Many Subway Cars in New York City Have Been Spray-Painted by Vandals. 05/1973)

It should also be noted that Keynesianism itself had relied on credit creation and innovation to increase its impact. Government deficit spending was a core policy tool to generate the necessary resource injections to plug temporary "output gaps" at the macro-level. But expanding consumer credit was a necessary input into making sure that consumers could readily finance their purchases of the quantity of goods produced in ever multiplying variety, and buying their own homes (with mortgages) in the new suburbs, in both cases aided by government subsidies and policies. These policies and instruments remained but now were detached from their former Keynesian mission.

28.9 Ongoing Implications of Neoliberalism

The flow-on economic, social and political effects of Neoliberalism have been, and continue to be, profound. "Market fundamentalism" is a *reductio ad absurdum* of the earlier theories of the Political Economists who believed in markets, but who also carved out a separate sphere for politics and civic engagement. There is now no distinction between the economic and noneconomic, everything presumed to be a commodity to be consumed by individual choice at the price dictated by the market and at the quantity preferred by each individual agent.

Whether Neoliberalism has been a positive or negative development is in part in the eye of the beholder. Of course very large business, the financial sector, high-income individuals and capital interests in general have benefited greatly, which, of course, was the intention. Average economic growth rates in the developed world were strong during the 1980s and 1990s, per capita GDP growth between 1973 and 1994 very good as compared to 1890–1950—not equal to the Golden Age, but not bad. Indeed, this economic performance, especially coming off the deep recessionary period at the end of the 1970s and beginning of the 1980s, was used to validate the doctrine and its adoption by both sides of politics. Much trumpeted has been the "Great Convergence" in which developing country growth in per capita GDP has accelerated to increasingly catch up to the high-income levels of the developed world. This pattern has been ascribed to both increased global integration and the widespread adoption of elements of the Neoliberal platform by countries across the globe.

However, there have been considerable downsides as well, including deindustrialisation in the global North (see Chapter 29), rising income and wealth inequality (see Chapter 30), social unrest and discontent (see Chapter 31), and recurrent financial and economic crisis throughout the world, at increasing scale and scope (see Chapter 30). Geopolitics has become particularly unsettled in the last decade, and environmentally the Earth Systems are deemed to be in crisis.

True, these developments, good and bad, are not just the results of Neoliberalism, springing in great measure from deep-seated crosscurrents of the modern economy itself. But Neoliberalism is notable for purposely removing the old (if imperfect) modulators of the market economy while accentuating some of its more destabilising elements. Economic growth along the narrow lines of per capita GDP continues, and spreads, but is becoming less congruent with the more subtle social and economic indicators beneath, especially those most difficult to measure. Whatever the merits of Neoliberalism, there are some pressing problems that it clearly is not suited to deal with.

References

Araghi, F. (2010). The end of "Cheap Ecology" and the crisis of "Long Keynesianism." *Economic and Political Weekly, 45*(4), 39–41.

Barr, N. (1988). The Phillips machine. *LSE Quarterly, 2*(4), 305–337.

Booth, A. (2001). New revisionists and the Keynesian era in British economic policy. *The Economic History Review, 54*(2), 346–366.

Bordo, M. D. (1993). The Bretton Woods international monetary system: A historical overview. In M. D. Bordo & B. Eichengreen (Eds.), *A retrospective on the Bretton Woods System: Lessons for international monetary reform*(pp. 3–108). University of Chicago Press.

Caldwell, B. (2008). *Hayek's challenge*. University of Chicago Press.

Christodoulakis, N. (2015). *How crises shaped economic ideas and policies.* Springer.

Crafts, N. (1995). The golden age of economic growth in western Europe, 1950–1973. *Economic History Review, 48*(3), 429–447.

Ferguson, R. A. (2017). *We demand: The university and student protests.* University of California Press.

Friedland, R., & Sanders, J. (1986). Private and social wage expansion in the advanced market economies. *Theory and Society, 15*(1/2), 193–222.

Frazer, W. (1982). Milton Friedman and Thatcher's monetarist experience. *Journal of Economic Issues, 16*(2), 525–533.

Gilman, N. (2015). The new international economic order: A reintroduction. *Humanity: An International Journal of Human Rights, Humanitarianism, and Development*, 6(1), 1–16.

Girón, A., & Correa, E. (1999). Global financial markets: financial deregulation and crises. *International Social Science Journal*, 183–194.

Goodfriend, M., & King, R. G. (2005). The incredible Volcker disinflation. *Journal of Monetary Economics, 52*(5), 981–1015.

Graff, M., Kenwood, A. G., & Lougheed, A. L. (2013). *Growth of the international economy, 1820–2015*. Routledge.

Harvey, D. (2007). *A brief history of neoliberalism*. Oxford University Press.

Hobsbawm, E. J. (1994). *Age of extremes: The short twentieth century*. Michael Joseph.

Huber, E., Ragin, C., & Stephens, J. D. (1993). Social democracy, Christian democracy, constitutional structure, and the welfare state. *American Journal of Sociology, 99*(3), 711–749.

Jones, D. S. (2012). *Masters of the universe: Hayek, Friedman, and the birth of Neoliberal politics*. Princeton University Press.

Kelly, P. (1992). *The end of certainty: The story of the 1980s*. Allen & Unwin.

Klitgaard, M. B. (2007). Why are they doing it? Social democracy and market-oriented welfare state reforms. *West European Politics, 30*(1), 172–194.

Maier, C. S. (1977). The politics of productivity: Foundations of American international economic policy after World War II. *International Organization, 31*(4), 607–663.

Moffitt, R. A. (2003). The negative income tax and the evolution of US welfare policy. *Journal of Economic Perspectives, 17*(3), 119–140.

Mozumi, S. (2018). The Kennedy-Johnson Tax Cut of 1964, the defeat of Keynes, and comprehensive tax reform in the United States. *Journal of Policy History, 30*(1), 25–61.

Offer, A., & Söderberg, G. (2016). *The Nobel factor: The prize in economics, social democracy, and the market turn*. Princeton University Press.

Powell, L. F. (1971). *Powell memorandum: Attack on American free enterprise system*. US Chamber of Commerce.

Romano, F. (2009). Clinton and Blair: The economics of the third way. *Journal of Economic and Social Policy, 10*(2), 79–93.

Rothschild, E. (1994). Adam Smith and the invisible hand. *The American Economic Review, 84*(2), 319–322.

Slobodian, Q. (2018). *Globalists: The end of empire and the birth of Neoliberalism*. Harvard University Press.

Temin, P. (2002). The golden age of European growth reconsidered. *European Review of Economic History, 6*(1), 3–22.

CHAPTER 29

Structural Change

C. Gordon, *Many Possible Worlds*,
https://doi.org/10.1007/978-981-19-9281-0_29

Fig. 29.1 Offshoring in action: West Java (Original caption: Rio Lecatompessy, Ciawi, Bogor, West Java, Indonesia Published on October 27, 2020. *Image source* Rio Lecatompessy [photographer]. Free to use under the Unsplash License, https://unsplash.com/photos/cfDURuQKABk)

29.1 Economic Modernisation and Economic Structure

Economic modernisation has both quantitative and qualitative dimensions. The major measure of its quantitative aspect is real GDP per capita, indicating the market value of total output across a given population. The qualitative dimension of economic change is generally captured by the structure of the economy, a term that indicates how output production processes are distributed across different economic sectors, typically classified as primary (e.g. agriculture and mining), secondary (e.g. manufacturing and construction industries), tertiary (e.g. services) and quaternary (e.g. highly sophisticated services such as high-technology). Two economies may have very similar levels of GDP per capita but very different economic structures and thus very different distributions of income, potential for future output growth, employment characteristics, organisations and institutions and so forth. Indeed, economic modernisation is characterised by ongoing changes in economic structure typically with profound social and economic impacts and implications (Constantine, 2017; Kuznets, 1966) (Fig. 29.1).

The First Industrial Revolution represented the first modern shift in economic structure from a dominance of primary sectors, agriculture in most every country, and mining, significant for a few countries with significant mineral deposits, supporting a much smaller secondary sector. There were some small nations, such as the Netherlands, or city-states like Venetia in Italy, that developed significant tertiary sectors in finance and trade during the Commercial Revolution of the high Middle Ages (Lopez, 1976). The Netherlands saw particularly rapid structural transformation after a severe "Black Death" (bubonic plague epidemic) in the second half of the fourteenth century (Van Zanden & Van Leeuwen, 2012). But while certain Italian principalities flourished, there is no evidence of significant changes to urbanisation rates (a proxy for modernisation in occupational structure) in the central and northern parts of the country between 1500 and 1700 (Malanima, 2005).

In 1500, while all countries possessed a basic secondary sector of manufacturing, as a percentage of total output and input use these tended to be small and largely operated primarily within households, and thus outside formal market exchange. The seventeenth century, on the other hand, was quite crucial for the structural transformation of the English economy (Wallis et al., 2018), and by around 1700 agriculture was already contributing less to English output than were the secondary and tertiary sectors (Broadberry et al., 2015, Table 9.01). Still, it would be safe to say that the overall world economy prior to industrialisation was agrarian, i.e. most inputs were employed in agriculture and the lion's share of output came from there.

Industrialisation changed all this dramatically by reducing the importance of primary activities, agriculture particularly, while increasing the share of output, income and employment coming from the secondary sector, especially manufacturing. Though complex in practice, the basic dynamic was one of the human economy shifting from mostly extracting things to mostly making things (though a tremendous amount of resources continued to be extracted, more efficiently and on greater scale than ever) over the course of the First and Second Industrial Revolutions and beyond.

29.2 A Postwar Shift to Services

Just before the Second World War, most of the world's manufacturing and trade was concentrated in Europe and its offshoots, while the rest of the planet remained agricultural and poor, a great deal of it still formally under European colonial role. Manufacturing was the engine of growth in the developed world, while agriculture, and in some places, mining, remained dominant in the developing nations. However, even in the North, agriculture was still a significant economic activity in relative terms as late as 1938. Amongst the advanced countries, only Belgium and the UK had a peasantry constituting less than 20% of the population. In the US and Germany 25% still worked in agriculture, while in France, Sweden and Austria, the share was between 35% and 40%. By the early 1980s much had changed, in both North and South. For one thing, agriculture was creating food abundance using far fewer people and resources than ever before. In the nations mentioned above, the percentages of population engaged in agriculture were by then down to around 3% each yet their food output was higher than ever (Hobsbawm, 1994, 289).

Over the same period, the global South had experienced rapid industrialisation and was increasingly displacing the North as the relative centre of manufacturing output. From 1750 to 1880 Britain's share of world manufacturing increased from 2% to 23%, but after that was overtaken by newly industrialising countries, first in the West and then later in the East. From 1880 to 1938 America and Germany took the industrial lead from England, their respective shares of world manufacturing reaching 33% and 24%, with Britain falling down to 13%. After the war, the centre of global manufacturing slowly began to shift South. By 2006 East Asia had become a centre of high-value add industry, Japan, Taiwan and South Korea having a combined 17% share of global manufacturing output, China a 9% share. These economies have all grown significantly (except for stagnating Japan) since then (Allen, 2011, 8).

Industry, once the powerhouse of advanced nations, more and more became the economic motor for those on the periphery. Though the rich countries still did a great deal of manufacturing in absolute terms, their real value-add more and more came from services. Table 29.1 provides detailed regional data of sectoral shifts within the world's major regions between 1970 and 2008.

In total value-add terms, services were the dominant sector globally as early as 1970, accounting for 52% of world production, with industry

Table 29.1 Sector distribution of total value added by region (percentage shares at current prices), 1970 and 2008

Region	*Agriculture*	*Industry*	*Services*
Africa			
1970	24.5	32.0	43.5
2008	16.5	40.7	42.8
Asia			
1970	21.7	37.9	40.4
2008	7.4	38.0	54.6
Europe			
1970	10.4	43.0	46.7
2008	2.2	27.9	69.9
Latin America and Caribbean			
1970	12.3	35.5	52.2
2008	5.9	34.5	59.6
North America			
1970	3.0	33.9	63.0
2008	1.1	22.4	76.4
Oceania			
1970	8.6	36.9	54.5
2008	3.4	28.2	68.4
World			
1970	10.0	38.3	51.7
2008	4.0	30.1	65.9

Note Total shares occasionally do not add up to 100% due to rounding
Data selected from Memedovic and Iapadre (2010), Tables 4(a) and 4(b), pp. 45–46

at 38% and agriculture at 10%. By 2008 the figures were 66% services, 30% industry and 4% agriculture. The increasing service-orientation of modern economies, whether developed or developing, is striking. Almost all regions increased their share of value-add from services during this time, Africa being the sole exception, its service sector slightly slipping in relative global importance. In total terms (not shown in the table), Asia's overall share of world value-add from all sectors grew from 15.5% to 28.5% between 1970 and 2008, while Europe went from 40% to 33% and North America from 35% to 27%. Latin America, Oceania and Africa accounted for the remainder during this period (Memedovic & Iapadre, 2010, 6–9).

The changes in the two most populous countries in the world, China and India, have been particularly striking. Table 29.2 provides one measure of this, for the relatively short period between 1990 and

Table 29.2 China and India selected global export and import shares, 1990 and 2004 (%)

World Export Share	*1990*		*2004*	
	China	*India*	*China*	*India*
- *Manufacturing*	1.9%	0.5%	8.3%	0.9%
- *Commercial Services*	–	–	2.9%	1.9%
World Import Share				
- *Manufacturing*	1.7%	0.5%	6.3%	0.8%
- *Commercial Services*	–	–	3.4%	2.0%

Source Data extracted from Tables 2.1, 2.2 in Yusuf et al. (2007)

2004, during which both countries implemented significant economic reforms after the end of the Cold War. In 1990 China and India respectively accounted for 1.9% and 0.5% of world manufacturing exports. Neither country rated at all in terms of commercial services share of world exports in that year. By 2004, both countries had commercial services exports accounting for between 2% and 3% of the world total, and both had significantly increased their share of manufacturing exports, India almost doubling its share, and China more than quadrupling its.

The shift of all economies toward services, and a proportionate shift of global manufacturing from North to South, continues. In 2019, China accounted for 28.7% of global manufacturing, well ahead of the US at second place at 16.8%. Of the top ten largest global manufacturers, five were in Asia, accounting for 43.9% of the total. China's expansion is truly remarkable. India has grown also, but much less, reaching a 3.1% share (Richter, 2021). Meanwhile, in 2020, China's share of commercial services exports was 5.7% (Ma, 2021).

29.3 The "Post-Industrial" Economy and Society

These gross figures obscure a few important things. Mining is included under the category of industry. While the modern mining sector is typically highly industrialised and uses very advanced technology, it still is accounted for as a "primary" extractive activity. In some cases, especially in Africa where there is significant mining activity, the figures might actually understate an economic shift towards the tertiary sector by not properly accounting for the service features of mining activity.

Also, services themselves have been radically transformed. Traditionally, part of the tertiary sector, these have now spawned a so-called quaternary sector of high-value add, highly mechanised, and highly technologised processes that in some ways resemble industrial manufacturing more than the labour-intensive service provision of old. At the same time, services have also deeply penetrated manufacturing. Thus the lines between manufacturing and non-manufacturing activities, and thus secondary, tertiary and quaternary activities, have blurred significantly. Additionally, the service sector in developed countries is increasingly using highly sophisticated, cutting-edge technology, yielding high labour productivity (Islam & Iversen, 2018, 8).

These developments have manifested in a number of ways. In 30 major economies across the world, one analysis found that manufacturing production between 1970 and 2006 showed a marked movement in value-add towards information and communication technologies (ICT), machinery, precision instruments, chemical, plastics and rubber products, while moving away, in relative terms, from more traditional industries such as consumption goods and metal products. The largest shift took place in the 1970s with the combined share of ICT and machinery rising from 10% to 19% during the decade, with a much slower shift after that to a share of 22% in 2006 (Memedovic & Iapadre, 2010, 12–13).

Services began to be industrialised around the middle of the twentieth century, routine tasks with little variability being the first to be mechanised, and service production being broken into minute specialised tasks conducted in an assembly line fashion. This essentially represented the application of the "Fordism" developed in manufacturing (and named after one of its pioneers, the automobile producer Henry Ford) to services. Fast food is a leading early example, but it has since been applied to many other sectors ranging from financial services, sales and product support, and medical diagnostics. More complex jobs requiring continuous contextual adjustment and/or fine sensory motor-coordination have been more resistant to standardisation and automation but advances in artificial intelligence (AI) and robotics are bringing big changes here as well, especially in middle-skill jobs (Mokyr et al., 2015, 44).

This rise of the service sector, and the radical changes within it, led to the coining of the term "post-industrial economy". In a narrow sense, this simply refers to the shift in industrial economies away from industry into services, and more specifically high value- add services, especially those based in information, knowledge and research. The broader social and political changes, together with as their more subtle economic ones, fall under the rubric of the "post-industrial society". Post-Fordism, Information Society, Knowledge Economy and Network Society are some of the many other labels used to refer to these changes. The main societal features include: the transformation of knowledge into a form of capital entering the production process, either as a separate input or as part of educated labour skill and ability referred to as "human capital"; the commodification of ideas and their reformulation as a primary and direct driver of economic growth; the changing structure of work along technical lines; the institutionalisation of knowledge rights (especially the rise of intellectual property); the wider use of behavioural and information sciences and technologies in production, consumption and distribution; and the continuing organisation of arts and culture and creativity along industrial lines (Vogt, 2016).

In his 1974 article, *The Coming of the Post-Industrial Society,* the sociologist Daniel Bell extrapolated from the American society of his day to argue that the shift into services had moved primacy away from making things to knowing things, and that the "game between persons", i.e. social relations in a functional and reputational sense, was elevated into central place as a result. The "professional" was now the key figure in making the economy run, and an important marker here was the education they received and the credentials they had. They were in charge of codification of information into a form that could be manipulated by technologised production processes amenable to systematic productivity increase generating constant "innovation".

One of the more contentious issues that Bell did not address much but which strongly emerged after his article came out is the nature and role of labour in a services economy. Vogt (2016) notes that service work can be highly skilled, or low skilled, highly paid, or low paid, knowledge-based or based on little knowledge. An assumption typically made, utopian in its implications according to Vogt, is that service work is "good" work requiring well-educated people, and that an increasing focus on services, therefore, means that economies are becoming better for people, or at least for better educated people. It is a short inferential leap to say that these better educated people are somehow intrinsically better than uneducated ones, and that those lagging behind, especially the unskilled and uncredentialed (or those with the "wrong" skills and credentials, including those acquired from "inferior" institutions), have only themselves to blame for their failure.

The historical record renders these various suppositions questionable. Even in the times of highest economic growth during the 1960s and early 1970s, it was becoming apparent that the mechanisation and standardisation of labour affected not just the lowest skilled categories, but middle-skill workers as well who, when displaced, ended up competing for lower-skill jobs. Service jobs have also become increasingly flexible, which also means that they are increasingly precarious and unpredictable. Since 2008 flexibility with regard to time and place of work has grown. This does allow workers to potentially make work-life balance choices best suited for them, and there is also evidence that those fields with the greatest flexibility have seen the largest narrowing in gender wage gaps. However, relative real wages and the reliability of working hours have also fallen in many areas so this wage compression may be a bad rather than a good development. Meanwhile, the rise of the "on-demand" economy, contingent labour and the so-called precariat has greatly increased the uncertainty around paid hours, and so there is no guarantee that a worker will receive enough work to cover their living expenses, or indeed any work at all during a given pay period. A 2014 study indicated that almost 50% of part-time workers received only one week of advance notice on what their schedule would be for the week ahead. The problem is most intense at the bottom of the scale, but middle and senior levels also complain of being "always on", unable to turn down the dial for fear of getting downgraded or fired (Mokyr et al., 2015, 44–46).

29.4 Managerialism

An increasingly technological ordering of society has been a constant accompaniment to industrialism, and this has become a more marked feature of wider social, economic and political organisation and thought. Norbert Elias (1995) captured this with his concept of technisation, which refers to the ability of a society to manipulate the physical world for desired ends. He argued that modernity has seen this process shape, compete with, and sometimes overtake the broader and more esoteric civilising process that humans are undergoing in their evolution towards a more interdependent social structure (see Chapter 5). For Elias these two things must be balanced, but the former appears to be winning out in the technocratic society (see Chapter 8).

Maier (1970) traces this process back to "Taylorism" which refers to the application of the ideas of Frederick Taylor's "Scientific Management" to the industrial workplace and then, in modified form, to other sectors that were soon organised along industrial lines. Taylorism applied machine-oriented engineering principles to labour relations, i.e. the use of supposedly impartial, technical and objective criteria that were said to govern in physical design problems (like building a bridge) that were then imposed upon human action and movement on the factory floor. Taylorism promised a move from management of men to administration of things, with efficiency being the common goal. Instead of fights between interest groups in different power relations to one another, work problems now were said to have optimal solutions that would present themselves once enough facts and experiences were collected. It then remained for managers to apply these solutions, which, since they maximised efficiency, were in the interest of both labour and capital to pursue and conform to. Maier notes that this frame of thinking generally was biased towards the managers at the top of the factory hierarchy, who themselves were hired hands of the owners whose primary concern was to squeeze as much return out of their invested capital, machine and human, as possible. Taylor himself designed his various incentive schemes to reward workers for productivity increases, but with a significant share of any such gain retained by the capital owners (Maier, 1970, 31–32).

Indeed, this is the essence of the "Progress" doctrine of the nineteenth century, and its successor "Productivism" of the twentieth, i.e. that human intelligence and technology should be devoted to innovations that increase efficiency and productivity, expanding the total amount of material resources and, in so doing, eliminating any need for social or economic conflict, which itself had been redefined in narrow material terms. A bureaucratic ideology of control based on task specification, hierarchy, promotion up through the ranks and objective criteria was the result, a set of ideas and institutions that hardened into the doctrine of "Managerialism" which posited everything, even human relations, as a technical problem to be optimised "rationally". To challenge an organisation based on the logic of machines was to be "irrational" since such organisation was assumed to be inherently more efficient, even though this was plainly not always the case and not everything important could be boiled down to it. Completely ignored was the actual fact of control exerted by one group over another, which might be resented and resisted even in cases where the total resource pool was actually growing and gains were actually being shared. Management interests were not any more neutral than those of labour nor were they generally identical. (Burris, 1989, 317–318).

29.5 Technocracy, Digitalisation and Changing Production Processes

Until relatively late in the twentieth century, the human economy, and human activity more generally, was still "analog", i.e. based on physical material forms such as the circuit, the engine, the printed page, etc. Services still involved embodied mutual contact of some sort. The rise of advanced computing technology gave birth to digital forms of goods and services, i.e. those based mainly or purely on the "ones" and "zeroes" of computer encoding. Humans still are, of course, material beings living in a material world. But now most value-add comes from digital activities of one form or another. And with technologies such as 3-D printing, even manufacturing processes are becoming digitalised in the sense that physical outputs are designed, produced and distributed from an almost purely information-based platform (Schwab, 2017).

Although this is often presented as a sharp break from the past, there is arguably more continuity than discontinuity. Fordism (an overall production system based on the assembly-line process managed by a large vertical corporation) and Taylorism (the idea that all human actions can be broken down into component parts to increase efficiency and greater throughput) are models that have not so much been wiped away as they have been adapted for current technological and social conditions. The surface aspects and forms are unrecognisable, but the economic and intellectual foundation has mostly stayed unchanged. The attitude that the economy, and perhaps the total society, is a complete system, based on technical and scientific principles, following predictable mechanical regularities, and requiring specialist managers to run everything to ensure optimal equilibrium, remains the essence of "technocracy", a phrase that has fallen into disuse somewhat but whose practice continues today, in an altered but perhaps even more intense form.

This has had ongoing social and organisational implications. It was not so easy to understand and manage a machine or a factory during industrialisation. Great technical skill was required. It is perhaps even harder, at least in a technical sense, to manage the modern information-based enterprises and technologies of today. In fact, so much information is generated and production and distribution processes are so fast that human beings cannot actually directly manage them any more at all. Complex software contains embedded human instructions often incompletely known even to their creators because of the extended teamwork and processing power required to design, run and test them, and the underlying complexity of the software itself, software often used to check other software. The technocrat is more important than ever, yet also more dependent on others, while the gulf between that technocrat and mere mortal workers is larger than before too (Vogt, 2016). In the old factories, staff, whether skilled or unskilled, worked with tangible, physical things, even in the administering offices with their paper ledgers and files. In the digitalised workplace, most things are in abstract form, allowing for easier handling in one sense, but behind the screens (literally) of technical systems that only technicians can manipulate in any fundamental way. The power dynamics remain, but are more obscured as a result.

Digitalisation has also accelerated the continuing extension and fragmentation of global supply chains, increasing the division of labour across multiple specialised entities and allowing the potential outsourcing of an entire production process, in places far and wide, including for services. From the 1980s onwards, North–South trade links have expanded considerably, with multinationals in advanced economies restructuring and offshoring significant components of their value chains to lower labour cost and less regulated areas. Developing countries have meanwhile leveraged this multinational investment to develop domestic production capacity and technological advances of their own. The world trade-to-GDP ratio has surged as a result of all this shifting of value-add across country borders, growing by 12.3 percentage points during the 10-year period from 1990 to 2000 (from 39.2% to 51.5%), though slowing considerably after that, growing only 0.4 percentage points between 2010 and 2020, suggesting a certain saturation. China was a major beneficiary and instigator of this trend, with the share of Chinese goods as a source of merchandise imports across 12 major economies rising for every one of them between 1990 and 2015, including Japan (a 21.2 percentage point rise), the US (19.0 percentage points), and Canada (11.5 percentage points), accompanied by shrinking shares of imports by China from these countries (Vu et al., 2020, 4–8). Digitalisation has not been the sole source of these changes, but they have played a significant role.

Taken together, digitalisation has definitively intensified and expanded long-standing processes of technical control, management and manipulation of the physical world, including of human beings themselves, and in so doing has radically changed their forms. Abstract representations of the world now dominate technisation, making it much more efficient and effective, but also more rapid, disruptive, unpredictable and deep. This cannot be said to be an entirely bad development. But neither is it entirely good.

29.6 Northern Deindustrialisation

The shift towards services and "post-industry" is in relative terms. In absolute terms, the large service economies of the global North remain very large manufacturers. For example, even with a sharp services-oriented structural change, between 1977 and 2005 the value of American manufacturing rose from \$1.3 trillion to \$4.5 trillion and in 2005 the US still accounted for a quarter of the world's manufacturing output (Setser, 2007) (As noted above, the US had a 17.6% share in 2019, a large fall but still indicating a very significant industrial sector). Thus the rich economies remain large productive makers of physical goods, especially very advanced goods at the frontiers of technological change.

However, labour-saving productivity and the relative decline of manufacturing as a share of the total economy have led to an absolute shedding of industrial jobs in developed countries. This trend started with increasing automation in the 1970s and built up speed with offshoring, i.e. the utilisation of overseas enterprises in domestic production. Manufacturing employment between 1990 and 2015 contracted by 2.6 percentage points in Japan, 2.0 percentage points in the US, 1.9 percentage points in Denmark, 1.4 percentage points in Italy and 1.3 percentage points in Canada (Vu et al., 2020, 11).

Over the longer term it is expected that these lost industrial jobs will ultimately be replaced by new non-industrial jobs in new emerging sectors, many of which cannot even be conceived of at present. But this is based on national averages. Manufacturing sectors tend to be concentrated in spatially concentrated local agglomerations and when these areas lose industrial activity and employment, they often do not get compensating replacements from growth in new sectors. Deindustrialisation, which generically refers to the structural shift away from industry, is a label also attached to the phenomenon witnessed in many local areas that lose long-term manufacturing jobs and experience both relative and absolute economic decline, depopulation, poverty and dislocation. Where the service sector does expand in such areas, it typically offers low-wage, low-skill jobs that pay far less than the lost jobs did. The result is long-term excess structural unemployment.

Global integration, national specialisation and gains from trade are said to result in virtuous economic circles, and indeed much wealth, income and growth have been generated by these processes in both global North and South. But there are inevitable winners and losers both between countries and within them. Deindustrialisation appears benign from the perspective of a shift to a more productive national service economy. But it appears very dark from the perspective of former industrial regions, especially if they fail to attract new business with comparable pay levels and productiveness. In its final and worst phases, a manufacturing hollowing-out can take place. This has swept across many parts of the developed world over the past several decades (Fig. 29.2). The links between these effects and globalisation are complex, with offshoring conducted for a number of reasons. In addition to the pursuit of labour cost minimisation, developed world firms also offshore to seek out business-friendly regulatory environments, avoid home country regulations (such as those regarding labour safety or environmental mitigation), and to operate inside rather than outside of tariff or investment barriers (Islam & Iversen, 2018, 9). These developments tend to disadvantage older and higher cost, higher regulation industrial enclaves and favour emerging areas in developing countries.

But even this is uneven geographically. China, India and some other Asian countries have seen net increases in high-productivity employment generated by structural change that has contributed to overall growth. But Latin America and sub-Saharan Africa have witnessed much less positive structural change with less secure employment driving significant numbers into the informal economic sector (McMillan & Rodrick, 2011, 50). Some developing world locations that had initially benefited from Northern offshoring have since lost out to other peripheral locations resulting in their own "hollowing out". Rodrik (2016) has noted that these changes in developing countries have caused deterioration in economy-wide productivity in some cases. Even in China growing local investment there has recently not appeared to be accompanied by a significant resurgence in industry.

Fig. 29.2 Industrial ruins of the global North (*Image source* Photo by Daniel Lincoln on Unsplash, https://unsplash.com/photos/23fk429Ayok Packard Plant, Detroit, Published on December 3, 2018. Free to use under the Unsplash License)

Wherever they are located, the social effects on the losers can be truly devastating. Case and Deaton (2020) noted that in the US the number of deaths from suicide, drug overdose and alcohol abuse was 158,000 in 2017. In the mid-1990s, the annual total of such deaths was closer to 69,000. The greatest increases have been amongst non-Hispanic whites without a four-year degree. The greatest concentration of deaths has been in the "hollowed out" areas, though it is a more general phenomenon as well. Americans in this demographic born in 1960 were at higher risk of dying from suicide, drug overdoses and alcoholic liver disease than people born in 1950, those born in 1980 at much higher risk than those born in 1960 and so on. A prime, though not the only, cause appears to be a long-term decline in wages for men without a four-year degree since 1979, driven by a loss of manufacturing jobs, replaced, if at all, by lower wage employment in low-skill service occupations. Case and Deaton refer to these as "deaths of despair" of the white working class. The problem occurs across the developed world, but its social dislocation is much greater in the US than in Europe because of the latter's more extensive safety net.

29.7 "Financialisation"

By contrast, one area of the developed world service sector that has grown prodigiously is the financial sector. Banking and other related services have grown proportionately faster than other parts of the economy. For example, the 1947 share of total value added by the financial sector to American GDP was 2.3%. By 2005 this had risen to 7.7%. In Britain, the sector accounted for 9.4% of GDP in 2006. Extremely high salaries and bonuses draw in more and more of the best-credentialed talent away from other sectors. In 1970, for example, approximately 5% of the men graduating from Harvard went into finance, a figure that by 1990 had grown to 15% (Ferguson, 2008, 4).

Leading up to the Global Financial Crisis (GFC), all major developed countries saw a substantial rise in the percentage of GDP taken up by activities in their financial sectors. Various other measures, e.g. the share of corporate profits earned by finance versus other sectors, absolute size of and growth in various financial activities such as derivatives trading, and so on, confirm these trends which the GFC interrupted but did not reverse. By the first quarter of 2021, the global market capitalization, i.e. the combined value of every listed banking company on every stock exchange in the world, was estimated to be $56 trillion or 14% of the global economy. This measure is an underestimate because it only includes share values of publicly traded banks and does not include banks that are government owned or privately held, or finance institutions that are not banks, e.g. insurance companies and pension funds, amongst others. The total "assets under management" (AUM), a measure of the total amount of assets managed by investment companies, was, in 2020, $103 trillion, representing around a quarter of total global wealth estimated at $431 trillion (Ross, 2021).

This trend has gone by various names including the "finance-led growth regime", "finance-dominated accumulation regime", or, most succinctly, "financialisation". Financialisation in simple terms refers to the increase in size and importance of a country's financial sector relative to its overall economy. This has occurred most strongly in the developed world as financial intermediation activities have grown in importance and manufacturing and industry has declined. However, the economic change is deeper than this broad definition suggests. Purely financial motives, markets, actors and institutions have become central to the operations of the domestic and international economies (Guttmann, 2008, 2/15).

Financial intermediation is an essential component of economic modernisation, allowing the accumulation and movement of funds between savers and investors and, to use economic parlance, efficiently trade-off between present and future consumption. The Industrial Revolution itself was preceded by the Commercial Revolution, which consisted of a series of innovations and improvements in institutions and instruments of finance that enabled large aggregations of private and public capital to fund new corporate enterprises and facilitate the growth of international trade and investment. This process continued throughout the 1800s and 1900s, providing firms with access to increasingly novel and large pools of money, and the ability to move them seamlessly and efficiently across markets (see Chapter 19). These were critical inputs into modern growth and would not have been so readily accomplished without a growing and increasingly sophisticated financial sector.

However, financial innovation is a double-edged sword, particularly when money gets too footloose across international boundaries and when financial markets and institutions make decisions that unnecessarily and adversely affect real economic activity. The over-heated asset bubble leading to the Great Crash and the Great Depression that followed is a prime example from the past. The Global Financial Crisis (GFC) of

2007–2009, followed by the so-called Great Recession, is a much more recent one. Indeed, the economist Hyman Minsky (1980) has gone so far as to say the modern financial intermediation inevitably generates financial crisis on its own, a position summarised as the "financial instability hypothesis". In this template credit creators are inherently shortsighted, banks and other institutions lending far too much in boom times due to the ease with which short-term profit can be made then. This credit boom then over-inflates asset prices. There is an inevitable adjustment in such prices at which point many loans go bad, and a contractionary cycle is set in motion, exacerbated by lenders going to the other extreme of cutting credit to both good and bad credit risks. Minsky does not conclude that financial intermediation is, therefore, a net negative; only that it contains these inherent cyclical dynamics which cannot be eliminated but must be regulated. The GFC has validated this theory, at least for certain circumstances, enough so that many central banks and asset funds have incorporated it into their risk models (Minsky, 2016).

This double-edge is what the post-war Bretton Woods system tried to manage through fixed exchange rates, the Gold Standard, global LOLRs, and the US dollar as a world reserve currency (see Chapter 28). Under that system capital flowed relatively freely but under constraints. The developed economies supported the system with their own domestic financial policies including regulated (and low) interest rates, managed money supply growth, and domestic banking sector regulation. Banks, rather than nonbank financial institutions, were put in a quasi-monopoly position as credit creators for the economy, with bank loans as the major vehicle for most domestic money creation. Economic growth was very high, supported by financial intermediation, but stability was the main underlying policy goal.

Bretton Woods slowly came undone, and along with it these conservative domestic policy regimes in most countries were largely unwound as well. Banks, and various nonbank institutions such as lending companies, had always aggressively sought to outwit their domestic regulators and the tight international capital flow constraints of Bretton Woods. One of many examples of this is the rise of the Eurocurrency market during the early 1960s when US balance-of-payments deficits flooded the world with dollars that banks had taken in as bank deposits and loans in currencies located outside of their country of original issue. Thus, for example, US dollar denominated deposits made in Paris could fund a Pound Sterling denominated loan originating in London, thus bypassing the oversight of any domestic central bank or the reach of any national regulation. Later the development of interbank clearance systems, such as the computerised SWIFT and CHIPS networks furthered this process, enabling easy movement funds in and out of countries, and making currencies a growing area of speculation, even within a framework of fixed exchange rates. These innovations further enabled banks to go around domestic interest rate and capital outflow regulations if they chose to (Guttmann, 2008, 4/15).

Bretton-Woods, like the Gold Standard regimes before it, was never going to last forever, depending as it did on a stable permanent hegemon with strong international control over global money supply and demand, and a willingness to sacrifice national interest on behalf of the needs of the system. And indeed the stability of the system was bought at some cost in terms of economic growth that could have been achieved if credit creation was more relaxed. In that light, many of these banking workarounds could be seen as ways of finding more efficient uses of surplus capital, and the fact that the regulatory system weakened may have been actually a good thing from the perspective of long-term growth. Also, increasingly sophisticated economies require higher levels of financial intermediation than less sophisticated ones given the increasing complexity, scale and scope of real economy production with a need for greater levels and subtlety of debt financing.

However, the line between allocation of misallocation of resources is not always easy to determine. The trade-off of this potential efficiency generally definitely seems to be lowered financial stability, and sometimes crisis, which imposes substantial costs of its own. Indeed the Bretton Woods system and its various domestic financial policy auxiliaries were designed to address the freewheeling international and domestic financial systems of the Interwar period that ended in utter and total collapse. The stability it generated actually supported arguably more growth overall than a less stable system would have, as Minsky, amongst others, maintain.

Additionally, banks and financial institutions are private institutions with private interests that nonetheless have broader systemic functions. That is, credit extension and money creation are necessary for the functioning of a modern economy and the reason these functions are traditionally privately outsourced to banks is that their profit motive makes them more efficient. But that does not mean that they are always going to do the right thing as far as the system is concerned. In fact, there are many examples of them doing the wrong thing in that regard, which is why regulation is required. This is the essence of the Minsky argument, although it also goes beyond that to argue that the "rent-seeking", inordinate political manipulation, and corruption that can come with any unbounded special interest group is inevitable in modern finance, with the need for strong government checks and balances to rein it all in.

The balance between efficiency and regulation is, therefore, dynamic and complex. Many have argued that the current levels of financialisation indicate that there has been too much leeway once again given to the private interests of banks and financial intermediaries. The post-Bretton Woods liberalisations of the financial sectors of the US, UK and other major Western countries, many of which accompanied Neoliberal political regimes, were justified on the basis that they would power economic growth. But, except for short-term economic boosts, especially in the 1990s, the longer-term results have been much more mixed (see Box 29.1).

Box 29.1 The "Great Moderation"

On a website on American central banking history, maintained by the US Federal Reserve System, that country's central bank, there is a page on the Great Moderation which begins with a photo of three "Fed" chairmen standing together for a group shot: Paul Volcker, who presided over a "Monetarist" phase of monetary policy in the late 1970s and early 1980s in which official short-term interest rates shot to close to 20%, precipitating a deep recession but also an end to the accelerating inflation that had plagued the country during the 1970s; Alan Greenspan, who had kept official interest rates low and presided over the boom economy of the 1990s and early 2000s; and Ben Bernanke, once a Princeton University professor and expert on Great Depression banking, who initiated the policy of "Quantitative Easing" (QE) of a long-term lowering of interest rates to zero and a mass purchase of private financial assets by the central bank to keep the financial system from seizing up during and after the Global Financial Crisis of 2007–2009. The narrative that follows this photo defines the Great Moderation as a time, roughly between 1982 and 2007, when US rates of inflation and the volatility of economic growth moderated significantly and with high average per capita GDP growth overall. While the data analysed are American, it is noted that this was a worldwide phenomenon (Hakkio, 2013).

Why did this occur? The story given by the Fed webpage is that a combination of good luck, good policy and good structural change was involved. Good luck is self-explanatory: unlike the Great Depression, there were no particularly bad breaks economically that were big or concurrent enough to throw the economic or financial systems off the rails. Good policy refers to a central banking regime that had learned the lessons of both the over-tight money of the Great Depression, and the over-loose money of the late 1960s and 1970s, getting things "just right", as Goldilocks might say. Good structural change refers to the macroeconomic effects of a shift away from a manufacturing towards a service and knowledge economy, with the latter being less volatile than the former because of the lack of large inventory cycles, and an ability, in a technologised and digitalised world, to adjust faster to real-time changes and events (Hakkio, 2013).

Although there are separate entries elsewhere on the website, on this particular page there is no mention of the US share market crash of 1987; the Savings and Loan crisis of the 1980s which required massive infusions of government money to resolve; the Latin American debt crisis of the same decade; the turmoil of the "transition" economies of the former Soviet Union and the Eastern bloc which were the scene of rapid and chaotic capital inflows and outflows and severe economic dislocation, especially in Russia; the real estate bubble in Japan and its subsequent collapse into a decades long recession, still ongoing; the Asian Financial Crisis (AFC) of 1998 which ravaged Asia and for a time threatened to become a global cataclysm; the collapse of the hedge fund Long-Term Capital Management (LTCM), one of whose founders was an economics Nobel Prize winner, awarded for his innovations in financial theory; or the so-called "dot-com" high-tech share market bubble in America and its subsequent collapse with Enron being one of many resulting and spectacular corporate failures (Gordon, 2013).

It is curious omission, for the period of 1982–2007 was in fact a time of great economic ferment, a time that the economist Robert Shiller (2015) would later refer to as one of "irrational exuberance". One explanation is that the volatility of the period was mostly in the financial markets, not the "real" economy, which was the focus of the Fed narrative, even though there were plenty of real economy repercussions of financial events. Another is that at least some of the worst economic turmoil occurred off American shores, such as with the AFC and Russia's post-Soviet implosion. Yet another is that the economic averages obscure more fine-grained and less positive changes of the time, especially for those at the lower end of the income distribution who tended to get hardest hit by financial shocks and other shifts that left many former manufacturing communities out of the Great Moderation entirely. Or perhaps this is just an example of the tunnel vision of the policy technocrat, from whose perspective the dial twisting is having the desired effect on the indicators on the board, while being largely unaware of what is happening in the field. It is probably a bit of all that. In any case, the Great Moderation was not as moderate or as great as the label suggests.

To summarise all this, at least three major issues surround the twin-phenomenon of financialisation and the financial deregulation, globally and domestically, that has powered it.

29.7.1 The "Hot Money" Problem

Capital is always seeking the best and quickest return and as greater amounts of capital flow more and more easily (and with less and less transparency) there can be costly disruptions to domestic economies. This is a problem that has plagued the modern economy from its inception, and even before then. In the more contemporary context, the Asian Financial Crisis (AFC) of 1998 was in large part created by "hot money", i.e. speculative funds seeking quick returns in international markets, which quickly flow in to an economy, create asset bubbles in real estate and other real and financial assets, then just as quickly flow out after profit-taking, leaving the affected economies with asset price collapses and devastated financial sectors denuded of liquidity (Haggard, 2000). Nobel Prize-winning economist Joseph Stiglitz (1999) is one of amongst many who have documented this problem in the Asian Financial Crisis in 1998, considering it more generally to be a significant negative external cost of untrammelled globalised financialisation.

29.7.2 The "Rentier" Problem

"Rentier" is an old French term denoting an economic class that lives off of unearned economic rents because of its control over an asset that generates returns but which makes no productive input into the economy. Unimproved agricultural land is the classic example of an asset that landlords can collect rents from simply because they own it. Many now argue that the financial sector is behaving and acting like a rentier class, squeezing monopoly returns, with out of control liquidity flows concentrated in particular monopolistic financial institutions. The result is not just economic inefficiency, as resources are diverted from productive real economy activities, but often systemic crisis, as uncontrolled risk-taking to chase rents causes overall financial collapse, as happened with the GFC. Palma (2009), amongst many others, makes this case, and he argues specifically that Neoliberalism, which inspired the financial deregulation that brought this about, did not take this problem into account and must thus be modified accordingly.

29.7.3 The "Political Economy" Problem

As historian Lord Acton famously said: "Power corrupts. Absolute power corrupts absolutely". One could say the same about money. The financial sector in most countries has become extremely politically influential and arguably able to tilt governmental regulation and other institutions in its favour. Thus the global policy response to the GFC is often said to have "privatised returns and socialised losses" in a way very different from the comparable Great Depression decades ago. A few institutions failed. A few "rogue" operators were punished. For a little while finance sector executive bonuses declined. But after only a few years, finance sector compensation and profitability has roared back and a new deregulatory trend seems to be arising—even though large government bailouts were required to save most of the big financial institutions during the GFC (Gordon, 2013).

29.8 The Production Possibility Frontier (PPF) Revisited

This discussion of structural change and financialisation rounds back to the concept and measure that arose with the first incarnations of the modern economy, namely productivity. Prior to industrialisation, this was not a concern, practically or theoretically. Economies had to provide for basic needs and possibly produce sufficient surplus beyond this to hopefully improve the quality of everyday life, though this latter outcome did not need to be accomplished consistently. With the Industrial Revolution, productivity became central. Regular growth in per capita GDP became a necessity rather than an optional nicety. To put it in economic terms, the PPF had to be constantly expanding and an economy needed to be on that ever-inflating frontier (see Chapter 9 on the PPF concept).

The Growth Model posits technological change as an *ipso facto* driver of productivity expansion. Part of this is driven by innovation, but another part is based on a structural change development paradigm that assumes that there is low labour and capital productivity in the primary sector and progressively higher labour and capital productivity in the secondary, tertiary and quaternary sectors. Thus growth leads to structural change and hence a structural shift of labour and capital from low- to high-productivity sectors that in aggregate raises aggregate productivity and is thus a source of growth all its own (Islam & Iversen, 2018, 4).

There have been both major technological and structural change across the world over the past few decades. But there is some reason to doubt that the PPF has shifted as thoroughly as it had in the past. As noted, structural change has costs as well as benefits, and many of the costs now seem quite substantial, such as excessive financialisation and deindustrialisation and other disruptions. Thus the shift from secondary to tertiary/quaternary sectors may not be as straightforward from a productivity perspective as earlier primary to secondary shifts were. And the noneconomic effects are complex, and in some instances, potentially increasingly problematic.

Also the technical improvements since the 1980s in particular have undoubtedly transformed the society and economy in profound ways, but they may not have been as productivity increasing as those of the First, Second and Third Industrial Revolutions (we are now said to be in the Fourth). In the United States from 2009 to 2015, for example, there was slow productivity growth during the GFC, in contrast to high growth during the late 1930s when a similar downturn was on. Gordon (2015, 2018) notes that innovations often take a long time to show up in productivity statistics because it takes much time for these to be diffused throughout the economy. Thus the invention of the combustion engine in 1879 had to be refined, implemented in the form of the automobile, and then cars had to be widely adopted before the engine boosted per capita growth and shifted out the PPF. Inevitably diminishing returns set in and it then took some other new technology, with similar lags, to boost productivity again. So just as the Second Industrial Revolution was waning, the Third Industrial Revolution emerged. Amongst the changes it wrought was a replacement of clerical labour with more productive mainframe computing power during the 1950s and 1960s. The Fourth

Revolution then had the introduction of the Personal Computer (PC) in the 1980s, and then the marriage of the PC with communications technology in cloud-distributed computer networks and the Internet. Weak productivity growth in the 1970s and 1980s was thus replaced with strong growth in 1996–2004 (Gordon, 2015, 55) (Fig. 29.3).

However, and significantly, technological productivity past is not necessarily prologue, and Gordon (2015) argues that the current "information revolution" is not contributing nearly as much to economic efficiency as prior revolutions. This round of technical change may well now have also not only reached diminishing returns but possibly may also be weakening the link between technological change and productivity. He asks how much of the ever-growing activity on computers and networks is productivity-oriented now. People may have found more entertainment and social connection, and may even be better off emotionally and psychically (though that is debatable). But this current change does not necessarily represent an economic enhancement to the outputs of their labours. Technologists always promise that the next PPF enhancing innovation is just around the corner, e.g. nanocomputers, biotechnology, driverless vehicles, etc. Certainly, this has been a recurrent feature of industrialisation so it may well be possible that the past pattern of increased economic growth returns will repeat. But this cannot be taken for granted.

Gordon (2015) also notes also that socioeconomic outcomes in the US have been decaying for the past few decades, with a rise of single-parent households amongst whites, rising prison populations and increasing inequality. This is also decidedly bad for productivity, to say nothing of being negative in its own right (56–57). Some of this is directly related to the hollowing out of deindustrialisation that has left behind persistent social ills in many areas. It is not a problem limited to America, though some of the worst manifestations are there, as Case and Deaton (2020) have noted.

The bargain of the past two and a half centuries has been that radical change to technology, society and economy will consistently deliver greater and more broadly distributed material growth in wealth and income. These changes continue, but the economic promise does not seem to be as consistently delivered any more, both in productivity and distributional terms. Meanwhile, the immaterial aspects of all this have been sidelined, and many noneconomic negatives are occurring, persisting

Fig. 29.3 Students in front of old style screens (Austria, 1954) (*Image source* Austrian National Library, under an Unsplash licence https://unsplash.com/photos/3c1Jv1EXYtc)

and growing. It can no longer be assumed, if it ever really could be, that the future of modernity will necessarily be better than its past.

References

Allen, R. C. (2011). *Global economic history: A very short introduction*. Oxford University Press.

Broadberry, S., Campbell, B. M., Klein, A., Overton, M., & van Leeuwen, B. (2015). *British economic growth, 1270–1870*. Cambridge University Press.

Burris, B. H. (1989). Technocracy and the transformation of organizational control. *The Social Science Journal, 26*(3), 313–333.

Case, A., & Deaton, A. (2020). *Deaths of despair and the future of capitalism*. Princeton University Press.

Constantine, C. (2017). Economic structures, institutions and economic performance. *Economic Structures, 6*(1), 1–18.

Elias, N. (1995). Technization and civilization. *Theory Culture and Society, 12*(3), 7–42.

Ferguson, N. (2008). *The ascent of money: A financial history of the world*. Penguin.

Gordon, C. (2013). Two theories of the subprime crisis: Governance failure or mere greed? *International Journal of Behavioural Accounting and Finance, 4*(1), 3–17.

Gordon, R. J. (2015). Secular stagnation: A supply-side view. *American Economic Review, 105*(5) (Papers and Proceedings of the one hundred twenty-seventh annual meeting, pp. 54–59).

Gordon, R. J. (2018). *Why has economic growth slowed when innovation appears to be accelerating?* National Bureau Of Economic Research Working Paper 24554, http://www.nber.org/papers/w24554

Guttmann, R. (2008). A primer on finance-led capitalism and its crisis. Introduction. *Revue de la régulation. Capitalisme, institutions, pouvoirs*, (3/4), 1–15.

Haggard, S. (2000). *The political economy of the Asian financial crisis*. Institute of International Economics.

Hakkio, C. S. (2013). The great moderation, 1982–2007. *Federal Reserve History*. https://www.federalreservehistory.org/essays/great-moderation

Hobsbawm, E. J. (1994). *Age of extremes: The short twentieth century*. Michael Joseph.

Islam, S. N., & Iversen, K. (2018). *From "structural change" to "transformative change": Rationale and implications*. United Nations Department of Economic & Social Affairs, DESA Working Paper No. 155, ST/ESA/2018/DWP/155, February 2018.

Kuznets, S. (1966). *Modern economic growth: Rate, structure and spread.* Yale University Press.

Lopez, R. S., & Lopez, R. S. (1976). *The Commercial Revolution of the Middle Ages, 950–1350.* Cambridge University Press.

Ma, Y. (2021). China's share of merchandise and commercial service exports in global exports in 2020. *Statista.* https://www.statista.com/statistics/256604/share-of-chinas-exports-in-global-exports/

Maier, C. S. (1970). Between Taylorism and technocracy: European ideologies and the vision of industrial productivity in the 1920s. *Journal of Contemporary History, 5*(2), 27–61.

Malanima, P. (2005). Urbanisation and the Italian economy during the last millennium. *European Review of Economic History, 9*(1), 97–122.

McMillan, M. S., & Rodrik, D. (2011). *Globalization, structural change and productivity growth.* National Bureau of Economic Research, Working Paper 17143.

Memedovic, O., & Iapadre, L. (2010). *Structural change in the world economy: Main features and trends.* United Nations Industrial Development Organisation, Research And Statistics Branch Working Paper 24/2009.

Minsky, H. P. (1980). Capitalist financial processes and the instability of capitalism. *Journal of Economic Issues, 14*(2), 505–523.

Minsky, H. (2016). *Can it happen again?: Essays on instability and finance.* Routledge.

Mokyr, J., Vickers, C., & Ziebarth, N. L. (2015). The history of technological anxiety and the future of economic growth: Is this time different? *Journal of Economic Perspectives, 29*(3), 31–50.

Palma, J. G. (2009). The revenge of the market on the rentiers: Why neo-liberal reports of the end of history turned out to be premature. *Cambridge Journal of Economics, 33*(4), 829–869.

Richter, F. (2021). China is the world's manufacturing superpower. *Statista*, https://www.statista.com/chart/20858/top-10-countries-by-share-of-global-manufacturing-output/

Rodrik, D. (2016). Premature deindustrialization. *Journal of Economic Growth, 21*(1), 1–33.

Ross, S. (2021). Financial services: Sizing the sector in the global economy. *Investopedia.* https://www.investopedia.com/ask/answers/030515/what-percentage-global-economy-comprised-financial-services-sector.asp

Schwab, K. (2017). *The Fourth Industrial Revolution.* World Economic Forum.

Setser, B. W. (2007). *The post-industrial economy?* "Follow the Money" Blog, Post, September 3, Council on Foreign Relations, https://www.cfr.org/blog/post-industrial-economy

Stiglitz, J. E. (1999). Reforming the global economic architecture: Lessons from recent crises. *The Journal of Finance, 54*(4), 1508–1521.

Van Zanden, J. L., & Van Leeuwen, B. (2012). Persistent but not consistent: The growth of national income in Holland 1347–1807. *Explorations in Economic History, 49*(2), 119–130.

Vogt, K. C. (2016). The post-industrial society: From utopia to ideology. *Work, Employment and Society, 30*(2), 366–376.

Vu, K., Haraguchi, N., & Amann, J. (2020). *Deindustrialization in developed countries amid accelerated globalization: Patterns, influencers and policy insights.* United Nations Industrial Development Organisation, Department Of Policy, Research And Statistics Working Paper 6/2020.

Wallis, P., Colson, J., & Chilosi, D. (2018). Structural change and economic growth in the British economy before the Industrial Revolution, 1500–1800. *The Journal of Economic History, 78*(3), 862–903.

Yusuf, S., Nabeshima, K., & Perkins, D. H. (2007). China and India reshape global industrial geography. In L. A. Winters & S. Yusuf (Eds.), *Dancing with giants: China, India and the global economy* (pp. 35–66). World Bank & Institute for Policy Studies.

CHAPTER 30

"2016"

C. Gordon, *Many Possible Worlds*,
https://doi.org/10.1007/978-981-19-9281-0_30

Fig. 30.1 No news or fake news (*Image source* Photo by Elvis Bekmanis on Unsplash Riga, Latvia, Published on April 8, 2019, Free to use under the Unsplash License. https://unsplash.com/photos/HORKkCWWBsM)

30.1 2016: An Unusual year

It is dangerous to put too much importance on the events of a single year. Many "historic" things have come and gone that in hindsight end up not being as significant as they appeared at the time; or they ended up being important in ways quite different than thought at the time. The exact times that events take place are generally due to historical accident, and the really crucial timing of causes are often the antecedents of such events, and/or their after-effects (Fig. 30.1).

In historiographical terms, the "historic year" can be seen as a micro-periodisation, with all the pitfalls entailed by that frame. Still, years that contain multiple occurrences of apparently remarkable events are nonetheless worth considering in more detail, as they may be indicative of deeper shifts in human ways of doing and being. For example, 1929 was a true watershed in economic history, just like 1914 was a much broader epochal marker. Of course the events of the year 2016 are still too close (as of this writing) to be considered with a genuinely detached perspective. But it is worth a try.

There was, for example, the fact of the first nomination of a woman candidate for President by a major American political party, of Hillary Clinton by the Democrats. But her accession above the popular insurgent candidate Bernie Sanders, with leaked documents showing the Democratic Party strongly partisan and manipulative in Clinton's favour, tainted this achievement and was indicative of a wider narrative of the corruption of American politics and its control by elites. The leaks themselves assumed controversial importance, with US intelligence agencies blaming Russian interference in the US election campaign, an investigation that itself became meme and theme for the following years (Megino & Pankhania, 2016).

The issue of "fake news" was a constant campaign refrain of the Republican candidate for President, Donald Trump, who used the phrase often to attack unfavourable media coverage of him, although his own candidacy and electoral success could be said to be an almost pure media product, the press feeding off of his outrageous statements and gaudy contradictions. Many remarked on the "reality TV" aspect of it all, a media product that had deeply blurred the already fuzzy lines between "fact" and "fiction", Trump having been a star of a popular program of that genre called *The Apprentice*. The election contest between Clinton and Trump contained many disclosures that in the past would have been politically fatal but which Trump showed could be brushed off if dismissed brazenly enough and replaced with an equally brazen distraction. The *coup de grace* here was the "Access Hollywood" tape, more than a decade old, in which Trump described himself groping women, using particularly offensive language to do so. Trump superficially apologised for his "locker room talk" but otherwise blustered right past it all and ended up victorious in November (Megino & Pankhania, 2016).

Rodrigo Duterte's election as President of the Philippines was a parallel event that seemed to confirm both the appeal of "strongman" right populism and the effectiveness of a certain kind of outrageous hyper-nationalist rhetoric in circumventing official media narratives and traditional political opposition. Narendra Modi's 2014 election as President of India and Jair Bolsonaro's 2017 accession to the Brazilian Presidency were in a similar vein. Duterte's claims to have personally killed some narco-terrorists when he was Mayor of Davao, was one of a number of provocative statements he made that only seemed to boost his appeal. President Recep Erdogan's long-standing autocratic rule in Turkey, and his success in crushing a coup against him in 2016, was pulled in as additional evidence of a distinct change in the tone of mass politics towards charismatic authoritarianism (Lindsay, 2016). Although the term was thrown around a lot, none of these developments were "Fascist" in the true sense of that word (see Chapter 23), but they did suggest a throwback to a certain style of challenge to the democratic status quo.

In June, "Brexit", the UK's referendum vote to leave the European Union, was given a narrow "yes" vote, against the expectations of pollsters. Pollsters had also predicted that Trump would lose in his bid for the Presidency, but instead he won. As a result pollsters and other "experts" were now seen less trustworthy than ever before, adding to an expanding wave of anti-elitism. Brexit revealed the waning appeal amongst the masses of an official program of globalisation and economic integration. Trump ran in favour of economic nationalism and against the Trans-Pacific Partnership (TPP) free trade deal so favoured by President Obama and the official Washington establishment. Hillary Clinton, previously a strong supporter of TPP, had to reverse her position in the face of Bernie Sanders' strong opposition which resonated with a white working class that had always felt such treaties hurt them, delivering benefits mainly to the rich, and to corporate interests. Multilateralism more broadly seemed to be in retreat. Trump ran against the Paris Climate Agreement and the Iran Nuclear Deal, both of which his government did indeed pull out of after he got into office. Anti-immigration themes, already widely resonant in electoral politics, were trumpeted even further by Trump, and also to varying degrees by most European governments still struggling against the influx of Syrian refugees fleeing from six long years of civil war (Lindsay, 2016).

Violence was an ongoing undercurrent. There was a January siege by Al-Qaeda-linked militants of a popular tourist hotel in Burkina Faso, a deadly bombing at the Brussels airport in Belgium, an suicide bomb attack on the Istanbul airport, a large truck deliberately driven through a crowd celebrating France's Bastille Day in Nice, and a similar truck attack at a popular Christmas market in Berlin. These were ideologically motivated attacks by individuals who claimed to believe in some version of the diverse doctrine referred to as "Radical Islam". The most egregious such attack that also brought in an anti-gay hate motive was that of a lone gunman entering Pulse, a gay nightclub in Orlando, Florida in the United States, and gunning down scores of people, in the type of mass shooting that took place on most days in America, but typically far less lethally. The gunman evoked support for a radical Islamist extremist organisation as justification for his crime (Wikipedia, 2016). Such terrorist attacks had been fairly regular occurrences, but their frequency this year suggested unresolved and worsening social conflict to some.

One event that would prove to be especially ominous when looked at in retrospect was the outbreak of a "new" virus, Zika, with Brazil being the epicentre, soon spreading elsewhere, including to the US. Zika was especially dangerous to the foetuses of pregnant women, and thousands of babies were born with Zika-related microcephaly, i.e. a small head and under-developed brain. Outbreaks of "strange" "new" diseases had become increasingly regular before this—Ebola in Africa, SARS, MERS, etc.—and COVID-19 in 2020 would show this to be a problem that was only growing worse (Linsday, 2016).

Another event that got some attention in America was the Flint, Michigan water crisis, in which US President Obama declared a state of emergency there a little less than two years after the local government had outsourced its water supply to a private company that had promptly switched the city's water source to the Flint River. This saved a bit of public money, but had caused an unprecedented public health crisis as acidic river water corroded the decaying municipal water pipes, leaching out lead into water consumed by a population mostly poor and Black. Prior to this the water had been provided municipally and was sourced from the cleaner Lake Huron and Detroit River. The switch in water supply had not been motivated by prior problems of quality, but of greed, with lucrative contracts signed by Michigan's Governor with private water contractors. The problem is still not adequately resolved and the crisis shed a spotlight on the ideology of rampant privatisation and institutionalised racism in America. Obama's state of emergency incidentally did little to correct the problem, bringing a sense of betrayal to the city's largely African-American community (Denchak, 2018).

Finally, a symbolically important death during 2016 was that of Cuban leader Fidel Castro, who had already handed over the Presidency to his brother Raul a number of years before. The Cold War had been over for three decades and the death of one of its leading icons suggested to some that this period was finally becoming a mere echo. Even though a few nominally Communist countries, most notably China, still existed, "Really Existing Socialism" and the people, associated with it, were now mostly no longer around at all (Weissenstein & Orsi, 2016).

30.2 Superficial Placidity and Technocratic Paradigms

These events are indicative of the fact that development of the modern economy has been marked by tremendous instability, turmoil, disruption and dislocation, the dark side of the "light" of rapid and spreading material growth. This seemed to be especially true of the twentieth century with its World Wars, depression and other lesser conflagrations. Even the "Golden Age" of the 1950s and 1960s was riven by Cold War and social discord in the economic core, and often much worse things in the periphery. In the 1970s, even this prosperous phase of capitalist modernity came to an end, with the breakdown of the Keynesian "consensus", the occurrence of stagflation, and the rise of Neoliberalism (see Chapters 24, 25, and 28).

But then the Cold War ended and Western capitalism was triumphant and the Western developed economies were treated to a decade of strong economic performance. Figure 30.2 shows that growth in the Western Capitalist bloc was in the decade immediately following the Cold War as prodigious, GDP per capita increasing almost 28% in Western Europe and almost 24% in the Western Offshoots. Outside this rich core, the growth picture was much less impressive, however. Eastern European GDP per capita contracted between 1990 and 2000 (though there were individual

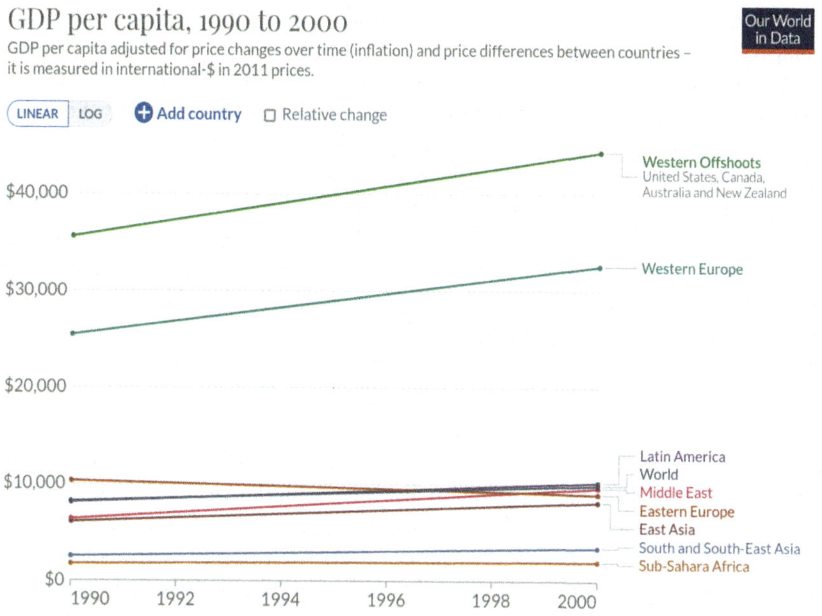

Fig. 30.2 GDP per capita growth in the 1990s, by global region (*Image source* Roser [2013]. Used under a CC-BY license)

country exceptions), while sub-Saharan Africa and South and South-East Asia essentially stagnated. These two regions were shaken by the collapse of Communism and the Asian Financial Crisis (AFC), respectively. The Middle East, East Asia and Latin America grew, but proportionately much less than the West and the overall world growth average was quite modest.

Many took this diverse performance as evidence that the rich West had "won" the Cold War because of its superior economic institutions, policies and experience. The 1990s and beyond for these winners was one of a "Great Moderation" in which business cycles were now smoothed over organically and largely automatically, along a permanent trend line of positive economic growth, delivered by the perfected modes of markets, permissive government policies, and private enterprise, and backed by wise central banking throughout the developed world (Graff et al., 2013, 309–310; 319). Policy and institutional "settings" were now "just right" in the Goldilocks sense, and all was right with the world (see Chapter 29).

As for the rest of the planet, its laggard growth was surely to due to poor institutions and policy decisions, especially in the formerly Socialist countries now in "transition". These and other countries needed to change their own policy settings towards the "Washington Consensus" of free markets, transparent institutional processes, political democracy and incentives for capital creation, accumulation and investment. It would take a bit of time, and some Western aid and assistance would be needed, but certainly they too would learn and reap the rewards of a post-ideological age (Williamson, 2013).

There was a consensus, domestically and internationally, that what was good for business was good for growth, individual initiative and the unleashing of free enterprise being the means to get there. The anti-hero corporate raider character, Gordon Gekko, of the 1987 film *Wall Street*, pithily summed this view up when he proclaimed "Greed is good". The policymakers provided the background ingredients of pro-growth and pro-business policies in which this competitive process could deliver its magic, tweaking their variables as needed. And the 1990s did, as noted, deliver a burst of GDP growth to the well-off nations. Since this was accompanied by deregulation, tax cuts and global integration, it seemed as if there was a positive causal connection between these policies and prosperity. A retrospective on the period by the World Bank had a title that said it all: *Economic growth in the 1990s: Learning from a decade of reform* (Zagha & Nankani, 2005). Governments had merely to adjust the dials correctly, and it was up to individuals to get out in the competitive market and make the best of all possible worlds.

30.3 Anger Movements

Yet even in the rich West, things were not as rosy as they appeared. Anger at the way things were had been long-standing in the Western democracies and the 1990s dulled this undercurrent a bit but did not end it. The tumult of the 1960s and the economic disorder of the 1970s had been a time of rising uncertainties and an already existing polarisation underlying even the Golden Age. In the US, for example, Richard Nixon had swept into office as President in 1968 on a wave of discontent and made an explicit pitch to the constituency of angry swing voters as he prepared to run for a second term. His Vice President, Spiro Agnew, was a willing attack dog, using his own peculiar rhetoric to lambast "liberals" and other enemies. Agnew spoke of newspapers disposing of their garbage by printing it, of a supposedly "positive" polarisation to maintain "decent" values and of an "artificial and masochistic sophistication" that kept people from being comfortably patriotic (Manchester, 1973, 1494). The tagline that Nixon himself used during his first term and 1972 election campaign was an appeal to the "Silent Majority" that economic and political elites had forgotten.

It was a politics of grievance. And although it was conducted against a background of relative prosperity, it fed off what appeared to be a betrayal of the implicit postwar development bargain of social peace, prosperity, rising wages and fixed 8-hour days in both factories and offices, with the feasibility for only one partner—the husband—to work, and yet still earn enough income to buy a house, support children and to have the whole family partake in a burgeoning myriad of leisure and consumption opportunities. All of this seemed in jeopardy with the rise of stagflation, the collapse of the Keynesian order, and the resurgence of the Third World and its apparent ability to hold the rich countries economically hostage by hiking the prices of their exports of raw commodities, this last fact manipulated by Western politicians into a sort of "humiliation" (see Chapter 28).

A rapidly changing world created a sense of powerlessness and social anxiety in the global North, something that Davis (2006) characterises as maladjustment to change (6). Change used to have promise; now it only had peril. And it was protection against peril that politicians offered as an antidote to fear and division, while sowing the same in their own self-interest. This was channelled in a number of directions. A symbolic nationalism was one redoubt. Hyper-patriotic America was especially prone to this. An American flag boom was kicked off in 1969 when the popular mass publication *Reader's Digest* sent small flag decals to its eighteen million subscribers setting off a craze in which tens of millions of people bought and displayed them everywhere and then bought new "America-Love It or Leave It" bumper stickers and other merchandise being churned out to meet the growing demand for patriotic display. It was Richard Nixon who began the trend of politicians wearing small flag lapel pins, soon *de rigeur* for any respecting politician or staff member (Reeves, 2001, 226).

Such patriotic impulses took flight in most of the other democracies, especially Britain, which once had a great Empire and now was struggling to keep its lights on and pay its international debts. The elections of Ronald Reagan as US President in 1980 and Margaret Thatcher as UK Prime Minister in 1979 were both products, in part, of a widespread sense that an old order had failed its hardworking "silent majorities" and sacrificed their respective nation's rightful places in the world in so doing.

The Reagan era is an interesting example to consider. The social movements that brought Reagan into power, first as Governor of California and then as an unlikely successful Presidential candidate, were unlike those of the past, motivated more by a desire to preserve a status quo deemed to be under attack rather than upend or reshape and improve it, as much of the 1960s tumult had been about. The 1970s American local "tax revolt" was a groundswell that powered an electoral reaction against both Democratic and Republican political party establishments. Centred in California, Reagan's political home, it unified middle- and upper-class landowners around an anti-bureaucratic, anti-welfare ideology. It also notionally pitted the suburbs against the cities, which were seen as full of "soft" liberal thinkers, ethnic minorities and other disaffected and dangerous people (Davis, 2006, 123). The result in California was a legislative cap on local property taxes, an innovation that rapidly spread to other states and helped buttress tax-cut and balanced-budget movements at the national level. Government, which used to be an engine of positive change, was now seen as an enemy to be forcibly limited by the electorate in its ability to exercise power and raise revenue for itself. It was captured in Reagan's 1980 campaign slogan: "Government is not the solution to our problem, government is the problem".

This was not, however, the old small state Liberalism of the nineteenth century, but a distinct aspect of the new ideology of Neoliberalism (see Chapter 28). An important political feature of it was an appeal to individual freedom, trumpeted in a negative rather than a positive sense, against a creeping activist state rather than as a fight for liberty of the person, although the rhetoric often misleadingly highlighted the latter. The call was to leave people alone, to live as they saw fit—as individuals. Collectives were out—the individual was in. It was summed up well by Nixon's 1973 informal reformulation of John F. Kennedy's inaugural theme of ask not what your country can do for you, but what you can do for your country: don't ask what your government can do for you, but what you can do for yourself (Reeves, 2001, 566).

30.4 A Passing of "Big Ideas"

The rightward shift fed by anger and grievance was unmistakable. But oddly this did not feed into any collective alliance behind an existing or new ideology. During the Cold War, Communism was at best tolerated in Western countries, more often suppressed. By the late 1970s and beyond increasingly it seemed to be a spent force, unattractive even to the dwindling numbers of idealists both East and West. Fascism, never a coherent ideology anyway, was now reduced to an epithet. The Second World War had pitted the inheritors of the humanist ideals of the Enlightenment and 1789 against those without such values, and it had been a close-run contest, though Enlightenment values won out in the end (Hobsbawm, 1994, 139). Or so it appeared on the surface. For what actually had triumphed was not a grand value system, despite the Cold War contest of ideas, but a worldwide quest for personal material comfort, ease and stability. Individual material fulfilment was the goal and not only in the Capitalist world. Technological and economic prowess seemed to have made it possible and it was the level of that prowess that mattered.

Indeed, "Big Ideas", as had formed and animated prior revolutions, whether those had been 1776, 1789, 1848, or 1917, were increasingly out of vogue. All they seemed to have brought in the past was high promise, followed by chaos and disappointment. And the world was now getting too complicated to change fundamentally anyway. What it really needed was to have the best management available to preserve growth and stability. With that a good individual life was at hand, as was national success. Without it life was difficult and, worst case, on the precipice. After the turbulence of the 1970s and 1980s, and the end of the Cold War, the main question for public policy now settled into adjustments within the narrow range of the Growth Model: how much taxes should be cut, or not, how much safety nets should be trimmed, or not, or which particular interest group should be favoured, or not. It was a decidedly small-bore politics, playing off of small group and individual lifestyle considerations, promising small increments of improvement.

As already noted the 1990s were good times in the West, at least according to the statistics of raw economic growth. But economic security was now a thing of the past and the one-earner household with a steady and growing standard of living supporting all the household members was impossible. These were replaced by the entrepreneurial possibilities that supposedly were everywhere, the chance for a quick profit for little effort now a tantalising, if elusive, possibility for everyone. Especially with the loosened up and booming financial markets and the hyper-networking of the Internet, the speculative opportunities were endless. Figure 30.3 shows the performance of share price indices across the Euro area between May 1991, just before the collapse of the Soviet Union, and June 2001, shortly before the attacks of 9–11 on the World Trade Centre. During this time, share prices rose by roughly 4 times in value. US share prices performed similarly. There were ups and downs and one could lose money investing in shares. But one could also potentially make much more than market averages too. If you had the capital anything was possible, it seemed.

It was not exactly that people were happy, or that there were no social divisions, or that there were no pressing problems. In fact, there was plenty of struggle and uncertainty beneath the surface. But a broad policy consensus existed on both sides of the establishment that economic growth was the main concern and that everything should be done to preserve rather than threaten it. There was some protest during this period, but much of it was episodic and directed at specific temporary

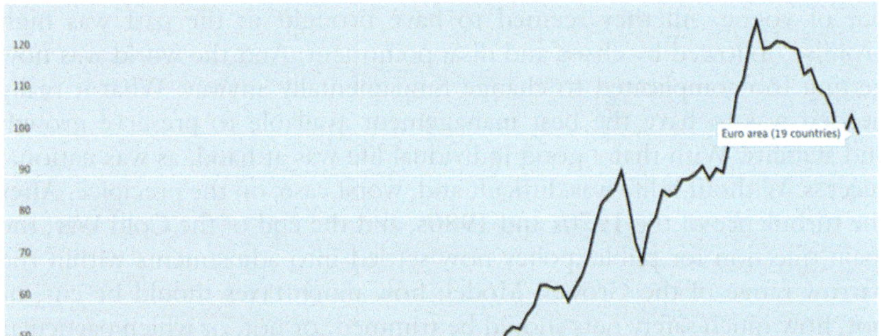

Fig. 30.3 Euro area (19 countries) share price average between May 1991 to June 2001 (2015 = 100) (*Image source* Data extracted from OECD [2021], Share prices (indicator). https://doi.org/10.1787/6ad82f42-en [Accessed on 14 November 2021]. Used under license granted for commercial use as per OECD terms and conditions)

causes, such as against particular wars or policies. There was little mass organisation in any sense that threatened the established orders, even within opposition parties or most of civil society. The Cold War's end had finally indicated that Communism had been a noble but failed experiment and that sweeping alternatives to the existing status quo were undesirable at best, impossible at worst, at least at a societal level.

30.5 Actions Without Equal and Opposite Reactions

In 1932, John Dos Passos had written, in the preface to his set of novels the *U.S.A. Trilogy*, of how the people who had have lived through the years after the First World War had seen the great illusions of the time uncovered, and were now faced with the "raw structure of history" that had to be dealt with immediately "before it stamps us out" (ix). Mass social movements had played a definitive role in driving reforms in the Capitalist democracies, and this was what Dos Passos was trying to say, that the people needed to organise to make sure they emerged ahead of the arc of fast-moving processes that would otherwise bury them as both individuals and as groups if they did not. This was what the extraordinary social and political ferment of the 1930s was about, as scary as it was at the time.

Contrast this with the 2007–2009 Global Financial Crisis (GFC) and the Great Recession that gripped much of the world, the developed countries the most. The crisis had many parallels with the 1930s, including a massive financial system implosion that was the result of reckless unregulated speculation. In its earliest stages, real and financial asset prices, GDP growth and employment actually fell faster in most places than they had during the Depression (Eichengreen, 2014). Figure 30.4 shows the fall in share prices across the Euro 19 area and the US between December 2004 and April 2009. Figure 30.5 shows changes in GDP per capita across selected countries between 2007 and 2011.

Both European and American shares had an impressive run up in overall share values of around 70% during a two-year period preceding the crisis, but then declined to around 40% of their peak values in the space of a year, a much sharper and faster fall than after the Great Crash. Real economy contraction was similarly sharp and fast. In the US and UK in particular, this was a deep growth recession, GDP per capita in both countries falling 5% or more between 2007 and 2009 and still not

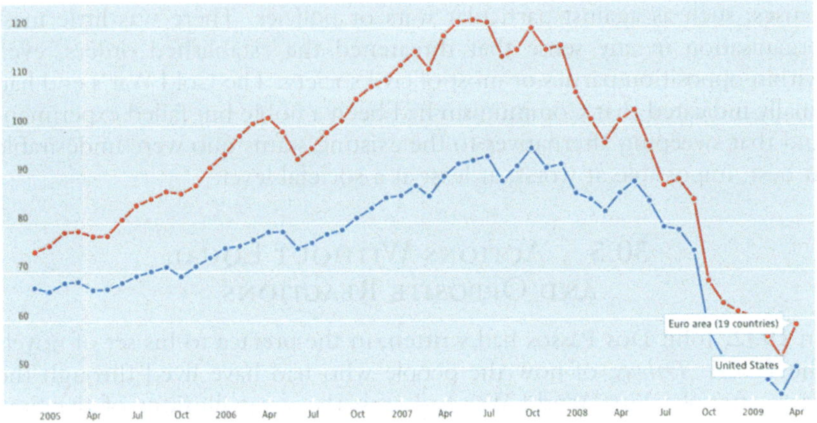

Fig. 30.4 Share price performance Euro area and the US, December 2004 and April 2009 (2015 = 100) (*Image source* Data extracted from OECD [2021], Share prices [indicator]. https://doi.org/10.1787/6ad82f42-en [Accessed on 14 November 2021]. Used under license granted for commercial use as per OECD terms and conditions)

recovering 2007 levels by 2011. These two nations were global financial centres and as it was a financial collapse that led to the greater crisis, it is no surprise that the contraction was greatest there.

The question arises, however, as to why, if 2007/2009 was, in many ways, worse than 1929/1930, there was not a similar social reaction in the latter case. This is even more surprising given that it came on top of several decades of relative slow-down in growth and increasing income inequality (see below). Social anger was already palpable and growing, and social conflict was simmering. Why wasn't there an explosion?

There is no straightforward answer to this. In part, policymakers had learned some of the lessons of the Depression, especially the need to quickly pump huge amounts of liquidity into the financial system to keep it from seizing up completely as it had back in the 1930s. Indeed, Ben Bernanke, chairman of the US Federal Reserve Bank at the time, was a noted scholar of Depression era banking collapse and his policies can be traced directly to his research in the area (Gordon, 2011). The US central bank set the tone for the rest of the world with the novel (and still ongoing) "Quantitative Easing" (QE) which involved the central bank

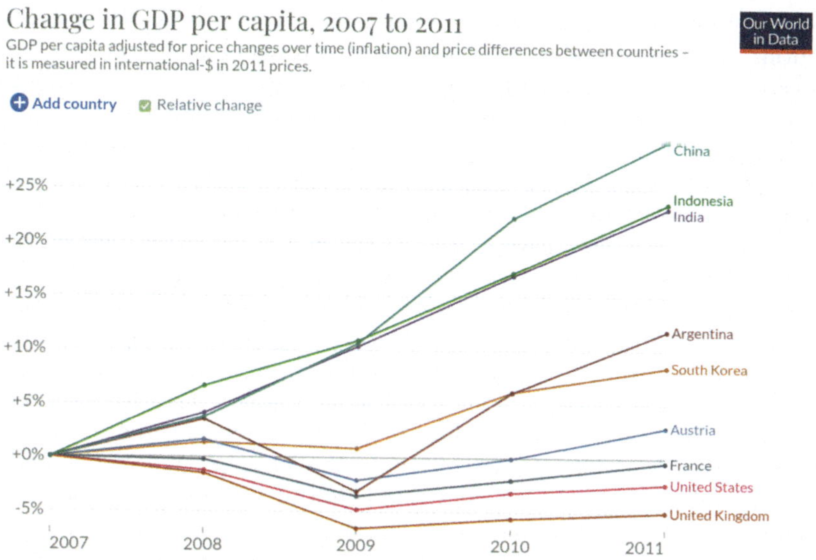

Fig. 30.5 Relative changes in GDP per capita, selected countries, 2007–2011 (2007 baseline) (*Image source* Roser [2013]. Used under a CC-BY license)

buying up distressed assets off of failing institutions, at prices well above their true value (which was often generally zero, or close to it), and paying for them with huge infusions of newly created money—not printed, as in the old days, but electronically transferred. Lowering interest rates to nothing and keeping them there accompanied this money supply expansion. In a few countries, interest rates even reached negative levels in nominal terms, meaning that to keep money in the central bank required the asset holder to pay for the privilege (Eisenshmidt & Smets, 2019). All of this did keep the financial system from falling apart, even though there were some close calls along the way. In particular, while some bank runs on a few major banks took place, governments completely protected depositors from any losses. This not only contained financial "contagion", but also limited a major source of public discontent and fear.

On the fiscal policy side, there was also a great deal of Keynesian "stimulus" spending to plug the "output gaps" of rapidly falling aggregate demand. However, while the amounts spent by governments were unprecedented in scale, in America and Europe especially the distribution of the monies generally did not much make it to the bulk of the population. Indeed in Europe the debt crisis that resulted as interest rates on sovereign debt spiked amidst a huge increase in government borrowing to fund the stimulus resulted in sharp cutbacks to public spending, including on pensions, public service wages and other categories that were exactly the opposite of the Keynesian prescription (Makin, 2019). Nonetheless, democratic government was responding in a way that it had not during the laissez-faire policy days of the 1930s and some mass support was acquired as a result. This was on top of existing safety nets that Neoliberalism had tattered but which were still more robust than had existed during the Depression. All this took some edge off the impacts of the crisis on those exposed to it and helped limit protest and unrest.

On the negative side of this social ledger, Varoufakis (2015) argues that the GFC broke the social contract that had arisen after the collapse of Bretton Woods and its Keynesian consensus between financiers, workers and the middle class, i.e. that anyone could buy a house with debt. In practical terms, this had decoupled the need for wage growth from the ability to finance asset purchases, or even major and minor consumption needs. Instead people could fill financial gaps with readily available credit, using their personal leverage to cash in on steadily growing asset prices, especially in houses. This depended, however, on nearly non-existent assessment of creditworthiness by lenders and never-ending increases in house prices. Neither of these could last forever. The resulting crash was predictable, but few saw it coming because credit was so essential for survival, both for the individual and for the financial sector. When it all fell down, the masses were understandably upset and felt betrayed.

While the fiscal and monetary measures did avoid the collapse of the financial sector, they did not do much to rescue the ordinary person. In fact, those most responsible for the crisis, the banks and nonbank intermediaries not only mostly avoided repercussion, they went back to big bonuses and profits within a couple of years. As mentioned above the fiscal stimulus packages trickled up for the most part, rather than down, even as home foreclosures rose and jobs evaporated. A leftist push-back came, some of them in the form of grassroots electoral political parties, such as Podemos in Spain, and Syriza in Greece. The biggest street movement was Occupy Wall Street (OWS), which consisted of people establishing residential encampments on various sites near financial markets and institutions (Varoufakis, 2015).

But these turned out to have no staying power. OWS was tolerated by authorities for around two years before being turned out by various local police forces, the strongest crackdown coming in New York, the home of the movement. The left parties had temporary gains, Podemos taking over the Madrid municipal government and gaining seats in the national and various regional assemblies, and Syriza taking power in Greece nationally for a few months. Here too, though, there was no sustained policy change, and not even much temporary alteration either. Even when a mass movement managed to take power or at least the balance of it in elections, they found themselves starved of cash to do anything (Varoufakis, 2015).

And outside of bringing out crowds to protests and ballot boxes, the deeper social infrastructure that had existed during the 1930s, such as labour unions and voluntary associations, which could sustain and focus the popular will, was much more threadbare. Even political parties had gone from being true mass organisations with many active members in the field, to professionally staffed organisations that mainly raised money from large donors. And the lack of a binding and compelling ideas system didn't help matters. In many ways, the left was reduced to a political program not dissimilar to that of the technocracy in charge, namely a raft of incremental proposals, a few perhaps innovative in themselves, but none of them adding up to a major alternative to the status quo. The "people" had lost their ability to pressure the powers that be, even when these were in deep crisis, and had little true alternative ideas to offer.

On other striking fact is the concentration of the economic crisis in the developed world. The Depression had been truly global. Figure 30.5 shows that while the developing nations were deeply affected, for various reasons China, India and Indonesia, the largest developing economies, did not suffer a growth contraction. They had paid their finance sector pipers back during the Asian Financial Crisis of 1998 and had learned at least some lessons from it, namely to make sure they had as much independence from Western finance as they could manage.

30.6 Broken Mirrors

Economic modernisation has brought along rapid changes in systematic mass communication, via an almost universal literacy delivered by compulsory public education and advances in technology. The late nineteenth century witnessed a proliferation of widely distributed and well-produced urban newspapers made possible by high-speed presses, the linotype and halftone photo reproduction. An associated step was the creation of global newsgathering organisations like the Associated Press that provided efficiencies in the creation of what we would now call "content", helping to formalise and standardise an emerging "news industry". In the US, for example, daily newspaper circulation increased 400% between 1870 and 1900, and similar increases were to be found in the other advanced economies (Henderson, 2005).

Daniel Boorstin (1971) created the term "Graphic Revolution" to refer to an industrialised capacity for image reproduction and mass diffusion. Photography was fundamental of course, but it was the ability to cheaply print photos that really made them take off. This was especially important in the creation of new forms of printed matter, such as magazines. Boorstin claims that it was this that helped create a celebrity culture focused mainly on how well known a person was rather than by any actual achievements they had. A demand for constant "news" aided this by a rising array of "pseudo-events" that were not happenings of any real sort, but manufactured occurrences designed solely for media coverage. The rising Public Relations industry became specialised in both image making and event-creating for mass media distribution.

Indeed, the use of mass-produced images had a dramatic effect on human understanding and experience of their collective experience. One art critic has noted that images are not mere adjuncts to words, but exist in parallel universes to them (Archer, 2002, 129). They are processed differently, evoke different emotional reactions, and the juxtaposition of word and text can have dramatically different meaning when taken together rather than separately.

The invention of film, the phonograph record, and the radio, accelerated and intensified these trends, and all of them rapidly became industries of their own and vehicles of mass entertainment, communication and opinion formation. The American recording industry saw sales grow by 600% between 1933 and 1938, even though this was in the depths of the Depression. Radios fell in cost, an average set costing around $35 in 1934, with 60% of all American households owning at least one. Radio was also live, unlike newspapers, and politicians discovered its unique power, as they had before with newspapers. Franklin D. Roosevelt proved to be an adept master of the medium, using his regular "fireside chats" to speak directly to his audience (Henderson, 2005). Television became an even more powerful medium of communication, fusing spoken words with moving images, an intoxicating combination. And now this has been further extended with the real-time, on-demand, "individualised" platforms of the Internet, most notably social media.

The effects of all this on human cognition and perception, both individual and collective, are still not fully known. The "rational actor" model proposes that the human being is a passive recipient of information who then processes it, weighs truth or falsehood, decides what is relevant and acts accordingly, as per initially held preferences and objectives that themselves might be revised according to what analysis has revealed. But Boorstin's "pseudo-events" are not always so easily distinguishable from "real" ones, and the veracity of "facts" is often unclear, distinctions that media outlets themselves often actively discourage, as per "reality TV". The sociologist Jean Baudrillard has argued that the pervasiveness of jarring and incoherent image-word combinations has led to a culture increasingly incapable of discriminating between reality and illusion (Henderson, 2005).

This may be going too far. But for sure the means for manipulating the masses has gone to new highs—and lows. The most notorious example is a document, widely believed to be by George W. Bush political adviser Karl Rove, in which it was claimed that the world is no longer is reality-based in the objective sense. Instead those in authority (referring to America in this case), when they act, will create their own reality, and change it again as required to stay ahead of those attempting to analyse what is happening a more factual way (Appy, 2015, 319). This is not apparently to be taken in a purely literal sense but more in the vein of "perception is reality". But how much distinction between the two is really left?

From the perspective of grassroots change, this all-encompassing and rather confusing media landscape has arguably absorbed the motive force of frustration and discontent that in the past might have gone into genuine social organisation that could serve as a counterweight to established centres of power. There are many mass movements out there, but they tend to be more "virtual" than real, capable sometimes of pulling out people into large protests or email campaigns, but not much more than that. Not that such activity is to be criticised. But the channelling of protest and dissent into media platforms may be one reason that the social and political turmoil of the GFC has not apparently been very successful at effecting meaningful systemic change. This is made worse by the fact that the mainstream political parties and other institutions do not represent much outside an official consensus of system management anymore and are impervious to elections, protests and the other officially allowed levers.

30.7 The Roots of 2016

Almost immediately after the fall of the Soviet Union, US President George H.W. Bush declared a "New World Order" (NWO) in which America would preside over a period of free enterprise and prosperity and political liberty. It was of in line with the general tenor of the "End of History" thinking that the end of the Cold War inspired (see Chapter 26). Although ideology had supposedly been trumped, the NWO was straight out of old Wilsonian "high principle" thinking fused with American exceptionalism (See Chapter 20). Academic analysts referred to this program as the "Washington Consensus" (Best et al., 2004).

This NWO was built on the hidden premises of the preceding Cold War. The American political scientist Richard Hofstadter wrote *The Age of Reform* in 1955, a book that recast traditional American history narratives to say that real reform was to be achieved more effectively by expertise and the elites working together on solving issues, rather than via pressure of the diverse rabble of class movements that had coalesced under the "Populist" banner of the late 1800s and early 1900s. Although written during the Cold War, the book came out of the common faith of both ideological blocs in the ability of "science" to manage society, cure its ills and constantly improve conditions. This "consensus" thinking about the power of expertise was actually strengthened because after the Cold War it was clear that there was no alternative to Capitalism and hence no deep politics. Now "non-political" experts were needed more than ever to get the settings correct.

Since the Americans had won, American experts were the ones to go to—hence the Washington Consensus. Yet this identification of expert advice with one country had the odd effect or bringing back a nationalist factor that the Cold War had submerged. True, America had always been a virulently patriotic nation. But one could not compete with the Soviet threat worldwide with American patriotism alone since the majority of people in the world were not Americans. The more effective appeal had to be to system superiority. The NWO now took this superiority for granted, but it now was unquestionably American as well. This element did not sit well with many non-Americans. The fall of the Eastern bloc in Europe had already unfrozen local nationalisms. The declaration of an American-designed system led by America as the best for everyone else, loosened it up for the rest of the world as well, understandably causing resentment and backlash against a unitary hegemon.

Meanwhile, even in the 1990s, things were not going so well for much of the global population. The plain economic facts are well-known: more and more of the developed world population had stagnating or falling wages and standards of living even as total wealth and income were increasing. Those countries that had implemented the greatest degree of Neoliberal policies to aid such growth seemed to have some of the thorniest side effects. Capitalism had always generated inequality, unless it was checked by external constraints such as government regulation and progressive taxation. There had been a peak in inequality coinciding with the height of the Second Industrial Revolution, that, combined with the Great Depression, had led to mildly redistributionist tax and spending policies during the Golden Age of third quarter of the twentieth century.

Neoliberalism wound back these policies and then some, and there was a return, with a vengeance, to inequality again. This second time around, though, government policies exacerbated rather than moderated the trend through regressive tax cuts, reductions in social welfare spending and financial deregulation. Figure 30.6 indicates that within the US and the UK in particular, but also in most other industrialised nations, the share of total wealth and income going to the top percentiles of the population (i.e. the top 1% or top 10%) increased steadily beginning in the 1980s. It had not yet reached the levels seen during the late nineteenth and early twentieth centuries as of 2014, but it was getting there, the process most advanced in the US. The larger "Latin" countries, such as France and Spain, had not reverted as fully to past regressive distributions, but income inequality was creeping back in there as well.

Such inequality might have been tolerable if at least there was strong economic growth. However, the GFC had already taken a great deal of wealth from the middle classes through unemployment and home foreclosures. The working classes, already hobbled by deindustrialisation, simply continued their downward spiral in living standards. Developing world growth, as Fig. 30.7 shows, was weak, even after pre-GFC levels of per capita GDP had been returned to around 2012. Indeed, the Western Offshoots, the best growth area in the developed world, nonetheless grew below the world average between 2010 and 2018. Granted, some countries in the developing world were growing much faster, seeming proof

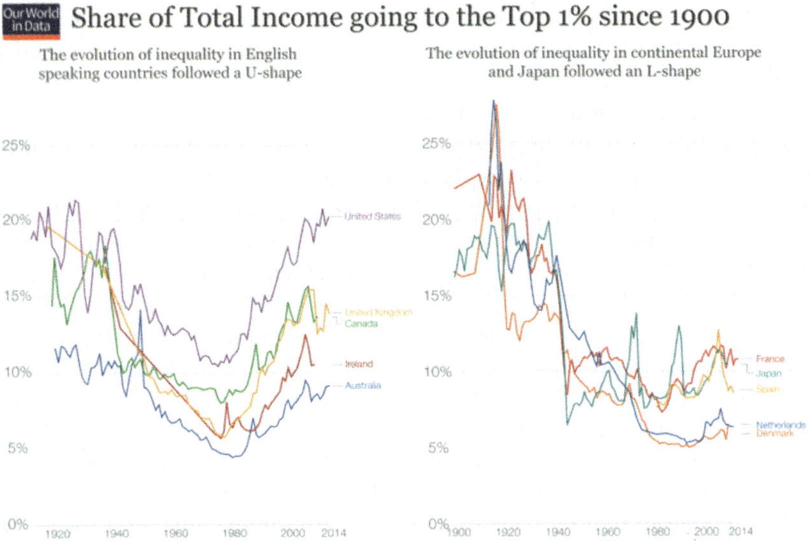

Fig. 30.6 Increasing inequality in the West (*Note* Online data are updated dynamically and may have been adjusted since this publication. Used under a CC BY license. *Image source* Roser and Esteban [2013])

of the promises offered by the global integrationists and free-marketers. But this was of little consolation to the greater and greater numbers of people being left behind in the wealthy countries where wealth got shared around less and less, to say nothing of the many developing world people who remained in poverty.

30.8 A Turning Point, But Nowhere to Turn?

There were no grand ideas to rally around anymore and no parties or movements to truly represent the people. Everything was a technical problem to be solved by experts and elites and it seemed as if they both had failed, as indeed they had. Almost every academic economist and financial analyst and government policy body missed the GFC, even though there had been numerous signs of systemic problems before these such as the dramatic collapse of the Enron Corporation (Gordon, 2013). And yet these many specialists had not paid the price for their mistakes,

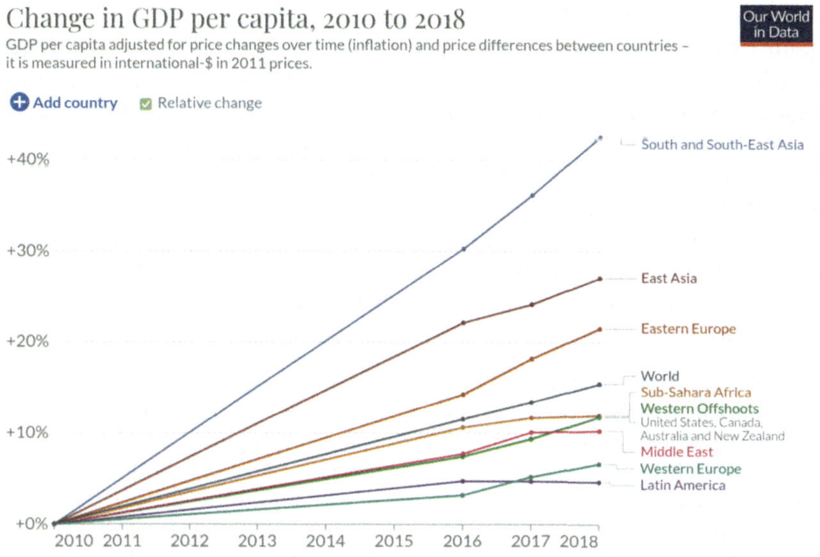

Fig. 30.7 Sluggish post-GFC growth in the developed world (*Note* Online data are updated dynamically and may have been adjusted since this publication. Used under a CC BY license. *Image source* Roser [2013])

nor did anyone in power responsible for the collapse. The "people" had paid instead. Not only had the technical growth paradigm ignored the politics that always come with any human relationships. It also ignored the possibility of elite failures of judgement and exercise of power of which the GFC was a major example (Frank, 2016).

During the 1930s, the Fascists had appealed to the displaced middle and working classes with a promise of writing the disenfranchised back into a social contract that many felt was only for the rich and privileged. Thus Mussolini said that capital would never exploit labour and imposed a social wage and full pensions to provide the masses with, if not wealth, then at least security. The Fascists also offered a form of meaning in the form of an exclusionary "nation" that was identified with the "people". These were ersatz and sometimes vile offerings. But they at least pretended to meet a genuine social need that the Liberalism of the time had not even been concerned with.

2016 was not a turning point in the sense that society had been turning against itself for some time. But it was indicative of a political, social and economic vacuum not dissimilar to that of the 1930s, like then an era after a global economic and financial crisis that had not been resolved, in the context of an order that most ordinary folks were now thoroughly dissatisfied with. Also like the 1930s, there was a backlash against economic integration simultaneous with a renewed sense of nationalism. What has been interesting this time is how this nationalism is sometimes expressed as a reaction against not just larger existing groupings (like the European Union) but also against existing nations in some cases (see Box 30.1).

Box 30.1 Modern day secession movements

The modern era has been a period of nationalism, consolidation, and integration. It also has been one of self-determination, popular sovereignty and human rights. These forces can pull in different directions, both towards, and away from, political and economic integration. Over the past fifteen or so years the trend has been away.

The 2010s especially saw rising disenchantment with, and distrust of, consolidations of political and economic power within large jurisdictions. This was most directed at supranational organisations and agreements, and unions of independent countries, both of which were deemed as involving cession of popular authority to distant elites who managed their domains for their narrow private interests rather than the general public. The legitimacy of the World Trade Organisation (WTO), the European Union (EU) and the Trans-Pacific Partnership (TPP) multilateral trade agreement, were prime targets, joining some traditional enemies like the United Nations and the International Monetary Fund. Such movements continue today.

Attacks on these institutional arrangements come from across the political spectrum, sometimes fusing "right" and "left" views. The most spectacular secession success was the Brexit referendum, which had inspired a whole range of "exit" neologisms, e.g. Grexit (for Greek's potential exit from the EU and Eurozone austerity programs) and "Irexit" for Ireland's leaving the EU. Quite a few subnational secession movements were inspired as well, such as "Wexit", which is a term that happens to refer both to a call for the democratic separation of the western provinces of Canada, i.e. Alberta, Saskatchewan, Manitoba, and British Columbia, to form their own independent and sovereign country; and for the Australian state of Western Australia to secede from that country. One could add "Texit" and "Calexit" to respectively refer to Texas secession and California secession in the US. Other secession movements that do not use an "exit" moniker include the Scottish independence movement and Catalan separatism in Spain.

Secessionism is nothing new, of course. But economic grievance and a discontented feeling that one would be better off outside a jurisdiction rather than within it have been more prevalent lately than in past times. Although Brexiteers would often appeal to British nationalism in their rhetoric, the movement was much more driven by distrust of economic and social elites and a sense of disenfranchisement by those most hard done by in the process of internationalisation, especially the poor regions outside of London and the poor neighbourhoods within it that provided the votes that made the difference between "yes" and "no". Distribution of resources and power have been the general motivating factor behind much current secessionism, in which some people feel that they are being ripped off by being part of a larger whole. There are some exceptions, such as the Scottish and Welsh autonomy/independence movements, where older idealistic nationalism is important. But even here, the arguments have had a flavour and language of economic net returns from staying in versus going it alone. In a thoroughly materialistic, economistic age, this is perhaps not surprising.

(The above discussion is drawn from Laczó and Rigo [2019], UK Parliament (2021), and Timsit [2016]).

History never repeats itself in a literal sense, but it does tend to throw up the conundrums that weren't addressed the last time around. This perhaps is what 2016 and its ongoing aftermath really signifies.

References

Appy, C. G. (2015). *American reckoning: The Vietnam War and our national identity*. Penguin Books.

Archer, M. (2002). *Art since 1960* (2nd ed.). Thames and Hudson.

Best, A., Hanhimäki, J. M., Maiolo, J. A., & Schulze, K. E. (2004). *International history of the twentieth century and beyond* (2nd ed.). Routledge.

Boorstin, D. (1971). *The image: A guide to pseudo-events in America*. Atheneum.

Davis, M. (2006). *City of Quartz: Excavating the future in Los Angeles* (New ed.). Verso Books.

Denchak, M. (2018, November 8). *Flint water crisis: Everything you need to know*. Natural Resources Defense Council. https://www.nrdc.org/stories/flint-water-crisis-everything-you-need-know

Eichengreen, B. (2014). *Hall of mirrors: The great depression, the great recession, and the uses-and misuses-of history*. Oxford University Press.
Eisenshmidt, J., & Smets, F. (2019). *Negative interest rates: Lessons from the Euro area* (Series on Central Banking Analysis and Economic Policies no. 26).
Frank, T. (2016). *Listen liberal: Or, what ever happened to the party of the people?* Picador.
Gordon, C. (2011). The great depression as a pedagogical theme for undergraduate business, economics and finance classes. *Australasian Journal of Economics Education, 8*(2), 1–17.
Gordon, C. (2013). Two theories of the subprime crisis: Governance failure or mere greed? *International Journal of Behavioural Accounting and Finance, 4*(1), 3–17.
Graff, M., Kenwood, A. G., & Lougheed, A. L. (2013). *Growth of the international economy, 1820–2015*. Routledge.
Henderson, A. (2005). From Barnum to "bling": The changing face of celebrity culture. *The Hedgehog Review* (Spring).
Hobsbawm, E. J. (1994). *Age of extremes: The short twentieth century*. Michael Joseph.
Laczó, F., & Rigo, M. (2019). New Versailles or a Velvet Revolution? Brexit and the exits of central and eastern European history, 1916–2016. *Contemporary European History, 28*(1), 57–60.
Lindsay, J. M. (2016, December 28). The 10 most significant world events in 2016. And how they'll reverberate in the coming year. *Atlantic Magazine*.
Makin, A. J. (2019). Lessons for macroeconomic policy from the global financial crisis. *Economic Analysis and Policy, 64*, 13–25.
Manchester, W. (1973). *The glory and the dream: A narrative history of America, 1932–1972*. Little Brown and Company.
Megino, L., & Pankhania, M. (2016, November 8). How we got here: A complete timeline of 2016's historic US election. *The Guardian*.
OECD. (2021). *OECD data—Share prices*. https://data.oecd.org/price/share-prices.htm. Accessed 20 October 2021
Reeves, R. (2001). *President Nixon: Alone in the White House*. Simon and Schuster.
Roser, M. (2013). *Economic growth*. Published online at OurWorldInData.org. https://ourworldindata.org/economic-growth
Roser, M., & Esteban, O. (2013). *Income inequality*. Published online at OurWorldInData.org. https://ourworldindata.org/income-inequality
Timsit, A. (2016). 5 US independence movements inspired by Brexit. *Politico*. https://www.politico.eu/article/5-us-independence-movements-inspired-by-brexit/
UK Parliament. (2021). *Brexit timeline: Events leading to the UK's exit from the European Union*. UK Parliament, House of Commons Library.

Varoufakis, Y. (2015). *The global minotaur: America*. Zed Books.
Weissenstein, M., & Orsi, P. (2016, November 27). Fidel Castro, who defied US for 50 years, dies at 90 in Cuba. *AP News*. https://apnews.com/article/5ef60f67cefb46869c5b6e5814588dec
Wikipedia (2016). 2016. Wikipedia.com. https://en.wikipedia.org/wiki/2016
Williamson, J. G. (2013). *Trade and poverty: When the Third World fell behind*. MIT Press.
Zagha, R., & Nankani, G. T. (Eds.). (2005). *Economic growth in the 1990s: Learning from a decade of reform*. World Bank Publications.

CHAPTER 31

Populism, Elitism and Identity

C. Gordon, *Many Possible Worlds*,
https://doi.org/10.1007/978-981-19-9281-0_31

Fig. 31.1 Meritocratic truths spoken through graffiti on a wall (*Image source* Photo by Arie Wubben on Unsplash, Red Factory, Zürich, Switzerland. Published on July 1, 2019 Free to use under the Unsplash License "A wise graffiti in the famous Red Factory Culture Centre in Zürich". https://unsplash.com/photos/YLPGqPgX3vo)

31.1 A Misunderstood Neologism

In 1957, the sociologist Michael Young published a book entitled *The Rise of the Meritocracy* ([1957] 1994). In it he imagined what Britain would be like in 2034, writing as if he were an official living in that year and looking back over the cumulative previous decades and attempting to predict what might occur during the following ones. Young invented the term "meritocracy", and as he wrote in his preface to a 1994 reprint, the book was intended as a satire and social commentary (xv), a point lost on most of the publishers he sent the manuscript to. It was finally published by a friend in 1957 and picked up by Penguin in 1958. After that the book took off in popularity and impact (Fig. 31.1).

Young noted that the right to a basic education, an enforced entitlement born with the Industrial Revolution, opened up a question: after that education was over, what then (xiv)? Mass literacy, skill and knowledge development were critical to expanding the productivity of an increasingly sophisticated economy, while the rise of mass democracy, itself quite different from the more exclusive and limited Republicanism of the Classical world, could only function if voting citizens could properly understand and assess the issues put before them. The economic and political planks of Liberalism in their different ways both relied on an educated populace.

From the imaginary future perch of his satirical piece, Young's narrator recounts how in England universal public education was established in 1870, followed later by patronage being replaced by competitive exams in the civil service, and finally a growing fight against the sway of inheritance, family influence and age in job succession. He noted the rise and increasing use of educational credentialing, standardised intelligence testing and workplace merit-rating systems as way of ensuring that the old informal forces of societal selection were kept at bay, to be ultimately rooted out and replaced with a system in which only the most qualified would be placed in positions of responsibility and power.

This all sounded reasonable. But by 2034, the fictional narrator recounts, the outcome ended up being anything but pacific, stable or just. Strikes, disturbances and political assassinations, partly fomented by the "Populist movement", which was led by women and a mostly male rank-and-file following, were now roiling the order of the day. The North of England, Scotland and Wales were lending great support to this pushback, chafing against the dominance of London and the South and its well-trained elites. While the motive force was coming from the lower classes, a dissident minority of the elite had allied with them, making for a powerful cocktail of explosive unrest.

Stepping out of the satire, Young argued that the public education of the industrial era had taken a critical turn in the twentieth century. Universal primary and secondary education provided of a basic floor of core abilities (such as literacy) that helped bind the larger society together and allowed liberal democratic institutions to function better. The expansion of tertiary education, its diffusion to large numbers of the population (though not everyone), and then the use of a tertiary degree as admission to higher-level work and status had the opposite effect. While it supposedly weakened the power of hereditary class, it replaced it with an educationally based hierarchy spawning a so-called meritocratic society, i.e. a social order based on measured achievement with merit-based classes, as opposed to what he termed the castes of agrarian society. Industrial mass democracy then used this template to justify inequality and provide rulers a technical justification for their being on top, and an equally technical justification for why those at the bottom were there:

essentially, they weren't good enough. They could improve themselves if they wanted to but that they didn't was their fault (xiii–xiv).

The book was oddly prescient in its scenario, if a bit off in its timing, the foretelling of social fraying a little late by about two or three decades. The book was written before Britain had joined what would become the European Economic Community, and yet it offers a foretaste of the Brexit movement fuelled by lower class and regional periphery discontent. What was even more striking was the background of the author himself. Young had been an active member of, and thinker in, the Labour Party after 1945, a reformer who was nonetheless attuned to the ongoing role of social power and class, however, its shape might be transformed over time. Years later, Young expressed disappointment that Labour Party Prime Minister Tony Blair had embraced the word Young had created, noting that while meritocracy was good for placing individuals in jobs, it was bad when it hardened into class privilege (Young, 2001). Young died a year after making those observations (Dean, 2002). He did not live to see how fully society would play out the script he satirically presented back in the late 1950s.

31.2 The Rise of Democracy

The idea behind classical Liberalism is twofold: free economic choice exercised through markets; and free political choice exercised through representative electoral democracy. This sounds good but hits at least two conundrums. One is the relationship between economic and political power, Liberalism assuming the two to be independent of one another (or perhaps more precisely the model requires these two to be separate for its major conclusions to follow). The other is the assumption that there are no aggregation effects in either sphere, in any form. That is to say, it is assumed that the outcomes of a sum of individual choices will simply add up to a collective total of the parts, whether they are votes or purchases, without any alteration arising from the effects of belonging to groups, crowds, etc., or mediated through distorting institutions, such as political parties or corporations.

Obviously, these are both highly unrealistic presumptions, especially in the volatile emotion-laden field of politics. The political philosophy of the ancient Greeks, which formed the basis for much Enlightenment thinking about government, was generally anti-democracy, seeing the democratic form as inevitably subject to demagoguery and manipulations of crowds by charismatic leaders that would override the purer and more rational impulses of individual citizens (Clayton, 2005). Even Athens was not a democracy in the modern sense but a city-state governed directly by a small core of elite white male citizens. The Romans scaled this concept up to the "republic", the word derived from the Latin *res publica* roughly translated as "public affair", which is a state governed by the "people", through elected representatives, and therefore directed towards the "public interest" rather than as a private concern of the rulers. But here too the definition of the "people" is malleable. In Rome, the number of citizens was far fewer than the number of subjects, even under the Republic, and this disjoint grew larger under the Empire, which was a non-Republican state that kept some superficial Republican forms, such as the Senate (Hodgson, 2016).

Republicanism receded in the West after Rome's fall, to re-emerge during the Renaissance. The evolution of England into a constitutional parliamentary monarchy and then the establishment of the new independent American republic were important institutional developments along republican lines. The signal event, however, was the French Revolution, which in one stroke established mass democracy in the modern sense, fusing Republicanism and Democracy in ways that remained merged into most of the twentieth century. The 1792 Constitution eliminated prior distinctions between types of citizens, making one mass category to include all men who were liable for military service and thus presumably allowed the right to choose the government for which they were fighting. There were some exclusions, such as vagabonds and criminals and servants, but most property-less wage earners were citizens, subject to their taking an oath to the Constitution. In 1793 old regime titles were mostly eliminated, making "citizen" the only sanctioned title of most Frenchmen, whether they supported the regime or not. Further extensions of citizenship, the franchise and the right to run for and hold elective office were added during the various permutations of the French Republic that followed in the nineteenth century (Tilly, 1995a, 223, 227).

To vastly oversimplify, one could say that while it was the English that led the modern economic revolution, it was the French that led the democratic political revolution, a mantle that would be taken up globally and explicitly by the Americans in the twentieth century. Yet Liberalism really takes the English system as its model on both fronts. England was not a mass democracy in any real sense until the beginning of the twentieth century, the country taking many decades to extend the franchise and more fully limit the power of the Crown in policymaking. Citizenship for a long time remained a more organic and informal affair, the country lacking a written constitution that spelled out its terms and conditions. The American system was a mix of both, paralleling the French in its use of a written Constitution and its first ten amendments spelling out a "Bill of Rights" for individual American citizens, but more British in its reliance on undemocratic institutions, such as the Electoral College for election of the President and the indirect election of the members of the upper legislative house, the Senate.

France's own revolution was driven by a rebellion against deep social and economic inequalities that subverted whatever political equilibrium was possible under the corporatist *Ancien Regime*. Egalitarianism was one of the principles of the Revolution, but the extension of the franchise to the property-less was the main solution offered to all inequality, economic and otherwise (Cobban, 1964). The British meanwhile had managed to avoid Revolution, but its own deep ongoing economic and social divisions remained, covered over by rapidly changing constellations of economic concentrations and power relations, especially amongst the labouring classes who ultimately formed their own party and finally successfully gained control of government in their own right in the early twentieth century. Class interest had played a large part in helping form English Liberalism in the first place and continued to shape its evolution. Perhaps because these stresses did not result in open rebellion, the English felt economic forces could be treated as background variables. But rising concentrations of economic power inevitably changed politics, especially in an era when the two were becoming more fused than ever.

31.3 Order Versus Chaos

All political systems, regardless of stripe, must face the issue of how to achieve desired objectives, whether good or ill, while also maintaining social stability. In authoritarian systems, this balancing act is conceptually (though not always practically) relatively straightforward since political authority explicitly rests in just a few hands. In democracy, such balancing is a much more complex undertaking. On the one hand, the wants and needs of the individual are sacrosanct, allowing for an implicit and automatic legitimacy when these are added up to a collective majority. On the other hand, there is no guarantee that such a majority, even if "rationally" arrived at, will be stable or sensible from the point of view of the true public interest. What if it is not possible to form a majority at all? What if majorities move from one extreme to another and back again?

This actually was an issue considered by the Greeks, most notably Plato, whose ideal government was one of philosopher kings, a sort of functional caste system in which each social order served the purpose that it was best suited for, with the rational people on top. What is particularly striking about Plato's idea is its finely articulated social engineering which includes giving the lower orders a set of false ideas that makes it easier to maintain the authority of rule of the philosophers for the good of the whole (Plato c. [375BCE] 2004). One could say that this was an early proposal for meritocracy, including the ideology needed to support it. So it is perhaps no surprise then that political thinkers and practitioners of the twentieth century arrived at rather similar notions of the need to control and manage mass democracy. The potential for chaos and regression, present even in the small-scale societies of ancient Greece, were even worse in a mass society, now with a mass economy to boot.

The bigger the masses were, the bigger the problem, which is perhaps why the Americans became the leading contributors to a revision of liberalism when applied to mass industrial societies. Edward Bernays, a nephew of Sigmund Freud's who had settled in America, came up with a model to deal with coordinating the populace under democracy. Bernays had joined the staff of what was colloquially referred to as the Creel Committee, set up in Washington DC to promote the war effort of America after it joined the Allies during the First World War after Woodrow Wilson had won a second term promising not to bring the country into it (see Chapter 15). Fordism was spreading throughout American production and something parallel was happening with the mobilisation of consumption to absorb all the plenty that the factories were churning out. If consumers could be manipulated to buy products that they might otherwise not touch, why couldn't citizens be manipulated to support and fight in a war that they were not that interested in fighting? Although not entirely original in his ideas, Bernays proved adept at applying the psychological concepts of his uncle in creating subliminal messaging and campaigns that would drive the masses to desired ends. In particular he justified the use of "propaganda", reviving a term that the Catholic Church had originated in its fight against Protestantism, redefining it as method of herding the people towards social objectives that as individuals, or as members of particular groups, they might not be inclined towards. This process would be benign, he argued, because rational experts would design its ends and means. Bernays considered himself an exemplar of such an expert. If the experts didn't step in, more nefarious operators would take over. Or, worse, there would be a chaos of clashing views and motives and actions (Justman, 1994; Olasky, 1984).

Contributing to this mix was a philosophy offered by the popular writer and public intellectual Walter Lippmann, in his book *Public Opinion* ([1922] 1965). Bernays had been interested in both private and public sales campaigns, and especially in the development of the new field of Public Relations, which was about influencing opinion-leaders and the press especially. Lippmann's brief was more focused on the formation of public ideas in purer sense. He also focused more on the press as an institution necessary for regulating democracy, rather than a separate entity through which to influence public opinion. Parallel to Plato's logic in the *Republic*, Lippmann argued that properly functioning democracy requires different classes of citizens. At the top was a small coterie of expert leaders who analysed society's problems and managed and implemented its solutions. The majority of the population outside this group was "the bewildered herd" which could function as an irrational, emotive and sometimes dangerous force. The expert few were to set themselves aside from the herd, devising programs and policies for the true common good, and then getting these implemented. In a democracy this required ensuring that the herd would pick the best leaders through elections. Once an election was over and the results were in, the herd's influence was over until the next election. It was an undemocratic idea, though supposedly set towards the democratic goal of ensuring formulation and execution of government actions for the true public will, as opposed to more half-baked schemes that the dangerous rabble might devise themselves. Its premise is that the masses cannot be trusted to manage either their own affairs or those of the common good (Lippman, [1922] 1965); Herbst, 1999) (Fig. 31.2).

Why would the masses stand for this? Lippmann, again echoing Plato, argued that the specialised class must have education that differs from that of the masses. In particular the responsible men have to know how the system actually works and how to keep it running in a "rational" fashion. The herd must be distracted much of the time and then guided during election times. Lippmann, like Bernays, thought that the techniques of mass persuasion are critical for both purposes. And both believed that the use of these techniques, in the hands of a separate expert class, was justified by a benign rational purpose of guiding the non-elites to

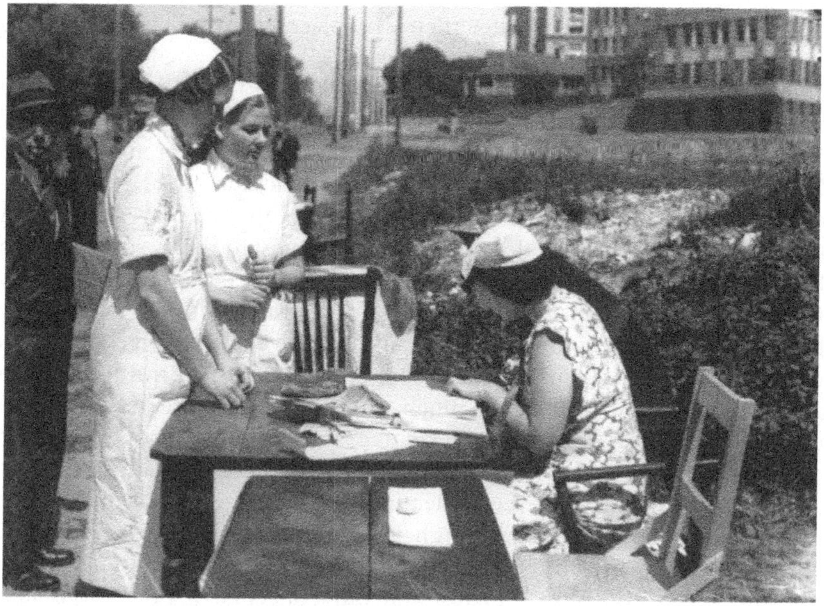

Fig. 31.2 The public right to vote—but not to decide? (see text) (*Image source* State Library of Queensland. hdl.handle.net/10462/deriv/82061 Original description: "Two nurses voting at an outdoor polling station on election day. The Queensland state elections were held on 12 April 1938. The buildings in the background appear to be those of the Royal Brisbane Hospital at Herston". No known copyright restrictions)

achieve a consensus outcome of social progress and order, and making the masses think that they had come up with such consensus by themselves (Chomsky, 1991).

31.4 Technocracy and the Ideology of Elitism

The increasing technological sophistication of capitalism buttressed the justifications for managing a political democracy. Chapter 29 has considered some of the technical challenges of managing and controlling "scientific" enterprise. Burris (1989) has argued that not only did economic organisational form and structure change with modernisation, but also that the ideas around their management changed too. New technical systems required people to alter their workplace behaviour to conform to mechanical prerogatives, and this involved substantial changes in collective and individual thought; in other words, it led to a new workplace ideology.

Technocratic systems organised people in radically different ways than before, giving primacy to particular forms of machine logic. This overlay did not, however, erase the ever-present reality of human power politics. A technocratic ideology was developed which suggested that re-organisation based around particular technologies was neutral because "technology is neutral" with new technology therefore always adopted supposedly because of its ever greater efficiency and effectiveness. Yet technology is usually never neutral in its social consequences, and institutional reorganisations of any sort are as much political as they are technical. To overcome political resistance to change and to push through desired agendas, supporting ideologies developed (not fully consciously) which justified the changes. These intellectual shifts were essential inputs into economic modernisation. Although just "ideas", they were as powerful and necessary as any purely material factors (Burris, 1989, 314).

During the 1800s and 1900s, the old concepts of professions and professionalism also were being altered. On the one hand, ever deeper specialisation and standardisation in various skills and activities was required, much like the parts of mass production modes. Yet the professional of the time also had a strong concept of an individual "collegial self", a social identity as a member of an elite fellowship of similarly trained colleagues, and an individual reputation based on meeting collectively defined "high" standards, thus offering a unique advantage over others outside the profession. There was something less formal but not dissimilar at the nonprofessional but craft-based worker level. Both classes were essential for industrial productivity but both also needed to be reformed into ways more useful for fitting into the increasingly impersonal corporation and shopfloor. Formalisation, classification and institutionalisation of both craft and profession were required, universities being the key legitimators of the process along with developing and offering the requisite credentials (Burris, 1989, 318–319).

This tension between individual autonomy and skill and the needs of a central organisation has been an ongoing challenge in capitalist development. Taylorism (see Chapter 29) was an early attempt to settle the balance in favour of the organisation, using the then rudimentary science of time and motion studies and cost accounting to appropriate and standardise worker craft to be overseen by a new professionalised managerial class supported by credentialed technical experts, with incentive pay offered to meet and beat management-defined "performance" goals. Taylor himself thought this would eliminate class conflict by keeping both sides of the new management equation working towards the same goals of productivity and efficiency. "Human Relations" was a later managerial idea-set designed to apply the principles of psychology to making the management of the organisation one big (functional) family (Burris, 1989, 319–321).

The technologised workplace has continued and elaborated this divide, along the lines of the expert and non-expert, a fundamental characteristic of technocracy. Knowledge, skill and information are the central variables of control, and rational manipulation of these lead to optimal solutions, with "irrational" or unskilled versions by definition leading to sup-optima. Such thinking claims that objectivity underlies meritocracy making it independent of politics. But this is the view from the top of the hierarchy. To challenge from below the "improvements" that managers bring in is to be irrational or retrograde since technology is always "progressive" and "correct" and can only be successfully implemented by "experts" (Burris, 1989, 321–326).

There is a counterpart to this thinking in Growth theory. Capital and Labour are inputs into a technical apparatus that yields output and the better the quality of the inputs and the technology, the more output that is yielded for a given amount of inputs. How should the rewards of this process be distributed? The theory says that each factor should receive the marginal return it creates, i.e. the marginal product of labour (MPL), the marginal product of capital (MPK) and any excess to these delivered back to the entrepreneur who has created the business enterprise employing them both. Distribution is thus purely technical and disembodied, with no power or politics to speak of. Any policy intervention should be about enhancing material growth potential as this increases the potential (though not the necessity) of making both labour and capital better off. Imbalances in power or resources, or immaterial needs such as a sense of meaning, don't even exist in this construct.

31.5 The California Ideology

Barbrook and Cameron (1996) argue that these tensions between individual person and technical system in the digital age have been altered by a contradictory mix of 1960s counterculture notions of individual expression (the "Hippie" movement of California being a prime example—see Chapter 24), and the ideas of the new entrepreneurs of Silicon Valley who combined "New Left" communalism and "New Age" individual human potential development (itself an odd juxtaposition) with individualistic libertarian leanings of digital inventors like Steve Jobs, the founder of Apple Computers. Borrowing ideas from media commentator Marshall McLuhan about the democratising forces of mass media, the digital revolution was posited as being a massive force for positive social change ("electronic media would break down old orders") while at the same time allowing a person to make as much money in the free market as they wanted, if they so chose. Digital technology would thus simultaneously make greater self-selected connection between people possible while supporting individual expression and enterprise. One could be whatever one wanted on the Internet and combine into communities of the like-minded quickly and easily. This is the "California Ideology" in a nutshell.

This utopia hasn't materialised. Instead, the new digital order is still dominated by the corporation, with the difference that the "creatives", formerly outsiders and nonconformists, are now brought fully into the fold of a whole that is fundamentally conservative as far as the broad array of background status quo powers. The names of the companies may change, but the company remains the owner and controller of the network in the background. Barbrook and Cameron add that the ideology ignores how much the government has helped private entrepreneurs to gain their wealth. The entire Internet was a creation of the US Defense Department, and many technology companies still get large contracts from this and other government agencies, providing crucial funding for their ongoing operations as going concerns.

Barbrook and Cameron's critique is not amenable to ready solutions and is only one a number of competing interpretations of the effect of the Internet on society and economy. But it is another paradigm that suggests that the sublimation and disguising of politics and political conflict within a technological-economic system that is dominated by a nexus of large corporations and government, and yet purports to be a free network of individual nodes, is a construct that conceals more than it reveals. Additionally, the premise of self-selection contained within the California Ideology arguably works against diversity and connection as much as it works for it since, in the extreme, digital platforms can lead to the formation of digital ghettoes that don't talk to one another, hardening ways of thinking of the members within them, and subject to algorithmic manipulation by platform owners, all things that have in fact transpired.

31.6 Networks Versus Hierarchies

A parallel notion is that the modern world is now a "networked society". There are various variations of this but a recent one is offered by Ferguson (2018) who claims that networks of individuals are now more powerful than old "hierarchical institutions", including States. For Ferguson, this is not actually historically novel. He notes, amongst many examples, that Enlightenment-era intellectual networks were critical in developing their ideas and challenging existing orders. Technology has simply hyper-charged this process, a development that Ferguson admits is not always benign. The role of networks, especially with social media, has led to greater polarisation and fragmentation across both networks and organisations. Thus networks can disconnect people as readily as they can connect them, an outcome not foreseen by the original Internet pioneers.

More libertarian thinkers dispute the more negative claims Ferguson makes about networks, claiming that healthy competitive forces within them will result in social optima. Others doubt his somewhat negative view of hierarchies, and question whether organisations of this type are necessarily bad. Still others add that the two types need each other, a clear fact of the Internet itself that relies on an extensive physical network of servers, cables and wireless connections maintained by hierarchical organisations.

Robert Putnam (1995) applies a concept meant to bridge this gap, namely "social capital" (see also Chapter 7). In some ways, this is merely a term for the well-known agglomeration effects that occur when people of similar and/or complementary minds and skills congregate or co-locate in specific areas, bringing a facilitation of close and regular social connections that inspire innovation. Silicon Valley itself is a prime example. Putnam goes beyond this to claim that the effectiveness of representative government is closely correlated with traditions of civic engagement, which includes active membership and participation in a diverse set of civil society groups ranging from choral societies to political parties. It is this sort of regular connection in organised form that helps build shared social capital, which, like its physical counterpart in economic production processes, is so important to yielding the social cohesion and coherence that democracy is so reliant upon. This social capital is accumulated through the strength, extensiveness and benign purpose of social networks that improve both the well-being of its individual members and provides a social "asset" that is an essential input into a well-functioning political, economic and social order.

In looking at America in the late 1990s, Putnam argues that it is the diminishing of civic engagement and social connectedness, i.e. social capital, that has helped lead to the growing political divisiveness and dysfunction in that country. The possible causes of this decline are diverse. Putnam himself puts great weight on the privatisation of entertainment, leisure and communication inculcated by mass media, which reduces the amount of time people congregate and work together in common social pursuits. Other possible causes include the increasing pressures of work life, mass consumerism and declining economic conditions for the working and middle classes.

If Putnam's construct is correct, it provides an answer to the conundrum of political democracy that Lippmann and Bernays argued needed to be filled through manipulation of the masses by benign expert elites. In Putnam's schema, it is social capital, arising from the masses forming themselves into civilly engaged groups with directions reflective of individual needs and wants and channelled into directions that will sustain and enhance the social fabric, that is critical to self-organisation of the public. Such a society will be resistant to demagoguery or chaos and will not need "experts" to shape it. Interestingly, John Stuart Mill and some of the early Political Economists were making similar points in their discussions of the critical importance of civil society to the workings of democracy (see Chapter 4).

Of course it is more than possible that elites and powerful interest groups can subvert social capital (and civil society) to its own ends, something that is an implicit premise of the California Ideology argument. And social capital, being an input into society, may not do much good if the society it is being input into has a fabric that is deeply compromised, just like the case where "good" labour or capital fed into a faulty production function may still yield only bad output.

31.7 The Elitism of the Professional Class

Still, there must be something in human society beyond the extremes of the atomistic individuality of Liberalism or the mass chaos and stupidity assumed by elitist conceptions of democracy. Human beings do connect to one another at scales between the two extremes. Corporatism is a traditional approach for organising politics that attempts to bridge the gap. Social capital and networks offer a couple of other constructs that can inform the unique balancing of individual and collective under representative democracy.

But none of these constructs, even Corporatism, really recognises the enduring presence of social and economic class. These have evolved dramatically with modernisation, but the reality of power dynamics remains. The confluence of theories of political democracy that emphasise the role of technical elites, the rise of the credentialed professional class needed to run the sophisticated technical apparatus of production, consumption and distribution, and the development of a practical ideology that reduces everything to finding the right combination of variables to produce a supposed "optimum" has had diverse and unintended consequences. Which is exactly what Young's meritocracy satire was meant to show. In many ways, the professional class, which is often not thought of as a class at all, has become more tightly connected within itself than ever before. The "one per cent" may own everything, but the "nine percent" just below them (taken collectively as the top ten per cent) helps run everything, just as Lippmann and Bernays said was desirable.

This has transpired in a number of ways. Whereas in the past corporate managers or politicians did not necessarily need to have a degree from a top university (although it certainly helped), and in a few cases did not have a degree at all, now one cannot hope to attain even entry-level work into the hierarchies of power without one. These institutions have also become much more insular in the socioeconomic profiles of their students and graduates than before, even within the select programs offered for priority admission to members of socially disadvantaged groups. And the income and social disparities between professionals and non-professionals have grown wider as well (Markovits, 2019; Sandel, 2020). Combined with a technocratic outlook that frames all problems in technical terms, this means that the gap between professionals, who have leading roles in policy decisions, and the rest of society has become a chasm. Indeed, even the label of "inequality" to describe the constantly enlarging maldistribution of wealth, income and position is a bloodless term that is far less evocative than the Victorian era phrase "the social question" which was used to frame the parallel problems of that time (Frank, 2016).

This is meritocracy in action. The elites are well trained and well educated, and superior in those narrow respects to their fellows. But how they got to where they are is not simply the result of their own actions, characteristics and accomplishments, but a product of a multiplicity of social, historical, economic and institutional factors. Yet the basic premises of their educational training justify their technical elitism as a natural, positive force and their own self-conception does not allow for the possibility that their privileged position, which they worked very hard for, is enabled even in part by factors other than their own will and exertion. Various data show that graduation from elite educational institutions is highly correlated with social class, and that the greatest single determinant of a person's wealth and income is now the wealth and income of the parents. This is not to deny genuine individual achievement, but it does suggest that the meritocracy is based on more than mere merit and that the meritocrats themselves tend to be most blind to this fact. Which creates a problem when it is these experts who are called on to correct the problem of "inequality" (Sandel, 2020).

31.8 The Degradation of Political Institutions

This rise of a professional merit elite class which has little consciousness of itself as a class has had numerous implications. Not least has been the degradation of the function of one of the industrial era innovations in mass politics, namely the political party. Parties in a democracy have always played an ambivalent role, on the one hand, organising groups into influential political blocs and enabling a greater coherence and influence for their views which can be translated into policy programs, actions and outcomes. On the other hand, these same parties have sometimes been barriers to the true expression of such views within the broader political process, especially when captured by small groups. This sort of imperfection is inevitable in any human arena. But the rising influence of a professional class and technocratic ideology has broadened the gap between political parties as power entities in and of themselves, and their mediating/organising representative function for broader groupings within society. This has been especially true for the mass parties of the centre-left, e.g. the Labour Party in the UK, the Democratic Party in the US and the various Socialist parties in Europe.

Traditional mass left politics had depended on class identity, consciousness and solidarity. Meritocracy subverted this, with level of education and expertise becoming the new social markers. Class itself did not go away but was masked and fragmented, and the parties of the working class got taken over by individual meritocratic stars that identified with others like them rather than their labouring counterparts. Rising to the top of the society, or staying on the bottom, was now seen as a function of educational merit, with the risers having justifiable pride, the losers justifiable self-blame (Hayes, 2012, Chapter 2).

This kind of thinking had always found a home in the individualistic culture of America. But it also became the norm in class-based Britain, hearkening back to the Victorian era doctrine of self-reliance so trumpeted by Samuel Smiles' book *Self Help* (see Chapter 9). This process was facilitated by the formulation of supposedly neutral public administration theories of the early twentieth century that became transformed by doctrines such as New Public Management (NPM) and supported by techniques of "Performance Management" in the late twentieth century, in which the running of government and delivery of public services was now treated as equivalent to, and just like, a profit-driven private enterprise in a private marketplace. Labour Prime Minister Tony Blair carried this to a logical extreme, though it became a widespread rhetoric across developed world democracies (Gruening, 2001).

Since every activity is like every other activity (according to these new managerial doctrines), elite education now was oriented towards training new leaders and managers in the management theory, knowledge and techniques that are purportedly applicable to almost any context or setting. Professional and experiential specialisation is still possible and desired by some. But such "narrow" subject matter focus tends to hamper the ability to move seamlessly from one diverse job to another, e.g. into government policy and planning, then into a corporate activity such as finance or consulting, and then back again. Managerial generalisation is much better for the career path. This erodes any conscious sense of class, or sometimes even identity with a specific profession, since those at the top are purportedly there mainly because of qualifications that allow the carrying out tasks to make the system work better whatever the context. It also creates a new mandarinate whose members think alike, have the same interests and have a set of connections between each other and lifestyle very distinct from the people being governed (Hayes, 2012, Chapter 2) (see Fig. 31.3).

◂**Fig. 31.3** The mandarinate: original version (see text) (*Note* an actual mandarin, in the original sense of a Confucian order, in this case emplaced in nineteenth century Vietnam. *Image source* Bibliothèque de l'ancien Musée des colonies [Paris], Créateur: Gsell, Émile, Éditeur: Studio photographique Gsell [Saigon]. Original notes: "Tong-King - Mandarin de la province d'Hay-Dzương /B'ăc Kỳ - Ông quan ở tỉnh Hải Dương. Date: 1877–1879. Description: Portrait d'un mandarin de la province de Hai Duong, revêtu de son costume d'audience solennelle. Le terme de mandarin est utilisé par les Occidentaux pour désigner un haut fonctionnaire lettré et éduqué dans la tradition de Confucius, mis au service de l'Empereur de Chine, à l'issue d'une sélection rigoureuse et très limitative des meilleurs candidats. Les mandarins ont aussi existé dans certains états voisins, dont le Vietnam". Public domain)

Moreover, if society simply becomes something to be managed, then efficiency in the production of coarse, measurable outputs (or "outcomes" using the Performance Management lingo) becomes the core objective above all else. Immaterial and ethical considerations may be spoken of, and often are. But these are marginalised as something to be taken care of later, after the economic achievement has been "maximised", since there is an overriding value of "more is better than less"; and with purportedly more resources overall as a result, there is potentially more to be diverted to such "side" issues after optimisation has been accomplished. (That this diversion rarely actually takes place tends not to be mentioned.) Conflicts of values or interests are also acknowledged. But here too optimisation techniques are applied. And in that process these too are put into purely material terms, turned into commodities whose price can be measured and whose quantities and qualities can be bought and sold in the (mimicked) marketplace and where there is a single optimal (material) outcome to be achieved.

This by itself is corrosive to the shared immaterial values necessary for any well-functioning society. It is positively poisonous in a democracy that purports to be based on political ideals and yet has no real ideals at all—not dissimilar in that respect to the corrosiveness that bedevilled the late Communist system which pronounced high-minded principles while sacrificing every one of them in practice. It is also not just a "Capitalist" problem, arguably bedevilling the lone remaining Communist superpower, China, which looks more like an authoritarian managerial capitalism every day.

31.9 The Imperfect Refuges of Identity and Populism

Yet each person remains inalterably individual in a deep sense, difficult to reduce to a concept or measure, but no less real for all that. Despite the pressures of mass systems, individuality needs to be expressed, and it needs to be done in a social context, given the deep innate sociality of the human animal. In the liberal democracies cynicism about politics, an inherently collective affair, runs deep. Politics by itself at present no longer seems satisfactory for finding an individual sense of purpose through melding into a larger group. Yet the need to have a sense of being an individual while also part of something larger remains. Modernity has changed the means for meeting this need, just as it has everything else.

31.9.1 Identity

The post-industrial age has seen a great variegation of social categories of identity that has altered most gender, sexual orientation, race, ethnic and many other group categories and the way in which individuals identify and select themselves into them. Essentialism, i.e. that doctrine that social categories are innate rather than socially constructed, is no longer seen as an acceptable philosophical or social default. Now complete freedom of choice to move in and out of identity categories, and invent new ones altogether, is the norm.

There continues to be much debate about the sources of these changes. An influential psychogenetic thesis (to use an Elias term—see Chapter 5) is that the human psyche has changed within late Western capitalism to become more self-centred. Using the word "self" in a neutral literal sense to refer to an inner character and cognition, this is not necessarily problematic. Many social and economic ills of the past have been products of rigid conformism to pre-set retrogressive categories, often based on a high degree of social suppression and repression, even to the level of outright persecution and discrimination. The social ferment of the 1960s was in part a reaction against the rigid template of suburban consumerism, patriarchal nuclear household, and corporate "organisation man" so dominant in the 1950s through much of the developed world (see Chapter 24). And in many ways individualism, seen as a liberating of the human being from social definition and direction by old, outmoded, social forces, runs straight back to the Enlightenment ideals that Western Civilisation so proudly trumpets.

One standard thread of analysis looks at this change in psychodynamic terms. This is not surprising given how influential Freudianism and the therapeutic modes that have grown up around it has been in the understanding and defining of modern identity categories in the first place. The depth psychology model promised individual awareness and liberation, an idea that the 1960s counterculture transformed into a political statement by claiming that self-discovery and self-expression, unadulterated, would overthrow the programming of existing oppressive orders. In this narrative, individual growth and freedom became politicised and, in the extreme, a replacement for the group politics of the past (Zaretsky, 2015).

This optimism proved to be premature, however. Individual awakening, to the extent it actually was occurring, proved not enough to change a society. Collèctive action was still required for that. Yet widespread disillusionment with social causes caused many to retreat into a cocoon of individualised experience, quite blatantly during the 1970s when the buzz of the 1960s was still lingering and the turmoil of the old order was reaching something of a fever pitch. Tom Wolfe (1976) went so far as to call the seventies the "Me Decade". A more weighty academic critique came with Christopher Lasch's 1978 book *The Culture of Narcissism*, which applied the diagnosis of a Freudian personality disorder to an entire society. This happened to be about America, but its exposition could be seen as applying more generally to late capitalist Western society. Lasch's critique is fairly wide-ranging, but it's basic thrust has two parts: (1) that the human psyche has changed over the course of the first three-quarters of the twentieth century, from the neurotic repressive Freudian "hysterical" personality type of the late Victorian age to a less repressed but equally anxious narcissistic type; and (2) that this has been driven by a growing psychologisation, educationalisation and academisation of everyday life, something to which he applies the rubric of "therapeutic culture" (Lasch, 1978, p. 153).

The Narcissist is typified by a person who pursues a course of hedonistic enjoyment to fill existential emptiness and finds one's identity through mirroring from celebrities and other public "successful" figures. The pathological version includes fear of competition yet seeking to be at the centre of things, accompanied by pseudo-self-insight and limitations in the ability to form of genuine relationships with others. Lasch claims that the old functional "economic man" of earlier capitalism, i.e. the economic agent who finds their place within the economic system and acts accordingly to survive and move forward within it, has morphed into a "psychological man" who moves away from relation to society to focusing on one's self; and from measuring oneself against a putative "objective", to experiencing the self according to one's shifting internal subjective state (De Vos, 2012, 51). Lasch made an interesting distinction between the Narcissist and the older "rugged individualist", both models that celebrated individualism (and, it must be said, in a very American fashion). He claimed that the latter sought meaning and self-image in conquering that "other" world, the "frontier" outside established society, while the former no longer had such external others to conquer and instead sought validation in the attentions of other people, especially those with celebrity or power (Lasch, 1978, 10).

Lasch actually finds the culture of psychological expertise to be part of the basic problem, that its domain has become too broad and that human ailments, including those that are purely subjective, are reduced to issues of treatment and intervention, becoming problems to be solved rather than a reality to be experienced, borne and learned from (Lasch 1978, 163). This critique could be extended to the culture of expertise more generally.

There is much to criticise in this view. Many have noted Lasch's bias towards white American men and a tendency to stereotype figures, such as feminists, African-Americans, gays and lesbians, who were legitimately and forcefully fighting white heterosexual masculine/patriarchal modes of sociality, the very groups that Lasch's 1970s intelligentsia audience felt most threatened by. Lasch's use of the Freudian model of the psyche has also been deemed as too narrow or too distorted. More generally, his use of psychological concepts to analyse what he refers to as the psychologisation of society can be seen as self-referential and self-fulfilling (De Vos, 2010, 534–537). His critique is quite time-, and culture-bound.

Having said all that there can be little doubt that the rise of a technical society, focused on expertise and technical models of inner and outer human processes, has likely caused significant change to individual thought and emotion. Even though "science" has mastered most problems (except, perhaps the ones that science itself creates), there is no longer any meaning of any lasting value. This remains a core need of most human beings and a central part of any identity they might have, social and otherwise. Science as a method can encompass everything, and has, including the human individual. But to do this it must narrow its frame of reference such that it often leaves the most important things out, especially the ineffable and immaterial. In so doing it leads to a sort of schism, on the one hand paying explicit attention to all phenomena, but on the other hand negating key parts of it at the same time. This can lead to both a divided self and society—and the creation and implementation of solutions that may miss the true point, and make things worse instead of better.

31.9.2 Populism

The individual search for identity, meaning and power always plays out in a larger group context. The modern political movement of Populism can be seen in this way. Its roots go back to Roman times when, during the Empire, the elites presided over and managed a teeming and sometimes fractious urban mass (especially in Rome itself) that periodically broke into disorganised and sometimes semi-organised rebellion that was most dangerous when it found a unifying theme under a leader that was out to protect the "people's" interests against those of their overlords. Class organisation was relatively simple, mainly peons versus aristocracy, with the usual auxiliary classes (such as minor functionaries and the Army) playing a key role in power shifts, as was the case near the end of the Western Empire. In this era, "populism" really was "of the people", which is why the Emperors focused so much on "Bread and Circuses" to keep the masses at least minimally satisfied and hence accepting of the regular injustice and exploitation of that society (Hodgson, 2016).

In more modern times, populism has become more complex since the "people" can no longer be treated as an undifferentiated mass. Although populist appeals sometimes act as if this is the case, in fact different segments of the population are typically played off against one another, which is why there is left-populism (in which the stated policy goals and rhetoric are those typically associated with leftist goals, e.g. redistribution and economic justice) and right-populism (e.g. nationalism and individual freedom). The common element is an appeal for solidarity within a supposedly oppressed "mass" against a ruling "elite" (Brubaker, 2017).

Meritocracy is obviously a prod to the appeal of populist politics, especially in the context of growing divides between professional and other classes, with workers slowly losing their job security and living wages, and with the educated classes gaining in theirs. Contributing to this has been a growing disconnect between the expressed views of the populace and the policies actually enacted by the political system. This last fact particularly points to a flaw in the Lippman and Bernays ideas about public opinion, i.e. that it needs to be moulded by experts to meet the true public interest rather than what its initial "raw" state throws up. This is a stance that treats the beliefs and values expressed even by majorities as illegitimate, something that is in contradiction to the whole notion of political democracy in the first place.

Right-populism and left-populism have both been especially ascendant during the past thirty years, but it is the former that has been mostly ascendant as far as electoral outcomes. Partly that is because many of the social democracy parties have been co-opted by narrow special interests, especially corporate interests that fund most major party operations to a large extent. These parties are now, as mentioned above, largely staffed and run by the elite professional classes, with increasingly tenuous connections to the lower classes, except in periodic election appeals and support from established but now relatively unrepresentative institutions such as labour unions. This has neutralised these parties as receptacles for genuine left discontent while their continued dominance of electoral politics has made it very difficult for any small left party to manifestly influence policy programs in most countries or even organise in the first place. Thus traditional mass Allies of the left now often respond more to the rallying cry of modern right politics, especially now that it is being couched more in terms of individualism and individual freedom from elite dicta, a stance that is more resonant with the anger of the disenfranchised, especially in a time of general disenchantment with organised politics.

31.10 Identity Politics, Citizenship and the Modern Liberal Democratic Challenge

Tilly (2004) argues that the European experience with successes and failures in developing democracy from 1650 to 2000 suggests that a number of mechanisms are critical for promoting democratisation. These include equalisation of wealth, income, power, prestige and political participation across major categories of the population; the creation of trust networks that are connected to the exercise of power, and the buffering of politics from those trust networks that are disintegrating; enhanced ability of the collective of political participants to direct and control government; and the existence of inhibitions to the arbitrary exercise of power by governmental agents (Tilly, 2004, 211–212).

Assuming that these are reasonably good starting points for fostering genuine political democracy, it should be clear that populism or identity group allegiances need not necessarily be antithetical to a working democratic political order. Identity politics has been a primary focus of social discourse and political debate over the past several decades at least. Typically defined as political activity or theorising based on a cultural, racial, gender, ethnic or other claims, it has been seen by some analysts as a filling of political vacuums created by the decline of both nation-state and the old class-based political parties and movements (De Vos, 2010, 532, fn. 5). If so, this indicates only a change in democratic Political Economy, not necessarily an undermining of it.

In fact, identity used in a political, in addition to a social and psychological sense, can arguably strengthen democracy, or at least the mutual tolerance for differences that is so critical to its smooth operation. Identity in this sense is the basis of multiculturalism, which, in its simplest form is the idea that different cultures can coexist peacefully, and profitably within a single country, even under a dominant culture. It has been adopted as official policy by various Western democracies such as Canada and Australia, and in a globalising world it seems to be an almost essential doctrine to allow for a basic political cohesion to remain solid within a rapidly integrating world (Siapera, 2006).

And yet there is a double-edge in this. In the past, essentialist thinking, usually distorted by racism and other ideology, challenged democracy, creating and sharpening conflict between different identity groups. Identity politics has lessened this particular threat (except as they arise in reactions against particular categories); but by making identity categories more fractured and more a matter of explicit choice, they also have the potential to fragment the common bonds needed for social cohesion. Social identities, especially in a political system, are seen by many to rest on shared common understandings and representations within a whole and identity politics has the potential to interfere with the formation of these common understandings.

Citizenship under democracy is one commonality that can contain both identity politics and multiculturalism, as it necessarily defines rights and responsibilities between States and their members and provides a framework for navigating through the differences of socially constructed categories, such as genders, races and nationalities amongst others. A good example of how this works has been around the shifting rights of gender under democracy. The initial tying of citizenship to military service in the first French Republic and in other states afterwards privileged males over females. Suffragist struggles ultimately got women the franchise and this act alone shifted the relational categories between male and female identities (Tilly, 1995b, 5–9). The legalisation of "gay marriage" is another example of how citizenship rights play a critical role in affecting identity and its politics and power relations. Many other examples could be given, e.g. rights of aboriginal peoples, racial exclusions and inclusions, property qualifications for voting, etc.

This is not to say that identity can or should be reduced solely to citizenship requirements and obligations. But democracy implicitly puts identity categories into the formulation of personal and collective sovereignty and identity politics could be said to simply be making that explicit and working it out through the larger political community. As with any political dynamic, it can be carried too far, such as papering over important social distinctions, even going so far as to "re-privilege" or "de-privilege" older orderings, sometimes deleteriously (e.g. class being relegated to subsidiarity to race and gender, even though class remains a reality that is sometimes more important than recognised). And the conflicts over identity can be intense enough to subvert political system functionality, as arguably has happened in some instances of the "Culture Wars". Then again, politics is inherently about conflict so the mere existence of it, or its reshaping into new forms, should not be seen as invalidating in and of itself.

A final point to be made is that identity is also bound up with what it means to be an individual, a concept that modernity has altered markedly and continuously (see Box 31.1).

Box 31.1 The contested concept of the human individual

The Enlightenment celebrated the sanctity and beauty of the human individual. Classical Liberalism built on this notion as a matter of policy, privileging the rights of the individual as the way to safeguard broader societal freedom, both political and economic. However, the twentieth century was an era in which the very notion of the existence of an individual self came into question.

Orthodox Marxist-Leninism held that there was no individual at all, only classes, and even those were entirely the result of social forces. This was antithetical to Liberalism and could thus be dismissed as a philosophy based on opposing terms that were arguably invalid. Less easy to dismiss were the strains of modern philosophy and science, supposedly politically neutral, that ran towards a similar conclusion about the unreality of the individual, if by different reasoning. Freud provided the first crack in the edifice of an autonomous objective self with his model of the human being as one buffeted by instinctual drives and unconscious complexes, both of which undercut the notion of free will and an immutable core of human personality. However, since Freud also believed that people could observe their own mental states with more certainty than anything in the outside world, one could say that he merely shifted the ground of individuality from objective to subjective and, in that sense, made the concept stronger (Lichtheim, 1972, 96).

Freud also introduced, however, some other seeds that undermined even a subjective self. The Freudian psyche was mechanistic and physiological at its base, consisting of an elaborate balancing system of nervous system energy. One could thus easily ask: why model the psyche at all? Why not just stick to the physiological dynamics and their associations with final actions, which are open to direct observation and study? This became the *modus operandi* of Behaviourism, most notably by J. B. Watson who said that the proper field of psychological investigation was the movements of the inner and outer body (e.g. limb movements, gland secretions, etc.) together with the environmental stimuli that could evoke such responses. Watson's theories were preceded by Pavlov's operant conditioning work (that won him the Nobel Prize), and it was striking enough to cause even liberal-minded psychologists to ask, *Does consciousness exist?*, the title of a 1904 work by the philosophical pragmatist and psychologist William James (Lictheim, 1972, 209–211).

Behaviourism was both simple and useful to those working in the emerging twentieth-century field of Industrial Psychology, which sought to better "adjust" workers to their assigned roles in capitalist organisations. They saw Freudian introspection as much inferior and much less useful than a laboratory and observation-based empiricism that yielded useful and applicable findings with definite economic returns. Some viewed introspection as a mere illusion, a meaningless and even misleading shadow of biophysical processes (Lictheim, 1972, 209–211).

These ideas were accentuated and elaborated during the mid-twentieth century when a stark philosophical divide opened up, accentuated by the Cold War dichotomy of a socially engineered scientific man versus a free society rugged individualist. One idea focused on the human search for meaning. While Kierkegaard invented the term "existentialism" in the nineteenth century, it became a full-blown philosophy at this time, with the French philosophers Jean-Paul Sartre and Albert Camus proclaiming the non-existence of any actual meaning in the world, a prognosis consistent with Marxism (Sartre himself converting to Communism later in his career), while fusing this with a radical individualism in which each human being makes their own meaning (something orthodox Marxism rejected). Wilhelm Reich did something similar but instead fused Freudian psychology with an emerging Marxist humanism, Erich Fromm and Herbert Marcuse working in somewhat similar veins (Lichtheim, 1972, 272–276).

There were also the hyper-capitalist notions of economic man as embodied in the "Objectivism" of Ayn Rand. Highly idealistic, Rand claimed rather radically that all human value could be reduced to money and market-determined prices, and that the unfettered competition of people within a truly free marketplace sorted out the human wheat from the chaff. Her heroes were total individuals who went completely against the grain of the crowd, winning out in the end because of their ruthless focus on achieving their material goals; or, if losing, showing the corruption of the world that defeated them. It was a heroic (and more extreme) artistic expression of the "Austrian" economics of Hayek and von Mises who maintained that free markets and minimal states everywhere were the only way to keep off the "road to serfdom", to use Hayek's evocative phrase. One could even say that it was Rand that put the individual back into primary focus, since Austrian school economists analytically focused more on competitive process as protective of individuals rather than on the individuals themselves (Peikoff, 1993).

The Cold War existence of a Socialist world provided an obvious counterpoint to this thinking, being explicitly socially determinist. If Socialism did indeed win out over Capitalism in the end, wouldn't this show that individualism was a cul-de-sac? Complicating this picture was the fact that, as already noted, there were strong anti-individualists in the Capitalist world, such as the Behaviourists. And the general rise of technocracy in the corporate and government realms seemed to indicate that individualism was rather beside the point. It was trumpeted but less and less practised, or even allowed in many domains. Thus the 1950s saw a running debate between Western philosophers, some of them emigres who had escaped from Eastern Bloc countries, about "Free Will" versus "Determinism". Like most such debates, there was no settling point, but certainly a great deal of heat (Magarey, 1987).

As the 1960s progressed, all of these strains seemed more and more unsatisfactory. Existentialism placed too great a burden on the individual.

Marxism and Behaviourism took too much away. And while Objectivism and the Austrian school had strong adherents, they were too doctrinaire for any but the most committed free market capitalist individualists, and thus too associated with existing political divides. Besides which, individual heroism, though regularly evoked, seemed out of date, as modernity seemed to have made individual existence contingent and unnecessary practically and theoretically. The 1960s counterculture, in its multiplicity of conflicting forms, can be seen as a set of social and individual responses to this unedifying state of affairs. Political unrest was often the spark, but the channels taken were generally along lines of personal expression and an improvisational attempt of people to work alternatives out for themselves, as their "true" selves.

This focus on individual expression and identity became more pronounced after the end of the Cold War, opening up a new personal freedom, set loose from a stultifying global ideological competition. The Personal Computer (PC) and the Internet promised to provide everyone the ability to interact with society on their own terms, forming groups of their own choosing and literally making their own "virtual" world. The Western boom times of the 1990s and early 2000s meanwhile promised that everyone had a chance to rise to the top of a competitive hierarchy. Oddly, philosophical discussions of what it actually meant to be an individual became much less pronounced at this time, with individuality taken for granted. Identity politics, in which individuals defined themselves, is what took over. It still is dominant in a time that is economically and politically much less rosy.

References

Barbrook, R., & Cameron, A. (1996). The Californian ideology. *Science as Culture, 6*(1), 44–72.

Brubaker, R. (2017). Why populism? *Theory and Society, 46*(5), 357–385.

Burris, B. H. (1989). Technocracy and the transformation of organizational control. *The Social Science Journal, 26*(3), 313–333.

Chomsky, N. (1991). *Media control: The spectacular achievements of propaganda* (1st ed.). A Seven Stories Presspublished in association with Open Media.

Clayton, E. (2005). Aristotle: Politics. In J. Fieser & B. Dowden (Eds.), *Internet encyclopedia of philosophy*. http://www.iep.utm.edu/a/aris-pol.htm

Cobban, A. (1964). *The social interpretation of the French Revolution*. Cambridge University Press.

De Vos, J. (2010). Christopher Lasch's the culture of narcissism: The failure of a critique of psychological politics. *Theory & Psychology, 20*(4), 528–548.

De Vos, J. (2012). Narcissism and the DSM-V: Christopher Lasch and the political leftovers of the debate. *Journal of Culture and the Unconscious, 8*(2), 49–61.

Dean, M. (2002, January 16). Lord Young of Dartington. *The Guardian.*

Ferguson, N. (2018). *The Square and the tower: Networks and power, from the Freemasons to Facebook.* Penguin Press.

Frank, T. (2016). *Listen liberal: Or, what ever happened to the party of the people?* Picador.

Gruening, G. (2001). Origin and theoretical basis of new public management. *International Public Management Journal, 4*(1), 1–25.

Hayes, C. L. (2012). *Twilight of the elites: America after meritocracy.* Crown Publishers.

Herbst, S. (1999). Walter Lippmann's public opinion, revisited. *Harvard International Journal of Press/Politics, 4*(2), 88–93.

Hodgson, L. (2016). *Res Publica and the Roman republic: "Without body or form."* Oxford University Press.

Justman, S. (1994). Freud and his nephew. *Social Research, 61*(2), 457–476.

Lasch, C. (1978). *The culture of narcissism: American life in an age of diminishing expectations.* W. W. Norton & Co.

Lichtheim, G. (1972). *Europe in the twentieth century.* Praeger Publishers.

Lippman, M. ([1922] 1965). *Public opinion.* The Free Press.

Magarey, S. (1987). That hoary old chestnut, Free will and determinism: Culture vs. structure, or history vs. theory in Britain. A review article. *Comparative Studies in Society and History, 29*(3), 626–639.

Markovits, D. (2019). *The meritocracy trap.* Penguin.

Olasky, M. N. (1984). Retrospective: Bernays' doctrine of public opinion. *Public Relations Review, 10*(3), 3–12.

Peikoff, L. (1993). *Objectivism: The philosophy of Ayn Rand.* Penguin.

Plato ([ca. 375BCE] 2004). *The Republic* (C. D. C. Reeve, Trans.). Hackett.

Putnam, R. D. (1995). *Bowling alone: America's declining social capital.* Simon & Schuster.

Sandel, M. J. (2020). *The tyranny of merit: What's become of the common good?* Penguin.

Siapera, E. (2006). Multiculturalism online: The internet and the dilemmas of multicultural politics. *European Journal of Cultural Studies, 9*(1), 5–24.

Tilly, C. (1995a). The emergence of citizenship in France and elsewhere. *International Review of Social History, 40*(Supplement 3), 223–236.

Tilly, C. (1995b). Citizenship, identity and social history. *International Review of Social History, 40*(Supplement), 1–17.

Tilly, C. (2004). *Contention and democracy in Europe, 1650–2000.* Cambridge University Press.

Wolfe, T. (1976, August 23). The me decade and the third great awakening. *New York Magazine.*

Young, M. ([1957] 1994). *The rise of the meritocracy.* Transactions Publications.

Young, M. (2001, June 28). Down with meritocracy. *The Guardian.*

Zaretsky, E. (2015). *Political Freud: A history.* Columbia University Press.

CHAPTER 32

Old Models, New Realities

C. Gordon, *Many Possible Worlds*,
https://doi.org/10.1007/978-981-19-9281-0_32

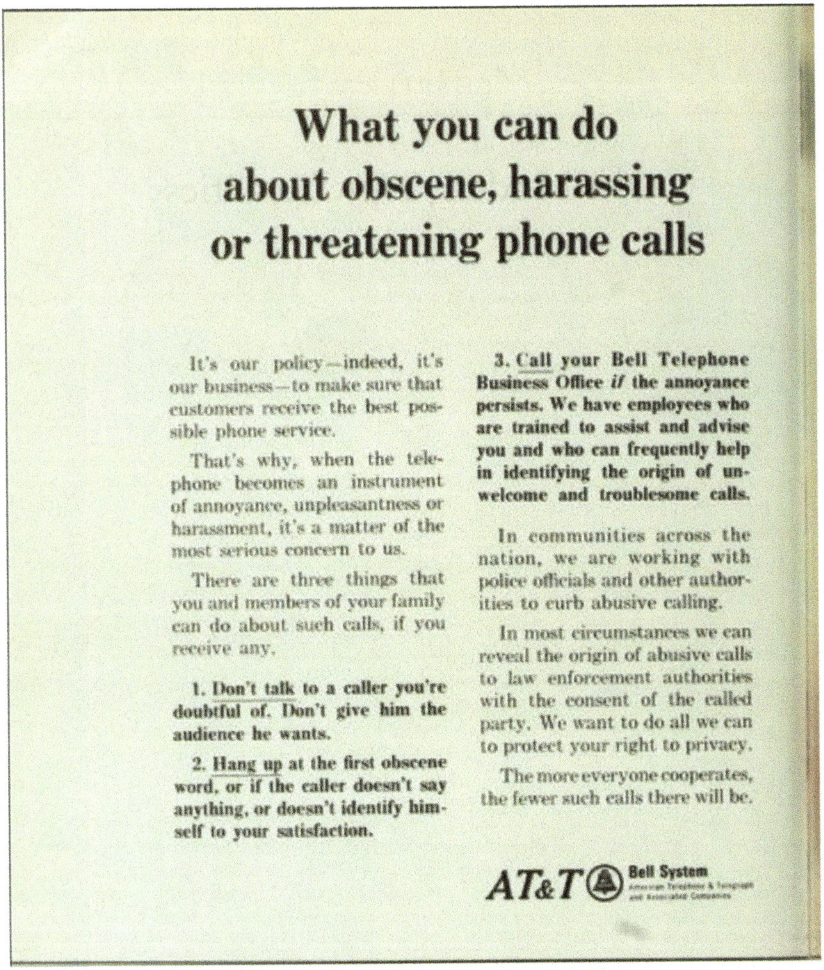

Fig. 32.1 The unintended consequences of modernisation (*Image source* Bell Telephone Magazine Summer 1966, back cover. American Telephone and Telegraph Company; American Telephone and Telegraph Company. Information Dept. Collection. Digitizing sponsor: Internet Archive. Contributor: Prelinger Library. No known copyright restrictions)

32.1 Two Mid-Century Visions of the Future

In October 1949, Aldous Huxley sent a letter to George Orwell, providing a few brief comments on Orwell's just published novel *Nineteen Eighty Four*. Huxley had written his own vision of a dystopian future in his 1932 novel, *Brave New World*, and after complimenting Orwell on his work, made a few brief observations about the differences between the two books.

In typical Huxley fashion, it is a short letter that makes some striking points. Huxley asserts that both their works are about "ultimate revolution...which aims at total subversion of the individual's psychology and physiology". He acknowledges that Orwell's model of infinite and continuing oppression by the State is one way to accomplish this, but believes it to be infeasible and too resource consuming over the long run. Instead, the "ruling oligarchy" will opt for easier ways to subsume the individual, likely through the combined use of hypnotism, psychoanalysis and drugs (he specifically mentions "barbiturates, which induce a hypnoid and suggestible state in even the most recalcitrant subjects"). Huxley also adds that "infant conditioning" will be added to this mix to create a servitude that people will become habituated to, ultimately embracing it due to continuous manipulation from above and an induced state of permanent "narco-hypnosis" (Huxley, [1949] 2012).

It does not appear that Orwell answered the letter. He had been diagnosed with tuberculosis while writing his novel, and his health deteriorated markedly as he wrote, made worse by the pressure of the work itself (a situation that no doubt contributed to a few noticeable inconsistencies that crop up with plot and character points, though these are not large enough to mar the work to any fundamental degree). Orwell the man would die just months after receiving the letter from Huxley (who himself would die of cancer in 1963) (Hollis, 1956; Murray, 2002).

The common theme of both Orwell and Huxley was the elimination of the individual as independent from society, a development that had been playing out in the real world for decades, through Depression, Communism and Fascism when Huxley published, and in the early Cold War polarity of Capitalism versus Communism when Orwell did. Being English, both men saw in their own society a rise of mass politics and mass economics that made even democracy give less room for the individual than ever before (Fig. 32.1).

People continue to debate about which vision was more prescient. To some degree they both made salient, but different points. Orwell presented an acute analysis of the degradation of language (in the form of "newspeak", a denuded and simplified official language to replace English, constantly manipulated and designed to limit creative thinking) and the constant emptying of terms of traditional meaning and replacing them with new meaning amenable to the aims of those in authority, a process managed in the novel by the "Ministry of Truth", the State's official propaganda agency. Huxley, on the other hand, demonstrated how natural human hedonism could be perverted and diverted into social channels that served political and economic interests of the few, including a blind objectified consumerism and a commodified sexual promiscuity. These were all penetrating points at the time and have become more so with each passing decade.

Still, there are some key points of difference between the two dystopias that cause ongoing debate. The world of *Nineteen Eighty Four* is run by three competing totalitarian empires in a constant state of war with each other. The reader is privy only to what is going on in one of these empires, Oceania, though presumably the State operates similarly across all three, conducting total surveillance of the citizens (especially of the elite apparatchiks), constant mass hate and fear campaigns, brutal repression and reprogramming of any sort of individual deviance from official directives, and a rigid, moralistic austerity tending towards prudishness, although the proletarian class is largely exempt and left in a sort of segregated animalistic existence of its own. The resemblance to Stalinist Russia is obvious and intentional.

Huxley's *Brave New World* is also internationally unified under an autocracy but the State structure is more vague (the world being divided into areas run under 10 "controllers"), and the focus is on the maximisation of consumption and production more than any particular political doctrine, though there is a self-justifying "Fordist" philosophy. Huxley's society is on the pleasure-seeking extreme, and sexual promiscuity and gratuitous sensation seeking are organised and encouraged. Conformity to norms is centrally coordinated, but more by means of incentives, propaganda, drugs and genetic engineering, helped by the fact that everyone is conforming to a lowest common denominator viscerally much easier to adhere to. Repression exists, and there are consequences for deviating into individualistic pursuits and attitudes, such as seeking a simpler, less materialistic life or sexual monogamy. But this generally is dealt with through social marginalisation, either informally or formally, with the main character in the novel being exiled to one a number of islands where non-conformist thinkers and actors are segregated into rather than tortured or killed as Orwell's hero is.

These novelistic differences can be taken as presenting a menu of ways that repression and suppression can be undertaken rather than interpreted as an either/or prediction. Huxley himself suggested as much in his letter to Orwell in which he posited that hard repression would ultimately have to shift to softer, less resource-intensive modes. Many contemporary commentators suggested that Orwellian totalitarianism was more of an "Eastern" mode, the Huxley version more "Western", though this is a very stereotyped Eurocentric view. Hedges (2010) looks back on these two authors and argues that there has been a trend line of increasing control that first took Huxleyan forms of seduction, and as these modes exhausted their returns, a more Orwellian surveillance and security state has increasingly taken its place. Of course one could as easily argue that the reverse progression applies, or some combination of both.

The technological world of Orwell's Big Brother is primitive enough to employ people to hand-edit newspapers, photos and other media and send them to various archives by means of a vacuum tube, means that were beginning to go out of date even in 1949, although the novel's two-way "telescreen" is decidedly ahead of its time. The film version of the book actually made in the year 1984 visually translates the book's technological environment very faithfully, offering a sort of "steampunk" landscape that jarringly offers a future that looks very much like the crumbling English infrastructure of Orwell's immediate postwar era. By contrast *Brave New World* uses the pharmaceutical, genetic engineering and social manipulation techniques that are high-tech, even by today's standards in many instances. In a technological sense, Huxley anticipates the future more accurately than Orwell.

These are, however, in the end, just novels, not prophecies. Their authors certainly intended to deliver cautionary messages and extrapolations based on what they saw during their own times. But the relevant question is not so much about which one made better forecasts, but how useful their imaginings are in understanding the world of the present and the past. From this standpoint, both books continue to have much to say.

32.2 A Scientific Paradise

In 1971, the psychologist and noted (some would say notorious) behaviourist, B. F. Skinner, published a book entitled *Beyond freedom and dignity*. Behaviourism in a very general sense argues that human actions are determined by the interaction between their environment and their genetics. The strongest version of the doctrine holds that actions are entirely the product of these two factors, weaker versions admitting other causes as well. Behaviourists sometimes add to this the idea that human subjective experience itself can be reduced to purely physiological processes. Since these processes are also patterned by genetics, and strong behaviourism assumes that actions result from environment and genes, some conclude that human psychology does not exist, and therefore neither does human agency (Herrnstein, 1977). These working premises informed the conclusions of his book in which he argued that free will did not exist, that thoughts and feelings were not particularly relevant to behaviour (and certainly bad bases for decision-making), and that individual and hence collective decisions were ultimately driven by the environment, genetics being taken as given and fixed. (The advances in genetic engineering since then would now allow this factor to be manipulated as well, which was one of the tools available to Huxley's dystopian planners.) Skinner then went a step further to argue that the development of "a technology of behaviour", that could alter human action consistently and systematically was both possible and desirable. And he went further than that to say that given the ills of the world at the time their deployment was absolutely necessary (Skinner, 1971).

Skinner's view was utopian, his methods scientific, and his dismissal of the individual as central to society was seen by many as reminiscent of the totalitarianism of the Nazis and the Soviets (Herrnstein, 1977). However, Skinner was not actually in favour of strong government control. Indeed, he anticipated the field of "Behavioural Economics" by several decades, arguing that modern technical knowledge and methods now allowed for targeted social interventions that were not coercive or intrusive, but which simply structured decisions in such a way that people would happily choose the optimal action over inferior ones. Still Skinner was certainly elitist, noting that "benevolent engineers" like himself would be necessary to do this structuring. He also admitted the possibility of such authority being abused, and while advocating against such misuse, he was not specific as to how this could be avoided (Skinner, 1971).

Skinner's choice of title was perhaps most provocative, suggesting that freedom and dignity were passé in some way. For Skinner, freedom was not relevant in the traditional philosophical sense since there was no true free will. Instead, freedom was not a positive attribute but the absence of pain and difficulty, an outcome best achieved by a well-structured environment. Dignity, meanwhile, Skinner defines as the positive and negative judgements people receive about their actions, an idea that he calls "pre-scientific" (assuming one accepts the rather unorthodox definition of the concept in the first place). Thus praise or scorn for individuals is not necessary, and one should instead look to the environment when interpreting their actions. Since the environment rather than the individual is largely responsible for actions, dignity, like freedom, is irrelevant (Skinner, 1971).

Skinner's original working title was simply "Freedom and dignity" but his editor suggested that he had so redefined these concepts that this did not adequately capture the book's contents. Hence, the addition of "Beyond" to the title, a change Skinner later said was unfortunate because it was too provocative and misleading. But in fact Skinner's overall conclusions are that society needs to abandon "values" (like those in his title) because these were formulated during times before the scientific method was used or perfected. This stance, too, generated a great deal of controversy, as did his inference that punishment needed to be dropped as an approach to maladaptive behaviours, since the individual will did not actually exist. For all this, or perhaps because of it, Skinner's book was a surprise hit, remaining on the *New York Times* best-seller list for 20 weeks (B.F. Skinner Foundation, 2021).

Skinner's book was one of a number of notable publications during the first half of the 1970s, including Ehrlich's *The population bomb*, the Club of Rome's "Limits to Growth" report, and Fuller's *Spaceship earth* (see Chapter 2). They all shared two commonalities. One was the idea that society had reached an existential crisis such as overpopulation, resource exhaustion, ecological collapse, nuclear war, social discord, etc. The other was that these problems were amenable to technical solutions. In fact, the individual did not figure prominently in any of these books, since they posited that "systemic" problems were in need of "systemic" solutions. Skinner stood out nonetheless because he explicitly rejected the role of the individual entirely.

32.3 The New Optimists

Fast-forward to the present age, and a book posthumously published in 2019 by international health expert Hans Rosling, with contributions from his son Ola Rosling and daughter Anna Rosling Rönnlund. Its title is quite suggestive: *Factfulness: ten reasons we're wrong about the world—and why things are better than you think*. The book defines "factfulness" as "only carrying opinions…[with] strong supporting facts", something that they say is not practised much. In actuality people across the world are mostly wrong about the actual state of global and local affairs, as indicated by vast majorities of people being negatively wrong when surveyed about basic statistics such as the percentage of the world population living in poverty, having access to vaccinations for communicable diseases and so forth.

Rosling et al. (2018) argue that there are two main reasons for this state of affairs. The first is the wide range of misinformation, both incorrect and negatively biased, that pervades the media and social discourse. Related to this is a basic ignorance about the actual statistics that official bodies such as the United Nations produce about global well-being. It is argued that human beings have ten perspective-distorting instincts, including a tendency towards negativity, drama and dualism (e.g. us versus them), all of which naturally lead us to underestimate the actual extent of positive change, and overstate the negative. These instincts and biases are unconscious and so we don't know what we don't know. Therefore, the average person around the world can systematically think that things are really bad even though the facts suggest otherwise. Their solution to this situation is twofold. First, make the facts readily accessible and present them in a compelling way; second, frame and present the facts differently, as needed, to reduce inherent instinctual misconception.

Hans Rosling was noted for his pithy, entertaining presentations and visualisations of data of all sorts that purported to show a general upward trajectory across most all indicators in most parts of the world, and set up a website (https://www.gapminder.org/) where such information could be accessed by all, with particular focus on educators. Rosling also re-sorted existing data, when it is reported along the dualistic lines of developing and developed worlds, into four levels based on income brackets, and also cutting down to fine levels of geographical detail, to show how much "development" there actually is in many "underdeveloped" countries (e.g. Shanghai being as wealthy as the wealthiest cities in the West—though the opposite comparison of "underdeveloped" areas in "developed" countries, such as deindustrialised cities, does not get the same level of attention).

As already noted, many economists, especially those using a Growth Model approach, have claimed that the Great Divergence of the Industrial Revolution has in turn become a Great Convergence in which all the nations of the world are converging towards a high-wealth, high-income, high well-being position that has never been attained before in human history (see Chapter 2). Rosling also shared this view, often referring to how more and more people are living in the so-called "healthy, wealthy corner" of the world. The start of our current millennium has seen many such analyses that use data to demonstrate the world is evolving around a positive trend, has been doing so for decades and is likely to continue to do so. Stephen Pinker's 2011 book, *The better angels of our nature: The decline of violence in history and its causes*, is one notable effort, in this case claiming that modern society is safer, more peaceable and less violent than ever before in human history, a claim that Morris (2014) also makes.

32.4 The World as It Is?

So how is the world doing? Is it steadily climbing the curve of modern technical progress or on the cusp of apocalypse? Or are we just muddling through? One could be forgiven for not being sure with all the competing confident visions out there. Even when confining oneself solely to the world economy, definitive prognostications are difficult to make.

Table 32.1, drawing on the concepts developed by Elias (see Chapter 5), maps out the moving pieces of the process of economic modernisation, along three broad categories cutting across three broad dimensions.

First, the modern economy has wrought profound changes in individual psychology (psychogenesis), which can be seen acting at levels of "heart" (emotion and intuition), "mind" (cognition and thinking) and "body" (physical sensation and corporeal processes).

Second, there are parallel, interacting and interrelated alterations to human social structure acting across the entire society (sociogenesis), within particular groups and institutions of varying scales ranging from small to large.

Table 32.1 A template of changes in social and individual psychic changes wrought by economic and social modernisation

Changes in individual psychic structure (psychogenesis)	*Changes in social structure (sociogenesis)*	*Changes in societal ability to manipulate material world (technisation)*
"Heart"	Macro/total	Social
"Mind"	Intermediate/group (institutions)	Technical
"Body"	Personal/social identity	Physical

Note These concepts are adapted from Elias (1969, 1982, 1995, 2000)

Table 32.2 Crosscutting issues for now and the future

Aspect	*Technisation*	*Sociogenesis*	*Psychogenesis*
Physical	(a) Limits to resources	(b) Limits to control	(c) Limits to knowing
Social	(d) Corporatisation, formalisation, bureaucratisation	(e) Instrumentalism versus Values	(f) Unintegrated meaning and immateriality
Individual	(g) Mediated reality	(h) "Mass everything"	(i) Freedom and identity

Third, technological change (technisation) has shaped human ability to manipulate the physical world in ways that are purely technical, purely social and purely individual and cutting across all three.

Table 32.2 meanwhile presents some "headline" crosscutting issues that have emerged over the course of economic modernisation and which arguably remain particularly relevant today. These are then sorted across the template categories of Table 32.1. Each element will be discussed in more detail.

32.4.1 Limits to Resources

As Chapter 2 discussed, the 1970s was a time when the ecological and environmental impacts of economic modernity were deemed as being at crisis level. No one doubted humanity's prodigious ability to extract and transform natural materials into consumables. But many sounded the alarm about the sustainability of this ongoing process. Before then, outside a few niche interests, such as conservationism, the rich countries saw no fundamental ecological problems with industrialisation. Certainly, there were significant flareups of "externalities" that had to be dealt with, such as toxic emissions and effluents, along with a rising flow of garbage. These sometimes resulted in acute episodes that literally could kill numerous people in a short period. For example, London's air pollution had been a severe problem as far back as the thirteenth century due to coal burning for home heating, prompting King Edward I to ban the burning of sea coal. The problem of coal burning obviously intensified with the Industrial Revolution and the severity of air pollution inside and outside of the city caused the passage of some of the first environmental regulations in history, along with the coining of the term "smog" in 1905, by a Londoner who used it to refer to the city's natural fog combined with its coal smoke (Urbinato, 1994).

However, while government policy moderated some of the worst effects and public-private efforts were devoted to managing some others (especially solid waste management) pollution of air, water, and land was essentially ignored, because intervention that was too strong would interfere too much with production. Also, industrial toxicity was not seen as a systemic threat but rather as a series of localised incidents to be dealt with, if at all, on a case-by-case basis. That the lower classes were generally worst affected further reduced its political importance in the minds of leaders. Of course any environmental devastation caused in the global "South" was deemed completely irrelevant.

Moore (2016) thus argues that until the 1970s, a "Green Arithmetic" paradigm dominated, based on a duality of "Society" and "Nature", further broken into sub-dualities of society without nature, and nature without humans, in which it is assumed that the workings of Society plus Nature will always add up to a sum of the parts. Problems in one part could thus be treated separately, ignoring flow-on effects to others, and if, say, "Nature" got too stressed, corrective actions, like tree planting, could be taken to restore the overall balance. Additionally, "Cheap Nature" was implicitly assumed, i.e. that Nature was always there to provide a source of endless raw materials into productive processes. Science and technology were utilised to squeeze more out of Nature and taking the edge off of any resulting ecological problems from doing so, something assumed to be always possible ad infinitum (3–4). This kind of attitude of "Man" over "Nature", with their separate domains, goes back centuries in the West and even has counterparts in non-Western thought and culture. Industrialisation and Science reinforced it mightily, especially since it seemed to "work", with output and technological advance powering ahead seemingly without limit, though with the occasional unpleasant ecological consequence.

After the Second World War, there was a shift to a more relational view of "humanity-in-nature", and "nature-in-humanity", fomented in part by the growth of social movements that were questioning long-standing assumptions about power relations and categories of race, gender, class and Western-centric thinking (see Chapter 24). Now humanity was seen as being in integral relationship with natural processes. Green Arithmetic was seen as no longer working because there was no longer an assumption of a simple additive process of two separate entities, but two intertwined parts of a whole that human action was increasingly throwing out of balance in disastrous and nonlinear ways (Moore, 2016, 4). This also was mirrored by the formulation of Nature as a complex "system" in which the whole could not be assumed to be a simple total arising from the sum of the parts.

"Cheap Nature" was meanwhile overthrown by the restiveness of the world's peripheral countries after decolonisation ended access to permanently abundant and inexpensive commodities and energy upon which international production rested, while the rising prosperity in the West diminished a long-standing tolerance of citizens for industrial environmental disamenities. An environmental movement based in the middle classes became very vocal in the developed core in the 1960s and 1970s and politicians had to respond with stricter regulations and more vociferous rhetoric on both sides of the political mainstream. This often added up to less than it seemed, however. For example, US President Richard Nixon created, by an Executive Order, a new Environmental Protection Agency (EPA) in 1970, coincident with the marking of the first "Earth Day" that year. However, the new agency's 5,650 employees and $1.4 billion budget were all reallocations of existing budget lines and people from other existing agencies. The major difference was that the new EPA reported directly to the White House rather than going through the Cabinet (Reeves, 2001, 238). Still some real action (in the US consisting of the passage of national clean air and water legislation around the same time) was taken, and a new mass issue had emerged.

Then as now, there were those who doubted that humanity really did face any systemic constraints that they couldn't get out of with their usual ingenuity. Economists in particular savaged the Club of Rome's "Limits to Growth" report as being inaccurate in its predictions and making the sort of "sky is falling" claims that ongoing economic growth had always seemed to invalidate (see Chapter 2). However, the report actually predicted an environmental existential crisis within the next century, i.e. by approximately 2070, so these pronouncements of inaccuracy are premature, and there are many environmental indicator trends attesting to its prescience in at least an ecological sense. Still, there is a strong view by some that technological change and superior human adaptation will refashion even a very complex nonlinear system back into a Green Arithmetic that will add up in the end.

A big area of debate is over the meaning of "limits". The old mechanical model of inputs and outputs against a resource constraint has been dropped by most analysts, though arguably not by many Growth Theorists. But even The Anthropocene model has been argued by some to be a "Promethean self-portrait" and an extension of a "neo-Malthusian" scenario, in which human needs and wants still sit outside Nature while exploiting it at the same time, the question remaining of how much Nature can meet these needs and wants before it breaks. Much of the current climate debate thus tends to be a technical one of numbers and models and variables extrapolated into the future, rather than, say, about the inherent value of Nature in and of itself, or Humanity as completely inseparable from Nature. Implicitly, Nature still has a "use" value and we simply are trying to cut back our use of it to "sustainable" levels (Moore, 2016, 6).

One alternative paradigm is the "Capitalocene" holding that capitalism is a way of organising nature into an entirely new world-ecology in which all nature, human and otherwise, is structured to work for free or at very low-cost, summarised as the "Four Cheaps" of food, energy, raw materials and human life. It is this reordering that is the problem, not adjustments to it. In its fullest sense, all species are included, moving away from what some argue to be the "human exceptionalism" of the Anthropocene model. Narrow capacity exhaustions are arguably maxing out, leading to stagnations in agricultural and labour productivity; but now there are also ecosystem collapses from over-exploitation and intrusion, which includes consequences like the COVID-19 pandemic (Moore, 2016, 7–11). Thus a mere "climate change" paradigm needs to be part of a broader set of multiple means of inquiry to determine proper means and ends—and values—that go beyond the current quagmire of technical debate.

32.4.2 *Limits to Control*

In fact, the entire paradigm of system "control" requires re-examination. Science has certainly grown increasingly sophisticated and powerful. And yet it still is based on an imagined "system", however complicated, that takes inputs, creates outputs, has definite underlying causes and effects, and discrete parts that at least potentially can be managed and kept in a desirable equilibrium and on a desired trajectory. Buckminster Fuller's Spaceship Earth analogy was exactly about this. And so too is most of the present discourse about the state of the planet and what to do about it.

The control model has yielded powerful results in terms of designing human interventions that are effective in narrow technical terms in narrow material domains. This even applies to various methods devised to deal with immediate negative impacts, such as waste management and emissions reduction. This model will always be needed, especially since the human social and economic world are now entirely dependent upon technical operations of one sort or another (Fig. 32.2).

There are, however, and always have been, real limits to both this framing, and the capacity to actually exert any kind of meaningful human power in the sense that the word "control" implies. Even when limiting the focus to local ecosystems, such systems are often so shape-shifting that they can be hard to define and describe much less control in any meaningful way. Take, for example, Los Angeles, California, a large urban agglomeration with a tremendous ecological footprint. The word "footprint" implies a stable, measurable impact on a stable setting, neither of which applies in "LA". Los Angeles has the longest "wild edge" of any major non-tropical city, at least 675 miles of enfolding wild habitats, with a primarily mountain edge containing many inaccessible pockets that remain wild even as human use around it intensifies, creating areas of what ecologists refer to as "sharp relief". Even the mere delineation of "wild" versus "urban" becomes problematic in this context. Although destruction of Los Angeles's natural habitat is undeniable, there is also a constant symbiosis between wild and urban areas, with naturalised alien plant and animal populations actually increasing biodiversity in some places, and entire new ecosystems arising in the boundaries between environs, so-called ecotones (Davis, 2006, 202–206). While specific interventions for specific issues can be temporarily applied in this context (e.g. invasive plant species reduction), in the end even this single urban ecology cannot be directed by human will nor fully understood by human intelligence.

Fig. 32.2 "Spaceship Earth" off course? (*Image source* US NASA, https://images.nasa.gov/, 3 February 1984. Original notes: "Mission Control activities during Day 1 First TV Pass of STS-11 S84-26297 [3 February 1984]—Robert E. Castle, Integrated Communications Officer [INCO], plays an important role in the first television transmission from the Earth-orbiting Space Shuttle Challenger. Castle, at a console in the Johnson Space Center's [JSC] Mission Operations Control Room [MOCR] in the Mission Control Center [MCC], is responsible for ground controlled television from the Orbiter on his shift. Here, the Westar VI satellite is seen in the cargo bay just after opening of the payload bay doors"). No known copyright restrictions

Imagine how much harder it is to track and categorise such changes across the whole planet.

Obviously, this is not to suggest that scientists are not aware of these complexities or avoiding dealing with them. Nor is complexity by itself a reason not to address pressing problems. But the scientific technical approach has two major limitations that generally grow larger with the scope of the problem being attacked: (1) the difficulty of control in a practical sense, even with sophisticated means available; and (2) the impossibility of control in an absolute philosophical sense, which confounds the whole aim of control that modern systems seek.

Regarding (1), the word "unintended consequences" says it all. Every scientific advance has brought with it new problems that are met with new advances that set off another round of new complications. There are myriad examples, ranging from the introduction of non-native plant, insect and animal species to control a particular threat (e.g. cane toads brought from Latin America into Queensland, Australia, to eat cane beetles that were destroying the sugar crop and then becoming a plague in their own right); to the widespread use of new synthetic chemicals to control native threats or to increase productivity which then create problems of their own.

One only has to consider the cautionary tale of Thomas Midgely, a prolific chemical inventor who, amongst other things, played a major role in developing leaded gasoline (Tetraethyllead), helped invent some of the first chlorofluorocarbons (CFCs), and was granted more than 100 patents over the course of his career. All of these inventions solved particular issues. Yet all of them also created vast negative environmental outcomes, so much so that many environmental historians refer to him as one of the single most environmentally destructive individuals in history. Though extreme, Midgely was a product of his mid-twentieth century times, which embraced all manner of innovations without a thought to their broader unintended impacts. The invention and widespread use of the pesticide DDT in the 1950s was part of a chemical industry-led campaign, in partnership with Big Agriculture, to declare a "war" on insects. Even though the ecological side effects of the chemical were known as early as 1953, it was tremendously effective in its intended purpose of controlling agricultural pests, just as CFCs and leaded gasoline had succeeded splendidly in their own narrow missions. But CFCs were found to be destroying the earth's ozone layer, while Rachel Carson's 1962 book *Silent Spring* pointed out the devastating effects of DDT on wildlife, especially birds. As for Midgely, after he was disabled with polio, he invented a pulley system to pull himself in and out of bed, and one day got strangled in it, dying as a result, a very apt, if macabre, metaphor (Curtis, 1992).

It is true that the immediate issues of CFCs, leaded gasoline and DDT, were addressed with policy fixes that were successful in dealing with the issues arising. But this was science dealing with problems that science created, after much damage had already been done. And not all problems created by science can be so easily addressed by it. The broader issue remains of the "Sorcerer's Apprentice" getting necessarily out of hand once set in motion. Putting aside the very real issue of intentional manipulation of expertise by industry and special interests (such as the hiding of the harmful effects of tobacco and manipulation of academic studies by the tobacco industry over the course of decades [Oreskes & Conway, 2010]), the ongoing parade of unintended scientific and technological consequences is a road paved with good intentions, but still often leading to an ever-closer and ever-hotter hell. Expert and non-expert alike know more than ever the limits of science and technical knowledge and the dangers of overconfident and hasty application of these modalities to real-world issues. And yet it is done over and over again. Like Midgely, we may be choking on our own technical apparatus and unable, and sometimes unwilling, to consider alternatives, even when faced with blunt-force common sense.

Disruptive and extensive interference with the environment is a basic characteristic of Sapiens, with its curious mind seeking to discover the secrets of the universe and disrupting their environment to find them out. Their big primate relatives also manipulate their environments much more than other mammals, though on a smaller scale than humans. But anthropological studies indicate that there is a wide variation in the relationships that different societies have with their surroundings, some of them quite pacific and noninterventionist in nature (Suzman, 2017). Certainly, the West has been on the interventionist extreme here, as the ancient Greek myth of Icarus and his corresponding character trait of hubris illustrate (Icarus builds an apparatus allowing him to fly but crashes to his death after ignoring a warning not to fly too close to the sun). But capitalism and industrialism have vastly accelerated, deepened and intensified both human manipulations and their consequences, making management of this element alone more difficult than ever, much less its understanding. The continuing opening of "Pandora's Box" is a trite commonplace in some ways. But its basic truth, and the need to face it squarely and re-adapt, in perhaps radical ways, remains.

Besides which, is "control" an attainable goal even in a conceptual sense? Watts (1957) notes that cybernetic systems aim for perfect self-control and yet inevitably must grow more self-frustrating as they approach it. He uses the analogy of wanting to have perfect command over the trajectory of a ball, yet attaining that only by holding on to the ball and not letting it go at all. Lest one thinks that one can nevertheless at least have a range of probabilistic supremacy by throwing the ball in a certain way after doing the requisite studies, Watts notes that even this "solution" will present new problems (e.g. how to get the ball back), which require further solutions etc. in a continuing and never-ending loop (48–49). To solve this overall issue, "Science", therefore, is always seeking out self-regulating systems that use feedback to equilibrate themselves. But feedback cannot control itself and there is no set point that provides perfect control without some final (human) authority that tells the loop to stop; as with a thermostat that is set to not go above or below 20 degrees Celsius exactly, which seems to offer perfect control but which will in practice tend to increasingly oscillate rather than equilibrate due to feedback loops (137–138).

Although "mechanism" is not generally explicitly adhered to like it was in the nineteenth century, its legacy lives on, and indeed, this is the very basis of the self-regulating system in the first place. Mirowksi (1989, 2001) notes how much the field of economics drew on the physics models of the First and Second Industrial Revolution expanding during the Third Industrial Revolution to the use of technical models such as Game Theory and computational math that were particularly shaped by Cold War politics and strategic doctrines. These were more "agent-based" and apparently sophisticated, but they still were based on mechanistic "atoms" following probabilistic, but no less mechanistic, rules.

A constant underneath all of this is the "scientific" notion of "Progress", i.e. a belief in the improvability of all things. Yet this necessarily requires the definition of "good" and "bad" and "worse" and "better" states along a continuum, which is by definition a false separation of the real into arbitrary forms through the use of human judgement. Furthermore, any form implicitly involves its opposite, in which, for example, the creation of a "softer" thing necessarily creates a new level of "hardness" simultaneously, even though unintended. "Progressing" things by getting more of a particular aspect automatically create more of its opposite aspect, an obvious futility (Watts, 1957, 116).

To reiterate, the technical and scientific "control" paradigm has its uses. But the mania of total control and especially "improvement" are not "objective" aims or categories but subjective human constructs and one gets tangled up in them if this is not realised. Watts speaks of the Zen approach of "suchness" in which one takes action as needed but not with a particular aim to "improve" things. This accords with Buddhist notions that the world as experienced by human beings is essentially all constructions of the mind. Thus there is the story of the old Zen master who said that men of former times were sharp in that they heard a single sentence speaking truth and they dropped all their study to just be with that truth. This is in contrast to the later situation where people sat and thought too much about such sentences, missing the whole point (Watts, 1957, 100). One does not need to adopt a Zen, Buddhist, or any other religious or philosophical perspective—or, alternatively, reject scientific method or rational approaches—to nonetheless conclude that some adjustment and transcendence of the current technical problem-solving approach is required.

32.4.3 Limits to Knowing

Of course the deepest belief of the Western canon is summed up in the epigram: "Knowledge is power". This notion flows directly from the Enlightenment ideas that all things are knowable, penetrable, and improvable through human inquiry and knowledge-directed action. The Scientific Revolution and the rise of big Science refined and expanded this sort of thinking and it remains embedded in the foundations of the modern economy's practice and ideology.

Yet in this age of "Big Data", "algorithms", "expert systems" and massive technical enterprise, there seems to be more "knowledge", but less "knowing" than ever before. Knowledge is a noun, while knowing is a verb, and putting aside its derivative definition of having knowledge, knowing refers to the quality of keen alertness, direct experience and awareness of the way things actually are. This is where data can increase knowledge but decrease knowing and in so doing confuse rather than clarify matters. This looms especially large in global warming policy in which the overarching problems are in some ways blatantly obvious but the details of how to resolve them collectively become obscured and deferred through bogged-down debates over measures and models, as occurred during the Kyoto conference that collapsed into recriminations about per capita emissions (with similar dynamics later besetting COP-26 in Glasgow) (Graff et al., 2013, 327–328).

Some of this occurs because of the deliberate intent and design of special interests, whose power can be enhanced by obscuring reality with complex technicalities, putting normal citizens and even politicians and leaders in the dark. But there is also the fundamental unknowability of past, present and future that cannot be encapsulated by technical metrics of uncertainty and probability. Dostoevsky ([1864] 1960) notes that "Reason only knows what it has succeeded in learning (some things, perhaps, it will never learn; this is a poor comfort, but why not say so frankly?), and human nature acts as a whole, with everything that is in it, consciously or unconsciously, and, even if it goes wrong, it lives" (203–204). Elsewhere he bemoans the scientific frame, so dominant in his own day: "A percentage! What splendid words they have; they are so scientific, so consolatory…Once you've said 'percentage', there's nothing more to worry about. If we had any other word…maybe we might feel more uneasy…But what if Dounia [an individual special to the narrator] were one of the percentage! Of another one if not that one?" (51–52; ellipses in the original).

The division between rationalist, scientific thought and other more humanistic varieties emerged most sharply with the Renaissance but such divisions have certainly increased with industrialisation. British scientist and novelist C. P. Snow (1963) went so far as to argue that there were "two cultures" of science and the humanities, respectively, which were not able to talk with one another. Although he later softened his views somewhat, in response to those who argued that this split was too simplistic, Snow was responding to a genuine phenomenon arising from complex technical specialisation in which knowledge and skill were more and more split into niches speaking their own languages, following their own trajectories and thus losing connection with and sight of the whole picture. The spiritualist Kahlil Gibran (1962) had a more humorous, but no less relevant, take on this rise of specialisation, writing in the early twentieth century during the height of the Second Industrial Revolution: "There are still more tribes and clans of gabbers, but they are too many to enumerate. Of these the strangest, in my opinion, is a sleeping denomination whose members trouble the universe with their snoring and awaken themselves, from time to time, to say, 'How erudite we are!'" (191).

All this may sound like mere cant, but it speaks to an ineffability that modernity and its methods is profoundly uncomfortable with, namely the fact that some things can only be understood through direct experience, which each person needs to acquire themselves. Dostoevsky ([1866] 1950) again: "Through error you come to the truth! I am a man because I err! You never reach any truth without making fourteen mistakes and very likely a hundred and fourteen. And a fine thing, too, in its way; but we can't even make mistakes on our own account! Talk nonsense, but talk your own nonsense, and I'll kiss you for it. To go wrong in one's own way is better than to go right in some one else's" (198–199).

One has to take care not to go too far here, of course, as the contemporary thicket of Postmodernism demonstrates. Postmodernism began as a critique of the objective and purportedly neutral grand overarching narratives of the modern world, especially, though not exclusively, "Science". It was not a denial of an objective "truth" but an interrogation of assertions about truth by established power structures, or incredulity about "metanarratives", to use Lyotard's (1984) terminology.

Indeed, most serious postmodern thinkers accept the ideal of objective truth but note that many arguments and conclusions claiming to be based on scientific truths often turn out to be power plays rather than truth. Foucault (1977) noted that scientifically "enlightened" ways of improving society were often covers for increasing power over people rather than about helping them. While the existence and utility of "facts" in the traditional sense, such as the number of troops in the Italian Army on 1 May 1941, are obviously not denied, their socially constructed aspects and the underlying intents behind them are offered as legitimate areas to study as well. Prado (2017) distinguishes between this and "Post-truth" which moves away from "objective" truth to relativisation of all "truth", based on how one feels about or perceives things.

In this respect, the postmodern frame can actually be seen as restoring a measure of value and validity to common sense, intuition and personal subjective experience that the scientific paradigm has too often sidelined or eliminated. One can look at knowing as taking in all modalities to get at the truth, not just one (e.g. "Science") or another (e.g. "Emotion").

32.4.4 Corporatisation, Formalisation, Bureaucratisation

Technocracy is a term bandied around a great deal when speaking of the modern world and the modern economy especially. But what does the term mean exactly? It has to mean more than bureaucracy, as this is as old as the State itself. And it also must be distinguished from the advance in technical means to manipulate physical forces and material things, which is simply the story of human technology (Lictheim, 1972, 397). Galbraith's (1967) concept of "technostructure" is certainly relevant in describing the increasing planning, management and direction of private corporate activity by technical expertise. Weber's concept of "rationalisation" is also relevant (see Chapter 11), elaborated on by Marcuse (1964), in referring to a complete formalisation of social and economic processes under an purportedly "objective order of things" (such as "Science" or "The Marketplace") that keeps generating higher and higher levels of organisation to achieve ever greater and larger scale outputs from a given level of input. Being "scientific", "optimal" and "productive", these elements of technocracy are said to transcend politics, at the level of both organisational management and society as whole. Technocracy refers to this mode of operation as well as the institutional ecosystem supporting it, consisting of large corporations, governments and civil society groupings devoted to shared and specific technical-cum-political purposes, e.g. the "military industrial complex" and other "iron triangles" (see Chapters 22 and 29).

Yet the term technocracy may now be out of date in its original sense. It is true that the digital age and "knowledge economy" have brought complicated technical approaches to everything, and in some ways have thus increased the depth and breadth of technocratic modes. But the nature, intent and form of technocratic institutions have changed in significant ways. Old dichotomies between "public" "public-private" and "private" entities have largely been eliminated in practical terms. The State has been effectively "hollowed out" in many cases through a vast network of private service contracts, paid for with public monies, that are used almost exclusively across the policy spectrum to include policy formulation, implementation and service delivery (Skelcher, 2000). Corporations and corporate and corporatised vehicles are the norm everywhere else across the economy and the society at large. Even individuals now consider themselves "enterprises", whether they formally incorporate or not, and more and more people are hired in this manner, as "casual" employees delivering services to a central entity—or a set of interrelated entities managed by one authority (Cunningham, 2016; Shah, 2011).

The private corporation itself has transmogrified. "Strategic alliances", "joint ventures" and other fragmented and dynamic power-sharing arrangements between separate and often "competing" companies are the norm in international business especially, often creating new "separate" entities in the process (Cantwell et al., 2010). Many of these companies are bought and directed for financial engineering purposes, funded and controlled by vast agglomerations of private capital with often obscure origins, an example being private equity funds that are now key players, as passive or active owners of major enterprises going well beyond traditional financial services, into real estate, infrastructure, media ventures and most everything else (Anker-Sorensen, 2016).

Maximisation of the private rate of return is, as always, the goal of those participating in this diverse organisational ecosystem. But it does not use the means or seek the ends of the older technocracy in terms of planning and managing grand outcomes or seeking system stability. The Galbraithian "technostructure" and the Keynesian state both had the goal of maximising production, smoothing business cycles and providing reasonable returns on investment along with a manageable range of regular wage growth. Real products were being made and there were tangible tasks of production, consumption and distribution to be accomplished and coordinated. Now the "real" is outsourced or offshored, often far down the supply chain from the point of view of the capital owners (or more properly speaking, in many cases, temporary lessors and lessees, since much capital is controlled, but not owned, by heavily leveraged entities working off someone else's capital) the profits often derived from pure financial manipulation. The "transaction" seems to be the end in and of itself, the more of them the better since these generate fees, profits, cuts and all other manner of financial wizardry outcomes, with, sometimes, actual production of actual new value-add incidentally involved. System instability from this perspective is often not a minus but a plus, because more money can be made in "micro-trades" on volatile price movements using complicated algorithms to operate financial engineering magic than within a stable system with more predictable price movements. "Long-term", which used to be years, now is minutes, days, or at most months for the larger mergers, acquisitions and asset sales and purchases primarily designed to provide yield on the "flip" (Lewis, 2011; Partnoy, 2003).

This is most obvious in the financial sector itself which has invested billions of dollars in their own proprietary trading networks, satellites, and underground and undersea cables designed to get proprietary information and execute trade fractions of milliseconds faster than competitors, enough time to achieve repeated micro-arbitrage that can add up to substantial sums. These "dark pools", more formally known as Alternative Trading Systems (ATSs), provide anonymous participants with trading venues executing hidden orders away from public markets, disclosure and regulation. In 2012, there were over 50 dark pools in the US, only 19 of them providing public information and accounting for over 14% of consolidated trading volume. Europe had 16, accounting for approximately 4.5% of volume (Buti et al., 2017, 244). This is part of a larger development within the finance sector referred to as "Fintech", i.e. the introduction of cutting-edge technologies in the financial sector, amounting to a sort of full digitisation of the industry. As mentioned, though, the outputs and outcomes of such innovation here are not always clear-cut, presenting some serious systemic, policy and regulatory issues (Gai et al., 2018; Nicoletti et al., 2017, 195–209).

Yet "Silicon Valley" is not all that different, in principle seeking to stimulate endless and repetitive "clicks" by its "users" (the fact that the same term "users" also can refer to narcotics addicts is often remarked upon). One should not conclude that there is no actual "value-add" from any of these arrangements. But much technical enterprise now is not set up to be "technocratic" in the old sense of system optimisation and planning, nor is much tangible actually produced. The relationship between "value" and the productive process is much more tenuous than a few decades back.

Also "power" no longer travels along clear and obvious channels. The standard analytical paradigm remains one of "State" versus "private" power, with a supposed balance between the two delivered by political systems and markets. But not only have the distinctions between the two blurred, as noted above, the emerging challenge may be more about identifying exactly who really exercises power over the economy and the society and how. Russia and China, for example, are often referred to as authoritarian systems, as they are. But in both places, the State has sometimes been used to contain and control the power of private enterprise rather than just being a mere channel for private interests as it often appears to be in the "liberal" democracies. The efficacy of these systems is very debatable. But so too is that of democratic systems. The general issue of economic and political power is highly contested across the world but much of the current discussion of these issues appears to be based on dynamics of a century ago.

32.4.5 Instrumentalism Versus Values

In Russia, roughly a hundred years after Dostoyevsky composed some of his greatest novels, Solzhenitsyn (1974) told the story of a non-political offender, Gennady Smelov, who started a lengthy hunger strike in 1960 while in prison. The prosecutor went to his cell and asked him: "Why are you torturing yourself?" To which Smelov replied: "Justice is more precious to me than life". The next day Smelov was taken to the

Leningrad Special Hospital (i.e. insane asylum) where the doctor told him: "We suspect you may be a schizophrenic" (473). That someone would give up one's life for a higher social value literally did not compute for the authorities.

The Communist system held up official ideals, such as equality and justice, and purportedly was devoted to perfecting society (and by extension, the individual, deemed to be a pure product of it) along "scientific" means. The Capitalist world was less explicitly idealistic, and less total, as well as more democratic in form. But both systems shared a modern industrial era belief in material outcomes being the ultimate measure of societal ends. Capitalism "won" the contest, but the instrumentalism that underlay both systems remains.

Instrumentalism in a general sense refers to the idea that the value of anything is summed up by the outcomes achieved as a result of it. The term also refers to a philosophical doctrine holding that ideas are useful instruments for structuring reality into concepts that allow for manipulation of that reality, and that the worth of an idea flows from its effectiveness in explaining and predicting phenomena. In the context of the scientific method, this view is agnostic as to whether scientific concepts are literally true, or correspond to reality in some way, instead evaluating them according to their power in making accurate empirical predictions or resolving internal conceptual consistencies. "Scientific realism" opposes this one-dimensional benchmark, holding that scientific theories must both generate reliable predictions and accurately describe the world (Stanford, 2015).

Combined with the rising strains of materialism, reductionism, mechanism and determinism (see Chapter 1) and Utilitarianism (see Chapters 4 and 17), modern society and everything in it has been essentially reduced, in intellectual terms, to uses and outcomes, under a rubric of instrumentalism. Long-standing values, morals and ethics are still nominally upheld, and sometimes even practised. But the measure of everything is its worth in the achievement of a desired material outcome (or avoiding an undesired one). Further, most everything is monetised, actually or conceptually or both, so that different courses of actions and their supposed outcomes can be compared, and the "best" (i.e. highest return) chosen.

Benefit-cost analysis (BCA) is one apotheosis of this sort of thinking, now widely conducted and applied to all manner of diverse phenomena, including the current COVID-19 crisis, where the monetised "costs" of various policies (lockdowns, social distancing, vaccinations, etc.) are compared against the economic "benefits" of same to arrive at a net societal gain or loss. While political heat is generated over issues of "principle", such as personal liberties of movement and action, the right of non-interference into one's body, and so forth, and much ink is split cogitating over the "balance" and "trade-off" between the personal and collective good, these issues nonetheless are in practice almost always reduced to the core, determinative BCA of policy and action. Whether such an analysis is actually conducted formally or not is another matter (it often is not). But everything is framed in BCA terms implicitly. Broader "values" are not given economic value and thus fall by the wayside. They are not even defined properly in most discourse, public or expert (e.g. "freedom", which seems now to have collapsed into a definition focusing on the extent of personal licence to engage in marketplace and social activities).

This development has both pros and cons. The shift towards instrumentalism can evade getting bogged down in debates about ideals that can be meaningless at best, and destructive at worst, and a standard of "what works best" can be liberating as well as practically effective. Such philosophical pragmatism can, and has, also opened up a social and political space of wider freedom and diversity and personal expression, since multiple approaches can often perform equally well in practical terms of outcomes relative to a given sacrifice.

However, the dark side is that ultimately nothing has any sanctity. Universal values and intrinsic measures of worth can be impractical and socially divisive. But they also can be supportive and protective of both society and individual. Just because they have sometimes been used in the service of rigidity and intolerance and ignorance in the past, does not mean that they have to be used this way now, or that they are old-fashioned. To take another COVID-19 example, vaccine mandates have been legitimately discussed in terms of trade-offs between public health and personal choice. Although the principle of personal sanctity over one's body is often rhetorically evoked by both opponents and proponents, within a purely extrinsic framework this is not a meaningful or relevant question since what matters—what always matters—is whether society is better off or not in taking a particular action and the answer to this question always depends on a shifting set of results.

There is something lost because of this. Indeed, the very language of "tradeoff" is based on relative outcomes. A prosaic problem with this is that prediction and measurement of outcomes is not always easy even during the best of times and can become near impossible during crisis times. And such assessments generally require complex expert analysis in which the experts, like us all, still remain flawed human beings operating under uncertainty. Outcome-based logic has a serious downside in that the ends literally justify the means. Technology, science and Capitalism have made this path easier to follow and while its material upsides may seem obvious, the downsides can be too easily forgotten. And even its material upsides should not be taken for granted.

32.4.6 *Unintegrated Meaning and Immateriality*

One distinguishing feature of the first Western "Modern Art" was to represent "reality" in new and novel ways, either "scientifically", as was the contention of Cubism in purporting to more truly show lines and dimensions that two-dimensional representational painting missed; or, with similar intent, to use subjectivity to more fully capture actual experience, as the Impressionists aimed to do with their breaking down of colour into components that people actually "see". In these and other cases, artists still sought to make statements about the nature of the world, even if, as with the "anti-art" Dada movement that arose after the end of the First World War, it was to say that statements of any sort were pointless. By the 1960s, however, even this perspective was eroding. While art used to have self-sufficiency in meaning, this was now said to be "contingent" on the how the audience viewed it. Individually and collectively the viewing crowd would bring its own meaning, just as they would to everything else (Archer, 2002, 59). Nothing was permanent or transcendent, even in art.

From here it was a short step to questioning the whole notion of an "Artist". If audiences brought the meaning, why couldn't they make the art too? Andy Warhol brought a certain literalism to this with the replication of manipulated mass advertising and communications images, and this was the more general spirit behind "Pop Art" and other movements that did something similar but on a more bespoke scale. Meanwhile, there were some who presented art as a set of instructions that could be carried out by anybody, possibly with different and interesting results depending upon who carried them out. This was the intent behind some art installations during the 1970s that provided instruction cards to gallery attendees directing them to manipulate spaces or surfaces that were provided (Archer, 2002, 96).

Performance art, interactive or otherwise, was another form that broke down barriers between artist and viewer, and between "art-space" (e.g. a museum) and general space (e.g. the street). Marina Abramovic, for example, sat publicly exposed and invited viewers to abuse her, in one case requiring outside intervention, while Valie Export and her *Tapp und Tast Kino* (Touch Cinema) invited passers-by to put their hands through the box covering her and touch her naked breasts. Not all performance art was this transgressive or grotesque. But they shared the common message that even the Enlightenment values, such as Reason and Objectivity, that had ultimately spawned Modern Art, were now to be rejected along with everything else. It was not just a case of the old being outmoded, to be replaced by newer, superior expressions, but a putting down of all "artistic" expression as phoney somehow. Western Rationalism and Classical forms were seen as anti-human and exclusive and in the 1960s this extended to "normal" Western middle class values, indeed any values at all, which was part of the reason for the appearance of vulgarity and prurience in some of the works of the period and afterwards (Archer, 2002, 104–107).

This "anti-expression" of the 1960s and 1970s soon became co-opted, however, by the marketplace, various movements picking up on the extensive commodification, commercialisation and instrumentality of everything, especially given the importance of visuals in mass marketing. Warhol, a deliberately ambiguous figure, sold exceptionally well, his mass production silk-screens allowing for a vast financial leveraging of his individual efforts. Irony masking cynicism became the norm, Edward Ruscha's art, for example, being referred to as "advertising art advertising itself as art that hates advertising", a "California Cool" that provided an aura of "post-hierarchy", with everything, including ideas, emotions and events, being of equal value and importance, and hence of no importance or value at all (Davis, 2002, 69).

All art has long had a commercial aspect to it, and forms of mass production were nothing new, greats such as Michelangelo and Da Vinci employing scores of workers to create their art and having rich patrons underwrite it. But their art sought to convey meaning and hierarchy expressed through a form that only some could create and perhaps not all could understand. Art now was another consumable, meaning whatever its purchaser thought it meant, being worth whatever the buyer was willing to pay for it. Art has always reflected the state of society, and meaninglessness in absolute terms (outside of the relative meaning of purchase and consumption), is now what is being reflected back.

Once again, this development is not an unalloyed "good" or "bad". Given the excesses of the "Age of Ideology" (see Chapter 15), the danger of collective meanings and messages now seems especially clear. License to be one's self, free of any trapping, old or new, is an inviting and potentially liberating prospect. Yet human beings remain what they are and meaning, something beyond the material and one's limited self, is something each one craves in their own way. Neither modernity nor post-modernity has been able to deliver this, but still the vacuum is there to be filled. The modern capacity to produce and consume, unrivalled in history, does not meet this genuine need either, though it does temporarily fill superficial gaps well.

32.4.7 Mediated Reality

Industrialism created a demand for literacy on a mass scale, and the provision of public education to supply it. Literacy, along with mass society, increased the distances between people and groups, both of which increased the abstraction of human relationships, increasing the importance of the brain's frontal cortex in navigating and understanding the world, while reducing the importance of the more "primitive" but more holistic hybrid mind-body apparatus (Fig. 32.3).

As already chronicled, mass media of all sorts has expanded and multiplied and pervaded to the deepest corners of collective and individual. Bingeing on anything used to be seen as bad. Not "binge-watching", however, which is presented as a necessary enjoyment and fulfilment for today's hard times.

This orgy of media has many effects, not least of which is an overload of human cognitive and sensory systems by stimuli and "content". This is an information society in which nobody seems to get the story straight. Rather than clarifying, this narrative multiplicity confuses and numbs. As author Ray Bradbury presciently said in his 1953 science fiction dystopia novel *Fahrenheit 451:* "Cram them full of noncombustible data, chock them so damned full of 'facts' they feel stuffed, but absolutely 'brilliant' with information. Then they'll feel they're thinking, they'll get a sense of motion without moving. And they'll be happy, because facts of that

Fig. 32.3 An early, and prescient, vision of a mediated future (*Image source* As shown in illustration. Public domain)

sort don't change. Don't give them any slippery stuff like philosophy or sociology to tie things up with. That way lies melancholy" (58).

Developments such as these loosen a stable sense of truth or meaning as already indicated. But they go beyond this and are not just confined to media experience. Everyday life, for the regular person and specialist alike, is now literally "screened" off via various electronic devices, the "smart" phone being the most ubiquitous example. Whereas mediation used to deal with mainly "far off" phenomena such as foreign affairs or the goings-on within certain power centres, caught up through reading newspapers and listening to the radio or watching a limited number of television channels, now most people will, for example, look at their weather "app" before looking out the window, and may even dispense with looking out the window entirely. Social media platforms do the same for social relationships.

The technical organisation of society places technical specialists into this mediated reality particularly deeply, ranging from doctors looking at computer records rather than directly at patients to make diagnoses, to loan officers guided by algorithms rather than personal relationships in extending credit. A bizarre manifestation is the practice of automated warfare at a distance. Drone operators in active battle situations are typically thousands of miles away from the drones they are operating via advanced computer and telecommunication systems. But their contact with the real world is not only mediated but actually not immediate due to "latency", which refers to the time it takes for information to make its way from the drone to a satellite tens of thousands of miles up in space, down again to a ground station, then switching to fibre-optic cable to reach the pilot's computer console. The scene on a pilot's screen may be between two seconds and five seconds old and once an instruction is given this too has a lag. Thus a separate team of pilots stationed close to the actual drone runway is needed to monitor flying in real time on the ground. Moreover, the pictures received are not always of very fine resolution and are easily degraded by zooms in and out, light conditions of the time of day, and dust in the air. Another buffer is imposed by the use of military jargon, often euphemistic, to describe the action, e.g. MAM (military-aged male) to refer to any military fighter regardless of age of actual role (Cockburn, 2015, 4–8).

Technical specialisation, mechanisation and digitalisation have had other effects as well. Just as the top of the hierarchy is managed more and more by "managers" who supposedly can "manage" anything, whatever the content, many line jobs at lower or middle levels require technical operators who have more area knowledge than a manager but whose main qualifications are in operating the technical systems (such as skills testing platforms) or general analytical skill (such as in "Big Data" analysis) rather than the specific business at hand. Data are data after all, and platforms are platforms, and what the data and platforms are actually about often makes little difference to the analysis or work to be done. Personal embodied experience in particular becomes largely irrelevant.

The pervasiveness of electronic mediation of all forms at all levels has added to the tendency of human beings to project on to the world and replace actuality with mental concepts. This capacity is vastly enhanced by technology and its diffusions, and becomes more uniform at the collective level too, sometimes by design, through social media and other digital platforms. The extent that people live in a true "hyperreality", i.e. the fabricated system of meaning created by mass culture and mass images, is a debatable point (Baudrillard, 1994). But certainly the distinction between manufactured and "real" experience is subject to more potent manipulation than ever before and is more confused as a result.

32.4.8 *"Mass Everything"*

At the heart of economic modernity is the ability to do everything at scale. Indeed, economic growth and productivity depend upon it. Mass processes do have that to recommend them. But this feature has some problematic elements from a political, social and human perspective. Spengler predicted that the modern megalopolis would make liberal democracy unworkable and the twentieth century presented a long march of events and changes that made the individual smaller and smaller in stature when put in a broader context. The First World War showed that technology and organisational ability, not individual heroism, mattered most in military matters, while mass production showed the same for the individual worker (though the individual entrepreneur, such as Henry Ford, kept their hero status, as they continue to do) (Lichtheim, 1972). The Second World War reinforced these inferences for war; the Golden Age of capitalism reinforced them in peace (Fig. 32.4).

32.4.9 *Freedom and Identity*

Yet individuality was proclaimed more loudly than ever even as its practical significance declined (see Chapter 31). As noted earlier, everyone was now their own boss, having the freedom (if they had the guts) to get out into the marketplace and make their fortune. This was especially prominent in the 1980s and 1990s in which aggressive capitalistic activity almost became a duty. Around this time, the author Budd Schulberg, in a postscript to the fiftieth anniversary edition of his famous send-up of Hollywood nihilism *What Makes Sammy Run*, wrote with surprise that people had turned his "angry expose" anti-hero, the Hollywood gofer who rises to studio head, Sammy Glick, a narcissistic and successful manipulator, into a "character reference" (Davis, 2006, 46).

This sort of attitude has waned as the prosperity of the 1990s has given way to the crisis and privation of the following decades. Yet the doctrines of individualism, and the freedom of the individual, have continued, but shifted. Now there are niche social spaces for everyone to be and express

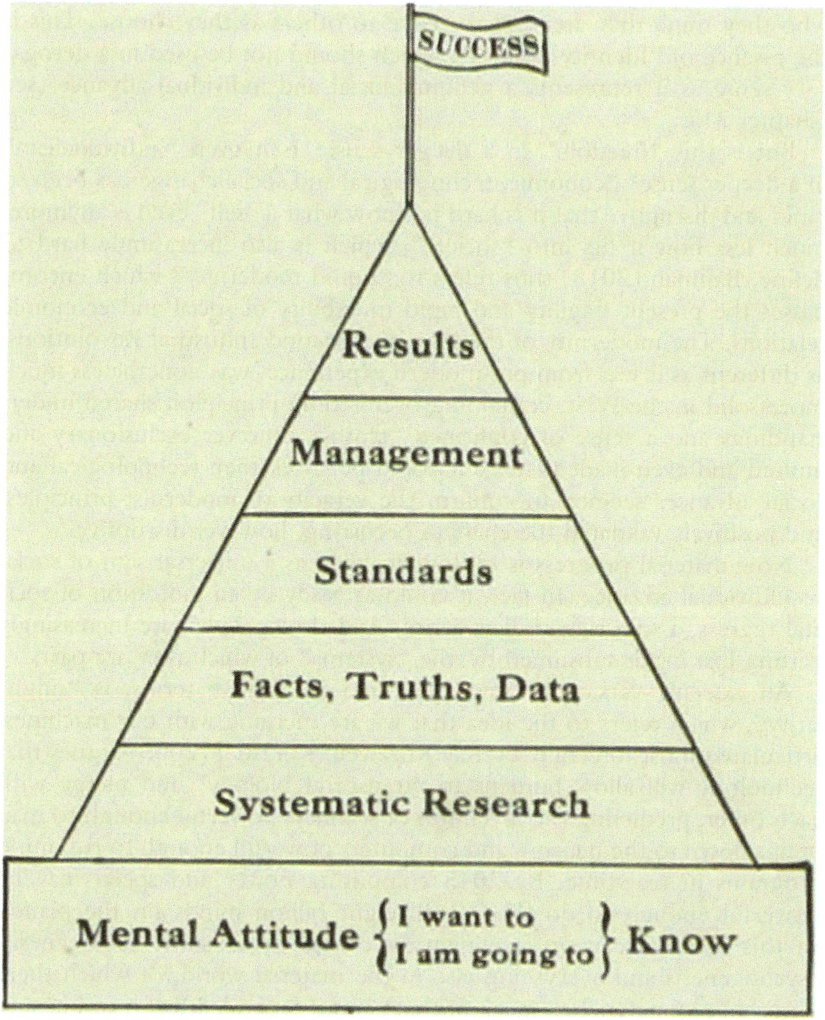

Fig. 32.4 The road to success is paved with mass intentions (*Image source* Kent, W. [1918]. *Bookkeeping and cost accounting for factories*. Wiley, p. 119. Contributing library: University of California Libraries. Digitising sponsor: Internet Archive. No known copyright restrictions)

who they think they are, and to relate to others as they choose. This is the essence of “Identity Politics”, which should not be used in a derogatory sense as it represents a genuine social and individual advance (see Chapter 31).

But is this “freedom” in a deeper sense? Is it even “individualism” in a deeper sense? Economic, technological and social change has been so rapid and disruptive that it is hard to know what a “self” even is anymore, much less how it fits into “society”, which is also increasingly hard to define. Bauman (2013) thus refers to “liquid modernity” which encompasses the present fragility and rapid mutability of social and economic relations. The modernity of the First and Second Industrial Revolutions, as different as it was from pre-modern experience, was nonetheless much more solid in the West, containing overarching principles, shared understandings and a sense of confirmed “truth”, however exclusionary and limited and even inadequate as it could be. Back then technological and social advances seemed to confirm the veracity of modernist principles, and positively validated the changes occurring, however disruptive.

Now material progress is no longer taken as a universal sign of social or individual advance. In fact, it could as easily be an indication of societal regress, a sure sign of decadence. And the “people” are increasingly getting lost in, or subsumed by, the “systems” of which they are part.

An extreme version of this, presented in positive terms, is “singularity”, which refers to the idea that we are merging with our machines, articulated most forcefully by Ray Kurzweil. Kurzweil (2005) argues that technology will allow humans to “transcend biology” and merge with each other, predicting the invention of scanners powerful enough to map brains down to the neuron, and computers powerful enough to run mind programs in real time. By 2045 computing power and speed may be powerful enough to do this for all eight billion minds on the planet. In this sort of scenario, technisation comes to subsume sociogenesis, psychogenesis and everything else in the material world, of which there is nothing immaterial to speak of that cannot be boiled down to bits and bytes.

But one person’s sweet dream is another person’s dark nightmare. Putting aside whether singularity is even possible, which many doubt (Edwards, 2011), is it desirable? What the trajectory of the economy since 1800 does definitely seem to show is that technology has wrought prodigious change and has become the central organising principle of human society, for better and for worse. Yet even the material world cannot be reduced to a technology, since social, psychological, biological and physiological dynamics are integral to the greater whole and irreducible in some fundamental ways. There are also the immaterial aspects to consider, which some dismiss, or reduce to the material, but which humanity grapples with either way.

32.5 Old Models, New Realities

Any narrative of things past implicitly carries within it the question of what comes next. It does not, however, necessarily carry any answers. For past is certainly not prologue and history never repeats itself exactly, though human beings do appear to need to re-experience certain things over and over, as individuals as well as collectively. Whether the economy, and the society in which it sits (or perhaps it is now the reverse), will be a utopia, a dystopia, a collapse or something else entirely is impossible for this author to say with any confidence, particularly with the addition of fast-breaking events occurring even as these words are being typed, in this case the Russian invasion of Ukraine.

One thing that can be said is that there have been dramatic changes in the nature of human psychology, social relations, ecology and economic modes of production, consumption and distribution over the past three centuries. Yet the models used to understand this change are far from adequate to understanding or explaining yesterday's reality, much less today's.

Consider the models of economics that purport to focus explicitly on the workings of the system of material productivity. Its first incarnation, the Political Economy of the late 1700s and early 1800s, was already made obsolete by developments unfolding within mere decades of its first formulation. It was an inadequate simplification to begin with in many respects, with its assumption of a small enterprise economy of competition between atomistic agents with relatively fixed self-seeking psychologies. But the already pronounced rise, by the middle of the nineteenth century, of a nexus of economically activist states, large private firms, oligopoly and monopoly markets, and the mobile capital of international financiers, rendered the theory, and its associated political doctrine of Liberalism, something of a caricature. It took the Great Depression and two World Wars to lead to widespread alterations to its idea structures, and even then these were modifications, not overhauls.

There have been some alterations to the methods and theories of economics since then, though substantial regression as well. But neither the Global Financial Crisis (GFC) nor the Coronavirus pandemic have yet led to the fulfilment of textbook predictions of sharp economic contraction, fall in prices of all sorts, especially assets, and then a subsequent reflation to re-equilibrate supply and demand at new "optimal" levels. The GFC did initially play out as textbooks predicted, with an economic depression deeper than that of the 1930s. But an unprecedented experiment in permanent free money, technically referred to as Quantitative Easing (QE), the nearly total rescue of a problematic financial sector, and, less importantly, the uneven application of large-scaled Keynesian fiscal "stimulus", though much more regressive in its distribution than past efforts, "ended" the GFC without systemic collapse.

Still, the textbooks suggested that QE itself might lead to unmanageable consequences, possibly strong hyperinflation, on the one hand, or stagnation, on the other. It seemed implausible that both zero per cent interest rates and the maintenance of huge central bank holdings of private and public financial instruments could last for over a decade, which it now has and only finally slowly being reversed as this book goes to publication. Moreover, although the fiscal stimulus packages were ultimately wound back, the overhang of government debt they incurred remained and these too were predicted to be ultimately disastrous if not attended to. Once more, though, the consequences were not at all what the standard models suggested. For this reason, the theories of Minsky (1980, 2016) and of "Modern Monetary Theory" (MMT) (Mitchell et al., 2016) have received much attention and credence, though more outside than inside the universities. Not that these models are more "correct" than the existing ones. But they do at least incorporate some salient bits of reality more than their official alternatives.

Meanwhile, real and financial asset prices have boomed through most of the COVID-19 crisis, and a depression has not resulted, even though the classic confidence-destroying conditions of high economic uncertainty and deep temporary dampening of production and consumption have prevailed over much of its course. Extraordinary stimulus packages definitely arrested the possibility of collapse at the most dangerous moments, so this seems to explain why depression did not take hold. But what is the cause of the unprecedented ongoing asset boom and will it ever "correct" itself? The existing models predict an eventual recalibration of asset markets, although the specialists also have to admit that they cannot be exactly sure how the workout period will look.

Some of the more interesting propositions have therefore come from outside the academy. For example, analysts within Citigroup in 2005 posited that the modern economy is now a "plutonomy" (a term they appear to think was original to them, though it was in use as early as the 1850s). This is largely as it sounds, i.e. that the economies of the US, UK, and Canada in particular, are more and more based on the spending by the top 1% or so, and that economic growth will actually increase as rising income inequality and profit share of total income does. In typical parochial Wall Street fashion, these analysts note that one should avoid buying shares in companies oriented towards the masses, as these will tend to lose value as their customers lose total spending power over time. Luxury and other pursuits of the idle rich are where the profits, and hence the rising share values, are. They also note that social and political risks to economic performance are high, e.g. unrest and electoral volatility. But if these are managed, there is no reason not to expect continued positive growth in GDP per capita, even though only a very few of the "capita" will be pocketing the gains (Kapur et al., 2005).

The Citigroup analysts are not economists and are not offering formal or even informal models. And they may well be wrong, admitting that they are offering a "provocative thesis". The point is that to get a proper sense of what is going on now, and what has been going on in the past, one has to go well beyond the current economic mainstream and try out formulations that at least appear to be much closer to what is actually real. A plutonomy may or may not exist, but it is a starting point that at least fits some of the facts in ways that more narrow economics constructs are very far from doing.

Lest one think that economics is being singled out here, other "standard" approaches of other disciplines also seem to be misfiring in obvious ways. Standard political science views of democratic process and democratic politics are obviously not convincing anyone and seem divorced from the way politics really gets done. Even political pollsters are getting a lot wrong these days, misled in part by class and social analysis based on outmoded paradigms. To take a different example, geopolitical theory of the standard sort is Eurocentric, and, especially Anglosphere-centric and often Cold War-centric, even though the Cold War has been over for three decades now. So China's current trajectory is treated in very conventional terms, generally with a self-serving bias attached to it depending on who is doing the analysis. But can China's rise be adequately understood in the context of a traditional system of nation-state competition? Is that model fully relevant anymore in a radically altered global institutional environment? This of course says nothing about present developments in Ukraine. One can be forgiven for being truly uncertain about how the geopolitical order will look in a decade, once ideological priors are dropped.

It is easy to throw stones, of course, and these critiques are offered more in the spirit of a call for humility and openness to views and constructs that are now generally treated as in competition with each other (e.g. economics versus sociology), when they should be treated as complements and helpful challenges to one another, as well as those that are sidelined or ignored (in particular, "working" wisdom such as that of the Citigroup analysts cited above). This is not a case of the truth being "somewhere in the middle" or approximating a single truth by privileging one analysis over others for all times and all places. Instead, and at a minimum, useful knowledge and understanding from various disciplines, academic and non-academic, needs to be marshalled together to better fit and explain the reality of a modern economy that is both constantly shape-shifting and yet is very consistent in some of its underlying aspects, all at the same time.

These tasks take a lot of work and patience and honesty, even though sharp disagreement is inevitable. But at least unnecessary (and sometimes intentional) muddle would be lessened. There were many possible worlds and some impossible ones that have been considered and conceived of over the course of history up to this point and it would helpful to know more about those to know where we really are and to make better guesses about where we might be heading.

References

Anker-Sorensen, L. (2016). Financial engineering as an alternative veil for the corporate group. *European Company Law, 13*(5), 158–166.

Archer, M. (2002). *Art since 1960* (2nd ed.). Thames and Hudson.

Baudrillard, J. (1994). *Simulacra & simulation* (S. F. Glaser, Trans.). University of Michigan Press.

Bauman, Z. (2013). *Liquid modernity*. Wiley.

B.F. Skinner Foundation. (2021, May 31). Beyond freedom and dignity. *Blog Large*. https://www.bfskinner.org/2021/06/01/beyond-freedom-and-dignity/

Buti, S., Rindi, B., & Werner, I. M. (2017). Dark pool trading strategies, market quality and welfare. *Journal of Financial Economics, 124*(2), 244–265.

Cantwell, J., Dunning, J. H., & Lundan, S. M. (2010). An evolutionary approach to understanding international business activity: The co-evolution of MNEs and the institutional environment. *Journal of International Business Studies, 41*(4), 567–586.

Cockburn, A. (2015). *Kill chain: Drones and the rise of high-tech assassins*. Verso.

Cunningham, I. (2016). Non-profits and the 'hollowed out' state: The transformation of working conditions through personalizing social care services during an era of austerity. *Work, Employment and Society, 30*(4), 649–668.

Curtis, A. (1992). Pandora's Box, Part 4: Goodbye Mrs Ant. *British Broadcasting Company (BBC) Channel Two.*

Davis, M. (2002). *Late Victorian holocausts: El Niño famines and the making of the third world*. Verso Books.

Davis, M. (2006). *City of Quartz: Excavating the future in Los Angeles* (New ed.). Verso Books.

Dostoevsky, F. ([1864] 1960). Notes from the underground. In *Three short novels of Dostoevsky* (Constance Garnett, Trans.). Doubleday and Co.

Dostoevsky, F. ([1866] 1950). *Crime and punishment* (Constance Garnett, Trans.). The Modern Library.

Edwards, C. (2011). The singularity isn't even close: Why Ray Kurzweil's predictions about the future are flawed. *Skeptic, 16*(2), 20–22.

Elias, N. (1969). *The civilizing process: The history of manners* (Vol. 1). Blackwell.

Elias, N. (1982). *The civilizing process: State formation and civilization* (Vol. 2). Blackwell.

Elias, N. (1995). Technization and civilization. *Theory Culture and Society, 12*(3), 7–42.

Elias, N. (2000). *The civilizing process: Sociogenetic and psychogenetic investigations* (Rev. ed.). Blackwell.

Foucault, M. (1977). *Discipline and punish: The birth of the prison* (A. Sheridan, Trans.). Penguin Books.

Gai, K., Qiu, M., & Sun, X. (2018). A survey on FinTech. *Journal of Network and Computer Applications, 103*, 262–273.

Galbraith, J. K. (1967). *The new industrial state*. Houghton Mifflin.

Gibran, K. (1962). *A second treasury of Kahlil Gibran* (A. R. Ferris, Trans.). Citadel Books.

Graff, M., Kenwood, A. G., & Lougheed, A. L. (2013). *Growth of the international economy, 1820–2015*. Routledge.

Hedges, C. (2010). A brave new dystopia. *Truthdig.com*. https://www.truthdig.com/articles/2011-a-brave-new-dystopia/
Herrnstein, R. J. (1977). The evolution of behaviorism. *American Psychologist, 32*, 593–603.
Hollis, C. (1956). *A study of George Orwell: The man and his works*. Henry Regnery Company.
Huxley, A. ([1949] 2012, March 6, Tuesday). 1984 v. Brave New World. *Letters of note*. https://lettersofnote.com/2012/03/06/1984-v-brave-new-world/
Lewis, M. (2011). *The big short: Inside the doomsday machine*. Penguin.
Lichtheim, G. (1972). *Europe in the twentieth century*. Praeger Publishers.
Lyotard, J. (1984). *The postmodern condition: A report on knowledge* (G. Bennington & B. Massumi, Trans.). University of Minnesota Press.
Kapur, A., Macleod, N., & Singh, N. (2005). *Plutonomy: Buying luxury, explaining global imbalances*. Citigroup Research. Industry note.
Kurzweil, R. (2005). *The singularity is near: When humans transcend biology*. Viking.
Marcuse, H. (1964). *One-dimensional man*. Beacon Press.
Minsky, H. P. (1980). Capitalist financial processes and the instability of capitalism. *Journal of Economic Issues, 14*(2), 505–523.
Minsky, H. P. (2016). *Can it happen again?: Essays on instability and finance*. Routledge.
Mirowksi, P. (1989). *More heat than light: Economics as social physics, physics as nature's economics*. Cambridge University Press.
Mirowksi, P. (2001). *Machine dreams: Economics becomes a cyborg science*. Cambridge University Press.
Mitchell, W., Wray, L. R., & Watts, M. (2016). *Modern monetary theory and practice: An introductory text*. Centre of Full Employment and Equity.
Moore, J. W. (2016). Introduction: Anthropocene or capitalocene? Nature, history, and the crisis of capitalism. In J. W. Moore (Ed.), *Anthropocene or capitalocene? Nature, history, and the crisis of capitalism*. PM Press.
Morris, I. (2014). *War! What is it good for? Conflict and the progress of civilization from primates to robots*. Farrer, Straus and Giroux.
Murray, N. (2002). *Aldous Huxley: A biography*. Martin's Press.
Nicoletti, B., Nicoletti, W., & Weis. (2017). *Future of FinTech*. Palgrave Macmillan.
Oreskes, N., & Conway, E. M. (2010). *Merchants of doubt: How a handful of scientists obscured the truth on issues from tobacco smoke to global warming*. Bloomsbury Press.
Partnoy, F. (2003). *Infectious greed: How deceit and risk corrupted the financial markets* (Rev. and updated ed.). Profile Books.
Prado, C. G. (2017). Post-truth. *The Philosophers' Magazine, 79*, 27–32.

Reeves, R. (2001). *President Nixon: Alone in the White House*. Simon and Schuster.

Rosling, H., Rosling, O., & Rönnlund, A. R. (2018). *Factfulness: Ten reasons we're wrong about the world—And why things are better than you think*. Flatiron Books.

Shah, H. (2011). Accountability: Has it been hollowed out in the modern state? *Journal of Political Studies, 18*(1), 77.

Skelcher, C. (2000). Changing images of the state: Overloaded, hollowed-out, congested. *Public Policy and Administration, 15*(3), 3–19.

Skinner, B. F. (1971). *Beyond freedom and dignity*. Knopf.

Snow, C. P. (1963). *The two cultures: And a second look: An expanded version*. Cambridge University Press.

Solzhenitsyn, A. I. (1974). *The gulag archipelago, 1918–1956: An experiment in literary investigation*. Harper and Row.

Stanford, P. K. (2015). Instrumentalism: Global, local, and scientific. In P. Humphreys (Ed.), *The Oxford handbook of philosophy of science*. Oxford University Press.

Suzman, J. (2017). *Affluence without abundance: The disappearing world of the Bushmen*. Bloomsbury Publishing USA.

Urbinato, D. (1994). London's historic "pea-soupers" (smog in London, England). *EPA Journal, 20*(1–2), 44–45.

Watts, A. (1957). *The way of Zen*. Vintage Books.

Bibliography

Acemoglu, D. (2008). Growth and institutions. In L. E. Blume & S. N. Durlauf (Eds.) *The new Palgrave dictionary of economics* (2nd ed.). Palgrave Macmillan.

Acemoglu, D. (2012). Introduction to economic growth. *Journal of Economic Theory, 147*(2), 545–550.

Acemoglu, D., Johnson, S., & Robinson, J. A. (2001). The colonial origins of comparative development: An empirical investigation. *American Economic Review, 91*(5), 1369–1401.

Acemoglu, D., Johnson, S., & Robinson, J. A. (2002). Reversal of fortune: Geography and institutions in the making of the modern world income distribution. *The Quarterly Journal of Economics, 117*(4), 1231–1294.

Acemoglu, D., & Robinson, J. A. (2006). *Economic origins of dictatorship and democracy*. Cambridge University Press.

Adair-Toteff, C. (1995). Ferdinand Tonnies: Utopian visionary. *Sociological Theory, 13*(1), 58–65.

Adalet, M. (2003). *Fundamentals, capital flows and capital flight: The German banking crisis of 1931* (Working Paper). University of California.

Addison, P., & Crang, J. A. (Eds.). (2006). *Firestorm: The bombing of Dresden 1945*. Random House.

Adelman, J. (2009). *Sovereignty and revolution in the Iberian Atlantic*. Princeton University Press.

Ahlskog, J. (2010). The political economy of colonisation: Carl Bernhard Wadström's case for abolition and civilisation. *Nordic Journal for Eighteenth-Century Studies, 7*, 146–167.

C. Gordon, *Many Possible Worlds*,
https://doi.org/10.1007/978-981-19-9281-0

Ahluwalia, M. (2002). Economic reforms in India since 1991: Has gradualism worked? *The Journal of Economic Perspectives, 16*(3), 67–88.

Aiginger, K. (2009). Comparing the current crisis to the Great Depression. *OECD Nero Conference*, Paris, September 21, presentation (OECD_crises_210909_short.ppt)

Aldrich, R. (1996). *Greater France: A history of French overseas expansion.* Macmillan International Higher Education.

Allen, L., & Belt, F. H. (1998). *The ABC-CLIO world history companion to capitalism.* ABC-CLIO.

Allen, R. C. (2009a). *The British industrial revolution in global perspective.* Cambridge University Press.

Allen, R. C. (2009b). The industrial revolution in miniature: The spinning jenny in Britain, France, and India. *The Journal of Economic History, 69*(4), 901–927.

Allen, R. C. (2009c). Engels' pause: Technical change, capital accumulation, and inequality in the British industrial revolution. *Explorations in Economic History, 46*(4), 418–435.

Allen, R. C. (2011). *Global economic history: A very short introduction.* Oxford University Press.

Almunia, M., Benetrix, A., Eichengreen, B., O'Rourke, K. H., & Rua, G. (2010). From great depression to great credit crisis: Similarities, differences and lessons. *Economic Policy, 25*(62), 219–265.

Alsan, M., & Goldin, C. (2019). Watersheds in child mortality: The role of effective water and sewerage infrastructure, 1880–1920. *Journal of Political Economy, 127*(2), 586–638.

Alvarez, E., Bogart, D., Satchell, M., Shaw-Taylor, L., & You, X. (2017). *Railways and growth: Evidence from nineteenth century England and Wales.* Cambridge University.

Amin, S. (2000). The political economy of the twentieth century. *Monthly Review (June), 52*(2), 1–17.

Aminzade, R. (1984). Reinterpreting capitalist industrialization: A study of nineteenth-century France: Proletarianization, small-scale industry and capitalist industrialization. *Social History, 9*(3), 329–350.

Anderson, B. (1991). *Imagined communities: Reflections on the origin and spread of nationalism* (Revised edition). Verso Books.

Angeles, L. (2008). GDP per capita or real wages? Making sense of conflicting views on pre-industrial Europe. *Explorations in Economic History, 45*(2), 147–163.

Anker-Sorensen, L. (2016). Financial engineering as an alternative veil for the corporate group. *European Company Law, 13*(5), 158–166.

Antonelli, C. (1997). The economics of path-dependence in industrial organization. *International Journal of Industrial Organization, 15*(6), 643–675.

Appy, C. G. (2015). *American reckoning: The Vietnam War and our national identity*. Penguin Books.

Aquinas, T. ([1237] 1997). Summa Theologica. In A. C. Pegis (Ed.), *Basic writings of St. Thomas Aquinas* (Vol. 2). Hackett Publishing.

Araghi, F. (2010). The end of "Cheap Ecology" and the crisis of "Long Keynesianism." *Economic and Political Weekly, 45*(4), 39–41.

Archer, M. (2002). *Art since 1960* (2nd ed.). Thames and Hudson.

Aristotle. ([ca. 350 BCE] 2000). *Nicomachean ethics*. (R. Crisp, Trans. and Ed.). Cambridge University Press.

Arnason, J. P. (2003) *Civilizations in dispute: Historical questions and theoretical traditions*. Brill.

Arnason, J. P. (2009). Civilizational analysis: A paradigm in the making. In R. Holton & W. R. Nasson (Eds.), *Encyclopedia of life support systems: World civilizations and history of human development*. EOLSS Publications (in cooperation with UNESCO).

Arnason, J. P. (2016). Revolutions, transformations, civilisations: Prolegomena to a paradigm reorientation. In J. P. Arnason & M. Hrubec (Eds.), *Social transformations and revolutions* (pp. 27–55). Edinburgh University Press.

Aronson, E., Wilson, T. D., & Akert, R. M. (2009). *Social psychology* (7th ed.). Prentice Hall.

Asbury, H. (1968). *The great illusion*. Greenwood.

Auden, W. H. (1939). September 1, 1939. http://poemdujour.com/Sept1.1939.html

Audoin, C. (2001). *The measurement of time*. Cambridge University Press.

August, T. (1986). Locating the age of imperialism. *Itinerario, 10*(2), 85–98.

Austen, R. A., & Headrick, D. (1983). The role of technology in the African past. *African Studies Review, 26*(3–4), 163–184.

Aya, R. (1978). Norbert Elias and "the civilizing process." *Theory and Society, 5*(2), 219–228.

B.F. Skinner Foundation. (2021). Beyond Freedom and Dignity. *Blog Large* (May 31). https://www.bfskinner.org/2021/06/01/beyond-freedom-and-dignity/

Bahçekapili, H. G., Yilmaz, O., & Sevi, B. (2019). *Evolutionary perspectives on religion*. Unpublished working paper.

Bailyn, B. (1967). *The ideological origins of the American Revolution*. Belknap Press.

Bairoch, P. (1976). Europe's Gross national product: 1800–1975. *Journal of European Economic History, 5*(2), 273–340.

Bairoch, P. (1982). International industrialization levels from 1750 to 1980. *Journal of European Economic History, 11*(2), 269–333.

Bairoch, P. (1988). *Cities and economic development: From the dawn of history to the present*. University of Chicago Press.

Bairoch, P. (1995). *Economics and world history: Myths and paradoxes*. University of Chicago Press.
Bairoch, P., & Goertz, G. (1986). Factors of urbanisation in the nineteenth century developed countries: A descriptive and econometric analysis. *Urban Studies, 23*(4), 285–305.
Bairoch, P., & Kozul-Wright, R. (1998). Globalization myths: Some historical reflections on integration, industrialization and growth in the world economy. In R. Kozul-Wright & R. Rowthorn (Eds.), *Transnational corporations and the global economy* (pp. 37–68). Macmillan Press.
Baker, D. (2006). The political economy of fascism: Myth or reality, or myth and reality? *New Political Economy, 11*(2), 227–250.
Baltzly, D. (2019). Stoicism. In E. N. Zalta (Ed.), *The Stanford encyclopedia of philosophy* (Spring 2019 Edition), https://plato.stanford.edu/archives/spr2019/entries/stoicism/.
Banti, A. M. (2020). *The nation of the Risorgimento: Kinship, sanctity, and honour in the origins of unified Italy*. Routledge.
Barber, W. J. (1970). *A history of economic thought*. Penguin Books.
Barbrook, R., & Cameron, A. (1996). The Californian Ideology. *Science as Culture, 6*(1), 44–72.
Barles, S. (2014). History of waste management and the social and cultural representations of waste. In M. Agnoletti & N. Serneri (Eds.), *The basic environmental history* (pp. 199–226). Springer.
Barr, A. H. Jr. (1946). *Picasso: Fifty years of his art*. The Museum of Modern Art.
Barr, N. (1988). The Phillips machine. *LSE Quarterly, 2*(4), 305–337.
Barraclough, G. (1967). *An introduction to contemporary history*. Pelican.
Barro, R. J., & McCleary, R. (2019). *The wealth of religions*. Princeton University Press.
Bartholomew, J. G. (1914). *An atlas of economic geography*. Oxford University Press.
Bassino, J. P., Broadberry, S., Fukao, K., Gupta, B., & Takashima, M. (2019). Japan and the great divergence, 730–1874. *Explorations in Economic History, 72*, 1–22.
Baudrillard, J. (1994). *Simulacra & simulation* (S. F. Glaser, Trans.). University of Michigan Press.
Bauernschuster, S., Driva, A., & Hornung, E. (2018). Bismarck's health insurance and the mortality decline. *IZA Institute of Labor Economics Discussion Papers*, No. 11628.
Baum, B. (2001). Freedom, power and public opinion: J. S. Mill on the public sphere. *History of Political Thought, 22*(3) (Autumn), 501–524.
Bauman, Z. (2000). *Modernity and the Holocaust*. Cornell University Press.
Bauman, Z. (2013). *Liquid modernity*. John Wiley & Sons.

Baumard, N. (2019). Psychological origins of the industrial revolution. *Behavioral and Brain Sciences, 42*, e189.

Baxandall, R. F., & Ewen, E. (2000). *Picture windows: How the suburbs happened*. Basic Books.

Bayly, C. A. (2004). *The birth of the modern world, 1780–1914: Global connections and comparisons*. Blackwell Publishing.

Beard, M. (2018). *Women & power: A manifesto* (updated). Profile Books.

Becker, G. S. (1971). *The Economics of discrimination*. University of Chicago Press.

Becker, J. F. (1961). Adam Smith's theory of social science. *Southern Economic Journal, 28*(1), 13–21.

Becker, S. O., Hornung, E., & Woessmann, L. (2011). Education and catch-up in the Industrial Revolution. *American Economic Journal: Macroeconomics, 3*(3), 92–126.

Beckert, S. (2015). *Empire of cotton: A global history*. Vintage.

Bell, D. (1960). *The end of ideology: On the exhaustion of political ideas in the Fifties*. Free Press.

Bell, D. (1976). The coming of the post-industrial society. *The Educational Forum, 40*(4), 574–579.

Bierman, H. (1999). The reasons stocks crashed in 1929. *The Journal of Investing, 8*(1), 11–18.

Berberian, H. (2019). *Roving revolutionaries: Armenians and the connected revolutions in the Russian, Iranian, and Ottoman worlds*. University of California Press.

Berg, A. S. (2013). *Wilson*. G.P. Putnam's Sons.

Berg, M., & Hudson, P. (1994). Growth and change: A comment on the Crafts-Harley view of the Industrial Revolution. *The Economic History Review, 47*(1), 147–149.

Berger, H., & Spoerer, M. (2001). Economic crises and the European revolutions of 1848. *The Journal of Economic History, 61*(2), 293–326.

Bergh, J., & Eichhorn, J. (2019). Introduction. In J. Eichhorn & J. Bergh (Eds.), *Lowering the voting age to 16: Learning from real experiences worldwide*. Springer Nature.

Bernanke, B. (1983). Nonmonetary effects of the financial crisis in the propagation of the Great Depression. *American Economic Review, 73*(3), 257–276.

Bernanke, B. (1995). The macroeconomics of the Great Depression: A comparative approach. *Journal of Money, Credit and Banking, 27*(1), 1–28.

Bernanke, B., & James, H. (1991). The gold standard, deflation, and financial crisis in the Great Depression: An international comparison. In R. G. Hubbard (Ed.), *Financial markets and financial crises* (pp. 33–68). University of Chicago Press.

Bernstein, M. A., & Wilson, M. R. (2011). New perspectives on the history of the military-industrial complex. *Enterprise & Society, 12*(1), 1–9.

Bértola, L., & Rodríguez Weber, J. (2015). Latin American economic history: Looking backwards for the future. In F. Boldizzini & P. Hudson (Eds.), *Routledge handbook of global economic history*. Routledge.

Best, A., Hanhimäki, J. M., Maiolo, J. A., & Schulze, K. E. (2004). *International history of the twentieth century and beyond* (2nd ed.). Routledge.

Bevins, V. (2020). *The Jakarta method: Washington's Anticommunist crusade and the mass murder program that shaped our world*. Public Affairs.

Bevir, M. (2001). The long nineteenth century in intellectual history. *Journal of Victorian Culture, 6*(2), 313–335.

Bezanson, A. (1922). The early use of the term Industrial Revolution. *Quarterly Journal of Economics, 36*(2), 343–349.

Blaut, J. M. (1999). Environmentalism and Eurocentrism. *Geographical Review, 89*(3), 391–408.

Bleich, E. (2005). The legacies of history? Colonization and immigrant integration in Britain and France. *Theory and Society, 34*(2), 171–195.

Blodget, H. (2014). The historical change in how we spend our time. *World Economic Forum Agenda*. https://weforum.org/agenda/2014/12/the-historical-change-in-how-we-spend-our-time

Blum, J., Cameron, R. E., & Barnes, T. G. (1970). *The European world: A history*. Little, Brown.

Blum, M., Eloranta, J., & Osinsky, P. (2014). Organization of war economies. In U. Daniel, P. Gatrell, H. J. Janz, J. Keene, A. Kramer & B. Nasson (Eds.), *1914–1918-online: International encyclopedia of the First World War*. Freie Universität Berlin. https://encyclopedia.1914-1918-online.net/article/organization_of_war_economies

Boarini, R., & d'Ercole, M. M. (2013). Going beyond GDP: An OECD perspective. *Fiscal Studies, 34*(3), 289–314.

Boden, R. (2008). Cold war economics: Soviet aid to Indonesia. *Journal of Cold War Studies, 10*(3), 110–128.

Bogart, D. (2013). *The transportation revolution in industrializing Britain: A survey* (p. 121306). University of California-Irvine.

Bogart, D., & Chaudhary, L. (2013). Engines of growth: The productivity advance of Indian railways, 1874–1912. *The Journal of Economic History, 73*(2), 339–370.

Bolt, J., Inklaar, R., de Jong, H., & van Zanden, J. L. (2018). *Rebasing Maddison: New income comparisons and the shape of long-run economic development*. Maddison Project Working Paper 10 (Maddison Project Database, version 2018).

Bolt, J., & van Zanden, J. L. (2020). Maddison style estimates of the evolution of the world economy. A new 2020 update. *Maddison Project Database*, version

2020. https://www.rug.nl/ggdc/historicaldevelopment/maddison/releases/maddison-project-database-2020

Bongaarts, J., & Potter, R. E. (2013). *Fertility, biology, and behavior: An analysis of the proximate determinants*. Academic Press.

Bongiorno, F. (2011). Australian labour history: Contexts, trends and influences. *Labour History, 100*, 1–18.

Booth, A. (2001). New revisionists and the Keynesian era in British economic policy. *The Economic History Review, 54*(2), 346–366.

Boorstin, D. (1971). *The image: A guide to pseudo-events in America*. Atheneum.

Bordo, M. D. (1993). The Bretton Woods international monetary system: A historical overview. In M. D. Bordo & B. Eichengreen (Eds.), *A retrospective on the Bretton Woods System: Lessons for international monetary reform*(pp. 3–108). University of Chicago Press.

Bordo, M. D., & Meissner, C. M. (2007). *Foreign capital and economic growth in the first era of globalization*. National Bureau of Economic Research, Working Paper 13577.

Bordo, M. D., & White, E. N. (1991). A tale of two currencies: British and French finance during the Napoleonic Wars. *The Journal of Economic History, 51*(2), 303–316.

Boserup, E. (1965). *The conditions of agricultural growth: The economics of agrarian change under population pressure*. Allen & Unwin.

Bosker, M., Buringh, E., & Van Zanden, J. L. (2013). From Baghdad to London: Unraveling urban development in Europe, the Middle East, and North Africa, 800–1800. *Review of Economics and Statistics, 95*(4), 1418–1437.

Bowers, B. (1982). *A history of electric light & power*. P. Peregrinus in association with the [London] Science Museum.

Bowers, B. (1998). *Lengthening the day*. Oxford University Press.

Boyer, G. R. (1998). The historical background of the Communist Manifesto. *Journal of Economic Perspectives, 12*(4), 151–174.

Bradbury, R. ([1953] 2012). *Fahrenheit 451*. Simon and Schuster.

Brainerd, E., & Siegler, M. (2003). *The economic effects of the 1918 influenza epidemic*. Centre for Economic Policy Research (CEPR) Working paper No. 3791.

Bråkenhielm, C. R. (2002). The idea of Europe in the perspective of world views and values. An Introduction. *SPIEL, 21*(2), 187–202.

Brandt, L., Ma, D., & Rawski, T. (2014). From divergence to convergence: Reevaluating the history behind China's economic boom. *Journal of Economic Literature, 52*(1), 45–123.

Braudel, F. ([1979] 1992). *The structures of everyday life: The limits of the possible*. University of California Press.

Braverman, H. (1974). *Labor and monopoly capital: The degradation of work in the twentieth century*. Monthly Review Press.
Briggs, A. (1955). *Victorian people: A reassessment of persons and themes, 1851–1867*. University of Chicago Press.
Brinton, C. ([1938] 1965). *The Anatomy of revolution* (Revised ed.). Vintage Books.
Broadberry, S. (2013). Accounting for the great divergence. *Voxeu*. https://voxeu.org/article/accounting-great-divergence
Broadberry, S., Campbell, B. M., Klein, A., Overton, M., & van Leeuwen, B. (2015). *British economic growth, 1270–1870*. Cambridge University Press.
Broadberry, S., & Harrison, M. (Eds.). (2005). *The economics of World War I*. Cambridge University Press.
Brown, D. (1970). *Bury my heart at Wounded Knee*. Henry Holt and Company.
Brubaker, R. (2017). Why populism? *Theory and Society, 46*(5), 357–385.
Brunton, B. G. (1988). Institutional origins of the military-industrial complex. *Journal of Economic Issues, 22*(2), 599–606.
Buchanan, T. (2002). Anti-fascism and democracy in the 1930s. *European History Quarterly, 32*(1), 39–57.
Burris, B. H. (1989). Technocracy and the transformation of organizational control. *The Social Science Journal, 26*(3), 313–333.
Buti, S., Rindi, B., & Werner, I. M. (2017). Dark pool trading strategies, market quality and welfare. *Journal of Financial Economics, 124*(2), 244–265.
Butler, E. (2015). *Classical Liberalism: A primer*. Institute of Economic Affairs/London Publishing Partnership.
Byrd, R. H. (1971). *Social Darwinism and British imperialism, 1870–1900* (Doctoral dissertation) Texas Tech University.
Byrne, P. (2013). *Natural religion and the nature of religion: The legacy of deism*. Routledge.
Cain, N., & Glynn, S. (1985). Imperial relations under strain: The British-Australian debt contretemps of 1933. *Australian Economic History Review, 25*(1), 39–58.
Caldwell, B. (2008). *Hayek's challenge*. University of Chicago Press.
Calomiris, C. W. (1993). Financial factors in the Great Depression. *Journal of Economic Perspectives, 7*(2), 61–85.
Calomiris, C. W., & Mason, J. R. (1997). Contagion and bank failures during the Great Depression: The June 1932 Chicago banking panic. *American Economic Review, 87*(5), 863–883.
Campbell, K. L., & Wood, J. W. (1988). Fertility in traditional societies. In P. Diggory, M. Potts & S. Teper (Eds.), *Natural human fertility: Studies in biology, economy and society*. Palgrave Macmillan.
Cannadine, D. (1984). The present and the past in the English industrial revolution 1880–1980. *Past and Present, 103*(1), 131–172.

Cantwell, J., Dunning, J. H., & Lundan, S. M. (2010). An evolutionary approach to understanding international business activity: The co-evolution of MNEs and the institutional environment. *Journal of International Business Studies, 41*(4), 567–586.

Capaldi, N. (1998). *The Enlightenment project in the analytic conversation*. Springer.

Carcopino, J. (2003). *Daily life in ancient Rome: The people and the city at the height of the empire*. Yale University Press.

Cárdenas, M., & Helfand S. (2011). Latin American economic development. In S. N. Durlauf & L. E. Blume (Eds.), *The New Palgrave dictionary of economics, online edition*. Palgrave MacMillan.

Carlos, A. M., & Frank, L. (1992). The profitability of early Canadian railroads: Evidence from the Grand Trunk and Great Western Railway Companies. In C. Goldin & H. Rockoff (Eds.), *Strategic factors in nineteenth century American economic history* (pp. 401–426). University of Chicago Press.

Carreras, A., & Josephson, C. (2010). Chapter 2: Aggregate growth, 1870–1914: Growing at the production frontier. In S. Broadberry & K. H. O'Rourke (Eds.), *The Cambridge economic history of modern Europe: Volume 2, 1870 to the present*. Cambridge University Press.

Carson, R. (1962). *Silent spring*. Houghton Mifflin Company.

Carson, R. L. (1977). *Comparative economic systems*. M.E. Sharpe.

Case, A., & Deaton, A. (2020). *Deaths of despair and the future of capitalism*. Princeton University Press.

Case, J. H. (1922). Preparation for war and the Liberty Loans. *The Annals of the American Academy of Political and Social Science, 99*(1), 121–129.

Carugati, F., & Levi, M. (2021). *A moral political economy: Present, past, and future*. Cambridge University Press.

Cebeci, M. (2019). Deconstructing the EU's "standards of civilisation." *Uluslararası İlişkiler/International Relations, 16*(64), 77–91.

Cerny, P. G. (1971). The mismatched President: LBJ and the USA. *Government and Opposition, 6*(2), 255–262.

Ceruzzi, P. E. (2005). Moore's law and technological determinism: Reflections on the history of technology. *Technology and Culture, 46*(3), 584–593.

Chakrabarty, D. (1998). Minority histories, subaltern pasts. *Economic and Political Weekly, 33*(9), 473–479.

Chakrabarty, D. (2009). The climate of history: Four theses. *Critical Inquiry, 35*(2), 197–222.

Chandler, A. D. (1977). *The visible hand*. University of Chicago Press.

Chandler, A. D. (1980). Industrial revolutions and institutional arrangements. *Bulletin of the American Academy of Arts and Sciences, 33*(8), 33–50.

Chandler, A. D. (1992). Organizational capabilities and the economic history of the industrial enterprise. *Journal of Economic Perspectives, 6*(3), 79–100.

Chapman, G. (1962). *Third Republic of France: The first phase, 1871–1894*. Palgrave Macmillan.

Chatterjee, P. (1995). *The nation and its fragments: Colonial and postcolonial histories*. Oxford University Press.

Cherny, R. W. (1997). *American politics in the Gilded Age, 1868–1900*. Harlan Davidson.

Chilosi, D., & Federico, G. (2015). Early globalizations: The integration of Asia in the world economy, 1800–1938. *Explorations in Economic History, 57*, 1–18.

Chilosi, D., Murphy, T. E., Studer, R., & Tunçer, A. C. (2013). Europe's many integrations: Geography and grain markets, 1620–1913. *Explorations in Economic History, 50*(1), 46–68.

Chomsky, N. (1991). *Media control: The spectacular achievements of propaganda* (1st ed.). A Seven Stories Press, published in association with Open Media.

Choudhri, E. U., & Kochin, L. A. (1980). The exchange rate and the international transmission of business cycle disturbances: Some evidence from the Great Depression. *Journal of Money, Credit and Banking*, *12*(4), Part 1, 565–574.

Chown, J. F., & Chown, J. (1994). *A history of money: From AD 800*. Routledge.

Christodoulakis, N. (2015). *How crises shaped economic ideas and policies*. Springer.

Clarence-Smith, W. G. (2012). The industrialization of the developing world and its impact on labour relations, 1840s to 1940s. In K. Hofmeester & P. de Zwart (Eds.), *Colonialism, institutional change and shifts in global labour relations* (pp. 29–66). Amsterdam University Press.

Clark, C. (2012). After 1848: The European revolution in government. *Transactions of the Royal Historical Society, 22*, 171–197.

Clark, G. (1994). Factory discipline. *Journal of Economic History, 54*(1), 128–163.

Clark, G. (2001). *The secret history of the Industrial Revolution*. Unpublished manuscript, University of California, Davis.

Clark, G. (2007). *A farewell to alms: A brief economic history of the world*. Princeton University Press.

Clark, G. (2010). *The consumer revolution: turning point in human history, or statistical artifact?* University California-Davis, Working Paper.

Clark, G., & Jacks, D. (2007). Coal and the industrial revolution, 1700–1869. *European Review of Economic History, 11*(1), 39–72.

Clark, K. (1969). *Civilization: A personal view*. Harper and Row.

Clayton, E. (2005). Aristotle: Politics. In J. Fieser & B. Dowden (Eds.), *Internet encyclopedia of philosophy*.

Cleveland, W. L., & Bunton, M. (2018). *A history of the modern Middle East*. Routledge.

Coase, R. H. (1960). The problem of social cost. *Journal of Law and Economics, 3*, 1–44.

Coatsworth, J. H. (1981). *Growth against development: The economic impact of railroads in Porfirian Mexico*. Northern Illinois University Press.

Cobban, A. (1964). *The social interpretation of the French Revolution*. Cambridge University Press.

Cockburn, A. (2015). *Kill chain: Drones and the rise of high-tech assassins*. Verso.

Cohen, E. A. (2004). History and the hyperpower. *Foreign Affairs, 83*(4), 49–63.

Cohen, I. B. (1976). The eighteenth-century origins of the concept of Scientific Revolution. *Journal of the History of Ideas, 37*(2), 257–288.

Cohen, L. (2003). *A consumers' republic: The politics of mass consumption in postwar America*. Knopf.

Colas, A. (2016). *Review of international studies, 42*(5), 840–857.

Conrad, S. (2003). Entangled memories: Versions of the past in Germany and Japan, 1945–2001. *Journal of Contemporary History, 38*(1), 85–99.

Constantine, C. (2017). Economic structures, institutions and economic performance. *Economic Structures, 6*(1), 1–18.

Conversi, D. (2018). In the shadow of the Belle Époque: Progress, decadence, and the rush to war. *The European Legacy, 23*(5), 564–570.

Coontz, S. (1992). *The way we never were: American families and the nostalgia trap*. Basic Books.

Cooper, R. N. (1992). Fettered to gold? Economic policy in the interwar period. *Journal of Economic Literature, 30*(4), 2120–2128.

Cosner, T. L., & Larson, G. L. (1980). Social fabric theory and the youth culture. *Adolescence, 15*(57), 99.

Cox, J. (2014). World's elites gather for Davos 2014: Contraception key in climate change fight: Gore and Gates. CNBC January 24. https://www.cnbc.com/2014/01/24/contraception-key-in-climate-change-fight-gore-and-gates.html

Cox, W. (2015). 500 years of GDP: A tale of two countries. *New Geography*. https://www.newgeography.com/content/005050-500-years-gdp-a-tale-two-countries

Crafts, N. (1995). The golden age of economic growth in western Europe, 1950–1973. *Economic History Review, 48*(3), 429–447.

Crafts, N. (1998). Forging ahead and falling behind: The rise and relative decline of the first industrial nation. *Journal of Economic Perspectives, 12*(2), 193–210.

Crafts, N. (2004). Productivity growth in the industrial revolution: A new growth accounting perspective. *Journal of Economic History, 64*(2), 521–535.

Crafts, N. (2020). *Slow real wage growth during the industrial revolution: productivity paradox or pro-rich growth?* Warwick Economics Research Papers #1268 (May).

Crafts, N. F., & Harley, C. K. (1992). Output growth and the British industrial revolution: A restatement of the Crafts-Harley view. *Economic History Review, 45*(4), 703–730.

Cranston, M. (2020). Ideology. In *Encyclopaedia Britannica*, https://www.britannica.com/topic/ideology-society, Accessed November 4, 2020.

Cromdal, J. (2006). Socialization. In K. Brown (Ed.), *Encyclopedia of language and linguistics* (pp. 462–466). Elsevier.

Cronon, W. (1987). Revisiting the vanishing frontier: The legacy of Frederick Jackson Turner. *The Western Historical Quarterly, 18*(2), 157–176.

Cuff, T. (2004). Historical anthropometrics. In R. Whaples (Ed.), EH.Net Encyclopedia, http://eh.net/encyclopedia/historical-anthropometrics/

Cunningham, I. (2016). Non-profits and the 'hollowed out' state: The transformation of working conditions through personalizing social care services during an era of austerity. *Work, Employment and Society, 30*(4), 649–668.

Curran, J., & Seaton, J. (2009). *Power without responsibility*. Routledge.

Curtis, A. (1992). Pandora's Box, Part 4: Goodbye Mrs Ant. *British Broadcasting Company (BBC) Channel Two.*

Custers, P. (2010). Military Keynesianism today: An innovative discourse. *Race & Class, 51*(4), 79–94.

Cypher, J. M. (2015). The origins and evolution of military Keynesianism in the United States. *Journal of Post Keynesian Economics, 38*(3), 449–476.

Dallago, B. (2004). Comparative economic systems and the new comparative economics. *The European Journal of Comparative Economics, 1*(1), 59–86.

Daniels, R. (2015). *Franklin D. Roosevelt: Road to the new deal, 1882–1939*. University of Illinois Press.

Dant, U. (2006). Material civilization: Things and society. *British Journal of Sociology, 57*(2), 289–308.

Daszkiewicz, W. (2007). Greek and Roman roots of European civilisation. *Studia Gilsoniana, 6*(3), 381–404.

Daudin, G., Morys, M., & O'Rourke, K. H. (2010). Globalization, 1870–1914. In S. Broadberry & K. H. O'Rourke (Eds.), *The Cambridge economic history of modern Europe: Volume 2, 1870 to the present* (pp. 5–29). Cambridge University Press.

David, P. A. (1969). Transportation innovations and economic growth: Professor Fogel on and off the rails. *Economic History Review, 22*(3), 506–525.

Davies, C. (2010). Jokes as the truth about Soviet socialism. *Folklore: Electronic Journal of Folklore*, (46), 9–32.

Davies, J. C. (1962). Toward a theory of revolution. *American Sociological Review, 27*(1), 5–19.

Davies, J. C. (1974). The J-curve and power struggle theories of collective violence. *American Sociological Review, 39*(4), 607–610.

Davies, N. (1994). The misunderstood war. *The New York Review of Books,* (June 9 issue).

Davies, N. (1996). *Europe: A history*. Random House.

Davies, N. (2006). *No simple victory: World War II in Europe 1939–1945*. Penguin Books.

Davis, M. (2002). *Late Victorian holocausts: El Niño famines and the making of the third world*. Verso Books.

Davis, M. (2006). *City of Quartz: Excavating the future in Los Angeles* (New Edition). Verso Books.

Davis, M. (2018). "Among the ordinary people": New Left involvement in working-class political mobilization 1956–68. *History Workshop Journal, 86*, 133–159.

Dawkins, R. (1976). *The selfish gene*. Oxford University Press.

De Boer, J. Z., & Sanders, D. T. (2005). *Earthquakes in human history: The far-reaching effects of seismic disruptions*. Princeton University Press.

De Bruhl, M. (2010). *Firestorm: Allied airpower and the destruction of Dresden*. Random House.

De Jong, H. J., & Palma, N. (2018). *Historical national accounting*. Maddison-Project Working Paper WP-12.

De la Escosura. (2005). *Colonial independence and economic backwardness in Latin America*. London School of Economics Working Paper 10/05.

De La Escosura, L. P. (2007). When did Latin America fall behind? In S. Edwards, G. Esquivel & G. Márquez (Eds.), *The decline of Latin American economies: Growth, institutions, and crises* (pp. 15–58). University of Chicago Press.

De la Escosura, L. P. (2009). Lost decades? Economic performance in post-independence Latin America. *Journal of Latin American Studies, 41*(2), 279–307.

De Vos, J. (2010). Christopher Lasch's the culture of narcissism: The failure of a critique of psychological politics. *Theory & Psychology, 20*(4), 528–548.

De Vos, J. (2012). Narcissism and the DSM-V: Christopher Lasch and the political leftovers of the debate. *Journal of Culture and the Unconscious, 8*(2), 49–61.

De Vries, J. (1984). *European urbanisation 1500–1800*. Methuen.

De Vries, J. (1994). The industrious revolution and the industrial revolution. *Journal of Economic History, 54*(2), 249–270.

De Tocqueville, A. ([1856] 1955). *The Old Regime and the French Revolution*. Anchor Books.

Dean, M. (2002). Lord Young of Dartington. *The Guardian*, January 16.

Deane, P. (1968). *Revolutionizing the sciences: European knowledge in transition, 1500–1700* (3rd ed.). Macmillan International Higher Education/Red Globe Press.

Deane, P., & Cole, W. A. (1969). *British economic growth, 1688–1959* (2nd ed.). Cambridge University Press.

Dear, P. (2005). What is the history of science the history of? Early modern roots of the ideology of modern science. *Isis, 96*(3), 390–406.

Degenne, A., & Forsé, M. (1999). *Introducing social networks*. Sage.

Dell, M. (2010). The persistent effects of Peru's mining mita. *Econometrica, 78*(6), 1863–1903.

DeLong, J. B. (1990). *"Liquidation" cycles: Old-fashioned real business cycle theory and the Great Depression*. National Bureau of Economic Research, Working Paper # 3546.

DeLong, B., & Eichengreen, B. (1991). *The Marshall Plan: History's most successful structural adjustment program*. Centre for Economic and Policy Research (CEPR) Discussion Paper Series 634.

Denchak, M. (2018). Flint water crisis: Everything you need to know. Natural Resources Defense Council, November 08. https://www.nrdc.org/stories/flint-water-crisis-everything-you-need-know

Dennison, T., & Nafziger, S. (2011). *Micro-perspectives on living standards in nineteenth-century Russia* (No. 2011-07). Department of Economics, Williams College.

Desai, R. (2020). Marx's critical political economy, 'Marxist economics' and actually occurring revolutions against capitalism. *Third World Quarterly, 41*(8), 1353–1370.

Diamond, J. (1997). *Guns, germs and steel: The fates of human societies*. Norton.

Diaz-Diaz, R. (1999). Abolition and emancipation. In Latin America and the Caribbean. In K. A. Appiah & H. L. Gates Jr. (Eds.), *Africana: The encyclopedia of the African and African-American experience* (pp. 5–9).

Dickinson, F. R. (2013). *World War I and the triumph of a new Japan, 1919–1930* (Vol. 39). Cambridge University Press.

Diehl, P. F., & Crescenzi, M. J. (1998). Reconfiguring the arms race-war debate. *Journal of Peace Research, 35*(1), 111–118.

Dincecco, M., & Wang, Y. (2018). Violent conflict and political development over the long run: China versus Europe. *Annual Review of Political Science, 21*, 341–358.

Djankov, S., Glaeser, E., La Porta, R., Lopez-de-Silanes, F., & Shleifer, A. (2003). The new comparative economics. *Journal of Comparative Economics, 31*(4), 595–619.

Donaldson, D. (2018). Railroads of the Raj: Estimating the impact of transportation infrastructure. *American Economic Review, 108*(4–5), 899–934.

Dos Passos, J. (1932). *Three soldiers*. The Modern Library.

Dostoevsky, F. ([1864] 1960). *Notes from the underground*. In *Three short novels of Dostoevsky* (C. Garnett, Trans.). Anchor Books: Doubleday and Co.

Dostoevsky, F. ([1866] 1950). *Crime and punishment.* (C. Garnett, Trans.). The Modern Library.

Dower, J. (1999). *Embracing defeat: Japan in the aftermath of World War II.* Penguin.

Driver, J. (2014). The history of utilitarianism. In E. N. Zalta (Ed.), *The Stanford encyclopedia of philosophy* (Winter 2014 Edition). https://plato.stanford.edu/archives/win2014/entries/utilitarianism-history/

Dubbelboer, M. (2015). Nothing ruins writers like journalism: Colette, the press and Belle Époque literary life. *French Cultural Studies, 26*(1), 32–44.

Duiker, W. J. (2010). *Contemporary world history* (5th ed.). Cengage Learning.

Dunn, W. C. (1941). Adam Smith and Edmund Burke: Complementary contemporaries. *Southern Economic Journal, 7*(3), 330–346.

Dunning, E., & Mennell, S. (1998). Elias on Germany, Nazism and the Holocaust: On the balance between "civilizing" and "decivilizing" trends in the social development of Western Europe. *British Journal of Sociology, 49*(3), 339–357.

Dunning, J. H. (1995). Reappraising the eclectic paradigm in an age of alliance capitalism. *Journal of International Business Studies, 26*(3), 461–491.

Durkheim, E. ([1897] 1951). *Suicide: A study in sociology* (J. A. Spaulding, & G. Simpson, Trans.). The Free Press.

Easterlin, R. (1995). Industrial revolution and mortality revolution: Two of a kind? *Journal of Evolutionary Economics, 5*(4), 393–408.

Easterly, W., & Fischer, S. (1995). The Soviet economic decline. *The World Bank Economic Review, 9*(3), 341–371.

Edelman, M. (2001). Social movements: Changing paradigms and forms of politics. *Annual Review of Anthropology, 30*(1), 285–317.

Edelstein, M. (1976). Realized rates of return on UK home and overseas portfolio investment in the age of high imperialism. *Explorations in Economic History, 13*(3), 283–329.

Edwards, C. (2011). The singularity isn't even close: Why Ray Kurzweil's predictions about the future are flawed. *Skeptic, 16*(2), 20–22.

Edwards, M. (2009). *Civil society* (2nd ed.). Polity Press.

Edwards, R. (2005). *New spirits: Americans in the Gilded Age, 1865–1905.* Oxford University Press.

Egger, V. O. (2018). *A history of the Muslim World since 1260: The making of a global community.* Routledge.

Ehrlich, P. (1968). *The population bomb: Population control or race to oblivion.* Sierra Club/Ballantine Books.

Eichengreen, B. (1992). The origins and nature of the great slump revisited. *Economic History Review (New Series), 45*(2), 213–239.

Eichengreen, B. (1995). Financing infrastructure in developing countries: Lessons from the railway age. *The World Bank Research Observer, 10*(1), 75–91.

Eichengreen, B. (1996). *Golden fetters: The gold standard and the Great Depression, 1919–1939*. Oxford University Press.

Eichengreen, B. (2014). *Hall of mirrors: The Great Depression, the Great Recession, and the uses-and misuses-of history*. Oxford University Press.

Eichengreen, B., & Flandreau, M. (1997). *Gold standard in theory & history* (2nd ed.). Routledge.

Eichengreen, B., & Sachs, J. (1985). Exchange rates and economic recovery in the 1930s. *Journal of Economic History, 45*(4), 925–946.

Eisenshmidt, J., & Smets, F. (2019). Negative interest rates: Lessons from the Euro area. *Series on Central Banking Analysis and Economic Policies no. 26*.

Eisenstadt, S. N. (2003). *Comparative civilizations and multiple modernities* (Vol. 1). Brill.

Eisenstadt, S. N., & Aizenshṭadṭ, S. N. (1996). *Japanese civilization: A comparative view*. University of Chicago Press.

Elias, N. (1969). *The civilizing process: The history of manners* (Vol. 1). Blackwell.

Elias, N. (1982). *The civilizing process: State formation and civilization* (Vol. 2). Blackwell.

Elias, N. (1995). Technization and civilization. *Theory Culture and Society, 12*(3), 7–42.

Elias, N. (2000). *The civilizing process: Sociogenetic and psychogenetic investigations* (Revised Ed.). Blackwell.

Eloranta, J. (2007). From the great illusion to the Great War: Military spending behaviour of the great powers, 1870–1913. *European Review of Economic History, 11*(2), 255–283.

Eloranta, J., & Harrison, M. (2010). Chapter 6: War and disintegration, 1914–1950. In S. Broadberry & K. H. O'Rourke (Eds.), *The Cambridge economic history of modern Europe: Volume 2, 1870 to the present*. Cambridge University Press.

Engel, J. A. (2011). Not yet a garrison state: Reconsidering Eisenhower's military—Industrial complex. *Enterprise & Society, 12*(1), 175–199.

Engerman, D. C., & Unger, C. R. (2009). Introduction: Towards a global history of modernization. *Diplomatic History, 33*(3), 375–385.

Engerman, S. L., & Sokoloff, K. L. (2000). Institutions, factor endowments, and paths of development in the new world. *Journal of Economic Perspectives, 14*(3), 217–232.

Epstein, E. J. (1986). Petropower and Soviet expansion. *Commentary, 82*(1), 23.

Estrin, S. (1991). Yugoslavia: The case of self-managing market socialism. *Journal of Economic Perspectives, 5*(4), 187–194.

Etherington, N. (1982). Reconsidering theories of imperialism. *History and Theory, 21*(1), 1–36.

Etzrodt, C. (2008). Weber's Protestant ethic thesis, the critics, and Adam Smith. *Max Weber Studies, 8*(1), 49–78.

Fairbank, J. K. (1986). *The great Chinese revolution, 1800 1985*. Harper & Row.

Faulkner, N. (2018). *A radical history of the world*. Pluto Press.

Featherstone, M. (1987). Norbert Elias and figurational sociology: Some prefatory remarks. *Theory, Culture & Society, 4*(2–3), 197–211.

Federico, G., & Tena-Junguito, A. (2017). A tale of two globalizations: Gains from trade and openness 1800–2010. *Review of World Economics, 153*(3), 601–626.

Felipe, J., & Mehta, A. (2016). Deindustrialization? A global perspective. *Economics Letters, 149*, 148–151.

Ferguson, N. (2008). *The ascent of money: A financial history of the world*. Penguin.

Ferguson, N. (2018). *The Square and the tower: Networks and power, from the Freemasons to Facebook*. Penguin Press.

Ferguson, R. A. (2017). *We demand: The university and student protests*. University of California Press.

Fernandez-Villaverde, J. (2001). Was Malthus right? Economic growth and population dynamics. SSRN Working Paper. https://papers.ssrn.com/sol3/papers.cfm?abstract_id=293800

Ferrero, G. (1941). *The reconstruction of Europe: Talleyrand and the Congress of Vienna 1814–1815* (T. R. Jaeckel, Trans.). G.P. Putnam's Sons.

Finley, T., Franck, R., Johnson, N., & Michalopoulos, S. (2017). Economic consequences of revolutions: Evidence from the 1789 French Revolution. *VoxEU/CEPR*. https://voxeu.org/article/economic-consequences-revolutions

Fiske, A. P. (1992). The four elementary forms of sociality: Framework for a unified theory of social relations. *Psychological Review, 99*(4), 689–723.

Fitzmaurice, A. (2003). *Humanism and America: An intellectual history of English colonisation, 1500–1625*. Cambridge University Press.

Fitzpatrick, M., Jones, P., Knellwolf, C., & McCalman, I. (Eds.). (2004). *Enlightenment world*. Routledge Press.

Flath, D. (2014). *The Japanese economy* (3rd ed.). Oxford University Press.

Flere, S. (2007). The broken covenant of Tito's people: The problem of civil religion in communist Yugoslavia. *East European Politics and Societies, 21*(4), 681–703.

Floud, R., Fogel, R. W., Harris, B., & Hong, S. C. (2011). *The changing body: Health, nutrition, and human development in the western world since 1700*. Cambridge University Press.

Fogel, R. W. (1964). *Railroads and American economic growth: Essays in econometric history*. Johns Hopkins University Press.

Fogel, R. W. (1979). Notes on the social saving controversy. *Journal of Economic History, 39*(1), 1–54.

Fogel, R. W. (1999). Catching up with the economy. *American Economic Review, 89*(1), 1–21.

Fong, E. (2014). *American exceptionalism and the remains of race: Multicultural exorcisms*. Routledge.

Forbes, C. (2014). *Australia on horseback: The story of the horse and the making of a nation*. Pan Macmillan Australia.

Ford, H., with Crowther, S. (1922). *My life and work*. Doubleday, Page & Company.

Ford, L., Klevisser, F., & Carli, F. (2008). Ethnic neighborhoods and urban revitalization: Can Europe use the American model? *Geographical Review, 98*(1), 82–102.

Foreman-Peck, J. (1983). *A history of the world economy: International economical relations since 1850*. Harvester Press.

Foreman-Peck, J., & Millward, R. (1994). *Public and private ownership of British industry, 1820–1990*. Clarendon Press.

Foucault, M. (1977). *Discipline and punish: The birth of the prison* (A. Sheridan, Trans.). Penguin Books.

Foucault, M. ([1978] 1998). *The history of sexuality: The will to knowledge*. Penguin.

Fouquet, R., & Broadberry, S. (2015). Seven centuries of European economic growth and decline. *Journal of Economic Perspectives, 29*(4), 227–244.

Frank, T. (1997). *The conquest of cool: Business culture, counterculture, and the rise of hip consumerism*. University of Chicago Press.

Frank, T. (2016). *Listen liberal: Or, what ever Happened to the party of the people?* Picador.

Frankl, V. ([1959] 2006). *Man's search for meaning*. Beacon Press.

Fraser, C. (2013). Decolonization and the Cold War. In R. H. Immerman & P. Goedde (Eds.), *The Oxford handbook of the Cold War*. Oxford University Press.

Frazer, W. (1982). Milton Friedman and Thatcher's monetarist experience. *Journal of Economic Issues, 16*(2), 525–533.

Freud, S. ([1929] 1962). *Civilization and its discontents* (J. Strachey, Trans.). W. W. Norton.

Friedland, R. (2009). The endless fields of Pierre Bourdieu. *Organization, 16*(6), 887–917.

Friedland, R., & Sanders, J. (1986). Private and social wage expansion in the advanced market economies. *Theory and Society, 15*(1/2), 193–222.

Friedman, M., & Friedman, R. (1990). *Free to choose: A personal statement*. Houghton Mifflin Harcourt.

Friedman, M., & Schwartz, A. (1963). *A monetary history of the United States, 1867–1960*. Princeton University Press.

Friedman, T. L. (2005). *The world is flat: A brief history of the twenty-first century*. Macmillan.

Fukuyama, F. (1989). The end of history? *The National Interest., 16*, 3–18.

Fukuyama, F. (1992). *The end of history and the last man*. Free Press.

Fuller, R. B. (1968). *Operating manual for spaceship earth*. Southern Illinois University Press.

Furet, F. (1981). *Interpreting the French revolution*. Cambridge University Press.

Fusfeld, D. R. (1998). Economics and the Cold War: An inquiry into the relationship between ideology and theory. *Journal of Economic Issues, 32*(2), 505–511.

Gabrial, B. (2008). History of writing technologies. In C. Bazerman (Ed.), *Handbook of research on writing: History, society, school, individual, text* (pp. 27–40). Lawrence Erlbaum Associates (Taylor & Francis Group).

Gabriel, S. (1998). Economy of great leap forward. *China Essay Series Mount Holyoke College*.

Gai, K., Qiu, M., & Sun, X. (2018). A survey on FinTech. *Journal of Network and Computer Applications, 103*, 262–273.

Galbraith, J. K. (1958). *The affluent society*. Houghton Mifflin.

Galbraith, J. K. (1967). *The new industrial state*. Houghton Mifflin.

Galbraith, J. K. (1972). *The Great Crash, 1929* (3rd ed.). Houghton Mifflin.

Gallardo-Albarrán, D. (2020). Sanitary infrastructures and the decline of mortality in Germany, 1877–1913. *The Economic History Review, 73*(3), 730–757.

Gallardo-Albarrán, D., & de Jong, H. (2021). Optimism or pessimism? A composite view on English living standards during the industrial revolution. *European Review of Economic History, 25*(1), 1–19.

Galor, O. (2005). From stagnation to growth: Unified growth theory. In P. Aghion & S. N. Durlauf (Eds.), *Handbook of economic growth* (Vol. 1, Part A, pp. 171–293). Elsevier.

Galor, O., & Weil, D. N. (1999). From Malthusian stagnation to modern growth. *American Economic Review*, 89(2), 150–154. Papers and Proceedings of the One Hundred Eleventh Annual Meeting of the American Economic Association.

Gambino, L., & Pankhania, M. (2016). How we got here: A complete timeline of 2016's historic US election. *The Guardian*. November 8, 2016. https://www.theguardian.com/us-news/2016/nov/07/us-election-2016-complete-timeline-clinton-trump-president

Gammon, E. (2010). Nature as adversary: The rise of modern economic conceptions of nature. *Economy and Society, 39*(2), 218–246.

Gandesha, S. (2020). The spectre of the 1930s. In J. Rayner, S. Falls, G. Souvlis & T. C. Nelms (Eds.), *Back to the '30s?: Recurring crises in capitalism, liberalism, and democracy* (pp. 1–34). Palgrave Macmillan.

Gardner, J. (2018). Beneath the rubble, the Crystal Palace! The surprising persistence of a temporary mega event. *World Archaeology, 50*(1), 185–199.

Garraty, J. A. (1986). *The great depression*. Harcourt Brace Jovanovich.

Gatrell, P. (2006). Chapter 14: Economic and demographic change: Russia's age of economic extremes. In R. G. Suny (Ed.), *The Cambridge history of Russia, volume 3: The twentieth century*. Cambridge University Press.

Gerschenkron, A. (1962). *Economic backwardness in historical perspective: A book of essays*. Belknap Press of Harvard University Press.

Gibran, K. (1932). *The wanderer: His parables and his sayings*. Knopf.

Gibran, K. (1962). *A second treasury of Kahlil Gibran* (A. R. Ferris, Trans.). Citadel Books.

Giddens, A. (1990). *The consequences of modernity*. Polity Press.

Gigerenzer, G, Swijtink Z., Porter, T., Daston, L., Beatty, J., & Krüger, L. (1989). *The empire of chance: How probability changed science and everyday life*. Cambridge University Press.

Gilding, P. (2011). *The great disruption: Why the climate crisis will bring on the end of shopping and the birth of a new world*. Bloomsbury Publishing USA.

Gilman, N. (2015). The new international economic order: A reintroduction. *Humanity: An International Journal of Human Rights, Humanitarianism, and Development, 6*(1), 1–16.

Gilmore, O. (2021). *The working week in manufacturing since 1820*. OECD.

Gimpel, J. (1977). *The medieval machine: The industrial revolution of the Middle Ages*. Penguin Group USA.

Girón, A., & Correa, E. (1999). Global financial markets: financial deregulation and crises. *International Social Science Journal*, 183–194.

Goldsmith, H. (2014). *The long-run evolution of infrastructure services*, CESifo Working Paper, No. 5073, Center for Economic Studies and Ifo Institute (CESifo), Munich. http://hdl.handle.net/10419/105088

Goldstone, J. A. (1982). The comparative and historical study of revolutions. *Annual Review of Sociology, 8*(1), 187–207.

Goldstone, J. A. (1996). Gender, work, and culture: Why the industrial revolution came early to England but late to China. *Sociological Perspectives, 39*(1), 1–21.

Goldstone, J. A. (2010). The new population bomb: The four megatrends that will change the world. *Foreign Affairs, 89*(1), 31–43.

Gollier, C., & Treich, N. (2013). The precautionary principle. In J. F. Shogren (Ed.), *Encyclopedia of energy, natural resource, and environmental economics*. Elsevier.

Goodfriend, M., & King, R. G. (2005). The incredible Volcker disinflation. *Journal of Monetary Economics, 52*(5), 981 1015.

Gordon, C. (2006). Assessing adequacy of America's transportation policies: Lessons from the debate about the role of railroads in the development of the American west. *Transportation Research Record, 1966*, 96–102.

Gordon, C. (2011). The Great Depression as a pedagogical theme for undergraduate business, economics and finance classes. *Australasian Journal of Economics Education, 8*(2), 1–17.

Gordon, C. (2013). Two theories of the subprime crisis: Governance failure or mere greed? *International Journal of Behavioural Accounting and Finance, 4*(1), 3–17.

Gordon, C. (2017). Carbarism: Civilising the automobile. *World Transport Policy and Practice, 23*(1).

Gordon, J. (1997). John Stuart Mill and the "marketplace of ideas." *Social Theory and Practice, 23*(2), 235–249.

Gordon, R. J. (2015). Secular stagnation: A supply-side view. *American Economic Review, 105*(5), 54–59. Papers and Proceedings of the one hundred twenty-seventh annual meeting.

Gordon, R. J. (2018). *Why has economic growth slowed when innovation appears to be accelerating?* National Bureau Of Economic Research Working Paper 24554, http://www.nber.org/papers/w24554

Gorski, P. (2019). *American covenant: A history of civil religion from the puritans to the present*. Princeton University Press.

Gottfried, P. (1973). Pessimism and the revolutions of 1848. *The Review of Politics, 35*(2), 193–203.

Graff, M., Kenwood, A. G., & Lougheed, A. L. (2013). *Growth of the international economy, 1820–2015*. Routledge.

Gray, C. S. (1971). The arms race phenomenon. *World Politics, 24*(1), 39–79.

Graves, R. ([1934] 1978). *I, Claudius*. Penguin Books.

Greco, M. (2005). On the vitality of vitalism. *Theory, Culture & Society, 22*(1), 15–27.

Green, N. L. (1986). *The Pletzl of Paris: Jewish immigrant workers in the "Belle Epoque"*. Holmes & Meier.

Greene, M. F. (2020). 30 years ago, Romania deprived thousands of babies of human contact. Here's what's become of them. *The Atlantic* (July/August).

Griffin, E. (2013). *The 'industrial revolution': Interpretations from 1830 to the present*. Working Paper, School of History, UEA, Norwich.

Gritz, J. R. (2017). The unsavory history of sugar, the insatiable American craving: How the nation got hooked on sweets. *Smithsonian Magazine* (May).

Grossman, D. (2014). *On killing: The psychological cost of learning to kill in war and society*. Open Road Media.

Grossman, R. S. (1994). The shoe that didn't drop: Explaining banking stability during the Great Depression. *Journal of Economic History, 54*(3), 654–682.

Gruening, G. (2001). Origin and theoretical basis of new public management. *International Public Management Journal, 4*(1), 1–25.

Guinnane, T. W. (2011). The historical fertility transition: A guide for economists. *Journal of Economic Literature, 49*(3), 589–614.

Guttmann, R. (2008). A primer on finance-led capitalism and its crisis. Introduction. *Revue de la régulation. Capitalisme, institutions, pouvoirs*, (3/4), 1–15.

Hacker, B. C. (2005). The machines of war: Western military technology 1850–2000. *History and Technology, 21*(3), 255–300.

Haggard, S., Kang, D., & Moon, C. (1997). Japanese colonialism and Korean development: A critique. *World Development, 25*, 867–881.

Haggard, S. (2000). *The political economy of the Asian financial crisis*. Institute of International Economics.

Hakkio, C. S. (2013). The great moderation, 1982–2007. *Federal Reserve History*. https://www.federalreservehistory.org/essays/great-moderation

Halberstam, D. (1973). *The best and the brightest*. Fawcett Publications.

Haldane, J. B. S. (1927). *Possible worlds and other essays*. Chatto and Windus.

Hancock, E. I. M. (1991). *National Socialist leadership and total war, 1941–1945*. Martin's Press.

Hanson, P. (1971). East-west comparisons and comparative economic systems. *Soviet Studies, 22*(3), 327–343.

Harari, Y. N. (2014). *Sapiens: A brief history of humankind*. Random House.

Hardach, G. (1977). *The First World War, 1914–1918*. Allen Lane.

Harley, C. K., & Crafts, N. F. (2000). Simulating the two views of the British Industrial Revolution. *Journal of Economic History, 60*(3), 819–841.

Harley, K. (2003). Growth theory and Industrial Revolutions in Britain and America. *The Canadian Journal of Economics/Revue Canadienne D'economique, 36*(4), 809–831.

Harris, T. (2006). *Revolution: The great crisis of the British Monarchy, 1685–1720*. Allen Lane.

Hart, M. (2016). Capitalist patriarchy. In A. Wong, R. Wickramasinghe, R. Hoogland & N. A. Naples (Eds.), *The Wiley Blackwell encyclopedia of gender and sexuality studies*.

Harrison, M. (1993). Soviet economic growth since 1928: The alternative statistics of GI Khanin. *Europe-Asia Studies, 45*(1), 141–167.

Harrison, M. (1998). The economics of World War II: An overview. In M. Harrison (Ed.), *The economics of World War II: Six Great Powers in international comparison* (pp. 1–42). Cambridge University Press.

Harvey, D. (2007). *A brief history of neoliberalism*. Oxford University Press.

Hastings, M. (2000). *Going to the Wars*. Pan.

Hatton, T. J., & Williamson, J. G. (1998). *The age of mass migration: Causes and economic impact*. Oxford University Press.

Hatton, T. J., & Williamson, J. G. (2005). *Global migration and the world economy: Two centuries of policy and performance*. MIT Press.

Hawk, B. (2015). *Law and commerce in pre-industrial societies*. Brill.

Hawke, G. R. (1970). *Railways and economic growth in England and Wales 1840–1870*. Oxford University Press.

Hawken, P. (Ed.). (2017). *Drawdown: The most comprehensive plan ever proposed to reverse global warming*. Penguin.

Hawking, S. W. (1988). *Brief history of time: From the big bang to black holes*. Bantam Books.

Hayden, F. G. (1982). Social fabric matrix: From perspective to analytical tool. *Journal of Economic Issues, 16*(3), 637–662.

Hayes, C. L. (2012). *Twilight of the elites: America after meritocracy*. Crown Publishers.

Hedges, C. (2010). A brave new dystopia. *Truthdig.com*, https://www.truthdig.com/articles/2011-a-brave-new-dystopia/

Hedges, C. (2011). *Death of the liberal class*. Vintage Books Canada.

Henrich, J., Boyd, R., Bowles, S., Camerer, C., Fehr, E., Gintis, McElreath, R., Alvard, M., Barr, A., Ensminger, J, Henrich, N. S., Hill, K., Gil-White, Gurven, M., Marlowe, F. W., Patton, J. Q., & Tracer, D. (2005). "Economic man" in cross-cultural perspective: Behavioral experiments in 15 small-scale societies. *Behavioral and Brain Sciences, 28*(6), 795–815.

Heilbronner, O. (2016). Music and protest: The case of the 1960s and its long shadow. *Journal of Contemporary History, 51*(3), 688–700.

Heller, M. (2002). Time of the universe. In G. F. R. Ellis (Ed.), *The far-future universe: Eschatology from a cosmic perspective* (pp. 53–64). Templeton Foundation Press.

Henderson, A. (2005). From Barnum to "bling": The changing face of celebrity culture. *The Hedgehog Review* (Spring).

Herbst, S. (1999). Walter Lippmann's public opinion, revisited. *Harvard International Journal of Press/Politics, 4*(2), 88–93.

Herrnstein, R. J. (1977). The evolution of behaviorism. *American Psychologist, 32*, 593–603.

Hewitson, M. (2014). *Germany and the causes of the First World War*. Bloomsbury Publishing.

Hickel, J. (2018). How Britain stole $45 trillion from India. And lied about it. *Aljazeera*. https://www.aljazeera.com/opinions/2018/12/19/how-britain-stole-45-trillion-from-india/

Hirst, P. (1997). The global economy-myths and realities. *International Affairs, 73*(3), 409–425.

Hobbes, T. ([1651] 2010). *Leviathan: Or the matter, forme, and power of a commonwealth ecclesiasticall and civill.* Shapiro, I. (Ed.). Yale University Press.

Hobsbawm, E. J. (1987). *The age of empire, 1875–1914.* Pantheon Books.

Hobsbawm, E. J. (1994). *Age of extremes: The short twentieth century.* Michael Joseph.

Hobson, J. A. ([1902] 2018). *Imperialism: A study.* Routledge.

Hodgart, A. (1977). *The economics of European imperialism.* Edward Arnold.

Hodgson, L. (2016). *Res Publica and the Roman republic: "without body or form."* Oxford University Press.

Hoefer, C. (2016). Causal determinism. In E. N. Zalta (Ed.), *The Stanford encyclopedia of philosophy* (Spring 2016 Edition). https://plato.stanford.edu/archives/spr2016/entries/determinism-causal/

Hofstadter, R. (1965). *The paranoid style in American politics: And other essays.* Knopf.

Hollis, C. (1956). *A study of George Orwell: The man and his works.* Henry Regnery Company.

Horesh, N. (2012). From Chengdu to Stockholm: A comparative study of the emergence of paper money in East and West. *Provincial China, 4*(1), 68–99.

Horesh, N. (2020). *Chinese money in global context.* Stanford University.

Horne, G. (2018). *The apocalypse of settler colonialism: The roots of slavery, white supremacy, and capitalism in 17th century North America and the Caribbean.* New York University Press.

Horsefield, J. K. (1944). The origins of the Bank Charter Act, 1844. *Economica, New Series, 11*(44), 180–189.

Huber, E., Ragin, C., & Stephens, J. D. (1993). Social democracy, Christian democracy, constitutional structure, and the welfare state. *American Journal of Sociology, 99*(3), 711–749.

Huberman, M., & Minns, C. (2007). The times they are not changin': Days and hours of work in Old and New Worlds, 1870–2000. *Explorations in Economic History, 44*(4), 538–567.

Humphrey, T. M. (1975). The classical concept of the lender of last resort. *Federal Reserve Bank of Richmond Economic Review, 61*, 2–9.

Huntington, S. P. (1993). The clash of civilizations? *Foreign Affairs, 72*(3), 22–49.

Huxley, A. ([1949] 2012). 1984 v. Brave new world. *Letters of note*, Tuesday, March 6, 2012, https://lettersofnote.com/2012/03/06/1984-v-brave-new-world/

IGBP. (2014). The Great Acceleration data (October 2014). International Geosphere-Biosphere Programme (spreadsheet), http://www.igbp.net/download/18.950c2fa1495db7081ebc7/1421334707878/IGBPGreatAccelerationdatacollection.xlsx

IGBP. (2015). *International Geosphere-Biosphere programme.* http://www.igbp.net

Ignatieff, M. (2005). Chapter 1. Introduction: American exceptionalism and human rights. In M. Ignatieff (Ed.), *American exceptionalism and human rights* (pp. 1–26).

Ikenberry, G. J. (2020). *A world safe for democracy: Liberal internationalism and the crises of global order.* Yale University Press.

Immerwahr, D. (2019). *How to hide an empire: A short history of the greater United States.* Random House.

Inglehart, R. (2005). *Modernization, cultural change, and democracy: The human development sequence.* Cambridge University Press.

Inglehart, R., & Baker, W. (2000). Modernization, cultural change, and the persistence of traditional values. *American Sociological Review, 65*(1), 19–51.

IPPC. (2007). *Climate Change 2007 : Impacts, adaptation and vulnerability, contribution of Working Group II to the fourth assessment report of the Intergovernmental Panel on Climate Change.* Intergovernmental Panel on Climate Change.

IPPC. (2019). *Climate change and land: an IPCC special report on climate change, desertification, land degradation, sustainable land management, food security, and greenhouse gas fluxes in terrestrial ecosystems.* Intergovernmental Panel on Climate Change.

IPPC. (2021). *Human Influence on the climate system: Contribution of Working Group I to the Sixth Assessment Report of the Intergovernmental Panel on Climate Change.* Intergovernmental Panel on Climate Change.

Ishay, M. (2019). *The Levant express: The Arab uprisings, human rights, and the future of the Middle East.* Yale University Press.

Islam, S. N., & Iversen, K. (2018). *From "structural change" to "transformative change": Rationale and implications.* United Nations Department of Economic & Social Affairs, DESA Working Paper No. 155, ST/ESA/2018/DWP/155, February 2018

Jackson, R. V. (1977). *Australian economic development in the nineteenth century.* Australian National University Press.

James, C. L. R. (1963). *Black Jacobins: Toussaint L'ouverture and the San Domingo revolution* (2nd ed., revised). Vintage Books.

James, J. A. (1984a). The use of general equilibrium analysis in economic history. *Explorations in Economic History, 21*(3), 231–253.

James, H. (1984b). The causes of the German banking crisis. *Economic History Review, 37*(1), 68–87.

Jean-Yves, H., & Loïc, V. (2013). *OECD insights: Economic globalisation origins and consequences*. OECD Publishing.

Jedwab, R., & Vollrath, D. (2019). The urban mortality transition and poor-country urbanization. *American Economic Journal: Macroeconomics, 11*(1), 223–275.

Jerven, M. (2011). A clash of disciplines? Economists and historians approaching the African past. *Economic History of Developing Regions, 26*(2), 111–124.

Johansen, S. (1996). The Great Exhibition of 1851: A precipice in time? *Victorian Review, 22*(1), 59–64.

Johnson, C. (1982). *MITI and the Japanese miracle*. Stanford University Press.

Johnson, D. G. (1997). Agriculture and the wealth of nations. *American Economic Review, 87*(2), 1–12.

Jones, D. S. (2012). *Masters of the universe: Hayek, Friedman, and the birth of Neoliberal politics*. Princeton University Press.

Jones, E. L. (2000). *Growth recurring: Economic change in world history*. University of Michigan Press.

Jones, S. E. (2011). A brief survey of Sir Isaac Newton's views on religion. In M. D. Rhodes & J. W. Moody (Eds.), *Converging paths to truth* (pp. 61–78). Religious Studies Center, Brigham Young University; Deseret Books.

Jordan, D. P., & Young, R. J. (1997). Transforming Paris: The life & labors of Baron Haussmann. *Urban History Review, 25*(2), 71.

Judt, T. (1992). The past is another country: Myth and memory in postwar Europe. *Daedalus, 121*(4), 83–118.

Jullian, P. (1982). *La Belle Epoque: An essay*. Metropolitan museum of art.

Jung, C. G. ([1959] 1969). *The archetypes and the collective unconscious* (Collected Works, Vol. 9, Part 1). Princeton University Press.

Justman, S. (1994). Freud and his nephew. *Social Research, 61*(2), 457–476.

Kamitake, Y. (2008). The formal structure of industrial revolutions. *Hitotsubashi Journal of Social Studies, 40*(1), 17–58.

Kammen, M. (1993). The problem of American exceptionalism: A reconsideration. *American Quarterly, 45*(1), 1–43.

Kampmark, B. (2011). Science and war: Remembering the military industrial complex. *New Zealand International Review, 36*(4) (July/August), 11–14.

Kapur, A., Macleod, N., & Singh, N. (2005). *Plutonomy: Buying luxury, explaining global imbalances*. Citigroup Research. Industry note.

Kardiner, A. (1941). *The traumatic neuroses of war*. Hoeber Inc.

Katz, P. (2015). *The partnership: Brecht, Weill, three women, and Germany on the brink*. Nan A Talese/Doubleday.

Kaviraj, S. (1995). *The unhappy consciousness: Bankimchandra Chattopadhyay and the formation of nationalist discourse in India*. Oxford University Press.

Keegan, J. (1976). *The face of battle*. Viking.

Keegan, J. (1989). *The Second World War*. Century Hutchinson.

Kelley, A. C., & Williamson, J. G. (1984). Population growth, industrial revolutions, and the urban transition. *Population and Development Review, 10*(3), 419–441.

Kelly, M., Mokyr, J., & Gráda, C. Ó. (2014). Precocious Albion: New interpretation of the British industrial revolution. *Annual Review of Economics, 6*(1), 363–389.

Kelly, P. (1992). *The end of certainty: The story of the 1980s*. Allen & Unwin.

Kendall, R. (2004). *Degas by himself*. Time Warner Books UK.

Kennedy, P. M. (1989). *The rise and fall of the Great Powers*. Random House.

Kershaw, I. (1991). Hitler: Profiles in power. *Pearson Education.*

Kershaw, I. (2005). War and political violence in twentieth-century Europe. *Contemporary European History, 14*(1), 107–123.

Keynes, J. M. (1919). *The economic consequences of the peace*. Macmillan & Co.

Keynes, J. M. (1936). *The general theory of employment, interest and money*. Macmillan & Co.

Kitcher, P. (2010). The climate change debates. *Science, 328*(5983), 1230–1234.

Kim, S. H. (2020). Max Weber. In E. N. Zalta (Ed.), *The Stanford encyclopedia of philosophy* (Winter 2020 Edition). https://plato.stanford.edu/archives/win2020/entries/weber/

Kindleberger, C. (1987). *The world in depression 1929–1939*. University of California Press.

Kindleberger, C., & Aliber, R. Z. (2005). *Manias, panics, and crashes: A history of financial crises* (5th ed.). John Wiley & Sons, Inc.

King, E. (2007). The Crystal Palace and Great Exhibition of 1851. *British Library Newspapers*. Gale.

Klein, H. (1999). *The Atlantic slave trade*. Cambridge University Press.

Klein, M. (2001). *Rainbow's end: The Crash of 1929*. Oxford University Press.

Kline, M. (1980). *Mathematics: The loss of certainty*. Oxford University Press.

Klitgaard, M. B. (2007). Why are they doing it? Social democracy and market-oriented welfare state reforms. *West European Politics, 30*(1), 172–194.

Knight, J., & Harrison, S. (2014). Limitations of uniformitarianism in the Anthropocene. *Anthropocene, 5*, 71–75.

Koc, T. C., & Teker, S. (2019). Industrial revolutions and its effects on quality of life. *PressAcademia Procedia, 9*(56), 304–311, Global Business Research Congress, May 30–31, 2019, Istanbul, Turkey.

Koch, H. W. (1984). Social Darwinism as a factor in the 'New Imperialism.' In H. W. Koch (Ed.), *The origins of the First World War* (pp. 319–342). Palgrave.

Kochan, L. (1970). *Russia in revolution*. Paladin.

Koestler, A. (1940). *Darkness at noon*. Macmillan.

Koh, H. H. (2003). On American exceptionalism. *Stanford Law Review, 55*, 1479–1527.

Kohn, M., & Reddy, K. (2017). Colonialism. In E. N. Zalta (Ed.), *The Stanford encyclopedia of philosophy* (Fall 2017 Edition). https://plato.stanford.edu/archives/fall2017/entries/colonialism/

Komlos, J. (2000). The Industrial Revolution as the escape from the Malthusian trap. *Journal of European Economic History, 29*(2), 307–331.

Komlos, J., & Snowdon, B. (2005). Measures of progress and other tall stories: From income to anthropometrics. *World Economics, 6*(2), 87–135.

Kornai, J. (1986). *Contradictions and dilemmas: Studies on the socialist economy and society*. MIT Press.

Kostantaras, D. (2020). *Nationalism and revolution in Europe, 1763–1848*. Amsterdam University Press.

Koubi, V. (2005). War and economic performance. *Journal of Peace Research, 42*(1), 67–82.

Kranzberg, M. (1986). Technology and history: "Kranzberg's Laws." *Technology and Culture, 27*(3), 544–560.

Kumekawa, I. (2017). *The first serious optimist*. Princeton University Press.

Kurlansky, S. (2004). *1968: The year that rocked the world*. Ballantine.

Kurzweil, R. (2005). *The singularity is near: When humans transcend biology*. Viking.

Kuznets, S. (1966). *Modern economic growth: Rate, structure and spread*. Yale University Press.

Landes, D. S. (1969). *The unbound Prometheus: Technological change and development in Western Europe from 1750 to the present*. Cambridge University Press.

Landes, D. S. (1999). The fable of the dead horse; or, the Industrial Revolution revisited. In J. Mokyr (Ed.), *The British industrial revolution: An economic perspective* (2nd ed., pp. 128–159). Westview Press.

Lange, M. (2017). *Killing others: A natural history of ethnic violence*. Cornell University Press.

Lapsley, D. K., & Steyld, P. C. (2011). Id, ego, and superego. In V. S. Ramachandran (Ed.), *Encyclopedia of human behavior* (2nd ed.). Elsevier.

Larkin, M. (1995). *Religion, politics and preferment in France since 1890: La Belle Époque and its legacy*. Cambridge University Press.

Lasch, C. (1978). *The culture of narcissism: American life in an age of diminishing expectations*. W. W. Norton & Co.

Lawson, G. (2011). Halliday's revenge: Revolutions and international relations. *International Affairs, 87*(5), 1067–1085.

Lawson, G. (2016). Within and beyond the "fourth generation" of revolutionary theory. *Sociological Theory, 34*(2), 106–127.

Laczó, F., & Rigo, M. (2019). New Versailles or a Velvet Revolution? Brexit and the exits of central and eastern European history, 1916–2016. *Contemporary European History, 28*(1), 57–60.

Lebergott, S. (1966). United States transportation advance and externalities. *Journal of Economic History, 26*(4), 437–461.

Lee, P. (2011). The curious life of in loco parentis at American universities. *Higher Education in Review, 8*, 65–90.

Lehning, J. R. (2013). *European colonialism since 1700* Cambridge University Press.

Leitenberg, M. (2006). *Deaths in wars and conflicts in the 20th century* (3rd ed.). Cornell University Peace Studies Program Occasional Paper #29.

Lenin, V. I. ([1917] 1939). *Imperialism, the highest stage of capitalism: A popular outline*. International Publishers.

Leonard, C., & Ljungberg, J. (2010). Population and living standards, 1870–1914. In S. Broadberry & K. H. O'Rourke (Eds.), *The Cambridge economic history of modern Europe: Volume 2, 1870 to the present* (pp. 108–130). Cambridge University Press.

Lewis, J. E., Jr. (2000). *The American union and the problem of neighborhood: The United States and the collapse of the Spanish Empire, 1783–1829*. University of North Carolina Press.

Lewis, M. (2011). *The big short: Inside the doomsday machine*. Penguin.

Liboiron, M. (2012). History of consumption and waste, U.S. 1800–1850. In C. A. Zimring & W. L. Rathje (Eds.), *Encyclopedia of consumption and waste: The social science of garbage*. SAGE Publications.

Lichtheim, G. (1972). *Europe in the twentieth century*. Praeger Publishers.

Lida, C. E. (2002). The democratic and social republic of 1848 and its repercussions in the Hispanic world. In G. Thomson (Ed.), *The European revolutions of 1848 and the Americas*. Institute of Latin American Studies.

Lin, N. (1999). Building a network theory of social capital. *Connections, 22*, 28–51.

Lindsay, J. M. (2016). The 10 most significant world events in 2016. And how they'll reverberate in the coming year. *Atlantic Magazine* (December 28).

Lindsey, T. (2021). Soeharto: The giant of modern Indonesia who left a legacy of violence and corruption. *The Conversation*. August 21, https://theconversation.com/soeharto-the-giant-of-modern-indonesia-who-left-a-legacy-of-violence-and-corruption-164411

Linklater, A., & Mennell, S. (2010). Norbert Elias, the civilizing process: Sociogenetic and psychogenetic investigations—An overview and assessment. *History and Theory, 49*(3), 384–411.

Lippman, M. ([1922] 1965). *Public opinion*. The Free Press.

Lipset, S. M. (1996). *American exceptionalism: A double-edged sword*. WW Norton & Company.

Litke, J. (2013). *Twilight of the republic: Empire and exceptionalism in the American political tradition*. University Press of Kentucky.

Livesey, J. (2001). *Making democracy in the French Revolution*. Harvard University Press.

Lizardo, O., & Stoltz, D. S. (2018). Max Weber's ideal versus material interest distinction revisited. *European Journal of Social Theory, 21*(1), 3–21.

Lobingier, C. (1918–1919). Napoleon and his code. *Harvard Law Review, 32*(2),114–134.

Lopez, R. S., & Lopez, R. S. (1976). *The commercial revolution of the middle ages, 950–1350*. Cambridge University Press.

Lovejoy, H. B., & Anderson, R. (2020). Introduction: "Liberated Africans" and early international courts of humanitarian efforts. In H. B. Lovejoy & R. Anderson (Eds.), *Liberated Africans and the abolition of the slave trade, 1807–1896* (pp. 1–24). Rochester University Press.

Lovell, J. (2019). *Maoism: A global history*. Random House.

Löwy, M. (2020). Revolutionary romanticism in the twentieth century: Surrealists and Situationists. In A. Hemmens & G. Zacarias (Eds.), *The Situationist International: A critical handbook* (pp. 138–146). Pluto Press.

Luna, E. (2002). Drug exceptionalism. *Villanova Law Review, 47*, 753–807.

Lyotard, J. (1984). *The postmodern condition: A report on knowledge* (G. Bennington, G., & B. Massumi, Trans.). University of Minnesota Press.

Ma, D., & Rubin, J. (2019). The paradox of power: Principal-agent problems and administrative capacity in Imperial China (and other absolutist regimes). *Journal of Comparative Economics, 47*(2), 277–294.

Ma, Y. (2021). China's share of merchandise and commercial service exports in global exports in 2020. *Statista*. https://www.statista.com/statistics/256604/share-of-chinas-exports-in-global-exports/

MacFarquhar, R., & Schoenhals, M. (2006). *Mao's last revolution*. Belknap Press of Harvard University Press.

MacIntosh, J. (2016). Mechanism, in modern philosophy. In *The Routledge encyclopedia of philosophy*. Taylor and Francis. https://www.rep.routledge.com/articles/thematic/mechanism-in-modern-philosophy/v-1

MacLeod, R. M. (1965). The Alkali Acts administration, 1863–84: The emergence of the civil scientist. *Victorian Studies, 9*(2), 85–112.

Macpherson, C. B. (1962). *The political theory of possessive individualism: Hobbes to Locke*. Clarendon Press.

Macpherson, W. J. (1995). *Economic development of Japan 1868–1941*. Cambridge University Press.

Maddison, A. (2007). *The world economy volume 1: A millennial perspective volume 2. Historical statistics*. OECD, Development Studies Centre OECD Publishing.

Madsen, D. L. (1998). *American exceptionalism*. University of Mississippi Press.

Magarey, S. (1987). That hoary old chestnut, Free Will and Determinism: Culture vs. structure, or history vs. theory in Britain. A review article. *Comparative Studies in Society and History, 29*(3), 626–639.

Magraw, R. (1983). *France 1815–1914: The bourgeois century*. Fontana.

Maier, C. S. (1977). The politics of productivity: Foundations of American international economic policy after World War II. *International Organization, 31*(4), 607–663.

Maier, C. S. (1970). Between Taylorism and technocracy: European ideologies and the vision of industrial productivity in the 1920s. *Journal of Contemporary History, 5*(2), 27–61.

Makin, A. J. (2019). Lessons for macroeconomic policy from the Global Financial Crisis. *Economic Analysis and Policy, 64*, 13–25.

Malanima, P. (2005). Urbanisation and the Italian economy during the last millennium. *European Review of Economic History, 9*(1), 97–122.

Malle, S. (1993). What are comparative economic systems today? *Aula, 15*(3), 95–102.

Malthus, T. R. ([1798] 1872). *An essay on the principle of population: Or, a view of its past and present effects on human happiness; with an inquiry into our prospects respecting the future removal or mitigation of the evils which it occasions*. Reeves and Turner.

Manchester, W. (1973). *The glory and the dream: A narrative history of America, 1932–1972*. Little Brown and Company.

Mann, C. C. (2018). The book that incited a worldwide fear of overpopulation. *Smithsonian Magazine* (January/February).

Mao, Z. (1967). *Quotations from chairman Mao Tse-tung* (2nd ed.). Foreign Languages Press.

Marangos, J. (2003). Was shock therapy really a shock? *Journal of Economic Issues, 37*(4), 943–966.

Marcuse, H. (1964). *One-dimensional man*. Beacon Press.

Margo, R. A. (1993). Employment and unemployment in the 1930s. *Journal of Economic Perspectives, 7*(2), 41–59.

Markie, P., & Folescu, M. (2021). Rationalism vs. empiricism. In E. N. Zalta (Ed.), *The Stanford encyclopedia of philosophy* (Fall 2021 Edition). https://plato.stanford.edu/archives/fall2021/entries/rationalism-empiricism/

Markovits, D. (2019). *The meritocracy trap*. Penguin.

Marks, S. (1978). The myths of reparations. *Central European History, 11*(3), 231–255.

Marx, K. ([1867, 1885, 1894], 1965). *Das Kapital: A critique of political economy* (F. Engels, & S. L. Levitsky, Trans.). H. Regnery.

Mason, D. S. (2011). *A concise history of modern Europe: Liberty, equality, solidarity* (2nd ed.). Rowman & Littlefield Publishers.

Mason, K. O. (1997). Explaining fertility transitions. *Demography, 34*(4), 443–454.

Massey, D. (1988). Economic development and international migration in comparative perspective. *Population and Development Review, 14*(3), 383–413.

Maxwell, G. (2010). WH Auden's "The age of anxiety". *The Guardian* (April 10), https://www.theguardian.com/books/2010/apr/10/auden-age-anxiety-leonard-bernstein

Mayhall, L. E. N. (2001). Feminisms. In P. N. Stearns (Ed.), *Encyclopedia of European social history from 1350 to 2000* (Vol. 4, pp. 44–54). Charles Scribner's sons (Gale).

Megino, L. & Pankhania, M. (2016, November 8). How we got here: a complete time line of 2016's historic US election. The Guardian.

McClelland, P. (1968). Railroads, American growth and the new economic history. *Journal of Economic History, 28*(1), 102–123.

McDonough, T. (1995). Lenin, imperialism, and the stages of capitalist development. *Science & Society*, 339–367.

McGee, R. W. (1989). The economic thought of David Hume. *Hume Studies, 15*(1), 184–204.

McGreevey, R. (2017). US Imperialism, 1898–1914. In *Oxford research encyclopedia of American history.* Oxford Research Encyclopedias.

McKeown, T. J. (1983). Hegemonic stability theory and 19th century tariff levels in Europe. *International Organization, 37*(1), 73–91.

McKeown, T., & Record, R. G. (1962). Reasons for the decline of mortality in England and Wales during the nineteenth century. *Population Studies, 16*, 94–122.

McLynn, F. (1998). *Napoleon.* Pimlico.

McMillan, M. S., & Rodrik, D. (2011). *Globalization, structural change and productivity growth.* National Bureau of Economic Research, Working Paper 17143.

McNeill, J. R. (2016). *The Great Acceleration: An environmental history of the Anthropocene since 1945.* Harvard University Press.

Meadows, D. L., Meadows, D. H., Behrens, W. W., & Randers, J. (1972). *The limits to growth: A report for the club of Rome's project on the predicament of mankind.* New American Library.

Meisner, M. J. (1999). *Mao's china and after: A history of the people's republic* (3rd ed.). Free Press.

Mercer, B. (2020). *Student revolt in 1968: France.* Cambridge University Press.

Meek, R. (1976). *Social Science and the ignoble savage.* Cambridge University Press.

Melville, H. (1853). Bartleby, the Scrivener (Part I: Nov 1853) + (Part II: Dec 1853). *Putnam's Magazine.*

Memedovic, O., & Iapadre, L. (2010). *Structural change in the world economy: Main features and trends.* United Nations Industrial Development Organisation, Research And Statistics Branch Working Paper 24/2009.

Meyer, A. G. (2013). *Leninism.* Harvard University Press.

Middleton, R. (2010). British monetary and fiscal policy in the 1930s. *Oxford Review of Economic Policy, 26*(3), 414–441.

Milanovic, B. (2016). *Global inequality.* Harvard University Press.

Miller, D. (1984). *Anarchism.* JM Dent & Sons.

Miller, W. R., & Thoresen, C. E. (2003). Spirituality, religion, and health: An emerging research field. *American Psychologist, 58*(1), 24–35.

Millward, R. (2005). *Private and public enterprise in Europe: Energy, telecommunications and transport, 1830–1990.* Cambridge University Press.

Minge-Kalman, W. (1978). The Industrial Revolution and the European family: The institutionalization of childhood as a market for family labor. *Comparative Studies in Society and History, 20*(3), 454–468.

Minsky, H. P. (1980). Capitalist financial processes and the instability of capitalism. *Journal of Economic Issues, 14*(2), 505–523.

Minsky, H. (2016). *Can it happen again?: Essays on instability and finance.* Routledge.

Mirowksi, P. (1989). *More heat than light: Economics as social physics, physics as nature's economics.* Cambridge University Press.

Mirowksi, P. (2001). *Machine dreams: Economics becomes a cyborg science.* Cambridge University Press.

Mishkin, F. S. (1978). The household balance sheet and the Great Depression. *The Journal of Economic History, 38*(4), 918–937.

Mitchell, B. R. (1992). *International historical statistics: Europe 1750–1988.* Stockton Press.

Mitchell, J. C. (1974). Social networks. *Annual review of anthropology, 3*(1), 279–299.

Mitchell, W., Wray, L. R., & Watts, M. (2016). *Modern monetary theory and practice: An introductory text.* Centre of Full Employment and Equity.

Moeller, R. G. (1996). War stories: The search for a usable past in the Federal Republic of Germany. *The American Historical Review, 101*(4), 1008–1048.

Moffitt, R. A. (2003). The negative income tax and the evolution of US welfare policy. *Journal of Economic Perspectives, 17*(3), 119–140.

Mohan, R., & Aggarwal, V. (1990). Commands and controls: Planning for Indian industrial development, 1951–1990. *Journal of Comparative Economics, 14*(4), 681–712.

Mohajan, H. K. (2019). The first Industrial Revolution: Creation of a new global human era. *Journal of Social Sciences and Humanities, 5*(4), 377–387.

Mokyr, J. (1999a). The Second Industrial Revolution, 1870–1914. In V. Castronovo (Ed.), *Storia dell'economia Mondiale* (pp. 219–245). Laterza Publishing.

Mokyr, J. (1999b). Editor's introduction: The new economic history and the Industrial Revolution. In J. Mokyr (Ed.), *The British industrial revolution: An economic perspective* (2nd ed., pp. 1–127). Westview Press.

Mokyr, J. (2009). *The enlightened economy: An economic history of Britain, 1700–1850* (pp. 83–84). Yale University Press.

Mokyr, J. (2016). *A Culture of growth: The origins of the modern economy.* Princeton University Press.

Mokyr, J., Vickers, C., & Ziebarth, N. L. (2015). The history of technological anxiety and the future of economic growth: Is this time different? *Journal of Economic Perspectives, 29*(3), 31–50.

Monfasani, J. (2016). *Renaissance humanism, from the middle ages to modern times.* Taylor & Francis.

Moore, J. W. (2016). Introduction: Anthropocene or capitalocene? Nature, history, and the crisis of capitalism. In J. W. Moore (Ed.), *Anthropocene or capitalocene? Nature, history, and the crisis of capitalism.* PM Press.

Morris, I. (2014). *War! What is it good for? Conflict and the progress of civilization from primates to robots.* Farrer, Straus and Giroux.

Moskos, C. C., Jr. (1974). The concept of the military-industrial complex: Radical critique or liberal bogey? *Social Problems, 21*(4), 498–512.

Mosse, G. L. (1990). The political culture of Italian futurism: A general perspective. *Journal of Contemporary History, 25*(2), 253–268.

Mozumi, S. (2018). The Kennedy-Johnson Tax Cut of 1964, the defeat of Keynes, and comprehensive tax reform in the United States. *Journal of Policy History, 30*(1), 25–61.

Murphy, T. E. (2015). Old habits die hard (sometimes). *Journal of Economic Growth, 20*(2), 177–222.

Murray, N. (2002). *Aldous Huxley: A biography.* Martin's Press.

Nadeau, R. (2010). The not so worldly philosophers: Why mainstream economics can't be green. *Synesis: A Journal of Science, Technology, Ethics, and Policy, 1*(1), T3–T10.

Naggar, T., & Naggar, A. K. (2005). Comparative economics: A reference guide. *The American Economist, 49*(2), 90–95.

Narsey, W. (2016). *British imperialism and the making of colonial currency systems.* Palgrave Macmillan.

Nash, K. (2009). *Contemporary political sociology: Globalization, politics and power.* John Wiley & Sons.

Neal, L., & Cameron, R. (2016). *A Concise economic history of the world: From paleolithic times to the present* (5th ed.). Oxford University Press.

Needham, J. (1965). *Time and Eastern man*. Royal Anthropological Institute of Great Britain & Ireland.

Nelson, C. (2014). *The age of radiance: The epic rise and dramatic fall of the atomic era*. Scribner.

Neumann, F. (1949). The war crimes trials. *World Politics, 2*(1), 135–147.

Newbery, D. M. (2002). *Privatization, restructuring, and regulation of network utilities* (Vol. 2). MIT Press.

Ney, A. (2021). Reductionism. *The internet encyclopedia of philosophy*, ISSN 2161-0002, https://www.iep.utm.edu/

Nicoletti, B., Nicoletti, W., & Weis. (2017). *Future of FinTech*. Palgrave Macmillan.

Nitzan, J., & Bichler, S. (2006). *Cheap wars*. MPRA Paper 5549, University Library of Munich, Germany.

Nolte, G., & Aust, H. P. (2013). European exceptionalism? *Global Constitutionalism, 2*(3), 407–436.

North, D. (1990). *Institutions, institutional change, and economic performance*. Cambridge University Press.

Norris, R. S. (1992). The Soviet nuclear archipelago. *Arms Control Today, 22*(1), 24–31.

Nowell-Smith, G. (1990). On history and the cinema. *Screen, 31*(2), 160–171.

Nozaki, Y. (2008). *War memory, nationalism and education in postwar Japan: The Japanese history textbook controversy and Ienaga Saburo's court challenges*. Routledge.

Nunn, N. (2008). The long-term effects of Africa's slave trades. *The Quarterly Journal of Economics, 123*(1), 139–176.

Nye, J. V. (1987). Firm size and economic backwardness: A new look at the French industrialization debate. *Journal of Economic History, 47*(3), 649–669.

Obadic, I. (2014). A troubled relationship: Yugoslavia and the European Economic Community in détente. *European Review of History—Revue européenne d'histoire, 21*(2), 329–348.

Ober, J. (1993). Public speech and the power of the people in democratic Athens. *PS: Political Science & Politics, 26*(3), 481–486.

O'Brien, P. (1983). Transport and economic development in Europe, 1789–1914. In P. O'Brien (Ed.), *Railways and the economic development of Europe* (pp. 1830–1914). St. Martin's Press.

O'Brien, P. (1988). The costs and benefits of British imperialism 1846–1914. *Past & Present, 120*, 163–200.

O'Brien, P. K. (1996). Path dependency, or why Britain became an industrialized and urbanized economy long before France. *Economic History Review, New Series, 49*(2), 213–249.

O'Brien, P. (2006). *Provincializing the First Industrial Revolution*. London School of Economics and Political Science, Department of Economic History.

O'Brien, P. (2013). Historical foundations for a global perspective on the emergence of a western European regime for the discovery, development, and diffusion of useful and reliable knowledge. *Journal of Global History, 8*(1), 1–24.

O'Brien, P. (2017). *Was the first industrial revolution a conjuncture in the history of the world economy?* London School of Economics Working Paper.

Ochs, E., & Solomon, O. (2010). Autistic sociality. *Ethos, 38*(1), 69–92.

OECD. (2006). Appendix B: World population, GDP and GDP Per Capita Before 1820, in *The World Economy: Volume 1: A Millennial Perspective and Volume 2: Historical Statistics*, OECD Publishing. Organisation for Economic Cooperation and Development.

OECD. (2021). *OECD data—Share prices*. https://data.oecd.org/price/share-prices.htm. Accessed October 20, 2021.

Offer, A. (1993). The British empire, 1870–1914: A waste of money? *Economic History Review, New Series, 46*(2), 215–238.

Offer, A., & Söderberg, G. (2016). *The Nobel factor: The prize in economics, social democracy, and the market turn*. Princeton University Press.

Ogle, V. (2019). Time, temporality and the history of capitalism. *Past & Present, 243*(1), 312–327.

Ohanian, L. E. (1997). The macroeconomic effects of war finance in the United States: World War II and the Korean War. *The American Economic Review, 87*(1), 23–40.

O'Hara, G. (2010). New histories of British imperial communication and the "networked world" of the 19th and early 20th centuries. *History Compass, 8*(7), 609–625.

Okrent, D. (2010). *Last call: The rise and fall of Prohibition*. Scribner.

Olasky, M. N. (1984). Retrospective: Bernays' doctrine of public opinion. *Public Relations Review, 10*(3), 3–12.

Olson, M. (1971). *The Logic of collective action: Public goods and the theory of groups* (Second Printing with a New Preface and Appendix). Harvard University Press.

Olsson-Yaouzis, N. (2012). An evolutionary dynamic of revolutions. *Public Choice, 151*(3/4), 497–515.

Oneal, J. R., & Oneal, F. H. (1988). Hegemony, imperialism, and the profitability of foreign investments. *International Organization, 42*(2), 347–373.

Oppelland, T. (2017). Governments, parliaments and parties. In U. Daniel, P. Gatrell, O. Janz, H. Jones, J. Keene, A. Kramer & B. Nasson (Eds), *1914–1918-online international encyclopedia of the First World War*. Freie Universität Berlin. https://encyclopedia.1914-1918-online.net/article/governments_parliaments_and_parties

Ord-Hume, A. (1977). *Perpetual motion: The history of an obsession*. Martin's Press.

Oreskes, N., & Conway, E. M. (2010). *Merchants of doubt: How a handful of scientists obscured the truth on issues from tobacco smoke to global warming*. Bloomsbury Press.

Organski, A. F., & Kugler, J. (1977). The costs of major wars: The phoenix factor. *American Political Science Review, 71*(4), 1347–1366.

O'Rourke, K. H. (2000). Tariffs and growth in the late 19th century. *The Economic Journal, 110*(463), 456–483.

O'Rourke, K. H. (1997). The European grain invasion, 1870–1913. *The Journal of Economic History, 57*(4), 775–801.

Orwell, G. (1949). *Nineteen Eighty-Four. A novel*. Secker & Warburg.

O'Shaughnessy, N. (2009). Selling Hitler: propaganda and the Nazi brand. *Journal of Public Affairs: An International Journal, 9*(1), 55–76.

Osterhammel, J. (2014). *The transformation of the world: A global history of the nineteenth century* (P. Camiller, Trans.). Princeton University Press.

Ostrower, G. B. (1996). *The league of nations: From 1919 to 1929*. Avery Publishing Group.

Oto-Peralías D., & Romero-Ávila D. (2017). *Colonial theories of institutional development: Toward a model of styles of imperalism*. Springer.

Outram, D. (2019). *The enlightenment*. Cambridge University Press.

Overy, R. (2000). Chapter 8: Warfare in Europe since 1918. In T. C. Blanning (Ed.), *The Oxford history of modern Europe* (pp. 214–233). Oxford University Press.

Oxford English Dictionary. (2020). Civilization. https://www.oed.com

Palma, J. G. (2009). The revenge of the market on the rentiers: Why neo-liberal reports of the end of history turned out to be premature. *Cambridge Journal of Economics, 33*(4), 829–869.

Palma, N. (2020). American precious metals and their consequences for early modern Europe. In S. Battilossi, Y. Cassis & K. Yago (Eds.), *Handbook of the history of money and currency* (pp. 363–382).

Pam, N. (2013). Sociality. *Psychologydictionary.org*, https://psychologydictionary.org/sociality/. Accessed September 10, 2020.

Parker, R. (2008). An overview of the Great Depression. In R. Whaples (Ed.), *EH. Net. Encyclopedia*. https://eh.net/encyclopedia/an-overview-of-the-great-depression/

Partnoy, F. (2003). *Infectious greed: How deceit and risk corrupted the financial markets (revised and updated edition)*. Profile Books.

Patton, M. (2016). U.S. role In global economy declines nearly 50%. Forbes.com (February 29), https://www.forbes.com/sites/mikepatton/2016/02/29/u-s-role-in-global-economy-declines-nearly-50/?sh=1d78117a5e9e. Accessed July 12, 2021.

Paul, C. (1900). *The history of the devil and the idea of evil; from the earliest times to the present day*. Open Court Publishing Company.

Paul, D. B. (2003). Darwin, Social Darwinism and eugenics. In J. Hodge & G. Radick (Eds.), *The Cambridge companion to Darwin* (pp. 214–239). Cambridge University Press.

Paxton, R. O. (2007). *The anatomy of fascism*. Vintage.

Pechatnov, V. O. (2017) The Soviet Union and the Bretton Woods conference. In G. Scott-Smith & J. Rofe (Eds.), *Global perspectives on the Bretton Woods Conference and the post-War world order*. Palgrave Macmillan.

Peikoff, L. (1993). *Objectivism: The philosophy of Ayn Rand*. Penguin.

Pelz, W. (2016). *A people's history of Modern Europe*. Pluto Press.

Perez, C. (2002). *Technological revolutions and financial capital: The dynamics of bubbles and golden ages*. Edward Elgar.

Perrin, F. (2011). Unified growth theory: An insight. *Historical Social Research/Historische Sozialforschung, 36*(3(137)), 362–372.

Persky, J. (1991). Retrospectives: Lange and von Mises, large-scale enterprises, and the economic case for socialism. *Journal of Economic Perspectives, 5*(4), 229–236.

Pfister, U. (2019). The inequality of pay in pre-modern Germany, late 15th century to 1889. *Jahrbuch für Wirtschaftsgeschichte/Economic History Yearbook, 60*(1), 209–243.

Pfister, U. (2020). The Crafts-Harley view of German industrialization: An independent estimate of the income side of net national product, 1851–1913. *European Review of Economic History, 24*(3), 502–521.

Pfister, U., & Fertig, G. (2020). From Malthusian disequilibrium to the Post-Malthusian era: The evolution of the preventive and positive checks in Germany, 1730–1870. *Demography, 57*(3), 1145–1170.

Pigou, A. C. (1928). *A study in public finance*. MacMillan and Co.

Piketty, T. (2014). *Capital in the 21st century*. Harvard University Press (*companion data at:* http://piketty.pse.ens.fr/en/capital21c2

Pinker, S. (2011). *The better angels of our nature: The decline of violence in history and its causes*. Penguin.

Plato. ([ca. 375BCE] 2004). *The Republic* (C. D. C. Reeve, Translator). Hackett.

Pleština, D. (2019). *Regional development in communist Yugoslavia: Success, failure, and consequences*. Routledge.

Poeze, H. A. (2009). The Cold War in Indonesia, 1948. *Journal of Southeast Asian Studies, 40*(3), 497–517.

Polanyi, K. (1944). *The great transformation*. Beacon Press.

Pomeranz, K. (2000). *The great divergence: China, Europe, and the making of the modern world economy*. Princeton University Press.

Porter, R. (1990). *The enlightenment*. Macmillan.

Post, R. C. (2007). *Urban mass transit: The life story of a technology*. Greenwood Publishing Group.

Potter, D. M. (1954). *People of plenty: Economic abundance and the American character.* University of Chicago Press.

Potter, D. M., & Fehrenbacher, D. E. (1976). *The impending crisis, 1848–1861.* Harper & Row.

Powell, L. F. (1971). *Powell memorandum: Attack on American free enterprise system.* US Chamber of Commerce.

Prado, C. G. (2017). Post-truth. *The Philosophers' Magazine, 79*, 27–32.

Pratt, J. (2008). Scandinavian exceptionalism in an era of penal excess, part 1: The nature and roots of Scandinavian exceptionalism. *The British Journal of Criminology, 48*(2), 119–137.

Pratt, J. (2013). Elias, punishment, and decivilization. In J. Pratt, D. Brown & M. Brown (Eds.), *The new punitiveness: Trends, theories and perspectives* (pp. 256–271). Routledge.

Price R. (Ed.). (1996). *Maroon societies: Rebel slave communities in the Americas* (3rd ed.). Johns Hopkins University Press.

PsPrint.com. (2021). *History of the printed newspaper.* https://www.psprint.com/resources/history-of-the-printed-newspaper/

Puffert, D. (2008). Path dependence. In R. Whaples (Ed.), *EH.net Encyclopedia*, http://eh.net/encyclopedia/path-dependence/

Pula, B. (2015). Postwar economic growth under central planning. *Global Field* (blog), https://globalfield.wordpress.com/2015/03/30/postwar-economic-growth-under-central-planning/

Putnam, R. D. (1995). *Bowling alone: America's declining social capital.* Simon & Schuster.

Rafael E. F. (2017). Philippine problems are problems of modernity, not of transition: A Luhmannian critique of Randolf S. David's theory of modernity. *Philippine Sociological Review* 65 (Special Issue: Imagined democracies), 151–170.

Ramesh, S. (2017). An economic history of India. In S. Ramesh (Ed.), *China's Lessons for India: Volume I: The political economy of development* (pp. 23–54). Palgrave Macmillan.

Rattansi, A. (2017). *Bauman and contemporary sociology: A critical analysis.* Manchester University Press.

Ravazzoli, E., Streifeneder, T., & Cavallaro, F. (2017). The effects of the planned high-speed rail system on travel times and spatial development in the European Alps. *Mountain Research and Development, 37*(1), 131–140.

Reeves, R. (2001). *President Nixon: Alone in the White House.* Simon and Schuster.

Reynolds, D. (2005). *In command of history: Churchill fighting and writing the Second World War.* Penguin UK.

Riall, L. (2002). *The Italian Risorgimento: State, society and national unification.* Routledge.

Ricardo, D. (1821). *On the principles of political economy* (3rd ed.). J. Murray.
Richards, T. (1990). *The commodity culture of Victorian England: Advertising and spectacle, 1851–1914*. Stanford University Press.
Richerson, P. J., & Boyd, R. (1998). The evolution of human ultra-sociality. In F. Eibl-Eibesfeldt (Ed.), *Indoctrinability, ideology, and warfare: Evolutionary perspectives* (pp. 71–95). Berghahn Books.
Richter, F. (2021). China is the world's manufacturing superpower. *Statista*, https://www.statista.com/chart/20858/top-10-countries-by-share-of-global-manufacturing-output/
Ridolfi, L., & Nuvolari, A. (2021). L'histoire immobile? A reappraisal of French economic growth using the demand-side approach, 1280–1850. *European Review of Economic History, 25*(3), 405–428.
Risch, W. J. (Ed.) (2015). *Youth and rock in the Soviet Bloc: Youth cultures, music, and the state in Russia and Eastern Europe*. Lexington Books.
Ritschl, A., & Straumann, T. (2010). Business cycles and economic policy, 1914–1945. In S. Broadberry & K. H. O'Rourke (Eds.), *The Cambridge economic history of modern Europe: Volume 2, 1870 to the present* (pp. 156–180). Cambridge University Press.
Roberts, J. (2000). Revolution from above and below. In T. C. Blanning (Ed.), *The Oxford history of modern Europe* (pp. 15–45). Oxford University Press.
Rodrik, D. (2016). Premature deindustrialization. *Journal of Economic Growth, 21*(1), 1–33.
Rodríguez, L. A. M. (2020). Bartolomé de Las Casas y el pensamiento decolonial: Debates y precisiones. *Estudios, 41*, 210–226.
Rogers, J. A. (1972). Darwinism and social Darwinism. *Journal of the History of Ideas, 33*(2), 265–280.
Romano, F. (2009). Clinton and Blair: The economics of the third way. *Journal of Economic and Social Policy, 10*(2), 79–93.
Romer, C. (1990). The Great Crash and the onset of the Great Depression. *Quarterly Journal of Economics, 105*(3), 597–624.
Romer, C. (1992). What ended the Great Depression? *Journal of Economic History, 52*(4), 757–784.
Romer, C. (1993). The nation in depression. *Journal of Economic Perspectives, 7*(2), 19–39.
Rose, P. (1983). *Parallel lives: Five Victorian marriages*. Penguin Books.
Rosen, G. (2015). *A history of public health* (Revised Expanded Edition). John Hopkins University Press.
Rosenberg, N., & Birdzell, L. E., Jr. (1986). *How the West grew rich: The economic transformation of the industrial world*. Basic books.
Roser, M. (2013) *Economic growth*. Published online at OurWorldInData.org. Retrieved from: https://ourworldindata.org/economic-growth

Roser, M., & Esteban, O. (2013). *Income Inequality*. Published online at OurWorldInData.org. Retrieved from: https://ourworldindata.org/income-inequality

Rosling, H., Rosling, O., & Rönnlund, A. R. (2018). *Factfulness: Ten reasons we're wrong about the world—And why things are better than you think*. Flatiron Books.

Ross, S. (2021). Financial services: Sizing the sector in the global economy. *Investopedia*. https://www.investopedia.com/ask/answers/030515/what-percentage-global-economy-comprised-financial-services-sector.asp

Rostow, W. W. (1960). *The stages of economic growth: A non-Communist manifesto*. Cambridge University Press.

Rothschild, E. (1994). Adam Smith and the invisible hand. *The American Economic Review, 84*(2), 319–322.

Rothstein, R. (2017). *The color of law: A forgotten history of how our government segregated America*. Liveright Publishing.

Roy, T. (1999). *Traditional industry in the economy of colonial India*. Cambridge University Press.

Roy, W. G. (1997). *Socializing capital: The rise of the large industrial corporation in America*. Princeton University Press.

Rublack, U. (2017). *Reformation Europe: New approaches to European history (Second edition)*. Cambridge University Press.

Ruttan, V. W. (2006). *Is war necessary for economic growth? Military procurement and technology development*. Clemens Lecture Series, Saint Johns University, October 9.

Rutterford, J. (2009). Learning from one another's mistakes: Investment trusts in the UK and the US, 1868–1940. *Financial History Review, 16*(2), 157–181.

Said, E. W. (1978). *Orientalism*. Pantheon Books.

Salomon, J. J. (1984). What is technology? The issue of its origins and definitions. *History and Technology, An International Journal, 1*(2), 113–156.

Salvatore, A. (2015). Modernity. In G. Bowering (Ed.), *Islamic political thought: An introduction* (pp. 135–151). Princeton University Press.

Sampson, A. (1995). *Company man: The rise and fall of corporate life*. Times-Business/Random House.

Sandel, M. J. (2020). *The tyranny of merit: What's become of the common good?* Penguin.

Sargent, L. T. (2017). Ideology and utopia: Karl Mannheim and Paul Ricoeur. In Z. Czigányik (Ed.), *Utopian horizons: Ideology, politics, literature* (pp. 19–39). Central European University Press.

Sawyer, S. M., Azzopardi, P. S., Wickremarathne, D., & Patton, G. C. (2018). The age of adolescence. *The Lancet Child & Adolescent Health, 2*(3), 223–228.

Scanlan, P. X. (2019). Emancipation and captivity in the British Empire. *History and Anthropology, 30*(5), 503–508.

Scanlan, P. X. (2020). *Slave empire: How slavery built modern Britain*. Robinson.

Shaw-Taylor, L., & Wrigley, E. A. (2014). Occupational structure and population change. In R. Floud, J. Humphries & P. Johnson (Eds.), *The Cambridge economic history of modern Britain* (Vol. 1, pp. 1700–1870, 53–88).

Shlapentokh, V. (1988). The Stakhanovite movement: Changing perceptions over fifty years. *Journal of Contemporary History, 23*(2), 259–276.

Schlesinger, A. M. Jr. (1960) *The age of Roosevelt: The politics of upheaval*. Houghton-Mifflin.

Schlosser, E. (2013). *Command and control: Nuclear weapons, the Damascus accident, and the illusion of safety*. Penguin Press.

Schoenhals, M. (2005). "Why don't we arm the left?" Mao's culpability for the cultural revolution's "Great Chaos" of 1967. *The China Quarterly, 182*, 277–300.

Schumpeter, J. (1934). *The theory of economic development*. Harvard University Press.

Schumpeter, J. ([1942] 1994). *Capitalism, socialism and democracy*. Routledge.

Schumpeter, J. (1954). *History of economic analysis*. Allen & Unwin.

Schwab, K. (2017). *The Fourth Industrial Revolution*. World Economic Forum.

Segesser, D. M. (2014). Controversy: Total War. In U. Daniel, P. Gatrell, O. Janz, H. Jones, J. Keene, A. Kramer & B. Nasson (Eds.), *1914–1918-online international encyclopedia of the First World War*. Freie Universität Berlin.

Selbin, E. (2013). *Revolution, rebellion, resistance: The power of story*. Zed Books Ltd.

Sessions, J. (2015). Colonizing revolutionary politics: Algeria and the French revolution of 1848. *French Politics, Culture & Society, 33*(1), 75–100.

Setser, B. W. (2007). *The post-industrial economy?* "Follow the Money" Blog, Post, September 3, Council on Foreign Relations, https://www.cfr.org/blog/post-industrial-economy

Shah, H. (2011). Accountability: Has it been hollowed out in the modern state? *Journal of Political Studies, 18*(1), 77.

Sheehy, G. (1991). *Gorbachev: A one-man revolution*. Mandarin.

Sherkat, D. E., & Blocker, T. J. (1994). The political development of sixties' activists: Identifying the influence of class, gender, and socialization on protest participation. *Social Forces, 72*(3), 821–842.

Shiller, R. J. (2015). *Irrational exuberance*. Princeton University Press.

Shimazu, N. (1998). *Japan, race and equality: The racial equality proposal of 1919*. Routledge.

Shonick, K. (2009). Politics, culture, and economics: Reassessing the West German guest worker agreement with Yugoslavia. *Journal of Contemporary History, 44*(4), 719–736.

Showalter, D. (2015). *The wars of German unification*. Bloomsbury Publishing.
Siapera, E. (2006). Multiculturalism online: The internet and the dilemmas of multicultural politics. *European Journal of Cultural Studies, 9*(1), 5–24.
Siegelbaum, L. H. (2008). Roadlessness and the "path to communism": Building roads and highways in Stalinist Russia. *Journal of Transport History, 29*(2), 277–294.
Simpson, M. (2020). The Anthropocene as colonial discourse. *Environment and Planning d: Society and Space, 38*(1), 53–71.
Singh, A. (2007). *Globalization, industrial revolutions in India and China and labour markets in advanced countries: Implications for national and international economic policy*. United Nations International Labour Organization (ILO), Working Paper 81, Policy Integration Department.
Sivasundaram, S. (2020). *Waves across the south: A new history of revolution and empire*. William Collins.
Skelcher, C. (2000). Changing images of the state: Overloaded, hollowed-out, congested. *Public Policy and Administration, 15*(3), 3–19.
Skinner, B. F. (1971). *Beyond freedom and dignity*. Knopf.
Skocpol, T., & Trimberger, E. (1977). Revolutions and the world-historical development of capitalism. *Berkeley Journal of Sociology, 22*, 101–113.
Skocpol, T. (1979). *States and social revolutions: A comparative analysis of France*. Cambridge University Press.
Skoll, G. R., & Korstanje, M. E. (2013). Constructing an American fear culture from red scares to terrorism. *International Journal of Human Rights and Constitutional Studies, 1*(4), 341–364.
Slobodian, Q. (2018). *Globalists: The end of empire and the birth of Neoliberalism*. Harvard University Press.
Smelev, N., & Popov, V. (1989). *The turning point*. Doubleday.
Smith, A. ([1776] 2000). *The wealth of nations* (E. Cannan, Ed.). Modern Library.
Smith, B. G. (2001a). The development of gender history. In P. N. Stearns (Ed.), *Encyclopedia of European social history from 1350 to 2000* (Vol. 4, pp. 3–13). Charles Scribner's sons (Gale).
Smith, B. G. (2001b). Women and femininity. In P. N. Stearns (Ed.), *Encyclopedia of European social history from 1350 to 2000* (Vol. 4, pp. 25–35). Charles Scribner's sons (Gale).
Smith, D. (1999). "The civilizing process" and "the history of sexuality": Comparing Norbert Elias and Michel Foucault. *Theory and Society, 28*(1), 79–100.
Smuts, J. C. (1926). *Holism and evolution*. Macmillan.
Snay, M. (1993). *Gospel of disunion: Religion and separatism in the antebellum South*. Cambridge University Press.

Snow, C. P. (1963). *The two cultures: And a second look: An expanded version.* Cambridge University Press.

Solzhenitsyn, A. I. ([1968] 1991). *Cancer ward* (3rd ed.) (N. Bethell, & D. Burg, Trans.). The Noonday Press/Farrar, Straus and Giroux.

Solzhenitsyn, A. I. (1974). *The gulag archipelago, 1918–1956: An experiment in literary investigation.* Harper and Row.

Somerwine, C. (2018). *France since 1870: Culture, politics and society* (3rd ed.). Palgrave.

Späth, J. (2019). Turning constitutional history upside down: The 1820s revolutions in the Mediterranean. In T. Hauswedell, A. Körner & U. Tiedau (Eds.), *Re-Mapping centre and periphery: Asymmetrical encounters in European and global contexts* (pp. 111–134). UCL Press.

Spencer, D. S. (1988). A short history of geopolitics. *Journal of Geography, 87*(2), 42–47.

Spengler, O. ([1918] 1932). *The decline of the West* (C. F. Atkinson, Trans.). Alfred A. Knopf.

Sperber, J. (2005). *The European revolutions, 1848–1851* (2nd ed.). Cambridge University Press.

Spolaore, E., & Wacziarg, R. (2013). How deep are the roots of economic development? *Journal of Economic Literature, 51*(2), 325–369.

Stanford, P. K. (2015). Instrumentalism: Global, local, and scientific. In P. Humphreys (Ed.), *The Oxford handbook of philosophy of science.*

Stearns, P. N. (2001a). *The encyclopedia of world history* (6th ed.). Houghton Mifflin Company.

Stearns, P. N. (2001b). Men and masculinity. In P. N. Stearns (Ed.), *Encyclopedia of European social history from 1350 to 2000* (Vol. 4, pp. 37–43). Charles Scribner's sons (Gale).

Stearns, P. N. (2003). *Western civilization in world history.* Taylor & Francis Group.

Stearns, P. N. (2016). World history, identity and political change. *Foundations of Science, 21*(1), 105–115.

Steele, V. (2004). Femme fatale: Fashion and visual culture in fin-de-siècle Paris. *Fashion Theory, 8*(3), 315–328.

Steffen, W., Broadgate, W., Deutsch, L., Gaffney, O., & Ludwig, C. (2015). The trajectory of the Anthropocene: The Great Acceleration. *The Anthropocene Review, 2*(1), 81–98.

Steffen, W., Grinevald, J., Crutzen, P., & McNeill, J. (2011). The Anthropocene: Conceptual and historical perspectives. *Philosophical Transactions of the Royal Society A: Mathematical, Physical and Engineering Sciences, 369*(1938), 842–867.

Steffen, W., Leinfelder, R., Zalasiewicz, J., Waters, C. N., Williams, M., Summerhayes, C., Barnosky, A. D., Cearreta, A., Crutzen, P., Edgeworth, M., &

Ellis, E. C. (2016). Stratigraphic and Earth System approaches to defining the Anthropocene. *Earth's Future, 4*(8), 324–345.
Stein, H. (1969). *The fiscal revolution in America.* University of Chicago Press.
Sterman, J. D. (1986). The economic long wave: Theory and evidence. *System Dynamics Review, 2*(2), 87–125.
Stevenson, R. (2010). Remembering the pleasant bits: Nostalgia and the legacies of modernism. *Novel: A Forum on Fiction, 43*(1), 132–139.
Stiglitz, J. E. (1999). Reforming the global economic architecture: Lessons from recent crises. *The Journal of Finance, 54*(4), 1508–1521.
Strachan, H. (2003). *The First World War.* Penguin.
Strachan, H. (2000). Military modernization. In T. C. Blanning (Ed.), *The Oxford history of modern Europe* (pp. 77–100). Oxford University Press.
Strasser, S. (1999). *Waste and want: A social history of trash.* Metropolitan Books.
Suny, R. G. (1997). Stalin and his Stalinism: Power and authority in the Soviet Union, 1930–53. In I. Kershaw & M. Lewin (Eds.), *Stalinism and Nazism: Dictatorships in comparison* (pp. 16–24). Cambridge University Press.
Suzman, J. (2017). *Affluence without abundance: The disappearing world of the Bushmen.* Bloomsbury Publishing USA.
Svec, M. (1988). The Prague spring: 20 years later. *Foreign Affairs, 66*(5), 981–1001.
Swedberg, R. (2008). Economic sociology. In S. N. Durlauf & L. E. Blume (Eds.), *The new Palgrave dictionary of economics* (2nd ed.). Palgrave Macmillan.
Swidler, A. (1986). Culture in action: Symbols and strategies. *American Sociological Review, 51*(2), 273–286.
Syvitski, J., Waters, C. N., Day, J., Milliman, J. D., Summerhayes, C., Steffen, W., Zalasiewicz, J., Cearreta, A., Gałuszka, A., Hajdas, I., & Head, M. J. (2020). Extraordinary human energy consumption and resultant geological impacts beginning around 1950 CE initiated the proposed Anthropocene Epoch. *Communications Earth & Environment, 1*(1), 1–13.
Tabb, W. K. (1982). *The long default: New York City and the urban fiscal crisis.* New York University Press.
Taibbi, M. (2019). *Hate Inc.: Why today's media makes us despise one another.* OR Books.
Tallis, F. (2001). *Hidden minds: A history of the unconscious.* Arcade.
Tarver, H. M., & Slape, E. (2016). *The Spanish empire: A historical encyclopedia.* ABC-CLIO.
Taylor, C. (1992). Modernity and the rise of the public sphere. *The Tanner lectures on human values* (Vol. 14, pp. 203–260). Stanford University
Taylor, M. (2000). The 1848 revolutions and the British empire. *Past & Present, 166*, 146–180.

Taylor, B. D., & Botea, R. (2008). Tilly tally: War-making and state-making in the contemporary third world. *International Studies Review, 10*(1), 27–56.

Temin, P. (1976). *Did monetary forces cause the Great Depression?* Norton.

Temin, P. (1993). Transmission of the Great Depression. *Journal of Economic Perspectives, 7*(2), 87–102.

Temin, P. (2000). A response to Harley and Crafts. *The Journal of Economic History, 60*(3), 842–846.

Temin, P. (2002). The golden age of European growth reconsidered. *European Review of Economic History, 6*(1), 3–22.

Tena-Junguito, A., Lampe, M., & Fernandes, F. T. (2012). How much trade liberalization was there in the world before and after Cobden-Chevalier? *The Journal of Economic History, 72*(3), 708–740.

Ther, P. (2016). *Europe since 1989: A history* (C. Hughes-Kreutzmüller, Trans.). Princeton University Press.

Thompson, E. P. (1967). Time, work-discipline, and industrial capitalism. *Past and Present, 38*, 56–97.

Thoreau, H. D. ([1845] 1917). Walden, or, life in the woods (J. C. Bowman, Ed.). Scott, Foresman and Company.

Thoreau, H. D. ([1849] 2016). *Civil disobedience.* Broadview Press.

Tilly, C. (1975). Western state-making and theories of political transformation. In G. Ardant (Ed.), *The formation of national states in Western Europe* (Vol. 8, pp. 601–638). Princeton University Press.

Tilly, C. (1984). *Big structures, large processes, huge comparisons.* Russell Sage Foundation.

Tilly, C. (1992). War in history. *Sociological Forum, 7*(1), 187–195.

Tilly, C. (1995a). The emergence of citizenship in France and elsewhere. *International Review of Social History, 40*(Supplement 3), 223–236.

Tilly, C. (1995b). Citizenship, identity and social history. *International Review of Social History, 40*(Supplement), 1–17.

Tilly, C. (2004). *Contention and democracy in Europe, 1650–2000.* Cambridge University Press.

Timsit, A. (2016). 5 US independence movements inspired by Brexit. *Politico.* https://www.politico.eu/article/5-us-independence-movements-inspired-by-brexit/

Tomasello, M. (2020). The adaptive origins of uniquely human sociality. *Philosophical Transactions of the Royal Society B, 375*(20190493).

Tooze, A. (2014). *The deluge: the Great War, America, and the remaking of the global order, 1916–1931.* Penguin Books.

Toynbee, A. J. (1884). *Lectures on the industrial revolution in England; Popular addresses, notes and other fragments.* Rivingtons.

Travlos, K. (2020). Chapter 1: Introduction. In K. Travlos (Ed.), *Salvation and catastrophe: The Greek-Turkish War, 1919–1922* (pp. 1–22). Lexington Books.

Turner, F. J. (1894). The significance of the frontier in American history. In *Annual Report of the American Historical Association for the Year 1893.*

Tyrrell, I. (1991). American exceptionalism in an age of international history. *The American Historical Review, 96*(4), 1031–1055.

Uebele, M. (2011). National and international market integration in the 19th century: Evidence from comovement. *Explorations in Economic History, 48*(2), 226–242.

UK Parliament. (2021). Brexit timeline: Events leading to the UK's exit from the European Union. *UK Parliament, House of Commons Library.*

Unger, C. R. (2018). *International development: A postwar history*. Bloomsbury Publishing.

UN. (1976). *World economic survey 1975.* Department of Economic and Social Affairs, United Nations Secretariat.

UN. (1999). *The world at six billion.* Population Division, Department of Economic and Social Affairs, United Nations Secretariat.

Urbinato, D. (1994). London's historic "pea-soupers." (smog in London, England). *EPA Journal, 20*(1–2), 44–45.

US LOC. (2021a). *New century celebrations: Topics in Chronicling America.* United States Library of Congress, https://guides.loc.gov/chronicling-america-new-century-celebrations

US LOC. (2021b). *Anarchist incidents (1886–1920): Topics in Chronicling America.* https://guides.loc.gov/chronicling-america-anarchist-incidents

US NASA. (2020). *Climate change: How do we know?* United States National Aeronautic and Space Administration, https://climate.nasa.gov/evidence/

US Space Force. (2020). United States Space Force. https://www.spaceforce.mil/About-Us/FAQs/Whats-the-Space-Force/.

Uvalić, M. (2018). *The rise and fall of market socialism in Yugoslavia.* University of Ljubljana, Slovenia, July.

Van Bavel, J., & Reher, D. S. (2013). The baby boom and its causes: What we know and what we need to know. *Population and Development Review, 39*(2), 257–288.

Van der Linden, M. (2017). *Transnational labour history: Explorations*. Routledge.

Van der Walt, L. (2016). Global anarchism and syndicalism: Theory, history, resistance. *Anarchist Studies, 24*(1), 85–106.

Van Zanden, J. L., Baten, J., Mira d'Ercole, M., Rijpma, A., Smith, C., & Timmer, M. (2014). *How was life?: Global well-being since 1820*. OECD Publishing.

Van Zanden, J. L., & Van Leeuwen, B. (2012). Persistent but not consistent: The growth of national income in Holland 1347–1807. *Explorations in Economic History, 49*(2), 119–130.

Varoufakis, Y. (2015). *The global minotaur: America, Europe and the future of the global economy*. Zed Books.

Veblen, T. (1919). *The place of science in modern civilisation*. B. W. Huebsch.

Vernon, J. R. (1994). World War II fiscal policies and the end of the Great Depression. *Journal of Economic History, 54*(4), 850–868.

Vialet, J. C. (1980). *A brief history of US immigration policy*. Congressional Research Service, Library of Congress, Report # 80-223 PW.

Vogt, K. C. (2016). The post-industrial society: From utopia to ideology. *Work, Employment and Society, 30*(2), 366–376.

Voltaire. ([1759] 1959). *Candide* (L. Bair, Ed. & Trans.). Bantam Dell.

Voth, H. J. (2003). Living standards during the industrial revolution: An economist's guide. *American Economic Review, 93*(2), 221–226.

Vu, K., Haraguchi, N., & Amann, J. (2020). *Deindustrialization in developed countries amid accelerated globalization: Patterns, influencers and policy insights*. United Nations Industrial Development Organisation, Department Of Policy, Research And Statistics Working Paper 6/2020.

Wallerstein, I. (1976). *The modern world-system: Capitalist agriculture and the origins of the European world-economy in the sixteenth century*. Academic Press.

Wallis, P., Colson, J., & Chilosi, D. (2018). Structural change and economic growth in the British economy before the Industrial Revolution, 1500–1800. *The Journal of Economic History, 78*(3), 862–903.

Ward, J. D., Sutton, P. C., Werner, A. D., Costanza, R., Mohr, S. H., & Simmons, C. T. (2016). Is decoupling GDP growth from environmental impact possible? *PLoS One, 11*(10), e0164733.

Warner, A. G. (2010). The evolution of the American brewing industry. *Journal of Business Case Studies, 6*(6), 31–46.

Washbrook, D. (1994). The commercialisation of agriculture in colonial India: Production, subsistence and reproduction in the "Dry South", c.1870–1930. *Modern Asian Studies, 28*(1), 129–164.

Waterhouse, B. C. (2017). The personal, the political and, the profitable: Business and protest culture, 1960s–1980s. *Financial History*, (Spring), 14–17.

Watson, D. R. (1983). Review: La Belle Époque: Domestic, military and foreign politics under the third French republic. *The Historical Journal, 26*(3), 761–768.

Watson, T. (2012). A (very brief) history of public relations. *Communication Director* (January), 42–45. European Association of Communication Directors (EACD).

Watts, A. (1957). *The way of Zen*. Vintage Books.

Weatherall, D. (1976). *David Ricardo: A biography*. Martinus Nijhoff.

Webb, S. B. (1984). The supply of money and Reichsbank financing of government and corporate debt in Germany, 1919–1923. *The Journal of Economic History, 44*(2), 499–507.

Webb, S. B. (1988). Latin American debt and German reparations after World War 1: A comparison. *Weltwirtschaftliches Arhiv, 124*(4), 745–774.

Weber, E. (1976). *Peasants into Frenchmen: The modernization of rural France, 1870–1914*. Stanford University Press.

Weber, E. (1986). *France: Fin de siècle*. Belknap Press of Harvard University Press.

Weber, M. (1930). *The Protestant ethic and the" spirit" of capitalism and other writings* (Parsons, T., Translator). Unwin University Books.

Weede, E., & Muller, E. (1998). Rebellion, violence and revolution: A rational choice perspective. *Journal of Peace Research, 35*(1), 43–59.

Weiss, J. (1967). *The fascist tradition: Radical right-wing extremism in modern Europe*. Harper & Row.

Weissenstein M., & Orsi P. (2016) Fidel Castro, who defied US for 50 years, dies at 90 in Cuba. AP News. November 27. https://apnews.com/article/5ef60f67cefb46869c5b6e58145 88dec

Wesseling, H. L. (1981). Colonial wars and armed peace, 1870–1914: A reconnaissance. *Itinerario, 5*(2), 53–73.

West, R. (1982). *1900*. Viking Studio Book.

Westad, O. A. (2017). *The Cold War: A world history*. Penguin Random House UK.

Weyland, K. (2009). The diffusion of revolution: "1848" in Europe and Latin America. *International Organization, 63*(3), 391–423.

Whale, P. B. (1944). A retrospective view of the Bank Charter Act of 1844. *Economica, New Series, 11*(43), 109–111.

Whaples, R. (1995). Where is there consensus among American economic historians? The results of a survey on forty propositions. *Journal of Economic History, 55*(1), 139–154.

Whaples, R. (2008). Cliometrics. In S. N. Durlauf & L. E. Blume (Eds.), *The new Palgrave dictionary of economics* (2nd ed.). Palgrave MacMillan.

Whatley, W., & Gillezeau, R. (2011). The impact of the transatlantic slave trade on ethnic stratification in Africa. *American Economic Review, 101*(3), 571–576.

White, C. M. (2013). *A global history of the developing world*. Routledge.

White, E. (1984). A reinterpretation of the banking crisis of 1930. *Journal of Economic History, 44*(1), 119–138.

White, S. (1986). Economic performance and communist legitimacy. *World Politics, 38*(3), 462–482.

Whitehead, H., & Rendell, L. (2014). *The cultural lives of whales and dolphins*. University of Chicago Press.

Whyte, W. H. (1956). *The organization man*. Simon & Schuster.

Whyte, W. H. (1988). *City: Rediscovering the center*. Doubleday.

Wicker, E. (1980). A reconsideration of the causes of the banking panic of 1930. *Journal of Economic History, 40*(3), 571–583.

Wiesner-Hanks, M .E. (2001a). Gender and work. In P. N. Stearns (Ed.), *Encyclopedia of European social history from 1350 to 2000* (Vol. 4, pp. 55–67). Charles Scribner's sons (Gale).

Wiesner-Hanks, M. E. (2001b). Patriarchy. In P. N. Stearns (Ed.), *Encyclopedia of European social history from 1350 to 2000* (Vol. 4, pp. 14–24). Charles Scribner's sons (Gale).

Wikipedia. (2016). 2016. Wikipedia.com, https://en.wikipedia.org/wiki/2016

Wilde, O. ([1895] 2003a). The soul of man under socialism. In *Complete works of Oscar Wilde* (5th ed., pp. 1174–1197). Collins.

Wilde, O. ([1897] 2003b). The Ballad of Reading Gaol. In *Complete works of Oscar Wilde* (5th ed.). Collins.

Wilde, R. (2020, 28 August). Belle Époque or the "Beautiful Age" in France. *ThoughtCo*. thoughtco.com/the-belle-epoque-beautiful-age-1221300.

Williams, A. (2007). *Failed imagination? The Anglo-American new world order from Wilson to Bush* (2nd ed.). Manchester University Press.

Williamson, J. G. (1974). *Late nineteenth-century American development: A general equilibrium history*. Cambridge University Press.

Williamson, J. G. (1975). The railroads and Midwestern development, 1870–1890. In D. C. Klingaman & R. K. Vedder (Eds.), *Essays in nineteenth century economic history*. University of Ohio Press.

Williamson, J. G. (1988). Migrant selectivity, urbanization, and industrial revolutions. *Population and Development Review, 14*(2), 287–314.

Williamson, J. G. (2000). What Should the World Bank Think about the Washington Consensus? *World Bank Research Observer, 15*(2), 251–264.

Williamson, J. G. (2006). Global migration. *Finance & Development*, *43*(3).

Williamson, J. G. (2013). *Trade and poverty: When the Third World fell behind*. MIT Press.

Williamson, O. E. (1985). *The economic institutions of capitalism: Firms, markets, relational contracting*. Free Press.

Winch, D. (2001). *That disputatious pair: Economic history and the history of economics*. Centre for Economics and History at the University of Cambridge Working Paper.

Winch, D. (2010). Arnold Toynbee's Industrial Revolution. Keynote address to *Before and After Toynbee,* Cambridge Victorian Studies Symposium (September 23), Cambridge University.

Winks, R. W., & Neuberger, J. (2005). *Europe and the making of modernity, 1815–1914*. Oxford University Press.

Winn, J. A. (2008). *The poetry of war*. Cambridge University Press.

Winnacker, R. (1938). Elections in Algeria and the French Colonies under the Third Republic. *The American Political Science Review, 32*(2), 261–277.

Wohlstetter, A. (1959). The delicate balance of terror. *Foreign Affairs, 37*(2), 211–234.

Wolfe, T. (1976). The me decade and the third great awakening. *New York Magazine* 23.

Wolfe, T. (1979). *The right stuff.* Farrar, Straus and Giroux.

Wong, J. (2004). The adaptive developmental state in East Asia. *Journal of East Asian Studies., 4*, 345–362.

Wright, E. O. (1997). *Class counts: Comparative studies in class analysis.* Cambridge University Press.

Wright, G. (1990). The origins of American industrial success. *American Economic Review, 80*(4), 651–668.

Wrigley, E. A. (1988). *Continuity, chance and change: The character of the Industrial Revolution in England.* Cambridge University Press.

Xu, M., David, J. M., & Kim, S. H. (2018). The Fourth Industrial Revolution: Opportunities and challenges. *International Journal of Financial Research, 9*(2), 90–95.

Yao, X., & Lin, Y. (2016). Emerging manufacturing paradigm shifts for the incoming industrial revolution. *The International Journal of Advanced Manufacturing Technology, 85*(5), 1665–1676.

Yeo-chi King, A. (2018). "Modernization" and "modernity": The construction of a modern Chinese civilizational order. In A. Yeo-chi King, *China's great transformation: Selected essays on confucianism, modernization, and democracy* (pp. 111–128). The Chinese University of Hong Kong Press.

Yilmaz, O., Bahçekapili, H. G., & Sevi, B. (2019). The evolution of human sociality. In T. Shackelford & V. Weekes-Shackelford (Eds.), *Encyclopedia of evolutionary psychological science.* Springer.

Young, A. (1997). *The harmony of illusions: Inventing post-traumatic stress disorder.* Princeton University Press.

Young, J. (2015). Infrastructure: Mass transit in 19th- and 20th-century urban America. *Oxford research encyclopedia of American history.*

Young, M. ([1957] 1994). *The rise of the meritocracy.* Transactions Publications.

Young, M. (2001). Down with meritocracy. *The Guardian* (June 28).

Younis, M. (2017). United by blood: Race and transnationalism during the Belle Époque. *Nations and Nationalism, 23*(3), 484–504.

Yusuf, S., Nabeshima, K., & Perkins, D. H. (2007). China and India reshape global industrial geography. In L. A. Winters & S. Yusuf (Eds.), *Dancing with giants: China, India and the global economy* (pp. 35–66). World Bank & Institute for Policy Studies.

Zagha, R., & Nankani, G. T. (Eds.). (2005). *Economic growth in the 1990s: Learning from a decade of reform.* World Bank Publications.

Zalasiewicz, J., Waters, C. N., Ellis, E. C., Head, M. J., Vidas, D., Steffen, W., Thomas, J. A., Horn, E., Summerhayes, C. P., Leinfelder, R., & McNeill, J. R. (2021). The Anthropocene: Comparing its meaning in geology (chronostratigraphy) with conceptual approaches arising in other disciplines. *Earth's Future*, *9*(3), p. e2020EF001896.

Zalasiewicz, J., Waters, C. N., Williams, M., Barnosky, A. D., Cearreta, A., Crutzen, P., Ellis, E., Ellis, M. A., Fairchild, I. J., Grinevald, J. M., Haff, P. K., Hajdas, I., Leinfelder, R., McNeill, J., Odada, E. O., Poirier, C., Richter, D., Steffen, W., Summerhayes, C., ... Oreskes, N. (2015). When did the Anthropocene begin? A mid-twentieth century boundary level is stratigraphically optimal. *Quaternary International, 383*, 196–203.

Zalasiewicz, J., Williams, M., Haywood, A., & Ellis, M. (2011). The Anthropocene: A new epoch of geological time? *Philosophical Transactions: Mathematical, Physical and Engineering Sciences, 369*(1938), 835–841.

Zaretsky, E. (2015). *Political Freud: A history*. Columbia University Press.

Zimmermann, E. (1990). On the outcomes of revolutions: Some preliminary considerations. *Sociological Theory, 8*(1), 33–47.

Zimring, F. E., & Hawkins, G. (1999). *Crime is not the problem: Lethal violence in America*. Oxford University Press.

Zinkina, J., Ilyin, I., & Korotayev, A. (2017). The nineteenth-century urbanisation transition in the First World. *Globalistics and Globalization Studies, 2017*, 164–172.

Zinn, H. (2005). *A people's history of the United States: 1492–present*. Harper Perennial Modern Classics.

Index

C. Gordon, *Many Possible Worlds*,
https://doi.org/10.1007/978-981-19-9281-0

B

D

F

H

I

J

K

L

M

O

P

T

SPRINGER NATURE

GPSR Compliance

The European Union's (EU) General Product Safety Regulation (GPSR) is a set of rules that requires consumer products to be safe and our obligations to ensure this.

If you have any concerns about our products, you can contact us on ProductSafety@springernature.com

In case Publisher is established outside the EU, the EU authorized representative is:

Springer Nature Customer Service Center GmbH
Europaplatz 3
69115 Heidelberg, Germany

The manufacturer's authorised representative in the EU is Springer Nature Customer Service Centre GmbH, Europaplatz 3, 69115 Heidelberg, Germany. If you have any concerns regarding our products, please contact ProductSafety@springernature.com

Printed and bound by CPI Group (UK) Ltd, Croydon, CR0 4YY
01/10/2026
02225873-0001